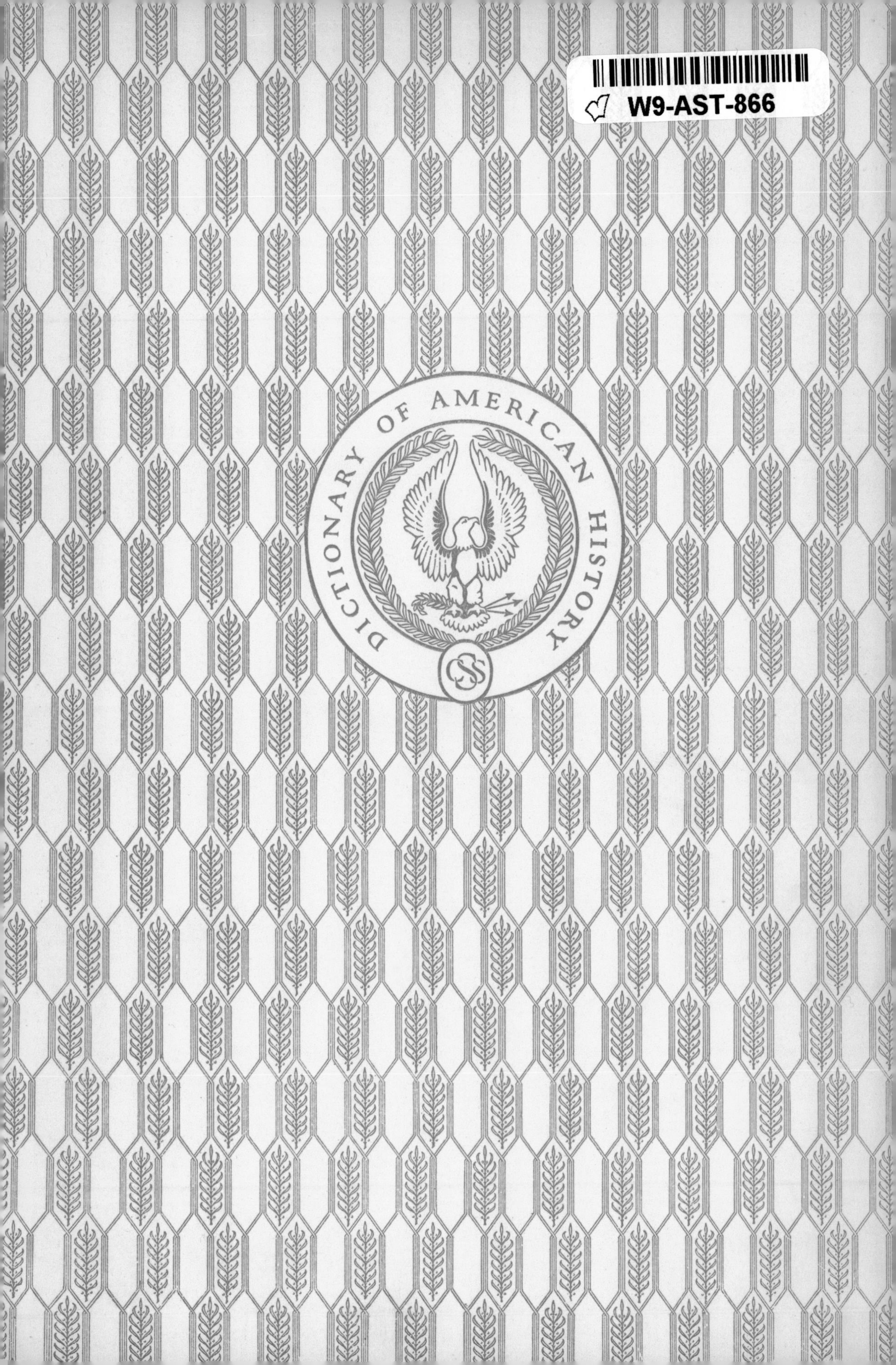
W9-AST-866
DICTIONARY OF AMERICAN HISTORY
CSS

DICTIONARY OF
AMERICAN HISTORY

VOLUME I

DICTIONARY OF AMERICAN HISTORY

JAMES TRUSLOW ADAMS
Editor in Chief

R. V. COLEMAN
Managing Editor

VOLUME I

NEW YORK
CHARLES SCRIBNER'S SONS
1940

Printed in the United States of America

A

Advisory Council

Foreword

AMERICA has never before been so interested in its history as it is today. The many tercentenaries in recent years have helped us to realize that we have a past and are no longer young. That past is essentially our own, different from that of other nations. We have developed a distinct American culture.

In the last few decades our history has been almost completely rewritten. New facts have been discovered; new interests have developed. A generation ago historians had done the merest spade work in many departments of our national life. They were still chiefly concerned with political and military events. Today our whole culture is their province, and the public which reads history has widened with the widening of the historian's vision. Moreover a knowledge of history has become essential to an understanding of much in the daily press and in the radio broadcasts, recording the events of our world hour by hour. Advertisers, sensitive barometers of public interest, have taken to using historical material in their advertisements. History is no longer the concern of a few. If the interests of scholars have broadened, so has the use of the results of their researches, until historical facts are sought for in business offices as well as in halls of learning.

Until now the facts of the new history have not been readily available. They are scattered through thousands of volumes of general histories or special studies. There has been an increasingly insistent demand for some one source to which an inquirer might go to find, and quickly, what he wishes to know as to specific facts, events, trends or policies in our American past, without searching for hours, perhaps unsuccessfully, through stacks of books, even should he have access to them. It is this need which the *Dictionary of American History* is intended to fill.

Work on it began in the latter part of 1936 and has progressed steadily ever since. The editorial program started with the compilation of a vast index of proposed subjects, in which several hundred historians, representing all interests and all sections of the country, together with many historical societies, co-operated. This preliminary step was followed by an intensive sifting process which resulted in a tentative list of some six thousand topics. This list, with the suggested number of words for each article, was then printed and again presented to all of those who were co-operating. On the basis of the advice and criticisms received, the list was again carefully revised, and the assigning of subjects to authors was begun.

More than a thousand historians, representing a cross section of American historical scholarship, have joined in the writing of the five to six thousand articles which will be found in the completed work. The intent has been to have each article written by the historian in whose field it properly falls. In the case of certain specialized subjects, the articles have been contributed by men in closest touch with the facts. Thus Admiral Byrd wrote the account of his Polar flights; General John J. Pershing wrote that of the American Expeditionary Forces; Gutzon Borglum wrote of his colossal sculptures in the Black Hills; and Doctor Arthur E. Morgan wrote the articles on Flood Control and the Tennessee Valley Authority.

Throughout the long and complicated editorial process, emphasis has constantly been placed on the fact that this is a "dictionary" and not a collection of essays or even an encyclopædia. In general, the articles are brief, each dealing with a separate, and definite, aspect of our history. There are, however, a considerable number of "covering articles," each of which not only presents its broader subject in an orderly sequence, but, by cross references, guides the reader to the various supporting or related articles in which the individual phases of the subject are treated in more detail. Thus, if the reader wishes to know only the general succession of events, he does not have to piece them together from scores of separate articles; but if, on the other hand, he wishes information about only one aspect of the subject he will find it, indexed under the name by which it is usually identified.

This arrangement, which it is hoped will be found extremely useful, has involved one of the most difficult and meticulously painstaking portions of the editorial work — that of making constant cross references either by exact citation or, more generally, by the symbol *qv* (*quod vide*, "which see"; *qqv* being used for the plural). Where in one article there may be even a casual reference to a related subject, the reader is referred to that article in case he desires to follow the line of investigation. Thus, on "International Law" the investigator will find a 1500-word covering article by Professor Charles G. Fenwick of Bryn Mawr College. As he reads the article he will find a reference to the "foreign policy" of the United States, from which a qv will carry him to an article on this subject by Professor Samuel Flagg Bemis of Yale University. A few lines farther along there is a reference to "recognition," from which a qv carries him to an article on the "Policy of Recognition" by Professor George D. Harmon of Lehigh University. Then the reader comes upon such aspects of international law as "neutrality," "belligerent," "contraband" and "blockade," to separate articles on which he is guided by the symbol qqv. Somewhat farther along, a cross reference takes him to an article on "Recognition of the Latin-American Republics" by Professor Dana G. Munro of Princeton University; while a reference to the Monroe Doctrine carries him to an article on that subject by Professor Dexter Perkins of the University of Rochester. "Naturalization" is mentioned, and a qv leads the reader to an article on the topic by Professor Robert Phillips of Purdue University. In the same way, he is referred to articles on "Continuous Voyage" by Professor Richard W. Van Alstyne of Chico State College, and on "The *Alabama*" by Professor Allan Nevins of Columbia University. A cross reference and a qv direct the reader to articles on the "Fourteen Points" and the "Treaty of Versailles," both by Professor Bernadotte E. Schmitt of the University of Chicago; also to an article on the "League of Nations" by Professor Harold S. Quigley of the University of Minnesota. From a reference to the "Open Door" the reader is led to an article on this subject by Doctor Stanley K. Hornbeck of the Department of State; and from a reference to the "Briand-Kellogg Pact" to an article on that topic by Professor Benjamin H. Williams of the University of Pittsburgh. In the last paragraph, where the "Pan-American Conferences" are referred to, there is a cross reference to an article on these conferences by Professor A. Curtis Wilgus of George Washington University. Similarly, in each of the articles to which the reader is referred he will discover references to yet other related subjects. Thus, without going outside these volumes the student will find an almost inexhaustible mine of collateral material — contributed in each case by a recognized authority.

This breaking down of larger topics into their component parts, for immediate reference, has also been one of the difficult editorial tasks. In every case we have tried to choose the caption which would most likely occur to the reader in searching for a subject of which he has a general idea but not specific knowledge. For example, if he should wish to learn about the frequently mentioned undefended frontier between Canada and the United States he would probably never find it were it indexed only under the heading "Rush-Bagot Agreement." He will find it in the *Dictionary of American History* not only from that caption but also from one reading "Canadian Boundary, Disarmament of." The system of breaking down articles in this way, for ready reference, has naturally called for conciseness in treatment if the work as a whole were not to become too bulky, but each author has had the opportunity of retaining his individual flavor within this necessary restriction.

It is obvious that every item in history could not find a place. Every town, city, college, and so on, could not be mentioned though each has its own story of local interest. Lines have had to be drawn. Although exclusions may occasionally appear arbitrary to some, they have been made only after the most careful consideration, and upon advice from competent scholars.

The items in the brief bibliographies have been selected, so far as possible, with a view to accessibility in the average library. References do not include volumes, chapters or page numbers if the subject may easily be found in the work referred to; but in those cases in which there might be difficulty, exact citations are provided.

We owe the deepest gratitude to the thousand and more scholars who have given us their unselfish and wholehearted co-operation. We have already spoken of the way in which great numbers of the articles have had to be made to dovetail into one another. Frequently the author of one has not seen some other closely connected with it. The fitting together has of necessity been part of the editorial duties and could not have been accomplished had not the contributors, many of them among the most eminent scholars in the country, shown understanding of the difficulties, and assisted, by their unfailing courtesy as well as unflagging patience. It is impossible to acknowledge our full debt to them.

We also wish to express to the members of the Advisory Council our great appreciation of their help in planning the work and shaping its policy, as well as for their advice and criticism in connection with the articles proposed for inclusion, and their constant oversight of, and interest in, the broad details of the work as it progressed.

We are deeply indebted to Mr. Paul M. Angle of the Illinois State Historical Library and to Doctor Will D. Howe for reading the entire proof of the five volumes and making most helpful suggestions.

As Editor in Chief I also desire to bear testimony to the invaluable work done by the Managing Editor, Mr. R. V. Coleman. His broad knowledge of American history, his understanding of the relations of its parts and periods, his wide acquaintance among the scholars and historical institutions of the country, and his editorial skill, have alone made this work possible.

We have happily been assisted by a most competent and loyal staff. As the volumes now near completion we wish to say how much we owe to the Associate Editors, Mr. Thomas Robson Hay and Doctor Ralph Foster Weld, and to assure them of our recognition of their constant and valuable assistance. A work of this sort, more complex than the user may realize, calls for the most watchful care in every detail to avoid those pitfalls which every historian realizes lie in his way. To those who have done so much to help us with these many problems we extend our appreciative thanks: to E. Graham Platt, Frances B. Gallagher, Marion G. Barnes and Roger Hart, who have been associated with the work from beginning to end; and to all those others who in one way or another and at one time and another have assisted.

To sum up, the *Dictionary of American History* is the result of the labor of some four years and of the collaboration of well over a thousand persons — historians and those who have made history — representing every part of the country and every phase of its life. We send it out now to the public with the hope that it will prove worthy of the scholarship of the nation and be useful to all its people, of all ages and of all vocations.

JAMES TRUSLOW ADAMS

Jan. 2, 1940

Note to the Reader

The symbols *q.v.* (*quod vide*, "which see") and *qq.v.* (the plural of *q.v.*) indicate that there are separate articles on the subjects so marked. In general, these articles should easily be found under natural phrasings of the titles, but, if there is difficulty, the Index may prove helpful.

DICTIONARY OF
AMERICAN HISTORY

A. B. Plot — Comstock Lode

A. B. Plot (1823–24). The political enmity between Sen. Ninian Edwards of Illinois and William H. Crawford, Secretary of the Treasury, produced this "plot." Crawford had employed the unstable western banks to collect public land revenues in fluctuating banknote currencies. This policy, though justifiable, resulted in losses to the government, while he doubtless used his banking connections to advance his political influence. In 1823 the Washington *Republican*, a Calhoun organ, published a series of articles signed A. B. which attacked Crawford for malfeasance in his relations with certain banks, and accused him of suppressing letters on the subject for which the House had called. These articles were written by Edwards; while some thought he desired to damage Crawford in the 1824 presidential campaign, J. Q. Adams believed the real object was to remove W. W. Seaton and Joseph Gales, Crawford supporters, from the post of public printers. Early in 1824, while on his way west as the newly appointed Minister to Mexico, Edwards sent formal charges against Crawford to the House. He was at once recalled to testify before an investigating committee of seven, resigning his ministership. The committee report not only exonerated Crawford but left Edwards' reputation severely blemished.

[T. C. Pease, *The Frontier State 1818-48, Centennial History of Illinois;* Ninian W. Edwards, *History of Illinois from 1778 to 1833 and Life and Times of Ninian W. Edwards;* J. E. D. Shipp, *Giant Days, or the Life and Times of William H. Crawford.*]

ALLAN NEVINS

A. B. C. Conference, The, met at Niagara Falls May–July, 1914, after Argentina, Brazil and Chile tendered mediation to prevent a conflict between the United States and the Huerta regime in Mexico (*see* Vera Cruz, 1914). The conference failed because Carranza, victorious in recent battles, rejected its proposal for a provisional government chosen by agreement between the contending factions. Huerta, however, resigned on July 15 and Carranza assumed the presidency on Aug. 22. (*See also* Mexican Relations.)

[*Foreign Relations of the United States,* 1914.]

DANA G. MUNRO

A. E. F. *See* American Expeditionary Forces.

Abbot Downing Coach. *See* Concord Coach.

Abenaki, The, were in colonial times a loose confederacy of Algonkian[qv] tribes occupying the present state of Maine and southern New Brunswick. In a restricted sense the term applied to the Indians of the Kennebec River (and sometimes in a wider sense it covered all the Algonkian tribes of the Atlantic coast). The New England settlers generally called them Tarrateens. Under missionary influence they were active allies of the French against the northern New England settlements, which they ravaged repeatedly, notably during King William's War[qv]. After the Peace of Utrecht[qv] the French maintained their influence, and in consequence of the resumption of irregular attacks on border settlements the New Englanders in 1724 destroyed Norridgewock[qv] on the Kennebec, the center of the French mission to the Abenaki. The Kennebec population was dispersed, mainly to Canada, where their principal settlement developed on the St. Francis River near its juncture with the St. Lawrence. The Penobscot and Passamaquoddy, and the Malecite to the east of them, did not move to Canada, and in 1749 the Penobscot made their peace with the English. Some Indians returned to Norridgewock, but it was attacked in 1749, and in 1754 its inhabitants migrated again to St. Francis, which, although ravaged in 1759 by Robert Rogers'

Rangers (*see* St. Francis, Rogers' Expedition Against), has remained the principal home of the remnants of the Abenaki tribe.

[F. W. Hodge, *Handbook of American Indians North of Mexico.*]

REGINALD G. TROTTER

Abilene, Kans., an early cow town, was established by Joseph G. McCoy in 1867 as a depot to which Texas cattle might be driven for shipment by rail to Kansas City (*see* Abilene Trail; *also* Chisholm Trail). Attempts of trail drivers[qv] to reach market in 1866 had largely failed due to the hostility of the settlers of Missouri and eastern Kansas, who feared the introduction of Texas fever. Located on the Kansas Pacific Railway[qv] west of all settlement, Abilene was for two or three years a popular shipping point until the westward advance of settlers forced the drovers to new cow towns[qv] farther west.

[Joseph G. McCoy, *Historic Sketches of the Cattle Trade and Southwest.*]

EDWARD EVERETT DALE

Abilene Trail, The, was a cattle trail leading from Texas to Abilene[qv], Kans. Its exact route is disputed owing to its many offshoots, but it crossed the Red River a little east of Henrietta, Tex., and continued north across the Indian Territory[qv] to Caldwell, Kans., and on past Wichita[qv] and Newton to Abilene. The first herds were probably driven over it in 1866, though it was not named until Abilene was established in 1867.

EDWARD EVERETT DALE

Ab-Initio Movement, The, was a controversy that originated during Reconstruction[qv] in Texas in 1866. In the constitutional convention of that year the question arose, "Was secession null and void from the beginning (*ab-initio*) or became null and void as a result of the war?" The staunch unionists or radicals took the position that it was null and void from the beginning and therefore all laws based upon secession were null and void and all public and private relations based upon such laws were null and void. This contention was rejected by the governor, military officers, both constitutional conventions and by the Republican State Convention, but it seriously divided the party of Reconstruction. Two brothers assumed leadership of the respective groups, Morgan Hamilton of the Ab-Initios and ex-Gov. A. J. Hamilton of the anti-ab-initios. This heated controversy continued over a period of three years. A. J. Hamilton and the conservatives finally emerged victorious but not until compromise had been made.

[C. W. Ramsdell, *Reconstruction in Texas.*]

J. G. SMITH

Ableman v. Booth, 1859 (21 How. 506), provided Chief Justice Taney with an opportunity for a masterly analysis of Federal and state powers. Sherman Booth, sentenced to jail by a Federal court for assisting in the rescue of a fugitive slave at Milwaukee, was released on a writ of habeas corpus[qv] issued by a judge of the Supreme Court of Wisconsin on the ground that the Fugitive Slave Act[qv] was unconstitutional. The case was carried to the United States Supreme Court[qv] which rendered a unanimous opinion pronouncing the Fugitive Slave Act valid and forbidding a state to interfere with Federal prisoners by habeas corpus writs.

[J. B. McMaster, *History of the People of the United States*, Vol. VIII; C. B. Swisher, *Roger B. Taney;* Homer Cummings and Carl McFarland, *Federal Justice.*]

JOHN G. VAN DEUSEN

Abolition Movement, The. The first recorded vote against slavery in the United States was that on Feb. 18, 1688, by the Monthly Meeting of the Germantown, Pa., Society of Friends (*see* Quakers). Long before that, even in 1624, protests were heard against slavery in the colonies, both in the South and in the North. When the Revolution came, it was plain to increasing numbers that slavery was inconsistent with the sentiments of the Declaration of Independence[qv]. In Jefferson's first draft of that document the slave trade[qv] was described as a "cruel war against human nature itself, violating its most sacred rights of life and liberty." Negroes were freed on enlisting in the Continental armies, in which many served.

The early formation of antislavery societies[qv] during and immediately after the Revolution showed the strength of the opposition to slavery which waxed until the invention of Eli Whitney's cotton gin[qv] in 1793 enthroned King Cotton[qv], made slaves valuable, and, together with the Missouri Compromise[qv], caused the dying out of antislavery sentiment. With each year of cotton prosperity the bitterness against all who attacked the human property of the South rose. Still James G. Birney, William Swaim, Cassius M. Clay, John Rankin, John G. Fee, and other Southerners worked steadily in the South for Abolition.

For the corresponding appearance in the North by 1830 of a militant antislavery movement[qv] there were various reasons, among them the general awakening of a more humanitarian[qv] spirit as shown by the reforming of jails, hospitals and orphanages, the growth of the temperance movement[qv], and the beginning of the agitation for women's rights and suffrage[qqv]. At this time there appeared a number of leaders and agitators, among the first being Benjamin Lundy, who in turn inspired William Lloyd Garrison, the founding of whose *Liberator*[qv], with his determined announcement: "I will be as harsh as truth and as uncompromising as justice . . . I will not retreat a single inch, and I will be heard," brought about instant repercussions in the South. Within a year the legislature of Georgia offered a reward of $5000 for Garrison's "arrest and conviction."

The Garrison wing was uncompromisingly for immediate emancipation, refused to act politically, violently denounced all who disagreed with its policies, had little to do with the Middle Western and political movements and was as offensive to the moderate wing as to the slaveholders. At first the Church in the North was hostile to the Abolitionists (*see* Slavery, Attitude of Churches to); every church in Boston was closed to them. But gradually there appeared a group of great preachers, such as Theodore Parker, William Ellery Channing, Samuel J. May, and, later, Henry Ward Beecher and others, to espouse the cause of the slave. Other outstanding leaders were Theodore D. Weld, Wendell Phillips, Albert Gallatin, and John Quincy Adams then in the House of Representatives, although he refused to ally himself directly with the Abolition movement. Soon Abolitionists entered Northern state legislatures and Congress, in which, prior to 1835, there was only one, William Slade of Vermont.

Thereafter Abolition was in politics to dominate everything until Emancipation[qv]. To this end the annexation of Texas, the war with Mexico, the Fugitive Slave Law, the Kansas-Nebraska Act, "Bleeding Kansas," the determination of the slaveholders to extend their "peculiar system"[qqv], all contributed and gave the Abolitionists their opportunity to appeal to the conscience of the nation and keep the country in a turmoil. To this, two books contributed enormously, Harriet Beecher Stowe's *Uncle Tom's Cabin*[qv] (1852) and Hinton Rowan Helper's *The Impending Crisis of the South*[qv] (1859). From 1850 on, the history of Abolition is the history of the nation, and John Brown's Harpers Ferry raid[qv] the curtain-raiser to the bloody years which ended in April, 1865.

[G. H. Barnes, *The Antislavery Impulse.*]

OSWALD GARRISON VILLARD

Abolitionist Literature extended from 1820 to the Civil War[qv] and included many varieties, namely: newspapers, published letters, the *Annual Reports* and other publications of the antislavery societies[qv], sermons and addresses condemning slavery[qv], the narratives and lives of escaped slaves and kidnapped free Negroes, William Lloyd Garrison's *Thoughts on African Colonization* (1832), a denunciation of the principles and purposes of the American Colonization Society[qv], some popular poems of John Greenleaf Whittier and James Russell Lowell and others, *The Liberty Minstrel* (a collection of songs by George W. Clark which passed through several editions), extended analyses and denunciations of the Fugitive Slave Act of 1850[qv] (some of which were reprinted several times), *Uncle Tom's Cabin*[qv] and subsequent works by Harriet Beecher Stowe, and the Rev. W. M. Mitchell's *Underground Railroad* (1860), which gave a glimpse at the secret methods of helping the runaways.

The great number of antislavery newspapers began with Charles Osborn's *Philanthropist* (1820) and Benjamin Lundy's *Genius of Universal Emancipation*[qv] (1821), both originating at Mt. Pleasant, Ohio, and *The Castigator* (1824) at Ripley, Ohio. *Letters on American Slavery* (1826) by the Rev. John Rankin passed through five editions by 1838. Having read the little book, Garrison became Rankin's "disciple." The Rev. Samuel Crothers, Rankin's contemporary and not distant neighbor, also abhorred slavery, as shown in his *Life and Writings* (1857). Antislavery societies became numerous in the North after 1832 and often had hundreds of members, by whom their *Annual Reports* were read. These abolitionists[qv] also read such publications as *The Anti-Slavery Almanac,* Theodore Dwight Weld's *Slavery as It Is, The Anti-Slavery Manual, The Cabinet of Freedom, The Liberty Bell,* Jay's *View of the Action of the Federal Government on Slavery,* Horace Mann's *Slavery: Letters and Speeches,* E. B. Chase's *Teachings of Patriots and Statesmen,* and the memoirs of escaped slaves, including Frederick Douglas' *My Bondage and My Freedom,* C. E. Stevens' *Anthony Burns,* the *Narrative of Henry Box Brown,* and J. R. Giddings' *The Exiles of Florida;* also the few but stirring memoirs of abductors of slaves. Occasionally a runaway's narrative sold up to 10,000 copies. *Uncle Tom's Cabin* (1852) quickly made a "mass appeal" and intensified Northern hatred of the Fugitive Slave Law of 1850. Mrs. Stowe's *Key to Uncle Tom's Cabin* (1853) fed fuel to the fire, and her *Dred* increased the excitement over the Kansas struggle[qv] and the assault on Charles Sumner (*see* Brooks-Sumner Affair).

[*Ohio State Archæological and Historical Quarterly*, July, 1937; A. B. Hart, *Slavery and Abolition;* Henry Wilson,

Rise and Fall of the Slave Power in America; and the publications referred to above.]

WILBUR H. SIEBERT

Abominations, Tariff of. *See* Tariff of Abominations.

Abraham, Plains of, on the west side of the city of Quebec, were named after Abraham Martin, a Quebec pilot, who once owned part of the land. They were the scene, in 1759, of the battle (*see* Quebec, Capture of) that brought an end to the dream of French empire in North America, and, incidentally, resulted in the death of two great generals, Wolfe and Montcalm. The site is now a Canadian national park.

LAWRENCE J. BURPEE

Abraham Lincoln, Fort, was built by Gen. George A. Custer in 1873, on the Missouri River, just below Heart River. Fort McKean, on top a hill above this fort, was an infantry post, and though built first, was usually considered part of Fort Abraham Lincoln. In 1895 the fort was abandoned. Fort Lincoln was authorized the same year to be built near the city of Bismarck, N. Dak., as an eight-company post. Buildings were constructed in 1903, but the post was abandoned until 1927. It is the only surviving military post in North Dakota.

[L. F. Crawford, *History of North Dakota.*]

CARL L. CANNON

Absentee Ownership, as commonly conceived, is a type of organization where management and direction are separated in whole or in part from actual ownership. Usually the owner is not present where operations are carried on, although, upon occasions, he may be on the spot. Such conditions are as old as the centuries. At the very beginning of American settlement there existed in colonization, or trading, companies, resident owners—in most cases largely a fiction—and directing owners, who lived in England. In very early times, in the southern colonies, the need of continually taking up new land imposed upon owners a system of direction by means of which some holdings were managed by overseers. These persons were often ex-indentured servants who had been trained to plantation conditions. In later plantation days, notably after the great development of cotton as a commercial crop, the management of plantations by overseers became a rather common occurrence. Some shipping ventures in New England properly belong in the class of agent direction. Captains and crews of merchant vessels were sometimes merely contract representatives of the actual owners, or operated under some kind of share system, by means of which they obtained some of the profits in the ventures.

It is in recent times, however, that the question of absentee ownership has become a live question. Two fields in which it is an issue are in farm tenancy[qv] and in the growth of the industrial corporation. The corporation idea is as old as Roman law, perhaps in its "entity" aspect, as old as the human race. The concept was preserved in the mediæval municipal corporation, and adapted, notably in the 19th century, to business practices. The significant fact in this development is that the corporation became a kind of little republic with management vested in representatives of stockholders (directors), the stockholders themselves taking no part in the management. In fact, stockholders may be dispersed over wide areas, as with such large organizations as General Motors[qv]. Such development has been made possible by the use of evidences of property—stock, bonds, notes, mortgages, leases. In American practice, at least in the earlier days of the Constitution, the corporate form was looked upon with suspicion, possibly as an outward and visible sign of monopoly[qv]. The earliest corporations in the United States were in turnpikes, banking, and shipping ventures, where the need of large capital and limited liability made this form desirable. The first organizations of this type came into existence under special charter; it was not until the decade 1840 to 1850 that the states began to grant charters of general incorporation. In the banking field, free banking[qv] is an illustration; but after 1860 the corporation was to an ever increasing extent adopted for industrial and commercial purposes. Out of the corporate idea has developed in quite recent times the concept of trusteeship. This applies not only to financial institutions, but more and more to industrial and commercial companies. That is to say, that the directors occupy a position of trust and confidence with respect to stockholders.

Some idea of the growth of the corporate form is seen by its use in manufacture. By the census of 1929 some 210,000 establishments were in this form. They turned out goods worth over $69,000,000,000. A similar condition exists in mining, forestry, commerce, finance, and transport. Another view is contained in the value of listed securities on the New York Stock Exchange[qv]. On June 30, 1938, the value of listed bonds was over $49,000,000,000. The total shares of listed stock were 1,426,800,000,000 with a market value of over $41,900,000,000. This says nothing about shares listed on the Curb and other exchanges.

Shortly before the panic of 1929[qv] corporate farming was beginning to make considerable headway. Stocks and bonds were sold in many communities. Such enterprises were organized after the manner of industrial corporations, with directors, general managers, superintendents, foremen, and general run of workers. In another aspect farming presents a case of absentee ownership, namely, in the various types of tenancy. This condition has been increasing over the last thirty years. In 1930, 42.4% of American farms were operated by tenants. Whether or not this condition is socially desirable is a debatable question. Some investigators have suggested that, in many cases, tenancy is only a temporary status. The young man starts as a tenant, gradually accumulates funds, and ultimately becomes an owner. Besides tenancy, in 1930, about 55,000 farms in this country were operated by managers. Mechanization of farms, the condition of the terrain in some areas, and the kinds of crops are factors in determining the type of management.

[P. A. Bruce, *Economic History of Virginia in the Seventeenth Century;* W. B. Weeden, *Economic and Social History of New England, 1620-1789*, Vol. II; *Hunt's Merchants' Magazine*, volumes from 1840 to 1850 relative to the Corporation.]

ISAAC LIPPINCOTT

Absentee Voting was first permitted to Union soldiers in the field during the Civil War, and some states today restrict such voting to persons in the military or naval service of the government. Beginning, however, with Vermont (1896) and Kansas (1901, 1911), nearly all states have enacted laws permitting civilians who expect to be absent from their home precincts on an election day—including traveling salesmen, government officials, railway and steamship employees, and college and university students—to cast ballots either before leaving home or *in absentia*. The more generous laws also permit absentee voting on account of illness or disability.

[P. O. Ray, *Introduction to Political Parties and Practical Politics*, 3rd ed.]

P. ORMAN RAY

Abundant Life, The More, a phrase of scriptural flavor used by President Franklin D. Roosevelt in his address before the Inter-American Conference for the Maintenance of Peace, Buenos Aires, Argentina, Dec. 1, 1936, to signify the improved living conditions and enlarged cultural and economic opportunities available to the whole world through the maintenance in the Western Hemisphere of constitutional representative government based on faith in God.

[F. D. Roosevelt, *The Public Papers and Addresses*, Vol. V.]

STANLEY R. PILLSBURY

Academic Freedom represents the traditional right of the scholar to study and teach as his conscience may dictate. It was reflected in the chartered special privileges of scholars and universities in Europe and England, and developed in the several countries in accordance with their general views regarding freedom.

In the United States the early colleges and universities[qv] were under ecclesiastical leadership, and occasionally difficulties arose from philosophical independence. However, some colonial colleges by charter provisions prohibited religious tests, and laid foundations for freedom not only from political but also from ecclesiastical authority.

During the 19th century four developments made academic freedom an important issue. First, the emphasis upon research which accompanied the change of many colleges into universities, either in organization or in spirit, raised controversial questions. Second, the impact of scientific research and philosophic speculation upon religious belief produced tension. The evolutionary theory[qv], for example, was a focal center of this issue for about fifty years. Third, the development of private philanthropy as the basis for the support of colleges and universities led in some instances to attempts to please actual or prospective donors by limitations upon teaching and research. Fourth, state support and control of universities raised problems when professors were critical of measures or policies of the state government. With local exceptions, however, the struggle for academic freedom was won.

A new phase occurred with the rise of the state and the growth of political control of social and economic matters. It reached an acute stage with the World War, and since that time has been chronic because of the appearance of the self-conscious totalitarianism of Communism, Fascism, and Nazism, all which reject the basic assumptions of academic freedom. These developments made the academic community more jealous of its rights; fears aroused by real or fancied penetration of Communistic or Fascist ideals, thought to be fostered by some members of faculties, led to conflicts and occasional incidents. Thus far, with relatively few local exceptions, academic freedom has been maintained.

HENRY M. WRISTON

Academies. There have been three types of secondary schools in the United States: the Latin grammar school[qv] of the Colonial Period; the academy which began about the middle of the 18th century and continued for nearly a century; and the public high school[qv]. The Latin grammar school was displaced by the academy and the academy was largely displaced by the public high school.

An early school of this kind grew out of the work of Benjamin Franklin in Philadelphia. Most of the early academies, however, seem to have been the fruits of denominational interests, and most of them were private institutions, although some states undertook to provide for county systems of academies. They were also under the control of self-perpetuating boards of trustees, were often chartered by the legislatures of the various states and had the right to own and control property, to receive gifts and endowments, and to engage and dismiss their teachers. These institutions went by a variety of names, such as academy, institution, seminary, collegiate institute, and sometimes college. There were academies for boys, academies for girls, and in some cases these schools were co-educational. Tuition fees were usually charged but occasionally the legislature would charter an academy or grant it other privileges with the provision that poor children should be taught gratuitously. The academy movement spread widely. It was reported that by 1830 there were 1000 such incorporated institutions in the United States and within two decades probably more than 6000, instructing more than 260,000 pupils.

The academies stimulated interest in the training of teachers and may be considered the forerunner of the normal schools[qv]. Many became the nuclei from which collegiate institutions developed. They served also to encourage the education of girls and women. Variants of the academy appeared in the manual labor schools and in military schools.

[Edgar W. Knight, *Education in the United States.*]

EDGAR W. KNIGHT

Acadia and the Acadians. The name Acadia, whether of European origin or a derivative of the Indian word *Aquoddiake,* was first applied in letters-patent to the grant obtained by Pierre de Guast, Sieur de Monts, from the King of France, Nov. 18, 1603. The boundaries of Acadia, never clearly defined, roughly embraced the North American coast from Cape Breton to the shores below the Hudson (40° to 46° N. Lat.) and overlapped considerably the land claimed by England by virtue of Cabot's discovery (*see* Cabot, Voyages) and Sir Humphrey Gilbert's possessory claim in the 16th century. Such was the basis for the conflicting claims of England and France to North America which resulted in a hundred and fifty years of predatory warfare, during which time Acadia, unproductive and desolate, was traded back and forth between the two powers as English and French diplomats sought to adjust the balance of losses and acquisitions elsewhere.

Although by the Treaty of Utrecht, 1713[qv], "all Nova Scotia with its ancient boundaries" was ceded to England, French empire builders saw the advantage of tacitly narrowing the indefinite limits of Nova Scotia to what is now the peninsula bearing that name, and England, faced with the necessity of holding the land from the Kennebec to the St. Croix, came to view the French inhabitants of the peninsula, the Acadians, with alarm. By 1755 new colonial wars had broken out. The Acadians, both the victims and oftentimes the participators in maundering warfare, charged by the English with disloyalty undoubtedly fostered by Jesuit priests, were believed to menace the English colonial possessions from within. By an act of extreme severity, immortalized by Longfellow in his *Evangeline*[qv], over 4000 of these Acadians were uprooted from their homes and dispersed to other English colonies, principally Maryland and Virginia. Some made their way to the West Indies and Louisiana (*see* Acadians in Louisiana). Many found their way back, however, and today their descendants may be found in Nova Scotia as well as in Madawaska, Maine.

[F. Parkman, *A Half-Century of Conflict* and his *Montcalm and Wolfe;* J. B. Brebner, *New England's Outpost.*]

ELIZABETH RING

Acadian Coast, THE, is the section of Louisiana along the Mississippi River settled by the exiled Acadians[qv] after about 1760. While applying particularly to the present parish of St. James, the term is sometimes used to designate the scattered Acadian settlements on the Mississippi as far as the mouth of Red River.

[C. Gayarré, *History of Louisiana;* A. Fortier, *Louisiana,* Cyclopedic.]

WALTER PRICHARD

Acadians in Louisiana, THE. It is not known that any of the Acadians came directly from their homeland to Louisiana. They came in irregular groups and at irregular intervals, having first attempted to settle at other places without success. Some came by ship to New Orleans from the New England and Atlantic seaboard colonies, but the majority came overland, from Maryland, Pennsylvania, and Virginia, by trail across the mountains and by flatboat[qv] down the Tennessee, the Ohio, and the Mississippi rivers. This accounts for the fact that some came after the first deportation, while others did not arrive until 1766. From New Orleans they were first sent some fifty miles up the river to what is now St. James Parish (county) and gave the name of Acadian Coast[qv] to that section of the river. Others pushed up the river as far as Pointe Coupée[qv], in the parish of that name. Later arrivals were sent westward into southern Louisiana, from 70 to 100 miles from New Orleans, along Bayou Lafourche and Bayou Teche, into the region protected by the frontier *postes* of Attakapas and Opelousas.

At the former *poste* they largely founded the town of Saint Martinville, which soon became and has remained the center of the Acadian life in Louisiana. Land was given them in this frontier region, they built their homes and furnished them largely with handmade furniture that may still be seen throughout south Louisiana. An industrious and prolific people, in this genial climate they rapidly increased in numbers and spread westward into the parish which bears their name, Acadia, and the surrounding territory. They and their descendants have been largely farmers, but some became merchants and stock raisers, while some entered the professions. In the region of the Teche and Lafourche they developed a characteristic culture that exists today despite modern changes.

Until the last three decades their language was almost entirely French, and they developed a characteristic dialect which has been the subject of recent interesting study. For many years their newspapers were published in French. However, public education has, during the present century, taken rapid hold among them, the speaking and study of English is compulsory in all schools, so that all of the present generation know and speak English, though French is still the family tongue. The French press has disappeared.

Saint Martinville is one of the most charming towns in Louisiana, and a Mecca for tourists. Here on the banks of the Teche stands the "Evangeline Oak," and nearby in the churchyard of Saint Martin is the grave of Evangeline[qv], marked by a life-size bronze statue, for here lived Emmeline Labiche, the original of Longfellow's heroine. Not far distant is the Evangeline State Park, a beautiful tract along the Teche, where there is preserved a typical Acadian farm dwelling, furnished as they originally stood.

No record was kept of the numbers of Acadians who arrived in Louisiana. Dudley LeBlanc, in his *True Story of the Acadians,* states that 2500 came by way of France, and that the total number was 5000. This appears to be an exaggeration for the total number deported is given as 5788, by Ficklin. In 1787, which was thirty-two years after the beginning of the deportations, Gov. Miro of Louisiana had a census of the Acadians taken, and reported the number in the province as 1587. It would appear that the number did not exceed 2000 altogether, or at most 2500. Today they number more than 300,000, and their region is the most densely populated section of the state.

[Alcée Fortier, *Louisiana Studies;* Margaret A. Johnston, *In Acadia;* Alcée Fortier, Acadians, in *Louisiana,* Cyclopedic; Charles Gayarré, *History of Louisiana.*]

J. FAIR HARDIN

Acceptance Business and Foreign Trade. A bank acceptance is a time bill of exchange[qv], drawn on a bank and accepted by it. The Federal Reserve Act[qv] granted member banks the privilege of accepting drafts against them arising from the domestic shipment or storage of goods, or from the exportation or importation of goods and the storage or shipment thereof in or between foreign nations.

The development of dollar acceptances during the World War enabled United States bankers to gain practically all of our import and export financing, and eventually to engage in the financing of trade between European nations. Since 1920 most of the foreign patronage has returned to European bankers, although American shippers continued to use dollar acceptances almost exclusively. Approximately 75% of current United States bankers' acceptances have arisen from the importation, exportation, or shipment of our goods in foreign trade.

[W. R. Burgess, *The Reserve Banks and the Money Market.*]

FRANK PARKER

Acceptance Speech. *See* Notification Speech.

Accidents. In an average year, only four diseases kill more people than accidents. Accidents lead all causes of death for both sexes between the ages of three and twenty-one, and among males from three to forty. Among males of all ages, heart disease alone kills a greater number, while among females, accidents rank between sixth and seventh as a cause of death. While man has always suffered from accidental injuries, with the introduction of factory systems and the development of machines, railroads, automobiles, and hundreds of mechanical devices, an era fraught with many new and unforeseen hazards was ushered in. It was not so many years ago, however, that serious thought concerning accident prevention started to supersede the old philosophy that mishaps were acts of God.

Probably the first step in the control of untoward events were mechanical safeguards. In 1833, Stephenson suggested steam whistles for locomotives. It was in 1868 that Westinghouse perfected the first air brake, and the first test of automatic car couplers was made in 1885. By 1893, standard safety equipment was required on all railroad trains through the adoption of the Federal Safety Appliance Act. It was not before 1900, however, that railroads began to organize definite campaigns against accidents.

It was about this time, shortly before the first workmen's compensation[qv] laws were passed, that some industrial plants began to practise organized accident prevention. In 1912, a small group of men interested in accident prevention met in Milwaukee, under the Association of Iron and Steel Electrical Engineers. This group decided that by exchanging ideas on a co-operative basis, much greater progress might be made in the control of accidents. Out of this meeting was evolved the idea for a national association that would act as a clearing house for the best ideas in accident prevention. At a convention called in New York City for the following year, the National Safety Council for Industrial Safety was formally organized. With the automobile had come the problem of public safety, and in 1915 the name was changed to the National Safety Council and the constitution altered to include a national program of public as well as industrial safety.

The motor age has brought an enormously increased accident toll. In 1937 there were 39,500 traffic deaths, 1,360,000 personal injuries and an economic loss of $1,700,000,000. This toll is four fifths as great as American losses in the World War, and is equivalent to the destruction of a city like Waltham, Mass., or Santa Monica, Calif.

Deaths from home accidents each year rank second only to traffic fatalities. In 1937 they caused 32,500 deaths and 4,700,000 non-fatal injuries. About 140,000 of these were permanent disabilities.

Each year since 1913 has seen considerable improvement in industrial safety. At that time there were about 35,000 workers killed yearly in occupational accidents, although fewer persons were working then than now. In 1937, there were 19,500 occupational deaths, a reduction of 44% since 1913.

[Stewart Holbrook, *Let Them Live.*]

W. H. CAMERON

Accomac. *See* Bacon's Rebellion.

Ackia, Battle of. On May 26, 1736, the Chickasaws[qv] decisively defeated the French under Bienville at Ackia, near present Tupelo, Miss. This defeat reduced French prestige in that quarter, where French and English traders were engaged in a contest for control of Indian trade. (*See also* Chickasaw-French War.)

[J. F. H. Claiborne, *Mississippi, as a Province, Territory and State;* Charles Gayarré, *History of Louisiana;* Dunbar Rowland, *History of Mississippi.*]

WALTER PRICHARD

Acoma is the name of both an Indian tribe and its pueblo, perched on a bold rock extending 357 feet into the air in Valencia County, N. Mex. It was discovered by the Spanish in 1539 and at one time had a large population. The Indians gained subsistence by cultivating gardens near the base of the rock which they reached by a dizzy trail cut in the rock. In 1599 the rock was scaled by the Spaniards who, after a three days' battle, killed about 1500 Acoma, or half the tribe.

[F. W. Hodge, *Handbook of American Indians.*]

CARL L. CANNON

Acre Right. *See* Cabin Right.

Act for the Impartial Administration of Justice, The (one of the Coercion Acts[qv]), passed by Parliament in May, 1774, provided that whenever the governor of Massachusetts doubted whether a person accused of misconduct in suppressing a riot or executing the law could secure a fair trial in Massachusetts, he might, with consent of the Council, transfer the trial to another colony or to Great Britain. This act—known in America as the "Murder Act"—aroused the colonists' apprehensions that the British government intended to establish a military despotism by giving British soldiers the privilege of shooting down Whigs with impunity.

[C. H. Van Tyne, *The Causes of the War of Independence.*]

JOHN C. MILLER

Acting. *See* Drama, The American.

Active Case, The, known as Olmstead et als. v. Rittenhouse's Executives, raised the question of prerogative as between Federal and state courts. Olmstead of Connecticut and others seized the British sloop *Active* (1777), which was later captured by the Pennsylvania armed brig *Convention,* commanded by Houston. Award of prize money[qv] to Houston and his crew by state courts of Pennsylvania was set aside by the Supreme Court (1809) after a bitter dispute regarding jurisdiction.

WHEELER PRESTON

Acts of Trade. *See* Navigation Acts, The.

Adair v. U. S., 1908 (208 U. S. 161). In violation of a Federal law of 1898, William Adair, acting for the L. & N. Railroad[qv], dismissed O. B.

Coppage because he was a member of a labor union. The Supreme Court declared this law unconstitutional because it violated the right of personal liberty and of property guaranteed by the Fifth Amendment[qv].

[Charles Warren, *The Supreme Court in the United States.*]

E. MERTON COULTER

Adams, Fort (Miss.), built 1798–99 by Maj. Thomas Freeman eight miles above the 31st parallel on the east bank of the Mississippi River (Loftus Heights[qv]), was an earthwork, magazine, and barracks for boundary defense (*see* Southern Boundary, Survey of the) against the Spanish, just removed from Natchez[qv] and confined to Louisiana and Florida (*see* Pinckney's Treaty). It was the United States port of entry on the Mississippi.

Here Gen. James Wilkinson negotiated a treaty with the Choctaws (Dec. 12, 1801) for resurveying the British line from the Yazoo southward marking limits of the Natchez District, and for a road (Natchez Trace) through Choctaw country to the Chickasaws, thence to Nashville[qqv]. Negotiations for a road to Mobile were opened but abandoned for fear of Spanish hostility. Wilkinson completed the resurvey in 1803. Congress appropriated $6000 for the Trace (1806). After American acquisition of Louisiana and Flordia[qqv], Fort Adams was abandoned.

[Dunbar Rowland, *Mississippi*, Vol. I; American State Papers, *Indian Affairs*, Vol. I; C. E. Carter, Territorial Papers of the United States, Vol. V, *The Territory of Mississippi.*]

MACK SWEARINGEN

Adams Express Company. In 1839 Alvin Adams, a produce merchant ruined by the panic of 1837[qv], began carrying letters, small packages and valuables for patrons between Boston and Worcester. He had at first a partner named Burke, who soon withdrew, and as Adams & Company, Adams rapidly extended his territory to New York, Philadelphia and other eastern cities. By 1847 he had penetrated deeply into the South, and by 1850 he was shipping by rail and stagecoach to St. Louis. In 1854 his company was reorganized as the Adams Express Company. Meanwhile, a subsidiary concern, Adams & Company of California, had been organized in 1850 and spread its service all over the Pacific Coast; but not being under Adams' personal management, it was badly handled, and failed in 1854, causing a panic which shook California to its depths. The South was almost entirely covered by the Adams express service in 1861, when the Civil War necessitated the splitting off of another company, which, for politic reasons, was given the name of Southern. There was a mysterious kinship between the two ever afterward, they having joint offices at common points. Southern stock was never quoted in the market, and it was even charged by some Adams stockholders that the Southern was secretly owned by the Adams. The parent company held a strong position from New England and the mid-Atlantic coast to the far Western plains. Its stock holdings were enormous. In 1910 it was the second largest stockholder in the Pennsylvania Railroad[qv] and the third largest in the New Haven, besides owning large blocks of American Express, Norfolk & Western and other shares. Its ante bellum employment of Allan Pinkerton to solve its robbery problems was a large factor in building up that noted detective agency[qv]. Along with the other expresses, it merged its shipping interests into the American Railway Express Company, but continued its corporate existence as a wealthy investment trust.

[Alvin F. Harlow, *Old Waybills.*]

ALVIN F. HARLOW

Adams-Onís Treaty, THE, signed at Washington, Feb. 22, 1819, by John Quincy Adams, Secretary of State, and Luis de Onís, Spanish Minister, closed the first era of United States expansion by providing for the cession of East Florida[qv], the abandonment of the controversy over West Florida[qv], which had previously been seized by the United States (*see* Mobile Seized, 1813), and a boundary delineation along the Sabine River from the Gulf of Mexico to the 32nd parallel, N. Lat., thence north to the Red River, along it to the 100th parallel, W. Long., north to the Arkansas, along it to its source, thence directly north or south as the case might be to the 42nd parallel, N. Lat., and west on that line to the Pacific Ocean (*see* Oregon Question, The). The United States assumed claims of its own citizens against Spain, prorating them down to a maximum of $5,000,000. Non-conflicting articles of Pinckney's Treaty of 1795[qv] were to remain in force. Spanish goods received certain tariff privileges in Florida ports.

Spain, weakened by European wars and colonial revolutions, was obliged to sacrifice her interests, especially after Andrew Jackson's seizure of Spanish property in the Floridas in 1818 (*see* Arbuthnot and Ambrister, Case of). Other nations declined to assist Spain in the negotiations. Ferdinand VII's ministers at first refused to ratify the treaty, using as a pretext the nullification of certain land grants made by Ferdinand in the Floridas. Evasion failed, and after a revolt made Ferdinand a constitutional monarch in 1820, his council was obliged to approve the treaty. Ratifications were exchanged at Washington on Feb. 22, 1821. (*See also* Louisiana Purchase, Boundaries of.)

[Hunter Miller, *Treaties and Other International Acts of the United States of America.*]

PHILIP COOLIDGE BROOKS

Adamson Act, THE, enacted under Administration pressure backed by a strike threat, was passed Sept. 2, 1916. It established, in place of a ten, an eight-hour day*qv* for railroad trainmen. The alternative of 100 miles of run remained unchanged. The railroads claimed the law raised wages rather than regulated hours, as normal operation required over eight hours work. The law was upheld, in Wilson v. New (243 U. S. 332), as hour legislation in the interests of interstate commerce*qv*.

[J. R. Commons and J. B. Andrews, *Principles of Labor Legislation.*]

JAMES D. MAGEE

Adding Machine. *See* Business, Mechanical Devices Used in.

"Address of the Southern Delegates" (1848). Southern delegates in Congress, aroused by hostile resolutions on slavery, called a caucus for Dec. 23, 1848. John C. Calhoun submitted an address "moderate in manner" but calculated to unite the South which, with three amendments that did not "affect the truth of its narrative, or materially change its character," was finally adopted on Jan. 22, 1849, after Berrien's substitute had been rejected. Calhoun's address relates entirely to the sectional contest over slavery and recounts the aggressions of the North on the South. These aggressions were of two kinds: nullification of constitutional guarantees for the return of fugitive slaves*qv*; and the exclusion of slavery and Southerners from the common territories (*see* Wilmot Proviso). Calhoun maintained that these aggressions threatened ultimate abolition and the complete overturn of Southern society unless the South united and brought them to an end. Less than half the Southern delegates signed the address and it accomplished little. (*See also* Tarpley Letter, The.)

[T. H. Benton, *Thirty Years' View;* John C. Calhoun, *Works,* Vol. VI; G. P. Garrison, *Westward Extension;* W. M. Meigs, *Life of John Caldwell Calhoun.*]

FLETCHER M. GREEN

Addyston Pipe Company Case, THE, 1899 (175 U. S. 211). The Supreme Court, by a unanimous decision based on the Sherman Anti-Trust Act*qv*, permanently enjoined six producers of cast-iron pipe from continuing an agreement eliminating competition among themselves. Justice Peckham, speaking for the Court, denied that the decision in the Knight case*qv* obtained, saying that here was a definite conspiracy to interfere with the flow of interstate commerce and a positive scheme to limit competition and fix prices. This decision indicated that the Sherman Anti-Trust Act possessed "teeth" and tended to restrain similar activities.

[Eliot Jones, *The Trust Problem in the United States;* W. Z. Ripley, *Trusts, Pools and Corporations;* L. B. Evans, *Leading Cases on Constitutional Law.*]

ALLEN E. RAGAN

Adena Prehistoric Culture, THE, a type of Mound Builder*qv* culture, takes its name from a mound at Adena, Ohio. It apparently existed in southern Ohio and adjacent parts of Kentucky, West Virginia and Indiana. The culture is characterized by shapely conical mounds, burials in log cists (usually without cremation), skill in carving small objects in the round, the use of tubular pipes, and a limited use of copper for ornamental purposes. No dwelling sites have been found.

[Henry Clyde Shetrone, *The Mound-Builders.*]

EUGENE H. ROSEBOOM

Adkins v. Children's Hospital, 1923 (261 U. S. 525), was a Supreme Court decision holding invalid an act of Congress creating a Minimum Wage*qv* Board to "ascertain" and "fix" adequate wages for women employees in the District of Columbia.

The question before the Court was whether the act of Congress constituted a deprivation of "life, liberty or property without due process of law" under the Fifth Amendment. The Court held by a vote of five to three that the act was an unjustified interference by Congress with the freedom of employer and employee to contract as they pleased. Taft, Sanford and Holmes, dissenting, took the view that the Fifth Amendment did not stand in the way of reasonable legislation calculated to correct admitted evils. The case was expressly overruled by West Coast Hotel Company v. Parrish*qv* (57 Sup. Ct. 578), 1937.

[Roscoe Pound and others, *The Supreme Court and Minimum Wage Legislation.*]

GEORGE W. GOBLE

Administrative Agency. *See* Congress, The Regulatory Powers of.

Administrative and Political Divisions. *See* Local Government.

Administrative Discretion, Delegation of. Delegation of discretionary power to administrative officials has accompanied the increase in functions of government, particularly regulatory functions, during the past half century. Legislative motives for the delegation have been numerous and varied—to avoid tedious, technical decisions necessary in regulation[qv], to employ a more expert personnel and less formal procedure in discovering facts than is possible in courts of law, to provide continuing, preventive regulation of an elastic character, and even to disguise legislative failure to make a clear-cut decision on questions of policy. Discretionary power has been delegated to the President, governors of states, and municipal executives; but more frequently, where regulation directly affecting the public is involved, authority has been granted to responsible heads of departments or to independent commissions. For example, the Secretaries of Agriculture and Labor, the Interstate Commerce and Federal Trade Commissions[qqv], state directors of banking, state public utility commissions, and local health officers or boards of health exercise important discretionary powers.

Although discretion is commonly labeled "quasi-legislative" or "quasi-judicial"[qv], the classification is chiefly one of convenience; for many (quasi-legislative) rules are made after investigation of a judicial character, and many administrative (quasi-judicial) orders to individuals serve to define a general rule of conduct by establishing precedents. According to American constitutional law, legislatures may not delegate discretionary authority without anchoring it to a basic policy and setting limits to the swing of judgment. As interpreted by the courts this rule has not been a serious check to delegation of power. However, the traditional review by law courts of administrative decisions affecting private rights has greatly curtailed the discretion of administrative officials (*see* Judicial Review). The courts have not only asserted their right to settle questions of law, but have freely substituted their judgment for that of designated officials in deciding questions of fact. Consequently the findings of expert bodies are not infrequently set aside, and their determinations commonly lack finality. Administrative regulation has tended to become a preliminary to the formal judicial prosecution and trial which it was intended to replace (*see* Administrative Justice).

[John Dickinson, *Administrative Justice and the Supremacy of Law.*] GEORGE A. GRAHAM

Administrative Justice or administrative adjudication is a term applied to the procedure whereby the rights of individuals are determined by administrative agencies[qv] rather than by regular courts of law. This procedure is sometimes referred to as "regulation by government" in contrast to "regulation by law."

To some extent, administrative adjudication has existed in the United States from the first. For example, the Patent Office, the Land Office, the Post Office Department and the Treasury Department[qqv] have throughout their existence exercised what amount to judicial powers in some instances. Since early history there have similarly been examples of administrative adjudication in the states, particularly in relation to such matters as taxes and public health.

Since about 1890 there has been a remarkable development of administrative justice. This has been due to the vast increase in the regulatory activity of both the state and Federal governments. As a result, by 1919 Massachusetts had 216 administrative agencies and New York had 187. Each of the other states usually had two score or more. These agencies became responsible for a vast amount of adjudication in relation to banks and other financial institutions, public utilities, sanitation and public health, employment of women and children, conditions of work, industrial accidents, taxes, and so forth. In the period since the World War there has been much improvement in the machinery of administration, at least in those states which have followed the lead of Illinois which in 1917 adopted a comprehensive plan for administrative reorganization. In the reorganized departments which are few in number (ten in Illinois), the practice has been to include special boards to perform quasi-judicial[qv] as well as quasi-legislative functions.

In the Federal Government likewise, there has been a rapid growth of administrative agencies exercising quasi-judicial functions. First are those which are located within other governmental organizations, as, for example, the Board of Appeals created in 1933 in the Veterans' Administration, and the Government Contract Board created in 1936 in the Department of Labor. Another classification consists of independent agencies whose chief function is regulation, such as the Interstate Commerce Commission created in 1887, the Federal Trade Commission set up in 1914, the Securities and Exchange Commission and the Federal Communications Commission both of which came into existence in 1934, the Federal Reserve Board created in 1933, and the National Labor Relations Board authorized by a 1935 act of Congress[qqv]. Under another classification are regular courts of law which have been assigned the functions of reviewing administrative decisions. For example, under the Radio Act of 1927, Congress assigned to the Court of Appeals of the District of Columbia the authority to review the decisions of the Federal Radio Commission. This function was continued in 1934 in relation to the Federal Communications Commission.

Under a separate classification is the United States Tariff Commission[qv] which was created in 1916. It exercises quasi-judicial power in relation to unfair practices in connection with imports. Still another classification includes those agencies in which are vested licensing powers. An example is the Civil Aeronautics Authority created in 1938 to replace a bureau within the Department of Commerce. A separate classification must be given to the Comptroller General[qv] of the United States who, since 1921, has performed a judicial function in reviewing governmental accounts. A separate classification should also be given to executive officials such as the Secretaries of Agriculture, the Interior, and of Labor who, in recent years, have been assigned important functions in connection with administrative adjudication.

Among the most important of the agencies are those which are referred to as independent administrative courts. These agencies perform no functions other than those of a quasi-judicial nature. These administrative courts are the Court of Claims[qv], created in 1855; the Court of Customs and Patents Appeals, created in 1929; and the Board of Tax Appeals, created in 1924.

The development of administrative justice has been not only rapid but haphazard. General procedural rules have not been developed. Rules of evidence vary from those used in regular courts to practically no rules at all. Some administrative agencies hold formal hearings while others are very informal. Most agencies assume jurisdiction of their own volition while in other instances administrative adjudication is initiated by formal or informal complaints by interested parties. Usually the decisions of administrative tribunals can be appealed to regular courts, but in some cases their findings are final, at least as to "fact" if not as to "law." Decisions of some agencies are self-enforcing while those of others require an order from a regular court in order to secure enforcement. Obviously, there is much need for reform in the whole field of administrative justice in the interest of uniformity, efficiency and fair dealing.

[Frederick F. Blachly and Miriam E. Oatman, *Administrative Legislation and Adjudication;* John Dickinson, *Administrative Justice and the Supremacy of Law in the United States.*]

ERIK McKINLEY ERIKSSON

Administrative Reorganization, THE MOVEMENT FOR, had its real beginning in 1910 when President Taft appointed a commission to study the matter. No action resulted. In 1918 Congress passed the Overman Act[qv] under which President Wilson accomplished some reorganization. In 1921 a committee was appointed to investigate proposals for administrative reform but again nothing important was accomplished. In his annual messages to Congress, President Hoover strongly urged on Congress the necessity of reorganization in the interests of efficiency and economy. On June 30, 1932, he was granted the right to reorganize subject to Congressional approval. In the following December he issued eleven executive orders, providing for extensive reorganization but, on Jan. 19, 1933, they were rejected by the House of Representatives. Subsequently, on March 3, 1933, President Hoover signed a bill empowering his successor for a period of two years to reorganize the administration as he saw fit. President Franklin D. Roosevelt issued forty-one executive orders under this law but failed to bring about any far-reaching reorganization. For a time the matter was dropped but on Jan. 12, 1937, the President again asked for broad reorganization powers. On March 29, 1939, Congress completed action on a bill granting him a limited power to reorganize.

[L. F. Schmeckebier, Organization of the Executive Branch of the National Government of the United States, *American Political Science Review*, XXVII-XXIX (1933-35); The President's Committee, *Administrative Management.*]

ERIK McKINLEY ERIKSSON

Admirals. The highest rank in the American navy until 1862 was captain, for commodore was merely a courtesy title for a captain in charge of more than one ship. Admiral was thought to savor of aristocracy. But in 1862, Congress, in order to honor Farragut for his victory at New Orleans (1862)[qv], made him a rear admiral, and after Mobile (1864)[qv], a vice admiral. In 1866 he was made an admiral for life. Three years after Farragut's death in 1870, David D. Porter, who had been a vice admiral since 1866, was appointed admiral, which grade he retained till his death in 1891. In 1899 George Dewey was made Admiral of the Navy and remained so until he died in 1917. Controversy over the battle of Santiago[qv] prevented the award of admiral or vice admiral to either Sampson or Schley.

When the navy was expanded in 1915, Congress made provision for the rank of admiral and vice admiral to be held temporarily by the officers in first and second command respectively of the principal fleets, and in 1916 the rank, pay, and privileges of an admiral were assigned to the Chief of Naval Operations, who was to outrank all the rest. As in the Spanish-American

War, the close of the World War brought disputes regarding the relative merits of the various fleet commanders and Washington bureau chiefs. These jealousies prevented any naval officer from being granted the coveted right to fly permanently the four-starred admiral's flag.

[L. P. Lovette, *Naval Customs, Traditions, and Usage.*]

WALTER B. NORRIS

Admiralty Law and Courts. In the American colonies in the 17th century admiralty jurisdiction was generally exercised by the ordinary common law courts, although governors had the right to commission courts of vice admiralty; but by the end of the century royal patents were being issued for the establishment of vice admiralty courts, beginning in New York in 1696. In addition to the jurisdiction of the English admiralty courts over such matters as prize, wreck, salvage, insurance, freight and passenger contracts, bottomry, charter parties and seamen's wages, the colonial vice admiralty courts enforced the Acts of Trade[qv]. Piracy, which originally was under the jurisdiction of the admiralty, was in the colonies normally dealt with by courts specially commissioned by the crown to deal with particular cases. Procedure in vice admiralty was *in rem* rather than *in personam.* As the vice admiralty courts exercised summary jurisdiction and did not have trial by jury, they attained a considerable degree of unpopularity among that element in the colonies opposed to the Acts of Trade, and in some colonies writs of prohibition were frequently issued by the common law courts against the vice admiralty on the ground that the latter court was incompetent to act in particular litigation. As a rule such writs were obeyed. Common law courts throughout the colonial period, as, for example, the Mayor's Court of New York City, continued to exercise a good deal of admiralty jurisdiction.

After the Revolution most of the states erected their own courts of admiralty, really continuing the provincial courts, but the Federal Convention gave to the Federal courts "all cases of admiralty and maritime jurisdiction." Among the anachronisms surviving down to the 20th century in American admiralty law has been the privilege of the shipowner to limit liability after a disaster to whatever the value of the vessel or wreckage may be after the occurrence of the act. The *Titanic* and *Morro Castle* are two notorious examples of the application of this rule. The evolution of the doctrine of continuous voyage[qv] by the Federal courts during the Civil War provided Great Britain during the World War with a convenient precedent to justify the seizure of our ships bound for neutral ports on the ground that their ultimate destination was Germany.

[C. M. Andrews, Introduction to the Records of the Vice Admiralty Court of Rhode Island, *American Legal Records*, Vol. III; H. J. Crump, *Colonial Admiralty Jurisdiction in the 17th Century;* F. R. Sanborn, *Origins of the Early English Maritime and Commercial Law;* C. M. Hough, ed., *Reports of Cases in the Vice Admiralty of the Province of New York and in the Court of Admiralty of the State of New York.*]

RICHARD B. MORRIS

Admission of States. *See* States, Admission of.

Adobe Houses are structures made of earth and used principally in the Rocky Mountain plateau and in southwestern United States. The method came from North Africa via Spain and was introduced by the Spanish conquerors into the Southwest in the 16th century. Most of the Spanish mission buildings were made of this material. Wet clay and chopped hay or other fibrous material were mixed and the mass tramped with the bare feet. This was moulded into brick and sun dried. The walls were laid up with mud mortar. In the Rocky Mountain plateau adobe houses were made by moulding clay directly into the wall instead of making it into bricks. Adobe was widely used to build forts and trading posts as far east and north as Nebraska. Adobe was corrupted to "dobie" by the Americans. Since 1900 there has been a revival of adobe construction.

EVERETT DICK

Adobe Walls, The Battle of, was fought at the buffalo hunters' trading post by that name, on the north side of the Canadian River, in the Panhandle of Texas, June 27, 1874. The hide hunt was on, and the Adobe Walls post, established by hunters and traders from Dodge City[qv], Kans., was the southern outpost.

The Comanche, Cheyenne and Kiowa[qqv] were concentrated in Indian Territory, but during the spring of 1874 made several raids into Texas. Concentrating on the hunters who were killing their source of food, clothing and shelter, several hundred Indians attacked Adobe Walls. But they could not stand up against the fire of the Sharp's[qv] buffalo guns, and though three of the hunters were killed, the Indians, after losing heavily, abandoned the attack.

[Olive K. Dixon, *Life of Billy Dixon;* R. N. Richardson, in *The Panhandle-Plains Historical Review, 1931.*]

J. EVETTS HALEY

Adult Education is the name, borrowed from English usage, given to an American movement having its origins in the tradition of free speech[qv] inherent in the New England town meetings[qv] of the 17th century. The movement may be traced through the rise of the mechanics institutes in the early 19th century, the flowering of the lyceum movement[qv] in the eighteen-thirties and eighteen-forties, the foundation of the Philadelphia Extension Society in 1876, and the subsequent growth of the free public library[qv] and university extension movements. The term "adult education" did not come into general use in the United States until 1924, when the Carnegie Corporation[qv] of New York initiated a series of exploratory studies based on considerations similar to those contained in the findings of the epoch-making British Ministry of Reconstruction Report of 1919.

Following the publication of the American studies, two national and four regional conferences of adult educators were held, resulting in the founding at Chicago in 1926 of the American Association for Adult Education. The Association acts as a clearing house for information, an agency for the sponsorship and conduct of experiments and demonstrations, of studies and researches, and as the publisher of various materials on the philosophy and methods employed in the movement. It also publishes the quarterly *Journal of Adult Education*. It is currently (1938) engaged in a five-year study of the social significance of adult education, the findings being published from time to time in book form. Some forty subfields of adult education are under examination.

It is estimated that some 27,000,000 Americans, one third of the adult population, participate more than sporadically in some form of adult education, enormous increases during the economic depression (*see* Panic of 1929) being attributable to increased leisure time due to shortened working hours and to the large relief[qv] effort of the Federal Government in this field. The range of activities extends from radio[qv] listening individually and in groups, at one extreme, to post-graduate professional courses and conferences, at the other. Wide variations exist in the program offerings, the movement including provisions for the illiterate and the barely literate as well as services for collegiate alumni. Commonly included in the adult education enrollment are those who take part in rural adult education through the agricultural extension offerings of the land-grant colleges and the U. S. Department of Agriculture (*see* Agricultural Education), 7,000,000 strong; library patrons pursuing reading according to plan, numbering 1,000,000; members of men's and women's clubs participating in educational activities, 1,250,000; lyceum, Chautauqua and lecture course members[qqv], 1,000,000; subscribers to private correspondence school courses, 1,250,000; indoor recreation groups, 2,100,000; participants in public school offerings, in the regular evening elementary and high schools involving both cultural work and vocational offerings, 2,000,000; and those taking part in emergency relief classes of all types, numbering 2,250,000.

In addition, the open forum movement includes 500,000; churches and religious groups enroll 300,000; university extension 350,000; and various forms of vocational education, mainly for younger adults, 600,000. Smaller but highly important groups comprise workers' education, museum course attendants, foreign-born organization memberships, music groups including orchestras and choral societies, parent education, Negro groups, settlement[qv] and neighborhood groups, little theater[qv] organizations exclusive of audiences, corporation school enrollees, Civilian Conservation Corps[qv] Camp members, prisoners in penal institutions, and students in thousands of special schools for adults, etc.

The development of adult education in America, having been chiefly in the hands of a large number of private voluntary organizations, has been on the whole free from troublesome problems of censorship and control. Such questions have arisen in late years, however, as the tax-supported ventures in the field suddenly assumed large numerical proportions. However, the more farseeing of the school administrators, in responding to the new demand for adult education, are wisely forming advisory committees and local councils representative of many adult interests. These groups are expected to influence the program offerings in the direction of liberality of point of view, allowing for the full and free discussion of controversial subjects.

Important beginnings have been made in conducting the basic psychological, sociological and educational research necessary for a full understanding of adult instructional problems. Important contributions have been made by Prof. E. L. Thorndike and his associates at Teachers College, Columbia University, in determining the learning ability of adults at various age levels and also in determining adult interests. Studies and researches at the University of Chicago have done much to identify the interests of adult readers. Sociological studies made in rural districts by Prof. Edmund deS. Brunner of Teachers College, Columbia, have likewise contributed to an increasing fund of knowledge of adult education needs as have also such urban studies as R. S. and H. M. Lynd's *Middletown*.

American adult education has been described

as a "bourgeois" movement in contrast with European adult education, which even in Great Britain is much more representative of the working classes than of the population generally. In the United States adult education is regarded more as a right than as a privilege, and opportunities are usually as much available to the "middle class" as to working men and their families. The much more widespread opportunity for free child education through the adolescent years even to young manhood and young womanhood is accountable for this difference from the European scene.

Proponents of the movement assert that it bears a direct and important relationship to the effective functioning of the democratic form of government envisaged by the founders of the United States, and trace their obligation to the public back to the considerations set forth by Jay, Hamilton, and Madison in the Federalist[qv] papers. Adult educators are outspoken in their support of a liberal position on political, economic, and social issues, but generally concur in the belief that their responsibility for the education of the adult student stops with due and careful preparation of the individual for social action rather than extending to social action itself. The leaders of the movement have conscientiously avoided any political flavor or affiliation in their adult education work.

[Dorothy Canfield Fisher, *Why Stop Learning?;* Morse A. Cartwright, *Ten Years of Adult Education;* Dorothy Hewitt and Kirtley Mather, *Adult Education—A Dynamic for Democracy;* Mary L. Ely, *Adult Education in Action.*]

MORSE A. CARTWRIGHT

Adulteration. The first federal recognition of the duty of the United States Government to protect consumers was evidenced by the Tea Inspection Act of March 2, 1897. Nine years later, the Pure Food and Drugs Act[qv] prohibited the adulteration of drugs, confectionery and foods, detailing those acts which constituted violation. The next step taken was the passage of an act forbidding transportation or sale of adulterated insecticides or fungicides within the territories as well as importation into the United States (36 U. S. 331). Shortly thereafter, the importation of adulterated grass and grain seeds was prohibited (37 U. S. 507). Various states forbid the adulteration of certain articles, e.g., California prohibits the sale or offering for sale of debased quicksilver.

[Publications of Consumers Research, Inc., and of Consumers Union, both give information concerning adulteration of specific items in commerce.]

ROBERT G. RAYMER

Adventists, OR MILLERITES, were followers of William Miller (1782–1849) who, during 1831–44, preached that, according to Daniel's and Ezra's prophecies, at Christ's second coming in 1844 fire would destroy the earth. The advent failing to materialize and opposition from existing sects becoming intolerant, a new church, Adventist, developed in 1845. The adherents believed in Christ's personal, visible return, the necessity for repentance and faith to obtain salvation, a physical resurrection, and a millennium spanning the period between the first and second resurrections. This organization finally disintegrated to form five extant groups, among them the Advent Christian Church and the Seventh-day Adventists[qv].

[I. C. Wellcome, *History of the Second Advent Message and Mission, Doctrine and People;* G. D. Hagstotz, *Seventh-day Adventists in the British Isles*, 1878-1933; M. E. Olsen, *A History of the Origin and Progress of the Seventh-day Adventists.*]

G. D. HAGSTOTZ

Adventure, THE, was a sloop built in the winter of 1791–92 at Clayoquot on Nootka Sound by Captains Asa Gray and John Kendrick of Boston who were on an exploring and trading expedition in the Northwest. It was the first American sailing vessel built on the Pacific coast.

[K. Coman, *Economic Beginnings of the Far West.*]

CARL L. CANNON

Adventurers. Colonization demanded labor and capital. Settlers had to be transported across a hostile sea, properly equipped to build life anew in a virgin land, and supplied with food until self-sustaining. Many were able to help themselves, venturing both life and money. Many others in their poverty were dependent upon financial assistance. The demands upon capital were heavy.

The term "adventurer" runs far back into English history when there appeared a body of traders known as "merchant adventurers." The very name, adventurer, denoted a new age and spirit in mercantile life. With money to invest, these enterprising merchants sought opportunities beyond England's shores. They adventured or risked their capital in foreign trade. Groups of merchant adventurers existed in Bristol, London, York, Chester and other leading ports.

These adventurers supplied the capital and enterprise which built up England's profitable commercial dominion in the Old World in the 16th century. The New World offered new opportunities. The merchants of Bristol aided Gilbert's futile colonial venture in Newfoundland in 1583 and a few London merchants assisted Raleigh[qv] in his ill-fated attempt to settle Roanoke Island in 1585. A larger capital was necessary and the familiar device of the joint-stock company was employed (*see* Trading Companies). Adventurers of Plymouth subscribed to the stock of the Plymouth Company^qv^ whose colonial effort in Maine in 1607 promptly failed. London adventurers took stock in the company which by persistent effort succeeded in making Virginia a permanent colony (*see* Virginia Company of London). A group of London merchants risked their capital in aiding the Pilgrims to settle the colony of Plymouth^qv^ in 1620. The colony of Massachusetts^qv^ originated in an association of merchants living in and about Dorchester^qv^, England. Not all those who risked their capital were merchants. The charter of 1609 to the Virginia Company of London incorporated fifty-six companies of the city of London and 659 persons gathered from various walks of life.

[C. M. Andrews, *Colonial Period of American History;* C. P. Nettels, *Roots of American Civilization.*]

WINFRED T. ROOT

Advertisements, Early American (1704–1830), were usually of the legal notice variety with a slight amount of display or illustration. The *Boston News Letter*^qv^ in its third issue, May 1–8, 1704, carried a notice of real estate for sale, and two notices of lost articles. Soon there were also runaways to be advertised, and slaves for sale. These were set solid as other matter, though with a larger initial letter. Franklin in 1735 used larger type at the head of a notice; and somewhat later began the use of small woodcuts—of ships, Negroes, horses, etc.—to give variety and interest to the page. Notices were usually column width, and the larger were elongated squares. Shortage of paper led printers to discourage large notices, and to set a limit to the size of cuts.

These advertisements furnish valuable information for social and economic history. Commodities listed by merchants and manufacturers show the variety of imports and extent of manufactures, as well as consumers' tastes. Details of transportation and communication are found in notices of the sailings of ships, of post-routes, and later of stage, canal, and steamboat schedules. Beginnings of the professions are indicated by such notices as Paul Revere's offer to make false teeth (1768), and those offering the services of barbers, school teachers and dancing masters. Morals of an earlier generation are revealed by advertisements for runaway apprentices and slaves, and by offers of slaves for sale, often with detailed descriptions; and when the head of a family inserted a notice for a wet nurse, or informed the public not to trust the wife who had left his "bed and board." Lotteries^qv^, theatrical entertainments, horse races^qv^, and exhibitions of animals were recorded in advertisements; while cultural advance was indicated by notices of schools, musical organizations, libraries and lists of books for sale.

[Frank Presbrey, *The History and Development of Advertising.*]

MILTON W. HAMILTON

Advertising, National. Up to the time of the Civil War, advertising in America was mainly local, in such forms as signs, posted bills, cards, pamphlets, handbills and brief notices in the newspapers. Many merely identified a seller and listed his wares. Others aimed to bring together a specific need and a supply, and were often inserted by the prospective buyer, as in "Lost and Found" and "Wanted" advertisements. Even retailers' advertisements seldom contained much salesmanship before the adoption of the one-price policy.

Among manufacturers, almost the only ones who advertised were the proprietors of patent medicines^qv^. Most families resorted to self-medication, especially in districts where doctors were scarce and not readily accessible. There was a lively demand for sarsaparillas, bitters, liniments, pills, and panaceas. Such items had a low transportation cost, a high profit margin to manufacturer and retailer, and enjoyed a good repeat sale. However, the task of inducing the first purchase required aggressive salesmanship. Medical advertising was usually full of sensational and exaggerated claims; much of it was fraudulent.

Medical advertisers used every available medium. A favorite form was the almanac^qv^, since it was likely to be kept for reference throughout the year. The newspapers^qv^ were almost the only periodicals available. Their values varied greatly and their rates were elastic. The difficulty of bargaining for space in them was partly solved by the emergence of the advertising agency^qv^. The agent could secure the lowest possible rate and handle the details of billing and checking; later he undertook other services.

After the Civil War the agricultural papers and religious papers^qqv^ enjoyed a brief importance. The general magazines at this period were not highly regarded as advertising media, and most of the influential ones did not welcome advertising. Some inserted only advertisements of books issued by their own publishing house. But in the eighteen-eighties, the magazines began to be more receptive to advertisers whose products and claims they considered acceptable. Because they had a country-wide circulation of well-to-do people, and were comparatively free from objectionable medical advertising, they rose rapidly toward a position of leadership in national advertising.

By this time American inventive genius had brought forth many new types of articles, and the network of railroads had made it possible to ship them to all the states of the Union. Manufacturers of cameras, fountain pens, typewriters, bicycles and a host of other new articles found the magazine a convenient medium for educating the public regarding their products. Manufacturers of new types of old articles like shaving soap, or of articles that were not habitually used, like chocolate and canned soup, widened their markets by magazine advertising. Brands of staple articles competed for the consumers' choice. Service industries used institutional advertisements to build good-will for their organizations and methods.

The growth of national advertising was aided by the constantly increasing efficiency of transportation, by the cheapness of periodicals, by the gradual transition from home-made to factory-made products, and by the change from buying in bulk to buying in packages. Advertising, in turn, exerted a reciprocal action in hastening these changes. This action was most obvious in the field of periodical publishing, where early in the 20th century advertising had become the chief source of income. It made possible 2-cent newspapers of forty-eight or more pages, and 5-cent weeklies with as much editorial content as the old 35-cent monthlies.

Advertising in the small "standard-size" (6″ x 9″) magazine soon reached a point of saturation. Advertisements in a thick segregated advertising section had a poor chance of being seen. Advertisers turned to the larger size flat publications, with reading matter distributed through the advertising section. Many of the older magazines changed their formats to meet the advertisers' wishes; others suspended. The losses were largely offset by the rise of new periodicals of various kinds, notably class publications with audiences selected on the basis of vocation or leisure interests.

The volume of national advertising continued to grow, with few setbacks, for the first three decades of the 20th century. During the World War it was an important aid in selling Liberty Bonds[qv] and in popularizing Government policies, including such policies as refraining from white bread and other articles needed for war purposes (*see* Food Administration, 1917–19). In 1929 the highest peak of national advertising was reached in an issue of the *Saturday Evening Post* containing 272 pages, of which about 168 were advertising pages (many in four colors) with a total cost of $1,579,408. The actual advertising cost per inch of space, on the basis of audience reached, was lower than that of most magazines of the 19th century, for the publication reached nearly three million families. The *Post* circulation has since then exceeded the three million mark, but its volume of advertising has never since equalled that of 1929.

The only medium that has consistently grown in volume of advertising since 1929 is the radio[qv]. This had first become available in 1922 but did not become significant until about 1930. Many advertisers have sponsored coast-to-coast broadcasts; a much larger number have had programs that reached all the thickly populated areas. Although radio advertising appeals through the ear and hence is not a direct competitor of advertising that appeals through the eye, it probably took parts of the advertising budget that would otherwise have been spent in newspaper, magazine and outdoor advertising. Nevertheless the newspaper continued to hold its leadership in manufacturers' advertising, with the magazine in second place, but by decreasing margins.

Even during the most prosperous period, national advertisers faced several obstacles that tended to lessen the efficiency of their advertising. Among them were: (1) the increased competition for attention; (2) the decline of public faith in advertising, due partly to the percentage of fraud and misrepresentation; (3) the competition of wholesalers and retailers.

The keen competition for the eye and ear of the public led to more scientific study. Market research was invoked to discover the number and character of consumers, their wants and habits, and the most efficient channels for reaching them. Psychologists examined buying motives and the ways to appeal to them. Methods of pre-testing copy were devised. Every part of the art and technique of advertising was analyzed. Courses in advertising were offered in universities. Before 1900 there was practically no literature of advertising, and only a few books before 1910. Since then, hundreds of volumes have been published covering every phase of the subject.

Although the better magazines and newspapers used every precaution to exclude fraudulent advertisers, these still found media for transmitting their messages. To eliminate them altogether, the Associated Advertising Clubs (later called the Advertising Federation of America) adopted the motto "Truth in Advertising" in 1911 and appointed a Vigilance Committee to see that fraudulent advertisers were prosecuted and punished according to law. This work was later systematized in the Better Business Bureaus in fifty-five cities, financed mainly by advertisers and publishers. Several states made false advertising a misdemeanor. The Federal Government, through the Post Office Department, the Department of Agriculture and the Federal Trade Commission[qqv], also stamped out some of the most serious evils. During the depression years, however, the frantic search for stimulants to buying caused some relapses into objectionable forms of advertising.

The competition of middlemen manifested itself most disturbingly in price-cutting on nationally advertised brands, and the promotion of private brands[qv]. Although the nationally advertised brands seldom allowed an abnormally large profit margin, they were frequently used as "loss-leaders" by large-scale dealers. This practice made them less acceptable to dealers who could not afford to meet the price cuts. A remedy was sought in Fair Trade Laws which legalized price maintenance[qv] of resale prices. Before the passage of these, however, many wholesalers and dealers (including some of the most drastic price-cutters) had established their own private brands. These usually required more personal sales effort, but were relatively free from price comparisons. Some manufacturers succeeded in getting the co-operation of dealers in making their advertising effective. In fields where price-cutting and private branding were not prevalent, national advertising did not usually result in an increase in the number of competitive brands. On the contrary, the number tended to decrease, as the brands that received little popular support were eliminated. The survivors were not invariably the most extensive or persuasive advertisers; often—as in automobiles and automobile accessories—they were those that had gauged more accurately the wants of consumers and adapted their product and messages to them.

[Frank Presbrey, *History and Development of Advertising;* Paul T. Cherington, *The Consumer Looks at Advertising;* H. J. Kenner, *The Fight for Truth in Advertising.*]

G. B. HOTCHKISS

Advertising Agency. The modern advertising agency appears to have originated in the activities of independent space brokers early in the 19th century. Some of these were free-lance advertising salesmen, or conveniently situated business men (such as post-masters) who as a sideline accepted advertisements for insertion in various newspapers. Probably the earliest to make space brokerage his sole business was Volney B. Palmer. Shortly after 1840 he had offices in Boston, New York and Philadelphia, and represented himself as a duly accredited agent to receive advertisements and subscriptions for "most of the best papers published in the United States and Canada." He assumed no responsibility for collecting money from the advertiser, but charged the publisher 25% for his service in selling the space.

Another agent, John L. Hooper, who began business in New York about the same time as Palmer, or a little later, inaugurated a policy that eventually became standard practice with agencies. He assumed the financial risk of paying the publisher himself and then collecting from the advertisers. By the time of the Civil War, at least twenty agencies were operating in the larger cities.

In 1865, George P. Rowell invented his "List System" which consisted in buying space at wholesale and selling at retail. His offer was "an-inch-of-space-a-month-in-one-hundred-papers-for-one-hundred-dollars." Similar methods were adopted by other agents and applied to other kinds of periodicals, such as religious papers, farm papers, and general magazines[qqv]. The system was an important factor in the early development of magazine advertising, but ultimately was abandoned, and the commission basis of payment was re-established.

Throughout the early period, the chief service of the agent was that of buying space more efficiently than the advertiser could do it. Newspapers varied tremendously in advertising values and the publishers' claims of circulation were notoriously unreliable. Only an expert space-buyer could determine the value of advertising space in a given medium, and buy it at the lowest price. Secret knowledge of values and rates, together with bargaining ability, remained the chief assets of the advertising agent until 1869. In that year appeared the first volume of Rowell's American Newspaper Directory. This listed 5411 publications in the United States and 367 in Canada, with estimates of their circulation. Subsequent issues of this directory, and other media directories and services, gradually made information about circulations more accessible and reliable. Space-buying had become a minor function of most agencies by 1914, when the Audit Bureau of Circulations was established to secure accurate and systematic information regarding the quantity and quality of circulation of periodicals.

In the meantime, the agencies were developing new and valuable services. Through their experience in placing advertising they accumulated funds of knowledge about planning and executing campaigns. They wrote copy, designed the pictorial and typographic display, supervised the art work, and handled the production of material used in the actual printing of the advertisements. Many agencies added research departments and departments for handling such media as industrial publications, direct mail, and radio. Although most of these services could be performed by the advertiser himself, the bulk of national advertisers and many local advertisers found it expedient to employ the expert knowledge of an agency.

Thus the advertising agents approached a professional status. However, they were in the anomalous position of regarding the advertisers as their clients, while receiving most of their compensation from the media in the form of a commission. The amount of this varied in the eighteen-eighties and eighteen-nineties, but ultimately became standardized at 15% for most newspapers and magazines. The amount of service rendered to the advertiser was not so easily fixed. Moreover, the competition for desirable clients resulted occasionally in "splitting commissions" or otherwise rebating a part of the compensation.

To correct such practices and other forms of unfair competition, local associations of agencies were formed, and in 1917 a national organization, known as the American Association of Advertising Agencies. This included in its membership the majority of the "fully recognized" agencies in the country. An agency was "recognized" by a publisher when he granted it the commission on space purchased through it. To secure such recognition, an agency usually had to demonstrate its financial strength, its expert ability, its possession of several substantial clients, and its freedom from alliances with either publishers or advertisers.

The Association of Agencies adopted a code of Standards of Practice in 1924 by which the members agreed to refrain from unfair competition or rebates, from submitting speculative plans or copy, and from preparing or handling any advertising of an untruthful, indecent, or objectionable character. The commission system remained a target for criticisms by large advertisers. At their instigation, the Federal Trade Commission[qv] brought suit against the Association, together with several publishers' associations, as a conspiracy in restraint of trade[qv], but after lengthy investigation and litigation the suit was dismissed. Nevertheless, the powerful Association of National Advertisers recommended a change to a more flexible system, and steps in that direction have been taken by some agencies.

[George P. Rowell, *Forty Years an Advertising Agent;* Frank Presbrey, *History and Development of Advertising.*]

G. B. HOTCHKISS

Aeolus. One of the early experiments in railroad cars, the yachtlike *Aeolus* was designed to sail before the wind. It was tried on the Baltimore & Ohio Railroad[qv] in 1830. On one occasion the *Aeolus* failed to stop when it reached the end of the finished track, and ran into an embankment.

[Edward Hungerford, *The Story of the Baltimore and Ohio Railroad.*]

FRANK FREIDEL

Aeronautics. *See* Aviation; Balloons.

African Company, Royal, THE (1672–1750), was one of a series of trading companies granted a monopoly of the African slave trade[qv]. In 1672 it took over the charter and African trading posts of the Company of Royal Adventurers to Africa established by the Duke of York and associates in 1662. In 1697 its monopoly was destroyed when independent merchants were permitted to engage in the trade upon payment for fourteen years of export duties which were turned over to the company to maintain its posts. From this time the trade was largely absorbed by the independents. During the 18th century most of the slaves were carried to the West Indies and North America in ships owned by Bristol, Liverpool and colonial merchants. The company endeavored to prevent independent traders from bargaining directly with native dealers. Most of the Negroes it secured were sold to the independents, to the English South Sea Company after it was granted the Asiento[qv] (1713), or even to foreign traders. The destruction of the monopoly, the competition of independent traders, the expense of maintaining its posts, and the imposition of poll duties on slave importations by Virginia, South Carolina, Jamaica and Barbados, all proved so disastrous to the company, that, in spite of annual grants by Parliament of £10,000 beginning in 1729, its affairs were wound up in 1750. By that year, of the 155 British ships in the trade, twenty were North American, nearly half from Rhode Island.

[L. H. Gipson, *The British Empire before the American Revolution.*]

CHARLES F. MULLETT

African Methodist Episcopal Church. The oldest and largest denomination of colored Methodists[qv], organized in 1816 with Richard Allen as its first Bishop. The origin of this body was the result of friction in St. George's Methodist Episcopal Church in Philadelphia, due to a feeling of race discrimination and a consequent conviction on the part of the colored members that they would enjoy a larger measure of freedom in worship and service by themselves. The denomination grew in the first decade slowly, reaching a membership of nearly 10,000, but after the close of the Civil War increased rapidly and now claims a membership of more than 500,000. In doctrine and polity it differs little from the mother church.

[Matthew Simpson, *Cyclopedia of Methodism;* Benjamin E. Mays and Joseph William Nicholson, *The Negro's Church.*]

C. H. STACKPOLE

Agamenticus. Successively known as Bristol (1632), Agamenticus (1641), Gorgeana (1642), and York (1652), this early Maine settlement, equidistant from Mt. Agamenticus and the Piscataqua River, has the distinction of being the first municipal corporation in America (1642), created so by Sir Ferdinando Gorges whose special favor the settlement enjoyed. Settled about 1624, it was one of the few substantial settlements in the province of Maine during the trying period of colonial wars[qv].

[C. E. Banks, *History of York, Maine.*]

ELIZABETH RING

Agent, Colonial. *See* Colonial Agent, The.

Agrarian Movement, THE. Efforts on the part of the rural classes to better their lot by concerted political action have been almost a constant quantity in American history. Even in colonial times the southern planters, forced to exchange their produce for British manufactures on terms that left them permanently in debt to British merchants, protested to the point of revolt against the imperial regulations that they blamed for their distress. From their point of view the American Revolution was a movement to free American agriculture from the tyranny of British commercialism. Independence was no sooner won, however, than in some of the northern states the debt-ridden farmers of the back-country launched a similar protest against the political power of the well-to-do seaboard merchants. The latter, frightened by such episodes as Shays' Rebellion[qv] in Massachusetts and the paper money craze in Rhode Island (*see* Trevett v. Weeden; Paper Money), joined with the creditor classes generally in a movement to provide a national government strong enough to keep order and protect property. The Constitution[qv] of the United States was the result.

Differences between the devotees of commerce and of agriculture speedily produced a two-party political system[qv] for the new republic. The Federalists[qv], under the effective leadership of Alexander Hamilton, made it their business to head off money inflation, establish the national credit, keep open the lanes of commerce, and minimize the rights of the states (*see* States' Rights), in which occasionally the agrarians had the upper hand. When the need for more revenue required the levying of an excise[qv] tax, they singled out whiskey[qv], a by-product of the back-country farms, to bear the burden. These policies the Republicans (*see* Republican Party, Jeffersonian), equally well led by the agriculturally minded Thomas Jefferson, criticized with increasing vehemence. When the "Revolution of 1800" made Jefferson President, the more offensive Federalist measures were repealed, and a new course, definitely favorable to agriculture, was charted. The purchase of Louisiana added new territory for the agricultural interest to exploit, while such measures as the Embargo and Non-intercourse[qqv] gravely jeopardized the welfare of commerce. Under Jefferson's successor, Madison, the War of 1812[qv] was fought, less to safeguard American commerce on the high seas than to end the British and Indian menace to the westward march of agriculture, and to pave the way for the conquest by farmers and planters of Canada and Florida.

Ironically, the commercial restrictions that preceded and accompanied the War of 1812 resulted in a new and formidable challenge to the supremacy of the agriculturalists. Domestic manufacturing, essential because commerce had languished, soon revealed possibilities of profit that could not be ignored. Factories, particularly in the Northeast, multiplied with amazing rapidity, and the agricultural interests, scarcely aware of what had been going on, awoke to find themselves almost displaced by factory owners and their satellites in the control of the Republican (Jeffersonian) party. Soon the very party that Jefferson had founded was chartering a new national bank (*see* Bank of the U. S., First and Second), adopting a protective tariff[qv] and giving serious consideration to a nation-wide program of internal improvements[qv]. Jacksonian Democracy[qv] was in no small degree the inevitable response of the agriculturalists to this challenge of the industrialists, and with the elevation of "Old Hickory"[qv] to the presidency—"the Revolution of 1828"—much of the lost ground was recovered. The Bank was destroyed, the tariff was reduced, and the burdensome problem of internal improvements was relegated to the states and to individuals.

The solidarity of the agricultural front was not to be maintained for long. The planters of the South, now obedient to the dictates of "King

Cotton"[qv] and devoted as never before to the syster of slave labor, had little in common with the small free farmers who owned the West. Both wished for expansion (*see* Manifest Destiny), and they cheerfully joined hands against the Indians and against the Mexicans to take what they wanted. But each hoped to exclude the other from the spoils of war. The small free farmers wished a small-free-farmer West; the slave-owning planters wished a slave-owning-planter West. The southern planters, however, were far more gifted at the game of politics than their western rivals, and for a generation after Jackson left office they maintained an unbroken ascendancy in the national councils.

Distaste for the policies of the slave-holding South at length drove the free-farmer West into an open alliance with the industrial Northeast. The fruit of this union was a new Republican party, which promised to the West free lands, to the Northeast a protective tariff, and to both a Pacific railroad[qqv]. Rather than submit to such a program the South fought, and lost, the Civil War. With southern protests stilled, the other sections voted themselves what they had promised, and, for good measure, a new national banking[qv] system as well. Slavery[qv] itself was abolished.

The leadership of the re-united nation fell naturally to the industrialists. This was not due solely to the War, for the rising tide of industrialism was world-wide, not merely national. In the United States, as elsewhere, population tended more and more to concentrate in cities; and whole new industries such as steel and oil[qqv], virtually unknown before the Civil War, extended the field of industrial operations far into the West and South. Against this growing strength of the industrialists the agriculturalists found it difficult to unite. Farmers in the industrialized sections ministered to the local city markets, and tended to accept without protest both the policies and the prices that were offered them, while the farmers of West and South, with their economic interests at best somewhat divergent, overcame with difficulty the rancors let loose by war.

The same forces that had been at work to transform industry, however, were bringing about a revolution in agriculture. The old system of production for use, to which the small free farmer had long been accustomed, gradually gave way to a system of production for sale. New machines transformed each farm into a kind of factory, designed often-times to turn out a highly specialized product. The farmers of the Northwest concentrated on wheat, or corn, or live stock, or dairy products[qqv]. The farmers of the South still pinned their faith mainly to tobacco and cotton[qqv]. Fruit-growers appeared in the Far West. All were dependent upon the railroads for transportation, upon the banks for credit, upon the merchants for all those necessities of life that farmers no longer produced for themselves, upon nation-wide or world-wide markets for the prices of the things they had to sell. Land values, thanks in part to the greater economy of production with the new machines and in part to the disappearance of the frontier[qv], rose persistently. But farm mortgages also mounted, tenantry increased (*see* Farmer, Tenant), and each cycle of depression left the rural classes worse off, relatively, than they had been before.

Out in the upper Mississippi Valley, where the cost of transportation ate up all the grain growers' profits, and down in the reconstructed South, where the crop-lien system had forced the cotton growers into virtual peonage, the "embattled farmers" began fumblingly and reluctantly to unite in their own defense. Through their experiences with the Granger movement, the Greenback movement, and the Farmers' Alliances[qqv], they learned that, if only they could stand together as voters, they might force the governments of state and nation to restrain the railroads and the trusts[qqv], to scale down debts by some form of money inflation[qv], and to protect in general the farmers' interests. They discovered, too, that by co-operation in marketing, in purchasing, and even in manufacturing they might hope, with adequate management, to help themselves. Efforts to unite the rural classes into a People's Party[qv] that would take over the government and administer it directly in the farmers' interest failed during the 1890's, but the drift toward closer organization and co-operation went on.

During the 20th century the rural classes brought persistent pressure upon state governments to attain desired ends. In Wisconsin, for example, the LaFollette progressives[qv], composed mainly of rural voters, captured the Republican organization, instituted the primary system[qv] of making nominations for office, established close supervision of railroads and public utilities[qv], and reformed the system of taxation. The Farmers' Nonpartisan League[qv] in North Dakota, Minnesota and other northwestern states attempted with less complete success to bring about state operation of elevators, flour mills, and other businesses deemed guilty of taking unfair advantages of the farmers. Alliances with labor became increasingly common, and paved the way for such organizations as the Farmer-Labor party of Minnesota[qv], and the Farmer-Labor-Progressive federation of Wisconsin. In the South the rural whites, increasingly rebellious against the exactions of country storekeepers and landlords, put their trust in the promises of such demagogic leaders as James K. Vardaman and Theodore G. Bilbo of Mississippi, the "Hon. Jeff." Davis of Arkansas, and Huey P. Long of Louisiana. Numerous agricultural organizations, such as the American Society of Equity, the Farmers' Union, and the American Farm Bureau Federation, appeared both in the South and in the West. Most of these orders emphasized almost equally the need of political pressure and of farmer-owned business co-operatives[qv].

On the national front the agriculturalists regained much of the unity they had known before the Civil War. Republican "insurgents" from the Northwest worked together with southern Democrats from agricultural regions against the high protective rates of the Payne-Aldrich tariff[qv], and during Wilson's administration helped inaugurate a generous Federal farm loan system[qv]. When the overexpansion of agriculture during the World War led to a drastic deflation at its close, a congressional "Farm Bloc," aided by pressure from a multitude of agricultural organizations the country over, began an agitation for farm relief that led eventually to the establishment under Hoover of the short-lived Federal Farm Board[qv], and under F. D. Roosevelt of the Agricultural Adjustment Administration[qv]. Both measures had as their main objective the stabilization of farm incomes at a high enough level to insure farmers a profitable return for their labor and investments. When in 1936 the United States Supreme Court held the "A.A.A." unconstitutional, the New Deal[qv] substituted for it a soils conservation[qv] policy designed to gain the same end in another way.

[Charles A. and Mary R. Beard, *The Rise of American Civilization;* Edward Wiest, *Agricultural Organization in the United States.*]

JOHN D. HICKS

Agricultural Adaptation to the Plains. The Great Plains, with sub-humid climate, wind, heat, high rate of evaporation, and lack of timber, presented agricultural problems new to the experience of settlers of Anglo-American descent. Three approaches were employed: pastoral, irrigation and dry land farming. The pastoral period was represented especially by the live stock boom (1865–1886). Next came the small farmer invasion of the 1880's. The drouth[qv] decade beginning in 1886 brought the irrigation[qv] boom. Especially difficult was the problem of the transitional country between humid and arid regions which could employ traditional methods during wet cycles but desperately needed the full technique of dry land farming in dry periods. Out of the conflict of ideals and objectives the inhabitants of the Plains worked out their destiny. No lasting stabilization had been reached, however, when the technological revolution of the 1920's and the drouth and depression of the 1930's brought a prolonged test of the soundness of current practices.

In a humid climate timber and water are available to all, and self-sufficiency is possible. The instruments to sustain life had to be brought to the Plains from outside: railroads, weapons (revolver and repeating rifle), barbed-wire fencing, windmills, fuel and farm machinery[qqv]—all products of the industrial revolution[qv]. Nature limited the variety of production and enforced specialization; cash crops were necessary to enable farmers to buy the necessities of life. Thus the Plains civilization was founded on regional interdependence.

The early phases of the live stock industry were abnormal, based on native cattle, the supply of which was soon exhausted, pastured upon public land[qv] without charge. Later came fenced public range and improved breeding. A permanent cattle and sheep industry required the transition to privately owned land, sometimes supplemented by public range; improved breeds of stock adapted to the region; and the production of some irrigated or drouth-resistant hay and feed crops for winter and drouth feeding. Significantly, in order to survive, the live stock interest found it necessary to compromise with field crop agriculture.

The small farmer invasion of the Plains in the 1880's was based on the 160-acre family size farm idea, with a mixed farm-crop program of the more humid East. Experience demonstrated that a larger unit was necessary. Farmers had to learn to ridge the soil against the prevailing winds or to leave it rough and trashy to prevent it from blowing. They had to devise means of working the soil quickly, when moisture was available, and to prepare it to receive and conserve moisture most effectively. Some systems involved summer-fallowing, some insisted on diversified farming, but no fixed procedure was applicable to all regions of the plains and intermountain area, and the extensive experimental work done during the drouth period of the 1930's superseded much of the earlier practices. Conventional moldboard plows gave way in part or altogether during the 1890's to disc machinery which left the ground relatively rough, the trash on top, and worked drier ground, or to the lister which ridged the ground. During the 1930's, the chisel tool, or the small bottomed lister, with damming attachment (sometimes called the basin tool or basin lister), found favor over the disc machinery or regular lister among many operators.

The problem of speeding up tillage operations was partly met by the lister, but not until the tractor[qv] was perfected and became available for general use after the World War could it be said to have been solved. As summer-fallowing became more widely accepted as part of dry land farming practice, tools for fallow cultivation were emphasized. Although some preferred the new type chisel tool, special tools or attachments for listers were developed such as the duck-foot, the spring-tooth and the rod-weeder. During the 1920's, extensive experimental work was done with seeding tools; deep-furrow and semi-deep-furrow drills, either disc or shoe types; the chisel tools; varying widths of spacing between the rows; varying widths of furrows in which the seed was scattered in the rows; varying degrees of ridging of ground between the rows to prevent blowing of the soil and to catch rain and snow until the crop made sufficient growth to cover the ground. Some of the most advanced machines of 1937 were combination tools, incorporating in one piece of machinery, the chisel or lister, the fallowing attachments, and the seeding accessories.

The harvesting of short-stemmed small grain required special machinery also. The header and, about the turn of the century, the convertible header-binder reached the size limits of horse-driven machinery. After the World War, mechanical power made practical the combine[qv] (header-thresher) which reduced harvesting and threshing to a single operation. It is significant that the farmers themselves and the implement makers achieved most of this adaptation and invention through a process of private trial-and-error experiment, governmental agencies contributing only a minor role, and even that only in the later stages and mostly in those departments where exact scientific knowledge, procedures and equipment were necessary, such as plant breeding and insect and disease controls. One of the most remarkable features of the history of the Great Plains region was the marvelous resourcefulness, persistence, and optimism of the inhabitants in adaptational experimentation.

The original crop program of the small Plains farmer was transplantation of his accustomed planning from the humid East, especially corn and oats[qqv] as the principal crops. Hard spring wheats[qv] eventually supplanted these as well as the soft varieties of wheat in the northern Plains during the late 1870's and 1880's, assisted by the development of the purifier and the roller grinding machinery for handling hard wheats in the flour mills[qv]. In the southwest Plains drouth-resistant hard winter wheat was introduced from Russia in 1873 (*see* Wheat, Turkey Red), spreading during the drouth period of the 1890's, and after 1900 was supplemented by new introductions and the development of varieties by both governmental agencies and private individuals. The sorghums came to provide forage and grain crops in place of corn, being introduced from Africa and Asia, a few varieties of the saccharine sorghums as early as the 1850's, and the grain types such as milo and kaffir later in the century, feterita in 1906 and sudan grass in 1909.

Irrigation was subject to drastic limitations, because the area from which water could be drawn was itself arid. In any event, only a small percentage of the area could have water from the surface supply and this type of project was restricted to the valleys near the sources of the streams. Ground water supplies were limited by the same moisture deficiency for the area, and by the depth of wells and the cost of pumping. Large scale pumping projects were not practical as they were for surface-water reclamation projects, therefore each farmer must install his own equipment if he practised irrigation farming. Thus the Plains area proper could receive little direct benefit from irrigation of either type. It was primarily either a live stock or a dry land farming area, or a combination of them. The indirect benefits of irrigation were nevertheless vital to supplement other economic activities and to achieve balances within the Plains and Mountain area as a whole.

[H. E. Briggs, The development of agriculture in territorial Dakota, *Culver-Stockton Quarterly*, 7 (1931): 1-37; L. C. Aicher, Damming attachments for listers, *30 Biennial Report* of the Kansas State Board of Agriculture, 35: 78-82; C. R. Bell, The history of American wheat improvement, *Agricultural History*, 4 (April 1930): 48-71; E. C. Chilcott, Dry farming in the Great Plains area, *Yearbook*, U. S. Dept. of Agric., 1907; E. C. Chilcott, Some misconceptions concerning dry farming, *Yearbook*, U. S. Dept. of Agric., 1911; E. C. Chilcott, Preventing soil blowing on the Southern Plains, *Farmers' Bulletin*, U. S. Dept. of Agric., No. 1771 (1937); John S. Cole, Implements and methods to control soil blowing on the Northern Great Plains, *Farmers' Bulletin*, U. S. Dept. of Agric., No. 1797 (1938); Carter Goodrich, et al., *Migration and economic opportunity;* A. L. Hallstead, Reducing risks in wheat growing, *30 Biennial Report* of the Kansas State Board of Agriculture, 35:98-110; Henrietta Larson, *The Wheat Market and the Farmer in Minnesota, 1858-1900;* C. P. Loomis, The human ecology of the Great Plains area, *Proceedings* of the Oklahoma Academy of Science, 1937; Angus McDonald, Erosion and its control in Oklahoma Territory, U. S. Dept. of Agriculture, *Misc. publication*, No. 301; James C. Malin, Adaptation of the agricultural system to sub-humid environment, *Agricultural History*, 10 (July 1936): 118-41; James C. Malin, The turnover of farm population in Kansas, *Kansas Historical Quarterly*, 4 (Nov. 1935): 339-72; John H. Parker, Wheat improvement in Kansas, *29 Biennial Report* of the Kansas State Board of Agriculture, 34: 39-64; H. S. Schell, Drought and agriculture in eastern South Dakota in the eighteen-eighties, *Agricultural History*, 5 (October 1931): 162-80; R. C. Smith, Upsetting the balance of nature with special reference to Kansas and the Great Plains, *Science*, 75 (June 24, 1932): 649-54; W. E. Smythe, *Conquest of Arid America;* A. T. Steinel and D. W. Working, *History of Agriculture in Colorado;* A. F. Swanson, The development of sorghum culture in Kansas, *29 Biennial Report* of the Kansas State Board of Agriculture, 34: 165-74; W. P. Webb, *The Great Plains;* E. J. Wickson, *Rural California;* John A. Widtsoe, *Dry Farming.*]

JAMES C. MALIN

Agricultural Adjustment Administration (1933). The Agricultural Adjustment Act of 1933 was an emergency^qv^ measure of the New Deal^qv^. In 1932 the platform of the Democratic party pledged the extension and "development of the farm co-operative movement and effective control of crop surpluses." Thus, it was at the instigation of Secretary of Agriculture Henry Wallace that President F. D. Roosevelt called representative farm leaders to Washington on March 10, 1933. Six days later the Chief Executive sent to Congress a bill drafted by the conference.

In his message of March 16, the President pointed out that while the measure followed "a new and untrod path," "an unprecedented condition" called for a "new means to rescue agriculture." By May 10 Congress had agreed to the provisions of the farm bill, and two days later the President signed the measure proposing to "relieve the existing national economic emergency by increasing agricultural purchasing power." The statute emphasized the emergency situation and attempted to increase farm income and to reduce farm surpluses. Using the years 1909–14 as a base period, the administrators hoped to establish and maintain a balance between production and consumption of agricultural products.

Included in the statute were provisions relative to credit extension and relief for farm mortgages; but more particularly the Secretary of Agriculture was given extensive authority to reduce productive acreage and to foster marketing quotas. To effect the program farm surpluses were removed from the market and prices were to be increased by placing restraints on production. Immediate payments were made to farmers participating in the program.

The much discussed tax levied upon processors was to "obtain revenue for extraordinary expenses incurred by reason of the national economic emergency." The tax was to help defray the administrative costs of carrying out the provisions of the enactment. And agreements drawn up by participating farmers were to prevent produce from burdening markets. To help administer the act, state and local committees, or associations of producers, were to assist the Federal officials. This was a concession to avoid the criticism of centralization. The entire plan was to be financed by an appropriation of $100,000,000.

After the Agricultural Adjustment Act was in operation three years the Supreme Court in 1936 declared, in U. S. v. Butler^qv^, that the statute was unconstitutional. (*See also* Rickert Rice Mills v. Fontenot.) It was held that the regulation of agriculture did not come within the jurisdiction of Congress, but was instead a function properly belonging to the states. Following this declaration, Congress enacted a Soil Conservation and Domestic Allotment^qv^ program for farm relief.

[Henry Wallace, *New Frontiers;* Edwin G. Nourse and others, *Three Years of the Agricultural Adjustment Act;* 48 U. S. Statutes at Large, p. 31.]

BENJAMIN F. SHAMBAUGH

Agricultural Adjustment Administration Act of 1938. This act was the result of the unconstitutionality of previous New Deal^qv^ farm legislation and the success of the Soil Conservation and Domestic Allotment Act^qv^ passed in 1936. During the first session of the Seventy-fifth Congress an extension of the soil conservation plan was given consideration. Through the summer of 1937 hearings of farm leaders were conducted in various states; but the second session adjourned while the farm bill was still in the hands of a conference committee.

In his message of Jan. 3, 1938, President F. D. Roosevelt emphasized the work of the conference committee and hoped that a "sound, consistent measure" would be adopted. After some debate in Congress the President, on Feb. 16, signed the measure providing "for the conservation of national soil resources."

The Soil Conservation Act was to be continued as a permanent farm policy; and to promote the program, national acreage allotments were to be fixed at a point "to give production sufficient for domestic consumption, for exports, and for reserve supplies." To induce farmers to operate within the allotments, payments were to be made by the Government. In order that "an adequate and balanced flow of agricultural commodities" might be maintained, the statute incorporated a method for storing produce in years of shortage. Four research laboratories are to be established at Peoria, Ill., in the New Orleans area, in the Philadelphia area, and in the San Francisco area, to study farm needs. And if two thirds of the farmers participating in the program agreed, marketing quotas in tobacco, corn, wheat, cotton, and rice might be fixed by the Secretary of Agriculture.

[*Laws of Congress*, 75th Cong., 3rd Sess., Chap. 30; *Congressional Record*, 75th Cong., 3rd Sess., Appendix, p. 810.]

BENJAMIN F. SHAMBAUGH

Agricultural Education has developed in four interrelated lines. Collegiate instruction while tried in a few states during the 1850's was definitely established by Federal endowment in the Morrill Land-Grant Act[qv] of 1862. Before 1890 curriculum and method were uncertain and relatively ineffective. Subject matter was not verified and organized and teaching methods were not systematized. Technical courses were grouped about the departments of agricultural chemistry, applied botany, and "agriculture" which included the various branches of farm organization and practice. The requirement of manual labor by most of the institutions emphasized training in practical skill at the expense of scientific principles.

By the 1890's transforming influences were in operation. Experiment stations[qv] were establishing information and differentiating it into special fields, and contributing to the extension and perfecting of the laboratory method. Textbooks and reference works based upon American conditions and needs were multiplying. Short courses, general and special, were set off from the regular course and met an increasing demand. A series of conventions culminating in the formation of the Association of American Agricultural Colleges and Experiment Stations (renamed Association of Land-Grant Colleges and Universities) in 1887 brought an interchange of ideas and experiences. The "Second Morrill Act" of 1890 gave more adequate endowment and encouraged the states to provide regular educational support.

Graduate study in agriculture has attained to standardized achievement through the research organization and technique of the experiment station. Agricultural research involving special application of the basic sciences has paralleled the growth of these sciences. With the recent emphasis upon the problems of rural economy and society especial attention has been given to the application of the social sciences.

Efforts to bring existing information directly to the farmers were made early in the 19th century by the agricultural societies[qv] through their exhibitional fairs and lecturers. From the 1870's the colleges combined with the state boards in conducting farmers' institutes[qv]. Early in the 20th century reading courses, demonstrational trains and co-operative regional projects were introduced. The whole extension program was modernized and unified by the Smith-Lever Act[qv] of 1914 (supplemented by the Capper-Ketcham Act of 1928) which makes the college the directing and clearing center for the main lines of extension effort: county agents, boys' and girls' clubs, extension specialists and home economics demonstrators.

From the manual labor schools of the 1820's efforts had been made from time to time to teach agriculture at the secondary level but it was only with the development of the agricultural phase of the vocational educational work provided for in the Smith-Hughes Act[qv] of 1917 (supplemented by the George-Deen Act of 1936) that this type of vocational high school was given assured place. Except for a limited utilization of materials in the teaching of the common branches agriculture has not entered the elementary curriculum.

[A. C. True, *A History of Agricultural Education in the United States;* E. P. Cubberley, *Public Education in the United States.*]

EARLE D. ROSS

Agricultural Experiment Stations were established to provide instructional materials for the colleges and to investigate occupational problems. Organization and method were modeled upon European stations and the work of state chemists. The first station was founded by Connecticut in 1875 and by 1887 fourteen states had definite organizations and in thirteen others the colleges conducted equivalent work. The Bussey Institution at Harvard (since 1871) and the Houghton Farm at Cornwall, N. Y. (1876–88), were privately endowed stations. Through the combined efforts of the colleges and the Department of Agriculture the Federal Hatch Act of 1887 provided an annual subvention for the stations. This aid has been increased by the Adams Act (1906) and the Purnell Act (1925).

[A. C. True and V. A. Clark, *The Agricultural Experiment Stations in the United States;* A. C. True, *A History of Agricultural Experimentation and Research in the United States.*]

EARLE D. ROSS

Agricultural Implements. *See* Farm Machinery.

Agricultural Societies, as an educational and as a political force, have vitally affected the progress of agriculture. During the post-Revolutionary years the low status of American agriculture prompted the forming of societies which, through meetings, premiums and publications, sought to stimulate improvement. The earliest society devoted exclusively to agriculture was the Philadelphia Society for Promoting Agriculture, organized in March, 1785. Washington and Franklin were members. In August, 1785, the Agricultural Society of South Carolina had its beginning. Agricultural societies followed in Maine (1787), in New York (1791), in Massachusetts (1792), and in Connecticut (1794). The Columbian Agricultural Society (D. C.), the first society to hold an agricultural exhibition, was formed in 1809. In 1817 the Albemarle (Va.) Agricultural Society was created under the leadership of Thomas Jefferson, with James Madison as its president.

The county agricultural fair[qv] received a great impetus as an educational agency in the Berkshire Agricultural Society movement, which, originating in 1810 on the initiative of Elkanah Watson, of Pittsfield, Mass., during the next twenty years swept New England and spread south and west. After a lull between 1830 and 1850, county societies experienced a renaissance in the decade 1850–60, when also many state societies began to exert an influence on legislation. The United States Agricultural Society, the first real national association, organized in 1852, was instrumental in the creation of the United States Department of Agriculture[qv], in 1862.

Economic disturbances following the Civil War occasioned the "agrarian movement"[qv], from which came organizations aimed at greater economic security for the farmer. Chief among these was the National Grange[qv], or Patrons of Husbandry, formed in 1867, through the efforts of Oliver H. Kelley. Engaging a secret fraternal ritual and embracing both men and women, the Grange undertook a program that was economic and political in purpose as well as educational and social.

Since 1900 the outstanding developments in agricultural organization have been: (1) farmers' co-operatives[qv], essentially economic in purpose, reported in the last census to have handled in 1929, for 825,000 farms, purchases and sales valued at over $1,000,000,000; and (2) the farm bureau[qv], primarily educational and partly political, whose county units became the local co-operating agencies of the agricultural extension service established by Congress in 1914.

[O. H. Kelley, *Origin and Progress of the Order of Patrons of Husbandry;* O. M. Kile, *The Farm Bureau Movement;* A. C. True, *History of Agricultural Education in the United States, 1785-1925;* R. H. True, *Sketch of the History of the Philadelphia Society for Promoting Agriculture;* R. H. True, *The Early Development of Agricultural Societies in the United States*, Agr. Hist. Soc. Papers, No. 3.]

CARL R. WOODWARD

Agricultural Wheel, THE, was a movement started in 1882, by W. W. Tedford, farmer and school teacher, to improve farming conditions. In 1886 it became the National Agricultural Wheel, and in 1889 merged with the National Farmers' Alliance[qv] and Co-operative Union of America.

[I. M. Tarbell, *Nationalizing of Business.*]

CARL L. CANNON

Agriculture. The nations of Europe that participated in the colonization of North America were influenced by various motives. A leading one with Spain was the hope of obtaining a generous supply of the precious metals. The dominant motive of France was the acquisition of wealth through the trade in furs and peltries, natural products of America's woods and streams.

Britain felt these motives too, and also another which affected her rivals as well, namely, the hope of making significant explorations leading to the nation's enrichment through commerce. But Britain in the 17th century had large groups of persons who for their own and the nation's benefit needed to emigrate. This fact differentiated her colonizing activity from that of the other powers and resulted in the establishment of agriculture as the leading industry in the British colonies.

This agriculture, in the first instance, was necessarily a kind of subsistence farming. Men were thrown upon their own resources in the presence of abundant, cheap, and fertile soil. By clearing and cultivating some of this land, keeping livestock to live on natural grasses and on browse, roots, nuts, acorns, etc., and by associating household industries with farming, men could hope to make a living in primitive fashion. The doing of this became the regular procedure of many thousands of colonists, especially those who settled in New England. The habits, the skills, the bodily strength and moral fiber guaranteeing survival under such conditions, were developed as fixed traits of American character, and became essential conditions of the westward movement which led to the conquest of the continent for agriculture, and ultimately for the culture appropriate to enlightened living. As population pushed westward toward new frontiers, the subsistence farmer was usually the true "pioneer"; however, his movements may have been suggested or directed by fur traders, promoters of transportation, or other commercial agencies.

Virginians, the first English colonists, began like those of Plymouth to farm for the sake of a livelihood. But the planting of tobacco[qv] quickly changed the agriculture of that colony in large part to the business type of farming under the planting and slave labor economy. The Virginians, in the item of tobacco, had hit upon a crop for which there was an adequate cash market in England, the necessary condition to make farming a business. Land was easy to procure; capital could be derived from the crops; labor was provided at first by indentured white servants[qv], drawn from the poorest class of immigrants, and finally by African slaves[qv]. The temptation to increase land holdings, enlarge the labor group, strengthen management, and multiply its profits was such that great plantations inevitably resulted with all the social, economic and political concomitants of such a system.

The plantation type[qv] of agriculture came to have a powerful appeal for social and political reasons, so that even when its economic soundness was in doubt it continued to flourish as movement westward in the Southern states took place. The greatest single economic cause of its expansion, after tobacco, indigo and rice[qqv] had reached the limits of profitable cultivation in Virginia, the Carolinas and Georgia, was the production of short staple cotton[qv], ginned by machinery. For that product the demand, during a certain period, seemed unlimited, cotton being the chief export of the United States; and plantations spread over the most available lands in all the states of the lower South. The number of small and moderate-size farms, mainly subsistence homesteads[qv], in that region was always much greater than the number of plantations, but the plantations and their owners dominated the area economically, socially and politically.

Planters and their families constituted a farming aristocracy modeled in colonial times upon the English country gentry. Pretentious houses, elegant furniture and rich plate, spectacular turnouts, and stables of superior saddle horses were among the evidences of their distinction. They dispensed a generous hospitality, visited much, leaving overseers in charge of their farming operations and their slaves; they devoted much time to public affairs, educated their children in the best schools and colleges. For many years, prior to the Civil War, the Southern planting class was the leading group in national politics as well as in the affairs of their several states. Washington, Jefferson, Madison, Monroe and Jackson, among the Presidents, belonged to the Southern planter class.

Both the primitive subsistence farming and big business farming of the plantation type exploited the soil[qv], robbing it of its fertility and causing it to waste away through erosion. By owning vast areas and continually opening up new fields, planters were able to maintain themselves for several generations during which "old fields," covered with weeds, bramble, and finally a crop of young timber, expanded apace. Northern subsistence farmers, on their smaller areas, followed courses not greatly dissimilar. New fields were opened until the entire area, in many cases, had been cleared and soon the farm as a whole was a reluctant producer. Before the close of the 18th century the farms of southern New England could no longer be made to yield profitable crops of wheat[qv], and so the people lived on bread made of a mixture of corn and rye, "rye and injun," as it was called. It was haphazard farming at best.

So long as the absence of a cash market for farm products deprived the people of an incentive to better farming, the primitive methods persisted. The change was brought about through the growth of towns and cities based on commerce and industry, the promotion of foreign trade, and the opening of roads, canals and other means of transportation[qqv] enabling farmers of the interior to reach the seacoast with their products. The planters of the South had an advantage in that ocean-going vessels could ascend the rivers, docking at the planters' wharves. Earliest improvement, of course, came to the farms nearest the port cities, Boston, New Haven, New York, Philadelphia. High prices for grain in Europe during the Napoleonic wars gave a notable stimulus to wheat growing, both North and South. The progress of manufacturing during and after the War of 1812, marked by the rapid growth of city populations, dependent for supplies upon the farms, gave a powerful and permanent impulse to agricultural improvement, "better farming." Now began the general agitation of the subject by organized groups known as agricultural societies[qv], the establishment of an agricultural press, the widespread attention to English books on farming, the beginnings of the importation from England of improved livestock, the general awakening of the American newspapers to the needs of their rural constituencies. The *American Farmer,* begun at Baltimore in 1819, was the first American farm journal[qv]. It soon had a large number of imitators, especially in the North.

This period, also, was marked by a particularly rapid movement of population into what was destined to become the greatest farming area of the United States, the Middle West. Indiana, Illinois and Missouri gained the status of statehood by 1820. Michigan, Iowa and Wisconsin were destined to follow within the space of a single generation. This extraordinary westward movement[qv] tended to revolutionize agricultural conditions. The Government's land laws were liberalized so that it was practically possible for settlers to buy good farm land at $1.25 per acre, and a pre-emption[qv] right was soon added as a further concession to settlers. New transportation agencies, the steamboat, perfected for use on western rivers by 1817, the great canals of which the most important was the Erie Canal completed in 1825, and the beginnings of railroads[qqv], partially removed the handicaps of western farmers and brought them, with their fresh fertile lands, in partial competition with farmers of the East. The latter could not survive, save on the lowest subsistence plane from which they had already gradually risen, without a determined and well-directed policy of agricultural improvement.

Such improvement, since Northeastern farms generally required fertilization, called for emphasis upon the production of livestock—cattle, hogs, sheep, and to some extent, horses. The demand of the cities for meat, for butter and cheese (*see* Dairy Industry), wool to feed the factory spindles, and horses to draw coaches and drays was such that a policy of livestock[qv] improvement and better management also could be logically based upon it. It seemed the way to save the agriculture of the Northeastern states. But a livestock economy required more land than did the primitive subsistence farming. The old 50, 75, or 100 acre farms were found to be uneconomical for keeping herds and flocks of sufficient size to pay dividends.

The conjunction of the new farming, based on livestock, in the Northeast, with the opening of vast new and fertile wheat-growing areas in the Middle West, was a principal cause of the large emigration from older states to newer in that period. Owners of farms that were too small sold to their neighbors and went west, as did the sons and daughters of thousands of farm households, attracted by the ease with which farms could be made on the open lands, and fortunes acquired through wheat growing. The latter industry, in turn, under the impulsion of new machinery for harvesting and cultivation, steadily tended toward an enlarged scale of operations (*see* Farm Machinery).

The phenomenon of open-land farming with wheat as the money crop was a new one. The valleys of the Delaware and Susquehanna rivers, the earlier wheat centers, had originally been wooded. The Genesee valley furnished the foretaste of what the West would supply in seemingly endless abundance—rich, level, grass-covered lands, easily subdued to cultivation. The difficulty was that such lands, equally with the timbered lands, quickly became conditioned against wheat, yielding ever more meager returns to the cultivator. Besides, the very ease of cultivation proved a disadvantage, for the open-land farmer was tempted to break up his entire farm in a few years in order to have the maximum amount of wheat to sell. Consequently, the wheat farms on the open lands "ran down," and in a short time became unprofitable.

The remedy was obvious: a different kind of farming, with livestock, feed crops, and fertilization as the watchwords (*see* Diversification, Agricultural). Thousands of the earlier wheat growers, wedded to their vocation, simply sold out and went farther west to raise wheat under more favorable, that is, newer, conditions, and on a larger scale. Genesee valley wheat farmers, not a few, removed first to Wisconsin or Iowa, then to Minnesota or the Red River valley, and finally to the Palouse country of Washington, increasing their holdings and their product at each remove. Others, realizing that soil robbery is a losing game, adopted the new farming and remade their former wheat farms into stock and dairy farms. Thus it was that agricultural improvement moved westward at the remove of about one generation behind the pioneer settlers.

The westward movement brought into view two new phases of big-business farming in addition to the planting system characteristic of the South. These were, first, large-scale cattle raising under the open ranching or grazing system and, second, bonanza wheat farming on the Great Plains by the machine method.

Ranching was a development, under new and favorable conditions, of practices which were already old at the middle of the 19th century. The business of cattle raising was normal to all peaceful frontiers, and in the piedmont[qv] district of Virginia, North and South Carolina, cowpens and cattle trails, as well as cowboys, were well understood phenomena of the 18th century. The vast supply of Spanish cattle which fell to the United States upon the annexation of Texas[qv], and the gradual pacification of Indian tribes over enormous stretches of the Great Plains, which were covered with nutritious grasses, gave the new impetus to the open-range cattle business[qv] which had its greatest development in the period 1865 to 1885. The cattle kings, owners of herds numbering thousands, lorded it over customary ranges embracing sometimes hundreds of thousands of acres of government land. Private control of a few hundred acres dominating watering privileges was all that was necessary to bring about such control.

Ranchers were the nabobs of the grazing states and territories, as the planters were of the cotton and tobacco states, although due to their sparse numbers and isolation they did not dominate all life in the manner of the planters, nor did they constitute an acknowledged aristocracy. In some respects the ranchers' position was quite as precarious as that of the planters. Not only did their profits depend on the price of beef and the cost of marketing, but quite as much on weather and on cattle diseases. Untimely rains in the fall spoiled the grass for winter feeding. But blizzards[qv] such as visited nearly the entire grazing area in the winter of 1885–86 decimated the herds and brought universal bankruptcy to the owners. Foot-and-mouth disease, Texas fever, and murrain to which ranch cattle were subject, and sometimes an epidemic of cattle thieving, played havoc with a business that, with luck, made surer profits than any other phase of agriculture.

Cattle ranchers also had to reckon with the sheep ranchers who were rival contenders for the range, especially in the rough land areas; and when the pressure of population made the Great Plains an object of desire to farmers, who had the legal support of the Federal Government, the doom of the open range became assured. Cattle ranching continues, but under far different conditions. The rancher now generally owns or leases his range lands. He puts up winter feed and protects his cattle against storms. His herd is no longer composed of lanky Texas longhorns[qv], but of blocky, compact beef-breed varieties like the Herefords, Shorthorns, or Galloways. The ranches have become big stock farms.

Sheep[qv] ranching at times was more profitable than cattle ranching. The mountain areas are best adapted to sheep, and under the herding system—a man with a wagon in charge of thousands of sheep—the cost of raising them was extraordinarily low, so that large profits rewarded good management.

The bonanza wheat farms[qv] were made possible by the existence in a few regions like the Red River valley, the Palouse country, and the Great Valley of California, of practically unlimited stretches of unusually enduring fertile soil, which could be counted on to grow profitable wheat crops for many successive years. With some thousands of acres of such land, bought at a cheap price, with capital to procure machinery, work stock, and labor, the manager could ordinarily count on very large profits. At least that was true during the period of very heavy European demand for American wheat, which lasted from the 1840's down to recent times. The substitution of tractors[qv] for horse power, with implements of cultivation adapted to the newer power, and the combine[qv] instead of the self-binder and the threshing machine to harvest the crop, have made profits possible on the cheaper lands even at very much less than the traditionary "dollar a bushel" for wheat.

Great improvements have been made in the process of wheat growing, as in cattle raising. Government research in seed breeding, and in the discovery of varieties best suited to different types of soil and climate like the dry and high plateau lands, also in methods of cultivation and conditions of marketing, have affected the business to a considerable extent. Recently, the Government's attempt at crop control has been an element to be reckoned with (*see* Agricultural Adjustment Administration). The chief problem under present world conditions is in the tendency of wheat growers to oversupply the market, foreign purchases having declined sharply since 1920 and the domestic market being insufficient to absorb the bumper crops of good years. Under adverse conditions, however, it is clear that the larger capitalistic growers have the advantage over small growers, their costs of production being lower. Nevertheless, the advance in farm land prices has resulted in breaking up many of the greatest wheat-growing units. There is no longer a Dalrymple farm in the Red River valley of North Dakota with its spectacular procession of scores of self-binders reaping a single great field. The size of big wheat farms in the Palouse area today is frequently gauged by the capacity of a unit of machinery, the combine setting the standard.

A major proportion of all wheat grown now is produced on farms that are under 1000 acres in extent. Farms over that size, however, exist to a considerable number, especially in the states of the Pacific Northwest. The annual production for a number of years prior to the World War was between 500,000,000 and 600,000,000 bushels. In 1938 the crop is estimated at 800,000,000.

Tremendous strides in agricultural improvement were made in England during the second half of the 18th century, in the benefits of which the United States shared in the 19th. The body of information accumulated in books became directly available to Americans, and in addition the intercourse of Americans with English farming enthusiasts had a certain influence toward inspiring the imitation of the better British farming methods. It was partly personal contacts that created the better farming agitation through the press, and through organization.

Nevertheless, most of this British material was a systematization of the results of common-sense practice rather than a body of scientific knowledge. It was not until the science of chemistry began to be applied to the problems of agriculture that we have the true beginnings of a science of agriculture. The practical commencement was made in 1803, when Sir Humphry Davy gave his lectures on "the connection of chemistry with vegetable physiology," published ten years later as *Elements of Agricultural Chemistry*. Boussingault in France and Justus Liebig in Germany, especially the latter, advanced the science enormously through experimentation and publication, and in 1843 J. B. Lawes founded the world-famous Rothamsted station in England, securing as chief coadjutor the chemist, J. H. Gilbert.

Americans quickly availed themselves of the scientific knowledge obtainable in England, Scotland, Holland, Germany and France; and, with their genius for organization, produced a magnificent system of agricultural schools and of experiment stations[qqv] which European countries have a right to envy. In short, before the close of the 19th century America was in possession of the equipment for making its agriculture as nearly professional as is possible in an activity compounded of science, business and habitual practice. Within the present century the progress of organization has gone forward till practically every farmer in every county of the forty-eight states has at his command not only the best scientific aids in print, but the advice of a scientifically trained farm expert, and schools in which his children can learn the science of farming.

Despite all this, despite the enormous outlay made by the Federal Government and by the states in the interest of improved and scientific agriculture, it is a truism to say that most Americans continue to farm in traditional ways instead of following the guidance furnished by science, although the proportion of these is gradually decreasing. The Government's land policies of the past have had much to do with conditioning unfavorably the agriculture of the present; for example, in permitting the homesteading[qv] of lands unfitted for permanent cultivation, permitting forest destruction, the overgrazing of grasslands and forest land, etc.

The Government's land policy[qv] was framed for farmers going into the fertile, well-watered, wooded, or open lands of the Middle West. It was ill adapted to the needs of cattle ranchers who wished to utilize the high plains for grazing, their best use. For the Middle Westerner a homestead of 160 acres would insure a family's living; a section, 640 acres, would constitute a large estate. The rancher, however, needed for his business, in order to make it pay, a township, possibly more than a township, covered with the sparse buffalo grass.

A multitude of problems must be solved before farming in America can be brought to its ideal perfection professionally, and as a way of living.

[Everett E. Edwards, *A Bibliography of the History of Agriculture*, Department of Agriculture Miscellaneous Publication No. 84, 1930; Percy Wells Bidwell, *Rural Economy in New England;* Percy Wells Bidwell and John I. Falconer, *History of Agriculture in the Northern United States, 1620-1860;* L. C. Gray, *History of Agriculture in the Southern United States to 1860;* U. B. Phillips, *Life and Labor in the Old South;* A. O. Craven, The Agricultural Reformers of the Ante-Bellum South, *American Historical Review*, 1928; Joseph Schafer, *The Social History of American Agriculture;* A. C. True, *History of Agricultural Education; Report of the Country Life Commission*, Washington, 1909; B. H. Hibbard, *A History of the Public Land Policies.*]

JOSEPH SCHAFER

Agriculture, Credit for. *See* Farm Credit Agencies, Federal.

Agriculture, Department of. A Federal organization devoted exclusively to agriculture was anticipated in the activities carried on by the Patent Office[qv] from 1836 to 1862. These activities were begun by the Commissioner of Patents, who, independently of his office, assumed responsibility for the distribution of new and valuable seeds among farmers in 1836. Three years later this work received official recognition when Congress made a small appropriation to the Patent Office for "collecting and distributing seeds, prosecuting agricultural investigations, and procuring agricultural statistics." For the first twenty years, the Patent Office was primarily concerned with the collection of agricultural statistics and the purchase and distribution of seeds. In 1854 the agricultural work received a scientific emphasis with the employment of a chemist, botanist and entomologist, and with the establishment of a garden for experiments.

Rapid urbanization, need for increased production during the Civil War, and pressure from agricultural societies[qv] caused the establishment, by the organic act of May 5, 1862, of a Department of Agriculture headed by a commissioner. Under the commissioners, from 1862 to 1889, the department passed through its formative period. The scope of its work was constantly extended, and as it became specialized, various administrative units were set up to carry out the functions theretofore performed by individuals, which later developed into the bureaus of the present day. The gathering and disseminating of agricultural information and the distributing of seeds was continued, while the scientific work of the divisions of Chemistry, Entomology and Botany, which were created shortly after the establishment of the department, was supplemented by the creation of new divisions, such as Microscopy in 1871, Forestry in 1880, Veterinary in 1883, Economic Ornithology and Mammalogy in 1886, Pomology in 1886, and Vegetable Physiology and Pathology in 1887. The success of the Bureau of Animal Industry, established in 1884, in combating animal diseases and its notable scientific achievements in the theory of diseases hastened the department's elevation to cabinet status in 1889.

With cabinet status, the department passed into its expansive period, in which its work came to cover almost every phase of agricultural endeavor. Its activities are carried on through an organization of ever-increasing complexity, which at present is headed by the Secretary, assisted by general administrative officers working through the following offices: Land Use Co-ordination, Personnel, Budget and Finance, Operation, Solicitor, Information, and Experiment Stations; through the following bureaus: Agricultural Economics, Animal Industry, Biological Survey, Chemistry and Soils, Dairy Industry, Entomology and Plant Quarantine, Federal Surplus Commodities, Home Economics, Plant Industry, Public Roads, and Weather; through the following services: Forest, Extension, and Soil Conservation; through the following administrations: Agricultural Adjustment, Commodity Exchange, Farm Security, and Food and Drug; and through the following corporations: Federal Surplus Commodities, and Federal Crop Insurance.

These activities, in general, fall into several classes: 1. Research activities, which predominate in most bureaus, and which relate to various physical phenomena, such as those connected with soils, climate, etc., to various biological phenomena, which in agriculture have been developed into highly specialized phases such as genetics, plant and animal pathology, agronomy, horticulture, dairying and animal husbandry, and to various social phenomena arising from the production, distribution and consumption of agricultural commodities. Planning activities are consolidated in the Bureau of Agricultural Economics, and incorporate erosion control, rehabilitation, price stability, marketing, production adjustment, security of farm tenure, forest wild life and soil conservation. As a result of the Hatch Act of 1887, the department through the Office of Experiment Stations co-ordinates and directs similar research activities of the agricultural colleges throughout the country. 2. Extension and information activities, which relate to the dissemination of information resulting from the research activities of the department and of state agricultural colleges, and which are carried out co-operatively by the Extension Service and the states through county agents, as a result of the Smith-Lever Act[qv] of 1914. 3. Eradication or control of plant and animal diseases and pests, attempted chiefly by the Bureau of Entomology and Plant Quarantine and the Bureau of Animal Industry. 4. Service activities, such as weather reporting by the Weather Bureau, which was transferred to the department from the War Department in 1891, crop reporting by the Bureau of Agricultural Economics, forest administration by the Forest Service, and wild-life-refuge administration by the Bureau of Biological Survey. 5. Administration of regulatory laws, which began with the inspection and quarantine of livestock in 1884 and which now include more than fifty laws, pertaining, among other matters, to the safeguarding of the food and drug supply, to the inspection of commodities in interstate shipment, to the maintenance of commodity standards, to the supervision of packers, stockyards, and of commodity exchanges. 6. Road construction, carried out co-operatively by the Bureau of Public Roads and the states, as a result of the Federal Aid Road Act of 1916[qv]. 7. Emergency-adjustment work carried on in consequence of numerous important Congressional enactments during the Roosevelt administration, resulting in various programs designed to promote the conservation of the basic resources of the country: greater security of tenure, and the efficient production, distribution and utilization of agricultural products.

[Francis G. Caffey, *A Brief Statutory History of the United States Department of Agriculture*, U. S. Department of Agriculture, Office of the Solicitor, Washington, 1916; Arthur P. Chew, *The Response of Government to Agriculture*, Washington, 1937; M. S. Eisenhower and Arthur P. Chew, *The United States Department of Agriculture: Its Structure and Functions*, U. S. Department of Agriculture, Miscellaneous Publication No. 88, 2nd rev., Washington, 1934; Charles H. Greathouse, *Historical Sketch of the United States Department of Agriculture: Its Objects and Present Organization*, U. S. Department of Agriculture, Division of Publication, Bulletin No. 3, 2nd rev., Washington, 1907; James M. Swank, *The Department of Agriculture: Its History and Objects*, U. S. Department of Agriculture, Report No. 7, Washington, 1872; William L. Wanlass, *The United States Department of Agriculture: A Study in Administration;* Edward Wiest, *Agricultural Organization in the United States*.]

T. R. SCHELLENBERG

Agriculture, European Influences upon. Having an abundance of land and a scarcity of labor the early settlers in America reverted, in general, to the system of extensive husbandry so common in Europe centuries earlier. The nucleated village plan was transplanted to New England and New France but elsewhere scattered homesteads were generally preferred. The modified feudal system introduced in the proprietary colonies broke down and the manors became great plantations. In the Illinois country[qv] the French established a form of the European land system with commons and cultivated common fields. The row culture, so characteristic of American agriculture, was adopted, along with maize, from the Indian. The field-grass system of Europe awaited more mature settlements. The field tools after the early 19th century were developed to fit local conditions and with slight influence from abroad.

The colonists on their rich lands generally disregarded the advanced English ideas on agriculture but when their soils[qv] began to show signs of exhaustion, the more progressive farmers turned to England for guidance. Except for Jared Eliot, who followed English thought, the principal agricultural writers who influenced America until well into the 19th century were Englishmen. Coke of Holkham was influential in introducing the agricultural county fair[qv] into America. He also sent Devon cattle, particularly for the foundation of the Patterson herd in Maryland. Sir John Sinclair and Arthur Young of the English Board of Agriculture were in correspondence with Washington, Jefferson and others and stimulated the formation of agricultural societies[qv] in America and the adoption of improved practices. After 1815, however, America turned its face inward and developed a strong feeling of nationalism and self-confidence. European influence waned but the work of the soil chemist, Johnston of Edinburgh, was widely known and highly regarded in America near the middle of the 19th century. Later in the century much breeding livestock[qv] was imported for the improvement of American flocks and herds.

[L. C. Gray, *History of Agriculture in the Southern United States to 1860;* N. S. B. Gras, *A History of Agriculture;* R. C. Loehr, The Influence of English Agriculture upon American Agriculture, 1775-1825, *Agricultural History,* 11:3-15.]

RUSSELL H. ANDERSON

Agriculture, Government Control of. In 1932 the index number of the Federal Bureau of Agricultural Economics, expressing the ratio of prices received by farmers for the commodities they sold in relation to prices paid for the goods they purchased, was 53 as compared with 100 on a five-year base, August, 1909–July, 1914. In his campaign utterances in the fall of 1932, Gov. Franklin D. Roosevelt of New York severely condemned the farm relief[qv] measures of the Hoover administration, and promised the farmers of the nation that if elected President he would immediately call their leaders together to formulate a plan upon which they could agree as best for the improvement of agricultural conditions. Toward that objective, the President-elect had Henry Morgenthau, Jr., who was at that time Chairman of the Advisory Committee on Agriculture in New York State, meet with some fifty agricultural leaders in Washington on Dec. 12, 1932. The results of this conference were presented in the form of amendments to the Jones Bill and came before the last lame duck[qv] Congress, but a House and a Senate hostile toward each other prevented any definite action.

On March 10, 1933, Secretary of Agriculture Henry A. Wallace called a meeting of representative farm leaders in Washington, and the deliberations of this group, together with the technical assistance of agricultural specialists, resulted in the Agricultural Adjustment Act[qv] which was approved by the President on May 12, 1933. This measure was composed of three parts: (1) that granting authority to the President, through the Secretary of Agriculture, to take steps to increase agricultural purchasing power by means of raising farm income; (2) another empowering the Farm Credit Administration (*see* Farm Credit Agencies) to lighten the load of farm mortgages; and (3) the granting of certain unusual powers to the President (*see* Presidents, Special Powers Granted to) with regard to the national currency and credit. The act provided, upon ratification by referenda of the farmers concerned, authority to establish quotas for limiting the production by individual farmers of certain leading agricultural commodities considered as basic. No penalties were provided in the act for those who did not care to enter into such a voluntary contract, but such penalties were established for the cotton grower in the separate Bankhead Cotton Act[qv] of 1934 and for the tobacco grower in the similar Kerr Tobacco Act. The principle employed in the act was that of rewarding the farmer by benefit payments for his compliance. The measure was self-financing through processing taxes collected by the Bureau of Internal Revenue from the first domestic processor of each of the basic commodities.

On Jan. 6, 1936, the original Agricultural Adjustment Act was declared unconstitutional by the United States Supreme Court on the grounds that agriculture is a purely local activity and that Federal attempts to control its production were in violation of the Tenth Amendment (*see* Constitution) and hence constituted an interference with rights the states had reserved to themselves. In place of the annulled measure, the Soil Conservation and Domestic Allotment Act[qv] was enacted by the Congress on Feb. 29, 1936. The emphasis in this measure was on soil conservation, and the objective was sought by rewarding the farmer for balancing his production between "soil depleting" and "soil conserving" crops and practices. Provision was made, however, for restoration of parity in the purchasing power of the farmer at as rapid a rate as the Secretary of Agriculture determined to be practicable; and, undoubtedly, it was hoped that the response of the farmers would be sufficiently general to bring about an effective control of agricultural production. That this hope was in vain was made apparent by a bumper crop of wheat in 1937, and in the same year, the largest cotton crop ever before produced in this country.

Faced again with the threat of overwhelming farm surpluses, the Congress on Feb. 16, 1938, replaced the Soil Conservation and Domestic Allotment Act of 1936 by the Agricultural Adjustment Act of 1938[qv]. This measure provided for the continuation of the soil conservation program inaugurated in 1936. In addition, however, it authorized national acreage allotments set at levels designed to bring about production ample for domestic consumption, for exports and for reserve supplies; marketing quotas for commercial producers of cotton, wheat, corn, tobacco and rice; the systematic storage, with the assistance of government loans, of food and feed surpluses in years of big yields and the release of these in lean years; and beginning in 1939, crop insurance for wheat, the premiums to be paid in kind. Marketing quotas were to be invoked upon the appearance of designated surpluses which promised to be burdensome, and were to be effective then only upon approval of a two-thirds majority of the farmers concerned. Once the marketing quotas were established, heavy penalties were provided for noncompliance. Funds for carrying out the provisions of the act were to be provided through appropriations from the Treasury of the United States.

[Mordecai Ezekiel and Louis H. Bean, *Economic Bases for the Agricultural Adjustment Act*, U. S. Dept. of Agriculture, December, 1933; Agricultural Adjustment Administration, *Achieving a Balanced Agriculture;* Reports of the Agricultural Adjustment Administration; Wilson Gee, *American Farm Policy; Agricultural Adjustment Act*, Publication No. 10, H. R. 3835, 73rd Congress, approved May 12, 1933; *Soil Conservation and Domestic Allotment Act*, Publication No. 461, S. 3780, 74th Congress, approved Feb. 29, 1936; *Agricultural Adjustment Act of 1938*, Publication No. 430, H. R. 8505, 75th Congress, approved Feb. 16, 1938.]

WILSON GEE

Agriculture, The Influence of Transportation on. In the opening of new settlements away from the coast this varied with the relative value of the products raised. Wheat, wool, butter and cheese bore the cost of transportation better than corn and oats[qqv] for example. Western Pennsylvania could haul whiskey but not grain to the seaboard (*see* Whiskey Insurrection).

Early settlers across the mountains complained bitterly when the Spanish interfered with their outlet down the Mississippi (*see* Mississippi River, Free Navigation of). Further development of this area led to a demand for a trade way which would permit a commercial agriculture, and trade connections with the East. The first such highway, the Erie Canal[qv], opened the wheat lands of western New York and led to a shift from grain to livestock in New England. But the highway which carried Genesee wheat brought settlers and a market to the lake country. The influx of settlers absorbed the produce for some years but exports of wheat began in 1835 from Ohio and steadily grew in volume, with profitable shipment limited to the area near Lake Erie.

The Cumberland Road[qv] greatly reduced the time of travel overland to the Ohio, but few products could bear the cost of hauling over the mountains. The road facilitated the entry of settlers and the steamboat[qv] supplied them with goods. The southern outlet gave the Mississippi and Ohio lands a marked advantage over the lake country until the opening of the Erie Canal. As connections were made between the systems, as the Illinois and Michigan Canal[qv], much of the traffic turned toward the lakes. Corn could bear the cost of wagon transport some thirty miles and wheat about fifty, thus much of the interior remained on a subsistence basis until the coming of the railway[qv] net which placed practically the whole Middle West within reach of a market. The South lacked such a network of railroads but had numerous navigable rivers.

Beyond the Mississippi such trails as the Oregon and Santa Fe[qqv] had fostered trade and led some settlers into the far West, but commercial agriculture in most instances awaited the railroad. When the railroad reached Abilene[qv], Kans., in 1867, it tapped the growing cattle empire of the Southwest which now spread to the northern plains (*see* Cow Country). Wheat raisers pressed westward and later, with the extension of the railroad into the Dakotas and the development of new milling machinery, they opened up the northern wheat belt.

When the railroads were opening up new markets, farmers welcomed them as outstanding benefactors. In the eighteen-seventies, when the farmers of the older sections began to suffer from low prices and relatively high freight rates, they sought to place the blame for their troubles upon the railroads and grain elevators[qv]. Illinois began the crusade against them with a regulating act in 1870 and other states followed with similar "Granger" laws[qv]. In their zeal the states overstepped their powers under the Constitution and the problem, outlined by the efforts of the states, was placed before Congress which passed the Interstate Commerce Act[qv] in 1887.

Since 1920 the motor truck[qv] has been an important factor in the transportation of farm products, particularly fruit, vegetables, livestock and milk. It has taken a commanding position within a range of 150 miles and has won much traffic at greater distances. In connection with radio marketing service it has had a stabilizing influence, reducing day-to-day fluctuations. The influence of the motor truck has been largely in the distribution of products although it has led to some shifts of producing areas by restoring more of the advantages of proximity to market.

[H. U. Faulkner, *Economic History of the United States;* R. H. Anderson, New York Agriculture Meets the West, *Wisconsin Magazine of History*, Dec. 1932,-Mar., 1933; S. J. Buck, *The Granger Movement.*]

RUSSELL H. ANDERSON

Aguayo Expedition, THE (1720–22). Marquis San Miguel de Aguayo, governor of Coahuila[qv] and Texas, left Monclova in 1720 with an expedition of 500 soldiers to re-establish the Spanish missions and presidios in East Texas which had been abandoned in 1719 because of trouble with the French at Natchitoches[qv]. Joined by eighty refugees at San Antonio, Aguayo continued northeastward, re-established six missions and fortified Adaes (now Robeline, La.) near the French. On his return in 1722, he erected a mission near the site of LaSalle's Fort St. Louis[qv]. Thus Aguayo in effect put an end to French claims in Texas.

[Eleanor Buckley, The Aguayo Expedition in Texas and Louisiana, *Texas Historical Quarterly*, Vol. XV.]

L. W. NEWTON

Ague, OR SHAKES AND AGUE, THE, was a disease of malarial origin prevalent on the frontier from the Appalachian to the Rocky Mountains. It was thought to be caused by the dew or by gases from newly plowed virgin soil. The patient was afflicted with chills lasting an hour or two, succeeded by a fever, severe headache, and delirium lasting six to eight hours. Then came a devitalizing sweat and temporary recovery only to be followed by the same process in from one to three days. Hardly a person in low territory escaped it. Quinine was the best of innumerable remedies.

[Everett Dick, *The Sod-House Frontier.*]

EVERETT DICK

Air Commerce Act of 1926, THE. *See* Civil Aeronautics Act.

Air Conditioning. The only air conditioning known in the 19th century consisted of hot air or steam heating and ventilating fans. Cotton mills, to keep down lint, learned to use a fine water spray, which both moistened and cooled the air. In 1897 Joseph McCreary patented an air washer which also cooled and humidified to some extent. In 1906 Stuart W. Cramer devised an automatic humidity control, and Willis H. Carrier invented an improved air washer which automatically controlled temperature. Other improvements followed. After 1920 artificial cooling of theaters in summer increased rapidly, and no large new theaters were erected without complete air conditioning. In other buildings the improvement came more slowly. After 1930 the conditioning of railway trains came to be more and more an expected service.

[Earl Vernon Hill, *Aerology for Amateurs and Others; Scientific American*, 1897-1938.]

ALVIN F. HARLOW

Air Mail. The first test of air-mail service was made in May, 1918, when the United States Army and the Post Office Department together set up an experimental line between New York and Washington, using army pilots. After three months, the Post Office assumed entire control of the line, and employed civilian aviators. This route was too short to give the plane much advantage over the railway, and did not continue long. Other disconnected lines were tried, between New York and Cleveland, Cleveland and Chicago, Chicago and Omaha, but all had the same fault—they were too short to attract mail at high rates. In 1920 the Post Office Department installed a service between New York and San Francisco, whereon the planes flew only by daylight, the mail being transferred from them at dusk to railway trains and rushed on, to take to the air again early next morning. This was replaced on July 1, 1924, by a continuous, day-and-night service across the continent. In 1926–

27 the Department turned the handling over to private corporations as contractors. Branch lines and north-and-south lines were rapidly added. In 1930 when two new routes—New York to Los Angeles via St. Louis and Los Angeles to Atlanta—were designated, there were only two bids for the former contract and one for the latter. Charging that there had been collusion among air-line owners in the bidding, Postmaster-General Farley on Feb. 9, 1934, canceled all air mail contracts, and for four months army planes carried the mail, while an official investigation was conducted. There were several fatal accidents to army fliers. New contracts were signed in June, and the service, which by this time covered the United States pretty thoroughly and connected with lines to Canada, the West Indies, Mexico, Central and South America, was returned to private planes.

In 1935 regular mail service was established across the Pacific between San Francisco and Manila, and in 1939 transatlantic service between New York and London.

[Alvin F. Harlow, *Old Post Bags;* Paul T. David, *The Economics of Air Mail Transportation.*]

ALVIN F. HARLOW

Air Navigation Agreements, International. The United States did not ratify the Convention Relating to the Regulation of Air Navigation, negotiated at the Paris Peace Conference in 1919, which created the Commission Internationale de Navigation Aérienne. In 1923, at the Pan-American Conference^qv in Santiago, the United States took a prominent role in negotiations that finally led to the signing of the Pan-American Convention of Commercial Aviation in 1928. While the United States has refrained from participation in multipartite agreements regarding public air law with European countries, it has participated in conferences for the codification of private air law such as the Warsaw Conference of 1930, and is usually represented on the Comité International Technique d'Experts Juridique Aériens. The United States has numerous bipartite agreements with such countries as Canada, Mexico, Cuba and the Latin-American states which regulate flights over the territories of the signatory powers.

[Kenneth Colegrove, *International Control of Aviation.*]

KENNETH COLEGROVE

Air Photography. The first American aerial photograph was a view of Boston taken from a captive balloon by J. W. Black on Oct. 13, 1860. Few attempts to follow up Black's work were made in the next fifty years, the balloon photographs of W. N. Jennings made in the early eighteen-nineties, and the development of kite photography by W. A. Eddy (1895) being the most important exceptions. The advent of the airplane resulted in further efforts. The earliest photographs from airplanes in this country were probably made in 1911. The first airplane photograph used as a newspaper illustration is said to have been a view of fire-destroyed Springfield, Mass., taken on Jan. 26, 1914.

During the World War, rapid developments in aerial cameras were made both at home and abroad. The marked improvement in aerial photographic technique resulting from these developments led, by 1920, to extensive photographic mapping by a number of public and private agencies. As a result, up to April 1, 1938, 1,505,100 square miles of continental United States had been mapped photographically for various bureaus of the Department of Agriculture, the United States Coast and Geodetic Survey and the United States Geological Survey.

[Robert Taft, *Photography and the American Scene;* Sherman M. Fairchild, Aerial Photography, *Annals of the American Academy*, 1927, Vol. 131, pp. 49-55; H. K. Baisley, Aerial Photography, *Annual Report of the Smithsonian Institution*, 1936, pp. 383-390; *Photogrammetric Engineering*, 1938, Vol. 4, No. 3, pp. 169-207.]

ROBERT TAFT

Airplane, The. *See* Aviation.

Airplane Disasters, in the United States, have accompanied the progress of aviation as indeed of all other modes of transportation. In 1908, while airplane flights were still in the experimental stage, Orville Wright crashed his plane, killing his passenger, Lt. Selfridge, in a demonstration before the War Department at Fort Myer. In 1911, John J. Montgomery, of Santa Clara College in California, whose experiments contributed much to the art of gliding, was killed in one of his machines. The conquest of the Atlantic and the Pacific was accomplished only after numerous disasters. Several fatal accidents attended the contest to win the Orteig prize for the first nonstop flight from New York to Paris over the Atlantic; in 1926, René Fonck crashed his plane when taking off from Roosevelt Field and two of his crew were burned to death, and in 1927 the French aviators, Nungesser and Coli, were lost over the Atlantic when attempting the more difficult east-to-west crossing. The Dole race (*see* Airplane Races) from Oakland to Hawaii in August, 1927, cost ten lives when several planes crashed, two disappeared over the Pacific and two planes were lost while searching for them. In 1937, the gallant woman aviator, Amelia Earhart, and her navigator were lost in the Pacific on a flight around the world when flying the lap between New Guinea and Howland Island. In January, 1938, the veteran Capt. Edwin C. Musick and his crew of six, on the *Samoan Clipper,* disappeared when making a trial flight for the new Pan-American Airways service from Pago Pago Harbor to Auckland, New Zealand.

In commercial flying, every year following the inception of scheduled routes has taken its toll of accidents and deaths. In the period of 1918–26, when the Post Office Department flew the mail, there were thirty-nine fatalities (thirty being pilots and nine passengers) in the 11,835,080 miles flown. In the ten years of 1928 to 1937, when the carriage of the mails as well as passengers was by transport companies, there were 353 fatalities in a total of 488,348,434 miles of flying over scheduled routes.

The death of Sen. Bronson M. Cutting, in 1935, in the crash of a transcontinental airliner in Missouri, led the United States Senate to cause an investigation of airplane accidents and to recommend more rigid governmental regulation. Previous to the Civil Aeronautics Act of 1938[qv], the Secretary of Commerce and the Director of the Bureau of Commerce were responsible for the enforcement of regulations for air safety, while investigation boards were appointed each time an accident occurred. Under the act of 1938 responsibility for regulation was concentrated in the Civil Aeronautics Authority, while a permanent Air Safety Board investigated and reported upon all accidents in air commerce.

[*Annual Report of the Director of Aeronautics to the Secretary of Commerce; Air Commerce Bulletin; Senate Report No. 185*, 75th Congress, 1st session.]

KENNETH COLEGROVE

Airplane Races played a prominent role in stimulating the development of aircraft as well as in arousing popular interest in aeronautical progress. At the first large air meet or exhibition held in the United States at Los Angeles in January, 1910, Glenn H. Curtiss made a new world's record for speed with a passenger in the plane, flying at a rate of fifty-five miles an hour. In the same year he won the prize of $10,000 offered by the *New York Herald* for the first flight from Albany to New York, while his pupil, Charles K. Hamilton, won the prize offered by the *New York Times* and the Philadelphia *Public Ledger* for the first flight between the two cities and return in twenty-four hours. The *New York Times* also offered a prize of $25,000 for the first flight between New York and Chicago completed in seven days, and the Chicago *Evening Post* duplicated the prize. For several years after the World War, the Pulitzer Trophy offered by the editor of the *St. Louis Post-Dispatch* and the *New York World* stimulated aeronautical achievement. In 1920, in a race under the auspices of the Aero Club of America, held at Mitchel Field, Garden City, Lt. C. C. Mosley won the trophy with a speed of 156 miles per hour over a closed course. In the race of 1921, at Omaha, the trophy and a world record were won by Bert Acosta with a speed of 176 miles, while in 1923, at St. Louis, the trophy was won by Lt. A. J. Williams at a speed of 243 miles per hour.

The Orteig prize of $25,000 for the first nonstop flight between New York and Paris over the Atlantic, offered in 1919, was not won until 1927 by Charles A. Lindbergh (*see* Lindbergh Flies Across the Atlantic). An innovation in aerial racing in America was the Dole race in 1927, when a planter of Hawaii offered prizes of $25,000 and $10,000 for the first and second airplanes to reach Hawaii from Oakland. In previous competitions, such as the Orteig prize, the competitors were unrestricted as to the time of departure; in the Dole race, all competitors were to take off at approximately the same time, on Aug. 12, which was postponed to Aug. 16 because of weather conditions. The race cost heavily in human lives. Three flyers were killed in preliminary flights. Two planes were lost over the Pacific, and two others disappeared in the search for them resulting in seven more deaths. Of the fifteen planes entering the contest only eight took off, and only two reached Hawaii. The winning plane was piloted by Maj. Arthur Goebel with Lt. William Davis as navigator, in a flight of twenty-five hours and seventeen minutes. The loss of life in the Dole race provoked so much criticism that proposals for similar races across the Atlantic were frowned upon by many aeronautic experts. In the Bendix Transcontinental Speed Dash, held each year since 1929, the contestants take off from Burbank at frequent intervals on the same day.

In 1922 the formation of the National Aeronautic Association placed air races upon a sound basis. The first national air races under its auspices were held in 1923 at St. Louis with an attendance of 50,000 on the last day of the races. Since then the air races have been held generally on the week-end of Labor Day each September. At the races in Cleveland in 1938 a crowd of 79,000 witnessed the three-day events. The principal trophies were the Bendix Transcontinental Speed Dash between Burbank, Calif., and Bendix, N. J., the Greve Trophy Race for speed in traveling 200 miles in twenty laps over a ten-mile course and the Thompson Trophy for speed in a race of 300 miles of thirty laps over a ten-mile course. The purses for these races totalled respectively, $30,000, $25,000 and $45,000.

[*Aircraft Year Book*, published by the Aeronautical Chamber of Commerce of America; *Aviation; Aero Digest.*] KENNETH COLEGROVE

Airports. The establishment of air routes for mail, passenger and express service in the years following the World War required the building of fields for the take off and landing of aircraft, and, at the terminals, hangars for storing and servicing the aircraft. Most of the fields used by the army and navy as well as those of the aeronautical manufacturers were not located convenient to large cities. To facilitate air traffic, in 1918, the municipality of St. Louis appropriated $28,000 to level a field. This was but a beginning and eventually several million dollars were devoted to the construction of a municipal airport. Among other cities which constructed, owned and operated airports were: Newark, Chicago, Pittsburgh, Cleveland, Wichita, Minneapolis, Oakland, San Francisco and Seattle. Other cities such as Philadelphia, Los Angeles (Burbank) and Miami depended upon commercially owned or operated airports. Within a decade every city that was a terminal of an air route was equipped with an airport having cement runways, large hangars and ground stations for radio communication. By 1927, there were 864 municipal and private airports. In that year, under the Air Commerce Act of 1926^qv^, the Department of Commerce assumed the regulation of the Federal system of airways, and the department undertook the encouragement of the development of airports, the building of intermediate landing fields and the encouragement of the airmarking of cities. At the same time the department conducted experimentation with aids to air navigation, such as the transmission by radio teletypewriter, carrying this device to the point where reliability equal to land wire operation was attained permitting the transmission of meteorological information to aircraft while in flight. By 1938, when the Civil Aeronautics Authority took over the regulation of the Federal airways, the governmental agency had established Airway Traffic Control offices and taken responsibility for the operation of such stations in the airports at Newark, Cleveland, Chicago, Pittsburgh, Detroit, Washington, Burbank and Oakland. At this time there were 2376 airports and landing fields in the United States. Of these, 787 were municipal airports, 49 were state-operated airports, 434 commercial airports, 267 intermediate landing fields, 637 marked auxiliary fields, 61 army airdromes, 25 naval air stations, 91 private fields and 25 government fields. For night flying, 717 airports were equipped. In the three years following 1935 the Works Progress Administration^qv^ expended over $93,000,000 of Federal funds on the improvement of airports.

[*Annual Report of the Director of Aeronautics; Annual Report of the Secretary of Commerce; U. S. Department of Commerce: Descriptions of Airports and Landing Fields in the United States, 1938; Aircraft Year Book*, published by the Aeronautical Chamber of Commerce; Joseph H. Wenneman, *Municipal Airports.*]

KENNETH COLEGROVE

Airways are air routes designated for regular travel by aircraft carrying mail, passengers and express and for itinerant aircraft between terminal cities and laid out over the best flying terrain. Prior to the World War, in the United States as in Europe, there were no air routes in continuous operation, save for a few seasonal short lines occasionally operated since 1911 in connection with air meets and exhibitions and other special arrangements. In 1918 an experimental air-mail^qv^ route was started by the Post Office Department between Washington, D. C., and New York. In 1920, the Department opened the transcontinental air mail route between New York, Chicago and San Francisco. A route from St. Louis to Minneapolis was initiated in 1920. In the same year foreign mail contract routes were opened between Seattle and Victoria in Canada, and between Key West and Havana in Cuba. Since then every year has witnessed extensions or improvements in the air-mail service. With the lighting of the airway between Salt Lake City and San Francisco, night-flying permitted the carriage of air mail by continuous flight from New York to the Pacific coast without the necessity of grounding the planes after sunset.

In 1926, under the Air Commerce Act^qv^, a Federal airways system was inaugurated, the Secretary of Commerce being charged with the establishment and maintenance of civil airways and their equipment, with intermediate landing fields, beacon lights, signal and radio range beacons, and other aids to air navigation. In 1926 the Federal Government relinquished the operation of the air mails to commercial companies which carried the mails under contract at pound rates on the same basis as that carried by land and water. The contract constituted a generous subsidy to encourage the development of passenger and express transportation in the air in addition to air-mail carriage. Today, practically all air routes are those over which not only the mails, but also passengers and express, are carried by commercial planes. In 1927 the Department of Commerce, with an appropriation of $300,000, controlled 1386 miles of lighted airways, with 32 lighted intermediate landing fields and 107 airway beacons, maintained by 134 employees. By 1937 the Department was authorized to expend some $5,000,000 per year on Federal airways, which now included 22,399 miles of lighted routes, 280 intermediate landing fields, 1916 beacon lights, 82 radio communication stations, 164 radio range stations, 55 radio marker stations and 13,885 teletypewriter circuits, maintained by 1538 employees. In 1923 the scheduled miles flown over American air routes were 5,870,489. By 1927 it had increased to 76,996,165. In 1938 the establishment and the supervision of the Federal airways were transferred from the Department of Commerce to the Administration of the Civil Aeronautics Authority.

Expansion of air routes beyond the United States received an impetus when, in 1927, the Pan American Airways Corporation inaugurated air lines to Latin-American countries. Soon it maintained regular schedules from New York to Bermuda, from Miami to the West Indies and along the east coast of South America to Buenos Aires, from Miami to Panama and to Santiago along the west coast of South America, and from Brownsville and Los Angeles to Mexico City. In 1934 Pan American Airways began operations in Alaska and Canada, and in 1935 a Pacific service, which soon included a regular schedule from San Francisco to Hong Kong and the Philippines by way of Hawaii, and to New Zealand.

[*Annual Report of the Director of Aeronautics; Annual Report of the Secretary of Commerce; Air Commerce Bulletin; Aircraft Year Book*, published by the Aeronautical Chamber of Commerce of America; *Annual Report to Stockholders of the Pan American Airways Corporation.*]

KENNETH COLEGROVE

Aisne Defensive, THE (May 27–June 5, 1918), was a sequel of the operations on the Somme in March, the Germans making a new attack southward between Soissons and Reims with the intention of drawing French reserves south so that they could renew their attacks in the north. The attack was successful even beyond their hopes, and reached the Marne near Chateau Thierry, only forty miles from Paris. The Germans then attempted to establish a bridgehead on the Marne, and also to push westward toward Paris; both efforts were unsuccessful. Two American divisions took part in the defense—the Third opposing the crossing of the Marne, and the Second being very heavily engaged at the Bois de Belleau[qv] and at Vaux, west of Chateau Thierry[qv].

[John J. Pershing, *Final Report as Commander-in-Chief, A.E.F.;* Oliver L. Spaulding, *The United States Army in War and Peace.*]

OLIVER LYMAN SPAULDING

Aisne-Marne Operation, THE (July 18–Aug. 6, 1918), was the Franco-American counter-offensive, following the German offensive of July 15 in the Marne salient (*see* Aisne Defensive). The French Tenth Army (Mangin) opened the attack, striking eastward into the salient just south of Soissons. The main attack was made by the XX Corps, with three divisions in front line, two American and one Moroccan. The Germans were taken by surprise, and their outpost line made little resistance, but the line soon stiffened and the fighting was severe. It was not until the 21st that control of the Soissons-Chateau Thierry highway was gained. The total penetration was eight miles.

From July 21 on, the armies farther east joined in the advance—the Sixth (Degoutte) and the Fifth (Berthelot), along both faces of the salient. With the Sixth Army there were two American corps headquarters—the I (Liggett) and the III (Dickman)—and eight American divisions. The Germans conducted their retreat skillfully, making an especially strong stand on the Ourcq on July 28. But early in August they were back behind the Vesle.

The operations since July 15 had changed the whole aspect of the war. A German offensive had been suddenly stopped in mid-career, and the advance changed to a retreat. The Marne salient had ceased to exist, and the Germans were never again able to undertake a serious offensive.

[John J. Pershing, *Final Report as Commander-in-Chief, A.E.F.;* Oliver L. Spaulding, *The United States Army in War and Peace.*]

OLIVER LYMAN SPAULDING

Aix-la-Chapelle, Treaty of (Oct. 18, 1748), ended the War of the Austrian Succession (*see* King George's War). The chief term which concerned American history was the restoration of Louisburg[qv] to France, which irritated the New Englanders who had been active in the capture. The peace was merely an intermission in the protracted struggle for control of the St. Lawrence and Mississippi basins. Its final phase, the French and Indian War[qv], began in 1754.

[*Cambridge History of British Foreign Policy*, Vol. IX.]

EDMUND K. ALDEN

Akron, THE. *See* Dirigibles.

Akron Law, THE (Feb. 8, 1847), resulted from a movement for a better public school system in Akron, Ohio. The Ohio General Assembly passed a special law for the city, which provided for an elected board of education of six members, the organization of the city as a single school district, free admission of all children to the public schools, the adoption of a system for the classification of pupils and their promotion by examinations, and local taxation for financing the schools. The law was broadened in 1848 to apply to any incorporated town, if the voters by a two-thirds vote chose to adopt the plan. In 1849 a general law, modeled on the Akron Law, reduced this requirement to a majority vote, required that schools be kept in operation not less than thirty-six nor more than forty-four weeks per year, and limited to four mills the amount of taxes to be raised for school purposes in any one year. In 1850 townships and special districts were permitted to make use of this system. Thus the Akron Law, with some modifications, came to be applied generally throughout the state.

[Edward A. Miller, The History of Educational Legislation in Ohio before 1850, *Ohio Archaeological and Historical Quarterly*, XXVII (Jan., 1918), 1-271.]

EUGENE H. ROSEBOOM

Alabama. The roots of Alabama's history reach back to the beginnings of contact between Europe and North America. Some of the earliest Spanish explorers visited the Alabama coast, and DeSoto[qv] in 1540 explored the interior of the state. Alabama was the patrimony of three of the celebrated royal houses of Europe. The Spanish founded at least two temporary settlements on its soil in 1559. The French occupied it from 1702 to 1763; the British from 1763 to 1783; and the Spanish again held the southern portion of it from 1783 to 1813. Spain held the strip below parallel 31° and the United States all above that line (*see* Southern Boundary, Survey of). The Spanish base at Mobile[qv] was crushed out in 1813. In 1817 the Alabama Territory was organized out of the Mississippi[qv] Territory, of which it had been a part since 1798, and was admitted to the Union as a state, Dec. 14, 1819.

Alabama was settled principally by farmers, planters and professional men. An unique incident in its settlement was the founding of a colony of prominent Napoleonic exiles at Demopolis in 1817. The social and economic life of the state prior to 1860 was like that of the cotton[qv] South generally. Agriculture was the dominant interest, and the plantation system[qv] flourished in all of its glory. Alabama ranked second as a cotton-producing state in 1860.

Prior to 1860 politics was colorful. Many professional politicians, who had held high official stations in other states, moved into Alabama and jousted with each other for position and leadership. The Democratic and Whig parties[qqv] sprang up and under able leadership stimulated a vigorous political life. The Democratic party dominated, but the Whigs kept up a spirited contest and exerted a large influence. Though local questions, such as the State Bank and state aid to railroads, gave rise to sharp contests, politics usually revolved around national questions. The people generally supported Jefferson's agrarian policies and the South's cause in slavery[qv]. Andrew Jackson was the idol of the masses but Calhoun and Clay had many followers. The states' rights[qv] sentiment grew apace after the Creek Indian[qv] controversy of 1832–33, and became robust under the impact of sectionalism[qv] between 1845 and 1860. William L. Yancey and his colleagues put the state in the front ranks of defense of southern rights. The exponents of sectional reconciliation, headed by Henry W. Hilliard, however, stayed the progress toward secession for a decade (*see* Compromise of 1850).

Alabama seceded from the Union in 1861, and the Confederate Government was organized and set up at Montgomery, since known as the "Cradle of the Confederacy." During the war that followed, its soldiers distinguished themselves in battle and prominent men held high places in the civil and military counsels of the Confederacy. The cost of the war was terrific. Property losses, including slaves, have been estimated at $500,000,000. The white population was frightfully decimated, and more than 437,000 slaves were freed and for many years had small part in rebuilding the state. When the war was over Alabamians earnestly sought restoration to the Union. They set up a state government under President Johnson's plan of reconstruction, but this plan was repudiated by Congress and the people were subjected again to enervating uncertainty and to military oppression (*see* Reconstruction). The state was restored to the Union under the Congressional plan in 1868. This plan resulted in six years of ignorant and corrupt government at the hands of adventurers from the North (*see* Carpet-Baggers) and poor local whites and Negroes, that in some respects was more costly than the war itself. When home rule was restored in 1875 the state debt amounted to $32,000,000 and the local debt to about $20,000,000, much of which was fraudulent and was repudiated.

Besides the debt load, reconstruction gave the state the one-party system. The Democratic party has dominated since 1875. The maintenance of white supremacy[qv] was the prime objective in politics prior to 1901. The populist[qv] outburst of the 1890's came dangerously near to giving the Negro voters the balance of power. This experience led to the disfranchisement of most of the Negroes by the Constitution of 1901, which also introduced some other notable changes. Besides the suffrage provisions, it extended the term of executive and legislative officials from two to four years and made executive officers ineligible to succeed themselves; it created the office of lieutenant-governor, reduced the powers of local government, and enlarged the powers of the legislature over corporations.

Politics since 1890, broadly speaking, has been an affair between the conservative and progressive wings of the Democratic party. These groups have battled over such public questions as taxation, education, prohibition, methods of nominating officers, and the regulation of corporations. In recent years the progress of the state in public health and child welfare work has been conspicuous.

Though there has been a notable rise in mining and manufacturing since 1900, agriculture still dominates, and the people are largely rural. Only 28.1% of the population was urban in 1930. Cotton is still the leading crop.

[T. P. Abernethy, *The Formative Period in Alabama;* A. B. Moore, *History of Alabama.*] A. B. MOORE

Alabama, THE. In June, 1861, Capt. J. D. Bulloch reached England as Confederate agent[qv] to contract with private builders for warships. He first obtained the *Florida*[qv], and on May 15, 1862, a second and more powerful ship, the *Alabama,* was launched at Liverpool. The United States Minister, C. F. Adams, who had previously demanded the detention of the *Florida,* now presented, on June 23, what he thought full evidence of the illegal character of the *Alabama;* but the British authorities were deplorably slow and the sudden insanity of a law-officer of the crown caused a five-day delay. Finally orders were telegraphed to hold the vessel, but she had already sailed under pretense of a trial trip. Earl Russell and other Cabinet members felt a sincere desire to keep her from leaving, and deeply regretted the evasion. Guns, munitions and coal were brought her at the Azores, and she became the terror of American vessels. Under Capt. Raphael Semmes, before her destruction in June, 1864, in the English channel (*see Kearsarge-Alabama* Fight), she sunk, burned, or captured more than sixty ships.

[Ephraim D. Adams, *Great Britain and the American Civil War;* Allan Nevins, *Hamilton Fish.*] ALLAN NEVINS

Alabama Claims, THE. American grievances against Great Britain during and just after the Civil War all clustered about this generic phrase; but they filled a broad category. The Queen's proclamation of neutrality, giving the South belligerent rights, was regarded by Secretary Seward and most Northerners as hasty and unfriendly. The Confederate cruisers, built or armed by Britons, not only destroyed American shipping, but did indirect damage by driving insurance rates high and forcing many American ships under foreign flags. The Confederates raised large sums of money in Great Britain and outfitted blockade runners[qv] there.

Early in the war Seward instructed Minister C. F. Adams to lay before the British Government, with a demand for redress, the losses caused by the *Alabama*[qv]. As a result the British authorities showed greater care. In April, 1863, they halted the *Alexandra* when Adams proved she was intended for the Confederacy; in September, Russell issued orders to detain the two armored rams which Laird[qv] was building. Only one other ship, the *Shenandoah*[qv], clearly violated the British neutrality laws and she only after refitting at Melbourne. Ultimately, the United States entered claims against Great Britain for damage wrought by eleven vessels, totalling $19,021,000. Of these the damage done by the *Alabama* was estimated at $6,547,609; that by the *Shenandoah* at $6,488,320; and that by the *Florida*[qv] at $3,698,609. The American claims were repeated from time to time but met no response until 1868. The Johnson-Clarendon Convention[qv], signed that year under Seward's close supervision, made no mention of the *Alabama* damages but provided for a settlement of all Anglo-American claims since 1853. Partly because of the unpopularity of the Johnson Administration, the Convention was overwhelmingly defeated by the Senate (April 13, 1869). Sumner seized the opportunity to make a speech reviewing the whole American case against Great Britain. He declared that the *Alabama* and other cruisers had not only done heavy damage, direct and indirect, but with the Queen's proclamation and other moral and material support given by England to the South had doubled the duration of the war. His object in thus implying that the total American bill reached $2,125,000,000 was to lay a basis for demands which could be met only by the cession of Canada. Fortunately Hamilton Fish, becoming Secretary of State in March, 1869, took a saner position. Playing for time, he soon adopted the view that the whole set of *Alabama* claims could be met by the payment of a moderate lump sum, an apology, and a definition of maritime international law meeting American wishes. When he mildly urged Canadian independence, the British Government refused to admit that the two questions could be connected. The impasse between the two nations was brief. Great Britain advanced to a more conciliatory position when Lord Granville succeeded Clarendon as Foreign Minister, and when the Franco-Prussian War and Russia's denunciation of her Black Sea pledges threatened European complications. Washington became more amenable when Canada showed distinct hostility to the United States, when the Santo Domingo[qv] controversy destroyed Sumner's influence over Grant, and when financial interests pressed for a settlement. With Sir John Rose, a Canadian prominent in London, acting as intermediary, Fish and Granville decided that a joint commission should settle the whole nexus of disputes—Canadian fisheries, northwestern boundary[qqv] and Alabama Claims. The Commission, meeting under Fish and Earl DeGrey, drew up the Treaty of Washington[qv] (signed May 8, 1871), which expressed British regret for the escape of the *Alabama* and other cruisers, laid down three rules of maritime neutrality, and provided for submission of the Alabama Claims to a board of five arbitrators, American, British, Italian, Swiss and Brazilian. This tribunal decided Sept. 14, 1872, that Great Britain had failed in her duties as a neutral, and awarded the United States $15,500,000 in gold to meet her direct damages, all indirect claims having been excluded. American opinion accepted the award as adequate.

[John Bassett Moore, *International Arbitrations*, I; S. F. Bemis, ed., *American Secretaries of State*, VII; Bancroft Davis, *Mr. Fish and the Alabama Claims;* Caleb Cushing, *The Treaty of Washington;* Allan Nevins, *Hamilton Fish.*]

ALLAN NEVINS

Alabama Platform, THE, adopted by the Democratic state convention in 1848 and approved by other southern groups, was W. L. Yancey's answer to Wilmot Proviso and squatter sovereignty[qqv] principles. It demanded congressional protection of slavery in the Mexican Cession. Rejected by the National Democratic convention of 1848, the principle was incorporated in the majority report at Charleston in 1860 (*see* Campaigns of 1848 and 1860). When that convention disrupted, it became the basic issue of the southern Democratic party.

[C. P. Denman, *The Secession Movement in Alabama.*]

WENDELL H. STEPHENSON

Alabamo, The Battle of (April 25, 1541). Breaking up winter quarters in the Indian village, Chicacilla, Ferdinand DeSoto[qv] marched his forces to seize the Indian fort at Alabamo, Miss., on the Yazoo River. After a bitter fight, he captured the fort and killed most of its garrison.

[Lambert A. Wilmer, *The Life, Travels and Adventures of Ferdinand DeSoto, Discoverer of the Mississippi;* Theodore Irving, *The Conquest of Florida by Hernando DeSoto.*]

ROBERT S. THOMAS

Alamance, Battle of. To punish and suppress the Regulators of North Carolina[qv], Governor Tryon ordered Gen. Hugh Waddell to Hillsborough with a force of about 1000 militia. The Regulators to the number of 2000 had assembled on the Alamance River, about one-half without arms, and with no officer higher than captain. The provincial army had artillery and was adequately equipped. The battle, fought May 16, 1771, lasted two hours and ended in disaster to the Regulators. The provincials lost nine killed and sixty-one wounded while the Regulators had about twenty killed and a greater number wounded. As a result of their defeat, many of the Regulators migrated to the trans-Alleghany region, to Tennessee[qv] in particular.

[E. W. Caruthers, *Life of Rev. David Caldwell.*]

SAMUEL C. WILLIAMS

Alamo, Siege and Fall of the (Feb. 23 to March 6, 1836). When the revolting province of Texas swept its soil clear of weak Mexican garrisons in 1835 the commander-in-chief, Sam Houston, ordered a concentration on the theory that the Mexicans would return (*see* Texas Revolution). He recommended the destruction and abandonment of the fortifications at San Antonio. For this cautious counsel Houston was deposed from command. A twenty-seven-year-old lawyer, Lt.-Col. William Barret Travis, found himself in joint command, with James Bowie, of about 145 men at San Antonio when on Feb. 23 Santa Anna appeared with between 6000 and 7000 men.

Travis and Bowie could have retreated safely. Instead they moved into the stout-walled Alamo Mission, answered a demand for surrender with a cannon shot and sent couriers for reinforcements. A message signed by Travis read: "I have sustained a continual Bombardment and cannonade for 24 hours and have not lost a man. . . . Our flag still proudly waves from the wall. I shall never surrender or retreat. . . . VICTORY OR DEATH." On the eighth day of battle thirty-two recruits crept through the Mexican lines, the last reinforcements the garrison was to receive. This brought their number to about 187. Though suffering from want of sleep, and with ammunition running low, the Texans had lost the services of only one man, Bowie, ill and disabled by a fall.

At four in the morning of March 6, the thirteenth day of battle, Santa Anna stormed the Alamo on all sides. The first and second assaults were broken up. Day was dawning when the Mexicans attacked again. The Texans' guns were hot, their ammunition nearly out and, though casualties had not been numerous, men were dropping from exhaustion. The walls were breached. From building to building and room to room in the mission compound the defenders fought, clubbing rifles and drawing knives. The last point taken was the church. There fell David Crockett and twelve volunteers who had followed him from Tennessee.

By eight o'clock the last of the 187 defenders was dead, though the Mexicans spared about thirty noncombatants. Mexican losses were about 1500 killed and died of wounds.

The first effect of the butchery was to sow panic through Texas, precipitating a flight of the civil population and of the government toward United States soil. Inwardly raging against Travis' disastrous stand, Houston gathered an army. Six weeks later, marching to meet Santa Anna, Houston paraded his men and in an impassioned address abjured them to "Remember the Alamo!" With that cry on their lips they vanquished the Mexicans at San Jacinto[qv], establishing the independence of the Texas Republic[qv].

[Marquis James, *The Raven.*]

MARQUIS JAMES

Alaska. The discovery and occupation of Alaska climaxed an eastward expansion trend of Russia, which, beginning about the middle of the 16th century, in a hundred years had gained a firm footing in the great river valleys of Siberia and given the Czar at least a shadowy claim as far east as Bering Sea.

From Okhotsk in the south and Anadirsk in the north, as centers of operation, the peninsula of Kamchatka was reduced to subjection and when rumors of the existence of another land, across a narrow sea, created a ferment of interest among navigators, Peter the Great set exploration in motion. As one of the last important acts of his reign, Peter inaugurated an expedition headed by Vitus Bering, a Danish sea captain, with the Russian Tchirikoff as second. The object was to determine the geographical relation of northeastern Asia to the American continent. On Aug. 8, 1728, three years after leaving St. Petersburg, Bering in the ship *Gabriel* rounded the northeastern point of Asia, proving that the continents of Asia and America were distinct and separate. That they were not far apart in that latitude was indicated by various signs.

A new expedition in 1741 resulted in the discovery of Alaska's mainland, together with some of the islands between Alaska and Kamchatka. Then followed the fur traders from Kamchatka whose activities quickly disclosed much of the Alaskan coast and her most obvious sources of wealth.

Independent Russian fur traders, bitter rivals for the profits of the trade, not only threatened to destroy the fur-bearing animals but made the coasts and inlets of Alaska frequent scenes of bloodshed. A natural result was the concentration of the business, at first in the hands of a few large companies and finally, in 1799, in a monopoly called the Russian American Fur Company[qv], chartered for a term of twenty years. The charter granted exclusive rights of trade from N. Lat. 55° to Bering Strait, including the "Aleutian, Kurile, and other islands situated in the northeastern ocean." The company was also empowered to make discoveries, north and south, and to occupy them for Russia; and to trade with neighboring people.

The company's success was due largely to its Alaskan manager, Alexander Baranoff. He established a central station at the island of Sitka, built ships for the trade and for expansion southward, finally occupying a port and territory in California. Failing in a plan to provide vessels for the China-Russian trade, he entered into an agreement with John Jacob Astor by which Alaska would be supplied with needed goods, including foodstuffs, in exchange for furs which Astor would sell in Canton. Later, the company made a similar agreement with the Hudson's Bay Company[qv]. Receiving full supplies of grain from Oregon, the California post, Fort Ross, was sold in 1841 to Capt. John A. Sutter.

When the company's charter was renewed in 1821, it professed to grant rights extending to N. Lat. 51°. This gave rise to controversies with both the United States and Great Britain, and finally to treaties with both delimiting the Russian claims (*see* Alaska Boundary Question).

The Russian government in 1867, disturbed over the prospect of war with Britain and not willing to extend the company's charter again, sold the territory to the United States (*see* Alaska, The Purchase of). The price paid was $7,200,000.

"Seward's folly," as American newspapers were fond of calling Alaska, was badly neglected by a government whose people generally regarded the country as a liability rather than an asset. One resource, the seal crop on the Pribilof Islands[qv], was leased to the Alaska Commercial Company[qv]. A better contract entered into with the North American Commercial Company in 1890 gave the Government a revenue from that source alone which guaranteed the repayment of the purchase price of Alaska. Pelagic sealing, however, has caused great losses and created international complications.

Sealing questions, and the fisheries (*see* Seal Fisheries), interested Congress. But the Klondike[qv] placer discoveries in 1896 caused a gold rush reminiscent of California in 1849. Alaskan streams began to be prospected in earnest, and great quartz deposits like those at Juneau were opened. Alaska became a land of adventure, romance and riches, which could no longer be neglected by the Government.

Control through army and navy had proved unsatisfactory. The first regular government was established in 1884. Alaska became a civil and judicial district, with an appointive governor, a judge, a district attorney, a clerk of court, a marshal and four United States commissioners. With some modifications, that arrangement continued down to 1912. Alaska was then given a senate and house of representatives elected from four judicial districts, each district choosing four representatives for two years, two senators for four years. Juneau is the capital of the territory. Alaska has had a delegate in Congress since 1906.

The leading industries of the territory are the fisheries, products of which in 1934 aggregated nearly $42,000,000; and mining, $16,721,000. A Matanuska colonization project was begun in 1936.

[H. H. Bancroft, *History of Alaska;* Joseph Schafer, *The Pacific Slope and Alaska.*] JOSEPH SCHAFER

Alaska, The Purchase of. Three alleged movements for the sale of Alaska before 1867 are disclosed by documents in the Soviet Foreign Office: in 1854, during the Crimean War, to prevent England from seizing the territory; in 1856, when Senator Gwin of California and Secretary of State Marcy proposed its sale to this country; and in 1860, when President Buchanan contemplated its purchase. There is no record of these movements in the Department of State.

On Dec. 28, 1866, Russia decided to sell Alaska to the United States because of the financial decline of the Russian American Company[qv] and Russia's disinclination to administer Alaska and inability to defend it, and in order to avoid future difficulties with the United States. *Ca.* March 9, 1867, the Russian Minister, Edouard de Stoeckl, broached the subject to Secretary of State Seward, who readily agreed. On March 30, 1867, a treaty was signed conveying Alaska to the United States for $7,200,000. The Senate on April 9 gave its advice and consent to ratification out of gratitude for Russia's having sent its fleet to American waters in 1863 (*see* Russian Fleets, Visit of), supposedly as a demonstration against England and France, which were sympathetic to the Confederacy. Ratifications were exchanged June 20, 1867, and the treaty was proclaimed that day. The formal transfer took place at Sitka, Oct. 18, 1867.

The motives which induced Seward to purchase Alaska are not altogether clear, but we know that prior to the Civil War he had envisioned the United States as coextensive with the North American continent and that after the War he had embarked upon a program of expansion. While he was engaged in this program, Stoeckl appeared with the offer of Alaska. As Alaska fitted into his plan of expansion, Seward probably purchased it for that reason.

[Victor J. Farrar, *The Annexation of Russian America to the United States;* Frank A. Golder, The Purchase of Alaska, in *American Historical Review*, Vol. XXV, April, 1920.] VICTOR J. FARRAR

Alaska Boundary Question, THE. Maps of Alaska, American, English, Russian, French or Spanish, dated after the treaty of 1825 between Russia and England, all represented southern Alaska as a thirty-mile-wide strip parallel to the coast. That is what the treaty stipulated in establishing a boundary between Russian territory and British. The line was to start from the southernmost point of Prince of Wales Island in N. Lat. 54° 40′, ascend along Portland Channel to latitude 56°, then follow a supposititious "range of mountains" running parallel to the coast to the intersection of the 141° of longitude; thence north on that parallel to the Arctic Ocean. If the supposed range of mountains at any point was found to lie more than ten marine leagues from the ocean, then the line was to follow "the sinuosities of the coast" and not more than ten marine leagues therefrom. Since such mountains were nonexistent, the thirty-mile strip was always reckoned as Russian, later American territory.

The Klondike[qv] placer mines, discovered in the upper Yukon country in 1896, were found to lie east of longitude 141°, therefore in British territory. The only practicable way to reach the

Klondike was by ascending Lynn Canal to its head, thence following one of several passes to the Yukon. It would have been of vast importance to British interests to gain a duty-free entrance through Lynn Canal which they would have if the inlet could be shown to extend far into British territory: impossible, however, on the theory that the line of demarcation ran, at the distance of thirty miles, parallel to the "sinuosities of the coast."

Now there began to appear Canadian maps representing an entirely different theory of the boundary line. This was based on a "coast" defined as international law defines the three-mile limit, namely, sinuosities except at inlets, then "headland to headland." This clash of theories made the Alaska boundary question. It was adjudicated under a treaty stipulating that the findings of a joint commission[qv], three American lawyers and three British, should be accepted as final. The commission met in London during the summer of 1903 and found by majority vote in favor of the American claim.

[*Alaskan Boundary Tribunal*, *Proceedings*, 58th Cong., 2nd Sess., Senate No. 102.] JOSEPH SCHAFER

Alaska Boundary Tribunal. The claim of the Canadians that the boundary of the Alaska panhandle should be so redrawn as to give them the heads of the principal salt-water inlets resulted in the convention of 1903 between Great Britain and the United States. By its terms provision was made for submitting the seven questions at issue to a tribunal of "six impartial jurists of repute." President Roosevelt, who was authorized to appoint three, chose George Turner, Henry Cabot Lodge and Elihu Root, all of disputed impartiality. His Britannic Majesty appointed two prominent Canadians, Sir Louis A. Jetté and A. B. Aylesworth, and Lord Alverstone, Lord Chief Justice of England. The Tribunal met in London, Sept. 3 to Oct. 20, 1903, and after considering lengthy written and oral argument voted (the two Canadians dissenting) against the main Canadian contention. In response to angry charges, Lord Alverstone insisted that his decision had been purely judicial. Although this may have been true, it is clear that President Roosevelt tried to influence his vote by strong indirect pressure.

[A. L. P. Dennis, *Adventures in American Diplomacy.*] THOMAS A. BAILEY

Alaska Commercial Company (incorporated 1869), a Pacific Coast enterprise with offices at San Francisco, was organized by groups of eastern and western capitalists for the exploitation of the seal fishery[qv] in Alaskan waters. Congress leased it a twenty-year monopoly (May 1, 1870) to kill seals on the Pribilof Islands[qv]. It is now (1939) a trading company.

[H. H. Bancroft, *History of Alaska.*] LLOYD C. M. HARE

Alaska-Pacific-Yukon Exposition, Seattle, 1909, was a notable achievement of the Pacific Northwest. The Federal Government spent $600,000 for exhibits on the Philippines, Hawaii and Alaska to reveal to the American people, by the first comprehensive demonstration, the peoples, arts and industries of these possessions. Japan presented the largest foreign exhibit she had ever attempted; China and Oceania were well represented. An estimated $20,000,000, secured by taxation, appropriations, gifts and revenues, was spent on the entire exposition. It was a minor, but a highly successful, American exposition.

FRANK MONAGHAN

Alaska Railroad, THE, was authorized by Congress March 12, 1914, to connect one or more of the open harbors on the southern coast of Alaska with the navigable waters, coal fields and agricultural lands of the interior. Commenced in 1915 under general supervision of the Secretary of the Interior and technical supervision of the Alaska Engineering Commission, the 612 miles of road was completed in 1923, and has since been in operation. The main line (470 miles) extends from Seward to Fairbanks. The enterprise has been financed, and is owned, by the National Government.

[Annual reports of the Secretary of the Interior; O. F. Ohlson, The Alaska Railroad, *Baldwin Locomotives*, IX, 19-30 (April 1931); *United States Daily*, March 20, 1930, p. 198.] P. ORMAN RAY

Albany. In September, 1609, Henry Hudson moored his ship, the *Half Moon*[qv], near the site of the present city of Albany. No serious attempt at settlement was made, however, until the spring of 1624, when the Dutch West India Company[qv] sent over a group of eighteen families, mostly Walloons[qv], who built Fort Orange on the site of the present steamboat square. During the years 1630–36 the colony was augmented by the arrival of groups of colonists sent over by Kiliaen van Rensselaer, who had been granted a large tract of land near Fort Orange. In 1652 the village of about 100 houses, which had grown up in the protection of the fort, was declared independent of the Patroon's colony, and became known as Beverwyck. Shortly afterward, the fur trade, which had been under the control of the

Dutch West India Company, having been thrown open to the citizens, rapidly increased.

On Sept. 24, 1664, Fort Orange surrendered to the English and Beverwyck became Albany, after the Scotch title of the Duke of York. On July 22, 1686, Governor Dongan granted the city a charter. For many years Albany was the key in the regulation of Indian affairs. Since the early days of the colony relations with the Iroquois[qv] had been friendly. During the period of the colonial wars many conferences including the famous Albany Congress[qv] of 1754 were held there. The fur trade continued to be important.

On the eve of the Revolution Albany was a prosperous city of 3000 inhabitants, laid out in a wide strip along the Hudson. The Albanians entered into the struggle with ardor. The position of the city made it strategically important, and throughout the war the inhabitants were in fear of attack. The year 1777 was an anxious one. Burgoyne advanced toward the city by way of Lake Champlain and St. Leger by way of the Mohawk (*see* British Campaign of 1777). At the request of Gen. Schuyler the lead window weights were melted down and made into bullets. The surrender of Burgoyne and retreat of St. Leger relieved the anxiety of the people, but conditions in the city were wretched. It was crowded with refugees and sick or wounded soldiers. In addition a conspiracy among the Negroes, British prisoners and Tories[qv] was feared. News of the Provisional Peace was received with great rejoicing, and the citizens set to work with zest to build up their neglected trade. By a law enacted on March 10, 1797, Albany became the capital of the State of New York. Fulton's steamboat, turnpikes, the Erie and Champlain Canals, railroads[qqv], improved highways and the creation of the Port of Albany have contributed to the city's modern historical importance.

[Codman Hislop, *Albany, Dutch, English and American.*]

A. C. FLICK

Albany Congress, THE (1754), called by order of the British government for the purpose of conciliating the Iroquois[qv] and securing their support in the war against France, was more notable for the plans that it made than for its actual accomplishments. In June commissioners from New York, Massachusetts, Rhode Island, Connecticut, Pennsylvania, New Hampshire and Maryland met with the chiefs of the Six Nations[qv]. Encroachment on their lands, the trade of Albany with Canada, and the removal of Johnson (later Sir William Johnson) from the management of their affairs had aroused a dangerous spirit of disaffection among the Indians. Gifts and promises were bestowed and the alliance renewed, but the Iroquois went away only half satisfied.

For the better defense of the colonies and control of Indian affairs it had long been felt that a closer union was needed than occasional meetings of governors or commissioners. Discussion of such a union now became one of the principal subjects of the congress. Massachusetts indeed had granted her delegates authority to "enter into articles of union . . . for the general defense of his majesty's subjects." The plan adopted was one proposed by Benjamin Franklin and frequently referred to at the time as the "Albany Plan." It provided for a voluntary union of the colonies with "one general government," each colony to retain its own separate existence and government. The new government was to be administered by a President General appointed by the crown and a Grand Council of Delegates from the several colonial assemblies, members of the Council to hold office for three years. This federal government was given exclusive control of Indian affairs including the power to make peace and declare war, regulate Indian trade, purchase Indian lands for the crown, raise and pay soldiers, build forts, equip vessels, levy taxes and appropriate funds. The home government disapproved this plan because it was felt that it encroached on the royal prerogative. The colonies disapproved of it because it did not allow them sufficient independence. Nevertheless this Albany plan was to have far-reaching results. It paved the way for the Stamp Act Congress of 1765 and for the Continental Congress of 1774[qqv]. And when, during the troubled days which followed, the need of a closer union was felt, there was a definite plan to serve as a guide in the deliberations of the representatives of the colonies.

[E. B. O'Callaghan, ed., *Documentary History of the State of New York.*]

A. C. FLICK

Albany Convention, THE (1689–90), was a convention of the civil and military officers of Albany, which, convening on Aug. 1, 1689, set itself up as an emergency government until the pleasure of William and Mary should be made known. Fearful of attack by the French, the convention sought a promise of aid from Jacob Leisler[qv], who had seized control of southern New York, but was rebuffed by Leisler, whose subsequent demand that he be recognized as commander-in-chief was rejected. Badly frightened by a French attack on Schenectady[qv], the convention sought aid from New England and in the spring yielded to renewed demands from Leisler.

[V. H. Paltsits, Transition from Dutch to English Rule, in Flick, *History of the State of New York*, Vol. II.]

A. C. FLICK

Albany Regency, THE, was the first American political machine^qv^. It was organized (1820) under Martin Van Buren, and acquired its name because his first aides, residing in Albany and nearby, managed the machine during his absence in the United States Senate. The Regency developed party discipline and originated the control of party conventions^qv^ through officeholders and others subservient to it. The spoils system^qv^ was the core of its philosophy. The Regency waned when Van Buren's star set in 1848.

[Denis Tilden Lynch, *An Epoch and a Man, the Times of Martin Van Buren;* Denis Tilden Lynch, *The Growth of Political Parties, 1777-1850.*]

DENIS TILDEN LYNCH

Albatross, THE, was the Yankee-owned ship which brought to W. P. Hunt, partner of the Pacific Fur Company^qv^, at its Astoria^qv^ post, news of the outbreak of the War of 1812. Hunt chartered the ship and removed the furs from Astoria to avoid possible British capture, thus abandoning the first American fur post on the Columbia River^qv^.

[H. M. Chittenden, *History of the American Fur Trade.*]

CARL L. CANNON

Albemarle, THE, Confederate ram^qv^, built on the Roanoke River, under command of James W. Cooke on April 19, 1864, sank the gunboat *Southfield,* put the *Miami* to flight, and captured Plymouth, N. C. On May 5 she fought indecisively Capt. Melancton Smith's seven blockaders at the mouth of the Roanoke. But on the night of Oct. 27 Lt. William B. Cushing, with fifteen men in a small launch, bearing a torpedo ingeniously attached to a spar, sank her.

[J. Thomas Scharf, *History of the Confederate States Navy;* E. M. H. Edwards, *Commander William Barker Cushing.*]

CHARLES LEE LEWIS

Albemarle and Chesapeake Canal, THE, was built by a corporation in 1856–60 to afford inland navigation between Chesapeake Bay and Albemarle Sound. It is really two canals, thirty miles apart; one eight and one-half miles long, connecting Elizabeth River with North Landing River in Virginia, the other five and one-half miles long, connecting Currituck Sound with North River in North Carolina.

ALVIN F. HARLOW

Albemarle Settlements. The first permanent settlement in what is now North Carolina was made in the Albemarle Sound region about the middle of the 17th century by Virginians, in quest of good lands. In 1653 the Virginia Assembly granted Roger Green a tract of land on Roanoke River south of Chowan, to be located "next to those persons who have had a former grant." In 1662 George Durant purchased lands from the Indians in this region, and there is evidence to indicate that others had done the same. When it was learned that the Albemarle settlements were not included in the Carolina^qv^ proprietary grant of 1663, a new charter was granted in 1665, which included them. Government was instituted in Albemarle in 1664 and within a decade settlements extended from the Chowan River to Currituck Sound. (*See also* Cape Fear River Settlements.)

[R. D. W. Connor, *North Carolina: Rebuilding an Ancient Commonwealth.*]

HUGH T. LEFLER

Albuquerque, N. Mex., originated, April, 1706, as the Spanish villa "San Felipe de Albuquerque," named for King Philip V and the Viceroy, Duke of Albuquerque. It was on the Chihuahua Trail^qv^ and dominated the Rio Abajo (down river) part of the province. Exposed to Apache and Navajo^qqv^ inroads, the settlers were "reduced" (1779) to the plaza arrangement which survives in "Old Town."

New Albuquerque started a century later (1880) a mile to the east, as a railroad center. That year, the Santa Fé system (*see* Atchison, Topeka and Santa Fé Railway) built down the Rio Grande and the Atlantic and Pacific^qv^ headed westward over the old United States survey (1853) along the 35th parallel. Connection southeast into Texas came only in 1907. In recent years the automobile and airplane also have made Albuquerque an important crossroads of transcontinental routes.

[L. B. Bloom, Albuquerque and Galisteo, in *New Mexico Historical Review*, X (1935); C. F. Coan, *A History of New Mexico.*]

LANSING B. BLOOM

Alcaldes, THE, were mayors of Mexican towns. Under the American provisional government in California these officers were recognized by military governors and continued in office until 1850.

[T. H. Hittell, *History of California.*]

WILLIAM S. LEWIS

Alcatraz, a thirty-five-acre island in San Francisco Bay, was first used in 1886 by the War Department as a place of confinement for long-term military prisoners. In 1907 it was designated Pacific Branch of the United States Military Prison; later, as Pacific Branch United States Disciplinary Barracks. Transferred to the Department of Justice in 1934, Alcatraz is now the penitentiary in which are confined the more dangerous and difficult types of persons convicted of federal crimes.

[C. M. Tuteur, Alcatraz—the Prison Island, *San Francisco Police and Peace Officers Journal*, XV; S. Bates, *Prisons and Beyond.*]
P. ORMAN RAY

Alder Gulch, Mont. Gold was discovered on Alder Gulch, and the first stampede reached there June 6, 1863. The people lived in brush wickyups, dug-outs[qqv] and rocks, but later a town sprang up which was named Virginia City[qv]. The diggings[qv] were the richest gold placer deposits ever discovered and in three years $30,000,000 was taken from them.

[G. Stuart, *Forty Years on the Frontier.*]
CARL L. CANNON

Aldrich Commission. *See* National Monetary Commission.

Aldrich-Vreeland Emergency Currency Law, THE, enacted May 30, 1908, as a result of the so-called "bankers' panic" of 1907[qv], aimed to give elasticity to the currency through the next six years, by permitting national banks[qv] to issue circulating notes on securities additional to Federal bonds. It permitted issuance, under strict supervision, of additional currency, on bonds of states, cities, towns and counties, and on commercial paper. A tax graduated up to 10% discouraged abundant issues. The Act also created a National Monetary Commission[qv] to investigate systems of money and banking abroad and to advise Congress of desirable changes in the American banking system.

[*U. S. Statutes at Large*, Vol. 35.]
JEANNETTE P. NICHOLS

Aleutian Islands, THE, were discovered in 1741 by Vitus Bering, commissioned in 1725 by Peter the Great to lead a Russian expedition to determine whether Asia joined America. Michael Novidiskoff, probably the first fur trader in Alaska, reached Attu in 1745. Then began a lucrative trade with the native Aleuts in the pelts of the fur seal and the sea otter[qqv]. The port of Unalaska[qv], founded in 1761, became one of the three Russian settlements in Alaska, and had 25 white and 125 half-breed inhabitants in 1867 when Alaska was purchased by the United States. In 1881, when the United States Government determined to protect the fur seals by prohibiting the pelagic or open-sea killing, the far-reaching extent of the Aleutian Islands was the basis of the American claim that the Bering Sea constituted a *mare clausum*[qv]. (*See also* Bering Sea Fisheries.)

[Henry W. Clark, *History of Alaska.*]
KENNETH COLEGROVE

Alexandria, Va., on the Potomac River, below Washington, was an important trading center until early in the 19th century, particularly as a tobacco warehousing and deep-sea shipping port. Incorporated in 1748, on an original grant of 6000 acres, awarded in 1669, the site was owned for a century by the Alexander family. It was situated on the main stage route, the King's Highway, running southward into Virginia. Braddock[qv] departed from there on his fatal expedition. The Fairfax Resolves[qv] were signed in Alexandria, July 18, 1774. From 1791 to 1846 Alexandria was under exclusive Federal jurisdiction as part of the District of Columbia. Jefferson's Embargo Act[qv] destroyed its tobacco trade. During the Civil War it was occupied by Union troops. Alexandria was the home of Lee and other prominent Virginia families. In recent years its colonial architecture has attracted much interest.

[Mary G. Powell, *The History of Old Alexandria, Virginia.*]
ETHEL ARMES

Alexandria Conference, THE (March 28, 1785), between Maryland and Virginia, concerned navigation and commerce in Chesapeake Bay and the Potomac and Pocomoke rivers. Scheduled for Alexandria for March 21, it actually met at Washington's invitation at Mount Vernon. Daniel of St. Thomas Jenifer, Thomas Stone and Samuel Chase represented Maryland, George Mason and Alexander Henderson, Virginia. In ratifying the agreement, Maryland urged the inclusion of Pennsylvania and Delaware, while Virginia urged a meeting of all the states to adopt uniform commercial regulations. This produced the Annapolis Convention[qv], the origin of the Convention of 1787[qv].

[J. Thomas Scharf, *History of Maryland.*]
WALTER B. NORRIS

Alfalfa. Spanish explorers probably first brought seed of this legume to the Americas in the 16th century. It was grown in Mexico and later became established in Peru and Chile. Attempts by colonists along the Atlantic seaboard to grow it met with indifferent success. George Washington planted a field of alfalfa in 1794.

Development of alfalfa as a great forage crop of the United States dates from about 1850, when seed from Chile or Peru was introduced into California by gold seekers. It moved into Utah, thence to Colorado, Kansas and Nebraska and by 1900 had reached Illinois and Ohio.

Alfalfa found its most favorable environment in the great Mississippi Valley and in mountain regions of the West. Of eleven and one-half million acres harvested in the United States in 1934, over seven and one-half million acres were grown in fourteen North Central States, bounded on the east by Ohio and by Colorado on the west. Value of the 18,742,093 tons of alfalfa hay produced in the United States that year was $268,-298,614.

Alfalfa, in common with other legumes, serves as a host for bacteria which possess the ability to extract nitrogen from the air and render it available in the soil to other plants. This soil-improving characteristic, combined with its forage value, makes it one of the great economic crops and favorably influences the development of a well-diversified type of agricultural and livestock production, essential to a stabilized and profitable farming industry.

[*Yearbook of Agriculture, 1937*, United States Department of Agriculture; *Alfalfa in Kansas*, Kansas State Board of Agriculture; Charles V. Piper, *Forage Plants and their Culture.*]

ARTHUR CAPPER

Algeciras, Conference at. France made agreements with England and Spain in 1904 which allowed her to increase her influence in Morocco. Germany, angered because she was not consulted, demanded a conference of the signatories of the Morocco agreement negotiated at Madrid[qv] in 1880. Among the signatories was the United States to whom the German government now appealed for an extension of the open-door policy[qv] to Morocco. President Theodore Roosevelt, in an attempt to obtain a peaceful solution, helped Germany by persuading England and France to attend a conference at Algeciras, Spain, in 1906. In the conference, however, the Germans appeared so uncompromising that Roosevelt supported France, which in the end won out by obtaining a privileged position in Morocco. The United States Senate ratified the resulting treaty but declared that this action was taken solely to protect American interests and should not be interpreted as an abandonment of a non-intervention policy[qv] toward Europe.

[E. N. Anderson, *First Moroccan Crisis;* A. L. P. Dennis, *Adventures in American Diplomacy.*]

LYNN M. CASE

Algiers, United States War with. *See* Barbary Wars, The (1801–05) (1815).

Algonquin (ALGONKIN), THE, is a generic term for a linguistic stock or basic group of Indians having a wide distribution, their territory reaching from Newfoundland to the Rocky Mountains and from isolated areas in California to Pamlico Sound. This great family embraced numerous tribes and groups of tribes having a common linguistic affinity. The Algonquin were first met in Canada where the Weskarini provided the name now applied to the whole. The western group embraced the Blackfoot confederacy and the Arapaho and Cheyenne[qqv]; the extensive northern division the Chippewa[qv], the Missasaga, Nipissing, Abittibi, Algonkin and probably the Cree[qv]. The northeastern division embraced the Montagnais group, the Abnaki[qv], including the Micmac, Malecite, Passamaquoddy, Arosaguntacook, Sokoki, and Norridgewock. The central division embraced the Sauk, Fox, Kickapoo, Mascoutin, Pottawatomie, the Illinois branch of the Miami group which included the Peoria, Kaskaskia, Cahokia, Tamaroa and Michigamea, the Miami group proper, including the Miami, Piankashaw and Wea[qqv]. The eastern division embraced all the Atlantic coast Algonquian tribes, such as the Pennacook, Massachusetts, Wampanoag, Narragansett, Nipmuc, Montauk, Mohegan, Mahican, Wappinger, Delaware, Shawnee[qqv], Nanticoke, Conoy, Powhatan and Pamlico.

The Algonquian tribes were the first to sustain the shock of French and English penetration and suffered greatly from wars with the Iroquois[qv]. Most of the tribes except those of the north were sedentary and carried on agriculture with varying degrees of intensity. They possessed a degree of manual skill and their mental qualities are not to be despised. Among their great leaders were such men as Tecumseh, Pontiac, Samoset, Massasoit, King Philip, Powhatan and Nimham. Many eastern tribesmen embraced Christianity early in the colonial period.

[Hodge, *Handbook of American Indians.*]

ARTHUR C. PARKER

Alien and Sedition Acts, THE, were enacted by Congress (1798) because of threatened war with France, and the desire of the Federalists[qv] to insure against Jeffersonian Republican[qv] success at the polls. The presence in the country of a considerable number of alien Frenchmen favorable to the Republicans, and intemperate newspaper opposition to the Federalists, were the principal factors in prompting these laws.

The act of June 18 decreed that instead of

five years, aliens must reside in the country fourteen years before naturalization, and must declare such intention five years before applying for citizenship. This law was repealed by the Republicans (Jeffersonian) in 1802. The act of June 25, which expired in 1800 and was not renewed, empowered the President to deport any aliens he deemed dangerous to public peace. The third act, of July 6, was the most defensible. It empowered the President, in time of war, to arrest, imprison, or banish aliens with whose motherland this country might be at war. In the two years of its existence, it was never applied, but many French were frightened into leaving the country. The principal objection to these laws was the arbitrary power they granted the executive.

The Sedition Act of July 14 made it a high misdemeanor "unlawfully to combine and conspire" in order to oppose legal measures of the Government, to interfere with an officer in the discharge of his duty, to engage in or abet "insurrection, riot, or unlawful assembly or combination." The penalty was a fine of not more than $5000 and imprisonment up to five years. The publication of false or malicious writing against the nation, the President or Congress, was punishable by a fine of not more than $2000 and imprisonment not exceeding two years. The anti-Federalists[qv] held that this act was unconstitutional. Of all the Federalist leaders, only John Marshall opposed it openly. A decision of the Supreme Court in 1882 supports the view that the Sedition Act was unconstitutional. It is noteworthy that the act was used to punish Republican editors who had criticized President Adams, while the diatribes of Federalists against Vice-President Jefferson were ignored. Ten individuals, all Republicans, were fined and imprisoned under the Sedition Act. The most notable was Dr. Thomas Cooper, later president of South Carolina College. He paid $400 and spent six months in prison for saying that when Adams took office he "was hardly in the infancy of political mistake: even those who doubted his capacity thought well of his intentions . . . nor had he yet interfered, as President of the United States, to influence the decision of a court of justice." Many others were tried but not convicted. In some cases the Federalist judges, especially Justice Samuel Chase, displayed violent partisan bias against the accused. As the public began to treat the victims of these prosecutions as martyrs and popular heroes, the Federalists realized their mistake and ceased to enforce the act. Four decades later, Congress refunded some of the fines.

The most conspicuous result of these four laws was the evocation of protests from many states. The extreme protest was voiced in the Virginia and Kentucky Resolutions[qv] written, respectively, by Madison and Jefferson.

[J. S. Bassett, *The Federalist System.*]

MILLEDGE L. BONHAM, JR.

Alien Contract Labor Law, THE, enacted by Congress Feb. 26, 1885, was supplemented by later ones, notably that of 1907, as amended by that of 1910. The object was to prevent the lowering of wage standards by importing indigent and dependent laborers. The original Act excepted certain groups, such as domestic labor, artists, and lecturers. The Act of 1903 extended the exceptions to any "recognized learned profession," including teachers. Violation of these acts involves both penal and civil liability.

C. SUMNER LOBINGIER

Alien Landholding. The common-law disability of aliens to inherit lands in the United States has always been removable by statute and by treaty. Alienage occasioned by the Revolution was excepted by the Definitive Treaty of Peace[qv], which also required Congress to "recommend to the State Legislatures" restitution of confiscated estates. The Jay Treaty[qv] went a step farther by guaranteeing existing titles wherever held, and treating British subjects, with respect thereto, as equal to citizens. But this did not hold for lands thereafter acquired, nor for other than British aliens. The Convention of 1800[qv] removed the disability of alienage for French citizens in all the states. A treaty with Switzerland (1850) similarly affected Swiss citizens. But in the absence of such a treaty state laws applied, as in Kansas where the disability was expressed in the state Constitution. In California, on the other hand, the Constitution authorized aliens to acquire, transmit, and inherit property equally with citizens; and this, like similar provisions in other states, was upheld by the Supreme Court. The vast increase in European immigration after the mid-19th century stimulated a contrary sentiment. In 1887 Congress passed an act prohibiting aliens (natural or corporate), from acquiring lands in the territories or District of Columbia "except . . . by inheritance or . . . in the ordinary course of justice." In Nebraska, where an Englishman named Scully had bought large areas, an act was passed in 1889 prohibiting non-resident aliens or foreign corporations, with certain exceptions, "from acquiring title to or taking or holding any lands." The Washington State Constitution prohibiting ownership of lands by aliens who have not declared their intention of becoming citizens was judicially upheld; but an Arkansas act of 1925, similar in scope, was annulled as infringing the state prohibition of "distinction . . . between resident aliens and citizens in regard to . . . property."

C. SUMNER LOBINGIER

Alien Property. During the Revolution several colonies sequestrated British debts[qv] and refused to restore right of suit (*see* Confiscation of Property). The United States in 1802 settled British claims, and subsequently by treaties with many countries affirmed the general doctrine of inviolability of enemy alien property during war. But in 1917 Congress authorized the conveyance of such property to a Custodian as trustee for management and "if necessary" for sale, to prevent its use by the enemy. Later the idea of trusteeship changed and the property was sold freely at very low prices, even after the Armistice. Several thousand coveted German chemical patents were bought (at $50 each!) by The Chemical Foundation, organized for this purpose by a former Alien Property Custodian and associates. By a series of acts since 1921, notably the Settlement of War Claims Act[qv] of 1928, Congress has compensated Austrians and Hungarians in full. Of German property seized by the Custodian, 80% has been returned. The balance was to have been settled out of bonds deposited by Germany by Agreement of 1930, but in default since 1931. For ships and certain other property used by the Government, Germans have been paid 50%, the remainder being held up as above.

[Annual Reports of the Secretary of the Treasury, 1930, 1934, 1936.] FRANK A. SOUTHARD, JR.

Aliens. *See* Naturalization.

Aliens, Legislation Regarding. The alien problem confronted the United States practically from the beginning. In its earliest form it concerned mainly natives and foreign-born who had elected to remain British subjects after independence (*see* Loyalists). The Definitive Treaty of Peace, 1783[qv], guaranteed immunity, to those electing to remain British, from prosecutions "for the part . . . taken in the war," from "loss or damage in . . . person, liberty or property" and from continued imprisonment on the same account. It likewise authorized creditors to recover debts which had been sequestered in the Colonies; but this was not carried out and the Jay Treaty[qv] waived for each signatory future rights of confiscation[qv]. Such waiver was likewise made in many subsequent treaties and those rights were not actually exercised by the United States for nearly a century and a quarter. The right of aliens to enter and settle was virtually unlimited by legislation before 1882 and that of naturalization[qv] was extended to aliens by the First Congress. American insistence upon the right of expatriation[qv] was in fact a cause of the War of 1812. The Fourteenth Amendment[qv] to the Federal Constitution, forbidding any state to "deny to any person within its jurisdiction the equal protection of the laws," purported to place aliens virtually on a par with citizens regarding civil rights[qv]. A lower Federal court in California declared unconstitutional a state statute forbidding Chinese to fish in streams of that state; but the Supreme Court upheld a Pennsylvania act of 1909 prohibiting resident aliens from killing wild game or owning firearms, as infringing neither the Fourteenth Amendment nor the Italian (1871) or Swiss (1855) Treaty. In some of the western states, e.g., Nebraska, aliens who had declared their intention to become citizens were permitted to vote; but such legislation was generally repealed during or after the World War.

C. SUMNER LOBINGIER

All American Canal, THE, scheduled for completion in 1939, at a cost of $38,000,000, will divert Colorado River water at Imperial Dam, 23 miles above the Mexican border, and carry it 80 miles to the Imperial Valley and 130 miles to the Coachella Valley, Calif., for irrigation, replacing a canal traversing Mexican territory. An apportionment negotiated by Secretary of Interior Ray Lyman Wilbur in 1930 entitles these areas to 3,850,000 acre feet annually, plus a share of any excess water. Mexico will not be served by this canal, but will divert from the river independently.

[Ray Lyman Wilbur and Northcutt Ely, *The Hoover Dam Contracts.*] NORTHCUTT ELY

All Quiet Along the Potomac, a poem first published as "The Picket Guard" by Mrs. Ethelind Eliot Beers in *Harper's Weekly,* Nov. 30, 1861. It refers to official telegrams reporting "all is quiet tonight" to the Secretary of War by Maj. Gen. George B. McClellan.

[George W. Stimpson, *Popular Questions Answered.*]

FRED A. EMERY

Allatoona Pass, Battle at (Oct. 5, 1864). After the fall of Atlanta[qv] Hood (C.) moved his army northward to destroy Sherman's (U.) communications. Sherman followed. Hood detached French's (C.) division to destroy a railroad bridge. On his march French stopped to destroy stores at Allatoona and attacked Federal troops stationed there, but without success. The popular song, "Hold the Fort," was based on messages exchanged between Corse (U.) at Allatoona and Sherman.

[*Battles and Leaders of the Civil War*, Vol. IV.]

THOMAS ROBSON HAY

Alleghenies, Routes across. The steep eastern escarpment of the Allegheny Mountains, about 3000 feet high, extending from the Mohawk valley to the Tennessee River was a serious impediment to the westward movement[qv]. Routes across the Alleghenies depended upon gaps and approaches to these along the tributaries of rivers. Probably buffalo first trod these routes. Later the Indians followed them as trails. In turn they were used by white explorers and fur traders.

The Susquehanna with its West Branch extending close to the Allegheny River furnished a route much used by the Indians, though whites other than fur traders made little use of it during the early period. The branches of the Juniata River led to two historic routes across the Alleghenies, one, the Frankstown Path, much used by Pennsylvania fur traders, and the other, the Traders Path, followed by Forbes' Expedition[qv] and the Pennsylvania Road. From the Potomac at Wills Creek ran the route over the Alleghenies, used by Gist, Washington, and Braddock. From the headwaters of the Potomac also ran a route over the mountains much used in later times as the Northwestern Pike. The headwaters of the James River determined a route overland to branches of the Great Kanawha, one branch of which, the New River, also provided a route from the headwaters of the Roanoke River. Farthest south Cumberland Gap[qv] offered easy passage from eastern Tennessee to central Kentucky making possible the much used Wilderness Road[qv]. In the light of the extensive use made of Forbes' Road, Braddock's Road[qqv] and the Wilderness Road in the westward movement, probably no routes in the United States are more properly known as historic highways.

Even in the age of railways and automobile highways, topography is dominant, and the transportation of the 20th century follows closely the old routes across the Alleghenies.

[Archer Butler Hulbert, *Historic Highways of America;* Alfred P. James, Approaches to the Early History of Western Pennsylvania, *Western Pennsylvania Historical Magazine*, XIX (1936), 203.]

ALFRED P. JAMES

Allegheny Portage Railway, THE, spanned the thirty-six miles between Hollidaysburg and Johnstown to link the eastern and western canals of the Pennsylvania System[qv]. Constructed in 1831–35 when the ascent of 1400 feet from Hollidaysburg to Blair's Gap, at the summit of the Allegheny Mountains, within 10.1 miles seemed a prohibitive gradient for a continuous roadbed, the railway consisted of eleven level stretches and ten inclined planes, five on each side of the crest. The planes were operated by stationary engines. Locomotives quickly replaced horses as motive power. In 1856 the planes were superseded by a continuous railway. The Portage Railroad was sold to the Pennsylvania Railroad[qv] in 1857 and shortly abandoned.

[W. B. Wilson, *History of the Pennsylvania Railroad Company.*]

E. DOUGLAS BRANCH

Allegheny River, THE, rises in Potter County, Pa., and flows in an arc through New York and back into Pennsylvania, where it unites with the Monongahela[qv] to form the Ohio. About 350 miles long, it is navigable by small steamboats for about 150 miles. It was considered by the French and early English explorers as a part of the Ohio River. The Delaware and Shawnee[qqv] settled along its course soon after 1720; white settlement followed after 1790. It was an important highway for settlers and freight in the keelboat and flatboat[qqv] era. Its name is probably a corruption of *Alligewi-hanna,* "stream of the Alligewi," from a tribe that Indian tradition says once inhabited the region.

LELAND D. BALDWIN

Alliance, Farmers'. *See* Farmers' Alliance, The.

Alliance, THE, was a Continental frigate[qv], thirty-six guns, built in Salisbury, Mass., 1778. She carried Lafayette and Thomas Paine to France. Her first commander, Landais, showed doubtful loyalty in the *Bonhomme Richard-Serapis* engagement[qv]. Barry cruised in her from 1780 through the last sea fight of the Revolution with the *Sybil,* March 10, 1783.

[G. W. Allen, *Naval History of the American Revolution.*]

WALTER B. NORRIS

Almanacs. In Colonial days the almanac was a publication of prime importance second only to the Bible and widely used by farmers. Beginning as a publication of astronomical information and prophecy, it later grew into one of culture, occupying the position in the 18th century later taken by the magazine.

The first almanac printed in America was entitled *An Almanac Calculated for New England,* by Mr. Pierce, printed by Stephen Daye at Cambridge in 1639; in 1676 an almanac was published in Boston; in 1686 in Philadelphia, Samuel Atkins, "A student in the mathematics and astrology," compiled *The American Messenger.*

Almanacs were published in New York in 1697, in Rhode Island in 1728, and in Virginia in 1731. In content these almanacs were similar to earlier ones in Europe containing prophecies concerning human beings and the weather, based on astrology. The early almanacs were preserved from year to year and the blank spaces used for diaries, recording accounts, and attempts at poetry.

The most famous of the early almanacs are *The Astronomical Diary and Almanac* published by Ames in Boston (1725–64); and *Poor Richard's Almanac*[qv] by Franklin in Philadelphia (1732–57). The latter was unequalled in reputation for proverbs, wit, and wisdom, not all original. Nathaniel Ames, in his *Astronomical Diary and Almanac,* furnished perhaps a greater versatility than appeared in any other almanac of the century. Its tide charts, solar table calculations and eclipses, and changes of the moon were definite assets.

Foreign language almanacs were widely used. A prominent example was *The Hoch Deutsch Americanische* in 1739 and various almanacs published by the Pennsylvania Germans[qv].

In the 19th century, almanacs were frequently issued for political and other propaganda and advertising purposes as indicated by the *Sun Anti-Masonic Almanac* (1831); *Harrison Almanacs* (1840–41); *Henry Clay Almanac* (1844); *General Taylor's Rough and Ready Almanac* (1848); *Cass and Butler Almanac* (1849); *Common School Almanac* (1842); *Temperance Almanac* (1834).

The Confederate Almanac and Register (1862) and *Uncle Sam's Union Almanac* (1863) gave military statistics somewhat as did *Hutchin's Almanac* of New York in the later 18th century.

Comic almanacs in the eighteen-thirties; *Josh Billings' Almanac* in 1870; *Fithian's Silk Growers Almanac* in 1840; *The Poultry Breeder's Almanac* of 1856 and the *Phrenological Almanac* of 1841 are typical of the times.

All the outstanding religious denominations published almanacs giving denominational statistics and other information. Medical almanacs of all types have been widely distributed. Encyclopedic information is well served by almanacs published by newspapers of which that of the *Tribune* (1846) and the later *World Almanac* are examples.

[Thomas, *History of Printing in America.*]

H. H. SHENK

Alphabetical Agencies. A term first applied to the numerous Government agencies set up under authority of Congress, beginning in March, 1933, to administer the New Deal[qv] relief and recovery measures. It soon became customary to refer to them by the initials of their respective titles, e.g., N.R.A. (National Recovery Administration), A.A.A. (Agricultural Adjustment Administration), F.C.A. (Farm Credit Administration), T.V.A. (Tennessee Valley Authority), S.E.C. (Securities and Exchange Commission), P.W.A. (Public Works Administration), W.P.A. (Works Progress Administration), C.C.C. (Civilian Conservation Corps)[qqv]. Later, Government agencies that antedated the New Deal were similarly referred to, e.g., I.C.C. (Interstate Commerce Commission), F.T.C. (Federal Trade Commission) and R.F.C. (Reconstruction Finance Corporation)[qqv].

[L. F. Schmeckebier, *New Federal Organizations;* S. C. Wallace, *The New Deal in Action.*]

P. ORMAN RAY

Alphadelphia Association, THE, was a Fourierist[qv] community established in Comstock township, Kalamazoo County, Mich., in 1844. A German, Dr. H. R. Schetterly, was the leading spirit. Three thousand acres of land were purchased, a large "mansion" built, and at one time probably 300 members were admitted. The common property was valued at $43,897.21 in 1846. It was disbanded in 1848.

[*Michigan Pioneer and Historical Collections,* Vol. V, 406-12.]

WILLIS DUNBAR

Alta California. Under Spain (1533–1822) California embraced the whole Pacific coast of North America from Cape San Lucas to the Oregon country. Till the middle 18th century it was frequently represented on maps as an island some 3000 miles long. Early in the 18th century the Jesuit Father Kino proved by actual exploration that the southern portion of the area was a peninsula and the rest of it mainland. Thereafter the peninsula came to be called Baja (Lower) and the rest Alta (Upper) California.

[C. E. Chapman, *California, The Spanish Period;* H. E. Bolton, *Outpost of Empire.*]

HERBERT E. BOLTON

Alta Vela Claim. This was a flimsy claim against the Dominican Government by American adventurers ejected on the eve of the unsuccessful Spanish reoccupation (1861–65) of the guano island by that name located some fifteen miles south of the Dominican Republic. It has both a sinister and an auspicious significance in United States political history because former Secretary of State Jeremiah S. Black resigned as defending counsel in the impeachment[qv] trial of President

Andrew Johnson in 1868 when the latter would not order Secretary of State Seward to approve the claim.

[Samuel Flagg Bemis, *Diplomatic History of the United States.*]

SAMUEL FLAGG BEMIS

Alton Petroglyphs. Near the present town of Alton, Ill., Marquette in 1673 saw painted upon the face of a rocky bluff the figure of a monster which terrified him and interested later travelers until its destruction about 1856. Called "Piasa" by the Indians, the figure was that of an imaginary bird legendary with many tribes.

[F. W. Hodge, *Handbook of American Indians.*]

CLARK WISSLER

Aluminum. From its discovery in 1825 to 1886, the year in which Charles Martin Hall perfected an electrolytic process for its reduction, aluminum was a costly metal. Its chief qualities were lightness, a high degree of resistance to corrosion, good electrical and heat conductivity, and good reflectivity for light and heat; it was considered as a material which would enjoy great usefulness if its price could be brought down. Prior to Hall's invention, aluminum sold for $8 a pound, and at one time had sold as high as $545 a pound. Now (1938) it costs approximately twenty cents a pound, and in 1937, 292,000,000 pounds of aluminum were made in the United States alone.

Hall, a native of Ohio and a graduate of Oberlin College, was twenty-two years old at the time he discovered the new process. After vainly attempting to interest a number of manufacturers, he went to Pittsburgh in 1888, and there discussed the possibilities of making aluminum on a commercial scale with Capt. Alfred E. Hunt, head of the Pittsburgh Testing Laboratory. Hunt immediately grasped the significance of the discovery, and in a few weeks was able to interest a group of men in forming a company to exploit the invention. The sum of $20,000 was raised for this purpose, and the Pittsburgh Reduction Company came into being.

The uses of the metal were at first confined to novelties, but constant research improved the product, and its applications were widened with every passing year. The addition of small amounts of other metals to aluminum produced various grades of alloys which could be used in an infinite number of ways, greatly widening the metal's sphere of influence.

In 1907 the name of the Pittsburgh Reduction Company was changed to that of the Aluminum Company of America, in order to identify the firm more closely with the product it manufactured. The virgin metal, of which this firm is the sole producer in the United States, is taken by thousands of fabricators and made into tens of thousands of commodities. The first large field which aluminum entered was that of cooking utensils, but today only a fraction of the annual tonnage is earmarked for this purpose. Aluminum and its alloys find their largest use in the field of transportation, where they are employed in the manufacture of airplanes, bus and truck bodies, stream-lined trains, street and subway cars, railroad cars, automobiles, vessels of various types, engines, outboard motors, motorcycles and bicycles.

Aluminum alloys of high strength are used in the construction of bridge floor systems, dragline booms and buckets, shovel dippers, heavy-duty dump trucks, hopper cars, flood bulkheads, mine skips, and man cages. Because it is inert to many chemicals, aluminum is used in the form of tanks, carboys, and other types of containers. Many dairies use aluminum tanks, while a number of important American breweries are equipped with aluminum fermenting and storage tanks, wort coolers, yeast tubs and beer barrels.

[Edwards, Frary and Jeffries, *The Aluminum Industry.*]

C. C. CARR

Amana Community, The. Consisting of approximately fifteen hundred people, living in seven villages and owning twenty-six thousand acres of land in one of the garden spots of Iowa, the Amana Community had for nearly a century conducted the most successful experiment in communism recorded in the annals of American history. Then in 1932 by unanimous vote this community reorganized as a joint stock company where stockholders are both owners and employees.

Born of religious enthusiasm, this unique community was founded in 1714 as the Community of True Inspiration in protest against the arbitrary rule of church and state. For mutual protection the Inspirationists congregated on several large estates in south Germany. But high rents and unfriendly governments forced them to seek a new home in America.

Under the leadership of Christian Metz the Inspirationists crossed the Atlantic in the early eighteen-forties and settled near Buffalo in Erie County, N. Y. Here they laid out six villages, called the place Ebenezer, built mills and factories, tilled the soil, and formally adopted communism as a way of life.

The rapid expansion of nearby Buffalo threatened that isolation which the Inspirationists had sought in the New World. And so, after twelve years at Ebenezer they moved to the frontier state of Iowa where they located in Iowa County, incorporated as the "Amana Society," and once more built houses, churches, schools, stores and mills, and continued their community life of "brothers all" through communism.

With the passing of years, the frontier disappeared, isolation became impossible, memories of the founding forefathers faded, the old idealism grew dim, spiritual enthusiasms waned, and in the midst of world depression in the early nineteen-thirties, the Community of True Inspiration faced a setting sun.

The crisis was met with intelligent leadership which realized that it would be impossible to maintain an 18th-century culture in the competitive gear of a machine age. And so, church and state were separated and the community was reorganized on the basis of co-operative capitalism in which the old communism is simply overtone.

[Bertha M. H. Shambaugh, *Amana, The Community of True Inspiration*, and *Amana That Was and Amana That Is*, published by The State Historical Society of Iowa.] BERTHA M. H. SHAMBAUGH

Ambassadors. The grade of ambassador is the highest rank in the diplomatic service[qv]. An ambassador has direct access, when desired, to a sovereign. The United States did not appoint officers of this rank until the close of the 19th century, contenting itself with ministers. The first ambassador of the United States was Thomas F. Bayard of Delaware, commissioned to Great Britain on March 30, 1893. The first ambassador to the United States was Sir Julian Pauncefote of Great Britain, who was presented to President Cleveland on April 11, 1893. Following this exchange of ambassadors between the United States and Great Britain, similar officers were appointed and received for the principal European powers. The first ambassador to Japan was Luke E. Wright of Tennessee, appointed Jan. 25, 1906; to China, Nelson T. Johnson of Oklahoma, appointed Sept. 17, 1935. The first ambassador of the United States to a Latin-American republic was Powell Clayton of Arkansas, who received his commission on Dec. 8, 1898. Although Matías Romero, who had long held the post of minister to the United States, had been appointed as first ambassador from Mexico with a commission dated Dec. 5, 1898, and arrangements had been made for the presentation of his credentials, his death prevented his reception; consequently the first ambassador received for a Latin-American republic was Manuel de Azpíroz of Mexico, who was presented to the President on March 30, 1899. Ambassadors today (1939) represent the United States in the following countries—the date of inception of the office is indicated in parentheses: Argentina (1914), Belgium (1919), Brazil (1905), Chile (1914), China (1935), Colombia (1938), Cuba (1923), France (1893), Germany (1893), Great Britain (1893), Italy (1893), Japan (1906), Mexico (1898), Panama (1939), Peru (1919), Poland (1919), Russia (1898), Spain (1913), Turkey (1906), and Venezuela (1938).

SAMUEL FLAGG BEMIS

Ambrister. *See* Arbuthnot and Ambrister, Case of.

Ambulance Companies. During Gen. Grant's attack on Fort Donelson[qv] in February, 1862, four ambulance companies and four field hospitals were organized by Surgeon H. S. Hewitt. As provisional organizations they were used to remove the wounded to field hospitals. Maj. Jonathan Letterman later fathered the formation of an expanded ambulance corps, large enough to serve for every battlefield need. In the World War, ambulance companies, organized with the assistance of the American Red Cross[qv], were successfully used as units of divisional sanitary trains.

[*The Medical Department of the United States Army in the World War; Medical and Surgical History of the War of the Rebellion;* both compiled in the Office of the Surgeon General, United States Army.]

ROBERT S. THOMAS

Amelia Island Affair. The Embargo[qv] Act (1807) and the abolishment of the American slave trade[qv] (1808) made Amelia Island, on the coast of Spanish Florida[qv], a resort for smugglers[qv] with sometimes as many as 300 square-rigged vessels in its harbor.

To Amelia in June, 1817, came one Gregor McGregor, styling himself the "brigadier general" of the United Provinces of the New Granada and Venezuela and general-in-chief of the armies of the two Floridas. He left for Nassau in September, but his followers were soon joined by Luis Aury, formerly associated with McGregor in South American adventures, but later leader of a piratical band on Galveston Island, Texas. Aury assumed control of Amelia, got a legislature elected, set a committee to drawing a constitution, and invited all Florida to unite in throwing off the Spanish yoke. The United States becoming tired of having its laws violated sent a naval force which captured Amelia Island Dec. 23, 1817, and put an end to the miniature republic.

The island was returned to the Spaniards prior to 1821.

[Carolina Mays Brevard, *History of Florida;* James Parton, *Andrew Jackson.*] W. T. CASH

Amen Corner was a celebrated niche in the corridor of the old Fifth Avenue Hotel (1859–1908), New York City, where politicians and reporters gathered to discuss coming political events. It was here that Sen. Thomas C. Platt's "Sunday School Class" was held in the late eighteen-nineties, and when the Senator announced his decisions his associates would say "Amen."

[*The Autobiography of Thomas Collier Platt,* compiled and edited by Louis J. Lang.]

HAROLD F. GOSNELL

Amendment Clause of the Constitution, THE, was adopted by the Convention of 1787[qv] with little controversy. It is contained in Article V of the United States Constitution. It provides two methods for the proposal of Amendments: either by a two-thirds vote of both Houses of Congress or, on the application of the legislatures of two-thirds of the states, Congress shall call a convention for proposing Amendments. In either case Amendments must be ratified in one of two ways: either by action of the legislatures of three-fourths of the states or by conventions in three-fourths of the same. Congress is empowered to provide either one of these methods of ratification.

During the entire one hundred and fifty years of our history under the Constitution the only method used for amendment, with but one exception, has been the proposal by Congress, and the ratification by the state legislatures. The exception was the Twenty-first Amendment[qv] which by direction of Congress was ratified by conventions in the states. From time to time changes in the method of ratification have been suggested in order that there might be some sort of popular vote upon the question. Up to the present time (1939) this has not resulted in any formal Amendment being passed by Congress.

[Edward S. Corwin, *The Constitution and What It Means Today.*] WILLIAM STARR MYERS

Amendments to the Constitution, to the number of twenty-one, may be said to have been made on seven different occasions.

Amendments I to X may be considered almost a part of the original Constitution. That document contained no Bill of Rights[qv]. The prevailing feeling in the Convention of 1787[qv] was that it was unnecessary to have one since the new government had no authority to interfere with the inalienable rights of individuals which already existed under the English Common Law. On the other hand, many states felt it to be necessary that definite provisions should be included in the Constitution which specifically would make safe the rights of individuals. For this reason the conventions in Massachusetts, New York and a number of other states ratified the Constitution (*see* Constitution, Ratification of the) with the recommendation that a Bill of Rights be added by the amending process when the new government was established. Various states proposed a total of 189 Amendments, many of which were upon like subjects. Twelve Amendments were finally proposed by Congress on Sept. 25, 1789. Ten of these were declared ratified by the necessary number of states on Dec. 15, 1791. They form a Bill of Rights and bind the National Government, but do not limit the powers of the states.

The Eleventh Amendment[qv] was proposed by Congress on Sept. 5, 1794, and was declared ratified on Jan. 8, 1798. It provided that the judicial power of the United States should not be construed to extend to any suit in law or equity against any one of the United States by citizens of another state or by citizens or subjects of any foreign state.

The Twelfth Amendment[qv] was proposed by Congress on Dec. 12, 1803, and declared ratified on Sept. 25, 1804. It was largely the result of the controversy following the tie in the election of Jefferson and Burr in 1800 (*see* Campaign of 1800), and provides primarily that presidential electors[qv] shall make a separate designation in their choice for President and Vice-President[qqv].

The Thirteenth, Fourteenth, and Fifteenth Amendments[qqv] were the result of the Civil War struggle and may be considered as part of the same process. The Thirteenth Amendment was proposed by Congress on Feb. 1, 1865, and declared ratified on Dec. 18 of the same year. It abolished slavery[qv] and involuntary servitude. The Fourteenth Amendment was proposed by Congress on June 16, 1866, and declared ratified on July 22, 1868. It provided that national citizenship be primary and state citizenship derived therefrom. The most important provisions deal with the privileges or immunities of citizens, "due process of law," and the equal protection of the laws[qqv]. Other sections are mainly of historical interest since they provide for matters arising immediately out of the Civil War. The Fifteenth Amendment resulted in the enfranchisement of the Negroes[qv]. It was proposed by Congress on Feb. 26, 1869, and was declared ratified on March 30, 1870.

The Sixteenth and Seventeenth Amendments[qqv] were the result of the so-called Progressive movement[qv] during the early years of the 20th century. The Sixteenth Amendment empowers Congress to levy a national income tax[qv], was proposed by Congress on July 12, 1909, and was declared ratified on Feb. 25, 1913. The Seventeenth Amendment provides for the election of the United States Senators[qv] by direct vote of the people. It was proposed on May 16, 1912, and was declared ratified on May 31, 1913.

The World War exerted a profound effect upon the thought of our people and it was during the time when its influence still was of primary importance that the Eighteenth and Nineteenth Amendments[qqv] were adopted. The Eighteenth or "Prohibition"[qv] Amendment was proposed on Dec. 18, 1917, and declared ratified on Jan. 29, 1919. The Nineteenth or Woman's Suffrage[qv] Amendment was proposed on June 4, 1919, and declared ratified on Aug. 18, 1920.

The latest two Amendments may be described as the direct results of the New Deal[qv] movement. The Twentieth Amendment[qv] provides that the terms of the President and Vice-President shall begin on Jan. 20 and those of senators and representatives on Jan. 3 of the appropriate years. It was proposed on March 2, 1932, and was ratified on Feb. 6, 1933.

The Twenty-first Amendment[qv] repealed the Eighteenth or "Prohibition" Amendment by means of conventions in the states. It passed Congress on Feb. 20, 1933, and was declared ratified on Dec. 5 of the same year. It is the only Amendment in which the ratification by state conventions has been authorized and required by the action of Congress.

[Edward S. Corwin, *The Constitution and What It Means Today.*] WILLIAM STARR MYERS

"America." *See* "My Country, 'Tis of Thee."

America, Discovery of. "Traditionally, the history of America begins with the 'discovery' in 1492. Now, that date does mark an important episode—the first piloting of sailing vessels across the Atlantic Ocean, an episode comparable with the first piloting of airplanes across the same sea. But neither was a feat of discovery." (Edgar Lee Hewett.) In other words, America was populated before the continents were "discovered" by western Europeans. It is the consensus of opinion of anthropologists at the present time, that man did not develop, indigenously, in America, but that early man came from the Mongoloid groups of central Asia and probably "discovered" and entered North America by way of Alaska, either by crossing Bering Strait, or possibly by an isthmus or other land bridge which may have existed at the time.

About the year 1000 A.D. roving Norsemen[qv], starting from the Scandinavian colonies in Greenland, may have reached the coast of North America anywhere between Labrador and the Chesapeake. If they did, they left no undisputed archæologic evidences of their visit. The legends of the voyages of Leif Ericsson and Thorfinn Karlsefne depend upon three manuscripts of sagas written more than three hundred years after the possible "discovery" of that part of America which Leif called "Vinland the Good." Admitting Leif to have been the "discoverer" of America, Edward Channing aptly said, "The history of America would have been precisely what it has been if Leif Ericsson had never been born and if no Northman had ever steered his knorr west of Iceland."

On the other hand, it is an undisputed historic fact that on Aug. 3, 1492, the Genoese, Christopher Columbus, sailed from Palos, Spain, under the authority of the King and Queen of that country. On Oct. 11, 1492, he saw, and the next day Columbus and his party landed on, some island in the Bahamas which the Indians called Guanahani, and which Columbus rechristened San Salvador. Its exact identity today has never been conclusively established, but many good scholars have accepted Watling Island as his first landfall. Following this Columbus made three other voyages to the New World (1495, 1499 and 1502), during which he touched the coasts of South and Central America. But it must be remembered there is a documented story that one of the factors which induced Columbus to make his voyage was his actually meeting with, or knowledge of, a Spanish pilot who brought back news of having been wrecked on an island far west of the Madeiras as early as 1484.

Possibly independently, John Cabot[qv] sailed from Bristol, England, in May, 1497, and some time in June probably discovered the continent of North America. In 1499, Alonso de Ojeda and Juan de la Cosa visited South America, and with them went Americus Vespucius who wrote such popular accounts of his own deeds that the German geographer, Martin Waldseemüller, coined the word "America"[qv] in a book published in 1507. The inevitability of the so-called discovery of America by Europeans is illustrated by the fact that the Portuguese, Pedro Cabral, in 1500, tried to reach India by way of the African coast, and was accidentally blown to the west where unintentionally he reached the coast of Brazil.

The island of Espagnola (Hispaniola-Santo Domingo) became the Spanish outpost from which further discoveries of the mainland were made. Thence Vasco Nuñez de Balboa went to Central America, crossed the Isthmus of Panama and discovered the Pacific Ocean, Sept. 25, 1513. The eastern coast of the mainland of North America had been seen and was cartographically traced by 1502. On Easter Sunday, 1513, Juan Ponce de Leon[qv], from Espagnola, found his way to the site of the present city of St. Augustine, Fla. Francisco Gordillo coasted as far north as Cape Fear (1521) and Lucas Vasquez de Ayllon[qv] followed and got as far as the James River in Virginia (1526). Meantime Hernando Cortés had landed in Mexico and conquered it in one of a series of the most amazing expeditions in all history (1519). Panfilo de Narvaez[qv] explored western Florida, and possibly Georgia (1528–36) while his treasurer Alvar Nuñez Cabeza de Vaca[qv] walked overland from Pensacola Bay, Fla., to the Gulf of California. In 1539 Hernando de Soto[qv] took an expedition from Tampa Bay, Fla., marched north to the Savannah River, turned west and proceeded overland until he reached the Mississippi in 1541.

By this time Antonio de Mendoza[qv] had become viceroy of New Spain (Mexico, as opposed to Peru) and from his bailiwick, Franciscan[qv] friars were pushing up into what is now "The Southwest"[qv] of the United States. Fray Marcos de Niza (1539) brought back such reports that Francisco Vasquez de Coronado[qv] started out in April of 1540 on an expedition which took him as far north as central Kansas (1541).

So much for the Spaniards. Meantime the French had entered the field of exploration. Giovanni da Verrazzano, acting under the favor of Francis I, came to North America in 1524 and possibly saw the Lower Bay of New York. Jacques Cartier coasted Labrador in 1534, and in the next year entered and explored the St. Lawrence to the La Chine Rapids above Quebec. The discovery of much of the present area of the United States from the north was the work of Samuel de Champlain[qv], who found Maine in 1603–4, and Cape Cod in 1605, and got as far as central New York State in 1615.

Last, but most effective of the discovering nations was England. The Hawkins—William, John, and James—roamed the West Indies. Sir Francis Drake[qv] doubled Cape Horn and reached the coast of California, near, if not at, San Francisco Bay in June, 1579. In 1602 Bartholomew Gosnold reached the coast of Maine near Cape Porpoise, skirted Cape Cod (which he named) and found Narragansett Bay. George Weymouth in 1605 sighted Nantucket and then headed north to find the coast of Maine in the neighborhood of Monhegan and the Gorges Islands.

Mention should be made of an alleged discovery of America by Swedes and Norwegians from Greenland in the 13th century, through Hudson Bay and the Red River of the North into the present State of Minnesota. This theory rests on an inscribed stone and certain artifacts which need further study (*see* Kensington Stone, The). There are also stories of pre-Columbian discoveries of America by the Chinese, Welsh, Irish, Phœnicians and others. These are all legendary.

[Justin Winsor, *Narrative and Critical History of America;* Edward Channing, *History of the United States*, Vol. I.]

RANDOLPH G. ADAMS

America, THE, is an American yacht which in 1851 won the trophy cup presented by the Royal Yacht Squadron, the famous America's Cup. She served later as a Confederate despatch boat, was captured, served as practice ship at the Naval Academy, defended the Cup in 1870, was sold to Gen. B. F. Butler in 1873, and in 1917 to Charles H. W. Foster of the Eastern Yacht Club. She was permanently docked at the Naval Academy in 1921.

[J. S. Hughes, *Famous Yachts;* W. M. Thompson, *The Yacht America.*]

LOUIS H. BOLANDER

America, The Name. The earliest explorers and historians designated America as the "Indies," the "West Indies," or the "New World," and these terms remained the favorites in Spain and Portugal for over two centuries. Amerigo Vespucci was little known there, but beyond the Pyrenees the chief source of information on the discoveries was his account of his voyages, translated into Latin. A coterie of scholars at St. Dié, in Lorraine, chiefly Martin Waldseemüller and Mathias Ringmann, printed this in 1507 in *Cosmographiae Introductio,* a small work designed to accompany and explain a wall map and globe executed by Waldseemüller. In their work two names were suggested for the new "fourth part" of the world, one *Amerige* (pronounced "A-mer-i-gay," with the *-ge* from the Greek, meaning "earth"), and the other *America* (in the feminine form, parallel to *Europa* and *Asia*). The latter form was placed on Waldseemüller's maps of 1507, and their wide circulation brought about the gradual adoption of the name. Waldseemüller was aware of only South America as a continent, but Mercator in 1538 extended the designation to both continents.

Although Vespucci was not responsible for the giving of the name, the injustice to Columbus has aroused a series of protests since 1535. Various impossible origins of America have been suggested—that it comes from a native Indian word, from a sheriff of Bristol named Richard Ameryk, etc. The etymology of *Amerigo* can be traced to the old Germanic, meaning "ruler of the home." The name America is today highly ambiguous, since it often, as determined by the context, refers to the United States alone.

[Edward Gaylord Bourne, The Naming of America, in *American Historical Review,* Vol. X (1904), 41–51.]

ALLEN WALKER READ

American Academy of Arts and Letters, THE, founded in 1904 to protect and foster literature and the fine arts[qv], limits its membership to fifty, chosen from the larger National Institute of Arts and Letters. Among past and present members are counted many of the most distinguished Americans in letters and arts, including music.

JAMES TRUSLOW ADAMS

American Antislavery Societies. The first two American antislavery societies were the New York "Society for the Promoting of the Manumission[qv] of Slaves" and the "Pennsylvania Society for Promoting the Abolition of Slavery, the Relief of Free Negroes unlawfully held in Bondage and Improving the Condition of the African Race." Under their auspices the first convention of Abolition societies was held in Philadelphia in January, 1794. The Pennsylvania society was created in April, 1775, less than a week before the clash at Lexington and Concord[qv]; Benjamin Franklin and Dr. Benjamin Rush were among its presidents. John Jay, later Chief Justice, was the first president of the New York society on its organization in 1785. Other state societies were organized in Delaware, 1788, Maryland, 1789, Rhode Island and Connecticut, 1790, Virginia, 1791, and New Jersey, 1792. There were also Abolition societies in Charlestown, Md., and Winchester, Va., and one for the State of Kentucky. The older societies withered and died after the Missouri Compromise[qv] of 1820.

The militant Garrisonian Abolition movement[qv] led to the formation of the New England Anti-Slavery Society[qv] later called the Massachusetts Anti-Slavery Society, on Jan. 6, 1832, and the National Anti-Slavery Society in Philadelphia, Dec. 6, 1833. The New York Anti-Slavery Society was mobbed on the day of its organization, Oct. 21, 1835. From then on such organizations multiplied rapidly throughout the North. In 1835 there were 200; by 1840, 2000 auxiliary societies with a membership between 150,000 and 200,000. The American Anti-Slavery Society came to life in 1833. (*See* Antislavery Movement.)

[G. H. Barnes, *The Antislavery Impulse, 1830-1844.*]

OSWALD GARRISON VILLARD

American Automobile Association, THE, was organized March 4, 1902, in Chicago, Ill., by representatives of nine automobile clubs. Winthrop E. Scarritt, of the Automobile Club of America (New York City), was chosen first president.

The purposes of the A.A.A., as outlined in the formal call for organization, included: enactment of liberal motor vehicle laws; protection of legal rights of motor vehicle users; improvement of public highways; "development and introduction of the automobile"; equitable regulation of racing and endurance tests; and the provision of a medium for "counsel and interchange of information, ideas, and suggestions tending to the development and advancement of the art."

One of the earliest activities of the A.A.A. was the sponsoring, during the period 1905–13, of national reliability runs, popularly known as the "Glidden Tours." The A.A.A. also sponsored the good roads movement[qv] which resulted in the establishment of the Federal aid system[qv].

Gradually the motor clubs lost nearly all of their early social aspect and became primarily service and civic organizations. At the close of 1937 there were approximately 750 motor clubs, state associations, and motor club branches, with about 800,000 members, federated under the A.A.A. banner.

RICHARD W. TUPPER

American Bible Society, THE, was organized in New York City in 1816 by delegates from thirty-one local societies. Elias Boudinot was elected president. Its purpose was to produce and distribute the Scriptures in all languages and in all lands. Its work has continually prospered and expanded, and is furthered by a number of auxiliary and co-operating societies.

By the close of 1936 the whole Bible had been published in 176 languages, the New Testament in 214, portions or selections in 601 more, so that the Scriptures have now been published in 991 languages and dialects. During the year 1936 through its various agencies at home and abroad the Society put in circulation, in upwards of forty countries, a total of more than 7,760,000 Bibles, Testaments, Gospels and portions. A much appreciated feature of the Society's service is its ministry to the blind[qv]. Since the beginning of such work more than 125,000 embossed volumes in twenty-five languages and systems have been published.

The Society has a number of well-organized agencies in home and foreign lands. It is interdenominational, is governed by its own duly elected officers, managers, and committees, and asks for the observance of a Bible Sunday each year.

[Annual Reports of the American Bible Society.]

C. H. STACKPOLE

American Bottom, THE, narrow Mississippi River flood plain extending roughly 100 miles between Chester and Alton, Ill., took its name jointly perhaps from the first American settlers in the Old Northwest[qv] and from serving as part of the territorial boundary before the Louisiana Purchase[qv]. Site of pre-eminent burial and ceremonial mounds[qv], the bluff-hemmed strip became a lifeline of white population in the wilderness with settlements at Cahokia, Kaskaskia, Fort de Chartres, Bellefontaine[qqv], and Prairie du Rocher among others. Frontier travelers found the pond-dotted flat "miasmatic" but "extremely fertile."

[L. C. Beck, *Gazetteer of Illinois and Missouri;* H. I. Priestly, *The Coming of the White Man;* W. K. Moorehead and M. M. Leighton, *The Cahokia Mounds;* C. W. Alvord, *Cahokia Records, 1778-1790.*]

IRVING DILLIARD

American Colonization Society, THE (1817–1912), labored to remove free Negroes[qv] from the United States to Liberia[qv], and in addition, aided in manumitting[qv] slaves and in suppressing the slave trade[qv]. Local branches in every state, the churches and, in some cases, state legislatures supplied the money necessary to buy slaves, transport them, and establish them in Liberia. The Society transported 6000 Negroes between 1821 and 1867. Lack of funds, internal dissension and the opposition of extremists, North and South, hampered the efforts of the Society after 1840. After 1865 the Society functioned chiefly as trustee for the Liberian settlement.

[E. L. Fox, *The American Colonization Society, 1817-1840.*]

ELIZABETH W. MEADE

American Eagle, THE. *See* Eagle, The American.

American Expeditionary Forces, THE. This term was used to designate the American troops serving in Europe during the World War. The declaration of war found us without plans for organizing a force that would be capable of offensive action in modern warfare. On May 26, 1917, Maj. Gen. John J. Pershing, who had been selected by President Wilson to command our land forces abroad, was directed to proceed with his staff to France. Shortly after his arrival, convinced that military assistance on a vast scale would be necessary to Allied success, Gen. Pershing cabled the War Department that its minimum undertaking should contemplate 1,000,000 men in France by the following May, and that plans should be based on an ultimate force of 3,000,000. When the Armistice[qv] came, approximately 2,000,000 men had been transported to Europe, where they were trained, subsisted and equipped through their own supply system, and took a decisive part in bringing the war to a successful conclusion.

In the spring and early summer of 1918 a series of powerful German offensives threatened defeat of the Allies. In the crisis Gen. Pershing placed the entire resources of the American Expeditionary Forces at the disposal of the Allied High Command, postponing until July 24, 1918, the formation of the American First Army.

The assistance we gave the Allies in combat began in May with the capture of Cantigny[qv] by an American division in the first independent American offensive operation of the war. This was followed early in June by the entrance into battle of two divisions that stopped the German advance on Paris near Chateau-Thierry[qv]. In July two American divisions, with one Moroccan division, formed the spearhead of the counter-attack against the Chateau-Thierry salient, which marked the turning point of the war. Approximately 300,000 American troops were engaged in this Second Battle of the Marne. In the middle of September the American First Army of 550,000 men reduced the St. Mihiel[qv] salient. The latter part of September our Meuse-Argonne offensive[qv] was begun. After forty-seven days of intense fighting, this great battle ended brilliantly for our First and Second Armies on Nov. 11. More than 1,200,000 American soldiers had participated.

With the cessation of hostilities, attention was immediately turned to repatriating the troops. By the end of August, 1919, the last American division had embarked, leaving only a small force in occupied Germany, and on Sept. 1, 1919, Gen. Pershing and his staff sailed for the United States. (*See* World War.)

JOHN J. PERSHING

American Expeditionary Forces in Italy. As tangible proof of American co-operation, the Italian Minister of War urged that American units be sent to Italy. The 332nd Infantry Regiment, the 331st Field Hospital, and the 102nd Base Hospital were so despatched. With headquarters at Treviso, the 332nd Infantry made numerous marches to the front line, there to be observed by Austrians and Italians. The regiment participated in the attack to force a crossing of the Piave River^qv (Oct. 26, 1918), and in the Battle of the Tagliamento River^qv (Nov. 4). In March, 1919, American troops sailed from Italy.

[Cablegrams exchanged between War Department and Gen. Pershing; Letters from Chief, American Military Mission to Italy; Records of Supreme War Council; Regimental records, 332nd Infantry; all on file in United States War Department.]

ROBERT S. THOMAS

American Express Company. In 1850 two express companies then operating in the Northeast, Wells, Butterfield & Company and Livingston, Fargo & Company, were united to form a joint stock association with a capital of $150,000 known as the American Express Company. Henry Wells and William G. Fargo were the real governing geniuses of the company, and Wells became its first president. It operated on important lines in New England, followed the Great Lakes into the Midwest and Northwest, and even thrust fingers into Canada. It played no small part in the commercial development of the State of Michigan. Its incorporators organized Wells, Fargo & Company^qv in 1852 as a sister organization for the western half of the country. The United States Express Company was organized in 1854 as a subsidiary, but in the course of two decades the two companies drifted apart and became sharp competitors. In 1915 the American operated on 61,500 miles of steam and electric railroads, water and stage lines, this being the second largest territory among the express companies. In 1918 all the companies merged their shipping interests in the American Railway Express Company, the American Express Company continuing as a banking and tourist bureau. In 1929 the Railway Express Agency, owned by the railroads, took over the American Railway Express Company.

[Alvin F. Harlow, *Old Waybills.*]

ALVIN F. HARLOW

American Federation of Labor. A federation of autonomous craft and industrial unions, chiefly the former, organized in 1886. The A. F. of L. was a reorganization of the Federation of Organized Trades and Labor Unions of the United States and Canada (1881). The object of the new federation was to promote vigorous independent trade unionism^qv based upon craft autonomy, as opposed to the centrally controlled unionism of the Knights of Labor^qv (1869). Each of the federation's constituent unions has its own government, determines its own policies, and conducts its own financial affairs. The federation has no powers except those conceded by its member unions through a written constitution and the annual convention. Craft autonomy with loose federation for the administration of common interests and the promotion of common purposes is the foundation of the A. F. of L. structure.

The organic unit of the federation is the local union. These locals are integrated in national or international unions. To achieve greater economic and political unity and power, A. F. of L. unions have formed city central labor unions or local federations. Even within the same industry, co-ordinating councils have been set up, such as the building trades councils. These deal with jurisdictional disputes between member unions and in other ways promote common interests. Crowning the structure of the federation is the Executive Council, consisting of a president, several vice-presidents, a treasurer and a secretary, which administers the affairs of the federation in the interim between conventions.

The general object of the A. F. of L. is continued improvement of the economic status of wage-earners. Thus far its accomplishments have been confined largely to the ranks of skilled workers. Its aim is attained chiefly through the medium of collective bargaining^qv in the industrial field. To secure and make effective the method of collective bargaining, such weapons as the strike, boycott, picketing^qqv and union labels are employed.

Sustained leadership has been a factor in the steady growth of the federation. Although serious losses in membership have occurred in each period of depression, the total membership increased from less than 200,000 in 1886 to approximately 4,100,000 in 1920. The membership in 1938 is estimated at 2,861,000. Since 1935 the leadership of the federation has been in serious conflict with the Committee for Industrial Organization^qv over the issue of industrial versus craft unionism.

[American Federation of Labor, *History, Encyclopedia, Reference Book;* Selig Perlman, *A History of Trade Unionism in the United States;* Samuel Gompers, *Seventy Years of Life and Labor;* Lewis L. Lorwin, *The American Federation of Labor.*]

GORDON S. WATKINS

American Flag. *See* Flag of United States, The.

American Forces in Germany. *See* Army of Occupation (1918–23).

American Fur Company, The, was incorporated for a period of twenty-five years, under the laws of the State of New York by an act passed on April 6, 1808. Its capital stock was not to exceed $1,000,000 for two years; thereafter it might not exceed $2,000,000. John Jacob Astor was the sole stockholder. From being a poor immigrant German lad in 1784, Astor had risen by 1808 to a position where he felt he could challenge unaided and successfully the two great fur-trading companies of Canada that were securing a large part of their furs within the limits of the United States—the North West Company[qv], with a capital of $1,200,000, and the Michilimackinac Company, capitalized at about $800,000. All that he needed was incorporation as a company. This might seem presumption on Astor's part, but events were to prove that his belief in himself was justified.

To get control of the fur trade of the Great Lakes[qv], the American Fur Company first came to an agreement with the North West Company and the Michilimackinac Company, whereby the South West Fur Company[qv], representing the three companies, was constituted Jan. 28, 1811, to last for five years. It was to confine its operations to the region south of the Canadian frontier. The War of 1812 stopped the normal course of the fur trade and by 1817 Astor was able to buy out his partners in the South West Company at a very low price. Thereupon the Northern Department of the American Fur Company was established, with headquarters at Mackinac[qv].

The next aim of the Company was to secure the St. Louis and Missouri River trade. In 1817 it made a tentative arrangement with powerful St. Louis firms, but it was not until 1822 that the Company established its own branch in St. Louis. This became known as the Western Department of the American Fur Company.

Still another obstacle to be overcome in securing monopoly of the fur trade of the United States was the abolition of the system of United States trading factories, which had been in existence since 1796 and which were a step in the direction of a safe, enlightened and humane Indian policy[qv]. However, they could compete successfully with Astor for the trade and so he determined to get rid of them. With the aid of such interested men as Lewis Cass and Thomas Hart Benton, he campaigned successfully. In 1822 the system was abolished (*see* Factory System, The Indian).

Private traders and other companies were treated in the same high-handed manner. Competition was stifled by fair means or foul. An act excluding foreigners from the trade was passed by Congress in 1816, probably at the instigation of the American Fur Company. In 1824 Congress passed another act, designating certain places at which trade might be carried on, which greatly hampered the Company's competitors while favoring the Company men.

In 1827 the greatest rival of the Company united with it—the Columbia Fur Company[qv]—which operated between the upper Mississippi and the upper Missouri, and known henceforth as the Upper Missouri Outfit of the American Fur Company.

By 1828 the Company had a virtual monopoly of the fur trade of the United States. In 1834, however, it became politic for the Company to withdraw from the Rocky Mountain area. In that year, too, Astor withdrew from the Company, whose charter had lapsed in April, 1833, though no notice had been taken of that fact. During the last decade of its existence, the Company made profits and declared dividends of over $1,000,000. After 1817 the Company had consisted (till 1823) of Astor, Ramsay Crooks, and Robert Stuart. After 1823 and until 1827 the only new partners were the St. Louis firms. In 1827 the Columbia Fur Company's men were added. In 1834 Astor sold out his interests: those in the Western Department to Pratte, Chouteau[qv] and Company; and those in the Northern Department to a group headed by Ramsay Crooks. This second group, of some ten stockholders, now became the American Fur Company. It lasted till 1842. During these eight years Ramsay Crooks was president of the Company. Its operations were confined roughly to the area between Detroit, the Ohio and the Red River of the North. It built vessels on the upper Great Lakes, established extensive fisheries on Lake Superior, marketed the furs of the St. Louis firm of Pratte, Chouteau and Company (after 1838 Pierre Chouteau, Jr., and Company), tried desperately to oust such important rivals as W. G. and G. W. Ewing of Fort Wayne and maintained something of a banking business throughout the area of its operations. After its failure in 1842 it seems to have been reconstituted once more in 1846 as a commission house. Its papers end for all practical purposes in 1847.

[Kenneth W. Porter, *John Jacob Astor, Business Man;* Grace Lee Nute, Papers of the American Fur Company, in *American Historical Review*, April, 1927.]

GRACE LEE NUTE

American Historical Association, The, was formed at Saratoga, N. Y., on Sept. 9, 1884, and incorporated by act of Congress on Jan. 4, 1889, with headquarters in Washington. From the first it exerted a constructive influence in the organization of research, classification of official archives and in promoting the study of neglected fields. Its activities have been carried on chiefly through the *American Historical Review* (founded in 1895, taken over in 1898) and through standing committees, like the Historical Manuscripts Commission (1895) and the Public Archives Commission (1899). Significant reports have been issued by special committees, notably the Committees of Seven and of Eight on history in the secondary and elementary schools (published, 1899, 1909), the Commission on the Social Studies (in fifteen parts, 1932–37) and the Committee on Bibliography (*A Guide to Historical Literature,* 1931). Important publications have also been made through the Littleton-Griswold, the Beveridge and the Revolving funds. In 1903 a Pacific Coast Branch was founded, which since 1932 has issued the *Pacific Historical Review.*

[*Papers of the American Historical Association,* 1885-91; *Annual Reports,* Government Printing Office, 1890; J. F. Jameson, The American Historical Association, 1884-1909, *American Historical Review,* XV, 1-20.]

HENRY E. BOURNE

American Iron and Steel Institute, with its predecessor organizations, is one of the oldest trade associations in the United States, dating back to 1855. It assumed its present form in 1908, with Judge Elbert H. Gary, chairman of the United States Steel Corporation*qv*, as its first president. Its development was in response to the need for a co-operative agency in the iron and steel industry*qv* for collecting and disseminating statistics and information, carrying on investigations, providing a forum for the discussion of problems and generally advancing the interests of the industry.

[Joseph H. Foth, *Trade Associations.*]

JOHN W. HILL

American Joint Commission to France. *See* France, American Joint Commission to.

American Labor Party, THE, arose during April, 1936, as a New York State unit of Labor's Non-Partisan League sponsored by John L. Lewis of the Committee for Industrial Organization*qv*, Maj. G. L. Berry of the Pressmen's Union and Sidney Hillman of the Amalgamated Clothing Workers. The Party acting independently aided the re-election of President F. D. Roosevelt and Gov. Lehman of New York in 1936, and contributed to Mayor LaGuardia's re-election in November, 1937. Primarily a pressure group*qv*, the American Labor Party has preferred to support those behind a program of social legislation rather than to enter independent candidates.

[P. W. Ward, The Coming Labor Party, *The Nation,* April 15, 1936.]

HARVEY WISH

American Legion, THE, is an organization of veterans of the World War. Any person who served in active duty in the army, navy, marine corps or coast guard*qqv* of the United States forces between April 6, 1917, and Nov. 11, 1918, and who received an honorable discharge, is eligible to membership. Also, the mothers, wives, daughters and sisters of Legion members are eligible to auxiliary membership. Col. Theodore Roosevelt, Jr., is given credit for first suggesting such an organization. On Feb. 16, 1919, some twenty men of the American Expeditionary Forces*qv* met in Paris, and had dinner together. "At that dinner the American Legion was born." Two subsequent organization meetings followed; one held in Paris, March 15–17, 1919; and the second in St. Louis, Mo., May 8–10, 1919. The Paris Caucus was attended by 1000 representative officers and enlisted men of the A. E. F. Col. Bennett C. Clark presided at this meeting, and an executive committee was appointed to confer with a similar executive committee in the United States to plan for the St. Louis Caucus. At the St. Louis meeting, May 8–10, 1919, final steps were taken to incorporate the American Legion. It was chartered by act of Congress, Sept. 16, 1919.

Early in its history, the American Legion announced the primary objectives for which it would strive. It declared itself a patriotic organization of the first order, and dedicated its efforts to "God and Country." Relief for the wounded and disabled veterans*qv* was placed first in its program. In 1922, it succeeded in having the United States Veterans Bureau*qv* established. Also, it secured the organization of a National Rehabilitation Service, to see that every veteran received proper hospital care and treatment, and adequate compensation. The Legion soon made itself felt as a pressure group*qv* in national politics. As early as 1920 the National Legislative Committee reported that it had secured the passage of bills embodying a fourfold bonus*qv* plan; a bill that raised the monthly allowance of disabled men; and an amendment to the Civil Service Law*qv*, giving preference to honorably discharged soldiers, sailors and marines, seeking Federal positions.

In 1922 the American Legion inaugurated a child welfare*qv* program, and in 1925 it turned its attention to the aid and care of orphans of veterans. Another activity sponsored by the Legion was that of community service. By 1926 this veterans' organization had some 10,000 local posts scattered throughout the country, and each post was called upon to assist in programs looking toward civic improvements. A list of the projects included the creation of parks and playgrounds, the building of hospitals, the enlargement of public welfare work, safety-first campaigns, the organization of Junior Baseball Leagues and similar undertakings. In 1928, the Legion undertook another form of activity, known as that of giving emergency relief. Chief aid was given to the flood sufferers of the Mississippi Valley following the devastating floods of 1927 and 1928 (*see* Floods). This same service was repeated during the later floods of 1936 and 1937. As the Legion grew older and increased in membership (it had 1,053,909 paid up members in 1931), it expanded its program of activities. It became especially active in a nation-wide child welfare campaign in 1929–30. It threw its influence behind the child labor[qv] amendment then pending in forty-four states, and urged the passage of a bill providing for universal service of all able-bodied citizens, and for the conscription of wealth in time of war.

Early in the depression years of the 1930's the Legion adopted a program calling for the immediate payment of the Adjusted Service Certificates at face value (*see* Bonus). In 1934 a large home in Washington, D. C., was purchased (the National Headquarters of the American Legion are in Indianapolis, Ind.), to house the rehabilitation and legislative activities of the Legion. The campaign for the immediate payment of the bonus was vigorously pushed throughout the sessions of the 74th Congress. The Vinson Bill, as the act came to be known, finally passed both House and Senate in January, 1936, only to be vetoed by President Roosevelt. The veto was, however, promptly overridden, the vote in the House being 346 to 59, and in the Senate 76 to 16–"Thus ending in victory the years of efforts on the part of the Legion to obtain immediate payment of the certificates as an act of justice to World War veterans." Following this victory, and with the approach of the twentieth anniversary of its organization, the Legion announced that it was dedicating itself anew to a nationwide program of public service. The aims listed include, Americanism, peace, national defense, neutrality, universal service, youth training, child welfare, community service, care of the disabled, protection of war widows and orphans, highway safety and the preservation of law and order.

[G. S. Wheat, *Story of the American Legion;* Marquis James, *History of the American Legion;* Marcus Duffield, *King Legion;* Knowlton Durham, *Billions for Veterans;* and *Reports of the Annual National Conventions of the American Legion.*]

JOHN W. OLIVER

American Liberty League, THE, was organized in August, 1934, with the express purpose of fighting radicalism[qv] and defending property rights and the United States Constitution. Among its organizers were many lifelong, though conservative Democrats, but it was clearly inimical to the "New Deal"[qv] and, because of this and its many wealthy members, was denounced by the F. D. Roosevelt administration as reactionary.

[Fifty-Eight Lawyers, *United States Law Review*, Vol. 69, pp. 505, 613; Vol. 70, p. 22.]

ALVIN F. HARLOW

American Management Association. A professional association for business executives. Organized in 1913 in personnel field. Took present name in 1923 and broadened scope. Personnel, Insurance, Financial, Marketing, Office, Production and General Management divisions hold annual conferences and publish papers. *Management Review, Personnel* and *Business Conditions and Forecasts* are published. The Association makes no profit, does no lobbying and advances no propaganda. Its interests are practical solution of management problems and development of the science of management.

[*The American Management Association and its Predecessors,* Special paper No. 17.]

ALVIN E. DODD

American-Mexican Mixed Claims Commissions, THE. Behind United States-Mexican relations lies the constant question of unsettled damage claims. The first joint commission (1839–42) settled American claims with awards totaling $2,026,139.68. Payments were interrupted by revolution, and Mexico failed to ratify another claims convention (1843). The question thus became a factor in the Mexican War[qv]. By the Treaty of Guadalupe Hidalgo[qv] the United States paid, through a special (American) commission, claims against Mexico for $3,250,000, including the fraudulent Gardiner award[qv]. A second joint commission (1869–76) settled 2025 claims arising 1848–68 with awards to Mexico of $150,498.41 (167 cases) and to United States $4,125,622.20 (186 cases), including interest on the Pious Fund[qv].

The Bucareli Conference (Mexico City, 1923), which arranged for recognition of the Obregon government, brought two joint commissions. A general claims commission (1923–31) awarded $2,599,166.10, plus interest, to the United States, and $39,000 to Mexico, and disposed of 148 out of 2781 claims arising since 1868. Agrarian claims were excluded when the commission was renewed (1932). By executive agreement (1934) the commission reported its findings to both governments (1937) for agreement by direct negotiations. The special (Revolutionary, 1910–20) claims commission met twice (1926 and 1931), hearing and dismissing two claims. Mexico refused (1932) to renew the commission, but settled the claims (1935) for $5,448,020.14. A special (American) commission was then established (1935) to settle with claimants by 1938.

[F. S. Dunn, *Diplomatic Protection of Americans in Mexico;* A. H. Feller, *Mexican Claims Commissions, 1923-34.*] HAROLD E. DAVIS

American (or Know-Nothing) Party, THE, enjoyed a meteoric career during the 1850's. It was founded in New York in 1849 as a secret patriotic society known as the Order of the Star Spangled Banner, but experienced little success until after 1852. Expansion from that time on was so rapid that by 1854 a national organization could be perfected.

This phenomenal growth was due partly to the charm of secrecy with which the party clothed itself. Members were initiated and sworn not to reveal its mysteries; their universal answer to questions was "I know nothing about it," thus giving their organization its popular name: the Know-Nothing Party. All who joined were pledged to vote only for natives, to work for a twenty-one-year probationary period preceding naturalization, and to combat the Catholic Church.

More important in accounting for the party's success was the period in which it thrived. Older party lines had been disrupted by the Kansas-Nebraska Act[qv] and many voters, unwilling to cast their lot either with proslavery Democrats or antislavery Republicans, found refuge with the Know-Nothings. At this time, too, anti-Catholic sentiment, long fostered by churches, societies and the press, was reaching its height. The American Party attracted thousands of persons who sincerely believed that Catholicism and immigration menaced their land.

These factors account for the startling strength shown by the party. In the elections of 1854 and 1855 it was successful in a number of New England and border states and its supporters fully expected to carry the country in 1856.

By this time, however, the slavery issue had caused a split in Know-Nothing ranks. A proslavery resolution, pushed through the 1855 convention by Southern delegates, caused a lasting breach and the American Party entered the election of 1856[qv] so hopelessly divided that its presidential candidate, Millard Fillmore, carried only the State of Maryland. This crushing defeat and the growing sectional antagonism over slavery brought about the party's rapid end.

[L. D. Scisco, *Political Nativism in New York State;* L. F. Schmeckebier, *History of the Know-Nothing Party in Maryland;* M. E. Thomas, *Nativism in the Old Northwest, 1850-1860;* Ray Allen Billington, *The Protestant Crusade.*] RAY ALLEN BILLINGTON

American Peace Society, THE (Washington, D. C.), was founded upon the initiative of William Ladd, in New York City, May 8, 1828. It was formed by the merging of many state and local societies, of which the oldest dated from 1815. Ladd was an advocate of a "Congress and High Court of Nations." Since 1828 the Society has regularly published a periodical, now called *World Affairs.* A. CURTIS WILGUS

American Philosophical Society, THE, was founded by Benjamin Franklin in 1743 "for the promotion of useful knowledge among the British plantations in America." It is the oldest learned society[qv] in America and from its foundation to the present time has included in its membership the leading scientists, scholars, statesmen and public servants of this country and some of the most illustrious of foreign lands. Membership is limited to 500.

Its publications are the *Proceedings,* the *Transactions,* the *Memoirs* and the annual *Year Book.* The Library includes more than 80,000 volumes, 50,000 pamphlets and 5500 maps in addition to a rich collection of MSS. including the largest existing collection of Frankliniana. During the years 1934–38 the Society distributed nearly 300 grants in aid[qv] of research of an aggregate sum of about $347,000. The total endowment is approximately $5,000,000. EDWIN GRANT CONKLIN

American Protective Association, THE, a secret anti-Catholic society, was founded at Clinton, Iowa, in 1887 by Henry F. Bowers. It grew slowly in the Middle West until the Panic of 1893[qv] brought home to natives the economic rivalry of second generation immigrants and this, combined with rural antagonism toward urban Catholics, the effective propaganda of nativistic[qv] newspapers and speakers, revived Catholic demands for a share in public school funds, and political instability following the Democratic victory in 1892 attracted a million members by 1896. This voting strength was utilized to gain control of local Republican organizations and carry elections throughout the Middle West but in 1896 the Association split over the question of supporting William McKinley, and its members deserted rapidly amidst the greater excitement of the free silver[qv] campaign. It lingered on despite steadily declining support until 1911.

[H. J. Desmond, *The A.P.A. Movement. A Sketch.*]

RAY ALLEN BILLINGTON

American Railway Association, THE, had its inception in meetings of General Managers and ranking railway operating officials known as Time Table Conventions, the first of which was held on Oct. 1, 1872, at Louisville, Ky. In 1875 the group changed its name to General Time Convention and in October, 1891, to American Railway Association. In January, 1919, ten separate groups of operating officers were amalgamated with the association and carried on their activities as divisions, sections or committees of the larger group.

[American Railway Association, Historical Statement; Present Activities, Aug. 15, 1921.]

HARVEY WALKER

American Railway Union, THE, was started by Eugene V. Debs[qv] in June, 1893, in an attempt to unite all railroad workers. In June, 1894, it ordered its members not to handle Pullman cars in sympathy with the Pullman shop strikers[qv]. Violence resulting, President Cleveland sent troops to stop interference with the mails. The union officers were jailed for violating an injunction secured by the railroads under the Sherman Act[qv]. The strike was lost, and the union collapsed.

[McAlister Coleman, *Eugene V. Debs.*]

JAMES D. MAGEE

American Republican Party, THE, a minor nativistic[qv] political organization, was launched in New York in June, 1843, largely as a protest against immigrant voters and officeholders. In 1844 it carried municipal elections in New York City and Philadelphia and expanded so rapidly that by July, 1845, a national convention was called. This convention changed the name to the Native American Party and drafted a legislative program calling for a twenty-one-year period preceding naturalization[qv] and other sweeping reforms in the naturalization machinery. Failure to force congressional action on these proposals, combined with the growing national interest in the Mexican problem, led to the party's rapid decline.

[L. D. Scisco, *Political Nativism in New York State;* Ray Allen Billington, *The Protestant Crusade.*]

RAY ALLEN BILLINGTON

American Republics, Bureau of. *See* Pan-American Union, The.

American Revolution. *See* Revolution, American.

American Sugar Refining Company, THE, has been since its incorporation in New Jersey, Jan. 10, 1891, the largest business unit in the sugar refining industry. Like its predecessor, the Sugar Refineries Company (1887), it consolidated most of the existing plants with a view to cost reduction and price control and for many years carried the popular sobriquet, "The Sugar Trust"[qv]. The Supreme Court declared in the much-cited Knight case[qv], March 24, 1894, that its purchase of the stock of competitors was not a combination in restraint of trade[qv]. The combination expanded horizontally for about twenty years as new competitors arose; later it expanded vertically, undertaking the production of cane and raw sugar in Cuba and acquiring lumber interests. The company was investigated by the Industrial Commission in 1900 and by a special congressional committee in 1911–12. Federal suit for its dissolution begun in 1910 was terminated by consent decree announced Dec. 21, 1921, when it was stated that its effective control of refined sugar had dropped from 72% to 24%.

[Jenks and Lauck, *The Trust Problem.*]

LELAND H. JENKS

American System, a term applied by Henry Clay, in his tariff speech of March 30–31, 1824, by which he sought to justify the greater measure of protection that he was trying to secure in the tariff bill under discussion. His object was to create a home market and "to lay the foundations of a genuine American policy"; he wished to check the decline of American industry and offered a remedy which, he said, "consists in modifying our foreign policy, and in adopting a genuine American system." By this he proposed to eliminate the dependence upon the foreign market with the result that American industries would flourish and a home market for the surplus of agricultural products would develop. Such a program was presumed to offer attractions not only to the eastern manufacturer but also to the western farmer. Implicit in the arrangement was the availability of more revenue for internal improvements[qv], upon which Clay had already taken a leading position.

Since Clay became known as "the father of the American system," the practice soon developed of applying this label to collateral measures for which he stood. With his tariff[qv] and internal improvement policies was combined his proposal to have the national government distribute among the states the proceeds of the sale of public lands[qv]. Clay's contemporary biographer, Calvin Colton, declared (I, 428) : "There are collateral measures, and measures of affinity, having more or less of an intimate connection. There are numerous measures of result emanating from this system. But internal improvement, and protection of American interests, labor, industry and arts, are commonly understood to be the LEADING measures, which constitute the AMERICAN SYSTEM."

[C. Colton, *The Life and Times of Henry Clay;* T. H. Clay, *Henry Clay.*]

ARTHUR C. COLE

American Telephone and Telegraph Company. Thomas Sanders of Haverhill, Mass., and Gardiner G. Hubbard of Cambridge each supplied one half the funds necessary to finance Alexander Graham Bell in the experiments which led to his obtaining patents on the telephone[qv] (1875–76) , with the understanding that the three owned the patents jointly. After the telephone became a workable instrument, the three patentees organized on July 9, 1877, a joint stock concern known as the Bell Telephone Company, with Hubbard as trustee, to whom all patent rights were assigned. Thomas A. Watson, who had been Bell's faithful assistant all through the experiments, was given a tenth interest. On Feb. 12, 1878, the New England Telephone Company was organized to control the business in that territory. The need for more capital and a better organization to cover the country led to the organization of a new Bell Telephone Company minus Hubbard's trusteeship and with a capital of $450,000 in the summer of 1878. Technical improvements devised by others were bought and incorporated with the Bell instrument. A group of new stockholders headed by William H. Forbes now came into virtual control of the company's policy and these desired unity of all telephone interests. Accordingly on Feb. 17, 1879, the National Bell Telephone Company, capitalized at $850,000, was organized and took over the existing Bell and New England companies.

A period of litigation over telephone patents followed, the Bell's chief opponent being the Western Union Telegraph Company[qv], which had bought Edison's and other patent rights. The Western Union capitulated to the Bell company on Nov. 10, 1879. A new and enormously larger corporation to control the nation-wide business through the ownership of many small companies was now desired. On March 20, 1880, the American Bell Telephone Company was organized, with a capital of $7,350,000. As the telephone became more efficient, the American Telephone and Telegraph Company was organized Feb. 28, 1885, with a capital of $100,000, to build and operate long-distance lines. For fifteen years the latter was a subsidiary company, but in 1900 the American Bell passed out of existence, and the American Telephone and Telegraph became a great holding company for city and regional organizations, as well as the owner of long lines. In 1909 this company took over the Western Union Telegraph Company, but the Government, under the Sherman Anti-Trust Act[qv], forced the separation of the two companies in 1913.

[Alvin F. Harlow, *Old Wires and New Waves.*]

ALVIN F. HARLOW

American Tobacco Case, THE. In this decision, 1911 (221 U. S. 106) , the Supreme Court, following the same line of reasoning as in the Standard Oil[qv] decision of the same year, found that the American Tobacco Company had attempted to restrain commerce and monopolize the tobacco business in violation of the Sherman Anti-Trust Act[qv]. "Restraint of trade"[qv], the Court declared, did not embrace "all those normal and usual contracts essential to individual freedom, and the right to make which was necessary in order that the course of trade might be free," but on the other hand, in view of "the general language of the statute, and the public policy which it manifested, there was no possibility of frustrating that policy by resorting to any disguise or subterfuge of form, since resort to reason rendered it impossible to escape by any indirection the prohibitions of the statute."

[E. D. Durand, *The Trust Problem;* J. A. McLaughlin, *Cases on the Federal Anti-Trust Laws of the United States;* W. W. Willoughby, *The Constitutional Law of the United States.*]

W. A. ROBINSON

American Tract Society, THE, organized in New York City (1825) for the dissemination of Christian literature in leaflet form, co-ordinated the activities of numerous local societies. It is interdenominational and is governed by an executive committee. It soon took rank with the American Bible Society[qv]. During its history a total publication of 834,873,708 copies of Christian literature has been produced and distributed. Colporteurs have visited two and one-half million families. Five hundred tracts in thirty languages have recently been put in circulation.

[*Methodist Year Book*, 1934.]

C. H. STACKPOLE

Americanism. By an Apostolic Letter, entitled *Testem benevolentiæ* (from the first two words of the text), addressed by Leo XIII to the American hierarchy on Jan. 22, 1899, the pontiff, while expressing praise for the progress Catholicism had made in the United States, took occasion to point out some dogmatic and moral tendencies which he signaled out for correction. The three main points of discussion were: the adaptation of Christian teaching to our advancing civilization, freedom of spirit in matters of faith and of Christian life, and the division of virtues into active and passive. Principal among these was the alleged effort on the part of some American ecclesiastics to have the Church adapt her teaching to contemporary religious thought. Hence the name as used in the Brief. The term "Americanism" is vague, although it was defined at the time as "a spirit that is democratic, tolerant, anti-mediæval, up-to-date, individualistic, believing chiefly in good works, and lastly, very ultramontane" (Adrian Fortescue, *Folia Fugitiva,* N. Y., 1907, 276). The Latin and English Text of the Brief will be found in the *American Catholic Quarterly Review,* XXIV (April, 1899), 184–201.

[Peter Guilday, The Church in the United States: 1870–1920, *Catholic Historical Review*, January, 1921.]

PETER GUILDAY

Americanization began on the first frontier. Traders and settlers, from the beginning, adapted their food, clothing, shelter, religion, warfare, education, agriculture, transportation and trade to the environment and to Indian modes. The process became more marked along the mid-18th century frontier where Scotch-Irish and Germans met pioneers from the eastern settlements and rubbed elbows with the Indians and with the Indian traders, producing a new American society in flux, characterized by religious emotionalism and by an optimistic democracy. The war spirit of the American Revolution and of the War of 1812 molded the diverse elements into a vigorous nationality.

Jacksonian Democracy[qv] after 1825 furnished a new instrument of Americanization in such local party organizations as Tammany Hall[qv]. The common school revival in the 1830's and the rapid spread of academies[qv] which followed caught up and Americanized the foreign-born in the movement for general education. From the earliest times foreign-born Americans like Albert Gallatin had pointed the way to Americanization, but beginning with the years immediately preceding the Civil War, the German foreign language press, led by such men as Francis Lieber, assumed an increasingly important but contradictory role of keeping alive German consciousness and directing it toward Americanization. Nativism[qv] in the 1850's emphasized the problem of Americanization but contributed nothing to its solution.

Civil War army service Americanized the German and Irish immigrants of the 1850's, and post-war expansion also assisted, especially by employment in railroad construction and in the growing industries. But increasing immigration[qv] and the change in the sources of the immigration after 1890 presented new problems of assimilation[qv]. Homesteaders living under frontier conditions were easily Americanized by the common schools, Protestant churches, the labor and dangers of pioneer life and democratic political organizations, but it was more difficult with the new immigrants herded into rapidly growing city slums or into mining and manufacturing towns. Since much of the new immigration was Roman or Orthodox Catholic or Jewish, Protestant churches came to play a less important part in its Americanization. During the 1880's settlement houses[qv] began to Americanize the community life of the slums with a program of neighborliness. Mutual benefit societies and national cultural organizations became common. But no consciously organized program of Americanization appeared, until attention was directed to the seriousness of the situation by the Immigration Commission (1911).

The World War found 15,000,000 European-born immigrants in the United States, including 3,000,000 adults who could not speak English, and 9,000,000 who read foreign newspapers exclusively. New York City alone had half a million non-English speaking inhabitants. The drive for Americanization started in Cleveland July 4, 1914, with the organization of the first Americanization day. By 1915 at least 150 cities observed such a day and in the same year a national Americanization Committee was organized. In April, 1918, a conference on Americanization was called by the Secretary of the Interior. Soon state and city committees were established, and Americanization schools appeared throughout the country. Trade unions[qv], instead of assisting in the process, discouraged Americanization by discriminating against foreign-born membership. Americanization seemed also to weaken family life by encouraging a second generation revolt against family and church and their Old World moral codes.

Two other aspects of Americanization may be noticed briefly: that of the Indians, accomplished through trade, missions, treaties, reservations, schools, finally culminating in the Dawes Act of 1887[qv], and the less conscious Americanization of the Negro through missions, schools, slavery and post-slavery economic exploitation.

[Emory Bogardus, *Essentials of Americanization;* J. W. Jenks and W. J. Lauck, *Immigration Problem;* R. E. Park and H. A. Miller, *Old World Traits Transplanted.*]

HAROLD E. DAVIS

American's Creed, The. In a nation-wide contest (1917) for "the best summary of American political faith," this 100-word composite of fundamental expressions by the builders of the republic was compiled by William Tyler Page, who received the award of $1000, which was offered by the city of Baltimore as "the home of the Star-Spangled Banner[qv]."

[*The Book of the American's Creed.*]

MATTHEW PAGE ANDREWS

America's Cup Races, The. *See* Yacht Racing.

Amiens, The Treaty of, signed March 27, 1802 (after agreement in October, 1801, on preliminary articles) between France and Great Britain, ended the war declared by France on Feb. 1, 1793, and terminated the first phase of the wars of the French Revolution. Its significance for American history is that it afforded a short breathing spell in the controversy with the belligerents over neutral rights, and offered an interval of peace during which Napoleon turned to the newly acquired province of Louisiana as a field for the building of a great colonial empire. On the eve of war again with Great Britain in 1803, he sold Louisiana[qv] to the United States to cash in on the territory before it should be captured by superior British sea power.

[Henry Adams, *History of the United States during the First Administration of Thomas Jefferson,* Vols. I, II.]

SAMUEL FLAGG BEMIS

Amish Mennonites, The, are followers of Jacob Amman. They separated from the Mennonites[qv] in Europe in the late 17th century because of a strict interpretation of the practice of "avoidance" and "shunning," i.e., ostracizing, socially and religiously, violators of church rule.

Ultraconservatism is the chief characteristic of their cult. They use hooks and eyes instead of buttons, wear beards but ban the mustache, the badge of the soldier.

They first appeared in Pennsylvania about 1714, and now (1939) have settlements in Pennsylvania, Iowa, Maryland, Indiana, Illinois, Ohio, Delaware, Kansas, Michigan, Missouri, Montana, Nebraska, Oklahoma, Oregon and Virginia.

[C. H. Smith, *The Mennonite Immigration to Pennsylvania.*]

H. H. SHENK

***Amistad* Case** (1839). The fifty-four slaves on this Spanish schooner mutinied near Cuba, murdered part of the crew, and caused the remainder to sail into Long Island Sound and the jurisdiction of American courts. Piracy charges were quashed but some salvage claims awarded by legal proceedings in Connecticut. In 1841 the Supreme Court declared the Negroes free. Private charity provided their transportation back to Africa. This case offers an interesting comparison with the *Creole* affair[qv].

[J. W. Barber, *A History of the Amistad Captives.*]

JARVIS M. MORSE

Amite, Battle of, was a skirmish fought on the Amite River in Mississippi Territory, August, 1808, between a party of nineteen frontier settlers and a marauding band of thirty Choctaw Indians[qv] who were committing depredations in that vicinity. Regular troops and militia were called out, but the Indians disappeared.

[Dunbar Rowland, ed., *Mississippi* (Cyclopedic), I.]

WALTER PRICHARD

Amnesty (1862–98). Proclamations issued by President Lincoln, primarily as war measures, and by President Johnson as aids to Reconstruction[qv], extended pardon and re-enfranchisement, with certain exceptions and restrictions, to those then in or who had been in rebellion against the United States Government (*see* Civil War). The constitutional meaning of amnesty was not clearly understood, but it was thought to be a sort of general or group pardon. Although the word does not appear in the Constitution, Congress, in the Confiscation Act[qv], July 17, 1862, granted to the President the right of "amnesty." Lincoln made no use of this privilege until after the Union victory at Chattanooga[qv], when, Dec. 8, 1863, he issued his first amnesty proclamation, supplementing it, March 26, 1864, with another restricting the scope of the first. On May 29, 1865, Johnson proclaimed amnesty and pardon to a degree sufficient to provide an adequate number of "rebels" to man the restored state governments. As Johnson's contest with the Radical Republicans[qv] became more bitter, Congress determined to reconstruct the South in its own way. On Jan. 7, 1867, it angrily repealed the amnesty grant authorized in the Confiscation Act, and then, in the third reconstruction act, July 19, 1867, repeated its stand that a presidential pardon did not re-enfranchise. Johnson, denying the right thus to abrogate his presidential power of pardon[qv], issued three more amnesty proclamations—Sept. 7, 1867, July 4, 1868, and Dec. 25, 1868—the last granting general amnesty without the formality of oath. These, however, were mere gestures so far as the franchise was concerned because Congress, in the Fourteenth Amendment[qv], adopted July 28, 1868, had finally secured control of the authority to grant amnesty, at least to the extent of restoring the right to hold office. Henceforth amnesty would be extended by legislative statute rather than by executive proclamation.

Under the Fourteenth Amendment over 150,000 persons were barred from holding office unless Congress, by a two-thirds vote, should remove their disabilities. During the next few years much time was spent in enacting individual amnesty acts, mostly applying to those ex-Confederates who were willing to join the radical party. In order to satisfy public demand and to aid in Grant's re-election (*see* Campaign of 1872), Congress, on May 22, 1872, passed a general amnesty act, which re-enfranchised all except between 500 and 750 who had been high officials in the Confederate Government. Thereafter, individual disability bills dribbled through each congressional session, the last being passed Feb. 24, 1897. By an act of June 6, 1898, final amnesty was granted, by removing the disabilities from those still barred by the provisions of Section 3 of the Fourteenth Amendment.

[J. T. Dorris, *Pardon and Amnesty During the Civil War and Reconstruction;* J. G. Randall, *Constitutional Problems Under Lincoln;* William A. Russ, Jr., *Congressional Disfranchisement,* an unpublished doctoral dissertation deposited at the Library of the University of Chicago.]

WILLIAM A. RUSS, JR.

Amnesty (1919 f.). Soon after the close of the World War the Federal authorities began liberating and amnesting the many conscientious objectors[qv] to military service and other violators (including deserters) of war-time legislation. From Fort Leavenworth[qv], where more than 2000 were confined, the Secretary of War discharged 113 in January, 1919. Other liberations followed and by 1922 the work was practically done. Sometimes prisoners' disabilities were removed by order of the President, as in the case of Harold S. Gray, whom President Wilson ordered "dishonorably" discharged from Alcatraz on Aug. 23, 1919. As late as March 5, 1924, President Coolidge granted "amnesty and pardon to all persons" under conviction, or who might thereafter be convicted, of desertion.

[Mrs. Lucy Robbins, *War Shadows: A Documentary Story of the Struggle for Amnesty;* Norman Thomas, *The Conscientious Objector in America; U. S. Statutes at Large,* Vol. 40, pt. 2.]

JONATHAN T. DORRIS

Amundsen Polar Expeditions. Roald Engelbregt Gravning Amundsen gained his first experience as an explorer in the Belgian Antarctic Expedition, 1897–99. He led the first expedition to sail through the Northwest Passage[qv] from the Atlantic to the Pacific, a feat he accomplished in the sloop *Gjöa,* 1903–6. He discovered the South Pole in December, 1911, beating Capt. Scott to the goal by a month. He sailed through the Northeast Passage from Norway to Alaska in the *Maud,* 1918–20, on an unsuccessful attempt to drift across the Pole from the New Siberian Islands. In an effort to attain the North Pole with Lincoln Ellsworth by airplane from Spitsbergen in 1925 he reached latitude 88°. With Ellsworth and Col. Nobile he navigated the airship *Norge,* from Spitsbergen to Alaska in 1926. He was lost in 1928 while flying across the Arctic wastes in search of the missing *Italia's* crew.

[Amundsen, *The North West Passage; The South Pole; Nordöst Passagen; My Life as an Explorer;* Amundsen and Ellsworth, *Our Polar Flight; First Crossing of the Polar Sea.*]

N. M. CROUSE

Amusements. In the early colonial period, the recreational opportunities available were naturally limited. The harsh conditions of pioneer life demanded of all classes a concentration on work which left little leisure for amusements, and under the stress of economic circumstance any "mispense of time" was rigorously prohibited in both Jamestown and Plymouth[qqv]. As conditions improved, a gradual change was effected but in New England normal recreational developments were further impeded by the religious prejudice of Puritanism[qv]. Colonial leaders in both Massachusetts and Connecticut vigorously attempted to suppress almost all kinds of amusements, with bans not only on the theater[qv], card playing, horse racing[qv], but also on tavern sports and dancing. No conflict between pleasure and conscience inhibited the fox-hunting, horse-racing, cockfighting[qv] planters of Virginia and South Carolina. They enjoyed such opportunities for diversion as came their way without thought as to whether they might be inspired by God or the Devil, but New Englanders tended to look with suspicion upon play in any guise whatsoever and indulged in recreation with sober restraint.

The spirit of Puritanism was, however, not proof against the growing demand for recreation, as economic security and leisure increased. Throughout the colonies a predominantly agricultural population found relief from the tedium of farm work in the festivities attendant upon training days and elections; at house raisings and husking bees[qv]; at country dances and at such tavern sports as bowling, shuffle board and quoits—activities which were always enlivened by a plentiful flow of spirituous liquors. Hunting and fishing were everywhere enjoyed; shooting matches had a great popularity and other rural pastimes found favor in New England as in the Middle and Southern Colonies. In the colonial cities and on southern plantations[qqv], the more wealthy enjoyed a social life in which elaborate dining and wining, card playing, concerts and frequent balls and assemblies were predominant features. The theater was restricted to New York, Philadelphia and the South, but otherwise New England had gone far toward discarding earlier restraints as the 18th century progressed and the colonial period drew to its close.

After the Revolution, and for the first quarter of the 19th century, there was no marked change in the recreational scene, but the gradual industrialization of the country and the growth of urban populations were soon to have far-reaching effects. Deprived of the simple pleasures of country life, the great mass of city dwellers became more and more dependent upon the commercial amusements which rapidly developed to meet this increasing need. The restraints of religious prejudice, inherent in what is called Puritanism, and the feeling, natural to a young and expanding country, that everything else should be subordinated to work, gave foreign visitors of the first half of the 19th century the impression that Americans took no time for play; but there was evidence to the contrary on every hand.

The theater[qv] became an important element in the amusement scene, not only in the larger cities but in smaller towns throughout the country. And it had a popular appeal, reflected in both admission charges and the type of entertainment it offered, which it had not had in colonial days. The second quarter of the century also witnessed the development of amusements even more frankly adapted to the popular taste: variety theaters, minstrel shows[qv], dancing halls and the beginnings of amusement parks. The peripatetic showmen and animal exhibitors of earlier days joined forces to produce the modern circus[qv], and traveling shows began to tour the country, bringing a new form of entertainment to rural as well as urban communities. For the wealthy, social life in the cities became more pretentious, summer resorts sprang up, but the really significant fact in the development of amusements in the first half of the 19th century was their increasing democratization. The new vogue for popular, commercialized entertainment was graphically symbolized in the career of P. T. Barnum[qv].

The rise of sports[qv] also began just before the Civil War, although it was in the 1870's and 1880's that they became really important. Informal sports had always been popular in rural communities but the cities called for organization, and the crowds which were attracted by the opportunity to get a vicarious satisfaction out of watching others play soon led to commercialization. Horse races on occasion drew as many as 50,000 spectators; boating and yachting races[qv] had an immense vogue, restricted as far as participation was concerned to the wealthy, but providing a spectacle for thousands; pedestrian races were popular, and while prize fighting[qv] had not yet escaped the odium which clung to it throughout the bare-knuckle days, it began to awaken intense popular interest. The 1850's saw the beginnings of baseball[qv], with amateur clubs springing up in New York and other cities, pointing the way to a development which was soon to make it the national game.

After the Civil War what we now term spectator sports made still greater advances, emphasized by the professionalization of baseball, but there was also far more widespread participation in sports. The successive introduction of new games provided healthy outdoor amusement for thousands. Archery, croquet, roller skating and then lawn tennis swept the country, for the first time bringing women into sports activity; football[qv] developed as a college sport with the adoption of national rules of play; and baseball was more widely played on sand lots and country fields. Bicycling[qv] became an outdoor activity for hundreds of thousands. The complaint that spectator sports were playing a far larger role in the life of the people than participant sports was widely heard before the close of the century, but great masses of people played themselves, favoring the games for which little or no equipment was necessary and organization not essential. Always there were hunting and fishing, skating and sleigh-riding in the winter, informal ball games, bowling, quoits, shooting matches, pitching horseshoes. . . .

At the same time, commercial amusements served to supplement to an increasing extent the informal activities of social life. Visits and entertaining, club life, reading, card playing, music, country excursions, picnics and the more elaborate functions of the socially elect constituted the non-athletic amusements of most of the people most of the time, as they always must, but city life was still responsible for needs of which commercial showmen took full advantage. There was further expansion of the theater in the last half of the 19th century, with stock companies and well-known players touring the country; concerts and opera, the establishment of vaudeville circuits, and bigger and better circuses. Dancing halls multiplied; amusement parks were established not only near the large cities but wherever trolley lines could bring together paying customers; there was a great increase in bowling alleys and billiard parlors. Amusement was becoming an important business.

For all this expansion, the beginning of the 20th century nevertheless brought about a further transformation in the general pattern of the country's recreational life more important than anything which had heretofore taken place. The machine which had made possible the new leisure of men and women of the working classes, and had thereby created the need for commercial amusements, was itself adapted to recreational activities. The automobile, the moving picture and the radio[qqv] were rapidly to become the principal sources of entertainment for the American people as a whole. Spectator sports drew ever greater crowds with baseball, prize fighting, college football, athletic meets and professional hockey gaining in popularity; participation in sports grew apace with the new popularity of tennis, golf and skiing; national parks[qv] and city playgrounds providing new facilities for outdoor recreation. But automobile pleasure riding, attendance at the movies and listening to the radio were to dominate the modern amusement scene. By the end of the third decade of the century, they accounted for by far the greater part of the national expenditure on amusements, a figure which has been estimated as high as $10,000,000,000 a year.

FOSTER RHEA DULLES

***Amy Warwick* Admiralty Case,** 1863 (2 Black 635). This was one of the Prize Cases[qv] in which the Supreme Court upheld the power of the President to recognize the existence of a civil war and thereupon to establish a blockade[qv], without awaiting congressional action.

[Charles Warren, *The Supreme Court in United States History.*]

CHARLES FAIRMAN

Anaconda Copper, one of the largest copper mining[qv] companies of the world, and the principal producer of the Butte district of Montana, was organized in 1881 as The Anaconda Silver Mining Company, Marcus Daly having persuaded James B. Haggin, Lloyd Tevis and George Hearst to purchase for $30,000 the small Anaconda silver mine, then only sixty feet deep. The ore contained just enough copper to facilitate the recovery of the silver for which it was being worked, but at greater depth it became evident that its principal content was copper. A copper smelter was erected in 1884 and 3000 tons of ore was being treated daily by 1889. Continuing to expand through the purchase of other mines it was reorganized as the Anaconda Mining Company in 1891, with a capital of $25,000,000. The Hearst interests were sold to the Exploration Company, London, and the company was reorganized in 1895 as the Anaconda Copper Mining Company, three quarters of the stock having been bought by the Amalgamated Copper Company. In 1910 its capitalization was increased to $150,000,000 to take over all the properties of the Amalgamated in the Butte district and some of the William A. Clark interests, the purchase being completed by 1915 and the Amalgamated dissolved. By 1937 it had an authorized capital of $600,000,000 and was operating in Chile, Peru and Poland as well as in the United States.

[H. J. Stevens, *The Copper Handbook.*]

T. T. READ

Anæsthesia. Though it had been known from ancient times that certain narcotic[qv] preparations would deaden pain and though Sir Humphrey Davy had suggested in 1800 that nitrous oxide (popularly called "laughing gas") might be used in surgery, no anæsthesia was ever administered in an operation until 1842. On March 30, 1842, Dr. Crawford W. Long used sulphuric ether on a patient in Jefferson, Ga., and removed without pain a tumor from the back of his neck. Though local prejudice was strong against this practice, Long later used ether in performing a number of other operations, but he published no statement of the fact. In December, 1844, Dr. Horace Wells, a dentist of Hartford, Conn., having likewise discovered that "laughing gas" was an anæsthesia, had it administered to himself and had a tooth extracted without pain. In 1846 Dr. W. T. G. Morton, a

Boston dentist and a former associate of Wells, using sulphuric ether, performed a like act. Soon thereafter he administered ether in an operation in the Massachusetts General Hospital. A long contest over the question of priority in the use of an anæsthesia has followed, complicated further by the claims of Charles T. Jackson, a Boston chemist.

[J. T. Flexner, *Doctors on Horseback;* Frances L. Taylor, *Crawford W. Long and the Discovery of Ether Anesthesis;* F. R. Packard, *History of Medicine in the United States.*]

E. MERTON COULTER

Anahuac, Attack on (June, 1832). Anahuac was a Mexican military post on the east shore of Galveston Bay. To effect the release of William B. Travis and other Americans held there, a group of American settlers in Texas attacked the place. The resulting negotiations led the Texans to declare for the Santa Anna party in Mexico. The incident was an important preliminary to the Texas Revolution[qv].

[E. C. Barker, *Mexico and Texas, 1821-1835.*]

E. C. BARKER

Ananias Club, The, was an expression employed by the press in 1906–7 to avoid the "short and ugly word" (liar) in connection with the "mutual accusations of inveracity" which arose between President Theodore Roosevelt and Sen. Tillman of South Carolina over the railway rate bill and later during the controversy between Roosevelt and the "nature fakers."

[Mark Sullivan, *Our Times,* Vol. III.]

ROSCOE R. HILL

Anarchists. The leading exponent of philosophical anarchism in the United States was Benjamin R. Tucker. In his magazine *Liberty,* published in Boston, he defined anarchism as the law of equal liberty, with self-interest the supreme law for man, abolition of the state to be achieved by education and passive resistance. His theories were set forth in *Instead of a Book* (1893). Another, an insurgent school, leaned to the Bakunin-Kropotkin theory that the state belongs to a low stage of evolution and must disappear since the trend of social progress is toward more and more liberty. It saw evolution and revolution as alternating processes, revolution and political assassination as an accelerated evolution and belonging to the unity of nature. While this school did not advocate deeds of violence it did not condemn, and sometimes condoned them. To it belonged John J. Most, who, after expulsion from Germany in 1878 and imprisonment in England for incendiary utterances in his periodical, *Freiheit,* made his home in New York. Until 1883, anarchists and socialists[qv] belonged to the same organizations, though theoretically they were diametrically opposed. In 1887, in Chicago, following the Haymarket riot[qv], four men who confessed themselves anarchists but denied bomb throwing were hanged. It was a young Russian immigrant, Emma Goldman, a gifted orator, who in 1889 became an active leader of the insurgent school. She championed an anarchist of the deed, Alexander Berkman, when, having attempted the life of Henry C. Frick, he was sentenced to twenty-two years' imprisonment. When President McKinley was shot, Sept. 6, 1901, by another anarchist of the deed, Leon Czolgosz, Emma Goldman became the object of suspicion when she published an essay explaining the deed in its social and psychological aspect. In 1906 she published an anarchist magazine, *Mother Earth,* which Berkman edited on his release.

In July, 1917, Berkman and Emma Goldman were sentenced to two years in the penitentiary, with $10,000 fine and deportation to Russia for their activities in the Anti-Conscription agitation. Since then the movement seems to have died.

[E. V. Zenkner, *Anarchism;* Dr. Paul Eltzbacher, *Anarchism.*]

CHARLES J. FINGER

Ancient, Fort, the name given a large prehistoric earthwork in Ohio. Earthern walls from six to twenty feet high enclose the top of an irregular plateau; area about 100 acres. Experts place it in the mound building[qv] period and consider it a ceremonial structure instead of a fortification.

[H. C. Shetrone, *The Mound Builders.*]

CLARK WISSLER

Andaste, The, so named by the Jesuit Fathers, were prominent in the 17th-century history of the Susquehanna basin which they entered earlier from the Ohio. Though of Iroquoian[qv] stock, enmity with Iroquois kinsmen aligned them with northern Hurons[qv]. Identified with Smith's *Sasquesahanoughs* (1608), Champlain's *Carantouannais* (1615), the *Minquas* of early Swedish fur trade (1637), the *Conestogas* whose fort formed the crux of Pennsylvania-Maryland boundary disputes[qv], in 1676 they precipitated Bacon's Rebellion[qv] and their own virtual extermination.

[J. S. Clark, *Aboriginal History of the Susquehanna.*]

ELSIE MURRAY

Anderson v. Dunn (6 Wheaton 204, 1821). The right of the House of Representatives to charge, hear and punish contempt[qv], and detain, arrest and imprison those so charged, was unanimously upheld on the analogy of the right of the judiciary to punish contempt—for the self-preservation of the institutions of the state.

PHILLIPS BRADLEY

Andersonville Prison (February, 1864–April, 1865) in Georgia was the largest and best-known of Confederate military prisons[qv]. Hastily established because the number of prisoners constituted a military danger and was a serious drain on the food supplies of Richmond, no adequate preparations were made for housing the captives. The proverty of the Confederacy, a defective transportation system and the concentration of all resources on the army, prevented the prison officials supplying barracks, cooked food, clothing or medical care to their charges. The prison consisted solely of a log stockade of sixteen and one-half acres (later enlarged to twenty-six acres) through which ran a stream of water. Rations to the prisoners generally consisted of corn meal and beans, and seldom included meat. Bad sanitary conditions, lack of cooking facilities, poor food, crowding and exposure soon produced respiratory diseases, diarrhœa and scurvy[qv]. The inadequate medical staff, without drugs, could not cope with the situation. During the summer the number of prisoners increased to 31,678. There are 12,912 graves in the National Cemetery at Andersonville. Estimates place the total number of deaths at even higher figures. In September, the approach of Sherman's army caused the removal of all well prisoners to Charleston, S. C. Only enlisted men were confined in Andersonville; commissioned officers were held at Macon, Ga.

To the prisoners and to their friends in the North it appeared that the Confederates were deliberately murdering the captives. As a result of this belief, Capt. Henry Wirz, commander of the interior of the prison, was tried in August, 1865, on charges of murder and conspiring with Jefferson Davis to murder. Although found guilty by a military commission, and hanged, Nov. 10, 1865, subsequent investigation has revealed much in Wirz's favor. For many years Andersonville prison was a vital element in the "bloody shirt"[qv] issue in politics.

[W. B. Hesseltine, *Civil War Prisons: A Study in War Psychology.*]

W. B. HESSELTINE

André Is Captured. Maj. John André, adjutant-general of the British Army in North America during the Revolution, was entrusted by Sir Henry Clinton with the correspondence between the British Headquarters and the American traitor, Brig.-Gen. Benedict Arnold[qv], in the years 1779–80. On Sept. 21, 1780, he met Arnold at Joshua Hett Smith's house, just south of West Point on the Hudson, to complete the arrangements for the betrayal of West Point[qv] to the British. He had arrived on the British vessel *Vulcan* which anchored opposite Haverstraw. While Arnold and André were in conference, American artillery fire compelled the *Vulcan* to fall down-stream. Having lost his means of transport, André was persuaded to change his costume for a disguise and carry the treasonable papers back overland by horseback. He crossed the Hudson, started down the east bank, and was captured (Sept. 23) by three American irregulars, John Paulding, Isaac van Wart and David Williams who searched him, discovered the papers and turned him over to the American army. André explained himself to Washington, and Sir Henry Clinton demanded his release on the ground that he had gone to consult with Arnold under a flag of truce, which was true. But, in fact, his conduct had made him a spy, as he said in his own words: "The events of coming within an Enemy's posts and of changing my dress which led me to my present Situation were contrary to my own Inclination as they were to your [Clinton's] orders. . . ." He was tried before a court-martial (Sept. 29), of which Maj. Gen. Nathanael Greene was the president, convicted of being a spy and ordered to be hanged. Washington refused to intercede in his behalf, and he was executed on Oct. 2, 1780, at Tappan, N. Y.

[W. Abbatt, *Crisis of the Revolution.*]

RANDOLPH G. ADAMS

Andrews' Raid. On April 12, 1862, twenty-two Union spies attempted to destroy the strategic railroad between Atlanta and Chattanooga. After a race in the engine *General* they were captured by men from the pursuing engine *Texas*. Eight were subsequently hanged.

[John R. Hornady, *Atlanta, Yesterday, Today, and Tomorrow.*]

HAYWOOD J. PEARCE, JR.

Andros Regime. *See* New England, Dominion of.

Anglican Church. *See* Church of England in the Colonies, The.

Anglo-American Relations properly date from the year 1783, when the Definitive Treaty of Peace[qv] was ratified. It was, at first, the hope of the British Ministry that some sort of an intimate alliance might be immediately worked out with the United States, for the old imperial relationship. This would leave the United States independent, in complete free trade with the Empire, bound by a close naval alliance to furnish seamen and ships. The peace commissioners at Paris proved unamenable to this, and it fell flat.

During the period of the Confederation[qv], 1783–89, the imperfect constitutional organization of the United States, and the resulting national weakness, placed it at the mercy of British commercial preponderance and diplomatic calculation. John Adams, first minister of the United States to Great Britain, tried in vain to secure a treaty of commerce, as well as an adjustment of issues connected with non-fulfillment of the Treaty of Peace. These comprised British retention of the strategic military posts on American soil along the newly established river-and-lake boundary (*see* Border Forts), the failure of the Federal Government promptly and perfectly to execute articles of the treaty relating to the payment of private pre-war debts (*see* British Debts) and the prevention of further confiscations and discriminations against returning Loyalists[qv]. The existing commercial situation was entirely satisfactory to Great Britain, with the Americans now taking nine-tenths of their imports from England but automatically excluded by the fact of independence from trade with the British colonial dominions. There was no danger of retaliatory tariffs or commercial discrimination against British commerce so long as the government of the Confederation lacked control over interstate and foreign commerce. Meanwhile the internal weaknesses of the Confederation presaged to secret British observers an impending break-up. In London there seemed no necessity for a treaty. Great Britain would not even send a diplomatic representative to the United States.

The political miracle of the Constitution[qv] and the establishment of the new national Government under President George Washington saved independence and crystalized American nationality in permanent form. The outbreak of the French Revolution at this same time presently gave rise to a series of European wars that completely absorbed British attention and energies for the next twenty-five years. Stiffened American nationality, with control over foreign and interstate commerce, and a resolution to police the Western Indians and reduce them to national authority, gave the British government more respect for the authority and independence of the United States and led to the exchange of diplomatic representatives in 1791. A movement in the new Congress for discriminatory tariffs against British goods and ships precipitated this despatch of a British minister to Philadelphia.

The instructions of the first British minister, George Hammond, were to talk the Government of the United States out of commercial discrimination and to offer to make a general treaty only on condition of the establishment of a neutral Indian barrier state[qv], under British influence. This plan was frustrated by the innate patriotism of even the pro-British elements in the United States, and by the exigencies of the international situation in Europe, where war broke out between England and France in 1793. The United States, on its side, wanted neutrality. The frontier situation and British arbitrary naval seizures produced a war scare in the spring of 1794 but this was settled by Jay's Treaty[qv], which was a decisive turning point in Anglo-American relations and indeed in the history of the United States. It was the price which Washington's Government, under Federalist[qv] advice, paid to British sea power for the redemption of American territory and for a breathing spell of peace to secure the newly established nationality and financial stability which depended on Anglo-American commerce for its revenues.

All attempts at a negotiated basis of Anglo-American relations during the Napoleonic wars fell down as the system of retaliations was built up between the Leviathan of the Seas and the Colossus of the Land, each trying desperately to destroy the other by the most deadly weapons at his disposal. American administration reprisals at British naval practice, such as the Non-Importation Act, the Embargo and the Non-Intercourse Act[qqv], only served to damage American commerce and to align the United States as a supplement to Napoleon's Continental System (*see* Napoleon's Decrees). The "retaliatory" British blockade and the practice of impressment[qqv], especially the latter, fired American public opinion with the old hostility to England, although not to the extent of war. It is to be noted that, when war was declared in 1812, the very coastal constituencies of Congress, which had been most oppressed by British naval practice, voted against war; this was presumably because war trade on British sufferance, as controlled by the British navy for British supply and profit, was to them preferable to war and the ruin of trade. What tipped the scales in favor of a declaration of war was the vote of the members from the Southern and the new Western states (*see* War Hawks). The United States was lucky to get out of the war without the loss of territory (*see* War of 1812).

The Peace of Ghent[qv], ratified in 1815, was really a compromise peace on the basis of the *status quo ante bellum*. It settled none of the issues, like impressment and the freedom of the seas[qv], which had helped to cause the war. But it did settle the permanence of the northern frontier, and England proved willing to extend the frontier, by the Convention of 1818[qv], on the line of 49° N. Lat. as far as the Rocky Mountains, leaving the opposing claims in the Pacific Northwest still unsettled (*see* Oregon Question). A naval limitations agreement in 1817 (*see* Great Lakes, Agreement for Disarmament on the), ratified subsequently by the Senate, demilitarized the Great Lakes. It has remained in effect ever since, and the principle of disarmament has been extended in practice all along the frontier.

Two other great diplomatic settlements were necessary in the generation after Ghent to harmonize completely Anglo-American frontier relations: the settlement of the Northeastern frontier dispute by the Webster-Ashburton Treaty of 1842[qv], and the termination of the long contention for dominion over Oregon. Webster's concessions in the Northeast were compensated by the victory of American diplomacy, on the eve of the war with Mexico[qv], in settling the Northwestern territorial question by the Oregon Treaty of 1846[qv], which continued the line of 49° N. Lat. straight through to the Pacific Ocean, reserving for British subjects trading with the Hudson's Bay Company[qv] the right to navigate the Columbia River[qv]. The achievement of this line was a diplomatic victory rather than the "compromise" that it is sometimes represented to be. The United States had always refused to take less than 49°. Great Britain had not consistently refused to take less than the line of the Columbia River, which was the basis of her claim. The exact line through the channels out to the open sea became a matter of dispute subsequent to 1846 and involved the sovereignty of the San Juan[qv] archipelago at the entrance to Puget Sound. These islands were adjudged to the United States by the Alabama Claims arbitration of 1871, provided for in the Treaty of Washington[qqv].

In the mid-century there were three other serious issues between the United States and Great Britain: the regulation of the suppression of the African slave trade[qv] on the high seas, the Texas question and the Isthmian question (*see* Panama Canal). Both countries had abolished the African slave trade. Great Britain had negotiated treaties with the principal maritime powers providing for the mutual right of visit and search[qv] of ships suspected of engaging in the slave trade. The United States refused to make such a treaty unless Great Britain would at the same time expressly abandon the practice of impressment. After much diplomatic discussion, the British government explicitly disavowed any right of visit and search in time of peace but insisted that it was proper to visit a vessel suspected of flying the American flag illegally; otherwise slavers could cover themselves by that flag with impunity. The United States consistently maintained that ships flying its flag illegally could be searched and even captured and punished but there must be no mistake made in molesting a real American vessel. This uncompromising attitude by both parties created incidents and obstructed the strict policing of this nefarious commerce.

Undoubtedly, the influence of the Southern slave states in the American Congress made it impossible for the Federal Government to reach an agreement with England, because in 1862, after the secession of the Southern states and the outbreak of the American Civil War[qqv], Secretary of State Seward promptly concluded a convention with Great Britain, providing for the mutual right of visit and search in specified waters off the coasts of Africa and Cuba, with mixed courts at Sierra Leone, Cape Town and New York, composed of an equal number of judges from each party for the trial of offenders. The passage of time and the growth of American power had wiped away any possibility of renewal by Great Britain of the obnoxious and humiliating practice of impressment.

Slavery, too, played a prominent part in the Texas question. It was the purpose of British diplomacy to prevent Texas from becoming annexed to the United States, and in a friendly way to press for the ultimate abolition of slavery there. An independent Texas would be an alternate source, indispensably needed, of cotton to keep British textile mills operating, in case difficulties with the United States should ever shut off that source. Further, Texas as a sovereign state would be outside the American tariff walls and, presumably, a free-trade market for British manufactures (*see* Webster-Ashburton Treaty). On the eve of the war between the United States and Mexico, British diplomacy had negotiated a treaty between Texas and Mexico, providing for Mexican recognition of Texan independence upon the condition of Texas never being annexed to any third state. This treaty was never ratified, and annexation[qv] in 1845 definitely ended the Texas question. Great Britain's attitude about Texas, however, did much to offset the appeasement of feeling wrought by the Webster-Ashburton settlement of 1842 and the Oregon Treaty of 1846.

The Isthmian question involved the control of the route of a future canal. American expansion into Texas, the war with Mexico and the alliance with New Granada (Colombia) annoyed Great Britain, which sought to block American influence on the Isthmus, by securing control of strategic points at both termini of the Nicaraguan canal route (*see* Bidlack-Mallarino Treaty). Anglo-American tension on the Isthmus reached almost the point of war in 1850, but was adjusted by the Clayton-Bulwer Treaty[qv] of that year, one of the most embarrassing international engagements which the United States has ever ratified. This treaty placed any future Isthmian canal under the joint control of the United States and Great Britain and provided that there should never be any discrimination in traffic charges against the citizens or subjects of either party to the canal treaty.

It was indeed a fortunate occurrence that on the outbreak of the Civil War Anglo-American relations had been cleared of any serious controversy, for the war served to embitter feelings between the two peoples. Great Britain allowed Southern cruisers to be constructed and fitted out from British ports, whence they proceeded to spread havoc in the merchant marine[qv] of the United States, the destruction of which would not displease British maritime interests. In the famous *Trent* case[qv] Great Britain protested to the point of an ultimatum against American seizure of disloyal subjects from British ships on the high seas. The conformance of the United States to British demands, albeit justified on technical grounds, saved peace with England and strengthened the American point of view against the old British practice of impressment. Although the cotton shortage, caused by the blockade of Southern ports, and Southern embargoes on cotton export, brought great hardship to the masses of British textile employees, Great Britain acquiesced in the imperfect Union blockade because it established a valuable Anglo-American precedent for the employment by Great Britain in any future contingency of an imperfect blockade of her own in a war in which the United States might be neutral. British diplomacy cashed in heavily on this precedent during the period of American neutrality in the first three years of the World War.

Despite their sufferings, the British working classes, to whom slavery was hateful, sympathized ardently with the cause of the Union. After the Civil War the United States successfully demanded the arbitration with Great Britain of British responsibilities for the equipment and consequent depredations of the Confederate cruisers, the *Alabama*[qv] and ships of her class. For this the Geneva Arbitration of 1871 awarded a total of $15,500,000. At the same time, various British claimants received $1,929,819, in awards of a General Claims Commission, and the Halifax Mixed Commission[qv] awarded $5,500,000 as additional compensation to Great Britain for fishery concessions in British territorial waters that had been extended without compensation in 1866, upon the expiration of the Canadian Reciprocity Treaty of 1854[qv].

The Geneva adjudication was one of several Anglo-American arbitrations which cleared away the controversies which arose during the generation after the Civil War. The attempt of the United States to control the seal fisheries[qv] in Bering Sea met the protests of the British against the exercise of sovereign rights on the high seas, even for the protection and preservation of marine life. The ensuing arbitration of 1892 gave a clear-cut decision against the United States, whose case had been greatly prejudiced by earlier traditional American protests in favor of the freedom of the seas.

In 1895 President Grover Cleveland startled the world with his spectacular ultimatum insisting that Great Britain arbitrate a long-standing boundary dispute between British Guiana and the republic of Venezuela. It was President Cleveland's conviction that Great Britain would violate the Monroe Doctrine[qv] if she exploited the boundary dispute to expand her territory on the American continents at the expense of an American republic. The rise of German naval power and its threat to the British Empire, graphically signalized by the Kaiser's telegram of congratulations to President Krueger of the Transvaal on the eve of the Boer War, together with the ever-present exposure of the Canadian flank of empire, speedily induced Great Britain to accept Cleveland's ultimatum and arbitrate her controversy (advantageously, it proved) with the United States (*see* Venezuela Boundary Controversy). Since then Great Britain has accepted the Monroe Doctrine as a permanent part of her foreign policy and has consistently striven for an *entente cordiale* with the United States, as a means of strengthening her diplomatic and even military resources to deal with controversies and wars that threaten her intimately in the Old World. This approach is illustrated by the cordial tone of British diplomacy and public opinion during the Spanish-American War[qv]. In line with the improvement of

Anglo-American relations and the new cordial tone, Great Britain prevailed upon Canada to submit to arbitration her dispute over the Alaskan boundary[qv]. At the same time, British policy profited heavily by the American Open Door policy[qv] in China, which was as British in its origin as it was American, and certainly more to the advantage of Great Britain than to the United States. There is no documentary evidence yet presented of an explicit bargain diplomatically, by which Great Britain got out of the Caribbean, and the United States got into the Far East, but it was implicit in the general situation.

The last great controversy to be cleared up between the United States and England was the historic dispute over fishing privileges on the Atlantic coast of British North America, which was compromised by the arbitral decision of 1910 (*see* Fisheries Dispute). Since then the United States and Great Britain have enjoyed general treaties of arbitration and conciliation and have been pledged to peace by the Briand-Kellogg Pact[qv]. Since both of them are powers whose vital interests dictate peace, and each of whom would have much to lose by the defeat of the other, they tend to drift together in the face of common danger.

The inveterate friendship of Anglo-American relations and the common outlook on danger made the United States and its people highly sympathetic to the British cause at the outbreak of the World War. Other factors inclined toward a neutrality more benevolent to Great Britain than to Germany and her allies: a common cultural background, a common tradition of liberal constitutionalism, a common language, highly conducive to skillful British propaganda (as contrasted with clumsy German propaganda and misunderstanding of American history), and an economic tie-up in the shape of munitions supply and heavy subscriptions to the war loans of Britain and her allies. These factors made the United States want Great Britain to win, rather than Germany, particularly because the United States had little to lose if Great Britain should win and much to lose if Germany, which had never recognized the Monroe Doctrine, should triumph. All of this predisposed the United States toward the Allied cause but the precipitation of war occurred only when Germany added the challenge of unrestricted submarine warfare.

During the World War the United States, as a belligerent, did not desert, technically speaking, its traditional stand for the freedom of the seas; but after the war, in 1927, by an exchange of notes, the United States, while carefully reserving its principles in the premises, released Great Britain from claims for maritime captures and interferences with American neutral commerce, 1914 to 1917.

Anglo-American relations since the World War, while cordial, have not been passionately friendly. The principal outstanding issues today are: discriminations against American commerce wrought by inter-imperial preference treaties (like that of Ottawa, 1932) and Great Britain's default on her pledge to pay her war debt[qv] while insisting that the United States observe its pledge, inherited from the old Clayton-Bulwer Treaty and reincorporated in the Hay-Pauncefote Treaty[qv] of 1902, not to levy any higher traffic charges on foreign ships than on American ships going through the Panama Canal[qv], control and defense of which, since 1902, consented to by Great Britain, is at the cost of the American taxpayer, as is also payment of the defaulted loans to Great Britain. It should always be remembered that of the approximately $4,277,000,000 loaned to Great Britain, $581,000,000 is a peace debt loaned after Nov. 11, 1918. To these grits in the present smoothness of Anglo-American relations must be added the disappointment experienced when Great Britain refused to act with the United States for the solution of the Manchurian crisis of 1931 to 1933. Many observers feel that here started the chain of aggressions which extended itself in the Rhineland, Abyssinia, Spain, Austria and Czechoslovakia at the expense of the democratic powers, and which seems to unleash a future of dismay for them.

The existing issues are small and capable of settlement by wise and resolute statesmen, if there are such. The commercial question has recently been adjusted, at this writing, by the new trade agreements of 1938: between the United States and Canada, and between the United States and Great Britain and her crown colonies. More than ever Great Britain and the United States need each other's friendship. More than ever each has much to lose by the other's defeat and little to fear from the other's prosperity and success. More than ever the culture, the freedom and the ideals of each great people are threatened by new ideologies and auguries in the international world.

[Samuel Flagg Bemis, *A Diplomatic History of the United States;* Ephraine D. Adams, *Great Britain and the American Civil War;* Frank L. Owsley, *King Cotton Diplomacy;* William Archibald Dunning, *The British Empire and the United States.*]

SAMUEL FLAGG BEMIS

Anglo-Chinese War (1839–42), American Interests in the, center about the initiative of Commodore Lawrence Kearny[qv] that led to opening several Chinese ports to American commerce. Arriving off Canton with the *Constellation* and *Boston* in March, 1842, Kearny found the war, precipitated by the opium[qv] dispute, nearly ended. He cultivated friendly relations with both sides and when the victorious British demanded special trade privileges, he pleaded with the Chinese for equal privileges being granted Americans. This principle was accepted by the Chinese and formed the basis of our first treaty with China negotiated by Caleb Cushing[qv] at Canton in 1844.

[C. O. Paullin, *Diplomatic Negotiations of American Naval Officers.*] DUDLEY W. KNOX

Anglophobia and Anglomania. Historically the attitude of mind described by these words goes back to the period of the Confederation[qv]; but these particular descriptive terms first became part of the American vocabulary in the decade between 1880 and 1890. The terms were exploited by partisans in the Democratic and Republican parties[qqv] alike. The anglomaniac was popularly described as an aristocrat, usually from the East, who aped English manners, read English books and favored an Anglo-American alliance. The Murchison letter[qv] episode of the presidential election of 1888[qv] indicates how the politicians took advantage of the feeling against the anglophile.

The anglophobe was more articulate than the anglomaniac and was much more in evidence in the 1890's. In the Middle West there existed the traditional anti-English attitude, supplemented by the political hostility of the Populist[qv] group. The cheap-money group declared that England alone stood in the way of universal bimetallism[qv]; and the Populist orators demanded war against this great "money empire." Racial groups, especially the Irish-American and German-American, were generally anglophobe, and their attitude of hostility toward England was especially notable during the Boer War.

The work of such statesmen as John Hay and James Bryce helped to soften some of the animosities developed by the anti-British group, but despite these efforts there was a strong outburst against England when the repeal of the Panama Tolls Act[qv] was before Congress.

Before America's entry into the World War the feelings of the two groups were intensified by events connected with the struggle over neutral rights. Ambassador Walter Hines Page was pictured as an anglomaniac by one faction while William Randolph Hearst was considered an anglophobe. America's entry into the war naturally brought a temporarary truce between the groups. Despite some recurrence of feeling in the post-war period, there has been no such intensive partisanship as that characterizing the turn of the century.

[B. A. Reuter, *Anglo-American Relations During the Spanish American War.*] THEODORE G. GRONERT

Anián, Strait of. A mythical strait, supposed to connect the Atlantic and Pacific, sought by the Spaniards in the 16th and 17th centuries. In 1601 they tried to find a harbor on it beyond Quivira[qv] for direct intercourse with Spain. Until 1742 the Gulf of California was believed by many to join the west end of the strait.

[C. E. Chapman, *A History of California: Spanish Period.*] LANSING B. BLOOM

Annapolis. *See* Naval Academy, United States.

Annapolis Convention, THE, was the precursor of the Constitutional Convention of 1787[qv]. On Sept. 11, 1786, twelve commissioners from New York, New Jersey, Pennsylvania, Delaware and Virginia met in the State House at Annapolis, Md., to discuss reform of the vexatious restrictions placed upon interstate commerce by the various states. Among those present were Alexander Hamilton, John Dickinson and James Madison. The convention took no action except to recommend that a larger convention be held in Philadelphia the following May.

[A. C. McLaughlin, *The Confederation and the Constitution.*] WALTER B. NORRIS

Annapolis Royal. *See* Port Royal (N. S.).

Annexation of Territory. No specific provision was made in the Constitution for the annexation of territory. It is doubtful that the Fathers in 1783 contemplated expansion across the empty continent beyond the ample boundaries set down in the Definitive Treaty of Peace[qv]. All the region beyond the Mississippi, north of the Great Lakes and south of 31° N. Lat., then remained in the hands of strong European monarchies. But Europe's distresses were America's advantage. The wars which followed the outbreak of the French Revolution and convulsed the Old World from 1793–1815 exhausted the energies of Great Britain and Spain, and also of France which had intervened in Louisiana in 1800–1803, and enabled the United States first to clear its own territory of foreign troops and then to expand. By the twin treaties of Washington's administration, Jay's Treaty with England (1794) and Pinckney's Treaty with Spain (1795)[qqv], the West was cleared. Practice discovered four different means of annexation, all of which proved to be constitutional. A lucky break in the European constellation of 1800–1803 enabled President Jefferson unexpectedly by treaty to purchase the vast territory of Louisiana[qv] and thus to annex it to the United States. After 1815 England was so exhausted that, as Castlereagh said, she needed a long period of repose; reposing she made a boundary treaty in 1818 (*see* Convention of 1818) which accepted the line of 49° N. Lat. to the Rocky Mountains and acknowledged the equal claim of the United States to the Pacific Northwest. Spain, harassed by South American revolutions, in 1819 gave up Florida to the United States in a treaty which also established a most favorable transcontinental frontier line from Texas to California (*see* Adams-Onís Treaty).

These new boundaries were soon expanded in both directions: to the southwest, by the annexation of Texas[qv], and by the purchase of Mexican territory in the Treaty of Guadalupe Hidalgo[qv], 1848, following a war the fundamental cause of which was the Texas question; to the northwest, by the Oregon Treaty[qv] in which England recognized full American sovereignty south of 49° to the Pacific Ocean. Great Britain was opposed to both of these expansions, but preferred to accept them because at that time she was not in a position really to fight, either for Texas or Oregon. In 1853 the United States bought from Mexico a comparatively small strip of territory, the Gadsden Purchase[qv].

It will be noted that this expansion of territory took place in three ways: by treaties of purchase; by treaties for frontier settlements; and by joint resolution of annexation, accepted by the republic of Texas reciprocally in 1845.

Two other treaties of purchase vastly expanded American territory: Alaska[qv], from Russia in 1867 (Russia preferred to sell an unprofitable colony rather than see it some day conquered by the British navy), and the Philippines[qv] from Spain in 1899, as a result of the war of 1898. In the same treaty of peace Puerto Rico and Guam[qqv] were ceded as an outright conquest. The Hawaiian Islands[qv] were meanwhile annexed by joint resolution of Congress, which was reciprocally voted by the Hawaiian legislature, as in the case of Texas. The Danish West Indies[qv] were acquired by a treaty of purchase in 1917. A number of small islands in the Atlantic and Pacific (*see* Pacific Islands) have been annexed by presidential proclamation (a fourth means of annexation). Annexation of the Philippines, accomplished by a treaty of peace and purchase, is being undone by an act of Congress (*see* Philippine Independence).

[Samuel Flagg Bemis, *A Diplomatic History of the United States.*]

SAMUEL FLAGG BEMIS

Antarctic Exploration. *See* Byrd's Polar Flights; Wilkes Exploring Expedition, 1838–42.

Antelope, THE, a Spanish vessel taken March, 1820, by an American privateer, was seized by a United States revenue cutter with a cargo of slaves captured from Spanish and Portuguese ships. Vessel and Africans were claimed by Spanish and Portuguese vice-consuls on behalf of their citizens. Chief Justice Marshall, declaring for the United States Supreme Court that the African slave trade was not contrary to the law of nations, that the American cruiser had no right of search[qv] and seizure in a time of peace, and that it was not the duty of the United States to execute the penal laws of another country, directed that the slaves be restored to the foreigner in possession at the time of the capture.

[10 Wheaton 66.]

LIONEL H. LAING

Anthracite, or hard coal, is a solid fuel characterized by a very high percentage of fixed carbon and a low percentage of volatile matter. Although anthracitic coals are mined in limited quantities in Arkansas, Colorado, New Mexico, Virginia and Washington, the term "anthracite" usually is applied only to the output from an elongated area of approximately 480 square miles in eastern Pennsylvania.

The existence of Pennsylvania anthracite was known to colonists as early as 1763. Obadiah Gore used it successfully in a smithy forge in Wilkes-Barre in 1769, and anthracite was shipped to the Carlisle arsenal in 1776. Jesse Fall, also of Wilkes-Barre, demonstrated its industrial fuel possibilities in nail manufacturing in 1788; twenty years later he put it in the domestic picture by burning it on an open grate with natural draft.

Progress, nevertheless, was slow. Wood, plentiful and cheap, was the preferred household fuel. Acceleration in industrial demand had to wait upon the manufacturing growth of the new nation. Canals, and later railroads[qqv], had to be developed as marketing adjuncts to mining operations. Between 1807 and 1820, total output aggregated only 12,000 net tons; the 1,000,000-ton mark was not reached until 1837 and annual production did not touch 10,000,000 tons until 1863.

Thereafter the long-term trend continued steadily upward, culminating in the war-time peak of 99,611,811 tons in 1917. Long before that peak, however, bituminous coal[qv] had far outstripped anthracite in the industrial markets. Today, anthracite is primarily a domestic fuel; over 85% of the output is used for heating services.

Here, too, competition is taking its toll. Strikes (*see* Anthracite Strike, 1902), increasing mine costs and transportation charges in the early years of the 20th century shrank the areal market while actual tonnage was showing no alarming downward trends. More recently, and particularly since 1927, competition with other fuels in what is now its major market—the New England and Middle Atlantic states—has still further curtailed anthracite consumption, scaling down output from established mines to 51,745,000 tons in 1937. In the campaign to stop these losses and recover vanished markets, the greatest gains have been made in the sale of the smaller sizes of anthracite adaptable for use in household stokers.

[*Mineral Resources of the United States*, U. S. Geological Survey, 1879-1923; U. S. Bureau of Mines, 1924-31; *Minerals Yearbook*, U. S. Bureau of Mines, 1932-38; Eliot Jones, *The Anthracite Coal Combination in the United States;* Hudson Coal Co., *The Story of Anthracite.*]

SYDNEY A. HALE

Anthracite Strike (1902). In May, 1902, after vain efforts to secure an agreement, 150,000 anthracite[qv] miners, members of the United Mine Workers[qv], under the leadership of John Mitchell, went on strike for higher wages, shorter hours and recognition of the union. Most of the mines were owned by corporations which also controlled the coal-carrying railroads. Though the strike forced a complete shutdown, practically paralyzing the industry, the owners refused any dealings with the striking miners. There was little violence and because they had real grievances, the miners won a large measure of public sympathy and support. As winter approached acute coal shortage developed. A widespread public demand arose for prompt settlement. Prices rose steadily. The coal operators still refused to meet the miners' representatives, their spokesman, George F. Baer, declaring in June: "We will give no consideration to any plan of arbitration or mediation or to any interference on the part of any outside party." On July 17 Baer wrote: "The rights and interests of the laboring men will be protected and cared for, not by the labor agitators, but by the Christian men to whom God in his infinite wisdom has given the control of the property interests of the country." Two months later, Baer again stated the operators would not yield. Soon afterwards President Theodore Roosevelt intervened and called for a conference of the warring elements. The operators resented this action and accused the President of failure to send troops to protect the mines from violence. Of this charge, the President was not guilty, as the governor of Pennsylvania had refused to call for Federal troops; instead he called out the Pennsylvania Guard. The situation was becoming dangerous. After a secret, but unsuccessful, attempt had been made to intercede through a commission of which ex-President Cleveland was to be chairman, the President was ready to send regular troops, even to take over and operate the mines. This determination was allowed to be known and as a result the owners and operators yielded and in a stormy conference agreed to a committee of arbitration to be appointed by the President. The miners returned to work and, March 18, 1903, the commission awarded them a 10% increase in wages and other concessions. This strike is notable in that it emphasized that in struggles between capital and labor, the interests of a third party, the public, are paramount.

[John R. Commons, *History of Labour in the United States.*]

THOMAS ROBSON HAY

Anthracite-Tidewater Canals. Anthracite was discovered in northeastern Pennsylvania in the latter 18th century, but for years it could be gotten to market only by floating it in arks or flatboats[qqv] down the turbulent streams flowing out of the coal region—a difficult and expensive method. Josiah White in 1818 improved the upper Lehigh River with dams, but this not proving adequate, he built the Lehigh Canal, completing it to the Delaware River at Easton in 1829. From there the Delaware Division of the Pennsylvania Canals continued the haul to tidewater at Bristol. Later, some of the coal crossed New Jersey to New York Harbor through the Morris Canal[qv], built 1824–32. The Schuylkill Canal, completed in 1825, was not conceived as a coal carrier, but it became one of the greatest in the country. The Delaware & Hudson[qv], built 1825–29, hauled coal out of the Lackawanna region, which was also served by the North Branch of the Pennsylvania State Canals[qv], following down the Susquehanna, transferring some of its coal at Middletown to the Union Canal[qv], whence it passed via the Schuylkill to Philadelphia and New York; or it carried on to Columbia, where the Susquehanna & Tidewater (built 1835–38) took over and hauled the coal down to Baltimore, sometimes through the Chesapeake & Delaware Canal[qv], Delaware River and Delaware & Raritan Canal[qv] to New York. These canals in their heyday, during the 1860's and 1870's, may each have carried from 1,000,000 to 3,000,000 tons yearly; but the greater speed of the railroads destroyed them, one by one. The Lehigh-Delaware was the longest-lived of all. In 1931, after it had transported nearly 50,000,000 tons of anthracite, not to mention other freight, all in horse-drawn boats, its traffic was abandoned.

[Alvin F. Harlow, *Old Towpaths.*]

ALVIN F. HARLOW

Anti-Bank Movement of the West, THE. Opposition to banks of issue existed from the beginning of such institutions in America in the late 18th century. It was a marked characteristic of the Jeffersonian[qv] movement. After the panic of 1837[qv], however, the sentiment reached the stage of a movement to abolish banks. It was rooted in Jacksonian fear, debtor distress, and a bullionist or "hard money"[qv] theory (*see* Jacksonian Democracy).

The movement was centered in the new Jacksonian states of the Mississippi Valley and reached its climax in the constitutional conventions of the 1840's and 1850's. Between 1845 and 1863 banks were abolished at one time in Illinois, Wisconsin, Iowa, Missouri, Arkansas, Louisiana, Texas and the Pacific Coast.

The movement is properly interpreted as an early example of agrarian[qv] protest similar to the Populist[qv] movement of a later date.

[L. C. Helderman, *National and State Banks: A Study of Their Origins.*]

L. C. HELDERMAN

Antietam, The Battle of (Sept. 17, 1862). Early in September, 1862, Gen. Lee's (C.) Army of Northern Virginia[qv] crossed the Potomac into Maryland (*see* Maryland, Invasion of). He concentrated at Frederick, then sent Jackson's corps south to take Harpers Ferry, and Longstreet's westward across the South Mountain[qv]. On the 14th McClellan's (U.) Army of the Potomac[qv] forced the mountain passes.

Lee began to concentrate toward the Potomac, and took position at Sharpsburg, on the Antietam Creek. While Longstreet was assembling here, Lee heard that Jackson had captured Harpers Ferry[qv], and took the bold decision to stand and fight behind the creek, with the Potomac at his back. Longstreet took the right of the line; Jackson's troops, as they arrived, the left.

McClellan planned to strike Lee's left with three corps (Hooker's, Mansfield's and Sumner's); to follow this blow with an attack by Burnside's corps on the Confederate right; and to hold Porter's and Frankin's corps, with Pleasonton's cavalry, in reserve in the center.

But Hooker, Mansfield and Sumner attacked successively, not simultaneously, and each in turn was beaten. Burnside's attack on the other flank came still later. Longstreet's line had been weakened to reinforce Jackson, for Lee had no real reserve; hence Burnside made some progress at first, but when fully engaged he was struck in flank by A. P. Hill's (C.) division, the last of Jackson's troops returning from Harpers Ferry. Burnside was driven back to the bridge by which he had crossed the creek, and darkness ended the fighting.

On the 18th Lee stood fast and McClellan did not renew his attack. On the 19th Lee effected his withdrawal across the Potomac. The numbers engaged are uncertain; perhaps a fair estimate is 50,000 Federal, 40,000 Confederate. But this was Lee's entire strength, and McClellan had 20,000 in reserve, never used. The losses may be estimated as 12,000 Federal, 9000 Confederate.

[Official Records, War of the Rebellion; *Battles and Leaders of the Civil War;* J. C. Palfrey, *The Antietam and Fredericksburg.*]

OLIVER LYMAN SPAULDING

Anti-Federalists, THE, were opponents of ratification of the Constitution[qv] (1781–88), who feared loss of individual liberty and state rights[qv]. After 1793 they became identified with the Jeffersonian Republican Party[qv].

WHEELER PRESTON

Anti-Horse Thief Association, THE, was organized at Fort Scott, Kans., in 1859 to provide protection against marauders thriving on border warfare[qv]. It resembled vigilance societies[qv] in organization and methods. After the Civil War gangs of outlaws made their hideaways in the inadequately policed Indian Territory[qv] and preyed on the livestock, chiefly horses, of the neighboring states. During the period 1869 to 1875 officers were unable to cope with the bandits, and few sheriffs ventured south of the Marion County line, 150 miles north of the Indian Territory. The organization spread to other sections of the state as necessity arose, and probably to other states, but eventually turned into a social organization.

[E. Dick, *Sod House Frontier;* J. A. McClellan, Joseph McClellan, in *Kansas Historical Collection,* Vol. 17.]

CARL L. CANNON

Anti-Imperialists. This term was applied to American leaders who opposed colonial expansion after the Spanish-American War[qv]. Sen. George Frisbie Hoar and other New England Republicans were strong Anti-Imperialists, but refused to desert their party on the issue. A number of liberals joined the Anti-Imperialism League, which in 1900 threw its support to William Jennings Bryan.

[W. R. Thayer, *Life and Letters of John Hay.*]

THEODORE G. GRONERT

Anti-Masonic Movements. Suspicion of secret societies[qv] was marked at an early date, but the fact that Washington and other patriots were Masons[qv] seemed proof that the Order was not dangerous. In 1826, however, when the Morgan Trials[qv] aroused western New York there was a widespread reaction, which assumed national importance with the organization of the Anti-Masonic party. Many Masons renounced their vows, membership in New York dwindling from 20,000 to 3000 between 1826 and 1836. The number of lodges was reduced from 507 before 1826, to 48 in 1832. In Vermont the Grand Lodge voted down a proposal for dissolution, but agreed to receive charters from chapters desiring to surrender them, and provided that funds of such lodges should go to the state public school fund. Many congregations were divided, especially Presbyterian, Baptist, Methodist and Congregational[qqv]. Masons were excluded from membership, and pastors were barred from their pulpits. In Pennsylvania, Anti-Masonry found favor among Quakers, Mennonites, Dunkards, Moravians and some Lutheran and German Reformed groups[qqv]. A Vermont law of 1833 forbade extrajudicial oaths; and elsewhere Masons were deprived of local office and dropped from jury rolls.

Anti-Masonic newspapers were an index of the rapid growth of the Anti-Masonic party. Charging intimidation of printers and suppression of facts of the Morgan Trials, party leaders urged the establishment of "free presses." Thurlow Weed, who in 1828 had started the Rochester *Anti-Masonic Enquirer,* was given financial backing in 1830 for his *Albany Evening Journal,* the principal party organ. In 1832 there were forty-six Anti-Masonic papers in New York and fifty-five in Pennsylvania. In September, 1831, a national Anti-Masonic convention was held at Baltimore, naming William Wirt of Maryland for President. This, the first "third party"[qv], only drew support from Clay, and helped the sweep for Jackson in 1832. It received seven electoral votes from Vermont. The party also gained adherents in Pennsylvania, Ohio, New Jersey, Massachusetts, Connecticut and Rhode Island; but only Pennsylvania, through the leadership of Thaddeus Stevens, and Vermont elected Anti-Masonic governors. In the late 1830's the excitement subsided, or was replaced by the antislavery[qv] agitation. By 1838 the party had merged with the Whigs[qv].

After the Civil War there was another movement directed against secret societies. The National Christian Association was founded at Aurora, Ill., in 1868 to oppose secret orders, "Jesuitism, Mormonism, atheism, spiritualism and free love"[qv]. It maintained a national organization and published a weekly, *The Christian Cynosure* (1867–71). This crusade was unsuccessful, and the 1880's and 1890's witnessed a great increase of fraternal orders.

[J. C. Palmer, *The Morgan Affair and Anti-Masonry;* Charles McCarthy, *The Anti-Masonic Party; The Anti-Masonic Scrapbook,* 1883.]

MILTON W. HAMILTON

Anti-Monopoly Parties (1873–76), sometimes called Independent or Reform parties, were organized by farmers, especially Grange[qv] members, in Indiana, Illinois, Michigan, Wisconsin, Minnesota, Iowa, Missouri, Kansas, Nebraska, California and Oregon. Their platforms demanded government reform, economy and reduced taxation; all but two also demanded state regulation of corporations, particularly railroads. In some states the new parties fused with the Democrats[qv]; thus they had some success in Iowa, and elected the whole state ticket in Wisconsin. In other states, as in Oregon, and to some extent in Illinois, they remained independent and won local victories. In Illinois, Kansas and California they secured the election of "Reformers" as United States senators. In Wisconsin, Iowa and Minnesota, in 1874, the Anti-Monopolists obtained enactment of "Granger" railroad laws[qv]. Though these were soon repealed or moderated, their passage evoked court decisions establishing the right of states to regulate railway corporations. The Anti-Monopoly parties did not survive the presidential campaign of 1876[qv].

[S. J. Buck, *The Granger Movement;* S. J. Buck, Independent Parties in the West, in *Essays in American History Dedicated to Frederick Jackson Turner.*]

SOLON J. BUCK

Antinomian Controversy, THE, was a theological dispute begun in Boston by Mistress Anne Hutchinson in the fall of 1636. She had been a parishioner and devout admirer of John Cotton in Boston, England, and with her husband followed him to the new Boston, where they were admitted to membership in the First Church. She was exceptionally intelligent, learned and eloquent, and began innocently to repeat on week days to small gatherings the substance of Cotton's sermons, but soon commenced delivering opinions of her own. At the height of her influence about eighty persons were attending lectures in her house.

She caused turmoil by putting a different conclusion from that maintained by the clergy upon the doctrine of the Covenant of Grace. The standard view held that the elect entered a Covenant with God on the condition of their believing in Christ, in return for which God contracted to give them salvation, but that thereafter the justified saints devoted themselves to good works, not in order to merit redemption, but as evidence of their having been called. Mrs. Hutchinson declared that stating the matter thus put too much emphasis upon "works" and denied the fundamental Protestant tenet of salvation by faith alone. Consequently she preached that the believer received into his soul the very substance of the Holy Ghost and that no value whatsoever adhered to conduct as a sign of justification.

This conclusion made for a disregard of morality such as Protestant theologians had everywhere endeavored to resist, and it could clearly lead to disastrous social consequences; the New England clergy, recognizing in her teachings a form of "Antinomianism," i.e., a discarding of the moral law, could not possibly have tolerated her. She made matters worse by accusing all the clergy except Cotton of preaching a Covenant of Works, so that Winthrop says it began to be as common in Massachusetts to distinguish the party of works and the party of grace "as in other countries between Protestants and papists." Thus she threatened to split the colony into factions, particularly when she was supported by her brother-in-law, the Rev. John Wheelwright, and the young governor, Harry Vane. The other clergy and magistrates believed that the existence of the whole enterprise was at stake; led by John Winthrop, and employing consummately clever tactics, they regained control of the government in May, 1637, then proceeded to disarm Anne's partisans and suppress the movement. Anne was examined by a synod of the ministers, which found her guilty of eighty erroneous opinions; John Cotton publicly repudiated her. Wheelwright was banished to New Hampshire; Anne was arraigned before the General Court, where she boasted of having received explicit revelations from the Holy Ghost, a possibility which no orthodox Protestant community could for a moment admit. She was excommunicated from the First Church in March, 1638, John Cotton pronouncing sentence upon her, and banished from the colony by the Court, whereupon she fled to Rhode Island.

[C. F. Adams, *Antinomianism in the Colony of Massachusetts Bay; Three Episodes of Massachusetts History;* Perry Miller, *Orthodoxy in Massachusetts;* E. S. Morgan, The Case Against Anne Hutchinson, *New England Quarterly*, X, 635-649, 1937.] PERRY MILLER

Anti-Poverty Societies supported Henry George's view that involuntary poverty resulted from human laws; they were formed in New York City (1887) and other cities.

WHEELER PRESTON

Anti-Rent Agitation, THE, which swept New York, 1839–46, was a culmination of the resentment of farmers against the leasehold system[qv], whereby the great landlords and land companies collected yearly tribute in produce, labor or money, and exacted a share ("quarter sales") of one quarter or one third of the amount realized from the sale of a leasehold. In 1839, when the heirs of Stephen Van Rensselaer tried to collect some $400,000 in back rent, the farmers rebelled. Gov. Seward called out the militia and issued a proclamation of warning. This sobered the rioters and ended the so-called "Helderberg War." Similar disturbances, however, soon broke out in the counties south of Albany.

In Columbia and Delaware Counties groups of men disguised as Indians tarred and feathered sheriffs and deputies who attempted to serve writs of ejectment. The murder of Deputy Sheriff Steele, August, 1845, led Gov. Wright to proclaim Delaware County in a state of insurrection. Anti-rent secret societies spread rapidly and became a political influence. The constitution of 1846 prohibited new feudal tenures and a court decision declared "quarter sales" illegal. There followed a general conversion of old leases into fee simple ownership.

[E. P. Cheney, The Antirent Movement, in A. C. Flick, *History of the State of New York*, Vol. VI.]

A. C. FLICK

Anti-Saloon League, THE, was founded at Oberlin, Ohio, May 24, 1893. Creating this statewide organization was the idea of the Rev. H. H. Russell. This "Ohio plan" was copied by many states and in 1895 a national organization, the Anti-Saloon League of America, was established at the Calvary Baptist Church, Washington, D. C. Soliciting and securing aid from the Protestant Evangelical churches, the league grew rapidly and came to regard itself as the "Church in Action Against the Saloon."

Theoretically, the co-operating churches possess the ultimate authority within the league. In fact, however, real control is exercised by the national executive committee and the national board of directors. The board, composed of not less than two nor more than five representatives from each state, is chosen by the state boards. The executive committee, when the board is not in session, exercises all the powers of the board. The General Superintendent, appointed by the board, exercises general supervision over national and state affairs and nominates the state superintendents who are theoretically selected by the state boards. Both state and national organizations employ legislative agents and attorneys who act as lobbyists for the league. Wayne B. Wheeler was national legislative superintendent from 1920 to 1927.

Prior to the Eighteenth Amendment[qv] the league centered its attention upon destroying the liquor traffic by legislation. To this end it sought and obtained local option[qv], county option, state prohibition, regulation of interstate liquor shipments and finally national prohibition[qv]. Following national prohibition the league sought by propaganda and pressure to achieve enforcement and the maintenance of this policy. For the first time in its history it was completely on the defensive. Accused of responsibility for the development of bootleg[qv] gangs, disrespect for law and all of the undesirable social practices of the post-war period, the league slowly lost support. The depression of 1929 brought a diminution in the league's revenues. Faced by a public willing to try anything which might re-establish prosperity, and weakened internally, it lost ground rapidly, suffering its final indignity in 1933 when the Eighteenth Amendment was repealed. Since that date it has not been significant in national politics and has returned to its original program of persuasion and local option.

[E. H. Cherrington, *History of the Anti-Saloon League;* Peter Odegard, *Pressure Politics;* Justin Stewart, *Wayne Wheeler, Dry Boss.*]

DAYTON E. HECKMAN

Antislavery. Antislavery sentiment varied all the way from the mildest doubts as to the wisdom of chattel slavery to a militant movement to abolish it without compensation and without delay. It was conditioned upon forces that worked in fields as diverse as the legal and political, the religious and moral, the social and economic and the more vaguely sentimental and humanitarian. An antislavery attitude was implicit in the English legal system as it stood on the eve of American colonization, by which time the remnants of slavery under the feudal system had disappeared. Even the early colonial statutes recognizing slavery[qv] put numerous qualifications upon its status. If Protestantism as such did not debar slavery, at least its more radically democratic sects, like the Quakers[qv] and various Puritan groups, did denounce it. They marshaled moral and religious arguments against the institution, the Quakers stressing the implications of the doctrine of human brotherhood. The influence of John Locke[qv] led 18th-century commentators to include personal freedom as one of the natural and inalienable rights of man; the exploitation of such theories during the American Revolution included a strong challenge to slavery on humanitarian grounds, which penetrated the ranks of many of the Southern slaveholders themselves.

From the earliest days of the institution there were those who condemned it on social and economic grounds, as a wasteful and more expensive system making for unwilling workmen and a prejudice against honest toil and one which degraded the poor and elevated a small slavocracy[qv]. In the ante-bellum period others attributed to slavery responsibility for the economic backwardness of the South and the "thriftlessness, desolation and debasement" (Abbott, *South and North,* 329–330) that prevailed in that section. In the 1850's Lincoln and others charged the extreme defenders of slavery with an attack, under their "mudsill" theory, upon the white man's charter of liberty, the Declaration of Independence[qv]. Slavery was also held responsible for the political situation under which an oligarchy of a few thousand slaveholders came to rule the million whites of the South and exercised a dominant influence in national politics. On this ground Northern sentiment came to be aroused to an attempt to check the spread of slavery and its political power, by preventing its further extension into the territories. (*See* Missouri Compromise; Compromise of 1850.)

Throughout the duration of slavery, particularly in its later years, there were those who sentimentalized over the unfortunate lot of the poor slave toiling in bondage; they pictured the cruelty and injustice of harsh masters and overseers and other evils, real or imagined, connected with the system. The horrors of the slave traffic, the hapless plight of the fugitive, hunted by bloodthirsty pursuers and their baying bloodhounds, the thrilling rescues of captives from proslavery mobs bent upon carrying their victims back into bondage became the stock in trade of sentimental arguments, literary and oral. (*See* Fugitive Slave Act; Dred Scott Case; *Uncle Tom's Cabin,* Influence of; Underground Railway.)

With the outbreak of the Civil War, Northern

sentiment increasingly charged slavery with responsibility for the attempt to destroy the Union. Out of this situation arose an increasing demand for the extinction of slavery, root and branch.

[J. Macy, *The Anti-Slavery Crusade.*]

ARTHUR C. COLE

Antislavery Literature became a force in the latter half of the 18th century as an expression of the egalitarianism then dominant in England. By 1800, through the essays of Quakers^qv like John Woolman, and of humanitarians^qv like Thomas Jefferson, Benjamin Franklin and Thomas Paine, the abstract right of the Negro slave to freedom on both religious and political grounds had become part of our literary tradition. During the next three decades the rise of cotton^qv and the opening of the Southwest to slavery^qv led to sectional^qv divergence. By 1832 Southern tradition viewed slavery as a permanent institution, while Northern opinion still condemned it "in the abstract." (*See* Proslavery; Antislavery.)

During the ensuing decade, militant organization of antislavery sentiment produced an enormous volume of antislavery tracts, but the controversy over immediatist doctrine^qv, imported here from the contemporary British movement, gave to most of them only ephemeral value. Aside from some brilliant writing in the antislavery periodicals, notably the *Liberator*^qv, effective work during this decade was largely done by the antislavery orators, such as Wendell Phillips and Theodore Dwight Weld.

By the 1840's, however, immediatism was triumphant; slavery was no longer an abstract wrong, but a concrete horror; and the Slave Power was the enemy of mankind. In this new tradition, Whittier wrote his greatest poems for freedom and James Russell Lowell published his *Biglow Papers*^qv. In 1851 Harriet Beecher Stowe embalmed the tradition for all time in her novel, *Uncle Tom's Cabin*^qv.

Toward the close of the 1850's economic tracts against slavery appeared to supplement the humanitarian literature: Helper's *Impending Crisis*^qv (1857) and Olmsted's travel narratives, especially his *Journey in the Seaboard Slave States* (1856). The Civil War put an end to significant antislavery literature.

[M. N. Work, *A Bibliography of the Negro in Africa and America.*]

GILBERT HOBBS BARNES

Antislavery Literature and the Mails. Antislavery literature was barred from the mails in the South in 1835. It was excluded by indirect means, and not by law, although a bill for the purpose was debated in the Senate, failing of passage on June 8, 1836, by six votes. The American Anti-Slavery Society^qv had mailed thousands of copies of its publications to individuals in the Southern states. On July 29 and 30, 1835, members of an indignant mob removed a mass of these papers from the post office at Charleston, S. C., and burned them. Postmaster-General Amos Kendall subsequently wrote the Charleston postmaster and others in the South, unofficially sanctioning their removal of antislavery papers. Postmasters or other citizens thereupon prevented the delivery of such literature. Feeling grew bitter throughout the country and violent means were used to silence unwelcome opinions. Denying the abolitionists^qv the use of the mails was unwise in that it enabled them to add to their basic arguments the issue of a deprivation of their civil rights.

[J. B. McMaster, *A History of the People of the United States*, Vol. VI.]

ROBERT P. LUDLUM

Antislavery Movement, The, in the United States may be defined as the history of organized propaganda against Negro slavery^qv. This movement was but one of a complex of forces affecting slavery, which included economic developments both North and South, the pull and haul of sectional politics (*see* Sectionalism), changing creeds in both religion and social philosophy, and even the fortuitous course of public events. Before 1830, one or the other of these forces so overshadowed earlier forms of antislavery organization as to make them negligible (*see* Missouri Compromise); but after that date a new type of organization appeared which made history. Begun originally to promote interdenominational enterprises such as the distribution of Bibles and tracts (*see* American Tract Society), this new type of organization during the previous decade had spread to temperance, prison reform^qqv and similar moral causes. By 1830 it had become a major force in the American scene.

Though each cause was organized separately as a national society, the whole movement was administered through interlocking directorates by a relatively small number of philanthropists and clergymen, who were regularly re-elected at annual conventions of delegates from the nation, which met in New York each May. Between conventions, the societies propagandized their reforms through tracts and weekly newspapers, and through traveling agents (*see* Antislavery Literature). Among the ruling philanthropists, the most influential were the brothers Arthur and Lewis Tappan, wealthy New York merchants;

and among the agents, incomparably the most eloquent and successful was Theodore Weld.

This whole movement was copied slavishly, in some cases even as to names, from like organizations in Great Britain. It was to be expected, therefore, that shortly after British philanthropists started a parliamentary drive, in 1830, for the immediate abolition of slavery in the West Indies (*see* Immediatism), the Tappans should organize a similar movement here. In June, 1831, they published plans for an American Anti-Slavery Society[qv]; during the next two years they laid its foundations throughout the North; and in December, 1833, they launched it at Philadelphia.

During its first two years, the Society's drive against slavery, in the form of a monster pamphlet[qv] campaign, met with little but hostility. This was largely because the pamphlets advocated immediate emancipation, which was everywhere interpreted as meaning "to turn the slave loose, regardless of consequences." Actually, the "watchword" of immediate emancipation was adopted in order to identify the American with the British movement; and the phrase was officially defined as meaning merely that "measures looking toward ultimate emancipation be immediately begun." But the failure of the pamphlet campaign clearly showed, as Channing, New England liberal, remarked, that "it is a fatal mistake for a party to choose a watchword which almost certainly conveys a wrong sense and needs explanation."

Meanwhile, however, Theodore Weld, at Lane Seminary in Cincinnati, at Oberlin and in New York, had been training a corps of agents in a new technique of antislavery agitation, revivalistic in character and essentially religious in its appeal. So successful were they that in 1836 the national society abandoned its pamphlet drive, and took over their support. During the remainder of the decade these new agents converted whole communities to the duty of denouncing slavery as a sin. (*See* Proslavery.)

The chief activity of these new converts was securing signatures from their neighbors on petitions to Congress for antislavery objects. The fact that Southern Congressmen opposed their reception in the House made petitions a prime means of propaganda; and when John Quincy Adams championed their cause in Congress, the question of their reception became a national issue (*see* Petitions, Antislavery). More and more of the efforts and resources of the converts went into local petition campaigns; and the national society, thus deprived of funds and functions, withered away. In 1840 it ceased in all but name.

Two years later, antislavery sentiment in districts converted by Weld's agents had become so strong that their representatives in Congress, led by Joshua Giddings, decided to break with the party program and attack slavery systematically upon the floor of the House. Under Weld's guidance—he was now in Washington—they succeeded, and thereby established still another type of antislavery organization, an insurgent bloc[qv] in Congress.

Though the insurgents' program in Congress was determined largely by the course of public events, they furthered systematic propaganda by means of a weekly newspaper, *The National Era*, which was established in Washington with Lewis Tappan's aid. Through its columns they directed antislavery workers in the field, and published effective tracts and documents. Here first appeared the greatest tract of the movement, *Uncle Tom's Cabin*[qv].

As the number of insurgents increased, friction with party leaders grew intolerable. The time inevitably came when they broke with their parties and established the final form of antislavery organization, first as the Free Soil party[qv], then as the antislavery wing of the Republican party[qv].

[G. H. Barnes, *The Antislavery Impulse*, 1830-44; F. J. Klingberg, *The Antislavery Movement in England.*]

GILBERT HOBBS BARNES

Antisuffragists, those opposed to suffrage for women. The first antisuffrage group was organized by women in Washington in 1871. Other groups were formed in Eastern states from time to time but the movement made little progress in the West. In 1911 women organized The National Association Opposed to Woman Suffrage and in 1913 the Men's Antisuffrage Association was organized in New York. The organizations disappeared with the ratification of the Nineteenth Amendment[qv] in 1920. (*See also* Woman Suffrage.)

[Ida Husted Harper, *History of Woman Suffrage*, Vol. V.]

HALLIE FARMER

Antisyndicalist Laws. Beginning with Idaho in 1917, criminal syndicalism laws have been passed in twenty-one states and two territories. These laws define criminal syndicalism[qv] as "the doctrine which advocates crime, sabotage, violence, or other unlawful methods of terrorism as a means of accomplishing industrial and political reform." The immediate cause of such legislation was the activity of the Industrial Workers of the World[qv], which advocated sabotage and other forms of direct action among the miners, lumber workers and agricultural laborers of the West and Northwest. During the period of the

World War obstruction by the I. W. W. was greatly feared. Following the war, considerable hysteria developed as a result of the organization of the Communist party[qv] of America. Antisyndicalist laws represented an attempt to suppress all subversive[qv] activities. Under these laws criminal syndicalism is a felony. State supreme courts have upheld these statutes and the United States Supreme Court has approved them as valid exercise of police power[qv]. Reversal of sentences by higher state courts has been common, and state executives have issued numerous pardons.

[P. F. Brissenden, *The I.W.W.: a Study in American Syndicalism.*]

GORDON S. WATKINS

Antitrust Laws. The industrial life in the United States started under a regime of *laissez faire*[qv] and, for many years, no attempt was made to regulate business of any kind. The rapid growth of population, the introduction of the factory system with large-scale production, the development of the corporate form of business organization, the extension of transportation systems and protection from foreign competition all contributed to the growth of what has generally come to be known as the trust[qqv]. In reality it has taken many forms, such as the trust proper, in which the shares of stock of several independent firms are placed in the hands of a trustee who manages the business for the good of the group; the holding company[qv], in which the parent company owns a controlling interest in subsidiary companies; the merger, in which the actual properties of former companies are consolidated into one business; and the trade agreement, in which several firms reach an agreement as to the business practices which they will follow. In the formation of these big businesses many unfair practices were used, such as cutthroat competition, rebates and repression of patents. The public reaction to such practices, together with the antagonism to the monopolies[qv] which resulted, led to the demand for regulation.

The Sherman Antitrust Act[qv], passed in 1890, was the first formal result of the demand for regulation. This declared all combinations in restraint of trade[qv] to be illegal and penalties were provided for violation. Because of the extreme provisions of the act, little was done in the way of its enforcement and the Supreme Court adopted the "rule of reason"[qv] in 1911. Under this the decree was set forth that the act applied only to those combinations in business which resulted in unreasonable restraints upon trade. Throughout these years of inactivity the trust movement grew rapidly.

The failure of the Sherman Act to accomplish satisfactory regulation resulted in the passage of the Clayton Act and the Federal Trade Commission Act[qqv] in 1914. These acts recognize that combinations in themselves are not necessarily evil, but that certain practices should be prohibited. The Clayton Act prohibited certain types of price discriminations and the use of tying contracts; regulations were placed upon the use of the holding company; under certain conditions, one person was not allowed to be a director in two or more companies engaged in commerce; and directors in corporations were to be held personally liable for illegal activities. The work of the Federal Trade Commission is that of investigation of business practices to the end that unfair competition may be prevented. It does not have final jurisdiction but can press its charges before the courts. It often acts, moreover, in an advisory capacity as to the legality of contemplated business practices.

The National Industrial Recovery Act[qv] was passed in 1933. Under this, codes were drawn for different industries which set forth the type of combination and business practices which each expected to use. Much dissatisfaction arose over the codes and many modifications would have had to be made had not the Supreme Court declared the act unconstitutional. At present (1939) the legislation of 1914 prevails although legislation has granted immunity from its application to certain types of business. In general, the present attitude is to recognize the possible advantages of big business, but to set up standards of conduct and to see that they are enforced.

[Gemmill and Blodgett, *Economics.*]

MERLIN H. HUNTER

Anza Expedition, THE (Oct. 23, 1775–Jan. 4, 1776), was sent out by Antonio Bucareli, Viceroy of New Spain, to provide Alta California[qv] with the white population essential to its occupation in face of English and Russian threats. Led by Juan Bautista de Anza, who in 1774 had proved that a route existed from Sonora to California, 244 persons crossed the Colorado desert and reached San Gabriel. Local jealousies prevented Anza from founding the city he laid out but his capable lieutenant, José Joaquin Moraga, Sept. 17, 1776, dedicated a presidio[qv] on the site of modern San Francisco and there, Oct. 9, 1776, was started the mission San Francisco de Asís.

[H. E. Bolton, *Anza's California Expeditions.*]

OSGOOD HARDY

Apache, Fort, Incident at (Sept. 13, 1886). Chiricahua and Mimbreno Apaches living near Fort Apache were believed aiding hostile bands in the summer of 1886. September 13, Col. J. F. Wade summoned the Apaches^qv^ to the fort, for counting, surrounded them with troops and shipped them wholesale to Fort Marion, Fla., to be interned.

[Nelson A. Miles, *Personal Recollections.*]

PAUL I. WELLMAN

Apache, THE, was a name applied to a number of banded warlike tribes in New Mexico, Arizona and west Texas, belonging to the Athapascan family. After the Spanish conquest the tribes increased and extended into northern Mexico. From their homes in the mountains they raided Mexicans and Americans alike, and became notoriously expert at hiding, trailing, ambushing and shooting. Apache campaigns were bloody and prolonged. Some bands were practically exterminated before they surrendered and the name has become synonymous with treachery and cruelty. F. W. Hodge believes some of their later hostilities were due to mismanagement. Their famous chiefs were Cochise^qv^, Victorio and Geronimo^qv^. The Chiricahua tribe held out longest; Geronimo was not captured until 1886, and a few bands were still at large in 1900.

[F. W. Hodge, *Handbook of American Indians.*]

CARL L. CANNON

Apache Pass Expedition (Feb. 4–23, 1861). Cochise, a chief of the Chiricahua Apaches, was arrested Feb. 5, 1861, by Lt. George N. Bascom, 7th Infantry, on an unproved charge of having captured a boy. He escaped, led attacks on a nearby stage station and on a wagon train, captured three men and offered to exchange one of his prisoners for Indians held by Bascom. Bascom demanded all three. On his way to Bascom's relief, Asst. Surgeon B. J. D. Irwin captured three Indians. It was later learned that Cochise had killed his prisoners, and six Indians were hanged in retaliation. This incident was the reputed origin of the long warfare (1861–74) against Cochise.

[Don Russell, in *Winners of the West,* December, 1936.]

DON RUSSELL

Apalache Massacre, THE (1704), was an episode in Queen Anne's War^qv^. Having failed to take St. Augustine, Fla. (1702), ex-Gov. James Moore of Carolina with 50 Englishmen and 1000 Indians invaded the Apalache district in western Florida, defeating Capt. Mexia's force of 30 Spaniards and 400 Apalaches, destroying all (i.e., 13) but one of the Franciscan^qv^ mission settlements and carrying off considerable loot including about 1400 Christian Indians.

[J. T. Lanning, *The Spanish Missions of Georgia.*]

FRANCIS BORGIA STECK

Apartment Houses. The word apartment has only recently come into its present use. In England it means a house let to tenants or lodgers. In the United States it is difficult to distinguish between apartments and tenements^qv^. In New England any house or apartment rented is called a tenement. The usual definition of an apartment is a division of a building designed to be used by an individual or a group of individuals living together. An apartment is usually of better construction, pays higher rentals and if over three stories is equipped with elevator^qv^.

The apartment has come into use in the United States within the last thirty-five years and prevails mainly in large cities where land values are high and congestion of population prevails. Families desiring to avoid the responsibilities connected with maintaining an individual home prefer apartments. The new methods of construction have made possible the building of large numbers of apartments on small lots and still provide light and air as well as many comforts.

There are no statistical figures which distinguish tenements from apartments. Nor is there a legal way of precise differentiation. Apartments being multifamily dwellings accommodating three or more families we can only present the conditions and trends regarding multifamily dwellings built within a certain period of time. In 255 of the largest cities of the country, of all dwellings built during 1921 only 24.42% were multiple dwellings while in 1928 the multifamily dwellings increased to 53.74% of all the dwellings built in that year. In the cities of the Middle Atlantic states the proportion of such construction increased from 35% in 1921 to 70% in 1928.

Families desiring to combine home ownership with the advantages of apartment house living bought co-operative apartments. There are (1938) about 200 such apartments in New York and many others throughout the country. In 1930 there were 3,615,379 families living in apartments or multifamily dwellings or 12.1% of all the families of the United States. The number is constantly growing.

The largest increase in multifamily dwellings has taken place in the cities of over 100,000 population, the great metropolitan centers and their suburbs and the cities between 25,000 and 50,000 population. The apartment hotel is a new development in the larger cities and embodies the advantages of an apartment with many of the services afforded by hotels.

[Reports of the Dodge Corporation; Coleman Woodbury, *Apartment House Increases and Attitudes Towards Ownership.*]

CAROL ARONOVICI

Apia, Disaster of. On March 16, 1889, one British, three American and three German warships were crowded into Apia Harbor, ready for hostilities due to the German attempt to set up a protectorate under a puppet native king. A hurricane swept in, destroying the German *Eber, Adler* and the *Olga,* with the loss of 134 men; the U. S. *Trenton* and the *Vandalia,* with a loss of fifty-two lives. The U. S. *Nipsic* was run ashore. The British *Calliope* escaped by steaming out to sea. The Berlin Conference followed, establishing for Samoa[qv] a tripartite government.

[G. H. Ryden, *The Foreign Policy of the United States in Relation to Samoa.*]

J. W. ELLISON

Apostolic Delegation, THE, was established in Washington, D. C., by Pope Leo XIII, Jan. 24, 1893. Archbishop Satolli, representative of the Holy See at the World's Columbian Exposition[qv], was appointed as the first Apostolic Delegate. Since an attempt to establish formal diplomatic relations with the United States had been prudently abandoned in 1837, Pope Leo XIII did not accredit the Apostolic Delegate to the Government, but to the Catholic Church in the United States.

[*Catholic Encyclopedia,* Vol. IX; *The Ecclesiastical Review,* December, 1936.]

T. E. HEWITT

Appalachian Mountains, As Boundary. *See* Proclamation of 1763, The; Quebec Act, The; Indian Barrier State (Proposed).

***Appam* Case,** 1917 (243 U. S. 124). On Jan. 15, 1916, a German cruiser captured the above named British merchantman on the high seas and took her into Hampton Roads, Va. There her British crew was released by order of the American Government and on February 16 the shipowner filed a libel in the proper United States District Court, which ultimately decreed restitution of ship and cargo. On appeal by the German government to the Supreme Court the decree was affirmed on the ground that the capture, being a prize[qv], of which the lower court had jurisdiction, the ship's detention in port was a breach of American neutrality, unauthorized by any treaty.

C. SUMNER LOBINGIER

Appeal of the Independent Democrats, THE, a manifesto issued in January, 1854, was inspired by the Kansas-Nebraska Bill[qv], then pending. The signers, led by Sen. Salmon P. Chase, were free soilers[qv]. Chase had tried to convert Northern Democrats into a Wilmot Proviso[qv] party. Now, by a master stroke, precisely timed, he helped to create the Republican party[qv]. The "Appeal" was sincere and effective, though it contained exaggerated statements and unsound prophecies relative to the possible influence of the Douglas measure on the spread of slavery.

[*Congressional Globe,* 33rd Congress, 1st Session, 281-282.]

WILLIAM O. LYNCH

Appeals from Colonial Courts. In the latter part of the 17th century the new colonial charters[qv], proprietary and royal, reserved for the King in Council the right to hear cases on appeal from provincial courts where the sum litigated exceeded £300 sterling. In the New England colonies particularly the appellate authority was at best grudgingly conceded, as the Connecticut and Rhode Island charters made no provision for judicial review. At times, as in the case of Frost v. Leighton (1739), an order of the Privy Council[qv] was deliberately ignored by the Massachusetts authorities. Pending appeals, executions of the colonial courts were suspended. Such appeals were both costly and protracted.

Through this appellate procedure the Privy Council sought to bring the legal systems of the colonies into conformity with that of England, particularly in such matters as the rules of evidence and the jury system. Major issues of colonial policy were reviewed in litigation brought on appeal, notably Indian relations, the colonial currency laws and intestate succession. Currency practices in the colonies were more generally dealt with by the Privy Council under its authority to disallow colonial legislation or by Parliament (*see* Royal Disallowance). In the suit of the Virginia clergy instituted to recover back salaries resulting from the disallowance of the "two penny act"[qv], the Council, in view of the constitutional storms raised by the Stamp Act[qv], was prompted by political considerations to dismiss the appeal on a technicality. In the notable case of Winthrop v. Lechmere the Council held the Connecticut custom of divisible descent of intestate estates[qv] invalid as contrary to the common law, but reversed itself in Clark v. Tousey and in the Massachusetts case of Phillips v. Savage, a great victory for egalitarian property concepts in New England.

[G. A. Washburne, *Imperial Control of the Administration of Justice in the Thirteen American Colonies;* R. B. Morris, *Studies in the History of American Law.*]

RICHARD B. MORRIS

Apple Culture. The apple *(Pyrus Malus)*, indigenous to southwestern Asia and adjacent Europe, thrives in temperate zones. Cultivated since the beginning of civilization, it is today the most important commercial pomological fruit. The world area in cultivated apples in 1932 was estimated at 6,940,000 acres, planted in about 415,000,000 trees, yielding a yearly average of 550,000,000 bushels. Thirty-five per cent of the world's acreage and crop is found in the United States.

Europe's best varieties were introduced in America by the early settlers. The French planted apples in Acadia and along the St. Lawrence about 300 years ago. The English and the Dutch introduced apples on the Atlantic seaboard as early as 1630. In Virginia, apples were grafted on wild stocks as early as 1647. In 1726 Chief Justice Dudley, of Massachusetts, wrote: "Our apples are, without doubt, as good as those of England, and fairer to look to." During the colonial period, Massachusetts, New York, Pennsylvania and Virginia grew quantities of apples for cider and for export as well. In 1790–91 the United States exported to England 12,352 barrels of apples, valued at $12,352. A number of new varieties were developed in America; in 1869 Charles Downing listed 1856 varieties.

Indians, traders, missionaries, settlers, carried the fruit to the frontier. Spanish missionaries planted apples in California in the 18th century. Apple culture in the Pacific Northwest was introduced in 1826, at Vancouver, Wash., by the Hudson's Bay Company. In 1847, Henderson Luelling brought his famous "traveling nursery" overland from Iowa. He established the first nursery in the Northwest, and introduced some of the best varieties of apples. During the gold rush, Oregon exported to California quantities of apples, which sold for as much as 75 cents to $5 each.

With the increase of population and adequate transportation facilities, the Pacific Coast and the entire country began to grow apples on a large scale. Practically every state grows apples; from twenty-five to forty states ship the fruit. The leading apple states in 1932 were: Washington, 30,960,000 bushels; New York, 22,197,000; Pennsylvania, 9,537,000; California, 9,045,000; Virginia, 7,830,000; Maine, 5,800,000; Ohio, 5,145,000; Oregon, 4,950,000; Idaho, 4,200,000; West Virginia, 4,191,000; New Jersey, 3,640,000; Massachusetts, 3,525,000. The apple industry, except on the Pacific Coast, is not as well organized as that of other fruits. It is confronted with severe competition on the domestic market and from tariff barriers abroad.

[L. H. Bailey, *The Standard Cyclopedia of Horticulture;* Bailey, *The Apples of New York.*]

J. W. ELLISON

Appleseed, Johnny. As the American frontier moved into Ohio, Indiana and Illinois, the settlers were deprived of fruit until orchards could be grown. Since the people lacked money, they could not have bought young trees were nurseries available; and horticulture languished. John Chapman therefore consecrated himself from 1801 to 1847 to the mission of bringing seed from Pennsylvania and planting flowers and fruits, especially apple seed in the forests to be ready for the free use of the settlers when they arrived. Meager documentary evidence and rich tradition have preserved Chapman's fame under the sobriquet of Johnny Appleseed.

[W. A. Duff, *Johnny Appleseed, an Ohio Hero;* Henry Chapin, *The Adventures of Johnny Appleseed; Kansas Horticultural Society Report*, 1922-23, pp. 137-40; *Harper's Magazine*, November, 1871, pp. 830-36.]

BLISS ISELY

Appointment, Council of. *See* Council of Appointment, New York, The.

Appointments and the Appointing Power. In the thirteen colonies appointment was a crown prerogative vested in the governor. In practice, however, the colonial assemblies[qv], in control of the purse, assumed the power of appointing the treasurer. In some colonies they came to control administration by appointing their own commissions of Indian affairs, intercolonial relations and military matters, even dictating the appointment and removal of military officers.

Long before the Revolution some legislatures were claiming the right to make all nominations by appropriating the salary not to the office but to a specified person. Independence removed virtually all restraint upon appointment by the legislature, even the governor being their appointee by all the first state constitutions except in Massachusetts and New York. By 1787 Americans generally thought of their executives as titular, political chiefs not properly concerned with administration and appointments.

The Federal Constitution[qv] departed radically from prevailing theory and practice in vesting the appointing power in the President[qv]. When the first Congress concluded that the Senate[qv] held no check on the President's power of removal[qv] his evolution into the administrative chief was inevitable.

Early Presidents made relatively few removals but the Four Years Law (1820) established a fixed term for numerous Federal officials. Taking advantage of consequent expirations President Jackson introduced (1829) rotation in office[qv] in order to democratize the official personnel by overthrowing the prevailing aristocracy of office holders. The practice rapidly degenerated into a vicious spoils system[qv] and persisted scarcely challenged until the Civil Service Reform[qv] movement secured passage of the Pendleton Act[qv] (1883) which authorized a classified list of Federal officials to be recruited on the basis of merit[qv].

In 1867 Congress had passed a Tenure of Office Act[qv] to prevent President Johnson from packing the civil service with appointees who might sabotage the congressional reconstruction program. It made each dismissal contingent upon the Senate's confirmation of a successor. Worsted in bitter controversies over dismissals by Presidents Hayes (1877–8) and Cleveland (1885), the Senate initiated a measure repealing (1887) the Tenure of Office Act.

In 1925 the Supreme Court in Myers v. U. S.[qv] (272 U. S. 106) confirmed the prevalent popular opinion that the President had unlimited power of dismissal of executive appointees, but in 1934 they modified their opinion in Humphrey's Executor v. U. S.[qv] (295 U. S. 602) by holding that he could dismiss members of a quasi legislative or quasi judicial agency[qv] such as the Federal Trade Commission[qv] only for reasons specified in the statute creating it.

[F. J. Goodnow, *Comparative Administrative Law.*]

W. E. BINKLEY

Appomattox, former courthouse (county seat) of the county of the same name in Virginia, and scene of the surrender of the Confederate Army of Northern Virginia to the Union Army of the Potomac[qqv], April 9, 1865, is twenty miles ESE. of Lynchburg. Gen. R. E. Lee, commanding the Confederate forces which evacuated Petersburg and Richmond[qqv] on the night of April 2–3, had planned to withdraw into North Carolina, via Danville, and to join Gen. Joseph E. Johnston; but on the third day of retreat, Lee found the Federals across his front at Jetersville, on the Richmond and Danville Railroad. As he was dependent on the railways for supplies, he determined to move westward across country to the Southside Railroad at Farmville, where he hoped to procure rations for a march to Lynchburg. Thence he would turn south again toward Danville. En route to Farmville, Lee was attacked heavily on April 6, at Sayler's (Sailor's) Creek[qv], where he lost about 6000 men. The next day at Farmville he was again assailed before he could victual all his troops. By that time, long marches without food had so depleted the Confederate ranks that Gen. Grant addressed Lee a proposal for the surrender of the army. Lee did not consider the situation altogether hopeless and pushed on toward Lynchburg by the Richmond Stage Road. When the army bivouacked around Appomattox Courthouse on the evening of April 8, the reflection of Federal campfires against the clouds showed that the surviving Confederates, now reduced to two small corps, were surrounded on three sides. Lee closed his column and prepared to cut his way out, but, when he found the next morning that the corps of John B. Gordon faced impossible odds on the Stage Road, he sent a flag of truce to Gen. Grant. A suggestion that the army break into small bands and attempt to slip through the enveloping lines was rejected by Gen. Lee on the ground that it would carry a hopeless struggle into country that had escaped the ravages of war. After some delay in communicating with Gen. Grant, who had made his dispositions with the greatest skill, Lee rode, about 1 P.M., into the village and, at the house of Maj. Wilmer McLean, formally arranged the surrender of all forces then under arms in Virginia. Gen. Grant's generous terms, which allowed officers to retain their side arms and provided for the parole of all surrendered troops, were executed with the least humiliation to the defeated army. A full day's rations were issued the prisoners of war. When the troops marched into an open field to lay down their weapons and their flags, April 12, the Federal guard presented arms. The number of Confederate infantrymen surrendered at Appomattox with arms in their hands was 7892; the total number of troops paroled was 28,231. In an interview with Lee on April 10, Grant sought to prevail on the Confederate commander to advise that all the remaining Confederate troops cease resistance, but Lee insisted that this was a question to be decided by the civil authorities.

[U. S. Grant, *Personal Memoirs*, Vol. 2; *Battles and Leaders of the Civil War*, Vol. 4; D. S. Freeman, *R. E. Lee*, Vol. 4.]

DOUGLAS SOUTHALL FREEMAN

Apportionment, Constitutional, signifies the distribution of legislative membership among established units of government, usually allocated with more or less exactness upon an equality of population. The Federal Constitution[qv] requires that representatives be apportioned among the several states according to population. Since 1842, they have been chosen in single member districts (*see* District, Congressional); the boundaries of these districts are fixed by state law. In the Senate[qv], the equality of states is a constituent element of American federalism. The result is greatly to overrepresent the agricultural sections of the country. The practice in respect to state legislative apportionment has been largely conditioned by the democratic idea of equality, which holds that representatives should be allocated among districts containing substantially an equal number of persons. The application of this theory, in earlier days, was reasonably satisfactory, as many counties and towns were equal in population and similar in interest. The basis of representation[qv] in the lower house of the legislature is usually the county. In simplest form, each county is a separated district with one representative. The town is the basis of representation in New England; the ancient practice survives of allowing each town, regardless of size, at least one representative. The upper house of the legislature is formed by a grouping of counties or by a division of the more populous ones into districts, with approximately equal population. In municipal government[qv], the ward was, for many years, the unit of representation, with one or two aldermen from each ward. The modern types of city government provide, however, for election-at-large of the municipal legislative body.

Periodic reapportionment for the House of Representatives[qv] is made after each census[qv]. Provision is made in most state constitutions[qv] for legislative reapportionment every ten years. Constitutional provisions in respect to this practice are mandatory in form, but no effective method exists to force a legislature to act if it does not wish to do so. The continuation of existing apportionment results; this often perpetuates a very unequal arrangement. Should the legislature fail to act, apportionment by state executive or by local officials is authorized in several states. Although emphasis upon a mathematically accurate population distribution of seats may be exaggerated, where counties or towns are given equality of representation, regardless of population, or where a limitation is placed on the number of representatives from one county, the basis of apportionment is decidedly unfair. Rural sections thus become overrepresented and extreme discrimination exists against urban areas. The legislative gerrymander[qv] develops various forms of discrimination, partisan, sectional or rural and urban in character. In application, therefore, a conflict often occurs in the theories of territorial representation and of population representation, with results thoroughly inconsistent with American principles of government.

[W. Anderson, *American City Government;* W. F. Dodd, *State Government*, 2nd Ed.]

THOMAS S. BARCLAY

Apprenticeship. A system by which a youth bound himself to a master workman for a period of years in exchange for maintenance and training in a craft. Known in ancient times, it was elaborated by the mediæval guilds. The general principles of an English act of 1562, defining the relations of master and apprentice, were adopted in the American colonies, where both voluntary and compulsory apprenticeship existed. In the latter case, poor children were bound out to masters for support and trade-training. Massachusetts Bay by a General Court Order (1642) required all masters to teach apprentices to read, as well as the principles of religion. This was the first compulsory education law in America, and was followed by similar enactments in Connecticut (1650), New Haven (1655) and New Plymouth (1671). It was extended to New York by the Duke of York's Laws[qv] of 1665.

The privileges and duties of master and apprentice were defined in a form of contract called an "indenture" (*see* Indentured Servants). During the 19th century the system gradually receded with the advance of machinery, factories and technical schools. It still continues in some degree, however, in certain skilled trades, as well as in trade-union regulations.

[R. A. Bray, *Boy Labour and Apprenticeship;* R. F. Seybolt, *Apprenticeship and Apprenticeship Education in Colonial New England and New York;* Samuel McKee, *Labor in Colonial New York.*]

RALPH FOSTER WELD

Appropriations by Congress. The Constitution gives Congress exclusive control over the public purse, the only limitations being restriction of army appropriations to a two-year period and the veto power[qv] of the President. The latter, however, is ineffective since it can be exercised only in regard to an entire bill.

Appropriations fall under three heads—permanently specific, permanent and annual. Theoretically the bulk of appropriations is of the last type, to insure close control of expenditures; but in practice many fall ouside this category. Permanent specific appropriations (rivers and harbors, public buildings, fortifications, etc.) are available until the amount provided is exhausted. Permanent appropriations (interest and sinking-fund charges, judicial salaries, etc.) continue annually until the authorizing act is repealed. Deficiency bills*qv* provide additional funds whenever appropriations prove inadequate.

Although there is no constitutional provision to the effect, it has been customary for such bills to originate in the House of Representatives. The Senate in 1856 unsuccessfully attempted to share this function. The first appropriation bill (1780), prepared by the House sitting as the Committee of the Whole*qv*, was thirteen lines in length and covered four items. To take financial leadership away from the Treasury where it had largely rested during Hamilton's secretaryship, the Committee on Ways and Means*qv* was established (1796) and given power to prepare and introduce financial measures. This group was superseded by the Committee on Appropriations in 1865. Thereafter special appropriation committees were appointed from time to time until finally (1880) eight additional committees were submitting appropriation legislation. Since there were by this time fourteen regular bills containing hundreds of items each, the division of authority and responsibility encouraged logrolling, pork-barrel*qqv* legislation, inconsistency and waste. This condition was furthered by Congressional insistence that its appropriations were mandatory, that the Government was required to spend the full amount of any fund provided, and that unexpended balances could not be shifted to other uses. The situation called for revision and reform, so in 1911 a commission was appointed to consider the advisability of a national budget. In spite of a favorable report the Budget and Accounting Act*qv* was not passed until 1921. This authorized the President, assisted by the Bureau of the Budget, to prepare and submit an annual budget to Congress. While acceptance of these estimates is optional, Congress in its appropriations has adhered rather closely to them. Congress has thus retained its final authority over expenditures while control has been unified and estimates based on demonstrated need.

[D. S. Alexander, *History and Procedure of the House of Representatives;* C. G. Haines and B. M. Haines, *Principles and Problems of Government;* D. R. Dewey, *Financial History of the United States.*]

W. B. LOCKLING

Aqueducts. Of both types of aqueducts—those carrying canals across streams and gorges and those supplying water to cities—America has constructed some notable specimens. On the many canals*qv* built in the United States before 1850 there were some fine stone-arched aqueducts, such as those by which the Erie*qv* crossed the Genesee River at Rochester and the Mohawk at Little Falls, the Morris Canal's*qv* crossing of the Passaic River and the Chesapeake and Ohio's*qv* over the Monocacy. Many canal aqueducts, however, were just huge, leaky wooden troughs supported by stone piers and wooden trusses or—in the case of two on the Delaware and Hudson*qv*—supported by cables; in effect, suspension bridges*qv*. Nearly all of these structures of both types have passed out of existence.

The first public water supply*qv* for cities, around the beginning of the 19th century, was obtained from wells*qv* or near-by streams. New York City in 1837–43 built the first great aqueduct in America for this purpose, a masonry conduit bringing 72,000,000 gallons daily from the Croton River, forty-one miles distant. A new Croton aqueduct was built in 1885–90—nearly all tunnel, well-nigh an air line, and only 30.87 miles long. At the time of construction, it was our greatest engineering feat. Both these were surpassed by the Catskill aqueduct, opened in 1917, which has its head in the Ashokan Reservoir, ninety-two and one-half miles from the city. It passes under the Hudson River by an inverted siphon which descends to 1100 feet below the surface of the water. The Los Angeles aqueduct, built 1908–13, is the longest in existence, bringing 259,000,000 gallons daily from the Owens River, 235 miles distant. For a quarter century after 1910, San Francisco toiled at completing the great aqueduct which conveys its water from the Hetch-Hetchy Valley, 168 miles distant.

ALVIN F. HARLOW

Aquidneck Island. An Indian name for Rhode Island*qv*, the largest of the islands in Narragansett Bay. The island's purchase from the Narragansett sachems was witnessed by Roger Williams on March 24, 1638.

[S. G. Arnold, *History of Rhode Island.*]

ARTHUR R. BLESSING

Arabian Gold in our colonies (after 1685)—mostly *pagodas,* from the India pagodas on their reverse side, or gold *mohurs* of India or Persia—was captured by our colonial pirates from Arabian or Indian ships in the Arabian Sea. New York merchants got much more by trading with the Madagascar pirates; and these "Arabian" gold coins were common in New York, Philadelphia and Rhode Island in 1690. Private Avery in 1698 brought his huge "Arabian" loot to the West Indies, whence our colonies got their supply of specie.

[F. W. Clarke, *Weights, Measures and Money of All Nations;* Charles J. Bullock, *The Monetary History of the United States;* George Francis Dow and John Henry Edmonds, *The Pirates of the New England Coast;* John Harris, *Collection of Voyages.*]

GEORGE WYCHERLEY

***Arabic* Case.** On Aug. 19, 1915, a German submarine torpedoed without warning the British White Star passenger liner, *Arabic,* with the loss of two United States citizens. This attack occurred soon after the exchanges of notes that followed the torpedoing similarly of the *Lusitania*[qv], in which the United States had insisted that the lives of noncombatants could not lawfully be put in jeopardy by the capture or destruction of unresisting merchantmen. The German act indicated that it was still uncertain whether Germany had accepted the American position. After seeking to justify the attack on the ground that the *Arabic* was attempting to ram the submarine, the German government disavowed the act and offered indemnity. Claims of United States citizens arising out of this and similar cases were eventually adjudicated by the Mixed Claims Commission, United States and Germany, following the war between the two nations. (*See also* World War.)

[*Foreign Relations of the United States, 1915 Supplement.*]

SAMUEL FLAGG BEMIS

Aranda Memorial, THE, was a statement said to have been presented by Pedro Pablo Abarca de Bolea, Count of Aranda, to Charles III of Spain in 1783 or 1784. In the Memorial appear statements of regret that Spain and France entered the war in behalf of the American colonies. It contains a striking prediction that the new "federated republic" will become an "irresistible colossus" endangering Spain's possession. Hence the author suggested that new kingdoms, bound to Spain by marriage and commercial ties, be created from the Spanish colonies. By some historians Aranda's authorship of the Memorial has been questioned.

[Arthur P. Whitaker, The Pseudo-Aranda Memoir of 1783, in *The Hispanic American Historical Review,* August, 1937; Almon R. Wright, The Aranda Memorial, Genuine or Forged, *ibid.,* November, 1938.]

ALMON R. WRIGHT

Aranjuez, The Convention of (April 12, 1779), provided for the entrance of Spain, as an ally of France, into the war against Great Britain (*see* Revolution, American), in case Great Britain should reject (which she did) Spain's impossibly intrusive offer of mediation. Spain and France made a pact to fight the war jointly, and not to negotiate peace separately, and in any peace Gibraltar was to go to Spain. Other desirable acquisitions were stipulated for both allies out of anticipated conquests from Great Britain.

[Samuel Flagg Bemis, *Diplomacy of the American Revolution.*]

SAMUEL FLAGG BEMIS

Arapaho, THE, a large and important plains tribe, and a branch of the Algonquin[qv] family, ranged from the head of the North Platte River to the Arkansas, when first encountered by the whites. Formerly they lived, according to tradition, east of the Missouri, probably in Minnesota. In warfare they associated themselves with the Cheyenne[qv] who were good fighters with a strong tribal organization and culture. Most white observers of the 1850's and 1860's found the Arapaho dirty, lazy and immoral to a degree. In war they were formidable enemies, especially under Cheyenne leadership, but they were more friendly and hospitable than their allies in times of peace. Some members of the tribe participated in the Fort Fetterman fight, raids in western Kansas, the Beecher Island fight, the Washita massacre, and a few were in the Custer fight on the Little Big Horn[qqv]. They attended the Medicine Lodge Treaty of 1867[qv] at which it was proposed to move them south of the Arkansas. In early days the Santa Fé trade[qv] was greatly harassed by raids from this tribe.

[F. W. Hodge, *Handbook of the American Indians;* G. B. Grinnell, *Fighting Cheyennes.*]

CARL L. CANNON

Arbella, THE, was flagship of the "Winthrop Fleet" on which, between April 8 and June 12, 1630, Gov. Winthrop, other members of the Company and Puritan emigrants transported themselves and the Charter of the Massachusetts Bay Company[qv] from England to Salem, thereby giving legal birth to the commonwealth of Massachusetts. (*See* Great Migration.)

[*Winthrop's Journal;* C. M. Andrews, *The Colonial Period of American History.*]

RAYMOND P. STEARNS

Arbitration, Commercial. The Charter of the New York Chamber of Commerce (1768) provided that the body could arbitrate business disputes. Its first arbitration plan failed because there was no method of enforcement; the second and third plans undertook too much. The fourth attempt profited by previous experiences and incorporated features from European commercial courts, stock exchanges, trading bodies and other organizations. This plan has become a model for such undertakings in this country. In the meantime, commercial arbitration was started by the Philadelphia Chamber of Commerce in 1801, the Boston Chamber of Commerce in 1836, the Boston Board of Trade in 1854, and by other bodies in Memphis, New Orleans, Chicago, Baltimore, St. Louis, Cincinnati, Indianapolis and elsewhere. When a dispute arises, a board selected from a list of arbitrators, with representatives of the disputants, hears evidence and renders a decision, which the parties have agreed in advance to respect. The award is set aside only because of fraud, corruption, misconduct or the exceeding of power by the arbitrators. Otherwise, it is adhered to as scrupulously as a court decision. The plan is generally regarded as an economical and effective substitute for litigation in commercial disputes.

[William George Bruce, *Commercial Organizations.*]

PAUL T. CHERINGTON

Arbitration, Industrial. Disputes between employers and employees are usually settled by joint conference under the terms of a trade agreement, mediation, conciliation*qv*, voluntary arbitration, compulsory investigation or compulsory arbitration.

Conciliation and mediation are essentially the same process. Mediation takes place when an outside person or agency intercedes to suggest a peaceable settlement. Conciliation usually takes the form of a joint conference of the representatives of the disputants, according to the terms of a trade agreement, but it may be the result of the good offices of an outsider. Arbitration may be voluntary or compulsory, depending upon whether or not the submission of the dispute to settlement is required by law.

Mediation, conciliation and voluntary arbitration are the predominant methods of settling labor disputes in the United States. The most important agency of mediation and conciliation here is the Conciliation Service of the United States Department of Labor, established March 4, 1913. State conciliation and mediation agencies have been relatively unimportant.

Most states provide for voluntary arbitration, but in this field also Federal agencies have been much more important. In peace times the latter have been developed largely in one industry—railroading. The settlement of labor disputes in this industry has been provided for under the terms of a series of significant laws including the Act of 1888, the Erdman Act of 1898, the Newlands Act of 1913, the Esch-Cummins Transportation Act of 1920*qv* and the Watson-Parker Act of 1926 (*see* Railroad Mediation Acts). Under the last-named law collective bargaining*qv* is recognized and a comprehensive system of adjustment is created. Temporary regional bipartisan Boards of Adjustment are established to encourage settlement of disputes by the parties themselves. Cases not settled by the Boards of Adjustment go to the Board of Mediation, which is composed of five salaried members appointed by the President of the United States and removable by him for cause. Although conciliation is stressed, voluntary arbitration is provided for. By consent of the disputants the controversy may be submitted to Boards of Arbitration created for each case and consisting of from three to six men, depending upon the decision of the parties. If either party protests the award, the case is argued in a circuit court the decision of which is final unless the disputants agree to modification. The act also provides that if the permanent Board of Mediation fails to conciliate the parties or to secure arbitration it must notify the President that an emergency exists which threatens disruption of interstate commerce. The President may, if he deems it necessary, appoint an Emergency Board of Investigation which has compulsory fact-finding powers and reports to him within thirty days. From the time such a board is created no strike, lockout*qqv* or change of condition in employment may take place for sixty days. The President may publicize the findings, if he sees fit, but they are not binding on the disputants after the specified time limit expires.

Compulsory investigation was first given prominence in the United States in 1915, when Colorado passed a law patterned after the Canadian Industrial Disputes Investigation Act of 1907. Under the Colorado Act the Industrial Commission is empowered to settle disputes in "public interest" industries through compulsory investigation of facts. Strikes and lockouts are prohibited for thirty days, the findings may be publicized, and public opinion is relied upon to force compliance with the findings of the commission. This act has been less successful than the Canadian law, but it has contributed to the growth of conciliation and peace. Many other states have statutes providing for compulsory investigation, but they have not been successfully executed.

Compulsory arbitration with compulsory acceptance of the award has been attempted seriously by only one state. In 1920 Kansas created a Court of Industrial Relations consisting of three judges appointed for three years by the governor. In all industries "affected with a public interest" lockouts, strikes, boycotts, picketing*qqv* and other methods of industrial warfare were prohibited. The court could require the submission of evidence and render a decision concerning wages, hours, working conditions, working rules and similar matters. The criteria established to guide the action of the court involved a "fair" wage and healthful employment conditions for employees, "fair" profits for employers, and "fair" prices for consumers. Any enterprise under its jurisdiction could be taken over and operated by the court, if necessary. The orders of the court were to be effective for at least sixty days, at the end of which time employers or employees could appeal for a rehearing either before the Industrial Court or the Supreme Court of Kansas. Unless the award was modified after examination of the new evidence, it was binding upon both parties. A fine of not more than $1000 or imprisonment of not more than one year, or both, was imposed on individuals guilty of willful disobedience of the court's orders; a fine of $5000 or imprisonment of two years, or both, was imposed on officers of unions and corporations or employers' associations guilty of instigating violations. Some parts of the act were declared unconstitutional by the United States Supreme Court, and continued opposition by employers and employees caused the legislature in 1925 to abolish the court and transfer its functions to the Public Service Commission, which has never exercised them. While the act still is on the statute books it is practically a dead letter.

[J. R. Commons and J. B. Andrews, *Principles of Labor Legislation;* International Labour Office, *The Conciliation and Arbitration of Industrial Disputes;* D. A. McCabe and G. E. Barnett, *Mediation, Investigation, and Arbitration in Industrial Disputes;* U. S. Bureau of Labor Statistics, Bulletin 322, *Kansas Court of Industrial Relations.*]

GORDON S. WATKINS

Arbitration, International, may be defined in general terms as the submission of a controversy to persons not parties to the dispute with the understanding that the decision of the arbitrators shall be regarded as final. It involves, therefore, a controversy which it has not been possible to settle by direct negotiation; the creation of a special tribunal to decide the dispute; an understanding in respect to the precise issues to be arbitrated; determination of the procedure to be followed; and in some cases an agreement upon the special rules of law to be applied to the decision of the case. In recent years arbitration has come to be distinguished from "judicial settlement" which is a similar reference of a controversy to a permanent court rather than to a tribunal constituted for the particular case.

The history of arbitration in modern times may be said to begin with the Jay Treaty[qv] of 1794 by which the United States and Great Britain agreed to submit to arbitration three groups of disputes arising from the terms of the Definitive Treaty of Peace[qv], 1783. While the arbitrations carried out in pursuance of the terms of the Jay Treaty could not all be described as successful, yet the precedent of recourse to arbitration was established, and the United States continued during the 19th century the policy of arbitrating disputes which seemed susceptible of settlement by that procedure. The successful arbitration of the Alabama Claims[qv] dispute not only strengthened the United States in its faith in the procedure of arbitration, but it had a wide influence in impressing upon other nations the possibility of the peaceful settlement of disputes by that method. Again in 1892 the United States and Great Britain agreed to arbitrate the Bering Sea seal fisheries dispute[qv], the results of which, while not immediately successful, led ultimately to a constructive solution of the problem of protecting the fisheries. Following the creation of the Hague Permanent Court of Arbitration[qv] a number of disputes were arbitrated by tribunals constituted by selection from the general list of the court, the most important of which were the Mexican Pious Fund Case[qv] and the North Atlantic Coast Fisheries Case. The recent arbitration of the *I'm Alone* Case[qv] was before a mixed commission[qv] of two members.

Side by side with the actual practice of arbitration has been the growth of an elaborate series of agreements looking to the arbitration of future disputes. As early as 1848, in the Treaty of Guadalupe Hidalgo[qv], the United States agreed with Mexico that if any disagreement should thereafter arise between them they would endeavor to settle it by peaceful negotiations and that, if these should fail, then "by the arbitration of commissioners appointed on each side," unless this procedure were incompatible with the nature of the difference or the circumstances of the case.

By the close of the 19th century numerous treaties of "general arbitration," as distinct from the arbitration of specific disputes, were entered into among the Latin American states. This movement received an additional impulse from the adoption at the Hague Peace Conference of 1899[qv] of a broad provision recognizing that in questions of a legal nature and in the interpretation and application of treaties arbitration was the most effective and equitable means of settling disputes which diplomacy had failed to settle. In 1903 Great Britain and France concluded a general treaty which served as a model for numerous subsequent treaties. The chief problem presented by treaties of this general character was that, since it was impossible to foresee what particular disputes might arise in the future, it was necessary to qualify them so as to leave loopholes of escape from the obligation in case a dispute arose which one of the parties would not be willing to arbitrate. In the so-called Root Treaties of 1908[q.v.] the United States agreed with the other contracting parties that differences which might arise of a legal nature or relating to the interpretation of treaties should be referred to the Hague Permanent Court of Arbitration, "provided, nevertheless, that they do not affect the vital interests, the independence, or the honor of the two contracting states and do not concern the interests of third parties." Three years later President Taft sought to conclude a new series of arbitration treaties in which the obligation to arbitrate was made to extend to "justiciable" disputes, which were defined as disputes susceptible of decision by the application of the principles of law or equity. These treaties failed of ratification because the President objected to a reservation entered by the Senate which would have made it necessary for the President to submit to the Senate in each particular case the question whether the character of the dispute came within the terms of the treaty.

In view of the difficulties met with by President Taft in the negotiation of an arbitration treaty along more liberal lines than the Root Treaties of 1908, Secretary Bryan undertook in 1913–15 to negotiate a series of treaties designated as Treaties for the Advancement of Peace (*see* Bryan Treaty Model). These treaties were phrased so as to cover all disputes not otherwise settled by negotiation; but instead of providing for arbitration, which would have necessitated exceptions and qualifications, they called for the submission of the dispute to a permanent international commission for "investigation and report."

At the close of the World War the United States took part in the formulation of the Covenant of the League of Nations[q.v.], Article XIII of which provided for the submission to arbitration of any dispute which the members of the League might recognize as being "suitable for submission to arbitration." The alternative to arbitration was the submission of the dispute to "inquiry" by the Council of the League. Four groups of disputes were enumerated as "generally suitable" for submission to arbitration. A subsequent amendment to this article offered the alternative of submission of the dispute to "judicial settlement." In the succeeding years it became the custom, in the conclusion of peace treaties such as those signed at Locarno[q.v.] in 1925, to tie up provisions for arbitration with provisions for conciliation and for judicial settlement, leaving to the parties the option of one or other of those methods of peaceful settlement. In the Briand-Kellogg Pact[q.v.] the agreement merely recites that the contracting parties will never seek the settlement of disputes "except by pacific means."

In 1929 the General Treaty of Inter-American Arbitration was signed by representatives of all of the twenty-one American republics except Argentina. The treaty calls for the submission to arbitration of questions "juridical in their nature," and it specifies under that head the four groups of disputes enumerated in Article XIII of the Covenant of the League of Nations and in Article XXXVI of the Statute of the Permanent Court of International Justice. Two exceptions are entered: controversies within the "domestic jurisdiction" of the parties and controversies affecting states not parties to the treaty. The terms of this treaty were incorporated into the Convention to Co-ordinate Existing Treaties signed at Buenos Aires in 1936 (*see* Peace Conference at Buenos Aires, 1936).

Closely associated with the development of the obligation to arbitrate have been the various efforts to create a permanent international court before which disputes might be brought for settlement. Most of the arbitrations of the 19th century were held before mixed arbitration tribunals, composed as a rule of an equal number of judges chosen by each of the disputants, with an umpire chosen by agreement between the national judges. The umpire was thus made to carry the responsibility for the decision; while the tribunals themselves were ephemeral in character, so that their decisions had little weight as precedents. At the Hague Peace Conference of 1899 the Convention for the Pacific Settlement of International Disputes was signed, which created the Hague Permanent Court of Arbitration, consisting of a list of judges appointed by the signatory powers to the number of four each. From this list special tribunals of five judges were to be constituted when a case for arbitration arose. At the second Hague Conference of 1907 the United States delegation endeavored to bring about the establishment of a more permanent court, known as the Judicial Arbitration Court, which would sit continuously and build up a system of international jurisprudence in the form of precedents having something of the force of law. Due to the failure to agree upon the choice of judges the court never became a reality; but the draft convention providing for it had influence upon the Advisory Committee of Jurists which met at The Hague in 1920 and prepared the draft of the Statute of the Permanent Court of International Justice. Reference of a dispute to the Permanent Court is described as "judicial settlement" as distinct from "arbitration"; and the court renders a "decision" as distinct from an arbitral "award."

[J. B. Moore, *A History and Digest of the International Arbitrations to which the United States has been a Party, 1898; International Adjudications*, Modern Series, 1929–.]

CHARLES G. FENWICK

Arbor Day, Origin of. On the motion of J. Sterling Morton the Nebraska State Board of Agriculture designated the tenth day of April, 1872, as a day to plant trees, naming it Arbor Day. Later the state legislature changed the day to April 22, the birthday of Morton, and made it a legal holiday[qv]. Other states followed this example.

[Addison E. Sheldon, *Nebraska Old and New.*]

EVERETT DICK

Arbuthnot and Ambrister, Case of. An incident of Gen. Andrew Jackson's raid into East Florida[qv] in 1818. Believing himself tacitly authorized to seize the Floridas in view of Spain's delay in diplomacy, Jackson attacked the Seminole Indians[qv] in Spanish territory. At St. Mark's, Fla., he captured Alexander Arbuthnot, a Scotch trader who had warned the Indians to escape. At the village of Chief Bowlegs on the Suwanee River he captured Robert Ambrister, an English trader, who had plotted an Indian uprising. After courts-martial, Ambrister was shot and Arbuthnot hanged, both at St. Mark's on April 29, 1818. The British government took no action, but Spain protested the invasion. Secretary of State John Quincy Adams vigorously defended Jackson in his published despatches to the United States Minister at Madrid, and thus helped to force Spanish signature of the Adams-Onís Treaty[qv] of Feb. 22, 1819, which included the cession of East Florida.

[John S. Bassett, *Life of Andrew Jackson.*]

PHILIP COOLIDGE BROOKS

Archæology, North American. In North America the term archæology covers research into the culture of native peoples living before the 16th century, the time level separating the historic from the prehistoric. In the study of living natives, or Indians, historical methods are used, but for those living before the 16th century the method is that of archæology. The primary objective is the discovery of time sequences in cultures and peoples. Such chronologies are expressed in successive changes in artifacts or in typological differences. The empirical determination of time sequence in artifacts is by super-position; i.e., when in undisturbed deposits, one type of artifact is found consistently above another, the lower one is the older. For example, in some rock-shelters and cave entrances east of the Mississippi, pottery[qv] is found in the upper levels only: certain shell heaps along the Atlantic coast show the same sequence. It is evident, therefore, that in this part of North America there is a pre-pottery period, followed by one of pottery, extending into the 16th century, or historic time. In southwestern United States a similar pre-pottery period has been demonstrated, but in parts of California and northward along the Pacific coast belt no pottery is found nor was any made in historic time.

Pre-pottery time can be subdivided in the Ohio Valley and the Ozark Mountains by the appearance of cultivated plants. Thus, in certain rock-shelters, seeds of the cultivated sunflower, gourd and pigweed appear at a given level, later these give way to maize[qv] and pottery. So the first people to occupy these shelters were hunters who may have gathered some wild seeds but knew nothing of agriculture; later, hunters who cultivated certain local plants for their seeds lived here. Finally, maize was introduced from the south, but this was also the period of pottery. Agriculture in southwestern United States seems to have begun with maize and pottery and on the Pacific side of the continent where no pottery is found, there was no agriculture.

In southwestern United States and in parts of Mexico it is possible to subdivide the pottery period because styles in form and decoration changed frequently. The super-position of these styles in refuse heaps gives the time order of their appearance. Thus for parts of Arizona and New Mexico, the following culture periods have been established: Basket-Maker III, Pueblo I, II, III, IV and V, as subdivisions of the pottery period. These are culture periods because many other types of artifacts change in unison with pottery styles. In other words, in this area, pottery styles are the indicators of culture sequence.

To integrate fully such archæological sequences in cultures with historical chronology, actual dates are necessary. Surprisingly enough, this has been found possible by the tree-ring[qv] method where timbers used in buildings have been preserved by favorable climate or by charring in fire. For contiguous parts of New Mexico and Arizona this method gives exact dates for artifacts and ruins grouped typologically, or in culture periods, as follows: Pueblo V, since 1700; Pueblo IV, 1350–1700; Pueblo III, 950–1350; Pueblo II, 600–950; Pueblo I, 100–600; Basket-Maker III, ?–100 A.D. Undated are Basket-Maker I and II.

In Mexico and Central America certain ruins and the cultures they represent bear inscription dates whose correlations with our own calendar are still in doubt. Hence, the one sure chronology for North America is the one given above. Whether the remainder of the United States can be correlated with this remains to be seen.

A sequence without dates has been established for the Mississippi Valley, as: (8) Historic Period; (7) Proto-historic Period; (6) Mississippi Culture; (5) Woodland Culture; (4) Maize and Pottery Culture; (3) Pre-maize Agriculture; (2) Hunters of modern fauna; (1) Hunters of extinct fauna. Periods 4 to 8 have been traced over most of the country between Kansas and the Atlantic, 3 and 2 are known in Kentucky and the Ozarks and 1 in New Mexico, Colorado, and Nebraska.

[Clark Wissler, *The American Indian;* Cole and Deuel, *Rediscovering Illinois.*] CLARK WISSLER

Archangel, American Troops at. After the Russian revolution (1917) the Allies sent a joint expedition, under British command, to co-operate with the White Russians at Murmansk and Archangel against the Bolshevist forces. By President Wilson's order American troops, eventually numbering 5100, participated. On Sept. 4, 1918, the 339th Infantry and auxiliary units reached Archangel with other Allied forces. The mission of the Allies was limited to protecting the ports and surrounding territory. The Americans guarded a front of 450 miles south and east of Archangel, and between September, 1918, and May, 1919, suffered more than 500 casualties. The last American troops withdrew from north Russia in July, 1919.

[*Final Report of General John J. Pershing; Order of Battle of the United States Land Forces in the World War.*]

JOSEPH MILLS HANSON

Architecture, American, has presented a succession of styles which, with one exception, were echoes of contemporary architectural fashions in England, France and Italy. Beneath this superficiality, American genius and energy have expressed themselves through vast resources of native raw building materials, the richest and most diversified in the world. As a result, the United States has produced an architecture varied in style and quality. It has made contributions to the science of building of which one, at least, is epoch-making: skeleton steel construction with its overwhelming daughter the skyscraper*qv*. In consequence of these abilities and opportunities, and its vast wealth, the United States, in the early years of the 20th century, achieved a pre-eminent position in world architecture which it is still holding, perhaps precariously.

The Spanish, Dutch, Swedish and English settlers of the eastern North American coast ignored such aboriginal models as huts and wigwams*qv*, and sought to reproduce the architecture of the fatherland. The predominance of English dominion and influence made the architecture of this region essentially English, which in the 17th century was Elizabethan and Jacobean. Our first houses had such English characteristics as the overhanging second story, steep gabled roofs, leaded glass casement sash, a huge central chimney and in all likelihood half-timbered walls, soon to be clapboarded against the rigors of New England climate. These are all mediæval characteristics hardly yet affected by the Renaissance. Typical examples are the Parson Capen House, Toppsfield (1683), the House of Seven Gables, Salem, and the Paul Revere House, Boston. Perhaps less than 100 remain. In the South the few surviving 17th-century buildings were built of brick*qv*, which eliminated the overhang, as in the John Rolfe House at Smith's Fort (1651), Bacon's Castle, Surry County, (1676), and St. Luke's Church, Isle of Wight County (1632), all in Virginia. The faint Dutch and Swedish influence in the Middle Colonies was shortly overwhelmed by the weight of English culture and tradition. We therefore find in succession, after the "Early American," echoes of the robust Renaissance of Sir Christopher Wren, as in the public buildings of Williamsburg*qv*; the simpler dignity of the early Georges in Independence Hall*qv* and Christ Church, Philadelphia; and the delicacy of the Adam period in the later days of George III, as in Homewood, Baltimore, the Russell House, Charleston, and McIntire's work in Salem; covering in all a period approximately from 1700 to 1800.

It must not be inferred that the American adaptation of these English fashions was without originality or power. In the transatlantic voyage all of the European styles have undergone a sea change that have made them in many cases representative of the New World. This is particularly true of the Colonial style. Here the modest scale of the buildings, the lack of money, the availability of pine, the absence of professional architects and a certain inherent taste shared by aristocrat and craftsman alike produced an architecture of which any land at any time could justly be proud.

The American Revolution, and Thomas Jefferson's residence in France from 1784 to 1789, profoundly influenced American architecture. The source of inspiration was turned from England to France, and beyond that to ancient Rome. The professional architect appeared in Bulfinch, Thornton and Hoban. Jefferson was a near-professional. His capitol building in Richmond (1789) introduced the columned and pedimented portico. His house, Monticello, and the University of Virginia (1818) made him the father of the Post-Colonial, Federal, or Republican style (as it is variously called) dated usually from 1790 to 1820. Other monuments of this style are the earliest portions of the Capitol in Washington, the old City Hall, New York (1803), the White House[qv] (1818), and the State House, Boston.

In the later years of the 18th century ancient Greek architecture was revived as a result of the published researches of the British architects Stuart and Revett. A furious vogue of the Greek style followed. It came to America through Benjamin Latrobe, an English architect, who built the Bank of North America[qv] in Philadelphia (1799–1801) in pure Greek style and started a fashion that spread throughout the land. The classic mania accompanied the pioneers. Its invasion of the wilderness is one of the most extraordinary phenomena in our architectural history. The covered wagon, along with rifle and plowshare, found room for the portico of the Parthenon. Although architects like Strickland, Mills and Walter built many state capitols, exchanges and institutes, the new style was essentially an architecture of the Handbooks, little volumes with drawings and minute directions for reproducing the Greek. They were on every gentleman's table and in the breeches pocket of every carpenter. Æsthetically its contribution was one of charm and dignity. Its best monument, perhaps, is Girard College, in Philadelphia, built by Thomas U. Walter in 1833. Churches usually followed the type established in colonial days, but with Greek detail. Among the government structures in the Greek style in Washington, the Treasury building is the best. There were a vast number of houses, a splendid example of which is the James F. D. Lanier House (1844), in Madison, Ind. Among the contributions to the science of building introduced in this period was "balloon construction," invented in Chicago (1837), which revolutionized frame construction for wooden buildings, and is universally used today. The Greek style was moribund in the 1850's, the Civil War finished it.

The ideals of the Greek Revival were completely repudiated in the architecturally chaotic years between 1855 and 1880. In the 1850's comfort and safety just achieved in ocean travel sent scores of our "merchant princes" and their families to Europe. They observed the Gothic Revival in full blast in England, and in France the sophisticated classicism of the Second Empire. Both were brought back to America along with the latest in clothes and cooking. It was a period of great material expansion and pride of purse, and there was a rush of building for a public whose attitude toward art, while enthusiastic, was naïve and provincial. The result demonstrated the difficulty of imitating and adapting such complicated models, especially by untrained architects. It is in fact the nadir of our national taste and in architecture has appropriately been called the Parvenu style. Its apotheosis was the Centennial Exposition in Philadelphia (1876)[qv]. The period has scarcely a single creative idea to its credit which has survived.

In the Parvenu period buildings inspired by contemporary French architecture came first. They are characterized by heavy mansard roofs, elaborate cornices, often of galvanized iron, debased detail and an indiscriminate use of the orders. The high and narrow ideal permeated the structure. Ornament and elaborations as evidence of cost were cachets of elegance and taste. The "cast iron front" appeared on our commercial buildings, and residences with "brown stone fronts" and high stoops lined our fashionable avenues. As the French type of classic was the favorite for masonry construction, so the English Gothic Revival, or Mid-Victorian, was used for lesser buildings, often of wood. It had the curious Italian tinge which the writings of Ruskin had given it. As used in Villa architecture and in the Cottage style it called upon the jig saw to perform wonders in intricate and often charming scroll work. The cupola and the porte-cochère were popular in both varieties of the Parvenu and the high and narrow motive prevailed as well. The performances of the Gothic type were much superior to the essays in European classic; Memorial Hall at Harvard and New Old South Church in Boston demonstrate this, as do countless modest houses.

Jibes at our domestic art by foreign guests at the Centennial Exposition in 1876, as well as examples of foreign craftsmanship exhibited there, gave us pause; and at this critical moment appeared H. H. Richardson, graduate of the École des Beaux Arts in Paris, who leaped into fame with the building of Trinity Church in Boston (1879). Its style was French Romanesque, practically unknown in America. The popularity of this new fashion was almost equal to that of the Greek Revival, although it was held at bay in New York City by Richard M. Hunt and the youthful firm of McKim, Mead and White, who held by the classic tradition, of which they almost alone were worthy interpreters.

The heavy Romanesque was essentially an architecture of stone. For the wooden house of the ordinary citizen our architects eagerly followed some talented young English architects in what was called Free Classic, or Queen Anne, alike, in its Romanticism, to the Romanesque Revival. The turning lathe replaced the jig saw, and our houses between 1880 and 1893 were picturesque jumbles of steep roofs, balconies, gables, dormers and many chimneys, built in all sorts of materials. Shingles for walls, stucco and plate glass windows made their bow and the high and narrow motive made way for the low and broad. With all its faults the Queen Anne style was more truly indigenous than any since the Colonial.

The great gift of the period, however, had nothing to do with style, unless begotten of the virile strength of the Romanesque Revival. In 1884, Maj. William Le Baron Jenney built the Home Insurance Building in Chicago. In this structure the front, rear and court walls above the second floor, as well as the floors, were supported by a skeleton of wrought and cast iron, beams and columns. In the Tacoma Building built by Holabird and Roche (1887), a steel skeleton extended from the ground, the steel columns resting on isolated foundations. These were the first skyscrapers, progenitors of a mighty brood.

When the World's Columbian Exposition[qv] was conceived, the Commission of Architects decided to build in the classic style. Although there were contributing factors such as the growth of architectural education, this great World's Fair of 1893 in Chicago was the principal cause of the revolt that made Romanesque and Queen Anne not only out of fashion but taboo. The classic urge which succeeded was really eclectic; any historic style if correctly done was *au fait*. The new dispensation included in addition to architecture landscape gardening, mural painting and sculpture. This Eclectic period extended through the World War and has been called the Golden Age of American architecture; not the purest but certainly the most sumptuous of our modes. Undisturbed by wars or rumors of wars in a period of unexampled prosperity, completely sure of itself, it revived not only the splendor that was Rome, but that which was Italy, France, England and Spain to boot! Whatever may have been false in its philosophy, it developed the science of building as had not been done since the Middle Ages.

Its largest product was the skyscraper[qv], which at the same time spelled an engineering triumph and an æsthetic failure. The job of adapting an ancient style to the great height of a modern steel skeleton was too much for the men of the Golden Age, and they admitted it. In other fields the eclectics were more successful. Being school men, their planning was excellent; so much so that norms were developed for office buildings, hotels, libraries, banks, railway stations, schools, churches, etc., which still persist. In buildings of moderate height where classic proportions were suitable, such as the Boston Public Library by McKim, Mead and White, almost perfection was achieved. A list of the masterpieces of the Golden Age would be extensive. To cite the Palace of Fine Arts, World's Fair, Chicago, by Charles B. Atwood; the Pennsylvania Station, New York; the Harkness Memorial at Yale, by James Gamble Rogers; St. Thomas' Church, New York, by Cram and Goodhue; Lincoln Memorial, Washington, by Henry Bacon, merely scratches the surface. Ralph Adams Cram and Bertram Goodhue revolutionized ecclesiastical architecture with a fresh and brilliant interpretation of the Gothic. D. H. Burnham, city planner, made architecture Big Business, and planned a new Chicago and San Francisco. The American city was rebuilt in those years of mellow fruitfulness. The first super-skyscraper, the Woolworth Building in New York, was built by Cass Gilbert in 1917. By following the Gothic principle of verticality it somewhat redeemed the many failures of the misapplied classic.

In 1922 the Chicago *Tribune* held a competition for its proposed building, thirty stories high. The second prize, by Eliet Saarinen, was generally accepted by architects as the long looked for solution of the riddle of the skyscraper. It became the chosen formula for skyscraper and super-skyscraper alike. The *Daily News* Building, by Raymond Hood; Rockefeller Center (seventy stories); Chicago Board of Trade, by Holabird and Root; and the Empire State Building (eighty-four stories), by Shreve, Lamb and Harmon, illustrated the new dispensation and mark, perhaps, its culmination.

An important element in the solution of the skyscraper was the Functional or International style, which saw its birth in the work and principles of Louis Sullivan of Chicago as first expressed in the Transportation Building in the World's Fair of 1893. Receiving no hearing during the Golden Age, though kept alive by Frank Lloyd Wright and the Chicago School, it assumed importance in Holland and Germany just before the World War, and returned to America triumphantly in our post-war building boom. The International style is puritan in its purpose. It would purge from architecture falsities in expression, the use of historic styles and all ornament, unless it be "significant." It revolutionizes the concept of architecture in that a building is not an expression of mass but of volume in which walls become but an enclosing skin for the rooms (volumes) within. Our architecture, which has been molluscan for thousands of years, now becomes vertebrate. Such a concept calls for new building materials, and the manufacturers, who in America have always marched side by side (and sometimes a step ahead) with the architects, are producing them ready to his hand.

The International style has conquered nearly every field in commercial building, though the Gothic in ecclesiastical architecture and Colonial in the domestic field hold somewhat precariously their lines. The restoration of colonial Williamsburg (1927–36) has greatly strengthened the Colonial in popularity. As the well-loved style has been somewhat chastened and streamlined, it may survive.

Nevertheless the Functional or International style seems to be elected to represent the new era. Its contributions in the utilities such as kitchen arrangement and equipment, furniture and lighting; in construction with its advance in reinforced concrete and prefabrication and in the creation of new building materials give it the leadership aside from style. Its greatest successes have been so far in buildings of specialized functions such as factories, airdromes, casinos, etc. Its abhorrence of ornament marks it as a "puritan movement" and especially adaptable for world expression. Hence its excellent name, the International style.

The last great expression of the spirit of the Renaissance, that beauty is its own excuse for being, occurred in the San Francisco Exposition of 1915 (*see* Panama-Pacific International Exposition). It is of arresting significance that the International style was selected without question for the great exposition in New York in 1939^{qv}, "The World of Tomorrow."

[M. S. Briggs, *The Homes of the Pilgrim Fathers in England and America;* H. D. Eberlein, *Architecture of Colonial America;* R. A. Cram, *American Church Building of Today;* G. H. Edgell, *American Architecture of Today;* T. F. Hamlin, *American Spirit in Architecture;* Fiske Kimball, *American Architecture,* and *Domestic Architecture of the American Colonies and the Early Republic;* Howard Major, *Domestic Architecture of the Early American Republic: the Greek Revival;* Lewis Mumford, *Sticks and Stones;* Rexford Newcomb, *Old Mission Churches and Historic Homes of California;* R. W. Sexton, *American Commercial Buildings of Today;* T. E. Tallmadge, *Story of Architecture in America.*]

THOMAS E. TALLMADGE

Archive War, THE, was a contest between Austin and Houston, Tex., in 1842, over the state archives. Austin had been designated as the capital in 1839 but President Houston, after a Mexican raid on San Antonio in 1842, fearing the archives might be lost, undertook to remove them to Houston. The citizens of Austin overtook the wagons and forced them to be returned to Austin.

[H. H. Bancroft, *History of the North Mexican States and Texas,* Vol. II.]

J. G. SMITH

Archives. The body of records and papers officially produced or received by a government, a governmental agency, an institution, an organization, or a firm in the conduct of its affairs and filed or preserved by it or its legitimate successors for record purposes constitutes its archives. The term is sometimes applicable to the papers of a family or an individual, but such collections usually lack the organic character of true archives. Collections of historical manuscripts assembled by an agency or individual rather than received or produced in the transaction of affairs are not archives, even though they contain official documents. Although archives are preserved primarily for administrative purposes, they constitute a fundamental basis of knowledge of the history, not only of the agency whose records they are, but also of the people in their social and economic relationships.

The national archives of the United States, consisting of the records of all the agencies of the Federal Government, are, of course, of outstanding importance for American history. Although most nations long ago made special provisions for the preservation and administration of their non-current records, the United States until recently left them in the custody of the agencies that had accumulated them, with the result that some were inadvertently destroyed and many were stored in unsuitable places where they were subject to deterioration and were practically inaccessible to scholars or officials. In 1926 Congress made provision for the construction of an Archives Building in Washington, which, though not fully completed until 1937, was occupied in 1935. The agency known as The National Archives was set up in 1934 to have the custody and administration of the records transferred to the building, and the Archivist was given authority to inspect any records of the Federal Government. Under his direction a comprehensive survey was made of the records in Washington, and a similar survey of Federal records outside Washington was made as a Works Progress Administration[qv] project with The National Archives as a co-operating sponsor. The mass of information assembled by these surveys is on file at The National Archives.

Among the more important records already (1938) transferred to the Archives Building are the Senate files to 1929 with some exceptions, most of the records of the State Department to 1906, the centralized records of the army to 1912, the records of the Attorney General and the Justice Department to 1903, records of the Office of Indian Affairs from 1795 to 1907, records of pensions based on military or naval service from 1817 to 1917, and records of most of the emergency World War agencies. With a few exceptions, the records at The National Archives are available for consultation, and photostatic or microfilm reproductions of them can be obtained at low cost. A guide to these records, revised from time to time, is published by The National Archives.

Most of the states preceded the Federal Government in making some provision for the centralization of non-current records, but these provisions are extremely diverse and frequently inadequate. Usually the functions of an archival agency are performed by the state historical society, the state library, a state department of archives and history, a state historical commission, or the Secretary of State. Independent archival agencies have recently been established in a few states, but they usually have historical as well as strictly archival functions. In Illinois, however, the archives agency, though a branch of the state library, is separately administered and has its own building. In most of the states vast quantities of non-current records remain in the custody of the offices that accumulated them. The Public Archives Commission set up by the American Historical Association[qv] in 1899 brought about the compilation and publication in the *Annual Reports* of the Association of guides to the archives of all but a few of the states; but most of these guides are now out of date. More comprehensive guides or inventories of state archives are now being compiled by the Historical Records Survey set up by the Works Progress Administration in 1936.

The non-current records of counties and other local governments have been sadly neglected. In a few states such records have been assembled in part in central depositories, and in a few they are inspected from time to time by a state official. Inventories have been published of the county records of Illinois and California, and more complete inventories of local records throughout the country now being compiled by the Historical Records Survey will serve to open up to historians a tremendous mass of original material for the history of the American people.

The archives of semipublic and private organizations have also been neglected, as a rule, after they ceased to be of current value; but a few religious organizations, educational institutions and business firms have made special provision for the preservation and use for historical purposes of their records. In this field again, the Historical Records Survey is rendering valuable services in inventorying church records and other non-public archival material throughout the country.

The archives of foreign governments also include material of great importance for American history. This is especially true of those of England, France and Spain for the colonial and Revolutionary periods; but students of the foreign relations of the United States find pertinent material in the archives of practically every country. Fortunately for the historian, a series of guides to material for American history in foreign archives has been compiled and published by the Carnegie Institution of Washington[qv], and much of this material is available in the form of reproductions at the Library of Congress[qv].

As a result of the establishment of The National Archives, the expansion of state archival activities and the work of the Historical Records Survey, interest in archival problems was greatly increased and the need was felt for a professional organization to promote their solution. This need was met by the establishment in 1936 of the Society of American Archivists, which launched a quarterly magazine, *The American Archivist,* in 1938.

[C. H. Van Tyne and W. G. Leland, *Guide to the Archives of the Government of the United States in Washington;* Archivist of the United States, *Annual Reports;* C. M. Gates, The Administration of State Archives, in *Pacific Northwest Quarterly*, January, 1938; Business Historical Society, *The Preservation of Business Records.*]

SOLON J. BUCK

Arctic Exploration. *See* Polar Expeditions.

Argonauts of California. *See* Forty-Niners.

***Argus-Pelican* Engagement** (1813). Off St. David's Head, Wales, on August 14, the British brig *Pelican,* captured the American brig *Argus.* The American loss was six killed and seventeen wounded; the British had two killed and five wounded.

[Theodore Roosevelt, *The Naval War of 1812.*]

CHARLES LEE LEWIS

Arickaree, Fight on the. *See* Beecher Island, Battle of, 1868.

Arikara, THE, Caddoan people, primitive inhabitants of central South Dakota, were strongly entrenched on Missouri River for centuries before white exploration. They lived in substantial houses in stockaded villages, and cultivated extensive gardens. They were expelled by the Sioux[qv] August, 1794, and settled near present Mobridge, S. Dak. A remnant is now at Fort Berthold.

[DeLand, *Aborigines of South Dakota,* Vol. 3, South Dakota Historical Collections.]

DOANE ROBINSON

Arizona, the forty-eighth state admitted to the Union, is the fifth in area. The southwestern one third of the state is chiefly low desert, sloping toward the Gila and Colorado rivers and the Gulf of California; the northeastern two thirds being the high mountain deserts and forest lands of the Colorado plateau. Arizona contains some of the oldest human habitations in the United States, some Indian towns and cliff dwellings[qv] dating back 1000 years or more. A considerable population of sedentary Pima[qv] and Yuma Indians occupied towns and irrigated lands in the Gila valley, wherein they were often on the defensive against the attacks of Apache[qv] and other highland tribes.

Opinions differ as to who were the first white visitors to Arizona. Padres Juan de la Asunción and Pedro Nazal are said to have reached it in 1538, and Fray Marcos de Niza probably entered it in 1539. It is certain that Francisco Vásquez de Coronado's[qv] Spanish army crossed it en route to Cíbola[qv] (Zuñi, in New Mexico), in 1540; while detachments from his expedition reached the Colorado mouth and discovered the Hopi[qv] Indian towns and the Grand Canyon[qv]. In 1583, Antonio de Espejo seems to have worked gold deposits near Prescott, and in 1604–6 Juan de Oñate[qv], conqueror of New Mexico, crossed northern Arizona and descended the Colorado to the Gulf. Franciscan[qv] missionaries were at work among the Hopis of northeastern Arizona between 1629 and 1680. Padre Eusebio Francisco Kino and other Jesuits[qv] penetrated southern Arizona from 1691 onward, founding Mission San Xavier del Bac in 1700 and other Pima missions soon afterward. A Pima revolt[qv] in 1750–53 led to the establishment of a Spanish presidio[qv] at Tubac[qv] in 1752, moved to the Spanish and Indian settlement of San Agustín de Tucson in 1776. The Jesuits, expelled in 1767, were replaced by Franciscans, who maintained a feeble hold upon the missions until about 1828. During Mexican rule, 1821–56, the only important white settlements in Arizona were at Tubac and Tucson in the Santa Cruz valley, nearly all others having been abandoned because of frequent Apache raids.

Anglo-American fur trappers penetrated Arizona by way of the Gila valley as early as 1826, and were fairly common visitors thereafter. The Mexican War[qv] saw the passage of a number of American military expeditions through the Gila valley from New Mexico to California, one of which, the Mormon Battalion[qv], captured Tucson Dec. 16, 1846. The Treaty of Guadalupe Hidalgo[qv], Feb. 2, 1848, left nearly all of Arizona south of the Gila a part of the Mexican state of Sonora. The region north of the Gila became part of New Mexico Territory under the act of Congress of Sept. 9, 1850. Explorations for a proposed Pacific coast railway, 1848–53, seemed to indicate the acquisition of the southern Gila valley as necessary for such a line. Accordingly, the Gadsden Purchase[qv] was negotiated with Mexico, Dec. 30, 1853, by which Arizona between the Gila and the present Mexican boundary was added to New Mexico, official possession being taken at Tucson, March 10, 1856.

In 1856 a convention at Tucson petitioned Congress to grant separate territorial status to Arizona, but the movement was defeated. Texan Confederate troops occupied southern Arizona for a few months in 1862; but after their expulsion, Congress, on Feb. 24, 1863, established the Federal territory of Arizona (including at first the southern tip of Nevada). A movement for statehood took definite shape on Oct. 2, 1891, with the framing of a constitution by the legislature, at Phoenix, the new territorial capital. Nearly twenty years later, Aug. 21, 1911, President Taft gave a new state constitution his approval, conditioned upon the elimination of a clause providing for the recall[qv] of judges; and the acceptance of this condition led to Arizona's formal admission as a state, Feb. 14, 1912, although the troublesome provision was soon restored. George W. P. Hunt was the first state governor, and served seven terms in that office.

[T. E. Farish, *History of Arizona;* J. H. McClintock, *Arizona, Prehistoric, Aboriginal, Pioneer, Modern.*]

RUFUS KAY WYLLYS

***Ark* and the *Dove*,** THE, were the two vessels which brought the first colonists, about 200 in number, to Maryland[qv]. These pioneers left England at the suggestion of and under instruction from Cecil Calvert, to whom, on June 20, 1632, Charles I had granted a charter which conferred proprietary powers and authorized the colonization of the territory in the vicinity of the Chesapeake Bay. Sailing from Cowes, on the Isle of Wight, on Nov. 22, 1633, the *Ark* and the *Dove* laid their course to the Chesapeake by way of the Canary Islands and the West Indies. Entering the Potomac during the first week in March, 1634, they explored the northern bank of this river until, on March 27, it was finally decided to make the first permanent settlement on a river which empties into the Potomac not very far from its mouth. This settlement was and still is known as St. Mary's.

[C. C. Hall, *Narratives of Early Maryland, 1633-1684.*]

RAPHAEL SEMMES

Arkansas. The first white man to visit the region known as Arkansas was DeSoto[qv] (1541). Next came Marquette and Jolliet (1673) and then LaSalle and Tonti (1682)[qqv], who came to take possession of the Mississippi Valley for the French. In 1686 Tonti founded Arkansas Post[qv], the first permanent settlement in the region. The name "Arkansas" is derived from that of a tribe of Indians living west of the Mississippi and north of the Arkansas rivers. It appears on a map of 1718 as "Akansas." Capt. Zebulon Pike spelled it "Arkansaw" (1811) and it so appears in some government documents, but "Arkansas" came into general use. The Arkansas legislature of 1881 adopted the pronunciation Ark' an saw.

This region became American territory with the purchase of Louisiana[qv] (1803). When the State of Louisiana was admitted to the Union in 1812 Arkansas District became a part of Missouri Territory and then a separate territory of the first type in 1819, when Missouri applied for statehood. Arkansas Post was the first capital, but Little Rock soon took its place. The growth of the population was slow at first, but some energetic leaders soon got the territory advanced to the third stage with a bicameral legislature[qv] elected by the people. The same class of ambitious leaders rushed it into statehood (1836), ahead of time, measured by the population. One reason for the rush was to get banks. The first legislature created two, a State Bank and the Real Estate Bank (private). These banks, which were underwritten by the state, soon failed and left a debt of $3,000,000 for the state to pay.

Most of the people who settled in Arkansas came from the older South. Some brought their slaves with them. Cotton growing became the leading industry. Henry M. Rector, a defender of slavery, was elected governor in 1860 and he moved for secession[qv]. The state convention submitted "secession" or "co-operation" to be voted on in August, but after the bombardment of Fort Sumter[qv] and Lincoln's call for troops, the convention reassembled and seceded with only one dissenting vote. Isaac Murphy cast that vote and he became the first loyal governor in 1864. Although the state government had been organized under Lincoln's plan of reconstruction, Arkansas subsequently had to endure four years of congressional Reconstruction which left the state and counties heavily in debt with no money in the state treasury (*see* Joint Committee on Reconstruction). A new constitution was drawn up in 1874 and Augustus H. Garland was elected governor. In politics Arkansas has always been Democratic except for the Reconstruction period, although the agrarian movement[qv] attained considerable strength in the 1880's and 1890's. A large part of the debt left by the Reconstructionists was repudiated in 1884 as illegal (*see* Repudiation of State Debts); also the unliquidated part of the debt of the Real Estate Bank for the same reason. The initiative and referendum[qqv] were adopted in 1910 and have been used extensively, sometimes for good, sometimes for ill. An extensive road-building program, since 1915, and other expenditures left the state with a bonded indebtedness of about $165,000,000, the heaviest debt per capita and in proportion to wealth in the Union. It was advantageously refunded in 1933 and the state soon began to call bonds before they were due.

The constitution of 1868 provided for a public school system and this has been carried out. The state has a university, four separate agricultural colleges and two separate teacher-training colleges.

[D. T. Herndon, ed., *Centennial History of Arkansas;* Josiah H. Shinn, *Pioneers and Makers of Arkansas History;* T. S. Staples, *Reconstruction in Arkansas;* David Y. Thomas, *Arkansas in War and Reconstruction;* David Y. Thomas, ed., *Arkansas and Its People.*]

DAVID Y. THOMAS

***Arkansas*, Destruction of the Ironclad** (1862). After the *Arkansas* passed through the Federal fleet before Vicksburg[qv] to co-operate in Breckinridge's attempt to recapture Baton Rouge[qv], her machinery became disabled when within five miles of her destination, and she was run ashore and blown up to escape Federal capture, Aug. 5, 1862.

[*War of the Rebellion Records*, Naval Series, XXIII, 293; A. Fortier, *History of Louisiana.*]

WALTER PRICHARD

Arkansas, French Post and Mission at. When LaSalle[qv] laid claim to the entire Mississippi Valley for France in 1682 he granted to Henry de Tonti a large concession at the Quapaw villages on the Arkansas River, and in 1686 Tonti established the Arkansas Post as the earliest French settlement in the lower Mississippi Valley. In 1689 Tonti established a Catholic mission at the post, and by 1700 Jean Couture[qv], who was left in command of the post, had developed an extensive trade with the English of Carolina. The subsequent history of the coast is obscure until the Western Company[qv] took possession of Louisiana in 1718 and John Law sent 700 German colonists to develop his large concession on the Arkansas River. But Law's venture collapsed a few years later, and his colonists abandoned the settlement and located at the "German Coast" (*see* Côte des Allemand) near New Orleans. When French Louisiana was divided into nine districts in 1721, Arkansas Post became the administrative center for the Arkansas District, and in 1722 Benard de la Harpe strengthened the stockade and placed a regular garrison there. Arkansas Post remained important until the end of the French regime in 1762 as the administrative and commercial center of the extensive Arkansas District and as the site of a Jesuit mission[qv].

[Dallas T. Herndon, ed., *Centennial History of Arkansas;* David Y. Thomas, ed., *Arkansas and Its People: A History, 1541-1930;* M. W. Benjamin, French History of Arkansas, in *Publications of the Arkansas Historical Association,* II (1908); Charles Gayarré, *History of Louisiana.*]

WALTER PRICHARD

Arkansas, Great Bend of the, was an important landmark on the Santa Fé trail[qv], marking the first point at which the river was encountered, 278 miles from Independence[qv], and roughly half way to Bent's Fort[qv], which was 530 miles. At Walnut Creek, which joined the Arkansas at the apex of the bend, travelers commonly encountered the first fringe of the buffalo[qv] herds, and Pawnee Rock[qv], fifteen miles beyond, was regarded as the beginning of the hostile Indian country. One hundred miles from Walnut Creek was the Cimarron Crossing where a short cut to Santa Fé could be obtained.

[Col. Henry Inman, *The Old Santa Fé Trail.*]

PAUL I. WELLMAN

Arkansas, THE. Akensas, Akansas, Acansa, a tribe of Indians belonging to the southwestern Siouan[qv] family. They called themselves O guahpa or Akapa, signifying "those going down stream." They were mound builders[qv]. By De Soto's[qv] time, 1541, they were in the lower Arkansas valley. DeSoto's chroniclers called them Pacaha and Capaha. The early French explorers called them Arkansea. LaSalle[qv] and Tonti found them living in three villages near the mouth of the Arkansas River, in 1683. The Arkansas were tall, well-shaped, non-warlike, agricultural people. From the Arkansas Post[qv], France controlled their trade and made alliances with them. As a result of the Anglo-American westward movement[qv], they were pushed west and south. The remnant of the tribe, now called Quapaw, is in northeastern Oklahoma.

[F. W. Hodge, ed., *Handbook of American Indians;* G. R. Thwaites, *Early Western Travels, 1748-1846.*]

ANNA LEWIS

Arkansas Post, Battle of. Arkansas Post (Fort Hindman) was fortified by the Confederates for the protection of Little Rock. After the repulse of Sherman's (U.) attack upon Vicksburg[qv] (Dec. 29, 1862) it was considered essential to capture the post. Gen. John A. McClernand, with 30,000 men backed by Admiral David D. Porter's fleet of ironclads[qv], forced Gen. Thomas J. Churchill to surrender Jan. 11, 1863.

[David Y. Thomas, *Arkansas in War and Reconstruction.*]

DAVID Y. THOMAS

Arkansas River, known to the early French as Rivière des Ark or d'Ozark, derived its name from the Arkansas Indians[qv] who lived on its banks. The river was first discovered and explored by DeSoto[qv] in 1541 on his journey into the Southwest. The French explorers, Jolliet and Marquette[qv], reached its mouth in 1673, in their search for a river "coming in from California on the southern sea." The Arkansas Post[qv], established in 1686 by Henry Tonti, was the first permanent settlement in Arkansas River region, and around the post centers the early history of the river.

Arkansas River to the French was the highway leading into the Spanish Southwest—Taos and Santa Fé[qqv]. French traders preferred waterways as highways. The headwaters of the Arkansas were in Spanish territory. The Spanish explorer Uribarri in 1696 called the upper Arkansas by the name Rio Napestle, probably of native Indian origin. This name was applied to the river by the Spanish until the 19th century. The treaty with Spain in 1819 (*see* Adams-Onís Treaty) made the Arkansas River west of the 100th meridian a part of the western boundary of the United States. The name Arkansas, which had applied only to lower reaches of the stream, was carried westward by American traders and trappers and succeeded in replacing the name Rio Napestle, or Napeste.

Arkansas River was navigable with keelboats[qv] as far west as Grand River. In early days "Arkansas" and "Ozark" were used interchangeably and were applied to Arkansas River, the mountains north of it and the post near its mouth.

[A. B. Thomas, *Spanish Exploration of Oklahoma, 1599-1792;* Anna Lewis, *Along the Arkansas.*]

ANNA LEWIS

Arkansas River Route, THE, was the mountain or Pikes Peak division of the Santa Fé Trail[qv], which avoided the dangerous Jornada[qv] desert of the Cimarron cut-off. Instead of turning south at Cimarron Crossing near the present site of Dodge City[qv], this route followed up the Arkansas River to old Bent's Fort[qv] near present-day La Junta and there turned southwesterly to the mountains and crossed the difficult Raton Pass[qv]. Choice was now open to continue southward rejoining the other Trail and going through Las Vegas to Santa Fé, or to proceed westward, past the Maxwell Ranch, along the base of the mountains and over the range to Taos[qv]. The Trail then followed the Rio Grande down to Santa Fé[qv]. The Arkansas River Route, though longer, was extensively used because of the importance of Bent's Fort, the trading center of the trappers and Indians; the presence of water and the demand for freight at the settlements along the way. Also it was the route to the Colorado goldfields of 1858 (*see* Pikes Peak Gold Rush) and later and to Denver-Auraria[qv].

[Henry Inman, *The Old Santa Fé Trail.*]

MALCOLM G. WYER

"Arkansas Traveler," THE, is not only the best-known piece of folklore that Arkansas can lay claim to but the favorite of all old-time breakdown fiddle tunes in America. The rollicky dialogue and the rollickier tune go back to the days of Davy Crockett, but the author of neither has been determined. Newspapers, books and articles of commerce have taken the title. As the tradition goes, a stranger traveling in Arkansas comes to a roofless tavern before which the proprietor sits fiddling. "Where does this road go?" asks the stranger. "It's never gone anywhar since I been here," the squatter answers, going on fiddling. Finally, after more such colloquy, the stranger asks, "Why don't you play the rest of that tune?" Immediately the squatter makes the stranger dismount and play. This "turn of the tune" brings forth civil, though still comical, answers, whiskey, food, shelter, horse provender, a hospitality having all the gusto of a country hoe-down.

[Fred W. Allsopp, *Folklore of Romantic Arkansas,* Vol. II.]

J. FRANK DOBIE

Arks were known also as flatboats[qv], broadhorns, Kentucky or Orleans boats, etc. These craft until 1860 carried a large part of the downstream traffic on the rivers of the West. They were cheaply constructed of green wood, shaped like boxes with raked bows, roofed over in whole or in part, and were sold for lumber or firewood at their destinations. They were steered by a long oar, and two or more sweeps, or broadhorns, were used to move them into or out of the current. Three to five men constituted the crew. They averaged about fifteen by fifty feet and held forty to fifty tons of flour.

[Leland D. Baldwin, *The Keelboat Age on Western Waters.*]

LELAND D. BALDWIN

Arkwright Machinery. A spinning machine developed, rather than invented, by Richard Arkwright in England about 1770. It was a marked improvement over earlier forms of spinning machines. The English government prohibited the exportation of machines or drawings but a young immigrant, Samuel Slater, carried the idea to Providence, R. I., and under his direction Almy and Brown constructed a set of Arkwright machines carrying seventy-two spindles. These were installed in 1790 in a small building at the Falls of Pawtucket which still (1938) stands. This introduced the modern factory to this country. (*See also* Machines.)

[Dexter S. Kimball, *Principles of Industrial Organization.*]

DEXTER S. KIMBALL

Arlington National Shrine is on the Virginia bank of the Potomac, directly opposite Washington, D. C. Originally part of the estate of George Washington, it passed to his adopted son, G. W. Parke Custis. In 1831 Robert E. Lee married Mary Ann Custis. Mrs. Lee inherited a life interest in the estate, which after her death was to go to her eldest son, G. W. Custis Lee.

Upon the outbreak of the Civil War, the estate was seized by the United States, which acquired an alleged tax title, built a fort and hospital on the site and used the grounds as a cemetery. In 1882, after suit which reached the Supreme Court, G. W. Custis Lee was declared the legal owner of the property. The matter was settled by paying Custis Lee $150,000 indemnity.

The estate has become the site of one of the most important shrines maintained by the United States. In the cemetery are buried the dead of every war since the Revolution. Arlington House has been restored and a Memorial Amphitheater erected. After the World War the Tomb of the Unknown Soldier[qv] was added.

[J. T. Faris, *Historic Shrines of America.*]

L. C. HELDERMAN

"Arm in Arm" Convention. *See* National Union ("Arm in Arm") Convention.

Armaments. *See* Defense, National.

Armed Neutrality, THE, had its origin (1780) at the Court of Catherine II, Empress of Russia, who desired to free neutral trade from the interference of belligerents. Her declaration sought to overturn the "Rule of 1756"[qv] and secure for neutrals the freedom of navigation even to the ports of belligerents; it restricted the category of contraband[qv] to munitions and the essential instruments of war; it asserted as an established rule of international law[qv] the principle that "free ships make free goods"[qv], and set forth a new theory of blockade[qv]. The declaration was followed by the arming of the neutrals of northern Europe to protect their commerce in accordance with the principles to which they had subscribed.

The United States on Oct. 5, 1780, accepted unreservedly the rules of the Armed Neutrality as a basis for its instructions to the commanders of its armed vessels. This action by Congress was intended to pave the way for the United States to become a party to the League of Neutrals. Francis Dana was appointed minister to Russia to secure the twin objectives of recognition of the independence of the United States and its admission "as a party to the convention for maintaining the freedom of the seas"[qv]. His mission was in vain. The United States could not, while a belligerent, become a party to the Armed Neutrality, and Catherine II refused to receive Dana as long as the independence of the colonies was not recognized by Great Britain. The Definitive Treaty of Peace[qv] in 1783 altered the situation, and the primary object of the mission to Russia was removed. Madison pointed out that, although Congress approved the principles of the Armed Neutrality, it would be "unwise to become a party to a confederacy which might thereafter complicate the interests of the United States with the politics of Europe." Congress finally resolved (June 12, 1783) upon a clear distinction between the principles of the Armed Neutrality and a confederation for their enforcement. That the United States should have escaped from participation in a confederacy of this sort was fortunate. All the members of the Armed Neutrality abandoned, upon the very next opportunity of their becoming belligerents, the creed which they had sought to enforce by arms when they were neutrals. Whatever advantage might have been gained for American commerce by membership in the league would not have compensated for the political embarrassments of such an alliance.

[W. S. Carpenter, The United States and the League of Neutrals of 1780, *American Journal of International Law*, XV, pp. 511-522.]

WILLIAM S. CARPENTER

Armies, Disbanding of the. *See* Demobolization.

Arminianism, the Reformed theology which arose in opposition to the prevailing Calvinism[qv], received its name from Jacobus Arminius (1560–1609), a mild and liberal-spirited Dutch theologian. It places chief emphasis upon man's freedom and holds that God's sovereignty is so exercised as to be co-operable with the freedom of man. Introduced into America in the early 18th century, its influence spread rapidly in spite of able opposition. Those who accepted it became the advocates of a larger tolerance. On the frontier it made even more rapid headway than elsewhere, since it emphasized the natural human duties rather than speculative theology and the equality of all men in the sight of God, rather than limited grace and the possibility of salvation only for the few, which was the Calvinistic position.

[G. L. Curtiss, *Arminianism in History.*]

WILLIAM W. SWEET

Armistice of November 11, 1918. On Oct. 4, 1918, the German government appealed to President Wilson for an armistice with a view to peace on the basis of the Fourteen Points[qv]. As a prerequisite, Wilson insisted on the practical democratization of the German government and hinted openly at the abdication of William II. Gen. Pershing, the American commander in France, wished to continue the war until Germany was thoroughly beaten, but the Allied commanders, including Marshal Foch, agreed to an armistice and Wilson accepted this view. On Nov. 5, the United States notified Germany that the Fourteen Points were accepted as the basis of peace, subject to two reservations: (1) the freedom of the seas[qv] was not to be discussed;

(2) Germany must make reparation for the damage done to the property of Allied nationals during the war. The terms of armistice were communicated to Germany on Nov. 8 and signed on Nov. 11 at 5 A.M., to take effect at 11 A.M. Germany had to evacuate all territory west of the Rhine, which was to be occupied by Allied troops; a neutral zone was established ten kilometers east of the Rhine. Germany surrendered large quantities of artillery, machine guns, airplanes, motor trucks and railway rolling stock, as well as most of her navy: it was made impossible for her to resume fighting. She had also to renounce the treaties of Brest-Litovsk and Bucharest and to withdraw her troops from Russia, Rumania and Turkey. The blockade was to continue until peace was made, and a blanket financial reservation was added that "any future claims and demands of the Allies and the United States of America remain unaffected." The armistice was for one month, and was renewed from time to time until peace was signed.

[Charles Seymour, *American Diplomacy during the World War.*]

BERNADOTTE E. SCHMITT

Armor Plate. Credit for the first proposal for an iron-plated ship (*see* Ironclad Warship, Development of) belongs to an American, Col. John Stevens, of Hoboken, N. J., who, early in the War of 1812, designed a floating battery[qv] protected with iron plates. In 1820 Col. Stevens fired thirty-two pound shot at seventy yards without damage against targets protected with iron one-half inch thick, and in July, 1841, his sons, Edwin A. and John C. Stevens, fired sixty-four pound solid shot at thirty yards without damage against targets protected with wrought-iron boiler plates riveted together to four and one-half inches thickness. Steel supplanted wrought iron for armor plate in 1876, the first all-steel plates being made at Creusot, France. The Creusot process was brought to the United States in 1887 by the Bethlehem Steel Company. In 1890 tests at Annapolis proved definitely the superiority of steel over compound (wrought iron faced with steel) plates. In 1891 the Harvey process increased the resistance of steel by nearly 50%, but was supplanted by the Krupp process in 1900.

[J. P. Baxter, *Introduction of the Iron-Clad Warship;* William Hovgaard, *Modern History of Warships;* United States Naval Institute, *Proceedings*, July, 1883.]

LOUIS H. BOLANDER

Armour and Company, one of the world's largest meat and slaughtering establishments, arose from the partnership of John Plankinton and Philip D. Armour in a meat-packing and grain business established at Milwaukee in 1863. Shortly after the Civil War Armour became interested in a grain commission business in Chicago. In 1868 a meat-packing plant was added to the Chicago business, which in 1870 took the name of Armour and Company. Its growth was due to a vast emporium of livestock, railway transportation systems, the vigor and ability of leaders, the building of stockyards and to the growing use of refrigerator cars in transporting meats. Armour's first plant outside of Chicago was opened at Omaha in 1898. Armour and Company of Delaware was formed in 1922 to facilitate financing and administration. Armour and Company of Illinois, incorporated in 1900, showed an inventory in 1936 of 14 packing, 17 produce and creamery houses, 203 branch places, 7 foreign branch houses, a working capital of $112,291,000 and annual sales of $749,000,000.

[Howard C. Hill, Development of Chicago as a . . . Meat Packing Industry, *Mississippi Valley Historical Review*, X, December, 1923.]

LOUIS PELZER

Armstrong, Fort (1816–36), was one of a chain of frontier defenses erected after the War of 1812. It was located at the foot of Rock Island[qv], in the Mississippi River, five miles from the principal Sauk and Fox[qqv] village on Rock River, Ill. Of stone and timber construction, 300 feet square, the fort was commenced in May, 1816, and completed the following year. It was garrisoned until 1836, usually by two companies of United States regulars.

[D. W. Flagler, *History of the Rock Island Arsenal;* Stephen H. Long, *Voyage in a Six-Oared Skiff to the Falls of Saint Anthony in 1817*, Minnesota Historical Society Collections, II, Part I.]

PAUL M. ANGLE

Army, Confederate. Officially, the "Army of the Confederate States of America" was the small regular force established by an act of the Confederate Provisional Congress, March 6, 1861, to consist of one corps of engineers, one of artillery, six regiments of infantry, one of cavalry and four staff departments (adjutant and inspector general's, quartermaster general's, subsistence and medical). This force, incompletely organized when war began, was soon overshadowed by the volunteer forces known officially as "the provisional army." Other acts of Feb. 28 and March 6 authorized the President to assume control over military operations, to accept state forces and 100,000 volunteers for twelve months. By the end of April President Jefferson Davis had called for 82,000 men. On May 8 Congress authorized enlistments[qv] for the war and on Aug. 8, four more states having joined the Confederacy, 400,000 volunteers for one or three years' service. After the passage of the first conscription act in April, 1862 (*see* Confederacy, Conscription in the; Conscription), men were taken into the provisional army directly without the necessary aid of the state authorities.

The highest office in the Regular Army was that of brigadier general until Congress, on May 16, 1861, established the rank of general in order to give higher Confederate commanders control over major generals of state troops in the field. On Aug. 31 Davis nominated and the Congress confirmed Samuel Cooper, Albert Sidney Johnston, R. E. Lee, Joseph E. Johnston and G. T. Beauregard as generals of the Regular Army. On April 12, 1862, Braxton Bragg became a general in that army and in May, 1864, E. Kirby Smith a general in the provisional army. Major generals in the provisional army, under the act of Feb. 28, 1861, were first appointed in May of that year. In September, 1862, the rank of lieutenant general in the provisional army was created.

Serious difficulties were encountered in arming, clothing and feeding the troops. Most of the arms available in May, 1861, were obsolete or inferior and even these could not supply all the men. There was little powder. Only one foundry could cast cannon and only one small powder mill was in operation. The chief reliance for improved arms was in purchases abroad, but getting them through the blockade[qv] was a slow, risky and expensive process. The Government made contracts with private firms for arms, set up its own arsenals and powder mills. Shoes, clothing and blankets were hard to procure, for wool and leather were scarce and importations did not fill requirements. Food supplies, much more plentiful in the South, were often reduced by weak transportation facilities. By 1863 horses and mules had become scarce, thus reducing the mobility of the cavalry, artillery and baggage trains. Although the Confederate soldier was often poorly armed, clothed and fed, discipline in the larger armies was good and morale high until near the end.

The Confederacy[qv] was divided into military departments, fluctuating in number and extent, under commanders responsible only to the War Department and the President. Prompt co-ordination between these departments was often lacking. Other than President Davis himself, there was no commander-in-chief until R. E. Lee was appointed on Feb. 6, 1865, although Lee had been Davis' military adviser for a short time early in 1862 and Braxton Bragg from February to October, 1864.

Because of incomplete surviving records the number of enlistments in the Confederate armies has long been in dispute. Southern writers have estimated them at from 600,000 to 800,000 men, some Northern students at from 1,100,000 to 1,500,000. This last figure is obviously too high for a white population of about 5,000,000. The United States Census for 1860 indicates approximately 1,100,000 men of military age in the seceded states, but these figures are deceptive. Many sections where hostility to the Confederacy developed furnished few soldiers; other large areas were soon overrun by the Union armies. Apparently more men from the seceded states went into the Union Army[qv] than came to the Confederate colors from the non-seceding slave states. Exemptions, details for industrial work and other evasions of service cut down enlistments. Probably between 800,000 and 900,000 actually enrolled, but so many were never in service at any given date. Consolidated returns in the War Department showed:

	Total present and absent	*Total present*	*Total effective present for duty*
Dec. 31, 1862	449,439	304,015	253,208
Dec. 31, 1863	464,646	277,970	233,586
Dec. 31, 1864	400,787	196,016	154,910

Liberal allowances for scattered commands not reported and for irregular organizations would not bring the total enrolled to more than 600,000 at any of these dates. The state militia, serving short terms, uncertain in number and of dubious value, probably fell short of 100,000 at any given date. Losses from battle, disease, capture and desertion so reduced the numbers with the colors that only 174,223 surrendered in April and May, 1865.

[*War of the Rebellion: Official Records of the Union and Confederate Armies; Statutes at Large of the Confederate States;* T. L. Livermore, *Numbers and Losses in the Civil War in America, 1861-65;* R. H. McKim, *The Numerical Strength of the Confederate Army.*]

CHARLES W. RAMSDELL

Army, Enlistment in. *See* Enlistment; Enlistment in the Union Army.

Army, Peace-Time Work. The work of the army in time of peace is so inconspicuous that the country at large seldom hears of it, and yet so multifarious that it is difficult to describe. It falls into two great classes—that work which the army does in its own preparation for war, and that which it does for others.

The activity which attracts the public attention is that concerned with parades^qv^, horse shows and similar displays. This all comes within the "preparation" class; for while winning horse show, polo or parade trophies does not prepare for war, the ability to win them makes for discipline and for maintenance of mobility in the field. But the more direct preparation is obscure. The public sees troop columns and truck trains on their way to maneuvers, but knows nothing of the long preparation and laborious execution of the maneuvers themselves. The same is true on a smaller scale of the ordinary daily field exercises of a regiment or garrison. And even the daily housekeeping duties of the army are no small task. The captain who is personally responsible for shelter, clothing, subsistence, discipline, training and recreation of a hundred or more men, the training and health of as many horses, the upkeep of a small fleet of motor vehicles and the accountability for $100,000 or more of Government property, is a busy man.

Such preparatory work is not done by the Regular Army for itself alone. It has always been charged with a somewhat vague responsibility for assisting the National Guard[qv], and for several generations has handled such military instruction as was given in schools and colleges. But since the World War it has been very definitely charged with responsibility for instruction and inspection of the National Guard; for the entire training of the newly formed Officers' Reserve Corps[qv], including the Air Corps Reserve, which furnishes so many of our commercial pilots; for systematic and uniform instruction of the Reserve Officers' Training Corps[qv]; and for the conduct of innumerable Citizens' Military Training Camps[qv].

The other phase of army peace-time work is connected with emergencies of all kinds. From the beginning of our history the Army has fixed the frontier line, guarded it, explored beyond it, pushed it forward as the advance of settlement demanded, established communications by road, rail, wire and radio, aided the civil authority in maintaining order, given relief in fire, flood, famine and catastrophes of all kinds, e.g., the Black Hawk War, the Union Pacific Railway, Sitting Bull, Geronimo, the opening and organization of Alaska, the San Francisco fire, the Panama Canal, the conquering of the yellow and typhoid fevers, the Civilian Conservation Corps[qqv].

[Oliver L. Spaulding, *The United States Army in War and Peace.*]

OLIVER LYMAN SPAULDING

Army, Union (1861–65). When Fort Sumter[qv] was fired on, the United States had an army barely exceeding 16,000 enlisted men and officers, and the effectiveness of this organization was soon lessened by the resignations of Lee and other Southern officers. Northern states were feverishly passing laws for the raising, equipping and training of volunteers[qv] for three years of the war. And by April, 1861, the governors had offered some 300,000 such troops to the Federal Government. But President Lincoln, though determined to restore the Union by force, would not assemble Congress before July 4. Without new legislation there was no authority for an increase in the army, so all the recruiting fervor of the early spring was wasted.

The 75,000 militia, called for on April 15, could be used for only three months, and hence were rushed into battle at Bull Run[qv] in a futile effort to show the strength of the Union before their enlistment should expire. The lesson of Bull Run finally aroused Federal activity as it had not been stirred by the earlier agitation in the states. On July 22, 1861, and following, Congress authorized the creation of a volunteer army of 500,000 men and legalized the President's call of May 3 for 42,000 three-year volunteers and 22,700 regulars. The Regular Army at an authorized strength of 42,000, which was halfway approximated, was used throughout the war for border defense against the Indians. The volunteer army, with which the war was fought, was officered mainly by political generals chosen by the governors, and in the early months, at least, by regimental officers elected by the enlisted men. The result was a needlessly slow development of discipline and efficiency. Also, the competition of state governments with the War Department in bidding for uniforms, munitions, food and supplies led to a scandalous series of contract grafts, high prices and shoddy products (*see* Army Contracts).

The volunteering spirit so cooled off after Bull Run that the remainder of 1861 had passed before an acceptable army could be whipped into rudimentary shape. By the middle of 1862 the first army had been so badly depleted by disease and battle that on July 2 an additional 300,000 volunteers were called for, the governors again being left to care for recruiting and management of the new contingents till they were mustered into service. The troops were urgently needed and on Aug. 4, when volunteering proved sluggish, a draft[qv] of 300,000 nine months' militia was ordered under terms of an act of July 17, 1862. As a direct means of getting soldiers this draft proved a failure, only about 65,000 men being provided. But Federal, state and local bounties lured enough volunteers during the next few months to tide over the emergency.

Early in 1863 it was seen that continued heavy casualties, desertions[qqv], the expiration of short-term enlistments and scanty volunteering was likely to cause a collapse of the army before the close of the year. Consequently, the Enrollment Act of March 3, 1863, was passed to provide men by draft. The act was intended mainly to stimulate volunteering by threat of conscription[qv], thus encouraging the states and localities to avoid this stigma by the offering of adequate bounties[qv]. Men of means were given an easy escape from the draft by the payment of a $300 commutation fee or the hiring of substitutes[qv]. By a later amendment the commutation fee was limited to conscientious objectors[qv], but substitution was permitted till the end of the war. The direct product of two years of repeated drafting was about 50,000 conscripts and 120,000 substitutes. But in the same period over a million volunteers were procured by bounties. Thus for the last half of the war the army was relieved from the constant danger of extinction which had threatened the first half.

The total effective strength of the army on Jan. 1, 1863, before Federal conscription was begun, was just under 700,000. On May 1, 1865, at its highest point, the number was nearly 800,000. Including all men not fit for active service, each of these figures would be increased by about 200,000. The commissioning of 2537 generals alone (including brevet brigadiers) for an army of this size may be taken as an indication of the part spoilsman politics played in army organization. Nevertheless, after the first year the weeding out of incapable officers in high positions went on apace, proved capacity began to replace political favoritism and regimental elections for minor officers, and a tolerable degree of discipline was evolved. Contract grafts continued to lessen the efficiency of the army, but in a diminishing degree. An obtuse policy of the War Department prevented the supplying of the soldiers with modern weapons, which were available to the Union but not to the Confederacy, thus further restricting military efficiency.

[F. A. Shannon, *The Organization and Administration of the Union Army, 1861-1865.*]

FRED A. SHANNON

Army, United States. The United States Army is distinctly different from other armies, in origin, organization and employment.

It is modeled primarily upon the English; for when English colonists arrived in America they brought with them not only their civil but their military institutions. In England, as elsewhere in Europe, the land forces were made up primarily of regular, that is to say professional, troops; of these there were several classes, but their distinguishing characteristic was that they were directly under the orders of the king, whether or not they were directly raised by him; and that they were available for service anywhere that he might direct.

Besides these there were in many countries, and notably in England, nonprofessional, part-time, militia troops, intended primarily for local use in defense of the territory.

When English colonies were established in America or elsewhere, they were entitled, as British territory, to defense by the king's troops; and garrisons of those troops were sent to them at the king's discretion. Each colony also raised its own militia[qv], for preservation of order and defense of the frontier. When a special emergency arose a special expedition was formed, made up of the king's troops, local militia and local irregulars formed for the occasion.

When the American colonies rebelled, the king's troops suddenly became not friends but enemies. Nothing was left to the colonies but their own militia, with such new troops as they might see fit to form. These troops were subject, not to any central government, but each troop unit to its own colonial government. When the New England contingents assembled at Boston there was no real command, but only voluntary co-operation—which might answer for a time, in an inactive situation, but could not work for long.

When Washington joined, a central command was assured, but there was still no permanency of forces. Each colony dealt with its own; discipline, training, pay and supply were all chaotic. The only answer was to form a new force, responsible to Congress only, not to any state. This new force was the Continental Army[qv], which now took the place corresponding to that of the old British regulars. The force at large continued a mixed force, including Continentals, separate militia for each colony and new levies of various kinds.

At the end of the Revolutionary War the militia regiments went back to their own states, where most of them were disbanded; but a few regiments now forming part of our National Guard[qv] are continuations of these Revolutionary units. The Continentals had always been looked upon as a wartime expedient, and the entire force was promptly disbanded, with one interesting exception. Certain military stores were on hand, at West Point and Fort Pitt[qqv], and it was necessary to provide for guarding them until they could be disposed of. Hence one company of artillery was retained in service for that purpose. The company selected happened to be the one formerly commanded by Alexander Hamilton; and Hamilton's Battery is still in service, as Battery "D," 5th Field Artillery.

But hardly had the Continental troops been discharged when it was found that the Federal Government needed troops of its own, not of any state. The Whiskey Rebellion[qv] in western Pennsylvania placed the Government in the humiliating position of having to borrow troops from the states to enforce its own laws; and the Indians on the northwestern frontiers, in Ohio, Indiana and Michigan, proved too serious a problem to leave to local forces. So a new Regular Army was built up. Our oldest infantry regiment, now numbered as the Third, dates back to 1784; and we have many troop units almost as old.

This gives us our traditional military system: a small Regular Army under the exclusive control of the National Government; varying forces of militia in each state, responsible solely to the state in peace, but capable of passing under Federal control in war. The limitation upon the use of British militia still remained among our state troops—they could not be ordered abroad. In our case, many of the militia construed this limitation so strictly that they even questioned the authority of the United States to order them outside their own states. This point was raised so often during the War of 1812[qv] that on one occasion Gen. Jackson, having raised some entirely new troops and offered them to the Government, explained that they were "volunteers and not militia, and had no constitutional scruples."

In the Mexican War[qv] the force of state troops required was not large. The Regular Army was expanded, and various new regiments were raised under the authority of the United States. These new regiments were called regular, because they belonged to no state, but they were not permanent troops, and were disbanded upon conclusion of peace.

In the Civil War[qv], on the other hand, the little regular force was not a drop in the bucket. All that existed were used, and the only complaint was that there were not more of them; but the war was fought chiefly by state troops, raised and officered by the states and then mustered into the Federal service. Many individual regular officers, of course, were assigned to duty with these troops, which helped the new forces, but contributed to the disintegration of the old.

This procedure, of disregarding regular troops and raising state troops, became thoroughly familiar to all the people during the Civil War. Without thinking of merits and demerits, the country at large came to look upon it as the natural and proper way of raising troops. The Spanish War was comparatively a small effort, and the leading men in the Government, both civil and military, were nearly all men of Civil War experience; the old plan was followed, as a matter of course, and apparently without conscious weighing of other plans.

A complication arose at the close of hostilities with Spain. We had inherited an insurrection in the Philippines[qv], and many of the troops sent there were state troops enlisted for the war with Spain. They continued, loyally and cheerfully, to serve in the insurrection, but palpably it was unfair to expect them to do so indefinitely; and we had recourse to the Mexican War expedient of raising temporary troops under Federal, not state, authority. In this case we called them, not temporary regulars, but United States Volunteers, and they served until additional regular troops could be authorized and raised.

We had become familiar, then, with four classes of troops; the Regular Army, always in service, subject to the Federal Government alone, and kept almost as busy in peace as in war; temporary regulars or United States Volunteers, like the regulars but authorized only by special acts of Congress for war times; state troops, under the jurisdiction of the states only; and state troops mustered into the service of the United States for specific purposes.

When it came to the great mobilization for the World War[qv] we utilized all these classes, and much in the same manner as before. The Regular Army was greatly expanded, and at the same time it was called upon for heavy details of officers and men to form a nucleus for the new troops, badly disrupting the old. State troops were called for, and mustered into the service of the United States; they were then so completely reorganized as to leave little sign of their old form. A new National Army[qv], of temporary troops under United States control, was formed. Such was the haste to get troops into the field that the possibilities of orderly expansion were overlooked; so many divisions were organized that when one was to go overseas it almost always had to be filled up by drafts from others, leaving those others to go through the whole organization process again.

At the close of the war a drastic reorganization was made, with a view to obviating the difficulties encountered. The state troops, now called the National Guard, were placed on a more systematic basis, and provision was made for more simple and rapid transformation into United States troops. The National Army, of course, had disappeared, but provision was made for a corps of reserve officers, to maintain its tradition and to prepare the way for the prompt mobilization of a new one. The Regular Army was given a new system of organization and command, and was reduced to a peace basis; but a large number of additional officers, not required by the Regular Army organization itself, was added to furnish instructors for the National Guard and for the reserve officers, and to set up a scheme of school training for officers and officer candidates. This expansion of the Regular Army lists, of course, did provide for the needs in question, but it enormously reduced the amount of troop duty that an officer can do, and threw more emphasis upon theoretical study and less upon practical troop work than we had ever tried before.

The school system just mentioned calls for a word of explanation. It consists of elementary professions schools in all regular troop units; special schools for officers of each arm; a command and staff school at Fort Leavenworth for selected officers of all arms; and a War College[qv] at Washington for instruction in the mechanism of the War Department staff and of the highest troop units in the field. To keep up the numbers of the reserve officers required under the general scheme the old system of military instruction in high schools and colleges was improved and systematized, taking the form of a Reserve Officers' Training Corps[qv]. To provide noncommissioned officers for any new force to be raised, the Citizens' Military Training Camps[qv] were formed, operating every summer. A few of the attendants at these camps, who attend for four summers, are commissioned as reserve officers, on the same basis as graduates of the R.O.T.C.

This whole system is in operation, and is under trial, particularly with respect to the number of troops that can be efficiently raised in a given time. It will be noted that while nearly all the details have been changed, the general scheme is that under which we have always raised our armies in past wars. It is still too early to predict how, in its present form, it will succeed under stress; or to judge to what extent, if any, the whole plan will require reconstruction to meet modern conditions.

[Oliver L. Spaulding, *The United States Army in War and Peace;* National Defense Act with Amendments, *House of Representatives Document*, 1935; Hearings on National Defense, House of Representatives, March, 1927; Burnside Report on Reorganization of the Army, *Senate Report 555*, Dec. 12, 1878.]

OLIVER LYMAN SPAULDING

Army, United States, Insignia of Rank in. The origin of insignia of rank in our army dates from the period of Washington's variously clad Continental Army[qv], wherein it became necessary to devise badges in order to indicate rank. Washington's order read, "As the Continental Army has unfortunately no uniforms, and consequently many inconveniences must arise from not being able to distinguish the commissioned officers from the privates, it is desired that some badges of distinction may be immediately provided; for instance that the field officers may have red or pink colored cockades in their hats. the captains yellow or buff, and the subalterns green. They are to furnish themselves accordingly. The sergeants may be distinguished by an epaulette or stripe of red cloth sewed upon their right shoulder, the corporals by one of green." Just prior to the issuance of this order, Washington directed that "the general officers and their aides-de-camp will be distinguished in the following manner: The Commander in Chief by a light-blue ribband worn across his heart between his coat and waistcoat; the Major and Brigadier General by a pink ribband worn in like manner; the Aides-de-Camp by a green ribband." Major Generals' sleeves were to be distinguished from Brigadier Generals' by a "broad purple ribband." Thus began the indications of rank in our army. Such markings now extend, through varying devices, from the Second Lieutenant's single gold bar to the General's four silver stars, and through a variety of chevrons for noncommissioned rank.

[Col. Robert E. Wyllie, *The Romance of Military Insignia.*]

ROBERT S. THOMAS

Army Contracts have been used as the chief instruments through which the American armed forces have been supplied with materiel since the Revolution. A dubious fame had been won by these contracts as early as 1777, when the states were urged by the Continental Congress[qv] to fix prices on clothing in order to forestall large profits gained from "sharping and extortion." In 1781, when the harassed Congress adopted the European system of supply, a single civilian contractor might become virtually dictator of the army's movements. Buying supplies and transporting them to the troops, the contractor was inclined not only to stint on quality but to await a favorable market and favorable weather. Bitter criticism during the War of 1812 and the Florida Indian campaigns led in 1818 to an attempt to halt corruption and to promote efficiency by the adoption of a strengthened staff system. Public notice and inspection were required and staff members were prohibited from profiting personally on purchases or sales.

But the first months of the Civil War saw collusion, fraud and favoritism at their worst. Contracts, made at exorbitant prices, were sold to subcontractors and the profits pocketed without risk; the Government bought its own cast-off arms; troops were clad in shoddy which disintegrated under their eyes. A congressional investigation resulted in restrictive legislation, passed early in 1862, requiring competitive bidding and written contracts, prohibiting subletting and subjecting contractors to court-martial in cases of indictment for fraud. Government inspection was tightened up, with the result that the worst abuses were eliminated, although unreasonable profits continued, laying the foundations of many American fortunes.

The effect of legislation and regulation produced by these experiences came to a head in the World War and proved as obstructive under modern conditions as their lack had earlier proved scandalous. The War Department unwound itself from peace-time red tape hardly a month before the armistice signaled the end of the war. Nevertheless, the World War was remarkably free from contract scandals. Although $17,480,000,000 was disbursed from April 6, 1917, to June 1, 1919, of which $9,850,000,000 was spent on contract by the Quartermaster Corps and Ordnance Department alone, Congress in 1919–20 found little evidence of graft or collusion. Congressional criticism centered around the cost-plus[qv] contract, an emergency instrument ultimately prohibited. To offset profits, price-fixing[qv] was attempted and excess-profits taxes[qv] were applied, measures which were only partially successful. In this war, however, the contractor was in no position to bargain on equal terms, for the Government, with its massive purchasing power, perfected propaganda techniques and the legal right to commandeer productive facilities, was in a position superior even to that of the giant corporation.

[L. C. Hatch, *The Administration of the American Revolutionary Army;* M. M. McKee, Service of Supply in the War of 1812, *Quartermaster Review,* Vol. VI; F. A. Shannon, *The Organization and Administration of the Union Army;* J. F. Crowell, *Government War Contracts.*]

WAYNE C. GROVER

Army General Staff, DEVELOPMENT OF THE. In the period of our colonial wars, when our military institutions were being formed from those of England, the staff of an army consisted primarily of a Quartermaster General and an Adjutant General, each with a staff of his own to handle details. The Quartermaster General assisted the commander in preparing operations plans, and in the execution of these plans collected information and arranged marches and quarters. The supply service (*see* Army Supply) was under his direction. The Adjutant General dealt with the internal economy of troop units.

During the 19th century the Quartermaster General became a supply officer only, while the term General Staff was used to signify all general officers and members of staff departments, not belonging to regiments. The staff departments reported direct to the Secretary of War, and the nominal Commanding General of the army had little authority over them.

In 1903, by act of Congress upon recommendation of Secretary Root, a General Staff Corps was formed. In place of a Commanding General of the army a Chief of Staff was provided, issuing orders to the whole army in the name of the Secretary of War.

This system being new to us, no really efficient organization was worked out for some years. Finally, in the American Expeditionary Forces[qv] in France, a system was adopted assimilating our General Staff organization very closely to the French. Meanwhile a different system had been adopted in the War Department[qv], and at the end of the war it became necessary to choose between the two. The A.E.F. system was decided upon, with some modifications.

Our General Staff now consists of five divisions, one dealing with personnel administration, one with military intelligence, one with organization and training, one with supply and transportation and one with war plans. It differs from the other types described above, in that they are essentially army agencies, dealing exclusively with intelligence and operations and having nothing to do with War Department administration. Ours is distinctly a War Department agency, controlling the entire administration of the army.

[Oliver L. Spaulding, *The United States Army in War and Peace.*]

OLIVER LYMAN SPAULDING

Army Hospitalization may be defined as the process of providing shelter, care and other environmental factors needed to restore the disabled to health and physical fitness. The Surgeon General of the army is the head of the Medical Department. He is charged among his other duties and responsibilities with the supervision of the administration of all establishments for the care, treatment and transportation of the sick and wounded personnel of the military establishment under the immediate direction of the War Department, as prescribed by the Secretary of War.

The first hospital for sick soldiers in the territory now known as the United States was established on Manhattan Island in 1658. During the American Revolution, because of the poverty and meager resources of the country, little was done in hospital building. The sick and wounded were at first evacuated to various types of houses. Later there were provided log huts so built that air could penetrate the crevices. These huts were without floors, the ground being hardened or baked with heat. Each hut accommodated eight to twelve men. During the War of 1812, in addition to previous hospital facilities, a general hospital was established constituting forty wards containing between 700 and 800 patients. The patients were segregated according to surgical cases and various other diseases. Profiting by the experience of the British government during the Crimean War, this country during the Civil War developed the most perfect system of army hospitals ever known up to that time. It consisted of the pavilion type of general hospital. Each pavilion constituted a single ward of not more than fifty beds, isolated from adjacent buildings. An improvement to this type of building was made at the time of the Spanish-American War. The Letterman General Hospital at San Francisco was among the best. Still greater improvements were made in the pavilion type of hospital during the World War, and today there are available for use at any time, plans and specifications for standardized pavilion hospitals appropriate for both the Zone of the Interior and the Theater of Operations requirements.

During peace only station and general hospitals care for army patients. The station hospital, varying greatly in bed capacity, serves only the local station or post. Its facilities depend in general upon the size of the command served. General hospitals provide general and special, rather than local and ordinary, needs. They are organized, equipped and staffed to afford better facilities than can be given in station hospitals. In time of war, peace-time hospitals are augmented by leasing existing buildings and sites and by the erection of new buildings in the Theater of Operations and the Zone of the Interior. All hospitals established in the Zone of the Interior to meet local mobilization needs are designated either station or general hospitals, while hospitals in the Theater of Operations are classed as mobile and fixed hospitals. The mobile hospitals (hospital companies or troops, surgical hospitals, evacuation hospitals and convalescent hospitals) accompany the armies in the Combat Zone and are equipped with sufficient tentage for sheltering patients, but utilize existing buildings when possible. The fixed hospitals (station hospitals, general hospitals, hospital centers and convalescent camps) are units in the Communication Zone to which the sick and wounded are sent for definitive treatment. Casualties requiring prolonged treatment or considered a permanent loss as a military asset are transferred to station and general hospitals in the Zone of the Interior.

[*The Medical Service of the Corps and Army*, published by the Medical Field Service School, Carlisle Barracks, Pa.; *The Medical Service of the Field Forces*, published by the Medical Field Service School, Carlisle Barracks, Pa.]

CHARLES M. WALSON

Army of Occupation (1918–23). As part of the Allied Army of Occupation, the American Third Army, commanded by Maj. Gen. Joseph T. Dickman, crossed into Germany in December, 1918, taking station in the North Sector of the Coblenz bridgehead. Units of the Third Army were stationed at various points within the American area and engaged in duties of occupation and training, including participation in civil administration of occupied territory, until July 2, 1919, when the Third Army was discontinued. It was succeeded by the "American Forces in Germany."

Maj. Gen. Edward F. McGlachlin, Jr., assumed command of this newly designated force until July 8, 1919, when its permanent commander, Maj. Gen. Henry T. Allen, reported. From January, 1920, Gen. Allen worked in conjunction with the Rhineland High Commission. At noon on Jan. 27, 1923, American troops having left the Coblenz area, Gen. Allen relinquished command of the American area.

[Henry T. Allen, *The Rhineland Occupation.*]

ROBERT S. THOMAS

Army on the Frontier. This term applies to the activities of the United States Army stationed near the frontier settlements from the beginning of national existence until about 1890, the end of the settlers' frontier. The principal functions performed by this army were: 1, guarding the frontier settlements from hostile Indians; 2, aiding the settlement of the West by developing and protecting the communication between the older settlements and the frontier, by exploring the West, constructing roads and defending the overland trails, water routes and later telegraph and railroad lines; and 3, policing the frontier until the civil governments could maintain order.

The western movement[qv] of settlers brought conflict with the Indians. Scores of Indian wars and campaigns were fought by the army. Some of the more notable Indian wars were: the Northwest Indians, 1790–95 and 1811–13; Seminole Wars in Florida, 1817–18, 1835–42 and 1856; Black Hawk War, 1832; Sioux War, 1862–67; War of the Plains Indians, 1863–69; Sioux and Cheyenne War of 1876–79; and Apache Wars, 1861–90[qqv]. These wars were fought by the regular infantry and cavalry regiments occasionally aided by state militia and volunteers. The frontier soldiers were usually stationed in posts at strategic points defending the routes of communications, settlements and Indian reservations. The strength of this army, about one half of the Regular Army in time of peace, ranged from 1423 troops in 1790 in the Northwest Territory[qv] to over 26,000 in 1868, which was the height of the Indian wars on the Great Plains. The frontier posts had on the average a garrison of 200 troops. By 1867 over 100 posts were scattered throughout the West. As the Indian wars ended, after 1870, these posts were rapidly abandoned.

The army supplies were carried by boats, steamboats, ox and mule trains, pack mules and horses and later by railroads, which stimulated the development of trade, farming and ranching. The difficulty of supplying these remote army posts encouraged farming and urban enterprises around the posts, the beginning of permanent settlements.

The daily life of the frontier soldier was a hardy one. The soldiers built their shelter, escorted travelers, emigrants, and wagon trains on the trails, aided and protected surveying parties, constructed thousands of miles of trails and roads, supplied needy emigrants, patrolled trails and railroad lines, guarded river navigation, protected government and private property from hostile Indians and outlaws, assisted and fed friendly Indians, fought hostile Indians and gave police assistance to the weak civil authorities on the frontier. Their shelters were usually log, stone, adobe or sod huts constructed largely by their own labor. The hardships of the soldiers, the miserable quarters, inferior food and the lonely life encouraged many desertions.

The army on the frontier disagreed with the Indian Bureau[qv] and the frontier civil authorities over the Indian policy[qv]. The frontiersmen in general demanded the destruction or removal of the Indians (*see* Indian Removals). The Indian Bureau attempted to protect the Indians, and the army to coerce them. When the Indians revolted the army made war upon the entire Indian tribe, punishing the innocent with the guilty, even to the extent of killing women and children in raids on villages or camps. The Indian Bureau and the army officials accused each other of being responsible for the Indian wars.

[C. Goodwin, *Trans-Mississippi West;* G. W. Manypenny, *Our Indian Wards;* N. A. Miles, *Serving the Republic;* F. L. Paxson, *History of the American Frontier,* and *The Last American Frontier;* R. E. Reigel, *America Moves West;* J. Winsor, *The Westward Movement.*]

RAYMOND L. WELTY

Army Posts, THE, of the United States Army[qv] played an important part in the westward extension of the frontier[qv]. In the older eastern states they became centers for recruiting and drilling troops and guardians of the coast line at strategic points. These older forts followed European models of construction, and accommodations for the soldiers, officers and their wives were usually comfortable. Not so those of the frontier, which were often in advance or on the fringe of the settled regions and were usually speedily constructed by the soldiers themselves. Jefferson introduced the factory or trading system[qv] in connection with the establishment of army posts as a means of dealing with the Indians. Settlements grew up around these posts and after their abandonment, usually after a period of a few years, towns of the same name frequently remained. Important treaties with the Indians were very often made at the forts, or at points near them under military protection. Many of these treaties were negotiated by the officers themselves.

A study of the extension of forts westward will show that they were usually slightly in advance of the frontier line of settlement and at some periods were constructed more rapidly than at others. The period after the War of 1812 was one in which forts were rapidly advanced throughout the old Northwest[qv] into territory formerly claimed by the British. As Spain and Mexico were pushed back in the Southwest, army posts followed, until by 1845 a line of eleven forts extended from Lake Superior to the Gulf of Mexico.

Indian raids during the Civil War on the Great Plains and the extension of mail routes and later railroads to the Pacific necessitated the buildings of forts at strategic points. Regular Army forts accommodating usually from two to six companies with artillery were supplemented by minor temporary or lightly held centers designated as camps or cantonments. These last were usually little more than huts or shelters and often merely wooded, grassed and watered areas suitable for a few days' stay.

The usual form for the larger posts, which indicates a fairly permanent station for troops, was in the form of a quadrangle constructed around a parade ground, with the officers' quarters, barracks, post traders and hospital on one side and the stables and quartermaster's supplies on the other. The ends of the quadrangle might be occupied by the guard house, company kitchens and work shops, and farther back by the laundress' quarters. Not all new forts had such elaborate equipment.

Despite the lack of the amenities, life at some of these frontier posts was pleasant—in peace times—for the younger set. Young West Pointers brought out their wives, who maintained as far as possible the social standards of their old homes, and "post hops," riding and hunting parties and card games were enjoyed. Wild game was often plentiful but this asset of the larder was supplemented when necessary by cattle drives[qv] from the east and south, thus introducing cattle to the Great Plains. Gardens and farms were laid out around the posts to provide vegetables, grains and forage, and thus it was demonstrated that the prairies were not sterile because they had no trees. Flour mills were constructed at certain posts such as Snelling and Atkinson[qqv].

Most garrisons had post schools, libraries, newspapers and magazines. Plays were given and some of the most accurate and colorful literature of the new territory appears in the memoirs of army officers and even of their wives. After the abandonment of a post the buildings were usually sold and the land ceded or auctioned off. In a few cases the area was made into a national reserve.

[H. P. Beers, *Western Military Frontier;* U. S. War Department, Surgeon General Official Circular No. 8, *Report of the Hygiene of the United States Army with a Description of Military Posts.*]

CARL L. CANNON

Army School System. Such schooling as was available in the United States Army prior to and following the Civil War was obtained in Lyceum courses: assemblies at which selected officers presented prepared papers. The army was then scattered throughout the country in small isolated garrisons, much of the time in actual field duty. There was no definite educational system or policy.

The Garrison School, supervised by the War Department, replaced the Lyceum system and continued until the World War. A school of artillery instruction was begun at Fortress Monroe in 1824. In 1881 a School of Application for Infantry and Cavalry, now Command and General Staff School, was established at Fort Leavenworth, Kans. This was the first definite step to secure a bona fide system of instruction and has served as the basis for the army's school policies. The Army War College[qv], Washington, D. C., established in 1901, laid the cornerstone of our modern military educational system.

World War experience brought about the establishment of branch schools—the Special Service Schools. These constitute the backbone of the system; in them the officer learns the fundamentals of his arm.

Schooling is compulsory and continuous throughout an officer's service. Troop Schools and Special Service Schools which provide basic courses are usually attended by all officers of the particular service.

The General Service Schools are the Leavenworth School, the Army War College and the Army Industrial College. Attendance is by selection.

Every officer aspires for Leavenworth. Courses are for regular officers, with shorter courses for the National Guard and Officer's Reserve Corps[qqv]. The school prepares officers for command and general staff[qv] duty.

Only a few attend the War College, graduation from which completes the officer's education; the mission of the War College is to train officers in the operations of the army and higher echelons; and to instruct in those political, economic and social matters which influence the conduct of war.

The Army Industrial College situated in Washington, D. C., is limited to officers of the Regular Army. It trains officers in the wartime needs of industrial organization and mobilization of material; technique of wartime procurement of military supplies, etc.

W. M. GRIMES

Army Supply. As now used in the American Army, the word "supply," in its broadest sense, indicates all military stores and services furnished by one branch of the army for the use of another. This includes food, clothing, shelter, transportation, weapons, ammunition, equipment of all kinds, purchase, pay, hospitalization[qv], labor, etc. These supply functions of the army are divided between the several branches of the staff known, generally, as the Supply Departments or the Supply Services and are grouped under the supervision of a General Staff^qv officer known as the Assistant Chief of Staff for Supply.

Beginning in the Revolution and until a comparatively recent date, the principal supply functions of the army, as above defined, were divided between the Quartermaster Department, the Subsistence Department, the Pay Department, the Corps of Engineers, the Ordnance Department and the Medical Department. The Signal Corps was added in 1863 and the Chemical Warfare Service in 1920.

The Corps of Engineers, the Signal Corps and the Chemical Warfare Service not only furnish supplies to other arms, but also perform a distinctive combat function of their own, so that, to this extent, they belong to the Line of the army.

Under the act of Aug. 24, 1912, the Quartermaster Department, the Subsistence Department and the Pay Department were merged into one branch, known as the Quartermaster Corps. Later, in 1920, the old Pay Department was taken away from the Quartermaster Corps and with added duties became the Finance Department.

During the World War the Supply Services, while continuing in a general way to perform their old duties, were largely superseded in the War Department by a branch of the General Staff known as the Division of Purchase, Storage and Traffic.

In France a somewhat similar organization was created under the name of the Services of Supply, with headquarters at Tours and entirely separated from Gen. Pershing's headquarters at Chaumont (*see* American Expeditionary Forces). During the course of the war, a number of changes were made in this organization, but, generally speaking, it provided for a redistribution of the old supply functions into the following groups: the Quartermaster Department, the Transportation Department, the Motor Transport Corps, the Army Service Corps, the Division of Construction and Forestry, the Division of Engineer Supplies, the Division of Light Railways, the Ordnance Department, the Gas Service, the Medical Department, the Finance Department, the General Purchasing Board and the War Risk Insurance.

After the World War there was another reorganization of the Supply Departments in Washington. In effect, they resumed their old functions under their old names, with the addition of the Chemical Warfare Service, but were coordinated by an Assistant Chief of Staff for Supply.

In addition to this there was created a procurement agency in the office of the Assistant Secretary of War which is charged with the general supervision of procurement of military stores in time of peace and with the mobilization of industry in time of war.

In the more restricted sense, the word "supplies" is used in the army to indicate military stores and does not include personal services.

[Gen. Johnson Hagood, *The Services of Supply.*]

JOHNSON HAGOOD

Army War College, THE, is the highest seat of instruction in, and culmination of, the educational system of the United States Army^qv; it trains selected officers for high command and the higher General Staff^qv duties; and ninety Regular Army and a limited number of Navy and Marine Corps officers pursue a one-year course. Organized in 1901 by Secretary of War Root, until creation of the General Staff of the army in 1903, it performed the functions of that body, continuing as a part thereof until the World War.

J. L. DEWITT

Arnold Betrays the Cause. Brig. Gen. Benedict Arnold of the Continental Army had fought gallantly for the American cause from Ticonderoga (1775) to Saratoga (1777)^qqv. But by the spring of 1779 several motives led him to open up a treasonable correspondence with the British headquarters in New York. These were (1) irritation at repeated slights by Congress, (2) resentment at the authorities of Pennsylvania who had court-martialed him, (3) need for money and (4) opposition to the French alliance of 1778^qv. Throughout the rest of 1779 and 1780 he transmitted military intelligence about the American Army to the British. July 12, 1780, he "accepted the command at West Point as a post in which I can render the most essential services" [to the British]. He demanded from the British £20,000 in case he could betray West Point and £10,000 in case he failed but himself went over to the British. Negotiations were carried on with Maj. John André^qv, adjutant general of the British army. The latter visited Arnold at a point between the British and American lines Sept. 21, 1780. On Sept. 23, when returning from this meeting, André was captured by the Americans, and the incriminating documents found in his stocking were sent to Gen. Washington, who happened to be in the neighborhood. News of André's capture was also sent to Arnold, thus giving him time to escape down the Hudson River to the British before he could be arrested for treason. He became a brigadier general in the British army, went to England after the defeat of the British and died there June 14, 1801.

[I. N. Arnold, *Life of Benedict Arnold;* W. Abbatt, *Crisis of the Revolution.*]

RANDOLPH G. ADAMS

Arnold's March to Quebec. In the summer of 1775 Col. Benedict Arnold went to Cambridge, Mass., and laid before Commander in Chief George Washington a plan for attacking Canada. Washington was sympathetic. The old classic route by way of Lakes George and Champlain and the Richelieu River was assigned to Gen. Richard Montgomery. News of another passage by way of the Kennebec and Chaudière rivers had reached Washington. This route was assigned to a force under Arnold. On Sept. 19 Arnold's command left Newburyport, Mass., and went by sea to and up the Kennebec where 200 bateaux had been ordered to be ready. With these Arnold headed up the river. Made of green wood and ill-adapted to the upper rushing waters of the Kennebec, these bateaux were a tactical blunder which, however, did not daunt Arnold. Neither did he hesitate when Maj. Roger Enos turned back with one-fourth of the little army. On up the Dead River, full of ice and through snowstorms, with insufficient food and clothing, Arnold led his force. Oct. 28 found them going across the carrying place which was actually the divide between the St. Lawrence and Atlantic watersheds. Arnold plunged ahead with an advance guard while the remainder were reduced to eating dogs and shoeleather. At Sertigan, Arnold arranged for supplies which refreshed his exhausted detachment so that they were able to go down the Chaudière and reach the St. Lawrence on Nov. 9, 1775. In the meantime Montgomery had reached Montreal, but Arnold went on across the St. Lawrence and was actually in front of Quebec before Montgomery arrived. Guy Carleton, the British commander at Montreal, evacuated that place and got into Quebec before Montgomery could join Arnold on Dec. 2. Carleton had 1200 men while the combined American forces numbered scarcely 1000. Nevertheless, in a blinding snowstorm, Montgomery and Arnold assaulted Quebec on the night of Dec. 31, 1775. The effort failed, Montgomery was killed and Arnold wounded. Arnold's march through the wilderness of Maine has been regarded as a classic of perseverance and determination in the face of extreme hardship.

[J. H. Smith, *Arnold's March from Cambridge to Quebec,* and *Our Struggle for the Fourteenth Colony.*]

RANDOLPH G. ADAMS

Arnold's Raid in Virginia. In December of 1780 Commander in Chief Sir Henry Clinton of the British armies in North America determined to send an expedition into Virginia. Its purpose was to conduct desultory raids into the tidewater region of that state and to block the mouth of the Chesapeake. The command was given to the traitor, Benedict Arnold, because Clinton admired his intrepidity and believed he could induce some more Americans to desert. Leaving Sandy Hook on Dec. 20–21 and arriving at Hampton Roads Dec. 30, Arnold seized the small boats on the James River and pushed up that stream to Westover. Sending Simcoe's Rangers ahead, the force was moved on to Richmond, which Arnold occupied after a skirmish on Jan. 5, 1781. He destroyed the iron foundry at Westham and the American stores at Richmond. Arnold then re-embarked on the James and fell down to Portsmouth, which he fortified and whence he sent various marauding and pillaging expeditions into the neighborhood until March, when he was joined and outranked by Maj. Gen. William Phillips. In April Phillips and Arnold started another expedition up the James, reaching City Point on the 24th, whence they proceeded overland to Petersburg where 1000 hogsheads of tobacco were destroyed, as were the small boats on the Appomattox. Arnold then returned to Osborn's on the James where he destroyed a small American fleet, marched to Manchester where 1200 hogsheads of tobacco were destroyed, thence to Warwick where the flour magazines and mills were burned. In May the force fell down to Westover, thence to Brandon. Throughout these movements the British were harassed by the inferior forces of Lafayette and Wayne. Phillips died at Petersburg on May 13, 1781, and the chief command momentarily devolved on Arnold again. But at this time Lord Cornwallis came up with his superior forces and joined the detachment of Phillips and Arnold to his for the campaign of the summer of 1781.

[J. G. Simcoe, *Journal of the Operations of the Queen's Rangers.*]

RANDOLPH G. ADAMS

Aroostook War, The, was an undeclared and bloodless "war," from February to May, 1839, occasioned by the failure of the United States and Great Britain to determine the boundary between New Brunswick and what is now Maine (*see* Northeast Boundary). In 1820 Maine became a state. Almost immediately, ignoring the British contention that all land north of Mars Hill, in Aroostook, was British, the Maine legislature, jointly with Massachusetts, made grants to settlers along both branches of the Aroostook River. In 1831 Madawaska, in the disputed area, was incorporated by Maine. Finally, in January, 1839, Rufus McIntire was appointed land agent, with authority to take a posse into the disputed area and oust Canadians. Within two months 10,000 Maine troops were either encamped along the Aroostook River or were on their way there. At the insistence of Maine congressmen, the Federal Government voted a force of 50,000 men and $10,000,000 in the event of war. To prevent a clash Gen. Winfield Scott was despatched to negotiate a truce with the lieutenant governor of New Brunswick. This he did, and Great Britain, convinced of the seriousness of the situation, agreed to a boundary commission, whose findings were incorporated in the Webster-Ashburton Treaty[qv].

[H. S. Burrage, *Maine and the Northeastern Boundary Controversy.*]

ELIZABETH RING

Arpent, The, is an old French unit of land measure, both linear and superficial, now standardized in Louisiana at 192 English feet, or a square of that dimension (equal to approximately five sixths of an acre). French colonial land grants were described as fronting a given number of arpents on a river or bayou by forty arpents in depth and containing a certain number of superficial arpents.

WALTER PRICHARD

Arrest. "The course of development (under the common law) seems to have been outlawry, vengeance, hue and cry[qv], arrest." The first three stages had passed before the colonization of America, though arrest without warrant "survives from the hue and cry" (not abolished in England until 1827) and is here the oldest form. Such arrest is still permitted by an officer or private citizen, of one who is about to commit, is committing or has committed a crime in the former's presence. In certain cases an officer may make such an arrest on suspicion. Suspected aliens were formerly arrested by immigration inspectors without warrant; but the practice was finally discontinued as "illegal." Arrest upon a warrant issued by a justice of the peace became the usual practice in England and the common law, as carried to the colonies, generally required a warrant.

But arrest was not confined to criminal procedure. The civil writ of *capias ad satisfaciendum,* e.g., was executed by imprisoning defendant until debt and costs were paid; that practice continued in England until 1869. "From time immemorial members of Parliament were privileged from arrest during the sessions of that body" (67 Neb. 75); but its act of 1770, sponsored by Lord Mansfield, limited the privilege to civil arrest (207 U. S. 438) and seven years later language of that act was embodied in the Articles of Confederation[qv] (V), a decade thereafter in the Federal Constitution[qv] (I, 6, paragraph I) and subsequently in many state constitutions; but in none does the exemption extend to other civil process (293 U. S. 76) in the absence of an express provision, which, however, has been enacted in some states. "When the Constitution was adopted arrests in civil suits were still common in America" (293 U. S. 83). Indeed, the United States Circuit Court for the Rhode Island district, with Chief Justice Jay presiding in 1792, annulled, as impairing the obligation of contracts[qv], a state statute exempting a debtor from arrest during a moratorium. Statutes are still in force in some states authorizing the arrest of a delinquent debtor, especially one guilty of fraud; but in others a state constitutional ban of imprisonment for debt has been held to preclude such arrest (106 Ala. 35), and it is not permitted in Federal courts except in enforcing a state law (U. S. Code § 843). Differing in its nature and origin from the common-law arrest is the "attachment" for contempt in disobeying an order of a chancery court (e.g., an injunction[qv]). Always obnoxious to the champions of labor, such jurisdiction in Federal courts has been somewhat curtailed by the acts of Congress of 1914 (Clayton Act[qv]) and 1932 (Norris-LaGuardia Act[qv]); but the power to "attach" for contempt remains and in some state courts even decrees for alimony are thus enforced, despite the constitutional prohibition of imprisonment for debt[qv].

[Wilgus, Arrest without a Warrant, *Mich. L. Rev. XXII,* 545; Warren, *History of the Supreme Court; Corpus Juris,* 2, VI, 568-712; Executions against the Body, etc., *Encyc. Pl. & Pr. VIII,* 584.]

C. SUMNER LOBINGIER

Arrest, Arbitrary, during the Civil War. Freedom from arbitrary arrest, guaranteed in the writ of habeas corpus[qv], has become synonymous in Anglo-Saxon tradition with civil liberty[qv]. The right to restrict this freedom nevertheless is recognized in England as a parliamentary function and in the United States as a constitutional exercise of power in time of "rebellion or invasion." Until 1861 this Federal right had never been exercised, but the Civil War brought widespread restrictions of civil liberty. In order to cope with antiwar activities (*see* Copperheads), President Lincoln issued several proclamations by which the privilege of the writ of habeas corpus was suspended, first within limited areas and later (Sept. 24, 1862) throughout the entire nation.

The President's control of arbitrary arrest was frequently questioned, especially by Chief Justice Taney, who held (*ex parte* Merryman[qv]) that the legislative branch rather than the executive had this constitutional authority. Lincoln ably defended himself against dictatorship charges in various open letters, however (*see* Birchard Letter; Corning Letter). Executive control was maintained and extended, even after Congress required (March 3, 1863) that political prisoners either be released or subjected to regular judicial procedure. The Department of State and later the War Department administered arrests. Passports were required, a secret service[qv] was organized and Union officers and local police co-operated in apprehending suspects. Political prisoners were detained without hearing and usually released after brief imprisonment. Trial by military commissions, such as in the Vallandigham and Milligan cases[qqv], was exceptional. Although the authority for such commissions was not questioned by the Supreme Court during the war, their use outside the war zone for the trial of civilians was declared unconstitutional after the war.

The number of arrests for antiwar activities is not known exactly. One official list with 13,535 names is incomplete, while on the other hand Alexander Johnston's guess of 38,000 is exaggerated. No authoritative total has ever been reached. One famous series of arrests included the mayor and a judge of Baltimore and certain members of the Maryland legislature. Equally important, however, was the imprisonment of a number of Northern editors and several public men including Congressman Henry May, ex-Gov. Morehead of Kentucky, the mayor of Washington and two of Buchanan's diplomats (C. J. Faulkner and G. W. Jones) returning from abroad.

The Confederacy likewise made summary arrests to suppress disloyalty. Success was small, however, not only because political prisoners became popular martyrs, but because Confederate policy met the additional resistance of state-rights[qv] opposition in numerous localities.

[J. G. Randall, *Constitutional Problems under Lincoln;* F. L. Owsley, *State Rights in the Confederacy.*]

MARTIN P. CLAUSSEN

Arrowsmith's Map. A MAP EXHIBITING ALL THE NEW DISCOVERIES IN THE INTERIOR PART OF NORTH AMERICA, was published in London, Jan. 1, 1795, by Aaron Arrowsmith, "Hydrographer to His Majesty." A large-scale map on a globular projection, it was printed on six sheets, measuring when joined 48½ x 57 inches. From notes furnished by members of the Hudson's Bay Company[qv], numerous additions and corrections were made on the basic map. More than seventeen editions were published between 1795 and 1850, first by the author and later by his two sons, which attest the accuracy and importance of the map.

[Charles O. Paullin's *Atlas of the Historical Geography of the United States.*]

LLOYD A. BROWN

Arsenals. An arsenal is primarily an establishment for the manufacture, repair, storage or issue of arms and all military equipment whether for land or naval service. The first arsenal in the United States was established at Carlisle, Pa., in 1776. In 1838 the Ordnance Department[qv] of the army was placed in charge of armories and arsenals. At present there are nineteen permanent stations maintained, six of which are manufacturing units, and, as such, are looked upon as arsenals in the strict sense of the word—these are Frankford, Pa., Picatinny, N. J., Rock Island, Ill., Springfield, Mass., Watervliet, N. Y., and Watertown, Mass. The remaining thirteen stations are designated not for manufacturing, but for handling, storage and issue of ordnance material for the army.

[*History of Arsenals*, Compiled and filed in the Office, Chief of Ordnance, War Department, Washington, D. C.]

ROBERT S. THOMAS

Art. Jeremiah Dummer (1645–1718) the first known American-born artist, added accomplishment as painter to proficiency in silversmithing. The names of many early immigrant artists are lost to record. Three generations of the Duyckinck family gave painters to the New York district, Evert Duyckinck (1621–1702) having arrived at New Amsterdam from Holland in 1638. Authenticated works of the following are well known: Pieter Vanderlyn (1687–1778), a Dutchman who painted portraits at Kingston and Albany; Gustavus Hesselius (1682–1755), a Swede who worked in Pennsylvania and Maryland; Jeremiah Theus (1719–74), an exceptionally gifted artist, Swiss-born, who worked in Charleston; and the Scot, John Smibert (1688–1751), who came from England under patronage of Bishop Berkeley and settled in Boston.

Through the same period there was widespread anonymous production of naively conceived or so-called "primitive" portraits, now appreciated for the special charm of their stiff but intuitively rhythmic design and their arbitrarily decorative coloring. These "folk art" masterpieces are considered by some as nearer to the beginning of a native tradition of art than the more numerous portraits painted in the European fashion. The primitive feeling can be traced continuously, in the works of such untutored painters as the Quaker preacher, Edward Hicks (1780–1849), and even into the 20th century in the naive canvases of John Kane.

Robert Feke and Joseph Badger were competent portraitists of the northern colonies in the middle 18th century. The fashionable native painters of the following fifty years were Ralph Earl (1751–1801); John Singleton Copley (1738–1815), who deserted America in 1774 and became a successful painter in London; and Gilbert Stuart (1755–1828), most talented of the native painters in the international tradition, who made a success in London, but returned in 1793 or 1794, and produced the portraits of Washington now seen, in originals or copies, in innumerable galleries. Benjamin West (1738–1820), born in America, went early to England, and succeeded Sir Joshua Reynolds as president of the Royal Academy. His paintings were unimportant, but he influenced American art through his teaching. Among his pupils were John Trumbull (1756–1843), painter of portraits and large-canvas historical scenes; Charles Willson Peale (1741–1827), whose sons Rembrandt and Raphael also became important painters; and the inventors, Robert Fulton and Samuel F. B. Morse (1791–1872).

In the early 19th century landscape became prominent, along with allegorical and historical pieces, still-lifes and even *genre*. Miniature painting was reaching its highest point; Edward Green Malbone (1777–1807) is considered the greatest American master, and Charles Fraser (1782–1860) his worthiest follower. Henry Inman, William Sidney Mount, Eastman Johnson, George Caleb Bingham and J. G. Brown exploited familiar native-scene and story-telling pictures.

The realistic portrait tradition was continued by Thomas Sully (1783–1872), Samuel Lovett Waldo (1783–1861), Chester Harding (1792–1866), and John Neagle (1796–1865). More creative was John James Audubon, with his *Birds of America*. Washington Allston was superlatively praised for his religious and historical canvases, but his reputation has declined. Landscape was developed by Thomas Doughty, Thomas Cole and Jasper Cropsey of the Hudson River School; by John Frederick Kensett; by Asher B. Durand; and by Frederick Edwin Church. With George Inness (1825–94) American landscape art touched maturity, in atmospheric works comparable to those of the Barbizon School in France. Alexander Wyant and Homer D. Martin were contemporaries of Inness.

Before the century-end, certain painters emerged as typically American in their vigor and forthrightness, most notably Winslow Homer (1836–1910) and Thomas Eakins (1844–1916). Greater in stature because more universal were the expatriate, James McNeill Whistler (1834–1903), deeply inventive, a pioneer of Modernism; Albert Pinkham Ryder, an unappreciated mystic, finally recognized as the most original artist in American history; and John H. Twachtman, who added to a brilliant but fragile Impressionism a formal magic almost Oriental. Others whose names survive were Ralph Blakelock, George Fuller, John LaFarge, Frank Duveneck, William Merritt Chase and Mary Cassatt.

Childe Hassam, Ernest Lawson and Frederick C. Frieseke carried on the ideals of the Impressionist school in the face of the growing post-Impressionist revolution of the early 20th century. The unchallenged fashionable painter of the time was John Singer Sargent, but his reputation later dwindled. By 1910 a vigorous revolt against fashionable elegance and sentimentality was staged by a group of realists led by Robert Henri, John Sloan, George Luks and, later, George Bellows. A more inventive group turned to follow the post-Impressionist trend (as marked out by the French leader Cézanne); John Marin, Walt Kuhn, Max Weber, John Carroll, Maurice Sterne and Henry Mattson, in particular, combining native originality with the new internationally developed æsthetic, served to bring the body of American art to unquestioned creative maturity.

The history of sculpture is far less significant as a native manifestation. In the colonial period such things as weather vanes and ships' figureheads were produced, along with the commoner architectural ornamentation and gravestones. In the early national period William Rush (1756–1833) was famous for his figureheads; John Frazee (1790–1852) was best known for tombstones and mantels; while the greatest figure was Samuel McIntire (1757–1811), celebrated for wood carving on furniture, doorways and mantels.

The sculptors born after 1800, affected by the neo-Classicism of European studios, were likely to spend their best years in Italy, as did Horatio Greenough, William Wetmore Story and Hiram Powers (1805–73), whose *Greek Slave* became internationally celebrated. These expatriates had little to do with American life, but a clay-modeller, John Rogers (1829–1904), scored with naturalistic depictions of everyday living. His enlarged mantelpiece compositions, known as Rogers groups, constitute the most distinctive American sculptured product up to 1880.

By that time a few monumental sculptors were finding a market, most notably John Quincy Adams Ward (1830–1910), and the French-trained Augustus Saint-Gaudens (1848–1907), the most graceful and proficient realist of his era and often named as America's foremost sculptor. Other figures of this group were Herbert Adams, Frederick MacMonnies, Gutzon Borglum, Lorado Taft, Paul Bartlett and Daniel Chester French. Borglum, with his colossal sculpture[qv], is now carrying on an experiment in mountainside rock carving. Most original sculptor of that generation was George Grey Barnard (1863–1938); but the transition to modern ideals was completed only in the work of Gaston Lachaise (1882–1935).

The early history of print-making is concerned less with art values than with topographical and other practical interests. Two phenomena of the mid-19th century are notable: the high artistic merit of the Currier and Ives prints[qv]; and the achievement of the American-born artist, James McNeill Whistler, as the foremost etcher of his time. Soon after 1900 Joseph Pennell was popular for his purely illustrational etchings and lithographs. Many painters turned their hands to the copper and stone mediums; among their works the lithographs of George Bellows are most original. There had been a time when American reproductive engraving on wood had been the world's finest, and there developed after 1910 an extension into finely creative work in this medium, as in the prints of Thomas Nason.

Many have felt that American originality and feeling for beauty have found expression chiefly in the utilitarian arts. Household utensils and furniture[qv] from the earliest colonial periods are marked by simple rhythmic beauty, with feeling for characteristic values in materials, whether wood or metal or clay. As the colonies advanced culturally, the imported classic style was adopted in ornamentation, with an accent recognizably American (as seen also in architecture[qv]). In the fields of commercial handicrafts, early American silverware and pewterware are outstanding, as is the native glass[qv]. Distinctive needlework and weaving developed among the home crafts.

When the machine took over task after task formerly accomplished by hand, the first result was a flood of mass-produced objects defaced with ornament badly copied from handicraft originals. Late in the 19th century there was a widespread attempt to improve standards, particularly by encouraging the purchase of handmade goods as against machine-made, an effort fostered by innumerable "arts and crafts" societies. A more rational approach to the problem has come since 1900 in the separation of the handicrafts from the mass-production crafts, which in turn have been recognized as having values and style-marks—even an æsthetic—of their own, so that a new profession, "industrial design," has emerged, concerned exclusively with the application of art principles to objects characteristically suited to duplication by the machine.

[H. Cahill and A. H. Barr, Jr., editors, *Art in America: a Complete Survey;* S. Isham and R. Cortissoz, *The History of American Painting;* F. F. Sherman, *Early American Painting.*]

SHELDON CHENEY

Art Collections of America. The Philadelphia Academy of Fine Arts, established in 1805 in Independence Hall (removed to a new building in 1876) was the first public art museum in the United States. The Boston Athenæum, opened in 1827, lent most of its collection to the new Museum of Fine Arts, opened in that city in 1876. The private collection of John Varden, begun in Washington about 1829, was transferred to the National Institution for the Promotion of Science in 1841 and thence to the Smithsonian Institution[qv] in 1862, becoming a part of the new United States National Museum. The Brooklyn Institute of Arts and Sciences, founded under another name in 1823, established a museum in 1889 and opened its large art building in 1897. Great expositions[qv] have displayed remarkable assemblings of art in permanent buildings which remained as museums—such as that at Philadelphia, 1876 (Pennsylvania Museum of Art); Buffalo, 1901 (Buffalo Fine Arts Academy); St. Louis, 1904 (City Art Museum, founded 1879); San Francisco, 1915 (San Francisco Museum of Art). Other great establishments are the Metropolitan Museum of Art in New York, those at Cincinnati, founded in 1869; Detroit (1882); Worcester, Mass. (1896), etc. The new American millionaire in the latter 19th century almost inevitably collected—often vicariously, by agents who scoured Europe and the Orient—some form or all forms of art, preferably paintings. Some of these private collections later enriched great museums—as that of J. Pierpont Morgan, the most of which went to the Metropolitan after his death in 1913 and that of William A. Clark, copper magnate (1839–1925), which fell to the Corcoran Art Gallery. Some by bequest became individual museums—notably those of W. W. Corcoran, founded in Washington in 1869 while the collector was still alive, of Charles L. Freer (died 1919) in Washington, of Henry E. Huntington at San Marino, Calif. (opened in 1928), of Henry C. Frick, New York, 1931, and Andrew W. Mellon, given to the National Government and endowed in 1937. Many were sold and dispersed after the owner's death; that of Charles T. Yerkes, traction magnate, sold in 1910, brought $2,707,866, a record sum. That of William Salomon in 1923 brought $1,288,705 and of Elbert H. Gary (1928), $2,297,763. So rapid was the movement of Europe's art treasures to public and private galleries in America around the beginning of the 20th century and thereafter that European art lovers were appalled by it. Lord Leverhulme's collection was even sent bodily to the United States and sold in 1926, bringing $1,274,000.

[Frederic A. Lucas, *Glimpses of Early Museums;* Lewis Barrington and L. C. Everard, *Handbook of American Museums.*]

ALVIN F. HARLOW

Article Ten of the League of Nations[qv] Covenant was of wholly American origin and was regarded by President Wilson as an extension of the Monroe Doctrine[qv] to the whole world. In Wilson's mind the undertaking "to preserve as against external aggression the territorial integrity and existing political independence of all Members of the League" was not a pledge to go to war in advance of congressional consideration and decision. He interpreted the obligations of the article as moral, not legal.

Opponents of the covenant in the Senate made Article X their principal target. They argued that it was not the proper business of the United States to guarantee either new boundaries or old empires or to intervene in cases of revolution against oppression. They contended that moral obligations would be found as binding as legal ones. Consequently the Senate adopted a ponderous reservation repudiating any obligation under the article except as the Congress should provide in any particular case. This was unacceptable to President Wilson not for its legal effect but for its embodiment of an attitude destructive to the principle of international responsibility. He contemplated territorial change accomplished through the peaceful operation of Article XIX rather than the traditional resort to violence.

[D. F. Fleming, *The United States and the League of Nations, 1918-1920.*]

HAROLD S. QUIGLEY

Articles of Confederation. The Continental Congress[qv] decided even before independence that it was necessary to set up a confederacy based upon a written instrument. Several plans appeared in the press and the subject was embraced in R. H. Lee's motion of June 7, 1776, on independence (*see* Declaration of Independence). On June 11 Congress voted to appoint a committee. This body set to work at once and on July 12 reported through John Dickinson a set of Articles of Confederation, of which eighty copies were printed for the use of members. Congress was so engrossed in war problems, however, that debates on the scheme dragged through more than a year. The principal disputes raged over the questions whether taxes should be apportioned according to the gross number of inhabitants counting slaves or excluding them—the South of course wishing them excluded; whether large and small states should have equality in voting; whether Congress should be given the right to regulate Indian affairs; and whether Congress should be permitted to fix the western boundaries of those states which claimed to the Mississippi. On Nov. 15, 1777, Congress finally approved a draft and sent it to the states, on the understanding that all must ratify it before it went into effect. This draft, declared a circular letter of Congress, "is proposed as the best which could be adapted to the circumstances of all; and as that alone which affords any tolerable prospect of a general ratification."

The Articles did not become the law of the land until March 1, 1781. Nine states ratified as early as July, 1778, but several of the smaller ones held back because of the question of western lands[qv]. Maryland in particular had urged that these lands be regarded as a common possession of all the states, and felt aggrieved when the Articles contained a clause declaring that no state should be deprived of territory for the benefit of the United States. She first declared that she would not ratify until her powerful neighbor, Virginia, ceased to advance extravagant western claims. But when New York had yielded and Virginia seemed certain to do so, Maryland on March 1, 1781, signed the Articles through her delegates, and made them effective.

Although the Articles have been harshly criticized and the very shrewdest critics at the time saw their inadequacy, they were generally regarded in 1781 as offering a sound national constitution. They provided for a "perpetual union" or "firm league of friendship" between the states. Each remained sovereign and independent, and retained every right not expressly ceded by the Articles to the general government. A single agency of government was established—a Congress; the states were to appoint from two to seven delegates annually to it, and each state was to have one vote. Rhode Island thus obtained a parity with New York or Virginia. The costs of government and defense were to be defrayed from a common treasury, to which the states were to contribute in proportion to the value of their surveyed land and improvements. The states were likewise to supply quotas of troops, in proportion to the white inhabitants of each, upon congressional requisitions. To Congress was entrusted the management of foreign affairs, of war and of the postal service; it was empowered to borrow money, emit bills of credit, and determine the value of coin; it was to appoint naval officers and superior military officers, and control Indian affairs. But none of these powers was to be exercised save by vote of a majority of all states, and the more important could not be exercised save by the vote of nine. On paper, almost every important national authority was turned over to Congress save three: the authority to raise money directly, the authority to enlist troops directly and the authority to regulate commerce. But the paper powers proved to be very different from actual power.

It soon became evident that Congress was doomed to fail in its attempts to make the Articles workable. These attempts consisted chiefly in requests to the states for money that was never paid, pleas for troops which filled no army ranks, and petitions for special powers which the states never granted. At various points the powers of the states were supposedly limited. They were forbidden to enter into treaties, confederations, or alliances, to meddle with foreign affairs, or to wage war without congressional consent, unless invaded. Most important of all, they were to give to free inhabitants of other states all the privileges and immunities of their own citizens. A citizen of South Carolina, for example, who removed to Boston, at once became a citizen of Massachusetts. Interstate extradition of criminals was also provided. The states could impose duties, but not any which conflicted with the treaty stipulations of Congress. They were required to "abide by the determinations of Congress" on all subjects which the Articles left to that body. The states did respect each other's rights to a considerable extent (when two or more of them fell out, any one could submit the dispute to Congress). But they failed lamentably to respect the needs and requests of the National Government. They refused to do what they should have done, especially in supplying money and men; they frequently did what they should have refrained from doing. A circular prepared by Congress not long after Maryland's ratification in 1781 declared: "The inattention of the States has almost endangered our very existence as a people."

Demands for amendment and invigoration of the Articles were made even before they became effective. New Jersey served notice on Congress Feb. 3, 1780, for example, that it was absolutely necessary to give the nation power to regulate commerce and to fix duties on imports. A committee which reported May 3, 1781, pointed to the chief defect of the Articles—the fact that they gave Congress no power to enforce its measures, and suggested a new article authorizing the employment of armed forces to compel recalcitrant states "to fulfill their Federal engagements." This would have led straight to civil war, and the plan failed. The years 1782–86 witnessed earnest efforts by Congress to obtain state consent to a Federal impost, which would have furnished a stable revenue; earnest efforts also were made to obtain from the states a sufficient control over shipping to enable it to wage commercial warfare with nations discriminating against the United States. But some states, notably New York and Rhode Island, long proved stubborn; others were tardy; and when they did act, their laws were found to conflict. Again, while the states were bound to respect the treaties made by Congress, several of them indulged in gross violations of the Definitive Treaty of Peace[qv]. The close of the year 1786 found the Articles of Confederation in widespread discredit, and many national leaders eager to find a wholly new basis for union. Yet the Articles, soon to give way to the Constitution[qv], should not be regarded with contempt. They had served as a stepping-stone to a new order; as John Marshall said later, they had preserved the idea of union until national wisdom could adopt a more efficient system. Had they not been agreed upon in time, the states might have fallen asunder after Yorktown.

[A. C. McLaughlin, *The Confederation and the Constitution;* Allan Nevins, *The American States During and After the Revolution.*]

ALLAN NEVINS

Articles of War, THE. These in general establish Federal military law, limited, personal and not territorial, criminal and punitive rather than civil, administered solely by military personnel, and not subject to review by civilian courts except to test jurisdiction (Swain v. U. S., 165 U. S. 553). Save for "any person" in contempt (Art. 32) or "found lurking or acting as a spy" (Art. 82), they affect only precisely defined "persons subject to military law." Entrance of such persons into service effects a definite "change of status" (*In re* Morrissey, 137 U. S. 157) and deprives them of many otherwise normal rights. Under Constitutional authority, Congress enacts

Articles of War for "the government and regulation" of the army, and the President by Executive Order specifies rules of procedure, modes of proof and limits of punishment. These Articles deal chiefly with strictly military offenses, although they also cover acts considered felonies in civilian courts (Arts. 92 & 93) and in addition "crimes or offenses not capital" (Art. 96).

June 30, 1775, the Continental Congress[qv] enacted our first Articles, based largely on British of 1765 and the Massachusetts of April 5, 1775. Amplified in 1776 and supplemented in 1786 regarding administrative details, Congress adopted them into Federal law Sept. 29, 1789 (1 Stat. 95), and by act of April 10, 1806 (2 Stat. 359) revised and adapted them into Constitutional conformity. These 1806 Articles, supplemented during the Civil War and restated in the Revised Statutes of 1874, remained in force until the acts of June 3 and Aug. 29, 1916 (39 Stat. 200 and 650) completely revised and modernized the full military code. Detailed study of World War experiences produced important amendments on June 4, 1920 (41 Stat. 759), which emphasized and extended legal rights of soldiers under charges and provided various means of obviating excessive trials.

[G. Glenn, *The Army and the Law; Manual for Courts-Martial, United States Army*, 1921.]

ELBRIDGE COLBY

Artillery, THE AMERICAN, dates from the Revolution, when a Massachusetts regiment and a Rhode Island company joined in the siege of Boston[qv], June, 1775. Its guns then, and long thereafter, were maneuvered by men hauling on drag ropes. A new regiment under Col. Henry Knox took over artillery duties in January, 1776. Knox transported from Ticonderoga[qv] the cannon which forced the evacuation of Boston (March 17). When Washington moved to New York, he left an artillery company in the captured coast defenses. Four regiments organized in 1777 constituted the regular artillery during the rest of the war.

An artillery battalion manned guns, but served chiefly as infantry, under Harmar, St. Clair and Wayne[qqv] against western Indians, 1790–94. Our first system of coast defenses[qv] brought new duties to the artillery (1794). When the War of 1812 came, small artillery detachments were scattered from Maine to New Orleans and Mackinac. There were three artillery regiments. One, of light artillery, was mounted as horse artillery, but soon lost its horses for want of forage. No coast defense succumbed to naval attack. In 1821 the artillery was reorganized into four regiments. One company in each was to be light artillery. The four companies were not mounted until 1838–39. They made brilliant records in the Mexican War. Gen. Scott mounted four more at Puebla (1847); but three fourths of the artillery served as infantry. In the Civil War fifty-six out of sixty companies were mounted, of which about twenty-two were horse batteries. In the Spanish-American War coast companies were mounted as siege artillery. In 1901 the artillery lost its regimental formation and became a corps under a chief. The Field and Coast were separated in 1907; the Coast was given a chief and the Field organized into regiments. The Coast was given a regimental organization for A.E.F. units in 1917 and for all units in 1924. A chief of Field Artillery was designated in 1918.

[William E. Birkhimer, *Historical Sketch of the Artillery, United States Army;* W. L. Haskin, *The History of the First Regiment of Artillery;* W. A. Ganoe, *History of the United States Army.*]

S. C. VESTAL

"As goes Maine, so goes the Union," a saying based upon the supposed accuracy of Maine's September election as a political barometer for the country, was originated by the Whigs after the presidential election of 1840[qqv].

[Claude E. Robinson, Maine—Political Barometer, *Political Science Quarterly*, June, 1932.]

ROBERT E. MOODY

Ash Hollow, Battle of (Sept. 3, 1855). To punish the Sioux Indians for the Grattan massacre on the California Trail, Gen. Harney left Fort Leavenworth[qqv], Kans., Aug. 5, with 1200 troops. Proceeding west of Fort Kearny[qv], Nebr., he encountered Little Thunder's band at Ash Hollow. The Indians fought desperately but were nearly exterminated, losing 136 killed.

[*South Dakota Historical Collections*, Vols. I and II.]

JOSEPH MILLS HANSON

Ashburton Treaty. *See* Webster-Ashburton Treaty of 1842.

Ashby's Gap. A pass in the Blue Ridge Mountains of Virginia leading from the Shenandoah Valley into eastern Virginia, often used by Confederate and Federal armies in the several valley campaigns. In June, 1863, J. E. B. Stuart's cavalry held this gap to prevent Hooker interfering with Lee's army in the march that led to Gettysburg.

[*Battles and Leaders of the Civil War*, III.]

W. N. C. CARLTON

Ashley Expeditions, THE, three in number, were for the purpose of launching the Rocky Mountain Fur Company in competition with the Hudson's Bay Company[qqv] and the older established American companies. The more important results were the exploration of vast areas of the Rocky Mountain Northwest, the firmer hold of American interests on the disputed Northwest country and the development of some of the more noted "mountain men,"[qv] including Jedediah Smith, Etienne Provost, Jim Bridger, Milton Sublette, Hugh Glass and Thomas Fitzpatrick.

Organized in St. Louis in 1822 the first expedition, commanded by Andrew Henry, Ashley's lieutenant, came to grief near Great Falls, Mont., where he was attacked by the Blackfeet[qv] and driven out of the country. Ashley headed another expedition in the following spring, only to be attacked by the Arikaras[qv], on the Missouri, and forced to retreat with heavy loss. Reinforced, the third expedition, in charge of Jedediah Smith[qv], pushed on to the Yellowstone, penetrated to the Green River Valley, the Utah trapping grounds, and learned from the Crow Indians the important location of South Pass[qv], the effective discovery of which dates from that time. The party returned with a rich cache of furs, and Ashley set forth on a return winter trip. He crossed the Continental Divide by Bridger's Gap, and reached the Green River near the crossing of the Oregon Trail[qqv]. Bridger in the previous autumn had discovered Great Salt Lake[qv]. The first mountain trappers' rendezvous[qv] was held in June and Ashley returned in the fall of 1825 with a fortune in furs.

[H. M. Chittenden, *History of American Fur Trade;* W. J. Ghent, *Early Far West;* H. C. Dale, *Ashley-Smith Expeditions.*]

CARL L. CANNON

Asia, Trade with, began immediately after the Revolution. The *Empress of China* sailed from New York for Canton on Feb. 22, 1784, and within a decade American vessels were calling regularly at Calcutta and Bombay, trading on the pepper coast of Sumatra, making port in Java and lading tea and silks from Canton. It was a trade which played an important part in reviving the commerce cut off by British navigation laws, and it brought new wealth to the enterprising merchants of New York, Philadelphia, Boston, Salem, Baltimore and Providence. Trade with the Far East[qv], from its very inception, held out the bright promise of bringing to the United States products which the colonies had depended on England to supply, and of providing a new market for American exports.

The trade with China[qv], concentrated in the port of Canton, was the most important branch of this commerce. Silks, nankeens and tea were the products sought by the American ships, with tea becoming virtually the sole import by the 1840's. In order to supplement American exports with other goods suitab'e for the Chinese market, American merchant seamen developed the fur trade of the Northwest Coast[qv] and scoured the islands of the South Pacific. Development of our early trade with China was an important factor in the settlement of Oregon[qv]. It led to the opening up of relations with Hawaii[qv], and served to build up that general interest in the Pacific[qv] which was an influential motive in our acquisition of California[qv]. The potentialities of the markets of the East as an outlet for American produce and manufactures won a hold upon popular imagination a century ago which bore little relation to the statistics of actual trade.

After its first period of dramatic growth, total trade with Asia underwent a relative decline. In the middle of the century, exports were valued at $3,028,000, or only 2.1% of our total exports in comparison with 3.6% in 1821, while imports, valued at $12,434,000, represented 7.2% of total imports in comparison with 9.8% in 1821. With the "opening" of Japan by Commodore Matthew C. Perry[qv], in 1854, a new market and a new source of imports became available. The rapid emergence of Japan as an economic and commercial power of the first rank provided the United States with a valuable outlet for its exports, primarily raw cotton, which was exchanged largely for silk. By the end of the century trade with Asia as a whole had regained its relative importance in our total commerce, and succeeding years witnessed its further growth to a position of the utmost importance. In the pre-depression period of 1926–30 average annual exports to Asia were valued at $573,973,000, or no less than 12% of our entire export trade, while average annual imports were valued at $1,192,632,000, or 29.6% of total imports.

The potentialities of the trade with China, despite disappointment in its actual development and the statistical evidence of Japan's greater importance both as a market and as a source of imports, have served as the primary factor in the formulation of our economic and political policies in the Pacific. The desire to promote this commerce was largely responsible for American territorial expansion in Alaska, Hawaii, Samoa and the Philippines[qqv]. It led to Secretary Hay's pronouncement of the Open Door policy[qv] in 1899. During the present century, the potential trade of China has intensified an interest in the preservation of that country's territorial and political integrity which has repeatedly brought the United States into serious controversy with Japan. American trade with Asia has been even more important in its bearing upon our political relations in the Pacific than in its significance for our general economic development.

[Tyler Dennett, *Americans in Eastern Asia.*]

FOSTER RHEA DULLES

Asiento, THE (1713), was a license granted to the English South Sea Company by the Spanish government, as a result of the Treaty of Utrecht^qv^, whereby the company was given the exclusive right to sell a total of 144,000 Negro slaves in the Spanish colonies during thirty years or at the rate of 4800 a year (*see* African Company, Royal). For this privilege the company paid the Spanish crown $200,000.

A. CURTIS WILGUS

Assassinations, Political, were all too frequent in the mid-West and far West in pioneer days, and in the South even in later decades. In 1839 a member of the Wisconsin territorial legislature, James R. Vineyard, shot another member, Charles C. P. Arndt, to death in the Assembly chamber. In Kentucky and some other states, politics engendered the most violent acrimony, and personal encounters, killings and duels were not uncommon. The assassination of President Lincoln^qv^ was the first of great political consequence in the United States. Two other Presidents were also murdered. Bitter quarrels among Republican leaders in 1880 over patronage had its effect upon the brain of a man named Charles J. Guiteau, who annoyed President James A. Garfield from the day of his inauguration, March 4, 1881, with importunities for a consular position. On July 2 he armed himself and shot the President down as he was passing through the Pennsylvania station in Washington, accompanied by Secretary Blaine. Mr. Garfield lingered for weeks, and finally, because of the heat of Washington, was removed to Elberon, N. J., where he died on Sept. 19. William McKinley was the third presidential victim. On Sept. 6, 1901, as he stood, shaking hands with a line of visitors to the Pan-American Exposition^qv^ at Buffalo, N. Y., he was shot by Leon Czolgosz, a young anarchist who had been influenced by the propaganda of Emma Goldman and others. Mr. McKinley died on Sept. 14. Among the most noted of American political assassinations was that of William Goebel^qv^, claimant to the governorship of Kentucky in 1900. Another was that of Edward W. Carmack, of Tennessee, who had just left the United States Senate and become editor of the Nashville *Tennesseean.* He was shot on a street in Nashville by Robin Cooper, son of a prominent political opponent, Col. Duncan Cooper, who accompanied his son to the killing. The Coopers were convicted of murder, but immediately pardoned by Gov. Malcolm Patterson. United States Senator Huey P. Long of Louisiana, a bizarre and dynamic character who had built a powerful political machine in that state and thereby aroused some violent antagonisms, was fatally shot in the Capitol building at Baton Rouge on Sept. 8, 1935, by Dr. C. A. Weiss, a dentist, son-in-law of a prominent anti-Long leader. Weiss was immediately shot dead by Long's ever-present bodyguard. Sen. Long died on the following day.

[E. Benjamin Andrews, *History of the United States.*]

ALVIN F. HARLOW

Assay Offices. Assaying is done at all the Federal mints^qv^, but special plants were established at New York in 1853, at Boise, Idaho, 1869; Helena, Mont., 1874; Deadwood, S. Dak., and Seattle, Wash., 1896, and Salt Lake City, Utah, 1908, for the receipt, testing, melting, and refining of gold and silver bullion and foreign coins, and recasting into bars, ingots or discs. The early mints established at New Orleans, La., Charlotte, N. C., and Denver, Colo., were later turned into assay offices.

[Jesse P. Watson, *The Bureau of the Mint.*]

ALVIN F. HARLOW

Assembly, The Right of, is guaranteed against interference by Congress in the Federal Constitution, and is supplemented by state constitutional provisions imposing similar restrictions upon state legislatures. In no place is the right absolute, but is subject to supervision in its exercise by local government officials. The right of assembly will not be sustained where its exercise threatens to disrupt the government or destroy the public peace. Here the assembly clearly becomes unlawful.

The Supreme Court in U. S. v. Cruikshank^qv^ (1876) held that the right of the people peaceably to assemble for lawful purposes, with the obligation on the part of the states to afford them protection, existed long before the adoption of the Constitution. It had existed in English law from "time out of mind" as a distinct, separate and independent right. That the right was so recognized was made evident by the numerous statutes which restricted and regulated its use.

A statute passed by Parliament in the reign of George I fixed the limitations upon the right of assembly which are still observed in this country. According to this act, the right of assembly cannot be maintained if the meeting is for an unlawful purpose or is conducted in a tumultuous manner. Most of the cases in which the right has been challenged fall into the second category. Four notorious cases of the last century which come under the heading of unlawful assembly involved four different motives. These were a meeting in Philadelphia of the proposed "Native American Party,"[qv] 1844 (*see* Philadelphia Riots, The); the "Astor Place Riots"[qv] in New York City, 1849, concerning a performance at the Astor Place Opera House; the disapproval of a stringent liquor law in the State of Maine, 1855, by a meeting in Portland, and the "Anarchists' Case" of 1886 (*see* Haymarket Affair, The), arising from an attempt of the workingmen in Chicago to introduce the eight-hour day. Each of these cases contained the essential elements of an unlawful assembly, in fact they were almost riots. In more recent years, most of the cases of unlawful assembly have developed from meetings of communists and strikers[qqv].

The practical decision whether or not an assembly is unlawful rests with the local police authorities. The chief of police or other official is supposed to exercise his fair and honest discretion. His action is subject to review by the courts but relief from the courts, if relief is merited, is at best uncertain (*see* Police Power).

[Jarrett and Mund, The Right of Assembly, *New York University Law Quarterly Review*, IX, pp. 1-38.]

WILLIAM S. CARPENTER

Assessment of Candidates. *See* Political Assessments.

Assimilation. As applied to immigration and cognate matters, the word is here used as signifying genuine absorption; the real incorporation of an individual into the idealistic and cultural fabric of American life, much as food is digested and becomes organically part of the human body. It is the culmination of a process which logically begins when the immigrant first sets foot on American soil, yet which may not end with the immigrant himself, but only with his children or even his children's children. Naturalization[qv], the legal act of conferring citizenship upon an alien, is only a step in the process, and often a very short step. The term Americanization[qv], being logically limited to the foreign born, does not fully coincide with assimilation in the word's larger meaning.

Despite the stoppage of mass-immigration for nearly two decades through a series of measures culminating with the Johnson Act[qv] of 1924, the assimilation of the foreign born and their progeny is far from complete. Many groups still exist, both in the cities and over the countryside, whose members remain essentially foreign-minded even unto the third generation. This, however, is a waning factor which promises to vanish in the relatively near future. More widespread and far more serious is the large element of native-born persons, especially in the large cities and industrial centers of the Northeast, who are cultural and spiritual nondescripts. Such persons usually speak English and have an American veneer in material externals such as clothing and forms of amusement. However, they are not American in the deeper sense. Though they have generally rejected the customs and ideas of their foreign-born forebears, and have thus lost their ancestral heritage, they have not acquired American culture and ideals.

These nondescript urban masses, with no genuine loyalties, traditional roots or cultural and idealistic standards, are not merely a heavy handicap on their local communities; they are likewise a grave problem for the nation as a whole. Inevitably restless and discontented, they are prone to crime and to ultra-radical agitation.

[Edward R. Lewis, *America: Nation or Confusion;* Gino Speranza, *Race or Nation.*]

LOTHROP STODDARD

Assiniboine, Fort (1834–35), post of the American Fur Company[qv], west of Fort Union, was, for a time, the head of steamboat navigation on the Missouri, and a depot for inland trade with the Assiniboine, Piegan and Blackfeet Indians[qqv].

[H. M. Chittenden, *The American Fur Trade of the Far West.*]

PAUL C. PHILLIPS

Assiniboine or Stone Indians, The, of Siouan[qv] stock, left the parent nation in the 17th century, and shortly after 1800 settled on the upper Missouri. By the Treaty of Fort Laramie in 1851[qv] they were assigned a reservation between the Missouri and Yellowstone rivers. In the 1870's they were moved to the Fort Peck and Fort Belknap[qqv] reservations.

[Edward T. Denig, Indian Tribes of the Upper Missouri, in 46th *Annual Report* of the Bureau of American Ethnology; F. W. Hodge, *Handbook of American Indians.*]

PAUL C. PHILLIPS

Assistance Clause, The. Election laws^qv^, providing for the choice of an "honest and capable man" from each major party to "assist any voter in the preparation of his ballot when from any cause he is unable to do so" (Delaware, 1891) or for the voter's choice of "any qualified voter in the election district" for the same purpose (Pennsylvania, 1891), soon facilitated the delivery of bribed votes. Party members, serving as assistants, influenced the marking of ballots and rewarded the "fixed" voters with the token (pin, tag, acorn) for which the promised bribe would be paid. The 20th century saw increasing state legislation to abolish the assistants and check fraud in connection with bona fide assistance to disabled voters.

[J. A. Woodburn, *Political Parties and Party Problems in the United States*, 3rd ed.; J. A. Salter, *Boss Rule.*]

BAYRD STILL

Assistant. The Massachusetts Bay Company Charter (1629)^qv^ provided eighteen assistants elected yearly by the "freemen"^qv^ (stockholders). Seven, with the governor (or deputy governor), constituted a quorum ("Court of Assistants") to manage the Company's ordinary affairs. When the Company became a commonwealth in Massachusetts, an assistant became a "magistrate." Until deputies were admitted (1634), the Court of Assistants was the colony's sole legislature. As the colony's constitution matured, the assistants held four functions, legislative, executive, judicial and "consultative" (i.e., the governor's "standing council" with extensive powers "in the vacancy of the General Court"^qv^). The Connecticut Charter (1662) provided twelve assistants with similar powers.

[H. L. Osgood, *The American Colonies in the Seventeenth Century.*]

RAYMOND P. STEARNS

"Associated Loyalists" of New England, or Loyal Associated Refugees, consisted of various associations formed by Col. Edward Winslow, Jr., in Rhode Island during its occupation by the British (December, 1776–October, 1779), to chastise the Americans for losses and indignities. They made several raids in Long Island Sound, capturing vessels, cattle and prisoners.

[W. H. Siebert, Loyalist Troops of New England, *The New England Quarterly*, IV, No. 1.]

WILBUR H. SIEBERT

Associated Power. Owing to traditional fear of entangling alliances^qv^ this was the official designation of our relationship to the Allies after entering the World War on their side in 1917.

JAMES TRUSLOW ADAMS

Associated Press. As early as 1827, the newspapers of New York had combined in sending reporters in rowboats to meet incoming ships off Sandy Hook, get European news and send it to the city by carrier pigeon or by semaphore telegraph from Staten Island or Coney Island, several hours before the ship docked. This combination became known as the New York Associated Press. After the invention of the electric telegraph^qv^ and the extension of the wires to Halifax, where the Cunard steamers touched, the association brought European news to New York two days sooner than by ship. The various telegraph companies installed news services of their own in the latter 1840's and fought the New York combination for several years; but gradually they yielded, and the Associated Press, at it came to be called, extended its service until it covered the country. After 1860 it had almost complete control of the news situation in the United States and Canada, and was bitterly vituperated in Congress and elsewhere as a ruthless monopoly. Between 1880 and 1900 there were wars and mutations, the United Press^qv^, a Chicago Associated Press and a Western Associated Press being involved. A new corporation was organized in 1900, and held the leadership of its predecessor. An attack upon it under the Sherman Antitrust Law^qv^ caused its membership rules to be made more liberal in 1915, and its members were permitted to use other press services also.

[Victor Rosewater, *History of Cooperative News-Gathering in the United States;* Melville E. Stone, *Fifty Years a Journalist.*]

ALVIN F. HARLOW

Associations represent one of the most effective pieces of revolutionary machinery used in the American Revolution. Before the Stamp Act^qv^ the colonies were already familiar through merchant societies and political clubs with the idea of organization by agreement and pledge of support for some particular purpose. It was therefore an easy step for them, after the passage of that act, to use the device in nonimportation^qv^ and nonconsumption agreements as a means of economic compulsion on the Mother Country, enforced by another form of association, the Sons of Liberty^qv^. Local organizations were early linked up through committees of correspondence^qv^ into an intercolonial association of the "true Sons of Liberty" whose chief aim appears to have been to keep a watchful eye on suspected enemies of the colonial cause. By 1773 nonimportation agreements and the Sons of Liberty had practically faded out of the picture, but came forcibly to the fore again when Parliament that year passed the act permitting the East India Company[qv] to export its tea to America without paying the usual English duties. Upon the passing of the Boston Port Bill following the Tea Party, the First Continental Congress[qqv] in 1774 adopted the famous "Association," the members pledging themselves and their constituents not to import, export or consume British goods until their grievances were redressed. The pledgers in this case provided the commercial boycott as sanction against both states and individuals who refused to join or broke their agreements. After the outbreak of hostilities, associations, both loyalist and patriot, were spontaneously formed, pledging the signers to serve their cause with their lives. During the course of the war, both England and her colonies found the association idea an effective device for recruiting troops.

[Carl Becker, *The Eve of the Revolution.*]

VIOLA F. BARNES

Associators, THE, were a military organization formed by Franklin, Nov. 21, 1747, to defend the Port of Philadelphia. Revolting against the pacific policy of the Quakers[qv], they formed military companies and erected two batteries on the Delaware. The Associators disbanded after the peace of Aix-la-Chapelle[qv] in 1748.

[Scharf and Westcott, *History of Philadelphia.*]

JULIAN P. BOYD

Assumption of, and Funding of, Revolutionary Debt. At the time of the organization of the American National Government under the United States Constitution it was found that the national debt consisted of the following: foreign debt, $11,710,378; to domestic creditors, $42,414,085, including $2,000,000 of unliquidated debt. Alexander Hamilton as Secretary of the Treasury proposed to pay this at par in order that the credit of the National Government might be established, though the domestic debt had been selling as low as 25%. This was finally agreed to after much popular opposition, since it meant that speculators who had bought up the securities would make large profits. In addition Hamilton also desired that the National Government should assume the payment of the debts incurred by the individual states in carrying on the Revolutionary War. This assumption of the state debts would increase the national debt by $18,271,786. From this proposal arose the celebrated "assumption" issue.

Some of the states had paid part of their Revolutionary War debt while others had paid but little, also some states were in far better financial condition than others, since they had suffered but little from the direct effects of the war. The State of New York was in peculiarly advantageous position if an assumption measure was proposed. It was among the largest of the debtors, but aside from this obligation was in an unusually strong financial situation, due to the sale of public lands and the careful investment of state funds. The Southern states whose population was smaller than that of the Northern states were especially hostile to this assumption, which would place increased taxation for its payment upon the entire country, themselves included. Hamilton rightly claimed that assumption of the state debts would cause the creditors holding these securities to look to the National Government for their payment, and thus increase their support of the new government at the expense of the states. He favored this as a strong believer in nationalism[qv].

At the same time quite a controversy arose concerning the location of the new national capital[qv]. The Southern states were especially anxious that it be placed on the banks of the Potomac River while other locations such as sites on the Susquehanna River in Pennsylvania and the Delaware River in New Jersey were advocated by the people of the Middle and Northern states. The issue of assumption was at first defeated in Congress but finally, with the assistance of Jefferson, Hamilton procured an agreement by which Southern votes in Congress were secured for the assumption of state debts in return for Northern votes to locate the national capital on the banks of the Potomac River at the present city of Washington, D. C. This agreement was accomplished by the adroit action of Thomas Jefferson, then Secretary of State, who invited the Secretary of the Treasury, Alexander Hamilton, to dine with him at his home. Also, a few other friends were present at this social meeting for an informal conference. Jefferson, himself, stated that reasonable men could form a compromise by mutual satisfaction, which compromise was to save the Union. Since it would take time to build the national capital it was further agreed that the Government, then located at New York, should be transferred to Philadelphia for ten to fifteen years, and after that to the present site of the national capital city at Washington.

As a result of this informal agreement both the measures with regard to the assumption of state debts and the location of the national capital were carried through Congress in the spring of 1790.

[J. S. Bassett, *A Short History of the United States;* Gilbert Chinard, *Thomas Jefferson;* S. McKee, ed., *Hamilton's Papers on Public Credit, Commerce, Finance.*]

WILLIAM STARR MYERS

Astor Fur Company. *See* American Fur Company, The.

Astor Place Riot, THE, in New York, May 10, 1849, grew out of long-standing jealousy between the American actor, Edwin Forrest, and the English tragedian, William Charles Macready, and was essentially an expression of anti-British feeling mingled with class hatred. When police failed to disperse a pro-Forrest mob outside the Astor Place Opera House where Macready was playing *Macbeth,* the militia was called out; violence and many casualties followed.

[M. J. Moses, *The Fabulous Forrest.*]

STANLEY R. PILLSBURY

Astoria. John Jacob Astor planned an organized fur trade[qv] on a continental scale some time before American occupation of the upper Missouri country. To his American Fur Company[qv], chartered in 1808, he added the Pacific Fur Company[qv], organized in 1810, and proceeded to extend his organization from St. Louis to the mouth of the Columbia[qv]. Two expeditions were sent to the latter point: one by sea, and the other along the route of Lewis and Clark[qv]. The sea-going party, under Capt. Jonathan Thorn, embarked Sept. 6, 1810, in the *Tonquin*[qv] and after a stormy voyage reached the Columbia, Mar. 23, 1811. Within three weeks Astoria was established under the direction of Duncan McDougal, acting resident agent. In June Capt. Thorn and a trading party were massacred by Indians in Nootka Sound, and the lone white survivor blew up the ship *Tonquin,* killing himself and many Indians.

July 15, 1811, a party of Canadians sent by the North West Company[qv] to forestall the Americans, arrived at Astoria. In January, 1812, a second party came from the rival North West Company post on the Spokane River. Then came the Astor Overlanders, thirty-four in number. They had left St. Louis March 12, 1811, under the leadership of Wilson Price Hunt, and had traveled up the Missouri and westward through the country of the Crows[qv], over the Continental Divide to the Snake River, thence to the Columbia and the Pacific, where they arrived Feb. 15, 1812. In May, the Astor ship, *Beaver,* arrived. Activities were extended inland to the mouth of the Okanagan, to the Spokane, and to the Snake River. Robert Stuart and a small party of eastbound Astor Overlanders set out with dispatches for Mr. Astor in New York, June 29, 1812, ascended the Snake River to its head, became the first white men to cross the South Pass[qv], wintered on the Platte, and arrived in St. Louis April 30, 1813. They did not return, for news of the War of 1812 sounded the doom of the Astor enterprise. While Hunt was absent, McDougal and his associates, whose sympathies were with the British, sold all the Astor interests on the Columbia to the North West Company. Hunt returned to find Astoria in rival hands, the post renamed Fort George, and the British flag flying where the Stars and Stripes had been. Astoria was restored to the United States in 1818 in accordance with the Treaty of Ghent[qv]. (*See* Oregon Question.)

[H. M. Chittenden, *The American Fur Trade of the Far West.*]

CARL P. RUSSELL

Atarés Massacre, THE, was the shooting of fifty men, mostly Americans, by the Spaniards, in Havana, Aug. 16, 1851. Belonging to the López filibustering expedition[qv] they were executed as pirates.

[H. Portell-Vilá, *Historia de Cuba en sus relaciones con los Estados Unidos,* Vol. I.]

HERMINIO PORTELL-VILÁ

Atchison, Kans., named for Sen. David R. Atchison of Missouri, was the headquarters of the proslavery movement in Kansas from its establishment in 1854. The *Squatter Sovereign,* published at Atchison, was the most outspoken of all the proslavery papers. Abolition sympathizers were tarred and feathered or driven from the vicinity by threats. Atchison citizens were active in the "Wakarusa War"[qv] and other border difficulties of 1855–57 (*see* Border War). They formed a unit of the proslavery "army" which, May 21, 1856, captured Lawrence[qv], the abolition headquarters, and destroyed the *Herald of Freedom* office, and the Free State Hotel.

[William G. Cutler, *The History of Kansas.*]

PAUL I. WELLMAN

Atchison, Topeka and Santa Fé Railway is the corporate title of one of the largest transport systems in America, owning 13,000 miles of main line stretching from Chicago into Kansas, across the southeast corner of Colorado into New Mexico, thence across Arizona to touch the coast at San Francisco, Los Angeles and San Diego. It has also a line branching to Galveston.

The initiative of Cyrus Holliday led to the chartering in Kansas, Feb. 15, 1859, of the Atchison and Topeka, rechartered in 1863 as the

Atchison, Topeka and Santa Fé Railroad. Actual building of the track beyond the Kansas border was begun in 1868, financed by T. J. Peters, of Cincinnati, who quickly sold securities to Eastern capitalists so that by 1869 control passed to Henry Keyes, of Newbury, Vt., as president of the concern. Later, Thomas Nickerson and W. B. Strong made the road a powerful factor in the development of the Southwest.

Increase in the cattle business helped the road to weather the Panic of 1873[qv] and in the later years of that decade building was resumed. As construction toward Santa Fé proceeded the road became involved in serious competition with the Denver and Rio Grande[qv] over territory. Santa Fé was reached in 1880, and a transcontinental link by connection with the Southern Pacific[qv] at Deming, N. Mex., was completed, March, 1881. Agreements with that company permitted building an independent track to Needles, where the Santa Fé bridged the Colorado River. West of that point, short lines already built were purchased and united to give entry to Los Angeles and San Diego, while a new track running northwest from Barstow, Calif., entered San Francisco.

The expense of construction into a newly settled country (long stretches of the line lie through deserts still very sparsely inhabited) coupled with the general financial depression of the early 1890's brought bankruptcy, which was followed by reorganization and sale to the Atchison, Topeka & Santa Fé Railway Company, chartered Dec. 12, 1895.

[R. E. Riegel, *The Story of the Western Railroads.*]

ROBERT G. RAYMER

Atherton Company. Maj. Humphrey Atherton, Gov. John Winthrop, the younger, and an incongruous intercolonial group of speculators formed a company which, by purchase from the Indians (1659) and foreclosure of a questionable Indian mortgage (1662), claimed title to nearly all the Narragansett country. Jurisdiction over the area was disputed between Connecticut and Rhode Island, whose charter claims conflicted; and the company, by supporting Connecticut and selling land to settlers, precipitated armed "incidents" and rendered vain all attempts at decision until the Board of Trade[qv] (1727) gave Rhode Island jurisdiction and left the company's heirs no tenable claims to the land.

[Edward Field, *State of Rhode Island and Providence Plantations . . .; Records of the Proprietors of the Narragansett, otherwise called the Fones Record.*]

RAYMOND P. STEARNS

Atkinson, Fort (Kansas) was one of the early posts located by the United States Government along the Santa Fé trail[qv]. It was built in Ford County on the Arkansas River by Maj. Hoffman in 1850, of sod. For this reason it was called Fort Sod and later Fort Sodom. It was besieged on one occasion by Comanches and Kiowas[qqv] but was relieved. Abandoned in 1853, it was later temporarily reoccupied, but was permanently abandoned in October, 1854. Other forts of this name were located in Florida, Iowa (near Council Bluffs), Nebraska and Wisconsin.

[F. W. Blackmar, *Kansas;* F. B. Heitman, *Historical Register of U. S. Army.*]

CARL L. CANNON

Atlanta, Capture and Burning of (1864). On Sept. 1, 1864, Gen. Sherman (U.) telegraphed President Lincoln: "Atlanta is ours and fairly won." Sherman had finally forced Hood (C.) out of the city (*see* Atlanta Campaign). The Confederate Army concentrated to the southward. All people remaining in Atlanta were deported. After a brief rest Hood started northward (*see* Hood's Tennessee Campaign). Sherman followed, but soon returned to Atlanta. On Nov. 16, 1864, the famous March to the Sea[qv] was begun.

Before setting out, Sherman ordered the complete destruction of the town. "Behind us," he wrote, "lay Atlanta smouldering and in ruins, the black smoke rising high in air and hanging like a pall over the ruined city." No city during the Civil War was so nearly completely annihilated.

[W. T. Sherman, *Memoirs*, Vol. II.]

THOMAS ROBSON HAY

Atlanta Campaign, The (May to September, 1864). The Union advance southward to Atlanta began, May 5, 1864, simultaneously with Grant's advance to Richmond (*see* Wilderness, Battles of the). Sherman's (U.) army numbered 110,000 men; Johnston's (C.) half that number. Sherman's superiority enabled him, with little risk, to maneuver Johnston from one position to another. If Johnston was to save his army and prevent Sherman from taking Atlanta, he could not afford to stand and fight unless conditions were favorable. He considered doing this at Cassville, half way to Atlanta, but his subordinate commanders believed the risk too great. Ten days later a fierce battle took place at New Hope Church[qv].

As the Confederates retreated nearer to Atlanta, fighting became more frequent. At Kennesaw Mountain[qv], Sherman made a frontal attack against prepared positions, but was everywhere repulsed. The flanking operations were resumed. By July 6 Sherman had moved so near Atlanta that Johnston transferred his army south of the Chattahoochee River, into prepared positions along Peachtree Creek[qv]. On July 17 Johnston was relieved by a subordinate, Hood (C.), because he had "failed to arrest the advance of the enemy" (*see* Davis-Johnston Controversy). On July 20 Hood violently attacked, but was repulsed with heavy losses. The attack was resumed, but was again repulsed. Sherman's renewal of his flanking movements to cut Hood's line of supply and force him out of Atlanta brought on the battle of Ezra Church[qv]. During August, Sherman edged closer to Hood's supply line. By the 31st he was across it. Hood evacuated Atlanta, Sept. 1; Sherman's troops moved into the city, Sept. 2 (*see* Atlanta, The Capture and Burning of). The campaign was over.

[*Battles and Leaders of the Civil War.*]

THOMAS ROBSON HAY

Atlantic and Pacific Railroad. This land-grant railroad was chartered on July 27, 1866, to run along the 31st parallel, from Springfield, Mo., by way of the Indian Territory[qv], northern Texas and Albuquerque and across the Colorado River at Needles. The road was to receive twenty sections of land per mile in the states traversed (except Texas) and forty sections in the territories. Railroad building had reached Vinita, Indian Territory, when the Panic of 1873[qv] brought an end to operations. In 1876 the company was reorganized as a part of the St. Louis and San Francisco, but still cash for construction was not forthcoming. Four years later the Atchison, Topeka and Santa Fé[qv] bought a half interest in the old Atlantic and Pacific. Before through trains were run from California to St. Louis in 1883 it was necessary to reach a settlement with the Southern Pacific[qv], which had built a line across California to Needles.

[Robert E. Riegel, *The Story of the Western Railroads.*]

DAN E. CLARK

Atlantic Cable. The laying of the Atlantic Cable was mainly due to the perseverance of Cyrus W. Field. A company was organized in 1854. A survey of the cable route followed. The British and American Governments loaned ships for the expeditions. A broken cable frustrated the efforts of 1857 and likewise efforts made in June of 1858. A later attempt in July met with success and by Aug. 5, 1858, the cable was laid. England and America rejoiced. President Buchanan and Queen Victoria exchanged greetings. Records of these early cable messages, cut in paper, are preserved at the Smithsonian Institution in Washington. Enthusiasm in America reached a culmination in early September when a great ovation was given Field in New York. But on Sept. 1 the cable ceased to function properly. For a time the experiment was much discredited.

During the Civil War capital was raised with great difficulty. Nevertheless, in July, 1865, the steamer *Great Eastern*[qv] began laying a cable which broke after two-thirds of it had been laid. Success crowned the efforts of 1866 and shortly after the cable of 1865 was recovered and operated. (*See also* Cables, Transatlantic; Pacific Cable.)

[Isabella Field Judson, *Cyrus W. Field—His Life and Work.*]

PHILIP G. AUCHAMPAUGH

Atlantic Coast Line Railroad, one of the most important railway systems of the South operating its main line between Richmond, Va., and Tampa, Fla. It was originally the Richmond and Petersburg Railroad, chartered by the State of Virginia in 1836 and received its present name in 1900 when other roads operating in the Southeast were consolidated with it.

[J. W. Starr, *One Hundred Years of American Railroading.*]

HALLIE FARMER

Atlantic Fisheries Dispute. *See* Fisheries Dispute, Arbitration of.

Atrocities in War. No war has been fought which did not produce its quota of brutality stories, narrations of savage, cruel and brutal deeds, shocking to those who, in the quiet calm of natural, peace conditions, read of them on the printed page. It is folly for any nation to try to dismiss the charge of perpetrating atrocities as complete falsehood. It is equally foolish to believe entirely the horror stories circulated during war. Upon investigation, these rumors frequently collapse entirely or are reduced to almost negligible minimums. Characterizations of atrocities extend throughout the gamut of human imaginations or fiendishness—bombardment of open towns, private houses, noncombatants, hospitals, orphan asylums and mercy stations; use of explosive bullets which burst within the human body and tear their way outward; employment of poison gas; massacre and mistreatment of enemy wounded and prisoners and of noncombatant civilians; rape; staking out of victims; crucifixion; eye gouging; tongue severing and splitting; hacking off of hands and feet; sexual mutilation; impaling and many other forms of brutality.

During the Revolution we suffered inhuman treatment of our men held prisoners aboard the nefarious British prison ships[qv] in Wallabout Bay, Long Island. In our naval wars, the record shows we were more sinned against than sinning and this is equally true of the Mexican War. If we discount the charge against us for the use of the "water cure"[qv] in the Philippine Islands, the Civil War brings out the worst charges and countercharges against us, charges in which we, perforce, stand self-accused since only our own people are involved. Stories of Libby Prison, Andersonville[qqv], Salisbury and others in the South are matched by tales of equal brutality in Northern prisons such as Elmira, Camp Chase and Rock Island[qqv]. In fairness, it should be remembered that, materially, the South was ill-equipped to handle great numbers of prisoners. A Southern writer commenting upon prison fare, shelter and the like stated that the only difference between Union prisoners in a Southern camp and Confederate soldiers in the ranks was that the latter were free. When Grant (U.) refused any longer to exchange prisoners, conditions in the already overcrowded Southern prisons rapidly became intolerable. To ascribe a systematic, preconceived policy of atrocity either to Union or Confederate Governments is ridiculous.

In the World War our late entry made us the scapegoat which automatically inherited credit or discredit for all the moth-eaten charges that had already gone the rounds. In the alien press, for purposes of propaganda, the American devil had ascribed to him all the fiendish acts with which the "Aussies" from down under, the "Ladies of Hell" from Scotland, the territorials from Morocco and our neighbors from Canada had been charged from 1914 to 1917—we were simply a new target for old ammunition. Solemn documentary proofs of outrages were printed in "Brown Books" to be refuted by the opposition in "White Books" with equally weighty statements. Usually, specific and thorough investigations of alleged atrocities committed disclosed a normal 90% error, sometimes revealing even that the charges were supported by forged documents and faked photographs.

The dum-dum or explosive bullet cannot be explained away; nor can the use of poison gas, but use of the former has never been authentically charged or proved against us and the latter was forced upon us as a weapon of war by Germany's first use of it in 1915 (*see* Chemical Warfare).

[Asa B. Isham, *Prisoners of War and Military Prisons;* R. Randolph Stevenson, *The Southern Side, or Andersonville Prison;* Southern Society Historical Papers, Vol. I, March and April, 1876; Jefferson Davis, *Andersonville and Other War Prisons;* Anthony M. Keiley, *Prisoner of War, or Five Months Among the Yankees;* The Right Flanker, MS. sheets circulated among Southern prisoners in Fort LaFayette, N. Y.; Henry M. Davidson, *Fourteen Months in Southern Prisons;* Clay W. Holmes, *The Elmira Prison Camp;* William H. Knauss, *The Story of Camp Chase;* Robert H. Kellogg, *Life and Death in Rebel Prisons;* Frank E. Moran, *Bastiles of the Confederacy;* Isaac W. K. Handy, *United States Bonds;* N. P. Chipman, *The Horrors of Andersonville Rebel Prison;* A. O. Abbott, *Prison Life in the South;* A. M. Reiley, *In Vinculis;* J. Ogden Murray, *The Immortal Six Hundred;* George Taylor, *Martyrs to the Revolution in the British Prison Ships;* Rev. R. Livesey, *A Relic of the Revolution;* Joseph Bedier, *German Atrocities;* Carl P. Dennett, *Prisoners of the Great War;* Foreign Relations of the United States, World War Supplement volume.]

ROBERT S. THOMAS

Attainder, now obsolete in all democratic governments, is a summary legal procedure whereby all the ordinary civil rights of the defendant are waived, the state proceeding against him by "bill," or legislative act. An attainted person suffered the loss of offices, property and usually life; his children losing the inheritance of the estate and their noble rank, if any. The Constitution of the United States specifically prohibits the enactment of bills of attainder.

[T. P. Taswell-Langmead, *English Constitutional History.*]

BEN R. BALDWIN

Attorney General of the United States. *See* Justice, Department of.

Aubry's Ride. Francis Xavier Aubry, after a successful trading venture in Santa Fé in 1848, determined to bring out a second caravan in the same year and allowed himself eight days to ride back to Missouri. Doubts being expressed by his friends, he wagered a considerable sum on his ability to do so. Riding hard, his horse gave out on the Arkansas, but he pushed on fifteen or twenty miles to Mann's Fort, secured a remount, pressed onward, was pursued by Indians near Pawnee Fork, but reached Independence within less than the time specified.

[G. D. Brewerton, *Overland with Kit Carson.*]

CARL L. CANNON

Auburn (N. Y.) Prison System. The details of the separate or silent system were originally worked out in the prison being erected by New York at Auburn in the years following 1819. An act of that year and another of 1821 called for individual cells to displace the discredited congregate system. Rows of cells, 3½ x 7 x 7 feet in size, were erected in tiers, back to back, forming a cell block which was inclosed by the outer walls of the building. The plan differed strikingly from the Pennsylvania solitary pattern[qv], but could trace a distant descent from the plans of the *maison de force* at Ghent. The cells provided separate sleeping quarters, from which the convicts marched in lockstep to the shops of contractors located in the prison yard. Strict rules of silence were enforced at all times. Religious services were conducted in chapels. The system was designed to isolate the convicts from each other and to encourage them to penitence without sacrificing the value of their labor. The fact that convict labor[qv] was thus available to the enterprising pioneers of the factory system in America helped to make Auburn the favorite pattern for state prisons[qv] during the next half-century.

[Blake McKelvey, *American Prisons.*]

BLAKE McKELVEY

Auctions. Sale by auction is a method of sale which was known to the Romans and at the time of the discovery of America the traders and merchants of European nations were familiar with its use. When the chief colonial cities reached some commercial importance, auctions became a part of their trading organizations. As early as 1729 Pennsylvania regulated auctions, New York followed in 1761 and Massachusetts enacted such a law in 1780. The Federal Government passed laws levying duties on sales at auction in 1794 and in 1813. From 1795 to 1801 the total value of goods sold at auction in the United States, with exceptions as provided in the law of 1794, was $64,996,278.

Auctions, however, were more important after the War of 1812 than they were before. This was due largely to the restrictions on commerce previous to and during the war which resulted in an unusual demand for goods. When peace was declared there was a rush for the American market and resort was had to the quickest and most convenient method of sale which often proved to be the auction. The preference for the auction method of sale seriously disturbed the business of American importers and jobbers. From one-half to three-fourths of the cargoes entering New York were on foreign account and instead of this merchandise passing through the trade channel of importer-jobber-retailer-consumer, it came accompanied by an agent and passed through the trade channel of auction-retailer-consumer, thus eliminating the importer and jobber.

The importers and jobbers did not sit idly by and watch this serious inroad on the business which they had customarily controlled. For fifteen years they attacked the auctions with petitions, pamphlets and ballots and although they were never successful in getting Congress to pass a bill restricting and regulating auctions, they were successful with the legislatures of the important commercial states.

The auction method of sale declined in importance after 1830 and did not again reach its former estate. The number of people following the occupation of an auctioneer, however, increased from 890 in 1850 to 4281 in 1930. The volume of sales made by 461 auction companies engaged in the wholesale distribution of commodities in 1929 was $373,775,525, about thirty-four times the total of all auction sales in 1800, but this amounted to only about one half of 1% of the total value of commodities sold at wholesale.

[Fred M. Jones, *Middlemen in the Domestic Trade of the United States 1800-1860.*]

FRED M. JONES

Audubon Societies, NATIONAL ASSOCIATION OF. This organization, for many years the foremost in the wild-life-conservation field, was incorporated Jan. 5, 1905. Primarily concerned with conservation education, it came into being as a federation of a number of dissociated state and local Audubon clubs which, in turn, had stemmed from the original "Audubon Society," first formed in 1886 by Dr. George Bird Grinnell, editor of *Forest and Stream.* This group consisted largely of school children, reached a total membership of about 50,000 and was abandoned in 1889 for lack of funds; memberships were based on pledges not to kill or injure "any wild bird not used for food" and not to make use of wild-bird plumage as an article of fashion or household furniture. No dues were charged.

One of the association's major projects has been the formation and maintenance of Junior Audubon Clubs, of which more than 150,000 have been established, with nearly 6,000,000 members. Each of these children has been provided, at less than cost, with literature designed to arouse an interest in wild life—especially birds—and its protection; the printed material has totaled more than 300,000,000 pages with more than 57,000,000 colored pictures. Besides this literature, the association distributes much miscellaneous printed material and publishes a magazine, *Bird-Lore.* Its adult education work has largely consisted in stimulating an interest in threatened forms of wild life and promoting an understanding of the biological principles behind their conservation. The association has also maintained a number of bird sanctuaries[qv].

[T. Gilbert Pearson, *Adventures in Bird Protection.*]

WILLIAM VOGT

Aughwick, Indian village on the Juniata River near the site of Shirleysburg, Pa., became in 1753 headquarters for George Croghan, trader and agent for Pennsylvania among western Indians. Friendly Indians, refugees from the vicinity of Fort Duquesne[qv], were maintained at Aughwick and left there to join Braddock's expedition[qv] in 1755.

[C. A. Hanna, *The Wilderness Trail;* C. Hale Sipe, *Indian Wars of Pennsylvania.*]

SOLON J. BUCK

Augusta, Fort, named for George III's mother. Constructed by Pennsylvania in 1756, at the site of present Sunbury, to defend the frontier after Braddock's defeat[qv], and to forestall the French who supposedly intended to fortify the forks of the Susquehanna, it protected frontiersmen from Indians and Tories until abandoned after 1780.

[*Report of the Commission to Locate the Site of the Frontier Forts of Pennsylvania,* 2 volumes, Harrisburg, 1896.]

WILLIAM A. RUSS, JR.

Augusta, Ga., was founded (1735) by Gen. James Edward Oglethorpe at the head of navigation on the Savannah River. Until 1773 it remained the northwestern outpost of Georgia, dominating Indian trade and relations. Largely loyalist, it fell twice into British hands (1779, 1780–81). For a short period, ending in 1795, it was the state capital. There a convention ratified the United States Constitution. Upland cotton and steam transportation made it, temporarily, the greatest inland cotton market in the world. A government arsenal and a large powder mill made it a major source of supply for Confederate armies during the Civil War.

[E. M. Coulter, *A Short History of Georgia.*]

CHESTER McA. DESTLER

***Augusta,* THE,** was a British vessel which, in 1777, led the attack against Commodore Hazelwood's fleet defending Fort Mercer[qv] on the Delaware. The Americans resisted, forcing a British retreat. Defense construction may have caused channel changes, and the *Augusta* grounded. The Revolutionists attacked and, on Oct. 23, the *Augusta* exploded, losing over sixty men.

[W. Allen Gardner, *Naval History of the American Revolution.*]

JULIAN P. BOYD

Augusta, The Congress of (1763), took place Nov. 5–10, in response to orders from the British government to the governors of Virginia, North and South Carolina and Georgia that they collect representatives of the southern Indians (Creeks, Cherokees, Choctaws, Chickasaws, and Catawbas[qqv]), inform them that the French and Indian War[qv] had ended, and bring about a general settlement on trade and boundary difficulties. The governors from these colonies (lieutenant governor from Virginia) and John Stuart, Superintendent of Indian Affairs[qv] in the Southern District, met 700 Indians at Augusta, signed a treaty of friendship, and secured therein important land cessions in Georgia from the Creeks.

[C. C. Jones, Jr., *History of Georgia,* Vol. II. W. B. Stevens, *History of Georgia,* Vol. II; *Journal of the Southern Congress held at Augusta in Georgia, 1763.*]

E. MERTON COULTER

Augusta, The Treaty of (1773), was made by Gov. James Wright, of Georgia, and John Stuart, Superintendent of Indian Affairs[qv] in the Southern District, with chiefs of the Creek and Cherokee nations[qqv], at the suggestion of the Indians, who were hopelessly in debt to various groups of white traders. By this agreement Georgia was ceded two tracts of land, one between the Altamaha and Ogeechee rivers and the other lying between the upper stretches of the Ogeechee and Savannah rivers, comprising in all more than 2,100,000 acres, and from the sale of these lands the traders were to be paid. A great influx of settlers was attracted here just before the Revolution.

[C. C. Jones, Jr., *History of Georgia,* Vol. II; W. B. Stevens, *History of Georgia,* Vol. II; George White, *Historical Collections of Georgia;* R. and G. Watkins, eds., *Digest of the Laws of the State of Georgia.*]

E. MERTON COULTER

Augusta County, Va., named in honor of Princess Augusta, wife of the Prince of Wales, was erected on Nov. 1, 1738, from that portion of Orange County lying beyond the Blue Ridge. The newly created county was to remain part of the parent county until the number of inhabitants warranted the establishment of a separate government, which was not until Oct. 30, 1745. Territorially it included the present states of Kentucky, Ohio, Indiana, Illinois, nearly all of West Virginia and a part of western Pennsylvania. Here the Virginians came into conflict with Pennsylvania's claims, for both colonies had settlers in those parts of Pennsylvania west of the Alleghenies. Becoming alarmed at the influx of Virginia settlers, Pennsylvania had erected, on Feb. 26, 1773, Westmoreland County, which included all of the present counties of Westmoreland, Fayette, Greene, Washington and parts of Allegheny, Beaver, Indiana and Armstrong. In

1774–75 Virginia created the District of West Augusta, which claimed the land of the newly created Westmoreland County. In 1776 Virginia attempted to strengthen title to these lands by dividing West Augusta into three new counties: Ohio, Yohogania and Monongalia. These conflicting jurisdictional claims produced the Pennsylvania-Virginia Boundary dispute[qv] which was not settled until 1780. The immense territory of Augusta County was thus cut down, first by the creation of Botetourt County in 1769, Fincastle in 1772, the three counties in West Augusta and later encroachments until it reached its present-day status.

[Jos. A. Waddell, *Annals of Augusta County, Virginia, from 1726 to 1871;* Edgar W. Hassler, *Old Westmoreland: A History of Western Pennsylvania during the Revolution;* Boyd Crumrine, *The County Court for the District of West Augusta, Virginia.*]

R. J. FERGUSON

Auraria (Colo.), established in October, 1858, was one of the towns started at the juncture of Cherry Creek and the South Platte, following gold discoveries earlier that summer (*see* Pikes Peak Gold Rush). In April, 1860, it was consolidated with Denver[qv], its rival, on the opposite bank of Cherry Creek.

[J. C. Smiley, *History of Denver.*]

MALCOLM G. WYER

Aurora, THE, a Philadelphia newspaper founded in 1790 by Benjamin Franklin Bache as the *General Advertiser.* When Freneau's *National Gazette*[qv] suspended, the *Aurora* took its place as the Jeffersonian Republican[qv] mouthpiece. It was notorious for its violent personal abuse and its attacks on Washington's administration, including the charge that the President had violated the Constitution and including also forged letters of Washington.

[B. Faÿ, *The Two Franklins.*]

JULIAN P. BOYD

Austin Colony, Texas. On Jan. 17, 1821, the Spanish authorities in Mexico granted to Moses Austin permission to settle 300 families in Texas. After the death of the grantee, and after Mexico's successful revolt from Spain, the Mexican provisional government confirmed this concession to Stephen F. Austin, the "Father of Texas." Subsequently the younger Austin obtained contracts to settle 900 additional families, most of whom he had introduced by 1833. Austin's colonies formed the nucleus of the Anglo-American occupation of Texas.

[E. C. Barker, *The Life of Stephen F. Austin.*]

E. C. BARKER

Austria, Treaty of Peace with (1921). After the Senate had refused to ratify the Treaty of Versailles[qv], the Treaty of Saint-Germain-en-Laye was not submitted to it. On July 2, 1921, a joint resolution of Congress declared at an end the state of war existing with Austria-Hungary since Dec. 7, 1917; it also affirmed the rights of the United States arising from its participation in the war, the terms of the armistice[qv] or the Treaty of Saint-Germain, and as one of the principal Allied and Associated Powers, and provided for the retention of all property seized in wartime until Austria had satisfied all claims for losses suffered by American nationals since 1914. The Treaty of Vienna (Aug. 24, 1921), based on this resolution, provided that the United States should enjoy the rights of Parts V, VI, VIII, IX, X, XI, XII, XIV of the Treaty of Saint-Germain, but should not be bound by Parts I (League of Nations), II, III, IV and XIII (Labor); further, the United States was privileged, but not bound, to participate in the Reparation Commission[qv]. The treaty was ratified by Austria on Oct. 8, 1921, and by the United States on Oct. 21, 1921.

BERNADOTTE E. SCHMITT

Auto Racing. The first road race occurred at Chicago in 1895, with a record of 7.5 miles per hour. Speedways were introduced in 1907–8. The classic 500-mile race is held each Decoration Day at the Indianapolis 2.5-mile paved track, constructed in 1909–10, where the record in 1938 was 117.20 miles per hour. Speed tests are made at Daytona Beach and Bonneville (Utah) salt flats. A record of 368.85 miles per hour was achieved (1939) at Bonneville. Over 150 races are held annually in the United States under rules of the Contest Board of the American Automobile Association.

ROSCOE R. HILL

Automobile, THE, was not invented by any one person but was evolved through the efforts of many experimenters in several nations. So early as 1787 Oliver Evans, of Philadelphia, petitioned the Maryland legislature for a patent on the manufacture and operation of steam-propelled vehicles, and in 1804 he ran through the streets of Philadelphia a strange vehicle consisting of a large wagon which carried, and was driven by, a steam-propelled flatboat. However, largely because of the atrocious roads of the period and because of concentration on railroad development, little progress was made in this country until almost the close of the 19th century and automotive development got its real start abroad.

In the 1830's steam-driven stage coaches–ponderous, clumsy and rough—were operating on regular schedules along several routes in England but eventually they were driven from the road by excessive toll charges and restrictive legislation. Most of the real progress was made in Germany: in 1876 Dr. A. N. Otto built a four-cycle internal combustion hydrocarbon motor, the same in principle as those used in motor vehicles today; in 1885 Gottfried Daimler built the first motorcycle, and in 1886 Carl Benz built the first automobile powered by a gasoline engine. The French quickly took up their ideas and by 1895 the French firm of Panhard & Lavassor was producing horseless vehicles on a commercial scale.

Meanwhile, activity in America was practically dormant, with most of the experimentation during the period being concentrated on heavy steam-propelled traction engines. After 1890, however, American pioneers began working in homes and workshops, borrowing heavily on the ideas of their European colleagues, and by 1900 they had laid the basis for a new industry. Authorities differ over the somewhat empty question as to which of the United States experimenters deserves precedence, but the weight of evidence places Charles and Frank Duryea first, in 1892; Henry Ford second in 1893, Elwood Haynes in 1894, with R. E. Olds, Alexander Winton and Charles P. King following closely. At any rate, the Duryea cars were the first American vehicles to prove themselves in competition: a Duryea road wagon won the first road race held in this country—the *Times-Herald* contest run over the snow-covered streets of Chicago on Thanksgiving Day in 1895—and the following year three of the four Duryea entries took all the money in the New York-to-Irvington race.

The first automotive trade journal, *The Horseless Age,* was launched with a good deal of temerity by E. P. Ingersoll in 1895, but the industry was to remain largely in the experimental stage until the close of the century. The next decade saw phenomenal advances in the art of road transportation. Twelve manufacturing firms in 1900 turned out 4000 vehicles; by 1910 there were sixty-nine companies in the field and their annual production had leaped to 181,000. This whole decade was marked by tremendous enthusiasm and intense activity: automobile clubs were formed; a dozen or more reliability runs were staged each year; a craze for speed contests of all kinds sprang up on both sides of the Atlantic—climaxed by the fantastic race around the world from New York to Paris in 1908; strenuous campaigns for construction of good roads[qv] were undertaken; legislators puzzled and wrangled over laws to govern the new form of transportation; extravagant claims for their products were made by the makers in screaming advertisements; and controversy between car owners and horse owners reached a furious crescendo.

Most of the firms started during this period operated on little more than a shoestring, using credit advanced by the supply companies, demanding advance payments and cash on delivery from dealers, and financing expansion through reinvestment of profits. The Ford Motor Company[qv] started business with a capital of $28,000; the Hudson Motor Car Company, with "considerably less than that." Very little actual manufacturing was done by these early companies; rather their job was to buy the parts ready-made, assemble them and sell the resultant vehicles as quickly as possible. Mortality among the automobile firms was very high: of the sixty-nine companies making cars in 1910, only eight still survived in 1938—Packard, started in 1900, Ford and Cadillac in 1903, Studebaker and Buick in 1904, Willys-Overland in 1908 and General Motors[qv] and Hudson in 1909.

Naturally enough, the tremendous profits realized by a few of the companies gave rise to many promotional ventures, based largely on hopes and extravagant claims, and a number of companies capitalized at many millions of dollars sprang into the picture only to crash and disappear almost immediately. Of all the large promotions, only two persisted for any appreciable length of time, and one of these—the Electric Vehicle Company—was sustained for some years by its ownership of the Selden patent[qv].

This patent was the storm center of a court battle that dragged on in the courts for eight years and was a vital factor in influencing the early development of the automobile industry. In 1879 George B. Selden, of Rochester, N. Y., filed application for a patent on a gasoline-propelled vehicle, but purposely kept the matter pending so that the patent was not granted until 1895. It eventually came into the possession of the Electric Vehicle Company which immediately began infringement proceedings. After one legal set-back, practically all the major manufacturers, with the exception of Ford, capitulated, forming themselves into the Association of Licensed Automobile Manufacturers. At length, the appeals court ruled that, while the patent was valid, it was not being infringed and therefore not enforceable. The principal effect of the Selden patent was to teach the manufacturers the value of co-operation and to give them a healthy fear of patent litigation, thus laying the groundwork for the cross-licensing agreement that has kept the automobile industry almost free of the patent difficulties which have plagued so many other lines of enterprise.

In 1910–11 the industry experienced a temporary set-back; twenty firms dropped out of existence and the curve of production increase slacked off considerably. Almost immediately, however, the automobile makers began improving production methods: mass-production[qv] techniques were perfected, phenomenal reductions were made in the man-hours of labor per car, and prices were slashed. Automobile purchasing again shot upward and by 1920 there were eighty-four firms engaged in automobile production, making in that year 1,906,000 cars valued at $1,809,000,000. During this period, American makers obtained dominance of the world markets, exports of passenger cars and trucks during 1920 totaling 142,000, while imports, which had begun back in 1895, dropped almost to the vanishing point.

The installment plan[qv] of car purchasing, instituted on a large scale shortly after the World War, proved a tremendous stimulant. The low prices obtaining in the used-car market aided in providing individual transportation for the lower-income groups and intensive road-building added further to the popularity of motor vehicles. Although the number of manufacturing firms dropped steadily, declining from a high of eighty-eight in 1921 to twenty in 1937, passenger car registrations continued rapidly upward, losing ground only during the depression years, 1930–33. In 1937, when more than 5,000,000 vehicles valued at nearly $3,000,000,000 were produced, there were approximately 30,000,000 motor vehicles registered in the United States, of which 25,500,000 were passenger cars. This represented 70% of all motor vehicles in use throughout the world and was equivalent to one vehicle for each four persons living in this country.

This tremendous motorization has profoundly affected many phases of American life. It has driven the horse from the highway, wrecking the $50,000,000 carriage and buggy-building industry in the process. It has brought about the construction of nearly 1,000,000 miles of improved highways. The motor vehicle has robbed the railroads of much of their passenger traffic and some of their freight, but it has provided them with 4,000,000 carloads of automotive freight annually and has given them a flexible instrument for delivery to and from the stations.

The automobile industry gives direct and semidirect employment to some 6,000,000 workers, with total wage payments since 1900 estimated at $82,000,000,000. It is the principal consumer of many important commodities such as steel, rubber, plate glass, nickel and lead, and is responsible for the tremendous expansion of the oil industry, which produces more than a billion barrels of crude petroleum a year.

Politically, the motor vehicle exerts continuous pressure for less local and more national governmental control. It produces more than a billion and a half dollars in taxes a year, most of which goes toward road-building. It has worked against sectionalism[qv] and provincialism and has been a major factor in integrating the nation. It has created a major social problem by causing some 40,000 deaths and 1,000,000 injuries yearly.

To the farmer, the motor vehicle has brought more centralized educational facilities, lower transportation costs on his produce, quicker medical attention, more social intercourse and greater ease in obtaining his supplies. To the city dweller, it has brought a new means of leisure-utilization, freedom from mass-transportation herding and a method of periodic escape from urban surroundings. It has hastened suburban development and is beginning to cause disintegration of congested business districts.

Practically every prosperous family owns a motor car; a startlingly large percentage of the poorest families own them. Like the bathtub, the telephone and the radio[qqv], it has become an essential element in the American way of living.

[J. R. Doolittle, *The Romance of the Automobile Industry;* R. C. Epstein, *The Automobile Industry.*]

RICHARD W. TUPPER

Auttose, The Battle of (Nov. 29, 1813). As an aid to Jackson in his campaign against the Creeks[qv], Gen. John Floyd, commanding 940 Georgia militia and several hundred friendly Creeks, crossed the Chattahoochee River into Alabama. On Nov. 29 he attacked Auttose, a Creek Indian village on the Tallapoosa River near Tookabatchee[qv], and drove the Creeks from their villages, burned their houses and killed 200, losing but 11 killed and 54 wounded himself.

[Henry Adams, *History of the United States of America.*]

ROBERT S. THOMAS

Avery Salt Mine is located near New Iberia, La. Although a brine spring was discovered in 1791, it was not until May, 1862, that the existence of a rock salt mass was revealed. The Confederate government worked the mine until the Union forces seized it in April, 1863.

ELLA LONN

Avery's Trace. In 1787 the North Carolina legislature provided for a lottery[qv] the proceeds of which should be used in cutting a way across the Cumberland Mountains in the Tennessee country in order to connect Washington District with the Cumberland settlements[qqv]. Peter Avery blazed and cut a trace through the sites of the present towns of Harriman, Monterey and Cookeville where the descent of the western escarpment of the Cumberland plateau began. The Cherokees[qv] claimed the region traversed by the trace and demanded toll for its use. Guards of militia became necessary where the party of travelers was not large or not well armed.

[W. E. McElwee, The Old Road, *The American Historical Magazine*, Vol. VIII.] SAMUEL C. WILLIAMS

Averysboro, Battle of (March 16, 1865). Hardee's corps of Gen. J. E. Johnston's Confederate Army, retreating through North Carolina, entrenched at this village and gave a portion of Sherman's (U.) Army, under Slocum and Kilpatrick, a determined resistance for several hours; but inferiority in numbers compelled his retreat during the night.

[*Battles and Leaders of the Civil War.*]

ALVIN F. HARLOW

Aviation. While Lilienthal and Pilcher were carrying on experiments with gliding in Europe between 1890 and 1900, Octave Chanute was doing the same in the United States. At precisely the same period, Ader in France, Maxim in England, and, in the United States, Samuel P. Langley, secretary of the Smithsonian Institution, were endeavoring to solve the problem of a power-driven glider. Ader and Maxim gave it up. Langley continued his experiments from 1887 until 1903, at which time the Government withdrew support from his experiments upon the wrecking of his last model. Wilbur and Orville Wright, operators of a bicycle repair shop in Dayton, Ohio, had about 1896 begun experiments, and in 1903 achieved short power-driven flights at Kittyhawk[qv] Island, N. C. On Oct. 5, 1905, they accomplished a flight of twenty-four miles, the aeroplane—as it was called for many years before the word was modified to airplane—remaining in the air thirty-eight minutes and three seconds. Wilbur Wright spent a part of 1908 in France and gave aviation a strong impetus there. The United States Government accepted its first plane (it had a speed of forty miles per hour) from the Wright brothers in 1909. This and all other machines constructed in America for a number of years thereafter were biplanes.

In 1908 the biplane of Glenn H. Curtiss won recognition, and in the following year won the prize in an international contest in France for the fastest time—15 minutes, 56⅕ seconds—over a course of 20 kilometers. In 1910 Curtiss flew from Albany to New York harbor, 142 miles, stopping three times for oil and fuel, at an average speed of forty-nine miles per hour. He produced a seaplane in 1911 which won for him the Aero Club of America trophy. At the beginning of the World War the United States was pre-eminent in seaplane construction. The Wright brothers had obtained broad patents, and there was much litigation with Curtiss and others, the Wrights' claims for the most part being upheld. Curtiss opened an aviation school and did much to spread the knowledge of the science. For several years all flights were either experimental or exhibitions at county fairs and elsewhere by individual aviators who owned their machines. A shocking number of these pioneers were killed in accidents (*see* Airplane Disasters).

In 1911 William R. Hearst offered a prize of $50,000 for a flight across the United States within thirty days, elapsed time. Galbraith P. Rogers attempted it with a plane having a 40-horse-power motor. He limped from town to town, his longest flight being but 133 miles, fell frequently, replaced many parts and finally, after sixty-eight days, reached California in another plane than the one with which he started. His elapsed time was forty-nine days. Thereafter, aviation began to make more rapid strides. May 2–3, 1923, Lts. Kelley and Macready of the United States Army flew nonstop from New York to San Diego in twenty-six hours and fifty minutes. In 1924 Russell L. Maugham reduced this to twenty-one hours forty-eight minutes, making six stops. In 1929 Frank Hawks crossed the continent eastward in a trifle over nineteen hours, and westward in seventeen hours thirty-eight minutes sixteen seconds. In 1930 he did the journey in twelve hours twenty-five minutes. In 1938 Howard R. Hughes flew from Los Angeles to Newark in seven hours twenty-eight minutes and twenty-five seconds. Lincoln Beachy's altitude record of 11,642 feet in 1912 was surpassed by Capt. Schroeder in 1918 with 28,000 feet, by the same man in 1920 with 36,000, by Lt. Macready in 1921 with 40,800 feet and by Lt. Soucek in 1930 with 43,166 feet.

The first plane to cross the Atlantic was the United States Navy's NC-4 (1919)[qv], one of three which attempted a flight via Newfoundland, the Azores and Portugal; the other two were wrecked en route. In June of that year two Englishmen, Alcock and Brown, flew the 1600 miles from Newfoundland to Ireland, but the 3600-mile solo flight of Charles A. Lindbergh[qv] from New York to Paris, May 20–21, 1927, was considered a milestone in aviation history. Two weeks later Clarence Chamberlin with a passenger flew nonstop from New York to a point in Germany, 3923 miles. For years European flyers tried in vain to cross the Atlantic in a westerly direction, and many were lost in the attempts; but by 1938 this had come to be a commonplace affair. In 1924 two army planes out of four (two being wrecked on the way) went around the globe, passing the Pacific via Alaska and Kamtchatka, and the Atlantic via Scotland, the Orkney Islands and Iceland. Their actual flying time was only 15 days and 11 hours, but they consumed 175 days, all told, in making the tour. In 1931 Wiley Post and Harold Gatty encircled the globe in eight days sixteen hours, and in 1933 Post did it alone in seven days eighteen hours and forty-nine minutes. This record was eclipsed by Howard R. Hughes, who, with a crew of four, accomplished the feat in July, 1938, in three days nineteen hours.

The United States Army used planes for scouting in the Mexican border troubles in 1916. Early in the World War several American flyers joined the Lafayette Escadrille[qv], and when the United States entered the war, American planes and men did notable work on the French and Italian fronts. Meanwhile, American factories were supplying many planes to other nations. It was during the war, on May 15, 1918, that the Post Office Department started the first experimental air-mail plane[qv] between New York and Washington. This carrying very soon passed into private hands, and the mail planes began carrying passengers—a traffic which grew within a few years to enormous proportions. The first goods other than letters to be sent by air were motion-picture news films carried by private planes. In 1927 the American Railway Express Company began carrying small packages by plane in a limited way. Rates at first were enormously high—at one time $10 per pound for 1000 miles—but they declined rapidly and the service developed with even greater speed. By 1934 not only small but heavy freight up to the size of an automobile was being carried all over the United States, and through Mexico and the West Indies to all parts of South America. After 1930 the great majority of machines built in the United States were monoplanes. Speeds had risen to 200 and even 300 miles per hour. On Jan. 1, 1930, there were 1279 airports[qv] in the United States; in 1938 there were 3000 such ports. Mail and passenger service was begun between the United States and South America in 1930, across the Pacific to Asia in 1935 and across the Atlantic in 1939.

[John Goldstrom, *A Narrative History of Aviation;* Chelsea Fraser, *The Story of Aircraft.*]

ALVIN F. HARLOW

"Awakening," Second, is the name usually given the great religious revival[qv] which swept over the United States in the latter 18th and early 19th centuries, following an era of extreme religious deadness. In the East it centered in the colleges where religion had been in sad plight with infidelity rampant among the students. President Dwight at Yale met the issue squarely and in chapel sermons and classroom discussions he won the respect of the students and prepared the way for a renewed religious interest. A revival began in 1802 which resulted in the conversion of a third of the student body. The Awakening spread to other colleges and soon a stream of young college graduates was entering every form of Christian work, particularly the Christian ministry and education and Home and Foreign mission[qqv] enterprises.

In the West the Awakening was attended with great emotional excitement, under the preaching of such evangelists[qv] as James McGready, Barton W. Stone and William McKendree. No churches were large enough to hold the vast crowds which assembled to hear the evangelists and as a result the camp-meeting[qv] evolved. While at first largely a Presbyterian movement, the revival soon became interdenominational and spread rapidly throughout the West. Though greatly increasing church membership and raising the standard of Western morals, there were some unfortunate results, such as excessive emotionalism and church schisms.

[Catharine C. Cleveland, *The Great Revival in the West, 1797-1805.*]

WILLIAM W. SWEET

Axes, Frontier. From the early contacts of Europeans with Indians in the 15th century, through all periods of fur trade and other commerce, the Indian demanded and received the iron axe and hatchet. The French in the 17th century distributed great numbers of axes with light polls and long blades, a type known as the French trade axe. Records show, however, that Holland and England both supplied this same "Biscay" hatchet. The tree-felling axe brought by Frenchmen for their own use was a large counterpart of the popular trade axe, with heavy blade and light poll. The axe taken to Jamestown and Plymouth differed little from that of the French, but before a century had passed, there had developed from this British tool a better-balanced Anglo-American implement with lengthened poll and somewhat shortened blade. Before 1776 American makers had developed the characteristic American axe with heavy squared poll that outweighed the bit, a tool unknown in other parts of the world. The Indian, however, refused to recognize the greater efficiency of this new axe and as long as frontier relationships endured the "French trade axe" persisted.

[Harold A. Innis, *The Fur Trade in Canada;* Henry C. Mercer, Ancient Carpenters Tools, *Old Time New England*, Vol. XV.]

CARL P. RUSSELL

Aylon, Expeditions of. In 1521 Vasquez de Ayllon sent from the West Indies an exploring expedition which visited the present Carolina coast, returning therefrom with a number of captured natives. In 1526 de Ayllon sailed in three caravels with 600 prospective settlers, Negro slaves, scores of horses and orders to seek the ever-elusive Northwest Passage[qv]. The name of his settlement, San Miguel de Gualdape, is recorded, but its site has yet to be determined, some scholars having placed it south of Cape Hatteras, while others have placed it within the Chesapeake, either on the James or the Potomac. Since the most extended account refers to severe cold, acceptance thereof would point to the more northerly site. The Spaniards suffered all the ills subsequently endured by the English at Jamestown[qv] in the form of malarial fevers, dissensions and Indian assaults. The settlement was abandoned and the survivors returned to the West Indies.

[Elroy M. Avery, *A History of the United States*, Vol. I.]

MATTHEW PAGE ANDREWS

Ayubale (Ayaville), Battle of (Dec. 14, 1703), was a frontier engagement between a force of 50 whites and 1000 Indians under ex-Gov. James Moore of South Carolina and the defenders of the Spanish mission at Ayubale, near Tallahassee. Moore, who as governor (1700–1703) had failed in an attempt to take the fort at St. Augustine, was given command of the expedition into Apalache[qv] to redeem his failure. He took Ayubale, devastated a wide area, badly crippled the Spanish in Florida and carried away 1300 Apalache Indian captives (or 600, according to the Spanish estimate), settling as Carolina dependents, on the east side of the lower course of the Savannah River, those not sold as slaves.

[D. D. Wallace, *History of South Carolina;* J. T. Lanning, *Spanish Missions in Georgia.*]

D. D. WALLACE

Ayuntamiento, THE, or ***Cabildo,*** is a Spanish and Spanish-American municipal council, with administrative, legislative and judicial functions. Citizens sometimes joined it in open meeting, or *cabildo abierto*. Many cities in the United States, including St. Augustine, Fla., San Antonio, Tex., and Los Angeles, Calif., have been governed by *ayuntamientos,* which still survive in republican Spanish America.

[C. E. Chapman, *Colonial Hispanic America: a History.*]

CHARLES EDWARD CHAPMAN and
ROBERT HALE SHIELDS

Azilia, Margravate of, designates the fantastic scheme of Sir Robert Montgomery to establish "a New Colony to the South of Carolina." Despite activities in Britain, he and others failed to settle the area between the Savannah and the Altamaha rivers, the Golden Islands region, within the three years conditioning his grant of 1717 from the Carolina proprietors[qv].

[V. W. Crane, *The Southern Frontier, 1670-1732.*]

H. B. FANT

Aztalan, an Indian village of moderate antiquity, was located near Lake Mills, Wis., on the Crawfish. The inhabitants, a people of Middle Mississippi Valley culture, lived on seeds, nuts, berries, molluscs, fish, birds and animals. Cannibalism was practised. Arts and crafts were well advanced, and pottery and implement manufacture was carried on. The village was protected by a wall of palisades with watch towers at regular intervals; within were rectangular and circular mud-plastered wooden houses. The earthwork enclosure was first described by N. F. Hyer in the *Milwaukee Advertiser* in 1836; it was surveyed and described by Dr. I. A. Lapham in *The Antiquities of Wisconsin* in 1855 and excavated by the Milwaukee Public Museum, 1919–20, 1932.

[Milwaukee Public Museum, *Aztalan.*]

CHARLES E. BROWN

Babcock Tester. *See* Dairy Industry.

Bachelor Houses. To protect the colony from being burdened with the indigent and to maintain moral standards, Connecticut as early as 1636 forbade heads of families from entertaining single young men without permission. Nor could an unmarried young man keep home alone without consent under penalty of a fine. The Connecticut Code of 1650 (*see* Ludlow's Code) and the New Haven laws of 1656 extended this prohibition to single persons of either sex. Similarly strict laws against strangers are found in the Massachusetts codes of 1641, 1648 and 1660.

[E. W. Capen, *The Historical Development of the Poor Law of Connecticut.*] RICHARD B. MORRIS

Backwoods and Back Country. The term backwoodsman was not applied to those who, in the first century of our colonization, settled in the wilder portions of New England. It did not become common until pioneers began advancing the frontier farther south–moving into and beyond the mountains of Pennsylvania, Virginia and the Carolinas, regions which came to be known to the Coast states as the back country. For generations after the great westward movement[qv] beginning about 1769–70, this back country, comprising the present Middle West, West Virginia, Kentucky, Tennessee and other inland areas farther south, was predominantly forest. Until after 1800 roads fit for wheeled vehicles were rare and short, and most traveling was done by water or mere horse trail. There were still only a few small cleared areas in what is now Kentucky in 1776 when the settlers chose two agents to ask protection of Virginia, with the result that "Kentucky County"[qv] was created, and in the following year sent two burgesses to the Virginia legislature. Backwoodsmen under George Rogers Clark (*see* Clark's Northwest Campaign) took Kaskaskia and Vincennes[qqv]. In Tennessee they first organized the Watauga Association and then the State of Franklin[qqv]. An undisciplined but, as usual, efficient army of them annihilated Ferguson's force at the Battle of King's Mountain[qv]. Later, under their idol, Andrew Jackson, they fought the Creek War and won the Battle of New Orleans[qqv]. Their prowess in war bred in them a group consciousness and pride. When Jackson was inaugurated in 1829 they flocked to Washington and made the occasion, including the White House reception, so turbulent and uproarious that old Federalists and Whigs[qqv] thought the era of mob rule had come. The word backwoodsman acquired during that period an opprobrium which it never afterwards lost.

[Theodore Roosevelt, *The Winning of the West;* E. Douglas Branch, *Westward;* Seymour Dunbar, *History of Travel in America.*] ALVIN F. HARLOW

Bacon's Rebellion (1675–76) had its roots in the autocratic government of Gov. Berkeley of Virginia and the resentment of the small landholders when Berkeley refused to defend the colonists adequately against murderous attacks by Indians. The building of forts and additional taxes did not satisfy those who desired direct action. When 300 men volunteered to go against the savages, Berkeley declared them rebels and ordered them to return. Although the majority, fearing the governor, obeyed, sixty followed Nathaniel Bacon, a planter who had settled on the western frontier of the province. Bacon attacked the Indians and killed 150.

Berkeley yielded to the popular demand for a new assembly, which inaugurated reforms giving the freeholders a greater share in government. Bacon, coming to Jamestown with 500 men, demanded a commission to fight the Indians and was supported by the House of Burgesses and the governor's council. Berkeley again yielded, but when Bacon departed the governor called upon the militia of two counties to suppress the upstart planter. Failing in this, Berkeley fled to Accomac County, across Chesapeake Bay, in the vain hope of finding supporters in that royalist section.

Bacon returned from his expedition against the Indians, assumed leadership and called a new assembly. During his absence on another expedition against the Indians, Berkeley returned to Jamestown with 600 men. Bacon hastened back, defeated Berkeley's force and the governor once more fled to Accomac. In the midst of Bacon's preparations for invading Accomac he was stricken with fever and died. After his death the rebellion collapsed. The aged governor executed some of Bacon's followers in spite of royal pardon. He was soon recalled by the king.

[C. M. Andrews, *Colonial Self-Government;* H. L. Osgood, *The American Colonies in the 17th Century.*]

PERCY SCOTT FLIPPIN

Bad Axe, Battle of (Aug. 2, 1832). The Sauk and Fox Indians[qqv], dissatisfied with lands to which the Federal Government had moved them, recrossed the Mississippi in April, 1832, and, under the leadership of Black Hawk[qv], revolted against the whites. They were finally penned up against the Mississippi River at the mouth of the Bad Axe River, midway between Prairie du Chien and La Crosse, Wis., and there completely defeated by an American force of 400 regular infantry and 900 militia, commanded by Gen. Henry Atkinson.

[Frank E. Stevens, *The Black Hawk War.*]

ROBERT S. THOMAS

Badlands of South Dakota were created by precipitation of volcanic ash, sand and Fuller's earth, perhaps borne by wind, from eruptions in the far Northwest which buried several hundred square miles more than 300 feet in depth. Water erosion carved this material into many fantastic forms. The precipitation engulfed vast herds of antediluvian monsters where they were feeding in the swamps, the remains of which were later exposed by erosion. The Federal Government has established the region as "The Badlands National Monument" and has built a system of highways into the more scenic regions of the park. The Badlands were discovered by fur traders early in the 19th century and for more than 100 years scientific societies, museums and educational institutions have been busily engaged in unearthing the paleontological treasures, so long entombed. Included in these relics are fossil mammoths, elephants, Brontotheriums, Protoceras, camels, horses and many of the Carnivora whose descendants are still extant. In these fastnesses the Sioux took refuge when pursued by the army in the Messiah War[qv] of 1890.

[The White River Badlands, *Bulletins 5 and 13*, South Dakota School of Mines.]

DOANE ROBINSON

Bagot-Rush Agreement. *See* Great Lakes, Agreement for Disarmament on the.

Bahama Islands, THE, although granted to the Carolina proprietors[qv] in 1670, were passed by during the most active age of colonization and had only a meager development before 1718. Pirates found their innumerable harbors most convenient. After 1718, with separation from the Carolinas, colonists increased and pirates diminished; nevertheless illegal trading still featured the economic life. In the preliminaries of the American Revolution, the islanders supported the American opponents of British policy and later aided them with military supplies. During the 19th century American interest in the Bahamas was sustained in numerous ways. They figured extensively in the blockade running[qv] during the Civil War. More recently, American investments in the islands' fruit production and an ever-increasing number of tourists have brought close relations. The prohibition[qv] experiment greatly stimulated American interest, and the islanders have sought by various attractions to maintain the contacts thus inaugurated.

[C. Atchley, *The West Indies.*]

CHARLES F. MULLETT

Bailey v. Drexel Furniture Company (259 U. S. 20) was a case in which the United States Supreme Court (1922) invalidated an act of Congress (1919) levying a tax of 10% upon the net profits of business concerns employing children under the age of sixteen. The Supreme Court held that the measure was not a valid exercise of the taxing power, since it was an attempt to bring under congressional control matters whose regulation belongs solely to the states. (*See also* Child Labor Cases.)

P. ORMAN RAY

Baker's Cabin Massacre, THE (April 30, 1774), a cause of Dunmore's War[qv], was the cold-blooded murder of some six or seven unarmed Mingo[qv] Indians by a party of unscrupulous whites at Baker's Cabin, about fifteen miles above present Steubenville, Ohio, on the Virginia side of the Ohio River. Logan[qv], the Mingo chief, went on the warpath, charging that his sister and other near relatives had been killed.

[R. G. Thwaites and Louise Phelps Kellogg, *A Documentary History of Dunmore's War.*]

EUGENE H. ROSEBOOM

Bakeshop Case, THE. *See* Lochner v. New York.

Balance of Trade. Following the mercantilistic[qv] tradition, an excess of merchandise exports over imports is usually called a "favorable" balance of trade, and the reverse an "unfavorable" balance, the original assumption being that the difference was paid in specie, the acquisition of which made a nation economically strong. This theory is fallacious but persistent. It confuses money with wealth and is incompatible with any demand-and-supply theory of the value of money. It leaves out of consideration all "invisible" items like capital loans, shipping charges, tourist expenditures, immigrant remittances and interest payments. Inclusion of these is necessary to calculate the more significant balance of international payments. In the long run the value of the wealth (including bullion[qv]) and services flowing out of a country tends to equal that of those flowing in except for excesses of bad debts or other losses in one direction or the other.

The American colonies had an "unfavorable" balance of trade because they were a new country and the settlers were constantly buying on credit or depending on England for capital for new undertakings. Mercantilistic England encouraged our extractive industries and discouraged manufacturing. In 1770 the colonies south of Pennsylvania had a nearly even trade balance with England; Pennsylvania and those north imported eight times as much from England as they exported to her, making up the difference largely by a very "favorable" trade balance with the West Indies[qv] and by their carrying business.

After the Revolution we still wanted English manufactures but found difficulty paying for them because England's markets were closed to many of our products and trade with the British West Indies was illegal. The new trade to China[qv], treaties with Prussia and Sweden and finally Jay's Treaty[qv] improved matters a little, but the development of cotton growing and the outbreak in 1793 of what soon became the Napoleonic wars helped much more. Both France and England bought heavily of our agricultural products and made increasing use of our shipping services. Between 1790 and 1807 our merchant marine[qv] engaged in foreign trade tripled. After 1806 England took successful steps to stop our commercial growth and from this the War of 1812[qv] developed. Following the war foreign manufactured goods flooded our markets and hurt our infant industries. Protection[qv] sentiment increased, producing progressively higher tariffs[qv] in 1816, 1824 and 1828. Thereafter rates fell (except in 1842). Higher tariffs here and abroad, a post-war depression and the greater interest in developing the West all cut down the rate of growth of our foreign commerce and its relative importance to domestic commerce. Foreign trade picked up after 1830. Europeans, particularly the English, invested approximately $250,000,000, much of it in our internal improvements[qv]. This ended abruptly with the Panic of 1837[qv] and defalcation by several states. Between 1838 and 1849 our trade balance was slightly "favorable." During the 1850's both imports and exports (notably cotton) expanded rapidly until the Civil War. Foreign trade[qv] declined during the war because of the Northern blockade[qv] and activity of the Southern cruisers.

During the prosperity following the war our foreign trade grew from $405,000,000 in 1865 to $1,164,000,000 in 1873. The Homestead Act[qv], wars in Europe, immigration[qv], railroad building[qv] and increasing use of agricultural machinery caused a rise in food exports. A five-year depression began in 1873. In 1874 our trade balance again became "favorable," largely because interest payments on foreign capital here exceeded new foreign investments. The annual balance has been "favorable" ever since 1876 except for 1888 and 1889. A great expansion of foreign trade began after 1897. Then our capital loans abroad grew nearly as fast as foreign loans to us. Tourist expenditures and immigrant remittances became important.

During the World War we supplied the Allies with enormous quantities of food and war materials. Between July 1, 1914, and Dec. 31, 1919, our trade balance was "favorable" by $18,600,000,000, $4,000,000,000 being paid in specie, $2,600,000,000 in returned securities, and the balance in capital loans, three-quarters governmental (*see* Debts, Foreign). In 1916 we ceased being a debtor nation and became a creditor.

The 1920's were a prosperous era. Since our high tariffs made imports difficult, the only way to continue to sell abroad was to make heavy loans. We loaned $12,000,000,000 during the decade, while foreigners invested $7,000,000,000 here. Of course a loss occurred from scaling down the war debts[qv]. Notable borrowers were Latin-American nations whose prospects were sometimes too optimistically regarded, and Germany, who was thereby helped to pay reparations[qv] to the Allies (*see* Dawes Plan; Young Plan), who in turn were able to pay us on their war debts. Then came the crash of 1929. Numerous Latin-American nations, largely dependent on the marketing of one or two commodities, defaulted. Our loans to Germany declined, and after the Hoover moratorium[qv] in 1931 Germany ceased paying reparations and the Allies gradually stopped paying their debts. Losses on foreign investments, however, were no greater proportionately than on domestic ones.

Foreign trade improved after 1933. Devaluation of the dollar stimulated exports, retarded imports and greatly increased our large stock of gold. Since 1934 numerous reciprocal trade treaties[qv] have lowered our tariff walls slightly and encouraged the flow of trade. This is desirable for many reasons, one being to help our debtors pay us. After a nation has been a creditor for some time it should usually receive back annually more in interest and returned principal than it makes in new loans. The United States is on the verge of having an "unfavorable" trade balance for this reason.

[J. P. Young, *International Trade and Finance;* E. L. Bogart, *Economic History of the American People;* C. Lewis, *America's Stake in International Investments;* Dept. of Commerce, *The Balance of International Payments;* also, *Statistical Abstract.*]

DONALD L. KEMMERER

Balcones Escarpment, THE, is a geologic fault extending across Texas from Del Rio to Red River west of Denison. Visible on the surface eastward from Del Rio and northeastward from San Antonio to Austin, it continues below the surface to the east of Waco and Fort Worth. It very nearly divides Texas into two geographical regions.

L. W. NEWTON

Balfour and Viviani-Joffre Missions (1917). After the United States entered the World War, a mission headed by Arthur James Balfour, British foreign secretary, and another by René Viviani, French minister of justice, and Marshal Joffre, former commander of the French armies, visited the United States. The British discussed questions of the purchase of war materials, military equipment, merchant tonnage and co-operation of the British and American navies; they proposed the sending of American troops to France to be trained and incorporated in the British and French armies. Joffre, on the other hand, urged the creation of an American Army, even though this might take longer, and this plan was adopted. Balfour discussed terms of peace with House and then with Wilson, but it is not clear whether he disclosed specifically the terms of the "secret treaties" between the Allies.

[Blanche E. C. Dugdale, *Arthur James Balfour;* C. Seymour, *The Intimate Papers of Colonel House;* Frederic Palmer, *Newton D. Baker;* W. G. Lyddon, *British War Missions to the United States, 1914-1918.*]

BERNADOTTE E. SCHMITT

Balize was a pilot village and fortification (1722), on the principal mouth (then usually called Southeast Pass) of the Mississippi, about a half-mile from the Gulf of Mexico and nearly a mile below the bar at the entrance (then) to the river proper, roughly 110 miles from New Orleans. Built by the French as first line of defense for Louisiana, it afforded slight protection because the mud would not hold strong works, there was frequent demolition by storms and floods and other passes were negotiable by light craft. The Spanish maintained it, but the United States abandoned it for defenses some thirty miles upstream (Forts Jackson and St. Philip[qv]).

[P. de Charlevoix, *Histoire et description générale de la nouvelle France,* Vol. VI.]

MACK SWEARINGEN

Ballads, American. When Prof. George Lyman Kittredge wrote, in the introduction of a volume of selections from Francis James Child's monumental work, *The English and Scottish Popular Ballads* (1904), that "A ballad is a song that tells a story or a story told in song" only one collection of American folk songs[qv] had been published (*Allen's Slave Songs of the United States,* 1867). Since that time more than 100 titles have been added to the literature of American balladry. Not all of the items in these books, of course, fit the definition of a ballad but they indicate the great richness of America's heritage of traditional balladry and an astonishing fertility in the production of indigenous folk songs. Versions of the so-called Child ballads have been found all over the United States, along with large numbers of the 18th and 19th century come-all-ye's. Often these ballads have been adapted to the locale that has preserved them and always new ballads have grown out of the traditional matrix. Among people, whether untutored or educated, whose lives are isolated, the desire for entertainment usually breeds songs that tell stories. American frontiers have been lonely.

In subject matter the ancient ballads and the indigenous product are generally widely different. The former sing of the highborn lady, the men of fortune and renown, while their American prototypes, composed by hard-handed miners, mountaineers, cowboys, sailors and lumberjacks, follow the pattern of the come-all-ye's and are peopled with working-class characters. Undoubtedly the most popular of indigenous types are the occupational ballads, the bad-man ballad, the murder ballad and the vulgar or bawdy ballad. In the occupational ballad the singer celebrates the hardships or the glories of some type of work or else he recounts a feat of daring, the tragic death of a worker, or some comic incident of camp life. "Foreman James Monroe," "James Bird," "The Buffalo Skinners," "Red Iron Ore," "Joe Bowers,"[qv] "Casey Jones" and "The Erie Canal" are familiar examples.

As the English loved Robin Hood because he took from the rich to give to the poor, so the American folk singer has commemorated Jesse James, Sam Bass, Pancho Villa and others. Indeed, the sympathies of the folk singer have always been with the rebel against society. Thus the 19th-century American ballad persistently attributes crime to the influence of a bad environment ("liquor and bad company") and then is likely to quote the criminal's confession where he apologizes for his deed. White ballads ordinarily run in this vein, although in the case of such horrible murders as that of Pearl Bryant or in the feud songs of the Southern mountains, the singers express their indignation at the deeds.

The vulgar ballad has, of course, not found its way into published collections, but there is no question as to the universal popularity of this type from the forecastle to the college campus. Transmitted by word of mouth and finding no occupational or class barriers, these ballads usually have fine tunes and are often couched in fresh and vigorous language.

American Negro ballads stand in a class by themselves, for while the main body of Negro songs are not strictly narrative in form, the race has produced America's most original and interesting narrative songs in English—"John Henry," "Frankie," "Casey Jones," "Po' Laz'us." Perhaps these Negro songs do not equal in grace and finish the older English lays, but in them are found the same fresh imagery, the same direct and incisive narrative technique along with new interest in the internal emotional problems of the characters. Certain work ballads, such as "Po' Laz'us" and "John Henry," orally composed and transmitted in big construction camps, have an epic vigor. Moreover, while the pioneer or occupational isolation that produced the best white ballads has been broken, the Negro community has kept its folk solidarity and has responded fruitfully to the influence of the radio and the phonograph by producing new songs of high quality.

America's heritage of Spanish, French and German ballads has been the subject of fruitful study in recent years. Surviving ballads in other foreign languages have received too little notice. The Library of Congress through aid from the Rockefeller Foundation and the Carnegie Institution has accumulated the music from field transcriptions of more than 5000 American folk songs and the work now goes forward from Government appropriations.

[Carl Sandburg, *The American Song Bag;* John A. and Alan Lomax, *American Ballads and Folk Songs.*]

JOHN A. LOMAX

Ballinger-Pinchot Controversy, THE (1909–11), was a bitter contention over the conservation[qv] of natural resources. Early in the Taft administration an order of former President Roosevelt withdrawing from sale certain public lands[qv] containing water power[qv] sites in Montana and Wyoming was cancelled. Chief Forester Gifford Pinchot protested and publicly charged Secretary of the Interior Richard A. Ballinger with favoritism toward corporations seeking water power sites. Pinchot defended L. R. Glavis, Land Office investigator, dismissed for accusing Ballinger of favoring the Cunningham syndicate's claims to valuable Alaskan mineral lands. Pinchot likewise was dismissed. A joint congressional investigating committee[qv] exonerated Ballinger. But failing to regain public confidence, Ballinger resigned. The incident widened the cleavage in the Republican party[qv].

[F. A. Ogg, *National Progress.*]

GLENN H. BENTON

Balloons. The first balloon ascent in America was made by a Frenchman, Jean Pierre Blanchard, Jan. 9, 1793, at Philadelphia, in the presence of President Washington. In 1795 an American, Dr. John Jeffries, with Blanchard, made the first balloon crossing of the English Channel. John Wise, of Lancaster, Pa., was the most prominent American balloonist before the Civil War. His most successful flight was in 1859 from St. Louis to Henderson, N. Y., covering a distance of 809 miles in twenty hours. In June, 1861, a balloonist, Thaddeus S. C. Lowe, offered his services to the Federal Government. He organized an aeronautic corps, built five balloons, and rendered useful service in reconnaissance at Bull Run, in the Peninsula Campaign and at Chancellorsville[qqv]. During the World War captive balloons were used by the army for field reconnaissance and fire control, and by the navy for spotting submarines below the water's surface. The United States Weather Bureau[qv] uses small, unmanned balloons for studying the direction and strength of air currents and for recording atmospheric conditions in the upper air.

[R. H. Upson and C. De F. Chandler, *Free and Captive Balloons; American Historical Review,* July, 1937.]

LOUIS H. BOLANDER

Ballot, THE. Originally derived from the Italian *ballotta,* a little ball used for secret voting, the word ballot is now applied to the voting papers, commonly called "tickets," used in elections. Historically ballots followed *viva-voce* choice of public officials. Common during colonial and post-revolutionary days the *viva-voce* method was defended as manly and open, placing a premium upon the practice of independent citizenship. It was attacked vigorously, however, because it permitted the wholesale intimidation of poorer electors. After innumerable state-wide controversies revolving around these opposing views, some of which persisted well into the 19th century, the older open method was everywhere supplanted by the ballot.

The ballots first used in American elections were provided by candidates or party committees. Occasionally they were tampered with in personal or factional interest ("phony ballots"); often they were voted under conditions making secrecy impossible. During the '70's and '80's of the last century election frauds of this character became rampant, especially in large cities. Reform was sought and in large measure achieved by the Australian ballot system under which ballots are provided and their genuineness guaranteed by the state. First used in the Louisville, Ky., municipal election of 1888, this system has now spread to all the states of the Union with four exceptions.

Owing to the inclusion of candidates for national, state and local offices, also to the choice by popular vote of executive and judicial as well as of legislative officials, the ballots used are long and complicated. Against this evil the Short-Ballot movement has made considerable progress. In form the ballots used in our states are either (1) of the party-column type, with or without emblems (*see* Emblems, Party); or (2) of the Massachusetts type in which candidates are grouped according to offices; or (3) of the Pennsylvania or hybrid type. Since 1892 voting by ballots has been giving way before the voting machine[qv] which is now in use in more than thirty states.

[E. C. Evans, *History of the Australian Ballot System.*]

ROBERT C. BROOKS

Ball's Bluff, Battle of (Oct. 21, 1861). Inconsequential as a military affair, this engagement had important results. Col. E. D. Baker (U.), Senator from Oregon, a personal friend of President Lincoln, was killed; the Union troops, through mismanagement, were defeated. Discontented Radicals[qv] and a critical public blamed McClellan (U.). Congress inaugurated the Committee on the Conduct of the War[qv] to investigate Ball's Bluff and other Union failures. McClellan, on orders from the Secretary of War, arrested Gen. C. P. Stone (U.), charged with responsibility both for the defeat and for Baker's death. No formal charges were ever made. After six months' imprisonment Stone was released by a special provision in the Confiscation Act, July 17, 1862[qv]. The Army of the Potomac (U.)[qv] questioned their leader's ability. "A fatal hesitation took possession" of McClellan. A movement against Richmond was deferred pending further preparation.

[*Battles and Leaders of the Civil War.*]

THOMAS ROBSON HAY

Baltimore, Battle of (Sept. 12, 1814). After the burning of Washington[qv], a British land force of 8000, commanded by Gen. Ross, attempted to capture Baltimore. Ross, killed in battle, was successfully opposed by a force of Maryland and Pennsylvania militia and volunteers.

[B. J. Lossing, *Pictorial Field Book of the War of 1812.*]

ROBERT S. THOMAS

Baltimore, Md. It was almost 100 years after the landing of the colonists at St. Mary's[qv] in 1634, the first settlement in Maryland, that Baltimore was founded, in 1729, on the Patapsco River, a tributary of the Chesapeake Bay. The new settlement was named in honor of Charles Calvert, fifth proprietor of Maryland, who held the hereditary title of Baron Baltimore, of Baltimore, in Ireland. While political and religious factors account in part for the founding of St. Mary's and of Annapolis, in 1649, the founding of Baltimore was due to the desire of the inhabitants of Baltimore County, in which the proposed town was located, to have a port in that vicinity. The site chosen on the Patapsco had an excellent harbor near grain and tobacco lands.

Although at first Baltimore grew very slowly, near the close of the 18th century the town ranked third in commercial importance, being surpassed in trade by only two ports, Philadelphia and New York. During the Revolution and the War of 1812, privateers[qv] built and manned in Baltimore played a conspicuous part. The bombardment by a British fleet of Fort McHenry[qv], which defended the town during the War of 1812, inspired Francis Scott Key to write the "Star Spangled Banner".[qv] After this war, the experience and knowledge gained by shipbuilders in that conflict and during the Revolution enabled them to develop a type of merchant vessel known as the Baltimore clipper[qv]. By the construction of the Baltimore and Ohio Railroad[qv], chartered in 1827, Baltimore retained much of the trans-Allegheny trade which the completion of the Erie Canal[qv] had threatened to divert. Baltimore prospered in the period between the War of 1812 and the Civil War. From the wealth acquired from trade, especially with the South, there arose a merchant class which dispensed a lavish but gracious hospitality.

[C. C. Hall, *Baltimore, Its History and Its People.*]

RAPHAEL SEMMES

***Baltimore* Affair,** THE (Oct. 15, 1891), was an attack by a Chilean mob in Valparaiso upon a party of 116 sailors on shore leave from the U. S. S. *Baltimore;* two Americans were killed and several others seriously wounded. This hostility emerged from the mistaken feeling that the United States had sympathized unduly with the *Balmacedistas* whom the Congressionalists had overthrown. The new government did not punish the assailants and offered neither apology nor explanation until President Harrison laid the matter before Congress. This was the nearest the United States has ever come to actual conflict with a South American nation.

[H. C. Evans, *Chile and Its Relations with the United States.*]

OSGOOD HARDY

Baltimore and Ohio Railroad, THE, was chartered Feb. 28, 1827, and built from Baltimore to the Ohio to counteract the prosperity that canals[qv] were bringing to the rival cities of Philadelphia and New York. It was planned originally to operate throughout its entire length by horsepower; with relay stations each ten miles for changes of steeds. The road was surveyed by United States Army engineers. Work on it progressed slowly and it was not until Christmas 1853 that it was completed to Wheeling, Va.

Steam power was first used in 1829–30. Interesting experiments were conducted in the development of locomotives and cars. The road played a dramatic role in the Civil War, particularly in and about Harpers Ferry[qv]. John W. Garrett, president of the road (1858–84), extended it westward to Cincinnati, St. Louis and Chicago; and eastward to Philadelphia and (by trackage rights) to New York.

[Edward Hungerford, *The Story of the Baltimore and Ohio Railroad.*]

EDWARD HUNGERFORD

Baltimore Bell Teams took their name from the small bells suspended in metal arches over the hames to speed the horses and sound warning on narrow, crooked roads. These teams hauled country produce to Baltimore and returned with goods for homes and local merchants. Such teams made regular trips from points as far southwest as Knoxville, Tenn., and operated till 1850 or later when they were superseded by canals and railroads. A few bell teams survive, chiefly on mountainous roads.

JOHN W. WAYLAND

Baltimore Clipper, THE, was a term applied to the fast topsail schooners developed in and around the Chesapeake Bay in the Revolutionary period and (later) to the square-rigged vessels having the same general lines which were built in the Chesapeake region. In post-Revolutionary days they came into general notice largely because their speed enabled them to be used effectively both in privateering[qv] and in the slave trade[qv]. *Ann McKim* (1833) was the ultimate expression of the type and by some is regarded as the link between the Baltimore clipper and the clipper ship[qv]. Her length (143 feet) was great by prevailing standards compared to her beam (31 feet). She had the characteristic Baltimore clipper drag in that she drew eleven feet forward and seventeen aft. Her stem was sharp but her greatest beam was so far forward that she was bluffer bowed than the later clipper ship. Her freeboard was low and her carrying capacity was small and hence she was primarily a speed model. The three masts were tall and light with a sharp rake, but she was ship-rigged with courses, topsails, topgallant sails and royals on each mast.

[Howard Irving Chappelle, *The Baltimore Clipper, Its Origin and Development;* Jacques and Helen LaGrange, *Clipper Ships of America and Great Britain.*]

HAMILTON OWENS

Baltimore Councils, Provincial and Plenary. Ecclesiastical legislation in the Roman Catholic Church[qv] of the United States began with a synod of the priests under Bishop John Carroll of Baltimore in 1791. The regulations adopted served to administer Church affairs until 1829, when the first Provincial Council of Baltimore was held. There were seven of these Councils (1829, 1833, 1837, 1840, 1843, 1846 and 1849). By the year 1852 the Church had been divided into several provinces and while provincial councils were held in these provinces under their archbishops, three plenary councils were held in Baltimore in 1852, 1866 and 1884. The legislation of these three national assemblies was concerned with explanations of Catholic faith, with regulations for the administration of the sacraments, with feasts and fast days, with clerical life and discipline, ecclesiastical property tenure and with Catholic education and social welfare agencies.

[Peter Guilday, *A History of the Councils of Baltimore: 1791-1884.*]

PETER GUILDAY

Baltimore Fire, THE (Feb. 7–8, 1904), the third greatest conflagration in American history, destroyed most of the central business district, over an area of 150 acres. Damages were estimated at $50,000,000 to $100,000,000. Better streets and more fire protection were indirect results.

[H. D. Northrup, *World's Greatest Calamities.*]

W. C. MALLALIEU

***Baltimore* Incident,** THE (Nov. 16, 1798). While convoying merchant vessels to Havana during naval hostilities with France[qv], Capt. Isaac Phillips in the United States sloop *Baltimore* encountered a British squadron. Facing superior force, and with strict injunctions to avoid conflict with British vessels, Phillips, under protest, submitted to the mustering of his crew and the removal of all seamen without papers showing American citizenship (*see* Impressment of Seamen). Fifty-five were taken off, but only five were finally retained. Phillips was afterward summarily dismissed from the navy, and stringent orders were issued requiring American national vessels to resist forcibly any similar insult to the flag.

[G. W. Allen, *Our Naval War with France.*]

ALLAN WESTCOTT

Baltimore Riot, THE (April 19, 1861), occurred when Pennsylvania and Massachusetts militia, en route to Washington, were attacked by Baltimoreans who considered them invaders. The railroad was not continuous through Baltimore, horses drawing the cars from one terminal to the other. After a few troops had gone through, the connecting tracks were blocked with anchors and other obstacles, which forced later contingents to march. The crowd pursued them with stones, bricks and a few pistol shots. The militia, who had broken into a run, fired backward over their shoulders and forward at the people lining the street ahead of them. The mayor endeavored to quiet the crowd and finally, near the Washington terminal, the police succeeded in holding the people back until the troops entrained. Four militiamen and twelve civilians were killed and an unknown number wounded.

[George W. Brown, *Baltimore and the Nineteenth of April, 1861.*] GEORGE FREDERICK ASHWORTH

Bandits. Highway robbery was comparatively rare before 1800, and usually consisted of the holdup of a traveler or a late walker by a solitary rough; the professional bandit was unknown. After 1800, holdups of mail coaches and post riders took place occasionally, sometimes with violence. A mail carrier was killed in Illinois in 1810 and a stagecoach driver near Baltimore in 1830. In the Middle West there were river pirates such as those of Cave-in Rock[qv], and between 1795 and 1800 the Harpe[qv] brothers in Kentucky, and a little later the murderous John A. Murrell in the same region—he was one of those who robbed travelers along the Natchez Trace[qv]—were much feared. The Gold Rush[qv] brought the scum of all the Western Hemisphere and Australia to California, and from 1850 on, robbery of stagecoaches[qv], mounted express messengers and others was common. With the opening of the Idaho[qv] gold mines in 1860, robbery began there and developed into a virtual reign of terror. From there, some of the outlaws moved to the new Montana gold mines in 1863, where they robbed and murdered until virtually eliminated by Vigilantes[qv] two years later. In the 1860's and 1870's robbery was a commonplace in California, among the widely scattered Nevada mining camps, and in the Sierra Nevada passes. "Shotgun messengers," cool and deadly marksmen, rode on stagecoaches beside the drivers, to protect express and mail, and there were some hot battles between them and the brigands. The opening of the Black Hills[qv] gold mines in 1876 launched another era of robbery, in which Sam Bass earned a reputation which he later enhanced by train robbery[qv] in Texas.

East of the Mississippi banditry was a minor evil before the Civil War (1861–65), money being handled casually by express with little thought of danger; but a wave of lawlessness followed the war. A party of amateur robbers concealed themselves in a supposedly locked express car leaving New York on a January night in 1866, and decamped from it in Connecticut with $700,000 in cash, bonds and jewels. The first train holdup of record was perpetrated Oct. 6, 1866, in southern Indiana by the four Reno brothers, who had drifted into crime during the war. They and their gang continued these attacks, thus becoming the first organized band of train robbers in history. Train robbery next appeared in western Tennessee and Kentucky and in Nevada; and in 1873 the James-Younger gang took to it. The career of this band continued for ten years thereafter, or until Jesse James' death in 1883 (*see* Northfield Bank Robbery). They were succeeded in that region by the Daltons, whose career was finally ended in their attempted robbery of the banks at Coffeyville, Kans., Oct. 5, 1892, when two Dalton brothers and two others of the gang were killed and another Dalton captured. Bill Doolin carried on a remnant of the gang for three years thereafter. During the 1880's the Southwest swarmed with bandits and rough characters; stage and train robberies were numerous, even cowboys and townsmen of hitherto honest record sometimes taking to crime. Rube Burrow, a farm hand, was one who attained great notoriety as a train robber in Texas, Mississippi and Alabama, 1886–91, his career being ended by death. Around the end of the century the Hole-in-the-Wall gang, from an impregnable lair in the Wyoming mountains, harassed the Union Pacific Railroad[qv]. Dynamiting of express cars held by stubborn messengers began. During the decade 1890–99, the *Express Gazette* said that there had been 261 train robberies, in which eighty-eight persons were killed and eighty-six wounded. Express cars now began to be built of heavier steel, carrying massive built-in safes, with time locks or combinations known only at terminals. "Arsenal cars," guarded by squads of heavily armed men, began running on important routes. Through these measures train robbery became more difficult and gradually less common.

The World War and the passage of the Eighteenth Amendment[qv] gave banditry a new impetus. Bootleggers[qv] were preyed upon by "hijackers," who, from the violent seizure of truckloads of liquor, proceeded later to the capture of loads of silks, cigars and other valuable freight. Bank and payroll holdups and the robbery of jewelers were of daily occurrence, frequently accompanied by murder—this partly due to the fact that the robbers were now often half-crazed from the use of heroin. Organized gangs, such as those of John Dillinger, Alvin Karpis and "Pretty Boy" Floyd, functioned again, turning their hands either to robbery or kidnaping[qv]. The Federal Bureau of Investigation[qv] and the new but well-organized state police forces began, however, to make crime more hazardous. Dillinger was killed by Federal agents in Chicago in 1934, as were more than a dozen others of the most notorious brigands in the country during that year and the previous one.

[Alvin F. Harlow, *Old Waybills;* Oliver G. Swan, *Frontier Days;* Herbert Corey, *Farewell, Mr. Gangster. America's War on Crime.*]

ALVIN F. HARLOW

Bank, Federal Reserve. *See* Federal Reserve System.

Bank Deposits. Prior to the Civil War, banks and note issue powers were considered as more or less synonymous, with deposits holding a place of secondary importance except in some of the large cities. Statistics of bank deposits are fragmentary for this early period. Some data, however, are available.

The First Bank of the United States (*see* Bank of the United States) had $8,500,000 of individual deposits in January, 1809, and $5,900,000 two years later. Deposits of the Second Bank of the United States fluctuated between $5,100,000 and $22,800,000 in the years 1817 to 1836 inclusive. Statistics for other banks are not available for this period. Between 1837 and 1860, deposits of state banks[qv] ranged between $56,000,000 and $260,000,000, being generally below $100,000,000 prior to 1850 and above that figure after 1850. These figures do not include savings deposits, which amounted to $149,000,000 in 1860.

Since the establishment of the National Banking System, commercial deposits have assumed a place of far greater importance than bank notes as a medium of exchange. Between 1866 and 1913 national banks[qv] were the most important group of commercial banking institutions. Deposits of these banks increased with a high degree of regularity from $564,617,000 in 1866 to $6,051,689,000 in 1913. The latter figure compared with national bank note issues of but $727,079,000.

After 1913, with the establishment of the Federal Reserve System[qv], bank deposits increased rapidly. In June, 1914, total deposits for all banks of the country were $18,566,000,000, the deposits of state and mutual savings banks totaling about twice those of national banks. Deposits of all banks grew steadily from 1914 to 1930, reaching a total of $54,954,000,000 in the latter year. Then, as a result of the great depression (*see* Panic of 1929), this figure shrank to just under $38,000,000,000 in June, 1933, since which date it has again increased to more than $52,000,000,000 in 1937.

The figures just given include deposits in savings banks, as well as savings and time deposits in commercial banks. Perhaps the best figures to show the extent to which checking deposits are used as a medium of exchange are those for "demand deposits adjusted," as calculated for member banks of the Federal Reserve System. Since Dec. 31, 1917 (when this figure is first available), these deposits have increased from $9,972,000,000 to $20,387,000,000 on Dec. 31, 1937.

[J. T. Holdsworth, *The First Bank of the United States;* A. B. Hepburn, *A History of Currency in the United States;* Annual Reports of the Comptroller of the Currency; Annual Reports of the Federal Reserve Board.]

FREDERICK A. BRADFORD

Bank Failures. American financial history has been characterized by the greatest instability of any nation. The record of its bank failures from the beginning of the Federal period to the bank crisis of 1933[qv] constitutes the severest possible indictment of our methods. Compared to that of England or Canada the record is one of an appalling failure of either private business to regulate itself or of government to regulate in the public interest.

The statistics of state bank[qv] failures (1789–1863) are inadequate, but the losses were unquestionably large. John Jay Knox estimated the losses to note holders, alone, at 5% per annum. Even the famous Free Bank System[qv] of New York (1838) showed a record of fifty-seven failures. It is not possible to estimate the losses to depositors and stockholders for the period. It must be noted, however, that the note issue function of banks was then the most important.

The establishment of the National Banking System[qv] did not materially reduce the disaster. Most of the failures since 1863, to be sure, have been state banks but the list of national bank failures leaves nothing about which to boast. By 1882 eighty-seven national banks were in the hands of receivers and over 400 had gone into voluntary liquidation. In 1893, alone, the number of failures was over 600. Between 1893 and the establishment of the Federal Reserve System[qv] not a single year passed without a failure. From the creation of the Federal Reserve System until 1920 only one year passed without a national bank failure, 1918.

In the prosperous period of the 1920's the record did not improve. The number of failures for the period 1920–33 continued to illustrate the glaring defects of the American system of private business and government regulation. The period saw 11,000 failures as against one in Canada and none in England. In 1930 came the largest bank failure in American history—the Bank of the United States in New York.

The new legislation since 1933, particularly the limited Federal insurance of deposits (*see* Federal Deposit Insurance Corporation), has made the greatest improvement in our record of bank failures. Our banking structure, however, is still far from perfect. The history of bank failures in America is a testimony to the patience of the American people.

[John Jay Knox, *History of Banking in the United States.*]

LEONARD C. HELDERMAN

Bank for International Settlements, The, evolved from the Hague Agreement of Jan. 20, 1930, which in turn was predicated on the report in March, 1929, of the Committee of Reparation Experts headed by Owen D. Young (*see* Young Plan). The bank was incorporated in and received its charter from Switzerland on Feb. 25, 1930. On March 31, 1937, there were thirty-nine stockholding banks, twenty-four scattered over Europe, fourteen in a syndicate led by the Industrial Bank of Japan, Tokio, and the First National Bank of New York. The bank began business May 17, 1930, with an authorized capital of $100,000,000, of which $25,000,000 was paid in at the outset. The board of directors is composed of the governors of the central banks of Belgium, France, Germany, Great Britain, Italy, Japan and a representative from the United States in addition to seven persons designated by each of the foregoing governors and nine directors elected by the other stockholding banks.

The chief objectives of the bank are to promote the co-operation of central banks, to provide additional facilities for international financial operations and to act as trustee in connection with international financial settlements entrusted to it. To achieve these objectives, the bank may perform practically all the functions ordinarily performed by a central bank, except that it is specifically interdicted from issuing notes, accepting bills of exchange, making advances to governments, or opening current accounts in the name of governments, or acquiring the predominant interest in any business enterprise.

[P. Einzig, *The Bank for International Settlements.*]

FRANK PARKER

Bank Notes have had wide use in the United States since the beginnings of the country. Prior to the introduction of national bank notes*qv* in 1863 the circulation consisted of state bank issues and notes of the United States banks (*see* Bank of the United States) during their chartered existences. Since 1866 state banks*qv* have been effectively prevented from issuing notes by a 10% Federal tax and, since 1913, Federal Reserve notes have assumed first place among bank-note issues of the country. Since 1935 the latter have been the only bank notes in general circulation.

[D. R. Dewey, *Financial History of the United States;* A. B. Hepburn, *A History of Currency in the United States.*]

FREDERICK A. BRADFORD

Bank of Augusta v. Earle, 1839 (13 Peters 519), involved the right of a Georgia bank to recover on a bill of exchange purchased in Alabama. The Supreme Court, speaking through Justice Taney, held that though a state might exclude the creature of another state, yet in the silence of any positive rule it would be presumed that foreign corporations were by comity permitted to make contracts. Taney's opinion became the leading authority on the law of foreign corporations.

[Charles Warren, *The Supreme Court in United States History;* G. C. Henderson, *The Position of Foreign Corporations in American Constitutional Law.*]

CHARLES FAIRMAN

Bank of Commerce v. New York City, 1863 (2 Black 620). The Supreme Court held that the state could not tax capital invested in Federal securities—thereby strengthening the financial position of the Government in the midst of the Civil War.

[T. R. Powell, Indirect Encroachment on Federal Authority by the Taxing Power of the States, 31 and 32, *Harvard Law Review;* Charles Warren, *The Supreme Court in United States History.*]

CHARLES FAIRMAN

Bank of North America, The, the country's first Government incorporated bank, was chartered by the Continental Congress*qv* in 1781 and commenced operations in Philadelphia on Jan. 7, 1782. Organized by Robert Morris, the bank supplied vital financial aid to the Government during the closing months of the American Revolution. Original depositors and stockholders included Thomas Jefferson, Alexander Hamilton, Benjamin Franklin, John Paul Jones, James Monroe, John Jay and Stephen Decatur.

[A. W. Whittlesey, *Highlights in the 125-Year History of The Pennsylvania Company.*]

A. W. WHITTLESEY

Bank of State of South Carolina, The. *See* South Carolina, The State Bank of.

Bank of the United States, First and Second. An act incorporating the subscribers to the Bank of the United States was approved by Washington and became law on Feb. 25, 1791. Under the provisions of the law the bank, which was to be located in Philadelphia, was to have a capital of $10,000,000, composed of 25,000 shares of $400 par value. One fifth of the capital was subscribed by the Government, the rest by private investors. Private subscriptions were limited to 1000 shares, and no shareholder was to have more than thirty votes. Foreign shareholders were not permitted to vote by proxy.

The management of the bank was vested in a board of twenty-five directors, elected by the shareholders. The board of directors was authorized to elect a president who was to receive compensation, the directors serving without pay. Only American citizens might be directors of the bank.

The bank was empowered to carry on a commercial banking business, was not permitted to deal in commodities or real estate and was limited in the interest it might charge on loans to 6%. The bank was authorized to issue circulating notes up to $10,000,000, the amount of its capital.

The Bank of the United States opened its doors for business on Dec. 12, 1791. It was efficiently managed and furnished the country, through its main office and eight branches, with sound banking service throughout its chartered life of twenty years. The bank served satisfactorily as fiscal agent for the Government and exerted a salutary controlling influence on the note issues of the state banks[qv] by refusing to accept state bank notes that were not redeemable in specie. In spite of the manifest advantages of a national bank, the charter of the First Bank was not renewed in 1811, doubt as to its constitutionality being the controlling factor. The bank therefore wound up its affairs, eventually paying shareholders $434 on each share held.

After a brief and unsatisfactory period of state banking, the Second Bank of the United States was incorporated under a law of April 10, 1816. The charter provisions were similar to those of the First Bank except that the capital and note issue limits were increased to $35,000,000. The President of the United States was also authorized to appoint five of the twenty-five directors.

The Second Bank was badly managed under its first president, William Jones, who retired in 1819. Langdon Cheeves, who succeeded Jones, spent his administration in getting the bank back to a sound position. In 1823 Nicholas Biddle assumed the presidency, and from then until 1833 the bank was well and capably managed, extending sound banking service to the country through its main office and twenty-five branches.

A dispute between Biddle and President Jackson led to the withdrawal of Government deposits in 1833 (*see* Removal of Deposits) and a severe contraction of the bank's business. Efforts to obtain a renewal of the Second Bank's charter proved futile and the institution ceased to function as a national bank upon the expiration of its charter in 1836.

[J. T. Holdsworth and D. R. Dewey, *The First and Second Banks of the United States;* R. C. H. Catterall, *The Second Bank of the United States.*]

FREDERICK A. BRADFORD

Bank of the United States v. Halstead, 1825 (10 Wheaton 51), concerned the applicability of state legislation regulating the procedural processes to Federal courts within the respective states. The Court upheld the power of Federal courts to alter forms of proceedings to meet changing conditions on general (implied) grounds relating to the judicial power and from specific legislative grants.

PHILLIPS BRADLEY

Bank of the United States v. Planters' Bank of Georgia (9 Wheaton 904). Mr. Chief Justice Marshall here (1824) enunciated the rule that a suit against a corporation chartered and partly owned by a state was not a suit against the state itself. "It is, we think, a sound principle that when a government becomes a partner in any trading company, it divests itself, so far as concerns the transactions of that company, of its sovereign character, and takes that of a private citizen." The rule was later applied to banks wholly owned by a state (*see* Briscoe v. Bank of the Commonwealth of Kentucky, 11 Peters 257).

[A. J. Beveridge, *John Marshall.*]

PHILLIPS BRADLEY

Bank Robbery. Bank burglars were but little heard of until the discovery of western gold in 1849. The Civil War gave another impetus to all forms of crime, including bank burglary. The burglars of those days occasionally rented a vacant store near the bank and from it tunneled underground to and through the vault wall; but they more frequently overpowered or corrupted the bank's night watchman and then picked or solved the vault's combination lock. The robbery of the Manhattan Savings Institution in New York of $2,747,000 in cash and securities in 1878 was a notable example of the last-named method. The introduction of the time lock by James Sargent in 1874 was a deterrent, and the gradual development during the next three decades of still better locks and almost impregnable steel vaults finally well-nigh eliminated bank burglary. In its stead, aided by the automobile, came the bank holdup, first introduced to America by the James gang at Liberty, Mo., in 1866. In two decades, 1914-34, 2500 banks were robbed in the United States—422 of them during the year ending Aug. 31, 1934. By that time, Federal and state police and detective agencies were reaching new high levels of efficiency and the yearly number of robberies began to decline. (*See also* Bandits.)

[Thomas Byrnes, *Professional Criminals of America;* Richard Wilmer Rowan, *The Pinkertons;* Herbert Corey, *Farewell, Mr. Gangster.*]

ALVIN F. HARLOW

Bankhead Cotton Act, THE, approved April 21, 1934, was designed to supplement the cotton production control provisions of the Agricultural Adjustment Act of 1933[qv]. While not actually placing limits upon the growing of cotton by individual farmers, the act established a national quota and levied a tax of 50% of the central market price (but not less than five cents per pound) upon cotton ginned in excess of the individual quota. This tax was the essence of the act. Following the decision of the Supreme Court invalidating the Agricultural Adjustment Act, Congress repealed the Bankhead Act (Feb. 10, 1936).

[Agricultural Adjustment, 1933 to 1935, U. S. Dept. of Agriculture. Washington: 1936.]

R. P. BROOKS

Banking. The fundamental functions of a modern bank are discounting, receiving deposits and lending its credit in the form of "created" deposits or bank notes.

There were no banks in this sense in colonial times, but there were loan offices or land banks, which made loans on real-estate security with limited issues of legal tender[qv] notes.

Robert Morris founded the first bank in the United States, the Bank of North America[qv], chartered Dec. 31, 1781. It greatly assisted the financing of the closing years of the Revolution. The second bank was the Bank of Massachusetts, chartered Feb. 7, 1784, and the third was the Bank of New York which began without a charter June 9, 1784. By 1800 there were twenty-six state banks[qv] and by 1811 there were eighty-eight.

Alexander Hamilton's financial program included a central bank to serve as a fiscal agent, provide a depository for public money, and be a regulator of the currency. Accordingly, the First Bank of the United States (*see* Bank of the United States), the fifth bank chronologically, was founded Feb. 25, 1791. Its sound but unpopular policy of promptly returning bank notes[qv] for redemption and refusing those of non-specie-paying banks, together with a political feud, were largely responsible for the narrow defeat of its recharter bill in 1811. Between 1811–16 people and Government were dependent on state banks whose number increased to 246. Nearly all but the New England banks suspended specie payments in September, 1814, because of the war and their own unregulated credit expansion.

The need for a new central bank was soon realized, and the Second Bank of the United States was established April 10, 1816, with a twenty-year charter. Like its predecessor it incurred the enmity of state banks by constantly requiring them to redeem in specie[qv]. This policy, President Jackson's prejudice against banks and monopolies and Biddle's tactless decision to let rechartering be an issue in the 1832 election (*see* Campaign of 1832) led to the bank's demise. After Sept. 26, 1833, the Government made all its deposits with the "pet banks"[qv] until the independent treasury system was set up.

The country, again without a regulator of bank currency, entered upon a period of loose banking practice. Banks loaned heavily on real estate and resorted to many subterfuges to avoid redeeming their notes in specie. Conditions were especially bad in Michigan where the term "wildcat bank"[qv] probably originated. Everywhere bank tellers had to consult newspapers for the current discounts on bank notes and turn to the latest bank-note detectors to distinguish the hundreds of counterfeits and notes of failed banks. In these "dark decades" of banking there were, however, a few bright spots which offered some protection to note holders. There were the Suffolk Banking System of Massachusetts (1819–56), which kept New England notes at par; the moderately successful Safety Fund (1829–66) and Free Banking[qqv] (1838–66) systems of New York, the latter copied in fourteen other states; the Indiana (1834–59) and Ohio (1845–66) state banks; and the Louisiana Banking System[qv]

(1842–62) which was the first to require a minimum per cent of specie reserve behind liabilities.

Secretary of the Treasury Chase began agitating for an improved banking system in 1861, one important motive for which was the desire to widen the market for government bonds[qv]. The National Currency Act creating the National Banking System[qv] was passed Feb. 25, 1863, and completely revised June 3, 1864. It was based on several recent reforms, especially the Free Banking System's idea of bond-backed notes. The reserve requirements for bank notes were high and real-estate loans were forbidden. State banks at first saw little reason to join, so in 1865 Congress levied a prohibitive 10% tax on their bank notes, effective July 1, 1866, which drove most of these banks into the new system. There were 1644 national banks by Oct. 1, 1866. The use of checks had been increasing in popularity in the more settled districts before the Civil War and the desire of all banks to evade the new restrictions on notes doubtless speeded up the shift to this more convenient form of bank credit. The proportion of state banks increased again, exceeding the national after 1894. Improvements of state banking laws began about 1887.

The National Banking System had two major faults. One was inelasticity of the bond-secured bank notes. The other was decentralization of deposit reserves. There were three classes of national banks, and the lesser ones kept part of their reserves in their own vaults and deposited the rest at interest with the larger, especially with the New York City banks which, in turn, loaned a considerable part on the call money market. In times of uncertainty the lesser banks demanded their outside reserves, call money rates soared, security prices tobogganed and many good as well as weak banks were ruined by runs.

After the panic of 1907 Congress passed the Aldrich-Vreeland Act to permit emergency bank note issues and established the National Monetary Commission to investigate foreign banking systems and suggest reforms[qqv]. The Aldrich Bill, proposed in 1912, provided for a central bank with fifteen branches, but was never passed. The Federal Reserve Act, passed Dec. 23, 1913 (*see* Federal Reserve System), was the product of many compromises. It created twelve regional central banks co-ordinated by a Federal Reserve Board. All national banks had to join: others might. Comparatively few but the largest have. To correct the fault of reserve decentralization member banks have to keep all legal reserves against deposits with their district Federal Reserve Bank. To provide a sound and elastic currency the act created the Federal Reserve notes, specifically backed by at least 40% gold and by other assets, originally intended to be chiefly short-time commercial paper. Federal Reserve banks can expand or contract credit by rediscount rate changes and open market operations[qv]. Some of these ideas were borrowed from Europe and aroused skepticism. The new system began operations Nov. 14, 1914, and convincingly proved its worth during the World War.

Although the system permitted limited real-estate and farm loans, it assisted chiefly commercial banking. Therefore agriculture was given twelve regional banks of rediscount for five- to forty-year loans by the Federal Farm Loan Act of July 17, 1916, and twelve more for nine months to three-year loans by the Agricultural Credits Act of March 4, 1923. These and other institutions were consolidated under the Federal Farm Credit Administration in 1933 (*see* Farm Credit Agencies, Federal).

Some authorities consider the easy credit policy of the Federal Reserve Board and the tendency of banks to invest, even speculate, heavily in capital securities, because of the unavailability of sufficient commercial paper, to have been an important cause of the 1928–29 boom and collapse. During 1921–29 there were 5714 bank failures[qv] and during 1930–32 there were 5102 more. Yet no reforms of consequence were passed. The Reconstruction Finance Corporation[qv], set up Jan. 22, 1932, helped stave off disaster temporarily, but the publicity of its loans and the strained condition of banks after four years of depression brought on the bank crisis of 1933[qv] culminating in the nationwide bank moratorium[qv] of March 6. The Franklin Roosevelt administration closed 2113 weak banks and enacted allegedly remedial legislation. The Banking Act of 1933[qv] divorced commercial and investment banking and set up a temporary Federal Deposit Insurance Corporation[qv]. The latter helped restore public confidence in banks. The Banking Act of August, 1935[qv], made deposit insurance permanent, eased restrictions on real-estate loans, enabling members to compete with state banks, lowered the quality of paper on which member banks might borrow, reorganized the Federal Reserve Board and renamed it the Board of Governors, and authorized it to increase legal reserves up to a maximum of doubling if necessary. Such a doubling was effected because our bank reserve percentages had increased so much, largely by reason of heavy gold imports and a small demand for bank loans, as to place a feared dangerous expansion of bank credit beyond the control of the Federal Reserve authorities. Legal reserves were reduced about one eighth after April 16, 1938, to induce credit expansion.

The recent trend in this country has been toward more government control of banking. A rapidly growing portion of banks' earning assets is in government bonds. At the end of 1938 two fifths of our 15,200 banks, holding over two thirds of the banking assets, were inside the Federal Reserve System, and 13,654 belonged to the Federal Deposit Insurance Corporation.

[H. White, *Money and Banking;* J. T. Holdsworth, *The First Bank of the U. S.;* R. C. Catterall, *The Second Bank of the U. S.;* D. R. Dewey, *State Banking Before the Civil War;* G. E. Barnett, *State Banks and Trust Companies;* E. W. Kemmerer, *The A B C of the Federal Reserve System,* 11th ed.; F. A. Bradford, *Money and Banking;* A. S. Pratt and Sons, *Digest of Federal Banking Laws; Annual Report of the Comptroller of Currency; The Federal Reserve Bulletin.*]

DONALD L. KEMMERER

Banking, Branch and Group. The First Bank of the United States (*see* Bank of the United States) had eight branches; the Second Bank had twenty-nine. Thereafter, what meager developments there were in branch banking before the 20th century took place under state authority.

The Federal Reserve Act of 1913 permitted foreign branches to a limited degree; in 1918 state banks having branches and wanting to join the Federal Reserve System*qv* were authorized to keep them; and the McFadden-Pepper Act*qv* of 1927 allowed national banks to set up a limited number of branches in the parent bank's city provided the state permitted branch banking.

During the 1920's hundreds of small state banks failed because of dependence on a single local crop or industry. Canadian and English experience indicated that branch banking offered a partial solution. Accordingly, the Banking Act of 1933*qv* permitted national banks to establish branches, under certain restrictions, in states allowing branch banking. This has attracted a few score state banks into the national system.

In 1936 eighteen states permitted state-wide branch banking, and seventeen permitted it within limited areas. California had the most highly developed systems. At the end of 1938 the 15,200 commercial banks in the United States had only 3581 branches, 1499 being national. Federal Reserve Banks had twenty-five branches.

Where branch banking is prohibited or discouraged, resort is sometimes had to group or chain banking, the distinction between them being that chains are owned by one or more individuals, and groups are owned by holding companies. The Banking Act of 1933 brought any group under Federal supervision if it owned even one member bank of the Federal Reserve System. At the end of 1937 there were 461 groups operating a total of 883 banks and having deposits of over $6,000,000,000.

[G. T. Cartinhour, *Branch, Group and Chain Banking;* D. R. Dewey, *State Banking Before the Civil War;* J. S. Lawrence, *Banking Concentration in the U. S.;* S. D. Southworth, *Branch Banking in the U. S.;* R. B. Westerfield, *Money, Credit and Banking; Annual Report of the Board of Governors of the Federal Reserve System;* F. A. Bradford, *Money and Banking.*]

DONALD L. KEMMERER

Banking, State. *See* State Banking.

Banking Acts of 1933 and 1935. The Banking Act of 1933, approved June 16, 1933, contained three groups of provisions as follows: (a) provisions designed to increase the power of the Federal Reserve Board*qv* to control credit, especially with respect to loans to brokers and customers secured by stocks and bonds; (b) provisions dealing with the commercial banks, of which by far the most important was the one providing for the insurance of bank deposits under the supervision of the Federal Deposit Insurance Corporation*qv*; and (c) provisions designed to separate commercial and investment banking functions by prohibiting commercial banks from operating investment affiliates and by prohibiting investment banking houses from carrying on a deposit banking business.

The Banking Act of 1935, approved Aug. 23, 1935, contained three titles. Title I amended the deposit insurance provisions of the Banking Act of 1933. Title II provided for a rather drastic reorganization of the Federal Reserve Board and changed the name of that body to the Board of Governors of the Federal Reserve System. Certain changes were also made in the management of the Federal Reserve banks. Powers over discount and open market operations*qv* of the Reserve banks were increased and centralized in the Board of Governors, and the discount base was very materially broadened. Title III contained a series of technical amendments to the banking laws governing the operations of the commercial banks.

[F. A. Bradford, *Money and Banking.*]

FREDERICK A. BRADFORD

Banking Crisis of 1933, THE, was the outcome of the large number of bank failures*qv* during the years 1931–32, combined with the wave of hoarding which swept the country and markedly weakened the banking structure. The attempts of the Reconstruction Finance Corporation[qv] to avoid final disaster were in large measure nullified by the publication of the names of borrowing banks, a procedure not calculated to restore confidence to frightened depositors.

Banking difficulties in Michigan finally caused Gov. William A. Comstock to declare a bank moratorium[qv] in that state on Feb. 14, 1933. Alarm quickly spread to neighboring states. Moratoria were declared in four other states by the end of February, and in seventeen additional states during the first three days of March. Finally, on March 4, banks in the remaining states closed their doors and the country was left devoid of banking facilities.

The situation was serious and prompt action was imperative. Congress, called in special session by President Roosevelt, passed the Emergency Banking Act of 1933 on March 9, thus providing machinery for reopening the banks. Under this act, only sound banks were to be reopened while those of questionable soundness were to be placed in the hands of conservators, to be opened later if conditions permitted.

The bank moratorium, which had been proclaimed by the President on March 6, was extended a few days to permit the provisions of the act to be put into effect. Sound banks were reopened on March 13, 14 and 15. By the latter date, banks controlling about 90% of the banking resources of the country were again in operation and the banking crisis of 1933 was at an end.

[J. I. Bogen and M. Nadler, *The Banking Crisis;* F. A. Bradford, *Money and Banking;* L. Sullivan, *Prelude to Panic.*]

FREDERICK A. BRADFORD

Bankruptcy Laws usually follow in the wake of a depression. The English bankruptcy legislation of Queen Anne's reign doubtless inspired the clause in the Federal Constitution (I, 8, 4) authorizing Congress "to establish . . . uniform laws on the subject of bankruptcies throughout the United States." This power, while it left the states free to pass insolvency legislation operative only within their respective limits, reserved the national field for Congress. It was nearly a dozen years, however, after the Federal Government was organized, before the power was exercised and then but meagerly. The act of 1800, mainly for bankers and merchants, failed to provide for voluntary bankruptcy and was repealed in 1803. Following the panic of 1837[qv], Congress passed a second act in 1841. It was an improvement on the first, in providing for voluntary bankruptcy, but was of even briefer duration, being repealed in 1843. The third act, that of 1867, remained in force until 1878. The panic of 1893[qv] and subsequent years furnished the background for the more elaborate and, as it has proved, permanent, legislation of 1898 (30 U. S. Statutes 544). Though amended in 1903, 1906, 1910, 1933, 1934 and 1938 its main provisions are still in force, after over forty years, and have been supplemented by rules and forms prescribed by the Supreme Court. The depression beginning in 1929[qv] occasioned substantial additions. The Municipal Bankruptcy Act of May 24, 1934, authorized local tax units to readjust their obligations where a substantial majority of creditors approve. The act of June 7, 1934, permits corporate reorganization under court supervision with consent of a majority of the creditors. (The amendment's moratorium clause was declared unconstitutional, 295 U. S. 555.) But the Chandler Act of June 22, 1938, has been pronounced "the first thoroughgoing revision" of the American bankruptcy statute in forty years. Sec. 77B of the original 1898 act, dealing with corporate reorganizations, was enlarged into a new chapter (X) and the S.E.C. (Securities and Exchange Commission) has created a new division which acts in an advisory capacity to the courts in such cases.

[*Collier on Bankruptcy*, 3d ed., 1934; *Am. Bar Ass'n Jnl.*, XXIV, 875, 880; U. of Chicago *L. Rev.*, V, I, 272, 398.]

C. SUMNER LOBINGIER

Banks, Land. *See* Farm Credit Agencies, Federal.

Banks, National, were first organized under the act of Feb. 25, 1863, entitled "An Act to provide a National Currency, secured by a pledge of United States stocks, and to provide for the circulation and redemption thereof." This act provided that any five or more natural persons might organize a national banking association by complying with certain routine requirements of the law and by fulfilling the minimum capital requirements which the law specified.

The act of 1863 was not a success. As late as Oct. 5, 1863, only sixty-six national banks had been organized, while the number of state banks[qv] was more than 1400. Consequently, the law was repealed and a new act, bearing the same title (the title National Bank Act was adopted in 1874), was passed and became law on June 3, 1864. It bore the same provisions relative to the organization of national banks as that of 1863.

Under the act of 1864 national banks might be organized with a minimum capital of from

$50,000 to $200,000, depending upon the location of the bank. Such banks might issue notes secured by government bonds and were authorized by law to carry on a strictly commercial banking business.

By October, 1864, the number of national banks had reached 508, but not until the passage of an act of March 3, 1865, imposing a 10% tax on the circulation of state bank notes, did the number of national banks increase rapidly. On Oct. 2, 1865, there were 1513 national banks, and the number had increased to 1644 a year later.

After 1866 the number of national banks increased steadily to 7509 in October, 1913, just prior to the passage of the Federal Reserve Act[q.v.]. At that time the national banks carried on the great bulk of the commercial banking business of the country. From 1913 on the number of national banks increased to 8249 in 1922, after which the number declined steadily to 5293 in June, 1937. However, the number of state and private banks[q.v.] also declined sharply. Total banking strength, as measured by total assets, of national banks increased slightly as compared with state and private banks between 1914 and 1937.

Since the establishment of the Federal Reserve System[q.v.], national banks have been permitted to carry on savings and trust business in order to allow them to compete with state banking institutions.

[C. F. Dunbar, *Theory and History of Banking;* F. A. Bradford, *Money and Banking;* Comptroller of the Currency, *Annual Reports.*] FREDERICK A. BRADFORD

Banks, Postal Savings. *See* Postal Savings Banks.

Banks, Private, the original form of banking historically, are strictly defined as individuals or partnerships engaged in any of the functions of banking—deposit, exchange, loan, discount or sale of securities. Like any private business their obligations were originally protected by the personal liability of the individual or partnership. They were the product of the era of *laissez-faire*[q.v.] and developed in America on the model of the great English "houses."

With the growth of social control of business—and banking was one of the earliest areas of economic life to yield to this—the number of private banks has declined. Some states prohibit their operations entirely and in all there has been an increasing tendency to subject them to the same control as corporations[q.v.] and curtail the field of their operations. The function of note issue has been taken over by the Federal Government.

They continued to exist because of a real need for their services, the lack of regulation, and a tradition of personal integrity. Perhaps the most famous "house" of private bankers in America has been that of J. P. Morgan.

Some of the banks which developed before the Civil War with charters for speculative businesses such as railroads, insurance companies, canal companies, etc., may be regarded as private banks. An example of these was The Manhattan Company, organized ostensibly for the purpose of supplying New York City with water. Another example was "George Smith's Bank" of Milwaukee, which, organized to carry on insurance, converted itself into a bank.

[L. C. Helderman, *National and State Banks.*]
LEONARD C. HELDERMAN

Banks, Savings. The earliest savings bank in the United States, and the first legally sanctioned savings bank in the world, was the Provident Institution for Savings in Boston, which received a charter on Dec. 13, 1816. The Philadelphia Savings Fund Society began business on Dec. 2, 1816, but did not receive a charter until Feb. 25, 1819. Between 1816 and 1820 nine mutual savings banks were chartered, two in Massachusetts, two in Rhode Island, two in New York and one each in Pennsylvania, Connecticut and Maryland.

From these early beginnings the number of mutual savings banks grew to 634 in 1914 (June 30) with deposits of nearly $4,000,000,000. Since 1914 the number of such banks has decreased to 564 (1937), but deposits have increased to slightly over $10,000,000,000. These banks are located in eighteen states, but four fifths of them are in New York and New England.

After the Civil War stock savings banks were organized in various states. By June 30, 1915, the number of these banks had reached 1529. By 1935, however, the number had declined to 341, since which year separate reports for such banks have not been published. The total of savings deposits in stock savings banks in 1935 was slightly over $700,000,000. Other savings deposits are held in the savings departments of national banks, state banks and trust companies.

[F. J. Sherman, *The Modern Story of Mutual Savings Banks;* Comptroller of the Currency, *Annual Reports.*]
FREDERICK A. BRADFORD

Banks, State. *See* State Banks.

Banks, Wildcat, were the unsound state banks[q.v.] on the frontiers after 1800 and especially in the

1830's and 1840's. Since they profited by keeping their bank notes in circulation, some of them located at remote places (among the wildcats) where it was difficult to present the notes for redemption. There were many evils. Charter granting was mixed with politics and sometimes graft. Capital was often composed of promissory notes. Many banks had little specie. Loans were made recklessly, particularly to land speculators. Redemption of notes was evaded. Circulation was unsatisfactory. Good bank notes were at a discount outside the town of issue, and there were counterfeits, raised notes and notes of closed banks. The confusion was so great that businessmen had to refer to "bank note reporters" to determine the value of a note. The crises of 1818, 1837, 1841 and 1857 were marked by failures of these banks.

[Horace White, *Money and Banking.*]

JAMES D. MAGEE

Bannock War, THE (1878), was the last major uprising of Indians in the Pacific Northwest. It was waged by approximately 1500 malcontents, principally Bannocks and Paiutes[qv]. Gen. O. O. Howard's troops engaged most of the hostiles, who, dissatisfied with reservation policies in Idaho and Oregon, fought under Chiefs Buffalo Horn and Egan. In the skirmishes, about eighty Indians and approximately fifty whites were slain. The majority of Indian prisoners were transferred to Yakima Reservation, Washington Territory, in 1879.

[G. F. Brimlow, *The Bannock Indian War of 1878;* R. Ross Arnold, *Indian Wars of Idaho.*]

GEORGE F. BRIMLOW

Baptists, the most numerous Protestant body in the United States, originated in England in the early 17th century and are not to be confused with the Anabaptists. They hold to five great principles: (1) separation of Church and State; (2) complete independence of the congregation; (3) the Scriptures as supplying the only standard of faith; (4) church membership based on a religious experience; and (5) immersion as the only Scriptural form of baptism. It has generally been held that Roger Williams was the father of the American Baptists and the church he founded at Providence (1638) was the mother church of the denomination in America. This is disputed, however, by recent Baptist historians, who have shown that Williams and his associates, though rebaptized, were not immersed. Rhode Island, however, became the center for the propagation of Baptist views and the first American college founded by Baptists was established at Warren, R. I., in 1764 (*see* Brown University). Baptists were severely persecuted in the New England colonies, outside Rhode Island, though after 1691 a larger degree of toleration was secured. Up until the Great Awakening[qv] Baptists flourished most in the Middle Colonies, due largely to English and Welsh immigration. The first Baptist Association in America, made up of five churches, was formed in Philadelphia in 1707. In 1742 this body adopted a Calvinistic Confession of Faith, and from that time forward the majority of American Baptists have been Calvinistic[qv] in their theology. By 1740 there were more than fifty Baptist churches in the colonies, the largest number being in New York, Pennsylvania, Maryland and Virginia.

As a result of the Great Awakening, the Separate, or revivalistic, Baptists, led by uneducated and unsalaried farmer-preachers, grew very rapidly in Virginia and North Carolina. This type of evangelism was particularly effective among the lower economic classes. By the end of the Revolution the southern Baptists were both numerous and influential. Separation of Church and State[qv] being one of the great Baptist principles, they naturally took a prominent part in the struggle to establish complete religious liberty in America. In both New England and Virginia, where that struggle was most severe, the Baptists were in the lead. Due largely to the farmer-preacher type of ministry, the Baptists proved one of the most effective of the churches in following moving population, and their churches were planted widely on every frontier.

In 1814 the General Convention of the Baptist Denomination in the United States for Foreign Missions was formed and in 1832 a similar organization for Home Missions was established. Opposition to missions[qv] developed on the frontier and after 1818 an antimission schism occurred, often called "Hard-Shells." Since Baptists were numerous in both North and South a slavery controversy arose, which in 1844–45 led to the formation of a Southern Baptist Convention. Since the Civil War the number of Negro Baptists has grown rapidly, largely due to the ease with which Baptist churches can be formed and the pageantry which they make of the rite of baptism by immersion. There are now more than 3,000,000 Negro Baptists, while white Baptists are twice as numerous in the South as in the North.

[A. H. Newman, *A History of the Baptist Churches in the United States;* W. W. Sweet, *Religion on the American Frontier: The Baptists.*]

WILLIAM W. SWEET

Baptists, Seventh Day. These literal Bible-followers, accepting the seventh day for Sabbath, started in Newport, R. I. (1671). A German group at Ephrata[qv], Pa., later joined them. They have 6807 members and sixty-eight churches in twenty-one states.

AUGUSTUS H. SHEARER

Bar Association, American, was organized in 1878, with members from all states in the Union, one of its primary objects being the improvement of legal education. It has exerted much influence in national legislation. To relieve pressure upon the Supreme Court calendar, it proposed and planned the United States Circuit Court of Appeals, created by Congress in 1891. It planned the consolidation of the United States Circuit and District Courts, accomplished in 1911. In 1920 it began taking an active part in the movement to provide legal aid for poor litigants. It fought the proposed Child Labor Amendment[qv] to the Constitution, but approved the uniform child labor laws of 1930.

[M. Louise Rutherford, *The Influence of the American Bar Association on Public Opinion and Legislation.*]

ALVIN F. HARLOW

Barataria is the name of a bay, a lake and a bayou on the Gulf coast of Louisiana, sixty miles south of New Orleans and forty miles west of the mouth of the Mississippi. The Barataria region is inseparably connected in history and legend with the smuggling operations of Jean and Pierre Lafitte, who maintained headquarters there from 1810 to 1815. Though regarded as pirates[qv] by the United States, the Lafittes claimed to operate as privateers[qv] under letters of marque and reprisal[qv] issued by the Republic of Cartagena, on the northern coast of South America, which had declared its independence from Spain in 1810. (*See also* Galveston Pirates.)

[Lyle Saxon, *Lafitte the Pirate.*]

WALTER PRICHARD

Barbados, settled in 1627, traded extensively—and not always legitimately—with New England, New York and Virginia throughout the colonial period, mainly exchanging sugar, cotton, molasses and ginger for foodstuffs. Moreover, many settlers went from Barbados to the Carolinas. Since the Revolution, the island has had little contact with this continent.

[C. Atchley, *The West Indies.*]

CHARLES F. MULLETT

Barbary Wars, The (1801–5; 1815). After the Revolution the United States, following the example of European nations, made annual payments to the piratical Barbary States, Morocco, Algiers, Tripoli and Tunis, for unmolested transit of merchantmen through the Mediterranean. Constant difficulties, however, ensued, such as the episode of the *George Washington*[qv], and in 1801 Tripoli declared war and seized several Americans and their vessels. The war, entirely naval except for the Derna Expedition[qv], was very feebly prosecuted by the commanders first dispatched, Commodores Dale and Morris, but in 1803 Edward Preble was sent out with the *Constitution, Philadelphia*[qqv] and several brigs and schooners. His arrival galvanized the entire force into vigorous action. Making a naval demonstration before Tangiers which brought the Emperor of Morocco to make amends for treaty violations, Preble set up a strict blockade of Tripoli itself. Here on Oct. 31, 1803, the *Philadelphia* ran on a reef just outside the harbor and was captured by the Tripolitans, who a few days later floated her and anchored her under the guns of the citadel. But on Feb. 16, 1804, Stephen Decatur and eighty other officers and men recaptured and burned her in a daring night attack.

During August and September, 1804, Preble, in addition to blockading, harassed the Tripolitan shipping and fortifications with frequent attacks, in which the small gunboats fearlessly entered the harbor to enable the crews to board and capture piratical craft while the larger ships kept up a protective fire on batteries. Such activity reached a climax on Sept. 4, when the *Intrepid*[qv] with its cargo of gunpowder and explosive shells was maneuvered into the harbor at night. Apparently the explosion occurred prematurely, for all the participants were killed and little damage was done to the Tripolitan shipping.

When, soon after, Preble was relieved by Commodore Samuel Barron, and he in turn the next spring by Commodore John Rodgers, the Bey was ready to conclude peace. He was partly induced to this by the success of the Derna Expedition, which had captured Derna and was threatening to march on Tripoli itself. The treaty, somewhat hastily concluded, June 4, 1805, abolished all annual payments, but provided for $60,000 ransom money for the officers and crew of the *Philadelphia.*

Although payments were continued to the other Barbary States, the absence of American naval vessels in the years preceding the War of 1812 encouraged Algiers to seize American merchantmen such as the *Mary Ann,* for which $18,000 was paid Algiers, and to threaten others such as the *Alleghany,* where an increased payment was demanded and secured. Immediately after the termination of the war, Decatur and Bainbridge were ordered to the Mediterranean with an overwhelming force (*see* Decatur's Cruise to Algiers). By June, 1815, within forty days from his departure from New York, Decatur, the first to arrive, had achieved his immediate mission. Capturing the Algerian flagship *Mashuda* in a running fight off Cape de Gat and appearing off Algiers, he demanded and secured a treaty humiliating to the once proud piratical state—no future payments, restoration of all American property, the emancipation of all Christian slaves escaping to American men-of-war, civilized treatment to prisoners of war and $10,000 for a merchantman recently seized. As Tunis and Tripoli were forced to equally hard terms and an American squadron remained in the Mediterranean, the safety of American commerce was assured.

[G. W. Allen, *Our Navy and the Barbary Corsairs.*]

WALTER B. NORRIS

Barbecue. An outdoor entertainment distinguished by the serving of meat cooked, often as whole carcasses, on racks over open pits of coals. Apparently originating in Virginia about 1700, probably in connection with local fairs where foot-races, dancing, fiddling contests and other sport and pastimes were engaged in, the barbecue was especially popular on the southwestern frontier. During the first period of nationalism the universal celebration of the Fourth of July[qv] did much to shape the barbecue as an institution. Beeves were donated, and meat, bread, condiments and often beer or lemonade were served free to all comers. There were oratory (*see* Frontier Oratory), music, dancing and various sports, including tournaments, roping contests and other equestrian games. Candidates for public office were invited to expound their platforms, and they and their partisans were quick to take advantage of the barbecue as a campaigning device.

The barbecue survives in the West and Southwest, largely as a social institution.

MODY C. BOATRIGHT

Barbed Wire. "Free grass" and the open range[qv] were doomed by advancing values and population. Without absolute control of his land and stock, no ranchman could afford extensive improvement. If he provided ample water, the stock belonging to other men would tramp out his range in getting to it; if he bought high-grade bulls, his neighbors would get the use of them, while at the same time scrub bulls of other brands ran with his cows. Colorado alone of the range states enforced laws against scrub breeders.

Cattle, some rovers always excepted, would after being located normally remain on a given range; but drouths and blizzards made them drift, a hundred—sometimes two hundred—miles. Moreover, open range meant open road for thieves. "Slick" wire would not hold range stock; plank fences were too expensive; hedges of *bois d'arc,* wild roses and other growth proved impracticable. Only small bunches of cattle could thrive under herd, and herding was costly; the line-riders of the big outfits were helpless when northers and blizzards struck.

Following various patents on barbed wire, in 1873 J. F. Glidden, a prairie farmer of Illinois, gave it commercial practicability and the next year sold the first piece. Factories developed. Fencing proceeded outward from privately owned land near settlements. John W. Gates in the late 1870's put up a "bob" wire fence on Alamo Plaza in San Antonio to demonstrate its being "bull proof and horse high." Before the plains were fenced into pastures, cowmen co-operated to build drift fences across long distances. By 1890 most of the range land under private ownership had been fenced, but it was decades later before some of the Federal and state lands of Western states were fenced.

With fencing came wire-cutting "wars" in Texas and elsewhere, brought on by men accustomed to using land without owning it and resentful of being shut out. Many big outfits fenced in vast tracts to which they had no right. Bigfoot Wallace used to say, "Bob wire played hell with Texas." But barbed wire came to stay. It revolutionized the whole range industry, cutting off trail driving[qv] and free grazing, making the improvement of breeds and the watering of the range by wells and tanks inevitable. It developed stock-farming. (*See also* Windmills.)

[W. P. Webb, *The Great Plains.*]

J. FRANK DOBIE

Barbed Wire Patent Case, The (143 U. S. 275, 1892), settled a long dispute as to patent rights for the invention of barbed wire (twisted wire with coiled barb) between the assignees of Joseph Glidden and Jacob Haish. The latter claimed that exclusive rights could not be set up because there were various types of barbed wire in local use at the time the Glidden patent was granted. The court decided, however, in favor of this patent on the ground that Glidden had "taken the final step in the invention which has turned a failure into a (commercial) success. In the law of patents it is the last step that wins."

PHILLIPS BRADLEY

Bargemen is a term that was used interchangeably with keelboatmen, bargers and keelers, and applied to men engaged in operating river boats that traveled upstream as distinct from flatboats. French bargemen and American bargemen employed on the Missouri and upper Mississippi were also hunters and trappers. Most full-time bargemen worked on the lower Mississippi and the Ohio and its tributaries. After 1820 they gradually disappeared as the steamboat, turnpike and railroad took over transportation.

The bargemen were traditionally the roughest element in the West, prodigious drinkers, fighters, gamblers, pranksters and workers, and the respectable elements along the rivers are said to have lived in terror of them. Their chief pleasuring resorts were New Orleans, Natchez, St. Louis, Shawneetown and Louisville. They wore red shirts as a sort of occupational badge. A number of bargemen were famous in their day and Mike Fink became the hero of a cycle of legends.

[Leland D. Baldwin, *The Keelboat Age on Western Waters.*]

LELAND D. BALDWIN

Barnburners was the nickname of a faction of the Democratic party*qv* in New York State in the 1840's. They were first called Radicals and were the progressive element in the party. The name "Barnburner" was given them as early as 1843, and accepted by them at the State Democratic Convention of 1847. It was based on the story of the Dutch farmer who was willing to burn his barn to get rid of the rats. They opposed further expenditures for canals*qv*, wanted a limitation on the state debt, and a direct state tax. They advocated a Constitutional Convention, and when it was called in 1846, they controlled it. In national affairs, they favored the Wilmot Proviso*qv* and opposed the extension of slavery*qv*. They seceded from the State Convention of 1847 and from the 1848 Democratic National Convention. They nominated Martin Van Buren for President and then united with the Free Soilers*qv*. This movement defeated Cass, the Democratic candidate. After this election they gradually returned to the Democratic party, but when the Republican party*qv* was formed most of the younger Barnburners joined, bringing elements of leadership and voting strength.

[H. D. A. Donovan, *The Barnburners.*]

AUGUSTUS H. SHEARER

Barn-raising is a custom representative of the combination of co-operative labor and social festivity common in frontier days. The custom still survives in some sections. (*See* picture and description of a barn-raising in York County, Pa., in *The Harrisburg Patriot,* Jan. 7, 1938.)

Before the day set for the barn-raising, carpenters cut the lumber. Great care is exercised, lest, on the day of the barn-raising, the pieces do not fit perfectly, and the carpenter's reputation be ruined in the sight of the men of the entire district.

On the day of the great event, all the neighboring farmers, with their families, assemble. In the morning all the men co-operate in erecting, with the simplest of tools, the framework of the barn. Prizes are sometimes offered for the exhibition of the greatest feat of strength. Dinner prepared by the combined efforts of the women present is then served. Later the occasion takes on a more strictly social aspect. The program usually includes games, athletic events and a dance. Wrestling, jumping competition and prize fighting have been common.

Barn-raisings have had most significance in sections of the Middle and West Central states where large structures were erected.

[Bristow, *Old Time Tales of Warren County, Pa.*]

H. H. SHENK

Barnstorming. In 1815, at the instance of N. L. Usher, of Lexington, Ky., a theatrical troup, which included Noah M. Ludlow, was led by Samuel Drake from Albany into the West. They often slept in barns and played in theaters that were little better than barns. William Turner, James Caldwell, Collins and Jones, Sol Smith, Mary Duff and Eliza Riddle were among the barnstormers who brought contemporary farce and melodrama as well as Shakespeare and Sheridan to Cincinnati, St. Louis, Nashville, New Orleans, and many smaller frontier centers in the days before railroads. By analogy, itinerant fliers and stunt pilots about 1912–22 were also called barnstormers.

[Noah Miller Ludlow, *Dramatic Life as I Found It;* William Dunlap, *A History of the American Theatre;* William Carson, *The Theatre on the Frontier.*]

HARVEY L. CARTER

Barnum's Museum. In December, 1841, P. T. Barnum bought Scudder's American Museum at Broadway and Ann Street, New York. This he enlarged as Barnum's American Museum, open weekdays at sunrise, with a single fee of twenty-five cents; exhibiting not only thousands of curios and relics but also living curiosities and "transient novelties"; with a "Lecture Room" seating 3000, in which plays were given. Fire destroyed building and contents, July 13, 1865. Barnum's less-famous New American Museum, opened Nov. 13, 1865, on Broadway between Spring and Prince streets, was also burned (1868).

[Bryan's edition of Barnum's autobiography, *Struggles and Triumphs.*]
G. S. BRYAN

Barrage. A curtain of fire, moving or stationary, designed to protect friendly troops while advancing or while in position. A *box* barrage forms three sides of a square and is customarily used to protect troops while making a raid on a portion of the enemy's line; a *rolling* barrage (referred to by the infantry as "creeping") is timed to lift its angle of fire and move forward as the infantry advances under its protection; an *anti-aircraft* barrage is defensive in character and is designed to protect a given area from enemy aircraft; a *balloon* barrage is a floating curtain of piano wire, suspended from captive balloons, used notably in the defense of London during the World War.
ROBERT S. THOMAS

Barrier Forts, Attack on (1856), was the first use of armed force against China by the United States. On Nov. 15, during intermittent warfare between the Chinese and the British, Commander Foote, in a small boat below Canton, was fired upon by the Barrier Forts. On the 20th, Foote retaliated by attacking the forts with a force of 287 sailors and marines, spiking the guns and blowing up the walls. The American loss was seven killed and twenty-two wounded. Although Secretary of State Marcy criticized the action as hasty, Foote's aggressiveness secured greater safety for Americans trading in China.

[J. M. Hoppin, *Life of Andrew Hull Foote.*]
WALTER B. NORRIS

Barron v. Baltimore. The issue in this case was whether the first ten amendments to the Federal Constitution[qv], and in particular the due process[qv] clause of the Fifth, were intended as restrictions on state as well as Federal authority. In 1833, in the last case participated in by John Marshall, the Supreme Court[qv] held that in view of the history of the adoption of the bill of rights[qv], the prohibitions were directed against the Federal Government but not against the states.

[A. C. McLaughlin, *A Constitutional History of the United States.*]
LEONARD C. HELDERMAN

Barter, strictly, is the exchange of goods for goods without using money, e.g., furs were obtained from the Indians for beads, liquor, firearms, etc. As the people on the frontier usually lacked money they bartered horses, farms, tobacco, etc. Less strictly but more importantly, barter is involved in transactions carried on in terms of money which utilize goods for part of the payment. The farmer's wife trades butter and eggs for groceries. The accounts are kept in money, but actually it is an exchange of goods for goods. Many real-estate deals are of this nature. The old radio or auto is part payment for the new one. Many security transactions involve giving old securities for new ones. Clearing houses of banks and stock exchanges involve a similar procedure. They offset the debits and the credits and pay only balances.

[B. M. Anderson, Jr., *The Value of Money.*]
JAMES D. MAGEE

Bartlett's (John Russell) Explorations were made in the years 1850, 1851, 1852 and 1853 in Texas, New Mexico, California and adjacent Mexican states, as United States Commissioner on the Mexican boundary question. Scientists accompanied the party and the results were published with interesting illustrations in 1854.

[H. R. Wagner, *Plains and the Rockies;* Bartlett, *Personal Narrative.*]
CARL L. CANNON

Bascom, Fort, was established on the Canadian River in New Mexico in 1868 by Gen. Getty acting under Gen. Sheridan's orders. Its purpose was to protect the frontier against raids of the Cheyenne, Kiowa, Comanche and Arapaho Indians[qqv]. It was abandoned in 1870.

[C. C. Rister, *Southwestern Frontier, 1865-1881.*]
CARL L. CANNON

Baseball evolved from the various bat-and-ball games which the early settlers in this country brought with them from England. It was the offshoot of a children's game actually called baseball in the 18th century, the old English game of rounders, and New England town ball. The origin of the modern game is often traced to new developments supposedly introduced by Abner Doubleday at Cooperstown, N. Y., in 1839, but there is no authentic evidence that he brought about any change in existing methods of play. A more important date in baseball's early history was the adoption in 1845 of a codified set of rules, embodying the more important features of the modern game, by the Knickerbocker Club of New York.

As in the case of every new sport introduced in the 19th century, baseball was at first a prerogative of the well-to-do, the gentleman amateur. But more democratic clubs than the old

Knickerbockers soon began to be organized in and about New York, and in the 1850's baseball was slowly reaching out to a wider public. It gradually superseded all older forms of the traditional ball game, although New England continued for some time to play town ball, and before the Civil War over fifty clubs were members of the National Association of Base Ball Players. Games were being played on regular schedule which attracted admission-paying spectators. When the champion Excelsiors, of Brooklyn, returned from a triumphal tour through the Eastern states, one of their games drew an estimated attendance of 15,000.

The Civil War interrupted this inter-club competition, but it provided a tremendous impetus for the growth of the game throughout the country. It was played everywhere behind the lines, and with the end of the war it was taken back by the demobilized soldiers to their home communities. Membership in the National Association jumped to 202 clubs in 1866. "The game of baseball," a contemporary sports writer stated in that year, "has now become, beyond question, the leading feature in the outdoor sports of the United States."

Professionalism began to invade the ranks of the players. The local club's desire to win led to the hiring of skilled players, and when the Cincinnati Red Stockings, a wholly professional team, toured the country in 1869 and won every game, the way was paved for the organization of baseball along new lines. The amateurs withdrew from the National Association and the professionals formed an organization of their own. Its failure to prevent gambling, the bribing of players, and operation of illegal pools for a time cast baseball under the shadow of intense public disapproval. The game was almost killed. But with the organization of the National League of Professional Baseball Clubs in 1876, made up of teams in New York, Philadelphia, Hartford, Boston, Chicago, Louisville, Cincinnati and St. Louis, professional baseball had a controlling body which effectively put its house in order. The National League stabilized the professional game, restored public confidence in the honesty of the regularly scheduled matches among league teams and gave all baseball a new standing in popular estimation.

Since that date it has continued to expand both as a professional game, drawing every year millions of spectators, and as an amateur sport played by thousands of teams throughout the entire country. While the National League worked out the immensely complicated system of major and minor leagues, franchises, player contracts and other business controls which still govern the professional game, colleges, high schools, Y. M. C. A.'s and local clubs organized amateur nines which competed with the keenest rivalry. Baseball became the national game because in its modern development it was a distinctively American product, and because it aroused both spectator and player interest to a greater degree than any other sport. While the professional has always held the spotlight, and in almost every way dominated the game, baseball has its roots in the small-town park, the village playing field and the city's vacant lot.

Until the opening of the 20th century, the National League had no real rival in the professional world. For a time it faced the competition of the American Association, and in 1889–90 the National Brotherhood of Base Ball Players represented a short-lived attempt on the part of the players themselves to take over control of the game. It was not until the organization of the American League ten years later, however, that two almost equally powerful major leagues were in competition. Their successful division of the field and the establishment, in 1903, of the National Commission brought about still further stabilization of the game, and inauguration that same year of the World Series, between the champions of the two leagues, added still more to popular interest in the game.

In the 1890's it was estimated that paid attendance at the games of the hundred-odd professional clubs organized under the National Agreement totaled approximately 8,000,000 annually. Two decades later A. G. Spalding placed the total for all major and minor league games at close upon 26,000,000, the majors accounting for 6,000,000. Neither estimate included attendance at college, high school or local amateur games. In the 1930's the broad, all-inclusive figure for annual attendance at baseball games has been estimated as high as 50,000,000. Obviously, exact statistics on the number of persons either playing or watching baseball are unobtainable. In recent years baseball has had to face far heavier competition from other sports, but its continuing popularity is attested on all sides. Among the contributing factors, both in baseball's growth and in its present standing, has been the immense publicity which has been given the professional game ever since the first reports of local contests began to appear in the New York papers of mid-century.

[A. G. Spalding, *America's National Game.*]

FOSTER RHEA DULLES

Basketball has the unique feature of being the

one popular sport played in this country which is truly American in its origins. It was invented, in 1891, by James Naismith, an instructor at the Y. M. C. A. Training School in Springfield, Mass. His purpose was to introduce an active but not too rough game which could be played indoors, without elaborate equipment, to take the place of outdoor sports curtailed by winter weather. It proved so practical that it spread rapidly. It was taken up by schools, colleges, athletic clubs and industrial organizations, while a modified game for women became equally popular in girls' schools and colleges. It today has its professional as well as amateur teams, although it remains primarily an amateur sport for young people, and it has been estimated that more people watch basketball than any other sport in the United States.

[John A. Krout, *Annals of American Sport.*]

FOSTER RHEA DULLES

Bateau, THE, was in general a keelless, flat-bottomed, sharp-ended craft, built of plank, and propelled by oars, setting poles or square sails and steered by oar or rudder. Large bateaux employed eighteen or twenty rowers and carried forty tons or more. Missouri bateaux were often called Mackinaw boats*qv*. Bateaux were superseded on the Ohio and Mississippi before 1800 by keelboats*qv*.

[Leland D. Baldwin, *The Keelboat Age on Western Waters.*]

LELAND D. BALDWIN

Bathtubs and Bathing. The first mention of the use of bathtubs in the United States dates back to the early 1820's. The most advanced installation took place in Philadelphia between 1832 and 1837 when the Stephen Girard Estate built a row of model houses. This was made possible by the water supply provided by the Schuylkill Water Works. The water rate for a bathtub in 1836 was $3.00 per year. In that year, despite an effort to ban them on sanitary grounds (their use was prohibited between Nov. 1 and March 15 as a health measure), Philadelphia had 1530 bathtubs. In 1845 Boston made their use unlawful, except on the advice of a physician. Hartford, Providence and Wilmington made heavy water charges for their use.

The "rain bath" was introduced during the middle of the 19th century. In 1850 Harper and Gillespie of Philadelphia installed the first bathtub in the White House, for President Fillmore. It was not replaced until President Cleveland's administration.

By 1860 most first-class New York hotels had bathtubs. In 1930 there were bathtubs in 16% of the farm homes and 87.5% of the non-farm homes in the United States.

CAROL ARONOVICI

Baton Rouge (La.). Founded by the French about 1720 as an important military and trading post, it became English in 1763, Spanish in 1783 and was annexed to the United States as a part of the Louisiana Purchase in 1810, after the successful West Florida Revolution (*see* Baton Rouge, Seizure of). In 1822 it became the United States military post and arsenal for the southwestern district, and remained such until 1877, except during a part of the Civil War (*see* Baton Rouge, Battle of).

[A. Fortier, *Louisiana*, Cyclopedic, I.]

WALTER PRICHARD

Baton Rouge, Battle of (Aug. 5, 1862). To regain control of the lower Mississippi, the Confederates planned to recapture Baton Rouge, La., then occupied by Union forces. Breckinridge's (C.) land forces were to be supported by the ironclad ram, *Arkansas*qv. He attacked the town from the east and forced the Union troops to the levee where their gunboats protected them. Unsupported by the *Arkansas,* which had broken down, Breckinridge withdrew.

[Alcée Fortier, *A History of Louisiana.*]

W. B. HATCHER

Baton Rouge, Seizure of (1810). Baton Rouge, on the Mississippi River, was in a portion of Spanish West Florida (between the Mississippi and the Perdido) to which the United States mistakenly asserted title as a part of the Louisiana Purchase*qv*, but of which it had not attempted to take possession. In September, 1810, American settlers in West Florida*qv* seized Baton Rouge, organized a convention, declared their independence of Spain, and invited the United States to annex their territory. President Madison disregarded their pretensions to independence, but promptly gave orders for the occupation of West Florida as territory belonging to the United States and Baton Rouge was occupied by American troops early in December, 1810.

[I. J. Cox, *The West Florida Controversy.*]

JULIUS W. PRATT

Battery, THE, southwestern tip of Manhattan Island and site of Dutch fortifications, so called because of the battery of cannon constructed there in 1693 by Gov. Fletcher. Later, it became a public park and was a popular pleasure ground and favorite promenade of New York citizens in the 18th and early 19th centuries. By 1858 it had fallen into disuse but by filling in it has been extended to an area of twenty-one acres including the Aquarium and historic landmarks.

[J. G. Wilson, *Memorial History of the City of New York.*]

A. C. FLICK

Battle Fleet, Cruise of the, Round the World (1907–9), was undertaken by order of President Theodore Roosevelt as a demonstration of national strength. The fleet, consisting of sixteen American battleships, sailed from Hampton Roads, Va., bound for San Francisco, on Dec. 16, 1907, under the command of Rear Admiral Robley D. Evans, by way of Rio de Janeiro and Magellan Strait. On May 6, 1908, the fleet reached San Francisco where, on May 9, Admiral Evans was relieved by Rear Admiral Charles M. Thomas. Five days later Admiral Thomas turned over his command to Rear Admiral Charles S. Sperry, who sailed from San Francisco for Hawaii on July 7. The squadron visited New Zealand, Australia, the Philippines, China and Japan, finally returning by way of the Suez Canal and the Mediterranean. It reached Hampton Roads on Feb. 22, 1909, after an absence of 434 days, of which 190 were spent in actual cruising. A month had been spent in Magdalena Bay in target practice and another month in Manila Bay in battle practice. The Battle Fleet visited every continent on the globe, sailed over every navigable ocean, and crossed the equator four times. The officers of the Fleet were entertained and feted by the rulers of nearly all countries visited, and naval greetings were exchanged with the warships of fourteen different nations.

[Franklin Matthews, *With the Battle Fleet;* Franklin Matthews, *Back to Hampton Roads;* R. D. Evans, *An Admiral's Log.*]

LOUIS H. BOLANDER

Battle Fleet, United States. *See* Fleet, The United States.

"Battle Hymn of the Republic," one of the most popular and inspiring of American patriotic hymns, was written (1861) by Mrs. Julia Ward Howe.

In the autumn of 1861 Mrs. Howe and her husband were in Washington, D. C., interested in hospital work under the Sanitary Commission[qv]. They had been outside the city on a mission in connection with their work and were returning in a carriage through an exceedingly dark night. They met a regiment of troops which was marching up the road and singing the familiar song known as "John Brown's Body," the music of which was written by William Steffe about 1852. Mrs. Howe remarked as the soldiers were passing that these were poor words to be set to such a glorious tune. Dr. Howe replied, "Julia, why do you not write better ones?" Mrs. Howe continued to turn the matter over in her mind and awakened from her sleep late that night when the words suddenly came to her, beginning "Mine eyes have seen the glory of the coming of the Lord." She arose and wrote down the entire hymn.

The poem was printed in the *Atlantic Monthly* for February, 1862. It at once became popular and spread over the entire country. Not only is it in all collections of patriotic American songs but is included in the hymnals of a number of churches as well.

[J. E. Richards and M. H. Elliott, *Julia Ward Howe,* Vol. I.]

WILLIAM STARR MYERS

Battleships. *See* Warships.

Battleships, Dummy. On Feb. 24, 1863, a scow with turret of tar-smeared barrel staves, wooden guns, clay furnace, pork barrel funnel and ludicrous mottoes painted across its false paddle box, floated down the Mississippi River by Federal seamen, caused the Confederates below Vicksburg to destroy the newly captured ironclad *Indianola.* A similar dummy released on a flood tide, Feb. 20, 1865, drew fire from Confederate batteries along Cape Fear River for several hours. The success of these facetious experiments was largely due to the sensation created by the monitor type of battleship.

[Richard S. West, Jr., *The Second Admiral, A Life of David Dixon Porter.*]

RICHARD S. WEST, JR.

Batts-Fallam Expedition (1671) was an expedition sent out from Fort Henry (site of Petersburg, Va.) by Col. Abraham Wood for the "finding out the waters on the other side of the mountains in order to discovery of the South sea." The leader was Capt. Thomas Batts, and the expedition was journalized by Robert Fallam. The party of five, including an Appamattox Indian chief, set out Sept. 1, 1671, crossed the Blue Ridge and the Allegheny range and pushed down the valley of Wood's (New) River to where that stream reaches the line of West Virginia, Sept. 17.

[C. W. Alvord and Lee Bidgood, *The First Explorations of the Trans-Allegheny Region.*]

SAMUEL C. WILLIAMS

Baumes Law, The, one of a series of amendments to the New York Penal Code, sponsored by Sen. Caleb H. Baumes of Newburgh, was passed by the legislature in 1926, to combat the so-called crime wave that swept the country in the aftermath of the World War. Its provision for a life sentence for fourth offenders was then widely acclaimed, but is now regarded as arbitrary and frequently unjustified.

[National Commission on Law Observance and Enforcement, *Report.*]

W. BROOKE GRAVES

Bay Path, THE, was a trail from the Connecticut River to Massachusetts Bay at or near Boston. Conversely, the same trail from the Bay to the Connecticut River would be the Connecticut Path. Some writers reserve the name Bay Path for such a trail in Massachusetts and that of Connecticut Path for one in Connecticut. There seems no question that from 1648 there was the New Path westward through Weston, Sudbury, Marlboro, Worcester, Brookfield and Brimfield to Springfield. Similarly, there is no question that after 1683 a Path ran southwestward from the vicinity of Boston to Woodstock, Conn., and thence westward to Hartford. Obviously the New Path was not used by the earliest settlers in the Connecticut Valley, but some claim that the second or southern route was the Old Path which was used by the Hooker party in 1636 and by the other early colonists. There is, however, considerable evidence that the Old Path followed a middle route coinciding in part with the eastern section of the second Path and with the portion of the New Path west of Brimfield. Competent recent authorities have tended to accept this middle route as the original Old Path used in the 1630's. But it must be admitted that the evidence is incomplete and not incontrovertible. On the other hand, the existence of the second route earlier than 1683 is not adequately supported by contemporary evidence. It is even possible that the original Old Path did not follow exactly any one of the three routes. All three routes assume a Path between Springfield and Hartford which would have been on the east bank of the Connecticut at least as far south as East Windsor.

[Florence S. M. Crofut, *Guide to History and Historical Sites of Connecticut;* Mathias Spiess in *Manchester* (Conn.) *Evening Herald*, Oct. 19, 1934; Levi B. Chase, *The Bay Path and Along the Way.*]

GEORGE MATTHEW DUTCHER

Bay Psalm Book, THE, so called from its origin in Massachusetts Bay Colony[qv], was the earliest book known to have been printed within the present boundaries of the United States. Begun in 1639 and finished in 1640, it was printed in Cambridge, Mass., by Stephen Daye, the first printer of the English colonies. Eleven copies are known to exist of which six are imperfect.

[C. Evans, *American Bibliography;* J. T. Winterich, *Early American Books.*]

CARL L. CANNON

Bayard-Chamberlain Treaty, THE, drafted by a joint commission at Washington, Feb. 15, 1888, was intended to clarify the respective powers and rights of Great Britain and the United States in the waters of Newfoundland and the adjacent provinces. The Treaty of Washington[qv], extending valuable privileges to American fishermen in Canadian waters, had been abrogated as of July 1, 1885, and more stringent and somewhat obscure provisions of the Convention of 1818[qv] were now effective. Rigorous enforcement by the Canadian authorities, seizure and forfeiture of American vessels, retaliatory legislation, jingoistic fulminations by press and politicians, had created a situation which threatened peaceful relations. The new treaty provided for a joint commission to define American rights in Canadian waters, recognized exclusive Canadian jurisdiction in bays whose outlets were less than six miles in width, remedied several minor American grievances and promised further concessions should the United States remove tariff duties on Canadian fish. The Senate rejected the treaty on Aug. 21, 1888, but more than twenty years later when the protracted fisheries dispute[qv] was arbitrated at The Hague, the substance of several of its more significant provisions appears in the award which that tribunal rendered against American claims.

[Joseph I. Doran, *Our Fishery Rights in the North Atlantic;* Allan Nevins, *Grover Cleveland.*]

W. A. ROBINSON

Bayard v. Singleton (N. C. Superior Court, 1787). This case is important because it is the first reported decision under a written constitution overruling a law as unconstitutional. (Four years earlier than cases cited in 1 Kent. Com., 450; State v. Glenn, 52 N. C. 324.) The defendant moved dismissal of the case according to an act of the legislature which required the courts to dismiss, upon affidavit, suits against persons holding forfeited Tory (enemy alien) estates. The court overruled the motion and declared that the constitution of the state gives every man a right to a decision concerning property by jury trial. If the legislature could thus alter or repeal the constitution it would thereby destroy its own existence, and might even take away, summarily, one's life.

[*North Carolina Reports*, I; H. T. Lefler, *North Carolina History told by Contemporaries.*] ROBERT W. WINSTON

Baynton, Wharton and Morgan (1763–98) was a firm of Philadelphia merchants which virtually monopolized the rich western trade at the close of the French and Indian War[qv] and which by its contacts in Philadelphia, Lancaster, Pittsburgh, Kaskaskia[qv] and London exploited the West in one of the most significant commercial enterprises of the day. Before the legal opening of Indian trade, it sent the first cargo of goods westward (1765) under protection of passes by George Croghan[qv], Deputy Superintendent for Indian affairs. This premature attempt to capture Indian trade infuriated the "Black Boys"[qv] who attacked the pack train and destroyed the shipment. Soon, however, the firm had 600 pack horses and wagons on the road between Philadelphia and Pittsburgh and some 300 boatmen on the Ohio.

Its unscrupulous business methods, Gen. Gage's curtailment of Indian trading posts and his restrictions on the Indian department, together with the collapse of trade due to illicit French suppliers and the growing competition of another Philadelphia firm, David Franks and Company, combined to cause a sharp decline in its fortunes during 1767. The company entered into voluntary receivership and withdrew completely from the Illinois trading venture in 1772.

To recoup its losses and those of the "Suff'ring Traders"[qv] of 1763, Baynton, Wharton and Morgan, with the firm of Simon, Trent, Levy and Franks, organized The Indiana Company[qv] to secure land grants for losses incurred through Indian attacks. Wharton and Trent represented their respective firms. Sir William Johnson's ingenious handling of the Indians at Fort Stanwix[qv] in 1768 resulted in the Six Nations[qv] ceding to this company 2,500,000 acres of land, now a part of West Virginia. Immediate objections arose, royal confirmation was withheld and Wharton and Trent were sent to London to negotiate for The Indiana Company. Here the claims of other groups brought about the formation of the Grand Ohio Company[qv] or Walpole Company (1769) in which the Indiana land grant was merged, but Wharton excluded Baynton and Morgan, thus incurring their bitter enmity. The outbreak of the Revolution caused this project to collapse. (*See also* Vandalia Company.)

[A. T. Volwiler, *George Croghan and the Westward Movement, 1741-1782.*] JULIAN P. BOYD

Bayonne Decree, THE. *See* Napoleon's Decrees.

Bayou Teche Expedition was a Federal raid directed by Gen. Banks in April and May, 1863, from Brashear City (Berwick Bay) to Alexandria, La., on Red River, to disperse the Confederate state government at Opelousas and to prevent Confederate reinforcements being sent from that quarter to Vicksburg[qv], then besieged by Gen. Grant.

[A. Fortier, *History of Louisiana*, IV.] WALTER PRICHARD

Beall's Raid on Lake Erie (Sept. 19, 1864) was an unsuccessful attempt to capture the revenue cutter *Michigan* and free Confederate prisoners on Johnson's Island[qv], Sandusky Bay, Ohio.

[J. F. Rhodes, *History of the United States from the Compromise of 1850*, Vol. V.] CHARLES H. COLEMAN

Bear Flag Revolt, THE (1846), climaxed a decade of suspicion and jealousy between the Anglo-Californians of the Sacramento Valley and the Mexican authorities. Unlike the American residents of Monterey and Los Angeles, many of whom were closely connected with prominent California families through business relations, friendship or even marriage, the American residents of northern central California formed a community by themselves. Restive under Mexican rule and over-anxious to assert their racial superiority, they had a deep-seated fear of their fate if the California authorities should get them completely under control.

Some color was indeed given to this fear by the treatment accorded the fur traders Smith and Pattie in the previous decade and especially by the deportation in 1840 of Isaac Graham and some forty of his friends. Accordingly it is not surprising that, when the settlers learned of the Hawk's Peak episode[qv] and Frémont's expulsion from California in March, 1846, they should have believed the rumors that the government planned to seize and expel all foreigners in the province.

Uneasiness gave place to alarm when the news came (later proved false) that 250 Californians were advancing on Sacramento. The Americans immediately repaired to Frémont's quarters at the Marysville Buttes where, in the middle of May, he had encamped on his return from Oregon. This much criticized defiance of the local authorities by Frémont was declared by him to be "the first step in the conquest of California." The next step was the seizure, early in June, by

Ezekial Merritt and a dozen other Americans of a large band of government horses which Gen. Castro had obtained from Gen. M. G. Vallejo at Sonoma and which were being driven to San José by way of Sutter's Fort[qv]. This was an act of war and it was decided that the third step must be the capture of Sonoma, the chief stronghold of the Californians north of the Bay Region. The actual capture of the quiet little pueblo at early dawn, June 14, 1846, was a rather ludicrous affair; "To whom shall we surrender?", demanded the kindly general's wife. After a scene of no little confusion and considerable imbibing of Vallejo's wine, simple articles of capitulation were arranged and signed.

Then followed the erection of the Republic of California under the leadership of William B. Ide. To signalize it, William Todd designed a flag from a piece of unbleached cloth five feet long and three feet wide. Facing a red star was a grizzly bear which gave both the flag and the republic its familiar name. A proclamation setting forth the justification and purposes of the revolution was prepared; but before the new government could get under way, July 10, 1846, the American flag was officially sent to Sonoma.

The actual accomplishments of the Bear Flag Revolt were thus of little importance, but had not the Mexican War[qv] intervened, either "Ide or Frémont might have stood out as the creator of a new republic, the Sam Houston of the Pacific Coast."

[R. G. Cleland, *A History of California: the American Period;* W. B. Ide, *Who Conquered California?*]

OSGOOD HARDY

Bear Paw Mountains, Indian Fight at (Oct. 3–5, 1877). At the end of their long campaign starting in Idaho, June, 1877, the Nez Percé Indians[qv] under Joseph (Hinmaton-yalatkit) were surrounded by Col. Miles' command in the Bear Paws of northern Montana. After a brave three days' resistance, Joseph surrendered, ending the Nez Percé War[qv].

[Nelson A. Miles, *Personal Recollections.*]

PAUL I. WELLMAN

Bear River, Calif., gold deposits were discovered in July, 1848, some six months after the strike at Sutter's[qv] mill. Some of the most picturesque mining camps in California collected on the river and its tributaries, including Red Dog, Dutch Flat and You Bet.

[O. C. Coy, *Gold Days.*]

CARL L. CANNON

Bear River, Utah, Battle of (Jan. 29, 1863). Indians, on friendly terms with the Mormons[qv], had preyed upon Overland Mail Route[qv] emigrants for fifteen years. To subdue and control them Col. P. E. Connor led California troops from Camp Douglas to Bear River. There, with scarcely 200 effectives, he fought four hours against 300 well-armed Indians, smashing their villages, capturing their animals and stores, and killing over 200 of them. His own loss was fifteen killed and forty-eight wounded.

[*War of the Rebellion—Official Records of the Union and Confederate Armies,* Series I, Vol. L, Parts I and II.]

ROBERT S. THOMAS

Bears, Bear Hunters and Bear Stories. When Lewis and Clark[qv] in 1806 returned from their historic expedition, they published to the world, along with other wonders, accounts of the grizzly bear and its ferocity. A naturalist named it *Ursus horribilis*—and in hunters' stories the grizzly has ever since been *horrible,* though his familiar names, "Old Ephraim" and "Moccasin Joe," indicate truthful modifications of the reputation. The grizzly certainly would fight when cornered, and often he imagined himself cornered when he wasn't. Stories like that of Hugh Glass and his hand-to-hand fight with a grizzly became an enduring part of American lore. The fights between bulls and grizzlies arranged by early Californians were an American counterpart to English "bear baiting" but more heroic.

The discovery of the grizzly increased the fame of the more widespread black bear, known, indeed, to have killed a few men, though the "bear hug" is a fable. Bear hunters became a type as distinct as keelboatmen[qv] or Indian fighters. In 1827 David Crockett of Tennessee was sent to Congress almost purely on his reputation as a "bar hunter"; he killed 105 bears in one season —and was soon talked of for the Presidency. Empowered by mother wit, he so narrated his exploits with bears that his autobiography remains an American classic. "Mighty hunters" like Wade Hampton of South Carolina followed Crockett. The tall tale has had no richer subject than the bear.

By 1925 dangerously approaching extinction, the grizzly lives on, not only in national parks but more nationally in the paintings of Western artists like Frederick Remington and Charles M. Russell, in many books, and in folk talk. Black Bruin's range has become exceedingly restricted, but he is known wherever nursery books and sportsman magazines are read or country people tell stories.

[J. Cecil Alter, *James Bridger;* Theodore H. Hittell, *The Adventures of James Capen Adams;* Joaquin Miller,

True Bear Stories; John G. Neihardt, *The Song of Hugh Glass;* Theodore Roosevelt, *The Wilderness Hunter;* Wm. H. Wright, *The Grizzly Bear.*]

J. FRANK DOBIE

Beaubien Land Claim, THE, was an effort to homestead a portion of the Fort Dearborn[qv] military reservation at Chicago. The claimant, Jean Baptiste Beaubien, had long lived on the tract as a trader, and in 1835 he entered some seventy-five acres of it at the land office. The commandant ignored this title and a prolonged legal contest ended in its rejection by the United States Supreme Court in 1839. Immense wealth hinged upon the issue and the contest aroused intense local public interest.

[*U. S. Reports,* 13 Peters, 498-518; Henry H. Hurlbut, *Chicago Antiquities.*]

M. M. QUAIFE

Beaufort, S. C., founded in 1711 on Port Royal Island in a region where Spanish, French and English had previously failed to maintain themselves, was the second permanent settlement in South Carolina.

[H. A. M. Smith, Beaufort, the Original Plan and Early Settlers, *S. C. Hist. and Gen. Mag.,* IX, 141-160, 1908.]

FRANCIS B. SIMKINS

Beauharnois, Fort, a French post and Jesuit[qv] mission, was erected in 1727 on Lake Pepin to keep the Sioux[qv] from attacking France's new line of communication between Lake Superior[qv] and the West; and to prevent the Sioux from allying with the Foxes[qv]. It was practically abandoned in 1728.

[Pierre Margry, ed., *Découvertes et Établissements des Français,* VI.]

GRACE LEE NUTE

Beaver Dam Creek, Battle of. *See* Mechanicsville, Battle of.

Beaver Dams, Battle of (June 24, 1813). Col. Boerstler with a detachment of about 600 men left Fort George[qv], the evening of the 23d, under orders to march by way of Queenston, Ont., to the De Cou house to disperse FitzGibbon's British irregulars and Indians. On the 24th the Americans were ambushed a little east of Beaver Dams and forced to surrender.

[Louis L. Babcock, *The War of 1812 on the Niagara Frontier.*]

ROBERT W. BINGHAM

Beaver Hats. America produced quantities of beaver fur, but men's beaver hats were all imported until the middle of the 17th century or after. Virginia in 1662 sought to stimulate manufacture by offering a subsidy of ten pounds of tobacco for every good hat made from native fur or wool. But once begun, hat manufacture grew rapidly. By 1731 the hatmakers of London were complaining to Parliament that New England and New York were producing 10,000 hats annually and exporting them not only to British possessions, but to Spain, Portugal, the West Indies, etc. In 1732 Parliament forbade American makers to export hats, even among the American colonies. Seven years' apprenticeship was also required and no Negroes were permitted to work at the trade. New England calmly ignored or evaded the law, which remained in force until the Revolutionary War. Silk hat manufacture began in earnest about 1835 and soon forced beaver out.

[H. H. Manchester, *Sixty Centuries of Hatmaking;* J. Leander Bishop, *History of American Manufactures, 1608-1860.*]

ALVIN F. HARLOW

Beaver Money (1849). Lack of currency in the Pacific Northwest led to the private coinage of gold dust into coins called "beaver money" because a beaver was pictured on each coin. They were also stamped with their weight, the initials of the partners of the issuing company, and the date 1849. These illegal, but useful, coins quickly disappeared from circulation because they contained 8% more gold than the United States coins.

[Charles H. Carey, *A General History of Oregon Prior to 1861.*]

ROBERT MOULTON GATKE

Beaver Trade. *See* various articles on the Fur Trade.

Becknell's Expeditions. William Becknell, sometimes referred to as the "Father of the Santa Fé Trail," set out from Franklin, Mo., for Santa Fé, N. Mex., June 10, 1821, on a trading expedition. He is believed by most authorities to be the first American merchant to reach the New Mexican capital after the establishment of Mexican independence. After a profitable trade he returned in January, 1822. His success was responsible for the rapid development of commercial relations with Santa Fé. He later made a second trip in which he departed from the regular trail by the Cimarron Division. This trip was memorable in that wagons were first used on the plains.

[W. J. Ghent, *Early Far West;* Wm. Becknell, *Journal of Santa Fé Expedition, 1821.*]

CARL L. CANNON

Bedford, Fort (Bedford, Pa.). Fort Raystown, built in 1757 by Col. John Armstrong as a frontier defense, was in July, 1758, much enlarged and strengthened by Col. Henry Bouquet for the use of the Forbes Expedition[qv]. Here Bouquet was joined in September by Gen. Forbes and the Virginia troops under Col. George Washington for the advance along the Forbes Road[qv], which began four miles westward. Rechristened Fort Bedford (1759), it was the principal depot for supplies and troops between Carlisle and Fort Pitt[qv]. The fort withstood a six weeks' siege during Pontiac's Conspiracy[qv], but in 1769 was bloodlessly yielded to James Smith's "Black Boys"[qv]. Dilapidated, it was abandoned before the Revolution.

[*Report of . . . the Frontier Forts of Pennsylvania*, I.]

E. DOUGLAS BRANCH

Bedini Riots, THE, were public demonstrations against the Papal Nuncio, Monsignor Gaetano Bedini, on Dec. 31, 1853, and Jan. 14, 1854, on the occasion of his visit to Cincinnati, Ohio. Nativistic, Know-Nothing[qqv] and anti-Catholic prejudice had been aroused by press and speeches, prior to his arrival. On the night of Dec. 31 a disorderly mob marched to the Cathedral Rectory, but was dispersed after rioting had broken out and one citizen and one policeman had been injured fatally. The demonstration on Jan. 14 was attended by no fighting, but an effigy of Monsignor Bedini was burned and threats were made against the Catholic clergy and churches.

[M. E. Thomas, *Nativism in the Old Northwest.*]]

ALFRED G. STRITCH

Beech Seal. A term applied to one of the popular methods of punishment employed by the Green Mountain Boys[qv] during the controversial days when Vermont was known as the New Hampshire Grants[qv] and the settlers rose in resentment against the efforts of New York to evict them from their lands, chastising offending agents with the pliable twigs of the wilderness, thereby ironically setting their seal, in allusion to the Great Seal of New Hampshire, upon their backs.

[Zadock Thompson, *History of Vermont.*]

LEON W. DEAN

Beecher Island, Battle of (1868). Col. George A. Forsyth, leading fifty experienced scouts, in search of Indians who had pillaged western Kansas, encamped, Sept. 16, 1868, on the Arickaree River, fifteen miles south of Wray, Colo. Attacked next morning by about 1000 Cheyennes and Sioux[qqv], led by Roman Nose, the scouts moved onto a sandy island and with butcher knives and tin plates scooped out rifle pits. In the first Indian charge, Roman Nose fell, Forsyth was wounded, and Lt. F. H. Beecher was killed. The Indians made several unsuccessful charges, then settled to a siege. Despite wounds, death and the stifling odor from their dead horses, the scouts held on. Emissaries eluded the Indians at night and sought help. On the ninth day troops arrived. Five scouts were dead, eighteen wounded and the remainder almost exhausted.

[Geo. A. Forsyth, *The Story of the Soldier.*]

LE ROY R. HAFEN

Beecher's Bibles was the term applied during the Kansas troubles[qv] to Sharps Rifles[qv]. In March, 1856, at New Haven, Henry Ward Beecher addressed a meeting at which a subscription was taken to equip a company of free-state emigrants to Kansas. Beecher said that for slave holders in Kansas a Sharps Rifle was a greater moral argument than a Bible. The first rifle was subscribed by Prof. Benjamin Silliman, of the Yale College faculty, the second by the pastor of the church in which the meeting was held and Mr. Beecher pledged the last twenty-five for Plymouth Church, Brooklyn.

[J. F. Rhodes, *History of the United States.*]

JAMES ELLIOTT WALMSLEY

Beef Trust Cases. In 1902 three large packers —Swift, Armour[qv] and Morris—formed the National Packing Company in an effort to secure control of packing houses in Kansas City, East St. Louis and Omaha. The Government promptly attacked these and three other concerns, charging monopolistic practices which had resulted in a large degree of control over the slaughtering and packing of meat. In 1905 the Supreme Court (196 U. S. 394) upheld the Government for the most part, but failed to order dissolution of the National Packing Company, and monopolistic practices continued. Thereupon the Government sought an injunction, but the individuals involved successfully pleaded immunity from criminal prosecution because they had previously been compelled to testify against themselves. In 1910 further attacks on the packers were again unsuccessful, but in 1920, after an extensive Federal Trade Commission[qv] investigation, the packers agreed to dispose of their varied stockyards interests, their retail meat markets and the wholesaling of lines not directly related to meat packing[qv].

[Harry W. Laidler, *Concentration of Control in American Industry.*]

R. E. WESTMEYER

Beekman Patent, The, granted April 22, 1697, by Gov. Fletcher to Col. Henry Beekman, was a tract sixteen miles square in Dutchess County, N. Y., embracing the present towns of Beekman, Union Vale, a portion of La Grange, and nearly all of Pawling and Dover. The death of Bellomont, Fletcher's successor, cut short an attempt to vacate the patent as an "extravagant grant." A new patent for the same land was issued by Cornbury in 1703.

[Frank Hasbrouck, *History of Dutchess County.*]

A. C. FLICK

Beer. *See* Brewing.

Bees, Husking, Quilting, etc. In the New England and Middle colonies and on the early and Midwestern frontiers various communal activities formed an important exception to the ordinarily individualistic habits of American farm families. The motivation was both economic and social. Log rollings and barn raisings[qv] necessitated collective effort; corn husking and threshing[qv] were most efficiently done by common endeavor. Machinery and specialized labor ended all these practices except for the threshing ring which continues where farms are not large and farming is diversified. Corn husking, cradling, threshing among men, sewing, quilting, apple paring among women, roused the competitive spirit, made sport of work, and gave public recognition to the champion worker. Courting opportunities were afforded the young people. The finder of a red ear at a husking bee was awarded an extra pull at the jug. Sociability, neighborliness and conversation were promoted. The educational counterparts of these activities were spelling bees[qv] and ciphering matches. Maple sugaring-offs in the North and cane sorghum boilings in the South made party occasions of work. The round-up in the cattle country was an adaptation of the same general principle. Competitive aspects survive in rodeos[qv] and various contests at agricultural fairs[qv].

[P. W. Bidwell and J. I. Falconer, *History of Agriculture in the Northern United States, 1620-1860.*]

HARVEY L. CARTER

Beet Sugar. Though sugar beets were grown experimentally near Philadelphia about 1830 there is no record that sugar was made from them. A small factory built in Massachusetts eight years later proved a failure. Soon afterwards Mormon[qv] pioneers erected a mill in Utah but only succeeded in making syrup. After the Civil War high sugar prices encouraged experiments with both sorghum and beets. Machinery was imported from Germany and France for beet factories in Illinois, Iowa and Wisconsin, where a few tons of sugar were made, and a larger project was promoted in California. During the 1870's Maine and Delaware offered a bonus for beet sugar manufactured within their limits, and factories were built at Portland and Wilmington. Small establishments were also erected elsewhere in the East, but none lasted more than a few seasons. By 1880, however, the industry was on a commercial basis in California, and soon thereafter Spreckles, a sugar millionaire from Hawaii, and the Oxnards, prominent refiners, erected factories in California and Nebraska. In 1892, when the output reached 14,000 tons, representatives of six companies met in San Francisco and formed an association to promote the industry.

By 1910 more beet than cane sugar was made in the continental United States. Ten years later the output exceeded 1,000,000 tons and in 1936–37 it reached nearly 1,700,000 tons.

Today eighty or more active factories in sixteen states buy beets under contract from nearly 90,000 farmers. Climatic and soil conditions, the varying profit of competing crops and distance from the coastal cane sugar refineries, which make a product chemically identical with beet sugar, favor the concentration of the industry in the mountain states, where Colorado leads the nation's output, and in California, Michigan and Nebraska. Beet pulp, a by-product of sugar manufacture, is used for feeding cattle and fits into the economy of stock-raising communities. Many minors and immigrants, especially from Mexico, work in the beet fields during the crop season. The United States ranks next to Russia and Germany as the largest beet sugar producing country and even under present quota limitations makes more than one-tenth of the world's supply.

[U. S. Census reports; U. S. Department of Agriculture reports; U. S. Beet Sugar Association, records; V. S. Clark, *History of Manufactures in the United States.*]

VICTOR S. CLARK

Belgian Relief (1914–19) was the means by which some 7,300,000 Belgian civilians, inside the German army lines during the World War[qv], received necessary food imports through the naval blockade. Created as a temporary committee in October, 1914, by a group of Americans, with the approval of their government, The Commission for Relief in Belgium (C.R.B.) became the neutral channel through which more than 5,100,000 tons of provisions and supplies passed into Belgium and were distributed by local Belgian committees. From 1915 some 1,800,000

French civilians in the occupied areas of northern France were included in the relief.

The functions of the C.R.B. were to secure basic foodstuffs by purchase or gift, to transport these commodities into Belgium and to guarantee their equitable distribution under the supervision of American or neutral volunteer workers. Delicate semidiplomatic relationships with belligerent and neutral powers, and public opinion widely mobilized, kept the door to Belgium open. Relief requirements were met by gifts amounting to $52,000,000 in cash and kind collected by volunteer committees in America, the British Empire and elsewhere, by British and French government subsidies totaling $314,000,000 and by American Government loans of $380,000,000 made to Belgium and France in 1917–19. Altogether the C.R.B. disbursed $894,797,000 with an administrative expense of less than half of 1% (.43%). The price level of breadstuffs in Belgium remained about 15% below commercial prices in surrounding countries.

From October, 1914, to July, 1919, Herbert Hoover, with his associates, directed and controlled the complicated operations.

[G. I. Gay and H. H. Fisher, *Public Relations of the Commission for Relief in Belgium;* G. I. Gay, *Statistical Review of Relief Operations.*]

PERRIN C. GALPIN

Belknap, Fort (Tex.), named for William G. Belknap, was built in 1850 on the Salt Fork of the Brazos River to afford frontier protection; also to guard the "Lower Indian Reserve" set aside by Texas. The tribes on the Reserve were the Caddo, Anadarkho, Waco, Tahwaccaro and Tonkawa.

[J. Pike, *Scout and Ranger*, ed. Carl L. Cannon.]

CARL L. CANNON

Belknap Scandal, THE (1876), was one of the series of scandals which marked Grant's second administration. Secretary of War W. W. Belknap's first wife agreed to secure a lucrative post tradership at Fort Sill^qv^ for C. P. March of New York on condition that she should receive one-half the profits. The trader at the post paid March $12,000 a year not to take the place and March paid $6000 to Mrs. Belknap. After her death he paid the money to the Secretary. Just before a House investigation committee moved to impeach him, Belknap resigned. The impeachment trial in April and May resulted in acquittal, largely on the ground that the Senate had no jurisdiction over a resigned officer.

[W. B. Hesseltine, *Ulysses S. Grant, Politician.*]

W. B. HESSELTINE

Bell Telephone Company. *See* American Telephone and Telegraph Company.

Belle Isle, an island in the James River at Richmond used as a prison for enlisted men captured by the Confederacy. In use continuously after the Battle of Bull Run^qv^, the prison held approximately 10,000 men by the end of 1863. At that time, because the prisoners constituted a drain on the food supply and were the objectives of several cavalry raids (*see* Dahlgren's Raid), the captives were sent to a new prison at Andersonville^qv^, Ga.

[W. B. Hesseltine, *Civil War Prisons.*]

W. B. HESSELTINE

Belleau Wood, Battle of (June 2–July 7, 1918). The German 7th Army, under von Boehn, driving southward from the Chemin des Dames toward Paris, on May 31 approached the Marne at Chateau-Thierry^qv^. Just west of there the American 2nd Division (Bundy) hastened into support of the French 21st Corps (Degoutte), the left corps of Duchesne's French 6th Army. Forcing back minor French units, by June 3 the Germans uncovered the American front line, which stood fast and stopped them. On June 6 the Americans assumed the offensive. Against bitter resistance the 4th (Marine) Brigade (Harbord) recaptured Bouresches and the southern edge of the Bois de Belleau, while on its right the 3rd Infantry Brigade (Lewis) advanced nearly to Vaux.

Continuing their local offensive, the Americans took most of Belleau Wood on June 8–11, and despite desperate counterattacks completed its capture June 21. At noon, July 1, following an intense artillery preparation, the 3rd Infantry Brigade stormed Vaux and La Roche Wood. The division front, everywhere established on favorable ground, was turned over to the American 26th Division, July 9, the 2nd Division retiring to a support position.

[Charles R. Howland, *A Military History of the World War;* Joseph M. Hanson, *History of the American Combat Divisions, The Stars and Stripes.*]

JOSEPH MILLS HANSON

Bellefontaine was the first permanent settlement of English-speaking people in the Old Northwest^qv^. The spring which gave it its name, "la belle fontaine," was located a short distance south of the present town of Waterloo, Ill. The first settlers, mainly veterans who had served with George Rogers Clark, established themselves with their families at Bellefontaine in the fall of 1779. At an election held there in 1782 fifteen Americans voted. The Federal census of 1800 enumerated 286 inhabitants, making Bellefontaine the third largest settlement in the Illinois Territory. As Illinois became more populous, Bellefontaine, never a compact village, gradually lost its identity.

[C. W. Alvord, *Kaskaskia Records, 1778-1790;* C. W. Alvord, *The Illinois Country, 1673-1818.*]

PAUL M. ANGLE

Bellefontaine, Fort or Cantonment (1805–26), on the south side of the Missouri, four miles from its junction with the Mississippi, was built under direction of Gen. James Wilkinson, in the fall of 1805, by Lt. Col. Jacob Kingsbury and two companies of the First Infantry. Constructed on low land near Coldwater Creek, where a fine spring gave name to the place, it was moved after the flood of 1810 to the top of the hill and there served as military headquarters for the Middle West until the erection of Jefferson Barracks[qv] in 1826.

[Kate L. Gregg, Building of the First American Fort West of the Mississippi, *Missouri Historical Review*, July, 1936.]

KATE L. GREGG

Bellevue War, THE. W. W. Brown, who kept a hotel at Bellevue, Jackson County, Iowa, was believed to be the leader of a gang of outlaws in that vicinity. When Sheriff William A. Warren attempted to arrest Brown and several other men on April 1, 1840, a fight resulted. Four of the posse and three of the alleged bandits (including Brown) were killed and thirteen of Brown's band were captured. The following day the citizens voted on the penalty, dropping white beans in a box for hanging, red beans for whipping. The red beans predominated and the men were flogged and sent down the river.

[Harvey Reid, *Thomas Cox;* John C. Parish, White Beans for Hanging, in *The Palimpsest*, Vol. I.]

RUTH A. GALLAHER

Belligerents are states or organized communities which are engaged in lawful warfare. Strictly speaking, only sovereign states are legally qualified to declare war and to acquire the status of belligerents and to exercise in consequence the rights of belligerents in respect to neutral powers. But international law[qv] has frequently recognized the *de facto* belligerent status of protectorates and other dependent states; and it has also found it necessary to accord belligerent status to colonies in rebellion against the mother country and to other "insurgent" communities which have been able to establish control over a definite area of territory and to maintain a separate government or *de facto* independence over a period of time. Recognition by third states of the belligerency of an insurgent community gives to the insurgents the right to apply in their regard the law of contraband and blockade[qqv] and otherwise to exercise the rights of land and naval warfare. The recognition by President Monroe in 1822 of the belligerency of certain of the South and Central American colonies preceded the recognition of their independence (*see* Monroe Doctrine). A sharp controversy developed between the United States and Great Britain in 1861 over the recognition by the latter of the belligerency of the Confederate States, Great Britain claiming that the earlier establishment of a blockade by President Lincoln had been itself a recognition of their belligerency (*see* Prize Cases; Alabama Claims). In the case of the *Ambrose Light* a United States Circuit Court held in 1885 that acts of warfare committed by unrecognized insurgents were acts of piracy; but this position has been sharply criticized. The recognition by the United States on Sept. 3, 1918, of a "state of belligerency" between the Czech army and the Central Powers was based upon the necessities of war rather than upon the *de facto* character of the Czech government.

[H. W. Briggs, *The Law of Nations: Cases, Documents and Notes;* C. G. Fenwick, *International Law.*]

C. G. FENWICK

Belmont, Mo., Battle of (Nov. 7, 1861), was Grant's (U.) first Civil War battle and first defeat. Frémont ordered the attack on Belmont to prevent Polk at Columbus, Ky., from aiding the Confederates in Missouri. Steaming from Cairo, Ill., Grant landed five miles above Belmont and drove Gen. G. J. Pillow's men to the river and set fire to their camp. Polk, crossing with re-enforcements and aided by the Columbus batteries, drove Grant to his transports.

[U. S. Grant, *Personal Memoirs; Battles and Leaders of the Civil War.*]

W. C. MALLALIEU

Beloved Woman. This was a title bestowed by the Cherokee[qv] Indians on an outstanding woman of the tribe, who was thereby entitled to speak in councils and to decide the fate of captives. The most famous of these was Nancy Ward who frequently, like her uncle the great Chief Attakullakulla, proved her friendship for the white people.

SAMUEL C. WILLIAMS

Belt, Indian. *See* Wampum Belt, The.

Beltrán-Espejo Expedition, THE. When the

soldier-escort of the Rodríguez expedition^qv^ returned from "New Mexico" (1582), the Franciscans^qv^ on the frontier at Santa Bárbara (southern Chihuahua) were alarmed for the safety of two missionaries who had remained at Puaráy. With fifteen volunteer soldiers Fray Bernardino Beltrán started north (November, 1582) to rescue his colleagues. Upon reaching the Pueblo country, he learned that they had been killed; but the soldiers refused to return before exploring the country.

We have no account from Beltrán regarding what happened; our knowledge rests on later statements of soldiers, especially Luxán and Espejo. The latter, desiring to emulate Hernán Cortés by developing a "new" Mexico, largely financed the expedition and tried to dominate it. His report added much detailed information of the Pueblo country and people; his exaggerations regarding population, resources and mining prospects were somewhat discounted by Luxán.

The expedition failed in its immediate objective, but its favorable reports of the country strengthened the resolve of secular and religious authorities to colonize and evangelize New Mexico.

[G. P. Hammond and A. Rey, eds., *Luxán: The Espejo Expedition into New Mexico;* H. E. Bolton, ed., *Spanish Exploration in the Southwest.*]

LANSING B. BLOOM

Bemis Heights, Battles of. *See* Freeman's Farm, Battles of.

Bender Family, THE, consisted of a middle-aged man and wife, son and daughter (though the parentage is questioned) who settled in a prairie cabin in southeastern Kansas in 1871. Here they fed and lodged passing travelers, and killed an occasional one for his money. Suspicion fell upon them and they fled in May, 1873, barely escaping a citizens' posse. They were pursued into the Indian Territory^qv^, but their fate remains a mystery. At least eleven bodies were found buried near their cabin.

[John T. James, *The Benders in Kansas.*]

ALVIN F. HARLOW

Benefactions and Gifts, strictly, include bequests but are best considered to be philanthropic donations made during the lifetime of donors. In 1889 Andrew Carnegie wrote: "The day is not far distant when the man who dies leaving behind him millions of available wealth, which were free for him to administer during life, will pass away 'unwept, unhonored, and unsung,' no matter to what use he leaves the dross which he cannot take with him. Of such as these the public verdict will be: The man who dies thus rich dies disgraced."

Carnegie distributed $350,000,000, or nine tenths of his wealth, during his lifetime in countless gifts including 8000 church organs, 3000 libraries, appropriations to 500 universities and colleges, and eight foundations (1896–1916) capitalized at $280,500,000. John D. Rockefeller's benefactions included $600,000,000 to five foundations (1901–23). The John D. Rockefellers, father and son, gave $50,000,000 to the University of Chicago; Sen. and Mrs. Leland Stanford $25,000,000 to Stanford University; George Eastman more than $25,000,000 to the University of Rochester and the Massachusetts Institute of Technology. The history of large American benefactions in the 1900's includes such other names as Jules S. Bache, George F. Baker, Curtis Bok, George G. and Ella S. Booth, Henry Buhl, Jr., Dr. Godfrey Cabot, James Couzens, James B. Duke, Henry Ford, Henry C. Frick, Charles Garland, Murry and Simon Guggenheim, Edward S. and Stephen V. Harkness, Charles Hayden, Anna T. Jeanes, Augustus Juilliard, W. K. Kellogg, Atwater Kent, S. S. Kresge, Lucius N. Littauer, John Markle, Israel Matz, Andrew W. Mellon, Gordon McKay, Gustav Oberlaender, Horace H. Rackham, Julius Rosenwald, Mrs. Russell Sage, Leopold Schepp, Caroline Stokes, Mrs. Henry A. Strong, Frank K. Sturgis, Charles R. Walgreen, Mrs. William Ziegler.

The donor of smaller sums contributes locally to various social welfare agencies and bodies, educational and religious institutions, perhaps a community trust or chest. For the decade 1921–30 the John Price Jones Corporation estimates the total charitable budget for the nation at more than twenty and three-quarters billions, of which foundations and community trusts may have contributed 9.16%. Of this huge sum, education received the largest share (43%); race relations, less than 1%. For the years 1930–37 American benefactions and gifts probably exceeded four and one-half billions. State and Federal distribution of great sums raised through borrowing and taxation has doubtless decreased but has not yet irreparably impaired the flow of private benefactions.

[Andrew Carnegie, *The Gospel of Wealth;* Frederick P. Keppel, *The Foundation, Its Place in American Life;* Hollis, *Philanthropic Foundations and Higher Education.*]

HOWARD J. SAVAGE

Benefit of Clergy was originally a plea exempting the clergy from criminal process of the

English royal courts, but ultimately it was a commutation of the death sentence in certain felonies for all prisoners who could read, which last requirement was dropped by the 18th century. In colonial times it was in general use in the South and occasionally in New England, notably in the famous "Boston Massacre"^{qv} case. Statutes abolishing this privilege appear after the Revolution, but until the eve of the Civil War it was still allowed in the Southern states, where its use meant sparing a master's valuable property in his slave.

[A. L. Cross, Benefit of Clergy in the American Criminal Law, Mass. Hist. Soc., *Proceedings*, LXI, 154-181.]

RICHARD B. MORRIS

Benning, Fort, Ga. Camp Benning (redesignated as Fort Benning in 1922) was established near Columbus, Ga., during the World War. By consolidation of the Small Arms Firing School (Camp Perry, Ohio), the Infantry School (Fort Sill, Okla.) and the Machine Gun School (Augusta, Ga.), the present model Infantry School was established at Benning in 1920.

[Charles J. Sullivan, *Army Posts and Towns;* William A. Ganoe, *The History of the United States Army.*]

ROBERT S. THOMAS

Bennington, Battle of (Aug. 16, 1777). Toward the middle of August Gen. Burgoyne^{qv} planned a raid on the American stores at Bennington. His purpose was fourfold: to encourage the loyalists^{qv}; frighten New England; replenish his stock of provisions; and mount a regiment of heavily equipped German dragoons. Accordingly, these dragoons, lumbering along on foot in their enormous jack boots and stiff leather breeches, were made the nucleus of the raiding force, which, under the command of the German Col. Baum, amounted, with Tories^{qv}, Canadians, Indians and a handful of English, to about 800 men. On nearing Bennington, Baum, learning that Gen. Stark had assembled about 1600 troops at Bennington to oppose him, sent to Burgoyne for reinforcements. Col. Breyman, with 500 men, was accordingly sent to his assistance. In the meantime Gen. Stark, hearing of Baum's advance, marched to meet him. On Aug. 15 it rained, and both armies remained in their lines. The following afternoon Stark attacked. Baum's command was too widely dispersed. His auxiliaries were scattered and his regulars, hastily entrenched on a hill overlooking the Walloomsac, were surrounded and most of them captured. In the meantime Breyman, ignorant of what was going on, approached. Stark, reinforced by Col. Warner with 350 men, re-formed and attacked. The Germans retreated and were pursued until dark. The Americans took about 700 prisoners. The fortunate outcome of the engagement did much to improve the morale of the American forces.

[H. B. Dawson, *Battles of the United States;* Hoffman Nickerson, *The Turning Point of the Revolution.*]

A. C. FLICK

Benton, Fort (1850–65). After 1830 the American Fur Company^{qv} established several trading posts near the navigation-head of the Missouri River. One of these, Fort Lewis (established 1844), a large, bastioned, log structure, was moved in 1846 to the site of the present town of Fort Benton, Mont., where it retained its original name until 1850, when it was renamed for Thomas Hart Benton, who allegedly saved the company from prosecution for selling whiskey to the Indians. The post was subsequently rebuilt with adobe bricks. During the Montana gold rush, beginning in 1862, Fort Benton became a main port of entry to the mines. A town with the same name sprang up around it and the fur company sold out to a mercantile firm in 1865.

[H. M. Chittenden, *The American Fur Trade* and *Early Steamboat Navigation on the Missouri River;* A. J. Craven, ed., Affairs at Fort Benton from Lt. Bradley's Journal, in *Contributions to Hist. Soc. of Mont.*, Vol. III.]

JAY MONAGHAN

Bentonville, Battle of (March 19, 1865). Gen. J. E. Johnston (C.), in command of the small Confederate force in the Carolinas, hoping to prevent a junction of Sherman (U.) and Grant (U.), here attacked the left wing of Sherman's army, which was moving rapidly northward (*see* Carolinas, Sherman's March through). Though outnumbered, Johnston succeeded in fighting a drawn battle, but lost at least 2600 men. Desultory fighting occurred during the next two days, but by the night of the 21st most of Sherman's army was concentrated at the spot, and Johnston retired.

[*Battles and Leaders of the Civil War.*]

ALVIN F. HARLOW

Bent's Fort, first known as Fort William, was founded by William Bent and partners about 1832, on the north bank of the Arkansas, some seven miles east of present La Junta, Colo. The founders are said to have previously built a temporary stockade farther up the river. Located on the mountain branch of the Santa Fé Trail^{qv}, Bent's Fort participated in both the mountain fur trade^{qv} and the overland commerce to Santa Fé, becoming the outstanding trading post of the Southwest. It was rectangular in form, about 180 by 135 feet. The walls, of gray adobe[qv], were two to four feet thick and fifteen high, with bastions at two diagonal corners. Within, low earth-roofed rooms faced an interior court. An adjoining adobe corral housed stock and equipment.

Cheyennes and Arapahoes[qqv] brought buffalo robes and skins for barter at the fort and from it white traders carried wares to Indian villages. An annual wagon train[qv] freighted furs to Missouri and returned with Indian goods. The fort outfitted trappers and traders, sheltered early travelers, was a depot for military expeditions before and during the Mexican War[qv]. William Bent married a Cheyenne woman, reared his family at the fort and became Colorado's first citizen. According to unverified tradition, the Government desired the fort, but offered an inadequate price. Bent thereupon deserted the fort and partially destroyed it in 1849. Moving forty miles down the river, he erected Bent's New Fort, 1853. This structure, built of stone, he leased to the Government in 1859. Next year additional barracks were built and the post was named Fort Wise, after the governor of Virginia. In 1861 the name was changed to Fort Lyon, honoring Gen. Nathaniel Lyon. Floods endangering the buildings in 1866, Fort Lyon was moved up the river to its present location.

[G. B. Grinnell, *Bent's Old Fort and Its Builders.*]

LEROY R. HAFEN

Berea College Case, THE (1908), upheld the right of a state to require the separation of Negroes and whites in private schools; held that the right to give instruction is a property right[qv] whenever such service is "rendered for compensation"; also held that it is a "part of one's liberty as guaranteed against hostile state action by the Constitution." Another case (1912), sometimes also referred to as the Berea College Case, dealt with tax exemption of service properties of educational institutions and held that the state cannot tax such properties.

[Berea College v. Kentucky, 211 U. S. 45; Commonwealth v. Berea College, 149 Ky. 95.]

EDGAR W. KNIGHT

Bergen Prizes (1779). Capt. Landais of the *Alliance*[qv], an American vessel of John Paul Jones' squadron in European waters, captured three British merchantmen (*Betsy, Union, Charming Polly*) in 1779. Bad weather forced Landais into Bergen, Norway. England requested and obtained restoration of the vessels from the Danish-Norwegian government. Jones, in person, demanded indemnification at Copenhagen. The Danish Premier, Count Bernstorff, negotiated with the United States for years. It was proved finally that an Anglo-Danish treaty (1660) obligated Denmark to England, hence under international law[qv] she could not be forced to indemnify the United States. Congress reimbursed Landais in 1806 and the heirs of Jones in 1848.

[S. J. M. P. Fogdall, *Danish-American Diplomacy, 1776-1920.*]

S. P. FOGDALL

Bering Sea Fisheries. *See* Seal Fisheries.

Berlin, The Treaty of (1921), is the separate peace treaty between the United States and Germany, entered into after the Senate rejected the Treaty of Versailles[qv]. This Treaty of Berlin is unique, first, because of its brevity, and secondly, because it is an "index-treaty," in that its provisions merely refer to provisions of the Treaty of Versailles which are either accepted or rejected by the United States. Provisions thus taken over were those with respect to colonies, disarmament, reparations and responsibility for the war. The most important features rejected were the League of Nations, the International Labor Organization[qqv] and the boundaries provisions. Approximately two thirds of the Treaty of Versailles, including its harshest provisions, was thus accepted by the United States through the Treaty of Berlin.

[Treaty of Berlin, in *U. S. Treaty Series,* No. 658; Treaty of Versailles, in *International Conciliation,* No. 142, September, 1919.]

CLARENCE A. BERDAHL

Berlin Decree. *See* Napoleon's Decrees.

***Bermuda* Admiralty Case.** In 1861 Confederate agents in Liverpool were loading a British steamer, the *Bermuda,* with munitions for the Confederate Army when United States Minister Adams learned of it, and notified Foreign Secretary Russell. Russell replied that the Crown Admiralty law officers found the evidence insufficient to warrant interference; their law applied only to the equipment of vessels to be used as transports or cruisers, and not to the nature of the cargo. The *Bermuda* sailed, and safely ran the blockade[qv] into Savannah (*see* Destination, Enemy, and Continuous Voyage).

[*Claims of the United States against Great Britain,* Civil War, Vol. I, pp. 759-61.]

ALVIN F. HARLOW

Bermudas, THE, have had close contacts with America from the first settlement by colonists shipwrecked on their way to Virginia in 1609 (*see* Somers' Voyage), down to the present day. From 1612 to 1615 the islands were included under the Virginia Company[qv] charter, but thereafter they had a separate history, first as a company colony and then under royal control. The settlers concentrated on tobacco (*see* Tobacco Contract, The) and the colony developed rapidly. Throughout the colonial period there was considerable trade with the mainland where, in addition, many Bermudans sought opportunities denied them in the islands. During the Revolutionary era the inhabitants opposed British colonial policy and sent delegates to the Continental Congress[qv] to secure relief from the trade embargo against loyal colonies. They achieved their end by furnishing powder and other supplies to the rebels.

[Hudson Strode, *The Story of Bermuda.*]

CHARLES F. MULLETT

Bernard, Fort, was a small trading post between Horse Creek and Fort Laramie[qv] on the Oregon Trail[qv]. It was noted by many overland emigrants before and after the California gold rush[qv] of 1849, but there is no definite information about the owner or how long it continued. A trappers' trail from Bent's Fort[qv] on the south joined the Oregon Trail at this post. Taos and Santa Fé[qqv] traders freighted flour here to trade to emigrants bound for the coast.

[A. B. Hulbert, *Forty-Niners.*]

CARL L. CANNON

Bessemer Steel. *See* Iron and Steel Industry.

Best Sellers. Any book which outsells its competitors, or the author of such a book, is named a best seller. Unhappily sharp trade practices and the suppression of actual sales figures tend to render the term meaningless in present-day publishers' advertising. Through the years, however, certain books have outdistanced others; their records are fairly well authenticated. *The Holy Bible*[qv], distributed in every known dialect, probably outdistances all other books; certainly its circulation in the United States is highest. Second in volume is Noah Webster's *Blue-Backed Speller*[qv] of which nearly 100,000,000 copies have been sold. Other schoolbooks, like *The New-England Primer,* "Peter Parley's" and *McGuffey's Readers*[qqv], sold beyond the million mark in the first half of the 19th century. Tract society publications frequently reached astonishing totals. Mason L. Weems' *Life of Washington* (1800), which the author peddled over the country, was reprinted some fifty times. The first American novel to reach a sale totaling a million copies was Harriet Beecher Stowe's *Uncle Tom's Cabin*[qv] (1852), often considered the firebrand of the Civil War. The largest sale of any work of fiction has been attained by the Rev. Dr. Charles Monroe Sheldon's *In His Steps* (1899), which, because of a defective copyright, was issued simultaneously by sixteen different publishers. Other novels with a circulation of a million and a half or more include Mark Twain's *Tom Sawyer* (1876), Lew Wallace's *Ben Hur* (1880), Owen Wister's *The Virginian* (1902), Jack London's *Call of the Wild* (1903), Harold Bell Wright's *The Winning of Barbara Worth* (1911) and Gene Stratton Porter's *The Girl of the Limberlost* (1909), *The Harvester* (1911), *Freckles* (1912) and *Laddie* (1913). Novels selling beyond a million copies include E. N. Westcott's *David Harum* (1898), J. W. Fox, Jr.'s *The Little Shepherd of Kingdom Come* (1903) and *The Trail of the Lonesome Pine* (1908) and Margaret Mitchell's *Gone with the Wind* (1936). Many other novels passed the half-million mark. Among college textbooks Edwin C. Woolley's *Handbook of Composition* (1907) and Richard T. Ely's *Principles of Economics* (1904) have sold more than a million copies and after thirty years still command large sales. Similarly leading its field is *The Boston Cooking School Cook Book* (1896). The book clubs in recent years have tended to bring into temporary prominence books thus distributed and to give them a factitious best-seller appearance.

HARRY R. WARFEL

Betharaba, the first town planted by German Moravians[qv] from Pennsylvania in Wachovia, N. C., was begun in 1753. Its early settlers were noted for advanced agricultural practices, especially their "Medicine Garden," which produced over fifty kinds of herbs. Betharaba grew slowly and today (1938) it is only a small village, known locally as "Old Town."

[J. H. Clewell, *History of Wachovia.*]

HUGH T. LEFLER

Bethel Community (1844–79) was a minor communistic experiment established in Shelby County, Mo., by William Keil accompanied by followers (chiefly German) from Ohio and Pittsburgh, Pa. Keil preached moral living, subscribing to no religious faith, and dominated an unincorporated, self-sustaining, orderly, prosperous community which expanded to four towns. Property and labor were shared, though private earnings were allowed. A sister colony was fostered in Aurora, Ore., in 1855. Both dissolved, dividing their property upon Keil's death.

[Robert J. Hendricks, *Bethel and Aurora.*]

FLOYD C. SHOEMAKER

Bethesda, House of Mercy, was what Rev. George Whitefield called the orphanage and school that he began to build near Savannah, 1740. Although his Georgia project outlived the great Awakener, it faltered before 1800. Savannah's venerable Union Society, sponsor of present Bethesda, revived the use of the site for orphanage purposes, 1855.

[E. W. G. Boogher, *Secondary Education in Georgia, 1732-1858.*]

H. B. FANT

Bible, THE. It is a fact of large historical importance that the appearance of the two most widely used of the early English translations of the Bible was contemporaneous with the beginnings of English colonization of America. The Genevan Bible, the work of exiled Protestant scholars who had fled to Geneva to escape Queen Mary's persecutions, was in fact the Puritan's Bible. Its convenient size and relative cheapness, together with its verse divisions and Calvinistic notes, gave it an immense popularity. From the date of its first publication in 1560 to 1640 it passed through 160 editions, and was, undoubtedly, the Bible most used by the first two generations of American Puritans[qv]. Even after the appearance of the King James or Authorized version (1611) the Genevan Bible continued to hold its own, though doubtless the Authorized version found greater favor outside New England. The availability of these two great versions from the beginning of colonization helps to explain the influence exerted by the Bible in American colonial life. Taking the colonial period as a whole the Bible was easily first in its moral and cultural influence upon the plain people of English speech.

The Bible in German, printed by Christopher Sower, Sr., the Dunker printer of Germantown, in 1740–43, the first Bible to appear in a European language in America, exercised a corresponding influence upon the growing number of German colonists.

The nation confronted no more serious problem after independence than that connected with the western movement of the population. Among the questions to be decided upon the immense stage of the West was whether the nation was to be Christian or pagan in its outlook. And no single factor had a larger part in determining what direction the nation would take than the widespread distribution of the Bible throughout the West, by such agencies as the American Bible Society (1816), the American Tract Society[qqv] (1825), and the American Sunday School Union (1824). These agencies, together with the direct influence exerted by the evangelical churches, made the Bible a necessity in almost every American home. As a result of the great revivals[qv] which swept over the nation from the beginning of the last century until near its end, Bible reading and study in the home as well as in the Sabbath Schools and denominational colleges was stressed as the best means of cultivating the Christian life. Family worship became a practice in tens of thousands of American homes, where a chapter of the Bible was read, a hymn sung, and a prayer offered as a part of the daily family routine. The Young Men's and Young Women's Christian Associations[qqv], from their formation, stressed Bible study.

The Bible has had an important part in advancing every reform movement in American history, as witness the antislavery, temperance and peace movements[qqv]. Unfortunately it has also been used to support glaring evils, to oppose progress, and has given birth to numerous erratic movements, and in too many instances to superstitious practices.

It is an opinion widely held at the present time that Bible reading and study has greatly declined and that there has been a corresponding decrease in its influence. Certainly the old emphasis upon Bible reading in the home has greatly lessened. If this is true, it is doubtless due in large part to the fact that the Bible is no longer considered the infallible guide in every department of life as it once was. Yet the Bible still is in great demand and exercising a wide influence, as indicated by the fact that the American Bible Society published 323,109 Bibles and 413,826 Testaments in 1933, and the Press-Radio Bible Service served newspapers having a daily circulation of more than 14,000,000 copies.

[P. Marion Simms, *The Bible in America.*]

WILLIAM W. SWEET

Bible Commonwealth is a term which has been applied by modern historians to the Puritan colonies of Massachusetts and New Haven, where the right to vote was limited to church members and an effort was made to bring all activities into harmony with the Bible. This effort is best illustrated by *An Abstract of the Lawes of New England . . .* (London, 1641), a code prepared by John Cotton which became the basis for the government of the New Haven Colony[qv]. With the exception of the chapters dealing with inheritance and crime, the provisions of this code were not biblical but were based upon the early practices of Massachusetts. Insofar as possible, however, all provisions were supported by marginal scriptural citations.

[I. M. Calder, *The New Haven Colony.*]

ISABEL M. CALDER

Bibles, Printing of. The first book printed within the limits of the present United States of which any copy survives was a portion of the Bible (the so-called *Bay Psalm Book*^{qv}, Cambridge, Mass., 1640). The first complete Bible produced was John Eliot's translation into an Algonquian language printed at Cambridge in 1663 (second edition, 1685). In 1688 William Bradford projected the printing of a Bible in Philadelphia, but nothing came of it or of John Fleeming's proposal in Boston in 1770. Partly because the printing of the King James version was an Oxford monopoly, three editions of Martin Luther's Bible in German appeared in America (Germantown, Christopher Sower, 1743, 1763, 1776) before any were printed in English. Robert Aitken published the first American Bible in English in Philadelphia, 1781–82. Isaiah Thomas is responsible for the legend of an English Bible printed surreptitiously in Boston about 1752, but no such book was attested by contemporaries, nor is any copy known to exist. Thomas printed the first Greek New Testament, Worcester, 1800. The first printing of the Douai version (Roman Catholic) was in Philadelphia in 1790.

[E. B. O'Callaghan, *List of editions of the Holy Scriptures . . . printed in America previous to 1860.*]

RANDOLPH G. ADAMS

Bicameral Legislatures. The bicameral system has always dominated in the United States, in both state and nation. In the Federal Congress, in addition to the established English precedent, there was the fact that the representative character of the two houses was quite different, as a result of one of the major compromises of the Convention of 1787^{qv}. The large states won representation on the basis of population in the House; the small states, fearful that this would place them at the mercy of the large states, won equality of representation in the Senate, as well as the constitutional guarantee that no state should be deprived of its equal representation without its consent—which means in fact, never. The bicameral principle is, therefore, firmly established in the Federal Government.

In the states, bicameralism has been universally in effect, with the specific exceptions here noted. After independence was achieved, three states set up or retained existing unicameral legislatures^{qv}; with the exception of Vermont, these lasted only a few years:

Georgia	1777–1789
Pennsylvania	1701–1789
Vermont	1776–1836

In the years immediately preceding our entry into the World War, there was considerable agitation for unicameralism; several governors recommended it, and several states voted on it, rejecting it by substantial majorities. The movement was resumed when Nebraska in 1934 adopted such a constitutional amendment, effective in 1937.

In the cities the bicameral system, with a large common council and a smaller select council, universally prevailed, down to the period of the Muckrakers and the Progressive movement^{qqv}. At present, all of the city councils are unicameral, nearly all with a small membership. The spread of unicameralism in the cities has been used as an argument for its extension among the states.

[Daniel B. Carroll, *The Unicameral Legislature of Vermont;* David L. Colvin, *The Bicameral Principle in the New York Legislature;* Hastings B. Lees-Smith, *Second Chambers in Theory and Practice;* Robert Luce, *Legislative Assemblies;* Dorothy Schaffter, *The Bicameral System in Practice;* John P. Senning, *The Unicameral Legislature;* W. F. Willoughby, *Principles of Legislative Organization and Administration.*]

W. BROOKE GRAVES

Bicycling. Invented largely in France and England, bicycles had their first vogue in America in the late 1860's. The sudden popularity soon collapsed but was revived a decade later when Albert A. Pope began importing them from England and later manufacturing them. Chiefly through his efforts, which included continuous propaganda for better roads, bicycling became, during the 1880's and 1890's, one of the most popular of American sports^{qv}. Change in design and model made bicycling more practical. Their use was thus widened to include business as well as pleasure. Bicycling as a sport reached its height in the late 1890's. After that it was pushed into the background by motor cycles and motor cars and by the development of golf, tennis, and other outdoor sports. The bicycle continued as an adjunct of business and in the middle 1930's it experienced a revival in both fields.

[*Thirteenth Census 1910,* Vol. X, pp. 825 ff.]

H. U. FAULKNER

Biddle Mission to Panama and Bogotá, THE. Charles A. Biddle, sent by President Jackson to Nicaragua, Guatemala and Panama to determine expediency of Isthmian canal negotiations, secured from New Granada a concession (June 22, 1836) for himself and associates to construct a trans-isthmian road or railway, and for steam navigation of Chagres River. Jackson, infuriated because of Biddle's use of a governmental mission to secure a private concession, disclaimed official connection with the affair. Biddle's death (Dec. 21, 1836) saved him a presidential reprimand.

[E. T. Parks, *Colombia and the United States, 1765-1934.*]

E. T. PARKS

Bidlack-Mallarino Treaty of 1846, THE, between the United States and New Granada (Colombia), removed tariff discrimination against American commerce, and provided for the guarantee of the neutrality of the Isthmus of Panama "with a view that the free transit . . . [across it] may not be interrupted." New Granada's rights of sovereignty over the Isthmus were also guaranteed.

On thirteen occasions (1856–1903) American troops were landed to protect the transit route. In 1903 President Theodore Roosevelt argued that this treaty "vested in the United States a substantial property right" in the Isthmus. When Panama[qv] seceded (Nov. 3, 1903) it was held by the American Government that the covenant ran with this land (*see* Hay-Bunau-Varilla Treaty, The).

[H. C. Hill, *Roosevelt and the Caribbean;* E. T. Parks, *Colombia and the United States.*]

E. T. PARKS

Big Black River, Battle at (May 17, 1863). After his defeat at Champion's Hill[qv], Pemberton (C.) retreated to the Big Black River. It was hoped the bridge could be held long enough to permit the army to cross before Grant (U.) could attack in force. Everything was in confusion; there seemed to be no leadership. On the morning of May 17 Grant's advance troops appeared. Pemberton was driven in retreat into Vicksburg[qv].

[F. V. Greene, *The Mississippi.*]

THOMAS ROBSON HAY

Big Bone Lick, THE, is in Boone County, Ky., one and one-half miles east from the Ohio River. The earliest known white man to visit this place was Capt. Charles Lemoyne de Longeuil, who came in 1729. Christopher Gist[qv] visited it in 1751; and in 1773 James Douglas, a Virginia surveyor, described the animal remains which he found on the surface. Here were found the bones of mastodon, Arctic elephant and other animals of the Glacial Age. In 1803 and 1806 Dr. William Goforth made a collection of fossils which he entrusted to the English traveler, Thomas Ashe. Ashe in turn sold these to the Royal College of Surgeons in London, and to private Irish and Scotch collectors. Thomas Jefferson made a collection of some of the bones, and natural history museums at Lexington, Cincinnati, Philadelphia and Boston collected the remaining skeletons. The large pre-historic animals were attracted to the Big Bone Lick by the seepage of brine from an underlying basal coal measure. Pioneers found that 500 gallons of this water made one bushel of salt.

[W. R. Jillson, *Big Bone Lick.*]

T. D. CLARK

Big Bottom Massacre, MUSKINGUM RIVER, OHIO (Jan. 2, 1791). Shawnee[qv] Indians surprised a new settlement on the Muskingum, stormed the blockhouse and killed eleven men, one woman and two children. Three settlers were captured while four others escaped into the woods. The Ohio Company of Associates[qv] acted immediately after this outrage to provide greater protection for settlers.

[*American State Papers,* Class II, Indian Affairs.]

ROBERT S. THOMAS

Big Brother Movement. In 1904, following an appeal by Ernest K. Coulter to the Men's Club of the Central Presbyterian Church of New York City, forty men each agreed to take an interest in and render assistance to one boy brought into the Children's Court. At present 355 volunteer Big Brother organizations enlist the services of 15,000 Catholics, Jews and Protestants in an intensive personal effort to prevent juvenile delinquency. In 1934 the movement aided 64,000 children in 100 cities in 36 states and 6 Canadian provinces, and claimed that 97% turned their back permanently on crime.

[William F. McDermott, When a Feller Needs a Friend, *Reader's Digest,* Sept., 1936.]

DONALD G. BISHOP

Big Hole, Battle of the, was fought in the Big Hole Basin, Mont., Aug. 9, 1877, during the Joseph campaign. Col. John Gibbon attacked Joseph's camp at daybreak, burning lodges and killing men, women and children. The surviving Nez Percés drove the soldiers back, captured a howitzer and ammunition, wounded Gibbon and disabled or killed sixty-nine soldiers; then withdrew during the night. (*See* Nez Percé War.)

[H. H. Bancroft, *History of Washington, Idaho and Montana.*]

WILLIAM S. LEWIS

Big Horn Mountains, THE, are a range of the Rocky Mountains lying mainly in north central Wyoming, but extending into southern Montana. Discovered in 1743 by Chevalier Vérendrye, they were early frequented by American fur traders. In 1811 they were crossed by Wilson Price Hunt and the overland Astoria[qv] expedition. Here in 1866 occurred the so-called Fetterman massacre[qv], and in 1876 Custer's force was annihilated in the Battle of the Little Big Horn[qv].

DAN E. CLARK

Big Knives or Long Knives was a term used by the western Indians to designate the English colonists. After 1750 it was restricted to the colonists of Virginia, in contradistinction to those of New York and Pennsylvania. George Rogers Clark[qv] spoke of himself and men as "Big Knives," or Virginians, in his speeches to the Indians in 1778 after the capture of Illinois. In the latter part of the Revolution, down to and during the War of 1812, the term was used to designate Americans. The origin is thought to have been the use of steel knives and swords by the colonists, perhaps contrasted with the stone knives of the primitive Indians.

[R. G. Thwaites, *Daniel Boone.*]

LOUISE PHELPS KELLOGG

Big Moccasin Gap, in extreme southwestern Virginia, admitted Daniel Boone and other pioneers through the Clinch Mountains into Kentucky. Not far from it were the blockhouses, built by Capt. John Anderson in 1777, where parties formed for the journey over the Wilderness Road[qv]. The line established by the Treaty of Lochaber[qv], 1768, and surveyed by John Donelson[qv] in 1770 crossed the road near this Gap.

[W. A. Posey, *The Wilderness Road;* A. B. Hulbert, *Boone's Wilderness Road.*]

JONATHAN T. DORRIS

Big Tree Treaty (1797). Robert Morris' agreement with the Holland Land Company[qv] required the acquisition of the Indian title. At Big Tree (Geneseo, N. Y.) with the sanction of the United States Government, the Senecas[qv], by a treaty concluded Sept. 15, ceded to Morris all of their land west of the Genesee River, except about 200,000 acres, for the sum of $100,000 to be invested in United States Bank stock.

[P. D. Evans, *The Holland Land Company.*]

ROBERT W. BINGHAM

Biglow Papers, THE. Originally these were nine satirical poems in Yankee dialect directed against the Mexican War, which, in the opinion of their author, James Russell Lowell, had as its object the acquisition of slave territory. From 1846 to 1848 the jingling rhymes like "What Mr. Robinson Thinks" spread from newspaper to newspaper. In 1848 Lowell gathered the nine poems into a collection, embroidering them with elaborations until the original intent of the lyrics was all but lost. To Hosea Biglow was added the pundit editor Parson Wilbur, who was endless in his comment. Written in haste, with youthful extravagance and zeal, the satires sparkle with fun and at times bite like acid.

Beginning in 1862, Lowell ran in the *Atlantic Monthly* a second series of the papers, this time satirizing the South. Some of the lyrics, like "Jonathan to John," display flashes of the old-time fire, but the poet, less youthful now, had to force himself into the satiric mood. The jingles of Hosea Biglow with their misspellings could not voice the national tragedy. As a result the final collection, 1867, with its chaos of embellishment, its beautiful nature poetry, and its long essay on Yankee dialect, is, unlike the first series, hardly to be rated as primarily satiric.

FRED LEWIS PATTEE

Bill of Rights. The first ten Amendments to the Constitution[qv] of the United States are generally referred to as the national Bill of Rights. At the time the Constitution was submitted to the people in 1787 (*see* Constitution, Ratification of the) there was much criticism of the document due to the fact that it did not contain a Bill of Rights. The explanation of this goes back to the original English common-law idea of government. According to this, individual rights exist of themselves as inborn and inalienable. The Constitution and government are merely an added protection to those rights which the people already possess. This idea underlies today the governments not only of Great Britain and the United States, but also those of the self-governing British Commonwealths.

In contrast to this should be mentioned the doctrine and belief that were and still are prevalent in other countries, such as the states of Continental Europe, which are under what might be termed a prerogative type of government. Even the most free of these countries in their written Constitutions make statements of individual rights that are based on the underlying thought that these rights are the gift of the state. Thus we find the Constitution of Switzerland (Article 55), "The freedom of the press is guaranteed. However, cantonal laws shall enact the necessary provisions to avoid abuse; these provisions shall be submitted to the approval of the Federal Council. The Confederation may also fix penalties in order to prevent abuses directed against itself or its authorities." This provision is characteristic of the most enlightened European democracies and is in direct contrast to the British and American common-law idea of protection for already existing, inalienable rights.

Naturally there was a general feeling among those who made the Constitution and who were advocating its adoption that a Bill of Rights was unnecessary, since it might grant rights that already existed or merely prohibit the Government from interfering with these rights, which it had no authority to do. Alexander Hamilton, in *The Federalist*[qv], No. 84, wrote: "'We, the people[qv] of the United States . . .' is a better recognition of popular rights than volumes of those aphorisms which make the principal figure in several of our State bills of rights, and which would sound much better in a treatise of ethics than in a constitution of government. . . . The truth is, after all the declamation we have heard, that the Constitution is itself, in every rational sense, and to every useful purpose, a bill of rights."

In contrast to this was a widespread popular feeling that it would be wise to make a definite statement of these fundamental rights since such a statement would have a beneficial and restraining influence on the minds of both rulers and the people and also might serve as a definite basis for future court decisions in protecting these rights. This feeling, amounting to a conviction, went back to the old British tradition inherited by the colonists from the Revolution of 1688. This great change in the government of England and her colonies had as one important result the Declaration of Rights of 1689 which formed the basis for the later American Bill of Rights.

Massachusetts, Virginia, New York and several other states ratified the new Constitution with the recommendation that a Bill of Rights be added which should specifically safeguard individual rights. This was done by the First Congress in the form of twelve proposed Amendments which, after some delay, were passed by that body on Sept. 25, 1789. Of the twelve Amendments submitted, ten were declared ratified by the necessary number of states on Dec. 15, 1791. They bind the National Government alone, but do not limit the power of the individual states. The material for these Amendments was drawn in large part from the Virginia Declaration of Rights[qv] which was adopted by a Virginia convention composed of members of the colonial House of Burgesses which met at Williamsburg in 1776. The preparation of this Declaration was in large part the work of George Mason. In a sense, it was intended to serve as an original compact for society by stating permanent and fundamental truths. Also, it was intended to be the basis for a new society and government to be independently organized in America. In plain language it stated specific and fundamental principles with regard to jury trial, cruel and unusual punishments, search warrants, freedom of the press, the subordination of military to civil power; the derivation of all authority from the people, who have an inalienable right to reform an evil government; the doctrine of the separation of executive, legislative and judicial powers; and it declared for a full grant of religious freedom. Likewise it stated that all men should have the franchise[qv] who had sufficient evidence of permanent common interests with the community.

Jefferson soon thereafter drew upon it when he wrote the Declaration of Independence[qv], and it not only became the basis for these first Amendments to the Constitution but also furnished a model for the various Bills of Rights adopted soon after by other colonies and offered the basis for the later Bills of Rights in many of the present state constitutions (*see* Bills of Rights, State).

The First Amendment provides that "Congress shall make no law respecting an establishment of religion, or prohibiting the free exercise thereof; or abridging the freedom of speech or of the press[qqv]; or the right of the people peaceably to assemble[qv], and to petition[qv] the government for a redress of grievances." These are among the most fundamental rights to be preserved in a free government. In contrast to the above quotation from the Swiss Constitution, they prohibit interference with individual rights that already exist.

More specifically they mean that the National Government has nothing to do with religion as such. The right of fair discussion of men and measures does not mean free license of utterance, but the right of a person to express his or her thoughts depends on the thoughts themselves and on time and place. The right on the part of citizens to meet peaceably for consultation in respect to public affairs and to petition for a redress of grievances is implied in the very idea of popular government. It is true that the right of petition has lost much both in use and influence during more recent years. This is due to the extension of the means for expression of

Bill of Rights

the popular will or protest, by universal suffrage. On the other hand, it still holds great potential value as a ready means of popular influence upon the course of legislation or administration in time of crisis.

Amendment II provides: "A well-regulated militia being necessary to the security of a free State, the right of the people to keep and bear arms shall not be infringed." This may be summarized as the right to bear arms in common defense but not to carry such arms as the individual may desire in order to use them in private conflict.

The Third Amendment provides: "No soldier shall, in time of peace, be quartered[qv] in any house without the consent of the owner, nor in time of war, but in a manner to be prescribed by law," and the Fourth Amendment provides for the security of the people "in their persons, houses, papers and effects, against unreasonable searches and seizures"[qv]. These two Amendments are designed to protect the people against any acts of illegal force by the National Government that may infringe their personal rights.

The four Amendments numbered V, VI, VII and VIII control legal proceedings in the Federal courts and constitute a statement of the rights of accused persons by guaranteeing to them the rule of common law.

The provisions of Amendment V are: "No person shall be held to answer for a capital, or otherwise infamous crime, unless on a presentment or indictment of a grand jury, except in cases arising in the land or naval forces, or in the militia, when in actual service in time of war or public danger; nor shall any person be subject for the same offense to be twice put in jeopardy of life or limb; nor shall be compelled in any criminal case to be a witness against himself, nor be deprived of life, liberty, or property, without due process[qv] of law; nor shall private property be taken for public use, without just compensation." The most important clause of this Amendment is that guaranteeing "due process of law" to every citizen under Federal law. This means "that the accused person be given the right to a fair hearing in a tribunal having jurisdiction of his case." (E. S. Corwin.)

Amendment VI lays down certain provisions that are designed to secure this due process of law. It provides that "in all criminal prosecutions the accused shall enjoy the right to a speedy and public trial, by an impartial jury of the State and district wherein the crime shall have been committed, which district shall have been previously ascertained by law, and to be informed of the nature and cause of the accusation; to be confronted with the witness against him; to have compulsory process for obtaining witnesses in his favor, and to have the assistance of counsel for his defence."

Amendment VII provides that "in suits at common law, where the value in controversy shall exceed twenty dollars, the right of trial by jury shall be preserved, and no fact tried by a jury shall be otherwise re-examined in any court of the United States, than according to the rules of the common law." This Amendment restricts the power of the Supreme Court of the United States in reviewing questions of fact upon appeal from lower Federal courts. Amendment VIII requires that "excessive bail shall not be required, nor excessive fines imposed, nor cruel and unusual punishments inflicted." The wording of this Amendment is taken almost verbatim from the English Bill of Rights of 1689.

The last two Amendments in the Bill of Rights numbered IX and X form a final restraint upon the National Government and require it to be one of enumerated powers only. Thus Amendment IX states that "the enumeration in the Constitution of certain rights shall not be construed to deny or disparage others retained by the people," and Amendment X states that "the powers not delegated to the United States by the Constitution, nor prohibited by it to the States, are reserved to the States respectively or to the people." It would seem that the sovereign people of the United States are ultimately the ones who enumerate the rights and reserve them to the states or to the people. In other words, as stated in the Preamble to the Constitution, "We, the people of the United States," did "ordain and establish" the Constitution, with the result that legally and politically it may be said that the United States *is* a Nation, rather than the more grammatical expression that the United States are a nation.

As may be imagined, the various provisions of the Bill of Rights have been called into question on numerous occasions, especially in time of war, but by origin, historic development and acceptance they have been rooted so deeply in the minds and consciences of the American people that their validity is essentially as strong and as universally accepted at the present time as in any period in our history. Any seeming infringement of them immediately arouses strong and overwhelming political opposition.

[F. W. Maitland, *The Constitutional History of England;* A. V. Dicey, *The Law of the Constitution;* E. S. Corwin, *The Constitution and What It Means Today;* Allan Nevins, *The American States during and after the Revolution 1775-1789;* Helen Hill, *George Mason.*]

WILLIAM STARR MYERS

Billeting, or quartering of military troops, was a European practice rarely resorted to in America. Regiments usually camped out or occupied forts and barracks erected at colonial expense. Increased troop arrivals during the French and Indian War made it an issue, beginning in New York and Philadelphia, in 1756. To shelter soldiers, the Mutiny Act[qv] of 1765 required colonial governments, when barracks did not avail, to billet troops in inns, barns and uninhabited houses, and furnish certain provisions. As "a common resort of arbitrary princes," billeting aroused resistance in Charleston (1764), New York (1766), and Boston (1768), largely arising from unwillingness to accede to any money legislation by Parliament and to any military enforcement of unpopular measures. This resistance fed on traditional British aversion to standing armies. Billeting, though paid for, led directly to the Boston Massacre[qv]. The Quartering Act[qv] of 1774, designed to permit billeting within Boston, had little to do with the final issue, which was already joined. Billeting was objected to in the Declaration of Independence[qv] and was prohibited in the Bill of Rights[qv] as stated in the Third Amendment to the Constitution.

[C. M. Clode, *Military Forces of the Crown;* C. H. Van Tyne, *Causes of the War of Independence;* G. O. Trevelyan, *The American Revolution;* W. C. Abbott, *New York in the American Revolution;* Edward McCrady, *History of South Carolina under the Royal Government, 1719-76.*]

ELBRIDGE COLBY

Bills of Credit is a term applied to non-interest-bearing government obligations which circulate as money, although commonly applied in this country to issues by the colonies and, later, by the Continental Congress[qv] and states during the Revolutionary War[qv]. Since the establishment of the National Government, such issues have been known as Treasury notes[qv] or United States notes.

Bills of credit in the colonies began with an issue of £7000, shortly increased to £40,000, in Massachusetts in 1690. This was followed by similar action by New Hampshire, Rhode Island, Connecticut, New York and New Jersey before 1711, South Carolina in 1712, Pennsylvania in 1723, Maryland in 1734, Delaware in 1739, Virginia in 1755 and Georgia in 1760. In most cases the bills were issued to excess and depreciated sharply in value. Parliament finally prohibited such paper currency, in New England in 1751, and in the other colonies in 1764.

As soon as the colonies broke away from the mother country, they again began to emit bills of credit in large amounts. The Continental Congress, unable to obtain necessary funds from other sources, authorized $241,552,780 of bills from 1775 to 1779 inclusive, while the various states put out $209,524,776 of bills during the same period.

[D. R. Dewey, *Financial History of the United States.*]

FREDERICK A. BRADFORD

Bills of Rights, State. In American history the Bill of Rights adopted by the State of Virginia in 1776 preceded those of the other states, and also was the model upon which the national Bill of Rights[qv], the first ten Amendments of the United States Constitution, was drawn up. The Virginia Declaration[qv], in large part, was the work of George Mason and was adopted on June 12 by the colonial House of Burgesses which met as a convention. The Virginia document was in large part a restatement of English principles drawn from such sources as Magna Carta, the Petition of Rights and the Bill of Rights. It still stands in practically the original form at the beginning of the sixth or present Constitution of the State of Virginia, which was formed in 1902.

While other and later constitutions of the various states have copied the Virginia provisions in large part, they also have added other provisions according to local or contemporary needs. The second great Bill of Rights in point of time was "The Declaration of Rights of the Commonwealth of Massachusetts" which was adopted in 1780. It was stated in thirty provisions while that of Virginia was stated in sixteen. The Massachusetts Bill of Rights goes into greater detail than that of Virginia, stressing such things as the right of the people to bear arms, a condemnation of *ex post facto* laws, bills of attainder[qv], and the quartering[qv] of soldiers in time of peace. The Puritan religious influence is shown in the statement that "it is the right as well as the duty of all men in society, publicly, and at stated seasons, to worship the Supreme Being, the great Creator and Preserver of the universe." The final article is a more lengthy and specific statement of the principle of Separation of Powers[qv]. This Bill of Rights also stands as a part of the original Constitution of Massachusetts and still remains in force today.

The Bills of Rights in other or later-formed states show the results of contemporary events and influence and are often much more lengthy. Thus, slavery is prohibited in the Bill of Rights of the State of Maryland; also in the State of Nevada, and in almost all the Southern states. This is a direct result of the Civil War and Reconstruction^qv period. Also, the Constitution of the State of New Mexico contains such an odd and legally questionable statement as the following, that "the people of the State have the sole and exclusive right to govern themselves as a free, sovereign and independent State."

While many of the Bills of Rights of the various states set forth matters which are never questioned and establish prohibitions of powers already beyond the competence of the state governments, yet there is no doubt that their effect in general is healthy and constructive. They specifically state and emphasize the fundamental principles upon which American government and society are founded.

[E. S. Corwin, *The Constitution and What It Means Today;* Allan Nevins, *The American States during and after the Revolution, 1775-1789.*]

WILLIAM STARR MYERS

Biloxi was the first establishment in and capital of Louisiana. Settled by Pierre le Moyne, Sieur d'Iberville, in 1699, with 200 French colonists, it has been relocated once at least, but still exists, approximately on its original site, on the Mississippi Gulf Coast, fifty miles west of Mobile Bay. When New Orleans was made Louisiana's capital in 1722, Biloxi ceased to be important. (*See also* Maurepas, Fort.)

[Robert Lowry and William H. McCardle, *A History of Mississippi.*]

MACK SWEARINGEN

Bimetallism. Under the coinage act of April 2, 1792, a system of bimetallism was established in the United States. The law provided for a gold dollar unit of 24.75 grains fine and a silver dollar of 371.25 grains fine. This thus established the mint ratio of gold to silver at 1 to 15. The act provided for the minting of gold coins of $10, $5 and $2.50 denomination, and silver coins of the denomination of one dollar, half-dollar, quarter-dollar, disme and half-disme. Copper cents and half-cents were also provided for.

In fundamentals the act of 1792 followed recommendations contained in Alexander Hamilton's report. This report, in turn, consisted in large measure of an able selection of the more workable proposals of earlier reports by Jefferson (1784), the Grand Committee (1785), and the Board of Treasury (1786). Strangely enough, Hamilton's chief creative proposal, for the elimination of foreign coins, was disregarded entirely in the act of 1792.

It seems probable that the adoption of a bimetallic system in 1792 resulted from a lack of knowledge regarding the principles of subsidiary coinage^qv. Hamilton, along with other financial experts of the time, could not conceive of fractional silver coins with a bullion^qv value less than their face value as money. Consequently, since fractional gold coins were impractical, Hamilton felt that the choice lay between a single silver standard and a bimetallic standard. As Hamilton in fact approved of a gold standard^qv, he recommended a bimetallic system, thinking that gold coin would be used for major transactions while silver would circulate in the fractional denominations. Moreover, when Hamilton submitted his report, the leading countries of the world had some form of bimetallism, the single gold standard not being adopted by England until twenty-five years later.

In accordance with the familiar principle of Gresham's Law, under which the cheaper metal drives out the dearer, gold did not circulate to any great extent after the adoption of the coinage act of 1792. After 1793, the market ratio of gold to silver was above 1 to 15 steadily in succeeding years. By 1812 the market ratio of gold to silver had reached 1 to 16, the mint ratio being fixed by law at 1 to 15. The mint ratio thus overvalued silver by making it worth one-fifteenth as much as gold (when used as money), while in the market silver was worth only one-sixteenth as much as gold. This being the case, it paid to take silver to the mint to be coined into money, while gold was more valuable for use as a metal or for shipment to foreign countries.

The United States was accordingly on a silver standard in practice from the early part of the 19th century on until 1834. The desire of Eastern business interests for a gold coinage plus a wish to develop newly discovered gold mines in North Carolina and Georgia were probably the chief forces leading to the passage of the act of June 28, 1834, which, by reducing the fine weight of the gold dollar to 23.2 grains, altered the mint ratio to 16.002 to 1. Nearly three years later the act of Jan. 18, 1837, for technical reasons, increased the fine weight of the gold dollar to 23.22 grains, thus changing the mint ratio slightly to 15.988 to 1.

The laws of 1834 and 1837 overvalued gold at the mint, but the discrepancy between the mint and market ratios was not sufficient to cause silver to disappear from circulation for some years. By the late 1840's, however, business was hampered by the disappearance from circulation of much of the fractional silver, which was full-weight coin and hence tended to be melted up and used as metal since the mint ratio overvalued gold. This difficulty was finally overcome by the passage of the coinage act of

Feb. 21, 1853, which provided for short-weight silver coins and thereby permitted the circulation of silver in the fractional denominations and gold coin for larger transactions. In practice the act of 1853 permitted the operation of a single gold standard, although legally the country still maintained bimetallism, since the law permitted the free coinage of silver dollars at the mint, even though it was not profitable to take advantage of this provision.

Because of the inflation[qv] following the issuance of greenbacks[qv] during the Civil War, both gold and fractional silver disappeared from circulation. In spite of the fact that the country remained on a paper (greenback) standard until 1879, the coinage laws were revised and recodified in 1873.

The act of Feb. 12, 1873, marked the end of legal bimetallism in the United States. The silver dollar was dropped from the list of coins which could be freely struck at the mint. Thus, with no free coinage of silver, the single gold standard was legally established in the United States.

The dropping of the silver dollar in 1873 was not the outcome of a design to put the United States on a gold standard. As a result of the overvaluation of gold at the mint, silver had not been presented for coinage into dollars for many years. Congress, accordingly, deeming this coin to be unpopular and unwanted, merely struck it off the list without giving a thought to the fact that this action legally established a single gold standard.

Shortly after 1873, the market ratio of silver to gold changed so that coinage of silver dollars would have again been profitable. The silver interests raised a hue and cry about "The Crime of '73,"[qv] which demonetized silver, although the accusation of a crime or conspiracy had no basis in fact.

From 1875 on, the silver interests have been strong enough to obtain silver legislation[qv] in their favor, although they have not succeeded in bringing back bimetallism. William Jennings Bryan ran for President in 1896 (*see* Campaign of 1896) on a platform advocating a return to bimetallism at the old ratio of 16 to 1 (accurately 15.988 to 1), but was defeated both in that year and in 1900.

In 1933, the silver interests obtained the inclusion (in the Thomas Inflation Amendment[qv] of May 12) of a clause permitting the President to re-establish bimetallism at such a mint ratio as he should designate. Fortunately, to date, no such action has been taken by the President.

[N. Carothers, *Fractional Money;* J. L. Laughlin, *History of Bimetallism in the United States.*]

FREDERICK A. BRADFORD

Bingham Purchase. In 1786, when Massachusetts, which then included Maine, disposed of large tracts of unsettled lands in Maine by lottery, William Bingham, a wealthy Philadelphia banker, drew several townships and purchased others, with a total area of 1,000,000 acres. Gen. Henry Knox had signed a contract to buy another tract of 1,000,000 acres, but his duties as Secretary of War prevented his developing it, and Bingham took that over also.

ALVIN F. HARLOW

Biographic Writing, American, reaches as far back as Cotton Mather's *Life of His Excellency Sir William Phips,* published in London in 1697; autobiographic writing may be said to date from Capt. John Smith's *True Relation* (1608). But unlike history, biographic writing produced no works of permanent importance until after the Revolution. The first three books worthy of notice—for Parson Weems' lives of Washington and Marion are not biographies but romances—are John Marshall's five-volume *Life of Washington* (1804–7); William Wirt's *Life of Patrick Henry* (1817); and Benjamin Franklin's *Autobiography* in the version presented by Temple Franklin (1817). Marshall's book, clumsily written, full of plagiarisms from various annalists and showing a strong Federalist[qv] bias, contains enough factual value to make it still useful; Wirt's volume, hasty, inaccurate and not devoid of inventions, was excellently written and for its time had real merit. Franklin's work is of course a classic. From these beginnings American biography rapidly multiplied the number of its titles, but before the Civil War yielded few works of permanent worth. Washington Irving's *History of the Life and Voyages of Christopher Columbus,* which appeared in four volumes in 1828, represented independent research in Spanish archives and was so beautifully written that it may still be read with pleasure. Jared Sparks set to work in the 1830's with more industry than literary talent or scientific method. His *Life of Gouverneur Morris* in three volumes (1832) and his *Life of Washington* in one (1837), were esteemed excellent in their day, but were without lasting qualities. His *Library of American Biography,* appearing in two series (1834–38, 1844–47) had more merit; a collection of brief filiopietistic memoirs of worthies of the colonial and early national period, it was naturally uneven, but filled a glaring gap and contained some biographies that are still of value. Meanwhile, George Tucker had written a two-volume life of Thomas Jefferson (1834) of more than mediocre quality. Irving's *Life of Washington* (five volumes, 1855–59) was thought worthy of its great theme and remained unsurpassed till the end of the century, though he dismissed the post-Revolutionary years briefly. Charles Francis Adams in the 1850's published a really admirable life of John Adams. In 1862–63 Pierre M. Irving's four-volume *Life and Letters of Washington Irving* furnished the first ample and spirited biography of an American writer.

After the Civil War biography rapidly became too ample and voluminous to permit of summarization. It attracted the talents of the ablest men of letters, as Oliver Wendell Holmes' memoirs of Emerson and Motley and Henry James' life of Hawthorne testify. Writers of note, the first being James Parton with his lives of Jefferson, Burr, Jackson, Greeley and others, gave their whole energies to it. With Henry Adams' *Life of Albert Gallatin* (1879) modern methods of historical research and criticism began to be applied to political biography; and with the ten-volume *Abraham Lincoln: A History* by John G. Nicolay and John Hay biography became more monumental in character. By the beginning of the 20th century it had easily eclipsed history in the interest of American readers.

[William P. Trent, John Erskine, Stuart P. Sherman and Carl Van Doren, eds., *The Cambridge History of American Literature*.]

ALLAN NEVINS

Birch Coulee, Battle of. Early Sept. 2, 1862, Sioux Indians attacked the camp near Birch Coulee, Minn., of a mixed force of 170 men commanded by Maj. Joseph R. Brown, despatched from Fort Ridgely to bury Sioux War[qv] victims. After thirty hours and sixty casualties, the detachment was relieved by Col. H. H. Sibley's main army.

[W. W. Folwell, *A History of Minnesota*.]

WILLOUGHBY M. BABCOCK

Birchard Letter, The (June 29, 1863), was a public letter to M. Birchard and eighteen other Ohio Democrats in which President Lincoln defended the administration's treatment of antiwar agitators, and offered to release C. L. Vallandigham[qv] if a majority of those to whom the letter was addressed would subscribe to certain pledges in connection with the prosecution of the Civil War.

[Nicolay and Hay, *Complete Works of Abraham Lincoln*.]

PAUL M. ANGLE

Birch-bark. The bark of the paper birch (*Betula papyrifera*) was used by Indians of the Great Lakes country and adjacent Canada for covering canoes, wigwams, food containers, and cooking vessels. A kettle of this bark will boil food safely, if it does not touch the flames. Small sheets of birch-bark were used for picture writing with a stylus by the Ojibway and a few other Indians. Its use for canoes and shelters extended into Alaska, thence to Siberia.

[W. J. Hoffman, *The Beginnings of Writing;* J. H. Saloman, *Indian Crafts and Lore*.]

CLARK WISSLER

Bird Sanctuaries may be defined as areas in which unnaturally favorable conditions are maintained, by manipulation of environment, for breeding, migrating and wintering birds. Their establishment began in the United States, in 1900, when William Dutcher, Chairman of the Bird Protection Committee of the American Ornithologists' Union, with funds provided by Abbott H. Thayer, the bird painter, employed wardens to protect gulls, terns and other water birds against millinery hunters, who had slaughtered these birds until they faced extermination.

From that time, prime movers in the establishment of bird sanctuaries have been the Audubon Societies[qv] and the Bureau of Biological Survey of the United States Department of Agriculture. Hundreds of sanctuaries have also been set aside by states and individuals but many of them scarcely deserve the name; a survey of nearly a hundred small bird sanctuaries, by Dr. L. E. Hicks, "showed that fully 80% actually contained less bird life after being so designated than before." This was usually the result of too great human interference.

It has been generally true that sanctuaries have been created in response to undeniable needs—initially to protect plume and millinery species, latterly for the harassed and reduced waterfowl.

Two methods have been used by the Audubon Societies in setting up sanctuaries. Permanent areas, such as the Paul J. Rainey Wild Life Sanctuary of 26,000 acres in Louisiana, have been intensively managed for the benefit of their denizens. In other regions the juxtaposition of birds and an Audubon warden has constituted sanctuaries; this system has the advantage of reducing costs consequent on land ownership, and making it possible for guardians to follow their flocks much as herders follow sheep. Under the ownership system, protection is based upon state and Federal conservation laws and trespass statutes; under the latter system, wardens depend entirely on conservation laws. At the present time (1938) a chain of twenty-four Audubon sanctuaries extends from Maine to Texas.

The Federal Government's bird sanctuary program, initiated in 1903, was given a tremendous impetus during the administrations of Franklin D. Roosevelt when more than 230 waterfowl refuges included more than 6,524,000 acres. Vast though this area seems, it is still an inadequate substitute for the more than 100,000,000 acres of once valuable wild-life habitats, turned into wild-life deserts by drainage.

[Anonymous, *Wildlife and the Land:* 75th Congress, 1st Session; T. Gilbert Pearson, in *Fifty Years' Progress of American Ornithology.*]

WILLIAM VOGT

Bird's Invasion of Kentucky (1780) constituted but one phase of an extensive series of operations planned by the British for the year 1780, whereby the entire West, from Canada to Florida, was to be swept clear of both Spaniards and colonists (*see* British Plan of Campaign in the West, 1780). From Detroit, Capt. Bird led an Indian army, accompanied by a few white men, against the settlers of Kentucky. The settlements of Martin's Station and Ruddle's Station were easily overwhelmed, but lack of provisions compelled a retreat. Over 300 prisoners were carried back to Detroit.

[M. M. Quaife, When Detroit Invaded Kentucky, in *Burton Historical Collection Leaflet,* IV, 17-32.]

M. M. QUAIFE

Bird's Point, Mo., neighbor to both Charleston, Mo., and Cairo, Ill., is opposite the mouth of the Ohio River. Of strategic importance in guarding both rivers, it was first fortified by the Spanish in 1795. Col. U. S. Grant was in command of this district for a time, and a few skirmishes took place here during the Civil War.

[Louis Houck, *History of Missouri;* U. S. Grant, *Personal Memoirs; War of the Rebellion Records,* Ser. I, Vol. 3.]

STELLA M. DRUMM

Birth Control. The American birth rate in 1800 was about 50 per 1000 population per year. It gradually fell to about thirty by 1900, and in recent years has approximated sixteen. While the motives leading to this change have arisen from our rising standards of living, the chief instrumentality of the change has been the increased use of mechanical and chemical contraceptives.

In 1802 Malthus taught that man must either limit his reproduction through "moral restraint" or suffer from vice, misery and starvation. In 1822 the "neo-Malthusian" movement began to advocate "preventives" in place of "moral restraint." This has come to be the modern "birth-control movement." Its most influential publication of the 19th century was *The Fruits of Philosophy,* by Dr. Charles Knowlton of Massachusetts, in 1832. The sale of this tract in England led to a famous trial which exonerated the distributors. But in the United States the propaganda was somewhat checked by the Federal Obscenity Law of 1873 and subsequent state enactments. Anthony Comstock was a leader in the suppression. Since 1914, when Margaret Sanger was arrested for distributing her *Family Limitation,* there has been continuous warfare between the birth-control movement and those who would use the obscenity laws to prevent the further spread of contraceptive information or devices. During all this time, despite the questionable legality, contraception has continued to spread. In recent years the legal restrictions have relaxed, mainly through judicial reinterpretations of the law rather than repeal. Nevertheless, the Massachusetts Supreme Court in 1938 compelled the closing of the Boston clinic. The American Birth Control League, the central organization of many local bodies which support clinics and which are commonly known as "maternal health," or "maternal welfare" leagues, in 1938 reported the existence of some 374 birth-control clinics in the United States. The number grows continually. In 1939 the American Birth Control League amalgamated with the other major national organization in this field, the Birth Control Clinical Research Bureau, to form the new "Birth Control Federation of America," with headquarters in New York City. The Roman Catholic Church, a major opponent of the movement, has given approval of the "rhythm method" of contraception.

[D. D. Bromley, *Birth Control, Its Use and Abuse;* N. H. Himes, *Medical History of Contraception.*]

JOSEPH K. FOLSOM

Bishop Hill Colony, a theocratic communistic colony, was founded in Henry County, Ill., in 1846 by Eric Janson who brought there some 1500 emigrants from Sweden where they had been persecuted because of their conversion to perfectionism[qv]. The colony was incorporated in 1853 and was dissolved in 1860. In 1879 many members of the former colony lost their farms to liquidate its debts and the costs of years of litigation.

[G. M. Stephenson, *The Religious Aspects of Swedish Immigration;* M. A. Mikkelsen, *The Bishop Hill Colony;* Johns Hopkins University, *Studies in Historical and Political Science,* Vol. 10.]

G. M. STEPHENSON

Bison. *See* Buffalo, The.

Bit. An archaic term for a currency value of one eighth of a dollar, used chiefly in the South and Southwest, when depreciation of colonial paper money, problems of exchange, coinage and lack of specie caused the circulation of the Spanish real, a silver coin of that value.

[Neil Carothers, *Fractional Money.*]

JOHN FRANCIS, JR.

Bituminous, or soft coal, the major source of power and heat in this country, is mined in twenty-nine states. Approximately 90% of the output, however, comes from thirteen states east of the Mississippi River, with two—Pennsylvania and West Virginia—producing about half the national total. Bituminous statistics usually include lignite and also anthracitic coals mined outside the Pennsylvania anthracite region. In 1936 coal in these two categories accounted for 3,630,000 tons out of a bituminous total of 439,-088,000 tons.

French explorers of the Mississippi Valley were the first to mention coal in this country. Jolliet[qv] and Marquette discovered coal between the present cities of Utica and Ottawa, Ill., in 1673. Commercial mining of bituminous coal, however, started in the Richmond Basin of Virginia about 1750. Illinois mining did not begin until sixty years later, with operations in Jackson County—many miles south of the original discoveries. A small tonnage was reported for Maryland in 1820, but continuous records do not begin until 1842. Kentucky officially entered the picture in 1828, Ohio ten years later and Pennsylvania in 1840.

Bituminous production did not pass anthracite[qv] in annual tonnage until 1870. From that time the general trend was steadily upward until the peak of 1917 when 579,386,000 tons were mined. Two major factors contributed to the phenomenal growth from the 17,371,000-ton total of 1870: these were the rapid development of rail transportation and the industrialization of the nation which set in after the close of the Civil War. Approximately 80% of the output of a normal year is consumed by the railroads, public utilities and general industry. From the standpoint of tonnage, however, the quantity of bituminous coal used directly or indirectly for heating services exceeds that of anthracite.

In recent years increasing competition from oil[qv] and hydroelectric power and the renascence of natural gas[qv] have served as checks upon the continued growth of bituminous coal. Probably even more important in turning down the production curve has been the increased efficiency in utilization by large industrial consumers. Despite these checks, bituminous coal was the source of 45% of the energy consumed in 1937. This percentage, however, understates the importance of coal since most of the crude petroleum and natural gas, which together contributed 40.2% of the total energy supply, do not come into direct competition with coal.

Steady progress in lightening the task of the worker has marked the history of the bituminous coal industry. An eight-hour day[qv] was written into union wage agreements in 1898 (*see* United Mine Workers). Many nonunion operators also adopted that standard so that by 1920, 97.1% of the workers were on an eight-hour basis. Even at the trough of the depression in 1932, the percentage held close to 92. With the advent of N.R.A.[qv], the percentage jumped to 99.8 and the standard work-week was cut from 48 to 40 hours under a government-sponsored agreement effective Oct. 2, 1933. On April 1, 1934, the maximum work-week was further reduced to 35 hours.

The mine mule is yielding to the electric locomotive; operations where animal haulage is now employed are exceptional. Pick mining also is disappearing; in 1891 only 5.3% of the tonnage was undercut by machine, by 1936 the figure was 84.8%. Even more spectacular gains have been made in replacing hand shoveling into cars underground with machine loading. Improvements in cleaning and sizing also have kept pace. Stripping, one of the earliest forms of mining, has assumed new importance with the development of large-capacity equipment.

[*Mineral Resources of the United States,* U. S. Geological Survey, 1879-1923; U. S. Bureau of Mines, 1924-31; *Minerals Yearbook,* U. S. Bureau of Mines, 1932-38.]

SYDNEY A. HALE

Black Ball Line, THE, was the first and most celebrated of the lines of transatlantic sailing packets[qv] from New York. Its popular nickname came from the black disc carried on the fore-topsail and the house flag. On Oct. 27, 1817, came the announcement of regular monthly sailings. Service started at Liverpool on Jan. 4, 1818, and at New York the next day. In 1822 it was increased to semimonthly sailings with eight ships. It was started by five New York textile and cotton merchants, all but one of whom were Quakers[qv]. Jeremiah Thompson is credited with the original idea. After 1834 it was operated by Capt. Charles H. Marshall. The line continued for exactly sixty years, terminating in 1878. During that time forty-three different ships were used.

[R. G. Albion, *Square-Riggers on Schedule.*]

ROBERT G. ALBION

Black Belt, The, is a crescent-shaped area extending along the Alabama River in Alabama and up the Tombigbee in northeastern Mississippi. About three fourths of its 5000 square miles lies in Alabama, including seventeen counties which make up nearly one fourth the entire area of the state. This region derives its name from the black soil which is prevalent here in contrast to the red clays to the north and south. The Black Belt is a prairie which lies much lower than the surrounding country due to the decomposition of the soft limestone rock which underlies the soil. This rock decomposition has given it a remarkably fertile soil which makes it one of the best agricultural regions of the entire South.

That portion of the Black Belt which lies in Alabama was first opened for settlement by the Creek[qv] cession of 1816. However, the pioneers were suspicious of the unusual black soil and it was not until the Jacksonian migration of the 1830's that the region began to be settled. The Mississippi portion was opened at this time, too, as the Choctaw and Chickasaw[qqv] moved west of the Mississippi. On account of the high fertility of the soil and the accessibility to market at Mobile it was inevitable that the Black Belt should become a plantation region producing great crops of cotton[qv] by slave labor. The slave population, in fact, at one time reached 87% of the whole, and thus afforded an additional justification of the name. From 1830 to 1860 the Black Belt of Alabama was the most prosperous portion of the state, held the most slaves, produced the most cotton, and was the bulwark of the Whig party[qv]. All the rivers of Alabama, except the Tennessee, water the region, and three of the five state capitals–Cahaba, Tuscaloosa and Montgomery–were located there.

With the coming of the Civil War, the Black Belt turned from cotton production to the raising of foodstuffs and furnished throughout the war a great part of the food supplies for the Confederate armies. As it had almost no railroad connections with the West or North it remained practically untouched by the Northern armies. After the war it again became the leading cotton-producing region of the South until 1880. In recent times, unable to meet the competition of Texas cotton, it has turned more and more to diversified farming and the raising of food crops, although still the principal cotton region east of the Mississippi.

[T. P. Abernethy, *The Formative Period in Alabama;* U. B. Phillips, *American Negro Slavery.*]

R. S. COTTERILL

Black Boys, The, were Pennsylvania frontiersmen who, in 1763, 1765 and 1769, came together under the leadership of James Smith to defend the frontier against the Indians, and who, in 1765, burned a pack-horse train belonging to Baynton, Wharton and Morgan[qv] engaged in the Indian trade (*see* Sideling Hill).

[A. T. Volwiler, *George Croghan and the Westward Movement;* Neil Swanson, *The First Rebel.*]

JULIAN P. BOYD

Black Codes, The, were laws passed in the ex-Confederate states in 1865–66, which dealt with the status of the Negro as affected by the abolition of slavery. As a rule, the laws were not organized as a separate code, in the usual sense of the word, but were statutes in the different states which dealt with vagrancy, apprenticeship, penalty for crime, property rights, etc. For the most part they adapted old principles on these subjects to the new conditions. The Negro was defined usually as "a person of color," one who had a certain degree of African blood, usually fixed at one eighth. Intermarriage between the races was forbidden. Marital relations and family responsibilities were legalized. Vagrancy laws attempted to force Negroes to work when many wished to "enjoy their freedom." Apprentice laws aimed to provide for orphans and the destitute young by hiring them out, usually to their former owners. Labor contracts provided means by which the Negroes might be held to steady labor, such as was required for the production of staple crops. Laws gave to the Negroes the ordinary civil rights to sue and be sued, and to give testimony in court, but only in cases involving Negroes. The laws varied greatly among the states, being most restrictive to the Negro in Mississippi and South Carolina, where the colored population largely outnumbered the white.

From the point of view of the South the laws were constructive measures to prevent complete chaos when the whole social system embodied in slavery was suddenly destroyed. From the point of view of the North the legislation expressed an attempt to revive slavery under another guise. The black codes furnished evidence to the already dissatisfied Radical Republicans[qv] that the state governments set up by President Johnson gave inadequate security to the permanence of Union victory, and so encouraged their demand for more thorough reconstruction[qv] by Congress (*see* Civil Rights Act; Fourteenth Amendment).

[W. A. Dunning, *Reconstruction, Political and Economic.*]

C. MILDRED THOMPSON

Black Friday (Sept. 24, 1869) was the climactic day of an effort by Jay Gould, James Fisk, Jr., Abel Rathbone Corbin and one or two associates to corner the ready gold supply of the United States. The nation then being on a paper-money basis, gold was dealt in as a speculative commodity on the New York exchange. Gould and Fisk first enlisted Corbin, who had married President Grant's sister; they then drew the new head of the New York Sub-Treasury, Daniel Butterfield, into the scheme, and unsuccessfully tried to involve Grant's private secretary, Horace Porter. On June 15, 1869, they entertained Grant on Fisk's Bristol Line steamboat, attempted to learn the Treasury's gold policy, and argued that it was important to keep gold high in order to facilitate sales of American grain in Europe. Grant was noncommittal. A gold corner did not seem difficult if government nonintervention could be assured, for New York banks in the summer of 1869 held only about $14,000,000 in gold, not more than a million was in local circulation and time would be required to bring more from Europe. On Sept. 2 Gould began buying gold on a large scale; on the 15th Fisk began buying heavily and soon forced the price from 135 to 140. The movement excited much suspicion and fear and on the 13th the *New York Tribune* declared it the "clear and imperative duty" of the Treasury to sell gold and break up the conspiracy. Secretary Boutwell visited New York but decided not to act; meanwhile Grant had gone to Washington, Pa., and was out of touch until he returned to Washington on Sept. 22. On the 23d, with gold at 144, the New York panic grew serious.

The climax of Black Friday found Fisk driving gold higher and higher, business profoundly disturbed throughout the nation, and the New York gold room a pandemonium as scores were ruined. As the price rose to 160 Boutwell in Washington urged the sale of three millions of the gold reserve, Grant suggested five, and the Secretary telegraphed an order to sell four. Gould, perhaps forewarned by Butterfield, had already begun selling and gold sank rapidly to 135; Fisk immediately found means to repudiate his contracts. The episode caused heavy indirect losses to business and placed an ugly smirch on the Grant administration.

[F. C. Hicks, ed., *High Finance in the Sixties;* G. S. Boutwell, *Reminiscences of Sixty Years in Public Affairs;* James Schouler, *History of the United States*, VII.]

ALLAN NEVINS

Black Hand. The Italian Mafia or Black Hand was a Sicilian secret society of a type fairly common since the Middle Ages. Its discipline was drastic, members being put to death for crimes against the society quite as ruthlessly as persons of whom the society disapproved. Attempts in Italy to suppress the organization caused many members to emigrate to the Southern states; it is best known here because of the famous incident in New Orleans, in 1891, caused by the ruthless murder of Chief of Police John C. Hennessey. (*See* Mafia Incident.)

[William E. Curtis, *The United States and Foreign Powers;* W. Brooke Graves, *American State Government.*]

W. BROOKE GRAVES

Black Hawk Purchase, THE, was the closing episode of the Black Hawk War[qv] and marked the first cession of land in Iowa. The treaty, negotiated by Gen. Winfield Scott and Gov. John Reynolds of Illinois, on the present site of Davenport, Iowa, was signed at Fort Armstrong[qv] on Rock Island on Sept. 21, 1832. Nine Sauks[qv] (including Keokuk) and twenty-four Foxes[qv] signed the treaty. Black Hawk was held captive in Jefferson Barracks[qv] at the time and did not sign the treaty which paid the red man fourteen cents an acre for 6,000,000 acres of land. The Indians ceded a tract about fifty miles wide along the Mississippi from the southern boundary of the Neutral Ground[qv] to the Missouri line. An oblong tract of 400 square miles was reserved for Keokuk and his followers as a reward for remaining out of the war. The Indians were to receive an annuity of $20,000 in specie for thirty years. The Government agreed to maintain one black- and gunsmith shop for three decades, and deliver forty kegs of tobacco and forty barrels of salt yearly for the same period. The treaty set aside $40,000 for the just debts of the Indians and restricted Black Hawk and his followers. The Indians agreed to remove by June 1, 1833, the date marking the beginning of legal settlement in Iowa.

[W. J. Petersen, The Terms of Peace, in *The Palimpsest*, 13: 74-89.]

WILLIAM J. PETERSEN

Black Hawk War, THE (1832), was waged chiefly in Illinois and Wisconsin between the United States and a faction of the Sauk and Fox Indians[qqv] led by Chief Black Hawk, whose home village was near Rock Island, Ill. In November, 1804, certain spokesmen of the two tribes had ceded to the Government their title to 50,000,000 acres of land, comprising the northwestern half of Illinois and much of southwestern Wisconsin and eastern Missouri. The validity of this cession was hotly denied by Black Hawk, who was supported by a formidable fraction of the two tribes. The issue became acute in 1831, when squatters pre-empted the site of Black Hawk's village, and the Chief threatened forcible resistance. An army of regulars and Illinois militia was embodied, however, and before this threat of force Black Hawk yielded and withdrew to the Iowa side of the Mississippi.

Early in 1832 he recrossed the river with several hundred followers, intent on joining the friendly Winnebago^{qv} and raising a crop of corn. Gen. Atkinson ordered him to return to Iowa, and since he did not comply, the war was on. Black Hawk slowly retired up Rock River, the white forces pursued, and numerous killings and minor activities took place. Before long Black Hawk perceived the futility of his foray into Illinois and made proffers of peace, which were ignored. The remnant of his despairing followers was pursued westward across southern Wisconsin to the mouth of Bad Axe^{qv} River, where, on Aug. 3, they were practically annihilated. At Fort Armstrong^{qv}, in September, Gen. Scott compelled the Winnebago to cede their possessions in Wisconsin and the Sauks and Foxes to cede all of eastern Iowa, by way of punishment for the war (*see* Black Hawk Purchase).

[*Autobiography of Black Hawk;* Frank E. Stevens, *The Black Hawk War.*]

M. M. QUAIFE

Black Hills, THE, lying chiefly in South Dakota and skirting over into southeastern Wyoming, are formed by an upthrust of the archean rock through the overlying strata to a maximum height of 7242 feet above sea level. Mount Harney is the granite (archean) core of the upthrust. Passing from the surrounding prairie through the foothills to Mount Harney, the explorer walks over the upcrop of each strata which rises in regular order: the shales, redbeds (gypsum), sandstone, schists, limestones, and granite as they are folded back, affording an unusual opportunity to study the geological formations underlying the region. The Black Hills were embraced within the Great Sioux Reservation as defined by the Laramie Treaty of 1868^{qv}. Gold was found in the Hills by miners accompanying Gen. Custer's expedition of 1874 which set out from Fort Abraham Lincoln^{qv} (Bismarck) to find a practicable highway to Fort Laramie^{qv}. The "discovery" created much excitement, but the Federal Government sought to protect the rights of the Indians until they had been duly extinguished by treaty. When early efforts to accomplish this release failed by reason of the refusal of the Sioux^{qv} to agree upon reasonable terms, the Government raised the embargo and gold hunters rushed into the diggings in vast numbers. This invasion led to the Black Hills War, the high feature of which was the destruction of Custer's army on the Little Bighorn^{qv} in June, 1876. After this affair the Government forced a treaty of relinquishment and civil government was established.

The miners first assembled at Custer, where 15,000 passed the winter of 1875–76. Gold having been found in Deadwood Gulch, there was a stampede from Custer to the new diggings early in 1876 and Deadwood became in a day the most exciting and picturesque gold camp on the continent. The diggings at that time were entirely in placer gravel, but before autumn the Homestake lead had been located and passed into the hands of San Francisco capitalists. The Homestake Gold Mine was developed and for sixty-two years has yielded fabulous sums. Its engineers believe its stores of ore cannot be depleted for scores of years to come.

There are extensive gold deposits in and about Keystone and that region is very heavily mineralized. Mica, spodumine, ambligonite, feldspar, arsenic, gold, silver and galena are produced in commercial values. More than 100 valuable minerals are present. Custer State Park is very extensive and scenically attractive. President Coolidge, with his staff, made it his summer home in 1927. The Needles Highway and Iron Mountain road within the park are nationally popular.

On Mount Rushmore, of the Harney Range, in the park, the Federal Government is nearing the completion of a colossal national memorial, consisting of massive sculptures of Washington, Lincoln, Jefferson and Theodore Roosevelt, by Gutzon Borglum^{qv}. The memorial is located essentially in the center of the North American Continent, upon the highest range between Pikes Peak and the Matterhorn.

DOANE ROBINSON

Black-Horse Cavalry, THE, is the name applied to a bipartisan group of corruptionists in the New York legislature which during the last quarter of the 19th century preyed particularly on corporations. It usually blackmailed by introducing bills against the corporations which would be killed if sufficient money were forthcoming.

[Theodore Roosevelt, *An Autobiography.*]

HAROLD ZINK

Black Jack, Battle of (June 2, 1856), was the first engagement of the Kansas Border War^{qv}. John Brown had committed the massacre of Potawatomie^{qv} Creek. In retaliation a Missouri band under Capt. Pate seized two of Brown's sons. Brown attacked Pate at Black Jack, near Baldwin, Kans. After minor casualties on each side Pate surrendered with twenty-one men. Both bands were dispersed by Col. Sumner of the Regular Army. Fighting revived, extended throughout the Border and merged at last in the Civil War.

[W. E. Connelley, *Standard History of Kansas and Kansans.*]

WILLIAM M. BALCH

Black Laws. Ohio enacted laws in 1804 and 1807, compelling registration of all Negroes in the state, forbidding any free Negro to remain without giving $500 bond against his becoming a public charge, denying validity to a Negro's testimony in trials where whites were involved, etc. These laws were an issue in the state campaign of 1846, and in the legislative session of 1848–49, with the Free Soil party[qv] leading the attack upon them, they were repealed.

[Charles B. Galbreath, *History of Ohio.*]

ALVIN F. HARLOW

Black Legion, The (*ca.* 1936), a secret organization which sought to usurp the functions of government in Michigan and adjoining states, first attracted public notice by its "execution," May 12, 1936, of Charles A. Poole of Detroit. The resultant criminal prosecutions and sweeping expression of public condemnation soon drove the order into obscurity and, possibly, to dissolution.

[See Detroit newspaper files, 1936-37, especially *Detroit News*, April 22, 1937.]

M. M. QUAIFE

Black Legs is a term now used in a general sense which once had a special significance, being associated peculiarly with the history of "Natchez-Under-the-Hill." It referred to professional gamblers possessing large capital, associated in perfectly organized gangs which robbed, murdered and plundered with impunity in the early period of the Old Southwest.

[Robert Coates, *The Outlaw Years.*]

JAMES W. SILVER

Black Patch War, The, resulted from attempts of Kentucky and Tennessee tobacco growers to overcome monopolistic control of markets and prices. By 1906 producers were sufficiently organized to threaten control of the "Trust." In the "Black Patch" or "dark fired" tobacco area, which embraced counties in southwestern Kentucky and adjoining districts in Tennessee, aggressive methods imposed by association members, and retaliation by non-members, resulted in much violence. During 1907 and 1908 "night riding"[qv] by the "Silent Brigade" was prevalent. Speculation in warehouse receipts, increased production in unrestricted areas, adverse court decisions and general friction, hostility and suspicion doomed the movement to deterioration.

[John G. Miller, *The Black Patch War;* B. H. Hibbard, *Marketing Agricultural Products.*]

FRED COLE

Black Rock, Bombardment of (Oct. 13, 1812). In reprisal for the capture of two British sloops by a small American naval force, Black Rock (at the northern end of the village of Buffalo) was subjected to a heavy bombardment. The short range of the guns on the American shore prevented an effective answer and considerable damage to the village was caused. During the bombardment news came of the American defeat at Queenston Heights[qv] and a week's armistice was arranged to permit the burial of the killed.

[L. L. Babcock, *The War of 1812 on the Niagara Frontier;* R. W. Bingham, *The Cradle of the Queen City.*]

JULIAN PARK

Black Swamp, The, is a term once applied to much of northwestern Ohio but more accurately to an area lying chiefly in the drainage basin of the Maumee River, including all or parts of a dozen present-day counties. Most of this region was once under the waters of Lake Erie. It is so level and swampy that drainage difficulties, the prevalence of malarial diseases and its general inaccessibility for a long time retarded settlement. After 1850, when drainage and transportation problems began to be solved, the region underwent a rapid development and today constitutes one of the richest farming sections of the state.

[Henry Howe, *Historical Collections of Ohio*, Vol. II.]

EUGENE H. ROSEBOOM

***Black Warrior* Affair,** The. The *Black Warrior,* a vessel in the American coastwise trade, touched at Havana, Cuba, Feb. 28, 1854, on her eighteenth voyage to New York. In technical conformity with law, but contrary to informal agreements, a cargo manifest was demanded. Failing this, the ship was seized, but was restored to her owners on payment of a $6000 fine, subsequently remitted. The controversy called forth able papers by William L. Marcy, Secretary of State, but the tactics of Pierre Soulé, American minister to Spain, temporarily threatened war. Linked somewhat with the Ostend

Manifesto^qv^, the issue hung fire until August, 1855, when Spain paid an indemnity of $53,000.

[*See* sketch of William L. Marcy, by H. B. Learned, in *The American Secretaries of State and Their Diplomacy* series, edited by Samuel Flagg Bemis, Vol. VI; A. A. Ettinger, *The Mission to Spain of Pierre Soulé.*]

LOUIS MARTIN SEARS

Blackburn's Ford, Battle at (July 18, 1861). On his advance to Bull Run^qv^ McDowell (U.) ordered Tyler's division to reconnoiter toward Manassas Junction. Tyler found Longstreet's (C.) brigade in position behind Bull Run at Blackburn's Ford, attacked, and was decisively repulsed. The morale of McDowell's army suffered from this initial reverse.

[*Battles and Leaders of the Civil War*, Vol. I; *Official Records, Union and Confederate Armies*, Vol. II.]

JOSEPH MILLS HANSON

Blackfeet, THE, a confederacy of the Siksika proper, Bloods and Piegan sub-tribes, so called because of the color of their moccasins, are members of the Algonquian^qv^ linguistic family and thus related to the eastern timber tribes. Acquiring the horse, they appear to have migrated to the Northwest, adopted the culture of the plains tribes and, existing chiefly on buffalo meat, come to occupy a territory some 300 miles in width along the eastern slope of the Rocky Mountains between the North Saskatchewan River, Canada, and the southern headwaters of the Missouri in Montana. They had great herds of horses and were in frequent conflict with neighboring tribes. While hostile to the white man in early days, they never waged actual war against the United States. In 1855 they were located in part on a reservation in northwest Montana where their descendants now reside.

[F. W. Hodge, *Handbook of American Indians;* G. B. Grinnell, *Blackfoot Lodge Tales.*]

JOHN FRANCIS, JR.

Blacklisting is the practice of circulating among employers the names of union members, labor agitators, strikers, or persons otherwise distasteful. Such information may be furnished one employer by another upon request, or possibly by an employers' association serving as a sort of clearinghouse. Blacklisting is a longstanding antiunion employer technique; the aggressive unionism of the 1830's faced a widespread blacklisting; the railroads maintained blacklists in the 1860's. In part, at least, the blacklist provoked the secret organizations of labor in the 1870's, the outstanding example of which was the Knights of Labor^qv^. Many states, beginning in the 1880's, at one time or another, endeavored to prohibit or restrict the practice, but the secret methods open to employers made detection virtually impossible. Proof was practically out of the question. Hence, in 1926, Commons and Andrews wrote "Blacklisting is legal in the United States to all intents and purposes." This remained the case so long as the right to discharge workers for union activity and membership remained legally unchallenged. The National Labor Relations Act^qv^ of 1935, which prohibited discharge for union activity, clarified this general situation.

[Commons and Andrews, *Principles of Labor Legislation;* A. G. Taylor, *Labor Problems and Labor Law;* Commons and associates, *History of Labor in the United States.*]

HERBERT MAYNARD DIAMOND

Blacksmith, THE. In colonial times the blacksmith was an important factor of the community. The first colony at Jamestown^qv^, Va., in 1607, brought over a blacksmith. Plymouth Colony^qv^ in 1626 enacted, "no smiths shall use their science or Trade . . . for any streangers . . . til . . . the necessity of the Colony be served." About 1635 Lynn assigned a blacksmith twenty acres. In 1642 Plymouth ordered smiths to "repaire armes speedyly," and to take corn for their pay. Secretary van Tienhoren in 1650 wrote that New Netherland^qv^ required "a blacksmith conversant with the treatment of horses and cattle." In 1694 a blacksmith's apprentice at Elizabeth, Va., after seven years' service, was to receive a full set of tools and clothing.

The blacksmith did the ironwork for implements, tools and the household. As roads were developed, horseshoes, horseshoeing and tires became important.

In 1810 Pennsylvania reported 2562 blacksmith shops, doing $1,572,627 worth of work. In 1850 the United States had 100,000 blacksmiths and whitesmiths, besides gunsmiths and machinists.

The blacksmith shop was the meeting place of all trades, where the blacksmith often led the discussions. Thomas Hazard, whose diary for 1777–81 is published, was a village philosopher. Nathanael Greene worked in his father's foundry before becoming a Revolutionary general. Elihu Burritt, the peace advocate, was called "The Learned Blacksmith." Longfellow wrote "The Village Blacksmith" in eulogy of his own ancestor. Henry Ward Beecher came from a line of blacksmiths. R. H. Stoddard, the writer, and Robert Collyer, the clergyman, started as blacksmiths.

HERBERT MANCHESTER

Blackstock's Hill, Battle of. *See* Enoree, Battle of.

Blackwater, Battle of (Dec. 18, 1861). While campaigning against the Confederate Gen. Sterling Price in Missouri, part of Gen. Pope's command, under Col. J. C. Davis, surrounded an enemy force south of Milford at the mouth of Clear Creek (vicinity of Warrensburg), and compelled its surrender. This was part of Pope's campaign to strip Price of supplies and munitions.

[*War of the Rebellion, Official Records of the Union and Confederate Armies*, Series I, Vol. VIII.]

ROBERT S. THOMAS

Bladensburg, Battle of (Aug. 24, 1814). Maj. Gen. Robert Ross, with 4500 British troops, landed on the Patuxent River in Maryland, Aug. 19–20, thus compelling Commodore Joshua Barney to destroy his gunboat flotilla in that river. The British force then turned toward Washington. About 6000 District and Maryland militia, a few regulars and Barney's seamen constituted the defensive force under Maj. Gen. William Winder. Ross reached Bladensburg Aug. 24. Across the river, on rising ground, Winder hastily and unskilfully posted his army, already worn down by three days' futile maneuvering, sleepless nights and scanty food. The British advanced steadily under artillery fire, drove back the American light troops after crossing the bridge, and approached the second line. Showers of Congreve rockets so terrified the raw militia that two regiments disintegrated immediately. A Baltimore regiment offered some resistance but broke when ordered to fall back. Barney's naval contingent, firing eighteen-pounders, checked Ross for a time, retreating only when its flanks were uncovered by fleeing infantry supports, its ammunition expended and Barney wounded. A general retirement, ordered by Winder, was effected in fair order, the British being too exhausted to pursue vigorously. Halting briefly at Capitol Hill, the Americans marched on to Georgetown. Ross entered Washington and burned the Capitol, presidential mansion and public buildings. President Madison, Secretary of War Armstrong, Secretary of State Monroe and Attorney General Rush were on the field during part of the battle. American losses were insignificant, those of the British rather severe. A congressional investigation whitewashed all concerned, but the uselessness of undisciplined militia against British regulars was again demonstrated. Winder was exculpated by a court of inquiry, and Armstrong, made the scapegoat by the public, was compelled to resign. Failure of the administration to adopt defensive measures in time may be considered the true explanation of the disaster. (*See also* Washington Burned.)

[J. S. Williams, *History of the Invasion and Capture of Washington;* American State Papers, Military Affairs, I, 524-599.]

CHARLES WINSLOW ELLIOTT

Bladensburg Duelling Field was five miles from Washington, but in the jurisdiction of Maryland, where statutes against duelling were more lax than in the District of Columbia. Thirty to fifty duels were fought there by statesmen, military and naval officers and civilians from 1802 until 1851. The most famous were the mortal wounding of Commodore Decatur by Commodore Barron (1820) and the killing of Sen. A. T. Mason of Virginia by his brother-in-law J. M. McCarty (1819).

[D. C. Seitz, *Some Famous Duels.*]

RICHARD J. PURCELL

Bland-Allison Act, The (Feb. 28, 1878), was the first of several United States Government subsidies to silver producers in depression periods. The five-year depression following the Panic of 1873^qv^ caused cheap-money advocates (led by Representative R. P. Bland of Missouri) to join with silver-producing interests in urging return to bimetallism^qv^. The silver dollar had been omitted from the list of coins by a mint reform act, which lent itself to the political soubriquet of "The Crime of '73,"^qv^ and silver^qv^ had depreciated with other commodities. The allies demanded restoration of free coinage of silver at "16–1," approximately $1.29 an ounce.

Free coinage, as the symbol of justice for the poor, was seized upon by greenbackers^qv^ and others determined to prevent resumption of specie payments^qv^ and to make government obligations payable in silver. When Bland's bill for free coinage, passed by the House, jeopardized Secretary of the Treasury Sherman's plans for resuming specie payments, Sherman substituted limited purchases for free coinage, through a Senate amendment sponsored by Sen. W. B. Allison of Iowa. The producers accepted the arrangement as likely to restore silver to $1.29.

The law required Government purchase, at market prices, of $2,000,000 to $4,000,000 worth of silver bullion monthly, and coinage into legal tender "16–1" dollars, exchangeable for $10 silver certificates receivable for public dues and reissuable. The President was directed to arrange an international bimetallic conference to meet within six months. These provisions signified:—victory for producers over inflationists, defeat of international bimetallists by national bimetallists, a drain on the Treasury through the customs in times of uncertainty and failure for the conference.

[H. B. Russell, *International Monetary Conferences.*]

JEANNETTE P. NICHOLS

Blast Furnaces, Early. From the earliest days of English colonization, Englishmen pointed out that the smelting of iron in the New World for England's manufacturers would be advantageous to the mother country in view of the diminishing English forests which furnished fuel for the production of iron. The first attempt to build blast furnaces in the colonies was made in Virginia by the London Company[qv]. The project was not successful. The Puritans[qv] in Massachusetts established the first successful ironworks as early as 1644 (*see* Iron Industry, Early, Furnaces and Forges). The colonial iron industry, however, made slow progress in the 17th century.

Not until the 18th century did the smelting of iron in America become important. The colonial iron industry then went through a process of remarkable development. By the outbreak of the American Revolution there were more blast furnaces in the American colonies than in England and Wales, and American furnaces produced more pig iron and castings than English furnaces.

Colonial blast furnaces were patterned after those of the mother country. Built of stone, they were usually about twenty-five feet square at the bottom and from twenty-five to thirty feet high. Although square, they were larger at the bottom than at the top; thus they resembled truncated pyramids. The blast, forced through a single tuyère into the furnace, was produced by large bellows driven by water power. Before 1800 blowing cylinders were substituted for bellows at a number of furnaces. American furnaces continued to use charcoal fuel and cold blast until just before 1840 when some ironmasters began using anthracite[qv] coal. Later, coke displaced anthracite and charcoal as a furnace fuel. The early iron industry was the foundation upon which the great iron and steel industry[qv] of the present was established.

[Arthur C. Bining, *British Regulation of the Colonial Iron Industry;* Arthur C. Bining, *Pennsylvania Iron Manufacture in the Eighteenth Century;* V. S. Clark, *History of Manufactures in the United States, 1607-1860.*]

ARTHUR C. BINING

Blease Movement in South Carolina, The, developed in the 1900's from the failure of the Tillman Movement[qv] to satisfy the ambitions of the white masses. By studiously imitating Ben Tillman's vehement attacks on Negroes, aristocrats and clerical politicians, Cole L. Blease became something of the popular idol Tillman had formerly been. Elected governor in 1910, his administration was bizarre, but not criminal. He pardoned extravagantly and answered the snubs of the opposition with abusive language. Although the combined opposition of Tillman and the upper classes could not prevent his reelection in 1912, his influence thereafter declined and his repeated attempts to win high office usually ended in failure. Blease lacked a constructive program and the prudence of a successful organizer. But his agitations had permanently quickened the political consciousness of the cotton-mill operatives and other poor whites.

[D. D. Wallace, *The History of South Carolina.*]

FRANCIS B. SIMKINS

Bleeding Kansas. *See* Border War, 1854–59.

Blennerhassett Island in the Ohio River below the mouth of the Little Kanawha River, an Indian rendezvous, was first known as Backus Island for Elijah Backus who purchased it in 1792. It is famous as the site of Blennerhassett House, where Aaron Burr and Harman Blennerhassett, who purchased the north end of the island in 1798, are alleged to have plotted treason against the United States. (*See* Burr Conspiracy, The.)

[William H. Safford, *The Life of Harman Blennerhassett.*]

CHARLES H. AMBLER

Blessing of the Bay, second seaworthy vessel built in what is now the United States, preceded only by the *Virginia,* a thirty-ton pinnace built by the Popham Colony[qv] at the mouth of the Kennebec River, Maine, in 1607. The *Blessing of the Bay,* a thirty-ton bark, mostly of locust, was built at a cost of £145 for John Winthrop at Mistick (now Medford), Mass., by Robert Molton and other shipwrights sent to New England in 1629 by the Company of the Massachusetts Bay[qv], and was launched July 4, 1631. She went to sea Aug. 31, 1631, and carried on a coastwise trade as far south as the Dutch town of New Amsterdam[qv] (New York).

[John Robinson and G. F. Dow, *Sailing Ships of New England;* W. B. Weeden, *Economic and Social History of New England.*]

R. W. G. VAIL

Blind, The. The first school for the blind to be set up in the United States was in New York City in 1832, and the second, though organized in 1829, was opened in Boston a few months later than the New York school. The third school was in Philadelphia in 1833. These three schools were all under private societies, with state appropriations to assist in their support. In 1837 a school was established in Ohio as a state institution; and from this time on nearly all the schools brought into being have been of like character. Besides the public institutions in which blind children are boarded and given care, there have been started in a number of cities day schools, more on the order of the regular public schools, the first being in Chicago in 1900. Home teaching carried into the homes of blind persons began formally in Connecticut in 1893. It is now carried on more or less definitely in about half of the states. Special industrial establishments or workshops number close to fourscore. The first one was in connection with the school in Boston in 1840. The initial independent shop was in Philadelphia in 1874. A little more than twenty special homes for the adult blind have been founded, the first being in Philadelphia, New York City and St. Louis, all started in 1868.

For the blind in general, there has been provided raised print, consisting in the largest part of a system of dots. In 1868 there was invented a special form known as New York Point, and in 1878 a system called American Braille, a modification of the original European Braille. In 1932 an agreement was reached calling for the use, with slight modifications, of English or European Braille.

In 1855 there was established at Louisville, Ky., the American Printing House for the Blind, which in 1879 began to receive an annual subsidy from the Federal Government. There are now several other printing plants. About twoscore periodicals are published in raised print, the chief of which is the *Matilda Ziegler Magazine for the Blind,* established in 1907. In 1868 a special library for the blind was begun at the Boston Public Library, a plan that has now extended to different cities. In 1896 a state library for the blind was inaugurated by New York. In 1897 a department for the blind was created at the Library of Congress at Washington.

Before the adoption of the Social Security[qv] law in 1936, pensions were provided by law in a little over one half of the states. The first were introduced in the city of New York in 1866, and in the state of Ohio in 1898. Through the Social Security law pensions are now available in the larger number of states. Private associations doing various forms of social service for the blind are found in many cities, the first in New York in 1905. Such bodies are also found in most of the states, Massachusetts coming first in 1903. Public commissions or other agencies for the blind, with like purposes, are found in a little more than half of the states, the first general one being in Massachusetts in 1903.

[Harry Best, *Blindness and the Blind in United States.*]

HARRY BEST

Blizzards. This word is applied to snowstorms or drifting snow accompanied by severe cold and strong winds. It probably first appeared in print in this sense about 1870, but was widely used by 1880.

The most famous blizzard in American history is that of March 11, 1888, in the northeastern states. The streets of New York City were piled with twelve feet of snow in many places; in Herald Square the drift was thirty feet deep. There were no means of transportation except sleighs. Fires started and burned themselves out because fire-fighting apparatus could not move through the streets. A food panic threatened, as thousands were marooned in their homes. The Stock Exchange suspended business, telegraph communication was cut, and railroads stopped running. For a while the East River was frozen over. This blizzard took an unknown number of lives, including that of Sen. Roscoe Conkling, and caused a property loss of $25,000,000.

Another famous blizzard was in Kansas in January, 1886. Almost 100 lives were lost, and stock by the thousands perished. Animals drifted with the storm until caught by fences or other obstructions, and froze to death in the drifts. After the storm bodies of stock, rabbits, antelope and even wolves were found huddled together.

More than 200 people were said to have perished in the Dakotas and adjoining states during the blizzard of Jan. 12, 1888. In that storm the wind attained a velocity of sixty miles an hour, the temperature falling 60° in twenty-four hours.

The storm of May 3–4, 1905, in the Dakotas, caught stockmen and homesteaders unprepared. Stock had already been turned out on the ranges and had shed their winter coats, and fruit trees were in blossom. When the blizzard came, great drifts were piled in the streets of Rapid City. Stock were driven blindly before the wind, over canyon walls, and into the draws where they were buried deep in the drifts. This storm caused greater livestock loss than any other in the history of the region.

On Dec. 4–5, 1913, Denver, Colo., experienced its worst blizzard. Due to the comparatively high air temperatures, however, there was little suffering as a result of the unusually heavy snowfall.

On Jan. 27, 1922, a severe snowstorm occurred on the Middle Atlantic seaboard. In Washington, D. C., it was known as the Knickerbocker storm, because the collapse of the roof of the Knickerbocker Theater killed nearly 100 persons.

The blizzard of Feb. 13–14, 1923, was one of the worst on record in the Dakotas and Minnesota, marked by unusually low temperatures. Notwithstanding ample warnings from the Weather Bureau, good telephone connections and better housing than in the old days, more than twenty people froze to death.

One of the worst blizzards since 1886 swept the Plains states on March 26–27, 1931, and was especially severe in Colorado and Kansas.

[*Bulletin of the American Meteorological Society*, *4*, p. 45; *9*, p. 55; *10*, p. 78; *11*, p. 47; *12*, p. 72. *Tycos-Rochester* Oct., 1928, p. 150; April, 1931, p. 70; April, 1932, p. 66; Jan., 1933, p. 34.]

RICHMOND T. ZOCH

Blockade is the effective cutting off of communications to a port by a blockading squadron to such an extent that communications are rendered dangerous. Since the close of the Revolution the blockade has played an important part in American naval and diplomatic history. The United States has always maintained that a blockade to be valid and binding must be maintained by a force strong enough to make it effective. This was first announced in the Treaty Plan of the Continental Congress of 1784. During the Napoleonic wars the United States protested to Great Britain and other Powers against blockades in name only. In his war message to Congress, June 1, 1812, President James Madison declared that "pretended blockades" under the name of "orders in council"*qv* had been used as a pretext for plundering American commerce. In 1814 he issued a proclamation against the "paper" British blockade of the Atlantic coast, claiming that it was not effective and formed no lawful obstacle for neutral shipping. The first American treaty to define a valid blockade was made with Colombia in 1824, when a blockaded port was defined as one "actually attacked by a belligerent force capable of preventing the entry of the Neutral."

At the outbreak of the Mexican War*qv* the naval commanders in the Gulf and on the Pacific coast were ordered to blockade as many Mexican ports as they could effectually. During the Civil War*qv* the Federal Navy maintained a blockade of the ports of the Confederate states*qv*, the most extensive in history. In the Spanish-American War*qv* the Navy maintained a blockade of all Cuban ports and of San Juan, Puerto Rico. The United States Naval War Code of 1900 reiterated the principle of a valid blockade as did the Declaration of London of 1909*qv*. In 1915 the British and French governments declared that they would "detain and take into port ships carrying goods of presumed enemy destination, ownership, or origin." This declaration was made effective by a British order in council of March 11, 1915, and by a French decree of March 13. The American Government on Oct. 21, 1915, protested against thus detaining American shipping, claiming that their blockade was ineffective and illegal, and that it involved a curtailment of neutral trading rights. When the United States entered the war the Navy assisted in maintaining the blockade of Germany's coast until the Armistice. (*See also* Foreign Policy.)

[U. S. Department of State, *Policy of the United States Toward Maritime Commerce in War*, 2 Vols.; C. C. Soule and C. McCauley, *International Law for Naval Officers*, 3rd ed.]

LOUIS H. BOLANDER

Blockade Runners, Confederate. With the number of violations of the blockade estimated at 8250 and the risk of capture averaging one in six, the trade proved highly lucrative. The value to the Confederacy is told in the record of 1,250,000 bales of cotton run out; in 600,000 small arms and other munitions, in the endless supplies of provisions, clothing, hospital stores, manufactures and luxuries run in. The goods entering the Confederacy were valued at $200,000,000. Except for the blockade runners the armies would more than once have been on the verge of starvation; except for the increasing stringency of the blockade they would probably have enabled the South to win its independence. They kept a Federal squadron of 600 vessels occupied. Furthermore, they afforded the one means of outside communication. On the debit side must be ranged the facts that the traffic drained away the gold, thus contributing to depreciation of Confederate currency; that it drew attention to the ports, probably precipitating attacks upon their defenses; that the yellow fever scourge in Wilmington was traceable to a blockade runner; and that the traffic, stimulating a hunger for speculation and the riotous living of the blockade-running gentry, demoralized many citizens.

[F. C. Bradlee, *Blockade Running During the Civil War;* F. L. Owsley, *King Cotton Diplomacy;* J. R. Soley, *The Blockade and the Cruisers.*]

ELLA LONN

"Blocks of Five." This phrase acquired notoriety during the Harrison-Cleveland election of 1888 when Dudley, Republican campaign treasurer, issued a circular on Oct. 24, to Indiana followers that they "divide the floaters into blocks of five" each in charge of a trusted leader with the necessary bribes who would insure the proper delivery of the vote.

[Ellis P. Oberholtzer, *A History of the United States Since the Civil War*, V.]

HARVEY WISH

Blocs, as the term is used in the United States, are members of legislative bodies who, disregarding party lines, agree to act together for certain special purposes, and set up an organization to accomplish these purposes. The co-operation of legislators with similar interests, such as the tariff or silver, has occurred throughout our history, but deliberately organized blocs are relatively recent, beginning with the Farm Bloc, organized in May, 1921.

This Farm Bloc consisted of about twenty-five senators from the West and South who organized for the purpose of promoting legislation on behalf of agriculture. Committees were appointed to deal with different subjects; and a program of legislation was worked out, involving at least twenty bills. At the same time a similar bloc was organized in the House with approximately 100 members who could be counted on to act together. These Senate and House blocs for a time held the balance of power in each house, and had considerable success in securing the legislation they desired. They gradually broke up, however, and by 1928 had practically ceased to exist as organized groups.

In December, 1922, a Progressive Bloc was organized, under the leadership of Sen. LaFollette (Rep., Wis.). With somewhat the same membership as the Farm Bloc, it operated differently in that it was a joint bloc of Senate and House members. It forced some modifications in congressional procedure and secured some concessions to the progressive viewpoint in legislation, but with the death of Sen. LaFollette in 1925 tended gradually to disintegrate.

After the election of 1934 another group of approximately 100 members of the House organized into a Progressive, or Liberal, Bloc, primarily to give militant support to President F. D. Roosevelt's New Deal[qv] program. Other blocs include a Bonus Bloc, a Farm Tariff Bloc, a Wet Bloc, a Dry Bloc and a Far Western Bloc.

[W. F. Willoughby, *Principles of Legislative Organization and Administration;* Arthur Capper, *The Agricultural Bloc;* Basil M. Manly, Organizing to Fight Corporate Rule, *LaFollette's Magazine*, Dec., 1922.]

CLARENCE A. BERDAHL

"Blood Is Thicker than Water." Commodore Tattnall, in command of the American Squadron in Far Eastern waters, made this adage a part of American history when explaining why he had given aid to the British squadron in an attack on Taku forts at the mouth of the Pei-ho, June 25, 1859, thereby infringing strict American neutrality.

[Tyler Dennett, *Americans in Eastern Asia.*]

KEITH CLARK

Bloody Angle, THE, at Spottsylvania (May 12, 1864), was the climax in the first phase of Grant's (U.) Wilderness Campaign[qv]. Union troop movements indicated Grant planned a heavy attack. Lee (C.) was uncertain where the blow would fall. Early in the morning Grant moved in force against "the salient," or "Bloody Angle" in Lee's line. Because of surprise, lack of artillery and the force of the onslaught "the salient" was overrun. To restore the broken line and save his army, Lee proposed to lead the counterattack. Officers and men remonstrated, crying "General Lee to the rear." Lee's example fired his troops with intense ardor. The opposing lines met; the Union advance was halted and forced back. Lee put in every available man. All day and far into the night the battle raged. Neither side could advance. Early next morning Lee retired to prepared positions. The fighting ceased.

[*Battles and Leaders of the Civil War.*]

THOMAS ROBSON HAY

Bloody Island was a sand bar in the Mississippi River, opposite St. Louis, Mo., which became densely wooded and a rendezvous for duelists. Appearing first above water in 1798 its continuous growth menaced St. Louis Harbor. In 1837 Capt. Robert E. Lee, of U. S. A. Engineers, devised and established a system of dikes and dams that washed out the western channel and ultimately joined the island to the Illinois shore.

[Stella M. Drumm, Robert E. Lee and the Improvement of the Mississippi River, in *Missouri Historical Society Collections*, Vol. 6.]

STELLA M. DRUMM

Bloody Marsh, The Battle of (July 7, 1742), was the principal and decisive engagement in the war of Jenkins' Ear[qv]. In the summer of 1742 a Spanish force collected in Havana and St. Augustine, consisting of about fifty sails and a number of men, estimated in contemporary accounts to be from 2800 to 4000, invaded Georgia. They made a landing preparatory to attacking Frederica[qv], the strongest English settlement in Georgia. Oglethorpe immediately marched out a hurriedly organized force and attacked. He routed the Spaniards, and in the retreat he posted in ambush on the edge of a marsh three platoons and a company of Highlanders. When a group of about 400 Spaniards unsuspectingly marched into the glade, Oglethorpe's forces attacked them and killed about 200 and forced the remainder to retreat to the south end of the island. A few days later the whole remaining force returned to Florida.

[W. B. Stevens, *A History of Georgia;* C. C. Jones, *A History of Georgia;* H. E. Bolton and M. Ross, *The Debatable Land; Collections of the Georgia Historical Society,* III.]

E. MERTON COULTER

"Bloody Monday" was the name given the election riots, Aug. 6, 1855, in Louisville, Ky. These riots grew out of the bitter rivalry between the Democrat and Know-Nothing parties[qqv]. Rumors were started that foreigners and Catholics had interfered with the process of voting. A street fight occurred, twenty-two persons were killed, scores were injured and much property was destroyed by fire.

[W. H. Perrin, J. H. Battle, G. C. Kniffen, *Kentucky, History of the State; The Louisville Journal,* Aug. 6-15, 1855.]

T. D. CLARK

Bloody Pond, N. Y., Battle of (Sept. 8, 1755). The British expedition, which under the command of Col. William Johnson was to capture Crown Point[qv], had proceeded no farther than the southern extremity of Lake George, when word was received of the approach of a body of French and Indians commanded by Baron Dieskau (*see* Lake Champlain in the French and Indian War). The following morning a detachment of 1000 men was sent out to reconnoiter, and a hasty attempt made to fortify the camp. The reconnoitering party fell into an ambush and the survivors retreated with difficulty to the English camp. A fierce attack on the camp followed, but was beaten off and the French were forced to retreat. Just before the final rout, several hundred Canadians and Indians left the field and returned to plunder the scene of the morning fight. They were resting near a forest pool when they were attacked by a scouting party from Fort Edward[qv]. After a short but bloody fight, the Canadians and Indians fled. The bodies of the dead were thrown into the pool, which henceforth was called Bloody Pond.

[F. Parkman, *Montcalm and Wolfe,* Vol. I.]

A. C. FLICK

Bloody Run, Battle of (July 31, 1763). Pontiac's siege of Detroit[qv] began May 9, 1763. On July 29 Capt. James Dalzel brought a detachment of 280 soldiers to the relief of the garrison. Dalzel was eager to attack Pontiac in his camp at the Grand Marais, and Maj. Gladwin, the commandant, reluctantly granted his permission. In the night of July 30–31, 250 redcoats marched eastward along the river road to surprise Pontiac. Instead, the column was itself furiously assailed at Parent's Creek (ever since called Bloody Run) and driven back to the fort in several hours of furious fighting. Dalzel was slain and sixty of his followers were killed or wounded.

[*See* Maj. John Duncan's narrative, in *Canadian Historical Review,* XII, 183-88.]

M. M. QUAIFE

Bloody Shirt, THE, usually found in the expression, "waving the bloody shirt." It is used to describe the attempts made in political campaigns (especially in 1872 and 1876) by radical Republicans[qv] to defeat the Democrats[qv] by impassioned oratory designed to keep alive the hatreds and prejudices of the Civil War period.

Perhaps the most reasonable explanation of the origins of the phrase is the Scotch tradition that after the massacre of Glenfurin, 220 widows rode to Stirling Tower, each bearing aloft on a spear the bloody shirt of her murdered husband, thus arousing the people to take vengeance on their enemies.

[W. A. Dunning, *Reconstruction, Political and Economic.*]

HALLIE FARMER

Bloomer Dress, THE, a loosely fitting costume of knee-length dress and "Turkish" trousers buttoned at the ankle, was introduced in Seneca Falls, N. Y., by Elizabeth Smith Miller in February, 1851, and popularized by Amelia Bloomer, editor of a feminist journal, *The Lily.* For its physical comfort and as a symbol of the suffrage movement[qv], the dress survived six years of ridicule but was extinguished by the revival of the hoopskirt.

[E. D. Branch, The Lily and the Bloomer, *The Colophon,* Dec., 1932.]

E. DOUGLAS BRANCH

Blount Conspiracy, THE, takes its name from William Blount, United States Senator from Tennessee in 1796–97. It was connected with the Yazoo land frauds[qv] of 1796 and its main purpose seems to have been to raise the value of Western lands by driving the Spaniards out of Louisiana and Florida[qqv]. This was to be accomplished by a land force of Western frontiersmen and Indians with the aid of a British fleet. The British minister in the United States, Robert Liston, gave the conspirators some encouragement and sent one of them to London. The conspiracy was exposed when an incriminating letter written by Blount to one of his agents fell into the hands of the administration and was transmitted by President Adams to the Senate (July 3, 1797). Blount was promptly expelled from that body. Impeachment[qv] proceedings against him were considered but dropped because of his expulsion. The exposure of the conspiracy had repercussions in the domestic politics and foreign relations of the United States, and there is some reason to believe that Aaron Burr's later conspiracy[qv] was connected with this one.

[Arthur P. Whitaker, *The Mississippi Question, 1795-1803.*]

ARTHUR P. WHITAKER

"Blue and Gray," THE, are familiar names for the armies of the North and South during the Civil War, derived from the fact that the Union Army wore blue uniforms while the Confederates wore gray. As sectional hatred has died, these terms have superseded the harsher names of the 19th century.

FRED B. JOYNER

Blue Eagle Emblem, THE, was a blue-colored representation of the American "thunder bird," with outspread wings, which was proclaimed on July 20, 1933, as the symbol of industrial recovery by Hugh S. Johnson, the head of the National Recovery Administration[qv]. All who accepted the President's Re-employment Agreement or a special Code of Fair Competition were permitted to display a poster on which was reproduced the Blue Eagle together with the announcement, "Member N.R.A. We Do Our Part." On Sept. 5, 1935, following the invalidation of the compulsory code system, the emblem was abolished and its future use as a symbol was prohibited.

[Hugh S. Johnson, *The Blue Eagle from Egg to Earth.*]

ERIK McKINLEY ERIKSSON

Blue Laws. Rev. Samuel A. Peters originated the account of the so-called Blue Laws of Connecticut in *A General History of Connecticut, by a Gentleman of the Province,* published in London in 1781. The term was taken up by various later editors of the laws to refer specifically to the legislation of the New Haven Colony[qv]. Such instances as punishments of a rebellious child by being forced to work for his father as a prisoner with a lock on his leg, and of a young unmarried couple by a fine of twenty shillings for kissing, were considered typical Blue Laws. Despite some distortions, it is perfectly true that rather rigid Sabbath, sex, and sumptuary regulations prevailed generally in Puritan New England. But Blue Laws were not original among the Puritans[qv] nor unique with them in this country. To some degree Blue Laws could be found in every one of the American colonies. Compulsory church attendance and laws forbidding sports, travel and work on the Sabbath were found in the South as well, perhaps the most sweeping Sunday law being the Georgia act of 1762. Blue Laws became in the main dead letters after the Revolution, but in more recent times there has been an attempt to revive them all along the line. National prohibition, anti-cigarette legislation, the activities of the Lord's Day Alliance and other groups attest to the survival of the Blue Law spirit to some degree.

[G. Myers, *Ye Olden Blue Laws;* F. E. Baldwin, *Sumptuary Legislation and Personal Regulation in England.*]

RICHARD B. MORRIS

Blue Licks, Battle of (Aug. 19, 1782). An engagement between 182 Kentucky pioneers and 240 Indians and Canadians, in the British service, raiding into Kentucky from the Ohio country and the vicinity of Detroit. It occurred near the Lower Blue Lick Springs on the Middle Fork of Licking River. A precipitate attack was launched by Kentuckians, from several pioneer "Stations," against the foe lying in ambush. After a fierce conflict of a few minutes, the right wing of the Kentuckians gave way and the entire body retreated in confusion, with a loss of about seventy killed and captured. The loss of the Indians and Canadians was never definitely ascertained. Notwithstanding the adverse outcome of the battle, no invasion by Indians in force ever afterwards occurred within the borders of Kentucky.

[Bennett H. Young, *History of the Battle of the Blue Licks;* Samuel M. Wilson, *Battle of the Blue Licks.*]

SAMUEL M. WILSON

Blue Lights. American frigates under Stephen Decatur prepared to run out of the harbor of New London, Conn., during the War of 1812[qv]. Decatur saw blue lights burning near the mouth of the river in sight of the British blockaders. Convinced that these were signals to betray his plans he abandoned the project. Suspicion was directed against the peace men and the odious epithet of "Bluelight Federalists" long was applied to extreme Federalists.

[James Schouler, *History of the United States of America.*]

CHARLES MARION THOMAS

Blue Lodges were secret proslavery societies formed in western Missouri during 1854 to thwart Northern antislavery designs to make Kansas a free territory under the Kansas-Nebraska Act^qv^. They not only promoted the migration of proslavery settlers to Kansas but occasionally crossed the border to participate in the election of proslavery members to the territorial government.

[L. W. Spring, *Kansas, the Prelude to the War for the Union.*]

ASA E. MARTIN

Blue Ridge Tunnel, THE, piercing the mountain under Rockfish Gap, between Afton and Waynesboro, Va., was constructed in 1850–58 by the Blue Ridge Railroad, the State of Virginia and the Virginia Central Railroad, at a cost of $488,000. It was for some time the longest tunnel in America. In 1870 it was acquired by the Chesapeake & Ohio Railroad.

[William Couper, *Claudius Crozet, 1789-1864.*]

JOHN W. WAYLAND

Blue Sky Laws. This term is applied to legislative enactments designed to prevent the fraudulent flotation or sale of corporate stocks and bonds. Kansas enacted the first Blue Sky Law in May, 1911, and this statute was followed by similar ones in forty-five other states. There are three types of these laws: (1) Fraud statutes, the principle of which is to follow and punish the security swindler under the criminal law; (2) Dealers-license statutes, which endeavor to prevent fraud by restricting security traffic to carefully selected professional dealers, as well as by revoking licenses for violation of the statute; and (3) Specific approval statutes, regulating and controlling only the securities sought to be sold within the state, through specific permits of sale. Blue Sky Laws have been supplemented by the Securities Act of 1933, and the Securities Exchange Act of 1934^qv^, which regulate and control interstate dealings in securities and the operation of the organized security exchanges respectively.

[*Corporation Manual,* U. S. Corporation Co.]

FRANK PARKER

Bluebacks, Confederate Paper Currency, were first issued under an act approved one month after the establishment of the Confederate Government. From an initial issue of $1,000,000, the Treasury notes grew to $800,000,000 by April 1, 1864, when deflationary measures were taken which reduced the outstanding currency to $480,036,095 on Oct. 1, 1864.

[*The Confederate Soldier in the Civil War*: a compilation, see appendix containing extensive reproductions of Confederate Treasury notes; *Reports of the Secretary of the Treasury to the Confederate Congress,* 1861-1865.]

WILLIAM M. ROBINSON, JR.

Bluegrass Country, THE, comprises some 8000 square miles of east central Kentucky. It is bounded by the Ohio River on the north and the Knobs on the east, south and west. The terrain, with some exceptions, has a gracefully undulating surface over a limestone foundation. The land is specially adapted to the growth of bluegrass, for which the region has been named. The inner portion with Lexington^qv^ at the center is a beautiful district of shaded, winding roads, fine farms and prosperous villages and towns.

To this region came the first settlers of Kentucky in one of the greatest migrations of American history. Over the Wilderness Road^qv^, by way of Cumberland Gap^qv^, trekked most of these multitudes. Here the pioneers, Daniel Boone and Simon Kenton became national heroes. At Harrodsburg^qv^ the first permanent settlement in Kentucky was made; at Boonesborough^qv^ the first Anglo-Saxon government west of the Alleghenies was organized; at Lexington the first college (Transylvania) in the West was established; at "Ashland" lived Henry Clay, the Great Pacificator; to Transylvania came Jefferson Davis to study; and to Lexington came Abraham Lincoln to court Mary Todd. These and many other places and incidents in the Bluegrass Country constitute a historic environment probably unequaled in the Mississippi valley.

[Thomas D. Clark, *A History of Kentucky;* Darrell Haug Davis, *Geography of the Blue Grass Region of Kentucky.*]

JONATHAN T. DORRIS

Bluestem Pastures, THE, prior to 1929 called Flint Hills, is a region in east central Kansas about 50 miles east-to-west (Wilson to Marion counties) and about 130 miles north-to-south (Potawatomie County to the south line), extending into Oklahoma to include that part of Osage County which lies between the Verdegris and the Arkansas rivers, where the region is called the Osage pastures. Originally all eastern Kansas was covered mostly with bluestem grasses, but because of the hilly character of the country and the presence of extensive outcroppings of limestone rock, settlement left this part of the area largely in grass. During the later 1880's the pastures were fenced and served not only the local herds but the transient herds from the Southwest, which by this time were moved by rail instead of by the long drive. The bluestem is unusually rich in feed value for grass-fattening livestock during the spring and early summer, and eventually the

region became the most important pasture country in the central prairie-plains area. Supplemented by the corn and alfalfa lands of the valleys, the region became also an important breeding center and the home of the great herds of W. J. Todd, Dan Casement and R. H. Hazlett.

As procedure became standardized, the shipments of southwestern cattle northward to the grasslands were made during April and May, and from pasture to market or feed lot from midsummer to fall. Some were pastured on lease by southwestern owners, some were bought outright by pasture owners and other were handled by commission houses. During the 1920's pasture rents varied from six to twelve dollars per head for the season, on the basis of three to five acres per head. The volume of this cattle movement from Texas alone during the years 1925–31 averaged 222,225 to the Kansas Bluestem and 122,319 to the Osage pastures. The peak shipments during the period were in 1927, when the numbers were 267,562 and 152,331 respectively. In 1930 the estimated cattle movement from the Southwest was: Texas, 360,000; New Mexico, 120,000; and Arizona, 90,000. The destination of most of these was the Kansas-Oklahoma pastures. The volume of this movement exceeded that of the old trail days, and when allowance is made for the number then diverted for stocking the northern ranges and for Indian and army contracts, the commercial beef shipments to packing centers through the bluestem pastures, although not so spectacular, represented annually several times as many cattle, as well as a finer quality of meat than the earlier period.

[F. A. Buechel, Eight years of livestock shipments in Texas, 1925-1932, Part I: Cattle and calves, *Bureau of Business Research*, Research Monograph No. 10, Austin, University of Texas, 1933; H. R. Hilton, The bluestem-limestone pastures of Kansas, *26th Biennial Report of the Kansas State Board of Agriculture*, 31, 1927-28, 187-194; T. W. Morse, In the Flint Hills of Kansas, *24th Biennial Report of the Kansas State Board of Agriculture*, 29, 1923-24, 171-175; R. H. Wilcox, et al., Factors in the cost of producing beef in the Flint Hills, *U. S. Department of Agriculture*, Department Bulletin 1454, Washington, Government Printing Office, 1926.]

JAMES C. MALIN

Bluffton Movement, THE (1844), in South Carolina, was an attempt to invoke "separate state action" against the tariff of 1842, after Calhoun's failure to secure the presidential nomination and the Northern Democrats' abandonment of the South on the tariff[qv] had apparently destroyed hope for relief within the Democratic party. Though many of the "Blufftonites" undoubtedly contemplated disunion, the object of their leader, Robert Barnwell Rhett, seems rather to have been a "reform" of the Union giving further safeguards to Southern interests. The movement collapsed within a short time, largely through its repudiation by Calhoun.

[Laura A. White, *Robert Barnwell Rhett; Father of Secession.*]

JAMES W. PATTON

Blunder, Fort. *See* Rouse's Point, Boundary Controversy.

Board of Trade and Plantations, THE, was the main British colonial office from its creation, May 15, 1696, until the eve of the American Revolution. It replaced the older committee of the Privy Council, called Lords of Trade and Plantations[qv]. It was a paid board of five members, the chief officers of state being also ex officio members. It had charge of poor relief in England, regular commercial relations with other nations, the enforcement of the trade and navigation acts[qv], the general supervision of colonial administration, the examination of colonial laws to see that they were not harmful to British interests nor contrary to the English common law. It heard and investigated complaints of merchants and recommended imperial legislation in its field. It supervised the negotiation of important commercial treaties and kept in touch with the regular consular service. Its voluminous records today are the chief source for American colonial history in its imperial aspects. (*See* Colonial Policy, The British.)

The Board was a part of the regular political party system and its members changed with the usual party shifts. Most of its business articulated with the office of the Secretary of State for the Southern Department, consequently the activities of the Board varied with the practices and desires of the Secretary of State. Under a dominant character like Newcastle it had little power—most of the business being transferred directly to Newcastle's office. In 1748 George Dunk, Earl of Halifax, was appointed president of the Board. He began at once to make his position important. Investigations were made and reports compiled of what had been going on in America for the past thirty years. Plans were developed for strengthening the position of the royal governors[qv]. Instructions were revised, judges were made dependent upon the crown for their salaries and their terms of office, and the struggle began between the agents of the crown and the leaders of the colonial legislatures. By his energy, Halifax made himself practically a secretary of state for the colonies, secured control of the colonial patronage and was admitted to the cabinet in

1756. His influence was powerful in colonial affairs many years after his retirement from the Board in 1761.

A group of rising young men received important political training as members of the Board under Halifax. Among these were James Grenville, Charles Townshend and Andrew Stone, the tutor of George III. Townshend was even president of the Board for a short time in 1763, to be followed by Lord Shelburne. He in turn was succeeded by Hillsborough, who became a full secretary of state for the colonies and was directly responsible for many of the unfortunate policies between 1764 and 1772 that ultimately led to the Revolution. His most offensive colonial activities were connected with his attempt to force Massachusetts to rescind its famous Circular Letter[qv] and his use of troops in Boston, culminating in the Boston Massacre[qv].

The permanent secretaries of the Board were among the best-informed men on colonial affairs in England. At the head of these were the Popples, William, William, Jr. and Alured, all related, who occupied the office from 1696 to 1737, and John Pownall, 1758–61. Another important officer was a solicitor and clerk of reports whose duties were to prepare all formal reports, to assemble information for use of the Board and to represent it before other departments of the government. The most famous of these was John Pownall, who served from 1745 to 1758 and personally prepared the reports associated with the work of Halifax. Another important officer was an attorney to whom all colonial laws were sent for examination and report as soon as they arrived from America. These reports on colonial laws subjected every American statute to a constitutional test. Three men, Richard West, Francis Fane and Matthew Lamb, filled this important position from 1718 to the end of the active work of the Board.

[O. M. Dickerson, *American Colonial Government, A Study of the British Board of Trade in Its Relation to the American Colonies.*]

O. M. DICKERSON

Boards of Trade. *See* Chambers of Commerce.

"Body of Liberties" (1641). *See* Massachusetts Body of Liberties.

Bog Iron Mining. Bog ore is a brown hematite deposited in pond and bog bottoms and was found by the early American settlers in the coastal lowlands from Massachusetts to Delaware. Since it was near water transportation and easily dug or raked from pond bottoms or picked up on marsh meadows it was the first important source of native iron supply, although superior but less accessible and tractable rock ores were also known to exist in America. These hematites were employed in the earliest New England works at Lynn and Braintree where they were smelted with charcoal in small furnaces which cast, directly from the ore, kettles and other hollow ware, as well as pig for refining into bars for nails and implements. American bog ore castings, such as kettles, were preferred in colonial households as tougher and lighter than imported ironware. Bog ores had been largely displaced by rock ores by the time of the Revolution and virtually ceased to be used toward the middle of the following century. The latest furnaces employing them extensively were built in Ohio on the south shore of Lake Erie about 1825 and shipped pig via the newly opened Erie Canal to Albany for casting stove plates.

[James M. Swank, *History of the Manufacture of Iron.*]

VICTOR S. CLARK

Boisé, Fort, was a fur trading post of the Hudson's Bay Company[qv] in Idaho. First built in 1834 on the Boisé River about seven miles above its mouth, it was relocated in 1838 near the confluence of the Boisé and Snake rivers. It was a small adobe-walled fort, famous as a stopping point on the Oregon Trail[qv]. Partially destroyed by flood waters in 1853, it was finally abandoned after the Indian War of 1855.

[C. J. Brosnan, *History of the State of Idaho.*]

CORNELIUS JAMES BROSNAN

Boll Weevil, a maggot which eats the buds and young bolls of cotton[qv], may have existed in Mexico and Central America for centuries. About 1892–93 it crossed into Texas, somewhere near Brownsville, and in 1894 was found in cotton fields 125 to 175 miles to the northward. Thereafter it advanced north and east at the rate of about 100 miles per year, until by 1923 it had reached the Atlantic coast. In 1930 it was said that 90% of the cotton-growing area was infested, though the fight upon it had decreased its ravages in the worst spots, and 1921 is called the peak year of the pest. During the ten previous years it was estimated to have destroyed an average of more than 2,200,000 bales annually. The cotton growers' woes were increased in 1916 by the appearance of the pink bollworm, another probable immigrant from Mexico.

[*An Annotated Bibliography of the Mexican Cotton Boll Weevil,* United States Entomology Bureau, Circular 140.]

ALVIN F. HARLOW

Bollman Case. In *ex parte* Bollman and Swartwout (1807) the Supreme Court upheld its power to issue a writ of habeas corpus[qv] to review a commitment by an inferior Federal court, and upon hearing ordered the release of two petitioners held on charges of treason as participants in the Burr conspiracy[qv]. Justus Erich Bollman and Samuel Swartwout, by separate routes, had carried copies of a letter in cipher from Burr to Gen. Wilkinson at New Orleans. Wilkinson arrested them and sent them to Washington, where they were committed for trial by the Circuit Court for the District of Columbia. While the case was pending in the Circuit Court President Jefferson attempted, unsuccessfully, to induce Congress to suspend the privilege of the writ of habeas corpus. In holding that the evidence had been insufficient to support a charge of treason, Chief Justice Marshall said for the Supreme Court that "there must be an actual assembling of men for the treasonable purpose, to constitute a levying of war." But, he added, if that be proved, then a conspirator, however remote from the scene of action, would be guilty. This dictum proved embarrassing when, a few months later, Marshall presided at the trial of Aaron Burr.

[A. J. Beveridge, *The Life of John Marshall;* Charles Warren, *The Supreme Court in United States History.*]

CHARLES FAIRMAN

Bolters are party members who do not support the regular nominee of their party. The "bolt" may occur at the convention as in 1912 when Theodore Roosevelt and his followers withdrew from the Republican party (*see* Progressive party) or it may occur after the convention or primary has been held.

[C. W. McKenzie, *Party Government in the United States.*]

C. H. HAMLIN

Bonanza Kings, THE, John W. Mackay, James G. Fair, James C. Flood and William S. O'Brien, organized the Consolidated Virginia Silver Mine near Virginia City, Nev., from a number of smaller claims on the Comstock lode[qv], in 1871. Later they added the near-by California mine. For three years after large ore bodies were uncovered in 1874 the two mines produced $3,000,000 per month. In 1876, for exhibition purposes, $6,000,000 was taken in one month from both mines. Production began to fall off in 1879 but in twenty-two years of operation the two mines yielded $150,000,000 in silver and gold, and paid $78,148,800 in dividends. The term bonanza was applied to the large ore body which lay in a vertical rift of the hanging wall of the Comstock lode.

[T. A. Rickard, *History of American Mining.*]

CARL L. CANNON

Bonanza Wheat Farming in the Red River Valley of the North during the period 1875–90 was an important factor in the settlement and development of the spring wheat region. The Cass-Cheney farm, first and most widely known of the bonanzas, was established in 1875 when George W. Cass, president of the Northern Pacific Railroad[qv] and E. P. Cheney, a director of the road, exchanged almost worthless Northern Pacific bonds for land held by the railroad in the Red River Valley. Cass took ten sections, Cheney eight and an experienced wheat farmer contracted to handle operations. Yields for the next decade were uniformly high. Capital was attracted to the region, and many Northern Pacific bondholders followed the example set by Cass and Cheney. By 1890 over 300 farms in the valley exceeded 1000 acres; a half dozen or more exceeded 15,000 acres. Some of the farms were individually owned; others were corporations. Few bonanzas were established after 1890 and most of the older farms were broken up within the next quarter century.

[H. E. Briggs, Early Bonanza Farming in the Red River Valley of the North, *Agricultural History*, VI, No. 1, January, 1932.]

ROBERT H. BAHMER

Bonds, Government. *See* Debt, Public; Liberty Bonds.

***Bonhomme Richard* and *Serapis,* Engagement between the** (Sept. 23, 1779), was one of the most notable of American naval victories. John Paul Jones' flagship the *Bonhomme Richard,* originally an Indian merchantman renamed in honor of Benjamin Franklin, was proceeding with Jones' tiny fleet up the east coast of England in quest of English cargoes. Although worn out and unseaworthy, she carried forty-two guns. About noon, Jones sighted two enemy ships of war, the *Serapis* and the *Countess of Scarborough,* convoying ships loaded with naval stores. He maneuvered his ship close to the *Serapis* and both opened broadside fire. Jones had placed some of his guns below, and two of the larger ones on his lower deck burst, killing and wounding several men. This catastrophe necessitated using only the lighter guns and musketry. The slaughter on both sides was terrible and the American ship was leaking badly. After an hour's fighting, Jones answered the British challenge to surrender: "I have not yet begun to fight." The two vessels became locked together and the battle raged for more than two hours longer. Jones was hampered by treachery of a captain in his own fleet, but finally by using British prisoners to man the pumps, he stayed afloat and wore down the enemy to the point of exhaustion and surrender.

[E. S. Maclay, *History of the United States Navy.*]

ARTHUR R. BLESSING

Bonito and the Chaco. A large prehistoric pueblo[qv] ruin known as Bonito stands in Chaco Canyon, N. Mex., northeast of Gallup. The shallow canyon contains eleven main ruins, part of them contemporary and all belonging to the prehistoric period known as Pueblo III, or the Grand period in pueblo culture. Bonito, as determined by the tree-ring[qv] method, was occupied during the interval 919–1130 A.D. It was originally four stories high, contained about 500 rooms, the architecture resembling that of modern Indian villages near Santa Fé. The ruin was partially excavated in 1896–99 by the Hyde Expedition, and in 1921–23 by the National Geographic Society.

[*National Geographic Magazine,* Vols. XXXIX, 1921, XLI, 1922, XLIV, 1923.]

CLARK WISSLER

Bonneville Dam, in the Columbia River forty-two miles from Portland, Ore., is one of numerous projects undertaken by the Public Works Administration under the National Recovery Act of 1933[qqv], with the fourfold purpose of improving navigation, controlling floods, reclaiming arid lands, and generating electric power. The Bonneville project includes a dam sixty-five feet high, a ship canal around the dam, an electric power plant, and a "fish-ladder" to enable salmon to make their annual run up the Columbia to spawn. The cost of the entire project is estimated at about $30,000,000.

[Reports of Chief Engineers, United States Army, 1934-1937.]

P. ORMAN RAY

Bonneville Expedition. Capt. B. L. E. Bonneville, U. S. Army, headed a party of trappers and traders in the Far West which started from Fort Osage, May 1, 1832. The well-known Platte-South Pass[qv] route was followed to Green River. Here, a few miles above the mouth of Horse Creek in a region favored by the mountain men[qv] as a place of annual rendezvous, Fort Bonneville was built. Abandoned shortly after completion, it was frequently called "Fort Nonsense." Bonneville moved to the headwaters of the Salmon, then continued to move during the most of the time that he was in the mountains. So thoroughly did he cover the Rocky Mountains and the Columbia drainage basin, and so good was his map making that he may be credited with having been the first to gain true geographic knowledge of the Far West. A branch expedition organized by Bonneville left Green River, July, 1833, under Joseph Reddeford Walker[qv], crossed Salt Lake Desert, descended Humboldt River, crossed the Sierras north of Yosemite Valley and spent the winter at Monterey. In the spring, it returned through the Sierras via Walker's Pass, across the Great Basin[qv], and up Bear River, joining Bonneville June 1, 1834.

Irving made of Bonneville's manuscript a compelling story, which ranks at the top of the literary contributions of the fur traders.

[Washington Irving, *The Adventures of Captain Bonneville.*]

CARL P. RUSSELL

"Bonnie Blue Flag, THE," was the title of a popular Confederate ballad that was sung throughout the South during the period of secession. Authorities disagree as to the author, as to where it was first sung and as to the meaning of bonnie blue flag. It was, however, sung often by Harry McCarthy; it was sung in New Orleans and in Richmond theaters in 1861; and the blue flag on the authority of Mrs. S. G. Stoney of South Carolina was the blue field of the United States flag bearing first a single star for South Carolina, which later, according to the song, "grew to be eleven," and was used before the adoption of an official flag.

[Mrs. S. G. Stoney, in Charleston, S. C., *News,* Oct. 16, 1904.]

CARL L. CANNON

Bonus. The policy of granting a bonus, a bounty, or a gratuity to ex-soldiers has undergone several changes within past centuries. There was a time when wars were looked upon merely as a business, however dangerous, in which the successful aggressor added to his personal possessions, and increased his power over his people. If the conquering general realized any gains or booty, they were divided among the soldiers. But in more recent times, with the rise of autonomous governments, the ex-soldiers discovered that they could, merely by their ballots, demand a share of their nation's riches. The idea that soldiers are entitled to some personal compensation over and above their monthly pay for fighting wars appeared early in this country. In 1778, the Continental Congress[qv] voted that all commissioned officers should, at the conclusion of the war, be given one half of their present pay for seven years, provided they lived that long. Noncommissioned officers were promised $80 flat bonus. Later in the war, additional demands and promises were made. The Continental Congress soon realized, however, that it could not meet all these demands. So a compromise was finally reached, whereby officers were given five years' full pay, and noncommissioned officers and privates a flat bonus. The ex-soldiers of the War of 1812, the Mexican War[qqv] and the various Indian wars were not treated so generously. At the close of the Civil War[qv] a bounty of $100 was granted to those who had served three years, and a lesser amount to those who had served shorter terms. Then in 1875 Congress passed an act to "equalize the bounty" of all ex-Union soldiers. It amounted in fact to an outright bonus. But President Grant vetoed the bill, and no later attempts were made to secure bonus payments for the Civil War soldiers (*see* Grand Army of the Republic). Neither did the ex-soldiers and sailors of the Spanish-American War[qv] receive special bonus payments. The practice of paying a bonus, or a bounty, or adjusted compensation, whatever the term may be called, had been completely abandoned, when, suddenly after the World War[qv], it was revived. The bonus, it should be emphasized, is something entirely different from a pension[qv]. The pension represents a regular payment, at stated periods, to a disabled person or dependents. The bonus represents the payment of a fixed, lump sum, and, in case of war veterans, is paid to *all* ex-soldiers, whether able-bodied or disabled.

The demands for a bonus payment to the veterans of the World War came early. It was first suggested in the St. Louis caucus of the American Legion[qv] in May, 1919, but was promptly voted down. It came up again at the fall convention of the Legion, 1919, at Minneapolis. Here, a new point of view, a "new terminology," was advanced. The point was made that the soldiers of the World War had not received sufficient compensation during the months they were in service. Had they remained at home, it was pointed out, they would have made more money. This difference in pay should be recognized, hence, they were entitled to "adjusted compensation." The Government should make up the back pay. At the same time, it was noted that certain members of Congress were eagerly soliciting the support of the ex-soldiers, and numerous bills had already been introduced aimed at giving the soldiers extra compensation for their services. A fourfold adjusted compensation bill which, among other things, provided for the payment of adjusted compensation, was passed in 1922. President Harding vetoed it. The measure was revived in 1923, and again passed both House and Senate, only to meet a second veto, this time at the hands of President Coolidge. However, both House and Senate repassed the bill over the President's veto, May 19, 1924. According to the bill, actual payment of the bonus (adjusted compensation) was deferred until 1945. Each veteran was awarded a dollar a day for each day's service in the United States, and a dollar and twenty-five cents for each day served abroad. With the exception of those whose credits fell below $50, the veterans were not given cash, but were awarded paid-up twenty-year endowment insurance policies, or Adjusted Compensation Certificates. Over 3,500,000 such certificates were issued. The face value of each certificate was equal to the amount of endowment insurance, procurable from a commercial insurance company for a net premium payment equal to the veteran's bonus credit plus 25%. The certificates bore interest at 4% compounded annually. The aggregate face values amounted to $3,500,000,000. This act was hailed as a real victory by the World War veterans. Many believed it would be the last demand made upon Congress. But not for long. In January, 1931, the American Legion led a movement asking for immediate payment of the certificates. As a result of these demands, a compromise measure was agreed upon. While the veterans were not permitted to cash their certificates in full, yet the Government would now lend each veteran 50% of the face value of his certificate, at 4½% interest. A bill, carrying these provisions, passed both House and Senate early in 1931. It, however, received an executive veto, this time from President Hoover. But it was repassed over his veto. Almost immediately the veterans made another demand, this time it was for the immediate and full payment of all certificates. The demand was attended by many spectacular events. Chief of these was the so-called "Bonus Army"[qv] that assembled in Washington in the spring and summer of 1932. A bill known as the Patman Bill, which provided for the printing of fiat money, and the immediate payment of $2,500,000,000 to the holders of Adjusted Compensation Certificates, passed the House in June, 1932. The Senate rejected it. The "Bonus Army" that had assembled in Washington, numbering from 12,000 to 15,000 men, caused some alarm and local authorities requested President Hoover to preserve order. Troops from the War Department and the local police ordered the Bonus marchers out of the city. Rioting developed and several were injured. Congress voted $100,000 to send the Bonus marchers back to their homes, and after a few days the men dispersed.

Following the inauguration of President Franklin D. Roosevelt in 1933, and the vast expenditures attending the New Deal[qv] program, a change in attitude was noted toward the immediate payment in full of soldier certificates. Many who had heretofore opposed the movement now agreed that the veterans had as valid a claim as any group in asking for the immediate payment of their bonus. In January, 1936, another bill providing for the immediate cash payment of their certificates passed the House by vote of 358 to 59. On Jan. 20 it passed the Senate by vote of 74 to 16. Four days later President Roosevelt vetoed it. But within an hour it was repassed by the House, the vote being 324 to 61, and three days later the Senate overrode the veto by a vote of 76 to 19. The result was that after some seventeen years of agitation the demands of the ex-soldiers that they be paid a special bonus, over and above their monthly pay for services rendered in the World War, were granted.

[Knowlton Durham, *Billions for Veterans;* Roger Burlingame, *Peace Veterans;* Marcus Duffield, *King Legion;* and official reports, leaflets, pamphlets compiled by the American Legion; *Congressional Record* of 73rd and 74th Congresses.]

JOHN W. OLIVER

Bonus Army, The. A spontaneous gathering of unemployed World War veterans who, late in May, 1932, began marching and hitch-hiking to Washington in small groups from all over the United States until about 15,000 were assembled there. The needy veterans, seeking some economic relief from Congress, eventually united in petitioning for immediate payment of the Adjusted Compensation, or "Bonus,"[qv] Certificates.

The problems of food, shelter and sanitation for the impoverished veterans embarrassed Washington, and there was latent danger of disorder. But the leader, Walter W. Waters, maintained almost military discipline and expelled communistic agitators, while patriotism permeated the ranks. Though the chief of police, Gen. Glassford, tried to provide quarters, most of the men built wretched hovels in which they lived.

In mid-June Congress, by a narrow margin, defeated the bonus bill, but the disappointed "Bonus Expeditionary Force" stayed on, haunting the Capitol grounds. Late in July Glassford ordered the veterans to evacuate. They failed to do so and on July 28, by instructions from the President, United States troops drove them forcibly from their quarters in public buildings and from their camps.

[Walter W. Waters, *B. E. F., The Whole Story of the Bonus Army;* E. Francis Brown, The Bonus Army Marches to Defeat, *Current History*, September, 1932.]

JOSEPH MILLS HANSON

Bonus Bill, Calhoun's. On Dec. 16, 1816, John C. Calhoun recommended that the House of Representatives appoint a committee to inquire into the expediency of creating a fund for internal improvements[qv] from the profits derived from the second National Bank[qv]. With the appointment of the committee, Calhoun, as chairman, introduced a bill on Dec. 23, 1816, to set apart as a permanent fund for internal improvements the $1,500,000 bonus exacted from the bank as a price of the charter and the profits from the $7,000,000 of the bank stock owned by the United States. Although the bill was passed, President Madison vetoed it, March 3, 1817, on the ground that it was unconstitutional, but suggested an amendment to the Constitution that would remove all doubts upon the subject.

[*Annals of Congress*, 14 Cong., 2 sess., 296, 361.]

GEORGE D. HARMON

Boodle (Boodler). A barroom or street term for money or booty applied by sensational newspapers (1884–86) to members of the New York Board of Aldermen who were charged with accepting bribes in connection with the granting of a franchise for a street railroad on Broadway. Thereafter, the term came into common use to signify bribery in general and particularly in municipal governments.

[M. Ostrogorski, *Democracy and the Organization of Political Parties.*]

P. ORMAN RAY

Book Auctions. The first recorded auction occurred in Boston (1713) and has been followed by 10,000 of which there are printed sales catalogues surviving. Earliest surviving catalogue is that of the Pemberton sale, Boston, 1717. Eighteenth-century auctions were conducted largely by booksellers, of whom Robert Bell of Philadelphia was most noteworthy. In the 19th century regular auction houses began. (Dates are those of the life of the house.) Cunningham in Boston (1824–41) was followed by Leonard (1842–78). C. F. Libbies continued in Boston, 1878 down to 1919. Royal Gurley was one of New York's earliest book auctioneers (1831–48) and closely paralleled by Cooley's which survived to 1856. Lemuel Bangs' name survived as Bangs, Platt & Co. and Bangs-Merwin, in New York (1838–1903). Bangs finally sold out to John Anderson whose name still survives in the merger of the Anderson Galleries with the American Art Association in 1929. George A. Leavitt's name spans the years 1855–92. Thomas E. Kirby began in New York in 1882 and founded the American Art Association which merged with the Anderson Galleries in 1929. But the story of New York cannot omit the name of Joseph Sabin, whose auctioneering led him to begin the compilation of his *Dictionary of Books Relating to America,* which was seventy years in being published (1867–1937). In Philadelphia Moses Thomas began the still surviving Samuel H. Freeman & Co. Stan V. Henkels' Philadelphia firm endured from 1882 to 1926.

[C. S. Brigham's introduction to G. L. McKay's *American Auction Catalogues, 1713-1934.*]

RANDOLPH G. ADAMS

Book Collecting and Book Collections. The systematic gathering of books in America must be associated with the names of great collectors. These may be divided into two groups, those whose collections went to found or to supplement institutional libraries, and those whose collections were broken up in an auction sale. The former added definitely to the cultural riches of the country. The latter did great service in preserving books until such time as a given book finally reached a great repository library.

In colonial times Increase Mather (1639–1723) and Cotton Mather (1663–1728) of Boston were noteworthy, and most of the surviving books which belonged to them are now at the American Antiquarian Society. Thomas Prince (1687–1758) built up his "American Library" with a view to writing his history of New England. The survivors of his collection are at the Public Library of the City of Boston. William Byrd (1674–1744) of Westover made one of the great libraries in Virginia, but it was scattered. The books collected by Benjamin Franklin (1706–90) were disposed of by sale, but they have been subjected to a good deal of study by George S. Eddy, and many can actually be located today in various institutional libraries. Possibly the most systematic of the colonial book collectors was Thomas Jefferson (1743–1826), whose library was sold to the United States and became the foundation of the Library of Congress[qv]. Almost as important was the library of James Logan (1674–1751) which is now, for the most part, at the Philadelphia Library Company.

The 19th century produced a host of collectors: Samuel G. Drake (1798–1875) of Boston; George Brinley of Hartford; Henry C. Murphy (1810–82) of Brooklyn; James Carson Brevoort (1818–87) of New York; William Menzies, of New York; Brayton Ives (1840–1914) of New York, and many more whose libraries ended on the auction block to the enrichment of others. The Brinley sale of 1876–93 was in many respects the "greatest Americana sale" ever held. But as these men were building up and breaking up their libraries another force was making itself apparent in the book-collecting world in America.

The Brown family of Providence, R. I., had collected since colonial times, but John Carter Brown (1797–1874) definitely forged to the front as one of the more significant. Under his guidance and that of his son, John Nicholas Brown (1861–1900), the John Carter Brown Library attained pre-eminence and was finally given to Brown University, where it is today. Paralleling the career of John Carter Brown was that of James Lenox (1800–1880) of New York, whose collection of Bibles, Americana and English literature is a foundation stone of what is now the New York Public Library. In the main, however, the 19th-century collectors were working for their own edification, and with but little idea of putting their work at the service of scholarship.

With the turn of the 20th century there came a new motive in American book collecting based on the ideas of Lenox and Carter Brown. That was the collecting of books to form permanent public or semi-public institutions. J. Pierpont Morgan (1837–1913) of New York led the field in the first decade of the century and his life work may be seen in the Pierpont Morgan Library, New York, today. Just before the death of the elder Morgan, Henry E. Huntington (1850–1927) of California forged to the front and during the remainder of his life could well be called the greatest American book collector. He collected not merely individual items but whole libraries. The Huntington Library at San Marino is his monument. At the same time Henry Clay Folger (1857–1930) of New York was collecting Shakespeare, and today the Folger Shakespeare Memorial in Washington, D. C., can count seventy-nine copies of the First Folio alone. From about 1900 to his death in 1934 William L. Clements (1862–1934) of Bay City, Mich., built up his collection of Americana which in 1923 was officially given to his alma mater, the University of Michigan. Edward Everett Ayer (1841–1927) of Chicago collected Americana, with special reference to the Southwest, and his collection is now at the Newberry Library, Chicago. William Smith Mason (1866–) of the same city specialized in collecting Benjamin Franklin. His collection is at Yale University. The Robert B. Adam library of Johnsoniana went to Rochester University. John H. Wrenn's collection of English literature, which was partly the work of the English bibliographer, Thomas J. Wise, is at the University of Texas. Hubert Howe Bancroft (1832–1918) collected the Pacific Coast, and after his death his library went to the University of California. Robert Cowan's collection of California is now at the University of California at Los Angeles.

At the same time, the work of important collectors was constantly being broken up by auctions. Among these were the Robert Hoe sale of 1911–12; the Levi Leiter sale of 1933; the Roderick Terry sales of 1934; the Ogden Goelet sale of 1935; the John B. Stetson sale of 1935. Bibliomania raged in the United States during the "hilarious decade" 1919–29, and the prices fetched were higher than ever before. Notable among the high points was the sale of the Americana of William C. Braislin of Brooklyn in 1927, and the English literature of Jerome Kern in 1929.

It has sometimes been said that a great scholar seldom forms a great library. Yet in America four historians have done so. The books of Jared Sparks (1789–1866) are at Cornell University; those of Peter Force (1790–1868) are at the Library of Congress; and the library of George Bancroft (1800–1891) is at the New York Public Library. Wilberforce Eames (1855–1937) made up and disposed of several great libraries.

[No general American treatise on this subject. See files of *Proceedings of the American Antiquarian Society; Bulletin* of the New York Public Library; *Publisher's Weekly;* A. E. Newton, *Amenities of Book Collecting;* A. S. W. Rosenbach, *Books and Bidders;* R. G. Adams, *Three Americanists.*]

RANDOLPH G. ADAMS

Book Publishing. Publishing, as it is now practised with the whole financial responsibility for the production and distribution of a printed work resting upon a firm or an individual other than the author, arose after the Revolution. From the establishment in 1638 of Stephen Daye's press at Cambridge, Mass., books were printed at the author's expense, the first being *The Bay Psalm Book*[qv] (1640). Hezekiah Usher in 1647 in Boston first imported books and took some risks in republishing successful British works. Partly because of state control of printing, few presses were set up. That at Cambridge had a monopoly for fifty years; printing was forbidden in Virginia until 1730. "After great Charge and Trouble I have brought the great Art and Mystery of printing into this part of America," wrote William Bradford, but he left Philadelphia in 1693 because of arrest and imprisonment; for thirty years he was the sole printer in New York. In 1712 Andrew Bradford went to Philadelphia; sixteen years later Benjamin Franklin opened his own shop. As towns developed throughout the colonies, printing offices with weekly newspapers were founded. Near Philadelphia in 1743 Christopher Sower began publishing German works from the first non-English press. From these presses came occasional books, the majority of which were religious in character and foreign in origin.

The successful War for Independence led to a call for native authorship and American books. Isaiah Thomas of Worcester, Mass., Mathew Carey of Philadelphia and Hudson and Goodwin of Hartford, Conn., issued nationalistic schoolbooks like Noah Webster's *Blue-Backed Speller*[qv]. Native poetry by the Hartford Wits[qv] and native fiction by Charles Brockden Brown failed to sell profitably. In 1801 Carey organized the American Company of Booksellers to foster book fairs and to stimulate American authorship. Yet, especially with the vogue of the novel after Scott's success in 1814 with *Waverley,* British books crowded American shelves, and publishers vied in securing first sheets and flooding the market with the writings of Scott, Bulwer-Lytton, Dickens, Thackeray and others. Until foreign publications were affected by the copyright[qv] law of 1891, they tended to dominate the market. Certain houses, like Carey's, Harper's and Putnam's, printed editions almost overnight to forestall competition. Only James Fenimore Cooper's and Harriet Beecher Stowe's novels competed successfully with oversea books.

Notable publishing changes were effected about 1815 by the employment of the stereotype process, which cheapened production and made possible a uniformity of editions of textbooks printed in different states. Railroad transportation, after 1840, tended to end the practice of leasing plates to printers and to centralize in one office the publication of a book. The vogue of annuals and gift books, with their beautiful "embellishments," gave rise to the arts of wood and steel engraving and lithography. By 1870 America led the world in the perfection of wood engraving[qv], but the development of photography[qv] and photo-engraving, an inexpensive process of reproducing pictures on metal, soon substituted mechanical for manual artistry. Since 1900, and especially since 1920, American publishers have paid great attention to the arts of design in manufacturing books, on the theory that beauty improves sales.

Attempts to provide good books at low prices to the masses were made by Harper's as early as 1830, but success first crowned the venture of Park Benjamin, the poet, who in the 1840's issued paper-bound quartos at prices below twenty-five cents a volume. Competitors with handier size and larger type soon ended the poet's experiment. From 1870 to 1891 a vast number of books, reprints and translations of foreign works as well as first editions of American writers flooded the market at prices ranging from twenty-five to fifty cents a copy. "The lesson of the year," declared the *American Booksellers' Guide* in 1873, "is that Americans want cheap books." Simultaneously dime novel series[qv], then never referred to as books, enjoyed enormous sales. Newspapers and magazines gave books as subscription inducements; the New York *Tribune* thus distributed thousands of copies of *Webster's Dictionary*[qv]. Door-to-door sale of religious, historical and encyclopedic books became profitable. Mark Twain, beguiled by the profits of publishing, lost a fortune in an ill-starred venture. Post-World War attempts to circulate books once a month through book clubs were resisted unsuccessfully by trade publishers. An extension of the publication of reprint editions of standard works at popular prices took place in the 1920's, when chain drug stores opened book counters and with their "dollar-ature" gave booksellers unexpected paralyzing competition.

In 1789 the Methodist Book Concern was established, the first church publishing house. Since then every sect and several interdenominational organizations have produced thousands of books to the extent of millions of copies. The American Tract Society[qv], for example, has published in 179 languages, dialects and characters. The American Bible Society[qv] has distributed millions of Bibles in many languages. Correspondence schools, like the International Correspondence School, have produced notable textbooks. To foster the printing of scientific writings, some twenty American universities have subsidized publishing houses. Other learned and professional societies similarly have created divisions for issuing writings of specialized interest. The Federal Government and state and territorial governments, as well as county and municipal divisions, issue books concerning their activities. Thus the production of books in the United States is large, that of trade publishers being probably less than half the total.

[H. W. Boynton, *Annals of American Bookselling, 1638-1850;* C. M. Depew, *One Hundred Years of American Commerce;* R. H. Shove, *Cheap Book Production in the United States, 1870 to 1891.*]

HARRY R. WARFEL

Bookshops, Old. In every large city there is at least one old bookshop with roots nourished by the literary tradition. Most notable is Boston's "Old Corner Book Store" with a sentimental history reaching back to 1812. Here Samuel G. Goodrich ("Peter Parley"[qv]) began his literary enterprises; here James T. Fields, later the publisher of the New England galaxy of writers, learned the book business as a clerk; here authors frequently congregated on their way to and from the dinners of the famous Saturday Club. In Charles Wiley's bookshop in New York City James Fenimore Cooper held court in a style becoming America's most popular novelist of the 1820's; Fitz-Greene Halleck, Joseph Rodman Drake, William Cullen Bryant and other celebrities joined the novelist. In New Haven, Hezekiah Howe, printer of Noah Webster's *American Dictionary*[qv] (1828), had an extensive collection of old books. His store became the rendezvous of Yale professors and scholars traveling overland between Boston and New York. These book dealers underwrote the publication of editions of desirable technical, professional and religious works; thus they frequently were publishers as well as booksellers. Many publishers maintained bookshops. Scribners and Putnams, among others, still conduct stores selling old and new books, although the tendency toward specialization in one department of the book business long ago set in.

Among the more notable dealers in old books in New York was William Gowans, who set up shop in 1829. At his death in 1871 his stock totaled 300,000 volumes. His customers included the noted literati of his generation. Until the middle of the 19th century old books came chiefly from England. Occasional shipments of folios and quartos and rare Americana stimulated a few dealers to specialize in rare, expensive works. In the 1850's interest grew in Americana, because Parkman, Bancroft, Cooper and Irving called attention to the pleasures of amassing collections relating to our country. Joseph Sabin, between 1864 and 1874, sold more than a million dollars' worth of such books. Sabin prepared *A Dictionary of Books Relating to America, from Its Discovery to the Present Time* (14 vols., 1868–84), a painstaking compilation, but permeated with a malevolent and saturnine spirit and marred with unscholarly remarks. In Philadelphia William Brotherhead capitalized the interest in Americana. He published several patriotic works, such as facsimiles of the signers of the Declaration of Independence.

Now that vast municipal and institutional libraries have replaced the scholar's personal library as a workshop, the antiquarian bookshop has lost some of its charm and much of its profit. The seller of old books has had to speed his pace by employing modern sales devices since the great personal libraries, like those of Lenox, Astor, Folger, Morgan and Huntington, have passed into the possession of institutions.

[H. W. Boynton, *Annals of American Bookselling, 1638-*

1850; William Brotherhead, *Forty Years among the Old Booksellers of Philadelphia;* W. L. Andrews, *The Old Booksellers of New York.*]

HARRY R. WARFEL

Boom Towns, those which sprang up like mushrooms as the result of some mineral or industrial development, were numerous in the 19th century. Rochester, N. Y., was one of the earliest notable examples, its growth after 1825 as the result of the building of the Erie Canal[qv] and the development of the Genesee water power being phenomenal for the period. There were a few boom towns in the Middle West, but the finest specimens began to be seen only with the discoveries of gold and silver[qqv] in the Far West. San Francisco itself in 1849–51 was a remarkable example. Simultaneously, in the gold regions, before there were any sawmills, villages of tents, with an occasional log hut, sprang up, and quickly formed city governments. By the time lumber began to be sawed, county governments were being organized and the crudest of small frame shacks became courthouses. Virginia City and other Nevada towns were mushroom growths from silver ore; meanwhile, in the 1860's, gold was producing many others in Idaho, Montana and Colorado, mostly ephemeral, though Helena, Mont., and Denver[qv], Colo., proved to be permanent. Gold brought Deadwood, N. Dak., into being in 1876. Two cities built on silver evolved swiftly in 1878, Tombstone, Ariz., a new foundation, and Leadville, Colo., long a somnolent hamlet, but whose population leaped from 300 to 35,000 in two years. Oil City, Pa., in 1859 was the first of a long series of petroleum boom towns, later continued in Ohio, Indiana, Oklahoma and Texas. The opening of a portion of the Indian Territory[qv] to colonization in 1889 created Guthrie and Oklahoma City almost overnight. Immediately afterward, new gold discoveries in Colorado did the same for Cripple Creek[qv] and Creede. Hopewell, Va., was a typical creation of World War munition plants, and other precocious towns arose in Florida during the land-speculation excitement of the 1920's.

[Alvin F. Harlow, *Old Waybills;* John M. Clampitt, *Echoes from the Rocky Mountains.*]

ALVIN F. HARLOW

Boomer Movement, The, is a term applied to attempts of settlers to occupy an area in Indian Territory[qv] during the period from 1879 to 1885. The Five Civilized Tribes[qv] of Indians formerly owned all of the present state of Oklahoma except the Panhandle (*see* Cimarron, Proposed Territory of). In 1866 as a punishment for having participated in the Civil War on the side of the South (*see* Indian in the Civil War), they were compelled to cede to the United States as a home for other Indians the western half of their domain. During the next ten years several tribes of Indians were given reservations on these lands but a fertile region of some 2,000,000 acres near the center of Indian Territory was not assigned to any tribe and came to be known as the "Unassigned Lands" or "Old Oklahoma."

Early in 1879 E. C. Boudinot, a railway attorney of Cherokee blood, published a newspaper article stating that this was public land, and so open to homestead entry. Widely reprinted, this article created great excitement. Later in the same year a colony of homeseekers under the leadership of C. C. Carpenter sought to enter the Indian Territory and occupy this area but was prevented by troops under Gen. Pope.

In 1880 David L. Payne became the leader of these so-called "Boomers." Payne organized the movement, charging a small fee for membership in his "Oklahoma Colony." During the next four years he and his followers made eight attempts to settle the region but in every case were ejected by soldiers. Upon his death at Wellington, Kans., in 1884 his lieutenant, W. L. Couch, led an expedition to the forbidden area, but was promptly removed by the military. The struggle was then transferred to the national capital and on April 22, 1889, the Unassigned Lands were opened to settlement under the provisions of an act of Congress.

[E. E. Dale and J. L. Rader, *Readings in Oklahoma History.*]

EDWARD EVERETT DALE

Boondoggling. On April 3, 1935, Robert C. Marshall, a witness before the Aldermanic Committee to Investigate the Relief Administration in New York City, testified that he taught various crafts, including "boondoggling," to workers on relief[qv], and described "boondoggles" as "gadgets" or useful articles made out of scrap material. The term boondoggling was thereafter rather loosely used by critics of the New Deal[qv] throughout the country to ridicule so-called useless made-work and unproductive educational, recreational and research projects of relief workers.

[L. P. Stryker, *Report to . . . the Aldermanic Committee to Investigate the Relief Administration in the City of New York; The Christian Science Monitor,* Weekly Magazine Section, Aug. 19, 1936; *The Literary Digest,* June 1, 1935, The Lexicographer's Easy Chair; *Scouting,* March, 1930, Vol. 18.]

STANLEY R. PILLSBURY

Boone, Jemima, and Callaway Girls Episode. The settlement of Boonesborough on the Kentucky River had been left in peace by the Indians until Sunday, July 14, 1776, when three girls were captured as they were floating in a canoe on the river. They were Jemima, daughter of Daniel Boone, and Elizabeth and Frances, daughters of Col. Richard Callaway. The settlement was thrown into a turmoil and a rescue party was organized by Boone. Meanwhile the girls were hurried north by their captors toward the Shawnee^qv towns across the Ohio. They attempted to mark their trail until threatened by the Indians.

The third morning, as the Indians were building a fire for breakfast, the rescuers came up. "That's Daddy's gun," cried Jemima, as one Indian was toppled into the fire. The others ran off leaving their plunder, which the whites took. The girls were escorted home in triumph. Jemima soon married one of the rescuing party, Flanders Callaway. Elizabeth Callaway married Samuel Henderson and Frances, John Holder. The episode served to put the settlers in the Kentucky wilderness on guard and prevented straying beyond the fort.

[George W. Ranck, *Boonesborough;* R. G. Thwaites, *Daniel Boone;* John Bakeless, *Life of Daniel Boone.*]

LOUISE PHELPS KELLOGG

Boone's Station was the stockaded home of Daniel Boone from 1780 to 1786. The place, which had been settled by Daniel's brother, Israel, in 1776, was on Boone's Creek in Fayette County, Ky., near the present village of Athens. Here John Filson interviewed Daniel Boone in 1784 for his *The Adventures of Colonel Daniel Boone.*

[G. W. Ranck, *Boonesborough.*]

JONATHAN T. DORRIS

Boone's Wilderness Road. *See* Wilderness Road, The.

Boonesborough, on the south side of the Kentucky River, in the present county of Madison, was founded April 2, 1775, by Daniel Boone. Despatched from the Watauga treaty ground by members of the Transylvania Company^qv to mark out a roadway to lands purchased from the Cherokees^qv, Boone and his companions blazed a trail across Cumberland Gap^qv and thence through the wilderness to the mouth of Otter Creek on the Kentucky. There they erected a stout stockaded fort which served as a rallying-point of defense for the harassed settlers throughout the Revolution. At Boonesborough, May 23–27, 1775, was held the convention called by the Transylvania proprietors to consider the needs of the colony. The novel proceedings and enactments were devoid of effective sanction, but they were timely and savored of the soil.

On July 14, 1776, three young girls, one a daughter of Boone, were captured near the fort by skulking savages, but within a day or two were rescued unharmed (*see* Boone, Jemima, and Callaway Girls Episode). On April 15, 1777, Boonesborough was subjected to a savage Indian attack, and on July 4 of the same year the assault was renewed on a larger scale. The fiercest siege and assault of all, however, occurred Sept. 7–20, 1778. The Shawnee^qv chiefs, Black Fish and Moluntha, together with the French-Canadian, Lt. Antoine Dagneaux de Quindre, were in command of a formidable body of Indians supported by a few British militiamen from Detroit and this combined force assailed the little fortress with all the arts of bravado and cunning. But neither force nor guile could bring about its downfall, and, finding their efforts futile, the invaders finally desisted and withdrew.

[George W. Ranck, *Boonesborough;* Lucille Gulliver, *Life of Boone.*]

SAMUEL M. WILSON

Boonton Iron Works, THE, were founded about 1770 by Samuel Ogden who, with others in his family, purchased a six-acre tract along the Rockaway River, near Boonton, Morris County, N. J. Here rolling and slitting mills were erected that engaged in the manufacture of nail rods and bar iron. With the building of the Morris Canal^qv in 1830 the New Jersey Iron Company was organized. This company built a new plant costing $283,000 and imported skilled mechanics from England. Under Fuller & Lord (1852–76) the enterprise tended to become an integrated industry with ore and timber reserves, canal boats, furnaces, mills and auxiliary plants. After 1881 the business slowly declined. The plant closed in 1911.

[C. S. Boyer, *Early Forges and Furnaces in New Jersey.*]

C. A. TITUS

Boonville, Mo., Battle of (June 17, 1861). In the first engagement of the Civil War in Missouri, troops of the Missouri state guard (pro-Southern) under Col. John S. Marmaduke were defeated by Brig. Gen. Lyon at Boonville, a strategic point on the Missouri River. The engagement began about five miles below Boonville. Union forces occupied Boonville and gained control of the river, and Confederate strength in Missouri was weakened.

[Walter Williams and Floyd C. Shoemaker, *Missouri, Mother of the West,* Vol. II.]

FLOYD C. SHOEMAKER

Booth v. U. S. (Feb. 5, 1934). In 1919 Congress passed an act permitting certain Federal judges to retire with full pay, at the age of seventy. On June 16, 1933, new legislation reduced their pay 15%. Retired Judge Wilbur F. Booth thereupon sued the Government. The Supreme Court unanimously ruled in his favor, holding that a retired judge did not "relinquish his office" and so, under Art. III, Sec. 1 of the Constitution, his pay could not be reduced.

[291 U. S. 339.]

ERIK McKINLEY ERIKSSON

Bootlegging is a term, derived from the early Indian traders'[qv] custom of carrying a bottle of liquor[qv] in the boot, especially applied to illicit deliveries of alcoholic beverages. The bootlegger is a peddler whose name differentiates his activities from those of the merchant who unlawfully purveys from a shop known variously as a "blind tiger," "blind pig" or "speakeasy"[qv]. The manufacture of illicit hard liquor is termed "moonshining"[qv] and the product, variously known, is perhaps most euphemistically described as "mountain dew."

Since the activity is illicit, no reliable estimates can be given as to the scope. In some sections of the country sentiment favors bootlegging as being a proper resistance to tyranny, in others it is regarded as completely reprehensible, all licensed retail liquor dealers holding the latter opinion quite determinedly. In those times and places in which alcoholic beverages can be obtained lawfully at reasonable prices the popular estimation of the bootlegger's business rapidly depreciates; but heavy taxation or legal efforts to prevent the traffic speedily render the purveyor a more respected member of society.

The profits derived from bootlegging depend somewhat upon the source of the beverage and somewhat upon the methods of retailing. To supply thirsty citizens in the days of the Eighteenth Amendment[qv] liquor was smuggled across the borders, alcohol lawfully possessed for manufacturing purposes was sold for beverages and a relatively small amount was distilled without license, the annual consumption from all sources averaging perhaps 100,000,000 gallons of hard liquor (1920 to 1932). In the larger cities powerful organizations arose to cater to the bibulous. These gangs, headed by an unusually astute or intelligent man, corrupted the agencies of law enforcement, arranged for a steady supply and set up a complete system of retailing both through luxurious speakeasies, known as "night clubs,"[qv] which furnished a variety of entertainment as well as food and illicit drink, and through the private calls of bootleggers upon regular customers. They tried to create a monopoly and were as ready to take a rival "for a ride" as they were thus to entertain a spy or a traitor. The unlucky recipient of this attention was likely to be found along an unfrequented road, filled with slugs from a machine gun; the methods of disposal were all quite final, however various. The St. Valentine's Day massacre of 1929 in a populous section of the Chicago North Side, within a few blocks of the great Newberry Library, was the slaughter of seven unarmed rivals by one of these bootlegging gangs. (*See also* Rum Row.)

To meet the rising tide of crime several steps were taken. An amendment to the National Prohibition Act was passed in February, 1929, raising the maximum penalty for bootlegging to a fine of $10,000 plus five years in prison, but this carried a rider stipulating that it was the intent of Congress to apply this drastic punishment to major offenders only. A year later, a Federal grand jury sitting at Chicago uncovered what was termed the largest liquor ring since the advent of prohibition[qv]. The indictment of 31 corporations and 158 individuals cited violations in New York, Chicago, Detroit, Cleveland, Philadelphia, St. Louis, Minneapolis, St. Paul, Los Angeles and North Bergen, N. J. This group was charged with the diversion of more than 7,000,000 gallons of alcohol in the seven years preceding indictment and were alleged to have done a total business in excess of $50,000,000. The State of Michigan went so far as to declare bootlegging a felony and to provide that on a third conviction for felony the convict might be sentenced to imprisonment for life.

Before the end of 1930 more than 200 persons had been killed in the process of enforcement of the Volstead Act[qv] and moderates were beginning to question if, after all, the game was worth the candle. The public revealed this attitude in a *Literary Digest* poll, May 24, 1930, by returning 30.5% of their votes in favor of continuance and strict enforcement of the prohibition amendment, 29.1% in favor of modification to permit light wines and beer and 40.4% for repeal.

A limited number of bootleggers has always operated and probably will continue, but since the quality of their merchandise and public support are both uncertain, their sales volume doubtless will remain relatively small.

[*Annals of American Association for the Promotion of Social Science*, Vols. XXXII, CIX, CLXIII.]

ROBERT G. RAYMER

Boots and Shoes. Boot and shoe making began in colonial America in the shops of village artisans working to order, in plantation shops employing slaves and with itinerant craftsmen who traveled from household to household to make the family footwear. Very early, however, coarse brogans were manufactured commercially in the northern colonies to ship to southern plantations. By the middle of the 18th century skilled craftsmen at Lynn, Mass., and other colonial centers were making finer footwear, especially ladies' shoes, for the general market. Little change occurred in the hand process of making shoes until about the time of the Civil War. For several decades before this, however, the industry had been developing a new organization to serve a larger commercial demand, especially in the West. Even before the Revolution, army contractors and wholesalers purchased shoes from makers working singly or in teams in "ten-footer" shops scattered through the more thickly settled parts of New England. Gradually, however, a system developed where shoes were produced in quantities by manufacturers, also principally in New England, who had warehouse-factories for cutting but who employed home workers served by wagon distributors and collectors to fit and sew uppers and to last and sole complete boots and shoes. During the 1870's and 1880's automatic machines for pegging and nailing soles, for shaping leather and for lasting were perfected. More important than this, the sewing machine was adapted to sewing uppers, welts and soles. These mechanical improvements, which were American inventions[qv], and the application of power to shoemaking machinery, caused all operations to be concentrated in factories many of which were grouped in shoe towns like Lynn, Brockton and Haverhill in Massachusetts and in larger cities. The new methods of manufacture encouraged styling and quantity production and, accompanied by improved tanning processes and a wider variety of leathers, enabled American footwear to conquer foreign markets. This development went hand in hand with the use of trade brands, extensive advertising and the practice of selling standard makes at fixed prices through chains of retail stores controlled by the manufacturer. From colonial times the principal shoemaking state of America has been Massachusetts, which still accounts for about one fourth of the billion dollars' worth of footwear made in the country. New York and Missouri, where St. Louis is a great shoemaking center, rank next to Massachusetts in this industry.

[Blanche Evans Hazard, *The Organization of the Boot and Shoe Industry in Massachusetts before 1875;* U. S. Census Reports.]

VICTOR S. CLARK

Borax. Until recently the principal source of borax in the United States was Death Valley[qv] and the adjacent mines in the Funeral Range. But the boring of a deep well near Kramer, Calif., revealed a richer deposit and the Death Valley properties were closed down.

The discovery of borax in Death Valley is credited to Aaron Winters, who sold out to William T. Coleman. He used Chinese to scrape up the "cotton-ball" borax, which he hauled 165 miles to the railroad at Daggett, Calif. The property was later taken over by F. M. Smith, the Borax King, who made the Twenty Mule Teams famous on the long haul to Mojave, Calif. Two of these huge wagons hooked together would haul 45,000 lbs. of borax, the capacity of an ordinary freight car.

[Dane Coolidge, *Death Valley Prospectors.*]

DANE COOLIDGE

Border Forts, The Evacuation of (1796). By the French and Indian War[qv] Great Britain conquered the western country, and by the Proclamation of 1763[qv] constituted it a permanent Indian preserve. This policy was reversed by the Quebec Act[qv] (1774) which annexed the entire Northwest to Quebec Province. Thereby the older colonies, which had fought to obtain the West, found themselves excluded from all share in it. During the Revolution they again renewed the struggle for the West, and at its close obtained it, with the Mississippi and the line through the middle of the Great Lakes-St. Lawrence system as the western and northern boundaries of the new nation (*see* Definitive Treaty of Peace, 1783).

Elsewhere in the treaty Great Britain agreed to evacuate all places held by her armies within the United States "with all convenient speed." These included Carleton Island (Fort Haldimand), Oswego (Fort Ontario), Niagara, Detroit and Michilimackinac, guarding the fur trade route between Montreal and the far Northwest, and serving as natural centers of control of the interior Indian tribes, allies of Great Britain in the late war. Both Gov. Haldimand and the Montreal traders were appalled by the boundary provisions of the treaty, the governor fearing the surrender of the posts would precipitate a general Indian uprising, the merchants foreseeing their own financial ruin. The early American overtures for the transfer were evaded, therefore, while their later appeals at London were met by the excuse that the Americans had not complied with the treaty in the matter of collection of debts owed to British merchants (*see*

British Debts, The), and the treatment accorded the Loyalists[qv].

For a decade Great Britain pursued a policy of opportunism, meanwhile retaining the posts and exercising *de facto* control over the Northwest. In 1793, however, she entered the continental revolutionary wars, while in America President Washington was prosecuting the conquest of the Northwestern Indian Confederacy (*see* Wayne Campaign). Faced with a war in Europe, the British Ministry had no stomach for another in America. By the Jay Treaty[qv] (ratified in 1795) the evacuation of the Western posts by June 1, 1796, was promised. The Americans proved less ready to receive than the British were to deliver them; Detroit was taken over July 11; Oswego on July 15; Niagara on Aug. 10; and Michilimackinac, Sept. 1. With the transfer American rule over the country adjacent to the Great Lakes was first established; west of Lake Michigan and on Lake Superior, however, British authority continued dominant until after the War of 1812.

[Alfred L. Burt, *The Old Province of Quebec;* Louise P. Kellogg, *The British Régime in Wisconsin and the Northwest;* A. C. McLaughlin, The Western Posts and the British Debts, in American Historical Association *Annual Report* for 1894.]

M. M. QUAIFE

Border Ruffians were citizens of western Missouri who endeavored to establish slavery in Kansas Territory. The term originated in 1855 with B. F. Stringfellow's assault upon Gov. A. H. Reeder, and was first used by the New York *Tribune*. Missourians readily adopted the name, and border ruffian stores, hotels and river boats capitalized upon it. Antislavery presses and orators soon expanded the term to include all proslavery Southerners in Kansas. Some of the "ruffians" were of the carousing type, but indiscriminate usage included such respectable leaders as Sen. D. R. Atchison. "Border ruffians" voted illegally in Kansas elections, raided Lawrence[qv] and other towns, stole horses, and in general molested free-state families (*see* Kansas Struggle, The). Much of their overzealous work was inspired by similar depredations committed by antislavery Kansans upon Missourians, and once such practices had begun a spirit of lawlessness prompted both groups to use extreme measures. (*See also* Border War.)

[W. E. Connelley, *A Standard History of Kansas and Kansans.*]

WENDELL H. STEPHENSON

Border Slave State Convention, The (1861), also called the Peace Convention or Conference, met in Washington, D. C., Feb. 4–27, 1861, on call by the Virginia legislature, in an attempt to satisfy the states of the far South on the slavery issue. Twenty-one states were represented, with the border states[qv] most active. The seven states which had already seceded did not send delegates, nor did Arkansas, Wisconsin, Minnesota, California, Oregon. Ex-President Tyler of Virginia, chosen president of the Convention, stated its purpose—"to bring back the cotton states and thereby restore the Constitution and the Union of the States." The Crittenden Compromise[qv] plan, which formed the basis of discussion, was so modified by further compromise in the course of the deliberations that the final recommendations of the Convention satisfied no one. The recommendations, submitted to Congress on Feb. 27, 1861, constituted the last attempt at conciliation on the slavery question in the territories.

[J. G. Randall, *The Civil War and Reconstruction.*]

C. MILDRED THOMPSON

Border State Representation in the Confederacy. *See* Confederacy, Border State Representation in.

Border States, The, was a designation applied to the tier of slave states bordering on the North, consisting of Delaware, Maryland, Virginia, Kentucky and Missouri. They were largely Southern in sentiment, though many of their economic ties were with the North. They owe their chief significance to their reaction toward secession and the Civil War[qqv]. None seceded except Virginia, from which West Virginia separated. Kentucky set up and maintained for a few months in 1861 the unique policy of neutrality, and all except Delaware sent considerable numbers of soldiers to the Confederacy. Kentucky and Delaware were the only states to cling to slavery until the Thirteenth Amendment[qv] abolished it.

[E. C. Smith, *The Borderland in the Civil War.*]

E. MERTON COULTER

Border War (1854–59), on the Kansas frontier, resulted from the opening of the territory to slavery, promoted emigration from the Northeast (*see* Emigrant Aid Movement, The), the arrival of squatters and speculators and the presence of an adventurous element recruited from both North and South. While claim jumping[qv] provoked dissension, the slavery issue was controlling. Recurring personal altercations led disputants to organize regulating associations and guerrilla bands. It is impossible to determine which side committed greater excesses in lynching, horse stealing, pillaging and pitched battles. The first eighteen months witnessed killings and robberies, but moderation and self-control prevented serious discord until the murder of a free-state settler, following a quarrel over a land claim, precipitated the bloodless Wakarusa War[qv], December, 1855. "Bleeding Kansas" soon became a grim reality. The "sack" of Lawrence[qv], May 21, 1856, by a posse of "border ruffians,"[qv] and John Brown's massacre of five proslavery men at Potawatomie[qv] three days later started a four months' reign of terror. Free-state men won victories at Black Jack, Franklin, Forts Saunders and Titus, Slough Creek and Hickory Point; their opponents pillaged and later burned Osawatomie[qv] but were prevented from destroying Lawrence by official intervention. A semblance of order restored by Gov. J. W. Geary in the fall was of brief duration. The Marais des Cygnes[qv] massacre of nine free-state men, May 19, 1858, was the last wholesale slaughter. In the same year disturbances in Linn and Bourbon counties reached critical proportions. Cessation of these early in 1859 terminated major conflict, albeit sporadic disorders continued until the Civil War inaugurated a new chapter in Kansas-Missouri relations. Anticipating a congressional appropriation which did not materialize, territorial commissioners approved claims for losses resulting from border trouble totaling over $400,000, which, though greatly exaggerated, give some notion of the extent of property damage.

[F. W. Blackmar, *The Life of Charles Robinson;* D. W. Wilder, *Annals of Kansas.*]

WENDELL H. STEPHENSON

Border War, The Religious Phase of (1857–59). Border conflicts were frequent after 1844–45 wherever the antislavery and proslavery wings of the churches met, as in Missouri, Kentucky and western Virginia. With the opening of Kansas, this conflict was extended there, and both Northern and Southern churches tried to occupy the territory. Church people were largely responsible for the formation and support of the New England Emigrant Aid Company[qv]. Thus the settlement of Kansas became for many a Christian crusade and the crusaders came singing Whittier's hymn:

> We cross the prairies as of old
>   The Pilgrims crossed the sea,
> To make the west as they the east,
>   The homestead of the free.

Such pious cant on the part of the antislavery party helps explain the fury with which the proslavery element resisted their control.

[W. W. Sweet, Some Religious Aspects of the Kansas Struggle, in *The Journal of Religion,* Vol. VII.]

WILLIAM W. SWEET

Borglum's Colossal Sculptures. The idea of carving a colossal head of Robert E. Lee on Stone Mountain, Ga., was first conceived, in 1915, by the Daughters of the Confederacy[qv], inspired by Mr. Borglum's colossal marble head of Lincoln in the Rotunda at the Capitol, Washington.

On visiting the mountain, in 1915, the sculptor refused to undertake the single head in dimensions insignificant for the mountain, and offered a design of the mobilization of the Confederate forces under their leaders, Lee, Jackson, Jefferson Davis and field officers, developing a wholly new treatment regarding memorials by departing from the conventional figure or grouping, and composing the subject into mass movement, stressing the importance of mass action relating to human events.

His conception involved the creation in the granite of Stone Mountain groupings in scale with the mountain itself. The composition contained infantry en masse marching in review before their commander, and some forty mounted general officers, supported by cavalry, and field guns. The horse and rider were approximately 160 feet in height, the length of the carving approximately 720 feet. All rough stone to a point within two feet of the finished surface was removed with dynamite and actual carving carried on with air drills and hand tools.

Stone Mountain developed a school of colossal sculpture and was progressing with great success when, in 1924, a sharp difference arose between Mr. Borglum and two members of the committee as to the degree of perfection and finish of the work, resulting in Mr. Borglum's abandoning the work and destroying his own models.

In 1930 at the call of the governor of the state, the sculptor went to Atlanta and agreed in public meeting to return as soon as the work on Mount Rushmore could spare him. The new plans for Stone Mountain will be doubled in dimensions, and in higher relief, following the highly successful carvings at Mount Rushmore.

The Mount Rushmore Memorial, begun in 1927, is located in the Black Hills of South Dakota. It is being carved on the apex of a great granite uplift. The figures, grouped in the form of a horseshoe, are scaled to the proportions of men 465 feet high, the sculptures fading into the precipice at the waistline. The first figure at the right is George Washington, commemorating the founding of the Republic. Next comes Jefferson, commemorating the development of our territorial greatness. In the center of the horseshoe is the figure of Theodore Roosevelt, commemorating the cutting of the Panama Canal. And on the left side of the horseshoe, opposite Jefferson, is the figure of Lincoln, commemorating the preservation of the Union. The horseshoe in which the figures are carved is cut back approximately 100 feet into the solid granite of the mountain and the distance between Jefferson and Lincoln is approximately 75 feet. The mountain itself is a great dyke, the front forming a vast amphitheater upon the west walls of which Borglum proposes to incise the Declaration of Independence and other national documents. The figures face southeast. The Memorial, first suggested by Doane Robinson, was sponsored by a group of patriotic individuals who had been impressed by Borglum's work on Stone Mountain. It is now entirely under the supervision of the Government of the United States.

GUTZON BORGLUM

Borgne, Lake, Battle of (Dec. 14, 1814), was the naval engagement preceding the Battle of New Orleans[qv]. The British, with a force of light barges commanded by Capt. Lockyer, captured the five American gunboats commanded by Lt. Thomas ap Catesby Jones guarding Malhereux Island Passage. This cleared the eastern approach to the city and avoided the fortifications along the river. The defeated Americans inflicted such heavy losses upon their captors as to contribute to the many delays which made it possible for the lately arrived Gen. Jackson to organize the defense of the city.

[A. T. Mahan, *The War of 1812 in Its Relations to Sea Power.*]

U. T. BRADLEY

Borough. Numerous colonial towns were patterned after the English borough, which was a trading community or town that had obtained some degree of corporate organization and certain rights of self-government. The colonial boroughs received their charters from the governors and were governed by a mayor and recorder, appointed by the governor, and aldermen elected by the freemen[qv]. Sitting as a common council, these officials passed bylaws regulating trade, industry and labor, binding out orphans, supervising poor relief, fixing the assize of bread and admitting the freemen, who in early days possessed a monopoly of retail trade, although in later times such regulations were generally relaxed. Sitting as a mayor's or sessions court, these same officials handled both civil and criminal business. After the Revolution borough charters were granted by the state legislatures. The suffrage was widened and the mayor came to be elected by popular vote and gained increasing authority in borough management.

[R. B. Morris, *Select Cases of the Mayor's Court of New York City;* A. E. Peterson and G. W. Edwards, *New York as an Eighteenth Century Municipality.*]

RICHARD B. MORRIS

Bosque Redondo, THE, was a reservation forty miles square on Pecos River, central New Mexico, to which 8000 Navajos[qv] were removed in 1863. Those who survived five years of disgraceful mismanagement were permitted by the Federal Government (1868) to return to their old habitat. Never since have the Navajos given any serious trouble.

[R. E. Twitchell, *Leading Facts of New Mexican History.*]

LANSING B. BLOOM

Boss, Political. Although not confined to the United States, the political boss has probably played a somewhat larger role in its political history, particularly since 1850, than in that of any other country. The boss has dominated city, county and state governments.

Cartoonists portray the boss as a coarse-featured, profane giant of a man who wears checked clothes and gaudy jewelry and constantly has a well-chewed cigar in his mouth. Actually there is wide variation in the physical, mental, moral and political characteristics of bosses. Usually a boss must start in precinct politics and through a process of survival of the fittest clamber to the top. He is more often than not a hard worker, courageous, a good judge of men, loyal to friends and generous to unfortunates. He may or may not be corrupt, harsh and indifferent to the public weal. As a rule he holds public office at some time, enjoys intimate relations with business and desires for himself great power or much money or both.

Tweed, Croker, Murphy, McManes, the Vares, Cox, Lundin, Prendergast and Ruef rank among notorious city bosses. Quay, Penrose, Platt, Taggart and Long are outstanding examples of state bosses.

[W. B. Munro, *Personality in Politics;* S. P. Orth, *The Boss and the Machine;* J. T. Salter, *Boss Rule;* Harold Zink, *City Bosses in the United States;* H. F. Gosnell, *Boss Platt and His New York Machine.*]

HAROLD ZINK

Boston. Capt. John Smith explored and mapped the vicinity of Boston in 1614. In 1621 a party from Plymouth visited the site of Boston, the peninsula called Shawmut by the Indians and other landmarks. Individual settlers in the next few years located there and across the Charles River. Following the Great Migration[qv] of 1630 John Winthrop's group first settled at Charlestown[qv], but soon moved over to the Shawmut peninsula. On Sept. 7 of that year it was ordained by the Court of Assistants, sitting at Charlestown, that the new town be named Boston. In 1632 it was made the capital of Massachusetts Bay Colony[qv] and that year the first meetinghouse was erected. The first post office was opened in 1639; in 1652 a mint began work and in 1686 the first bank in Boston as well as the first in the colonies was established. A printing press was set up in 1674 (though there had been one in Cambridge[qv], across the Charles, since 1638) and in 1704 the *Boston News-Letter*[qv] appeared. By this time Boston was becoming the largest and most important town in America. Its population in the middle 18th century was about 15,000. It was one of the earliest and chief centers of rebellion against the government of England and the first armed conflicts of the Revolutionary War (*see* Bunker Hill; Lexington and Concord) took place in its environs. But Washington forced the British to evacuate it in March, 1776, and thereafter its peace was undisturbed during the war.

In government it was merely a town administered by selectmen until 1822, when it received a city charter. During the 19th century it became the cultural center of the continent and took pride in its nicknames, "the Hub" and "the Athens of America." The names of Agassiz, Alcott, Aldrich, Dana, Eliot, Emerson, Hawthorne, Holmes, Howells, Longfellow, Lowell, Motley, Parkman, Prescott, Thoreau, Ticknor, Whittier and others which almost concurrently graced its golden age, its institutions of learning, its numerous literary, historical, scientific and musical societies, clubs and coteries, its Beacon Hill crowded with the homes of old, aristocratic families, its numerous colonial landmarks, all these gave it an unique distinction and atmosphere. It was the nation's leading port until well into the 19th century, when it lost the supremacy to New York[qv] because of its lack of water communication to the westward—though it still retained a considerable foreign commerce. The city suffered numerous disastrous fires in the 17th and 18th centuries, but the worst in its history was that of 1872, when sixty acres in the business portion were swept, with a loss of $60,000,000. By the filling in of tidal marshes and inlets, the original area of 783 acres was by 1930 expanded to 1800 acres. Gradual absorption of suburbs brought the city's area by that date to 47.3 square miles and its population to 781,188.

[Justin Winsor, *The Memorial History of Boston;* Van Wyck Brooks, *The Flowering of New England.*]

ALVIN F. HARLOW

Boston, Siege of (1775–76). On the day after the battle of Lexington[qv] (April 19, 1775) the Massachusetts Committee of Safety[qv] called out the militia. On April 22 the Massachusetts Provincial Congress[qv] resolved that an army of 30,000 men should be raised, Massachusetts to furnish about half, the other New England colonies the rest. Progress was slow; the old militia regiments could not be held together and new ones had to be raised. On June 17 was fought the battle of Bunker Hill[qv], which, while technically a British success, had the moral effect of an American victory.

On July 3 Washington, chosen as commander-in-chief by the Continental Congress[qv], assumed command. He found the British holding Bunker Hill and Boston Neck; the Americans faced them, their left in Somerville, their right in Roxbury and their center in Cambridge. It was evident that the makeshift force could not be relied upon; so in the face of the enemy a beginning was made upon organizing a Continental Army in place of the colonial contingents (*see* Washington's Eight Months Army).

During the winter no serious operations were undertaken. The Americans needed all their energies for organization; moreover, they were practically without artillery and ammunition. On the British side, the commanders could see no advantage in starting a campaign which they could not press to a finish.

In January, 1776, the guns captured at Ticonderoga[qv] (May 10, 1775) reached Cambridge. On March 4 Washington seized Dorchester Heights, from which his guns commanded the city and harbor. The British forces were now in an untenable position and on the 17th they embarked for Halifax. The Americans immediately occupied Boston.

[Richard Frothingham, *The Siege of Boston.*]

OLIVER LYMAN SPAULDING

***Boston-Berceau* Action** (Oct. 12, 1800). Off Guadeloupe during naval hostilities with France, the U. S. frigate *Boston* (thirty-six guns), Capt. George Little, captured the French corvette *Berceau* after a twelve-hour chase and a stubborn engagement extending intermittently from 4:30 till after 10 P.M. Though almost completely dismantled, the *Berceau* was towed into Boston as a prize.

[G. W. Allen, *Our Naval War with France.*]

ALLAN WESTCOTT

Boston Committee of Correspondence. A revolutionary body of propaganda and administration which became an important factor in promoting American unity and made possible the first Continental Congress[qv] through the spread of committees elsewhere. The parent body was appointed by Boston town meeting, Nov. 2, 1772, upon motion of Samuel Adams. It formulated public opinion, played a role in the early conduct of hostilities and facilitated the transition of Massachusetts from royal government to independent statehood.

[William V. Wells, *The Life and Public Services of Samuel Adams.*]
LLOYD C. M. HARE

Boston Common, bought by the city in 1634 as a pasture and parade ground, occupies forty-eight rolling acres between Beacon and Tremont streets, just below the State House. This beautiful park is the city's chief pride. Where the British troops were entrenched in 1775 her citizens now walk under the trees while their children ride in the swan boats on the Frog Pond. From the Common, her soldiers have marched away to all the wars; here famous preachers and orators have spoken; and here, in the Central Burying Ground, lies many a citizen as well as the British soldiers killed at the battle of Bunker Hill[qv]. Monuments to her famous citizens, including the St. Gaudens memorial to Col. Robert Gould Shaw, border the paths; and here band concerts and an open-air library give pleasure to the people.

[M. A. DeWolfe Howe, *Boston Common;* S. G. Drake, *Old Landmarks and Historic Personages of Boston.*]
R. W. G. VAIL

Boston Manufacturing Company was organized during the War of 1812 by Boston merchants previously engaged in the India trade. It built at Waltham the first complete textile factory in America, combining power spinning and weaving, on looms invented by one of the proprietors. This proved a pilot plant for the larger factories later built at Lowell.
VICTOR S. CLARK

Boston Massacre (March 5, 1770). Irritated by the presence of British troops in the city and emboldened by the weakness of the royal governor, an irresponsible mob of some sixty rioters set upon a squad of ten soldiers, under the command of Capt. Thomas Preston, which had gone to the rescue of a sentry attacked by the mob. While defending themselves, some of the soldiers, without orders, fired into the mob, killing three and wounding eight, two of whom later died. Public feeling ran high. To prevent further trouble, the two regiments of royal troops were withdrawn from the city. Capt. Preston and his squad were tried; the captain and six soldiers acquitted; two found guilty of manslaughter were branded in the hand and discharged. Public feeling, already aroused, was fanned to flame by such patriots as Samuel Adams and John Hancock. Biased propaganda, including the famous but historically inaccurate picture of the "massacre" issued by Paul Revere, was widely distributed. This minor outbreak, in which the rioters were largely at fault, was the first powerful influence in forming an outspoken anti-British public opinion and a demand for American independence.

[Justin Winsor, *Memorial History of Boston;* Randolph G. Adams, New Light on the Boston Massacre, in American Antiquarian Society *Proceedings,* Oct., 1937.]
R. W. G. VAIL

"Boston Men," a term derived from the hailing place of the first Yankee ships trading along the northwest coast of America, acquired universal use there to designate Americans, as distinguished from other white men or "Kling Chautsh" men (Englishmen and Canadians). The expression was so incorporated and used in the Chinook jargon[qv].

[G. Gibbs, *Dictionary of the Chinook Jargon.*]
WILLIAM S. LEWIS

Boston News-Letter, THE, was the first newspaper published without interruption during the colonial period. Number 1 included the week April 17 to 24, 1704. The original publisher was John Campbell, postmaster, and the first printer was Bartholomew Green. In 1727 Green became the owner and changed its name to *The Weekly News-Letter.* In 1763 the title was changed to *The Boston Weekly News-Letter and New England Chronicle* and there were later changes of title. Publication ceased in 1776 with the evacuation of Boston by the British troops. No complete file is known but the New York Historical and Massachusetts Historical Societies both have comparatively good files.

[James Melvin Lee, *History of American Journalism.*]
CARL L. CANNON

Boston Police Strike. About three quarters of the Boston police force went on strike, Sept. 9, 1919, when the police commissioner refused to recognize their right to affiliate with the American Federation of Labor[qv]. Mayor Andrew J. Peters and a citizens' committee headed by James J. Storrow made compromise proposals relating to pay and working conditions in order to prevent the strike, but the police commissioner rejected them. The strike thus precipitated left Boston almost unprotected and riots, disorders and robberies occurred.

The Boston police commissioner is appointed,

not by the mayor of the city, but by the governor of the state. Before the strike occurred Calvin Coolidge, then governor, was urged by the mayor and the Storrow Committee to intervene, but refused to act. When the rioting occurred Mayor Peters called out the Boston companies of the militia, restored order and broke the strike. With the city already under control, Gov. Coolidge ordered the police commissioner again to take charge of the police and called out the entire Massachusetts militia, declaring: "There is no right to strike against the public safety by anybody, anywhere, any time." This action gave Mr. Coolidge a reputation as a courageous defender of law and order, which led to his nomination for Vice-President (1920) and his eventual succession to the Presidency.

[*Report of the Storrow Committee*, Oct. 3, 1919, manuscript copy in University of Illinois Library; William Allen White, *A Puritan in Babylon: The Story of Calvin Coolidge; The Autobiography of Calvin Coolidge.*]

CLARENCE A. BERDAHL

Boston Port Act, THE (one of the Coercion Acts[qv]), was passed by Parliament on March 31, 1774. To punish Boston for the Tea Party[qv], the act ordered the port of Boston closed on June 1, 1774, until the townspeople paid for the tea destroyed on Dec. 16, 1773, and proved to the crown's satisfaction they were peaceable subjects. Because Boston alone was punished, Lord North believed the colonies would not "take fire." It was a costly mistake: the cry was raised in America that the Port Act was merely a prelude to a "Massacre of American Liberty"; the colonies rallied to Boston's aid; and the Continental Congress[qv] was called to concert opposition to the mother country.

[J. T. Adams, *Revolutionary New England;* C. H. Van Tyne, *The Causes of the War of Independence.*]

JOHN C. MILLER

Boston Resolutions, THE, were an expression of the longing of many Massachusetts patriots to restore puritanic simplicity in New England and strengthen patriotism by barring the importation of British luxuries. In 1767, when New England's declining prosperity made economy essential and the Townshend duties[qv] threatened fresh British oppression, Sam Adams secured the passage in the Boston town meeting of resolutions pledging the citizens to abstain from the use of many British manufactures, chiefly articles of luxury. Outside of New England, however, the movement had little success and it was soon merged with the nonimportation agreement[qv].

[C. H. Van Tyne, *The Causes of the War of Independence.*]

JOHN C. MILLER

Boston Resolutions, THE, of Feb. 9, 1810, were a forecast of New England separatism in the approaching War of 1812[qv]. In them the Massachusetts legislature condemned the severity of President Madison toward Francis James Jackson, the notorious British minister, exculpated Jackson and endeavored to compel renewed diplomatic intercourse with Great Britain.

[Henry Adams, *History of the United States, 1801-1817*, V.]

LOUIS MARTIN SEARS

Boston Tea Party, THE, took place on the night of Dec. 16, 1773, when 342 chests of tea belonging to the East India Company[qv] were thrown into Boston harbor by the patriots. This audacious destruction of British property was caused by the Boston Whigs' fear that if the tea were landed, its cheapness would prove an "invincible temptation" to the people. This, it was believed, would give the East India Company a monopoly of the American tea trade and establish the right of Parliament to raise a colonial revenue by means of port duties. Therefore, when it was learned at the town meeting of Dec. 16 that Gov. Hutchinson was determined to refuse the patriots' demand that the tea ships be permitted to return to England without paying the duty required by law, Sam Adams exclaimed that the meeting could do nothing more to save the country. His words were the signal for a war whoop from the "Indians"—Sons of Liberty[qv] disguised with blankets and dusky complexions—waiting outside the meetinghouse. With the cry of "Boston harbor a tea-pot this night," the braves streamed down to the waterfront, where, surrounded by an immense crowd of spectators, they made short work of the tea.

The Tea Party was "the boldest stroke which had yet been struck in America." It marked the beginning of violence in the dispute, hitherto waged chiefly with constitutional arguments, between mother country and colonies, and it put the most radical patriots in command throughout America. The efforts of the British government to single out Massachusetts for punishment, instead of isolating the Bay colony, served only to unite the colonies and hasten them into war with the mother country.

[C. H. Van Tyne, *The Causes of the War of Independence;* John C. Miller, *Sam Adams, Pioneer in Propaganda.*]

JOHN C. MILLER

Boston Ten Townships (N. Y.), THE, was a tract of 230,400 acres north of the Susquehanna River, including parts of Broome, Tioga and Cortland counties, claimed by both New York and Massachusetts until, by the Treaty of Hartford[qv] in 1786, a compromise was effected whereby New York was granted sovereignty and Massachusetts right of pre-emption of the soil. Subsequently, in 1787, right of purchase from the Indians was granted by Massachusetts to Samuel Brown and ten associates. (*See* Phelps-Gorham Purchase.)

[R. L. Higgins, *Expansion in New York.*]

A. C. FLICK

"Bostonnais," also "Bastonais." A term once applied by French-Canadians to Americans. It dates back to the invasion of Canada[qv] under Montgomery in 1775, and possibly to that of Sir William Phips in 1690. Meaning "People of Boston," it was given to all English colonists on the Atlantic seaboard and finally to all Americans.

LAWRENCE J. BURPEE

Botanists, Early. The earliest American botanists were field workers, who collected specimens of seeds and plants and transmitted them to European scientists, receiving many European specimens in return. Among those who carried on such a correspondence were Cotton Mather, Cadwallader Colden and John Bartram. Bartram's association with the English naturalist, Peter Collinson, is the most famous of such scientific partnerships. Other 18th-century botanists were Alexander Garden of South Carolina; John Mitchell of Virginia; Jane Colden, daughter of Cadwallader Colden of New York; Humphry Marshall of Pennsylvania; and John Bartram's son William, whose *Travels*, published in 1791, is the chief literary work of the early botanists, just as his father's garden, now in Philadelphia's park system, is their most important relic.

[William Darlington, *Memorials of John Bartram and Humphry Marshall;* R. Higgston Fox, *Dr. John Fothergill and His Friends.*]

RALPH FOSTER WELD

Bouchard Expedition, THE (1818), was an effort on the part of the Buenos Aires revolutionary authorities to bring into the anti-Spanish liberal cause the inhabitants of California. Hippolyte de Bouchard, with the *Argentina* and *Santa Rosa*, came to California by way of the Hawaiian Islands, and Nov. 20, 1818, captured Monterey. Other landings at Santa Barbara and Capistrano showed that the Californians were not anxious for freedom. Accordingly, Bouchard sailed for Chile, and California remained in the Spanish empire until April 11, 1822, when a special junta declared it dependent upon Iturbide's Mexican empire.

[C. E. Chapman, *A History of California: the Spanish Period.*]

OSGOOD HARDY

Boulder (Hoover) Dam, located in Black Canyon on the Colorado River between Arizona and Nevada, 422 miles above the mouth of the Colorado River, was authorized by the Boulder Canyon Project Act in 1928, for flood control, navigation improvement, irrigation, storage and power, subject to the Colorado River Compact; dedicated as Hoover Dam by Secretary of the Interior Ray Lyman Wilbur at the start of construction in 1930; and completed in 1936 by Six Companies, Inc., contractors for the United States Bureau of Reclamation. It rises 727 feet from bedrock, elevates the water surface 584 feet, creates a reservoir (Lake Mead) with a capacity of 30,500,000 acre feet and will generate 1,835,000 horse power of electric energy. The cost was approximately $130,000,000. In advance of construction, Secretary Wilbur secured power contracts disposing of 4,330,000,000 kilowatt hours annually, adequate to liquidate the Government's investment within fifty years, with large excess revenues. The City of Los Angeles and the Southern California Edison Company, lessees of the power plant, which was placed in regular operation June 1, 1937, will generate for ten allottees of energy, including the states of Arizona and Nevada and the Colorado River Aqueduct[qv].

[Wilbur and Ely, *The Hoover Dam Contracts;* Reports of the Secretary of the Interior, 1930-32 inclusive.]

NORTHCUTT ELY

Boundary Disputes, International. *See* Northeast Boundary, 1783–1842; Northwest Boundary Controversy; Mexican Boundary, The; Florida Boundary, The; Alaska Boundary Question, The; Haro Channel Dispute.

Boundary Disputes between the States. Disputes concerning more than one fourth of the present 109 interstate boundaries in the United States (including District of Columbia-Maryland and District of Columbia-Virginia in the total) have been submitted to the U. S. Supreme Court or to Congress—a few only for confirmation of an agreement already reached by the states themselves. At the time of the adoption of the Constitution controversies were pending between eleven of the thirteen states respecting their boundaries (37 U. S. 657, 723–24).

Most of the disputes have arisen concerning boundaries established by colonial grants and charters, or by treaties (1783–1848), which have become boundaries between the states. Disputes relating to boundaries established by Congress in the creation of new states (where portions of former treaty lines were not utilized) have

Boundary Disputes

been few; of these boundaries nearly all have been meridians or other straight lines, or parallels of latitude, which, though they disregard physiographic and human use factors, have occasioned relatively little difficulty as boundaries of states between which there are no tariff and migration barriers.

Some of the disputes concerning boundaries of colonial origin persisted more than a century. Those that have been decided by the U. S. Supreme Court include Virginia v. Tennessee (part of Virginia-North Carolina boundary until 1790), 1893; Maryland v. West Virginia (part of Virginia until 1863), 1910; Georgia v. South Carolina, 1922; Vermont v. New Hampshire, 1933; and New Jersey v. Delaware, 1934. The Massachusetts-Rhode Island boundary controversy, which originated in the Plymouth colony grant of 1630 and the Rhode Island charter of 1663, was not definitely settled until the two states agreed in 1860–61 upon a conventional line, confirmed by Supreme Court decree in 1861, part of which the states replaced in 1899 by a line which could be more readily marked. The Connecticut-New York boundary dispute, which began before 1650, was settled by the two states in 1880 and the agreement was approved by Congress in 1881. The North Carolina-South Carolina colonial dispute of 1729–87 was ended by the survey of 1815, extending the 1772 line to the Georgia corner. Similarly, the Massachusetts-New Hampshire boundary controversy, which originated in the Massachusetts charter of 1629, was finally settled by the adoption of the Mitchell-Hazzen line essentially as then monumented, in 1889–90 and 1895.

It may seem surprising that many state boundaries owe their origin to international treaties. The Mississippi River was established as a boundary by treaty between France, Spain and England, in 1763, "and this line, established by the only sovereign powers at the time interested in the subject, has remained ever since as they settled it" (Missouri v. Kentucky, 78 U. S. 395, 401). By the Definitive Treaty of Peace of 1783[qv] with Great Britain, the Mississippi River became the western boundary of the United States; it now constitutes nine interstate boundaries, two of them only in part. The northern boundary of Florida, and the Chattahoochee River as part of the Alabama-Georgia boundary, also owe their origin to the Treaty of 1783. The Oklahoma-Texas boundary (except the Panhandle portion) originated in the 1819 treaty with Spain (*see* Adams-Onís Treaty)—as did also the southern boundaries of Oregon and Idaho, concerning which there have been no outstanding disputes. The Rio Grande portion of the New Mexico-Texas boundary, decided by the Supreme Court in 1927, constituted part of the United States-Mexico boundary from the time of the Treaty of Guadalupe Hidalgo[qv], 1848, until the Gadsden Purchase[qv], 1853.

Boundaries between states of the Union are to be determined according to principles of international law (Wisconsin v. Michigan, 295 U. S. 455, 461). In rivers and bays the Supreme Court has held that the doctrine of the *thalweg,* or main channel of navigation, is applicable between states of the Union, where the boundary has not been fixed in some other way—as by agreement, practical location, prescription; and it applies even as between states that existed before the doctrine became fully established in international law (New Jersey v. Delaware, 291 U. S. 361, 383).

Water boundaries, in rivers and bays, have given rise to many more disputes than land boundaries. Disputes concerning river boundaries have been the most numerous and the most complicated. The 1783 treaty boundary in the Mississippi River was the middle of the river. The Supreme Court has held, however, that the middle of the principal navigable channel, or *thalweg,* and not the line equidistant from the two banks, constitutes the boundary (Arkansas v. Mississippi, 250 U. S. 39). Mississippi River boundary cases decided by the Supreme Court include: Missouri v. Kentucky, 1871; Iowa v. Illinois, 1893; Arkansas v. Mississippi, 1919; Louisiana v. Mississippi, 1931. Boundaries in the Missouri River which have been in dispute include: Nebraska v. Iowa, 1892, and Missouri-Nebraska, 1904, both relating to river changes by avulsion. The boundary in the Ohio River was decided in 1890 to constitute the north or right bank at low water, based upon the cession by Virginia to the United States of territory "to the northwest of the river Ohio." In the construction of this grant it was held that Virginia (territory now comprising Kentucky and West Virginia) must have intended to retain the river (Indiana v. Kentucky, 136 U. S. 479). The boundary in the Chattahoochee River is the west or right bank at average or mean stage during the entire year (Alabama v. Georgia, 64 U. S. 505). In the Connecticut River the boundary is on the right bank at low-water mark (Vermont v. New Hampshire, 289 U. S. 593). In the Potomac River the Maryland-Virginia and Maryland-West Virginia boundaries are on the south or right bank at low water; the grant to Lord Baltimore embraced the Potomac River to high-water mark on the Virginia shore, but "the evidence is sufficient to show that Virginia, from the earliest period of her history, used the South bank of the Potomac as if the soil to low water mark had been her own" (Maryland v. West Virginia, 217 U. S. 577, 579–80). The Georgia-South Carolina boundary is on the water midway between the main banks of the three boundary rivers, but the islands belong to Georgia (257 U. S. 516). The boundary in the St. Louis River, emptying into Lake Superior, was decided by the Supreme Court in 1920 (Minnesota v. Wisconsin, 252 U. S. 273).

Boundaries in waters other than rivers have been subject to dispute, and in several instances an economic factor was involved. Oyster beds have been at least partly the cause of disputes decided by the Supreme Court: Louisiana v. Mississippi, 1906 (from mouth of Pearl River to the high sea); and New Jersey v. Delaware, 1934 (Delaware River and Bay). Oyster beds were also involved in the Massachusetts-Rhode Island dispute, Rhode Island taking action to protect the oysters in 1844; and in the Maryland-Virginia dispute in Chesapeake Bay just before the Civil War. The Michigan-Wisconsin boundary in Green Bay and Lake Michigan constitutes a portion of another boundary which has been in dispute (Supreme Court decisions in 1926 and 1935), where fishing rights were among the questions involved.

Disputes which have been settled by Congress have related chiefly to boundaries originally established between territories by act of Congress; it has been intended that pending disputes be settled before the second of the two states ultimately concerned was admitted to the Union. The Ohio-Michigan dispute[qv] was notable. It was finally settled by an act of Congress in 1836 "to establish the northern boundary of the state of Ohio, and to provide for the admission of the state of Michigan into the Union"; as recompense for its loss of the disputed territory Michigan was given the upper peninsula of that state. The Illinois-Wisconsin dispute was also protracted, ending with the admission of Wisconsin into the Union in 1846. Congress has confirmed several boundary agreements reached by states, and has authorized certain states on the Mississippi River to modify their boundaries by direct agreement where tracts of territory become separated from the main body of land by sudden changes in the course of the river.

The Oklahoma-Texas boundary has given rise to the most numerous and complicated boundary questions ever submitted to the Supreme Court. Three separate problems, relating to the Red River and the 100th meridian, have presented themselves. In 1896 the Supreme Court decided the so-called Greer County[qv] question. In three decisions in 1921, 1922 and 1923 the boundary in the Red River was established on the south "cut bank"; oil wells in the bed of the stream made precise boundary location very important. In 1926 the Court decreed the true 100th meridian to be part of the Oklahoma-Texas boundary, instead of the line which had been erroneously marked.

In a number of instances two states concerned have submitted to the Supreme Court separate disputes concerning different parts of their boundary and sometimes two or more disputes concerning the same portion of boundary. There may be cited the Wisconsin-Michigan Supreme Court boundary decisions of 1926 and 1935; the Illinois-Iowa boundary decisions of 1893 and 1906; and the Oklahoma-Texas boundary questions already mentioned.

A case concerning the Arkansas-Tennessee boundary is still pending in the Supreme Court (1938). The District of Columbia-Virginia boundary, presumably at high-water mark on the south bank of the Potomac, is still in dispute. Other disputes may be anticipated, chiefly regarding boundaries in rivers and other waters.

Disputes have been somewhat heated in a few instances. When Georgia organized Walton County in 1803, the area being also claimed by North Carolina, there were riots and dissensions concerning conflicting jurisdiction. The Ohio-Michigan dispute, 1818–36, mentioned above, was one of the bitterest. The Federal Government tried unsuccessfully in 1838 to settle the Iowa-Missouri dispute; in 1839 both ordered out the militia, and hostilities were narrowly averted. But in 1846 Iowa was admitted to the Union and in 1847 the two states agreed to settle their controversy by means of an amicable suit in the Supreme Court, the decision being rendered in 1849. In general, boundary questions between states of the United States, as distinct from regional disputes, have never had a disrupting effect. (*See also* Pennsylvania-Connecticut Boundary Dispute; Pennsylvania-Maryland Boundary Dispute; Pennsylvania-Virginia Boundary Dispute; Texas Cession of 1850.)

[Paullin, *Atlas of the Historical Geography of the United States*, pp. 72-87; U. S. Geological Survey, Bulletin 817; U. S. Supreme Court Reports; James Brown Scott, *Judicial Settlement of Controversies between States of the American Union.*]

S. WHITTEMORE BOGGS

Bounties, Commercial, have played an important role in American economic development. In the colonial period Great Britain paid bounties on the export from the American colonies of hemp, flax, tar, potash, indigo and a number of other commodities in an effort to stimulate their production and to diminish her previous dependence for them on foreign nations. North and South Carolina profited the most from these bounties, and the production of naval stores and indigo became, with rice cultivation[qqv], their chief occupation. After the Revolution the loss of these bounties brought disaster to those engaged in the production of naval stores and indigo.

The colonial governments also offered bounties to encourage the manufacture of such goods as linen, woolens, iron, glass, brick and salt, and after 1775 they redoubled their efforts to build up domestic manufactures by combining cash bounties, financial subsidies and tariff protection.

In the national era bounties have been offered for various commercial purposes, the most important of which has been to encourage the production of beet sugar[qv]. In 1890 the United States offered a bounty of two cents a pound on sugar produced within the country and numerous states have likewise given bounties to the beet-sugar industry. Such bounties, coupled with high tariff protection[qv] and large expenditures in the Far West for reclamation[qv] projects on which one of the chief crops is sugar beets, have been responsible for the growth of the beet-sugar industry in the United States.

The Southern states which felt that up to 1860 bounties, tariff protection and subsidies to internal improvements[qv] had chiefly benefited other sections, incorporated a provision in the Confederate constitution which forbade them.

[G. L. Beer, *British Colonial Policy, 1754-1763;* H. L. Osgood, *American Colonies in the Eighteenth Century;* F. W. Taussig, *Some Aspects of the Tariff Question.*]

PAUL WALLACE GATES

Bounties, Fishing. *See* Fishing Bounties.

Bounties, Land. *See* Land Bounties.

Bounties, Military. When war forces were raised by volunteering instead of by conscription or militia obligations[qqv], bounties stimulated recruiting. For Indian and French campaigns, colonies offered cash inducements, sometimes solely to induce enlistments[qv], sometimes for bringing clothing or weapons into service. The practice was adopted during the Revolution by both Congress and the states. In January, 1776, \$6⅔ was offered to fill the Canada expedition; in June \$10 for three-year enlistments or re-enlistments; in September \$20 and 100 acres for enrollments "for the war." To fill militia quotas, states offered their own bounties, so that states and Congress bid against one another and sums mounted until Congress was offering \$200 and New Jersey \$1000. Bounty-jumping and re-enlisting were prevalent.

With the peace, bounties shrunk to \$6 in 1791 for Indian campaigns, but climbed after the Whisky Rebellion[qv] to \$16, three months' pay and 160 acres. During the War of 1812 cash offers increased to \$124 and 320 acres. They were abolished in 1833 but were resumed in 1847 to raise and re-enlist men for the Mexican War. Civil War bounties[qv] repeated Revolutionary history. Disappearing after Appomattox[qv], recruiting bounties were expressly forbidden by the Selective Service Act[qv] of 1917. (*See also* Land Bounties.)

[E. Upton, *Military Policy of the United States;* W. A. Ganoe, *History of the United States Army;* T. Cross, *Military Laws of the United States;* War Department, *Military Laws of the United States.*]

ELBRIDGE COLBY

Bounties, Military, in the Civil War. The earlier system of land grants was not followed except for the favored position of service men under the Homestead Act[qv], but from the start in 1861 states and localities stimulated recruiting by grants of money. This practice reached large proportions during the militia draft of 1862 when even the Federal Government offered \$25 for nine-month and \$50 for twelve-month volunteers. Since July, 1861, Congress had allowed \$100 for three-year men and the latter bounty was offered during the draft[qv], even to conscripts who would volunteer for the longer term.

The climax was reached after the Enrollment Act of March 3, 1863, which legalized the earlier practice of giving \$100 to conscripts and substitutes. Also, since those able to do so could avoid the draft on payment of \$300, for several months an equivalent sum was given to all three-year and \$400 to all five-year volunteers. But, since these bounties were divided over the term of service and were included in the monthly pay, they merely served as an addition to the legal wages. A worse system prevailed for state bounties. It was considered a disgrace for any congressional district to have to submit to a draft, so funds were raised to the utmost limit to fill the quotas before the wheel was set in motion. In consequence, the richer districts by offering \$1000 or more could entice volunteers from poorer localities and fill their quotas with ease, whereas the low-bounty regions were badly depleted of man power by the exodus and then had to give an additional quota by draft. Furthermore, a loathsome profession of bounty brokers arose, who not only recruited men and then robbed them of much of their bonus, but also resorted to bribery to secure the muster of broken-down derelicts who had to be discharged later. The problem of the bounty-jumper[qv] was greatly aggravated by these practices.

In four years' time the Federal Government paid over $300,000,000 in bounties, and in the last two years alone the states and localities paid about the same amount. The total mercenary fees for the war, including local bounties in the first two years and substitute fees, amounted to about three quarters of a billion dollars.

[F. A. Shannon, *Organization and Administration of the Union Army.*] FRED A. SHANNON

Bounty-Jumper, THE, was a product of the system of military bounties[qv] in the Civil War. Aided and abetted by bounty brokers, men would enlist, collect bounties, desert and then re-enlist elsewhere, repeating the process until finally caught. One deserter was sentenced to four years' imprisonment after confessing to jumping bounties thirty-two times. The large initial bounty payments was one of the major causes of the more than 268,000 desertions from the ranks of the Union Army.

[F. A. Shannon, *Organization and Administration of the Union Army.*] FRED A. SHANNON

Bouquet's Expedition (1763–65). At the outbreak of Pontiac's War[qv] Col. Henry Bouquet was sent with 500 regulars to relieve Fort Pitt[qv]. Leaving Carlisle, he marched westward, and after defeating the Indians at the battle of Bushy Run[qv] he relieved the beleaguered fort. Bouquet's force was too small to march against the Delaware and Shawnee[qqv] in the Ohio country, but in 1765 the Pennsylvania Assembly voted an adequate force for the expedition. Desertions from the militia, however, forced Bouquet to call for Virginia volunteers to meet him at Fort Pitt. After many delays he collected some 1500 men and in October, 1765, marched unopposed to the Muskingum River, near the mouth of the Tuscarawas. There he was met by chiefs bringing in eighteen white prisoners and suing for peace. Bouquet demanded the return of all the captives; and, taking the principal chiefs as hostages, he moved south to the forks of the Muskingum in the heart of the Indian country. Here he waited until some 200 prisoners had been surrendered to him.

He then made peace with the Indians, directed them to go to Sir William Johnson to make treaties (*see* Indian Policy, Colonial) and took hostages for the performance of this obligation and for the delivery of about 100 prisoners still in the hands of the Shawnee. He returned to Fort Pitt, and the Indians subsequently kept their promises and delivered there the remaining captives. Bouquet's expedition overawed the Indians and ended the reign of terror on the border. (*See also* Bradstreet's Expedition to Lake Erie.)

[Francis Parkman, *The Conspiracy of Pontiac.*]

SOLON J. BUCK

Bourbon County was established by Georgia in 1785, on the Mississippi River, lying north of the 31st parallel and extending to the mouth of the Yazoo River, above Natchez[qv]. Being largely a land speculation, it was to be governed by fourteen men mentioned in the act; and when a land office should be opened, the price per acre should not be more than twenty-five cents. As Spain had not yet evacuated this territory and as the United States disputed Georgia's claim to these western lands, the act was repealed three years later.

[A. P. Whitaker, *Spanish-American Frontier;* E. C. Burnett, Papers relating to Bourbon County, Georgia, 1785-1786, in *American Historical Review*, XV.]

E. MERTON COULTER

Bourgeois. The term was one used in the fur trade[qv], especially in the Northwest, and was applied to the leader of a unit. The bourgeois was governor of the pack train, master of the canoe brigade and despot of the trading post. His word was law and his orders were implicitly obeyed. His was the responsibility for the well-being of the men and the success of the trade venture. When the great companies were organized the bourgeois were the wintering partners. A collection of their diaries was published at Quebec in 1889 under the title *Les Bourgeois de la Compagnie du Nord-Ouest,* by L. E. Masson.

[Grace Lee Nute, *The Voyageur.*]

LOUISE PHELPS KELLOGG

Bourgmont's Explorations (1706–24). Etienne Veniard de Bourgmont, first French scientific explorer of the Missouri River, commanded Fort Detroit[qv] in 1706. By 1712 he was exploring the lower Missouri Valley. His "Route to follow to mount the Missouri River" (*ca.* 1714), dryly topographic, and "Exact Description of Louisiana" (*ca.* 1717), show he reached the Platte River. Search for a route to the fabulous silver mines of New Mexico and activities of the Spanish made imperative a French post in Missouri. Authorized by Louis XV, in 1723 Bourgmont led an expedition up the Mississippi from New Orleans and with the help of friendly Missouri Indians built Fort d'Orleans[qv] on the north bank of the Missouri River in Carroll County, probably two miles above the Wakenda, opposite Waverly, Mo. In 1724 he conducted an overland trip to the village of the Kansas Indians[qv] near present Doniphan, Kans., effecting peace with them and, further to the southwest, with the Padoucas.

[G. J. Garraghan, *Chapters in Frontier History.*]

DOROTHY PENN

Bouweries. When the Dutch West India Company[qv] took over Manhattan Island[qv] in 1626 (*see* New Netherland), it divided a large tract of land in what is now New York City's lower East Side into six bouweries or farms, placed buildings on them and leased them to tenants. One large farm, "the Company's Bouwerie," just west of these, was retained and operated to aid in providing for the company's officers and servants. Other tracts of forest land were granted to individuals, who cleared them and created their own bouweries.

[J. H. Innes, *New Amsterdam and Its People.*]

ALVIN F. HARLOW

Bowditch's *American Practical Navigator* was published in 1802 and has remained the textbook of American seamen. It has played the important part of guiding the navigator in every American adventure on the sea.

One edition followed another bringing up-to-date methods to the mariner. In 1866 the copyright and plates were bought by the Hydrographic Office of the Navy. It is not only a notable book but is one of our nautical institutions.

GERSHOM BRADFORD

Bowery, The, in New York City. First known in the 17th century as the Bowery Lane or Bowery Road, because it led from New Amsterdam[qv] out to the bouwerie[qv] or farm of Gov. Stuyvesant. Later it was the beginning of the road to Boston, and the first mail between New York and Boston started over it in 1673. By 1800 the slums[qv] growing up around it determined its future character. Some famous theaters were located on it; but it eventually attained world-wide notoriety because of the swindling, political chicanery, prostitution, crime and gang warfare carried on in its vicinity. It is now an ordinary business street.

[Alvin F. Harlow, *Old Bowery Days.*]

ALVIN F. HARLOW

Bowie Knife. Perhaps devised by Rezin P. Bowie, perhaps by his brother James, who died in the Alamo[qv], the knife both in origin and use has been the subject of a cycle of heroic folk tales. It achieved fame in the Sandbar Duel[qv] in 1827. Although supplanted largely by the six-shooter[qv], it was for four decades a part of the regular equipment of frontiersmen and backwoodsmen from Florida to California. The Mountain Men[qv] used a modified form of it. The Texas Rangers[qv] rode with it. The "pirates" of the Mississippi disemboweled their victims with it. Its steel of superb temper, the blade well guarded, handle and blade so balanced that it could be thrown as well as wielded, it was both economical and practical for skinning, cutting up meat, eating, fighting duels, stabbing enemies, hammering and performing other services.

J. FRANK DOBIE

Bowles' Filibustering Expeditions. William Augustus Bowles, after an adventurous life among the Creek Indians[qv], turned up in the Bahamas where he became acquainted with Lord Dunmore, governor of the islands, and with the trading house of Miller (Millar), Bonnamy (Bonamy) & Co. Here was the mainspring of his subsequent activities, for he became the agent of this commercial house, re-enforced with the benevolent and probable financial interest of Lord Dunmore, and in this capacity he sought the trade of the Creeks, which at this time was rather securely held by another English firm, Panton, Leslie & Co.,[qv] who had secured their concessions from Spain and from Alexander McGillivray, the half-breed Creek chief.

In pursuance of his aims, Bowles appeared on the west coast of Florida in 1788 with a cargo of goods which he liberally distributed among the Indians, without arousing the suspicion of McGillivray, but suspected of evil designs by the Spaniards. It was probably Bowles' purpose to attack the Spaniards through Indian allies, but the desertion of some of his men caused him to leave. In 1791, the year after McGillivray[qv] had made the Treaty of New York with the United States, Bowles returned to Florida with the idea of supplanting him in Creek leadership, being aided by the unpopularity of that agreement. Cunningly he plundered the storehouse of Panton, Leslie & Co., at St. Marks, but fell a prey to Spanish duplicity when he agreed to go to New Orleans to treat with the authorities there. For the next few years he was held prisoner in Havana, Madrid, Cadiz and in the Philippines. Escaping he returned to Nassau, in 1799, and soon put out for Florida on his third and last filibustering expedition. The next year he attacked the Spanish fort at St. Marks, successfully seized it, and held it for a few months. Being forced out he escaped into the hinterland, where for the next few years he was a menace to the Spaniards. At the suggestion of the United States, the Spaniards offered a reward of $4500 for him and in May, 1803, he was seized on American soil through a ruse connived in by American authorities, Spain and Great Britain. He died two years later in Morro Castle, Havana. Bowles' whole career in Florida had been directed assiduously against the Spanish power and in the interest of Great Britain generally, but more specifically to promote the commercial ambitions of Miller, Bonnamy & Co. (*See also* Spanish-Indian Relations.)

[A. P. Whitaker, *The Mississippi Question, 1795-1803;* J. W. Caughey, *McGillivray of the Creeks;* G. White, *Historical Collections of Georgia;* A. Stephens, ed., *The Life of General W. A. Bowles.*]

E. MERTON COULTER

Bowling Green in New York was originally a small open space before the fort at the foot of Broadway, sometimes called The Parade. It was leased for a bowling green in 1733. The leaden statute of George III was erected there in 1770, and destroyed by the populace at the outbreak of the Revolution in 1775.

[I. N. Phelps Stokes, *The Iconography of Manhattan Island.*]

ALVIN F. HARLOW

Bowyer, Fort, Attack upon (Sept. 15, 1814). From this fort, commanding the entrance to Mobile Bay, Maj. William Lawrence, with 130 troops, inflicted a mortifying defeat upon a British combined land and sea force of 6 vessels and 1300 men, under Capt. Henry Percy, killing 162 and wounding 70 British while losing only 8 Americans killed and wounded.

[Oliver L. Spaulding, *The United States Army in War and Peace;* William A. Ganoe, *The History of the United States Army.*]

ROBERT S. THOMAS

Boxer Rebellion, THE, was an antiforeign uprising in China beginning in May, 1900. A total of 231 foreigners and many Christian Chinese were murdered. On June 17 began the siege of the legations in Peking. The United States concerted with Great Britain, Russia, Germany, France and Japan to conduct a military expedition for the relief of the legations, sending 5000 troops for this purpose. The international relief expedition marched from Taku to Tientsin and thence to Peking, raising the siege of the legation on Aug. 4. The United States, however, did not join in the punitive expedition under the German Commander in Chief Count von Waldersee. In July Secretary of State John Hay issued a circular note to "preserve Chinese territorial and administrative entity," and during the Peking Congress^{qv} (Feb. 5–Sept. 7, 1901) the United States opposed the demand for a punitive indemnity which might lead to the dismemberment of China. The Boxer Protocol finally fixed the indemnity at $332,000,000, provided for the punishment of guilty Chinese officials, and permitted the Powers to maintain legation guards at Peking and between the capital and the sea.

[H. B. Morse, *The International Relations of the Chinese Empire;* Tyler Dennett, *Americans in Eastern Asia.*]

KENNETH COLEGROVE

Boxing. *See* Prize Fights.

Boy Scouts of America, THE, was incorporated Feb. 8, 1910, and granted a Federal charter from Congress in 1916. It was based on the English principles modified to meet the needs of American youth. The membership, Dec. 31, 1938, was as follows: total men, 261,396; total boys, 957,-217; total membership, 1,271,900, including 33,-174 members of the Philippine Islands.

The purpose is to develop character and to train for citizenship. The organization consists of a younger boys' program for boys from nine to eleven, who are known as Cubs; boys from twelve years upward are Scouts, and boys fifteen years of age and upward, Senior Scouts.

It supplements the work of the home, church and school, provides a constructive program of leisure-time activities, very appealing to boys. It aims, through outdoor projects, such as camping, hiking, signaling, cooking in the open and nature study, to teach boys to be self-reliant and resourceful and, through knowledge of first aid, life saving, swimming, etc., to enable them to be of service to others.

Volunteer leadership is a fundamental element in the Boy Scout scheme. Scouts are organized in Patrols, under a boy leader, and Troops, under a volunteer leader known as a Scoutmaster. The boy enters scouting as a Tenderfoot. As he advances in skill he advances in rank, receiving recognition. The official scout uniform is protected by Congress.

Since the beginning of the organization 8,411,-949 persons have been connected with the movement. The world scout membership is 2,774,323 (Jan. 1, 1937), divided among some seventy-three different lands.

[*The History of the Boy Scouts of America*, published by the National Council of the Boy Scouts of America; The Twenty-ninth Annual Report of the Boy Scouts of America.]

E. S. MARTIN

Boycotting. A boycott is a collective refusal to purchase commodities or services from a manufacturer or merchant whose employment or trade practices are regarded as unfair. Occasionally the economic boycott has been used by consumers against aggressor nations. Its chief use is by organized workers to secure better conditions of employment. Means for effecting a boycott include the distribution of cards, handbills, fair lists, unfair lists and picketing*qv*.

In the United States the courts have made a distinction between "primary" and "secondary" boycotts. The former involves refusal of patronage by employees directly concerned in an industrial dispute; the latter involves attempts to persuade or coerce third parties to boycott an employer.

Considerable uncertainty and confusion characterize the law of boycotts in the United States, but a few general principles are fairly well established. In most jurisdictions it is not unlawful for an association of aggrieved workers to withhold patronage. Moreover, it does not appear to be unlawful in the several states for such workers to ask or persuade others to assist in their cause. It is illegal, however, to use physical violence, coercion or intimidation. The behavior of pickets must be peaceful and customers must be accorded complete freedom in entering and leaving the boycotted establishment.

The pivotal point in the law of boycotts is the use of pressure against third parties. Because most manufacturers do not distribute their goods directly but through wholesalers and retailers, organized labor can make a boycott effective only by bringing pressure upon such dealers. This is in essence a secondary boycott, which is regarded as unlawful in most jurisdictions. In Arizona, California and Oklahoma, however, all peacefully conducted boycotts have been held legal, and some of the lower courts of New York have sustained them. In Missouri and Montana the printing and distributing of circulars for purposes of boycott may not be directly enjoined by the courts.

The boycott was held unlawful in the United States as early as 1886. In 1908 the United States Supreme Court in the Danbury hatters case*qv* decided that the secondary boycott constitutes a conspiracy in restraint of trade under the provisions of the Sherman Antitrust Law*qv* (1890). The Court held that treble damages might be recovered for losses sustained by the manufacturer through the interstate boycott. In the Buck Stove and Range Company case*qv* (1911), the same tribunal decided that all means employed to make effective an unlawful boycott are illegal, even though in themselves such means are innocent. Disregard of an injunction in this case by certain officials of the American Federation of Labor*qv* resulted in citation for contempt and jail sentence for one year. Although the sentence was subsequently set aside, the decision greatly discouraged the use of the boycott in labor disputes.

An attempt to escape from the restrictions of the Sherman Act was made through Section 20 of the Clayton Antitrust Act*qv* (1914), which prohibits the use of the injunction*qv* to restrain employees from picketing, boycotting and advising others to withhold patronage from an employer when such activities are carried on by peaceful and lawful means. In the Duplex Printing Press Company case (1921), however, the United States Supreme Court ruled that all methods employed to make effective interstate boycotts involving third parties are unlawful.

[Francis B. Sayre, *Cases on Labor Law.*]

GORDON S. WATKINS

Boydton Plank Road (also known as Hatcher's Run, Va.), ENGAGEMENTS AT (Oct. 27–28, 1864). While moving Union troops on the Boydton Plank Road where it crossed Hatcher's Run, a gap opened between Hancock's Second Corps and Warren's Fifth Corps. Confederates pushed into this opening and attacked Hancock's right and rear, provoking a bloody battle.

[*Battles and Leaders of the Civil War;* War of the Rebellion, *Official Records of the Union and Confederate Armies*, Series, I, Vol. XLII and Vol. LI.]

ROBERT S. THOMAS

Bozeman Trail, THE, was traced by John M. Bozeman, 1863–65, as the shortest and easiest route for emigrants to the Virginia City*qv* gold fields. The trail continued the route from the South Platte at Julesburg (Fort Sedgwick), past Fort Laramie, where it crossed the Oregon Trail, to the Powder River Crossing at Fort Connor*qqv*. Thence it passed eastward of the Big Horn Mountains to the Yellowstone River and westward to Virginia City.

The first caravan used the trail in the summer following the Powder River Campaign*qv* (*see* Indian Commissions, The). Notwithstanding the Treaty of Laramie*qv* in 1851 the Sioux Indians resented the invasion and when Forts Reno, Phil Kearny and C. F. Smith*qqv* were established for emigrant protection they went on the warpath. Red Cloud's War*qv* followed. By 1868 all posts along the trail had been abandoned (*see* Laramie, Fort, Treaty of, 1868).

Following suppression of the Sioux in 1877 (*see* Sioux Wars) the Bozeman Trail became an important route for cattle moving north from

Texas into Wyoming and Montana (*see* Cattle Drives).

[Brininstool and Hebard, *The Bozeman Trail.*]

PAUL I. WELLMAN

Bracito, Skirmish at. *See* Brazito Battle, Mexican War.

Braddock's Expedition (1755). After the battle of Great Meadows[qv] England and France prepared for war. Gen. Edward Braddock, appointed commander of all the British forces in America, was dispatched with two regiments for a campaign the first objective of which was Fort Duquesne[qv]. The regulars and the colonial forces rendezvoused at Fort Cumberland[qv], to start for Fort Duquesne by the route later called Braddock's Road[qv]. Wagons and horses were secured from Pennsylvania with Franklin's aid; Indian allies came from Aughwick[qv], but most of them deserted when Braddock ordered their families home.

The army, 2200 strong, started west June 7, but had advanced only to Little Meadows (near Grantsville, Md.) by June 16. Then, on the advice of Washington, his aide-de-camp, Braddock pushed on rapidly with some 1200 men and a minimum of artillery, leaving a command under Col. Dunbar to bring up the heavier goods. On July 9 the expedition crossed and recrossed the Monongahela near Turtle Creek. Up to this point every precaution had been taken against surprise, but apparently the officers now grew overconfident. A hill commanding the route was left unoccupied and the troops marched in an order too close for safety.

From Fort Duquesne Capt. Beaujeu led some 250 French and 600 Indians to oppose Braddock. He had not laid his ambush when the two parties unexpectedly met. The British opened fire, putting most of the French to flight and killing Beaujeu. His subordinate Dumas, however, rallied the Indians to seize the hill that Braddock had neglected and to surround the British line. The van of the English, falling back, became entangled with the main body so that order was lost and maneuvering was impossible. For three hours the British stood under a galling fire; then Braddock ordered a retreat. The general was mortally wounded; many of the officers were killed; the retreat became a rout. Washington, sent to Dunbar by Braddock, reported the defeat and dispatched wagons for the wounded.

Dunbar, now in command, ordered quantities of stores destroyed, and retreated rapidly to Fort Cumberland. Refusing the request of Virginia and Pennsylvania that he build a fort at Raystown (Bedford, Pa.) and defend the frontier, he marched to Philadelphia in August and left the border to suffer Indian raids. Though Braddock's expedition failed, it demonstrated that an army could be marched over the Alleghenies, it taught the troops something of Indian fighting and its very mistakes contributed to the success of the Forbes Expedition[qv].

[Francis Parkman, *Montcalm and Wolfe*, Vol. 1; Stanley Pargellis, Braddock's Defeat, in *American Historical Review*, January, 1936.]

SOLON J. BUCK

Braddock's Road ran from the Potomac at Will's Creek (Cumberland, Md.) to the Monongahela at Turtle Creek. The section from Will's Creek to the upper Youghiogheny River was opened by the Ohio Company[qv], probably in 1752. In 1754 Washington improved the road to Great Meadows[qv] and extended it to Gist's plantation (six miles northeast of the present Uniontown, Pa.). In 1755 Braddock's Expedition[qv] used the road and extended it almost to Fort Duquesne[qv]. After Braddock's defeat the road facilitated Indian raids; still later it became a highway for western emigration and part of it was incorporated in the National Road[qv]. (*See also* Cumberland Road.)

[A. B. Hulbert, *Historic Highways of America*, Vols. 3 and 4; J. K. Lacock, Braddock Road, in *Pennsylvania Magazine of History and Biography*, 1914.]

SOLON J. BUCK

Bradford Oil Field (Pa.), THE, is the most important of the Appalachian oil fields. Though not far from where the first well drilled for the purpose of producing petroleum was sunk in 1859, the early wells in this pool were not drilled deep enough to reach the producing sand and it was not until after 1874 that effective production began. By 1881 it was producing four fifths of the total production of Pennsylvania, nearly 25,000,000 barrels yearly, but thereafter steadily declined, until in the early 1900's its output was only about 5% of the peak. Experiments with flooding the sands with water to drive out more oil (a new technique) proved so successful that thirty years later it was again one of the most active of the eastern fields.

T. T. READ

Bradstreet's Expedition against Fort Frontenac (1758). After the disaster at Ticonderoga[qv] in July, 1758, Lt. Col. John Bradstreet led a successful raid which went far to restore American morale.

Taking command in early August of 2600 men secretly mobilized in the Mohawk Valley, Bradstreet moved swiftly forward along the waterways. He reached Oswego on the 24th and, crossing Lake Ontario, effected a surprise which enabled him to capture the fort at Cataraqui (present Kingston) on the 27th. Both the post and the French shipping were put to the torch. This bold campaign broke the French hold of the water routes by which the western posts were supplied, contributing to the evacuation of Fort Duquesne[qv] later in the same year and to the surrender of Fort Niagara[qv] in 1759.

[*Documents Relative to Colonial History, State of New York; Papers of Sir William Johnson;* George W. Schuyler, *Colonial New York,* Vol. II.]

ARTHUR POUND

Bradstreet's Expedition to Lake Erie (1764). Col. John Bradstreet emerged from two wars with high credit, first as Sir William Pepperell's capable assistant at the capture of Louisburg[qv] in 1748, and later as the conqueror of Fort Frontenac in 1758 (*see* Bradstreet's Expedition against Fort Frontenac). Unfortunately, his record suffered from his next assignment, command of the expedition of 1764 to the Great Lakes area to place Indian relations on a peace footing following the uprising under Pontiac[qv].

On the shores of Lake Erie, Bradstreet revealed ignorance of Indian affairs by concluding improper treaties with unimportant delegations of Delawares and Shawnees[qqv]. In this he went beyond his instructions; worse yet, he did not recover possession of all prisoners held by the former foes. To Col. Bouquet[qv], advancing from the Forks of the Ohio[qv], fell the duty of pushing far into Ohio to restore white prestige.

Bradstreet proceeded to Detroit, where he was only partially successful. While returning, he failed to carry out instructions to move on mutinous Scioto villages, a dangerous situation in that quarter being saved by Bouquet's steadiness. Delaying too long on the Sandusky shore, Bradstreet's forces, near to mutiny, encountered severe hardships. His reputation as a popular hero did not survive.

[*Johnson Papers; Documents Relative to Colonial History, State of New York;* A. Pound, *Native Stock.*]

ARTHUR POUND

Brady Photographs, THE. A collection of over 7000 photographs (two negatives, in most cases) taken by M. B. Brady and his associates during the Civil War at an expenditure of over $100,000. They included portraits of officers and soldiers and scenes at the front and in the rear, along the battle lines from Washington to New Orleans.

After the fighting ceased one set passed into the Government's possession; the other, after many adventures, was largely included in the collection printed in the ten-volume *Photographic History of the Civil War.*

[F. T. Miller, *The Photographic History of the Civil War.*]

THOMAS ROBSON HAY

"Brain Trust." Prior to his nomination as the Democratic candidate for the Presidency in 1932 (*see* Campaign of 1932), Franklin D. Roosevelt had brought together three close advisers, Raymond Moley, Rexford G. Tugwell and Adolph A. Berle, Jr., all professors in Columbia University. These three continued to aid Mr. Roosevelt during his campaign for election and, after his inauguration on March 4, 1933, they became prominent in the councils of the chief executive. To keep them in Washington they were given salaried offices, Mr. Moley in the Department of State, Mr. Tugwell in the Department of Agriculture and Mr. Berle in the Reconstruction Finance Corporation. They and all professors or "intellectuals" who subsequently joined the administration were indiscriminately dubbed the "Brain Trust," whether or not they were close to the President. The impression was created that they were responsible for everything that was done, so the expression "Brain Trust" became a symbol for all New Deal[qv] experimentation.

[Ernest K. Lindley, *The Roosevelt Revolution;* Unofficial Observer, *The New Dealers.*]

ERIK McKINLEY ERIKSSON

Brands, Private and National. From the beginning of American commerce, much merchandise offered for sale has been identified by marks of origin, ownership or sponsorship. On casks, boxes, etc., they were literally "brands," but the term was loosely used to cover other kinds of craftsmen's or merchants' marks. Only recently have the trade-marks[qv] of merchants or other distributors been set apart as a class called "private brands" to distinguish them from the trademarks of manufacturers. The manufacturer's trade-marked merchandise may be distributed and advertised nationally; the private-branded merchandise usually has only sectional distribution.

The rivalry between the two classes originated in the latter part of the 19th century, but did not become clearly evident until the 20th. The earliest manufacturers of trade-marked products who used national advertising[qv] to stimulate consumer demand met little opposition from wholesalers and dealers. Their articles were usually of a new type or manifestly superior to unidentified bulk goods. But gradually, nationally advertised brands entered commodity fields where the dealer's influence had been dominant. Here he already had his own "private brand," or an unadvertised brand that allowed a larger margin of profit. The manufacturer's brands, procurable through other channels, weakened his hold on his customers.

For this reason and others, the large department stores, mail-order houses and chains^qqv^ promoted the sale of private brands they controlled and established new ones. Some of these private brands were made by manufacturers who marketed their own nationally advertised brands. Often the only important difference was that one was sponsored by a manufacturer and bore a craftsman's mark, the other by a distributor and bore a merchant's mark.

[Maynard, Weidler and Beckman, *Principles of Marketing.*]

G. B. HOTCHKISS

Brandy Station, Battle of (June 9, 1863). Ordered by Hooker (U.) to ascertain whether Lee's army was moving northward, Pleasonton threw the Federal cavalry, 7981 strong, with 3000 infantry, across the Rappahannock. At Beverly Ford, Buford's division drove part of Stuart's (C.) 10,292 cavalry toward Fleetwood Hill and Brandy Station. Gregg's and Duffie's divisions, crossing below, attacked Stuart's rear at Fleetwood. Stuart hurried troops thither, precipitating the greatest cavalry conflict of the war. The Confederates retained the field, but Pleasonton learned that Lee was marching toward Maryland.

[John W. Thomason, Jr., *Jeb Stuart; Official Records, Union and Confederate Armies,* Vol. XXVII, Parts 1, 2.]

JOSEPH MILLS HANSON

Brandywine, Battle of the (Sept. 11, 1777), was fought near Brandywine Creek, Chester County, Pa. The British and Hessian^qv^ troops commanded by Howe, Cornwallis and Knyphausen composed a force of 18,000. The American Army under Washingon numbered 11,000, of whom a large number were militia. Following a feint attack by the Hessians upon the Americans at Chad's Ford, the British crossed the East Brandywine at Jefferis' Ford, continued southward and suddenly attacked Sullivan's troops near Birmingham Meetinghouse. The Americans, though outnumbered, fought gallantly, but were compelled to retire. Washington had received faulty news concerning the approach of the British. At night Washington withdrew his army without demoralization to Chester, Pa.

[C. W. Heathcote, *History of Chester County.*]

CHARLES W. HEATHCOTE

Brattleboro. *See* Dummer, Fort.

Brazil, Confederate Expatriates to. Perhaps nearly half of the eight or ten thousand Southerners who emigrated to foreign lands after the Civil War went to Brazil. The expatriates formed associations and sent agents to the southern empire to make arrangements and to select lands for homes. Coming from every Southern state and some Northern states, they represented every social class and profession. Many had been leaders in the Old South. At first the chief embarkation point was New Orleans; later it became New York. Rio de Janeiro received nearly all the immigrants, though the colonists settling on the Amazon went via Pará.

The greater number settled in colonies located in the wilderness of the provinces of Paraná, São Paulo, Rio de Janeiro, Espirito Santo, and Pará. Most of them tried agriculture and stock raising. They were comparatively successful at Villa Americana, in the hinterland of São Paulo, which at its peak was a thriving community of several hundred families. The experiments as a rule were not successful and broke up after a few months' or at most a few years' endurance, the colonists going to São Paulo, or, more often, returning to the United States. The failures were due to lack of access to markets; unsatisfactory labor supply (the Brazilian Negro could not be kept in isolated interior communities); climatic conditions, tropical insects and disease; lack of capital and the ordinary social institutions; and homesickness for friends and relatives. Yet many traces still remain of these Southern expatriates in Brazil.

[Lawrence F. Hill, The Confederate Exodus to Latin America, *Southwestern Historical Quarterly,* October, 1935, January and April, 1936.]

LAWRENCE F. HILL

Brazito Battle, Mexican War (Dec. 25, 1846). Reaching the Rio Grande east bank by midafternoon, Doniphan, with 500 Missouri volunteers, received Ponce de León's messenger, under a black flag, demanding surrender. In the ensuing thirty-minute fight, the Americans' superior fire and tactics triumphed. Ponce fled in disorder, losing a hundred killed and wounded to the American loss of seven slightly wounded.

[Justin Smith, *The War with Mexico.*]

ROBERT S. THOMAS

Breda, Treaty of, signed July 21/31, 1667, by England and France after the naval war between England and Holland in which France joined the latter, provided in Article 10 for the restoration of Acadia to France. King Charles II's order (1668) for its return was delayed by the claims of Thomas Temple to part of the region, based on a grant from Cromwell (1656). Restoration took place in 1670, France returning to England at the same time part of the island of St. Christopher.

[F. G. Davenport, ed., *European Treaties Bearing on the History of the United States*, Vol. II.]

ROBERT E. MOODY

Breed's Hill. *See* Bunker Hill.

Brewing. There is evidence of brewing by Europeans in America almost immediately after their first harvest of grains. Members of Sir Walter Raleigh's "Lost Colony"^qv^ brewed beer from Indian corn as early as 1587 in Virginia. One of the first commercial breweries of record operated in 1623 in New Amsterdam^qv^. An early New England brewery was operated by Capt. Sedgwick in Massachusetts Bay Colony^qv^ in 1637. A brewery was established in 1638 as a community enterprise of Roger Williams' colonists in what is now Portsmouth, R. I.

The Swedes arrived on the Delaware^qv^ in 1638 and although no date has been fixed for the establishment of their first brewery, the records of the colony allude to beer as one of its commodities and articles of commerce. William Penn was the first English brewer of that region. He erected his brewery in 1683 in Pennsbury, Bucks County, Pa.

When Gen. James Oglethorpe colonized Georgia, he introduced brewing to further moderation in drinking. Many other colonizers and leaders encouraged beer and ale as temperance beverages either by setting up their own breweries or advocating lower taxes to foster production. Samuel Adams, George Washington and Gen. Israel Putnam were among the famous colonial leaders proud of their brews. Most of the colonial manors maintained private breweries, for beer was not only a daily article of diet but also an ingredient in many tasty dishes.

The middle of the 19th century found brewing assuming new industrial importance, as brewers developed scientific control of their product to give it greater uniformity and stability. Lager brewing was introduced to America about 1840 permitting the better storage of American beers. In 1876, Louis Pasteur announced the epochal results of his studies on fermentation of French beer and his findings quickly became basic for American beer. Modern air-conditioning^qv^ grew from a brewery installation in Alexandria, Va., in 1880, providing pure air and even temperature, so vital in the fermentation and aging process.

American beer and ale reached a record consumption of 66,000,000 barrels—21 gallons per capita—in 1914. National prohibition^qv^ in 1920 suspended beer brewing for thirteen years and cereal or near-beer was produced in this period. On April 7, 1933, beer was relegalized, gaining in consumption with each passing year, due chiefly to its growing favor as a home beverage. Consumption for the first five years has totaled 223,000,000 barrels, with a retail value of about $7,000,000,000.

[The Research Library, United Brewers Industrial Foundation, New York, N. Y.]

HUGH HARLEY

Briand-Kellogg Pact, THE, was signed in Paris by fifteen nations on Aug. 27, 1928. Eventually forty-eight other governments adhered to the treaty. It grew out of negotiations which were begun between the United States and France. Article I provides that the parties renounce war as an instrument of national policy in their relations with one another. Article II provides that the settlement of disputes between the parties shall never be sought except by pacific means. Connected with the text of the pact are certain interpretations of Secretary of State Kellogg which were included as a part of the negotiations and which made clear that the treaty did not prevent wars of self-defense, that it was not inconsistent with the Covenant of the League of Nations^qv^ and that it did not interfere with the rendering of aid under the Locarno treaties^qv^ and the so-called treaties of neutrality.

[J. T. Shotwell, *War as an Instrument of National Policy and Its Renunciation in the Pact of Paris;* D. H. Miller, *The Peace Pact of Paris, a Study of the Briand-Kellogg Treaty.*]

BENJAMIN H. WILLIAMS

Briar Creek, Ga., Battle of (March 4, 1779). Gen. Augustine Prevost, British commander, trapped and routed a force of about 1200 Southern militia and regular Continentals under Col. John Ashe at Briar Creek, in Severn County. American loss was 150 killed and wounded; 189 captured. The British lost but 16, killed and wounded.

[Charles Stedman, *History of the American War.*]

ROBERT S. THOMAS

Bricks were made in Virginia as early as 1612. The first brick kiln of which we have any record in New England began work in Salem, Mass., in 1629. Up to that time, most dwelling-house chimneys had been built of wood, coated with clay. In that year, 1629, 10,000 bricks were imported from England to Massachusetts, where they were used principally for chimneys and fireplaces. The first brick house in Boston was built in 1638. Brick making was begun by the Dutch settlers near Albany in 1656. But in that century and the next, quantities of bricks continued to be imported from England and Holland, builders of fine residences believing, whether rightly or not, that a better quality of brick was made abroad than in America. As late as 1790, about as many bricks were being imported as were made in this country. Importation was curbed, however, in 1794 by the imposition of a 15% duty. Meanwhile, exportation had begun; in 1791 we shipped 743,000 bricks, mostly to the West Indies. The first patent on a brick-making machine was taken out in 1800, but not until 1829 did successful manufacture by machine begin, this in New York.

[J. Leander Bishop, *A History of American Manufactures.*]

ALVIN F. HARLOW

Bridge, then called Bridge Whist, was first played in America, in its original Russian form, with no bidding, before 1900. In 1907 Auction Bridge was introduced, coming from England, and by 1909 magazine articles deploring the craze were appearing. The first American code for Auction was drawn up in 1910. In 1925, on a coastwise steamer, Contract Bridge was first played, Harold S. Vanderbilt, capitalist, being given credit for its invention. After this innovation, the bridge fad assumed enormous proportions. Bridge discussions by radio were introduced in 1925. Expert players became wealthy from teaching and writing on the subject. No other indoor game in history was ever so popular.

[R. F. Foster, *Foster's Complete Hoyle.*]

ALVIN F. HARLOW

Bridger, Fort, was a frontier trading post and later a fort of the United States Army, located on Black's Fork, Uinta County, Wyo. It was named after James (Jim) Bridger, trapper and scout, who with his partner, Louis Vasquez, built it in 1843 and operated it for a number of years.

Although trading in pelts was carried on, Bridger's post is best known as a way station and supply point for emigrants bound for Oregon, Utah and California (*see* Oregon Trail). Its establishment marks the beginning of caravan travel to the Pacific Coast. The post was taken over by Mormon[qv] colonists from Utah about 1855; was burned by the Mormons on the approach of United States troops in the Mormon War[qv] of 1857; was rebuilt as a military post by the United States Army in 1858; and was finally abandoned in 1890. For many years it was famous as a mail, express and telegraph station.

[Cecil B. Alter, *James Bridger.*]

RUPERT N. RICHARDSON

Bridges. The earlier bridges in America were all of wood, many of them—when they crossed marshy streams or inlets—being supported by wooden piles or cribs of logs. Farther inland, stone piers were frequently built, and in the latter 17th century small stone arches began to appear. Spans were short and bridges were all open to the air until shortly after 1800, when trusses began to be devised, making longer and higher spans possible; and then the covered, completely boxed-in bridge appeared. The covering had two uses: it protected the trusses from the weather and consequent decay, and it prevented horses from being frightened if the bridge was high above the stream. Palmer, Town, Wernwag, Burr and Howe, inventor of the Howe Truss, were noted builders in wood. They became so adept that some covered truss spans of 200 and 250 feet length were built. Many of these bridges were private toll[qv] monopolies and very remunerative. The early traveler on rare occasions encountered a floating bridge—just thick planks fastened together by wooden stringers and floating on the water surface, sinking slightly as horse and vehicle passed over them. Wooden bridges and viaducts—those across deep gorges containing hundreds or thousands of heavy timbers—were used by railroads through a considerable portion of the 19th century; new ones were built in the West and South even after 1870. Serious wrecks, sometimes with great loss of life, were caused by the occasional burning of such bridges.

Wrought-iron bridges began to be built about 1800, chain suspension[qv] spans (the first one built in 1796) being the earliest type using iron. A little later came iron arches and trusses, mostly cast. The first iron truss bridge, a mixture of wrought and cast metal, was erected over the Erie Canal[qv] at Frankfort, N. Y., in 1840. Squire Whipple was the first real exponent and developer of the iron truss in America, though Fink (designer of the mile-long iron railroad bridge over the Ohio Falls at Louisville, built 1867–70), Bollman, Pratt, McCollum, Post, Warren and others designed trusses of great utility. In the 20th century bridge building became an exact science, and through the genius of such engineers as Gustav Lindenthal, Ralph Modjeski, O. H. Ammann and Joseph B. Strauss, bridges rapidly became more gigantic in capacity and span. With the crossing of the Hudson at New York in 1931, the James near Norfolk in 1928 and the Mississippi at New Orleans in 1935, the last of the streams once considered unbridgable was conquered. The crossing of San Francisco Bay[qv] (1936) and of the Golden Gate[qv] (1937) were still more colossal achievements.

Reinforced concrete began to be used cautiously in bridge building before 1900, but did not come into wide use until the second decade of the present century. Thereafter, some long and often very beautiful bridges and viaducts were built of this material.

[Wilbur J. Watson, *Bridge Architecture;* Henry Grattan Tyrrell, *History of Bridge Engineering.*]

ALVIN F. HARLOW

Bridges, Steel. James B. Eads[qv] first used steel in American bridge building when (1868–74) he designed and erected the great arched structure crossing the Mississippi at St. Louis. The supporting ribs of its three 500-foot arches are steel tubes, 18 inches in diameter, fabricated by a company headed by Andrew Carnegie, who had just introduced the Bessemer process into America. When rolled steel began to be produced in quantity in the early 1880's, it rapidly came into favor for all types of bridges. The cantilever railroad bridge across the Niagara River, with its 975-foot span, built during that decade, used the new material. The Washington Bridge across the Harlem River, completed 1889, with two beautiful 508-foot arches, was a fine product of the period. Another arch, this one of 840 feet, was thrown across the Niagara gorge in 1898 and was the wonder of the period. But the steel arch was still growing. Gustav Lindenthal's Hell Gate Bridge at New York, completed 1916, with a 1000-foot span, was overshadowed in 1932 by the Kill Van Kull Bridge at Bayonne, N. J., with a 1675-foot arch. A notable American example of the cantilever type was the Queensboro Bridge over the East River at New York, completed in 1903, whose longest span measures 1182 feet. The Southern Pacific Railroad over the Pecos River, 320 feet high, completed in the early 1890's, was built with the aid of a traveling crane which thrust out one half of the great central span as far as it could go and was then dismantled and shipped by rail over a 1200-mile detour so that it might build the other end of the bridge. The less spectacular steel truss was being greatly developed during those decades, one of its most remarkable manifestations being Lindenthal's bridge over the Ohio at Sciotoville, with one continuous truss, 1550 feet long, supported on three piers. (*See also* Bridges, Suspension.)

[Archibald Black, *The Story of Bridges.*]

ALVIN F. HARLOW

Bridges, Suspension. James Finley, an attorney, designed the first suspension bridge in America in 1801, a seventy-foot span across Jacob's Creek in western Pennsylvania. He took out a patent, and several bridges were erected under it. His bridges were suspended by "chains" of iron eye-bars from three to eight feet in length. The first wire suspension bridge was swung across the Schuylkill River near Philadelphia in 1816 —a footbridge supported by six 3/8-inch wires. Charles Ellet, Jr. and John A. Roebling, a German immigrant, did much to develop the cable suspension bridge in America. Ellet built bridges across the Schuylkill (1842), the Niagara (1847), and the Ohio at Wheeling (1849). Roebling built the second bridge across the Niagara (1855), bridged the Ohio at Cincinnati (1867) and then designed the Brooklyn Bridge[qv] (1869), the greatest of his achievements. This was followed by Lindenthal's Williamsburg (1903) and Manhattan (1909) bridges across the East River at New York. Twenty years later vastly greater spans were appearing. The George Washington Bridge across the Hudson at New York (1927–32) with a main span of 3500 feet was soon surpassed by the Golden Gate Bridge[qv] at San Francisco, with a 4200-foot span and 740-foot towers, built with amazing speed in less than four years, 1933–36. In almost the same time San Francisco Bay was bridged to Oakland with five miles of steel structures, including a 1400-foot cantilever, 19 truss spans and a double suspension bridge with 2 spans of 2310 feet each.

ALVIN F. HARLOW

Bridgewater, Battle of. *See* Lundy's Lane, Battle at.

Briscoe v. Bank of the Commonwealth of Kentucky, 1837 (11 Peters 257). The Bank of Kentucky was entirely owned by the state and its officers and directors were appointed by the state legislature. The question was whether notes issued by such a bank constituted a subterfuge by which the state in effect was emitting bills of credit[qv] in the sense forbidden by the Constitution. The court found the notes to be backed by the resources of the bank and not the credit of the state and the bank to be a separate entity suable on its own account; therefore, such notes were not bills of credit in the prohibited sense. This case "completely repudiated" the decision in Craig v. Missouri[qv].

[A. J. Beveridge, *John Marshall.*]

HARVEY PINNEY

Bristoe Campaign (Oct. 9–22, 1863). Lee (C.) crossed the Rapidan, Oct. 9, turning Meade's

(U.) right flank, and advanced toward Washington. Using parallel roads Meade marched rapidly to cover the capital. He reached Centreville first, his rear guard, under Warren (U.), severely repulsing A. P. Hill's (C.) corps at Bristoe Station, Oct. 14. A battle under favorable conditions proving impossible, Lee returned to the Rappahannock.

[Douglas S. Freeman, *R. E. Lee*, Vol. III; *Official Records, Union and Confederate Armies*, Vol. XXIX.]

JOSEPH MILLS HANSON

Bristol Trade. During the early 16th century Bristol found its location in southwestern England a great advantage in capturing trade with America; by the 17th century it had become the foremost English port. Throughout the 16th century Bristol merchants showed a steady willingness to support overseas expansion, alike in the realms of trade, fisheries and exploration. Hakluyt the geographer, Ferdinando Gorges*qqv* and a Newfoundland fishery syndicate, not to mention other important elements in American development, had Bristol contacts. Moreover, prevailing winds and ocean currents enabled the city's traders to share in the profitable Caribbean commerce. In the later 17th century Bristol became the port of departure for many American colonists. Although the city lost its commercial priority in the 18th century, it still shared heavily in western enterprises, especially through the slave trade and the fisheries*qqv*. On the eve of the American Revolution it was the second city in Britain, and its merchants greatly influenced British colonial policy*qv*.

[*Cambridge History of the British Empire*, Vol. I; C. P. Lucas, *The Beginnings of English Overseas Enterprise*.]

CHARLES F. MULLETT

British Campaign of 1777. As the year 1776 ended, the British ministry came to think of the problem in America as one of reconquest, rather than of policing. A reasoned procedure was evolved in consultation with Gen. Sir John Burgoyne, lately returned to London from Canada. The plan decided on provided for an expedition to proceed from Montreal southward along the familiar Champlain-Hudson route. A large army moving up the Hudson from New York would meet Burgoyne at Albany, after which a subsidiary force might proceed eastward down the Connecticut River. As Burgoyne moved from Montreal, an auxiliary force would go up the St. Lawrence River to Oswego and, with Indian aid, would strike into the Mohawk Valley. It was also proposed that a force of Southern Indians, Negroes and British regulars be used "to awe the Southern provinces." A "numerous fleet" would "sweep the whole coast." It was believed that the plan, properly concerted and carried out, "might possibly do the business [of ending the colonial revolt] in one campaign."

To carry out this plan, the British force in the colonies would be re-enforced from England. American auxiliaries of every description—Tories*qv*, Canadians and Indians—would be recruited and foreign regular troops would be hired for service in America (*see* Hessians, The). An unusual complement of guns was to be taken, as it was expected some of the numerous forts along the proposed route of invasion would need to be besieged and reduced by gunfire.

Because the active theater of war was comprised in a long narrow band along the North Atlantic seaboard, bisected from north to south by the Champlain-Hudson route, it was clear that if this route could be occupied and held, the revolt would soon come to an end. In fact, such occupation was "the indispensable first step in reconquering the colonies."

The reasoning was correct, but the plan failed because of the shortcomings of the commanding general, because of the physical barriers of river, forest and terrain, which impeded transport and troop movements, and the difficulty of securing adequate supplies of food and munitions. Final important causes were the uncertain allegiance of Canada and of the American Tories, and the overrating of Indian co-operation. The American opposition, at opportune moments, capitalized on these handicaps and was finally able to win a decisive victory. (*See* Burgoyne's Invasion; Highlands, The; Oriskany, Battle of; Bennington, Battle of.)

[Hoffman Nickerson, *The Turning Point of the Revolution*.]

THOMAS ROBSON HAY

British Debts, THE, were the debts owed by the American colonial merchants and planters to British merchants before the Revolution and which, obviously remaining unpaid during the war, continued a subject of dispute between the United States and England till 1802. The debts were a natural consequence of the economic system prevalent in the colonies. The merchants of the Northern colonies and the planters of the Southern colonies bought practically all of their manufactured articles from English merchants. The merchants of the northern colonies depended on their trade and the planters upon their prospective crops to pay the balances due in England. The result, from 1763 to 1775, was a rather constant indebtedness of some £3,000,000—most of which was owed by the Southern planters.

Stoppage of payment on these debts was frequently resorted to by the colonies in their fight against the colonial legislation of Parliament in the period, 1763–75. And the possibility of wiping out the indebtedness by war was one of the contributing causes of the Revolution.

During the Revolution all of the states enacted laws affecting these debts. In the states north of Maryland most of the debts were due to Loyalists[qv], while in the Southern states most of the debts belonged to the British merchants. Some of the laws confiscated Loyalist estates, including debts (England later claimed that debts due to Loyalists should be included with those due to British merchants); some laws sequestered the debts due to British merchants; others confiscated such debts; while still others banished or restricted the activities of the agents of the British merchants; other laws, such as paper money legislation, just as effectively abolished or barred the collection of the debts. In Maryland £144,536 of debts due to British merchants were paid into the state treasury; in Virginia about £287,000; and in North Carolina over £50,000.

These debts were an important problem in the negotiation of the Definitive Treaty of Peace in 1782–83[qv]. At one time the British ministers were ready to make peace without any guarantee for the Loyalists and merchants. However, John Adams, more interested in the fisheries[qv] than in the debts of the planters and having "no notion of cheating anybody," was responsible for the provision (Article IV) that the debts due before the war were to be paid in sterling. Article V required that Congress should recommend to the several states the restoration of the confiscated estates of the Loyalists. Article IV met with determined opposition in the Southern states and Article V in all of the states. Practically all of the states either delayed or refused compliance. British merchants and their agents were denied admission to some states; courts were frequently closed to the debt cases; installment laws were passed; wartime interest was disallowed; and in some cases the debts were declared to have been terminated by the war and the wartime legislation of the states. On the other hand, American Negro slaves were carried off by the British troops; American posts along the Canadian border were occupied by the British (*see* Border Forts, The Evacuation of); and Indians were incited to attack the frontier.

With the adoption of the Constitution, opposed by many of the debtors, a new chapter in the debts controversy opened. The Federal courts facilitated the collection of many of the debts; and the new administration was able to negotiate more effectively with England relative to the infractions of the treaty of peace. After Gouverneur Morris' mission to London an English minister, George Hammond, was sent to the United States. However, the Jefferson-Hammond negotiations failed to settle the debt question. Nothing more was done till the strained relations of 1792–93 led to the mission of John Jay and the famous Jay's Treaty[qv]. By Article VI of this treaty the United States accepted liability for such of the debts as could not at that date be recovered due to legal impediments imposed by the states. A five-man commission, to adjudicate the claims, sat at Philadelphia from May 29, 1797, till July 31, 1799. Claims to the amount of £5,638,629 8s. 1d. were received. The commissioners, however, were unable to agree on such important matters as: the jurisdiction of the commission; the nature of legal impediments; the question of the solvency of debtors; wartime interest, etc. The entire matter, therefore, fell again into the regular diplomatic channels. A final settlement was negotiated by Rufus King and the Addington Ministry on Jan. 8, 1802. By the terms of this settlement the United States was to pay, in lieu of its liability under Article VI of Jay's Treaty, the lump sum of £600,000. An English commission sat till 1811 adjusting the claims. It found only about 20–25% of the claims good, but even so was able to pay, with the £600,000, only about 45% of the approved claims.

[J. B. Moore, *International Adjudications*, Vol. III; unpublished work by the writer on *The Debts Owed by Americans to British Merchants, 1763-1802*, to be found at Indiana University.]

BEN R. BALDWIN

British Florida (1763–83). *See* Florida, British.

British Plan of Campaign in the West (1780). British authorities, during the spring of 1780, were prepared to carry out a comprehensive plan for the recapture of the Illinois country[qv] and to attack St. Louis, New Orleans and other Spanish posts on the Mississippi. Spain, allied with France, was then the enemy of Great Britain. Four simultaneous movements were begun. Col. Henry Bird with a force from Detroit was directed to "amuse" George Rogers Clark at the Falls of the Ohio[qv]. Gen. John Campbell, from Pensacola[qv], after taking New Orleans was to proceed up the Mississippi to Natchez[qv] where he was to be joined by a force which was to have captured St. Louis. Capt. Charles de Langlade was to advance down the Illinois River while another party was ordered to watch Vincennes[qv].

No part of the plan proved successful. Col.

Bird[qv], after taking two small posts in Kentucky, retreated. Gen. Campbell, frightened at the display of strength by Gov. Bernardo de Galvez at New Orleans, remained at Pensacola. A force of British and Indians from Michilimackinac[qv], after their first repulse at St. Louis[qv], withdrew. Capt. Langlade retreated precipitately upon learning of the approach of Illinois cavalry.

[James A. James, *The Life of George Rogers Clark.*]

JAMES A. JAMES

British Travelers in the United States, Early. Precisely because the British and American peoples have so much in common, British travelers were quick to note points of difference. Few failed to mention with disapproval the great use of ice and iced drinks, the sallow unhealthy look, the lack of recreation, the addiction to boarding houses and the omnipresent rocking-chair habit. American men bore additional charges of constant tobacco chewing, indiscriminate, though admittedly accurate, spitting, and sprawling with feet on chairs and tables. Of our abstract social traits, we were credited with hospitality, good nature and high sexual morality, but condemned for low political and business ethics, dollar chasing, hurrying, social equality, inquisitiveness, bragging and hypersensitiveness to British criticism.

Wansey (1794) and especially Melish (1806–11) made valuable observations concerning economic life in the East and South. Birkbeck (1818) and Flower (1818–21) viewed the Western frontier realistically but with confidence in its future development. The actor, Bernard (1797–1811), excelled in genial anecdotal description. The irrepressible journalist, Cobbett (1792–99; 1817–18), was no more critical of us than of his own native country. Fearon (1817–18), a trustworthy and penetrating observer, who covered 5000 miles, concluded that the United States was the poor man's land of opportunity. On the other hand, Weld (1795–97) and Ashe (1806) were neither favorable nor always reliable; Janson (1807) was often mendacious; Faux (1815) was a deliberately abusive faultfinder.

After 1825 professional commentators began to replace the earlier incidental observers. British condescension toward Jacksonian democracy[qv] became evident. Mrs. Frances Trollope (1827–31) was ill-tempered in tone and her generalizations concerning particulars which she disliked led her many European readers to unfair conclusions and infuriated Americans. Hall (1827–28) wrote with an aristocratic political bias and even a capable observer like Marryat (1837–39) could not approve our "mob government." Harriet Martineau (1834–37) commended our good points and condemned our shortcomings with excellent judgment. In common with nearly all British travelers she wrote scathingly of slavery. Dickens (1841–42), our most famous visitor, made justifiable criticisms, but Americans overlooked the fact that he had not spared his own country and resented it that he should criticize us at all. With the coming of such impartial observers as Buckingham (1837–40), the geologist Lyell (1841; 1845–46) and Mackay (1846–47), the pendulum of opinion swung back in our favor. America must have had its attractions to change Isabella Bird (1855) from antagonism to admiration and induce Beste (1852) to travel for pleasure by canal, river, rail and wagon with a wife and eleven children. (*See also* French Travelers in the United States.)

[Allan Nevins, *American Social History as Recorded by British Travelers;* H. T. Tuckerman, *America and Her Commentators;* Jane L. Mesick, *The English Traveler in America, 1785-1835.*]

HARVEY L. CARTER

Broad Seal War. Following the closely contested election of 1838 two groups sought admission to Congress from New Jersey. Both held commissions bearing the great (broad) seal of the state; only the Whig[qv] commissions, however, were legally executed and signed by the governor. Charging their opponents with fraud and facing loss of control of the House, the Democratic[qv] majority refused to seat all but one Whig. When it was proved that the county clerks in Cumberland and Middlesex counties had suppressed the returns in certain townships that would have given the Democrats a majority, the House, on Feb. 28, 1840, seated the five Democratic claimants.

[I. S. Kull, ed., *New Jersey, A History.*]

C. A. TITUS

Broadsides. A name given to sheets printed on one side only. In 17th-century America broadsides were used for poetical effusions, news items and political propaganda. In the Revolution they were used for political purposes, often reprinted in the printer's newspaper. Later they were used in political, antislavery and temperance campaigns; also for song sheets, especially during the Civil War. Parodies often resulted. Broadsides were also used for memorials, obituaries, accounts of trials, executions, sometimes in crude poetry. Newspaper carriers used them for New Year's offerings. They have also been used for official proclamations and posters. Broadsides are ephemeral, become scarce and increase in value. Good collections are in a few libraries. Recently newspapers and radio[qqv] have superseded broadsides, but they were used in the World War.

AUGUSTUS H. SHEARER

Broadway. Most of the lower course of Broadway is said to follow the routes of old Indian trails. In New Amsterdam[qv] its first quarter mile of existence was called the Heerewegh or Heere Straat. The name was anglicized to Broadway about 1668. Two public wells were dug in the middle of it in 1677 and abolished in 1806. The first paving, a ten-foot strip of cobblestones on each side of an earthen center, was done in 1707. The first sidewalks, four blocks on both sides, were laid in 1790. Washington for a time during his Presidency lived at 39 Broadway. In 1852 a franchise was granted for a cable car line on Broadway, then the city's chief residential street. The line, which was fought in the courts for more than thirty years, was finally built in 1885, but long before that time the street had ceased to be residential and had become the main business thoroughfare of the city. As it progressed northward, it followed in general the line of the Bloomingdale Road to 207th Street. Beyond the Harlem River it becomes a part of the road to Albany. The first subway line under it was begun in 1900. In the latter 19th century theaters congregated along it, first below and then above Longacre (now Times) Square, until its name became a symbol for the American theater. The first "arc" electric street lights in New York were placed on Broadway in 1880 and the brilliant lighting in the early 20th century brought it the nickname of "The Great White Way."

[Stephen Jenkins, *The Longest Street in the World.*]

ALVIN F. HARLOW

Brodhead's Allegheny Campaign (1779). Col. Daniel Brodhead set out from Fort Pitt[qv], Aug. 11, 1779, with 600 regulars, volunteers and a few Delaware[qv] warriors against the Seneca[qv] on the upper Allegheny. A party of Indians coming downstream was defeated, but warned the villages, and the inhabitants fled. After destroying their houses and corn, Brodhead returned to Pittsburgh. The spell of the Iroquois[qv] had been broken and provisional treaties were made with the Wyandotte[qv] and a branch of the Shawnee[qv] which for a short time saved the frontier from invasion. (*See also* Sullivan-Clinton Campaign.)

[Louise P. Kellogg, *Frontier Advance on the Upper Ohio,* and *Frontier Retreat on the Upper Ohio.*]

JAMES A. JAMES

Bronco, a Spanish word, was early used in America to characterize hostile savages as opposed to *Indios mansos*—gentle Indians. In time the Spaniards applied the adjective to wild horses, a usage peculiar to America. Frontiersmen borrowed the adjective and converted it into a noun, often misspelled *bronk* or *broncho.* The mustang[qv] is not synonymous with the bronco until caught and more or less broken. Loosely, a bronco is a range horse, a cow horse; more specifically and accurately, a range horse that pitches or bucks. Through Wild West shows, Rodeos, Cowboy Reunions, Frontier Days celebrations, the Calgary Stampede, etc., he is familiar to the American public; he is found in the *remuda*[qv] of every sizable ranch. The range horse is basically of Spanish (Andalusian and Arabian) stock, but in the Americas he developed a buck virtually unknown in Europe or Asia. There horses are traditionally "gentled"; but by Indians, cowboys[qv], vaqueros and gauchos they are "broken," usually a rough process hardly conducive to gentleness.

[William H. Carter, *The Horses of the World;* William R. Leigh, *The Western Pony.*]

J. FRANK DOBIE

Bronson v. Rodes, 1868 (7 Wall. 229), was an action on a New York executor's bond of 1851 to repay a loan "in gold or silver coin." In 1865 the obligor tendered payment in United States notes, which Congress had declared "lawful money and a legal tender[qv] in payment of debts." The tender was refused and the obligor sued to cancel a mortgage securing the bond. Decrees in his favor by two state courts were reversed by the United States Supreme Court, which held "that express contracts to pay coined dollars are not debts which may be satisfied by the tender of U. S. Notes."

[Carson, Great Dissenting Opinions, *Albany Law Journal,* L, 140.]

C. SUMNER LOBINGIER

Brook Farm Institute of Agriculture and Education, The, grew out of the realistic social criticism of the day, touched by German Transcendentalism. George Ripley was the indefatigable and brave center of the group which moved to a farm of 200 acres in West Roxbury, Mass., in April, 1841. The members undertook to build a co-operative community in which manual and intellectual labor might be united and men and women live in a simple but cultivated society. They worked hard, erected new buildings and did their best with the poor soil.

Ripley came to believe more organization was necessary and an adaptation of the Fourier[qv] phalanx was adopted in 1845, with the primary departments of agricultural, domestic and mechanic arts. Since communal living and centralized efficiency were basic to their new doctrine, they built a large phalanstery. Fire destroyed it in 1846 while the members were celebrating its completion. Money was depleted, they could not pay the promised 5% on investments, and the experiment had to end, but not in great debt.

Though not a financial success, Brook Farm was a great social success. Gaiety, entertainment, music, spirited talk, a successful progressive educational program with outside pupils and a generous economic democracy were there. Although the great Transcendentalists[qv] had too little faith in external reform to join the group, Hawthorne, Charles A. Dana and John S. Dwight were members and the famous of Boston and Concord came often to talk or lecture. Their interest has kept the farm in memory.

[Lindsay Swift, *Brook Farm;* J. R. Codman, *Brook Farm.*]

ALLAN MACDONALD

Brooklyn, N. Y. The first settlements within the present boundaries of Brooklyn were made at Gowanus and the Wallabout in 1636 and 1637. In 1642 a ferry was established connecting Long Island with New Amsterdam[qv], and within four years a hamlet called Breuckelen, after a village in Holland, was laid out about a mile from the ferry slip. This community, with its neighboring settlements, was organized as the town of Breuckelen in 1646. The name finally became Brooklyn, although for a century there were variant spellings. The district near the slip, called "the Ferry," became a market for Long Island agricultural products. After the Revolution there was an influx of non-Dutch settlers. In 1801 Brooklyn Navy Yard[qv] was established at the Wallabout. A district covering a square mile, with the Ferry as its nucleus, having a population of about 4000, was chartered as Brooklyn village in 1816. Growth was now very rapid. In 1834 Brooklyn township, numbering 24,000, was chartered as a city. During the quarter century before the Civil War Brooklyn's population multiplied more than eleven times. In 1854 the city of Williamsburgh was annexed. A residential suburb of New York—the "city of homes and churches"—it was also a great manufacturing, shipping and commercial center. By 1896 Brooklyn had expanded to take in the entire county of Kings, and on Jan. 1, 1898, as the borough of Brooklyn, it became part of the city of New York[qv]. It is now the largest borough of the city, with an estimated population (1939) of 2,792,600. Ferry lines, subway tunnels and three great suspension bridges connect Brooklyn with Manhattan.

[Henry R. Stiles, *A History of the City of Brooklyn;* Ralph Foster Weld, *Brooklyn Village, 1816-1834.*]

RALPH FOSTER WELD

Brooklyn Bridge was the first bridge built across the East River between New York and Brooklyn, and at the time the longest of all suspension bridges[qv]. There had been talk of bridging the river as early as 1840. The corporation to build the structure was organized in 1867, the city of Brooklyn subscribing for $3,000,000 stock and New York for $1,500,000. John A. Roebling was chosen chief engineer, but he died in 1869, and his son Washington completed the task. The bridge was thirteen years in building, and cost $15,500,000. It was opened on May 24, 1883.

[E. F. Farrington, *History of the Building of the Great Bridge.*]

ALVIN F. HARLOW

Brooklyn Heights, Battle of. *See* Long Island, Battle of.

Brooklyn Navy Yard, The (officially the New York Navy Yard), is situated on Wallabout Bay, East River. Here were moored the *Old Jersey* and other prison ships during the Revolutionary War[qv]. Many deceased American prisoners of war were buried on the adjacent shore. In 1801 Jackson's shipyard comprising about thirty acres was purchased by the Federal Government for a Navy Yard, and Lt. Thorne appointed commandant. Additional land was acquired subsequently. Extensive improvements were begun in 1806. During the War of 1812[qv] over 100 vessels were fitted out. The ship-of-the-line *Ohio* was launched in 1820. The first granite dry dock was completed in 1851. During the Civil War[qv] over 400 vessels were fitted out and 14 built; the employees increasing from 1650 to over 6000. In later years the yard has been constantly expanded to keep pace with the growth of the Navy and to become the largest naval industrial establishment. It now has very extensive facilities for fitting out, repairing, docking and building all classes of warships, including battleships of the maximum size. Since 1895 ten battleships and many smaller vessels have been constructed. During the World War[qv] about 17,500 men were employed.

[*Long Island Historical Society Proceedings*, 1877.]

DUDLEY W. KNOX

Brooks-Baxter War, The, was a dispute between Elisha Baxter, Arkansas governor (1873–74), and his political opponent, the Rev. Joseph Brooks, who, refusing to accept the election returns marched with followers on the State House and took possession. The State Supreme Court decided in favor of Brooks, but President Grant ruled that decision rested with the state legislature which supported Baxter's claims, May 11, 1874.

CHARLES J. FINGER

Brooks-Sumner Affair (May 22, 1856). Sen. Charles Sumner, in the course of his famous speech, "The Crime Against Kansas," ridiculed Sen. Andrew P. Butler of South Carolina for his devotion to "the harlot, Slavery." Three days after these remarks, during Butler's absence from Washington, his nephew, Preston S. Brooks, a member of Congress from South Carolina, sought out the Massachusetts senator at his desk and, rebuking him for his insult, struck him over the head repeatedly with a cane. When the attack ended Sumner sank to the floor with injuries that incapacitated him for some years. This demonstration, and the investigation ordered by the House, heightened the tension of the sectional controversy. Brooks, who was saved from expulsion by the two-thirds rule, was praised in the South and rewarded with re-election.

[Rhodes, *History of the United States*, II.]

ARTHUR C. COLE

Brotherhood of Locomotive Engineers. *See* Railroad Brotherhoods.

Brown, Fort, at Brownsville, Texas, was established in 1846 by Gen. Zachary Taylor and named for Maj. Jacob Brown, who was killed later in that year in its defense against a Mexican attack. It was captured and held for a short time in 1859 by the Mexican brigand Juan Cortina, and in the last year of the Civil War was taken from the Confederates by Federal troops. Since 1865 its 288 acres have been occupied by a United States garrison.

L. W. NEWTON

Brown University, founded in 1764 as Rhode Island College, and located at Warren, R. I., is the seventh oldest institution of higher learning in the United States. Brown was established under the fostering care of the Baptists but with the aid of other Christian denominations admitted to a share in the corporate control. The charter was most liberal—the embodiment of a spiritual heritage from Roger Williams—declaring that "all the Members hereof shall forever enjoy full free absolute and uninterrupted Liberty of Conscience."

The first president, James Manning, was elected and the first students were admitted in 1765. The first class was graduated in 1769. In 1770 the college was moved to Providence.

The college was closely associated with the struggle for independence. It was closed from 1776 to 1782 and University Hall was occupied as hospital and barracks by American and French troops.

In 1804 the college was named Brown University in honor of Nicholas Brown, a generous benefactor.

Brown has developed from a small English colonial college into a collegiate university consisting of three major subdivisions: The College, an undergraduate college for men; Pembroke College, an undergraduate college for women; and the Graduate School, for men and women.

[W. C. Bronson, *The History of Brown University, 1764-1914.*]

JAMES P. ADAMS

Brown v. Maryland, 1827 (12 Wheaton 419), which related to the right of a state to control the sale of imported merchandise, afforded Marshall an opportunity to supplement his first opinion on the meaning of the commerce clause[qv] of the Constitution as originally stated in Gibbons v. Ogden[qv].

Affirmed by the Court of Appeals, the case came to the Supreme Court on a writ of error. Marshall's opinion reversed the affirmation on the ground that the Constitution prohibits a state from levying imposts or duties on imports or exports, except what may be "absolutely necessary for executing its inspection laws." The principles stated have been upheld by nearly all courts that have dealt with the subject of commerce.

[A. J. Beveridge, *John Marshall*, Vol. 4.]

THOMAS ROBSON HAY

Brownists, a term applied to groups in England (*ca.* 1580–1660) which openly separated from the established church, was derived from Robert Browne, author of *Reformation without tarrying for anie*, 1583. Browne advocated an essentially Congregational[qv] polity, a church made up only of the visible elect who were to choose and install their own officers. Later Separatists[qv], including the Pilgrims[qv] at Plymouth, probably owed much to Browne, as also did the settlers of Massachusetts Bay[qv], although the latter always insisted that they had never "separated" from the Church of England.

[Henry Martyn Dexter, *Congregationalism of the Last Three Hundred Years;* Perry Miller, *Orthodoxy in Massachusetts.*]

PERRY MILLER

Brown's, John, Raid. *See* Harpers Ferry Raid, The.

Brownstown and Detroit Treaties (1807–8). At Detroit, Nov. 17, 1807, Gov. William Hull negotiated the cession of the Indian title to the southeast quarter of Michigan plus the portion of Ohio lying north of the Maumee. Between this tract and the settled portion of the United States lay an extensive area still in Indian possession.

Accordingly, at Brownstown, Nov. 25, 1808, Hull negotiated a second treaty whereby title to a roadway 120 feet wide, running from Maumee Rapids to Lower Sandusky (modern Fremont) and thence southward to the Greenville Treaty[qv] line, was secured. The object of the Brownstown Treaty was to make possible travel by land to Detroit, without trespassing upon the Indian domain.

[*See* U. S. Statutes at Large, VII, for the treaties; C. C. Royce, *Indian Land Cessions*, House Docs., 56 Cong., 1 Sess., Vol. 118, for analysis of treaties and maps of cessions made.]

M. M. QUAIFE

Brownstown and Monguagon Battles (Aug. 5, 9, 1812). Gen. Hull invaded Canada from Detroit in July, 1812. The British, operating from Fort Malden[qv], cut his line of communications with Ohio, which ran along the Detroit River. Two successive efforts to reopen it failed. In the first, Maj. Van Horne's 200 dragoons were routed by Tecumseh (Brownstown, Aug. 5). In the second, Col. Miller's force of 600 men won a victory (Monguagon, Aug. 9) but were unable to follow it up. The road remained closed, compelling Hull to withdraw from Canada a few days later.

[M. M. Quaife, The Story of Brownstown, in *Burton Historical Collection Leaflet*, IV, 65-80.]

M. M. QUAIFE

Brownsville Affair. About midnight of Aug. 13, 1906, unidentified Negro soldiers of Companies B, C and D, 25th U. S. Infantry at Fort Brown, Brownsville, Texas, angered at slights from white civilians, marched into town and shot into houses and at citizens indiscriminately, killing one man and wounding a policeman. Their officers investigated next morning but learned nothing. President Roosevelt ordered a thorough investigation which resulted in proof that the guilty men were from these companies but failed to identify them because no soldier would give evidence against his comrades. On Nov. 5 the President ordered 159 privates and non-commissioned officers from these companies and eight others "discharged without honor from the Army" and "forever debarred from the Army or Navy" because of their "conspiracy of silence." Sen. J. B. Foraker championed the cause of the discharged men; but after the Senate Committee on Military Affairs had conducted a lengthy investigation the majority sustained the President.

[U. S. Documents 5252-6; 5888-9.]

CHARLES W. RAMSDELL

Brussels Monetary Conference, THE (Nov. 22–Dec. 17, 1892), authorized by the Sherman Silver Purchase Act[qv], failed because Great Britain rejected American proposals for increasing silver coinage; the Americans rejected the British plan for small European silver purchases. This, with other circumstances, caused the repeal of the Sherman Act.

[International Monetary Conference, *Report and Journal.*]

W. C. MALLALIEU

Bryan-Chamorro Treaty, THE, between the United States and Nicaragua was signed Aug. 5, 1914. It granted to the United States in perpetuity the exclusive right to build an interoceanic canal in Nicaragua[qv], subject to a subsequent agreement regarding details of construction and operation; and also a ninety-nine-year lease of Great and Little Corn Islands and a right to establish a naval base in the Gulf of Fonseca. Nicaragua received $3,000,000.

Costa Rica and El Salvador protested against the treaty. Costa Rica claimed that an arbitral award by President Cleveland in 1888 had bound Nicaragua not to make grants for canal purposes without consulting her, because of her interest in the San Juan River. El Salvador asserted that the waters of the Gulf of Fonseca belonged jointly to El Salvador, Nicaragua and Honduras. Both appealed to the Central American Court[qv] which decided that Nicaragua had violated her neighbors' rights and should take steps to restore the legal status existing before the treaty. It did not declare the treaty itself invalid, because it had no jurisdiction over the United States. Nicaragua refused to accept the decision and the treaty remained in force. The proposed naval base has not been established and the Corn Islands remain under Nicaraguan jurisdiction, except for a small area occupied by the United States for a lighthouse.

[I. J. Cox, *Nicaragua and the United States, 1909-1927.*]

DANA G. MUNRO

Bryan Treaty Model ("Cooling-Off"), THE, was used in the treaties for the Advancement of Peace negotiated by William J. Bryan, Secretary of State (1913–15). By separate negotiations, thirty treaties were signed in which the essential features are, (1) submission of all controversies to investigation before proceeding to arbitration or satisfaction of honor, (2) a permanent international commission to make the investigation, (3) one year to be allowed for investigation and no hostilities to occur before report is made and (4) reservation by each nation of the right to decide, after the report, what action it should take. Ratifications of twenty-two treaties were exchanged, and commissions were appointed; however, no questions have been submitted under the terms of these treaties.

[Carnegie Endowment for International Peace, *Treaties for the Advancement of Peace.*]

ROSCOE R. HILL

Bryan's Station, Ky., was established in 1779 by four Bryan brothers from North Carolina. The occupants of this parallelogram of some forty cabins withstood several Indian attacks, the most important of which occurred in August, 1782, when they were besieged by about 300 Indians and Canadians under Capt. William Caldwell and Simon Girty. The battle of Blue Licks[qv] occurred about sixty miles northeast three days later.

[Reuben T. Durrett, *Bryan's Station,* Filson Club Publication, No. 12.]

JONATHAN T. DORRIS

Buccaneers, or Freebooters, called by the Dutch *Vlijbooters,* are terms commonly applied to the adventurers who infested the West Indies in the 16th, 17th and 18th centuries. Among themselves they were known as "Brethren of the Coast." It seems probable that a group of Normans early settled on an island, perhaps Tortuga, and organized themselves into a small band, living off wild animals and preying upon the neighboring Spanish colonies. They formed a picturesque lot, traveling in pairs, living in the open, dyeing their clothes in blood and going about armed to the teeth. The Spaniards early began to attack these groups and to destroy the wild cattle and swine which were their principal source of food. Driven to self-defense and finally to open warfare with Spain, they took to the sea and began a career of piracy[qv], plunder, murder and rapine, attacking Spanish commerce and colonial towns. This life appealed to many individuals of various nationalities and the number of buccaneers increased rapidly. But about 1670 a partial stop was put to this piracy in the Caribbean and some of the buccaneers went to the Pacific to continue their profession. Finally by the Treaty of Ryswick[qv] in 1697 buccaneering was practically suppressed. Among the picturesque leaders of the buccaneers were Pierre La Grand, François l'Olonnais, Henry Morgan, Van Horn, Jacques Cassard, Edward Teach (Blackbeard), Bartholomew Roberts, François Thurot, Jean d'Albarade and Montbars "The Exterminator."

[Maurice Besson, *The Scourge of the Indies;* Alfred Sternbeck, *Filibusters and Buccaneers.*]

A. CURTIS WILGUS

Buck Stove and Range Case. In 1906 the metal polishers in the Buck Stove and Range Company, St. Louis, struck for a nine-hour day. The American Federation of Labor[qv] put the company on their "unfair list," whereupon the company obtained a sweeping injunction forbidding this boycott[qv]. For refusal to obey, Samuel Gompers, John Mitchell and Frank Morrison were sentenced to prison for contempt, but did not serve. The case was outlawed in 1914 by the Supreme Court under the statute of limitations (*see* Clayton Act).

[H. W. Laidler, *Boycotts and the Labor Struggle.*]

H. U. FAULKNER

Buckboards. Originally designed for personal transportation in mountain regions, these distinctively American four-wheeled vehicles, with one seat resting upon elastic boards fastened directly to the axles, were widely used in newly settled sections.

[Buckboards may be seen in many museums and institutes.]

HARVEY L. CARTER

Buckland Races. Near Buckland Mills, on Broad Run, J. E. B. Stuart (C.), with Wade Hampton's cavalry division, covering Lee's retirement from Bristoe to the Rappahannock[qqv], on Oct. 19, 1863, turned on Kilpatrick's pursuing Federal cavalry, while Fitzhugh Lee's division charged the Federal flank. Kilpatrick was routed, fleeing five miles to Haymarket and Gainesville. The Confederates derisively called the affair "Buckland Races."

[J. W. Thomason, Jr., *Jeb Stuart; Official Records, Union and Confederate Armies,* Vol. XXIX.]

JOSEPH MILLS HANSON

Buckshot War (1838). As a result of the state election of 1838, both parties claimed control of the Pennsylvania House of Representatives. Two speakers were elected. A mob, largely from Philadelphia, assembled in Harrisburg, threatened violence and forced Thaddeus Stevens, Charles B. Penrose and Thomas H. Burrowes to escape from the Senate chamber through a window. Gov. Ritner called for United States troops which the President refused, whereupon the governor called out the Philadelphia militia, requisitioning among other equipment thirteen rounds of buckshot cartridges, whence the name "The Buckshot War." Three Whigs voted with the Democrats enabling them to organize the House, whereupon order was restored.

[Mueller, *The Whig Party in Pennsylvania.*]

H. H. SHENK

Bucktails, THE (1818–26), were a New York State party opposed to the canal policy of Gov.

DeWitt Clinton; named from a Tammany insignia, a deer's tail worn in the hat.

[J. D. Hammond, *Political History of the State of New York.*]

MILTON W. HAMILTON

Budget, Director of the, is an official created by the Budget and Accounting Act[qv] passed by Congress in 1921. The Director, who is the head of the Bureau of the Budget, is appointed by the President alone and for an indefinite term. Although nominally attached to the Treasury Department[qv], the Director enjoys complete freedom from control either by Congress or by any of the executive departments, being responsible to the President alone, as his personal agent. Annually, the Bureau of the Budget obtains from the various branches of the Government their respective estimates of funds needed for the ensuing fiscal period. These estimates the Director and his staff examine carefully in consultation with the agencies concerned. The revised estimates are then gone over by the President and Director, and may undergo further and drastic revision. When in final form, they become the basis for the annual budget submitted to Congress each January.

[W. F. Willoughby, *The National Budget System;* C. G. Dawes, *The First Year of the Budget in the United States.*]

P. ORMAN RAY

Budget and Accounting Act of 1921. Several states began experimenting with budgetary procedures around 1910, and President Taft's Commission on Economy and Efficiency recommended them for the Federal Government in 1911. After much discussion, Congress passed a bill in 1919, but it was vetoed, for technical reasons, by President Wilson. The adoption of such legislation was made a campaign issue by the Republicans in 1920; a budget bill was enacted in 1921 and signed by President Harding. Drafted by W. F. Willoughby and other experts in fiscal procedure, the act has two main parts : (1) that providing for the Bureau of the Budget, under a Director[qv], appointed by the President for an indefinite term and responsible to him; (2) that providing for the General Accounting Office, under a Controller General, appointed by the President for a term of fifteen years and intended to be entirely independent.

[Daniel T. Selko, *The Administration of Federal Finances;* W. F. Willoughby, *The National Budget System with Suggestions for Its Improvement.*]

W. BROOKE GRAVES

Buena Vista, Battle of (Feb. 22–23, 1847). During the Mexican War[qv] Gen. Zachary Taylor had advanced his army of 4700 men from Monterrey[qv] to a mountain pass south of Saltillo. Near the hacienda of Buena Vista he encountered a Mexican force under Santa Anna three times the size of his own. Though the Americans lost ground the first day, they won a brilliant victory on the second and the Mexicans withdrew. Taylor gained a reputation which made him President, but the further conquest of Mexico was entrusted to Gen. Scott.

[N. W. Stephenson, *Texas and the Mexican War.*]

L. W. NEWTON

Buenaventura River Myth was based on erroneous early Spanish and American maps which showed a river flowing from the Rockies into Great Salt Lake and emptying into the Pacific Ocean. Some overland emigrant parties even expected to reach California in boats. As late as 1844 Frémont was searching for this fabulous river.

[Allan Nevins, *Frémont, the West's Greatest Adventurer.*]

JEANNE ELIZABETH WIER

Buffalo, N. Y., was named for Buffalo Creek, which in the French occupation was known as Rivière aux Chevaux. There are many theories to account for the "translation" from Chevaux to Buffalo; none have been fully substantiated, but it is reasonably certain that the native habitat of the buffalo was never so far east. When in 1799 Dutch land speculators (the Holland Land Company[qv]) bought most of the Phelps-Gorham Purchase[qv], consisting of a million acres west of the Genesee River, they commissioned Joseph Ellicott to survey and offer for sale lots in a village on Buffalo Creek, to be called New Amsterdam. The Dutch name, however, never was generally used and when the village became the county seat in 1807 it officially took the new name. The town was completely destroyed by the British and Indians in December, 1813, but was rapidly rebuilt, became the terminus of the Erie Canal[qv] in 1825 and was a city by 1832.

[F. H. Severance, *An Old Frontier of France;* R. W. Bingham, *The Cradle of the Queen City.*]

JULIAN PARK

Buffalo, THE, or more properly the American bison, at the time of the discovery occupied about one third of the continent from 63° N. Lat. in Canada to about 25° N. Lat. in Mexico, and from the Blue Mountains of Oregon to the western portions of New York, Pennsylvania, Virginia and the Carolinas. The chief habitat was, however, the plains between the Missouri River and the Rocky Mountains. Fossil remains date to the mid-Pleistocene period.

Easily hunted and of large size—the males reaching 2000 pounds—the buffalo were everywhere a favorite source of food for the Indians and frontier whites. As civilization advanced westward the animals were exterminated and by 1850 few if any remained east of the Mississippi. The dry plains, however, still contained numbers so vast as to be almost impossible of computation. Gen. Phil H. Sheridan, in 1866, estimated 100,000,000 buffalo in the region between Camp Supply, I. T., and Fort Dodge, Kans., and this was only part of the western buffalo.

Plains Indians based their civilization and religion to a large extent on the buffalo, as those farther east based theirs on the maize. Methods of killing included stalking, stampeding herds over cliffs, and driving them into *cul de sacs*. When horses were introduced in the plains, the methods of pursuit and the surround were added. Every part of the buffalo was useful to the Indians, who depended on the bison for food, shelter, weapons and clothing. Natural increase, however, kept pace with the slaughter until the advent of the white man.

Building of the Union Pacific and Kansas Pacific railroads[qqv], the early trains of which were sometimes stopped by herds crossing the tracks, led to the disappearance of the animals in the central plains and by 1875 there were two distinct groups, the northern and southern. The railroads furnished transportation outlets and in the 1870's hide and meat hunters began a systematic and wholesale destruction, shipping robes and meat to the East. By 1878 the southern herd was practically extinct, although the four last survivors were not killed until 1889. Similarly the northern herd was exterminated by 1884, except for a few individuals. Buffalo bones, gathered by settlers, later were important in commerce.

Dr. William T. Hornaday, of the National Museum, first called the nation's attention to the virtual disappearance of the buffalo in 1886. He made a census in 1889 which showed a total of only 1091 American bison existing throughout the world. This was the low ebb. Many individuals became interested and in 1905 the American Bison Society was organized. Through its efforts public consciousness was aroused and today the danger of complete extinction seems ended.

In 1903 a census revealed in the United States 41 herds in 24 states, with 969 animals, and a total in the world of 1644. The 1933 census showed 121 herds in 41 states, with 4404 animals, while Canada contained 17,043 and the world total was 21,701.

[Martin S. Garretson, *The American Bison;* E. Douglas Branch, *The Hunting of the Buffalo.*]

PAUL I. WELLMAN

Buffalo Chips was the dried excrement of the American bison. It was widely used for fuel by the first white men on the Great Plains.

EVERETT DICK

Buffalo Hunters' War (1877). Comanche[qv] malcontents led by Black Horse (Tu-ukumah) left the Indian Territory[qv], December, 1876, for the Staked Plains[qv] of Texas. Feb. 22, 1877, they attacked buffalo hunters' camps in the Red River country of the Texas Panhandle, killing or wounding several. Forty-five hunters left Rath's trading post on Double Mountain Creek a few days later, and trailed the Indians, whose camp was attacked near Thompson's Canyon, Texas, March 18. The hunters were repulsed and the Indians escaped. One white man was killed and several were wounded; the Indian loss is not known. The inconclusive battle ended Comanche attacks.

[John R. Cook, *The Border and the Buffalo;* Paul I. Wellman, *Death on the Prairie.*]

PAUL I. WELLMAN

Buffalo Trails. The first thoroughfares of this continent, save for the time-obliterated paths of mastodon, musk-ox and Moundbuilder, were the traces made by buffalo and deer in seasonal migration and in quest of—or between—feeding-grounds and salt licks[qv]. Many of these routes, hammered by countless hoofs instinctively following watersheds and the crests of ridges in avoidance of lower places' summer muck and winter snowdrifts, were followed by the Indians as courses to hunting grounds and as warriors' paths; were invaluable to explorers and adopted by pioneers. Buffalo traces were characteristically north and south; yet their major east-west trails —through Cumberland Gap[qv]; along the New York watershed; from the Potomac through the Allegheny divide to the Ohio headwaters; through the Blue Ridge Mountains to upper Kentucky—anticipated the courses of trunk railways. And in Sen. Thomas Benton's phrase saluting these sagacious pathmakers, the buffalo blazed the way for the railroads to the Pacific.

[A. B. Hulbert, *Historic Highways of America,* I.]

E. DOUGLAS BRANCH

Buffer State. *See* Indian Barrier State (Proposed).

Buffington Island Skirmish, THE (July 19, 1863), in Meigs County, Ohio, contributed to the capture of the Confederate raider, Gen. John Morgan, who was seeking to escape across the Ohio River at a ford opposite Buffington Island (*see* Morgan's Raids, The). Delayed overnight, he was almost surrounded by Federal cavalry next day and the battle ended in a rout. Morgan and some 1200 men escaped but the raid finally ended in his capture at Salineville on July 26.

[Whitelaw Reid, *Ohio in the War*, Vol. I.]

EUGENE H. ROSEBOOM

Buford Expedition (1856). As a part of the effort to make Kansas a slave state (*see* Border War; Kansas Struggle), Col. Jefferson Buford of Eufaula, Ala., in April organized and equipped for settlement, mainly at his own expense, 400 men largely from Alabama, Georgia and South Carolina. In Kansas, Buford's men participated in many of the conflicts between the free and slave state factions.

[W. L. Fleming, The Buford Expedition to Kansas, *American Historical Review*, VI, 38-48.]

HENRY T. SHANKS

Building and Loan Associations, started in Frankford, Pa., in 1831, are the most successful form of co-operative credit in the United States. There have been various forms: (1) the terminating, ending when the given group all have their homes; (2) the serial, which start new groups at intervals; (3) the permanent, where one may start any time; (4) the Dayton, Ohio, plan started in 1870, where the payments do not have to be made regularly. At their best they permit doing business at low cost, making use of the knowledge of the members and what amounts to an amortization plan in paying back the loans. In the 1890's national associations failed and after 1931 there were more failures. The Reconstruction Finance Corporation[qv] has aided associations by lending them money. The Federal Home Loan Bank Act of June 13, 1933, permits them to get Federal charters and become Federal Savings and Loan Associations[qv].

[R. L. Garis, *Principles of Money Credit and Banking.*]

JAMES D. MAGEE

Building Materials. The first settlers in America naturally had to depend upon timber for a quick building material, and thatched, clay-chinked log cabins[qv], with greased-paper windows if any at all, were the first houses. Hand-split shingles (clapboards or shakes) soon began to be riven from four-foot blocks of wood with mallet and frow. Such roofs, usually of white oak, may still be seen upon a few houses in our Southern hill region. The first chimneys were of rough stone, sometimes topped with wood and clay. In later years pioneer cabins where stone was scarce often had the fireplace only of stone, the chimney from there upward being a pen of hand-split, two-inch oaken sticks, laid log-cabin fashion, chinked and lined with clay. A few such chimneys still survive.

The next type of house was of lumber, often hand-sawn. When sawmills were brought from Europe we could turn out our own plain lumber, but for many decades we continued to import for the finer houses columns, pilasters, molding, newel posts, balustrades, panelling, etc., not to mention glass and brass door hardware. Laths were split by hand until about 1825.

The Dutch and German settlers showed a liking for stone, with the result that eastern and southern New York, New Jersey and eastern Pennsylvania are still dotted with sturdy dwellings, barns and water mills of rough stone. On Long Island, where stone was scarce, most Dutch houses had all-shingled exteriors, like some on the New England coast. The Dutch stone houses often had weatherboarded gables. Many an old house, rebuilt or enlarged, shows a commingling of materials—this outer wall of stone, that one of brick, perhaps another one weatherboarded. The first brick[qv] were imported from England and Holland. Careful New England builders immersed their brick in boiling oil to make them damp-proof. Hollow wooden columns were sometimes filled with rock salt to guard against moisture and worms.

Although there was a short-lived attempt at glass making at Salem, Mass., about 1640, and though glass making was more soundly established at New Amsterdam in 1645, many American communities saw no glass windows until 1700 or afterward. The industry grew rapidly in the 18th century. Until after 1800 such glass as was used in the Ohio Valley crossed the Alleghenies on pack horses. Hand-wrought nails were a very early product in America. By 1790, machine-made nails were beginning to appear, coming first from England; but wrought nails were still being used long after 1800. By the middle of the 19th century we were producing our own brick, nails, glass, millwork, iron door hardware, and fire irons.

No buildings of American marble were erected until the latter half of the 19th century. Marble mantels were imported from Italy for the finer houses as long as the wood fireplace prevailed. The hob grate for burning coal was introduced about 1750, and as a finish around it, pictorial glazed tiles were brought from Holland. Wallpapers, highly pictorial, began to be imported from Europe about 1735. Pennsylvania's slate quarries were producing in the 18th century and roofing many of the better houses of that region. Metal roofing appeared in the 19th century—first, sheet copper, then tin, then—toward the close of the century—galvanized iron, accompanied by tarred paper and gravel. Composition shingles containing asbestos and other elements are 20th-century devices. Tile roofs were rare in America until this century.

The adobe*qv* house of the dry Southwest, usually built of huge, sun-dried earthen bricks—though sometimes with one-piece, molded walls—was an early feature of the landscape which has been returning to favor in that area since 1900. Protected on the outside with stucco, it makes a durable and comfortable house.

Brick and stone were laid in lime mortar until after 1818, when cement-making rock was discovered in central New York and soon afterwards in other places. A house of reinforced concrete beams and slabs was built in 1875 and in the latter 1880's and 1890's some small poured concrete or monolithic buildings were erected, reinforced with hoop iron and wire rope. Concrete blocks began to be manufactured about the same time.

Some wrought-iron beams and girders were brought to this country from Europe about 1840 and mixed with timber in building construction. Cooper Institute in New York, built 1854–59 by Peter Cooper, who manufactured bridge iron, was probably the first building in America with floors resting entirely upon iron frames. Even in the 1870's and 1880's buildings eight and ten stories in height were being supported entirely on masonry walls, which of course must be inconveniently thick near the ground. The production of steel beams, begun in 1885, brought about the birth of the skyscraper*qv* about five years later. With it came metal lath and the hollow terra-cotta wall. Quartz glass, which admits the ultra-violet rays of the sun, glass bricks, which make translucent walls possible, and the all-steel frame house, cut for assembly on the site of the proposed house, are among the most important products of the third and fourth decades of the 20th century.

[J. Leander Bishop, *A History of American Manufactures.*]

ALVIN F. HARLOW

Buildings. *See* Architecture, American.

Bull Boats. When Hudson's Bay Company*qv* traders first visited the Mandan Indians*qv* in 1790 they found that tribe possessed of tublike boats with framework of willow poles, covered with raw buffalo hides. Later, frontiersmen who ascended the Missouri noted this light, convenient craft. From 1810 to 1830, American fur traders on the tributaries of the Missouri regularly built boats eighteen to thirty feet long, using the methods of construction employed by the Indians in making their circular boats. These elongated bull boats were capable of transporting two tons of fur down the shallow waters of the Platte.

[Phil E. Chappell, *A History of the Missouri River.*]

CARL P. RUSSELL

Bull Garrison House, The (Dec. 15, 1675), was located on Tower Hill, South Kingstown, R. I. During King Philip's War*qv* it was attacked and burned by the Narragansett Indians*qv*, fifteen of its defenders losing their lives.

[*Rhode Island Historical Society Collection*, January, 1918, and July, 1925.]

HOWARD M. CHAPIN

"Bull Moose" Party, The, was a popular nickname given to the Progressive party*qv* of 1912–16 which nominated Theodore Roosevelt for the Presidency at a national convention in Chicago, Ill., in August, 1912. The Progressives seceded from the Republican party*qv* following the renomination of President William H. Taft. The name itself was a tribute to Mr. Roosevelt who often used the term "bull moose" to describe the strength and vigor of a person.

Thus he wrote, following his nomination for the Vice-Presidency on the Republican ticket in 1900, in a letter to Sen. M. A. Hanna, "I am as strong as a bull moose and you can use me to the limit." Also, when shot by a would-be assassin in Milwaukee, Wis., on the evening of Oct. 14, 1912, he insisted on immediately filling an engagement to speak, saying to the audience, "It takes more than that to kill a Bull Moose."

The party was in large part reunited with and reabsorbed into the Republican party during the campaign of 1916*qv*, after the nomination of Charles E. Hughes, who was acceptable to Mr. Roosevelt and the leading Progressives.

[J. B. Bishop, *Theodore Roosevelt and His Time.*]

WILLIAM STARR MYERS

Bull Run, First Battle of (July 21, 1861). This, the first major engagement, has been described as "the best planned and worst fought battle" of the Civil War. The principal Union army, under Gen. Irvin McDowell, was mobilized about Washington. Gen. Robert Patterson (U.), with a smaller army, was sent to "retain" Gen.

Joseph E. Johnston (C.) in the Shenandoah Valley. Gen. P. G. T. Beauregard (C.) occupied the line of Bull Run Creek, which lies across the main highways from Washington southward. His advanced force under Gen. M. L. Bonham was based on Fairfax Courthouse to watch McDowell's army. McDowell had available about 30,000 men and 49 guns; Beauregard, about 24,000 and 35 guns; Johnston, about 9000 to Patterson's 12,000. None of these armies was thoroughly organized or disciplined.

Public opinion compelled President Lincoln to order McDowell to move forward. The Federal advance guard drove in Bonham's pickets on July 17. In accordance with previous orders, Bonham withdrew to Centreville, waited until dark, then retired behind Bull Run where the road from Washington to Richmond crossed at Mitchell's Ford and where Beauregard expected the main attack. The Confederates were disposed as follows: Ewell held the right at Union Mills Ford below the Orange and Alexandria Railroad; D. R. Jones protected McLean's Ford two miles upstream; Longstreet held Blackburn's Ford a mile above; Bonham was a mile and a half farther; Cocke guarded Ball's and Lewis' fords, one and one half and two and a half miles above Mitchell's; a mile farther Evans held the Stone Bridge where the Warrenton Turnpike crossed Bull Run. Thus the Confederate line extended about eight miles behind a shallow, meandering creek. Ewell was supported by Holmes' brigade, while Early was behind Jones and Longstreet. Tyler (U.), commanding McDowell's advanced force, on his own initiative, made a reconnoissance in force on July 18, but was sharply repulsed by Longstreet and Bonham aided by Early (*see* Blackburn's Ford, Battle at).

Eluding Patterson, Johnston and part of his army reached Bull Run on Saturday, July 20. Though the ranking officer, Johnston did not assume personal direction of the Confederate operations till the middle of the ensuing battle, meanwhile stationing his troops on the slope behind Beauregard's line. McDowell and Beauregard planned to turn each other's left flank. Ewell, on the Confederate right, was to cross Bull Run at daylight of July 21, the other brigades to follow. Beauregard's order did not reach Ewell. Longstreet, after crossing, waited in vain for word of his attack. By 7 A.M., when Jones received his orders, Sherman (U.) and Schenck (U.) were attacking the Confederate left at the Stone Bridge, Burnside (U.), at the same time, attempting to flank this end of the Confederate line. Evans, at the Stone Bridge, promptly deployed his scant half brigade to meet these movements. Johnston sent Jackson (C.) and Imboden (C.) to support Evans and soon Bee (C.) and Hampton (C.) followed. Fierce fighting raged from Bull Run to the Henry House plateau, to which the Confederates were driven. Here Bee lost his life and Jackson won his name of "Stonewall." The arrival of another portion of Johnston's army turned the tide in favor of the Confederates. The Federals were driven across Bull Run in disorder, pursued along the Warrenton Pike. No fighting of any consequence had taken place on the Confederate right.

When the break took place on the Federal right, Johnston ordered Bonham and Longstreet to move in pursuit. The Federal withdrawal turned into a rout as the troops streamed back in the direction of Washington. The Confederate pursuit started from Mitchell's Ford in the direction of Centreville at which point it was halted, the Confederates later returning to Bull Run. Bitter controversy afterwards ensued between Davis and Johnston and Beauregard as to the responsibility for not pursuing the defeated Federals into Washington. Military critics think this was not feasible. The staff work and courier service on both sides was miserable and a heavy rainstorm added to the confusion and uncertainty. From some 13,000 men actually engaged, the Federals lost about 500 killed, 1000 wounded and 1200 missing; the Confederates, with about 11,000 engaged, lost about 400 killed, 1600 wounded and 13 missing. They captured 25 guns and much other material. But it was a Pyrrhic victory. The South was made overconfident, while the North was spurred to earnest effort.

[R. M. Johnston, *Bull Run: Its Strategy and Tactics.*]

MILLEDGE L. BONHAM, JR.

Bull Run, The Second Battle of, was initiated by the decision of Gen. R. E. Lee, Aug. 24, 1862, at Jeffersonton, Va., to send the 23,000 troops of Lt. Gen. T. J. ("Stonewall") Jackson to break the communications of Maj. Gen. John Pope's Army of Virginia[qv], which was unassailably placed on the upper stretches of the Rappahannock River, Virginia. Jackson started before daylight, Aug. 25, passed Thoroughfare Gap and, on the evening of the 26th, reached Bristoe Station. The next day Jackson plundered Pope's base at Manassas Junction and proceeded to Groveton Heights, five miles N.W. of Manassas. There, on the 28th, he attacked King's division. On Aug. 29 Pope in turn attacked Jackson, who with difficulty beat off repeated assaults. Lee, meantime, had brought up the remainder of his army, 32,000 men, and had formed them on Jackson's right. By nightfall of the 29th Lee's line formed an obtuse angle from N. to S. (Longstreet) and thence S.W. to N.E. (Jackson). Pope, re-enforced by a large part of the Army of the Potomac[qv], renewed the attack on Jackson on the 30th, but failed to confront Longstreet with sufficient force. Lee accordingly ordered a general attack which swept Pope from his positions. Heavy rain on Aug. 31 delayed pursuit and made possible the retreat by Pope within the Washington defenses. Pope blamed his defeat on FitzJohn Porter[qv], who was cashiered and was not vindicated until 1886, but Pope himself was not again trusted with field command. His losses, Aug. 16–Sept. 2, were 14,462; those of Lee were 9112.

[J. C. Ropes, *The Army under Pope;* D. S. Freeman, *R. E. Lee*, Vol. 2.] DOUGLAS SOUTHALL FREEMAN

Bull-Whacker. *See* Mule Skinner.

Bulldoze. During the Reconstruction[qv] period a Federal marshal was investigating an attempt to assassinate a registrar of voters in East Feliciana Parish, La. (1875). The natives refused him all information, and as the marshal stood pondering he was approached by a half-witted German who shouted, "Bull dooza mit der hooza!" The expletive had no meaning whatsoever, but to the frightened marshal it sounded like a threat from the Ku Klux Klan and he fled, which result was so satisfactory that the term "Bulldoze" came into general use throughout the South, with the generic meaning to intimidate in a bullying manner.

[T. Jones Cross, The True Etymology of Bulldoze, *Proceedings of the Historical Society of East and West Baton Rouge*, 1918.] MILLEDGE L. BONHAM, JR.

Bullion. Although both silver and gold were standards of value from 1792 to 1834, bimetallism[qv] did not prevail in practice, the circulating medium continuing to be a mixture of foreign and domestic coins and notes. The mint ratio overvalued silver, which would theoretically have caused silver imports and gold exports. Lack of gold and other factors prevented this, and in the years prior to 1806 silver dollars were exported as rapidly as minted until their coinage was discontinued.

Congress changed the mint ratio to approximately 16 to 1 in 1834, but this overvalued gold. Silver dollars, however, were slow to disappear, and from 1834 to 1844—the only such period in our history—silver and gold circulated interchangeably.

After 1844 silver dollars disappeared from circulation, and in 1851 silver was made a subordinate monetary metal, which it has ever since remained. From 1862 to 1879 the actual standard was paper. In 1873 Congress dropped the long unfamiliar "standard silver dollar" and provided for a "silver trade dollar" for export purposes, a gesture to mining interests. The increasing output of American silver mines, however, demonetization in Europe and the consequent declining market price of silver soon made free coinage of silver a national political issue. The "Crime of '73"[qv] was discovered. Free coinage of silver was demanded.

A compromise, the Bland-Allison Act[qv] (Feb. 28, 1878), resulted in the purchase and coinage during twelve years of 291,000,000 oz. of silver at a cost of $308,000,000. However, the price of silver was not thereby stabilized. On June 17, 1890, Congress passed the Sherman Silver Purchase Act[qv], increasing the monthly purchases to 4,500,000 oz.; but the act was repealed Nov. 1, 1893, after 169,000,000 oz., costing about $156,000,000, had been bought. Depression fostered further inflation sentiment. Silver featured the 1896 election campaign, but such factors as transition to world-power status, returning prosperity and discovery of new gold fields, discouraged bimetallism and the act of March 14, 1900, specifically fixed the gold dollar as "the standard unit of value."

During the World War the gold standard was temporarily suspended through an export embargo. The sale of up to 350,000,000 oz. of silver coin to Great Britain and its subsequent replacement was authorized by the Pittman Act of 1918[qv]. March 6, 1933, gold payments and exports were again suspended; on April 5 gold circulation was discontinued and the metal nationalized. The "Thomas Amendment"[qv] of May 12, 1933, granted the President important currency powers. On June 5, 1933, all forms of United States currency[qv] were made unlimited legal tender[qv]. At London in July a silver agreement providing *inter alia* for United States Treasury purchases of silver was reached between eight countries, and on Dec. 21, 1933, President Roosevelt, by proclamation, opened the mints to the full American mine production of silver for four years on a basis yielding the domestic producer 64.64¢ an oz., or a substantial premium over the market price. This proclamation was several times amended, and extended through June, 1939. By congressional action completed July 5, 1939, domestic-mined silver was given a Treasury market at 71.11¢ an oz. on a permanent basis.

On Jan. 30, 1934, the Gold Reserve Act[qv] temporarily authorized the President to fix the dollar at from 60% to 50% of its former gold content. The President thereupon proclaimed its content at 15 5/21 grains of gold 9/10ths fine. The official price of gold was thus fixed at $35 an ounce and the dollar was externally linked to gold, although left internally inconvertible. The Gold Reserve Act created a $2,000,000,000 Stabilization Fund. It also continued to vest in the Secretary of the Treasury broad, permanent powers to buy and sell gold without price or other restriction.

The Silver Purchase Act of 1934[qv], approved June 19, called for indefinite purchases of silver until one fourth of the total national stock of gold and silver at their monetary values shall consist of silver, unless the price of silver should previously reach its monetary value ($1.29 + an ounce). Under this act over 1,673,100,000 oz. of silver had been acquired through May 31, 1939, and under the proclamation of Dec. 21, 1933, as amended, 277,100,000 oz.

[Neil Carothers, *Fractional Money;* Charles J. Bullock, *Monetary History of the United States.*]

HERBERT M. BRATTER

Bummers. A nickname applied to foragers of Sherman's army during its March to the Sea[qv] and north through the Carolinas[qv].

[*Battles and Leaders of the Civil War,* Vol. IV; B. H. Liddell Hart, *Sherman; Soldier, Realist, American.*]

JOSEPH MILLS HANSON

Buncombe is a term which, by 1828, had come into general use in political Washington to mean speechmaking designed for show or public applause. It is reputed to have originated a few years earlier in connection with a speech which Felix Walker made in Congress to please Buncombe County, N. C., in his congressional district.

[*Niles' Weekly Register,* XXXV, 1828, p. 66; J. H. Wheeler, *Historical Sketches of North Carolina, from 1584 to 1851,* II.]

E. MERTON COULTER

Bundling, a mode of courtship in colonial days where the parties instead of sitting up together went to bed together, with their clothes on. This custom, inherited from Europe, apparently originated as a matter of convenience and necessity where space and heat were lacking. It was confined largely to the poorer classes. Its prevalence seems to have ended in the late 18th century with the general improvement of living conditions.

[Henry Reed Stiles, *Bundling; Its Origin, Progress and Decline in America.*]

HUGH T. LEFLER

Bunker Hill (June 17, 1775). To force the British from Boston, on the night of the 16th of June the American militia besieging the town sent 1200 men to seize Bunker Hill, on the peninsula of Charlestown. Instead, the detachment built a small redoubt on Breed's Hill, nearer Boston[qv] but easily flanked. Working silently, they were not discovered until daybreak, when British warships, anchored below, opened an ineffective fire. Col. William Prescott, commanding in the redoubt, strengthened his left flank, toward the Mystic River, by a breastwork, a rail fence stuffed with hay, and a slight defense of stones on the beach. The defenders of these were joined by perhaps 2000 men, and were commanded by Maj. Gen. Israel Putnam, while in the redoubt Brig. Gen. Joseph Warren served as a volunteer. Meanwhile, under the command of Maj. Gen. Sir William Howe, 2000 British infantry, with a few field guns, landed below the redoubt.

Dividing his men into two wings, early in the afternoon Howe attacked both the redoubt and the rail fence, expecting first to turn the fence by a column along the beach, which would make it easily possible to storm in front. The attack was bloodily repulsed by the provincials, chiefly New Hampshire men under John Stark, and the remainder of the British withdrew after being but briefly in touch with the Americans. At the second attack the British advanced on both wings with great courage; but the provincials, as before holding their fire until the regulars were close, cut them to pieces and forced their withdrawal. Still trusting to the desperate frontal attack, in the final attempt Howe merely feinted against the fence, and for the first time attacked the redoubt with the bayonet. For the first time, also, his fieldpieces got within effective range and drove the defenders from the breastwork. What would have happened had the Americans had enough powder cannot be known; but Prescott's men were out of ammunition and, after a first severe fire, on his order, quitted the redoubt. In this assault fell Maj. Pitcairn, British commander at Lexington, and Joseph Warren. The defenders of the fence covered the American retreat. After an engagement lasting less than two hours, the British were masters of the peninsula, but with heavy casualties of 1054, while the Americans lost, in killed, wounded and prisoners, but 441. At first regarded by the Americans as a defeat, Bunker Hill, because of the way in which militia resisted regulars, came to be regarded as a moral victory, leading to a dangerous overconfidence in unpreparedness.

[*Historical Magazine,* June, 1868; S. A. Drake, *Bunker*

Hill; Richard Frothingham, *Siege of Boston;* Allen French, *First Year of the American Revolution.*]

ALLEN FRENCH

Bunker Hill Monument, commemorating the Revolutionary battle, its cornerstone laid by Lafayette in 1825, was dedicated in 1843, Daniel Webster being chief orator.

ALVIN F. HARLOW

Burchard Incident, THE, arose when Rev. S. D. Burchard, speaking from the same political platform as the Republican candidate, James G. Blaine, Oct. 30, 1884, described the Democracy as the party of "rum, Romanism and rebellion." Blaine's failure to offset the diatribe cost him Irish support and the election.

[David S. Muzzey, *James G. Blaine.*]

JEANNETTE P. NICHOLS

Bureaucracy. The term bureaucracy is used in both a narrow and a broad sense. Used narrowly, it means a system of conducting government through special bureaus each headed by a chief. Thus, in the national Treasury Department is the Bureau of Engraving and Printing, in the Department of Justice is the Bureau of Prisons, in the Navy Department is the Bureau of Navigation, in the Department of the Interior is the Bureau of Mines, in the Department of Agriculture is the Bureau of Animal Husbandry, in the Department of Commerce is the Bureau of the Census, while in the Department of Labor is the Children's Bureau, to mention only a few.

As generally used, however, the term has a much broader meaning, embracing within its scope all government officials. In this broad sense, bureaucracy in the United States includes not only the officials of the Federal Government but also those who conduct the affairs of the state and local governments.

From small beginnings, American bureaucracy has developed until it has attained gigantic proportions. The thirteen original states, each with simple machinery of government, have expanded to forty-eight, each with a complex governmental setup, requiring the services of about 250,000 persons. Within these states, over 175,000 local units of government have been developed, each having the powers to borrow money and to tax and each having a set of officials to carry on the functions of its particular unit. Altogether more than 900,000 persons are employed by these local governmental agencies. This figure does not include those engaged in public education, of whom there are over 1,000,000.

Likewise, the Federal Government has developed from a simple organization in 1789 to the complex establishment of today. From a mere handful of employees at first, the Federal civil service increased to about 3000 in 1800 and then grew until it reached 841,664 on June 30, 1937. This last figure was the highest in American history with the exception of the World War period.

Congress took the first steps to create a Federal bureaucracy in 1789 when it created the departments of State, Treasury and War, together with the office of Attorney General. By 1938 the Federal administrative machinery included approximately 140 different agencies. Among these were ten departments; a number of executive agencies under the President, but not connected with any of the regular departments, such as the Civil Service[qv] Commission which was created in 1883; and a group of about a dozen independent regulatory organizations, the first of which was the Interstate Commerce Commission[qv], created in 1887.

During the World War and again during the New Deal[qv], the Federal organization was complicated by agencies, known as councils, commissions, boards, administrations and governmental corporations[qv], which were set up for special purposes. Most of these were placed under the direction of the President in the executive branch of the government.

As the various governments, local, state and national, have assumed new functions, adding new officials to perform each function, the evils associated with bureaucracy have tended to become more pronounced. The more complex an organization is, the more likely it is to be involved in red tape. Action is impeded by a multitude of rules and regulations drawn up by the agency itself. Traditions, precedents and paper work become all important. Again there is a tendency to avoid responsibility. Each official is afraid to act without the approval of his superior. "Buck passing" is a common characteristic of bureaucrats.

In a bureaucracy the tendency is for officials to forget that they are in office to serve the people rather than to be served. They tend to become arrogant and arbitrary in their official conduct. Concerned with self-perpetuation in office they too often ignore the public welfare and become mere "time servers." Usually the public is too apathetic or indifferent to make any attempt to remedy the condition.

To prevent these evils the theory of rotation in office[qv] was early developed. Under this theory, officeholders were to be replaced before they developed an attitude of proprietorship toward their offices. Unfortunately, in practice, rotation in office degenerated into the spoils system[qv] and resulted in "amateurism" in government.

Experts in administration now are generally agreed that the evils of bureaucracy can be avoided by the establishment of a real career service in government. Admission to the service would be on the basis of ability, special training would be provided and promotions would be made in accordance with the manner in which the duties of office were performed. The chief policy determination, instead of being delegated to administrative officials, would properly be left to the legislative body while secondary discretion in carrying out policies would be exercised by a comparatively small group of elected officials.

[James M. Beck, *Our Wonderland of Bureaucracy; Better Government Personnel Report* of the Commission of Inquiry on Public Service Personnel.]

ERIK McKINLEY ERIKSSON

Burgesses, House of. *See* Colonial Assemblies.

Burghers were those citizens of an incorporated city who, under the Dutch (1657), enjoyed great or small burgher rights, and under the English were entitled by birth or admission by the magistrates to the designation of freemen[qv]. In New York and Albany only freemen, who had paid the required fees, could do business or ply a trade.

[A. C. Flick, ed., *History of the State of New York.*]

A. C. FLICK

Burgoyne's Invasion. In late spring, 1777, Gen. Burgoyne prepared to invade New York from Canada by the Lake Champlain-Hudson River route (*see* British Campaign of 1777). Lt. Col. St. Leger was given command of a small expedition which was to ascend the St. Lawrence, cross Lake Ontario and advance on Albany by the Mohawk Valley. Both commanders were instructed that their principal objective was junction with Sir William Howe. An order was prepared, but, through a mischance, never sent from England, commanding Howe to proceed up the Hudson. In spite of this fateful blunder, Howe knew the British plans, for he had received a copy of Burgoyne's instructions.

Burgoyne's army was made up of 3700 British regulars, 3000 German troops, 250 Canadians and Tories and 400 Indians. With his well equipped force he proceeded up Lake Champlain in late June and on July 1 was within four miles of Ticonderoga[qv], which, with Mt. Independence east of the lake, was garrisoned by about 2300 Continentals under Gen. St. Clair. In spite of militia reinforcements St. Clair wisely abandoned the fortress the night of July 5–6. Engagements with pursuing British at Hubbardton[qv], Skenesborough (now Whitehall) and Fort Ann did not prevent St. Clair from saving his army to form the nucleus of later resistance. The taking of Ticonderoga increased the confidence of the British and was at first a severe shock to the patriots; later, it proved a stimulus to resistance.

Burgoyne's progress now became very deliberate. He was retarded by his extensive baggage and by the fact that the transportation of his artillery up Lake George required all available boats, while his army proceeded overland. To oppose him there were 2000 Americans under Gen. Schuyler at Fort Edward; but Schuyler was reinforced July 12 by about 1700 from St. Clair's command and 600 Continentals from Peekskill. Retreating before Burgoyne's slow advance, Schuyler felled trees across the roads and encouraged the country people to burn their standing crops and drive off their cattle. His steadiness was of the utmost value to the American cause.

Meanwhile Howe, evidently believing the rebellion nearly crushed and that Burgoyne did not require his active co-operation, left Clinton at New York to make a sortie up the Hudson with such troops as could be spared from the garrison and went to Philadelphia.

Fortune now began to turn against Burgoyne. A raiding force despatched to secure patriot stores at Bennington[qv] was overwhelmed, Aug. 16, by Stark's New Hampshire militia and Warner's small force. St. Leger, besieging Fort Stanwix[qv], managed, at Oriskany[qv], to repulse a relieving body of militia under Herkimer, but his Indian allies fled in panic at news of the approach of a patriot force under Benedict Arnold and he abandoned his campaign.

Gen. Gates, now in command of the American army near the mouth of the Mohawk, had about 6000 effective troops. Reinforced by Morgan's Virginia riflemen, he moved northward and entrenched at Bemis Heights, about eight miles south of the hamlet of Saratoga[qv], now Schuylerville. Burgoyne, whose Indian scouts had fled, was close upon the American army before he realized its presence. The first battle of Freeman's Farm[qv] was fought Sept. 19. Both armies remained in position and Burgoyne waited, hoping for news of Clinton's expected advance up the Hudson. Clinton got no farther than the Highlands[qv], however. Meanwhile Gates' numbers were increasing, bodies of New England militia were gathering in Burgoyne's rear and the British supplies were running dangerously low. It was necessary to fight or to retreat. By Oct. 7 Burgoyne's effective troops numbered about 5000, while the Americans in front of him were nearly 8000. A reconnaissance in force to examine the American left was repulsed, the British were driven back into their lines and a determined attack led by Gen. Arnold threatened their whole position (*see* Freeman's Farm, Second Battle of). Burgoyne now had no alternative and fell back toward Saratoga (Schuylerville). His movement was so deliberate that the Americans were able to surround him, and on Oct. 17, finding himself opposed by over 17,000 regulars and militia, with less than 3500 infantry ready for duty, he surrendered his army to Gates. (*See also* Convention Army; Franco-American Alliance of 1778.)

[Hoffman Nickerson, *The Turning Point of the Revolution.*]

RALPH FOSTER WELD

Burke Act, THE (1906), was designed to correct certain defects in the Dawes Act[qv] of 1887, under which the land in the Indian tribal reservations was to be broken up and distributed in severalty to the individual Indians. Because of the unpreparedness of most Indians for citizenship it provided that citizenship be granted on the final validation of their trust patents at the end of the probationary period of twenty-five years instead of on the receipt of the trust patents as stated in the Dawes Act. Thus the Government, when advisable, could continue paternalistic control as a safeguard against exploitation and debauchery.

[Robert E. Riegel, *America Moves West.*]

ASA E. MARTIN

Burlingame Treaty, THE (July 28, 1868), consisted of articles added to the Reed Treaty of 1858[qv] between the United States and China. These acknowledged Chinese territorial jurisdiction in China, left trade privileges in China to the discretion of the Chinese government and established free immigration between the countries (*see* Chinese Exclusion Acts). It placed China on the "most favored nation"[qv] plane with regard to treatment of consuls, immunity and privileges in travel, residence and education of Chinese subjects in the United States. It guaranteed nonintervention by the United States in Chinese domestic administration. It was signed in Washington by William H. Seward, Secretary of State, Anson Burlingame, acting as "Envoy Extraordinary and Minister Plenipotentiary" of the Emperor of China, and two Chinese envoys.

[Frederick Wells Williams, *Anson Burlingame and the First Chinese Mission to Foreign Powers.*]

ROGER BURLINGAME

Burlington Company, THE, was a group of eight investors of Burlington, N. J., which absorbed various mortgages of George Croghan between 1768 and 1770. The mortgages, issued to Gov. William Franklin and assigned by him to the company, included one for £3000 on 40,000 acres of Croghan's Otsego[qv], N. Y., purchase. Franklin, besides personal loans to Croghan, had purchased a 50% stock interest in the company for £1500 (1772). The remaining original shareholders sold their stock and rights, including Franklin's mortgages, to Andrew Craig and William Cooper who, without notifying Franklin, instituted sheriff's sale proceedings under a judgment of 1773 and, by questionable methods, purchased the Otsego tract for £2700 (January, 1786). Efforts of Franklin and Croghan's heirs to contest title proved fruitless.

[A. T. Volwiler, *George Croghan and the Westward Movement, 1741-1782.*]

C. A. TITUS

Burlington Route. *See* Chicago, Burlington & Quincy Railroad, The.

Burlington Strike, THE. On Feb. 27, 1888, locomotive engine men of the Burlington Railway, members of the Brotherhood of Locomotive Engineers[qv], struck for higher wages and abandonment of the system of classification. The strike was supported by the Knights of Labor[qv]. As it dragged on, violence flamed, trains were wrecked, men were shot and property was burned or otherwise destroyed. The Brotherhood finally gave in, but the railway damage was enormous. Since this time no serious railway strikes have been permitted. By Feb. 1, 1889, train operations were normal.

[John R. Commons, *History of Labor in the United States*, Vol. II.]

THOMAS ROBSON HAY

Burning Spring, THE, was located in present Kanawha County, W. Va., at or near Malden and was referred to by pioneers as "one of the wonders of the world." It is not known when this "boiling pot," which could be ignited and extinguished at will, was first seen by white persons, but in 1755 Mrs. Mary Ingles, a captive, assisted Indians in making salt there. The 250-acre tract on which the spring was located was patented by Generals George Washington and Andrew Lewis, but Washington never saw it. It was his intention to give the spring site to the "public forever," but instead it went to his nephew, Lawrence Augustine Washington who, in turn, sold it to Dickinson and Shrewsberry, who incorporated it in their salt plant.

[West Virginia Geological Survey, *Kanawha County,*

Wheeling, 1914, pp. 296-298; John P. Hale, *Trans-Allegheny Pioneers.*]

CHARLES H. AMBLER

Burns Fugitive Slave Case (1854) was one of three famous fugitive slave cases arising in Boston, Mass., after the enactment of the Fugitive Slave Law of 1850[qv]. Part of the Vigilance Committee (1850–61) planned to rescue Anthony Burns, an escaped slave, from an upper room of the courthouse. They battered in a door of the building at night, May 26, entered and one of them shot and killed Marshal Batchelder. Despite the committee's efforts, United States Commissioner Edward G. Loring remanded Burns to his owner, Suttle, of Alexandria, Va. On June 2 throngs witnessed the slave's departure. Several rich citizens paid $1300 and got him back early in 1855.

[C. E. Stevens, *Anthony Burns;* T. W. Higginson in *Atlantic Monthly,* March, 1897; W. H. Siebert, *The Underground Railroad in Massachusetts.*]

WILBUR H. SIEBERT

Burnt Corn, The Battle of, was an encounter between the Creek Indians[qv] and the Alabama frontiersmen, July 27, 1813, on Burnt Corn Creek in Conecuh County, Ala. On their return from Pensacola[qv] where aid had been received from the British, a party of Creeks led by Peter McQueen were attacked by three companies of frontiersmen under command of Col. James Caller and aides. The Indians, having at first been dispersed, later rallied and defeated the Alabamians who had busied themselves seizing Indian pack horses and plunder. Two frontiersmen were killed and fifteen wounded, Capt. Sam Dale being among the latter.

[W. G. Brown, *History of Alabama;* J. C. DuBose, *Alabama History;* A. J. Pickett, *History of Alabama.*]

JOHN B. CLARK

Burnt District, THE. On Oct. 3, 1864, when Gen. Philip H. Sheridan's army was encamped around Harrisonburg and Dayton, Rockingham County, Va., Maj. John Rodgers Meigs was killed in a fight with Confederate scouts. Sheridan, told that Meigs had been shot by bushwhackers[qv], ordered all buildings burned within a radius of five miles. This order was countermanded before it was fully carried out.

[John W. Wayland, *Virginia Valley Records.*]

JOHN W. WAYLAND

Burr Conspiracy, THE, is one of the most involved and mysterious episodes in early American history. Because it climaxed the dramatic struggle for power between Jefferson, the President, and Aaron Burr, a discredited political adventurer, it bulks large in the history of the period. Essentially it was a compound of personal and political rivalry, discredited ambition and land hunger.

Burr's exact intentions probably cannot ever be known. Following his duel with Hamilton (*see* below) he became a creature of circumstances, always hoping and scheming to regain at least something of his one-time popularity and power. To accomplish this he chose what he considered the most likely road to wealth and power—land conquest or seizure in Spanish territory west of the Mississippi.

Burr's first act was an attempt to attach England to his cause. Failing in this, he served out his term as Vice-President, meantime intriguing with those who might be of help, yet never disclosing his exact intentions. He went to the West, down the Mississippi to New Orleans and back overland, seeking friendly help and necessary funds. Returned to the East he sought successively to draw France and then Spain into his web of intrigue, but to no avail. Without the hope of foreign help, he was ready to accept funds from whatever source. Blennerhassett[qv], a trusting, visionary Irishman, who lived on an island in the Ohio River, was only one, though the most bizarre and reputedly the heaviest of the contributors to this weird venture.

Before leaving Philadelphia in the summer of 1806, Burr wrote his friend Gen. James Wilkinson, who commanded the American army on the Mississippi, that the expedition would start for New Orleans before the end of the year. But Wilkinson, thoughtful for his own safety and uncertain as to Burr, declined to be involved. Instead, when Burr's advance flotilla reached the lower Mississippi, Wilkinson ordered its members arrested. As Burr came down he, too, was seized and then paroled. He attempted to escape to Spanish territory, but was again captured and taken East for trial (*see* below). Burr was acquitted, but the "conspiracy" had already collapsed.

[W. F. McCaleb, *The Aaron Burr Conspiracy.*]

THOMAS ROBSON HAY

Burr-Hamilton Duel, THE, was the culminating point in the early partisan struggles of New York. It grew out of aspersions by Hamilton upon his rival's character. Burr, some weeks after his defeat, in 1804, for the governorship of New York, asked for an explanation and when Hamilton sought to evade the issue, Burr peremptorily challenged. Hamilton, in principle opposed to duelling[qv], averred that "peculiar necessity" forced him to accept the challenge. He wished to be useful, he explained, in those future crises which might affect the public weal. This enigmatical expression may be interpreted as a wish to break up plans to disrupt the Union. By facing Burr he may have thought to prevent his opponent from becoming a leader of disaffected New England Federalists[qv]. An alternative explanation was the prospect of war with Spain, which would carry with it leadership in the emancipation of Mexico (*see* Burr Conspiracy; Miranda's Intrigues). Both Hamilton and Burr wished to achieve this honor, and it seems to present a more compelling motive for the challenge and its acceptance.

The outcome of the duel at Weehawken, N. J., July 11, 1804, was fatal to both. Each fired once although Hamilton's friends claim that his shot was intentionally discharged in the air. Burr's reached its mark and his victim, mortally wounded, died the next day. Bankrupt in fortune and reputation and under indictment in New York and New Jersey, Burr thenceforth became a political outcast.

[Wandell and Minnigerode, *Aaron Burr.*]

ISAAC J. COX

Burr Trial, The Constitutional Aspects of the, have to do largely with the interpretation of the constitutional provision concerning treason[qv]. Aaron Burr was indicted for treason in 1807 (*see* Burr Conspiracy) and brought to trial in the United States Circuit Court at Richmond, Va., before Chief Justice John Marshall sitting as a circuit judge. The political passions of the times and the friction between President Jefferson and Chief Justice Marshall carried over into the trial and render appraisal difficult. An early incident of the trial was the Marshall opinion that a Federal court might issue a subpœna *duces tecum* to the President of the United States. In guiding the jury as to the law of treason the Chief Justice gave an interpretation so restricting the meaning of the words "levying war" that in the case at hand only the assemblage at Blennerhassett's Island[qv] could come within it. Burr, however much he may have counseled, advised or planned that assemblage, was not present. Under the Marshall interpretation his absentee connection was not sufficient to render him guilty of treason. Marshall held that the broader definition asked by counsel for the prosecution would include the English doctrine of constructive treason, which the phrasing of the constitutional provision was intended to exclude. This statement of the law resulted in a verdict of acquittal. The Chief Justice was sharply criticised for inconsistency and bias, in that in a dictum in an earlier case in the Supreme Court involving two of Burr's messengers (*see* Bollman Case) he had stated the law in a way which seemingly should have linked Burr with the treasonable assemblage.

[*Reports of the Trials of Colonel Aaron Burr for Treason and for a Misdemeanor;* Albert J. Beveridge, *The Life of John Marshall.*]

CARL BRENT SWISHER

Bushwackers. This term, originally used as far back as Washington Irving's day to describe a backwoodsman, came during the Civil War to be applied by Federal soldiers to Confederate guerrilla[qv] fighters, with a distinct implication of private plunder. Used in Missouri as synonymous with "Border Ruffians,"[qv] it was more commonly applied in the mountain sections of Virginia and Kentucky.

JAMES ELLIOTT WALMSLEY

Bushy Run, Battle of (Aug. 5, 6, 1763). Bouquet's expedition[qv] was attacked by Indians near Bushy Run, twenty-five miles east of Pittsburgh. After indecisive fighting until nightfall, the men rested on their arms, suffering greatly from thirst. In the morning Bouquet, feigning retreat, drew the Indians forward to receive a flanking fire from companies ambushed for the purpose. The Indians, completely routed, fled. Though the British loss of over a hundred officers and men probably exceeded that of the Indians, the victory relieved Fort Pitt[qv] and heartened the colonists.

[Francis Parkman, *Conspiracy of Pontiac.*]

SOLON J. BUCK

Business. *See* Trade, Domestic; Trade, Foreign.

Business, Big. The term "Big Business" first came into use in a symbolic sense subsequent to the Civil War, particularly after 1880, in connection with the combination movement that began in American business at that time (*see* Corporations; Trusts). Although the term has become common, there has never been general agreement as to what constituted "bigness." The large consolidated railroad and public utility systems have commonly been considered "big" because of the size of their fixed investments and their gross incomes. Industrial companies have been considered "big" both because of the absolute size of their assets and because of the size of their assets relative to the assets of other firms, especially competitors. The term has also been used in connection with the volume of sales of a particular business, especially when the sales of one concern were a substantial portion of the industry's sales. In a more sophisticated sense "bigness" has had reference to the extent to which an individual company, either by virtue of its size or for other reasons, was able to influence substantially the ruling prices in the trade. Certain banking houses have generally been acknowledged to be "big" not so much because of the size of their resources as because of the influence their members could exert on many companies and in many fields of activity.

The social consequences of the concentration of economic power in the hands of those persons controlling "Big Business" has been a constant concern both of economists and of politicians since the end of the 19th century. Various attempts have been made to investigate the effects of "bigness" upon labor, consumers and investors, as well as upon prices and competition. "Big Business" has been accused of a wide variety of misdeeds that range from the exploitation of the working man to the corruption of politicians and the fomenting of war. At the same time it has been generally admitted that much of the technological progress since 1850 has been dependent on and fostered by the growth in size and the increase in financial strength of individual business units. The long series of statutes and legal decisions designed to control or to regulate business, that begin with the Interstate Commerce Act and the Sherman Antitrust Act[qqv] and which have not yet come to an end, are in effect an attempt by society to mitigate the evils of "Big Business" while preserving its benefits.

[A. A. Berle and G. C. Means, *The Modern Corporation and Private Property;* Louis D. Brandeis, *The Curse of Bigness;* Eliot Jones, *The Trust Problem in the United States;* Henry R. Seager and Charles A. Gulick, *Trust and Corporation Problems.*] CHARLES C. ABBOTT

Business, Mechanical Devices Used in. The first really important step toward the use of mechanical devices for business came in 1873 when the first commercial typewriter[qv] was manufactured by Remington. While this was a distinctly elementary machine, working like a sewing machine with foot pedal, and typewriting only capital letters, it started the forward development of machinery for office use.

From that point on, the history of the use of mechanical devices in business offices has progressed at a very rapid pace. The production of card-indexing methods and filing systems followed in the period from 1880 to 1885. In 1893 at the World's Fair in Chicago the first filing cabinet was on display. These two factors in office equipment development set the pace for further developments in the creation of office devices.

The adding machine in its early stages and even today follows the principle of registering and printing characters through ribbon just as they are printed on a typewriter. The first bookkeeping machines were merely extensions of the carriages on typewriters. Many of that type still remain.

Practical duplicating machines and devices made their appearance during the period from 1910 to 1920. The principles upon which duplicating machines were developed resulted in the perfection of addressing machines and other devices which reproduce both drawings and type matter.

The more complicated requirements of business called for more complicated machinery for accounting and bookkeeping problems. The most modern device for accounting procedure is the punch card accounting and tabulating machine. This was developed between 1900 and 1910, and was first used by the United States Government in census work. Subsequently it was applied to all the complicated business of accounting. These machines operate through the use of punched cards whereon the holes indicate specific information relating to inventory, prices, payments, debts, etc.

Dictating machines are a direct result of the invention of the phonograph[qv] and are coming into more frequent use as timesavers.

The development of radio and wireless telegraphy has made possible interoffice communication by voice through the mere turning of a switch. Large offices are now equipped with devices whereby voices of executives can reach all parts of large factories from offices, or all parts of large offices themselves.

Another development is the photographing machine for offices where photographic copies of records are required speedily in quantity. The photostat machine, the dexigraph and other photographic record machinery are now available to and used by many hundreds of large organizations. These devices apply the principles of photography to the use of business, and have now been developed to the point where photographs are made on strips of film like the films used in motion pictures. These are projected frame by frame on a screen.

Retail business utilizes the adding machine principle in the form of the cash register. Other devices now used in business are numbering and dating machines, stapling machines, stenotype machines, devices for sealing, stamping and folding letters, machines for wrapping packages quickly, cash and change-making devices, etc.

LOUIS M. COTTIN

Business, Public Control of. In mediæval England many trades and professions were classed as public callings, and persons engaged in them were required to serve all who applied for service. The surgeon was thus classed, because of the importance of his services and the scarcity of surgeons. Likewise the smith, for if a horse cast a shoe, the rider was at the mercy of the nearest farrier. For similar reasons were classed the innkeeper, the victualer, the baker, the miller, the common carrier, ferryman and wharfinger. This was the common law. But Parliament also took a hand and regulated wages and the price of wool and food. Such statutes were in force in England when America was settled and the colonists brought to America with them the idea of legislative supervision of trades and professions. Hence, the prices of board and staple commodities like tobacco, bread and corn were regulated by most of the colonial assemblies[qv].

When the Federal Constitution and the various state constitutions were adopted, it was in accordance with "due process of law" for legislatures to regulate those businesses which had been regulated at common law[qqv]. But the types of business classed as common callings changed with economic conditions. The tailor, surgeon and smith, for example, soon ceased to be so classed, but the ferryman, wharfinger, innkeeper and common carrier continued in the category, with the addition in the 19th century of proprietors of turnpikes, bridges and canals[qqv]. But the popularity of *laissez-faire*[qv] economics during the first half of the 19th century caused governmental regulation to reach its lowest ebb during that period.

About the middle of the 19th century the business corporation[qv] began to emerge and for a time the view seemed likely to prevail that unless the state, in granting a charter of incorporation to a business, had imposed upon it a duty of public service, or granted it a special or monopolistic franchise, the corporation was free to conduct its business as it liked, though it partook of the nature of a public calling. But with the growth of business corporations controlling products or services upon which people greatly depended, the pendulum began to swing the other way, and, in a series of decisions beginning with the historic case of Munn v. Illinois[qv] in 1874, the United States Supreme Court developed the doctrine that all businesses, regardless of their franchise or charter powers, were liable to legislative regulation, if they were "affected with a public interest."

Statutes regulating the sale of foods and drugs, stock-yard transactions, insurance rates, insurance agents' commissions and rents were passed and held valid. In 1890 the Sherman Antitrust Act[qv], making monopolies illegal, was enacted by Congress and its validity upheld. The distinction between a public utility[qv] and a private business seemed to be breaking down in favor of a rule that any business is subject to regulation to the degree required by the public need. To the objection raised in each case that the "due process" clause of the Constitution was being infringed, the courts replied that the "due process" clause must yield to the police power[qv], when regulatory legislation seemed reasonably calculated to correct recognized economic or social evils. There were occasional setbacks, but the march of state regulation was relentless. Recent illustrations of the trend are statutes regulating the price of milk and of handling and selling leaf tobacco (Nebbia v. New York[qv], 291 U. S. 502, 1934; Townsend v. Yeomans, 57 Sup. Ct. 842, 1937).

With the creation of the Interstate Commerce Commission[qv] in 1887, with power to regulate the rates and conditions of railroad service (and since 1935 interstate motor carrier service), there was inaugurated the policy of administrative regulation of public utilities. Since then, most states have created public utility commissions, charged with the duty of determining reasonable rates and conditions of service of light, heat, power, water and telephone companies, and have set up administrative officers to regulate insurance, banking, mining, etc. In 1920 Congress created the Federal Power Commission[qv], at first composed of the Secretaries of War, Interior and Agriculture, but since 1930, of five commissioners appointed by the President. The commission has power to regulate the licensing of water-power rights on public lands, and since 1935, "the transmission of electric energy in interstate commerce." Congress has also created the Federal Communications Commission[qv] (acts of 1927 and 1934) with wide regulatory powers over radio broadcasting and other agencies of communication. Usually such commissions have power to find the facts, but their acts are subject to judicial review[qv] on matters of law.

The Federal Trade Commission and the Clayton Acts, passed in 1914, and the Robinson-Patman Act[qqv], passed in 1936, extended the principle of administrative regulation to businesses usually classed as private, i.e., not public utilities. These acts, re-enforcing and extending the Sherman Antitrust Act, made monopolies illegal, and prohibited interlocking directorates, price discrimination, "tying" contracts and other methods of "unfair" competition calculated to promote monopolistic control. Into this class of legislation also falls the National Labor Relations Act[qv] passed in 1935 (declared valid in National Labor Relations Board v. Jones and Laughlin[qv]), which prohibits employers from resorting to unfair labor practices and sets up a board for administering the law; and also the Securities Exchange Act of 1934 which created the Securities Exchange Commission[qv] with power to regulate security sales on stock exchanges and, since 1935, all securities issued or dealt in by public utility holding companies.

An act of Congress may be invalid not only because it infringes the "due process" clause of the Constitution, but because it is not among the powers expressly delegated to Congress. Since power to regulate business has not been expressly granted to Congress, regulatory acts of this nature are valid only if they come within some other congressional power, such as that to regulate commerce among the states or to tax for the general welfare. This is illustrated by the abortive attempt of Congress in 1932 to set up the National Recovery Administration[qv] with power to impose upon business codes of fair competition, minimum wages and maximum hours for employees. The act was held invalid (Schechter Poultry Corp. v. United States[qv]) not because of violation of the "due process" clause, but because its subject matter did not come within the power of Congress over interstate commerce, or any other congressional power. Similarly the Agricultural Adjustment Act[qv] of 1933, designed to regulate agricultural production, fell because it involved an improper exercise of the taxing power (United States v. Butler[qv]).

Many other Federal and state acts have been passed regulating various aspects of business, and proprietors have complained that much of the Government's intervention has been unjustifiable and oppressive and has operated to discourage and curtail individual initiative and enterprise. Whether or not governmental regulation has extended too far for the common weal, it has been one of the most significant political and economic developments of the last half century.

[Bruce Wyman, *Public Service Corporations*, Vol. I; National Industrial Conference Board, *Competitive Regulation of Competitive Practices.*]

GEORGE W. GOBLE

Business Clubs, such as Kiwanis, Lions and Rotarians[qv], were first organized on an international scale during the second decade of the 20th century. Rotary was the pioneer, dating its international beginning back to November, 1910. Kiwanis followed in 1916, and Lions in 1917.

These leaders among the business clubs have similar aims and purposes. Typical among them are civic improvement and beautification of various kinds, aid to underprivileged children, cultivation of high ideals of civic life, the promotion of a friendly spirit among business competitors and, in general, the making of one's home town a better place in which to live. Rotary advertises a motto, "Service above Self"; Kiwanis insist that "We Build"; and the Lions are named from the initial letters of "Liberty, Intelligence, Our Nation's Safety." These and similar organizations have international officers and conventions.

Rotary has the best claim to the adjective international and is the largest as well as the oldest of the groups. On March 1, 1938, there were approximately 4500 Rotary clubs including 187,000 individual members in "70 or more countries and geographical regions." There were more than 2800 Lions clubs numbering slightly less than 100,000 members in eight countries. The 1900-odd Kiwanis clubs of 95,000 members were confined to the United States and Canada. The club magazine for each group is sent to every active member and keeps the individual alive to the activities, aims and achievements of his organization.

In addition to the three larger fraternities there are many others of the same nature. Among these should be mentioned: Altrurians; American Business Club; Association of 20–30 Clubs; Civitan; Coöperative Club; Gyro; National Exchange; National Monarch; Optimist; Round Table; and National Metro Clubs.

[Charles F. Marden, *Rotary and Its Brothers.*]

S. S. McKAY

Business Cycles, i.e., recurring phases of depression, revival, prosperity and crisis or recession, have characterized the annals of American business since the beginnings of the country. Although the different phases of the business cycle have usually followed each other in the order noted, their intensity and duration have varied in marked fashion from cycle to cycle. At times, moreover, the revival or prosperity phases have been interrupted by minor recessions or depressions in business, while crises, which usually mark the termination of a speculative boom, have occasionally occurred in a period of depression.

The first major depression in this country occurred in the half-decade 1784–89 as a result of dislocations attributable to the Revolutionary War[qv]. A period of prosperity, interrupted by a minor depression in 1807–10, ensued and lasted until after the War of 1812[qv] when a severe depression, lasting from 1815 to 1821, set in (*see* Panic of 1819). This was followed, after a few years of moderate prosperity, by another depression of mild character which ran from 1825 to 1829. Prosperity followed, culminating in the Panic of 1837[qv] and a long depression which continued to 1843. The next major depression took place in 1857–58 (*see* Panic of 1857), shortly before the Civil War[qv].

Extended wars always breed depression and the Civil War was no exception. A depression in industry occurred in 1865–66, according to some authorities, or in 1866–67, according to others. This was followed by recovery and prosperity which finally ended with a Panic in 1873[qv]. The long depression of the 1870's, lasting until 1879, ensued. The subsequent recovery was interrupted by the depression of 1883–85, which began as a minor recession but was prolonged and intensified by the crisis of 1884. By 1887 prosperity had returned and continued until 1893 with the exception of a short depression in 1890–91. The Panic of 1893[qv] ushered in a severe depression which lasted, with the exception of a few months of prosperous conditions in 1895, until 1897, when business again turned upward. The prosperity which followed was broken briefly by a very mild recession in 1900 and, later, by the "Rich Man's Panic" of 1903–4. The latter was a financial rather than an industrial depression. The Panic of 1907[qv] was the forerunner of a comparatively short but severe depression which ran into the following year. Recovery from this depression carried business through until 1913, although there was an extremely mild recession in 1910–11.

The depression beginning in 1913 started out to be a comparatively mild one, but the outbreak of hostilities in Europe intensified it considerably. By 1915, however, war demands had induced renewed prosperity which continued, with the exception of a slight readjustment in 1919, until the late spring of 1920 when a crisis occurred followed by a rapid recession in business (*see* Panic of 1920).

The depression of 1920–22 was severe, although not unduly extended. Recovery brought a long stretch of prosperity to the country, broken by minor depressions in 1924 and 1927, which ended with the stock-market crash in the fall of 1929 (*see* Panic of 1929). There followed a long and severe depression from which recovery did not set in until after the Banking Crisis of 1933[qv]. The ensuing recovery was not regular but was interrupted by recessions in 1933, 1934 and 1935, followed by a fairly severe depression in 1937–38 (*see* Recession of 1937).

[E. C. Bratt, *Business Cycles and Forecasting;* C. Snyder, *Business Cycles and Business Measurements.*]

FREDERICK A. BRADFORD

Business Forecasting, as it is known today, would not be possible without the collection and dissemination of business statistics by government and trade agencies. Since the beginning of the 20th century, numerous services have come into existence for the sole purpose of forecasting business but all of them have, at one time or another, been found wanting. More recently, almost all attempts have been futile and must continue so as long as international markets are unsettled and government attempts to control or direct economic movements.

The earliest attempts to forecast business were, perforce, based upon the scanty basic statistics of interest rates, bond yields and such reports of current production as were available, mainly pig iron. For some years, the number of iron furnaces in blast had a vogue because orders for pig iron were a certain reflection of demand. This "index" failed to function after the World War because the erection of very large blast furnaces in place of many smaller units destroyed its flexibility.

The current vogue in business forecasting is concerned with the delineation of past business cycles as a measure of present-day movements. Graphical comparisons are frequently resorted to in the attempt to fit current cycles to some bygone cycle in order to establish some basis to forecast completion of the current cycle. Most of the statistics are thrown into the form of index or relative numbers and the various series are then combined into a single index number of business.

The oldest regularly published annual business forecast is only thirty years old. Many of the better known forecasts are published in connection with advisory services with which business forecasts are incidental. All, or nearly all, large corporations attempt to forecast business for short intervals.

Never before has so much factual data been available nor have we been so well and so promptly informed of what is going on. Formerly, the behavior of various indices could perhaps be the basis for forecasting business but now that developments may be determined by the direct influence of persons in power, business predictions are futile.

WILLIAM WREN HAY

"Busy Bees of Deseret," THE, were the Mormon settlers (1848) in what became Utah; Deseret is the "land of the honeybee" of the Book of Mormon.

WHEELER PRESTON

Bute, Fort, or Manchac Post, named for the British Prime Minister, was established in 1763 at the junction of Iberville River (Bayou Manchac) with the Mississippi, and remained an important British military and trading post in West Florida[qv] until captured by Spanish forces under Bernardo Galvez of Louisiana on Sept. 7, 1779.

[Alcée Fortier, *History of Louisiana*, II.]

WALTER PRICHARD

Butler's General Order No. 28. Gen. B. F. Butler established himself as military commander in New Orleans, May 1, 1862. The marked hostility of the inhabitants of the city to the Federal Government was exhibited in insults to which Federal officers and men were subjected by the women. Accordingly on May 15 Butler issued an order to the effect that any female insulting or showing contempt for any officer or soldier of the United States should be treated as a woman of the town plying her avocation. The order evoked a storm of protest at home and abroad, and was a cause of Butler's removal from command of New Orleans, Dec. 16, 1862.

[James Ford Rhodes, *History of the United States*, Vol. IV.]

JAMES E. WINSTON

Butler's Rangers (1777–84) was a regiment of Loyalists[qv], recruited by Col. John Butler with the consent of Sir Guy Carleton to serve with the Indians against the colonists. Eight companies were recruited. Their uniforms consisted of a green coat and waistcoat faced with red, buff breeches, white leggings and a hat of the Foot Regiment pattern. From their headquarters at Fort Niagara[qv], the Rangers embarked on forays which spread terror throughout New York and Pennsylvania. They perpetrated the Wyoming massacre[qv] in July, 1778, and took part in Johnson's raid on the Mohawk settlements in 1780. The regiment was disbanded in June, 1784.

[E. Cruikshank, *The Story of Butler's Rangers.*]

ROBERT W. BINGHAM

Butte des Morts Council (1827). Lewis Cass, governor of Michigan Territory, and Thomas L. McKenney, United States Indian commissioner, held a council with the Chippewa, Menominee and Winnebago Indians[qqv] at Little Butte des Morts, north of Lake Winnebago, near where the Fox River flows out. A treaty was signed there Aug. 11, 1827, adjusting boundaries and the relations of these tribes with the Indians migrating to Wisconsin from New York.

[Kappler, *Indian Treaties of the United States.*]

LOUISE PHELPS KELLOGG

Butter. *See* Dairy Industry.

Butterfield Claims (1854–90). The name is derived from the firm that handled the negotiations. In 1854 two ships, loaded with war materials, cleared at New York for St. Thomas. Suspicion arose that they were destined for Venezuelan rebels. Because of lack of evidence they were cleared in a libel suit. When they arrived at St. Thomas, Danish West Indies, trouble arose again because of their suspicious character. The owners presented a large claim for damages because the vessels were detained by the Danish government. Thirty-four years of negotiations ended in a Danish-American arbitration treaty (1888), as a result of which the claim was disallowed on the ground that the Danish government had observed strictly the neutrality laws involved.

[S. J. M. P. Fogdall, *Danish-American Diplomacy, 1776-1920.*]

S. P. FOGDALL

Butterfield Overland Dispatch. Because of much travel to Colorado after the discovery of gold there, D. A. Butterfield, backed by New York capital, organized a joint-stock express and passenger carrying service between the Missouri River and Denver. In July, 1865, the route via the Smoky Hill River was surveyed and soon thereafter coaches were in operation. Ben Holladay, acting for a competing organization, bought the Butterfield Overland Dispatch in March, 1866, when Eastern express companies threatened to take it over and establish a service between the Missouri River and Sacramento, Calif.

[LeRoy Hafen, *The Overland Mail.*]

C. C. RISTER

Butterfield Overland Mail. *See* Southern Overland Mail.

Byrd's Polar Flights. On April 5, 1926, Commander Byrd sailed on the S.S. *Chantier* for Kings Bay, Spitzbergen, which he intended using as the base for a flight to the North Pole. The vessel arrived in the bay on April 29. The only pier in the harbor was occupied by a Norwegian gunboat; therefore, it was necessary to ferry the big trimotored Fokker airplane, *Josephine Ford,* ashore through the drifting ice, which choked the bay, on a raft constructed from four ship's boats. This operation was successfully accomplished, and preparations for the flight commenced. After being held up by defects in the skis for some days, Byrd and his pilot, Floyd Bennett, eventually took off for the Pole shortly after midnight on May 9. The flight proceeded uneventfully until the airplane was one hour's flight short of the Pole, at which time a leak was discovered in an oil tank. In spite of this they continued onward. At 9:02 A.M., Greenwich Civil Time, the Pole was reached. After circling around it, the coarse was set for Spitzbergen. The return flight was uneventful, and the motors continued to function in spite of the oil leak.

Early in the Antarctic spring of 1929 Byrd made a flight from his base at Little America to the foot of the Queen Maud Mountains and laid down a gasoline base. On Nov. 29, 1929, at 3:29 P.M., the polar flight party took off in the Ford airplane, *Floyd Bennett,* for the Pole. At 9:15 they started up the Liv Glacier Pass for the Polar Plateau. The plane was so heavily loaded that she could not gain enough altitude to clear the head of the glacier. It was necessary to dump several hundred pounds of emergency food to lighten the plane enough to clear the "Hump." Once over the plateau the plane made good time. At 1:14, Greenwich Civil Time, the Pole was reached. A few minutes later the course was changed to head back to the mountains. This part of the flight developed into a race against clouds moving in from the east. The party just managed to get down Axel Heiberg Glacier before it was enshrouded. After a short flight to the eastward the plane was landed at the fuel base. At six o'clock the return journey to Little America began. Shortly after ten the party landed at the camp.

R. E. BYRD

Cabanne's Trading Post, located ten miles above Omaha on the west side of the Missouri River, was established between 1822 and 1826 for the American Fur Company[qv] by John Pierre Cabanne. Between 1833 and 1840 the post was moved to Bellevue, Nebr., and placed under the management of Peter A. Sarpy.

[Hiram Chittenden, *The American Fur Trade of the Far West.*]

EVERETT DICK

Cabeza de Vaca, Alvar Núñez, Travels of. In 1527, at about the age of thirty-seven, Cabeza de Vaca went to America as treasurer of the expedition led by Pánfilo de Narváez[qv], which landed near the present city of Tampa, Fla., in April, 1528. After a brief and disastrous exploration of the country the colonists built five horsehide boats and sailed for Cuba. A hurricane sank all but the one commanded by Cabeza de Vaca, and soon it was wrecked on the Texas coast. From the fall of 1528 to the spring of 1536 Cabeza de Vaca and his companions endured untold hardships in a 6000-mile journey through the American Southwest and northern Mexico. Finally safe in New Spain, Cabeza de Vaca returned to Old Spain to request of Charles V the governorship of "La Florida." Instead he was given the governorship of Paraguay. His account of his travels was printed in 1555 at Valladolid, Spain, under the title *Relación y Comentarios.*

[Morris Bishop, *The Odyssey of Cabeza de Vaca.*]

A. CURTIS WILGUS

Cabildo, THE, was the Spanish governmental organization for the province of Louisiana. It was established by O'Reilly in 1769, superseding the French Superior Council, and was abolished by Laussat when France regained possession of the province in 1803. Besides the governor, who presided, it consisted of two ordinary *alcaldes* (judges in New Orleans), *alferez real* (royal standard-bearer), provincial *alcalde* (judge outside New Orleans), *alguacil mayor* (high sheriff), depositary-general (treasurer and storekeeper), receiver of fines (collector), attorney-general-syndic (public prosecutor), *mayordomo-de-propios* (municipal treasurer of New Orleans) and *escribano* (clerk). It met in the Government House (*Casa Capitular* or *Principal*), commonly known today as the "Cabildo."

[J. S. Kendall, *History of New Orleans,* I.]

WALTER PRICHARD

Cabin Rights. At an early period in the settlement of the West, pioneers asserted their claims to parts of wild lands by blazing trees around the desired boundary, and later comers customarily recognized the claims: tomahawk rights[qv], they were called. Building a cabin and raising a crop, however small, of grain of any kind, led to "cabin rights," which were recognized not only customarily but by law. The laws of the colonies and states varied in their requirements of the settler. In Virginia the occupant was entitled to 400 acres of land and to a preemption[qv] right to 1000 acres more adjoining, to be secured in either case by a land-office warrant, the basis of a later patent or grant from colonial or state authorities.

SAMUEL C. WILLIAMS

Cabinet, THE, of the President[qv] is the result of custom and was created neither by the Constitution[qv] nor by statute law (*see* Revolutionary

Committees). The Constitution says (Article II, Section II) that the President "may require the Opinion, in writing, of the principal Officer in each of the executive Departments, upon any Subject relating to the Duties of their respective Offices." These offices were created by act of Congress at various times and their holders were considered to be the personal assistants of the President in the work of administration. Washington tried to carry out the intentions of the makers of the Constitution that the Senate[qv] should serve as a privy council on the British model, but he dropped the method of personal attendance and conference with the Senate when he found that this was creating friction with certain members of that body. Also in 1793 he tried to secure the advice of the United States Supreme Court[qv] at a time of crisis in our relations with France. He submitted to the Court a number of questions with regard to the interpretation of our treaties with France, but the justices refused to answer these questions on the ground that they lay outside their duties. Washington then turned to his three secretaries or department heads of State, War and Navy, and called them, along with the attorney general into a council of four. This conference in time was recognized by the public as the official council or cabinet of the President.

The name "cabinet" was first used about the year 1793. Congressional debates show that the term was used in Congress in 1798 and again in 1802, but it was only some twenty years after the establishment of the national government that the idea and name of a cabinet council was understood and accepted by the people. The name "cabinet" was not recognized in Federal statute law until the act of Feb. 26, 1907, which provided for an increase in the salary of those "heads of the Executive Departments who are members of the President's Cabinet." Thus it may be repeated that the name and establishment of the President's cabinet originated in custom as in England and in process of time became an accepted part of the National Government. Washington, at first, undertook to conduct his administration on a nonpartisan basis and his first cabinet was chosen equally between the two wings of his supporters—those who were of strong nationalist[qv] and those who were of states' rights[qv] tendencies. Finding that the emergence of vital issues of policy made necessary united support of his department heads or cabinet, he changed its membership so that it became united in support of his views.

At the time of the death of President William Henry Harrison his cabinet resigned and his successor, Vice-President Tyler, reconstructed his administration according to his own views. It has now become the understanding that the members of the cabinet are the personal appointees and advisers of the President, and Congress[qv] usually confirms a presidential nomination to one of these offices. Furthermore, while certain cabinet members, as the head of the Treasury Department or of the Department of Commerce, usually are business men especially fitted for the work of that department, yet in general cabinet positions are given upon a basis of geographical or political influence in order to consolidate party support behind the administration of a President. The actual influence of a cabinet depends in large part upon the desires and intentions of the President himself. In certain cases the cabinet may be a collection of political leaders, at another time of executive administrators. Also the personality of a specific cabinet member and his personal influence with the President may count for much. In recent years the creation of numerous departments or independent commissions has weakened cabinet influence. In addition, the private unofficial advisers of a President may have more influence than the cabinet as a united body. The so-called Brain Trust[qv] of Franklin D. Roosevelt is an illustration of this situation.

At the present time there are ten members of the cabinet, each one of whom presides over his respective department. These departments are State (foreign affairs), Treasury, War, Navy, Post Office, Interior, Justice, Agriculture, Commerce and Labor[qqv]. Each department has one or more "under secretaries" or "assistant secretaries" who act as assistants to or under the direction of the cabinet member. They may attend cabinet meetings in the absence of the head of the department or upon special occasions, but generally are not considered part of the "Ministry" as would be the case in Great Britain. The salary of each member of the cabinet is $15,000 a year. The term of office is four years or at the pleasure and discretion of the President.

At various times there has been discussion of the advisability of the President inviting the Vice-President[qv] to attend cabinet meetings. But this seems to have been the custom only in the administration of President Harding who in 1921 invited the regular attendance of Vice-President Calvin Coolidge, otherwise the attendance of the Vice-President has been merely casual and for some special purpose.

[H. B. Learned, *The President's Cabinet;* M. L. Hinsdale, *A History of the President's Cabinet.*]

WILLIAM STARR MYERS

Cables, Transatlantic. The submarine cable was scarce invented (1844), and its first successful experiment concluded across the English Channel (1850), when Atlantic cables[qv] were projected. Success came in 1866. Since that time, transatlantic cables have been taken as a matter of course, as a matter of necessity, completely demonstrated when storms and quakes disturb the depths and break the wires, as in 1929.

The conformation of the Atlantic sea bottom makes cable laying more possible, cable maintenance more practical than is true in other oceans. A "telegraph plateau," broad, level, relatively shallow, lies convenient where cables can rest—perhaps the "lost continent"—but in any event facilitating communication between Europe and America, in business, in diplomacy, in amity. It carries more than a score of cables, directly to North Europe, by "ports of call" in the Azores to South Europe.

The United States, which had been eager for cables, became absorbed after the Civil War in the lands of the West and in land telegraph[qv]. Germany and France and later Italy entered the field; but from the lack of imperial necessity, lack of capital and through the effects of the Great War, the majority of transatlantic cables are British-owned, the majority American-leased.

American government control operates through the granting of landing licenses, with anti-monopoly provisions, an executive function exercised by all Presidents since Grant, but under law only since 1921. To this extent only does the Government assume any authority over international submarine cables. It is a signatory to the international convention of 1884.

[Keith Clark, *International Communications;* George A. Schreiner, *Cables and Wireless;* Eugene W. Sharp, *International News Communications.*]

KEITH CLARK

Cabot Voyages (1497–99). Early in 1496 a petition was placed before Henry VII in the name of John Cabot and his three sons, Sebastian, Lewes and Sancto, for the privilege of making explorations in the New World. Letters patent dated March 5, 1496, were granted to the Cabots, and in the spring of 1497 they sailed west. Coasting southward they discovered Cape Breton Island and Nova Scotia. The following year (1498) letters patent were granted to John Cabot alone, authorizing him to make further explorations along the eastern coast of North America. The discoveries made on this voyage were supposedly recorded on a map and globe made by the explorer. Both are now lost. Because there is no firsthand data concerning the Cabot voyages, Sebastian Cabot has been called the "Sphynx of North American history." His identity is often confused with that of his father, John. Important contributions to geographical knowledge were made by the Cabots, though "the descriptions of the regions they explored apply to no portion of the United States."

[C. H. Coote in *Dictionary of National Biography;* Justin Winsor, *Narrative and Critical History of North America.*]

LLOYD A. BROWN

Cabrillo Expedition, THE (June 27, 1542–April 14, 1543). In the hope of finding a direct route from Spain to the East Indies through Spanish waters, Juan Rodríguez Cabrillo and Bartolomé Ferrelo sailed from Navidad, Mexico, and, Sept. 28, 1542, reached a port, "closed and very good, which they named San Miguel." They were in fact at San Diego and thus were the discoverers of California[qv]. After getting as far north as Drake's Bay they were forced back to the Santa Barbara Islands where Rodríguez died. Ferrelo carried on and is believed to have reached the vicinity of the Rogue River in Oregon.

[H. E. Bolton, *Spanish Explorations in the Southwest, 1542-1706.*]

OSGOOD HARDY

Cabusto, Battle of (November, 1540). Cabusto, an Indian (Chickasaw?) town situated, apparently, on the Black Warrior River near old Erie (Ala.), was the scene of one of DeSoto's[qv] conflicts with the Indians. A series of engagements were fought round about the old town in which it is claimed that about 8000 Indians participated. With Cabusto as a base, DeSoto broke through the palisaded defenses of the Indians north of the river and advanced up the Tombigbee valley.

[A. B. Meek, *Romantic Passages in Southwestern History.*]

A. B. MOORE

Cahaba Old Towns was a cluster of villages along the Cahaba River, some six miles northeast of Marion, Perry County, Ala. From Fort Claiborne in Monroe, Col. Gilbert Russell in the spring of 1814 was sent northward to Cahaba Old Towns in a futile effort to provide defense against the hostile Creek Indians[qv].

[W. G. Brown, *History of Alabama;* A. J. Pickett, *History of Alabama.*]

JOHN B. CLARK

Cahokia, the first permanent white settlement of consequence in Illinois, was founded in March, 1699, when priests of the Seminary of Quebec established there the Mission of the Holy Family. Their chapel, which became the nucleus of the village, was located near the left bank of the

Mississippi a short distance south of the present city of East St. Louis. Cahokia took its name from the adjacent Indian village, which in 1699 contained about 2000 Tamaroa and Cahokia.

The mission at Cahokia quickly attracted French settlers, principally from Canada, occasionally from Louisiana. Their number, however, was never large. A census in 1723 enumerated only twelve white residents, while at Kaskaskia and Fort de Chartres[qqv], the other principal settlements, 196 and 126 were counted. In 1767, after many French had removed to St. Louis[qv] because of the cession of the Illinois country[qv] to Great Britain, Cahokia contained 300 whites and 80 Negroes–about half the population of Kaskaskia. By 1800, however, its population had increased to 719, while that of Kaskaskia had dropped to 467.

Throughout the 18th century Cahokia exemplified several of the features of a typical French village. There was a common pasture land and a large common field divided into strips for cultivation. The church was the center of village life and the priest the most influential resident. Although a few families were distinguished by education and cultivated manners, most of the inhabitants were *coureurs de bois, voyageurs*[qqv] and traders who mingled freely with the Indians. English and American travelers usually criticized their squalor and lack of enterprise, but they noted also a carefree gaiety impervious to the hardships and uncertainties of their way of life.

Although Cahokia became the seat of St. Clair County, the first county organized in Illinois, its growth was not commensurate with that of the territory. With the removal of the county seat in 1814, decline commenced. By 1900 all vestiges of village life had disappeared.

[Gilbert J. Garraghan, New Light on Old Cahokia, *Illinois Catholic Historical Review*, Oct., 1928; C. W. Alvord, *Cahokia Records, 1778-1790; History of St. Clair County, Illinois.*]

PAUL M. ANGLE

Cahokia Mounds is a group of eighty-five prehistoric Indian mounds[qv] four miles northeast of East St. Louis, Ill. This group is the nucleus of a larger group, which is believed to have numbered originally between 200 and 300. Monks' Mound, 100 feet high with a rectangular base 1000 feet by 700 feet, is not only the largest mound in the group, but also the largest prehistoric monument in the United States. The Cahokia Mounds are believed to have been built between 1200 and 1500 A.D., perhaps much earlier.

[Warren K. Moorehead, et al., The Cahokia Mounds, University of Illinois *Bulletin*, Vol. XXVI, No. 4.]

PAUL M. ANGLE

Cahuenga Capitulation, THE (Jan. 13, 1847), ended California's part in the Mexican War[qv]. After preliminary negotiations, at the old Cahuenga ranch house, John C. Frémont and Andrés Pico signed a document, the liberal terms of which were in complete accord with Polk's conciliatory policy.

[R. G. Cleland, *A History of California: the American Period.*]

OSGOOD HARDY

Cairo, Ill., the "Eden" of Dickens' *Martin Chuzzlewit,* was founded in 1837 by the Cairo City and Canal Company, after an earlier effort (1818) had failed. For fifteen years the town grew slowly, but the sale of lots, which commenced in 1853, and the completion of the Illinois Central Railroad[qv] attracted settlers, with the result that by 1860 the population exceeded 2000. During the Civil War Cairo was of great strategic importance and for several months both Grant and Foote had headquarters there (*see* Belmont, Battle of). Because of its low elevation, its existence depends upon extensive levees, but even these have failed to prevent several severe inundations.

[John M. Lansden, *A History of the City of Cairo, Illinois.*]

PAUL M. ANGLE

Cajans. A local term applied in southeast Mississippi and southwest Alabama to designate a people of mixed bloods whose racial integrity is not determined. Physical aspects indicate a conglomeration of Gulf Coast Creole blood of the better type with Indian, African and Central American Negro and pure white. Socially they are not accepted by the better whites and refuse to be classed as Negroes. It has now become necessary for the educational systems of the states to provide school facilities and classify them other than White or Colored. The term is hardly more than forty years old, adopted to differentiate the group from a large colored Creole population. These people should not be confused with ones of Teche Louisiana called Acadians[qv].

PETER A. BRANNON

Cajon Pass, THE, the best route from the Mojave Desert to southern California, was probably first known to white men when, March, 1776, it was traversed by Father Francisco Garcés. The first American to discover it was Jedediah Smith[qv] (November, 1826). Shortly afterwards it became a part of the route between California and Santa Fé.

OSGOOD HARDY

Calamity Howler, a slang phrase contemptuously hurled by political opponents of the discontented Populists^qv and agrarians during the late 1880's and 1890's, signifies a noisy pessimist, particularly one who disagrees with the measures and policies of the ruling political party and who foretells the economic ruin of a section or the nation. The term first appeared in print, it is thought, in the *Congressional Record,* March 2, 1892, page 1654, column 1. Representative Jeremiah Simpson of Kansas, in speaking to a bill appropriating funds for charitable institutions in Washington, D. C., said, "If the destitution is so great here in the capital of the country, what must it be in the other portions of our Union? It seems to me time that we had some 'calamity howlers' here in Washington as well as in Kansas."

HARRY R. WARFEL

Calaveras Skull, THE, was allegedly found, in 1886, in auriferous gravels which would imply a very great antiquity. Unfortunately the circumstances attending the discovery, in Calaveras County, Calif., are not entirely satisfactory notwithstanding the claim made that the skull was found in the gravels of Bald Mountain at a depth of approximately 130 feet. Even if in comparatively recent years there has accumulated evidence to demonstrate that man in America existed in late Pleistocene times, nothing has been found approaching the antiquity postulated for the Calaveras skull. The skull, which is now in the Peabody Museum, is patently of Indian type not differing essentially from modern Indians of California. This in itself is a telling argument against hoary antiquity.

[Calaveras Man, in *Bulletin 30*, Bureau of American Ethnology; Skeletal Remains Suggesting or Attributed to Early Man in North America, *Bulletin 33*, Bureau of American Ethnology, Chap. IX, pp. 21-28.]

TRUMAN MICHELSON

Calder v. Bull, 1798 (3 Dallas 386). The *locus classicus* wherein the Supreme Court defined an *ex post facto* law: one which makes criminal an act not punishable when committed; or retrospectively increases the punishment; or alters the rules of evidence in order to convict the offender. Thus it was not unconstitutional for the Connecticut legislature to grant a retrial in a civil case.

CHARLES FAIRMAN

Calendar, THE. In 1582 Pope Gregory III, to correct the errors of the Julian calendar (established by Julius Cæsar), which made the year about eleven minutes too long, gave Europe (except Russia, Greece and the Near East) the Gregorian calendar which we still use, often referred to as New Style to distinguish it from the Julian calendar or Old Style. To correct the error, which by that time had amounted to ten days, the Pope ordained that the year 1582 should have the days between Oct. 4 and 15 stricken from the calendar. By providing bissextile or leap year, he further corrected the calendar so that three days are saved in every 400 years, leaving only an error of one day in 5200 years. This New Style of reckoning was not officially adopted (though frequently used) in Great Britain and her colonies until Sept. 3, Old Style, or 14, New Style, 1752, by which time the correction had increased by another day. According to the New Style, the year 1700 had only 365 days, while according to the Old Style it had 366 days. This discrepancy of one day has caused many errors in reducing Old Style to New, for it has not always been understood that events before 1700 require a correction of only ten days, while those from 1700 to 1752 require eleven days. For example, the Pilgrims landed at Plymouth on Dec. 11, 1620 O. S. (Old Style) or Dec. 21, N. S. (New Style) but at the time of the first local celebration of that event, the day was erroneously reckoned as Dec. 22, N. S., since the mistake was made of adopting the correction of eleven days, in use after 1700, not realizing that the event took place in the previous century when only ten days' correction was required. Many dates in American colonial history and biography have been recorded incorrectly in similar fashion.

From the 12th century until the adoption of New Style in 1752, the Civil, Ecclesiastical and Legal Year began in Great Britain and her colonies on March 25, while from 1582 the Historical Year was often unofficially figured from Jan. 1, as provided in the Gregorian calendar. Both styles of reckoning were in use at the same time and so it became customary to annex the date of the Historical to that of the Legal Year when referring to any date between the 1st of January and the 25th of March. When double-dating occurs, the upper or first figure indicates the Legal and the lower or last figure the Historical Year, as 162$\frac{1}{2}$ or 1621/2. In the Julian calendar the months were numbered, beginning with March (a practice followed by the Quakers who preferred not to use the pagan names of the months), so we frequently find a date written thus: "10th: 11th mo.; 1621," that is, the 10th day in the 11th month in the Civil Year 1621, which corresponds with Jan. 10 of the Historical Year 1622. Double-dating was always used in referring to time between the last day of February and March 25, when the year commenced on the latter date, since it would not otherwise be possible to tell to what year the date referred.

[N. B. Shurtleff, *A Perpetual Calendar for Old and New Style.*]

R. W. G. VAIL

Calhoun's *Disquisition on Government* represents John C. Calhoun's reasoned views on government as seen from the point of view of the permanent minority. Begun in 1843, finished to Calhoun's own satisfaction in five years' time, it elaborates the doctrine of his *Exposition*^qv^. Its keynote is the idea of a concurrent majority. Simple majority government always results in despotism over the minority unless some way is devised to secure the assent of all classes, sections and interests.

The argument is close-knit and convincing if one accepts the belief of Calhoun that the states retain absolute sovereignty over the Constitution and can do with it as they wish. This doctrine could be made effective by nullification^qv^. But Calhoun believed that the clear recognition of rights on the part of the states (*see* States' Rights) on the one hand and of the national majority on the other would prevent matters ever coming to a crisis. South Carolina and other Southern states, in the three decades preceding the Civil War, had provided legislatures in which the vested interests of land and slaves dominated in the upper houses, while the popular will of the numerical majority prevailed in the lower houses. This was done in conscious acceptance of the doctrine of the *Disquisition*.

[Richard K. Cralle, ed., *Works of John C. Calhoun*, Vol. I.]

JAMES ELLIOTT WALMSLEY

Calhoun's *Exposition* (1828). After the passage of the "Tariff of Abominations"^qv^ the South Carolina legislature resolved that it was "expedient to protest against the unconstitutionality and oppressive operation of the system of protective duties" and appointed a committee to report thereon. At the request of William C. Preston of the committee, John C. Calhoun prepared his *Exposition* in which he declared the tariff of 1828 "unconstitutional, unequal and oppressive; and calculated to corrupt public virtue and destroy the liberty of the country." Drawing on the "Resolutions of 1798" (*see* Virginia and Kentucky Resolutions), Calhoun proposed nullification^qv^ as the constitutional remedy. South Carolina should call a convention which should interpose the state's veto, to be binding upon its citizens and the general government unless three fourths of the states should amend the Constitution. Amended and published, although not adopted, by the legislature, Calhoun's *Exposition* was applied four years later in the nullification of the tariff acts of 1828 and 1832.

[Frederic Bancroft, *Calhoun and the South Carolina Nullification Movement;* John C. Calhoun, *Works*, Vol. VI; D. F. Houston, *A Critical Study of Nullification in South Carolina;* Gaillard Hunt, *John C. Calhoun;* W. M. Meigs, *Life of John Caldwell Calhoun.*]

FLETCHER M. GREEN

Calico Railroad, THE, was the derisive name applied to the Lyons, Iowa, Central Railroad which was to have been built across Iowa from Lyons, Iowa, to Council Bluffs. The company was organized in 1853. Iowa residents purchased stock and Iowa counties voted bonds to help build the road. Early in 1854 work on the track between Lyons and Iowa City was begun and progressed rapidly. The funds, however, were inadequate and some were misappropriated. As a result, work was stopped in June and engineers, contractors and laborers, involving some 2000 persons in all, were left without their pay and without work. The Iowa counties, however, were compelled to redeem their bonds. The railroad company had a store at Lyons and the goods (including a supply of calico) were distributed in partial payment to the workers; hence the name.

[Ruth Irish Preston, The Lyons and Iowa Central Railroad in the *Annals of Iowa*, Third Series, Vol. IX.]

RUTH A. GALLAHER

California, American Immigration to (1826–48). The few Americans in California before 1826 were deserters from New England trading ships. Overland immigration began with the arrival of Jedediah Smith^qv^ in 1826. During the next fifteen years, about thirty different groups came to California. The majority of these were trappers from the Hudson's Bay Company^qv^ post in Oregon, or traders from New Mexico. Probably about 300 Americans had established themselves in California by 1841, the year that home seekers began their trek across the plains.

During the winter and spring of 1840–41 numerous small groups along the frontier, particularly in Missouri and Arkansas, discussed the advisability of a move to California. As a result, in May, 1841, small parties assembled at Sapling Grove, a few miles west of the present site of Kansas City, and organized under the leadership of John Bartleson and John Bidwell. These pioneers crossed the Sierras in the vicinity of the headwaters of the Stanislaus River and reached various destinations in California by Nov. 1. Meanwhile another company, the Workman-Rowland, traveling over the Gila-Colorado route, arrived in Los Angeles.

Apparently there was no organized overland

expedition from the East to California in 1842, but the following year the movement was resumed. The Chiles-Walker party of 1843; the Stevens-Murphy Company of 1844 (the first immigrants to bring wagons into the settled part of California, and probably the first to enter California by way of the Truckee River route); the McMahon-Clyman, the Swasey-Todd, the Grigsby-Ide, the Hastings-Semple, the Sublette and probably other companies of 1845; various expeditions bringing approximately 500 people in 1846, including the ill-fated Donner party[qv], can only be mentioned here. In the latter half of 1846, following the outbreak of the Mexican War[qv], many immigrants to California were sailors or soldiers. The treaty of Guadalupe Hidalgo[qv], ending the war, was concluded Feb. 2, 1848, and California became a part of the United States. After that the account of immigration to California merges into that of the gold rush[qv] period.

[R. G. Cleland, *A History of California: The American Period;* Cardinal Goodwin, *The Trans-Mississippi West, 1803-1853.*]

CARDINAL GOODWIN

California, Russians in. It was fear of Russia which caused Spain to occupy California in 1769. Eventually the fear was justified. By the end of the 18th century Russian fur-trading posts were extended down the Alaska[qv] coast, a new Russian American Fur Company[qv] was established with Count Rezánof at its head and Baránof as chief factor at Sitka, the new capital. Shortage of supplies being a vital problem, Rezánof visited California (1806) with a view to opening trade in foodstuffs, but his success was only partial. His diplomacy included betrothal to Doña Concepción Arguello, daughter of the commander at San Francisco. This romance has been popularized by Bret Harte in a poem and by Gertrude Atherton in an historical novel. Rezánof died on his way back to St. Petersburg, but Russian interest in California continued. Without Spain's permission Kushkof in 1811 established north of San Francisco Bay the post called Fort Ross, which became the center of an agricultural colony and a base for an extensive sea-otter trade[qv] all down the California coast. A smaller settlement was founded on Bodega Bay. As a defensive move, first Spain, then Mexico, established settlements north of San Francisco Bay (San Rafael, 1817, and San Francisco Solano, or Sonoma, 1823). In 1824 Russia yielded all territorial claims south of 54° 40′ (*see* Oregon Question). By this time profits in the sea-otter trade had dwindled and Mexico's liberal trade policy enabled Russia to purchase supplies in California, thus lessening the agricultural importance of Fort Ross. As a result, in 1841 the establishment was sold to Sutter[qv] of New Helvetia (Sacramento) and Russia withdrew. Considerable ruins of Fort Ross are still to be seen.

[H. H. Bancroft, *History of California;* C. E. Chapman, *California: the Spanish Period;* H. Chevigny, *Lost Empire;* E. O. Essig, A. Ogden and C. J. DuFour, *The Russians in California;* Gertrude Atherton, *Rezánof,* a novel.]

HERBERT E. BOLTON

California, Spanish Exploration of. The discovery and early exploration of California were the work of the conqueror Cortés and his agents. Jiménez, one of his mariners, discovered the Peninsula in 1533. Two years later Cortés himself led a colony to the Bay of La Paz. In 1539 Juan de Ulloa, also sent by Cortés, rounded the Peninsula from the head of the Gulf to Cabo del Engaño, near N. Lat. 30°. Three years later Juan Rodríguez Cabrillo[qv] explored the entire outer coast of the Peninsula, discovered San Diego Bay (calling it San Miguel), the Channel Islands, Monterey Bay and perhaps Point Reyes, then returned to the Channel Islands, on one of which he died. The voyage was continued by Ferrelo (Ferrer), Cabrillo's second in command, who reached the vicinity of the Oregon border, returning thence to Mexico.

Because of English ravages on the Pacific (Drake[qv] and Cavendish) and the heavy toll of scurvy on the Manila galleons, Spain conceived the idea of founding a settlement on the Alta California[qv] coast to serve for defense and a port of call. California would be a cabbage patch for the support of the Manila trade. On this errand Sebastián Vizcaíno sailed from Mexico in 1602. He retraced the route of Cabrillo, changed the name of San Miguel Bay to San Diego[qv], explored and overpraised Monterey Bay and continued north to the vicinity of the Oregon border, about where the Cabrillo expedition had turned back. Plans to colonize Monterey Bay failed to mature and for nearly 170 years the California coast was seen by Spaniards only on the merchant galleons returning (southbound) from Manila. Under Spain (1769–1822) the interior of Alta California was extensively explored north from San Diego to Upper Sacramento valley and east to the Sierra Nevada.

[C. E. Chapman, *California: the Spanish Period;* H. E. Bolton, *Spanish Exploration in the Southwest;* H. R. Wagner, *Spanish Voyages to the Northwest Coast of America.*]

HERBERT E. BOLTON

California, The Conquest of (1846–7), is divided into two distinct phases. The first is characterized by considerable scurrying of men, by frequent raising of flags and by an absence of fighting. Frémont took over the command of the men at Sonoma on July 5, 1846, and ten days later led them through the streets of Monterey. Commodore Sloat raised the American flag at Monterey on July 7; it was unfurled at San Francisco and at Sonoma July 9 and two days later at Sacramento. On July 29 Frémont landed with his company at San Diego and Commodore Stockton succeeded Sloat as commander of the Pacific squadron and issued an offensive proclamation. On Aug. 4 and 6 Stockton raised flags over Santa Barbara and San Pedro respectively. On the 13th he met Frémont in Los Angeles (*see* California Battalion), raised the flag and four days later issued another proclamation. The first phase of the conquest was over.

In the second phase there was fighting and bloodshed. It began in the early morning of Sept. 23, with an attack by Californians (Mexicans) on the American garrison stationed at Los Angeles under the command of Capt. Gillespie. Capt. Mervine, sent by Stockton from Monterey with 350 troops, joined Gillespie's defeated forces at San Pedro and attempted a march on Los Angeles, but was driven back following an engagement with Capt. Flores' Californians. Both Santa Barbara and San Diego were quickly retaken by the Californians. Annoying guerrilla warfare in the north culminated in the battle of Natividad, Nov. 16, between Californians and a band of American frontiersmen on their way to join Frémont. The Californians retreated and the Americans moved south with Frémont to aid in recapturing Los Angeles.

Out of the inhospitable desert on Dec. 2 came Gen. Stephen W. Kearny to Warner's ranch with about 100 exhausted United States soldiers (*see* Kearny's March to California). On Dec. 5 he was joined by thirty-five men sent from San Diego by Stockton. On the following day Kearny fought the battle of San Pascual[qv]—the most stubborn engagement of the period. The Americans were left in possession of the field, but their loss was about a score killed and an equal number wounded. Among the latter was Gen. Kearny. Additional troops sent by Stockton arrived Dec. 10 and relieved the Americans. Two days later Kearny joined Stockton in San Diego. The united forces moved north and after two minor engagements (*see* San Gabriel, Battle of) again raised the American flag over Los Angeles. Three days later, Jan. 13, 1847, papers were signed at Cahuenga Rancho by Gen. Andrés Pico and Col. Frémont. This concluded the second and final phase of the conquest just seven months, lacking one day, after the occupation of Sonoma.

[R. G. Cleland, *A History of California: The American Period;* Cardinal Goodwin, *John Charles Frémont, an Explanation of His Career.*] CARDINAL GOODWIN

California Alien Land Law. To check the increasing competition of Japanese immigrant farmers, the California legislature passed the Alien Land Law of 1913. The act was amended and extended by popular initiative in 1920, and by the legislature in 1923 and 1927. These laws expressly permit aliens who are eligible to American citizenship to acquire, enjoy and transfer real property in the state to the same extent as citizens of the United States. On the other hand, individual aliens who are not eligible to citizenship and corporations in which a majority of members are such aliens, or in which a majority of the capital stock is owned by them, are permitted to hold real property only as may be stipulated in existing treaties between the United States and their respective countries.

[*Statutes of California* . . . 1913, Chap. 113; *ibid.*, 1921, lxxxiii; *ibid.*, 1923, Chap. 441; *ibid.*, 1927, Chap. 528; *So. Calif. Law Rev.*, III, 423-428, June, 1930; *Calif. Law Rev.*, XIX, 295-303, March, 1931; Porterfield v. Webb, 263 U. S. 225, 1923; People v. Cockrill, 268 U. S. 258, 1925; Tashiro v. Jordan, 256 Pacific, 545, 1927.]

P. ORMAN RAY

California Bank Notes. In 1822 began the hide and tallow[qv] trade through which California became well known to the New England states. Californians depended on "Boston Ships" for all goods of foreign manufacture and generally paid for them with hides, commonly known as "California bank notes," and averaging $1.50 to $2.00 in value.

[R. H. Dana, *Two Years Before the Mast.*]

OSGOOD HARDY

California Battalion, The. On July 5, 1846, at Sonoma, Capt. John C. Frémont absorbed into his command most of the American settlers and adventurers who had begun the Bear Flag Revolt[qv] on June 14. The total of 234 men was, at Monterey on July 23, enlisted by Commodore Robert F. Stockton, U. S. N., as the "Navy Battalion of Mounted Riflemen." Augmented to some 400 volunteers, the California Battalion served through the remainder of the American campaign against the Spanish Californians, participating under Frémont in Stockton's first capture of Los Angeles[qv], Aug. 13, and later receiving the final surrender of Gen. Andrés Pico's Californians to Frémont at Rancho Cahuenga on Jan. 13, 1847. It was mustered out of service, unpaid, April 1–19, 1847. The question of merging the Battalion with the regular United States forces under Gen. Stephen W. Kearny was an important part of the Kearny-Frémont controversy[qv] which led to Frémont's later arrest and court-martial.

[H. H. Bancroft, *History of California*, Vol. V; J. C. Frémont, *Memoirs of My Life;* Allan Nevins, *Frémont, the West's Greatest Adventurer.*]

RUFUS KAY WYLLYS

California Gold Rush. Gold was discovered by James W. Marshall at Coloma on the south fork of the American River on Jan. 24, 1848 (*see* Sutter's Fort). Further discoveries were made in the surrounding country during the month of February. The earliest reports to reach the communities along the coast were received dubiously, but by the end of May all uncertainty was removed. By the middle of June people were deserting homes and towns for the gold fields. Already, on June 1, United States Consul Larkin had forwarded official news of the discovery and his information reached Washington by the middle of September. Further dispatches, carried by Lt. Beale and dated a month later, were also received in the national capital. On June 12 Gov. R. B. Mason left Monterey to inspect the mines. About the middle of August he sent his report to the adjutant general, accompanied by a sample of gold. From $30,000 to $50,000, "if not more," he estimated were taken daily from the mines, and "there is more gold in the country drained by the Sacramento and San Joaquin rivers than will pay the cost of the present war with Mexico a hundred times over." A pick, a shovel and a tin pan were all that was required to obtain it. Mason's report, with its sensational observations, was included with the President's message to Congress on Dec. 5, 1848, and was published in the principal newspapers throughout the country.

The effect was immediate. By Jan. 18, 1849, sixty-one vessels, each carrying an average of fifty passengers, left Boston, Salem, New York, Philadelphia, Baltimore and Norfolk for the Pacific coast. Other ships carrying an unknown number of gold seekers sailed from Charleston and New Orleans during the same period. In February sixty ships were booked to leave New York and seventy from Boston and Philadelphia. The demand for accommodations to California had become so great that vessels were diverted from various services to provide passage for eager emigrants.

Both in Europe and in Asia populations were aroused by sensational reports from the gold fields. Five California trading and mining companies were organized in London at a cost of more than £1,250,000. Notices regarding the departure of vessels from the principal ports of Great Britain and from ports in France, Spain, Holland and Germany were published in foreign newspapers and magazines. Among the Asiatic peoples those most affected by the gold malady were the Chinese. The *Alta Californian* for May 10, 1852, estimates the number of Chinese in the territory Feb. 1, 1849, at fifty-four. By Dec. 31 of the same year there were 791. A year later there were more than 4000. The Japanese apparently heard of the discovery with stolid indifference. But in Australia the excitement was given free play. Shipmasters circulated reports and streets of the principal cities were placarded with announcements of "Gold! Gold!" in California, and soon it became difficult to secure passage on departing vessels. Even the inhabitants of the Marquesas Islands were affected. Members of the French colony who were free departed immediately and were quickly followed by the soldiers, leaving the governor alone to represent the government.

The spring of 1849 brought overland migration from Mexico and from the United States. "The mania that pervades the whole country, our own camp included," wrote an army officer regarding Mexico, "is beyond all description or credulity. The whole state of Sonora is on the move. . . ." Four thousand left for the gold fields before the beginning of summer, while in various rendezvous along the Missouri River numerous parties had gathered by the first of April. Bancroft estimates the number at 20,000. Bayard Taylor thought 30,000 crossed the plains and reached the gold fields before the beginning of winter. Throughout the summer of 1849, he says, the rich meadows of the Platte "were settled for the time, and a single traveler could have journeyed for the space of a thousand miles, as certain of his lodging and regular meals as if he were riding through the old agricultural districts of the middle states." Peter H. Burnett, later to be elected the first governor of the State of California, thought that at least "two thirds of the population of Oregon capable of bearing arms" migrated to the gold fields.

Probably more than 80,000 people came to California during 1848 and 1849. The Federal census for 1850 gives the total population, excluding Indians, as 92,597, but these figures do not include returns from San Francisco, Contra Costa and Santa Clara counties. The returns from the first were destroyed by fire and those of the last two were lost. Whatever the number, it was sufficient to create more intricate social, economic and political problems than had confronted any former frontier settlements in the history of the United States.

[Hubert Howe Bancroft, *The Works of*, Vol. XXIII; R. G. Cleland, *A History of California: The American Period;* Owen Cochran Coy, *The Great Trek.*]

CARDINAL GOODWIN

California Missions. California has no "old" missions and never had any. California was the very last province occupied, at the end of three centuries of mission founding, all the way from Buenos Aires to San Francisco and Jamestown. The missions founded by the Jesuits[qv] in Lower (Baja) California in the 17th and 18th centuries were taken over by the Franciscans[qv] in 1768. Next year the Franciscans advanced into Upper (Alta) California and three years later withdrew entirely from the southern district, yielding it to the Dominicans[qv]. The California Franciscans were members of the College of San Fernando in Mexico City, by which they were governed. The founder and moving spirit of the California missions was Father Junípero Serra. San Carlos Borromeo (Carmel) was his capital. Nine missions were founded in his presidency (1769–84) and nine under Lasuén (1785–1803), three more being added by 1823. They were established in the following order: San Diego, 1769; San Carlos, 1770; San Antonio, 1771; San Gabriel, 1771; San Luís Obispo, 1772; San Francisco de Asís, 1776; San Juan Capistrano, 1776; Santa Clara, 1777; San Buenaventura, 1782; Santa Bárbara, 1786; La Purísima Concepción, 1787; Santa Cruz, 1791; Soledad, 1791; San José, 1797; San Juan Bautista, 1797; San Miguel, 1797; San Fernando, 1797; San Luís Rey, 1798; Santa Inés, 1804; San Rafael, 1817; San Francisco Solano (Sonoma), 1823 (under Mexico).

The missions were both Christian seminaries and training schools in the rudiments of European civilization. The native Californians, except the Yumas, had no agriculture whatsoever and few of them had fixed abodes. Under the missionaries they became skilled in raising grain and fruits, tending cattle, horses and other stock; in building, spinning, weaving, tanning, leather work, blacksmithing, soap-making and many other crafts. Under the direction of the missionaries they built a score of beautiful missions. A complete mission plant comprised church, living quarters for the friars, the Indian village, shops, irrigation works, tallow vats, orchards, fields and vast pastures for flocks and herds. At each mission there were usually two priests and a small soldier guard.

At their height in 1821 the missions had in residence over 21,000 neophytes. By 1846 the total number of baptisms had reached 98,000. Under Mexico the California missions fared badly. Laws providing for secularization brought on a struggle which ended in the dispersion of the neophytes and the passing of most of the mission property into the hands of secular owners. The buildings fell into decay. Most of the churches are still (or again) used for religious purposes, but the rest of the buildings have largely disappeared. At some sites extensive restorations have been made or are in progress.

[Fr. Zephyrin Engelhardt, O.F.M., *Missions and Missionaries of California;* Nellie V. Sánchez, *Spanish Arcadia;* H. H. Bancroft, *History of California;* Helen Hunt Jackson, *Ramona*, a novel.]

HERBERT E. BOLTON

California since 1848. With the signing of the Treaty of Guadalupe Hidalgo[qv], Feb. 2, 1848, California, along with other lands wrested from Mexico by war (*see* Mexican War), was formally annexed to the United States. Thus was climaxed a half century of United States commercial and diplomatic interest in the region. The hide, tallow and fur trade[qqv] had brought Americans to California during the Spanish and Mexican periods[qqv]; organized American migrations had begun in the 1840's; Presidents Jackson, Tyler and Polk had futilely attempted the territory's purchase; annexation was the logical and inevitable outcome.

Two weeks before California formally became a part of the United States, gold was discovered in the Sierra Nevadas and soon pastoral California was invaded by a host of adventurers, among whom the vicious element was inevitably large (*see* California Gold Rush). By 1852 the population had jumped from 10,000 in 1846 (including 4000 Americans) to 250,000, centered mostly in San Francisco and the gold fields. This turbulent influx and the resultant clash between native Californian and Anglo-American custom rendered inadequate the military government set up during the Mexican War. The establishment of effective civil authority was imperative. Yet Congress, harassed by the question of slavery in the Mexican Cession, for two years remained deaf to California's plea for territorial government. At length, exasperated Californians took the initiative, devising a state constitution, ratified Nov. 13, 1849. This emergency document outlawed slavery[qv], wherefore Southern congressmen blocked Federal recognition of California's act for nearly a year. At last, on Sept. 9, 1850, President Fillmore signed the bill admitting California as a free state, as part of the Compromise of 1850[qv].

During the hectic decade which followed, California struggled to adjust herself to rapidly changing conditions. Crime was rife, leading several times to vigilante[qv] action. Anglo-American antipathy toward Spanish-Americans, whose numbers increased sharply during the gold rush, and toward the small but growing Chinese element led to frequent race riots. A further complication was added by the lack of homogeneity between the mining and commercial north and the pastoral south. Politics was corrupt and left by public indifference in the hands of a few. Concerned mainly with problems peculiar to herself, the state was for years but little affected by national issues. In 1860, however, the nationwide rift in the Democratic party[qv] extended to California, resulting in a Republican electoral victory. During the Civil War[qv], an active minority of Southern sympathizers endeavored to aid the Confederacy[qv], but sentiment predominantly favored the Union, to which were contributed both money and men.

One of California's most vital needs was communication with the East. In the absence of a transcontinental railway, long delayed by sectional differences and disagreement as to route, the Overland Mail[qv] was established in 1857 and the Pony Express[qv] in 1860. Construction of the railroad was at length undertaken during the Civil War and when the Central Pacific[qv], the California enterprise, met the Union Pacific[qv] near Ogden, Utah, May 10, 1869, a new era for California had begun.

Meanwhile economic and social changes were going on apace. The mining population dwindled, cities grew and the cattle industry declined sharply after the severe drought of 1864, thus paving the way for agricultural growth.

During the 1870's California was swept by a wave of popular discontent, in keeping with similar developments in other parts of the West (*see* Greenback Party; Granger Movement), but with causes which were in some respects peculiarly Californian. The presence of numerous Chinese antagonized white labor, leading to bloody anti-Chinese riots and, eventually, to the Federal Chinese Exclusion Act[qv] of 1882. Large agricultural estates, as well as confused land titles, produced especially by the survival of Spanish and Mexican land grants[qv], caused further dissatisfaction. More particularly, however, popular grievances turned upon the Central Pacific's monopoly of railroad transportation, its huge land investments and its political dictation. To remedy these and other evils, a new constitution was adopted in 1879, one of whose significant features was the extension of public control over the railroads, especially by the provision for a state Board of Railroad Commissioners.

Nearly thirty years elapsed before the state experienced another major political upheaval. Meanwhile, many of the conditions which prompted the agitation of the 1870's had disappeared. Government remained corrupt, however, and the railroads and other large corporations continued to incur public odium because of their political activities, real or alleged. By 1910 a popular reform movement, gaining impetus from a clean-up of municipal government in San Francisco and Los Angeles, had won control of state politics as well. Then followed various measures to render government more responsible to public will and to curb the political influence of the railroads.

Striking 20th-century developments were the rapid population increase of Los Angeles and southern California and the growth of a highly diversified agriculture, involving the reclamation[qv] of desert areas. By the second decade of the century, California, long absorbed in her own unique problems, had definitely entered the current of national affairs.

[R. G. Cleland, *A History of California: The American Period.*]

CHARLES EDWARD CHAPMAN AND ROBERT HALE SHIELDS

California Trail. A term applied to various through trails to California, the earliest ones being up the peninsula (1769) and northwest from Sonora (1774). From Santa Fé[qv] the Old Spanish Trail, made known (1776) by the Escalante expedition[qv], followed the Chama River, crossed Colorado into Utah and later was extended southwest to Los Angeles. Early traders and trappers also went west through Zuñi; then southwest by Salt River and west by the Gila[qv]; or (later) from Zuñi west to the Mohave country. Still others followed the Rio Grande south, then struck west to the headwaters of the Gila. In the 1840's gold-seekers converged in the Salt Lake Valley via the Platte River, Pueblo-Fort Bridger[qv], and Frémont trails[qv]; then continued west into northern California.

[R. P. Bieber, The Southwestern Trails to California in 1849, in *Mississippi Valley Historical Review*, XII, 1925.]

LANSING B. BLOOM

California under Mexico. For a quarter century, after 1822, California was a province of the Republic of Mexico. Outside of the missions this was a period of rapid and promising material development, whose direction was changed by the American conquest and the discovery of gold.

Of nearly 1000 so-called "Spanish" land grants, all but about a score were made under Mexico. Mexican colonists entered the province in considerable numbers, obtained vast ranches, built substantial country homes, raised great herds of cattle, horses and other stock, sold hides and tallow[qv], engaged in sea-otter[qv] hunting, enriched themselves by obtaining the property of the secularized missions and led a carefree pastoral life.

During this period California was invaded by foreign intruders on all sides. Sailors deserted their ships and remained in the province; Hudson's Bay[qv] trappers (Scotch, French and half-breeds) came yearly from the north. Stockton, for example, was founded by them as French Camp. American hunters and rovers came overland, without asking leave; English and American hide and tallow traders visited the California ports and set up the large establishments described by Dana in *Two Years Before the Mast.* Many of these foreigners settled in the country, married señoritas, acquired ranches, engaged in business or mechanical pursuits. Some of them became citizens of substance and influence. In 1841, contemporaneously with the movement of the covered wagon[qv] into Oregon, American immigrants began to come to California in caravans[qv], no less than fifteen of which arrived before the Gold Rush[qv]. Thus the forty-niners were by no means the pioneer Americans in California.

Politics were turbulent in these years. Mexico was disturbed and exercised little authority in the distant province. Governors sent from Mexico were generally unpopular and sometimes were ousted by local patriots. But native governors fared little better, because of the sectional rivalries between north and south California. Prominent in the politics of the period was the question of the secularization of the missions and the division of the plunder (*see* California Missions). The outstanding native Californian of this era was Gen. Mariano Vallejo, lord of the Sonoma March. Immigrants entered politics and became involved in the disturbances. After 1840 Sutter's vast estate, called New Helvetia (*see* Sutter's Fort), became the center of a quasi-independent community of Anglo-American immigrants, who had come with or without permission. Thus the way was being prepared for the Bear Flag Revolt[qv] and conquest by the United States.

[R. G. Cleland, *California: The American Period;* Nellie V. Sánchez, *Spanish Arcadia;* H. H. Bancroft, *California Pastoral;* R. H. Dana, *Two Years Before the Mast.*]

HERBERT E. BOLTON

California under Spain. In the 17th century Baja (Lower[qv]) California and Pimería Alta (now southern Arizona) were colonized by Spain, largely through the work of the Jesuit[qv] missionaries. After the expulsion of the Jesuits in 1767 their work was taken over by the Franciscans[qv]. There had been frequent talk of extending the settlements from these two bases northward into Alta (Upper) California[qv], but the step was not taken until foreign danger threatened. As a result of Bering's explorations in the North Pacific (1728–41), Russian fur traders established posts on the Aleutian Islands and began their southward march down the Alaska coast (*see* California, Russians in). Fearing the loss of Alta California, Spain now decided to occupy the province. The plan was carried out under the vigorous direction of José de Gálvez, Inspector-General of New Spain. He made use of men and means at hand. Gaspar de Portolá, governor of (Lower) California, was put at the head of a colony and Father Junípero Serra, president of the (Lower) California missions[qv], accompanied him with missionaries. Part of the colony went by sea, part overland up the peninsula. They met at San Diego Bay, and there founded the mission and presidio of San Diego[qv]. Continuing up the coast by land, over what is essentially the main railroad route, Portolá reconnoitered Monterey Bay and discovered San Francisco Bay, which all earlier explorers seem to have missed. Next year (June 3, 1770), Portolá and Serra founded the presidio and mission of San Carlos (Monterey), which became respectively the military and missionary capitals of the province. Within two years the missions of San Antonio, San Gabriel and San Luis Obispo were founded at intermediate points between San Diego and Monterey.

Two important problems were now solved by Juan Bautista de Anza, captain of the presidio of Tubac, in Pimería Alta (now southern Arizona). With twenty soldiers, Indian guides, cattle for food and Fathers Garcés and Díaz as diarists, in 1774 Anza[qv] explored a land route from the Mexican mainland over the mountains to San Gabriel. Next year he raised in Mexico a colony of settlers for San Francisco Bay, and led them over the same trail to California. His leadership was superb. Starting with 240 persons, he arrived at Monterey with 242, one death on the way being more than offset by the birth of three children. With this colony San Francisco[qv] was begun in June, 1776. Next year Felipe de Neve became the first governor of Alta California, which hitherto had been nominally ruled from Loreto, in Baja California.

When fully developed California under Spain was divided into four military districts (San Diego, Santa Barbara, Monterey and San Francisco). There were twenty missions, extending from San Diego to San Rafael (on the north shore of San Francisco Bay). Another, San Francisco Solano, was added in the rule of Mexico. Most of these mission colonies have become towns or cities. Three municipalities were founded, San José 1777, Los Angeles 1781 and Branciforte, now Santa Cruz, 1798. The chief industries of the province were agriculture, stock raising, and trade in sea-otter[qv] skins, the greater part of which was carried on by the missions. Spain's rule in California came to an end in 1822, independence being officially celebrated at Monterey on April 11.

[C. E. Chapman, *California: the Spanish Period;* Nellie V. Sánchez, *Spanish Arcadia;* H. E. Bolton, *Outpost of Empire.*]

HERBERT E. BOLTON

California v. Central Pacific R. R. Co. (1888). The Supreme Court held that, under the commerce and other clauses, Congress has power to construct interstate means of transportation directly or by charter through corporations; and that California could not tax the franchise thus granted by the United States.

[Charles Warren, *The Supreme Court in U. S. History.*]

JAMES D. MAGEE

Callabee Creek, Battle of (Jan. 27, 1814). In Macon County, Ala., fifty miles west of Fort Mitchell, Gen. Floyd, with 1200 Georgia volunteers, a company of cavalry and 400 friendly Indians, repulsed a night attack of the Red Stick Indians[qv] on his camp. Floyd lost so many in this hostile country that he immediately withdrew to the Chattahoochee.

[Benson J. Lossing, *Pictorial Field Book of the War of 1812.*]

ROBERT S. THOMAS

Calomel (monochloride of mercury) was throughout the 19th century a popular medication, especially for malarial fevers. Although known in colonial days, calomel first came to be widely used as a result of its administration by Benjamin Rush in the Philadelphia yellow-fever[qv] epidemic of 1793. Rush, believing the fever due to gas from decaying vegetation, attempted to remove the poison by bleeding and strong purgatives (calomel, rhubarb and jalap), a practice borrowed from John Mitchell of Virginia (1741). One of Rush's pupils, John Esten Cooke, extending the theory to practically all diseases, gave wide currency to the practice through his lectures and writings at Transylvania University (1827–37). He advised repeated and strong doses, even a dram in extreme cases. At the Louisville Medical Institute (1837–44) Cooke found complaints against his teaching, which finally caused his resignation. A milder dosage known as "Cooke's pills" (1–2 grams of calomel with aloes, rhubarb and soap) was popular for many years. In the army it was customary to take a pint of blood from each new recruit and give him Rush's "ten and ten." While W. A. Hammond was surgeon general (1862–64), calomel and tartar emetic were banned from the supply list, but later restored. Calomel is still used in acute malarial fevers as a preliminary purgative.

[F. R. Packard, *History of Medicine in the United States;* Robert Peter, *History of the Medical Department of Transylvania University.*]

W. C. MALLALIEU

Calumet, The. *See* Pipe, Indian.

Calumet and Hecla Mine, THE. A copper mine in the Keweenaw Peninsula of Lake Superior in northwest Michigan. For some years previous to its discovery by Edwin J. Hulbert in 1859 copper exploration and mining had been taking place in the region. Hulbert uncovered the conglomerate lode in 1864. The geological deductions which led to this result were based upon the discovery of masses of breccia scattered upon the ground, which suggested to Hulbert a search for the mother lode. The Calumet and the Hecla mines opened as separate undertakings under Hulbert's management, but soon afterwards Alexander Agassiz was sent out from Boston to superintend the initial stages of development. The problem of separating the conglomerate copper from its rock matrix was solved with great difficulty. The country was then very remote and wild, having only water transportation in the summer and none in the winter. In spite of difficulties the two original mines paid dividends in 1869 and 1870, and were consolidated into the Calumet and Hecla Mining Company in 1871. Other mining companies were opened in the vicinity, at first under distinct corporations, but by 1923 most of them had consolidated with the Calumet and Hecla Company.

Several shafts reached a depth of over a mile on the vertical and considerably over that on the vein or incline. Early milling methods did not recover all the copper from the rock, and the old tailings have been reworked with modern methods with remarkable results. By 1933 the aggregate tonnage of ore mined and treated had been 165,000,000. The various mines of the Calumet and Hecla have produced 4,808,000,000 pounds of copper metal, which sold for $771,000,000.

[T. A. Richard, *A History of American Mining.*]

LEW A. CHASE

Calvinism in its broadest sense is the entire body of conceptions arising from the teachings of John Calvin. Its fundamental principle is the conception of God as absolutely sovereign. The statement of Calvinism most influential in America was the Westminster Confession[qv] (1647). Its doctrinal portion was accepted by the New England Congregationalists[qv] and embodied in their Cambridge Platform[qv] (1648). American Presbyterians[qv] coming from Scotland and North Ireland were sternly Calvinistic. The Synod of Philadelphia, the oldest general Presbyterian body in America, passed the Adopting Act in 1729, which required all ministers and licentiates to subscribe to the Westminster Confession. Other Calvinistic bodies in America are the two Reformed Churches, the Dutch and the German, and all other Presbyterian bodies.

[W. W. Sweet, *Story of Religions in America.*]

WILLIAM W. SWEET

Calvo Doctrine, The, enunciated in 1885 by C. Calvo, the Argentinian international jurist, held that the use of neither force nor diplomatic pressure is justifiable in the prosecution of claims or indemnities with respect to either public or private debts or losses, resulting from civil war or other causes. The Calvo Doctrine is to be distinguished from the Drago Doctrine[qv] given validity by the Hague Convention[qv] of 1907 prohibiting the use of force in the collection of public debts.

[A. S. Hershey, The Calvo and Drago Doctrines, *American Journal of International Law*, 1907, 1926.]

PHILLIPS BRADLEY

Cambridge, Mass., was settled in 1631. Originally intended as the seat of government of the Massachusetts Bay Colony[qv], the town was early abandoned by Gov. John Winthrop and others in favor of Boston[qv], leaving Deputy Gov. Thomas Dudley and Simon Bradstreet as the principal founders of the "newe towne," as it was first called. For a time Rev. Thomas Hooker's company settled there (1632–36) before removing to Connecticut[qv]. Their places were taken by the company of Rev. Thomas Shepard, who became the first permanent minister of the town. The name of Newtown was changed to Cambridge when Harvard College[qv] was founded there in 1638. The following year the college set up the first printing press in North America with Stephen Day as printer.

[L. R. Paige, *History of Cambridge;* S. A. Drake, *History of Middlesex County;* Hannah Winthrop Chapter, D. A. R., *Historic Guide to Cambridge.*]

R. W. G. VAIL

Cambridge Agreement, The (1629), was the decision made and signed by Puritan[qv] members of the Massachusetts Bay Company[qv] that if the charter and company could be legally transferred to New England, they would migrate thither with their families. By accepting the agreement and overcoming the legal obstacle concerning removal, the company, originally organized for purposes of trade, shifted its emphasis of interest from commerce to religion. Although the joint stock remained under the direction of English business men for some time afterward, henceforth the control of the plantation was in the hands of Puritans, who, dissatisfied with the prospect of religious and political reform at home, looked to the Massachusetts project as an opportunity to establish a Calvinistic utopia. The sequel to the Cambridge Agreement was the Great Migration[qv] of March, 1630, when more than 1000 Puritans transferred families and effects to New England for the purpose of building a colony based on their ideas of close union of church and state.

[C. M. Andrews, *The Colonial Period of American History*, I.]

VIOLA F. BARNES

Cambridge Platform, The, was drawn up by a synod of ministers from Massachusetts and Connecticut (August, 1648), which met pursuant to a request of the Massachusetts General Court[qv]. The New England authorities desired a formal statement of polity and a confession of faith because of the current Presbyterian ascendancy in England and the activities of local Presbyterians[qv] such as Dr. Robert Child. The declaration endorsed the Westminster Confession[qv] and for ecclesiastical organization upheld the existing Congregational[qv] practice. The Cambridge Platform remained the standard formulation in Massachusetts through the 18th century and in Connecticut until the Saybrook Platform[qv] of 1708.

[Williston Walker, *The Creeds and Platforms of Congregationalism;* Perry Miller, *Orthodoxy in Massachusetts.*]

PERRY MILLER

Camden, Battle of (Aug. 16, 1780). Following Lincoln's disaster at Charleston[qv], Gates was given command of the Southern army consisting of 1400 regulars under DeKalb and 2052 militia. Marching southward from Hillsborough, Gates occupied Rugelys Mill, a strong position about thirteen miles northeast of Camden which had been occupied by the British under Lord Rawden. Gates unwisely sent 400 regulars to aid Sumter cut the British lines of communication far to the southeast (*see* Hanging Rock, S. C., Action at). Then failing to attack promptly, he allowed Cornwallis time to arrive with reinforcements. The two generals decided to suprise each other. Cornwallis, with 2000 veterans, marched northward and met Gates marching southward early in the morning of Aug. 16. The Americans were exhausted from long marches, many helpless with dysentery, and more than half were militia who had never been under fire. At the first attack the militia fled. The regulars, standing their ground, were surrounded and almost annihilated. DeKalb was captured, mortally wounded. The Americans lost 2000 killed, wounded and captured, seven cannon, 2000 muskets and their transport. The British loss was 324. Gates fled to Hillsborough and vainly attempted to rally his demoralized army and call out more militia, but his day was over. Dec. 2 he was replaced by Greene. Many Americans fled to the swamps and mountains and carried on guerrilla warfare (*see* Southern Campaigns, 1780–81).

[John W. Fortescue, *History of the British Army*, III; Edward McCrady, *The History of South Carolina in the Revolution.*]

NELSON VANCE RUSSELL

Camden-Yorke Opinion. A written opinion, professional and not judicial in character, was given in 1769 by Lord Camden, who was at the time Lord Chancellor of Great Britain, and Charles Yorke, who was later to be raised to the same eminent position. It related to the rights of private persons who had taken conveyances of lands from native tribes of India, and supported such titles, grants from the king not being necessary. It was held that the king only had sovereignty over the inhabitants as English subjects. The opinion was seized on by certain western land companies in America as applicable to any purchases they might make from the aborigines as proprietors of the soil. Many public men and lawyers in America concurred in the soundness of the opinion, Patrick Henry among them. However, when the matter came to judicial test in this country after the Revolution, the contrary view prevailed: titles to lands acquired from the Indian tribes were void when the state had not given consent; the real title was held to be in the state as sovereign.

[C. W. Alvord, *Mississippi Valley in British Politics.*]

SAMUEL C. WILLIAMS

Camels in the West. At the close of the Mexican War the United States added 529,189 square miles to its area. This territory contained no railroads and the difficulties of transportation were so great that an effort was made to establish across this new country fast express routes by using camels. Congress (1855) appropriated $30,000 to purchase camels in Egypt and Asia. Seventy-six camels were brought to Texas. Twenty-eight of them were taken to California (1857) to be used on mail and express routes through the desert country, but after a few trips their use was discontinued. They were later (1864) sold at auction, most of them being taken to Nevada and used to carry freight to and from the mines. Those remaining in Texas were sold to circuses and zoölogical gardens. The only other importation of camels was in 1860–62. Forty-five animals were brought from Siberia to San Francisco by Otto Esche, a German merchant, who planned to use them on eastbound express routes. He never started this service, but sold most of the camels to a mining company in British Columbia. Years later wild camels were occasionally seen in the Northwest, in Nevada, and especially in Arizona. All are now (1939) extinct.

[Lewis B. Lesley, Uncle Sam's Camels, *California Historical Society Quarterly*, December, 1930.]

A. A. GRAY

Camino del Diablo (the Devil's Highway), an old and difficult trail connecting a series of desert water-holes northwestward from the Rio de Sonóita to the Gila River near its confluence with the Colorado. Apparently it was first traced by white men when the Jesuit[qv] missionary, Padre Eusebio Francisco Kino, traversed it in February, 1699. The trail crossed the present international boundary some forty miles northwest of the border town of Sonóita, and thence crossed the Tule Desert westward to the southeastern end of the Gila Range, following the latter's eastern slope to the Gila River. As a short-cut from the settled portion of Sonora through the lands of the Pápago Indians to the Colorado and thence into California, it was frequently used by travelers, including Juan Bautista de Anza's[qv] exploring party of 1774 to California.

[H. E. Bolton, *Rim of Christendom*, and *Outpost of Empire;* K. Bryan, *Guide to Desert Watering Places.*]

RUFUS KAY WYLLYS

Camp Butler (1861–66), concentration camp for Illinois volunteers, was established in August, 1861, and used until June, 1866. It was located six miles east of Springfield. Here nearly a third of the Illinois regiments were mustered into the

Federal service and later discharged. After the capture of Fort Donelson[qv], Camp Butler was used also as a prison camp[qv], housing at one time as many as 3600 captured Confederates.

[Helen E. Sheppley, Camp Butler in the Civil War Days, *Journal of the Illinois State Historical Society*, January, 1933.]

PAUL M. ANGLE

Camp Chase, located just west of Columbus, Ohio, served the dual purpose of training camp and military prison during the Civil War. As the war continued, its importance as a prison camp[qv] increased and Confederate prisoners continued to be received in large numbers until the cessation of hostilities. The high tide of prison population was reached in 1863 when some 8000 Confederate soldiers were confined there. In 1864 a Confederate plan to release the prisoners at Johnson's Island[qv] in Lake Erie, seize Sandusky and release the prisoners at Camp Chase, miscarried.

[William H. Knauss, *The Story of Camp Chase.*]

FRANCIS R. AUMANN

Camp Douglas (1861–65) was established in September, 1861, for the concentration and training of Illinois volunteers. It covered sixty acres near the then southern limit of Chicago. After the fall of Fort Donelson[qv], Camp Douglas served also as a prison camp[qv], 30,000 Confederates being confined there at one time or another. It was dismantled in November, 1865.

[A. T. Andreas, *History of Chicago.*]

PAUL M. ANGLE

Camp Followers. There were various types of camp followers in our early wars—peddlers, sutlers, gamblers, Indians, Negroes; but most surely present of all were the women—sometimes wives of officers and soldiers, but more often not. The *Memoirs* of Baroness Riedesel tell how she and her children followed her husband with Burgoyne's army to Saratoga[qv], and war diaries and army orders tell of quite another type of woman, often the lowest imaginable. They became a problem in the French and Indian War[qv] though it is humorously noted that if an army settled down in a far northern camp for the winter, most of the women disappeared before December. Washington's orders in that war permitted a limited number, finally fixed at six to every hundred men, in camp and on the march, and even to draw rations, on condition that they behaved themselves well and did washing for the soldiers. Later, cooking was added to their duties. They were omnipresent in the Revolutionary War, the British army having more than the American because of its better pay and rations. The American army before Boston in February, 1776, sternly drummed two women out of camp (David How's *Diary*), but later relaxed its attitude. Several times, however, Washington had to issue orders against their being permitted to ride on the wagons when the army was on the march. When the army passed through Philadelphia, Aug. 23, 1777, Washington ordered that "Not a Woman belonging to the Army is to be seen with the troops on their march through the City." The women were therefore herded through alleys and back streets. A few women even participated in Arnold's dreadful march to Quebec[qv], including a squaw, the mistress of Aaron Burr. Some Indian men became hangers-on in the French and Indian War, drawing rations but giving little or no service in return. One finds sutlers and peddlers frequently whipped during that war for selling liquor to the soldiers. In the Carolinas during the Revolution, Negroes forsook the plantations by hundreds to follow Cornwallis' army, apparently regarding the British as their deliverers from slavery, but incidentally drawing free rations and having an adventure without work. The War of 1812 presents a somewhat similar picture, though Indians figure in it more largely. Just before the Battle of Lake Erie[qv], the British commissaries were feeding 14,000 Indians, men, women and children, of whom not even all the men could be depended upon to give service when it was desired.

[George Washington, *Writings;* Journal of Capt. Samuel Jenks, *Massachusetts Historical Society Proceedings*, March, 1890.]

ALVIN F. HARLOW

Camp Grant Massacre (April 30, 1871). An attack on Aravaipa Apaches[qv] at Camp Grant, Arizona Territory, by a party of Mexicans, Americans and Papago Indians from Tucson and San Xavier, who attributed to the Camp Grant Indians a series of murders and outrages, particularly a raid on San Xavier in which horses and mules were stolen. Twenty-seven bodies were found, nearly all women and children, and twenty-eight children were carried off, seven of whom were recovered. The leaders were acquitted in a jury trial.

[Frank C. Lockwood, *The Apache Indians.*]

DON RUSSELL

Camp Jackson Affair (May 3–10, 1861). Capt. Nathaniel Lyon, in command of United States Arsenal in St. Louis, imbued with the idea that Missouri authorities were planning to capture the arsenal, collected and armed a number of politico-military organizations as Home Guards. With over 8000 of these, mostly Germans and other foreigners, Capt. Lyon seized, on his own initiative and without resistance, the 669 militiamen encamped at Camp Jackson, St. Louis. While being marched away several miles to prison, these men were fired upon, three of them killed, about twenty-eight civilians killed and many men, women and children wounded. Many of the militiamen were opponents of secession and all were subsequently released on parole, subject to exchange as prisoners of war. (*See* Confederacy, Border State Representation in.)

[*War of the Rebellion: Official Records of the Union and Confederate Armies*, Ser. II, Vol. I; *Missouri Republican*, May 11-14, 1861.]

STELLA M. DRUMM

Camp Meetings. Outdoor religious meetings were a feature of the evangelical revival[qv] in both England and America in the 18th century. Baptists[qv] held meetings similar to the later camp meetings during the American Revolution. The meeting conducted jointly by Presbyterian and Methodist[qqv] ministers in Logan County, Ky., in July, 1800, is generally accepted as the first regular camp meeting. Held in a wood, near a supply of water, the encampments usually lasted four days or longer. There were several services each day and sometimes four or five ministers spoke at the same time from different parts of the camp ground. The animated evening services of the frontier assemblies, accentuated by pine knots flickering in the dense darkness, were usually tense with excitement and frequently marked by emotional irregularities such as jerking, falling, barking, rolling and dancing.

Camp meetings were not confined to the frontier, but extended throughout the United States during the early 19th century. Steamboats carried many hundreds of people at excursion rates from Eastern cities to near-by camp meetings. In many cases cottages replaced tents and permanent auditoriums were erected. During the late 19th century popular educational movements, such as Chautauqua[qv], and summer resort communities, such as Ocean Grove, N. J., developed from camp-meeting beginnings. Many summer assemblies still function as outgrowths of the camp meeting.

[Catherine C. Cleveland, *The Great Revival in the West, 1797-1805.*]

W. B. POSEY

Camp Supply. *See* Supply, Camp.

Camp Wild-Cat was a natural fortification in the Rockcastle Hills of Laurel County, Ky., where Union troops, under Col. T. T. Garrard, decisively repulsed Gen. Zallicoffer on Oct. 21, 1861.

[*War of the Rebellion: Official Records of the Union and Confederate Armies*, Ser. I, Vol. IV.]

JONATHAN T. DORRIS

Campaign Literature is the term used to cover all varieties of material circulated during a political campaign to influence the voter. This includes campaign textbooks, which contain a miscellaneous collection of information, statistical tables, documents and arguments particularly for the use of the party worker; biographies of the candidates; special pamphlets on the issues of the campaign; news stories and press releases; pictures, lithographs and cartoons; campaign songs and slogans; letters and postcards; posters, windshield stickers and other similar material, all of which has increased enormously with the growth of the electorate. In 1896 about 100,000,000 pieces were shipped from the Chicago headquarters of the Republican National Committee, while in 1936 at least 370,000,000 pieces were issued from the same headquarters and probably almost as much from the Democratic headquarters.

[Robert C. Brooks, *Political Parties and Electoral Problems*, 3rd edition; Ralph D. Casey, Party Campaign Propaganda, *Annals of the American Academy of Political and Social Science*, Vol. CLXXIX; Burton Bigelow, The Machinery behind Political Pamphleteering, *Journalism Quarterly*, Vol. XIV.]

CLARENCE A. BERDAHL

Campaign of 1788 and of 1792, The, had no formal nominations, only one presidential candidate, and little opposition to the second choice. The Constitution ratified, the Continental Congress[qv] delayed three months before fixing the first Wednesday in January, 1789, for choosing electors, the first Wednesday in February for their voting and the first Wednesday in March for starting the new government. Pennsylvania, Maryland and Virginia elected electors; Massachusetts' legislature chose hers from elected electors; New Hampshire's election failed and her legislature, as did those of the remaining states, appointed electors. Thirteen states could cast ninety-one votes; but two states had not ratified and one (New York) failed to elect or appoint; four electors failed to vote. Washington received the entire sixty-nine votes cast. John Adams received thirty-four as second choice and the other thirty-five were scattered among ten different candidates. In 1792 fifteen states could cast 132 electoral votes, when Hamilton's financial measures and the consolidation of national power (*see* Federalist Party) roused an opposition (Jeffersonian antifederalists) which centered its efforts on the defeat of Adams by the antifederalist[qv] George Clinton, as to defeat Washington was seen to be futile. The attempt failed. Washington's vote was again unanimous, and Adams defeated Clinton by seventy-seven to fifty.

[Edward A. Stanwood, *A History of the Presidency.*]

JOHN C. FITZPATRICK

Campaign of 1796, THE, was the first national election in American history to be contested by political parties. The French Revolution, Genêt and the Jay Treaty[qv] resulted in bitter partisanship. Without the modern machinery of nomination the Federalists[qv] informally agreed upon John Adams as Washington's successor; with him they chose Thomas Pinckney. With more enthusiasm the Republicans (*see* Republican Party, Jeffersonian) chose their leaders, Thomas Jefferson and Aaron Burr. Electors were chosen in sixteen states—in six by popular vote, in ten by the legislature. Of the total electoral votes Adams secured seventy-one, Jefferson sixty-eight, Pinckney fifty-nine, Burr thirty and the remaining forty-eight were divided among nine others, several of whom were distinctly not candidates.

[Edward A. Stanwood, *A History of the Presidency.*]

FRANK MONAGHAN

Campaign of 1800 and of 1804, THE. The election of 1800 forms a turning point in American political history. Its preliminaries were expressed in the famous Virginia and Kentucky Resolutions[qv], proffered by Jefferson and Madison as a party platform. Its party machinery, still more essential to success, was directed by Aaron Burr with supplemental support in Pennsylvania and South Carolina.

Burr had already established the nucleus of a political machine[qv] that was later to develop into Tammany Hall[qv]. With this organization he swept the City of New York with an outstanding legislative ticket, gained control of the state assembly and secured the electoral votes of New York for the Republicans (*see* Republican Party, Jeffersonian). He had already secured a pledge from the Republican (Jeffersonian) members of Congress to support him equally with Jefferson. Hence the tie vote which gave him a dubious chance for the Presidency.

Publicly disclaiming any intent to secure that office, Burr was, nevertheless, put forward by the Federalists[qv] in order to defeat Jefferson and bring about another election (*see* Jefferson-Burr Election Dispute). A slight majority in the House of Representatives enabled them to rally six states to Burr and divide the vote of two others, thus neutralizing the vote of the eight states that supported Jefferson. The contest was prolonged through thirty-five fruitless ballotings; on the thirty-sixth, by prearrangement, a sufficient number of Federalists cast blank ballots to give Jefferson ten states and the Presidency.

This narrow escape from frustrating the popular will led the incoming administration to pass the Twelfth Amendment[qv] to the Constitution. Jefferson covertly helped eliminate Burr in New York, and the party caucus brought George Clinton forward as candidate for the Vice-Presidency. Burr, already divining his political ostracism, attempted to recover ground as an independent candidate for governor of New York. Representative Federalists of New England sought his support in their plans for disunion, but he refused to commit himself to such a program. Jefferson, pre-eminently successful in the more important measures of his administration, was triumphantly re-elected in 1804 as President with George Clinton as Vice-President, the first to be elected as such under the new amendment.

[Edward A. Stanwood, *A History of the Presidency.*]

ISAAC J. COX

Campaign of 1808 and of 1812, THE. Candidates for the Republican (Jeffersonian)[qv] nomination in 1808 were James Madison, the choice of Jefferson; James Monroe, somewhat tainted by affiliation with John Randolph and the "Quids"[qv], who were anathema to the outgoing administration; and George Clinton, a New Yorker not favored by the "Virginia Dynasty."[qv] Jefferson's own refusal to consider a third term confirmed the two-term tradition for a President. At the party caucus[qv] Madison received eighty-three votes; his rivals three each.

The Federalist[qv] opposition was led by Charles Cotesworth Pinckney and Rufus King, but the chief obstacle to the Madison slate came from his own party, notably in Virginia and Pennsylvania, where William Duane, a powerful journalist, was unreconcilable. The malcontents finally voted the party ticket, however, and in the electoral college Madison obtained 122 out of 176 votes. Clinton ran behind the ticket by 9 votes to be Vice-President. Defeated for the Presidency, the Federalists nevertheless made serious inroads upon the Republican majority in the House of Representatives.

In 1812 Madison secured his renomination by a tacit rather than a formal yielding to the demands of Henry Clay and the "War Hawks."[qv] The vice-presidential nomination, tendered first to John Langdon of New Hampshire, went to

Elbridge Gerry of Massachusetts. Opposition to the party slate was led by DeWitt Clinton of New York, who finally accepted nomination from the Federalists, with Jared Ingersoll of Pennsylvania as his running mate. The electoral college gave Madison 128 votes, as against 89 for Clinton. Vermont and Pennsylvania stood by Madison, but New York was led by Martin Van Buren into the Clinton column. Gerry and the ticket could not carry the candidate's own state of Massachusetts, notwithstanding his recent election as governor. Thus, on the eve of the War of 1812[qv], the Republican party was seriously divided.

[Edward Channing, *The Jeffersonian System;* K. C. Babcock, *The Rise of American Nationality.*]

LOUIS MARTIN SEARS

Campaign of 1816 and of 1820, The. There was no campaign by parties in 1816 worth the name, none at all in 1820. President Madison's choice was James Monroe, old Jeffersonian protégé, Secretary of State and War. Some Republicans (Jeffersonian)[qv] favored Gov. Tompkins of New York. Younger Republicans, interested in nationalist measures following the War of 1812, including a bank, protective tariffs and internal improvements[qqv] to speed the development of the West, preferred Crawford, Secretary of the Treasury, a citizen of Georgia. They gave him 54 votes in the congressional caucus[qv] to 65 for Monroe. Here was the election of 1816, for in the electoral college Monroe overwhelmed Rufus King, signer of the Constitution and statesman of note, but a Federalist[qv] whose party now was thoroughly discredited by the Hartford Convention[qv]. Monroe was given 183 votes to 34 for King. Newer sectional conflicts and rivalry among the younger leaders embittered the "Era of Good Feeling,"[qv] but President Monroe was secure. He was re-elected in 1820, with only one dissenting electoral vote. Federalists saw a greater menace to their propertied interests rising with the democracy of the West; it was to dethrone "King Caucus" and the "Virginia Dynasty"[qv] in the free-for-all campaign of 1824.

[Edward A. Stanwood, *A History of the Presidency.*]

ARTHUR B. DARLING

Campaign of 1824, The, preparations for which began with the second inauguration of Monroe, marked the beginning of the transition from federalism to democracy with resulting voter realignment under new party emblems. The five candidates were prominent in national affairs and represented sections or factions rather than parties. In general, the politicians supported Crawford; John Quincy Adams represented business; Calhoun, the South and the rising slavocracy[qv]; Clay, the expanding West; Jackson, the people everywhere. The first three were Cabinet members, Clay was Speaker of the House and Jackson was the country's most popular military figure.

Crawford was virtually eliminated by sickness; Jackson was brought in late by his friends; Clay's support was never impressive; Calhoun withdrew and became candidate for Vice-President on both the Adams and Jackson tickets. No candidate received a majority electoral vote. Jackson secured the greatest number, 99; Adams, 84; Crawford, 41; and Clay, 37. Selection was made by the House. Adams was chosen. Jackson's supporters could only charge a "Corrupt Bargain"[qv] and bide their time. (*See* Campaign of 1828.)

[Bennett Champ Clark, *John Quincy Adams;* Marquis James, *Andrew Jackson: Portrait of a President.*]

THOMAS ROBSON HAY

Campaign of 1828 and of 1832, The. In 1828 President John Quincy Adams stood for re-election and Andrew Jackson of Tennessee made his second campaign for the Presidency. Designated the people's candidate by the action of friends in the legislature of his own State of Tennessee, Jackson won and held the necessary support of influential leaders in New York, Pennsylvania and South Carolina. The campaign was waged throughout the administration of Adams. It was not marked by any clear-cut declaration of political principle or program and Jackson came to think of it as a personal vindication. Of the twenty-four states, Delaware and South Carolina still expressed their choice by vote of the legislature. In twenty-two states the elections were held in the period from late October to early December. There was a great increase in the popular vote cast and both candidates shared in the increase; 643,000 being cast for Jackson and 507,000 for Adams. The electoral vote stood 178 for Jackson to 83 for Adams. John C. Calhoun of South Carolina was again elected Vice-President. In many parts of the nation there was evidence of a more effective organization of the vote than in any previous contest, yet, over and above all considerations in this election was the appeal that the frontier hero made to an increasing body of democratically minded voters. Jackson, himself, was the cause of an alignment of public opinion in the years that followed (*see* Jacksonian Democracy). Jackson men controlled the Congress, and platforms and programs were supported by leaders and sections and groups, but not by clearly defined political parties^qv^. Naturally Jackson stood for re-election although he had spoken in favor of a single term, and the campaign to renominate him began at once. After December of 1831, when Henry Clay returned to the Senate, he, rather than Adams, received the support of most of those who were opposed to Jackson. This did not include Calhoun, who in 1830 had broken with Jackson. Clay was formally presented by a national convention that met in December of 1831. He was endorsed by a national convention of young men which prepared a platform in a meeting held in May of 1832. In that month a national convention of Jackson supporters nominated Martin Van Buren of New York for the Vice-Presidency. In this election the recently gathered Anti-Masonic party^qv^ supported William Wirt of Maryland. The campaign not only witnessed the general use of the national party convention^qv^ but platforms^qv^ were presented and cartoons^qv^ freely used, and there was concentration of popular attention upon the pageantry of parades^qv^. Aside from the personal contest between Jackson and Clay the issue between the two centered upon Jackson's attack upon the United States Bank^qv^ and particularly upon his veto of the bill for the recharter of the bank, a bill which had the backing of the supporters of Clay in both Houses of Congress. Twenty-four states participated in this election and all except South Carolina provided a popular vote. The electorate endorsed the administration of Jackson, for the distribution of the vote in twenty-three states gave Jackson 707,000, Clay 329,000 and Wirt 255,000. In the electoral college the vote stood Jackson 219, Clay 49, Wirt 7, with 11 votes representing the vote of South Carolina cast for John Floyd of Virginia. Jackson had a greater proportion of the popular vote in 1832 than he had had in 1828.

[S. R. Gammon, *The Presidential Campaign of 1832;* Claude G. Bowers, *Party Battles of the Jackson Period.*]

EDGAR EUGENE ROBINSON

Campaign of 1836, The. Made up chiefly of Anti-Masons^qv^, National Republicans^qv^ and anti-Jackson Democrats, the Whig party^qv^, formed in 1834, naturally lacked unity. Because of this, the Whig leaders decided to put forward several sectional candidates in the 1836 presidential campaign. Accordingly, Judge Hugh L. White was entered in the race through nomination by legislative caucuses in Tennessee and Alabama, held in January, 1835. At about the same time, Judge John McLean was nominated by a legislative caucus in Ohio, but he withdrew from the race in the following August. Sen. Daniel Webster was nominated by a Massachusetts legislative caucus, also in January, 1835. Still another candidate of the Whigs was Gen. William H. Harrison, who was formally nominated by both Anti-Masonic and Whig state conventions in Pennsylvania in December, 1835.

Meanwhile at a national convention held in Baltimore on May 21–22, 1835, Martin Van Buren, who was President Jackson's personal choice, had been unanimously nominated for the Presidency by the Democrats^qv^. No platform was adopted by the convention, but a committee was authorized to draw up an address. Published in the party organ, the Washington *Globe,* on Aug. 26, 1835, this address presented Van Buren as one who would, if elected, continue "that wise course of national policy pursued by Gen. Jackson." For all practical purposes, this address may be regarded as the first platform^qv^ ever issued by the Democratic party.

When the election returns were finally in, it was found that Van Buren had won the Presidency with 170 electoral votes and a popular vote of 761,549 to 736,656 for his opponents. White received 26 electoral votes, Webster 14, and Harrison 73, while South Carolina bestowed its 11 votes on W. P. Mangum. No candidate for the Vice-Presidency received a majority of the electoral vote, so on Feb. 8, 1837, the Senate chose the Democratic candidate, Richard M. Johnson, over his leading rival, Francis Granger.

[Edward A. Stanwood, *A History of the Presidency.*]

ERIK McKINLEY ERIKSSON

Campaign of 1840, The. Distinctive in American history as the first national victory of the Whig party^qv^, the campaign of 1840 was unique for its popular and emotional appeal, organized on an unprecedented scale. To the Whigs belongs the credit of introducing into a presidential battle every political device calculated to sway the "common man."

The Whig convention, assembled at Harrisburg, Dec. 2, 1839, nominated Gen. William Henry Harrison of Indiana for President, and John Tyler of Virginia for Vice-President. No attempt was made to frame a platform^qv^; indeed, the only bond uniting the various groups under the Whig banner was a determination to defeat the Democrats^qv^. The Democratic convention held at Baltimore, May 5, 1840, was united on Martin Van Buren for President, but left to the state electors the choice of a Vice-President. A platform on strict construction^qv^ lines was adopted.

The Whigs conducted their campaign at a rollicking pitch. Harrison was adroitly celebrated as the "Hard Cider and Log Cabin" candidate, a phrase which the Democrats had used in contempt. Popular meetings, "log cabin raisin's," oratory, invective against Van Buren the aristocrat, songs and slogans ("Tippecanoe and Tyler Too"[qv]) swamped the country. In the election Harrison polled an electoral vote of 234, a popular vote of 1,275,016; Van Buren received 60 electoral votes and 1,129,102 popular votes. A minor feature in the campaign was the appearance of an abolition (the Liberty[qv]) party, whose candidate, James G. Birney, received 7059 votes. Although the causes for Van Buren's defeat should be traced back to opposition to Jackson, the Panic of 1837[qv] and the unpopular Seminole War[qv], the campaign methods employed by the Whigs contributed largely to Harrison's success.

[Edward A. Stanwood, *A History of the Presidency;* D. B. Goebel, *William Henry Harrison.*]

DOROTHY BURNE GOEBEL

Campaign of 1844, The. No outstanding Democratic[qv] candidate could muster the necessary two-thirds vote[qv] in the convention, so James K. Polk of Tennessee, the first "dark horse,"[qv] was nominated, with George M. Dallas of Pennsylvania as running mate, on a platform demanding "the re-annexation of Texas and the re-occupation of Oregon" and in favor of tariff reform. The Whigs[qv] nominated Henry Clay of Kentucky and Theodore Frelinghuysen of New Jersey, on a platform favoring protective tariff and a national bank but quibbling on the Texan annexation issue, which alienated some of the Whigs. Polk carried New York by a small popular majority and was elected, with 170 electoral votes to .105 for Clay. The popular vote was: Polk, 1,337,243; Clay, 1,299,062.

[Edward A. Stanwood, *A History of the Presidency.*]

WALTER PRICHARD

Campaign of 1848, The, resulted in the election of the Whig[qv] nominee, Zachary Taylor, who side-stepped the burning issue of slavery[qv] extension and coasted to victory on his military reputation. His Democratic[qv] opponent, Lewis Cass, straddled the slavery extension question by advocating state sovereignty[qv]. The new Free Soil party[qv], specifically opposed to extension and headed by Martin Van Buren, split the Democratic vote in New York and thus contributed materially to Taylor's triumph. Taylor carried half the states, eight in the South and seven in the North. The popular vote was: Taylor, 1,360,099; Cass, 1,220,544; Van Buren, 291,263. The electoral vote was: Taylor, 163; Cass, 127.

[Edward A. Stanwood, *A History of the Presidency.*]

HOLMAN HAMILTON

Campaign of 1852, The. The Whig party[qv] was apathetic and demoralized, so Democratic[qv] victory seemed almost certain. The question of greatest interest was who would be the Democratic candidate. After many ballots, the leading Democrats, Cass, Buchanan and Douglas, were eliminated and a "dark horse,"[qv] Franklin Pierce of New Hampshire, was nominated with William R. King of Alabama. The Whigs nominated Gen. Winfield Scott; and the Free-Soilers[qv], John P. Hale. Both major parties endorsed the Compromise of 1850[qv], so there were no issues and little contest. Pierce carried all states save Massachusetts, Vermont, Kentucky and Tennessee, though in the popular vote he received scarcely 30,000 majority. The popular vote was: Pierce, 1,601,274; Scott, 1,386,580; Hale, 155,825. The electoral vote was: Pierce, 254; Scott, 42.

[R. F. Nichols, *Franklin Pierce.*]

ROY F. NICHOLS

Campaign of 1856, The. The Republican party[qv] in this, its first presidential campaign, nominated John C. Frémont. Its platform opposed slavery expansion and condemned slavery and Mormonism[qqv] as twin relics of barbarism. The American, or Know-Nothing, party[qv] nominated ex-President Millard Fillmore. The Democrats[qv] nominated James Buchanan. Their conservative platform stressed States' Rights[qv], opposed sectionalism[qv] and favored a somewhat ambiguous plank, giving Popular Sovereignty[qv] to the territories. The electoral vote was Buchanan, 174; Frémont, 114; Fillmore, 8. The popular vote was Buchanan, 1,838,169; Frémont, 1,341,264; Fillmore, 874,534. The Republicans rejoiced in their showing, while the Democrats congratulated themselves upon having saved the Union.

[A. K. McClure, *Our Presidents and How We Make Them.*]

PHILIP G. AUCHAMPAUGH

Campaign of 1860, The. The Democratic[qv] national convention met amid great excitement and bitterness at Charleston, S. C., April 23, 1860. The delegates from the eight states of the far South demanded the inclusion of a plank in the platform providing that Congress should guarantee slave property in the territories. This was refused, and after several days of useless wrangling and failure to unite the convention upon a candidate an adjournment was taken to Baltimore on June 18 following. At this meeting the convention nominated Stephen A. Douglas of Illinois for President, and later the national committee nominated Herschel V. Johnson of Georgia for Vice-President. The platform pledged the party to stand by the Dred Scott decision[qv] or any future Supreme Court decision that dealt with the rights of property in the various states and territories. Seceding Democratic delegates met at Baltimore on June 28 and nominated John C. Breckinridge of Kentucky for President and Joseph Lane of Oregon for Vice-President. The platform reaffirmed the extreme Southern view with regard to slavery[qv]. Meanwhile, the remains of the "old-line" Whigs and American ("Know-Nothing") parties[qqv] had met in a convention at Baltimore on May 9 and adopted the name of the Constitutional Union party[qv], also the platform of "the Constitution of the Country, the Union of the states and the enforcement of the laws." They nominated John Bell of Tennessee for President and Edward Everett of Massachusetts for Vice-President and attempted to ignore the slavery and other sectional issues, with a plea for the preservation of the Union.

Also, the Republican[qv] national convention had met in Chicago on May 16. By means of the platform issues of nonextension of slavery and of a Homestead law[qv] and by advocacy of a protective tariff[qv], the agricultural elements of the northern and western parts of the country and the industrial elements of Pennsylvania, New England and other northern and eastern sections of the country were united. At first it seemed that the convention would nominate either William H. Seward of New York or Salmon P. Chase of Ohio, but a deadlock between their respective supporters being threatened the convention nominated Abraham Lincoln on the third ballot. Hannibal Hamlin of Maine was nominated for Vice-President on the second ballot.

The split in the Democratic party made possible the election of Lincoln. He received 180 electoral votes as against 72 for Breckinridge who carried the extreme southern states, and 39 for Bell who carried the border states[qv]. Douglas received but 12 (9 from Missouri and 3 of the 7 from New Jersey). The popular vote was far otherwise since it totaled 1,857,610 for Lincoln, 1,291,574 for Douglas, 850,082 for Breckinridge and 646,124 for Bell. The combined opponents thus received 930,170 over Lincoln who was a minority President during his first administration.

[Edward A. Stanwood, *A History of the Presidency;* W. S. Myers, *The Republican Party, a History.*]

WILLIAM STARR MYERS

Campaign of 1864, The. A national convention was called in the name of "the executive committee created by the national convention held in Chicago on the sixteenth day of May 1860." The use of the name Republican[qv] was carefully avoided. The convention met in Baltimore on June 7, 1864, and named itself the Union National Convention. The Republican leaders desired to appeal to Union sentiment and do away as far as possible with partisan influence. The platform, which was unanimously adopted, was a statement of "unconditional Union" principles and pledged the convention to put down rebellion by force of arms. Abraham Lincoln was nominated for a second term by the vote of every delegate except those from Missouri who had been instructed to vote for Gen. Grant. The nomination then was made unanimous. Andrew Johnson of Tennessee, a leading Southern Democrat who had been staunch in his loyalty to the Union, was nominated for Vice-President.

The Democratic party[qv] met in convention on Aug. 29, at Chicago. Its platform declared the war a failure and advocated the immediate cessation of hostilities and the restoration of the Union by peaceable means. The convention nominated Gen. George B. McClellan for President and George H. Pendleton for Vice-President. McClellan accepted the nomination but at the same time virtually repudiated the platform, for he was thoroughly loyal to the cause of the Union.

At first it appeared that the Democrats might defeat Lincoln, but the victories of the Union Army in the field proved that the war was not a failure and rallied the people to the support of Lincoln and Johnson and the Union cause. The election took place on Nov. 8. For the first time in our history certain states, those of the South, deliberately declined to choose electors for the choice of President. Lincoln carried every state that took part in the election but New Jersey, Delaware and Kentucky. He received 212 electoral votes. McClellan received 21. Lincoln was given a popular majority of only 494,567 in a total of 4,166,537. This election was one of the most vital in the history of the country since upon its result might depend the perpetuation of the national Union.

[W. S. Myers, *General George B. McClellan;* Edward A. Stanwood, *A History of the Presidency.*]

WILLIAM STARR MYERS

Campaign of 1868 and of 1872, The. The issues in 1868 were Southern reconstruction[qv] and the "Ohio Idea."[qv] Horatio Seymour of New

York and Frank Blair of Missouri, the Democratic[qv] nominees, ran on a platform calling for a restoration of the rights of the Southern states and payment of the war bonds in greenbacks[qv]. Alarmed by Democratic victories in 1867, the Republicans[qv] nominated the war hero, Grant, and Schuyler Colfax of Indiana. Their platform acclaimed the success of reconstruction and denounced as repudiation the payment of the bonds in greenbacks.

Personal attacks on the candidates and Republican "waving the bloody shirt"[qv] featured the campaign. An effort to replace the Democratic nominees in October failed but foreshadowed defeat. Grant received 214 electoral votes to Seymour's 80, and nearly 53% of the popular vote, receiving 3,012,833 votes to 2,709,249 for Seymour. Seymour carried eight states. The result was a personal victory for Grant rather than for Republican policies.

Dissatisfaction with the reconstruction policy and a desire for reform led to a Liberal Republican[qv] organization, supported by tariff and civil-service reformers, independent editors and disgruntled politicians. The new party nominated Horace Greeley, with B. Gratz Brown of Missouri, to oppose Grant's re-election in 1872. Its platform demanded civil-service reform[qv], universal amnesty and specie payment[qv]. The tariff[qv] issue was straddled to please Greeley, a protectionist. The Democrats accepted the Liberal Republican platform and nominees. The Greeley campaign lacked enthusiasm, and he was mercilessly lampooned. Grant received 286 electoral votes to Greeley's 66, and over 55% of the popular vote, receiving 3,597,132 votes to 2,834,125 for Greeley.

[C. H. Coleman, *The Election of 1868;* E. D. Ross, *The Liberal Republican Movement.*]

CHARLES H. COLEMAN

Campaign of 1876, The, is memorable because it resulted in the famous disputed presidential election. The leading aspirant for the Republican[qv] nomination was James G. Blaine of Maine. His name was presented to the national convention at Cincinnati by Robert G. Ingersoll in a striking speech in which he dubbed Blaine "the Plumed Knight." Among the other candidates were Benjamin H. Bristow of Kentucky, Roscoe Conkling of New York, Oliver P. Morton of Indiana and Rutherford B. Hayes of Ohio. For six ballots Blaine led the field, but on the seventh a stampede to Rutherford B. Hayes resulted in his nomination. William A. Wheeler was named as his running mate. The platform indorsed the Resumption Act[qv] and eulogized the Republican party for its work during the Civil War and Reconstruction[qqv].

Thomas F. Bayard of Delaware, Allen G. Thurman of Ohio, Winfield Scott Hancock of Pennsylvania and Thomas A. Hendricks of Indiana sought the Democratic[qv] nomination, but the logical contender was Gov. Samuel J. Tilden of New York, who was named on the first ballot. Hendricks was then nominated for the Vice-Presidency. The scandals of the Grant administration were denounced in unsparing terms (*see* Crédit Mobilier; Whisky Ring; Sanborn Contracts) and "Reform" was declared to be the paramount issue. Repeal of the clause of the act of 1875 providing for the resumption of specie payments[qv] was advocated, but Mr. Tilden personally was known to be a sound-money man rather than a Greenbacker[qv]. The platform also declared in favor of civil-service reform[qv].

In the campaign the Democratic speakers dwelt heavily upon the scandals under Republican rule and contended that only through a change of men and parties could there be any real reform. Republican orators resorted to "bloody shirt"[qv] tactics—that is, revived the Civil War issues—questioned Tilden's loyalty during that conflict and praised Hayes' military record: four honorable wounds and a brevet major generalcy. In the North the campaign was a quiet one, but in some of the Southern states attempts to intimidate Negro voters produced violent disorders and considerable bloodshed.

Early returns on election night indicated the election of Tilden, but presently it appeared that the result would be in doubt. When the electoral colleges met and voted, Tilden received 184 unquestioned votes, Hayes 165; with 4 votes of Florida, the 8 votes of Louisiana, the 7 votes of South Carolina and 1 vote of Oregon claimed by both parties. After a protracted, bitter dispute, Congress created an Electoral Commission of five Senators, five Representatives and five judges of the Supreme Court to help decide the result. Of the Senators, three were to be Republicans and two Democrats; of the Representatives three were to be Democrats and two Republicans; four of the judges, two Republicans and two Democrats, were designated by their districts and they were to choose the fifth judge. It was expected that the fifth judge would be David Davis, but his election to the Senate by the Democrats in the Illinois legislature gave him an excuse to decline the thankless task. The choice then fell upon Joseph P. Bradley, who had been appointed to the bench as a Republican, but some of whose decisions made him acceptable, temporarily, to the Democrats.

In case the two Houses of Congress voting separately refused to accept any return the dispute was to be referred to the Commission, whose decision was to be final unless it was rejected by both Houses. The two Houses, voting separately on strict party lines, did disagree. Decision, therefore, rested with the Commission, which, in all cases, by a vote of 8 to 7 (Bradley voting with the majority), refused to go behind the election results as certified by the state authorities (in the case of Oregon by the Secretary of State) and declared in favor of the Republican contenders. In each case the Senate accepted this decision, the House rejected it. All the disputed votes were therefore counted for Hayes and Wheeler and they were declared elected.

[P. L. Haworth, *The Hayes-Tilden Election;* J. H. Dougherty, *The Electoral System of the United States.*]

PAUL L. HAWORTH

Campaign of 1880, THE, took place during a business revival and with no definite issue before the country. It was routine politics. The Republicans[qv] overcame a serious split between groups headed by James G. Blaine and Roscoe Conkling respectively, by nominating James A. Garfield, a member of neither faction, over President Grant, supported by the Conkling wing for a third term. Against Garfield the Democrats[qv] nominated Winfield Scott Hancock, a nonpolitical Civil War general; but their party had no positive program, was discredited by its factious opposition to the Hayes administration and was defeated by a close vote. The Republicans carried the "doubtful states" and regained control over Congress. The popular vote was: Garfield, 4,454,416; Hancock, 4,444,952. The electoral vote was: Garfield, 214; Hancock, 155.

[E. E. Oberholtzer, *United States Since the Civil War,* Vol. IV; T. C. Smith, *Life of James A. Garfield.*]

THEODORE CLARKE SMITH

Campaign of 1884, THE, fought primarily between James G. Blaine and Grover Cleveland as Republican and Democratic[qqv] candidates respectively, was one of the most vituperative in American history. There were several reasons why it became relentlessly personal in character. From the moment of Blaine's nomination at Chicago on June 6 he came under heavy fire from the reform element of all parties. He was believed to be allied with the spoils element in Republican politics; he had an unhappy record for baiting the South; he favored certain big business interests; and his railroad transactions had raised a suspicion that he had used his official position for personal profit. To divert attention from these attacks certain Republicans published evidence that Cleveland, nominated on July 10 at Chicago, was the father of an illegitimate son born in Buffalo some ten years earlier. Of serious issues between the two parties there were virtually none; both had good reason not to meddle seriously with the currency question or tariff[qv], and international affairs attracted little attention. One leading feature of the campaign was the secession of a large body of Republicans who could not stomach Blaine and who became Cleveland Democrats or Mugwumps[qv]. Another feature was the open enmity of Tammany Hall[qv], under Boss John Kelly, for Cleveland, and the success of it and other malcontents in carrying many Irish voters over to Blaine or to the new Anti-Monopoly party[qv] headed by Benjamin F. Butler. After exchanges which one observer compared to the billingsgate of quarreling tenement dwellers, the two parties approached election day running neck and neck. Democratic victory was finally decided by the vote of New York state, in which the Rev. Dr. Burchard's[qv] "Rum, Romanism and Rebellion" speech at a reception to Blaine, the "Belshazzar's Feast" of Republican millionaires and politicians at Delmonico's just before election and Roscoe Conkling's knifing of Blaine all played a part. Cleveland obtained a popular vote of 4,874,986 against Blaine's 4,851,981, and an electoral vote of 219 against Blaine's 182. Butler's popular vote was just over 175,000, and that of John P. St. John, Prohibition[qv] candidate, was just over 150,000.

[Allan Nevins, *Grover Cleveland—A Study in Courage.*]

ALLAN NEVINS

Campaign of 1888, THE, turned chiefly on the tariff[qv] issue, and resulted in the election of Benjamin Harrison over Grover Cleveland by a majority of the electoral college[qv] but not of the popular vote. The Republicans[qv] had approached the election with scant hope of victory, for Cleveland had proved an admirable President, when his annual message of 1887, devoted entirely to arguments for tariff reform, gave them new heart. The issue was one on which they could rally nearly all manufacturers, most general business and perhaps a majority of workingmen. Benjamin Harrison, who represented extreme high-tariff demands, was nominated by the Republicans at Chicago on June 25, after Blaine had withdrawn for reasons of health, and John Sherman and Walter Q. Gresham, whose tariff views were moderate, had failed to gain strength. Levi P. Morton was named for Vice-

President. Harrison, supported by Blaine, by manufacturing interests who were induced by the Republican Chairman, Matthew S. Quay, to subscribe large campaign funds and by Civil War veterans hungry for pension^qv^ legislation, waged an aggressive campaign. His speech-making abilities made a deep impression on the country. Cleveland, who was renominated by the Democrats^qv^ at St. Louis early in June, felt that his presidential office made it improper for him to do active campaigning; his running-mate, Allen G. Thurman of Ohio, was too old and infirm to be anything but a liability to the party; and campaign funds were slender. Worst of all for the Democrats, their national chairman, Sen. Calvin S. Brice of Ohio, held high-tariff convictions, was allied with big business and refused to put his heart into the battle. Two weeks before election day the Republicans published an indiscreet letter by Lord Sackville, the British minister, hinting to a supposed British subject that Cleveland would probably be more friendly to England than Harrison; and though Cleveland at once had Sackville recalled, the incident cost him many Irish votes (*see* Sackville-West Incident). Cleveland received 5,540,329 popular votes, Harrison but 5,439,853; but Cleveland had only 168 electors against Harrison's 233. Charles B. Fisk of New Jersey, Prohibition^qv^ candidate, polled 249,506 votes; Alson J. Streeter of Illinois, Union Labor nominee, 146,935.

[Edward A. Stanwood, *A History of the Presidency.*]

ALLAN NEVINS

Campaign of 1892, THE, brought the re-election of Grover Cleveland over Benjamin Harrison by a majority the size of which surprised observers of both parties. Cleveland had been named on the first ballot at the Democratic^qv^ convention in Chicago, although David B. Hill of New York had made a demagogic attempt to displace him. Harrison, who had estranged the professional politicians of his party, who had quarreled with its most popular figure, Blaine, and who had impressed the country as cold and unlikable, was reluctantly accepted by the Republicans^qv^ at Minneapolis on June 10. It was impossible to repudiate his administration. However, the McKinley Tariff^qv^ of 1890 had excited widespread discontent, the Sherman Silver-Purchase Act^qv^ of the same year had angered the conservative East and heavy Federal expenditures had caused general uneasiness. Cleveland's firm stand on behalf of the gold standard and low tariffs^qqv^ and his known strength of character commended him to large numbers of independent voters. One factor adverse to the Republicans was the great strength manifested by the Populists^qv^, who polled 1,040,000 votes for James B. Weaver of Iowa and James G. Field of Virginia; most of this coming from old Republican strongholds in the Middle West. Another factor was the labor war at Homestead^qv^, Pa., which showed that the highly protected steel industry did not properly pass on its tariff benefits to the worker. Cleveland, with a popular vote of 5,556,543, had 277 electors; Harrison, with a popular vote of 5,175,582, had 145; while Weaver won 22 electoral votes.

[Allan Nevins, *Grover Cleveland—A Study in Courage.*]

ALLAN NEVINS

Campaign of 1896, THE, ended a twenty-two-year period in which neither major party had been able to control the National Government for more than the life of a single Congress; it ushered in a period of Republican^qv^ domination which lasted until 1911.

Favored by Mark Hanna's cannily managed campaign, William McKinley of Ohio was named on the first ballot by the Republican convention meeting at St. Louis. The traditional party platform was adopted with the exception of a declaration for the gold standard^qv^ until bimetallism^qv^ could be secured by international agreement. A bloc of Western delegates bolted and organized the Silver Republican party^qv^.

There was no dominant candidate for the Democratic^qv^ nomination. The important contest was over the platform. As presented to the delegates, it was an anti-administration document favoring free silver^qv^ at the sixteen-to-one ratio, criticizing the use of injunctions^qv^ in labor disputes and denouncing the overthrow of the Federal income tax^qv^. In its support William Jennings Bryan delivered his "Cross of Gold"^qv^ oration and endeared himself to the silver delegates by his effective answers to the criticisms of the administration orators.

The enthusiasm growing out of that speech gave impetus to Bryan's candidacy for the presidential nomination. Back of this was also the long campaign he had waged by personal conferences, speeches and correspondence with the inflationist delegates from the South and West. Another factor was the bolting Republicans and the Populists^qv^, who saw themselves being forced to support the Democratic nominee and demanded some one not too closely identified with the regular Democracy. Bryan appealed to the delegates as the Democrat who could unite the silver and agrarian factions.

The Populists, Silver Republicans and National Silver party members joined the Democrats in support of Bryan. The administration Democrats placed a National Democratic ticket in the field to hold conservative Democratic votes away from him.

The campaign was highly spectacular. The Democrats exploited Bryan's oratory by sending him on speaking tours back and forth across the country during which enormous crowds came out to hear him. In sharp contrast, the Republican management kept McKinley at his home in Canton, Ohio, where carefully selected delegations made formal calls and listened to "front porch" speeches by the candidate. More important were the flood of advertising, the funds for building local organizations and the large group of speakers on the hustings, which were maintained by Hanna's organization. The metropolitan press, like the other business groups—except the silver miners—was essentially a unit in opposing Bryan. The results showed a sharp city-versus-rural division, with Bryan carrying the Solid South[qv] and most of the trans-Missouri states. The remainder, including California, Oregon, North Dakota, Kentucky and Maryland, went to McKinley. With him were elected a Republican House and a Senate in which various minor party members held a nominal balance of power. The popular vote was unusually large, each candidate receiving larger totals than any previous candidate of his party, McKinley's vote being 7,098,474 and Bryan's 6,379,830. Their electoral vote was 271 and 176 respectively.

[E. E. Robinson, *The Evolution of American Political Parties;* Marian Silveus, *The Antecedents of the Campaign of 1896*, unpublished thesis, University of Wisconsin, 1933.]

ELMER ELLIS

Campaign of 1900, THE, carried over the presidential candidates and most of the issues of 1896. With the trend of prices upward, the pressure for inflation[qv] had declined, and the expansion of American control over new territories had created the issue of imperialism[qv].

At the Republican[qv] convention in Philadelphia a combination of circumstances forced Hanna and McKinley to accept Theodore Roosevelt as the vice-presidential candidate. The party's position on the new territories was defined as American retention with "the largest measure of self-government consistent with their welfare and our duties."

When the Democrats[qv] met at Kansas City, they were unwilling to accept the conservatives' proposal to forget the last platform and make anti-imperialism the only issue. The 1896 platform was reindorsed, an antitrust plank added and imperialism designated the "paramount issue."

The campaign lacked the fire of 1896. The Republicans emphasized the "full dinner pail"[qv] and the danger threatening it from the Democratic platform; the Democrats stressed the growth of monopolies[qv] under the McKinley administration and the danger of imperialistic government. The result was a more emphatic Republican victory than in 1896, one generally interpreted as an endorsement of both McKinley's domestic and foreign policies. The popular vote was: McKinley, 7,218,491; Bryan, 6,356,734. McKinley obtained 292 electoral votes to 155 for Bryan. This election made Roosevelt's elevation to the Presidency automatic upon McKinley's death in 1901.

[E. E. Robinson, *The Evolution of American Political Parties;* Edward A. Stanwood, *A History of the Presidency.*]

ELMER ELLIS

Campaign of 1904, THE. Theodore Roosevelt, who succeeded to the Presidency on the death of McKinley in 1901 (*see* Assassinations, Political), ardently hoped to be nominated and elected "in his own right." The death of Marcus A. Hanna of Ohio, whom the "big business"[qv] interests of the country would have preferred, made possible the President's nomination by acclamation when the Republican[qv] convention met in Chicago, June 21. Charles W. Fairbanks of Indiana was chosen for second place.

The Democrats[qv], meeting at St. Louis, July 6, pointedly turned their backs upon "Bryanism" by omitting from their platform all reference to the money question (*see* Free Silver) and by nominating for President, Alton B. Parker, a conservative New York judge, who at once pledged himself to maintain the gold standard[qv], and for Vice-President, Henry Gassaway Davis, a wealthy West Virginia octogenarian. Business leaders, however, more afraid of the Democratic party than of Roosevelt, contributed so heavily to the Republican campaign chest that Parker rashly charged "blackmail." Corporations, he said, were being forced to contribute in return for the suppression of evidence that the Government had against them. Roosevelt, indignantly denying the charge, won by a landslide that reclaimed Missouri from the Solid South[qv], gave him 336 electoral votes to Parker's 140 and a popular plurality of 2,540,067. Prohibitionist, Populist, Socialist and Socialist-Labor[qqv] candidates received only negligible support.

[Edward A. Stanwood, *A History of the Presidency.*]

JOHN D. HICKS

Campaign of 1908, THE. Theodore Roosevelt, though at the height of his popularity, refused to be a third-term candidate in 1908, but swung his support in the Republican[qv] convention to William Howard Taft, who was nominated.

The Democratic[qv] convention was as completely dominated by William Jennings Bryan, who became its nominee. Party differences were not significant. After an apathetic campaign Bryan carried only the Solid South[qv], Kansas, Colorado and Nevada, though he received 43% of the popular vote, securing 6,409,106 to Taft's 7,679,006. Taft's electoral vote was 321; Bryan's 162. The Republicans won the Presidency and both Houses of Congress.

[Samuel Eliot Morison and Henry Steele Commager, *The Growth of the American Republic.*]

CHESTER LLOYD JONES

Campaign of 1912, THE, marked the culmination of the progressive movement[qv] in national politics and resulted in the return of the Democrats[qv] after sixteen years of Republican[qv] Presidents.

The struggle for the Republican nomination became a sanguinary battle between the progressive and conservative wings, aided in each case by personal followings and some division of support from large interests. In the beginning it was the progressive, LaFollette, against the incumbent, Taft. But former President Theodore Roosevelt, who had been largely responsible for Taft's nomination in 1908, entered the race to rally behind him Republicans who believed Taft had been too friendly with the conservative Old Guard. The influence in Taft's hands was sufficient to return delegates pledged to him in most cases where they were named by conventions, but Roosevelt or LaFollette were successful in all states save one where presidential primaries[qv] were held. The conservative controlled National Committee placed Taft delegates on the temporary roll in all contests and the small majority resulting gave Taft the nomination. Roosevelt was later nominated by the newly organized Progressive party[qv], consisting largely of Republican bolters.

The contest for the Democratic nomination was also hard fought with both of the leading candidates accepted as progressives. Champ Clark led from the beginning and had an actual majority in the convention for a time, but when Bryan transferred his support to the second progressive, Woodrow Wilson, a shift began which resulted in the latter's nomination. All three party platforms[qv] were unusually favorable to progressive policies. Wilson, backed by a united party, won easily and Roosevelt was second. There was an unusual amount of shifting of party loyalties, although most Democrats voted for Wilson and most Republicans for Roosevelt or Taft. Wilson's popular vote was 6,296,547, Roosevelt's was 4,126,020 and Taft's was 3,486,720. Their electoral vote was, respectively, 435, 88 and 8. The Democrats won majorities in both branches of Congress. In spite of the three-way contest, a fourth candidate, Eugene V. Debs, Socialist, secured approximately 900,000 votes, the highest percentage of the total vote his party ever received.

[Edward A. Stanwood, *A History of the Presidency;* E. E. Robinson, *Evolution of American Political Parties.*]

ELMER ELLIS

Campaign of 1916, THE, reunited the Republican party[qv] and determined that American foreign policy should be left in Wilson's hands. The Republicans reunited when, after the nomination of Charles Evans Hughes, Theodore Roosevelt, already nominated by the rapidly declining Progressive party[qv], announced support of the ticket.

There was no opposition to Wilson's renomination. The Democrats[qv] defended the policies of the administration, especially the Underwood Tariff[qv] and the measures for the regulation of business. They also praised the foreign policy[qv] as one which had kept us out of war and preserved national honor.

The Republicans attacked the policies of the administration, promised a "stronger" foreign policy and were supported by the more extreme partisans of both alliances in the European war.

The results were in doubt for several days because of the close vote in several states. Wilson won the Presidency, carrying Ohio, New Hampshire, the South and most of the border and trans-Missouri states, including California, with an electoral vote of 277, against 254 for Hughes. The popular vote was: Wilson, 9,127,695; Hughes, 8,533,507. Congress remained Democratic only because independent members of the House were friendly.

[E. E. Robinson, *Evolution of American Political Parties.*]

ELMER ELLIS

Campaign of 1920, THE. The debate on the League of Nations[qv] determined the alignment of political forces in the spring of 1920. The Republicans[qv] were confident; the wounds of the intraparty strife of 1912 had been healed; the mistaken strategy of 1916 admitted; and the conservative mood of the country was easily interpreted. They met in convention in Chicago, could not agree upon any one of the leading preconvention candidates, Frank O. Lowden, Hiram

Johnson or Leonard Wood, and nominated Warren G. Harding, Senator from Ohio, on the tenth ballot. Calvin Coolidge, Governor of Massachusetts, was nominated for the Vice-Presidency.

The Democrats[qv] met in San Francisco. None of the discussed candidates, William G. McAdoo, Alfred E. Smith, John W. Davis, A. Mitchell Palmer or James M. Cox, commanded a great following. The last-named was nominated on the forty-fourth ballot, with Franklin D. Roosevelt as vice-presidential nominee.

Neither platform was unexpected or significant on domestic issues. The Republicans attacked the President and opposed American entrance into the League.

The Socialist party[qv], meeting in May, nominated Eugene Debs for the fifth time. A Farmer-Labor[qv] ticket appeared also. The Democratic national committee supported Wilson's appeal for a "solemn referendum" on the covenant of the League; Cox waged a persistent and vigorous campaign; Harding, remaining at his home for the most part, contented himself with vague generalizations. Neither candidate had been nationally known at the outset of the contest, and no clear-cut issue developed and no real contest transpired. The total vote cast was 26,748,224. The Nineteenth Amendment[qv] had been proclaimed in August and in every state women were entitled to vote. Harding had 60.35% of the total vote cast. Cox won the electoral vote in only eleven states, receiving 127 electoral votes to Harding's 404. The Socialist vote was 902,310, but the strength of all the third parties totaled only 5.52%.

[E. E. Robinson, *The Presidential Vote, 1896-1932.*]

EDGAR EUGENE ROBINSON

Campaign of 1924, The. As in 1920, so in 1924, the candidates were new in a presidential canvass. The Republican[qv] convention meeting in Cleveland, with a few scattering votes in dissent, nominated Calvin Coolidge, who as Vice-President had succeeded to the Presidency in the summer of 1923. The vice-presidential nomination, refused by several, was accepted by Charles G. Dawes. The platform was marked by extreme conservatism.

The Democrats[qv] met in New York and were in almost continuous session for two and a half weeks. Not only was there serious division upon the matter of American adherence to the League of Nations[qv] and upon the proposed denunciation of the Ku Klux Klan[qv], but also upon the choice of the nominee. Each of the two leading candidates, Alfred E. Smith and William G. McAdoo, was sufficiently powerful to prevent the nomination of the other, and finally on the 103rd ballot the nomination went to John W. Davis. Charles W. Bryan of Nebraska was nominated for Vice-President. The platform called for a popular referendum on the League of Nations.

A Conference for Progressive Political Action brought about a series of meetings and eventually a widespread support of Sen. Robert M. LaFollette[qv] in his independent candidacy, with Burton K. Wheeler as his running mate. LaFollette's platform, in which appeared most of the progressive[qv] proposals of the previous twenty years, was endorsed by the Socialist party[qv] and the officers of the American Federation of Labor[qv]. So real did the threat of the third party candidacy appear to be that much of the attack of the Republicans was upon LaFollette, who waged an aggressive campaign.

The total vote cast exceeded that of 1920 by two and a third million, but because of the vote cast for LaFollette (nearly 5,000,000) that cast for Republican and for Democratic tickets was less than four years earlier, Coolidge securing 15,718,211 votes, and Davis, 8,385,283. LaFollette carried Wisconsin. Coolidge topped the poll in thirty-five states, receiving 382 electoral votes, leaving the electoral vote for Davis in only twelve states, or 136 votes.

[E. E. Robinson, *The Presidential Vote, 1896-1932.*]

EDGAR EUGENE ROBINSON

Campaign of 1928, The. On Aug. 2, 1927, President Calvin Coolidge announced that he "did not choose to run" for President in 1928. The majority of the leaders of the Republican party[qv] were undecided with regard to the candidate they should support. A popular movement having its strength in the rank and file of the voters forced the nomination of Herbert Hoover on the first ballot at the Republican National Convention which met at Kansas City, Mo., on June 12, 1928. The platform contained strong support of the usual Republican policies such as a protective tariff[qv] and sound business administration. It advocated the observance and rigorous enforcement of the Eighteenth Amendment[qv]. Charles Curtis was nominated for Vice-President.

The Democrats[qv] met at Houston, Texas, and on June 28 nominated Alfred E. Smith for President. They then nominated Joseph T. Robinson for Vice-President. The platform did not differ strikingly from that of the Republicans. The contest became one between rival personalities. Gov. Smith, an avowed "wet," took a stand in favor of a change in the Prohibition Amendment, and advocated that the question of prohibition and its enforcement be left to the determination of the individual states.

At the election on Nov. 6 Mr. Hoover was overwhelmingly successful. He carried forty states, including five from the old South, with a total of 444 electoral votes. Gov. Smith carried eight states with an electoral vote of 87. The popular plurality of Mr. Hoover over Gov. Smith was 6,375,747 in a total vote of 36,879,414.

[W. S. Myers, *The Republican Party.*]

WILLIAM STARR MYERS

Campaign of 1932 and of 1936, THE. The presidential campaign of 1932 began in earnest with the holding of the Republican National Convention at Chicago on June 14–16. President Herbert Hoover and Vice-President Charles Curtis were renominated on the first ballot. The platform praised the Hoover record including his program for combatting the depression[qv]. After a long debate a "wet-dry" plank on prohibition[qv] was adopted which favored giving the people an opportunity to pass on a repeal amendment.

The Democratic National Convention was also held at Chicago, June 27–July 2, 1932. On the fourth ballot, Gov. Franklin Delano Roosevelt of New York was nominated for the Presidency, defeating Alfred E. Smith and ten other candidates. The platform pledged economy, a sound currency, unemployment relief, old-age and unemployment insurance under state laws, the "restoration of agriculture" and repeal of the Eighteenth Amendment together with immediate legalization of beer[qqv].

After a campaign featured by Mr. Roosevelt's promise of "a new deal,"[qv] the elections were held on Nov. 5. The popular vote for each party was as follows: Democratic, 22,821,857; Republican, 15,761,841; Socialist, 884,781; Socialist-Labor, 33,276; Communist, 102,991; Prohibition, 81,869; Liberty, 53,425; and Farm-Labor, 7309. The electoral vote was 472 for the Democrats and 59 for the Republicans.

In 1936 the Republican National Convention was held at Cleveland beginning on June 9. Gov. Alfred M. Landon of Kansas and Frank Knox, Chicago publisher, were nominated for the Presidency and Vice-Presidency, respectively. The platform strongly denounced the "New Deal administration," from both constitutional and economic viewpoints. It pledged the Republicans "To maintain the American system of constitutional and local self-government" and "To preserve the American system of free enterprise."

The Democratic National Convention assembled at Philadelphia on June 25 for what proved to be a ratification meeting for the New Deal. President Roosevelt and Vice-President Garner were renominated without opposition. The platform vigorously defended the New Deal and pledged its continuance.

When the election was held on Nov. 3, the Democrats again won an overwhelming victory, carrying every state except Maine and Vermont. The popular vote for each party was as follows: Democratic, 27,476,673; Republican, 16,679,583; Union, 882,479; Socialist, 187,720; Communist, 80,159; Prohibition, 37,847; and Socialist-Labor, 12,777. The Democrats received 523 electoral votes while the Republicans received only 8. The popular vote was the largest ever polled in an election in the United States.

[*American Year Book*, 1933, 1936; *World Almanac*, 1933, 1934, 1937, 1938.] ERIK McKINLEY ERIKSSON

Campaign Pledges. Campaigns of the modern type are usually dated from that of 1840[qv], when the famous slogan, "Tippecanoe and Tyler Too," inaugurated the era of political fanfare and mass appeal. Prior to the election of Jackson, nomination of presidential candidates had been by congressional caucuses[qv], which had issued addresses to the people, the forerunners of the later party platforms. When the national nominating conventions[qv] began to develop after 1831, the custom became general of stating the party program in specific statements of the parties' objectives if returned to power. Today the platform[qv] has become an important element in campaign strategy. Platform pledges are generally of two kinds. On the more noncontroversial issues, parties tend to be precise in their advocacy of, or opposition to, particular proposals. On questions on which there is widespread popular disagreement, the platform pledges frequently become vague and noncommittal. Sectional[qv] issues, whether geographical, racial or economic (if these can be distinguished), are likely to fall in the latter group. Questions of a political nature, on which national opinion has crystallized, are likely to be treated with fervor and directness. The influence of the minor parties, and of many pressure groups[qv], in advocating specific reforms and so educating public opinion on them, has been important in developing party policy on many questions, such as regulation of public utilities or woman suffrage.

Beside the general campaign pledges enunciated in party platforms, candidates for office often make specific campaign pledges implementing the platforms or recognizing and accepting responsibility for national or local demands. Presidential candidates rarely go beyond the frontiers of their party's pledges in defining their position, but on controversial questions sometimes clarify their personal position. Congressional candidates not infrequently have to state their attitude toward specific planks in order to conciliate local interests. It is significant to note that a specific campaign pledge is one of the two exemptions allowed Congressmen in failing to uphold a caucus decision on the floor of the House of Representatives.

PHILLIPS BRADLEY

Campaign Resources and Uses. Prior to 1888 little attention was paid to the matter of conducting political campaigns. In that year, with the tariff[qv] as the chief issue, the era of large campaign funds began. During the 1892 campaign the Republicans spent about $1,500,000; while in 1896, during the free-silver campaign, they raised $3,500,000. During the same campaign the Democrats raised a fund estimated at from $650,000 to $1,700,000. These amounts were not exceeded until 1916. The year 1920 saw campaign funds rise to a new high peak. In 1921 there was published a report on this campaign compiled by the Senate Committee on Privileges and Elections of which William S. Kenyon was chairman. This report showed that the two major parties spent a total of $10,338,509 during the campaign. Of this amount, the Republicans spent $8,100,739 and the Democrats, $2,237,770. The report included the expenditures of the national, senatorial, congressional and state committees but did not include the amounts spent by district, county and city committees or the sums collected and spent by non-party committees, such as the League to Enforce Peace.

In dealing with the subject of campaign expenditures, one must give consideration to the uses made of the money. While these expenditures have increased much faster than the size of the electorate, the costs of campaigning have also multiplied. Generally speaking, more money is spent for publicity than for any other purpose, whether the election is national, state or local. Enormous sums are required for newspaper and magazine advertisements, billboard posters, pamphlets, buttons, banners and placards. Another important item of expense is the maintenance of headquarters for party organizations ranging from the national committee down to the city or even precinct committees. Money raised by the national committee must be apportioned, in part, to the state committees. Beginning especially with the campaign of 1924, radio[qv] has become an indispensable part of political campaigns, and large sums are required to purchase time. Furthermore, speakers must be secured for meetings in all parts of the country. In addition, heavy expenditures are required for field workers, for election-day expenses and for miscellaneous items such as the preparation of registration lists and traveling expenses.

Because of the general belief that corruption and large campaign funds go hand in hand, both the state and Federal governments have passed regulative laws, usually referred to as "corrupt practices acts." Beginning with New York in 1890 all the states except Illinois, Mississippi, Rhode Island and Tennessee had, by 1926, enacted some sort of legislation to deal with campaign funds. While they differ considerably, all the laws have provisions dealing with bribery. Only thirty-three states have laws which may be described as fairly comprehensive. These usually require publicity regarding receipts and expenditures; limit the expenditures by candidates; prohibit expenditures for any purpose except those enumerated in the laws; prohibit contributions to campaign funds by corporations; and define persons and committees who may receive and spend money in political campaigns. As a whole the state corrupt practices acts are defective in that they lack adequate publicity and enforcement provisions. Nevertheless, the legislation has raised "the moral tone" of elections.

Except for a provision in the Civil Service Act of 1883 (*see* Pendleton Act, The) which prohibited contributions for political purposes by civilian employees of the United States, the Federal Government enacted no corrupt practices legislation until 1907. Then a law was passed prohibiting national banks and corporations from making contributions to the campaign fund of any candidate for a national office. In 1910 the first law was passed by Congress to require publicity for the campaign funds of Congressmen. This Campaign Expense Act was amended in 1911 by extending its provisions to Senators; by limiting the amount that could be spent; and by extending Federal regulation to nominations as well as elections. This last provision was invalidated, however, by the Supreme Court, which in 1921, in the case of Newberry v. U. S.[qv], ruled that a primary is not an election and therefore not subject to regulation by Federal legislation. In 1925 Congress enacted the "Federal Corrupt Practices Act" which applies exclusively to elections. It is largely a consolidation of previous Federal legislation. Periodic reports of expenditures are required, not only from party committees but also from non-party committees. The total expenditures by candidates for the United

States Senate or House in general may not exceed the maximum fixed by state laws.

Unquestionably, the Federal corrupt practices legislation, together with the state legislation, has eliminated many evils previously connected with political campaigns. Like the state laws, the Federal legislation is defective in its publicity and enforcement provisions. The legislation has not proved adequate to prevent all political contributions by governmental employees, especially through such devices as party dinners for which a price of $5 to as high as $100 is charged. Nor has the legislation prevented campaign books containing the President's autograph from being sold at high prices to corporations. The extension of governmental activity after 1929 created new campaign resources not always to be measured in terms of dollars. The party in power, by liberal Federal "benefits" to farmers, by relief to the unemployed through the Works Progress Administration and other agencies, by grants for public works through the Public Works Administration[qqv], as well as other devices, created groups whose self-interest would dictate political support for that party. In 1934 and 1936 these new "vested interests" unquestionably were an important source of strength to the party controlling the Federal Government. Because of repeated protests, particularly against playing politics with relief workers, the Senate, in 1938, created a Campaign Investigating Committee headed by Sen. Morris Sheppard of Texas. Prior to the elections on Nov. 8, 1938, the committee received about 1000 complaints of improper political activity. It carried on investigations in sixteen states. Most of the complaints were discarded as groundless but 300 charges involving 183 cases were retained on the committee's docket. As a result, Congress, in February, 1939, prohibited political activity on the part of the officials of the Works Progress Administration. (*See also* Hatch Bill.)

[James K. Pollock, *Party Campaign Funds;* Edward M. Sait, *American Parties and Elections.*]

ERIK McKINLEY ERIKSSON

Campaign Songs are partisan ditties used in American political canvasses and more especially in presidential contests. The words were commonly set to established melodies like "Yankee Doodle," "Hail, Columbia," "Rosin the Bow," "Hail to the Chief," "John Brown's Body," "Dixie" and "O Tannenbaum" ("Maryland, My Maryland"); or to tunes widely popular at the time, such as "Few Days," "Champagne Charlie," "The Wearing of the Green" from "Arrah-na-Pogue" or "Down in a Coal Mine," which served for "Up in the White House." Perhaps the best known of them was "Tippecanoe and Tyler Too,"[qv] in which words by Alexander C. Ross (1812–83) were adapted to the folk tune, "Little Pigs." First heard at Zanesville, Ohio, this spread rapidly over the country, furnishing a party slogan. It has been said: "What the Marseilles Hymn was to Frenchmen, 'Tippecanoe and Tyler Too' was to the Whigs of 1840." In 1872 an attempt was made to revive the air for "Greeley Is the Real True Blue."

The words, sometimes with music, of campaign songs were distributed in paper-covered song books or "songsters." Among these were the *Log Cabin Song Book* of 1840 and *Hutchinson's Republican Songster for the Campaign of 1860,* compiled by J. W. Hutchinson. For many years national campaigns included itinerant stump-speakers[qv], live animals, fife-and-drum corps, red fire, floats, transparencies and rousing mass meetings in courthouses and town halls. Glee clubs were organized to introduce campaign songs and to lead audiences and marchers in singing them. The songs were real factors in holding the interest of crowds, emphasizing issues, developing enthusiasm and satirizing opponents. With changes in the methods of campaigning, the campaign song declined as a popular expression.

[S. L. Cook, *Torchlight Parade.*]

G. S. BRYAN

Campaigns, Political. A political campaign is a drive for votes made by parties, their various auxiliary organizations and candidates, the aim being to achieve the election of the latter by a majority or plurality as required by constitutional or other legal provisions. Campaigns are also waged for nominations in conventions or direct primary[qqv] elections, and for or against initiative and referendum[qqv] projects. In the last-mentioned case they are seldom hotly contested since the element of party or personal rivalry is absent.

So far as the areas involved are concerned political campaigns in the United States range all the way from the quadrennial national contests to small township or borough affairs. Since the beginning of our national history the number of voters who must be reached has increased enormously, partly of course as a result of the growth of population, but also because of the extension of the right of suffrage[qv] to poorer white males prior to 1850, to Negroes[qv] following the Civil War, and finally to women culminating with the adoption of the Nineteenth Amendment[qv] to the Constitution in 1920. Estimates of the proportion of the total population qualified to vote are as follows: in 1789, 4%; at present from 40 to 45%.

With expansion on so gigantic a scale confronting them, party organizations in the United States developed *pari passu* until they have become by far the largest and most complicated in any democratic country. As the active agent in campaigns they parallel the structure of our constitutional government from the National Committees which act for the Democratic and Republican parties in Federal contests to the Executive Committees which take charge in each of the forty-eight states, and so on down to innumerable district, county, city and precinct committees. More or less dormant at other times, these committees collect large funds (*see* Campaign Resources and Uses), call into being many auxiliary bodies and develop tremendous activity during the course of campaigns and particularly just before elections.

Coincident with the above organizational development, elaborate techniques have been worked out, often aided by new inventions such as the motion picture and the radio[qqv], which enable party workers to reach the masses of voters. Appeals are made to individual voters—canvassing, "buttonholing," "door-bell ringing"; also and more largely to voters in the mass by public meetings of every description. Partisan newspapers are called into the service; "campaign literature,"[qv] optimistically so-called, involving every combination of emotional and rational exhortation and ranging in format from fat official textbooks to small pamphlets and dodgers, is distributed in enormous quantities. Every propagandist device is employed to present in the most favorable light to each element of the electorate: first, the traditions and record of the party, especially during the recent past; second, the principles and policies of the party particularly as expounded in its current platform[qv]; and, finally, the life and character of the candidates. In close contests much depends upon party strategy, i.e., the choice of a paramount issue, the distribution of funds and orators in various sections of the country, and the like. Third parties enter into the fray to the limit of their straitened resources. Knowing their candidates foredoomed to defeat, they are more interested than the major parties in preaching party doctrines.

Practical politicians are accustomed to say that the next campaign begins the day after an election has been held. However, the general public takes little interest in their "fence-building" until the pre-primary contest starts, namely, prior to early February of a presidential election year. Following the pre-primary campaign the pre-convention campaign continues until nominations are made at the national conventions in late June or early July. Thereafter the presidential campaign[qv] proper gets off to a slow start in dog-days but gathers speed up to the climactic finish on "the first Tuesday after the first Monday in November."

[Charles A. Beard, *The American Party Battle.*]

ROBERT C. BROOKS

Campaigns, Presidential, have occurred in the United States every fourth year, beginning in 1788, and will so continue as long as the present constitutional provisions remain in force. Each campaign has been ushered in since the 1830's by the holding of national party conventions[qv] to select presidential and vice-presidential candidates and to draw up platforms[qv]. The method of selecting delegates to these conventions was for a long time wholly extra-legal, and determined by local party traditions, but in many states presidential primaries are now held, by means of which the voters may register their preference for the supporters of a particular candidate. Each convention represents the various political units of the nation approximately according to population.

Sometimes, as in the case of a popular President desiring renomination, there is no contest in the convention, but often the nomination is awarded only after long balloting and much excitement. State delegations rally around their "favorite sons," and win or yield votes in accordance with backstage deals and promises. Doubtful states, that is, states that may vote either way in the election, have a decided advantage over the rest; New York and Ohio, for example, have furnished a disproportionate share of the presidential nominees. If the contest is not decided on an early ballot, a "dark-horse" candidate, one not previously regarded as a serious contender for the place, sometimes wins out. Until 1936 Democratic conventions required a two-thirds majority[qv] to nominate, but at that time the Democrats adopted the rule long current in Republican conventions that a simple majority would be sufficient. While military heroes, Congressmen, cabinet members and judges have all been accorded presidential nominations, in general the governor of an important close state has an advantage over all other contenders.

After the nominations are made the Chairman of the National Committee, an officer personally selected by the presidential candidate, takes command of the party forces. Under his direction the campaign treasurer raises and expends huge sums of money to send "stump speakers," campaign literature and funds for less circumspect purposes into the doubtful states (*see* Campaign Resources and Uses). In earlier times presidential candidates either stood aloof from the campaign, or made only dignified and sedate appearances, such as were a part of McKinley's "front-porch" campaign of 1896. Of late, however, presidential candidates have become themselves the chief campaigners. Frequent "swings around the circle" take them to every part of the country and the radio[qv] reports their every utterance to millions of listeners. Indeed, "radio appeal" has become one of the most important assets a candidate can have.

Campaign speeches and documents are usually formulated with a view to pleasing the maximum number of voters and real issues are often sidetracked in favor of blind appeals to partisanship. Thus "waving the bloody shirt"[qv] was the chief reliance of Republican orators for a long time after the Civil War, while the desire to maintain white supremacy[qv] outweighed all other considerations in the "Solid South."[qv] On the other hand, Bryan's battle for "free silver" and his attack on "imperialism," Wilson's advocacy of the "New Freedom" and Franklin D. Roosevelt's defense of the "New Deal"[qqv] are instances in which important policies were set before the electorate for acceptance or rejection.

[Edward A. Stanwood, *A History of the Presidency.*]

JOHN D. HICKS

Campbellites. *See* Disciples of Christ.

Campo Bello Fiasco, THE (April 9–28, 1866), was an attempt by the O'Mahony Fenians to seize the island of Campo Bello, New Brunswick, for Ireland. The British, aware of the plan, sent a vessel to Eastport, Maine, and increased their garrisons. Three United States vessels and troops under Gen. Meade successfully intercepted shipments of Fenian[qv] arms and prevented violations of our neutrality laws. Disheartened, the Fenians returned home to plan anew.

[J. Stephens, *Fenian Brotherhood.*]

EZRA H. PIEPER

Camps and Cantonments, World War. To build the camps and cantonments required for housing and training of our World War National Guard and National Army[qqv] divisions, the Construction Division of the army was created in May, 1917. This unit, later known as the "Cantonment Division," was first commanded by Brig. Gen. Isaac W. Littell—later by Brig. Gen. R.C. Marshall, Jr., under whose administration it became a part of the office of the Chief of Staff.

The Secretary of War (Hon. Newton D. Baker) ordered the building of sixteen cantonments with wooden barracks for the new National Army and, in addition, sixteen National Guard camps where troops would be quartered in tents with wood floors, with wooden buildings for kitchens and mess halls. Projected dates for calling conscripted men to the colors forced construction work to be crowded practically within a ninety-day period.

Each National Army cantonment contained, in addition to the barracks, quarters and administration buildings, a hospital, warehouses, railroad tracks, permanent highways, water supply, electricity, sewerage, refrigeration, welfare buildings, sewage-disposal plant, remount depot, target range and, in many cases, a power station. Each cantonment could accommodate a "Pershing" division, approximately 28,000 men.

The National Guard camps, in addition to tent facilities above described, included the principal installations of the National Army cantonments, but on a limited scale.

With the exception of two donated parcels, land for cantonments was purchased; sites for National Guard camps were all loaned gratis or rented.

By Sept. 1, 1917, the thirty-two construction projects were housing troops and a month later all tent camps were substantially complete. On Nov. 15 the same was true of the cantonments.

Physical work of building was done by civilian labor (reaching a peak of 200,000 men), employed by contractors working on a "cost plus"[qv] emergency contract. The average cost of construction per cantonment was $11,600,000, exclusive of land; for the National Guard tent camps, the average was $2,400,000.

National Army cantonments built were: Custer, Battle Creek, Mich.; Devens, Ayer, Mass.; Dodge, Des Moines, Iowa; Dix, Wrightstown, N. J.; Funston, Fort Riley, Kans.; Gordon, Atlanta, Ga.; Grant, Rockford, Ill.; Jackson, Columbia, S. C.; Lee, Petersburg, Va.; Lewis, American Lake, Wash.; Meade, Admiral, Md.; Pike, Little Rock, Ark.; Sherman, Chillicothe, Ohio; Taylor, Louisville, Ky.; Travis, San Antonio, Tex.; and Upton, Yaphank, Long Island, N. Y.

National Guard camps built were: Beauregard, Alexandria, La.; Bowie, Fort Worth, Tex.; Cody, Deming, N. Mex.; Doniphan, Fort Sill, Okla.; Frémont, Palo Alto, Calif.; Greene, Charlotte, N. C.; Hancock, Augusta, Ga.; Kearney, Linda Vista, Calif.; Logan, Houston, Tex.; MacArthur, Waco, Tex.; McClellan, Anniston, Ala.; Sevier, Greenville, S. C.; Shelby, Hattiesburg, Miss.; Sheridan, Montgomery, Ala.; Wadsworth, Spartanburg, S. C.; Wheeler, Macon, Ga.

Total capacity in men for the National Army cantonments was 654,786; for the National Guard camps, 438,042.

In addition to the above, three embarkation camps were built: Merritt, Tenafly, N. J.; Stewart and Hill, Newport News, Va. Two Quartermaster camps were constructed: Ordway, Washington, D. C.; and J. E. Johnston, Jacksonville, Fla.

After cessation of hostilities, the Government salvaged a vast quantity of material and disposed of all remaining installations either at auction or by sales preceded by advertising for sealed bids.

[Annual Reports of the War Department, Chief of Construction Division, 1918 and 1919.]

ROBERT S. THOMAS

Canada, American Invasion of, 1775–76. In attempting the conquest of Canada, the Continental Congress[qv] wished not only to effect a diversion favorable to the colonial operations around Boston (*see* Boston, Siege of; Bunker Hill), but, still more, to deprive Britain of a base for attack upon the revolutionary colonies. The idea was encouraged by the capture of Ticonderoga and Crown Point[qqv], which secured the route northward. Hopes of success were increased by the knowledge that there were few regular troops in Canada, and the plausible expectation of a rising of the French Canadians. After some hesitation, Congress authorized Gen. Schuyler (June 27, 1775) to undertake the invasion if he found it practicable. Active direction of the expedition fell to Brig. Gen. Richard Montgomery.

A first hasty enterprise against Montreal resulted only in the capture of Ethan Allen by the British (Sept. 25, 1775). The real gateway of Canada, St. Johns[qv] on the Richelieu, held by a large proportion of Canada's regular garrison, fell after a siege lasting from Sept. 17 to Nov. 2, during which the invaders were strengthened by ammunition and provisions obtained by the capture of Fort Chambly[qv]. Montreal was occupied Nov. 13, 1775.

Gen. Guy Carleton, governor of the province, fled to Quebec, which was already threatened by the force which Arnold had brought up by the tremendously difficult Kennebec route (*see* Arnold's March to Quebec); but even after Arnold's junction (Dec. 2) with Montgomery's depleted army, the colonial troops available for the siege of Quebec numbered only about 1000. The one assault which was attempted (Dec. 31) failed completely, Montgomery being killed; and in spite of considerable reinforcements toward spring the siege ended abruptly with the opening of navigation, when the first of 10,000 regulars arrived from England (May 5, 1776). On May 16 a British force from the west captured 400 Americans at Cedars, above Montreal; on June 7 part of the American main force, strengthened by a brigade under Gen. John Sullivan, who assumed command, met disaster at Three Rivers[qv]. On June 15 Montreal was evacuated. Sullivan's force and the small body under Arnold from Montreal were reunited at St. Johns. On June 18 the last Americans left that fortress. Carleton's pursuit was delayed while he built a fleet, which destroyed Arnold's (*see* Valcour Island, Battle of), but it was too late in the season for further operations, and invasion of the colonies was postponed until 1777 (*see* Burgoyne's Invasion).

The failure of the American invasion was due to inadequate military measures, to British sea power, and to the generally neutral attitude of the French-Canadians. It has been argued that the campaign was advantageous to the revolutionary cause in the end by forcing the British to divert the reinforcements of 1776 to the St. Lawrence, thus causing a dispersion of the royal forces which led to the decisive success at Saratoga[qv] in the following year.

[Justin H. Smith, *Our Struggle for the Fourteenth Colony;* G. M. Wrong, *Canada and the American Revolution.*]

C. P. STACEY

Canada, Attempts to Win, to American Revolution. For strategic reasons, if for no others, it seemed to the revolutionists essential to win Canada to their cause. On Oct. 24, 1774, accordingly, the Continental Congress[qv] despatched a letter appealing to the Canadians, dwelling upon their supposed grievances against the British government and inviting them to send delegates to the next Congress; it added that if they refused to be friends they would be treated as foes. Massachusetts made similar overtures on her own account, appointing a committee to correspond with the Canadians and early in 1775 sending John Brown to Canada to advance the cause. In the absence of any actual rising in the province, Congress later in the year decided to seize it by force (*see* Canada, American Invasion of, 1775–76); and in 1776 it supplemented its military effort by sending to Montreal a mission composed of Benjamin Franklin, Samuel Chase and Charles Carroll, and equipped with a printing press to assist in spreading revolutionary propaganda. The mission made little impression upon Canadian opinion and retired from Canada at the end of May, after the siege of Quebec had been raised by troops from England. The failure to win the French-Canadians to the American cause was due in great part to traditional animosities, largely based on religion, which were reinforced by resentment aroused by the exactions of the American Army; while even the English-speaking merchants, bound by close commercial ties to London, were unfavorable to actual secession from the Empire. Various proposals for enterprises toward Canada made later in the war were thwarted by the mutual jealousy of the French and Americans; neither party wished its ally to gain control of the colony.

[A. L. Burt, *The Old Province of Quebec;* Justin H. Smith, *Our Struggle for the Fourteenth Colony.*]

C. P. STACEY

Canada, Confederate Activities in, directed against Northern prison camps[qv] were reported as early as November, 1863, but had little basis until after arrival in Canada of Confederate commissioners Jacob Thompson, J. P. Holcombe and C. C. Clay in May, 1864.

A peace movement[qv] in July and a "Northwest Conspiracy"[qv] in August having failed, an effort was made to seize Federal ships on Lake Erie in Beall's raid[qv] in September and an attack was made on St. Albans[qv], Vt., in October, 1864. About this time plans to release Confederate prisoners in Northern prison camps uniformly failed.

Plots to burn Northern cities, including New York[qv] and Cincinnati, followed. In New York eleven hotels and Barnum's Museum[qv] were fired on Nov. 25, 1864, but the blazes were quickly extinguished. A train-wrecking effort near Buffalo in December, to release captured Confederate generals, failed and one plotter was executed.

Confederates in Canada supplied cash for buying gold, shipping it to England and selling it in order to depress Federal currency values. Two million dollars were thus shipped with no permanent result. About $300,000 was spent by Confederates in Canada in promoting these various futile schemes.

[John W. Headley, *Confederate Operations in Canada and New York.*]

CHARLES H. COLEMAN

Canada, Immigration to and Emigration from. Acadians[qv], expelled from Nova Scotia in 1755, went in some hundreds to southern Louisiana. Replacing the Acadians, emigrants from New England, New Jersey and Pennsylvania moved into Nova Scotia. The American Revolution caused a second considerable wave of northeastward migration when "Loyalists"[qv] fled to the Maritime Provinces. Many "Loyalists" also crossed the upper St. Lawrence and the Niagara frontier. A post-Loyalist movement, chiefly into Upper Canada, essentially part of the trans-Appalachian westward movement, gained momentum till the War of 1812, slackening thereafter in face of stimulated British immigration and diminished Canadian hospitality. By the 1840's Upper Canadians were overflowing to United States frontiers of settlement beyond Detroit and after 1880 French-Canadians emigrated to New England mill towns. Gold discoveries in British Columbia in 1858 attracted Amercan miners; and the Canadian prairies, after American wheat lands were occupied, drew at the turn of the century heavy American immigration, partly of Canadian ancestry. Emigration from older parts of the Dominion to American cities persisted for nearly a century though recently restricted. By censuses of 1930–31 there were 344,374 American-born in Canada, 3.3% of the population, rather evenly distributed, and 1,278,421 Canadian-born in the United States, mostly concentrated in Northern states. Perhaps a third of all persons of Canadian ancestry are in the United States.

[M. L. Hansen, R. H. Coats, et al., Movements of Population, in R. G. Trotter, A. B. Corey, W. W. McLaren, eds., *Proceedings of Conference on Canadian-American Affairs, June, 1937.*]

REGINALD G. TROTTER

Canada, Invasion of, 1812–14. Since the destruction of British power in Canada was a primary object of those responsible for bringing on the War of 1812 (*see* War Hawks) it was inevitable that the United States in the course of the struggle should attempt the conquest of the colony. In 1812 an attempted invasion on the Detroit frontier resulted in disaster (*see* Detroit, Surrender of) and an enterprise on the Niagara met the same fate (*see* Queenston Heights, Battle of). The next year brought more success; Perry's victory (*see* Erie, Lake, Battle of) permitted a successful invasion of western Upper Canada (*see* Thames, Battle of the) and the Detroit frontier region remained in American hands until the end of the war. Farther east, the Americans successfully raided York[qv], but initial successes on the Niagara (*see* George, Fort) were followed by a check at Stoney Creek[qv] and no permanent foothold was gained; while the campaign against Montreal was a total failure (*see* Chrysler's Field and Chateaugay). In 1814 invasion was again attempted on the Niagara, but though the American troops now gave a better account of themselves (*see* Chippewa; Lundy's Lane; and Erie, Fort) no conquest of territory resulted.

Among the causes of the American failures, the military unpreparedness of the United States and the large degree of skill with which the defense was conducted by the British regular troops in Canada are important. The determined resistance of the Canadian population was contrary to American expectations and was also a powerful factor. Finally, the American strategic plans were in general decidedly unsound, in that they wasted the country's military resources in ill-conceived enterprises against Canada's western settlements, instead of concentrating them in an effective offensive movement against the essential British line of communication in the St. Lawrence Valley.

[Sir C. P. Lucas, *The Canadian War of 1812;* A. T. Mahan, *Sea Power in its Relations to the War of 1812;* Julius W. Pratt, *Expansionists of 1812.*]

C. P. STACEY

Canada, Proposed Expedition against (1778). The opposition to Washington did not subside with the exposure of the Conway Cabal[qv]. In the hope of achieving control, Gates and his friends fixed on an invasion of Canada. Lafayette's interest and support were enlisted; he was to be leader of this fantastic "irruption into Canada" in the dead of winter. In February, 1778, he went to Albany. Nothing had been done. Lafayette was enraged and humiliated. By April he was back with Washington. Gates and his friends had blundered again. Six months later they attempted, unsuccessfully, to revive the plan.

[Justin H. Smith, *Our Struggle for the Fourteenth Colony.*]

THOMAS ROBSON HAY

Canadian-American International Joint Commission. *See* International Joint Commission.

Canadian-American Reciprocity. In order to help offset annexation sentiment and relieve economic distress in Canada Lord Elgin[qv], the Governor-General, negotiated a reciprocity[qv] agreement with the United States in 1854. There was no formal treaty, but it was agreed that certain agricultural, forest and mineral products, as well as those of the fisheries, should be imported from one country to the other on a reciprocal basis. The agreement did not apply to manufactures. American vessels were also permitted to navigate the St. Lawrence in return for a like privilege for Canadian vessels on Lake Michigan. The agreement was to operate for ten years and might then be terminated by one year's notice by either party. It was so terminated by the United States in 1866, largely as a result of diplomatic friction on issues growing out of the American Civil War (*see* Fisheries Dispute, Arbitration of).

Canadian statesmen of both political parties tried at different times to obtain another reciprocity arrangement with the United States. Such an agreement was made in 1911, but the Laurier government in Canada, which negotiated the agreement, was overthrown in a general election and the proposal was thereby rejected by Canada.

[Haynes, *The Reciprocity Treaty with Canada of 1854;* Allin and Jones, *Annexation, Preferential Trade and Reciprocity.*]

WILSON PORTER SHORTRIDGE

Canadian-American Relations. The present relationship of mutual confidence between the United States and Canada is of comparatively recent growth. In their earlier history issues arising between the republic and the British Empire produced not only an era of armed conflict (ending in 1815) but a long period of mistrust and difficulty thereafter.

Canadian-American relations in their earliest phase took the form of the chronic hostility, fanned by four intercolonial wars, which existed between the French Catholic settlers of New France and the English Protestant inhabitants of the thirteen colonies. Though the last of these wars (*see* French and Indian War) brought Canada under the British flag, the traditional animosities survived, and in the American Revolution[qv] which followed they undoubtedly tended to restrain the French-Canadians from active co-operation with the Americans (*see* Canada, American Invasion of, 1775–76; Canada, Attempts to Win, to American Revolution). The Definitive Treaty of Peace, 1783[qv], partitioned the continent between the new republic and a group of continuing British colonies in the north; and the arrival in those colonies of perhaps 40,000 Loyalists[qv] expelled from the States, who founded the provinces of New Brunswick and Upper Canada (now Ontario), went far to render the division permanent, for the views of these men, inevitably strongly anti-American, colored the political life of their communities for generations.

Relations between republic and colonies were stormy from the beginning. The allied questions of the western posts on American soil which the British persisted in retaining, despite the treaty, until 1796 (*see* Border Forts, Evacuation of), and of the alliances which, as part of the Canadian defense system, they kept up with Indian tribes within the United States (*see* Defiance, Fort; Fallen Timbers, Battle of; Wayne Campaign), rendered British rule in Canada obnoxious to the American frontiersman; and the latter factor was probably more instrumental than the problems of impressment[qv] and neutral rights at sea in producing the American declaration of war in 1812. The repeated unsuccessful invasions of Canada that followed (*see* Canada, Invasion of, 1812–14) only strengthened anti-American prejudices in the provinces. Memories of this war contributed materially to the growth of Canadian nationalism; for just as American national feeling was largely founded on antipathy to England, that of Canada was nurtured on antipathy to the United States. Though the Treaty of Ghent[qv] in general merely restored the *status quo,* the provision of Jay's Treaty[qv] which had permitted British intercourse with American Indians was not renewed and one historic cause of Anglo-American friction was thus greatly weakened. The Rush-Bagot Agreement[qv] of 1817 prevented a perpetuation of the wartime naval rivalry on the Lakes, but no limitation was imposed on land armaments, nor has any such limitation ever been negotiated.

Increasingly pacific relations were abruptly interrupted in 1837 when rebellions in Canada inaugurated another period of strain. The activity of American "sympathizers" and filibusters (*see* Hunters' Lodges) produced serious border incidents, notably that of the *Caroline*[qv], and these difficulties were soon reinforced by those over the Maine boundary (*see* Northeast Boundary), which led in 1839 to troop movements and apprehension of war (*see* Aroostook War). These matters were resolved by the Webster-Ashburton Treaty[qv], but the Oregon question[qv] prolonged the troubles to 1846. The next fifteen years, on the whole peaceful, were marked by the large development of commercial intercourse fostered by the Elgin-Marcy Reciprocity Treaty[qv] of 1854. The Senate's acceptance of this treaty has been attributed to Southern politicians' desire to avert the increase of free-soil territory by the annexation of Canada, which was represented as inevitable unless commercial concessions were made. An annexation movement which temporary commercial distress had produced in Montreal in 1849 gave color to this argument.

With the Civil War there commenced a decade of extreme danger in Anglo-American relations[qv]. The *Trent* Affair[qv] of 1861 caused the most serious threat of war since 1815 and the state of the border thereafter was one of armed and precarious peace. The *Alabama* Affair[qv] and similar incidents inflamed Northern opinion, and there was talk of annexing Canada in revenge. In 1864 the Confederates made attempts at using Canada as a base of operations against the North (*see* Canada, Confederate Activities in) and fortification projects undertaken on both sides of the border in this and the following year reflected the increasing tension. At the end of the war the recrudescence of filibustering in the form of the Fenian Raids[qv] maintained this dangerous atmosphere, and the abrogation of the Reciprocity Treaty by the United States in 1866 embittered it. Fear of American attack lent impetus to the movement for federation of the several British provinces, which bore fruit in the organization of the Dominion of Canada (July 1, 1867). The British government was more than willing to transfer its own responsibilities in America to the new government at Ottawa, which henceforth played an increasingly important role in negotiations with Washington.

The year 1871 is an important turning point. In that year the Treaty of Washington[qv], by providing for arbitration of the *Alabama* claims, ended ten years of tension, and simultaneously the withdrawal of British troops from central Canada encouraged the growth of a less military atmosphere along the border. The fundamental territorial controversies between the two communities had now been settled; furthermore, the abolition of slavery in the United States and the attainment of responsible government in Canada had removed domestic problems which had invited foreign interference. As memories of old conflicts faded, the influence of common racial and political traditions was freer to assert itself and to open the way for more peaceful relations; and from 1871 it is possible to speak with some truth of the Canadian border as an "unguarded" frontier, for no fortifications have since been built. The worst difficulties of the next period were the chronic Atlantic Fisheries dispute[qv] and the Bering Sea fur-seal question[qv], both ultimately decided by arbitration; but the repeated refusal of the United States (now committed to high protection[qv]) to consider a renewal of reciprocity caused constant irritation and influenced Canada's own decision to turn to protection (1878) and the subsequent maintenance of this policy. In 1895 the Venezuela Boundary crisis[qv] aroused fears of war, and President Theodore Roosevelt's handling of the Alaska Boundary question[qv] (1903) further revived old animosities. In 1911 these helped to defeat President Taft's project of a new reciprocity treaty; traditional Canadian patriotism, fearing American penetration, now combined with the influence of new business interests which had grown up behind the Canadian tariff to bring about the rejection of Sir Wilfrid Laurier's government in a general election on this issue (*see* Reciprocity). In these same years, however, there was created (1909) the International Joint Commission[qv] on boundary waters, which ever since has done unostentatious but valuable work in settling disputes arising along the border.

American neutrality in the early stages of the World War[qv] did not increase the popularity of the United States with Canadians; but the improvement in Anglo-American relations, produced by this conflict in the end, prepared the way for a new era in Canadian-American relations also. In the post-war years, the complete and obvious abandonment by the United States of any expansionist ideas combined with growing national self-confidence in Canada to create a more frank and generous atmosphere. The gradual growth of Canada's international status culminated in 1927 in the inauguration of direct diplomatic intercourse between Ottawa and Washington by an exchange of ministers; since that year all Canadian-American issues have been dealt with through these channels. The most unpleasant incident so treated has been that of the sinking of the *I'm Alone*[qv] (1929), and the mutually satisfactory manner in which it was disposed of by arbitration (1935) is evidence of the existing state of relations. Commercial friction, it is true, continued, and the American Hawley-Smoot tariff[qv] and the Canadian emergency tariff of 1930 amounted to an exchange of economic blows. Such episodes, however, did not prevent an increasing assimilation of the economic systems of the two nations.

[J. M. Callahan, *American Foreign Policy in Canadian Relations;* H. L. Keenleyside, *Canada and the United States.*]

C. P. STACEY

Canadian-American Waterways. The use by white men, as means of transportation, of the system of waterways that extends from the Gulf of St. Lawrence into the heart of North America, began with the second voyage of Jacques Cartier in 1535. In that year he not only discovered the St. Lawrence River, but, first in a small sailing ship, and finally in longboats, made his way upstream to the island of Montreal. His successors—explorers, missionaries, fur-traders, soldiers and settlers, by canoe, boat or sailing ship—finally traveled to every corner of the Great Lakes. The first sailing vessels on the Lakes, the *Frontenac* and the *Griffon*[qv], were built by La Salle, the former at Fort Frontenac[qv], now Kingston, Ontario, in 1678, and the latter near the present Buffalo in 1679. About 1737 LaRonde built a small sailing ship at Sault Ste. Marie and used her on Lake Superior in a search for copper mines. It was not until 1816 that the *Frontenac,* the first steam-driven craft on the Lakes, was launched near Kingston, on Lake Ontario. Two years later the *Walk-in-the-Water*[qv], the first steamboat on the upper lakes, was launched not far from the place where LaSalle had built the *Griffon.* When the need arose to carry large quantities of ore and grain down the Lakes from Superior and equally immense cargoes of coal from Erie ports up to Duluth and Superior, special types of lake vessels were designed of unprecedented capacity and the traffic up and down the Detroit River grew by leaps and bounds until it exceeded 100,000,000 tons annually of a value of more than $1,000,000,000. A suggestion of the growth of transportation facilities on these waters may be got by comparing LaSalle's 10-ton *Frontenac* with the *Lemoyne,* built at Midland, Ontario, in 1926, 613 feet long, and carrying a cargo of 570,000 bushels of wheat.

Navigation between Lake Superior and the sea was, in a state of nature, limited by waterfalls, rapids or shallows in the connecting streams and in the upper St. Lawrence. Since 1783, when the first canals were opened for navigation on the Canadian side of the St. Lawrence, the United States and Canadian governments have spent several hundred millions of dollars in improvements to navigation between Duluth, Fort William or Chicago and the sea, notably in building the American and Canadian canals at Sault Ste. Marie and the Welland ship canal[qv] connecting Lakes Erie and Ontario. Since the opening of the latter in 1930 the largest freighters can travel from the head of Lake Superior to the foot of Lake Ontario. From there to the sea the Canadian canals are only fourteen feet in draft.

To determine the practicability of deepening this remaining section of the waterway from the upper lakes to the Gulf, the International Joint Commission[qv] carried out an investigation and reported favorably in 1921. Subsequently the engineering side of the problem was reviewed by a board of American and Canadian government engineers and the economic aspects by American and Canadian committees, all of which reported favorably. A treaty to carry out the project, which also involved the development of water power on the upper St. Lawrence[qv], was signed at Washington in 1932, but failed to win the approval of the United States Senate. In 1938 a revised treaty, dealing also with works designed to improve the scenic beauty of Niagara Falls and to govern diversions at Chicago, was submitted by the United States Government to Canada. In 1936 the International Joint Commission investigated the feasibility of a deep waterway from the St. Lawrence by way of Lake Champlain to the Hudson and reported adversely.

[Geo. A. Cuthbertson, *Freshwater;* Moulton, Morgan and Lee, *The St. Lawrence Navigation and Power Project;* G. W. Stephens, *The St. Lawrence Waterway Project.*]

LAWRENCE J. BURPEE

Canadian and United States Boundary Disputes. *See* Northeast Boundary; Northwest Boundary Controversy; Alaska Boundary Question.

Canadian Annexation Movement, THE (1849), was sponsored by urban and commercial interests, primarily in Montreal, to offset the serious decline in trade, prices and property values in Canada which resulted from the capture of western trade by the Erie Canal route[qv], granting of bonding privileges by the United States, repeal of the Corn Laws and imperial preference, and failure of the United States to satisfy the Canadian demand for reciprocity[qv] in natural products in 1848 and 1849. An annexation manifesto, issued on Oct. 10, 1849, received over 1000 signatures among which were some of the most prominent political and financial leaders of Montreal. Widespread opposition, counter manifestoes and return of prosperity ended the movement within six months.

[C. D. Allin and G. M. Jones, *Annexation, Preferential Trade and Reciprocity.*]

ALBERT B. COREY

Canadian Boundary, Disarmament of. *See* Canadian-American Relations; Great Lakes, Agreement for Disarmament on the.

Canadian River, THE, is a part of the Arkansas River[qv] system. Early French traders and explorers followed its course west into the Spanish territory. The name Canadian possibly was given to the river by early French hunters and traders who came from Canada. The upper part was called by the Spanish, Rio Colorado. By the Treaty of Doak's Stand[qv] in 1820, Canadian River was made the northern boundary of the Choctaw[qv] nation. Early emigrants to California followed the south bank of the Canadian on to Santa Fé.[qv]

[Thoburn and Wright, *History of Oklahoma;* Grant Foreman, *Pioneer Days in the Early Southwest.*]

ANNA LEWIS

Canal Boats, THE. On the early American canals[qv], the blunt, horse-drawn boats were of three general types—freight boats carrying from 25 to 100 tons each of various commodities; passenger "packets"; and so-called line boats, which carried both freight and passengers, the latter getting poorer accommodations than on the packets. On the passenger boats the traveler both dined and slept in a central "saloon," a species of narrow canvas hammocks being affixed to the walls in tiers at night for berths.

[Alvin F. Harlow, *Old Towpaths.*]

ALVIN F. HARLOW

Canal Building was an early phase of the struggle to provide transportation facilities adequate to develop and to unite the country. The first problem was to get around the falls of the rivers flowing into the Atlantic (*see* Fall Line, The). To accomplish this, some canals were completed by private companies between 1789 and 1802. The second problem was to connect the coast with the Ohio and Mississippi River valleys and the rivers with the Great Lakes[qqv]. During this second phase, the mania for canal building by the states (with some Federal aid) can be understood only in the light of the success of the Erie Canal[qv] and the widespread speculation and wildcat banking[qv] which characterized frontier enthusiasm for the development of the resources of the West.

The Erie Canal, started in 1817 by New York state, and completed in 1825, gave the first low-cost transportation from the coast to the interior of the country. Following the lowest crossing of the Appalachians along the course of an old Indian trail, it was a great success. It carried a vast traffic, it was largely responsible for the development of New York City and the towns along its course and it paid for itself in a brief time.

Other states believed that the same success would crown their efforts. Canal building seemed essential both to those who wished to exploit the resources of the country and to those primarily interested in speculation. Wildcat bankers took long chances and viewed hopefully projects which now seem fantastic. Foreign investors carelessly assumed that state credit was as good as that of the Federal Government, which was practically out of debt in the 1830's. Thus the sound position of the Federal Government played a strange role, encouraging foreigners to buy state bond issues, the proceeds of which went into canal construction. In 1825 Ohio, with a population of about 700,000, undertook canal projects estimated to cost approximately $5,800,000, one tenth of its taxable wealth. In the end they cost more. By 1838 the debts of twelve states for canal construction amounted to over $60,-

000,000. The actual construction appears all the more remarkable when we remember that the builders had only human and horse power to remove soil, only black powder[qv] for blasting and that holes for blasting had to be drilled in the rock with hand drills.

The canals, together with the natural waterways, aided greatly in the development of the country. In fact, the superiority of the railroad[qv] over the canal was not clearly evident until the late 1860's. The peak load on the Erie Canal was in the late 1880's. The financial results, however, were not so favorable. Unlike the Erie, few of the canals were profitable, and there were defaults by states on canal debts as follows: Indiana, 1841–47; Maryland, 1841–48; Pennsylvania, 1842–45; and Illinois, 1842–47 (*see* Repudiation of State Debts).

The Federal Government has played a large role in more recent canal building. The St. Mary's River Canal[qv] between Lake Superior and the other Great Lakes, built by Michigan in 1853–55, was improved by the United States in 1870–71. In 1880 the Federal Government took over the whole project. The Cape Cod Canal makes traffic to and from Boston possible without going around the Cape. The building of the Panama Canal[qv], completed by the Federal Government in 1914, was marked by the utilization of modern machinery in moving vast quantities of earth and in the triumph of medical science over tropical diseases (*see* Yellow Fever).

The greatest state project in recent years (1903–18) is that of New York in rebuilding the Barge Canal system.

[Alvin F. Harlow, *Old Towpaths.*]

JAMES D. MAGEE

Canal Lands. Congress granted 4,424,073.06 acres of the public domain[qv] to the states for canals between 1824 and 1874, as follows:

Indiana	1,457,366.06 acres
Ohio	1,100,361.00 acres
Illinois	290,915.00 acres, plus 210,132.00 (1841) for general internal improvements, used for canal purposes
Wisconsin	325,431.00 acres
Michigan	1,250,000.00 acres

These canal lands were about 8% of the total of 52,251,937.19 acres granted during the same period for all internal improvements[qv].

Canal lands in Ohio were sold quickly (except the right of way and terminal grounds). Within twenty years (1848) 908,003 acres had been sold for $1,408,812.73. Ultimately Ohio received $2,-257,487, about one seventh of the building cost. Indiana records are inadequate, but the total receipts from land sales and canal tolls were $5,477,238. Illinois received (to 1871) $5,858,-547.47 or five sixths of the total construction cost. Speculation in canal lands contributed to the land speculation preceding the panic of 1837[qv]. Eighty acres of canal land in the heart of Chicago sold for $1.55 per acre in 1830. Six years later 375 canal lots brought $1,355,755. Ohio, Indiana and Illinois still have a small income from the canal rights of way.

[T. C. Donaldson, *Public Domain;* A. F. Harlow, *Old Towpaths.*]

HAROLD E. DAVIS

Canal Ring, THE. A group of corrupt contractors and politicians who conspired shortly after the Civil War to defraud the State of New York by overcharging for repairs and improvement of the state's canal system. It defied an "investigation" in 1868 and for years was powerful enough to prevent interference and to defeat unfriendly candidates for office.

[D. S. Alexander, *Political History of the State of New York.*]

ALVIN F. HARLOW

Canary Islands, THE, served as a way station for Spain's New World voyages, besides supplying wine for Spanish America and skilled workers for West Indian sugar plantations. New England early began a profitable intercourse with the Canaries, together with Portugal's Madeiras and Azores, involving mainly the exchange of lumber and fish for wine. Although illegal according to English interpretation of the Navigation Act[qv] of 1663, trade with the Canaries continued until the 1770's, causing much friction between New England and royal authorities.

[G. L. Beer, *The Old Colonial System, 1660-1754;* W. B. Weeden, *Economic and Social History of New England, 1620-1789.*]

CHARLES EDWARD CHAPMAN AND
ROBERT HALE SHIELDS

Candles lighted most American homes, public buildings and streets until kerosene lamps and gas replaced them. The housewives made many kinds, namely—bear grease, deer suet, bayberry, beeswax (expensive, for state occasions largely), tallow dip (commonest), from well-rendered mutton fat, and spermaceti (the waxy solid from the head of whales). Every autumn the housekeepers filled their leather or tin candle boxes to last through the winter. It was a long, hard task to dip or mold several hundred candles by hand. First, women prepared wicks from rough hemp, milkweed or cotton spun in large quantity. The homemaker was the only manufacturer until the 1700's when an itinerant candle-maker could be hired. Later, professional chandlers prospered in the cities. Although factories were numerous after 1750, the home-dipping was continued as late as 1880. There was a large market for sperm candles in the West Indies. In 1768 they bought over 500,000 lbs. of sperm and tallow candles from the colonies. The total production from both factories and homes reached an estimated $8,000,000 in 1810. The New England factories, which produced most, imported supplies of fat from Russia. There were large plants, also, in New Orleans, St. Louis, and Hudson, N. Y. South Carolina and Georgia produced quantities of seeds and capsules from tallow trees used extensively for candle-making in the South. Allied industries grew rapidly for making metal and pottery candle holders.

[Marion Nicholl Rawson, *Candle Days;* Alice Morse Earle, *Home Life in Colonial Days,* and *Customs and Fashions in Old New England;* Arthur H. Hayward, *Colonial Lighting;* Victor S. Clark, *History of Manufactures in the United States.*]

LENA G. FITZ HUGH

Cane Ridge Revival, THE, was the culmination of a great spiritual awakening in Kentucky, which began at the close of the 18th century (*see* Great Revival). This special manifestation of religious fervor occurred in August, 1801, at a camp meeting[qv] near the Cane Ridge Meeting House in Bourbon County. The number attending has been estimated at 20,000. Those under conviction exhibited peculiar physical and vocal exercises that indicated an abnormal religious experience. The Disciples[qv], or Christians, developed from the intellectual quickening of the movement.

[James R. Rogers, *The Cane Ridge Meeting House;* Alonzo Willard Fortune, *The Disciples in Kentucky.*]

JONATHAN T. DORRIS

Canning Industry, THE, has expanded in America due to simultaneous advances in the technic of manufacturing cans, agricultural research, the invention of automatic machinery and the art of canning. These have progressed rapidly during the past 140 years and the United States is in the forefront of canning nations, leading in volume and variety of canned products. Some 300 food products are canned and the enterprise has become one of the billion-dollar industries.

Pioneers of American canning were Thomas Kensett, Sr., and Ezra Daggett of New York, 1819, and William Underwood at Boston, 1821. They used the Appert process (sealing in airtight containers and immersing in boiling water) on oysters, meats, fruits, berries and vegetables, packing in glass. The tin can[qv], its name derived from the original English canister, was introduced here by Peter Durand in 1818. Underwood and Kensett changed from glass to tin in 1839. Canning sprang up rapidly thereafter in Maryland, Maine, New Brunswick, New York and Delaware, with new products added. Methods of obtaining higher temperatures were evolved, the cooking time thus shortened and pack volume rose.

The Civil War produced the first "boom" and canneries sprang up in the Midwest, to supply the armies. From about 5,000,000 annual cans, the national pack increased sixfold. Canning was introduced in California, now a leading producing state, in 1862. Two years later George W. Hume and A. S. Hapgood, Maine salmon canners, transferred their activities to the Pacific Coast. David S. Page, Dixon, Ill., made the first condensed milk can in Switzerland in 1865, paving the way for a major expansion in that product, carried forward later by Gail Borden and others (*see* Dairy Industry).

In the following decades machinery inventions and development led the way, while can-making refinements continued. Andrew K. Shriver, Baltimore, patented the first closed steam-pressure kettle in 1875. R. P. Scott of Ohio and Messrs. C. P. and J. A. Chisholm of Ontario evolved an automatic pea podder in 1885. William H. Sells, in 1892, built the first automatic corn husker, deriving his idea from the principle of the clothes wringer. Other revolutionary improvements in machinery were made.

Early in this century the can itself was radically improved. Solid food particles had been forced into the can through a hole in the top, over which a metal disc was soldered. Mutilation of food was common. An open-top can was developed by Charles M. Ams, W. Y. Bogle and George W. Cobb, Sr., which, known as the "sanitary can," has become the standard, modern tin container for food. Soon after this, scientific research laboratories sprang up throughout the industry, launching programs of investigation as to causes of spoilage and contamination. Nutritive values were analyzed and proved. Raw products research led to refinements in planting, growing and harvesting canning crops. Popular prejudices against canned foods waned and public acceptance grew, as the results of this work became trade practice. At the present time, in a normal year, between eight and nine billion cans of food are produced in the United States.

[J. H. Collins, *The Story of Canned Foods;* E. C. May, *The Canning Clan.*]

NELSON H. BUDD

Cannonism, a term common during Joseph G. Cannon's tenure of the Speakership of the House (1903–11) when the great powers of that office were used in the interest of the ultraconservative elements.

[D. S. Alexander, *History and Procedure of the House of Representatives.*]

W. A. ROBINSON

Canoe, The. When one mentions the canoe in American and Canadian history, it is usually with the understanding that a craft made of the rind of the white birch tree is meant. On occasions other materials were used for canoes, but never, apparently, if birch-bark could be secured.

The Algonquian Indians[qv] had learned both the secret of making and of guiding canoes expertly before white men reached North America. The latter adopted the canoe immediately. Until ailroads became common—about 1850—the canoe was the chief vehicle for reaching much of northern North America. Thus it became the usual craft in the transportation of furs and is always associated with the great explorers and the fur traders[qv]. It was admirably adapted to the waterways of the continent, being light enough to be portaged easily, responsive enough to be guided with precision through rapids and over low waterfalls, and so built as to be capable of repair at almost any place on the route from materials to be found along that route. Besides bark these materials were cedar for the frame and paddles, wattape (tree-root fibers) for sewing pieces of bark together and for lashing the bark to the gunwales, and resin for gumming the seams. No metal was used in its construction.

There were several kinds of canoes: the Montreal canoe, or *canot du maître,* from thirty to forty feet long, manned by ten to fourteen men; the *canot du nord,* or North canoe, from twenty to twenty-five feet in length, manned by four to eight men; a half canoe, somewhat smaller; and Indian canoes, still smaller. A light canoe was usually an express canoe without freight aboard. The Montreal canoes weighed about 300 lbs. and carried about five tons' weight of men and freight. They were used primarily on the St. Lawrence and the Great Lakes[qv]. The North canoes were used beyond the Great Lakes, in smaller rivers and on lesser lakes.

[Grace Lee Nute, *The Voyageur.*]

GRACE LEE NUTE

Cantigny, Americans Attack at. The American 1st Division (Bullard) on April 25, 1918, joined the French First Army. It occupied the sector facing Cantigny, held by the German XVIII Army. To test the Americans' offensive ability in their first active sector, the French command ordered the new division to capture Cantigny. After careful preparations the 28th Infantry attacked at 6.45 A.M., May 28. The assailants, assisted by French tanks, took all objectives, with 250 prisoners, in forty-five minutes. Thereafter the Americans repulsed several violent German counterattacks, losing 1067 killed and wounded, but maintaining their position.

[C. R. Howland, *A Military History of the World War;* J. M. Hanson, History of the American Combat Divisions, *The Stars and Stripes.*]

JOSEPH MILLS HANSON

Canton, The Fur Trade with, developed from the search for some staple, other than specie, which American merchants could exchange for the teas and silks of China. Furs met with a ready sale; the cargo of the first American vessel to Canton, Feb. 22, 1784, included furs. But only such rare furs as otter, seal, beaver and fox were acceptable. Boston merchants decided to seek sea-otter[qv] skins on the Northwest coast. The *Columbia* (Sept. 30, 1787–Aug. 9, 1790) returned with a cargo of teas—product of sea-otter skins bartered from the natives. Others hastened to follow. By 1796 American vessels were engaged in contraband fur trade with the Californians and by 1804 were borrowing Aleutian sea-otter hunters, on shares, from the Russian governor at Novarkhangelsk. In 1783, in the Southern Pacific, had begun the mass slaughter of the fur seal. When, after the War of 1812[qv], the fur trade with Canton was renewed, the growing scarcity of the sea otter, increased competition and a consequent decline in profits reduced the American vessels engaged from thirteen in 1821 to two in 1830. Trading in furs with Canton became merely one aspect of a more general "Pacific trade." ". . . by 1837 the old Northwest fur trade . . . was a thing of the past."

[F. R. Dulles, *The Old China Trade;* K. W. Porter, *John Jacob Astor;* Samuel Eliot Morison, *Maritime History of Massachusetts, 1783-1860.*]

KENNETH WIGGINS PORTER

Cantonments. *See* Camps and Cantonments, World War.

Canvass. The word is used to describe two political processes. First it means to ascertain by direct personal approach how citizens intend to vote at a coming election. During earlier decades such canvasses were often made ninety, sixty and fifteen days before the election. The practice is somewhat less common now partly because of the expense involved, partly because of the increasing tendency of voters to refuse information and finally because of the polls made locally by newspapers and nationally by magazines of wide circulation. Second, in a somewhat looser sense, to canvass means to make a campaign for the support of a given candidate or ticket.

ROBERT C. BROOKS

Cape Ann, Mass., was known in 1605 to Champlain as Le Cap aux Isles, and the next year he entered the cape's harbor. Capt. John Smith in 1614 called it Cape Tragabigzanda, after a Turkish lady, but it was renamed Cape Ann for the wife of James I. In 1623 the Dorchester Company[qv] of merchants in England established a fishing station at the cape, to which came disaffected settlers from Plymouth and Nantucket. Among these Roger Conant was a leader. In 1624 he quieted friction over fishing rights asserted for Plymouth by Myles Standish. For ships of that time the fishing grounds were too distant and the soil was poor, so that the enterprise failed in 1626. For twenty years the settlement languished, till Rev. Richard Blynman came in 1642. Then, under the name Gloucester, it began to grow as a deep-sea fishing port, absorbed Portuguese and Italian crews, and has never lost its eminence.

A moorland section of the cape, called Dogtown, was abandoned after the 18th century and its odd settlers became figures of rather sordid romance. Other sections, Annisquam and Pigeon Cove, are now given over to artists. Their works, together with Kipling's *Captains Courageous* and J. B. Connolly's *Out of Gloucester,* have kept Cape Ann in the public eye. Off the shore of West Gloucester is the reef of Norman's Woe, scene of Longfellow's "Wreck of the Hesperus."

[Charles B. Hawes, *Gloucester by Land and Sea.*]

CHARLES KNOWLES BOLTON

Cape Breton Expedition. *See* Louisburg Expedition, The (1745).

Cape Cod was a landmark for early explorers, possibly the "Promontory of Vinland"[qv] of the Norse voyagers (985–1025). Verrazano in 1524 approached it from the south, and Gomez the next year called it Cape St. James. Gosnold in 1602 gave it the name that survives. Champlain charted its sand-silted harbors in 1606 and Henry Hudson landed there in 1609. Capt. John Smith noted it on his map of 1614 and at last the Pilgrims[qv] entered the "Cape Harbor" on Nov. 11, 1620. Aside from Barnstable and Sandwich (1638) and Yarmouth (1639) the cape's fifteen towns developed slowly. Provincetown was a group of huts until the 18th century. A channel from Massachusetts Bay to Buzzards Bay is shown on Southack's map of 1717, but the present canal had a troubled development (*see* Cape Cod Canal) from 1870 to 1914. The Federal Government purchased it in 1928.

Whaling and cod fishing[qqv] arose in the 18th century and lost out to New Bedford and Gloucester, but oysters and clams still bring wealth to Wellfleet. Salt[qv] by evaporation of sea water became an industry before 1800. Cranberry growing started about 1816 at North Dennis. At Falmouth and elsewhere shipbuilding flourished before and after the Revolution. Sandwich was famous from 1825 to 1888 for its glass works. Whaling started migration of Portuguese from Lisbon, from the Azores and the Cape Verde Islands (*Bravas*). The cape has a long chronicle of shipwrecks, to which the ancient gravestones bear testimony. Ribs of the *Sparrow-Hawk* (1626) are at Pilgrim Hall. The United States submarine "S4" sank off Wood End, Dec. 17, 1927, when her crew of forty slowly died of suffocation, while sending out messages by the Morse code.

[Jeremiah Digges, *The Cape Cod Pilot;* Henry C. Kittredge, *Cape Cod: Its People and Their History.*]

CHARLES KNOWLES BOLTON

Cape Cod Canal, THE, connects Buzzards Bay and Cape Cod Bay and saves going around the cape. After many proposals and many failures, the eight-mile-long canal was built (1909 to 1914) by the Boston, Cape Cod and New York Canal Co. The Federal Government now operates it without tolls, having bought it in 1928. It forms part of the intracoastal waterway system.

[Henry C. Kittredge, *Cape Cod: Its People and Their History.*]

JAMES D. MAGEE

Cape Fear, Action at, 1865. *See* Fisher, Fort, Capture of, 1864–65.

Cape Fear River Settlements (N. C.). In 1664 and 1665 several hundred Barbadians planted a colony on the lower Cape Fear, which was abandoned in 1667. Little interest was shown in this region until after the removal of the Indian and pirate menace during the second decade of the next century. About 1723 settlers from South Carolina and from Albemarle[qv] began to move in, and in 1725 the town of Brunswick was laid out on the west bank of the river, about fourteen miles from the sea. Eight years later Wilmington was begun and became the colony's chief port. From 1735 to 1775 thousands of Scotch Highlanders settled on the upper Cape Fear. Naval stores and rice[qqv] became the most important products of the region.

[R. D. W. Connor, *North Carolina: Rebuilding an Ancient Commonwealth*, I.]

HUGH T. LEFLER

Cape Girardeau. As early as 1765, a bend in the Mississippi River about sixty miles south of the French village of Ste. Genevieve[qv] had been referred to as Cape Girardot or Girardeau. The settlement there dates from 1793 when the Spanish government, which had secured Louisiana in 1762, granted Louis Lorimier, a French-Canadian, the right of establishing a trading post. His grant gave him extensive trading privileges and a large tract of land surrounding his post. Lorimier was made commandant of the district and prospered from the returns of his land sales and trade with the Indians.

[Louis Houck, *History of Missouri.*]

W. J. HAMILTON

Cape Horn, southernmost point of the American continent, lies practically due south of Eastport, Maine, easternmost point of the United States. Traditionally the most dreaded of ocean headlands both because of the almost ceaseless storms for which it is noted and the fact that it lies within the southern ice line, Cape Horn was first sighted by the Dutch navigators le Maire and Schouten when on a voyage toward the East Indies in 1616. These were the first to enter the Pacific Ocean by way of Cape Horn, previous navigators having used the Straits of Magellan. William Schouten named the point Cape Hoorn after the town of Hoorn in Holland where he was born. The difficulty of making the west-bound passage of Cape Horn in sailing ships played a part in retarding the growth of California, but the discovery of gold[qv] on Sutter's[qv] ranch near Sacramento in the latter part of 1848 stimulated both the passage of the cape and the growth of the American mercantile marine. Because of the necessity always to contend with the rigors of Cape Horn when making a coast-to-coast voyage, American shipbuilders were compelled to produce fast, weatherly and immensely strong vessels. The stimulus given by the rapid growth of the trade to California went far to put American square-rigged ships in the forefront of the world. Famous Cape Horn ships of this period include the *Flying Cloud, Andrew Jackson* (which shared the record of eighty-nine days, New York to San Francisco), *Sea Witch, Great Republic, John Gilpin, Flying Fish, James Baines* (which logged the fastest speed ever recorded under sail, twenty-one knots). The rigors of the Horn passage, the growth of intercontinental trade, the greater development of the American Navy, the difficulty of adequately protecting the Pacific and the Atlantic coasts turned the attention of the United States to the building of the Panama Canal[qv]. From that time the importance of the route around Cape Horn, used long previously only by freight ships, most of them steamers, rapidly declined. The last American sailing ship to beat round Cape Horn is probably the schooner *Wanderbird,* in 1936. The last American Cape Horner in existence is the wooden ship *Benjamin Packard,* now in an amusement park at Rye, N. Y.

ALAN VILLIERS

Capital, National, The Location of, played an important part in Hamilton's successful establishment of the national credit. Immediately after the Continental Congress[qv] hastily adjourned (1783) from Philadelphia to New York, because of Pennsylvania's failure to protect it from the insults of mutinous soldiery (*see* Mutiny of Pennsylvania Troops), agitation was begun in Congress for establishing a permanent seat of government. Nearly every one of the Eastern and Middle Atlantic states offered a location, or urged a claim. The struggle continued for five years and carried over into the Congress under the Constitution. In 1790 Hamilton, cleverly using the desire of the Southern states to obtain the capital, traded, through Jefferson, Pennsylvania support for the Potomac River location, in return for Virginia support for his plan of the assumption[qv] of the states' Revolutionary War debts. The location act was approved July 16, 1790, and Virginia fulfilled her bargain by voting for the act (approved Aug. 4) making provision for the public debt.

[Claude G. Bowers, *Jefferson and Hamilton.*]

JOHN C. FITZPATRICK

Capital Gains Tax, 1936 and 1938. In the taxation of personal incomes one troublesome problem has been how satisfactorily to handle capital gains, that is, the gain from the sale of capital assets. Changes have been made in many of the revenue acts but a satisfactory method seems difficult to find. In the 1936 law gains and losses from sales of capital assets were to be taken into account in the calculation of taxable income. If the asset had been owned one year or less before sale, then the entire gain was to be included; ownership between one year and two years, 80% of the gain or loss was to be included; between two and five years, 60%; between five and ten years, 40%; and if ownership were more than ten years, only 30% of the gain was included. Realized losses were deductible in an amount equal to the capital gains and might be allowed beyond this to an amount of $2000. Any capital gains of corporations were taxed in full while losses were allowed only to the extent of gains plus $2000.

With an attempt better to differentiate between what might be considered investment and speculative gains, changes were made in the 1938 act. Profits from the sale of assets which have been owned for one and one-half years or less are to be taxed in their entirety, but if the ownership has been between one and one-half and two years only two thirds of the gains are taxable while ownership for more than two years makes but one half of the gain subject to taxation. Losses within the one-and-one-half-year period may be deducted from the gains and, if greater than the gains may, under certain restrictions, be carried forward to the next period. Losses in the longer period may also be deducted from gains, but no carry-over of losses is permitted. The provision for corporate gains and losses remains the same as in the 1936 act.

[R. H. Montgomery, *Income Tax Procedure.*]

MERLIN H. HUNTER

Capital Punishment. Prior to the Revolutionary War, most felonies were punishable by death. Popular thought held that a criminal deliberately chose to be wicked and was, therefore, entitled to no mercy. In harmony with this general attitude, executions were public exhibitions, and conducted as such, to deter others from crime.

Gradually, however, the states began to limit the number of capital offenses. In 1788 Ohio effected the first substantial reform by making murder the only crime punishable by death. Although this modification in severity was not as extensive in other jurisdictions, there was a definite tendency toward leniency after Ohio set the example. Today, murder is subject to the death penalty in all states applying capital punishment; rape in some Southern states; and burglary, robbery and arson in a few jurisdictions.

Compatible with the more humane instincts and, possibly, because some concluded that the death sentence was not a powerful deterrent, executions commenced to be held privately. New York abolished public hangings in 1835 and since then other states have followed suit. However, in a few Southern jurisdictions, those guilty of rape are still publicly executed.

During the middle of the 19th century the humanitarian spirit impelled many to seek the abolition of capital punishment. Michigan was the first to wipe out the death penalty in 1847. Other states followed although in a few instances the death penalty was re-established. Those jurisdictions without it today are Maine, Michigan, Minnesota, North Dakota, South Dakota, Rhode Island and Wisconsin.

A great number of other states allow the judge or jury to recommend life imprisonment instead of execution. However, there are still a great many who contend that capital punishment is the most effective measure as a safeguard against crime.

LEWIS E. LAWES

Capitalism is an economic system in which the ownership and control of land, capital and natural resources, the production and marketing of goods, the employment of labor and the organization and operation of the system as a whole are entrusted to private enterprise working under competitive conditions. Private property, contract, freedom of enterprise and profit making are basic rules; acquisition of consumption goods (food, clothing, etc.) is the goal; and accumulation, control and use of capital, as the essential instrument, is the way the goal is most quickly reached.

Most economists think of capital as "produced goods intended for further production." Tools, machines, coal, oil, lumber, unfinished or unsold goods, supplies are all examples. Cash and bank deposits are sometimes called "liquid capital" because they may be directed to any use the possessor wishes, but they are really only titles to capital. Capital is man-made and can be created only through some one's saving. Interest is the rental price for the use of capital. Throughout history the capitalistic or indirect process of production—creating capital to make consumption goods, such as making a net to catch fish—has been found more efficient than the direct method, involving no capital, such as catching fish by hand. Generous use of capital is the secret of the economies of mass production[qv], and the nations with the most capital per person have the highest standards of living.

Virginia and Plymouth were handicapped at the outset by lack of capital, lack of artisans and lack of the profit motive. The Pilgrims did not bring a horse, cow or plow, and their fishhooks and nets were too large for cod. When the meager supplies soon gave out there was a period of "starving" because there was little incentive in either colony for the individual to work hard to build up a surplus since the settlers were expected to put all their produce into a common fund from which all would be supported and out of which the companies financing the expeditions would receive repayment and profit, a system bordering on communism so far as the settlers were concerned. John Smith remarked "When our people were fed out of the common store and laboured jointly together . . . the most honest among them would hardly take so much true paines in a weeke, as now for themselves they will doe in a day: . . ."

When the settlers were permitted greater freedom of enterprise and allowed to accumulate private property, colonies grew and prospered. Although the English urged Virginia to produce wheat and naval stores, tobacco was far more profitable, so the Virginians grew it. All along the eastern seaboard capital was created when land was cleared, fenced and otherwise improved, sawmills, tobacco warehouses, corn cribs, indigo vats, blast furnaces, rope walks and ships were built; or when men fashioned countless household tools in the leisure moments of the evening. Usually the profits from their occupations were plowed back into the business, and since people were "skimming the cream" off the resources of a virgin continent, the profits were frequently sizable.

An outstanding factor in our economic development until the 20th century was the plentifulness of land and the scarcity of labor and capital, the reverse of conditions in Europe. Since most men preferred to work for themselves, even if only on a log-cabin farm, labor for hire was scarce and there were thousands of small capitalists. The problem of the dearth of labor was met by the indentured servant system and by Negro slavery[qqv]. The lack of capital was not so well handled. Many confused capital with money and, presuming that the interest rates were high owing to a scarcity of money, urged the Government to provide more money somehow. Whether the consequent inflation[qv] in the colonies greatly retarded the inflow of capital, or whether it put to quicker use savings that would otherwise have been uselessly hoarded is still disputed. The absence of banks of deposit and discount to pool and distribute the community's savings made the flow of "liquid" capital sluggish when its efficient use was highly desirable.

British interference with the operation of our capitalistic system was a major cause of the Revolution. Parliamentary taxation took private property without our leave; enforcement of trade and navigation acts, especially the Sugar Act of 1764 which threatened a profitable triangular trade[qqv], restricted our freedom of enterprise; and the laws forbidding legal-tender paper money seemed to dry up the supply of capital.

When our weakly confederated Government broke down, propertied men were largely instrumental in drawing up and securing the adoption of the Constitution which restored some sanctity to contract, put an end to legal-tender paper money and gave increased protection to private property.

Numerous factors affected the growth of capital in the next few decades. European wars augmented the demand for our agricultural products and led to a tripling of our foreign merchant marine between 1790 and 1807. After the embargo[qv] and other decrees reduced the supply of foreign manufactures the North diverted its savings to manufacturing and after the war higher tariffs were imposed to protect this new capital. Meanwhile the invention of the cotton gin and the power loom[qqv] at the close of the 18th century stimulated the demand for the South's cotton and revived slavery. Southerners grew cotton[qv] to buy more land and slaves to grow more cotton to buy more land and slaves, etc. By the middle of the century the supply of new cotton land had been greatly reduced, much land had been exhausted and little capital invested in its restoration, the output of the slave had not increased much, for that form of capital is not easily improved, and the South had little mechanical capital to show for its efforts, a fact that lost it the Civil War.

This demand for food and cotton was a chief cause of the westward movement[qv]. Thomas Jefferson had estimated in 1800 that it would take 1000 years to fill up the region east of the Mississippi but thanks to improvements in transportation the period was much shortened. Turnpikes, canals and then railroads[qqv] enabled people to market their goods more cheaply and brought about regional specialization. Growing knowledge of how to make iron and steel, the use of coke and the standardization of parts made possible larger-sized machines, which the small capitalist or artisan could not afford, and helped cause the shift from the domestic to the factory system. Yet without the corporation[qv] with its distinguishing features of limited liability and perpetual life, capital for railroads and factories could hardly have been obtained. Now that laborer and capitalist were no longer one, or working close together, their interests diverged. Skilled labor gradually organized to deal with organized capital. Reaction to the discipline of more specialized jobs stimulated interest in the 1840's in communistic experiments like the Brook Farm[qv].

The period following the Civil War was one of tremendous business expansion. A good index of capital increase is the amount of power used in industry which grew from 2,300,000 horsepower in 1870 to 22,300,000 in 1914. The number of iron and steel establishments increased about 63% between 1860 and 1910, their output 14,730% and the number of their wage earners 1296%, indicating the greater average size of the plants and the extent to which capital had enabled labor to accomplish more in a day. Profits were large: because regulations were few; many resources were being exploited for the first time; high tariffs[qv] kept foreign competition out of the great free-trade area within the nation; and our patent system and the relative scarceness of labor stimulated invention. Most of the capital for this expansion was drawn from within the nation. Jay Cooke[qv] set the precedent by selling government bonds to the general public during the Civil War and stocks later, and thus did much to arouse the interest of people of moderate means in securities. In 1886 New York stock exchange[qv] transactions first exceeded a million shares a day.

This get-rich-quick era produced giant railroad companies and industrial combinations known as "trusts,"[qv] which frequently used unfair methods of competition against rivals, exploited the people and corrupted governments. Both the Interstate Commerce Act, appointing a commission to regulate the railroads, and the Sherman Antitrust Act[qqv], to break up the "trusts" and make the members compete, were at first rendered ineffective by court decisions. According to the census of 1900 there were 185 "trusts" comprising a half of 1% of all establishments in the country but owning 15% of the capital and turning out 14% of the products. Public reaction, under the leadership of Theodore Roosevelt, produced a "trust busting" and reform era. The trusts fought state laws to regulate them and to give labor and the public some measure of protection by citing the clause in the Fourteenth Amendment providing that a person may not be deprived of his property without due process[qv] of law. Attempts to establish by law the ten-hour day in bakeries (Lochner case[qv]) or set a minimum wage for women (Adkins case[qv]) were deemed by the courts to interfere with freedom of contract[qv]. Yet in the end human rights received greater recognition without capitalists suffering seriously. An increasing number and variety of businesses were declared "affected with a public interest" and put under commission supervision. The income-tax[qv] amendment and laws made inroads on former rights of private property. It is noteworthy that the Socialist presidential candidate in 1912 polled nearly a million votes, a sixteenth of the total cast in an election where there were two liberal candidates.

War is hard on capitalism, for it results in the destruction of capital and necessitates the curtailment of individual rights of private property, freedom of enterprise and contract if the economic forces of the nation are to be organized for victory. Men were drafted into the army, a war industries board[qv] set prices and restricted non-war production and the railroads were run by the Government. With peace the nation attempted to return to "normalcy," however.

The decade following the war was one of great prosperity and at such times capital accumulates rapidly. The sale of Liberty bonds[qv] had made the public security-minded and now corporation stocks came to be more widely held. Between 1919–29 the number of common stockholders of the American Telephone and Telegraph Company[qv] increased from 116,721 to 458,135 and private corporations issued $64,000,000,000 of new capital securities and reinvested about $20,000,000,000 of savings. The horsepower of the average manufacturing industry increased 49% and the number of wage earners declined about 7%. Many economists believe that overinvestment in plant and equipment was largely responsible for the depression beginning in 1929 but this theory also has many critics.

During a depression savings are drawn upon heavily. The 1934 income-tax report shows that over the four years, 1931–34, industrial corporations as a whole operated at a loss of above $11,000,000,000. Between 1931–36 private corporations acquired only $10,000,000,000 of new capital from the securities markets. After 1933 the F. D. Roosevelt administration made some radical experiments. Adopting the policy advocated by the English economist, J. M. Keynes, it tried to spend the country out of depression and in six years doubled the national debt. Under the short-lived National Industrial Recovery Act[qv] minimum wages and maximum hours were set, and trade associations were told to draw up codes of fair practice and permitted to control prices and determine production. Utilities were faced with government competition; laborers were encouraged to believe that they had a property right in their jobs; and corporate saving was discouraged by the corporations undistributed profits tax, the avowed policy of price raising and abrogation of the gold clause[qv] in debt contracts. Most of these new developments represent a departure from the conditions under which the $120,000,000,000 of capital of the country has been built up, under which, for example, Henry Ford made his great and useful fortune, and under which real wages were quadrupled between 1791 and 1933.

[B. M. Anderson, Eating the Seed Corn, *Chase Econ. Bull. XVI*, 2; C. A. Beard, *An Economic Interpretation of the Constitution of the U. S.;* E. L. Bogart, *Economic History of the American People;* V. Clark, *History of Manufactures in the U. S.;* A. M. Earle, *Home Life in Colonial Days;* H. G. Moulton, *The Formation of Capital;* C. Nettels, *The Roots of American Civilization;* E. G. Nourse, *America's Capacity to Produce; Statistical Abstract of the U. S.;* A. C. Pigou, *Capitalism versus Socialism;* B. Wootton, *Plan or No Plan;* S. S. Kuznets, *National Income and Capital Formation, 1919-35;* E. A. Keller, *A Study of the Physical Assets, Sometimes Called Wealth, of the United States, 1922-33;* C. F. Ware and G. C. Means, *The Modern Economy in Action.*]

DONALD L. KEMMERER

Capitation Taxes. The Federal Government is forbidden by Article I, Section 9, of the Constitution from levying a capitation or other direct tax, "unless in Proportion to the Census of Enumeration" laid down in Section 2. Section 9, however, in accord with colonial practices of placing taxes on the importation of convicts and Negro slaves, permits a tax or duty to be imposed on persons entering the United States, "not exceeding ten dollars for each person." The poll-tax restriction does not apply to the states. Following colonial precedents, the states have employed this tax, generally placed on all males above twenty-one, sometimes sixteen, regardless of income or property. In Southern states the poll tax has often been made a prerequisite to the exercise of the suffrage, thus disqualifying the Negro or controlling his vote.

[H. Walker, The Poll Tax in the United States, National Tax Association, *Bulletin,* Vol. IX.]

RICHARD B. MORRIS

Capitol at Washington, The. In a disappointing public competition in 1791 of amateur and professional plans, Stephen Hallet's, though not satisfactory, was judged the best. Dr. William Thornton, by permission, submitted a more artistic design and Hallet was employed to make working drawings of it, and to superintend the erection. Accused of substituting his own plan for Thornton's, he was dismissed in 1794 and George Hadfield, an English architect, succeeded him. The cornerstone was laid with Masonic ceremonies by President Washington, Sept. 18, 1793; but the center portion had not been erected when the British burned the public buildings in 1814 (*see* Washington Burned). Rebuilding commenced in 1815, under Benjamin H. Latrobe, and the center portion of Acquia freestone with a low dome, designed by Charles Bulfinch, was finished in 1827. The present north and south wings of Massachusetts marble (the fluted pillars are from Maryland) were begun in 1851, from designs of Thomas Ustick Walters, and finished in 1857–59. The present dome of cast iron, an adaptation of Michelangelo's St. Peter's (Rome) and Sir Christopher Wren's St. Paul's (London), was begun in 1856 and finished in 1865. It is surmounted by Crawford's heroic bronze of Freedom, 19½ feet high. The dome is, roughly, 300 feet in height.

[W. B. Bryan, *History of the National Capitol.*]

JOHN C. FITZPATRICK

Capper-Volstead Act, The (Feb. 18, 1922). As a consequence of the depression of agricultural prices subsequent to the World War, farm organizations intensified their drive for government aid and managed to get a farm bloc established in Congress. Sen. Capper was a member of this bloc and the Capper-Volstead Act was a part of the farm legislative program. The act authorized various kinds of agricultural producers to form voluntary co-operative associations for purposes of producing, handling and marketing farm products—that is, it exempted such associations from the application of the antitrust laws. The Secretary of Agriculture was given power, on his own motion, to prevent such associations from achieving and maintaining monopolies. He could hold hearings, determine facts and issue orders ultimately subject to review by Federal district courts. The act is an example of legislative aid to agricultural co-operatives and of the delegation of adjudicative power to an administrative agency[qv].

HARVEY PINNEY

Capron Trail, The, one of the important east and west trails of Florida, was probably first run about 1850, the date of the establishment of Fort Capron (St. Lucie in St. Lucie County). It passed from Fort Capron through Fort Vinton, Fort Drum, Fort Kissimee, Fort Clinch, Fort Meade to Fort Brooke (Tampa). Fort Capron and the Capron Trail commemorated the valor of Capt. Erastus A. Capron who was killed Aug. 20, 1847, at the battle of Churubusco[qv], Mexico.

[Frederick W. Dau, *Florida Old and New.*]

KATHRYN T. ABBEY

Capuchins, The, a branch of Franciscan[qv] Friars Minor, came to America when Richelieu assigned them missions in New England (1630) and Acadia (1632). In 1722 the order was given ecclesiastical jurisdiction over Louisiana. They built (1728) St. Louis Church, the first permanent church building in Louisiana, and established the first school in the Mississippi Valley (1725). When the Jesuits^{qv} came (1726) a controversy over jurisdiction began, involving the civil authorities; it continued until the Jesuits were expelled (1763). The Capuchins have been inactive in Louisiana for a century, but their work continues elsewhere in America.

[Claude L. Vogel, *The Capuchins in French Louisiana, 1722-1766;* Otto Jeron, The Capuchins in America, *Historical Records and Studies*, V.] MACK SWEARINGEN

Caracas, Mixed Commissions at, were established subsequent to the 1902 crisis in the Venezuelan debt controversy^{qv}. After negotiations at Washington in which the United States played a decisive part, protocols were signed in February and March, 1903, between Venezuela and ten creditor powers (Great Britain, Germany, Italy, France, Belgium, The Netherlands, Norway-Sweden, Mexico, Spain and the United States), providing for settlement of claims by commissions consisting of one member appointed by each party and a neutral umpire. Venezuela allotted 30% of customs revenues at La Guayra and Puerto Cabello for payments awarded. The commissions sat at Caracas (June–December, 1903) and awarded sums ranging from over 10,000,000 bolivars (francs) to Belgium to 174,000 bolivars to Norway-Sweden. The United States received about 2,250,000 bolivars. All claims were drastically cut down except for those of Belgium and Mexico. Great Britain, Germany and Italy (the blockading powers) were given priority in payment by an arbitration tribunal at The Hague^{qv}.

[U. S. Department of State, *Papers Relating to the Foreign Relations of the United States, 1903, 1904.*]

CHARLES C. GRIFFIN

Caravan Traffic of the Great Plains existed from approximately 1825 to 1875 and reached its maximum development during the first few years after the Civil War. During this period both immigrant and trade caravans were employed, particularly after the beginning of the Oregon movement (1842), the Mormon migration (1847) and the discovery of gold in California (1848)^{qqv}.

The first important caravan traffic across the Great Plains^{qv} was via the Santa Fé Trail^{qv}. William Becknell drove the first wagon from western Missouri to Santa Fé in 1822. This was eight years before Jedediah Smith^{qv}, David L. Jackson and William Sublette took a party of eighty-one men and ten large wagons (drawn by five mules each) from St. Louis to the trappers' rendezvous^{qv} on the Wind River; and it was ten years before Capt. B. L. E. Bonneville^{qv} conducted still another wagon train across South Pass^{qv}. Caravans of twenty-five wagons or more were used largely to transport trade goods over the Santa Fé Trail to the value of $35,000 in 1824, $90,000 in 1826 and $150,000 in 1828. The distance traveled from Franklin, Mo., to Santa Fé was 870 miles. After the first few years, Lexington, some 60 miles farther west, was the point of departure; and still later, Independence^{qv}, 100 miles farther west, was the starting point.

Caravan movements over the Oregon Trail^{qv} were equally significant, although perhaps not so important commercially. Elm Grove, about twelve miles southwest of Independence, was a favorite starting point; and later West Port. At the former place, beginning in 1842, immigrants came in covered wagons^{qv} each spring, elected their captains, guides and other officers and began the long trek westward via the Oregon Trail. The caravan of 1842, organized by Dr. Elijah White, traveled as far as Fort Hall^{qv} before the wagons were abandoned. From here the immigrants traveled on foot, horseback or by raft down the Snake and Columbia rivers^{qqv}. The following year upward of 1000 immigrants moved over the same route in many wagons, some of which reached the banks of the Columbia.

During the 1850's, caravans, large and small, were thronging all roads across the Great Plains. Randolph B. Marcy conducted a caravan of 100 wagons from Fort Smith^{qv} to New Mexico via the Canadian River^{qv} in 1849, on the first leg of its journey to California; and agent William Bent (for the Comanches and Kiowas^{qqv}) estimated 60,000 immigrants to have crossed the plains along the Arkansas route^{qv} in 1859. Heavy freight caravans plied the routes between San Antonio and Chihuahua, between Santa Fé and Chihuahua; and from points in Nebraska, Kansas and Colorado to the far West by 1860. From Council Bluff to the Great Salt Lake via Fort Bridger^{qv} was a well-known road over which thousands of Mormon^{qv} pilgrims traveled from 1847 to 1860.

The Army Appropriation Bill of 1853 made available $150,000 to be spent by the Secretary of War, Jefferson Davis, to survey routes for western railways, and soon thereafter four surveys were made. This promised a new era that was formally initiated by the first Union Pacific^{qv} Act of 1862. Seven years later the first transcontinental line was completed. But caravan trade and travel were to remain for a decade yet until railroads could offer adequate facilities.

[Josiah Gregg, *Commerce of the Prairies;* Alexander

Majors, *Seventy Years on the Frontier;* Col. Henry Inman and Col. William F. Cody, *The Great Salt Lake Trail;* F. L. Paxson, *History of the American Frontier;* W. J. Ghent, *The Early Far West, A Narrative Outline, 1540-1850.*]

C. C. RISTER

Caravans, Outfitting of. A visitor to the West in 1860 estimated that 20,000 wagons were in use transporting immigrants and supplies, requiring around 100,000 oxen and 40,000 mules to pull them. Western towns such as St. Louis, Fort Smith, Little Rock, San Antonio, Denver and Salt Lake City[qqv] did a thriving business in consequence. At one of these (or others equally active), immigrants bound for the far West had a last opportunity to purchase necessities. Food (such as meal, flour, sugar, coffee and bacon), clothing, blankets, guns and ammunition, farm implements (such as an ax, hoe, shovel or an occasional plow) were a few of the purchases. In addition, immigrant wagons were generally burdened with certain household goods (a bedstead, a framed picture of grandfather or grandmother, a favorite chair and perhaps one or more heirlooms), and other sundry things considered as necessities. Many an immigrant traveling the Oregon Trail[qv] to the Columbia or the Platte route to California discarded much of his impedimenta before he arrived at his destination. In consequence many intermediate towns and communities profited. Settlers at Salt Lake City and in the Great Basin[qv] did a thriving exchange trade with the Forty-niners[qv], buying worn-out horses and cattle, or exchanging potatoes and flour for their excess burdens. Likewise Denver was to profit as a supply center during Colorado's gold-rush days, 1858–65 (*see* Pikes Peak Gold Rush).

The great rush for western lands following the enactment of the Federal homestead law[qv] of 1862 greatly increased caravan traffic[qv]; and in every town of considerable size along the frontier was one or more well-known supply firms. Guns and ammunition were generally bought. During the period of the destruction of the bison (*see* Buffalo, The) from the southern plains, a general supply store at Fort Griffin[qv], Texas, during a one-day period (1877), sold goods to the value of better than $4000, of which $2500 represented guns and ammunition. Other supplies were plows, farm tools, staple groceries, wagons, kerosene, dry goods, seed and feed for livestock. Such quantities of supplies were required that numerous freighting firms were organized and long trains of wagons were on every well-traveled road.

[Alexander Majors, *Seventy Years on the Frontier;* F. L. Paxson, *History of the American Frontier.*]

C. C. RISTER

Cardiff Giant, THE. A human figure weighing 2966 lbs. cut from Iowa gypsum in Chicago for George Hull, transported to Cardiff, N. Y., and secretly buried on the Newell farm. In 1869 it was "discovered" and exhibited as a petrified prehistoric giant, creating much excitement and deceiving many people until the hoax was revealed.

[*Autobiography of Andrew Dickson White.*]

DEXTER S. KIMBALL

Carey Desert Land Grant Act, THE (Aug. 18, 1894), authorized the President to grant to each public land state[qv] not exceeding 1,000,000 acres of desert lands in the public domain[qv] within its boundaries for sale to settlers, and for irrigation, reclamation, cultivation and occupancy, in tracts not exceeding 160 acres each, of which 20 acres in each tract must be cultivated on penalty of reversion of the tract to the public domain. Surplus derived by states from such land sales, in excess of cost of reclamation, was to be held as a trust fund for reclamation of other desert land in the state.

[William H. and Richard Olney Mason, *Mason's United States Code, Annotated.*]

FRED A. EMERY

Caribbean Policy. The special interest of the United States in the Caribbean, manifest from the earliest days of the Republic, greatly increased after the Spanish-American War[qv]. Puerto Rico[qv] had become an American colony and Cuba[qv] under the Platt Amendment[qv], a quasi-protectorate. The construction of the Panama Canal[qv], begun soon afterward, greatly increased the strategic importance of the lands which controlled its approaches. At the same time, political disorder and the resulting inability to meet obligations to foreigners exposed the smaller Central American and West Indian republics to increasingly frequent foreign intervention. This situation led President Theodore Roosevelt in 1905 to enunciate his so-called corollary to the Monroe Doctrine[qv]: that the United States could not prevent European intervention in the weaker American republics unless it took steps itself to correct conditions which invited such intervention.

The policy of Roosevelt and his immediate successors appears to have been based on this principle. Roosevelt himself occasionally interfered in the affairs of the Caribbean countries when serious crises occurred, as in the adjustment of the debts of the Dominican Republic[qv], the second intervention in Cuba and the Central-American disturbances of 1906–7. The Taft administration intervened forcibly in Nicaragua[qv], and in other countries adopted the so-called preventive policy, giving advice or exerting diplomatic pressure to prevent the development of situations which might make intervention necessary. The Wilson administration went farther, seeking to persuade several of the more disorderly countries to agree to the reorganization of their military forces under American instructors and the control of their expenditures as well as their revenues by American fiscal experts. The failure of these efforts was followed by the actual military occupation of Haiti[qv] and the Dominican Republic. The United States continued during this period to exercise much influence in the internal politics of Nicaragua, Panama and Cuba.

Under Presidents Harding and Coolidge, the general trend was toward less interference. Crowder's special mission in Cuba terminated, and the military government was withdrawn from the Dominican Republic. On the other hand, the United States made more definite its policy of refusing to recognize revolutionary governments in Central America and the withdrawal of the American marines from Nicaragua in 1925 was followed by the second intervention there. This latter event caused a strong reaction against "imperialism"[qv] both in the United States and in Latin America. Influenced by this sentiment, the Hoover administration adopted a definite policy of nonintervention. American forces were withdrawn from Nicaragua and American control in Haiti was greatly restricted.

President Franklin Roosevelt announced in December, 1933, that "the definite policy of the United States from now on is one opposed to armed intervention." In pursuance of the "Good Neighbor Policy"[qv] new treaties have been signed superseding those authorizing American intervention in Cuba and Panama, and the American marines have been withdrawn from Haiti. The policy of not recognizing revolutionary governments appears to have been largely abandoned. A measure of financial control, for the protection of bondholders, still exists in Haiti and in the Dominican Republic.

[Council on Foreign Relations, *Survey of American Foreign Relations, 1929;* Chester Lloyd Jones, *The Caribbean Since 1900.*]

DANA G. MUNRO

Carillion, Fort. *See* Ticonderoga, Fort.

Carlisle, Pa., founded 1751, became the center of the Scotch-Irish[qv] settlement in the Cumberland Valley. At the crossroads of important Indian trails, and the site of Fort Louther, it was a refuge and trading center for pioneers.

[C. P. Wing, *History Cumberland County, Pa.*]

MULFORD STOUGH

Carlisle Commission. *See* Peace Commission of 1778 (British).

Carlisle (Pa.) Indian School was established in 1879 by Capt. R. H. Pratt, under whose twenty-five-year direction it grew from 136 to 1000 pupils (boys and girls), the equipment expanding accordingly. Instruction included practical training in farming, horticulture, dressmaking, cooking, laundering, housekeeping and twenty trades. A distinctive feature was the "Outing System." Pupils were urged to spend a year working on farms, in homes or industries of the neighborhood. The school was closed in 1918.

[Elaine Goodale Eastman, *Pratt, The Red Man's Moses.*]

MULFORD STOUGH

Carlotta, Confederate Colony of. In 1865 many ex-Confederates left their native land for Mexico. Emperor Maximilian encouraged this exodus by appointing Commodore M. F. Maury Imperial Commissioner of Immigration. Military and civil colonies were to be established along the railway between Vera Cruz and Mexico City. The best-known colony, comprising 500,000 acres, was Carlotta, in the Cordova Valley, named in honor of the Empress. Among reasons for failure were a hostile American press; lack of funds; improper colonization methods; forcible land seizure and occupation; disturbed political condition in Mexico; local hostility; and opposition of the United States Government.

[George D. Harmon, Confederate Migration to Mexico, *Hispanic American Historical Review,* November, 1937, pp. 458-88.]

C. C. RISTER

Carlsbad Caverns, southeastern New Mexico, discovered by Jim White, Texas cowboy, in 1901, became a national monument in 1923 and a national park in 1930. The caverns occupy a tract of 720 acres. Largest of the explored part of the caverns is the "Big Room," more than three quarters of a mile long, 625 feet wide and 350 feet high.

[Ford Sibley, *My Trip Through Carlsbad Caverns.*]

S. S. McKAY

Carmelites, THE, were one of the Roman Catholic monastic orders which came to Louisiana in the early days of French settlement. When the province was divided into three ecclesiastical districts on May 16, 1722, they were given charge of all the region east of the Mississippi, from the Gulf of Mexico to the Wabash River, with headquarters at Mobile. Their administration was short-lived, for their jurisdiction was added to that of the Capuchins[qv] on Dec. 19, 1722, and they returned to France.

[A. Fortier, *History of Louisiana.*]

WALTER PRICHARD

Carmelo River, THE, which enters the Pacific Ocean from the southeast about five miles southwest of Monterey[qv], Calif., was discovered in 1602 by Sebastián Vizcaíno who exaggerated it to the proportions of a mighty river. It was long sought by subsequent explorers.

OSGOOD HARDY

Carnegie Corporation of New York, established by Andrew Carnegie in 1911, is for the advancement and diffusion of knowledge and understanding among the people of the United States and the British Dominions and colonies. Its endowment consists of two funds totaling $135,000,000, of which $10,000,000 is applicable in the British Dominions and colonies. The income only is subject to the disposal of the trustees.

For the first eight years of the Corporation's history, and until the time of his death, Mr. Carnegie was the president of the governing board of trustees and the administration of the Corporation was, in those years, chiefly under his personal direction and authority. Shortly after his death the trustees provided for a president who should give his whole time to the service of the board and should be its executive officer.

Before creating the Carnegie Corporation Mr. Carnegie had founded and endowed separately five other agencies in the United States: Carnegie Institute of Pittsburgh, Carnegie Institution of Washington[qv], Carnegie Hero Fund Commission[qv], Carnegie Foundation for the Advancement of Teaching[qv] and the Carnegie Endowment for International Peace.

The present program of the Corporation includes the support of educational and scientific research, publications of professional and scholarly societies and associations, fine arts education through educational institutions and national organizations, adult education, library service and training, and support of various related projects which give promise of providing new knowledge through (1) research, (2) studies which, through examination of existing conditions, may point to better conditions in the future, or (3) demonstrations, local or regional, of how new knowledge may most effectively be applied.

[Frederick Paul Keppel, *The Foundation; Its Place in American Life;* Robert M. Lester, *The Corporation; A Digest of Its Financial Record, 1911-1936.*]

ROBERT M. LESTER

Carnegie Foundation for the Advancement of Teaching, THE, established in 1905 by Andrew Carnegie, was incorporated by act of Congress approved March 10, 1906, "to provide retiring pensions for the teachers of Universities, Colleges, and Technical Schools in our Country, Canada, and Newfoundland" and "in general to do and perform all things necessary to uphold and dignify the profession of the teacher and the cause of higher education." Initial endowment of $10,000,000 from Mr. Carnegie was increased in 1908 to $15,000,000 to include publicly controlled higher institutions of education. Other gifts have come from Carnegie Corporation of New York[qv]. The self-perpetuating board of trustees consists of twenty-five members. Retiring allowances are provided only within a list of specified persons. The Foundation has disbursed (1938) more than $33,000,000 for allowances and widows' pensions in 168 institutions for 2755 individuals comprising 1855 retired college teachers and administrative officers and 900 widows.

In 1913 an endowment of $1,250,000 for its Division of Educational Enquiry was accepted from Mr. Carnegie. Studies made in or for the Division have dealt with medical, legal, engineering and dental education, college athletics, teacher training and the relation of colleges and secondary schools in Pennsylvania, etc. Results have been issued in twenty-nine bulletins, thirty-two annual reports and thirty-seven miscellaneous publications. Resources (1938) are $28,052,465. The Foundation offers no fellowships or scholarships of any kind.

[Annual Reports, 1906-37.]

HOWARD J. SAVAGE

Carnegie Hero Fund Commission, THE, was created in 1904 for the purpose of making annual awards from a trust income of $5,000,000, given by Andrew Carnegie, to recognize acts of heroism in the United States, Canada and Newfoundland. The Commission awards medals to heroes and gives out of this trust fund financial assistance when needed by those it recognizes for heroic acts, and for education, purchase of homes, liquidation of debts and pensions for dependents, according to merits of each case.

FRED A. EMERY

Carnegie Institution of Washington, THE, was founded in 1902 by Andrew Carnegie "to encourage in the broadest and most liberal manner investigation, research, and discovery, and the application of knowledge to the improvement of mankind."

The Institution attempts to advance fundamental research in fields not normally covered by the activities of other agencies and to concentrate its attention upon specific problems, with the idea of shifting attack from time to time to meet the more pressing needs of research as they develop with increase of knowledge. Constant efforts are made to facilitate interpretation and application of results of research activities of the Institution.

JOHN C. MERRIAM

Carnegie Steel Company. *See* United States Steel Corporation.

Carnifex Ferry, Battles at (1861). An Ohio regiment posted at this river-crossing in West Virginia was routed on Aug. 26 by a Confederate brigade under Gen. John B. Floyd, who thereupon entrenched and remained there until attacked on Sept. 10 by Rosecrans' small army. After a sharp action, Floyd, slightly wounded, retreated with his command during the night.

[*Battles and Leaders of the Civil War.*]

ALVIN F. HARLOW

"Carolana" was a colony projected by Daniel Coxe, a British physician and land speculator, who by 1698 had acquired title to the Sir Robert Heath grant[qv] of 1629, under which he claimed the region in the rear of the Carolina settlements and including the lower Mississippi Valley. The expedition sent out to plant the colony landed at Charleston (S. C.), but one ship sailed up the Mississippi River for 100 miles, turning back when Bienville informed the captain, on Sept. 15, 1699, that the French already occupied the region (*see* Louisiana, as a French and Spanish Colony). Coxe reasserted his claim to the territory, but his colony never materialized.

[Edward McCrady, *The History of South Carolina under the Proprietary Government, 1670-1719;* Samuel A. Ashe, *History of North Carolina;* R. G. Thwaites, *France in America, 1497-1763;* Grace King, *Jean Baptiste LeMoyne, Sieur de Bienville;* Alcée Fortier, *History of Louisiana;* Charles Gayarré, *History of Louisiana.*]

WALTER PRICHARD

Carolina, The Fundamental Constitutions of, the most pretentious of the attempts to establish a feudal aristocracy in English America, were drawn up in 1669 by John Locke under the direction of his employer and patron the Earl of Shaftesbury. Between that date and 1698 four revisions were issued by the Lords Proprietors. Outstanding features were the provisions for a provincial nobility of proprietors, landgraves and caziques[qqv] having permanent ownership of two fifths of the land; for a Grand Council made up of proprietors and their councilors which should have the executive and judicial authority, and—through its control of the initiative—should likewise control legislation; for an established Anglican Church and religious toleration; and for serfdom and slavery.

Shelving the top-heavy system for a time at the beginning of settlement, the proprietors set up revised Grand Councils in North and in South Carolina, but in the former the Fundamental Constitutions had little weight. In South Carolina they greatly strengthened the tendency toward a dominant landed aristocracy, and to them may be traced the ballot and certain land ownership requirements for voting and officeholding. The attempts of the proprietors to force the complete system upon the assembly came to a climax and failure about 1690.

[Edward McCrady, *The History of South Carolina under the Proprietary Government;* S. A. Ashe, *History of North Carolina.*]

R. L. MERIWETHER

Carolina Proprietors. The first Carolina patent was granted by Charles I to Sir Robert Heath[qv] in 1629. By its terms the province extended from ocean to ocean between the 31st and 36th parallels. This patent was declared forfeited on the ground of nonuse by Charles II, who in 1663 issued a charter with the same bounds to eight joint proprietors: Edward Hyde, Earl of Clarendon; George Monk, Duke of Albemarle; William, Lord Craven; John, Lord Berkeley; Anthony Ashley Cooper, Lord Ashley (later Earl of Shaftesbury); Sir George Carteret; Sir John Colleton; and Sir William Berkeley. In 1665 the boundaries were extended to include the territory from 29° to 36° 30′ N. Lat. "Declarations and Proposals," the first organic law, issued by the proprietors in 1663, promised land to settlers who should emigrate within five years, representation of freeholders in a provincial assembly and liberty of conscience. The Fundamental Constitutions of Carolina[qv], formulated by John Locke in 1669, never went into effect in the colony.

The enterprise resulting in loss, proprietary neglect became chronic. Great discontent was caused by the indifference of the proprietors during the war with the Tuscaroras (1711–12), and the Yamasee War (1715–16)[qqv] and by their lack of support when the province was threatened from the West Indies by the French and the Spanish (1706, 1719) and when it was attacked by pirates (1718). Proprietary orders destructive of provincial interests brought about a revolutionary movement in South Carolina[qv] (1719), which the crown thereupon took over as a royal colony, leaving North Carolina^qv^ to the proprietors until purchase of the proprietorship of both provinces for the crown (1729). Lord Carteret retained his interest in the form of a strip of land lying south of Virginia and estimated at an eighth of the original grant (*see* Granville Grant).

[S. A. Ashe, *History of North Carolina;* R. D. W. Connor, *History of North Carolina;* Edward McCrady, *The History of South Carolina under the Proprietary Government;* D. D. Wallace, *History of South Carolina.*]

D. D. WALLACE

Carolina Road. *See* Virginia Path, The.

Carolinas, Sherman's March through the. In February, 1865, Sherman's (U.) army left Savannah[qv] on its way northward "to make South Carolina feel the severities of war" and to unite with Grant (U.) in Virginia. By Feb. 17 it was at Columbia[qv], S. C., which was burned. None in Sherman's army ever admitted responsibility for this act. On March 10 the army was at Fayetteville, N. C. As Sherman advanced, opposition became stronger. At Bentonville[qv] on March 19 the advance was delayed several days, but by the 25th Sherman was at Goldsboro. On April 13 he had reached Raleigh.

The news of Lee's surrender[qv] caused Gen. J. E. Johnston (C.) to negotiate for the surrender of the Confederate Army. A conditional agreement was signed, April 18, but was repudiated because of too liberal terms. On the 26th Johnston surrendered on the same terms Lee had received.

Sherman marched nearly 500 miles in about eight weeks, impeded as much by the multitude of slaves and their families who mingled with the marching troops as by the weak and unorganized Confederate opposition.

[*Battles and Leaders of the Civil War.*]

THOMAS ROBSON HAY

Caroline, Fort. *See* Florida, French in.

***Caroline* Affair.** In November, 1837, William Lyon McKenzie launched a rebellion in Upper Canada. Defeated by the government forces, McKenzie and his followers fled to Navy Island in the Niagara River. Sympathizers on the American side of the river supplied them with food, arms and recruits. In this service the steamer *Caroline* was employed. On the night of Dec. 29 a body of Canadian troops crossed to the American side and seized the *Caroline,* killing Amos Durfee, an American, in the struggle. The steamer was towed into midstream, set afire and turned adrift. President Van Buren caused the State Department to protest vigorously to the British minister at Washington and to lodge a protest at London, all of which was ignored. For a time feeling ran high on both sides of the border and steps were taken to forestall invasion from Canada and to prevent Americans from violating the frontier. However, the case dragged on for some years and meanwhile became complicated by the arrest, in New York, of Alexander McLeod[qv] for the murder of Durfee. As an adjunct of the Webster-Ashburton Treaty[qv] the affair was settled in 1842 by an expression of regret on the part of England that there had not been an immediate explanation and apology for the occurrence.

[*Canadian Historical Review,* June, 1931; *New York History,* April, 1937; J. B. McMaster, *History of the People of the United States,* VI.]

MILLEDGE L. BONHAM, JR.

***Carondelet,* The,** was a Mississippi River steamboat with a sloping iron casemate and thirteen guns, built at St. Louis by Eads, which fought at Fort Henry and Fort Donelson[qqv]. In April, 1862, under Commander Henry Walke it forced the evacuation of Island Number Ten[qv] by running past the batteries at night to safeguard Union troops crossing below.

[*Battles and Leaders of the Civil War.*]

WALTER B. NORRIS

Carondelet Canal, The, named for the Spanish governor who sponsored it in 1794 as a navigation and drainage project, extended a mile and a half from New Orleans to Bayou St. John, thus opening water communication between the city and Lake Pontchartrain and eliminating the necessity of the long Mississippi River voyage.

[J. S. Kendall, *History of New Orleans.*]

WALTER PRICHARD

Carondelet Intrigue. Hector, Baron de Carondelet, was one of the governors of Spanish Louisiana who intrigued with western communities of the United States, notably Kentucky, for the purpose of detaching them from the Union. His purpose was to thwart the policy of the United States to secure unchallenged access to the Mississippi River[qv], a tendency which made Spanish colonial officials fear for the safety of Louisiana and New Spain. The movement came to an end with the ratification (1795) of Pinckney's Treaty[qv].

[Arthur Preston Whitaker, *The Spanish American Frontier, 1783-1795;* Samuel Flagg Bemis, *Pinckney's Treaty.*]

SAMUEL FLAGG BEMIS

Carpenters' Hall, Philadelphia, on Chestnut Street between Third and Fourth streets, was built by the Carpenters' Guild in 1770 as a meeting place for its members. It was here the first Continental Congress[qv] convened, on Sept. 5, 1774.

[Minutes Carpenters' Company, 1873; J. T. Schraft, *History of Philadelphia.*]

CHARLES W. HEATHCOTE

Carpet Manufacture. Carpetings first appeared in American homes around 1700. For over a century the meager domestic supply was a product of households, itinerant handicraftsmen, or small shops operated under a putting-out system. Aided by favorable tariff rates, transition to the factory organization began in 1791 when William P. Sprague set up a plant in Philadelphia. The linking of the Jacquard[qv] apparatus to the hand looms in 1828 gave a further impetus to this movement; and by 1835 the industry was dominated by sizeable mills located chiefly in the eastern coastal states. At this early date practically all varieties of modern floor coverings were being produced. Inventions by Erastus B. Bigelow and Halcyon Skinner between 1840 and 1875 made power weaving possible and by the latter date production was organized along modern lines in large plants, employing in some instances over 1000 workers. Lowered production costs and increasing national wealth combined to make the use of carpetings almost commonplace after 1870.

[A. H. Cole and H. F. Williamson, *The American Carpet and Rug Industry.*]

HAROLD FRANCIS WILLIAMSON

Carpetbaggers were persons from the North who went to the South after the Civil War[qv] and who, through affiliation with the Republican party[qv], became exploiters of the South, sometimes as financial adventurers, but more often as officeholders. Carpetbagger was an epithet of opprobrium applied by Southerners of the antebellum dominant class to these newcomers who were presumably settlers so transitory and propertyless that their entire goods could be carried in carpetbags, the characteristic hand luggage of the period. The term was used primarily of the Reconstruction[qv] period, 1865–77, but especially after the Reconstruction Acts of 1867 brought the states of the former Confederacy under radical control.

Many of the carpetbaggers were young men who had served in the Union Army during the war or in the Treasury Department and who, at the close of the war, became agents of the Freedmen's Bureau[qv]. Some were missionaries sent from the North to minister to the needs of the Negroes. Others went South not in any official capacity, but in search of their fortunes. All groups found their chance for political activity when the Reconstruction Acts of 1867 demanded a thoroughgoing reorganization of all the former Confederate states, except Tennessee. Because the old officeholding class was disqualified and because the new electorate was not experienced in holding office, there was opportunity for leadership which the newcomers avidly seized. Even before 1867 some of these newcomers in each state had become experienced in political activity as organizers of the Loyal Leagues[qv], which attempted to bring the Negroes and the former white unionists together in loyalty to the Republican party.

In the constitutional conventions elected in 1867–68 in the South, carpetbaggers were strongly represented and took active part in shaping the new state constitutions. In the seven states which were restored to the Union in 1868, four of the governors were carpetbaggers. In Congress there were many carpetbaggers in the delegations from the newly reconstructed states, twenty out of thirty-five members in 1868 in the House of Representatives and ten of the fourteen members of the United States Senate. Among the newcomers from the North there were a few Negroes who rose to conspicuous position as leaders of their race. Such were Hiram R. Revels, a colored preacher who succeeded Jefferson Davis as Senator from Mississippi, and Robert Elliott, who rose to power in state politics in South Carolina. Within the states, as in Congress, carpetbaggers generally supported the various schemes of fraudulent bond issues and other extravagant and corrupt financial programs which helped to bring the radical reconstruction governments into ill repute. After the political machinery of radical reconstruction in the South collapsed in 1876 or earlier, many carpetbaggers returned to the North; others who remained in the South ceased to live by public office and were absorbed in the ordinary class of work-a-day citizens. With the restoration of home rule in the South carpetbaggers as a class disappeared.

[E. P. Oberholtzer, *History of the United States since the Civil War*, Vol. II.]

C. MILDRED THOMPSON

Carriage Making. Horse-drawn vehicles were made in the colonies from their settlement. Prior to the Revolution, however, pleasure vehicles were rare and confined to towns. Most country travel was on horseback on account of poor roads.

Extensive road building and a rapid increase of horse-drawn vehicles began with the birth of the Republic, testifying to the territorial expansion of the country, the greater mobility of its population and the democratization of travel. Famous builders of wagons and stagecoaches established themselves at strategic points like Troy, N. Y., and Concord, N. H. (*see* Concord Coach).

After carriages for the well-to-do, such as the fifty-nine owned in New York in 1770, ceased to measure the demand for personal wheeled transportation, private conveyances developed along popular lines typical of American manufactures. The first example of this was the "one-horse shay," a light vehicle with two high wheels adapted to the rough roads and numerous fords of the still undeveloped country. For fifty years these were so popular that proprietors of carriage shops were usually known as chaise-makers.

By the middle of the last century the chaise was superseded by the four-wheel buggy, the most typical American vehicle prior to the cheap motor car. It was simpler, lighter, stronger and cheaper than other corresponding conveyances and culminated the 100-year era of horse-drawn transportation in the United States.

Carriage making, long since a factory industry, reached the height of its development in 1904. Since then it has declined rapidly. The number of horse-drawn vehicles of all kinds made annually in this country is less than 50,000, compared with 1,700,000 thirty years ago, and the number of wage earners engaged in making such vehicles has fallen to less than 5% of the number at the opening of the century.

[Ezra M. Stratton, *The World on Wheels;* Chauncey M. Depew, *One Hundred Years of American Commerce;* Victor S. Clark, *History of Manufactures in the United States.*]

VICTOR S. CLARK

Carriage Tax, Constitutionality of. In the case of Hylton v. U. S. (3 Dallas 171, 1796) the question of whether a tax on carriages imposed by an act of Congress (June 5, 1794) was a direct tax, and therefore subject to the rule of apportionment, was decided in the negative. Three justices, Chase, Paterson and Iredell, sitting without their colleagues, decided unanimously that the tax was an excise or duty and not a direct tax[qqv]. The case is chiefly interesting as the first in which the constitutionality of an act of Congress was directly reviewed by the Court.

[Charles Warren, *History of the Supreme Court of the United States.*]

PHILLIPS BRADLEY

Carrion Crow Bayou (Bayou Carencro), Battle of, was fought on Oct. 14–15, 1863, when the Confederates attempted to turn back a Federal raid up the Teche from Berwick Bay (Brashear City) to Opelousas and Washington, La. Other skirmishes occurred there on Nov. 3, 11, 18, 1863, during the return of the Federal raiders to New Iberia.

[*War of the Rebellion Records*, Series 1, XXVI, Part I, 332-395; C. A. Evans, ed., *Confederate Military History*, X, 105-106.]

WALTER PRICHARD

Carrizal, Skirmish of (June 21, 1916). Two troops of the 10th Cavalry, on a reconnaissance mission, attempted to force passage through the town of Carrizal, Chihuahua, Mexico (*see* Mexico, Punitive Expedition into). Four hundred Carranzistas, representatives of the Mexican government, resisted. In the skirmish that followed the American troops were defeated and forced to withdraw, leaving two officers and forty-three enlisted men killed, wounded or taken prisoner. This incident resulted in an exchange of sharp notes between the two governments and the massing of troops for quick action. However, further conflict was avoided by the appointment of a joint commission and the eventual withdrawal of American troops from Mexico.

[Frank Tompkins, *Chasing Villa.*]

C. A. WILLOUGHBY

Carrying Trade. *See* Shipping, Ocean; Freight; Motor Truck Transport.

Cartagena Expedition, THE, organized in England and composed of 30 ships of the line, some 90 other vessels, 15,000 sailors and 12,000 land troops, was designed to capture the great Spanish stronghold of the Caribbean region (*see* King George's War). At Jamaica the expedition was re-enforced by 3600 troops from the colonies, consisting of 5 companies from Massachusetts, 2 from Rhode Island, 2 from Connecticut, 5 from New York, 3 from New Jersey, 8 from Pennsylvania, 3 from Maryland, 4 from Virginia and 4 from North Carolina. The attacks on Cartagena, from March 9 to April 11, 1741, failed, and about two thirds of the land force was lost from illness and in battle.

[H. L. Osgood, *The American Colonies in the 18th Century.*]

PERCY SCOTT FLIPPIN

Carter v. Carter Coal Company, 1936 (298 U. S. 238). In this case the Guffey Coal Act[qv] regulating wages, hours, conditions of work and prices in the coal industry was declared unconstitutional on grounds that the production of coal is not within the interstate commerce power and that the act also made an unconstitutional delegation of legislative power. The price-fixing provisions were not passed upon. Seven states presented briefs on behalf of the act, arguing that the problems of the coal industry could not be solved by independent state action.

HARVEY PINNEY

Carter's Valley Settlement. John Carter, later leader in the Watauga settlement^qv^, located a trading house on the west side of the Holston River below Long Island and south of the Virginia line in 1770, and that section of the Holston Valley has ever since borne the name of Carter's Valley. Carter sold supplies to emigrants who came to Long Island to begin the water journey to the Natchez district, and also to the Cherokee Indians^qv^ out on hunts. The Indian chiefs objected to this trading post and in 1772 it was robbed by the Indians and abandoned by Carter, who removed to the Watauga. In the early part of 1776 another settlement of the valley was attempted only to be broken up in the summer of that year. Settlements by the hardier of the pioneers were renewed in 1777, and they thereafter held the fertile region in fair security.

[S. C. Williams, *Dawn of Tennessee Valley and Tennessee History.*]

SAMUEL C. WILLIAMS

Carthage (Mo.), Battle of (July 5, 1861). Defeated at Boonville^qv^ by Gen. Nathaniel Lyon, the secessionists under Gov. Jackson and Gen. Sterling Price retreated into southwest Missouri (*see* Price in Missouri), hoping for reinforcements from Arkansas. Anticipating this, Lyon sent Col. Franz Sigel to Springfield. Sigel advanced to check the retreating enemy until Lyon arrived. Near Carthage on July 5, although greatly outnumbered, he attacked Jackson. Defeated, Sigel retreated to Springfield. Impeded by high waters, Lyon arrived a week later. Encouraged by victory and reinforcements, the secessionists prepared to advance on Springfield.

[E. M. Violette, *A History of Missouri.*]

GLENN H. BENTON

Cartoons, Political. Early cartoons were woodcuts or engravings. Benjamin Franklin printed his "Join or Die" snake cartoon in the *Pennsylvania Gazette*^qv^, May 9, 1754; and it was widely copied in the colonial period. Paul Revere and other artists depicted the effects of the Stamp Act, the Boston Massacre^qqv^, etc., in separately issued engravings. The ratification of the Constitution^qv^ was celebrated by Benjamin Russell with the rising columns of the "Federal Edifice" cartoon in the *Massachusetts Centinel* (1788); but woodcut cartoons were used sparingly in newspapers. From the Jackson period through the Civil War many poster cartoons, wood engravings and lithographs were produced. These often contained portraits of political figures, with lettering issuing from their mouths. Civil War cartoons appeared in periodicals such as *Harper's Weekly* and *Vanity Fair.* The modern cartoon, a pen drawing with effective caricatures, was the creation of Thomas Nast^qv^ of *Harper's Weekly* in the post-war period. He popularized such symbols as the Republican elephant and the Tammany tiger. The first newspaper editorial cartoons were those of Walt McDougall used by the New York *World* in 1884; and were followed by those of Homer Davenport and Frederick Opper, creators of the dollar-marked suit and bloated "trust" figures in the *Journal.*

[William Murrell, *A History of American Graphic Humor, 1747-1938*, 2 vols.]

MILTON W. HAMILTON

Carver Claim, THE, grew out of the assertion that at St. Paul on May 1, 1767, the Sioux^qv^ nation granted to Jonathan Carver an extensive tract embracing approximately the northwestern one fourth of modern Wisconsin. The American Government rejected the claim over a century ago, but until recent decades credulous individuals have continued to press land titles based upon it.

[M. M. Quaife, Jonathan Carver and the Carver Grant, in *Mississippi Valley Historical Review*, VII, 3-25.]

M. M. QUAIFE

Carver's Travels (1766–68). The first Englishman to visit and publicly describe the region of the upper Great Lakes and the upper Mississippi was Capt. Jonathan Carver of Massachusetts. His tour, performed in 1766–68, was described in his *Travels,* first published in London in 1778. The book proved immensely popular, and many editions, in several different languages, were issued. In recent decades the reliability of the narrative has been keenly debated by scholars; examination of Carver's manuscript journal establishes that it differs in important respects from the published version. More recent research points to the conclusion that while Carver actually made the tour he describes, he suppressed the fact that he performed it as a hired agent of Maj. Robert Rogers, who was intent on finding the Northwest Passage^qv^ to the Pacific Ocean, rather than on his own responsibility.

[Louise P. Kellogg, *British Régime in Wisconsin and the Northwest*, 49-75.]

M. M. QUAIFE

Cary's Rebellion, an uprising in colonial North Carolina occasioned by the disfranchisement of the Quakers^qv^, a numerous sect in that province. In 1707 Thomas Cary, deputy governor, was deposed at the solicitation of the Quakers, but for two years refused to abandon his office. When the proprietors sent Edward Hyde as governor, Cary revolted, though he had promised to support Hyde. With Virginia aid, Cary was defeated, captured and sent to England on a treason charge, but was never tried.

[R. D. W. Connor, *North Carolina.*]

HUGH T. LEFLER

Cascades of the Columbia, THE, are falls or rapids in the Columbia River near where the Bonneville Dam^qv now stands. They were a cause of great difficulty to the explorers and fur traders, and were especially dreaded by the settlers, who often preferred the toil and hardships of crossing mountain passes to the dangers to life and property encountered in descending these cascades.

[Lewis A. McArthur, *Oregon Geographic Names.*]

DAN E. CLARK

Casco, Treaty of (1678), brought to a close the war between the eastern Indians and the English settlers of Massachusetts Bay^qv and sought to re-establish the friendly relations between the Indians and English that had characterized the northern settlements previous to the outbreak of King Philip's War^qv in 1675. By the terms of this treaty all captives were to be surrendered without ransom. The treaty also stipulated that the English should give the Indians one peck of corn annually for each family settled on Indian lands, with the exception of Maj. Phillips of Saco, a great proprietor, who was required to give a bushel.

[Francis Parkman, *A Half-Century of Conflict*, Vol. I.]

ELIZABETH RING

Casco, Treaty of (1703), was an unsuccessful attempt made by Gov. Dudley of Massachusetts Bay^qv to prevent further Indian hostilities from breaking out along the northern frontier. War was already going on in Europe between England and France (*see* Queen Anne's War) and the eastern Indians from whom trouble was expected were under the influence of French Jesuits^qv. Accordingly, Gov. Dudley appointed a meeting of the several chiefs and their tribes to confer with him and his councilors to reconcile whatever differences had arisen since the last treaty. They met in Casco, Maine, June 20, 1703. The Indians made the customary professions of peace, disavowing any conspiracy with the French to exterminate the English. They then presented the governor with a belt of wampum^qv and ended the ceremony with an exchange of volleys. The Indians undoubtedly intended to make the white leaders their victims on the spot, but the white and Indian leaders were so placed that one group could not be destroyed without the other. Within two months the eastern Indians were again on the warpath and the people of New England prepared for another period of surprise attacks from Indian enemies.

[J. G. Palfrey, *History of New England*, Vol. III.]

ELIZABETH RING

Casimir, Fort. *See* New Castle.

Casket Girls were women imported into Louisiana by the *Compagnie des Indes* as wives for settlers. Their name derives from the small chests (*cassettes*) in which they carried their clothes. They were conspicuous by reason of their virtue. Normally women were supplied to the colonists by raking the streets of Paris for undesirables, or by emptying the houses of correction. The Casket Girls, however, were recruited from church charitable institutions and, although poor, were practically guaranteed to be virtuous. For this reason, says Gayarré, it later became a matter of pride in Louisiana to show descent from them rather than from the more numerous prostitutes. Aside from providing respectable ancestry for some Creoles, the Casket Girls are not important. The first consignment reached Biloxi^qv in 1719; and New Orleans^qv in 1727–28. They inspired Victor Herbert's *Naughty Marietta.*

[Charles Gayarré, *History of Louisiana;* Dunbar Rowland, *Mississippi, the Heart of the South.*]

MACK SWEARINGEN

Castine, a town on the east side of Penobscot Bay, incorporated 1796, occupies a peninsula called by the French Pentegoet^qv and by the English Majorbagwaduce. Strategically located in respect to the Penobscot Indians and their trade and within the area in dispute between the English and the French, the place was a center of international rivalry from the earliest days. The trading post established in 1630 by Edward Ashley and the Plymouth colonists in the right of the Beauchamp and Leverett patent passed into the control of the French in 1635 by the Treaty of St. Germain^qv. English again by conquest in 1654, it was returned to the French in 1670 by the Treaty of Breda^qv, the trade being dominated by the Baron de St. Castin^qv until his return to France in 1701. From the beginning of the Indian wars in 1688 until 1759, the Indians, instigated by the French, prevented settlement by the English. Soon after 1763 the first English settlers took possession.

[George A. Wheeler, *History of Castine, Penobscot and Brooksville.*]

ROBERT E. MOODY

Castle Thunder was a tobacco warehouse in Richmond, Va., used (1861–65) by the Confederates to confine political prisoners and occasional spies and criminals who were charged with treason. Similar in general purposes to the "Old Capitol" prison in Washington, it enjoyed an unsavory reputation and its officers were accused of unnecessary brutality toward their charges. Upon the fall of Richmond[qv] the prison was used by the Federal authorities to house Confederates charged with crimes under international law.

W. B. HESSELTINE

Castorland Company, The, was organized in Paris in 1792 as the *Compagnie de New Yorck* to colonize French aristocrats and others dissatisfied with conditions following the French Revolution. Land in Lewis County, N. Y., part of the Macomb Purchase[qv], was bought from William Constable. Settlers arrived in 1796; within four years the colony had failed. The transplanted French people, unfitted for the vigorous open life and hard work of the frontier, preferred more civilized communities.

[A. M. Sakolski, *The Great American Land Bubble.*]

THOMAS ROBSON HAY

Casualties during Wars are often sketchily recorded, in so far as the major conflicts of the United States are concerned. During the Revolutionary War 231,721 Continental army enlistments were noted and about 145,000 for the militia; but, as many served several enlistments, it is probable that these figures represent not more than 250,000 individuals. The Adjutant General's Office has accounted for only 4044 killed and 6004 wounded, considerably below the real numbers. No disease deaths are recorded.

Multiple enlistments enlarge the figures for those engaged in the War of 1812 to 527,654, of whom 1877 were killed in action and 4000 wounded. The number of deaths resulting from disease is not known.

For the War with Mexico, a figure of 115,847 enlistments may be reduced to about 111,300 individuals, of whom 1192 were killed in action, 529 died of wounds, 11,155 of disease and 361 of other causes, giving a total of 13,237 deaths from all causes. The number of wounded who did not die is not available.

Union enlistments during the Civil War totaled 2,865,028, a figure which may have represented 2,250,000 individuals. Sixty-seven thousand and fifty-eight were killed in action, 43,012 died of wounds, 224,586 of disease and 24,872 of other causes, a total of 359,528 deaths. Because of the loss and destruction of records, Confederate statistics are far from complete. Probably 800,000 to 900,000 men served the Confederacy, of whom the Adjutant General's Office records 52,954 killed in action, 21,570 died of wounds and 59,297 of disease, giving a total of recorded deaths of 133,821. These figures are incomplete, that for disease deaths being far below actual losses from this cause. Total actual deaths in the Confederate service would probably be about twice as large as those given.

During the War with Spain, 280,564 men wore the uniform and 45,590 of these served abroad, of whom 498 were killed in action, 202 died of wounds, 5423 of disease and 349 of other causes, a total of 6472. Wounds, not mortal, amounted to 2974.

For army service in the World War, the United States uniformed 4,000,000 men and sent 2,086,000 to France, of whom 1,390,000 were engaged. Of these, 37,568 were killed in action and 12,942 died of wounds, a total of 50,510 killed in battle. Disease caused 62,670 deaths on both sides of the Atlantic and 6776 died from other causes. Men to the number of 182,674 suffered 193,663 wounds. Total casualties were 119,956 dead and 182,674 wounded.

[The Adjutant General's Office, Department of War; Francis B. Heitman, *Historical Register and Dictionary of the United States Army;* Leonard P. Ayres, *The War with Germany.*]

GEORGE FREDERICK ASHWORTH

Cat Nation, The, or the Erie (cat or panther), was an Indian tribe of Iroquoian stock, but not a member of the confederacy. During the 17th century they lived south of Lake Erie, from the Genesee and Allegheny valleys to about the present western boundary of Ohio. Their two principal towns were Gentaienton (meadows lying together) and Riqué (place of panthers) near the present Erie, Pa. The Iroquois Confederacy[qv] annihilated them between 1653 and 1655. Remnants of the tribe were absorbed into the Senecas.

[Francis Parkman, *Jesuits in North America.*]

HAROLD E. DAVIS

Catalina Island, Santa, located about twenty-five miles southeast of Los Angeles harbor, was discovered Oct. 7, 1542, by Juan Rodríguez Cabrillo[qv]. The chief bay, Avalon, during the Spanish and Mexican period was one of the most frequented ports of refuge for smugglers, sea-otter and seal hunters, and hide and tallow traders[qqv].

[J. N. Stewart, *Catalina's Yesterdays;* C. F. Holder, *The Channel Islands of California.*]

OSGOOD HARDY

Catawba, THE, from the first contact with Europeans have had their village or villages on the river of that name just below the North-South Carolina boundary. Wasted by rum, disease and their feud with the Iroquois, which latter was a plague to those colonies through which the war trail led, they had by 1760 declined to less than 100 fighting men. Save for their defection in the Yamasee War[qv] of 1715 they were the steadfast friends of South Carolina. Since 1840 they have resided on a square mile of their original lands and have subsisted largely on the bounty of the state.

[James Mooney, *Siouan Tribes of the East; Reports and Resolutions of the General Assembly of South Carolina.*]

R. L. MERIWETHER

Catholic Parochial School System. The Jesuits[qv] who attended the small Maryland and Pennsylvania missions assumed teaching soon after their arrival but it is impossible to give the date of the beginning of the first parish school. The school in connection with St. Mary's Church, built in Philadelphia in 1763, became the prototype of later parochial schools. Its history can be definitely traced from 1782 when a new schoolhouse was completed. In 1810 Mother Elizabeth Seton and her companions began the first free parochial school for boys and girls taught by Religious: St. Joseph's School, Emmitsburg, Md. Parochial schools became more numerous with the increase in Catholic population that began about 1848, and by 1870 this type of school was recognized as the accepted means of providing early education for Catholic children. The Third Plenary Council of Baltimore (1884) made the founding of a school obligatory on every parish, and to this school all children of the parish were to be sent; exceptions to the rule might be granted by the various bishops. Toward the close of the 19th century parish schools began to expand to include secondary schoolwork. In 1930 there were 7923 Catholic elementary (mostly parish) schools with an enrollment of 2,222,598 pupils.

[J. A. Burns and Bernard J. Kohlbrenner, *A History of Catholic Education in the United States.*]

BERNARD J. KOHLBRENNER

Catholicism in the United States. Organized Catholic life in the new Republic dates from the appointment of Father John Carroll as Prefect-Apostolic of the American Church in 1784. Six years later (Aug. 15, 1790) Carroll was consecrated first Bishop of Baltimore with spiritual jurisdiction over all Catholics in the nation; probably 40,000. The growth of the Church warranted (1808) a division of Bishop Carroll's labors, and suffragan Sees were erected at Boston, New York, Philadelphia and Bardstown, Ky. Since that time the Church in the United States has developed to an extent without parallel in the history of any other nation. From one ecclesiastical unit in 1808, there are today eighteen such provinces presided over by as many archbishops; from one diocese in 1789, there are today ninety-one; from twoscore priests in Carroll's day, there are now about 32,000; from an organization of 40,000 members a century and a half ago, the latest (1938) official figures give a total of about 21,000,000. The peaks of this growth came in the decades: 1840–50 (increase of one million); 1850–60 (increase of two millions); 1870–80 (increase of three millions); and 1900–1910 (increase of five millions).

Such tremendous vitality, due mainly to natural increase and to immigration, in one single religious group was bound to create rivalries, if not antagonisms; and the impact of such a powerful organization as the Catholic Church on the social, economic and political life of what is still popularly believed to be a Protestant nation may justly be recognized in the various attempts to curb both the religious and political freedom of American Catholics. From the founding of the first of these anti-Catholic societies, the American Protestant Association in New York in 1830, down to the recent activities of the Ku Klux Klan[qv], scarcely a decade has passed without a revival of various charges, chief of which is the alleged incompatibility of Catholic principles with American democratic ideals. This was the main theme of those public debates in the 1830's between Hughes and Breckinridge and between Purcell and Campbell. It was the principal weapon of attack by the strongly entrenched Protestant religious press of the country. It was during the same period that the Catholic Church made one of its most important contributions to the stability of the American nation—that of assimilating the millions of Catholic immigrants from other lands to a proper understanding of American social and political ideals and to American standards of living. No religious organization ever faced a problem more fraught with the possibility of failure; for, sharp difference of language, customs, traditions and racial characteristics threatened to retard for generations the Americanization of the newcomers. Fortunately, the American Church possessed all through this critical period leaders of uncommon courage and sagacity. Even in the midst of violent antagonism, bishops, priests and laity went quietly on with their work of making loyal Americans out of these millions of Catholics from abroad.

Although formal education is not a primary part of the Church's work in the world, nevertheless, it has been her policy in the United States, since the first legislative act of the Synod of 1791, to build up a school system exclusively Catholic. This has been accomplished at great odds. Generally speaking, Catholics have been of the poorer class; and with only a few and very minor exceptions (and then only for a short time in a few cities), they have carried the double tax burden of their own and of the public schools (*see* Catholic Parochial School System). The official statistics for 1938 reveal a total attendance in the Catholic elementary schools of 2,170,065; a total of 1984 Catholic high schools, 105 Catholic colleges for women and 56 for men, with a total student body of 288,684. There are 23 Catholic universities. The Catholic University of America, Washington, D. C., the principal link in this chain of educational institutions, was founded in 1889.

The very rapidity of the development of the Church in the United States during the past 150 years has necessitated a strict observance by the episcopate over the uniformity of Church discipline. Consequently, meetings of bishops with their priests in diocesan synods, meetings of bishops with the archbishop of a single province in provincial councils and meetings of the entire hierarchy in national or plenary councils have been held for the purpose of enacting canonical legislation on many aspects of Catholic life. During the years when the entire country was within the single province of Baltimore (1808–49), there were seven provincial councils (1829, 1833, 1837, 1840, 1843, 1846, 1849), the legislation of which was made known to the clergy and laity by joint Pastoral Letters. On three occasions (1852, 1866, 1884) the entire episcopate has held plenary councils in Baltimore and the legislation passed in these assemblies governed the Church in the United States, until the revised Code of Canon Law was issued by the Holy See in 1918 for the universal Church.

A striking fact in the recent history of the Church in the United States is the continuance of the War Council, created by the bishops and archbishops under the chairmanship of Cardinal Gibbons in 1917 to centralize all Catholic forces during America's participation in the World War, as the National Catholic Welfare Conference, located in Washington, D. C. Apart from societies of Catholic men and women which have become national in scope, legislation for the entire body of Catholics can only be enacted in a national or plenary council in which all the members of the hierarchy participate. Such a council can only be held with the permission of the Holy See, and is presided over by an Apostolic Delegate appointed by the Pope. The National Catholic Welfare Conference, the N. C. W. C. as it is popularly called, is not a legislative body, but is purely informational and administrative. It has at present six departments: education, the Catholic press, social action, legislation, i.e., the safeguarding of Catholic interests in state or Federal legislation, Catholic lay action and information. Each of these has a chairman, a member of the episcopate, and once a year, in November, the hierarchy meets at the Catholic University of America to hear reports from these episcopal officials. The National Catholic Welfare Conference News Service to the press (Catholic and secular) has become a powerful influence for the dissemination of truth on all mooted Catholic questions. The death of Pius XI and the election of Pius XII (Cardinal Pacelli, who visited the United States in 1936) accentuated the attention of the nation to the papacy and to the Church as stabilizing agencies for world peace.

[There is no complete guide to the sources for American Catholic history. The four volumes of the *History of the Catholic Church in the United States*, by John Gilmary Shea, is authoritative, though its value ceases with 1866. Partial catalogues of archival and printed material will be found in Guilday, *John Carroll* (to 1815), *John England* (to 1842), *John Gilmary Shea* (to 1892), and Recent Studies in American Catholic History: 1892-1930, *Ecclesiastical Review*, May, 1931. Selected bibliographies will be found in the series, *Studies in American Church History* (28 vols. to date) issued by the Department of History in the Catholic University of America, Washington, D. C. A short account of Church legislation will be found in Guilday, *History of the Councils of Baltimore.*]

PETER GUILDAY

Catlin's Indian Paintings. From 1830 to 1838 George Catlin, a young, self-taught artist, roamed the trans-Mississippi wilderness, sketching and painting some 600 Indian portraits, scenes of native life and landscapes. His expedition up the Missouri by the steamboat *Yellowstone*[qv] and downstream by canoe in the summer of 1832 with a long stay at Fort Clark produced a splendid Mandan[qv] ethnological series of portraits and ceremonies. In 1834 he accompanied the First Dragoons into Texas and the Comanche[qv] country, and spent the following two seasons on the upper Mississippi and Minnesota rivers among the Sioux[qv] and other northern tribes. Catlin exhibited his collection in Europe for years after 1838 and added the 603 items of the so-called Catlin Cartoon Collection. The original collection was presented to the Smithsonian in 1879 by Mrs. Joseph Harrison, Jr. While not a great artist, Catlin faithfully depicted the primitive Indians, their lives and surroundings.

[George Catlin, *Letters and Notes of the Manners, Customs, and Condition of the North American Indians;* Washington Matthews, *The Catlin Collection of Indian Paintings*, Smithsonian Institution, 1892.]

WILLOUGHBY M. BABCOCK

Catskill Mountains, N. Y., THE, took their name from the many wildcats roaming their hemlock-wooded slopes during the early days of New Netherland[qv]. The Dutch thought the mountains haunted. Rip Van Winkle's[qv] long sleep, after his tipsy encounter with the crew of the *Half Moon*[qv], as told by Washington Irving, is supposed to have occurred in Schneider's Hollow.

[H. A. Haring, *Our Catskill Mountains.*]

A. C. FLICK

Cattle Associations is a term applied principally to organizations of cattlemen after 1865 on the Western ranges. In scope these were local, district, sectional and national and, like miners' associations and squatter claim clubs[qqv], functioned on the frontiers. The Colorado Cattle Growers' Association was formed as early as 1867. The Southwestern Cattle Growers' Association of Kansas and the Montana Stock Growers' Association began in 1884. The Wyoming Stock Growers' Association, organized in 1873, had memberships of 400 in 1886 from nineteen states. Its 2,000,000 cattle, real estate, plants and horses were valued in 1885 at $100,000,000. In 1884 the National Cattle and Horse Growers' Association was organized at St. Louis.

A president, secretary, treasurer and executive committee were the usual officials to administer an association's affairs and to make reports at the annual or semiannual meetings. In the Wyoming Stock Growers' Association brand inspectors supervised the sale and transportation of 1,000,000 cattle in 1885. Roundup districts were laid out, rules for strays or mavericks adopted and thousands of brands recorded. Associations cooperated with local and state officials and were alert to urge favorable legislation by Congress.

[Louis Pelzer, *The Cattlemen's Frontier;* Ora B. Peake, *The Colorado Range Cattle Industry.*]

LOUIS PELZER

Cattle Brands, although traceable back to Egypt before Christ, are peculiarly associated with ranching. The institution of ranching[qv] as taken over from Mexico by Texas and California included brands. They are burned on range horses also. Attempted substitutions for fire-branding have proved impracticable. After all, suffering from the process is brief and not intense. The brand is a mark of ownership. If names and addresses were not so long, they would be branded on stock. Every legitimate brand is recorded by either state or county, thus preventing duplication within a given territory. Identification of range stock is necessary among honest people as well as against thieves, in fenced pastures as well as on open range[qv].

In form, brands are made up of (1) letters, (2) figures and (3) geometric designs, symbols, or representations of objects. Combinations are endless. Because brands reduce the value of hides and also induce screw worms, they are now generally smaller and simpler than they were when cattle were less valuable. They may or may not signify something peculiar to the originator; usually they have a significance. A seaman turned rancher gave the Anchor brand; a cowman who won a big game of poker on a hand of four sixes adopted 6666 as his brand; a rancher honored his wife Ella with "E Bar." Brands are the heraldry of the range. Reading and calling them is an art known only to range men. A straight line burned on the side of a cow may be a "Dash," a "Bar," a "Rail." The letter H set upright cannot be misread; lying on its side, however, it is "Lazy H"; in an oblique position, "Tumbling H"; joined to a segment of circle under it, "Rocking H"; separated from the segment, "H Half-Circle," etc. Happily, the art of running out, or blotting, brands—burning one device into another—is obsolescent.

[J. Frank Dobie, *On the Open Range.*]

J. FRANK DOBIE

Cattle Drives. Contrary to popular conception, long-distance cattle driving was traditional not only in Texas but elsewhere in America long before the Chisholm Trail[qv] was dreamed of. The Spaniards, always to be remembered as establishers of the ranching industry, drove herds northward from Mexico as far back as 1540. In the 18th century and on into the 19th the Spanish settlements in Texas derived most of their meager revenue from horses and cattle driven into Louisiana, though such trade was usually contraband (*see* Natchitoches). Meantime in the United States herds were sometimes driven long distances. In 1790 the boy David Crockett helped drive "a large stock of cattle" 400 miles from Tennessee into Virginia; twenty years later he took a drove of horses from the Tennessee River into southern North Carolina. In 1815 Timothy Flint "encountered a drove of more than 1000 cattle and swine" being driven from the interior of Ohio to Philadelphia. The stock in the states was gentle, often managed on foot. The history of trail driving[qv] involves horses as well as cattle.

Notwithstanding antecedent examples, Texans established trail driving as a regular occupation. Before they revolted from Mexico in 1836, they had a "Beef Trail" to New Orleans. In the 1840's they extended their markets northward into Missouri—Sedalia, Baxter Springs, Springfield and St. Louis becoming the principal markets. During the 1850's emigration and freighting from the Missouri River westward demanded great numbers of oxen, the firm of Russell, Majors and Waddell[qv] in 1858 utilizing 40,000 oxen[qv]. Texas longhorn[qv] steers by the thousands were broken for work oxen. Herds of longhorns were driven to Chicago; one herd at least to New York.

Under Spanish-Mexican ownership, California as well as Texas developed ranching and during the 1830's and 1840's a limited number of cattle were trailed thence to Oregon. But the discovery of gold in California[qv] arrested for a while all development there of cattle industry and created a high demand for outside beef. During the 1850's cattle were occasionally driven to California from Missouri, Arkansas and perhaps other states; the big drives, however, were from Texas. Steers worth $15 in Texas were selling in San Francisco for as high as $150. One Texas rancher in 1854 hired for $1500 a famous Indian fighter to captain his herd of 1000 steers to California; thirty-five armed men accompanied it. These drives were fraught with great danger from both Indians and desert thirst.

During the Civil War Texas drove beeves here and there for the Confederate forces. At the close of the war she had probably 5,000,000 cattle —and no market. Late in 1865 a few cowmen tried to find a market. In 1866 there were many drives northward without a definite destination and without much financial success; also to the old but limited New Orleans market, following mostly well-established trails to the wharves of Shreveport and Jefferson (Texas). In 1867 Joseph G. McCoy opened a regular market at Abilene[qv], Kans. The great cattle trails, moving successively westward, were established and trail driving boomed. In 1867 also the Goodnight-Loving Trail[qv] opened up New Mexico and Colorado to Texas cattle. By the tens of thousands they were soon driven into Arizona. In Texas itself cattle raising was expanding like wildfire. Caldwell, Dodge City, Ogallala, Cheyenne[qqv] and other towns became famous on account of trail-driver patronage.

During the 1870's the buffaloes[qv] were virtually exterminated and the Indians of the Plains and Rockies were at the same time subjugated, penned up and put on beef rations. An empire was left vacant. It was first occupied by Texas longhorns, driven by Texas cowboys. The course of empire in America has been west, but over much of Oklahoma, Kansas, Nebraska, the Dakotas, Wyoming, Montana and parts of Nevada and Idaho the precursors of this movement were trail men from the South. The Long Trail[qv] extended into Canada. In the 1890's herds were still driven from the Panhandle of Texas to Montana, but trail driving virtually closed in 1895. Barbed wire, railroads and "nesters"[qqv] closed it. During three swift decades it had moved over 10,000,000 cattle and 1,000,000 range horses, stamped the entire West with its character, given economic and personality prestige to Texas, made the longhorn the most historic brute in bovine history, glorified the cowboy[qv] over the globe and endowed America with its most romantic tradition relating to any occupation—a peer to England's tradition of the sea.

[Andy Adams, *The Log of a Cowboy;* J. H. Cook, *Fifty Years on the Old Frontier;* E. E. Dale, *The Range Cattle Industry;* J. Evetts Haley, *Charles Goodnight;* J. M. Hunter, *The Trail Drivers of Texas;* E. S. Osgood, *The Day of the Cattleman;* W. M. Raine and Will C. Barnes, *Cattle;* Walter P. Webb, *The Great Plains.*]

J. FRANK DOBIE

Cattle Industry, THE, was introduced into what is now the United States about 1600 by Spanish colonists from Mexico. During the next two centuries Spain's liberal land grants to settlers (*see* Empresario System) caused the industry to expand rapidly northward and by 1821, at the close of the Spanish regime in North America, large numbers of the lean, long-horned[qv] Spanish type of cattle were reared in California, Arizona, New Mexico and Texas.

In the meantime the early English colonists along the Atlantic seaboard brought over cattle of the breeds common to northern Europe. As English settlement advanced westward cattle growers tended to occupy lands along the frontier where pasturage was readily available. Once the Appalachians had been crossed the industry grew rapidly, since farm products could not be transported profitably across the mountains. Accordingly, the Westerners fed their surplus grain and hay to cattle which, when fully grown and fat, could be driven to market. By 1860 the cattle industry was very important in Kentucky and the states of the Old Northwest and had extended across the Mississippi into Missouri, Iowa, Arkansas, Indian Territory and eastern Kansas.

In the Southwest the Republic of Mexico, as well as the Texas Republic, had continued the liberal land policy of Spain. Texas, when annexed to the United States in 1845, retained possession of its own unoccupied lands and often sold large tracts to cattle raisers. By 1860 Texas had more than 3,500,000 head of cattle.

During the Civil War the number of cattle in most states was reduced from 30 to 50%. Texas, little touched by the war, however, was at the close of that struggle overflowing with cattle. In 1866 Texas ranchmen began to drive large herds north to railway points in Kansas and Nebraska known as "cow towns."[qv] Here, the fat, mature animals were shipped to market for slaughter while young cattle were sold to stock new ranges on the Central and Northern plains. By 1885 some 5,500,000 cattle had been driven north from Texas and the so-called range area had come to cover a vast region reaching from Mexico to Canada and extending from eastern Kansas far beyond the Rocky Mountains.

Shipments of dressed beef to Europe, which began in 1875 and grew to over 17,000,000 lbs. in 1884, gave impetus to the industry and helped to bring much European capital into the business. By 1885 the cattle industry in the United States had grown to gigantic proportions. The range area supplied the corn-growing states with enormous numbers of cattle to be fattened for market and received from these states many registered or high-grade breeding animals to improve its own herds. Great packing plants and stockyards[qqv] were built at the important market centers, as Chicago, Kansas City and Fort Worth. Cattle brokerage companies and banks specializing in cattle loans were established to finance the industry and railways provided specially equipped cars for the shipment of cattle and meat products.

After 1885 the character of the industry began to change. Much of the range area was occupied by settlers, necessitating smaller scale operation. The Department of Agriculture through its Bureaus of Animal Industry and of Agricultural Economics, did much to promote better breeding, care and feeding of cattle, and the same is true of the various agricultural colleges. The cattle industry is still very important, but the great ranches[qv] have with few exceptions given place to smaller ones, or livestock farms, producing by scientific methods cattle of high quality that can be marketed for slaughter at a far earlier age than was formerly done.

[E. E. Dale, *The Range Cattle Industry.*]

EDWARD EVERETT DALE

Cattle Rustlers, or cattle thieves, have been a problem wherever cattle have been run on the range upon an extensive scale. They drove off cattle in herds when Texas was a republic; they carry them off in trucks in Montana, today. Their methods have varied from open and forceful taking of cattle in pitched battles, to that of sneaking away with "dogie" or motherless calves. The former method, never prevalent, passed with the open range[qv]; the latter is still a favorite resort.

Cattle are branded to distinguish their ownership, but rustlers sometimes changed the old brand by tracing over it with a hot iron to alter the design into their own brand—a practice known as "burning brands" (*see* Cattle Brands). The taking of large and unbranded calves from the cows and then placing them in the rustler's brand was and is a favorite method. But the principal loss by rustlers today is through their use of automobiles and trucks. They kill cattle on the range and haul away the beef, and they load calves in their trucks of a night and are hundreds of miles from the scene by morning.

Laws for the recording of brands for the protection of livestock owners have long been rigid. But when the laws proved insufficient, cowmen came together in posses, in vigilance committees and finally in local and state associations to protect their herds (*see* Cattle Associations). The greatest deterrent in the early days (decade of the 1880's) was the fencing of the land with wire. That retarded the mobility of the rustler, but the automobile and the opening of roads greatly accelerated it and plenty of rustlers are still on the range.

J. EVETTS HALEY

Cattle Tick, THE, was the worst plague of the Western range during the trail-driving[qv] days (1865–95). It caused widespread outbreaks of what was variously known as Spanish, Texas and tick fever and pleuro-pneumonia, though for years the cause was unknown. Many states established quarantines against the Texas longhorns[qv]. The tick has now been virtually eradicated by dipping.

J. EVETTS HALEY

Caucus, Congressional (1796–1824), was the earliest method of nominating presidential candidates. No nominations were made for the first two presidential elections, since Washington was the choice of all. His retirement having been announced, the Federalist[qv] members of Congress met in secret conference in 1796 and agreed to support John Adams and Thomas Pinckney for President and Vice-President. Shortly afterwards the Jeffersonian Republican[qv] members agreed on Jefferson and Burr. In 1800 the respective party members met again for the same purpose.

After that date the congressional caucus was no longer secret, but an open meeting. Since the Federalist party was almost wiped out by the election of 1800, there was no Federalist caucus after that year, the Republican caucus nominations becoming practically nominations by Congress itself.

The system became increasingly unpopular. Many thought it contrary to the spirit of the Constitution for members of Congress thus virtually to select the President. The friends of Andrew Jackson were particularly bitter against the caucus and it was denounced by mass meetings throughout the country. In 1824 only about a fourth of the members of Congress attended, nominating William H. Crawford, who stood third in the electoral vote (*see* Campaign of 1824). The caucus never met again, being succeeded in the next decade by the national convention^qv^ system.

[Edward A. Stanwood, *A History of the Presidency;* Frederick W. Dallinger, *Nominations for Elective Office in the United States.*]

CLARENCE A. BERDAHL

Caucus, Party, in Congress, is a meeting of the respective party members in either House for the purpose of determining their attitude toward legislation and other matters. The Federalists^qv^ in the House certainly caucused as early as 1796; the membership of Senate committees was thus arranged by secret party conferences in 1797; and the Jeffersonian Republicans^qv^ in the House used this method to nominate John Rutledge for Speaker in 1799. The caucus was probably used even earlier and was firmly established by 1825.

In general the caucus has these purposes or functions: (1) to nominate candidates for Speaker and other House or Senate offices; (2) to elect or provide for the selection of the party officers and committees, such as the Floor Leader, Whips, Committee on Committees and Steering Committee; (3) to decide what action is to be taken with respect to legislation, either in broad terms or in detail. Caucus decisions are generally accepted by the respective party members, since bolting is likely to bring punishment in the form of poorer committee assignments, loss of patronage and the like; and hence the caucus has become a most important, although extraconstitutional, device in legislative organization and procedure.

[W. F. Willoughby, *Principles of Legislative Organization and Administration;* W. G. Haines, The Congressional Caucus Today, *American Political Science Review,* Vol. IX, pp. 696-706.]

CLARENCE A. BERDAHL

Caucus, Primary, is a general meeting of the party members in a local community, for the purpose of nominating candidates for local office, or for electing delegates to county or state conventions. Such a caucus is ordinarily open to all voters in the community who consider themselves members of the particular party involved, and it constitutes the first formal step in the nominating procedure. The caucus was used in the colonies at least as early as 1725 and particularly in Boston, where several clubs, attended largely by ship mechanics or caulkers, endorsed candidates for office before the regular election and which came to be known as "caucus clubs." The gentry also organized their "parlor caucuses" and this method of nomination soon became the regular practice within the political parties. It was entirely unregulated by law until 1866, became subject to considerable abuse and during the early 1900's was subjected to more drastic regulation by the state. Now the caucus has in many cases been completely supplanted by the direct primary^qv^.

[F. W. Dallinger, *Nominations for Elective Office in the United States;* Harold R. Bruce, *American Parties and Politics,* 3rd edition.]

CLARENCE A. BERDAHL

Cavaliers is a term applied to adherents of the Stuart kings of England, who fled to Virginia^qv^ after the fall of Charles I (1647–49). They introduced luxury and greater refinement into the colony, set the tone of its society, in sharp contrast to that of New England, gave a stimulus to the slave trade^qv^ and founded a sort of aristocratic oligarchy.

[George Bancroft, *History of the United States.*]

ALVIN F. HARLOW

Cavalry, Horse, a branch of the United States Army^qv^, has figured prominently in American history. During the American Revolution it was usually employed as a raiding weapon, only occasionally being used in a pitched battle. Cavalry, particularly on the Plains and in the Southwest, escorted settlers, punished Indian marauders and did police duty along the frontier. As the settlers continued westward into Indian hunting grounds, Indian opposition increased and both the demand and the need for protection became more urgent. In 1855 the cavalry was substantially increased and for the next forty years it was engaged constantly in Indian warfare.

The development of horse cavalry, in the modern sense, first appeared in the Southern forces during the Civil War. The great efficiency of the Southern cavalry, able to make sustained, rapid marches across country, expert in scouting and equally prepared to fight mounted or dismounted in battle, soon was realized by the Northern leaders who, by the end of the Civil War, utilized masses of horse cavalry with destructive effect. In the succeeding years of continuous fighting with the Indians in the West (*see* Sioux Wars) and in guarding our Southwestern frontier, the characteristics of mobility, fire power and shock, as well as the adaptability to all types of fighting, were further developed. Because of combat conditions during the World War[qv] only four American cavalry regiments were sent to France. (*See* Cavalry, Mechanized.)

[O. L. Spaulding, *The United States Army.*]

FENTON S. JACOBS

Cavalry, Mechanized, a branch of the United States Army[qv], consists of manned fighting vehicles, constructed with a view to securing a combination of maximum mobility, fire power and shock, *together with protection,* for employment in the execution of *cavalry* objectives. It is a post-World War development. Its role is essentially that of horse cavalry[qv], making combined action of horse and mechanized cavalry possible and desirable. To obtain the maximum efficiency and effect, however, each must be used in conjunction with the other. Motor-wheeled vehicles (motorization) have a limited cross-country mobility, but a high road mobility; whereas, tracklaying vehicles (mechanization) have a comparatively high cross-country mobility. These terms should not be confused. Fighting vehicles intended to close with the enemy are tracklaying. Fighting vehicles (armored cars and scout cars) intended primarily for reconnaissance, and only secondarily or incidentally for combat, are of the wheeled type. Armored fighting vehicles can derive only partial protection from the armor carried, for the use of armor must result in a compromise between the opposing factors of protection and mobility.

American mechanized cavalry units, based upon tracklaying vehicles, and with the necessary complement of wheeled vehicles, have a high tactical as well as strategical mobility. Such vehicles have many obvious limitations, however, because of the development of antitank weapons, portable mines and antitank auxiliaries. Nevertheless, the light fast tank and its cavalry counterpart, the combat car, are among the most redoubtable weapons of modern armies. They are tactically self-contained and capable of independent employment as well as operating in conjunction with horse cavalry or infantry.

[U. S. Cavalry Association, *Cavalry Combat.*]

FENTON S. JACOBS

Cave-in-Rock is a cave in Hardin County, Ill., on the Ohio River, about thirty miles below the mouth of the Wabash. In pioneer times it was used as an inn patronized by flatboatmen[qv]. It often served as a rendezvous for outlaws who robbed flatboats going down the river. Among its early occupants were Sam Mason[qv] and his gang of river pirates and highwaymen and the bloodthirsty Harpe[qv] brothers.

[Otto A. Rothert, *The Outlaws of Cave-in-Rock.*]

OTTO A. ROTHERT

Cayuse, THE, inhabited the Blue Mountain region in northeastern Oregon. They were a powerful, warlike tribe, allied to the Umatillas and Walla Wallas with whom they participated in the Whitman massacre[qv] and the early Indian wars of Oregon and Washington. They were noted for their wealth in horses. The tribal name has entered American dictionaries as denoting the sturdy type of Indian pony. The tribe now resides on the Umatilla reservation.

[H. H. Bancroft, *History of Oregon.*]

WILLIAM S. LEWIS

Cayuse War, THE (1847–50). Following the Whitman massacre[qv] (Nov. 29, 1847) volunteer troops were equipped to the extent of the meager resources of a pioneer settlement that war might be waged against the Cayuse Indians[qv] responsible for the massacre. The declared objective was to punish the guilty tribe and to force the surrender of the murderers. After enduring a severe winter the troops pursued the Cayuse during the spring and summer without having any decisive engagements. The discouraging and indecisive struggle dragged on until the spring of 1850 when it was ended by the voluntary surrender of five confessed murderers who thus made the close of the war possible. These Indians were later tried and hanged at Oregon City.

[George W. Fuller, *A History of the Pacific Northwest.*]

ROBERT MOULTON GATKE

Cazique **(*Cacique*)** was the Indian title for chieftains of the petty tribes on the Carolina coast. It was adopted by the Lords Proprietors for the third rank of their proposed provincial nobility and was conferred upon a dozen individuals.

[A. S. Salley, *Narratives of Early Carolina;* E. McCrady, *South Carolina under the Proprietary Government.*]

R. L. MERIWETHER

Cedar Creek, Battle of (Oct. 19, 1864). Following the battle of Fisher's Hill[qv], the Union and Confederate armies marched up and down the Shenandoah Valley (*see* Shenandoah Campaign), the former destroying property and crops as it went. Sheridan (U.) finally halted his army across Cedar Creek, east of Fisher's Hill. Shortly afterward he went to Washington. The Confederate Army unexpectedly attacked and after defeating the Union troops halted unnecessarily. The delay was fatal. Returning from Washington, Sheridan rode (*see* Sheridan's Ride) from "Winchester, twenty miles away," rallied his men and led them back into battle. The Confederates were defeated, suffering heavy losses. A Confederate victory was turned into a rout. Thereafter, both armies were transferred to Richmond.

[*Battles and Leaders of the Civil War;* John B. Gordon, *Reminiscences of the Civil War.*]

THOMAS ROBSON HAY

Cedar Mountain, Battle of (Aug. 9, 1862), the first encounter in the Second Bull Run campaign^qv^. Pope's (U.) advance under Banks (U.) at Cedar Run, near Culpeper, Va., was opposed by Jackson's (C.) troops, under Ewell (C.) and Winder (C.). Though outnumbered, Banks advanced, but, after bitter fighting, his troops were repulsed everywhere. Following a brief pursuit Jackson withdrew to join Lee's (C.) army. The Confederates, numbering over 20,000, lost about 1300; the Federals, numbering about 8000, lost nearly 2400.

[*Battles and Leaders of the Civil War.*]

THOMAS ROBSON HAY

Céloron's Lead Plates (1749) mark one step in the French-English rivalry over the Ohio Valley. By 1749 the English were pressing across the Alleghenies into the rich valley beyond the mountains. Unable to make reply in kind, the governor of New France sent an army, led by Pierre Joseph Céloron, to enforce its authority on the Ohio. He descended the river as far as the Great Miami, where he turned northward toward Detroit. En route, in frequent councils, he urged the natives to cease all intercourse with the English and warned the latter to leave the country. At strategic points along the Ohio, lead plates were planted, bearing an inscription reciting the French monarch's title to the country. One of them was found prior to 1821 at Marietta, Ohio, and is now owned by the American Antiquarian Society (Worcester, Mass.). Another plate was found at Point Pleasant, W. Va., and since 1849 has belonged to the Virginia Historical Society at Richmond. Both the English and the Indians ignored the admonitions of Céloron; the ownership of the Ohio Valley remained to be determined by the French and Indian War^qv^.

[M. M. Quaife, Pierre Joseph Céloron, in *Burton Historical Collection* Leaflet, VII, 33-48; Margry, *Découvertes et Etablissements des Français dans L'Amérique Septentrionale*, VI, 666-726; Information supplied by Librarian of American Antiquarian Society and by Corresponding Secretary of Virginia Historical Society.]

M. M. QUAIFE

Cement. In newly discovered lands adventurers seek gold; colonists seek limestone to make cement. American colonists made their first dwellings of logs, with log fireplaces and chimneys plastered inside, caulked outside, with mud or clay. To replace these the first brick^qv^ were imported. Brick masonry requires mortar; mortar requires cement, which was first made of lime burned from oyster shells. In 1662 limestone was found at Providence, R. I., and manufacture of "stone" lime began. Some limes made better cement than others, but not until 1791 did John Smeaton, English engineer, establish the fact that argillaceous (silica and alumina) impurity gave lime improved cementing value. Burning such limestones made hydraulic lime—a cement that hardens under water. Some of the colonial limes unwittingly may have been hydraulic, but it was after the beginning of the country's first major public works, the Erie Canal^qv^, 1817, that American engineers learned to make and use a true hydraulic cement (one that had to be pulverized after burning to slake or react with water). The first masonry on the Erie Canal was contracted to be done with common quick lime; when it failed to slake a local experimenter pulverized some and discovered a "natural" cement, that is, one made from natural rock. Canvass White, subsequently chief engineer of the Erie Canal, pursued investigations, perfected manufacture and use, obtained a patent and is credited with being the father of the American cement industry. During the canal and later railway building era, demand rapidly increased and suitable cement rocks were discovered in many localities: 1818, Fayetteville, N. Y.; 1828, Rosendale, N. Y.; 1829, Louisville, Ky.; 1836, Cumberland, Md.; 1838, Utica, Ill.; 1850, Siegfried's Bridge (Coplay), Pa.; 1875, Milwaukee, Wis.; 1883, Mankato, Minn., to mention a few. Cement made at Rosendale, N. Y., was the most famous, that at Coplay, Pa., the most significant, because it became the first American Portland cement. The name Portland cement was given by an English bricklayer, Joseph Aspdin, in 1824, to a cement made by burning and pulverizing briquets of an artificial mixture of limestone (chalk) and clay, because the hardened cement resembled a well-known building stone from the Isle of Portland. Manufacture of Portland cement developed abroad at the same time the manufacture of natural cements was spreading in America. Soon after the Civil War, Portland cements, because of their more dependable qualities, began to be imported. Manufacture was started at Coplay, Pa., about 1870, by David O. Saylor, by selecting from his natural cement rock such as was approximately of the same composition as the Portland cement artificial mixture. The Lehigh Valley around Coplay contained many similar deposits, and until 1907 this locality produced annually half (at first much more) of all the cement made in this country. By 1900 the practice of grinding together ordinary limestone and clay, burning or calcining the mixture in rotary kilns and pulverizing the burned clinker, had become so well known that the Portland cement industry spread rapidly to all parts of the country and by 1935 there were 165 plants in thirty-five states. Production increased from 350,000 bbls. in 1890 to 176,000,000 bbls. in 1928, the year of peak demand. At first cement was used only for mortar in brick and stone masonry. Gradually mixtures of cement, sand, stone or gravel (aggregates) and water, known as concrete, poured into temporary forms where it hardened into a kind of conglomerate rock, came to be substituted for brick and stone, particularly for massive work like bridge abutments and piers, dams, foundations, etc. Today it is hardly possible to conceive of constructing subways, waterworks, power plants, pavements, bridges and other public utilities without cement.

[Robert W. Leslie, *History of the Portland Cement Industry in the United States.*]

NATHAN C. ROCKWOOD

Cemeteries, National. Soldiers, sailors, marines and officers and men of the Coast Guard dying in the service of the United States, or dying in a destitute condition after having been honorably discharged from the service may be buried in any national cemetery free of cost. With the consent of the Secretary of War, any citizen of the United States who served in the army or navy of any government at war with Germany or Austria during the World War and who died while in such service or after honorable discharge therefrom also may be so buried (act of July 17, 1862; April 15, 1920). Provision for the acquisition of lands for national cemetery purposes was made in an act of Feb. 22, 1867. Ninety-one cemeteries have been established in twenty-nine states and the District of Columbia. Interments in these Federal burying grounds in 1935 totaled 436,189, of which some 10,700 were those of Confederates. Eighteen national cemeteries are found in the State of Virginia; the largest and most notable is the Arlington[qv] Cemetery. In the permanent American cemeteries in Europe, 30,895 veterans of the World War are buried. At Mexico City, Mexico, the remains of 1563 officers, soldiers and citizens of the United States who fell in battle or died in and around that city rest in an American cemetery established in 1873.

In 1933 the following national cemeteries were transferred from the War Department to the National Park Service of the Interior Department: Antietam, Md.; Battleground, District of Columbia; Chattanooga, Tenn.; Fort Donelson, Tenn.; Fredericksburg, Va.; Gettysburg, Pa.; Poplar Grove, Va.; Shiloh, Tenn.; Stones River, Tenn.; Vicksburg, Miss.; and Yorktown, Va.

[The Code of the Laws of the United States of America, Washington, 1935, pp. 1-3026. See pp. 47, 49, 991-994.]

CARL P. RUSSELL

Censorship. There is no record of censorship in the armies of the United States prior to the Civil War. Even during the first year of the Civil War censorship was not effective; this oversight enabled the Confederates to know the strength and disposition of the Union Army simply by reading the Northern newspapers. Original efforts to correct this evil were undertaken by the State Department. The War Department became equally interested as a result of an article appearing in the New York *Tribune* concerning the advance on Manassas[qv]. This article appeared the very morning the movement was to take place. Gen. Scott, Assistant Secretary of War, realized the seriousness of this situation and ordered that the telegraph convey no messages concerning military operations except those authorized by himself. The State Department also issued instructions which would not permit newspapers to publish military matters before being censored by them. When Edwin M. Stanton became Secretary of War he demanded that this function be under complete military control; he obtained this authority and from then on censorship was vigorously enforced and offenders were severely punished.

During the World War censorship was rigidly enforced within the army. Regulations issued to our army in France were based on those used by the British and contained implicit instructions as to letter writing, addressing envelopes, method of censoring outgoing letters and restrictions on photographs and telegraphic communications. Soldiers were forbidden to carry on their person any documents or written matter which would in any way aid the enemy, including letters received from home. While on leave, officers and soldiers were not permitted to discuss military matters of any nature. In order to reduce the task of censoring all letters written in the field, a green envelope was authorized in which letters could be forwarded for mailing; this green envelope bore a certificate which had to be signed by the sender; letters placed in this unsealed green envelope were ordinarily not censored at the base but were sealed, stamped and forwarded.

The army was especially sensitive on the subject of newspaper publicity; press articles were censored before leaving the theater of operations and were subject to further censoring before final publication.

[A. H. Meneely, *The War Department, 1861;* Censorship Orders for Troops in the Field, American Expeditionary Force.]

C. A. WILLOUGHBY

Censures of the President by Congress. Congress had vested in the Secretary of the Treasury discretion as to the deposit of government funds in the Bank of the United States^qv^. In order to compel removal of such deposits^qv^ from the bank, President Jackson dismissed one Secretary of the Treasury and appointed another (1833), whereupon the Senate passed a resolution censuring him for assuming "authority and power not conferred by the Constitution and laws and in derogation of both." The Senate refused to receive the President's "Protest," but four years later expunged the censure from its journal. After President Tyler's veto of a tariff measure (1842) a select committee of the House of Representatives reported a resolution censuring the President for strangling legislation by misuse of the veto power and refused to receive his protest. A censure of President Cleveland was implied in a Senate resolution (1885) expressing "condemnation of the refusal of the Attorney-General under whatever influence, to send to the Senate copies of the papers sent for. . . ."

[W. E. Binkley, *Powers of the President.*]

W. E. BINKLEY

Census. Article I of the Federal Constitution, which provides that Representatives "be apportioned among the several States . . . according to their respective numbers," provides also for a decennial census to furnish the necessary basis for such apportionment. It was only as an incident to the establishment of its democratic political machinery that the United States in 1789 became the first nation in the world to provide by law for a periodic enumeration of its people.

The first two censuses, those of 1790 and 1800, gathered little more than the necessary population figures, distinguishing colored from white and slave from free because slaves were to count as three fifths the same number of free persons in apportioning representation (*see* Compromises of the Federal Constitution). The census of 1810 was the first in which an effort was made to collect statistics on matters other than population, notably manufactures, but the results were uneven and incomplete. In 1840 an attempt, perhaps overambitious, was made to collect information on mines, agriculture, commerce, manufactures, occupations, schools, illiteracy, insane and idiots, pensioners and other subjects. The accuracy of the census figures for many of these subjects has been questioned, although the information gathered is of great value to the historian. In 1850 there was still further expansion of the categories to include, among others, newspapers and periodicals, libraries, religious bodies, criminals and mortality figures. The censuses of 1860 and 1870 were taken under the same law as that for 1850. Because of the difficulties of Reconstruction^qv^ in the South, the results of the 1870 census for that region are somewhat under suspicion.

All censuses prior to that of 1880 were taken under the supervision of United States marshals who hired assistants of their own to do the actual work of enumeration. Very little control from Washington was possible over these temporary political appointees and the results became less reliable as the schedules grew more complicated. The act providing for the 1880 census substituted a field force of supervisors and enumerators directly under the control of the Superintendent of the Census. The census of 1880 was vastly larger in scope, its results being published in twenty-four volumes, whereas five volumes had sufficed for any previous census. The census of 1890 was still larger. It was the first in which use was made of punch cards and electric tabulating machines, inventions which made possible tabulations of many combinations which were previously impracticable.

After long agitation, a permanent Census Office was established by act of March 6, 1902. Previously, every ten years since 1830, when the returns were first checked in Washington, a temporary organization had been called into existence to compile, edit and publish the results. This temporary Office, after 1849, was always set up in the Interior Department, and the permanent Office was placed there too, only to be transferred in 1903 to the newly established Department of Commerce and Labor, where it gradually came to be known as the Bureau of the Census. From 1913 it has been in the Department of Commerce.

Since it has become a permanent organization,

the Bureau has endeavored to restrict the scope of the decennial census by shifting some of its special inquiries to the in-between years. A census of manufacturers is now taken every two years and a census of agriculture every five years. A recent innovation of importance is a census of the distributive industries. The Bureau also regularly collects and publishes statistics on crime, births and deaths, finances of states, cities and local governments and on a large number of special industries and commodities. The permanently preserved Census records are of inestimable value to historians and social scientists since they constitute a practically complete record of the population of the nation for the 150 years of its existence and of that population's social and economic life.

[W. Stull Holt, *The Bureau of the Census*, 1929.]

OLIVER W. HOLMES

Cent, First American Use of. Our cent came from the adoption of the dollar[qv] as the unit and its division decimally. Colonial accounts were kept in pounds, shillings and pence but the circulation was mostly Spanish dollars. A privately issued coin dated 1783 (called the Washington cent) had the word cent on it. Vermont and Connecticut in 1785 coined cents, but Massachusetts, in 1787, was the first state to have the word on its coin. The "Fugio"[qv] cent in 1787 was the first cent issued under the authority of the United States. Cents were minted regularly by the Federal Government starting with 1793.

[Neil Carothers, *Fractional Money.*]

JAMES D. MAGEE

Centennial Exposition, Philadelphia (1876), celebrating the one hundredth anniversary of the Declaration of Independence, was the first great international exposition held in America. It was ten years in the planning and building; it covered more than 450 acres in Fairmount Park; its total cost was more than $11,000,000. Thirty-seven foreign nations constructed pavilions, many in their native architectural styles. The 167 buildings of the exposition housed more than 30,000 exhibitors from 50 nations. The gates were opened on May 10 and during the 159 days that followed there were 8,004,274 cash admissions. There were seven principal divisions in the exposition: mining and metallurgy, manufactured products, science and education, fine arts, machinery, agriculture and horticulture. The Woman's Building, an innovation in expositions, demonstrated the relative emancipation of women in America.

There was no midway or similar amusement, for nothing could have competed with the intense public interest in the working models of many new machines and processes. The architecture was confused, but impressive. The influence of various foreign exhibits evoked a new interest in interior decoration in America. In this exposition the world, for the first time, saw industrial America on display. Americans realized that the Machine Age had arrived and that their country was, in many ways, at last coming of age. The Centennial was honest, homely and revealing; it provided an immense stimulus to the growing æsthetic, social and industrial consciousness of America.

[J. S. Ingram, *Complete History of the Centennial Exposition;* James D. McCabe, *History of the Centennial Exposition.*]

FRANK MONAGHAN

Centinel of the North-Western Territory, The, published in Cincinnati by William Maxwell, was the first newspaper in the Northwest Territory[qv]. It appeared Nov. 9, 1793, and weekly thereafter until June, 1796, when it was merged with *Freeman's Journal.* Subscription was "250 cents" per annum, and 7 cents a single copy. The motto of the *Centinel:* "Open to all Parties —but influenced by none," expressed the publisher's aims: to afford an isolated community a medium to make known its varied wants and to record local happenings, as well as those of the outside world. A complete file is in the library of the Historical and Philosophical Society of Ohio in Cincinnati.

[*Proceedings*, American Antiquarian Society, New Series, Vol. XXIX, p. 141.]

BEVERLEY W. BOND, JR.

Central American Court of Justice, The, was a tribunal established by the five Central American republics in accordance with a treaty signed at the Central American Peace Conference held in Washington in 1907 under the sponsorship of the United States and Mexico. It consisted of five judges, one selected by each signatory state. It was given jurisdiction over all controversies arising among the signatories regarding which a diplomatic understanding could not be reached. The court was also authorized to hear cases of an international character brought by a citizen of one of the five republics against one of the other governments. The court was installed at Cartago, Costa Rica, on May 25, 1908. In 1916 and 1917 suits were brought in the court by Costa Rica and Salvador to prevent Nicaragua from carrying out the terms of the Bryan-Chamorro Treaty[qv] of 1914 between the United States and Nicaragua regarding a canal route.

The court decided both cases against Nicaragua. Since Nicaragua refused to accept the decision and since the United States failed to support the court, the tribunal was in a futile position. When the period of ten years for which the court was established expired in 1918 nothing was done to renew it and the court was dissolved.

[M. O. Hudson, *The Permanent Court of International Justice.*]

BENJAMIN H. WILLIAMS

Central Overland, California and Pikes Peak Express, The, was chartered by the Kansas legislature in February, 1860. It absorbed the stage lines running from Missouri to Denver and to Salt Lake City. Through its president, William H. Russell (*see* Russell, Majors and Waddell), it launched the famous Pony Express[qv]. In May, 1860, it succeeded to the Chorpenning contract for mail service from Utah to California. Maintenance of frequent stage service and heavy losses from the Pony Express brought embarrassment to the C. O. C. & P. P. Express. Employees dubbed it "Clean Out of Cash and Poor Pay." On March 21, 1862, Ben Holladay purchased the holdings at public sale for $100,000.

[L. R. Hafen, *The Overland Mail.*]

LeROY R. HAFEN

Central Pacific Race with the Union Pacific. This was a construction contest between the two companies bidding for government subsidies, land grants[qv] and public favor. The original Pacific Railway Act, 1862, authorized the Central Pacific to build east to the California line and the Union Pacific[qv] to build west to the western Nevada boundary. This legislation was unpopular with the railroad companies and they planned to build beyond the designated boundaries. Their attitude led to amendments to the Pacific Railway Act, 1865–66, and the roads were authorized to continue construction until they met. The amendments precipitated the now historic race, 1867–69, because the company building the most track would receive the larger subsidy.

The competing companies projected their lines 300 miles in advance of actual construction, which was technically within the law. But when surveys crossed and recrossed the railroad officials got into legal battles and the crews into personal ones. When the two roads were about 100 miles apart, Congress passed a law compelling the companies to join their tracks at Promontory Point[qv], Utah, some fifty miles from the end of each completed line. The final, and most spectacular, lap of the race was made toward this point in the winter and the spring of 1869, the tracks being joined on May 10. Nobody won the race because there was no definite goal on Promontory Point that had to be reached. The race was a dead heat if anything because both tracks reached the immediate vicinity about the same time.

[Gen. G. M. Dodge, *The Dodge Records.*]

J. R. PERKINS

Central Route, The, is a term frequently applied to the overland route used most extensively during the twenty years following 1848, by immigrants bound for California. There were many deviations. From Independence[qv] or other points on the Missouri the immigrants followed the Platte, went through South Pass[qv] in Wyoming, went around to the north of Great Salt Lake[qv], followed the Humboldt to the sinks and proceeded to California by different passes through the Sierras. Beginning with 1851, mail service was maintained over this route.

[Cardinal Goodwin, *The Trans-Mississippi West;* LeRoy Hafen, *The Overland Mail.*]

RUPERT N. RICHARDSON

Centralization. In national affairs, this term usually refers to the growing concentration of authority in the Federal Government over fields which formerly were occupied only in part, or not at all, by the state governments. Centralizing tendencies have been most conspicuous since the adoption of the Fourteenth Amendment[qv], which gave a veto upon state legislative acts to the Federal courts and thus placed in their hands the protection of fundamental property rights. But centralization has been stimulated mainly through congressional legislation regulating and protecting interstate commerce[qv], particularly through investigative and regulatory agencies centering in Washington (*see* Interstate Commerce Commission; Federal Trade Commission). More clearly has centralization been accelerated through Federal appropriations of money for a great variety of state enterprises or needs, called grants-in-aid[qv]. For example, Congress may not require a state to construct and maintain a system of highways of specified length, width and materials, or to maintain a state highway department. Yet, through its power to appropriate money and to prescribe conditions with which a state must comply if it wishes to share in the Federal funds, the National Government, through the Bureau of Public Roads in the Department of Agriculture, is able to do indirectly what it cannot do directly.

Centralization is viewed with alarm by some, who fear the ultimate reduction of the states to mere administrative areas of the National Government, like the French *départements.* By others, centralization is viewed as inevitable once national unity has been attained and social and economic interests have developed to a point where they overlap state boundaries.

In state affairs, centralization refers to the expanding activities of state governments, whereby they have assumed supervision, direct control, or actual performance of activities previously carried on inadequately, if at all, by counties, cities or other local governments. Such centralization has appeared notably in connection with the support of schools, highway construction and maintenance, charities and corrections and public health protection.

[F. A. Ogg and P. O. Ray, *Introduction to American Government*, 6th edition; A. F. Macdonald, *Federal Aid*, and *American State Government and Administration;* W. B. Graves, The Future of the American States, *American Political Science Review*, XXX, 24-51, February, 1936; L. W. Lancaster, *Government in Rural America.*]

P. ORMAN RAY

Centralized Purchasing. The rise of large-scale business, which early found central purchasing advantageous, brought the practice to the attention of governments. By the close of the World War most of the states and large cities had set up central purchasing offices staffed by expert buyers. The executive departments and independent offices of the National Government continued independent buying, with some co-ordination in the purchase of items needed by a number of agencies, until June 10, 1933. Then the President, by executive order, set up a procurement division in the Treasury Department^qv^. This division now buys all articles needed by two or more departments in the District of Columbia except the War Department, the Navy Department^qqv^ and the District government. The division is gradually extending its jurisdiction in the field services and to items required by only one agency. By 1937 centralized purchasing was in use in 36 states and more than 200 cities in the United States.

[Russell Forbes, *Governmental Purchasing.*]

HARVEY WALKER

Century Dictionary of the English Language, THE, was completed in eight volumes between 1889 and 1891 under the editorship of William Dwight Whitney. Its 450,000 entries define all the ordinary words and phrases of the English language, including those generally omitted from such works as obsolete, dialectal, provincial or technical. The distinguishing merit of the work lies in its encyclopedic method; in addition to the definitions and purely philological matter, there is much technical, historical and practical information. The same method was applied to proper names—names of persons, places, characters in fiction, books—in *The Century Dictionary of Names* (1894). In 1897 an Atlas formed the tenth volume. In 1909 a two-volume supplement to the dictionary appeared, and the whole work was reissued in twelve volumes. In 1927 an abridged, condensed and popular rendering of the great work was published, in two volumes, as *The New Century Dictionary.*

[M. M. Mathews, *A Survey of English Dictionaries.*]

HARRY R. WARFEL

Century of Progress International Exposition, Chicago (1933–34), was the greatest financial success in the recent history of world fairs. It was planned during a period of prosperity and successfully held in the midst of a great depression. It was designed to celebrate the one hundredth anniversary of the founding of the City of Chicago^qv^ and to demonstrate a century's progress in many fields. The original plans were frequently scaled down to meet the exigencies of shrinking budgets. During the 170 days beginning May 27, 1933, there were 22,565,859 paid admissions; during the 163 days beginning May 26, 1934, there were 16,486,377; a total of 39,052,236. Official foreign participation was extremely limited. The schematic pattern of the fair was vague and confusing. The modernistic architecture of the exposition has exerted much influence and the color effects have made themselves clearly evident in commercial design.

FRANK MONAGHAN

Cerro Gordo, Battle of (April 18, 1847). Advancing to the interior after taking Vera Cruz^qv^, Gen. Scott found a Mexican army under Santa Anna entrenched on the National Road, eighteen miles below Jalapa. Twiggs' division stormed two fortified hills after a turning movement suggested and guided by Capt. R. E. Lee. Shields' brigade gained the rear of the position and the Mexicans fled. Santa Anna escaped, leaving 3000 prisoners, guns, baggage and $11,000 in specie. The American loss was 431.

[Justin H. Smith, *The War with Mexico.*]

CHARLES WINSLOW ELLIOTT

Chad's Ford. *See* Brandywine, Battle of the.

Chain Gangs were occasionally used by Southern sheriffs in ante-bellum days, much as they had been used by the wardens of debtor prisons in the North and in England during the latter part of the 18th century. But the wide and systematic use of this form of convict labor did not appear until it was employed by the lessees who took full control over most of the convicts in the Southern states during the first decades following the Civil War. In place of the old ball-and-chain, the lessees substituted shackles fastened to both ankles of each convict and joined by a chain that permitted only short steps; a long chain was then strung through one of the links of each short chain, thus binding scores of convicts together. Compelled to work, eat and sleep together, the basest sort of conditions were maintained.

In the late 1880's protests against the convict leases (*see* Convict Labor Systems) led to their gradual abandonment in favor of penal plantations which usually dispensed with the chains. But it was not long before an increasing demand for good roads prompted the county sheriffs to hold a larger portion of the convicts for labor on the local roads, reviving the chain-gang system for this purpose. By the late 1890's the major portion of the convicts of Georgia, Florida, North Carolina, South Carolina and other Southern states were coupled together in road gangs. Humanitarian protests gradually led to state inspection of the county road gangs in several states and to state operation of the system in Georgia. The introduction of road-making machinery antiquated the chain gang and enabled the reformers to carry their opposition to the system to partial success in most of the states, but chain gangs still persist in many counties throughout a large section of the South.

[Blake McKelvey, *American Prisons;* J. F. Steiner and R. M. Brown, *The North Carolina Chain Gangs.*]

BLAKE McKELVEY

Chain Stores. This term may be applied to any organization made up of two or more stores in the same general business. The United States Bureau of the Census, however, in defining chains, excludes all organizations having less than four stores and also specifies that chain operation normally includes central buying and warehousing. Organizations of department stores[qv], although centrally owned, are rarely operated under central buying and warehousing and are consequently termed "ownership groups." Leased departments of stores, operated by utility companies, retailing household appliances to increase the use of gas and electricity, are considered as chains.

Chain stores are usually classified as "local" if their units are located in and around one city; "sectional" if located in two or more cities within a limited geographical area; and "national" if located in more than one section of the country.

The growth of chain-store systems has occurred chiefly within the past half century. The Great Atlantic and Pacific Tea Company[qv], largest chain in the United States, began as a single store in 1859. The F. W. Woolworth Company, oldest and largest of the variety chains, made its first unit beginning in 1879. Many of the other well-known chains made their beginnings, often in obscure little shops, in the 1890's and early 1900's. Chain stores introduced many improvements in retailing, including greater emphasis on light, fresh air and cleanliness, better and fresher stocks of merchandise and lower costs of operation.

The most rapid progress in chain-store development took place in the decade following the World War. This was a period of rapid retail trade expansion for the country as a whole. Total retail sales gained by at least 50%. All channels of distribution benefited, and while chains probably gained more than other types of retailers, it is probable that most of their growth was due to the general increase in business. The rising importance of the chains, however, aroused their competitors to serious efforts to protect their position. Independent retailers, dependent for their supplies of goods upon wholesalers, have had to meet chain-store competition in a number of constructive ways, such as in improvement of their stores in appearance, cleanliness, merchandise displays, lighting, advertising, accounting, personal salesmanship, closer study of consumer demand, better selection of merchandise and purchasing goods in quantities in co-operation with other retailers handling the same line of goods.

In recent years independent retailers have sought to remove chain-store competition by placing legal handicaps upon the chains, thus raising their costs of operation artificially. Such legislation has generally taken the form of discriminatory taxes, graduated according (a) to the total gross sales of the chain, or (b) to the number of store units operated in the state. The Indiana antichain-store tax law (1929), basing its discrimination against chains on the latter principle, was the first law of this nature to withstand the test of the courts (State Board of Tax Commissioners of Indiana v. Jackson, 283 U. S. 527). Later a Kentucky law assessing a graduated discriminatory tax based on volume of gross receipts, was declared unconstitutional (Steward Dry Goods Co. v. Lewis, 294 U. S. 550). The Louisiana act of 1934 established a new principle in that the tax was graduated according to the number of chain-store units operated regardless of location. This principle was approved by the United States Supreme Court in 1937 (Great

Atlantic & Pacific Tea Co. v. Grosjean, 301 U. S. 412) and has since been widely advocated by the enemies of chain stores.

The Patman bill, introduced in Congress in 1938, and again in 1939, sought to carry anti-chain taxation into Federal law and with such severity as to wipe out of existence all chains having stores in more than one state. Any remaining chain systems doing business solely on an intrastate basis could then be dealt with in any manner seen fit by the states. (*See also* Super-Market.)

[J. P. Nichols, *Chain Store Manual;* P. H. Nystrom, *Economics of Retailing;* J. P. Nichols et al., *Retailers' Manual of Taxes and Regulation;* Commerce Clearing House, *Tax Systems of the World.*]

PAUL H. NYSTROM

Chair Making. Among the numerous woodworking industries in the American colonies furniture making soon reached a point where it supplied articles for export to the South and to the Caribbean. The most common product was chairs, which are often recorded in coastal and sugar island cargoes. Their manufacture, which was already specialized before the Revolution, was recognized as a distinct branch of furniture making in the census of 1810. Rockers, said to be an American invention, were popular in Spanish America. Vessels leaving Baltimore for points around the Horn (*see* Cape Horn) in a single day of 1827 carried 12,000 chairs.

An expanding commercial market early invited quantity production and the use of mechanical aids in manufacture. Philadelphia chair shops had steam-driven machinery before 1825. About 1850 a Fitchburg factory producing principally for export had a capacity of sixty-five dozen chairs a day, and employed special machines to shape interchangeable parts[qv] which were boxed separately for shipment and assembled at their destination. Until after 1890 Massachusetts made more chairs than any other state. Towns like Ashburnham, Gardner and Westminster were centers for their production.

Chair design has accommodated itself to period fashions. Nevertheless popular types like the Windsor chair have remained in general use since introduced at Philadelphia about 1700, where they were known at first as Philadelphia chairs. Windsors were advertised during the 18th century by cabinetmakers who specialized in them.

Chairs are not as large a fraction of furniture[qv] output today as they were when household equipment was less elaborate. Modern statistics record them by groups like household, office, public building, wood, wicker and metal chairs. Today New York manufactures far more chairs than any other state and an increasing but still modest share of the annual output is made of metal.

[Thomas H. Ormsbee, *The Story of American Furniture;* Victor S. Clark, *History of Manufactures in the United States; United States Census of Manufactures.*]

VICTOR S. CLARK

Chalmette Plantation. Four or five miles below New Orleans[qv], on the east bank of the Mississippi, is the imposing Chalmette Monument which marks the site of Jackson's battle of 1815. The extensive sugar plantation was the property of Ignace de Lino de Chalmette, a wellborn French Creole. For Jackson's military convenience, Chalmette and his wife abandoned their plantation home. After the battle, only the charred ruins of their dwelling remained and many of the fine oaks with their drooping Spanish moss were missing. Chalmette died three weeks later.

[Grace King, *Creole Families of New Orleans.*]

L. W. NEWTON

Chambers of Commerce may be described as voluntary associations of businessmen approaching the problems of the community from the business angle. The Chamber of Commerce of the State of New York is the oldest such organization in this country, its original charter having come from King George III in 1768.

In general, American chambers of commerce follow the British, rather than the Continental, types and usually are broader in the scope of their activities than even the British prototype.

Although in many American cities the chambers of commerce were started as such, in most of the older cities they were derived from either one of two types of previous organizations. The first of these was the Board of Trade, established originally for the purpose of regulating or supervising trading activities. In Boston, Baltimore, Minneapolis, Milwaukee, St. Louis and Cincinnati as well as in other cities the present Chamber of Commerce has, as at least one of its component parts, a former trading body and some even continue this activity.

In the chambers growing out of trading bodies the growth usually has been effected by merger with other types of organization, the basis of combination being a common concern with civic affairs.

The second type of older American chamber is the organization characterized by having been originally a group of tax-paying businessmen—a Tax-Payers' League or a Civic Association, etc.

—united for defense, or to foster some civic interest.

The most common activities engaged in by American chambers of commerce include industrial and commercial development and expansion, and dealing with problems connected with agriculture, transportation, publicity, charity solicitation (community chests), regulation and promotion of trade and commercial arbitration[qqv].

The Chamber of Commerce of the United States (which was established in 1912) is a federation of local chambers and other business organizations and individuals to apply similar principles to national affairs. One of its principal activities is the conducting of referenda on legislative matters and other public questions.

[Wm. George Bruce, *Commercial Organizations.*]

PAUL T. CHERINGTON

Chambersburg, Pa., Burning of (July 30, 1864). Gen. Hunter (U.), defeated by Early (C.), in the course of his retreat up the Shenandoah Valley[qv] wantonly burned crops, homes and villages. In retaliation, Early dispatched a cavalry force under Gen. John McCausland to Chambersburg, in adjacent Union territory, to demand a ransom of $100,000 in gold or $500,000 in greenbacks[qv], failing the delivery of which, he was ordered to burn the town. McCausland went as directed. No ransom of the amount demanded could be paid. The town was burned.

[R. H. Early, ed., *Gen. Jubal A. Early: Autobiographical Sketch and Narrative.*]

THOMAS ROBSON HAY

Chambly, Fort, at the foot of the Richelieu River rapids, was built by the British, 1775, on the site of Fort St. Louis (erected 1764). Captured Oct. 20, 1775 (*see* Canada, American Invasion of, 1775–76), it was held until the spring of 1776 when it was evacuated and burned, as the Americans retreated southward to Ticonderoga[qv].

[J. H. Smith, *Our Struggle for the Fourteenth Colony.*]

ROBERT S. THOMAS

Champ d'Asile, THE. In 1817 a group of Napoleonic exiles under the leadership of Generals Lallemand and Rigaud made a fortified camp in Texas on the Trinity River, about thirty leagues from the coast, calling it Champ d'Asile. It was charged that they hoped to take Mexico and rescue Napoleon from St. Helena. Scarcely were the forts and dwellings completed when the Spanish, who claimed the territory, forced the colonists to withdraw to Galveston Island. There they remained for weeks, the victims of hunger, sickness and tropical storms. At last, aided by Lafitte the Pirate, they made their way to the French settlements in Louisiana.

[Jesse R. Reeves, *The Napoleonic Exiles in America, 1815-1819;* Anne Boreman Lyon, The Bonapartists in Alabama, in *The Gulf States Historical Magazine,* March, 1903.]

FANNIE RATCHFORD

Champagne-Marne Operation (July 15–18, 1918). This German offensive had several objectives. One was to correct their faulty supply in the Marne salient; another was to draw reserves to assure success in the offensive planned against the British in Flanders. The attack was made by three armies of the German Crown Prince Group. The plan was for the 7th Army (Boehn) to cross the Marne east of Château-Thierry and advance up the valley to Epernay. The 1st Army (Mudra) and 3rd Army (Einem) were to attack east of Reims in the direction of Epernay, swing south of the forest of Reims and capture Epernay and Chalons. The attack was definitely halted east of Reims on the first day by the efficient defense plans of the 4th French Army (Gouraud). West of Reims some fourteen divisions crossed the Marne but, unaided by the attack east of Reims and without artillery support, this attack soon bogged down. Orders were given on the 17th for their withdrawal, preparatory to a general withdrawal, from the Marne salient. The 3rd, 42nd and part of the 28th American Divisions participated. The approximate number of Americans engaged was 85,000. The 38th Infantry Regiment (3rd Division) here won the sobriquet, "Rock of the Marne" (*see* Aisne-Marne Operation, The).

[Girard L. McEntee, *The Military History of the World War.*]

GIRARD L. McENTEE

Champaign County Rescue Cases, THE, arising from an attempt to enforce the Fugitive Slave Act[qv], involved the conflict of state and Federal authorities. In April, 1857, Udney Hyde harbored, on his farm near Mechanicsburg, Champaign County, Ohio, a fugitive slave from Kentucky. The owner sent three United States deputy marshals and five Kentuckians for the chattel on May 21. The Negro nearly shot a marshal. Friends summoned by Hyde from Mechanicsburg scared the posse away, but it returned six days later and carried off four citizens. At South Charleston it assaulted an Ohio sheriff for trying to serve a writ of habeas corpus[qv], but next morning was overtaken by officers and a crowd and bound over to the Common Pleas Court of Clark County. Proslavery sympathizers appealed to Judge Humphrey H. Leavitt of the United

States District Court at Cincinnati, who assumed jurisdiction and released the defendants as having rightfully performed their duties and not being amenable to the state's laws. The payment of $950 by Hyde's neighbors for the slave's manumission terminated Federal suits against leading obstructors.

[*Ohio Archæological and Historical Publications*, XVI, 293-309; *Ohio Archæological and Historical Quarterly*, XLIII, No. 3.]

WILBUR H. SIEBERT

Champion's Hill, Battle of (May 16, 1863). When Pemberton (C.) at Edward's Station learned that Grant's (U.) army was about to move westward from the vicinity of Jackson toward Vicksburg[qqv], he decided to attack. He must defeat Grant to prevent being shut up in Vicksburg. By the morning of May 16, 1863, the Confederates had moved eastward to Champion's Hill. While Grant concentrated his army, Pemberton, uncertain as to what to do, halted his troops to await the expected attack. Grant handled his troops with energy and decision. The Union attack was successful. After several hours of battle, Pemberton's army was driven from the field toward Vicksburg.

[F. V. Greene, *The Mississippi.*]

THOMAS ROBSON HAY

Champlain, Lake. *See* Lake Champlain.

Champlain Fires a Shot. In 1608 Champlain made an alliance with the Indians of the St. Lawrence and with the Hurons[qv] from the interior; in 1609 their chiefs called upon him to assist them in a campaign against their enemies, the Iroquois[qv]. Champlain, with a small contingent of Frenchmen, accompanied the Indian war party up Richelieu River, and through Lake Champlain. At its southern end in a battle, July 29, three chiefs were killed by bullets from Champlain's arquebus. The Iroquois, astonished at the firearms, broke and fled.

It has been asserted by many early historians of Canada that the Iroquois thenceforth became the enemies of the French colony, and that by this act Champlain endangered his life work. This view attributes too much influence to a single battle, although Champlain in 1610 and again in 1615 attacked the Iroquois enemies with his Algonquian[qv] and Huron allies. The strategic position of the Iroquois and their ability to obtain firearms from the Dutch at Albany created a situation that made the Iroquois the natural enemies of New France. Champlain could not have foreseen that the Dutch would settle on the Hudson River and his obligation to help his allies created the situation. Had he not kept his promise to them, he could not have maintained his position at Quebec.

[H. P. Biggar, ed., *Champlain's Works*, Vol. II, 96-101, 134; L. P. Kellogg, *French Régime in Wisconsin and the Northwest.*]

LOUISE PHELPS KELLOGG

Champlain's Voyages. A sojourn of two years in Mexico and the West Indies (1599) prepared Samuel de Champlain for his first Canadian voyage (1603) when he served as geographer for the DeChastes expedition, authorized by Henry IV of France to make a general survey and fix settlements. Champlain justified his appointment by vigorously prosecuting a cartographic survey of the St. Lawrence region including the gulf, Gaspé and Isle Percé and the Saguenay River, resulting in a report prolific in valuable information. In 1604 under DeMonts, he explored Nova Scotia. A year later he explored the New England coast, mapping 1000 miles of coast line. Returning to France several times with his reports, he repeatedly voyaged to Canada, after 1607 being Lieutenant Governor. Other voyages of 1610, 1611, 1613 made him the acknowledged master of all that related to New France. A final voyage in 1633 ended in his effort to win the friendship of the Iroquois, whom he had previously attacked (*see* Champlain Fires a Shot).

[Edmund F. Slafter, in Winsor's *Narrative and Critical History of America.*]

ARTHUR C. PARKER

Champoeg Convention. On May 2, 1843, Oregon settlers met at Champoeg in the Willamette Valley to create a civil government which was to continue until either Great Britain or the United States established control (*see* Oregon Question, The). The plan was contested by the British settlers who looked upon it as pro-American. This provisional government was the only one in the Pacific Northwest until the Oregon territorial government was established by the United States on March 3, 1849.

[Charles H. Carey, *A General History of Oregon Prior to 1861.*]

ROBERT MOULTON GATKE

Chancellorsville, Battle of (May 2–4, 1863). In April Hooker (U.), with almost 130,000 men, lay across the Rappahannock River from Fredericksburg, Va. Intrenched behind Fredericksburg Lee (C.) awaited another attack such as that of Burnside (U.) in the previous December. In the absence of Longstreet's (C.) divisions in southeastern Virginia, Lee had approximately 60,000 men.

Beginning April 27, Hooker in rapid movements got four army corps across the Rappahannock on Lee's left flank, while maintaining his old lines and sending an army corps of 20,000 men under Sedgwick across the river below Lee's right flank. On May 1, with the forces on Lee's left, Hooker advanced across the river beyond Chancellorsville, only to retire behind Chancellorsville on the approach of the enemy. Lee, threatened by Hooker's movements, ran the risk of having his communication with Richmond cut and of being caught in an encircling trap. The greatest danger being on his left, Lee, leaving a force of about 10,000 men at Fredericksburg under Early, marched with the remainder of his troops toward Chancellorsville. The opposing armies, late in the day of May 1, took position for battle on lines nearly perpendicular to the Rappahannock. At night Lee and Stonewall Jackson (C.), conferring upon their dangerous situation, decided on a daring measure, that of dividing their forces and having Jackson with about 30,000 men march the next day around Hooker's right flank, while Lee with less than 20,000 men held the line in front of Hooker. Accordingly on May 2, while Lee deployed his men in skirmishes against Hooker, Jackson moved rapidly around Hooker's right flank.

In spite of adequate information of Jackson's movement, the army corps on Hooker's extreme right were unprepared when Jackson, late on May 2, fell upon them with irresistible fury. Howard's (U.) corps was routed and another corps badly demoralized. In the confusion and darkness greater disaster might have happened had not Jackson been dangerously wounded by the fire of his own troops and carried from the battlefield. In the renewed conflict of May 3 a cannon ball struck a column against which Hooker was leaning. Dazed by the effect and in doubt about the security of his army, Hooker withdrew his troops to the banks of the river, where they remained throughout May 4 in disorder and uncertainty.

Lee, meanwhile, turned back to deal with Sedgwick's corps, which had routed the Confederate force under Early and was rapidly approaching Chancellorsville. Under the fierce attack of Lee's veterans, Sedgwick likewise retired to the Rappahannock, which he crossed during the night of May 4. When, on May 5, Lee advanced again beyond Chancellorsville, Hooker withdrew the Union forces north of the river. In the battle Hooker lost 17,287 men and Lee 12,423. But Lee suffered the irreparable loss of Jackson, who after days of intense suffering died of his wounds.

[*War of the Rebellion, A Compilation of the Official Records of the Union and Confederate Armies*, Vol. XXV; John Bigelow, *The Campaign of Chancellorsville.*]

ALFRED P. JAMES

Change, Social, in America has been influenced chiefly by economic circumstances. The middle-class Englishmen who settled Massachusetts Bay organized their towns for purposes of good neighborhood and protection against the Indians. The self-contained communities which centered about the New England churches fostered an intense provincialism. By way of contrast, the first settlements in Virginia were early abandoned as the plantations drew people away from the towns. Agriculture on a broad scale, cultivated by slave labor, left few people in the towns, except those who were engaged either in the government of the colony or in its external commerce. The New England clergy strove to keep the people within the tidewater[qv] towns without success. The frontier[qv] beckoned with its allurements of free lands and less burdensome taxation. People refused to remain within the seaboard towns where they might be nonproprietors or at most proprietors of a tiny acreage, when by moving westward they could become proprietors of unlimited soil.

At the close of the Revolution the frontier had already become an important factor in social change. The Northwest Territory[qv] was thrown open to settlement as a part of the public domain[qv]. A joint-stock company had been formed by two enterprising citizens of Massachusetts to promote the settlement of the unoccupied lands (*see* Ohio Company of Associates); eager, impoverished veterans of the war were ready to go and take possession. In the Convention of 1787[qv] the propertied and commercial classes were anxious lest the tidewater sections be outvoted in the new government by the men of the interior. Elbridge Gerry, who feared the influx of Scotch-Irish, French Huguenots and Germans[qqv] along the frontier, pleaded that those who remained on the Atlantic seaboard might not "be at the mercy of the emigrants." Gouverneur Morris insisted that "the busy haunts of men, not the remote wilderness, was the proper school of political talents. If the western people get the power into their hands they will ruin the Atlantic interests."

Profound changes followed the expansion of the frontier (*see* Westward Movement). The growth of democracy[qv] in the United States was accompanied by an intensive cultivation of the principle of individualism. The abundance of free land, the extent and richness of the natural resources, the enterprise and optimism of the people and the scope for individual initiative combined to give the country an era of unparalleled prosperity. In such a society there was little place for aristocratic pretensions. The South with its slave economy stood apart from this democratizing influence, despite the efforts of Southern statesmen to link their section with the growing West. The Civil War, because it destroyed slavery[qv], ended the isolation of the South, but it was not until the present century that this section recovered from the ravages of the war sufficiently to partake of the national prosperity.

The end of the Civil War found the United States well on its way to becoming a great industrial nation. New social classes arose embracing those persons who worked for wages (*see* Labor). Free land[qv] disappeared and there was no further opportunity for the enterprising to seek independence by moving westward. Cities grew rapidly until more than 50% of the population dwelt in urban communities. Large aggregations of capital engaged in the exploitation of the natural resources and in transportation and commerce drove small competitors out of business to become employees of great corporations. When the economic collapse of 1929 came, the United States had passed through three centuries of development and had justified the fears of Thomas Jefferson when he warned of the dangers which would follow if agriculture gave place to industry.

[J. B. McMaster, *History of the People of the United States.*]

WILLIAM S. CARPENTER

Chantier in the fur trade signified the place near the larger posts where lumber was made up, boats and canoes built and other craftsmanship necessary for the post performed. The word comes from the French meaning shipyard.

[H. M. Chittenden, *History of the American Fur Trade of the Far West.*]

CARL L. CANNON

Chantilly, Battle of (Sept. 1, 1862), occurred during Pope's (U.) withdrawal to Fairfax Courthouse (Va.) after his defeat at the second battle of Bull Run[qv]. Jackson (C.), seeking to command the road on which Pope was retreating, encountered Federal troops protecting the line of retreat. A sharp engagement followed, accompanied by a terrific thunderstorm. Losses were heavy, Generals Isaac I. Stevens (U.) and Philip Kearny (U.) being killed. Jackson could not interrupt Pope's retreat, the Federals reaching Fairfax Courthouse without further disaster.

[*Battles and Leaders of the Civil War*, II.]

W. N. C. CARLTON

Chaparral, from Spanish *chaparro,* as used by Mexicans, who gave the word to the Southwest, generally means any kind of thick or thorny brush, but never timber. In California, chaparral is specifically the manzanita oak; in parts of Texas, the black chaparral. Chaparral peculiar to arid and semi-arid regions of the Southwest includes juajillo, granjeno, mesquite, all-thorn and huisache, the bushes often interspersed with various kinds of cacti, agaves and yuccas. Only dogs, horses and men used to the chaparral can run in it, and the "brush popper," armored in leather and ducking, is a distinctly different type from the plains cowpuncher. The leaves of chaparral growth are as slender as the thorns are sharp, preventing evaporation. Some varieties afford good browsing; others are as bitter as gall. Before the era of overgrazing, a solid turf and frequent grass fires kept the brush down. Now it usurps millions of acres once prairie. Cattle ranging in it tend to become wild. It hides rattlesnakes, coyotes and other "varments."

[J. Frank Dobie, *A Vaquero of the Brush Country.*]

J. FRANK DOBIE

Chapbooks were cheap popular pamphlets, generally printed on a single sheet and folded to form twenty-four pages or less, often crudely illustrated with woodcuts, sold by chapmen (Anglo-Saxon *céap* [trade] *men*) or peddlers. Published by tens of thousands in America to about 1850, they were most numerous from about 1800 to 1825. Famous authors and peddlers of American chapbooks were Rev. Mason Locke Weems of Virginia (author of the Washington cherry-tree story), Josiah Priest of New York state and Chapman Whitcomb of Massachusetts. Prominent among the publishers were Andrew Steuart of Philadelphia, Isaiah Thomas of Worcester, Fowle and Draper and Nathaniel Coverly of Boston, Samuel Wood & Sons and Mahlon Day of New York. The beginning of popular literature in the United States, with emphasis on the wonderful, the sad and the humorous, they were for over 100 years the only literature available in the average home except the Bible, the almanac and the newspaper[qqv]. They included fairy tales, lives of heroes and rascals, riddles, jests, poems, songs, hymns, speeches, shipwrecks, Indian captivities, highwaymen, deathbed scenes, executions, romances, astrology, palmistry, etiquette books, letter-writers, valentine-writers, moral and (sometimes) immoral tales.

[H. B. Weiss, *Catalogue of the Chapbooks in the New York Public Library;* same, *American Chapbooks; Catalogue of English and American Chapbooks in Harvard College Library;* W. W. Watt, *Shilling Shockers of the Gothic School.*]

R. W. G. VAIL

Chaplin Hills, Battle of. *See* Perryville, Battle at.

Chapultepec, Battle of (Sept. 13, 1847). The western approaches to Mexico City were commanded by Chapultepec, a rocky eminence, 200 feet high, crowned with stone buildings. After vigorous bombardment, Scott launched Pillow's division against the southern slopes. The garrison resisted desperately, but the Americans mounted the walls on scaling ladders and carried the *Castillo*. Quitman's and Worth's divisions then attacked the Belén and San Cosme gates, and the city surrendered the next morning. The American loss (for the day) was 138 killed, 673 wounded. Mexican casualties are unknown, but 760 were captured.

[Justin H. Smith, *The War with Mexico*, II.]

CHARLES WINSLOW ELLIOTT

Charity Organization Movement, THE. Private and secular charity organizations existed in America as far back as the Scots Charitable Society of Boston (1657). After the American Revolution such societies appeared in the principal cities, but the New York Society for the Prevention of Pauperism (1817) was the first to propose a general attack upon the problem of destitution. A movement led by Joseph Tuckerman, under the influence of William Ellery Channing's Unitarianism[qv], culminated (1832–34) in the organization of the Association of Delegates from the Benevolent Societies of Boston. Handicapped by their sectarianism, these societies declined into almsgiving agencies.

Rapid industrialization following the Civil War accelerated the growth of cities and increased pauperism, especially among immigrants crowded in slums[qqv]. This brought a large increase in organizations attacking special aspects of the problem, and, eventually, a movement to coordinate them which was influenced by the work of Frederic Ozanam in Paris, Dr. Thomas Chalmers in Edinburgh, Count Rumford in Bavaria and Edward Dennison and Octavia Hill in London, as well as by the municipal plans of Elberfeld and Hamburg in Germany.

The charity organization movement prided itself on its "scientific" character. It planned to eliminate poverty and crime by the reconstruction and rehabilitation of individuals and families and the suppression of mendicity. All the resources of organized private philanthropy were to be focused upon the problem through the Charity Organization Society. The first city-wide society thus organized was in Buffalo (1877). From there the movement spread within five years to all the principal cities, and by 1904 there were 150 societies, leaving only 45 cities with population over 25,000 unorganized. In many cities, United Charities buildings were erected. The movement produced notable periodicals, such as the Philadelphia Society's *Monthly Register* (1880); Alexander Johnson's *Reporter of Organized Charity,* Chicago, 1888–89; and the *Charities Review,* started in 1891 in New York.

Beginning in the late 1880's this program of individual and family rehabilitation was supplemented by settlement work[qv] inspired by Toynbee Hall, in London. Organized charity had much in common with the contemporary development of state boards of charity and it also stimulated the development of such welfare agencies as wayfarers' lodges, penny provident funds and fuel societies.

The movement assumed national proportions in the National Association of Societies for Organizing Charities (1888) and the National Council of Charity Officers, both in connection with the National Conference of Charities and Corrections, founded 1873. Working relations were established with such organizations as Hebrew Charities, the Society of St. Vincent de Paul, the Red Cross[qv] and the Salvation Army[qv].

In the early years of the 20th century social workers gradually lost faith in the elimination of poverty by organized charity. Professionalization, beginning with the New York School of Philanthropy (1904), set more practical limits to social work. The American Association for Organizing Family Work took the place of the American Association for Organizing Charities, and child welfare agencies and courts of domestic relations[qv] assumed many of the functions of family work.

Post-war disillusionment brought doubt whether organized charity was not aggravating the situation by its "relief from above." On the other hand, welfare agencies increased in numbers and activity, particularly those supported from public funds. When organized charity proved inadequate to deal with relief in the early 1930's government agencies of direct relief, work relief and social security[qv] took over much of the burden. Although organized private charity has continued, it remains to be seen how much its basic structure will be changed by the new developments. (*See* Relief.)

[F. D. Watson, *Charity Organization Movement in the United States;* A. Johnson, *Adventures in Social Welfare.*]

HAROLD E. DAVIS

Charity Schools. In the early days, free education generally meant instruction for the poor and underprivileged children. Numerous schools were established in the American colonies and many were found also in the American states that were organized and supported by benevolent persons and societies, a practice which served to fasten on the idea of free education an odium that was difficult to remove. The pauper-school conception came directly from England and persisted far into the 19th century. Infant-school societies, Sunday-school[qv] societies and other organizations engaged in such work. Schools were sometimes supported also in part by rate bills, charges levied upon parents according to the number of their children in school. Declaration of poverty exempted parents from the payment of rate bills, which also often put the element of charity in certain educational practices. In the history of education in the United States philanthropy and charity have played important parts, on the theory that the level of life among the masses could thus be raised and their moral, religious and economic conditions be improved. As a result many kinds of charity schools were established in this country, and in some instances the children were not only instructed but provided with food, clothes and lodgings. Generally the curriculum was of the most elementary character.

[Frank P. Graves, *A Student's History of Education;* Edgar W. Knight, *Education in the United States.*]

EDGAR W. KNIGHT

Charivari. A French word of unknown origin meaning rough music. Corrupted into *shivaree* in America it designates an old custom, particularly in the Middle West, of serenading newly wedded couples with every type of noise-making device, the object being to exact a "treat." Refusal to serve the serenaders with refreshments resulted in some form of hazing, the groom often being compelled to "ride a rail." The *shivaree* was a manifestation of mob instinct, and like the barn dance was a popular form of rural entertainment. In New England the custom took the name of *serenade* or *callathump.*

[*American Speech,* April, 1933, Vol. VIII.]

W. J. BURKE

Charles River Bridge Case, 1837 (11 Peters 420). In 1785 the Massachusetts legislature incorporated the Proprietors of the Charles River Bridge, for the purpose of erecting a toll bridge between Boston and Charlestown. In 1828, long before the expiration of the charter, the legislature incorporated the Warren Bridge Company to build another bridge a few rods from the first. The new bridge was to become free to the public within six years. Was the second charter unconstitutional as impairing the obligation of the first? (*See* Contract Clause.)

The case was carried from the highest court in Massachusetts (6 Pick. 376, 7 Pick. 344) to the Supreme Court of the United States, where it was first argued in 1831. Chief Justice Marshall would have held the second grant invalid; but because of absences and disagreement it was impossible to reach a decision until 1837. By that time new appointments had worked a transformation in the Court, which now upheld the constitutionality of the second charter with only two dissenting votes. In an opinion which marked that leaning against monopolistic power which characterized Jacksonian political philosophy (*see* Jacksonian Democracy), Taney, the new Chief Justice, developed the rule that corporate charters are to be construed strictly in favor of the public.

[C. B. Swisher, *Roger B. Taney;* Charles Warren, *The Supreme Court in United States History.*]

CHARLES FAIRMAN

Charleston, Capture of (May 12, 1780). In March, 1780, the British, under Gen. Clinton and Admiral Arbuthnot, besieged Charleston by land and sea. The Americans, commanded by Gen. Benjamin Lincoln, made little use of the bar at the entrance of the harbor and the adjacent sea islands, the natural defenses of the town. The fall of Charleston, after a brave but futile resistance, for a time paralyzed the American cause in the Carolinas. (*See also* Southern Campaigns, 1780–81.)

[E. McCrady, *South Carolina in the Revolution, 1775-1780.*]

R. L. MERIWETHER

Charleston, S. C. In 1670 an English expedition under Gov. William Sayle founded a settlement—the first permanent one in the Carolinas[qv]—on the Ashley River, three miles from the present center of Charleston, and named it Charles Towne, in honor of King Charles II. Other immigrants settled on the present city site, and in 1680 the public offices were removed thither. This soon became the largest and wealthiest town south of Philadelphia. A definitely French tinge was imparted to its population by the coming of Huguenot[qv] refugees from France in 1685–86, of 1200 Acadian[qv] exiles in 1755 and 500 French Revolutionary refugees from Santo Domingo in 1793. In 1706 the city withstood an attack by a combined Spanish and French fleet. In February, 1776, the Provincial Congress met here and adopted the first state constitution. The city was unsuccessfully attacked by the British in 1776 and 1779, but fell into their hands in 1780 (*see* Charleston, Capture of) and so remained until 1782. Until it received a city charter in 1783 it was governed by ordinances of the legislature, which were administered in part by provincial officials, in part by the churchwardens. It continued as the state capital until 1790. It was the center of the nullification^qv^ agitation of 1832–33, and of the secession^qv^ spirit of 1860. The first fighting of the Civil War^qv^ took place in its harbor *(see* Sumter, Fort). In the decades following the war, its beautiful old homes and churches, its aristocratic pride, its serenity and mellow atmosphere of the past gave it a charm all its own. It has suffered many calamities—not only sieges and bombardments, but hurricanes in 1699, 1752 and 1854, epidemics in 1699 and 1854, fire in 1740 and, on Aug. 31, 1886, the great earthquake which damaged nine tenths of its buildings. The foreign commerce of its port increased greatly after the World War.

[Mrs. St. Julien Ravenel, *Charleston, the Place and the People;* William A. Courtenay, *Charleston, S. C., the Centennial of Incorporation.*]

ALVIN F. HARLOW

Charleston, Siege of (1861–65). This popular term is a misnomer, for Charleston was never besieged, nor was any serious effort made either to fortify it or to invest it on the land side. The operations consisted in a blockade begun in May, 1861, with land and sea attacks upon the harbor fortifications. The harbor was well fortified and great ingenuity was displayed by the defenders in constructing an ironclad flotilla, a system of torpedo defense and even submarine boats. The wooden blockading fleet could not close in and even when Federal monitors arrived they could accomplish little against the land works. In 1863 Fort Sumter^qv^ was bombarded and almost destroyed, but the ruins could not be taken. Battery Wagner^qv^ was taken by formal siege operations, but no further progress could be made. It was in the course of these operations that the famous "Swamp Angel," an eight-inch 200-pounder Parrott rifle, was emplaced on a platform floated on deep mud, and fired five miles into the city, but burst on the thirty-sixth round. The city held out until February, 1865, and was finally evacuated on account of Gen. Sherman's advance northward from Savannah after his March to the Sea^qv^ *(see* Carolinas, Sherman's March through the).

[John Johnson, *The Defense of Charleston Harbor; Battles and Leaders of the Civil War,* IV.]

OLIVER LYMAN SPAULDING

Charleston, Spanish Expedition against. *See* South Carolina, Spanish Expeditions against.

Charleston, W. Va., took its name from Charles Clendenin, whose son George acquired lands at the junction of the Elk and Kanawha rivers in the year 1787. Here was located Fort Lee, a refuge for wilderness settlers for a generation following the French and Indian War. Here Gen. Andrew Lewis halted his army in his march from Lewisburg to Point Pleasant^qv^ in Dunmore's War^qv^. In 1791 Daniel Boone lived in a cabin in the suburbs of the present city and represented the county in the Virginia Assembly.

Charleston was a pivotal point in the early part of the Civil War and changed hands between the Confederates and Union forces a half-dozen times.

[Phil M. Conley, *West Virginia Encyclopedia;* Roy Bird Cook, *The Annals of Fort Lee.*]

MORRIS P. SHAWKEY

Charleston and Hamburg Railroad. *See* South Carolina Railroad, The.

Charleston Gardens. The Revolutionary and Civil wars took heavy toll of the 18th- and 19th-century gardens of Charleston and the neighboring parishes. Middleton Place has the only surviving colonial garden, laid out about 1740 by Henry Middleton. Its formal terraces rise from the west bank of the Ashley River and the camellias and evergreens planted by the botanist Michaux are its special pride. Magnolia Gardens, on the Ashley, were created during the 1840's by the Rev. John Grimke Drayton. Informal in style, their charm lies in the brilliance of massed azaleas, considered the finest in the world. Cypress Gardens, near Summerville, is the outstanding 20th-century garden achievement. The winding waterways of the old Dean rice plantation are utilized as its setting.

MARGARET B. MERIWETHER

Charleston Harbor, Defense of (1776). On June 1, 1776, a British squadron, led by Sir Henry Clinton and Peter Parker, anchored off Sullivan's Island, at the entrance to Charleston Harbor, S. C. The city was held by 6000 militia, while a much smaller force, led by Col. William Moultrie, was stationed on the island. On June 28 the British tried to batter down the island fort, only to find that their shots buried themselves in the green palmetto logs of the crude fortification. After the loss of one ship, the British retired and soon sailed for New York. Thus the Carolinas averted the threatened British invasion of the South.

[Edward McCrady, *South Carolina in the Revolution.*]

HUGH T. LEFLER

Charleston Indian Trade. As the only considerable English town on the southern coast, Charleston was from the beginning in position to reap a golden harvest from the trade to the Indians in English woolens, tools, weapons and trinkets. These goods, cheaper and better than those of the Spanish and French, soon became indispensable to the Indians and made the trade not only the first road to wealth in the colony but likewise the chief means by which the Carolinians drove back the Spanish and, after 1700, competed with the French for control of the region from the Tennessee River to the Gulf.

At first the proprietors and planters contended for the trade, but by 1700 it was the Charleston merchant who financed the traders and received the profits. After the French and Indian War[qv] the growth of Savannah and the acquisition by the British of Pensacola caused the center of the Southern Indian trade to shift westward.

[V. W. Crane, *The Southern Frontier.*]

R. L. MERIWETHER

Charleston (Ill.) Riot, THE, on March 28, 1864, between soldiers on leave and Copperheads[qv], resulted in nine killed and twelve wounded. Fifteen Copperheads were held for military trial but on Lincoln's order were released to the civil authorities. Two were indicted, tried and acquitted. Others involved escaped arrest.

CHARLES H. COLEMAN

Charlestown, Mass., was founded July 4, 1629, by Thomas Graves, Rev. Francis Bright, Ralph, Richard and William Sprague and about 100 others, who preceded the Great Migration[qv]. John Winthrop's company stopped here for some time in 1630, before deciding to settle across the Charles River at Boston.[qv]

[Richard Frothingham, *History of Charlestown;* J. F. Hunnewell, *A Century of Town Life: A History of Charlestown, 1775-1887;* Justin Winsor, *Memorial History of Boston.*]

R. W. G. VAIL

Charlevoix's Journey (1721) to America was an attempt on the part of the French authorities to discover a route to the Western Sea, through the continent of North America. The regent of France, not wishing to have his purpose known, disguised the journey as a tour of inspection of the posts and missions of interior America. Charlevoix left France in July, 1720, arrived at Quebec in September, too late to join the flotillas that ascended to the "Upper Country." In May, 1721, he went around the Great Lakes, arriving in Mackinac[qv] in time to accompany the new commandant at La Baye[qv] to his post. There he conversed with Sioux Indians[qv] on their knowledge of the Western Sea. Finding it too late for an excursion into Lake Superior, Charlevoix decided to visit Louisiana[qv]. He entered Illinois[qv] by the St. Joseph-Kankakee route, and at Kaskaskia[qv] spent the winter interviewing traders from the Missouri. Thence he went down the river to New Orleans[qv] where he spent fifteen days, and continued to Biloxi[qv] where in February, 1722, he fell ill. Not being able to remount the Mississippi as he had planned, he returned to France, where he arrived in December, 1722. His recommendations to the regent resulted in a post among the Sioux, established in 1727. His experiences in America he wrote in *Journal Historique* which was published in 1744, first translated into English in 1761 and republished and edited for the Caxton Club, Chicago, 1923, by the author of this sketch.

[Louise Phelps Kellogg, *French Régime in Wisconsin and the Northwest.*]

LOUISE PHELPS KELLOGG

"Charlotina" was the name proposed for a colony, the establishment of which was suggested in a pamphlet appearing in Edinburgh in 1763, entitled *The Expediency of Securing our American Colonies by Settling the Country Adjoining the River Missisippi, and the Country upon the Ohio, Considered.* Had such a colony been erected it would have included the region lying between the Maumee, Wabash and Ohio rivers, the upper Mississippi and the Great Lakes.

[C. W. Alvord and C. E. Carter, *The Critical Period, 1763-1765.*]

WAYNE E. STEVENS

Charlotte, Fort, was the name given to the French Fort Condé at Mobile[qv] when the English took over the town at the close of the French and Indian War[qv] in 1763. Fort Charlotte was captured by the Spaniards in March, 1780, and was held by them until United States troops under Gen. Wilkinson took possession in April, 1813 (*see* Mobile Seized). After the purchase of Florida by the United States in 1819 (*see* Adams-Onís Treaty), Fort Charlotte was of no further importance and was gradually demolished.

[P. J. Hamilton, *Colonial Mobile.*]

R. S. COTTERILL

Charlotte, The Treaty of Camp (October, 1774), ended Dunmore's War[qv] with the Shawnee[qv]. The site was on Pickaway plains, Pickaway County, Ohio; Dunmore marked the name with red chalk on a peeled oak. Here Chief Cornstalk, defeated by Col. Andrew Lewis at Point Pleasant[qv], made a treaty, agreeing that the tribe would give up all prisoners, would not hunt south of the Ohio, and would obey trade regulations of the British government.

[Ohio Archeological and Historical Society *Publications*, XXXVII, 1928.]

LOUISE PHELPS KELLOGG

Charter Colonies were promoted through private enterprise under charters from the crown. They were founded by trading companies, by lords proprietors and by squatters later incorporated. Colonies of the first type for the most part either disappeared or changed their status early. The Virginia Company[qv] lost its charter in 1624, the New England Council[qv] surrendered its patent in 1635, the Providence Island colony[qv] was conquered by Spain in 1641 and the Massachusetts Bay Company[qv] became a theocracy, leaving the Bermuda Company as the only one of its kind in control of a colony through the greater part of the 17th century. Connecticut and Rhode Island[qqv], founded as squatter colonies by dissenters from Puritan Massachusetts, received charters of incorporation early in the Restoration Period. The predominating type throughout the 17th century was the proprietary colony. Of this sort was Carlisle's Caribbean grant, Maryland and Maine, in the early part of the century, and after 1660 the Carolinas, New York, the Jerseys, the Bahamas and Pennsylvania.

Similar institutions of government developed in all of the charter colonies. All ultimately had governor, council and house of representatives, the two former chosen by company or lord proprietor, and in the corporation colonies, indirectly by the people. The house of representatives, first the voluntary concession of the trading company, as in Virginia and Bermuda, later became a generally accepted institution in all chartered colonies except New York. Government in the corporation colonies was the freest from outside control. Perhaps because they were settled without the mediation of trading company or proprietor, the inhabitants of those colonies from the beginning cherished a conception of government based on sovereignty of the people.

When the restoration English government turned its attention to the building of a colonial policy, it found charters obstacles in the path. Several colonies were royalized, and, with the view of ultimate consolidation of all colonial possessions into a few large units, the Dominion of New England[qv] was established. Its failure brought temporary reaction in favor of charter colonies, but throughout the 18th century the process of royalization went on until by 1776 only two proprieties, Maryland and Pennsylvania, and two corporation colonies, Connecticut and Rhode Island, remained. Except in the corporation colonies the people seem to have preferred royal rule.

[C. M. Andrews, *Colonial Period of American History.*]

VIOLA F. BARNES

Charter Oak, THE. *See* Connecticut: Charter of 1662.

Charter of Liberties (1683), drafted by New York's first assembly, was approved by James Duke of York as an instrument of government for his province. Recalling the rights of Englishmen and the principles of the great liberty documents, this charter described the framework of government, the functions of governor, council and a legislative assembly representative of the qualified freeholders, and guaranteed the freedom of the assembly, which was to meet at least once in three years, trial by jury, due course of law in all proceedings, protection of the property of women, freedom from feudal exactions, exemption from quartering of soldiers and especially religious toleration for all Christians.

[J. R. Brodhead, *History of the State of New York.*]

RICHARD J. PURCELL

Charter of Privileges, granted by William Penn to Pennsylvania, Oct. 28, 1701, guaranteed freedom of worship to all who professed faith in "*One* almighty God." All who believed in Jesus Christ were eligible to office. A unicameral legislature was established and the Council ceased to be a representative body.

[W. R. Shepherd, *History of Proprietary Government in Pennsylvania;* J. Paul Selsam, *The Pennsylvania Constitution of 1776.*]

J. PAUL SELSAM

Chartered Companies played an important part in colonization in the New World, though they did not originate for that purpose. The joint-stock company was already in existence in many countries in the 16th century as an effective means of carrying on foreign trade and when the New World attracted the interest of merchants, companies were formed for purposes of trade in that direction. Since production of certain desired articles required the transportation of laborers, colonization became a by-product of the trading company[qv]. The first English company to undertake successful colonization was the Virginia Company[qv], first chartered in 1606 and, through two sub-companies, authorized to operate on the Atlantic coast between 34° and 45° N. Lat. By later charters in 1609 and 1612 to the London branch of the Virginia Company, and in 1620 to the Council for New England[qv], the successor to the Plymouth branch, the original project was somewhat enlarged and developed more in detail. Down to the Puritan Revolution this method of sponsoring colonization predominated. The Newfoundland Company of 1610, the Bermuda Company of 1615, an enlargement of an earlier project under the auspices of the Virginia Company, the Massachusetts Bay Company*qv* of 1629 and the Providence Island Company*qv* of 1630 represent the most important attempts at trade and colonization. After the Puritan Revolution, the Lord Proprietor superseded the trading company as preferred sponsor of colonization, both king and colonists becoming increasingly distrustful of corporations. Massachusetts and Bermuda, the last of the companies in control of colonization, lost their charters in 1684, but the former had long since ceased to be commercial in character.

[C. M. Andrews, *The Colonial Period of American History*, I; H. L. Osgood, *The American Colonies in the Seventeenth Century*.]

VIOLA F. BARNES

Charters, Municipal, are legal constitutions which incorporate communities, set up organs of government, distribute powers, create rights and obligations. American city charters reflect theories prevalent in four distinct historical periods—namely the Colonial, Post-Revolution, Post-Civil War and Twentieth-Century eras.

Early American charters followed their English prototype. Prior to 1688 borough charters were granted by the king through the royal governors and proprietors. Between 1688 and 1776, the British Parliament and the colonial assemblies*qv* gained the power of amendment at the expense of the king.

Immediately after the Revolution, American municipal charters began to depart from their English pattern. State legislatures replaced the king as the charter-granting agency. Thus to this day American cities are creatures of their respective states. Checks and balances, separation of powers*qv* became the theory of municipal as well as of state and Federal governments. Post-Revolution charters were characterized by elected mayors, bicameral councils, popularly elected judiciaries, extended franchise, short terms, rotation in office and low salaries.

Following the Civil War, municipal charters reached their lowest point of efficiency. Responsibility was divided among numerous unco-ordinated administrative heads. Powers of mayors were curtailed while powers of councils were unduly inflated.

Reaction resulted in fundamental reforms in 20th-century charters. Home Rule*qv* which had been granted by Missouri to its cities as early as 1875 was taken up by other states. Civil Service*qv* became an integral part of the administrative structure. Executive powers again expanded. Councilmanic power decreased. Bicameral councils gave way to unicameral bodies. Centralization of power and responsibility became the accepted theory. Longer terms and better salaries were provided. The initiative, referendum and recall*qqv* were added.

Contemporary municipal charters are divided into mayor-council, commission*qv* and city-manager*qv* types. The majority of American cities are still operating under the old mayor-council system, while approximately 400 cities have commission charters and 450 have city-manager charters.

[National Municipal League, *A Model City Charter;* Joseph D. McGoldrick, *The Law and Practice of Municipal Home Rule, 1916-1930.*]

FRANCES L. REINHOLD

Chartres, Fort de (1719–72), seat of civil and military government in the Illinois country*qv* for more than half a century, stood near the present village of Prairie du Rocher in Randolph County, Ill. Named in honor of the son of the Regent of France, it was commenced in 1719 and completed the following year. Built of wood, and exposed to the flood waters of the Mississippi, the fort quickly fell into disrepair. In 1727 it was rebuilt, but by 1732 it was so dilapidated that St. Ange, the commandant, built a new fort with the same name at some distance from the river. By 1747, when a general Indian uprising seemed imminent, this too had fallen into such bad condition that repair was considered impossible and the garrison was withdrawn to Kaskaskia*qv*.

In 1751 the French government decided to build a new fort at Kaskaskia, but the engineer in charge, Jean Baptiste Saucier, decided on a location near the old fort. Foundations were laid in 1753; three years later the structure was substantially finished. Costing 200,000 livres, the new Fort de Chartres was an irregular quadrangle with sides 490 ft. long and stone walls 2 ft. 2 in. thick. Ten years after its completion a competent English officer described it as "the most commodious and best built fort in North America." It was capable of housing 400 men, although its garrison rarely exceeded half that number.

Fort de Chartres, transferred to the British on Oct. 10, 1765, was the last French post in North America to be surrendered under the Treaty of Paris*qv*. Renamed Fort Cavendish, it was the seat of British rule in the Illinois country until 1772 when it was abandoned and destroyed.

[C. W. Alvord, *The Illinois Country, 1673-1818.*]

PAUL M. ANGLE

Chartres, Fort de, Treaty (1766), is the name given to an agreement made by George Croghan, deputy superintendent of Indian affairs, with the Western Indians, by which the Indians acknowledged the authority of the king of England, and agreed to return prisoners and stolen horses and to permit the establishment of trading posts. The conference was held at Fort de Chartres*qv*, beginning on Aug. 25, 1766. Twenty-two tribes, including the Kaskaskia, Piankashaw, Kickapoo, Miami, Sacs and Foxes*qqv*, were present; later three other tribes adhered to the pact. The peace established at this conference lasted for the duration of British rule in the Illinois country.

[A. T. Volwiler, *Croghan and the Westward Movement.*]

PAUL M. ANGLE

Chase Impeachment Trial, The (June 2–March 1, 1805), was generally considered as part of a concerted Republican (Jeffersonian)*qv* effort to curb the power of the Federal bench. Justice Chase, an arbitrary personage with an abusive tongue and an unswerving confidence in the righteousness of the Federalist party*qv* which had elevated him to the bench was charged in the articles of impeachment with unbecoming conduct and disregard of law. The outcome of the trial before the Senate hinged largely on the question whether his conduct, admittedly objectionable, constituted "a high crime or misdemeanor." His acquittal, March 1, 1805, was probably a distinct gain for judicial independence.

[Charles Warren, *The Supreme Court in United States History.*]

W. A. ROBINSON

Château-Thierry Bridge, Americans at. Having broken the French front on the Aisne*qv*, the Germans entered Château-Thierry on May 31, 1918. Gen. Foch, rushing troops to stop them, sent the American 3rd Division (Dickman) to the region of Château-Thierry, where, aided by French Colonials, the Americans prevented the enemy from crossing on May 31 and June 1. The German attacks then ceased.

[De Chambrun and De Marenches, *The American Army in the European Conflict;* J. M. Hanson, History of the American Combat Divisions, in *The Stars and Stripes.*]

JOSEPH MILLS HANSON

Chateaugay (Canada), Battle of (Oct. 25, 1813). During the autumn of 1813, Maj. Gen. Wade Hampton advanced along the Chateaugay River into Canada with over 4000 troops. On Oct. 22 he halted about fifteen miles from the St. Lawrence. Here, three days later, he attempted to dislodge 800 hostile troops barring his farther progress. In this engagement the British suffered only twenty-five casualties, the Americans double this number. Hampton retired to United States territory.

[Henry Adams, *History of the United States,* Vol. VII.]

JAMES RIPLEY JACOBS

Chattanooga Campaign (Oct.–Nov., 1863). Before the battle of Chickamauga*qv* the Union troops under Grant, released by the capture of Vicksburg*qv*, had begun to move eastward. Bragg (C.) had failed to follow through after Chickamauga. All he could do was to "besiege" Rosecrans' (U.) army in Chattanooga. Grant, placed in general command of all Union forces in the West, replaced Rosecrans by Thomas and instructed him to hold Chattanooga "at all hazards." Food was running short and supply lines were constantly interrupted. Grant's first act was to open a new and protected line of supply, via Brown's Ferry*qv*. Re-enforcements arrived. Vigorous action turned the tables on Bragg, whose only act was to weaken himself unnecessarily by detaching Longstreet (C.) on a fruitless expedition to capture Knoxville*qv*. Bragg then awaited Grant's next move. President Davis (C.) visited the army and tried, unsuccessfully, to restore confidence.

On Nov. 24, 1863, Hooker (U.) captured Lookout Mountain*qv* on the left of Bragg's line. The next day Grant attacked all along the line. The Confederate center on Missionary Ridge*qv* gave way; the left had retreated; only the right held firm and covered the retreat southward into northern Georgia. A brilliant rear-guard stand at Ringgold Gap*qv* halted Grant's pursuit. The Union troops returned to Chattanooga; the Confederate Army went into winter quarters at Dalton, Ga.

[*Battles and Leaders of the Civil War,* Vol. III.]

THOMAS ROBSON HAY

Chautauqua Movement, The, had its beginning in an assembly held at Chautauqua, on the shore of Lake Chautauqua, N. Y., Aug. 4–18, 1874. Here John H. Vincent, a Methodist clergyman of New York, later Bishop, and Lewis Miller of Akron, Ohio, who were interested in developing Sunday schools*qv*, planned a course of meetings to give instruction in Sunday-school organization, management and teaching, and study of the Bible. They also arranged to include some recreation and a few lectures not actually relating to Sunday schools. The visitors were at first housed in a sort of camp, which rapidly grew into a permanent summer colony. In 1876 the session was lengthened to three weeks and later, with the introduction of new subjects, it extended to two months. In 1878 the Literary and Scientific Circle (home-study courses) was launched, and 7000 persons took this work in the first year. At times in after years as many as 25,000 were enrolled at once. At the assembly grounds in 1879 a school for teachers in secular subjects was opened, also a school of languages, later known as the College of Liberal Arts. Other developments, year after year, were Schools of Mathematics and Sciences, of Library Training, Domestic Science, Music, Arts and Crafts, Expression, Physical Education, Practical Arts and —in co-operation with Cornell University in 1912—Agriculture. The growth of the institution was rapid. Although founded by Methodists, many churches were represented at the first gathering and there was never any disposition to make the teaching of religious subjects denominational. One after another there came to be built on the grounds lecture halls with seating capacities of from 200 to 5000, a theater, clubhouses, gymnasiums, a memorial church, memorial library, a colonial market place, etc. Between 1924 and 1932 (when the attendance fell off considerably because of the industrial depression) about 45,000 persons attended the general assembly each season. A magazine, the *Chautauquan,* was published from 1880 to 1914.

Hundreds of local assemblies appeared within two or three decades in the United States and Canada, imitating in a limited degree the Chautauqua plan and often calling themselves "Chautauquas." At least two of these, the Catholic Summer School at Lake Champlain and the Jewish Chautauqua Society at Atlantic City, N. J., have been permanent and extensive in their programs. Shortly after 1900 the traveling Chautauqua appeared—promoted by a lecture bureau, moving from town to town, giving a week or more of lectures, concerts and recitals, from two to three programs a day, usually in a large tent. This had a considerable popularity for more than a decade.

[John H. Vincent, *The Chautauqua Movement;* J. L. Hurlburt, *The Story of Chautauqua;* J. S. Noffsinger, *Correspondence Schools, Lyceums, Chautauquas.*]

ALVIN F. HARLOW

Check Currency is the term applied to bank deposits subject to check. Although checks were used in making payments in New York and other large cities for years before the Civil War, extending back as far as the beginning of the 19th century, it is only since the Civil War that the widespread use of check currency in all parts of the United States has had its major development. Various estimates indicate that since 1900 from 85% to 90% of all payments in the United States are made by check.

[D. Kinley, *The Use of Credit Instruments in Payments in the United States.*]

FREDERICK A. BRADFORD

Checkoff, THE, is a system under which the employer by agreement with a union deducts union dues and assessments from the pay of union members. Funds thus collected are turned over to union officials. Coal mining provided the background of the checkoff. Deductions from the pay of the miner for advances by the employer of powder, tools, supplies, etc., were a regular feature of the industry from the outset. Such a practice readily lent itself to the union insistence on the checkoff. The practice had undoubtedly appeared earlier, but the United Mine Workers[qv] organized in 1890 sponsored the checkoff on a nationwide basis. In the unionized bituminous[qv] areas the demand was generally gained. The anthracite[qv] industry resisted the checkoff successfully until the 1937 agreement with the United Mine Workers. The checkoff has appeared in other industries, notably among the hosiery workers, but on nothing like so extensive a scale as in mining. The checkoff is frequently coupled with a demand for the closed shop[qv]. Its advantages to the union are the automatic collection of dues from the members and the enforcement of the closed-shop policy. Employers have usually resisted the demand for the checkoff. Fragmentary evidence would indicate further extension of the checkoff system since 1933.

[*Monthly Labor Review,* January, 1930; A. Haring, *The Checkoff in the American Coal Industry,* an unpublished dissertation available at the Yale University Library.]

HERBERT MAYNARD DIAMOND

Checks and Balances is the term used to denote the "separation of powers"[qv] of government that was the underlying principle upon which the Government of the United States was created by the Convention of 1787[qv]. This theory became popular in America in large part due to the writings of Montesquieu and William Blackstone. It consists in setting off legislative and executive departments from each other and the courts against both. Each department of government is supposed to operate as far as possible within a separate sphere of administration, but the co-operation of all three is necessary for the conduct of the government.

The makers of our Constitution were aware of the weakness of the Continental government under the Articles of Confederation[qv]. This consisted in the complete conduct of the government by the Continental Congress^{qv} with practically no executive or judicial departments. For this reason the office of President of the United States was created and largely modeled upon the kingship of Great Britain. In order to prevent executive aggression, such as had caused the misgovernment of George III, the system of checks and balances was introduced and also provision was made for a Federal judiciary[qv]. Furthermore it was provided that the Senate and House of Representatives should act as checks upon each other in the national Congress[qv].

[W. Wilson, *Constitutional Government in the United States.*]

WILLIAM STARR MYERS

Chemical Warfare. Before the World War, suffocating gases were used but these were nonlethal. On April 22, 1915, where the French and British lines joined in the Ypres salient, the Germans, waiting until wind conditions were favorable, launched a chlorine gas attack which inflicted fearful casualties. Dec. 19, 1915, they attacked again, this time with phosgene. These offensives were made by lining up cylinders on the battle front and releasing therefrom gas to be carried by the wind to the enemy. Should the wind change, the attacker suffered from his own weapon. In 1916 this form of gas attack gave way to the use of artillery shell filled with gas agents. In 1917 and 1918 British methods still further modified gas warfare by the introduction of the Livens projector and the Stokes mortar.

Aug. 17, 1917, Gen. Pershing requested authority to make Lt. Col. Amos A. Fries Chief of Gas Service in the American Expeditionary Forces[qv]. This was done five days later and Fries began the work which later became our Chemical Warfare Service abroad. The duties of this service were chemical research, development and manufacture; filling of shell and other containers with poisonous gases, smoke and incendiary materials; purchase and development of gas masks and other protective materials; supply of chemical agents in the field; training army personnel in chemical warfare duties, offensive and defensive; organizing, equipping and operating special gas troops. Schools were established in France at Langres and at Hanlon.

In America a Chemical Service Station was authorized Oct. 16, 1917. By May 11, 1918, the date when Maj. Gen. William L. Sibert was appointed Director of Chemical Warfare Service, with Fries in charge overseas, a condition had arisen wherein the Medical Corps directed gas defense production; the Ordnance Department, certain other defense functions; the Signal Corps controlled alarm devices; the Engineers had the "Gas and Flame" regiment; and the Bureau of Mines directed the Research Section. Sibert's appointment coalesced and co-ordinated activities at home and abroad and the 30th Engineers, a six-company regiment, became our First Gas Regiment. Edgewood Arsenal, originally known as Gunpowder Neck, Maryland, became the center of our chemical warfare production at home, and continues today as the center of such production, training and experimentation.

Abroad, the First Gas Regiment, which took part in every big battle from the second Marne to the Armistice[qv], was subsequently expanded into an 18-company organization; and two additional, similarly constituted, chemical warfare regiments were authorized to be formed. The signing of the Armistice precluded this action.

[Official Cablegrams exchanged between War Department and the American Expeditionary Forces; General Orders of the War Department and of the A. E. F.; Brig. Gen. Amos A. Fries, *Gas in Attack and Gas in Defense;* Brig. Gen. Amos A. Fries and Maj. Clarence J. West, *Chemical Warfare;* Col. Harry L. Gilchrist, *A Comparative Study of World War Casualties from Gas and other Weapons;* James T. Addison, *The Story of the First Gas Regiment; A History of DuPont Company's Relations with the United States Government* prepared by that company; Maj. S. J. M. Auld, *Gas and Flame.*]

ROBERT S. THOMAS

Chemistry, Industrial. The manufacture of tar, potash and glass was attempted in Virginia in 1608 and leather, salt and iron were made there on a small scale in 1620. All these enterprises were wiped out in the Great Massacre of 1622[qv]. Salt[qv] making began in the Plymouth colony the next year; but the projects of John Winthrop, Jr., in Massachusetts, beginning in 1633, are generally regarded as the initiation of industrial chemistry in America. It has kept pace with the growth of the nation and has utilized a vast store of natural resources. The production of sugar, fertilizers, iron, paints, the vulcanization of rubber and many other important advances mark its course. The history of American manufactures throughout the 19th century is closely related to this development.

The inorganic chemical industry had become well established before 1900 and developed rapidly thereafter. The 20th century witnessed the beginning of the synthetic organic chemical industry in this country. Both phases of chemical development have grown to great proportions, assuming world leadership in many specialties. In 1900 came the contact process for sulfuric acid and the production of carbon disulfide by an electric process. The commercial expansion of chlorine began in 1901, since when this basic chemical has enjoyed a great ascendancy with the development of chlorinated products and its wider use in bleaching and in public health. The first patent for synthetic resins, Bakelite, was issued in 1907. The industry has expanded enormously and developed hundreds of new types from a great range of raw materials. Carbon black, an important substance in tire compounding, was introduced in 1915; accelerators for vulcanization in 1906; and rubber[qv] antioxidants in 1925. The direct use of rubber latex began in 1921, electrodeposition of rubber in 1927 and the use of rayon[qv] cord in tire construction in 1937. In 1922 ethylene glycol came on the market and America began to synthesize ammonia by the fixation of atmospheric nitrogen, to be followed later by synthetic sodium nitrate[qv] capable of competing with Chilean nitrate in the world market. Nineteen nineteen was marked by the production of butanol and acetone by fermentation, leading later to the development of the first of the lacquers of the Duco type and producing something of a revolution in the protective coating industry. Chromium plating and solid carbon dioxide, introduced under the name of "dry ice," came in 1925 (*see* Refrigeration); the development of a quick freezing process for the preservation of foods in 1926; safety glass in 1927 and synthetic phenol and aniline in 1928. The hydrogenation of petroleum was begun in 1929; the polymerization of refinery gases to produce high antiknock gasolines in 1936; isooctane fuel, especially for aviation[qv], became commercial in 1934; solvent refining of lubricating oil in 1933; the Dowell process for increasing the production of old oil wells by the use of corrosion-inhibited acid in 1932; and tetraethyl lead, the well-known antiknock reagent, in 1922.

Dichlorodifluoro methane, a nontoxic, nonflammable refrigerant, was made in 1930. Alphacellulose of high purity was produced from wood pulp[qv] in 1927; camphor was synthesized from turpentine in 1933; bromine was separated from sea water on a commercial scale in 1934; and kodachrome for amateur motion pictures[qv] was introduced in 1935. Vitamin B_1 was synthesized in 1936. Other vitamins have been crystallized by American workers and hormones have been synthesized. The outstanding industrial development of 1938 was Nylon, the first truly synthetic fiber. First used commercially in bristles for tooth brushes, it promises to become of the utmost importance in the textile[qv] field, since it surpasses natural silk in important characteristics.

The chemical industry has served agriculture by supplying fertilizers[qv], insecticides and fungicides, methods of food processing and industrial outlets for such products as starch, cellulose and building boards such as Celotex. Manufacturing has been aided by such things as alloys, dyes, acids, alkalies and many specialties. Chemistry has supplied to buildings an unending variety of new materials, colors and shapes. Public health has benefited by disinfectants, germicides and bactericides, as well as by pharmacy and medicinal chemistry.

[E. E. Slosson, *Creative Chemistry;* H. E. Howe, ed., *Chemistry in Industry;* H. E. Howe, *Chemistry in the World's Work.*]

H. E. HOWE

Chequamegon Bay, on the southern coast of Lake Superior, is noted as the site of the first dwelling occupied by white men in what is now Wisconsin. The French traders, Groseilliers and Radisson[qv], built a hut somewhere on the west shore of the bay, probably in 1658. Other traders dwelt on this bay 1660–63 and were visited in the spring of 1661 by Father Ménard, first missionary to the Northwest. In 1665 Father Claude Allouez built a mission house near the southwest end of the bay. There his successor, Father Jacques Marquette[qv], came in 1669 and remained for two years.

In 1693 the largest island, now known as Madeline, at the mouth of the bay, was occupied by a fort built by Pierre LeSueur. This was abandoned before the close of the century. In 1718 a French fort was built on the island, where Louis Denis de la Ronde had an establishment for fur trading and exploration for copper mines. The post was called La Pointe, and a French garrison was maintained there until 1759. The first English trader to reach this distant post was Alexander Henry, whose French partner, Jean Baptiste Cadotte, founded a permanent trading post at this place. In 1818 two Massachusetts traders, Lyman and Truman Warren, came thither, married daughters of Michel Cadotte and became the leading fur traders of the region. Truman Warren died early; Lyman maintained his home at La Pointe until his death in 1847. A village of retired *voyageurs* and fur traders grew up here during the early 19th century and the American Fur Company[qv] had a post here for many years. The first Protestant mission was begun here in 1831.

[L. P. Kellogg, *French Régime in Wisconsin and the Northwest;* R. G. Thwaites, The Story of Chequamegon Bay, in *Wisconsin Historical Collections*, VIII.]

LOUISE PHELPS KELLOGG

Cherokee, THE, at the beginning of the 18th century, occupied or claimed all that region south of the Ohio and west of the Great Kanawha rivers, extending as far as the northern parts of South Carolina, Georgia and Alabama. DeSoto's[qv] march in 1540 gave them their first contact with white men. During the last quarter of the 17th century, first the Virginians and then the South Carolinians established commercial relations with them, and by 1700 French traders had come in. In 1730 Sir Alexander Cuming allied them to the British in a treaty and sealed it by taking a group of chiefs on a visit to England. In 1757 the British built for the Cherokees Fort Loudoun[qv] on the Tennessee River. During the French and Indian War[qv] the Cherokees remained true to their alliance, until near the end when trouble broke out which resulted in a fierce war lasting for two years (1760–61), in which the Cherokees captured Fort Loudoun and massacred many of the prisoners. During the Revolution they took up hostilities against the Americans, and for some years thereafter bloody encounters continued (*see* Cherokee Wars).

Beginning in 1721 the whites gradually whittled away by treaties the Cherokee country until, by 1819, the Indians were reduced to a small fragment of their former domain, most of which now lay in Georgia, but with small areas in North Carolina, Tennessee and Alabama. The Cherokees now determined to stand on their treaty rights and cede no more land. Under the tutelage of missionaries from New England and by the aid of the Federal Government they had already begun to take on much of the civilization of the white man, and in 1827 they organized a government with a written constitution. With an alphabet which Sequoyah[qv] devised, they published a newspaper, the *Cherokee Phoenix*, and issued from their printing press at New Echota many pamphlets. Unable to tolerate the organization of a nation within her borders, Georgia demanded the Cherokee country and the removal of the Indians to the reservations beyond the Mississippi. A bitter legal fight took place between Georgia and the Cherokees aided by the United States Supreme Court in two decisions, Cherokee Nation v. Georgia and Worcester v. Georgia[qqv], both of which the state ignored. With President Andrew Jackson sympathizing with Georgia, a treaty of cession was made in 1835 (*see* New Echota, Treaty of) and within the next three years all the Cherokees with the exception of a few in North Carolina were removed to the Indian Territory[qv].

[C. C. Royce, The Cherokee Nation of Indians, in *Fifth Annual Report of the Bureau of Ethnology to the Secretary of the Smithsonian Institution, 1883-84;* J. P. Brown, *Old Frontiers;* V. W. Crane, *The Southern Frontier, 1670-1732;* G. Foreman, *Indian Removal;* U. B. Phillips, *Georgia and State Rights.*]

E. MERTON COULTER

Cherokee Nation v. Georgia (5 Peters 1). In 1791 the Cherokee[qv] made a treaty of cession with the United States (*see* Holston Treaty) wherein they were guaranteed the remainder of their territory. When Georgia, in 1802, ceded her western lands to the Federal Government (*see* Georgia Compact, The) she received the promise that all Indians should be removed from her limits as soon as it could be done peaceably and on reasonable terms. Embittered by the failure of the Government to effect removal and by the organization of an independent Cherokee government within her borders, Georgia in 1828 and 1829 extended her laws over the Indians and began to occupy their territory. The Cherokees could get no protection from President Jackson (*see* Indian Removals) and therefore appealed to the Supreme Court, filing an original bill (Dec. 12, 1830) for an injunction restraining Georgia from interfering with the Cherokees or enforcing her laws within the Cherokee Nation. Georgia refused to defend the suit. The sympathies of the Court were with the Cherokees, but the majority opinion was that since the Cherokees were not citizens of the United States, nor, as contended by them, a foreign nation, they were not competent to appear as a party to a suit in the Supreme Court. (*See also* Worcester v. Georgia.)

[U. B. Phillips, *Georgia and State Rights;* Charles Warren, *The Supreme Court in the United States.*]

E. MERTON COULTER

Cherokee River, THE, was the early name for the Tennessee, so called because it ran through the Cherokee Indian[qv] country.

[James Adair, *History of the American Indians.*]

E. MERTON COULTER

Cherokee Strip, THE, is a term improperly applied to an area officially designated as "a perpetual outlet, West." Both the terms "Strip" and "Outlet" are used. Guaranteed to the Cherokee Indians[qv] by treaties of 1828 and 1833 as an outlet, it was not to be occupied for homes.

The area comprises about 12,000 square miles, and lies between 96° and 100° W. Long., and 36° and 37° N. Lat. The Treaty of 1866 compelled the Cherokee Nation to sell portions to friendly Indians.

The Strip was leased by the Cherokee Nation in 1883 to the Cherokee Strip Livestock Association for five years at $100,000 a year; the lease was renewed, but was terminated before expiration by the United States. In 1891 the United States purchased the Cherokee Strip for $8,595,736.12. Opened by a "run" on Sept. 16, 1893, it became part of the Territory of Oklahoma^qv^.

[George Rainey, *The Cherokee Strip.*]

M. L. WARDELL

Cherokee Trail, THE, sometimes called the "Trappers' Trail," was laid out and marked in the summer of 1848 by Lt. Abraham Buford in command of Company H of the First Dragoons, though it had previously been followed by trappers en route to the Rocky Mountains. It extended from the vicinity of Fort Gibson^qv^ up the Arkansas River to the mouth of the Cimarron and up the latter stream to a point in the northwestern part of what is now Oklahoma. From here it ran west to the Santa Fé Trail^qv^, which it joined at Middle Cimarron Spring. It was followed by numerous Cherokees^qv^ and many whites from northeastern Arkansas on their way to the gold fields of California^qv^.

[Ralph P. Bieber, ed., *Southern Trails to California*, Southwest Historical Series, Vol. V.]

EDWARD EVERETT DALE

Cherokee Wars, THE (1776–81). In April, 1776, commissioners of the Continental Congress^qv^ held a conference with the Cherokee^qv^ at Fort Charlotte with the purpose of conciliating the tribe, restless because of continued encroachment on its lands. Notwithstanding this, the Cherokee, disregarding the advice of the British agents among them, and yielding to the incitement of Shawnee^qv^ and other northern Indians, attacked the frontiers of Georgia and the Carolinas. Their most ambitious attacks—against Watauga and the upper Holston settlements^qqv^—were beaten off, and in return, South Carolina, aided by Congress, arranged for retaliatory expeditions converging from Georgia, the Carolinas and Virginia. Against these the Cherokee, dispirited because of the refusal of the Creeks^qv^ to aid them, offered little resistance; practically all their towns were destroyed, several hundred of them forced to find refuge in Florida, and the tribe purchased peace from the four states in treaties of June and July, 1777, only by extensive land cessions in the two Carolinas.

From 1776 to 1781 Cherokee affairs were under the supervision of North Carolina and Virginia, each of which appointed a Cherokee agent. James Robertson, the Carolina agent, resided at Echota^qv^, the Cherokee "capital," and exerted sufficient influence to keep the Cherokee at peace, except a disgruntled element which had built new towns down the Tennessee on Chickamauga Creek where the British agents established their headquarters. The Chickamauga^qv^, aided by some of the Creek towns, constantly raided the frontiers and in 1779 entered into an alliance with the northern Indians to aid Lt. Gov. Henry Hamilton in his campaign against George Rogers Clark. At Clark's suggestion a company of Virginia militia moving down the Tennessee to Illinois stopped off at Chickamauga Creek and, with the aid of Watauga forces, destroyed the Indian towns and carried off great quantities of supplies gathered there by the British. The towns were rebuilt and the Indian attacks continued, with the result that in the fall of 1779 another joint expedition from Virginia and North Carolina repeated the destruction of the preceding spring.

In the fall of 1779 Robertson left Echota for the new settlement Henderson was establishing on the Cumberland^qv^ and, with his influence withdrawn, the Overhill Cherokee relapsed into hostility, joining the Chickamauga and the Creeks in co-operating with Gen. Cornwallis and Maj. Patrick Ferguson by attacking the frontier. Joseph Martin, the Virginia agent, was unable to keep the Indians quiet, and again Virginia and North Carolina had recourse to a joint expedition, following the battle of King's Mountain^qv^. The devastation this time was as complete as in 1776. In the spring of 1781 Gen. Greene, now Federal Indian superintendent in the South, appointed commissioners to make peace with the Cherokee, which was done in April. This treaty, confirming the land cessions made at the treaties of DeWitt's Corner and Long Island in 1777, was thereafter steadily adhered to by all the Cherokee except the Chickamauga. Against the latter John Sevier led constant expeditions in 1781 and 1782 with the result that they moved farther down the Tennessee, where they built their Five Lower Towns and continued their hostility

[A. V. Goodpasture, Indian Wars and Warriors of the Old Southwest, in the *Tennessee Historical Magazine*, Vol. IV, March, 1918; W. H. Mohr, *Federal Indian Relations, 1774-1788;* H. L. Shaw, *British Administration of the Southern Indians, 1756-1783.*]

R. S. COTTERILL

Cherry Valley Massacre, THE (Nov. 11, 1778), in which Butler's Rangers^qv^, with Indians under Brant, attacked this important outpost in the upper Susquehanna Valley, was marked by special Indian savagery in retaliation for their losses at Oriskany^qv^. Whole families were surprised in their homes. A few escaped, thirty were killed, while seventy-one, taken prisoners, were mostly released next day. All the buildings were burned and cattle taken. Sixteen soldiers were killed but the remainder held the fort and cared for the returning refugees.

This massacre directly determined the Sullivan expedition[qv] against the Iroquois (1779).

[F. W. Halsey, *The Old New York Frontier;* Howard Swiggett, *War out of Niagara.*] FRANCES DORRANCE

Chesapeake and Delaware Canal. As early as 1764 a survey was made for a canal route between Chesapeake and Delaware bays. A company was organized in 1803, but languished and was not revived until 1822. The canal, 13⅝ miles long, with three locks, was finally built 1825–29. It had cost $165,000 per mile, making it the most expensive waterway of its time. A cut ninety feet deep through earth and stone was the heaviest engineering project yet undertaken in America. In 1919 the Government purchased it and made it into a sea-level ship canal.

[Alvin F. Harlow, *Old Towpaths.*]

ALVIN F. HARLOW

Chesapeake and Ohio Canal, THE, popularly known as "the Old Ditch," was a joint project of the United States, Maryland and Virginia. It was the legal successor of the Potomac Company[qv] in the attempt to connect the Chesapeake Bay with the Ohio River by a system of water transportation. The plan was to construct a series of locks and canals around the rapids and falls of the Potomac from Georgetown to Cumberland. From there the Ohio was to be reached at one of its tributaries, the Youghiogheny. Ground was first broken on July 4, 1828, and the canal was completed to Cumberland by 1850. Funds were contributed principally by Maryland, the terminal cities and the United States. The fifty shares of stock in the Potomac Company which George Washington had donated to a proposed National University[qv] were also invested and lost, for the corporation was not successful in reaching the Ohio. It failed on account of the inherent difficulty of the task, and because of competition from the Baltimore and Ohio Railroad[qv], which reached Wheeling about 1852. Continuing as a local enterprise on the Potomac River, it was placed (1889) in the hands of receivers, who still operate it.

[George W. Ward, *The Early Development of the Chesapeake and Ohio Canal Project.*]

LEONARD C. HELDERMAN

Chesapeake Capes, Battle of (1781). A naval engagement, Sept. 5–9, which led to the surrender of Cornwallis at Yorktown[qv]. When a British fleet of nineteen ships arrived at the entrance of the Chesapeake with reinforcements for Cornwallis, it found a French fleet of twenty-four ships, under DeGrasse, already there. The battle was fought on an easterly course in converging lines. The British lost one ship and had several badly damaged; as a result they could not attack again and Barras' French squadron of eight ships, transporting siege guns from Newport for the attack on Yorktown, was enabled to enter the Capes. The British fleet returned to New York and Cornwallis was trapped.

[A. T. Mahan, *Major Operations of the Navies in the War of American Independence.*]

WALTER B. NORRIS

***Chesapeake* Captured by *Shannon*.** On June 1, 1813, the United States frigate *Chesapeake,* 38 guns, Capt. James Lawrence, with an untrained crew sailed out of Boston on a cruise. At 5:45 P.M. she met H. B. M. frigate *Shannon,* 38 guns, 330 highly trained men, Capt. Philip Vere Broke commanding. In the opening maneuvers, Lawrence lost an opportunity to rake his enemy and exposed his own ship to a terrible bombardment at pistol range. By 5:55 all the American officers were killed or wounded and the crew was in a panic. Lawrence, dying, gave his last order "Don't give up the ship."[qv] Leading his crew personally Broke boarded, and at 6:05 had taken the *Chesapeake.*

[Theodore Roosevelt, *Naval War of 1812.*]

MARION V. BREWINGTON

***Chesapeake–Leopard* Incident** (1807). On June 22, off Hampton Roads, the American frigate *Chesapeake* was stopped by the British ship *Leopard,* whose commander demanded the surrender of four seamen, claiming them to be deserters from the British ships *Melampus* and *Halifax* (*see* Impressment of Seamen). Upon the refusal of the American commander, Capt. James Barron, to give up the men, the *Leopard* opened fire. The American vessel, having just begun a long voyage to the Mediterranean, was unprepared for battle, and to the repeated broadsides from the British replied with only one gun which was discharged with a live coal from the galley. After the *Chesapeake's* hull had been struck with fourteen round shot, her mainmast and mizzenmast had been "irreparably injured" (Decatur's letter to Secretary of Navy, July 4, 1807), her rigging had been greatly damaged and her crew had lost "three men killed and twenty wounded" (Log of *Chesapeake*), Barron surrendered his vessel.

The British boarding party recovered only one deserter, the others having left the *Chesapeake* before she sailed; but three American seamen were also removed by force. The British captain refused to accept the *Chesapeake* as a prize, but forced her to creep back into port in her crippled condition. Barron was court-martialed, found guilty of "neglecting, on the probability of an engagement, to clear his ship for action" (*Proceedings . . . Court-Martial . . . Barron*), and suspended from the navy for five years without pay. England's offer to make reparations enabled President Jefferson to avert war, in spite of the widespread anger throughout the United States. Negotiations were prolonged by Great Britain until 1811 when she formally disavowed the act and returned two of the men, one having meanwhile died and another having been hanged as a deserter.

[Charles Lee Lewis, *The Romantic Decatur.*]

CHARLES LEE LEWIS

Cheyenne, THE. An important tribe of Algonquian[qv] Indians, their name being a corruption of the Dakota *Shahiyena,* "people of alien speech." Originally living in Minnesota, from where they visited LaSalle's Illinois River fort in 1680, they were pushed out on the plains by the Sioux[qv], being reported by Lewis and Clark[qv] in 1804 as living west of the Black Hills[qv].

They early confederated with the Arapahoes[qv], but fought constantly with the Sioux, Crows[qv] and Hidatsas. In 1835 William Bent, who married a Cheyenne woman, induced about half the tribe, including part of the Arapahoes, to move south to the Arkansas River[qv] and hunt and trade near Bent's Fort[qv]. This artificial division between "Northern" and "Southern" Cheyennes still continues.

After Gen. W. S. Harney's Ash Hollow[qv] campaign of 1855, the Cheyennes joined the Sioux in hostility and from 1860 to 1878 were the most implacable foes of the whites, losing, according to James Mooney, more lives in fighting them than any other plains tribe, in proportion to their numbers.

They participated in the destruction of the commands of Capt. William J. Fetterman[qv], Dec. 21, 1866, and Gen. George A. Custer, June 26, 1876 (*see* Little Big Horn Battle). They were terrifically punished when their villages were destroyed by troops at Sand Creek, Nov. 29, 1864; Washita River[qqv], Nov. 27, 1868; Sappa Creek, April 23, 1875 and Crazy Woman Creek, Nov. 25, 1876. Other notable actions included Beecher Island[qv], Sept. 17, 1868; Adobe Walls[qv], June 27, 1874; Rosebud River, June 17, 1876, and the entire Dull Knife campaign[qv] of September, 1878, to January, 1879.

Throughout their wars the Cheyennes were characterized by desperate valor and they did perhaps more than any other tribes, save the Sioux and Apaches[qv], to hold back settlement of the West.

[George Bird Grinnell, *The Fighting Cheyennes;* George W. Manypenny, *Our Indian Wards.*]

PAUL I. WELLMAN

Cheyenne, Wyo., was established in 1867 by the advancing Union Pacific Railroad[qv]. After a brief boom as "Hell on Wheels"[qv] it became the chief outfitting point for the hordes of gold seekers flocking into the mining booms in the Sweetwater region and the Black Hills[qv], and, as home of the Wyoming Stock Growers' Association, "the administrative and social metropolis of the immensely larger cattlemen's range" of the Northern Plains. The collapse of the cattle boom of the 1880's ended its great days of glamour and romance.

[Louis Pelzer, *The Cattlemen's Frontier.*]

LAURA A. WHITE

Chicaca, Indian Town. A principal village of the Chickasaw Indian in north Mississippi, where, in March, 1541, Hernando DeSoto[qv] fought a disastrous battle with southern Indians. He lost over forty of his men, about fifty horses and the greater part of his herd of swine. Some historians place the village on the Yalobusha River.

[*Spanish Explorers in the Southern United States,* in Original Narratives of Early American History Series.]

SAMUEL C. WILLIAMS

Chicago, Burlington & Quincy Railroad, THE, sprang from the urgent need of prairie settlers for transportation. Between 1849 and 1855 four small ambitious pioneer lines in Illinois–Peoria & Oquawka, Northern Cross (from Quincy), Central Military Tract (Galesburg) and Aurora Branch–were joined in one system centering at Galesburg. The Oquawka terminal was shifted to Burlington and the railroad assumed its present title in 1855, popularly known as the "Burlington Route." Eventually it was extended west of the Mississippi, by construction and by the purchase of 203 small roads. Giving access to eastern markets, it played a major role in the development of the prairie states.

[Albert J. Perry, *History of Knox County, Ill.;* H. G. Greenleaf, *John Murray Forbes.*]

EARNEST ELMO CALKINS

Chicago, Ill. The name, an Indian word variously spelled and defined, was first associated with the portage (*see* Chicago Portage) between the Des Plaines River and the shallow prairie stream flowing into Lake Michigan at this point, thus linking the Great Lakes with the Mississippi. The portage was a trail center and the principal objective of early travelers. The first white man of record to sojourn on the site of the present city was Father Marquette who, overcome by illness, spent four months, December, 1674, to March, 1675, on the bank of the little river. By the Treaty of Greenville[qv], 1795, the United States acquired a tract six miles square at the river mouth on which Fort Dearborn[qv] was built in 1803. Evacuation of the fort at the opening of the War of 1812[qv] led to an attack by a band of Potawatomis[qv] on the retreating garrison in which thirty-eight of the sixty-seven soldiers, besides two women and twelve children, were killed, and a number taken captive, Aug. 15, 1812. The first white settler was James Kinzie, the "father of Chicago," a Canadian trader who came in 1804. After the Black Hawk War[qv] and the subsequent extinction of Indian titles, settlers began to arrive in numbers. On Aug. 4, 1830, the first official date in Chicago annals, the Illinois and Michigan Canal[qv] Commissioners published a plat for the "Town of Chicago" on part of the easternmost of the sections of land granted by the United States to the State of Illinois in aid of the canal. This was the first use of the name as a topographical designation. Organization of a village was voted Aug. 4, 1833, with an electorate of 28 and a population of 150, and on March 4, 1837, Chicago was incorporated as a city with a population of 4071. The canal, first suggested by Jolliet in 1673, was not completed until 1848, when it was quickly superseded by the railroads, the first of which, the Galena and Chicago Union, opened a ten-mile section westward, Oct. 28, 1848. Eastern roads built into Chicago in 1851, and by 1857 eight railways had entered the city. An era of expansion followed, population rising from 29,963 in 1850 to 300,000 in 1870. On Oct. 9–10, 1871, more than half the city was destroyed by a great fire which burned over 2200 acres, consumed 15,768 buildings and caused the loss of $188,000,000 and 300 lives (*see* Chicago Fire). Recovery was rapid and Chicago was rebuilt in stone and steel in place of the jerry-built pioneer town that had met a long-foreseen fate. Expansion was resumed on a wider scale and firmer foundation. Commerce and industry flourished, accompanied by labor disputes and social unrest issuing in several serious conflicts, among them the railroad strike of 1877, the Haymarket riot, May 4, 1886, and the Pullman strike of 1894[qqv]. Annexation of surrounding suburbs, especially between 1880 and 1890, increased the city's area from the original fraction of one section to 205 square miles. In the same decade the population was doubled, from 503,185 to 1,099,850. The World's Columbian Exposition[qv] brought Chicago to international attention as more than a commercial metropolis and incidentally exerted lasting influence upon its own development. The Chicago Plan Commission, engaged in a continuous program of city planning, is the direct issue and heir of the Exposition and, in general, the period since the "World's Fair" has been characterized by an awakened public spirit manifested in numerous organizations and activities concerned with the promotion of civic progress. The Century of Progress Exposition[qv], 1933, marked the centennial of the organization of the village of Chicago.

[A. T. Andreas, *History of Chicago;* B. L. Pierce, *History of Chicago.*]

C. B. RODEN

Chicago, Milwaukee & St. Paul Railway Co. v. Minnesota, 1890 (134 U. S. 418). An act of the Minnesota legislature, in 1887, established the Minnesota Railroad and Warehouse Commission and defined its duties in relation to common carriers. The supreme court of the state held that rates recommended and published by the Commission should be final as to what were equitable and reasonable charges; that there could be no judicial inquiry as to the reasonableness of such rates; and that a railroad company, contending that such rates were unreasonable, was not entitled to submit testimony on the question.

The United States Supreme Court declared the act unconstitutional because it deprived a railroad of property without due process of law and deprived it of equal protection of the law, substituting therefor the action of a commission without judicial functions or the machinery of a court of justice. The findings of the state court were therefore reversed.

JULIUS H. PARMELEE

Chicago, Milwaukee, St. Paul & Pacific Railroad, THE, operates 11,097 miles of road in twelve states between the Great Lakes and the Pacific Northwest. Its original predecessor company, the Milwaukee & Waukesha Railroad, chartered in 1847, was the first road in Wisconsin, and the first to operate through trains between Chicago and the Twin Cities (1867). It was extended to Omaha, 1882; Kansas City, 1887; Black Hills, 1907; Seattle-Tacoma, 1909. The Chicago, Terre Haute & Southeastern Railway was leased, July 1, 1921. Six hundred and fifty-six miles of main line in Montana and Washington are electrified. Its traffic, in order of volume, comprises mine products, manufactures, agricultural, forest and animal products.

[F. H. Johnson, *The Milwaukee Road, 1847-1935.*]

F. H. JOHNSON

Chicago and North Western Railway was organized on June 6, 1859. Its actual beginning reverts to 1836 when the Illinois legislature incorporated the Galena and Chicago Union, the first railroad built west of Chicago and Lake Michigan. By 1855 the G. and C. U. tapped the Mississippi at Dunleith and Fulton. When it merged with the North Western on June 2, 1864, the consolidated line comprised 860 miles of track. The North Western was completed to Council Bluffs early in 1867, the first railroad connection with the Union Pacific*qv*. By 1910 a maze of 118 corporations and 144 proprietary companies formed the gigantic cyclops substantially as it existed in 1939.

[W. J. Petersen, The North Western Comes, in *The Palimpsest*, Vol. XIV; *Yesterday and To-day: A History of the Chicago & North Western Railway System.*]

WILLIAM J. PETERSEN

Chicago and Rock Island Railroad, the first railroad constructed to the Mississippi, was incorporated by the Illinois legislature in 1847 as the Rock Island and LaSalle Railroad Company. The name was changed to Chicago and Rock Island in 1851. Completed to the Mississippi on Feb. 22, 1854, it linked the Atlantic with the Mississippi by its connection with the Michigan Southern and Northern Indiana Railroad. The first bridge across the Mississippi was completed in 1856. The Missouri was reached at Council Bluffs, Iowa, in 1869, and opposite Atchison, Kans., in 1871. Further consolidation led to the assumption, in 1880, of the present title, The Chicago, Rock Island and Pacific Railway Company. By 1922 the Rock Island network approximated 8000 miles.

[W. J. Petersen, The Rock Island Comes, in *The Palimpsest*, Vol. XIV.]

WILLIAM J. PETERSEN

Chicago Board of Trade. *See* Pit, The.

Chicago Crime Commission, THE, is an Illinois corporation organized in 1919 by the Chicago Association of Commerce and supported by private subscriptions. Its purpose is to promote the efficiency and activity of all state and local officers charged with the enforcement of criminal laws.

[*Bulletins of the Chicago Crime Commission*, 1919- .]

P. ORMAN RAY

Chicago Drainage Canal, THE. The geography of Chicago is such that the problems of water supply and drainage have always been extremely difficult. In 1886 the city council created a special commission, whose investigations ultimately resulted in the construction (1893–1900) of the Drainage Canal from Chicago to Lockport, whereby the flow of the Chicago River was reversed and the city sewage, diluted with water from Lake Michigan, was sent down the Illinois. The canal answered the city's needs for many years, but the diversion of the lake water provoked the increasing opposition of adjoining states and Canada, finally inducing the Federal Government to compel the city to provide other means of sewage disposal. (*See also* Chicago Sanitary District Case.)

[Curry, *Chicago: Its History and Its Builders*, III.]

M. M. QUAIFE

Chicago Fire, THE (Oct. 8–9, 1871). Modern Chicago began its growth in 1833; by 1871 it had a population of 300,000. Across the broad plain which skirts the river's mouth buildings by the thousand extended, constructed with no thought of resistance to fire. Even the sidewalks were built of resinous pine and the single pumping station which supplied the mains with water was covered with a wooden roof! The season was one of excessive dryness. Up from the plains of the far Southwest blew week after week a scorching wind which withered the growing crops and made the structures of pine-built Chicago dry as tinder. A conflagration of appalling proportions awaited only the starting spark.

It began on Sunday evening, Oct. 8. Where it started is clear; how it started no man knows. Living in a hovel at the corner of Jefferson and DeKoven streets was a poor Irish family by the name of O'Leary. The traditional story is that Mrs. O'Leary*qv* went out to the barn with a lamp to milk her cow; the lamp was upset and cow, stable and Chicago were engulfed in one common ruin. But Mrs. O'Leary testified under oath that she was safe abed and knew nothing about the fire until she was called by a friend of the family.

Once started, the fire moved onward resistlessly to the north and east until there was nothing more to burn. Between nine o'clock on Sunday evening and ten-thirty the following night an area of three and one half square miles, including the business center of the city, was burned, over 17,000 buildings were destroyed, and 100,000 people were rendered homeless. From Taylor Street to Lincoln Park, from the river to the lake, the city lay in ruins. The direct property loss was about $200,000,000. The loss of human lives, while never known, is commonly estimated at about 300. The mass of misery and the indirect material losses entailed by the fire were never measured; but the cost of the lesson Chicago learned on that October night and day was exceedingly high.

[Sheahan and Upton, *The Great Conflagration.*]

M. M. QUAIFE

Chicago Portage, THE. The Des Plaines River runs close to the head of the Chicago River and over the intervening portage the traveler could transport his boat from the Great Lakes–St. Lawrence to the Mississippi River system. The development of Chicago is primarily due to her strategic location at the head of Lake Michigan and on this natural thoroughfare to and from the Mississippi.

The length of the Chicago Portage varied greatly with the seasons. During a spring flood boats might sometimes pass between Lake Michigan and the Illinois River without any land carriage, while in dry seasons a portage of 100 miles, to LaSalle, was often necessary. The importance of this route was recognized by Jolliet[qv], who in 1673 pointed out the need of a canal across the Chicago Portage, but not until 1848 was the Illinois and Michigan Canal[qv] completed. With the advent of the canal and the railroad, the importance of the Chicago Portage ceased; already, however, it had determined the location of America's second metropolis.

[M. M. Quaife, *Chicago and the Old Northwest;* Robert Knight and Lucius H. Zeuch, *The Location of the Chicago Portage Route of the Seventeenth Century.*]

M. M. QUAIFE

Chicago Road, THE, is the ancient highway from Detroit to Chicago. For uncounted generations it was an important Indian trail, the explorer LaSalle in 1680 being probably the first white man to travel it. The disasters suffered in the War of 1812 taught the Government the bitter lesson that it could not defend the western country without highways over which to move its armies. In 1824 Congress appropriated money for the survey of roads of national importance (*see* Survey Act of 1824, The General), and the President allocated one third the entire sum to surveying a military highway connecting Detroit with Fort Dearborn[qqv] at Chicago. From about 1830 on, an ever-increasing flood of settlers poured into the Northwest and thousands of them traveled the new highway leading to Chicago, which has ever since been called the Chicago Road. Its route is approximately represented today by United States Highway 112.

[M. M. Quaife, *Chicago's Highways Old and New,* 29-50.]

M. M. QUAIFE

Chicago Sanitary District Case, THE (Wisconsin v. Illinois, 289 U. S. 395, 710) involved the question of whether the equitable power of the United States can be utilized to impose positive action on one of the states in a situation in which nonaction would result in damage to the interests of other states. The immediate problem was the increasing diversion of Great Lakes waters by the city of Chicago to carry off sewage through the long-established drainage canal (*see* Chicago Drainage Canal). It was claimed that the increasing amounts of water diverted, made necessary by the growth of the city, was lowering lake levels, thus impairing the transportation facilities of the bordering states. After exhaustive hearings, the Supreme Court had fixed (281 U. S. 696) maximum diversion at a point below that necessary to continued utilization of the drainage canal system alone, thus requiring the construction of sewage disposal works, but the city and state procrastinated. The opinion of the Court settled finally the question of the authority of the United States to intervene to enforce action by a state in such a situation. "In deciding the controversy between States, the authority of the Court to enjoin the continued perpetration of the wrong inflicted on the complainants, necessarily embraces the authority to require measures to be taken to end the conditions, within the control of the defendant state, which may stand in the way of the execution of the decree."

PHILLIPS BRADLEY

Chicago Treaties, THE (1821, 1833). In August, 1821, 3000 Indians assembled at Chicago to confer with Lewis Cass and Solomon Sibley, spokesmen of the United States Government, which desired to procure from the Potawatomi and allied tribes the southwestern part of Michigan, extending from Grand River to the south end of Lake Michigan. The Indians proved amenable and their title to this portion of Michigan was surrendered.

Twelve years later, a second and more imposing council was convened at Chicago. This time the Government wished to acquire from the Potawatomi and their allies several million acres of land lying between Lake Michigan and Rock River in northeastern Illinois and southeastern Wisconsin and to remove these Indians to new homes west of the Mississippi. Several thousand Indians attended the council and the picturesque conferences were extended many days. Eventually, everything was arranged and the Indians bade their native land a sad farewell; the future of Chicago belonged to the white race.

[M. M. Quaife, *Chicago and the Old Northwest.*]

M. M. QUAIFE

Chickamauga, Battle of (Sept. 19–20, 1863). The Army of the Cumberland[qv], under Gen. W. S. Rosecrans (U.), maneuvered an inferior Confederate force under Gen. Braxton Bragg out of Chattanooga, an important railway center, by threatening it from the west while sending two flanking columns far to the south. On finding that Bragg had evacuated the city and was retreating, Rosecrans pushed his forces eastward in a "general pursuit" until he found that the main Confederate Army had halted directly in his front. In order to unite his scattered corps he moved northward to concentrate in front of Chattanooga. Bragg attacked on the morning of Sept. 19 in the valley of Chickamauga Creek, about ten miles from Chattanooga. The effective strength was: Confederate, 66,000; Union, 58,000.

The fighting began with a series of poorly coordinated attacks in *echelon* by Confederate divisions which were met by Union counterattacks. From the start it was the concern of Rosecrans to keep open his communications with Chattanooga and this made him constantly anxious for the situation on his left wing. On the second day the battle was resumed by the Confederate right in such a way as to make Rosecrans fear a turning movement. A needless transfer of troops to the Union left, plus a blundering order which opened a gap in the center, so weakened the right that it was swept from the field by Longstreet's attack. Rosecrans and his staff were carried along by the routed soldiers. Thomas (U.), commanding the Federal left, with the aid of troops under Granger, held the army together and after nightfall withdrew into Chattanooga. Both commanding generals lost heavily in reputation, Rosecrans because of his ill-considered orders and his flight from the battlefield, Bragg because of his failure to follow up his subordinates' success and his subjecting his troops to needless slaughter. Rosecrans was presently superseded by Grant, but President Davis sustained Bragg, against his corps commanders' protests until after his defeat by Grant at Chattanooga[qv].

[*Battles and Leaders of the Civil War*, Vol. III.]

THEODORE CLARKE SMITH

Chickamauga, THE, was a lawless tribe of Indians, composed in largest part of Overhill Cherokees[qv], who seceded in 1777 under Chief Dragging Canoe, removed from the towns of the Little Tennessee River and settled on Chickamauga Creek near the site of the present Chattanooga. Later the seceders were joined by discontented or outlawed Creeks[qv]. Their villages were at and near the Suck of the Tennessee. In this natural stronghold they gave much trouble to emigrants going down the Tennessee, and to the Cumberland settlements[qv], as well as the whites in east Tennessee.

[J. P. Brown, *Old Frontiers.*]

SAMUEL C. WILLIAMS

Chickasaw, THE. An important Muskhogean tribe closely related to the Choctaw[qv] in language and custom, though formerly these tribes were mutually hostile. From their earliest history their habitat was northern Mississippi. They were noted from remote times for bravery, independence and warlike disposition toward surrounding tribes (*see* Chickasaw-Creek War; *also* Chickasaw-French War). Early in the 19th century they began sending their youth to Eastern schools, and mission schools in their nation, and in time became a literate people. As the result of white intrusion in their country, these Indians in 1832 entered into a treaty ceding their country to the United States (*see* Pontotoc, Treaty of). In 1837 they purchased from the Choctaw the western half of their domain in the Indian Territory[qv] and in that year the 6000 members of the tribe began emigration to the West. They first settled among the Choctaw and shared in a common government until 1855. The Chickasaw, considerably intermarried with the whites, possessed a constitutional government, a school system and became known as one of the Five Civilized Tribes[qv]. Early in the present century their communal land holdings were allotted in severalty to the individual members and tribal government was dissolved (*see* Burke Act). Their citizens and land are now included in the State of Oklahoma.

[F. W. Hodge, *Handbook of American Indians.*]

GRANT FOREMAN

Chickasaw Bluffs. The high bank of the Mississippi at the mouth of the Wolf River, where LaSalle built Fort Prudhomme[qv] (1682) and Bienville built Fort Assumption (1739). Much intrigue with the Chickasaws[qv] centered around this post, especially during the Spanish occupation of Louisiana. Gayoso built Fort Ferdinand there in 1797; later that year the United States successfully claimed it and built Fort Pickering, near which John Overton settled the town of Memphis[qv] in 1820.

[John W. Monette, *History of the Discovery and Settlement of the Valley of the Mississippi.*] MACK SWEARINGEN

Chickasaw Bluffs, Battle of (Dec. 29, 1862). Sherman's (U.) attack from the Chickasaw Bayou, off the Yazoo River, was part of a threefold Federal plan to reduce and capture Vicksburg[qv]. Porter's (U.) co-operating gunboats could not be brought within range; and Grant (U.), instead of keeping Pemberton (C.) in check near Granada, was compelled to fall back on Memphis when Van Dorn (C.) captured his depot at Holly Springs[qv]. The repulse of Sherman's troops at Chickasaw Bluffs demonstrated the futility of any attack against Vicksburg from the Yazoo.

[Richard S. West, Jr., *The Second Admiral, a Life of David Dixon Porter.*] RICHARD S. WEST, JR.

Chickasaw Council House, The Treaty of (Sept. 20, 1816), was negotiated by Andrew Jackson and other commissioners. By its terms the United States promised annuity to Chickasaw Nation, money and land to chiefs and warriors; engaged to exclude pedlars from their country. Chickasaw Nation ceded to United States land on both sides of Tennessee River.

[Charles J. Kappler, *Indian Affairs, Laws and Treaties.*] GRANT FOREMAN

Chickasaw-Creek War, THE (1793). On Feb. 13, 1793, a Chickasaw[qv] national council declared war against the Creek[qv], to avenge the murder of two Chickasaw hunters; on Feb. 14 Chief Tatholah and forty warriors started on the warpath. Chief Piomingo, attributing the murders to Creek resentment at the Chickasaw refusal to join an alliance against the Anglo-Americans, sought American aid. Gov. Blount, of the Southwest Territory[qv], favored such aid, to divert the Creek from attacks upon the Cumberland settlement[qv]; Indian Agent Seagrove, in Georgia, promised the Creek American support in return for "peace and friendship with us." The Federal Government, however, committed from motives of idealism and economy to a moderate Indian policy, using force only as a last resort, refused armed intervention; though Blount was allowed to give the Chickasaw part of the Federal treaty annuity supplies.

Much talk, little fighting ensued; Spanish officials of Louisiana and West Florida[qqv], following their Indian-solidarity and Indian-buffer policy, held intertribal hostilities to a minimum, and on Oct. 28 engineered at Nogales[qv] a treaty of alliance of the Chickasaw, Creek and other Southern tribes with one another and with Spain. Outstanding points in this incident are: (1) Indian anti-American confederation; (2) difficulties of Federal Indian policy.

[*American State Papers, Indian Affairs,* I; Serrano y Sanz, *España y los Indios Cherokís y Chactas en la Segunda Mitad del Siglo XVIII.*] ELIZABETH HOWARD WEST

Chickasaw-French War (1736–40). Prominent among the great events which the 18th century witnessed was the contest between England and France for the control of the Mississippi Valley[qv]. By 1725 an ultimate French victory seemed certain. One of the few obstacles to their policy of uniting their St. Lawrence settlements with those on the Gulf of Mexico by a series of forts throughout the intervening valley was the hostility of the Chickasaws[qv], smallest but most warlike of the Southern Indian tribes and one which had an undying hatred for the French.

Incensed by several decades of irritating and effective opposition from this valiant tribe, which was entrenched along the eastern bank of the Mississippi south of the Ohio, Bienville, governor of Louisiana[qv], at length decided that its extermination was imperative. The Chickasaw-French War which followed (1736–40) consisted of two unsuccessful military efforts. The first resulted in the wiping out of D'Artaguette's[qv] expedition from Illinois and Bienville's defeat at the battle of Ackia[qv] (1736) on the upper Tombigbee (present northeastern Mississippi). The second consisted in the assembling of 3600 soldiers during the winter of 1739 at Fort Assumption on the lower Chickasaw Bluff[qv]. For some strange reason no attack was attempted and with this ignominious fiasco Bienville's "war" against the Chickasaws ended.

[F. X. Martin, *History of Louisiana;* S. C. Williams, *Beginnings of West Tennessee.*] GERALD M. CAPERS, JR.

Chickasaw Old Fields were located on the north bank of the Tennessee River, four miles below the mouth of the Elk River, in the present Madison County, Ala. At this place the Chickasaw, according to their traditions, fixed their easternmost villages when they migrated east of the Mississippi although their chief towns were in northern Mississippi. The Chickasaw defended their claim to the adjacent land by driving out the Shawnee[qv] in 1714 and by overwhelming the Cherokee[qv] in 1769. The villages in Madison County seem to have been occupied until the American Revolution, and then abandoned, due to pressure from the Cherokee, who were extending their towns down the Tennessee. The Old Fields were claimed by the Chickasaw until 1805, when they were included in a land cession to the United States.

[F. W. Hodge, *Handbook of American Indians;* J. R. Swanton, Early History of the Creek Indians, Bulletin 73, *Bureau of American Ethnology.*] R. S. COTTERILL

Chickasaw Treaty, The (1783), was negotiated by Virginia's commissioners with the Chickasaws[qv], under the great Piomingo and other chiefs, at Nashborough (Nashville). This treaty removed the claim of that tribe to the territory between Cumberland River and the ridge that divided the waters of that stream from those of the Tennessee, to the south of Nashborough. The primary purpose of the Virginia government was to obtain a cession of western Kentucky, between the Tennessee and the Mississippi. That failed, and the remarkable result was that, at Virginia's expense, her commissioners, treating on North Carolina soil, cleared for North Carolinians the Indian title from one of the most fertile stretches of land in the West. Another result was the cementing of a firm friendship between the Cumberland settlers[qv] and the Chickasaws, a tribe ever noted for its fidelity.

[T. P. Abernethy, *Western Lands and the American Revolution.*]

SAMUEL C. WILLIAMS

Chicora was a portion of northern Spanish "La Florida," located in the present-day Carolinas, thought to have been inhabited in the 16th century by Indians of great wealth but of queer form, some having tails, others having feet so large they could be used for umbrellas, and some having an eye in the middle of their chests. In 1523 Lucas Vásquez de Ayllón[qv] obtained from Charles V a grant to the region to search for a giant king.

[Herbert E. Bolton, *The Spanish Borderlands.*]

A. CURTIS WILGUS

Chief Joseph's Campaign. *See* Nez Percé War (1877).

Chihuahua Trail, The. In the late 16th century Spanish exploration and colonization had advanced from Mexico City northward by the great central plateau to its ultimate goal in Santa Fé[qv]. Until Mexican independence (1821) all intercourse of New Mexico with the outer world was restricted to this 1500-mile trail. Over it came ox carts and mule trains, missionaries and governors, soldiers and colonists. When the Santa Fé Trail[qv] sprang up, traders from the United States extended their operations southward over the Chihuahua Trail and beyond to Durango and Zacatecas. Superseded by railroads, the ancient Mexico City–Santa Fé highway has recently been revived as a great automobile highway of Mexico. The part in New Mexico, State Highway 85, pioneered by Franciscan missionaries in 1581 (*see* Rodríguez-Chamuscado Expedition), may claim to be the oldest highway in the United States.

[L. B. Bloom, The Chihuahua Highway, in *New Mexico Historical Review*, July, 1937.]

LANSING B. BLOOM

Child Labor statistics were not available prior to 1870. Knowledge of the extent of juvenile employment at earlier periods is fragmentary. The seed of the child labor system may first have appeared in the spinning schools established early in the colonies. Textile[qv] mills founded after the Revolution promptly utilized the labor of children. Contemporary opinion did not disfavor such employment, and undoubtedly in early years no acute problem existed. Yet hours were excessively long. As the 19th century advanced child labor became prevalent. Two fifths of the factory workers in New England were alleged to be children in a report in 1832. Agitation for compulsory school attendance had appeared in the previous decade. In the 1840's laws of Connecticut, Massachusetts and Pennsylvania limited the hours of child habor in textile factories.

Hence by the time of the census of 1870, which reported the employment of three quarters of a million children between ten and fifteen years of age, the problem had grown to the point of national significance. From 1870 to 1910 the number of children reported as gainfully employed steadily increased as did also their percentage of the total number of children in the population. Aroused to action, the Knights of Labor[qv] projected a campaign in the 1870's and 1880's for child labor legislation and many states enacted laws. Conditions in canneries, the glass industry, anthracite mining and other industries began to attract attention in the closing years of the century.

Very early in the 20th century aggressive campaigns for the enactment of restrictive legislation developed. Conditions in the South, where the number of child laborers had multiplied threefold in the decade ending in 1900, aroused public sentiment for child labor laws. In the North, insistence upon improved standards of legislation and adequate enforcement of child labor laws led to the organization of the National Child Labor Committee in 1904. This committee investigated conditions in various states and in various industries. Child labor legislation was pushed in the various state legislatures. Conspicuous success attended its efforts. The results of this activity appeared in the absolute and relative declines in child labor reported by the 1920 and 1930 census enumerations. This trend probably also continued in the 1930's.

However, the backwardness of certain states, the lack of uniformity of state laws and the competitive difficulties arising therefrom led to demands for Federal regulation of child labor after 1910. Endeavors at congressional regulation were set aside by the United States Supreme Court in 1918 and 1922 (*see* Hammer v. Dagenhart; Bailey v. Drexel Furniture Co.). Undaunted by this failure, efforts were now made by child-labor reformists for a Child Labor Amendment*qv*. In 1924 the Amendment was submitted to the states for ratification, which has not yet been achieved. However, the Fair Labor Standards Act*qv* of 1938 prohibited child labor in the industries affected by its provisions and will materially affect factory employment of children. Problems remaining in the field of child labor, however, include the employment of children in agriculture, street trading, industrial homework and other areas in which effective regulatory measures are not yet universal or applicable.

[U. S. Bureau of Labor Statistics, *Bulletin* No. 604; *History of Wages in the United States from Colonial Times to 1928;* Commons and associates, *History of Labor in the United States*, Vols. I and IV; Millis and Montgomery, *Labor's Progress and Problems*, Vol. I.]

HERBERT MAYNARD DIAMOND

Child Labor Amendment, THE, submitted to the states for ratification in June, 1924, followed two unsuccessful attempts to achieve uniformity of child labor standards throughout the nation: the Child Labor Act of 1916, which invoked the interstate commerce power of the Federal Government, and the law of 1919, based upon the taxing power. Both were held unconstitutional, as improper exercise of the power invoked. (*See* Child Labor Cases.) The apparent impossibility of circumventing judicial hindrances to Federal legislation brought about the submission of a Constitutional amendment which would give Congress power "to limit, regulate and prohibit the labor of persons under 18 years of age." The use of the word "labor" instead of "employment," which was designed to permit whatever child labor legislation Congress might see fit to enact, and the coverage of persons between sixteen and eighteen years of age, were responsible for much of the opposition aroused. By the end of 1938 twenty-eight states had ratified, eight less than the number necessary to make the amendment part of the Federal Constitution.

ROYAL E. MONTGOMERY

Child Labor Cases. The United States Child Labor Law was enacted in 1916 to become effective Sept. 1, 1917. The act prohibited shipment in foreign and interstate commerce of goods produced in factories and canneries which within thirty days preceding removal of such goods had employed children under fourteen years of age, or children between the ages of fourteen and sixteen for more than eight hours a day or six days a week, or after 7 P.M. and before 6 A.M. The same restrictions were imposed on articles produced in mines and quarries employing children under sixteen years of age.

Upholding the decision of the Western District Court of North Carolina (1917), the United States Supreme Court on June 3, 1918, declared the law unconstitutional as an invalid use of the commerce power of the Federal Congress to infringe freedom of contract and prevent child labor within the respective states (*see* Hammer v. Dagenhart).

The revenue act of 1919 included almost the identical provisions of the 1916 Child Labor Law, except that a 10% tax on the net profits of employers violating the provisions was imposed. In May, 1922, the United States Supreme Court again upheld the decision of the same district court in declaring the measure an unconstitutional use of the Federal taxing power in regulation of something entirely within the police power of the several states (*see* Bailey v. Drexel Furniture Company).

[J. R. Commons and J. B. Andrews, *Principles of Labor Legislation.*]

GORDON S. WATKINS

Child Life and Welfare. In the writings of 18th-century philosophers of democracy came the first modern expression of the importance of child life in its influence upon society. There followed a succession of thinkers whose recognition of the worth of the child has had lasting influence in this country. With the advent of industrialization the desire to improve the environment of children adversely affected by factory, slum and sweatshop conditions gave rise to a mass of remedial legislation. In recent years health measures (*see* Hygiene) have lowered the infant death rate as well as the proportion of deaths from tuberculosis and diphtheria, and nutrition work and behavior clinics have lessened the hazards of childhood in other regards. The value of recreational programs has been recognized, and improved nursery school, kindergarten and experimental school methods have been developed to give the child his full chance.

The White House Conferences of 1909 and 1919 on the care of dependent children exercised a wide influence on subsequent legislation. In 1913 Ohio enacted a unified children's code, and has been followed by twenty-nine other states. Today many governmental and private organizations are engaged in child welfare activities, including churches, neighborhood houses, homes for wayward girls, health conferences for mothers and children, public health nurseries, children's hospitals, dental clinics, child guidance clinics, fresh air camps, traveling health conferences and public schools. The Child Welfare League of America, the Child Study Association, the National Child Welfare Association, the American Child Health Association, the National Congress of Parents and Teachers and hundreds of other organizations carry on various phases of child welfare work. The Federal Children's Bureau and many state departments of child welfare engage in research and education. The state agencies, sometimes supplemented by county boards, supervise the administration of institutions for delinquent and handicapped children and the care of dependent children, and administer child labor and illegitimacy laws.

[Sophonisba Breckenridge, American Sociological Society, *Papers and Proceedings*, Vol. XII; Paul H. Furfey, *Social Problems of Childhood;* M. V. O'Shea, ed., *The Child, His Nature and Needs;* Janet E. Lane Claypon, *The Child Welfare Movement;* George H. Payne, *The Child in Human Progress;* Philip Van Ingen, The History of Child Welfare Work in the United States in American Public Health Association, *A Half Century of Public Health*, ed. by M. P. Ravenel, pp. 290-332; James A. Tobey, *The Children's Bureau;* Grace Abbot, *Federal Aid for the Protection of Maternity and Infancy; Standards of Child Welfare*, Publication No. 60, Children's Bureau, Washington, 1919; *An International Handbook of Child Care and Protection*, compiled by Edward Fuller.]

FRANCIS R. AUMANN

Children's Books, American. The earliest American children's books were aids to piety, such as John Cotton's *Spiritual Milk for Boston Babes* (1684) and *The New-England Primer*[qv]. In the later 18th century Isaiah Thomas reprinted attractive British books, such as *The History of Margery Two Shoes* and *Babes in the Wood.* Mother Goose and tales of giants and of monsters became popular, and epitomes of British novels circulated widely. The exploitation of American scenes and character began with Irving's *Rip Van Winkle*[qv], while Cooper romanticized Indians, trappers and seamen. More popular than frontier tales were travel stories by "Peter Parley"[qv] and Jacob Abbott (1803–79), whose Rollo series was begun in 1834. Nathaniel Hawthorne's *Grandfather's Chair* (1841), *A Wonder-Book* (1852) and *Tanglewood Tales* (1853) demonstrate the truth that the best children's books are written by famous authors.

Mary Mapes Dodge's *Hans Brinker* (1865) was followed by Louisa M. Alcott's *Little Women* (1867), Thomas Bailey Aldrich's *The Story of a Bad Boy* (1870), Mark Twain's *Tom Sawyer* (1876) and *Huckleberry Finn* (1884) and John Bennett's stories of American home life and pioneer adventure. After 1880 the books of Horatio Alger vied with dime novels[qv] of adventure, detection and military exploit. The most memorable combination of picture and prose was attained by the artist Howard Pyle, in stories based upon old tales and romances of chivalry. Supreme among dialect stories were the Uncle Remus books of Joel Chandler Harris.

[A. W. S. Rosenbach, *Early American Children's Books, 1682-1840.*]

HARRY R. WARFEL

Children's Courts. *See* Juvenile Courts.

Children's Magazines, American. The first American periodical for juveniles was *The Children's Magazine* (Hartford, 1789), a work designed to supplement schoolwork between the ages of seven and twelve and to lead children "from the easy language of the spelling books up to the more difficult style of the best writers." The rising Sunday-school[qv] movement produced *The Youth's Friend and Scholar's Magazine* (Philadelphia, 1823–64), the first of hundreds of such papers, some interdenominational and some denominational, devoted to the inculcation of religious truth in fiction, verse and essay. Samuel G. Goodrich ("Peter Parley"[qv]) founded *Parley's Magazine* in 1833; eleven years later it was merged with *Merry's Museum for Boys and Girls* (1841–72), edited in 1867 by Louisa M. Alcott and attractively illustrated with woodcuts. Most famous of all children's magazines was *The Youth's Companion* (1827–1929), founded by Nathaniel Willis, a conservative Congregationalist anxious with an old man's extreme piety to exert a positive religious influence. Beyond all compare the most notable monthly children's publication was *St. Nicholas, An Illustrated Magazine for Young Folks,* founded in 1873 and edited for over thirty years by Mary Mapes Dodge. To it Kipling contributed his Jungle Stories. Other contributors included Mark Twain, Tennyson, Bryant, Longfellow, Bret Harte, Robert Louis Stevenson, Joel Chandler Harris, Jack London, Edna St. Vincent Millay, William Faulkner, Elinor Wylie and, to close the list, Ringgold Lardner. *The Little Corporal* (Chicago, 1865–74), under the editorship of Edward Eggleston and Emily H. Miller, attained an extraordinary popularity; its career ended in a merger with *St. Nicholas.* Other popular 19th-century magazines were *Harper's Young People* (1879–95) and the *Golden Argosy* (1882–88).

Among the most successful periodicals of the 20th century is *The American Boy* (1899–), devoted chiefly to fiction, whose editor declared: "The American boy is a boy of action. . . . He wants the literature of achievement." This point of view, emphasizing the contemporary scene, characterizes such juvenile magazines as the official scouting papers, *Boys' Life* (1911–) and the *American Girl* (1917–). Best among the younger children's magazines was *John Martin's Book* (1912–33), a colorful, cheery monthly edited by Morgan Shepard, who also compiled the several issues of *John Martin's Annual. Scholastic* (1920–), sturdiest of classroom aids, is a semimonthly embracing all high-school interests.

The life of nearly every independent children's magazine, in comparison with that of the adult journal, has been short, due to the fact that the audience grows up.

[F. L. Mott, *A History of American Magazines.*]

HARRY R. WARFEL

Chillicothe was the name of one of the four tribal divisions of the Shawnee[qv], but it was also used for the chief town of the tribe. Since the Shawnee in Ohio changed their location, several "Chillicothes" existed, a cause for confusion and controversy among local historians. Some half a dozen places bore this designation. Three were located in the lower Scioto Valley in present Pickaway and Ross counties as follows: one on the west side of the river about four miles south of present Circleville; a second three miles north of the city of Chillicothe; the third on the present site of the village of Frankfort. The first of these is the Chillicothe of Dunmore's War[qv]. Better known was the "Old Chillicothe" on the Little Miami, three miles north of present Xenia. It was attacked by Bowman in 1779 and destroyed by the Indians themselves on Clark's approach in 1780. Boone, Kenton and others were captives here. Another Chillicothe, located on the Great Miami at Piqua[qv], was destroyed by Clark in 1782.

[F. W. Hodge, ed., *Handbook of American Indians;* articles in *Ohio Archæological and Historical Society Publications,* especially Vols. XI and XII.]

EUGENE H. ROSEBOOM

Chillicothe Junto, THE, was a term applied to a group of Chillicothe (Ohio) Jeffersonian Republican[qv] politicians who brought about the admission of Ohio as a state (1803) and largely controlled its politics for some years thereafter. The best known were Thomas Worthington, Edward Tiffin and Nathaniel Massie.

[E. H. Roseboom and F. P. Weisenburger, *A History of Ohio.*]

EUGENE H. ROSEBOOM

Chimney Rock. A landmark visible at forty miles from any direction in western Nebraska east of the point where the River Platte cuts a way into the highlands and to the plains, listed by Johnson and Hunter in their *Guide Book to Emigrants,* 1847, as being 595 miles from Independence, Mo., and "where the trail leaves the river."

CHARLES J. FINGER

China, American Attitude toward. American contact with China began (1784) with trade. Its second chapter opened (1811) with the sending from the United States to China of missionaries. From the outset there were involved special problems of regulation, including safeguarding of life and mimimizing of friction between peoples of different backgrounds and different temperaments. The American Government in 1843 enjoined upon American nationals respect for the rights and susceptibilities of the Chinese; and it asked for and obtained from the Chinese government in its first treaty with China (1844) equality of treatment for American nationals and the right of extraterritorial[qv] jurisdiction.

The people and the Government of the United States have consistently been well disposed toward China. From this country there have gone to China a large number of missionaries and a large investment in cultural and philanthropic institutions. To this country there have come from China and from it there have returned to China large numbers of students. During recent years, in the foreign trade of China, this country has ranked first both in imports and in exports.

In 1899 Secretary of State John Hay gave expression to the doctrine of equality of commercial opportunity in the so-called "Open Door"[qv] notes; and in 1900 this Government suggested that the powers all pledge themselves to respect China's territorial and administrative integrity. In 1922 the American Government led the way in the elaboration, at the Washington Conference[qv], of a group of treaties and agreements whereby the principal powers undertook to respect China's sovereignty, to refrain from interference in China's internal affairs, to foster the principle of equal commercial opportunity in China and to refrain from action in China prejudicial to each other's rights and interests.

In 1932, in identical notes to the Chinese and the Japanese governments, Secretary of State Henry Stimson gave renewed and clear utterance to the principle of "nonrecognition"[qv] as enunciated by Secretary of State William Jennings Bryan in 1915, in regard to treaties, agreements or situations brought about in violation of existing rights in international law or under the treaty provisions.

In relations with China, the American Government has consistently been guided by the attitude and wishes of the American people as indicated in the national support of the positions taken as outlined above.

[Tyler Dennett, *Americans in Eastern Asia;* Stanley K. Hornbeck, Has the United States a Chinese Policy? *Foreign Affairs,* July, 1927; Stanley K. Hornbeck, *China Today: Political;* H. B. Morse, *The International Relations of the Chinese Empire;* W. W. Willoughby, *Foreign Rights and Interests in China.*]

STANLEY K. HORNBECK

China Clipper, THE, was the first hydroplane in the San Francisco–Manila transpacific service. This airliner, with Capt. Edwin C. Musick at the controls and a crew of seven, took off from Alameda, near San Francisco, for the first transpacific mail flight on Nov. 22, 1935, and reached Manila seven days later, having touched at Honolulu, Midway Island, Wake Island and Guam on the way. On Oct. 7, 1936, the same ship inaugurated the first passenger service to Manila, and in April, 1937, a fortnightly service to Hong Kong.

[*New York Times,* Nov. 30, 1935.]

KENNETH COLEGROVE

***China* Incident,** THE, was a World War analogue of the *Trent* Affair[qv]. A British cruiser (February, 1916) removed thirty-eight enemy aliens, including fifteen reservists, from the American ship *China* in the Yellow Sea. The prisoners were released on American demand, but the British assertion that enemy reservists were legally liable to seizure from neutral vessels remained untested.

[T. A. Bailey, World War Analogues of the Trent Affair, *American Historical Review,* XXXVIII.]

RICHARD W. VAN ALSTYNE

China Trade. Cut off from the West Indian Trade[qv], important in the colonial period, American merchants in the years following the Revolution sought new opportunities. Such were discovered in the China trade, which grew rapidly after the *Empress of China* returned to New York in 1785 from a successful voyage. Although New York sent the first vessel, the merchants of Philadelphia, Boston, Baltimore, Providence, Salem and lesser ports were quick to grasp the new possibilities. In the early years the routes generally followed were from the Atlantic ports, around the Cape of Good Hope, across the Indian Ocean and by way of the Dutch East Indies to China. Until after the Treaty of Nanking (1842) the only Chinese port open to foreign trade was Canton.

The early cargoes carried to China comprised chiefly silver dollars and ginseng[qv], a plant erroneously believed by the Chinese to have curative properties. When in 1787 Capts. John Kendrick in the *Columbia* and Robert Gray in the *Lady Washington* sailed from Boston for the northwest coast of America, and Gray with a load of sea-otter[qv] peltries continued to Canton where his furs found a ready sale, the problem of a salable commodity for the Chinese market was solved (*see* Canton, The Fur Trade with). For the next two decades Americans exchanged clothing, hardware and various knickknacks in the Northwest for sea otter and other furs, thus developing a three-cornered trade route. As sea otters gradually disappeared traders shifted to seals, found in large numbers on the southern coast of Chile and the islands of the south Pacific. Sandalwood, obtained in Hawaii and other Pacific islands, also became early an important item of trade. In return American sea-captains brought back tea, china, enameled ware, nankeens and silks. The China trade was characterized by long voyages and frequently by great personal danger in trading with Indians and South Sea islanders. Success rested largely on the business capacity of the ship's captain. The profits, however, were usually large. At its height in 1818–19 the old China trade (combined imports and exports) reached about $19,000,000.

After the Opium War (1840–42) between Great Britain and China, the latter nation was forced to open four additional ports to British trade. Similar rights for Americans were demanded by Commodore Lawrence Kearney and, shortly after, by the Treaty of Wanghia (1844) (*see* Cushing's Treaty), such privileges were obtained.

[F. R. Dulles, *The Old China Trade.*]

H. U. FAULKNER

Chinch Bugs rank with Hessian flies, gypsy moths, boll weevils and grasshoppers as "economic enemies." Discovered in North Carolina in 1785, chinch bugs were first described in 1831 by Thomas Say. In 1871 they caused $30,000,000 crop damages and $79,000,000 in 1887. One sixth of an inch long, black with white markings, they develop on Ohio, Mississippi and Missouri valley grasses—wheat, oats, rye; but not on legumes —clover, alfalfa, garden crops. They are attacked by spraying, burning, dusting and raising crops not eaten by them.

[W. P. Flint, The Chinch Bug and How to Fight It, *Farmers' Bulletin,* 1498, United States Department of Agriculture, June, 1926.]

LOUIS PELZER

Chinese Exclusion Acts. After the discovery of gold in California[qv] in 1848 workers were scarce, and the immigration of Chinese laborers was welcomed. The Burlingame Treaty of 1868[qv] facilitated this immigration. But the completion of the transcontinental railways brought more white laborers to the West, who now complained of Oriental competition. In 1871 in a San Francisco riot twenty-one Chinese were killed. The agitation for exclusion came to be led by Dennis Kearney, president of the Workingman's party. In 1877 a committee of the United States Senate reported in favor of modification of the Burlingame Treaty and in 1879 Congress passed an act restricting Chinese immigration, which was vetoed by President Hayes as a violation of the treaty. Two years later, the Angell Commission negotiated a treaty with China permitting restrictions upon the immigration of laborers, but exempting teachers, students, merchants and travelers. This was followed by the Exclusion Act of 1882. Subsequent acts of 1888 and 1892 contained flagrant violations of the treaty of 1880, partly induced by the failure of China to ratify the Bayard Treaty of 1888, sanctioning a prohibition of immigration of laborers for twenty years. A new treaty with China, in 1894, permitted for ten years the absolute prohibition of the entrance of Chinese laborers into the United States. The act of 1894 enforced this severe prohibition. In the following years, many Chinese laborers entered the United States (and after 1898 the Philippines) on fraudulent certificates issued by Chinese officials. In 1904 the Chinese government refused to renew the treaty of 1894, while harsh enforcement of the immigration laws in the United States led in 1905 to a boycott of American goods in China. Nevertheless, the laws excluding Chinese laborers remained on the statute book. Chinese resentment of this treatment was more than offset by the good will resulting from American friendly relations in the events following the Boxer Rebellion[qv] in 1900 and the establishment of the republic in 1911, and friction over the exclusion policy soon disappeared. In the meanwhile the number of Chinese in the United States declined from 107,488 in 1890 to 71,531 in 1910.

[M. R. Coolidge, *Chinese Immigration;* E. T. Williams, *China: Yesterday and To-day;* J. B. Moore, *Digest of International Law.*]

KENNETH COLEGROVE

Chinese Immigration and Labor. Beset by wars and famine at home and attracted by the story of gold in California[qv], Chinese began to come to America in large numbers in the middle of the 19th century. The first recorded Chinese immigrants reached San Francisco in 1848, though the first really significant immigration occurred in 1852, when some 18,000 Chinese arrived in San Francisco, which then had fewer than 37,000 inhabitants. The need for unskilled labor, created by the Civil War and the construction of the Union Pacific Railroad[qv], paved the way for the Burlingame Treaty[qv] of 1868 which, among other things, recognized the reciprocal rights of Chinese and Americans to immigrate at will. Until 1882, when coolie immigration was shut off, the yearly average of Chinese arrivals was around 16,000. Approximately 375,000 had entered the United States by that year (*see* Chinese Exclusion Acts).

Barred from staking claims or working virgin properties in California, the majority turned to other fields. At one time, of the 25,000 mechanics and laborers employed by the Central Pacific Railroad Company[qv], 15,000 were Chinese. In the 1870's and 1880's many turned to the land for a living. In 1870, 90% of the agricultural labor in California was Chinese; in 1880, 75%; in 1930, less than 1%. The second generation moved from the land and by 1920 there were but 57 Chinese-owned farms in the United States. In lumbering camps and mills Chinese were cutters, scalers and road builders. Today they have almost disappeared from the industry. They were once important in Pacific coast fisheries, as late as 1890 constituting one half of the 2000 permanent employees of canneries and 7000 to 9000 of the seasonal labor. Today less than 1000 Chinese work in fisheries and canneries. Chinese entered manufacturing and commerce: woolen mills, shoe and cigar factories, underwear factories, pork-packing and fish-drying industries, banking, wholesaling and retailing, exporting and importing. In coastal states approximately 100 important Chinese firms are now engaged in importation and sale of Oriental goods and wares.

With the completion of the Union Pacific Railroad thousands of Chinese were left without employment and so many white settlers had come to California that in 1871 there were said to be three men for every job. In the 1870's Chinese competition at low wages with white labor caused anti-Chinese feeling, expressed by boycotts[qv], "que" and laundry ordinances, antialien land laws, police taxes, etc. Typical of the times was the agitation led by Dennis Kearney in 1877 (*see* Kearneyites; Chinese Riots).

In 1880 the Burlingame Treaty was modified and China recognized the right of the United States to "regulate, limit or suspend . . . but . . . not absolutely prohibit" immigration of Chinese laborers. The way was now paved for the Exclusion Law of 1882, marking the beginning of the policy of Chinese exclusion from the

United States, which was extended to Hawaii and the Philippines in 1900 and 1902. Chinese are also subject to the general immigration[qv] laws of 1917 and 1924. Under the latter act all aliens not eligible to citizenship are excluded from the country. This applies to Chinese, as the courts have ruled that aliens of Asiatic race are ineligible for American citizenship. Allowances are made for students, business executives and visitors. American-born Orientals possess all the legal rights of citizenship.

Since the 20th century the Chinese in the United States have concentrated in large cities and are chiefly engaged in the laundry and restaurant businesses. They generally live in "Chinatown," an area where they maintain their own system of internal government and observe Oriental customs and holidays. A few enter the professions and many find employment in domestic service, retail shops, cafés, unorganized trades and establishments in Chinatown. The 1930 census records 74,954 Chinese, including 30,868 American-born, in the country. Of the 44,086 foreign-born, 38,377 live in urban centers, and men outnumber women 39,109 to 4977.

[Ira B. Cross, *A History of the Labor Movement in California;* Eliot G. Mears, *Resident Orientals on the Pacific Coast;* California's Attitude Towards the Oriental, *The Annals*, Vol. CXXII; G. T. Renner, Chinese Influence in the Development of the Western United States, *ibid.*, Vol. CLII; G. M. Stephenson, *A History of American Immigration;* W. C. Van Vleck, *The Administrative Control of Aliens.*]

LUTHER GULICK

Chinese Indemnity. *See* Boxer Rebellion, The.

Chinese Riots. Ill feeling against the Chinese began in California as early as 1852, when they were sometimes ejected from mining towns. In 1871 there was a serious riot in Los Angeles, when fifteen Chinese were hung and six shot to death. Hard times and the labor troubles of 1877 brought anti-Chinese feeling to the fore again in San Francisco, where it was fomented by the Kearneyites[qv], and in July, 1877, several laundries in San Francisco were wrecked and a number of Chinese killed. Upon the publication of the Morey Letter[qv] a mob attacked the Chinese quarter in Denver, Oct. 31, 1880, and did much damage before it was dispersed with fire hose.

[E. Benjamin Andrews, *History of the Last Quarter-Century in the United States.*]

ALVIN F. HARLOW

Chinook Jargon, THE, is a medium of communication composed of a combination of about 300 Indian, French and English words. It was employed generally by Indian traders, missionaries and miners and known to Indian interpreters along the Pacific coast from northern California to Alaska. Several Chinook-English dictionaries and religious tracts have been published.

[G. C. Shaw, *The Chinook Jargon.*]

WILLIAM S. LEWIS

Chinook Winds, peculiar to the Pacific Northwest, took their name from the Chinook Indian tribe. Blowing west and southwest from the Pacific during winter and early spring, they penetrate far into the interior and even to the eastern slope of the Rocky Mountains, melting and evaporating ice and snow and bringing sudden relief from the most severe winter weather.

[H. J. Winser, *The Great Northwest.*]

WILLIAM S. LEWIS

Chippewa, Battle of (July 5, 1814). On the north bank of Chippewa Creek, Gen. Riall had under his command a British force numbering about 2000. Gen. Jacob Brown with 4000 Americans was encamped near by. Riall began his attack at 4 P.M. Simultaneously, Brown ordered an advance of his left. The Americans were repulsed. Winfield Scott's brigade and the artillery were moved forward and engaged the British on the plain south of Chippewa Creek. Superior maneuvering and the effectiveness of the American artillery soon compelled the British to retire in confusion.

[Louis L. Babcock, *The War of 1812 on the Niagara Frontier.*]

ROBERT W. BINGHAM

Chippewa, THE. This tribe, the name a corruption of Ojibwa, meaning "to pucker up," of Algonquian linguistic stock was living, about 1640, in the Sault Ste. Marie area of Michigan. During the first half of the 18th century, gradually moving westward along both shores of Lake Superior, they decisively defeated the Fox and the Sioux[qqv] of northern Wisconsin and Minnesota and seized their lands. Meanwhile certain groups, such as the Ottawa and Potawatomi[qqv], split off to occupy the Lake Michigan area.

Typical forest culture Indians, using the dome-shaped bark and matting wigwam[qv] and the birch-bark canoe[qv], the Chippewa eventually controlled splendid hunting, fishing and wild-rice areas. Although wars with the Sioux continued sporadically until 1858, no further territorial advances beyond the compromise Prairie du Chien Treaty[qv] line of 1825 were made. Successive treaties with the United States Government in 1837, 1854, 1855 and 1863 gradually transferred most of the Chippewa lands to the whites and restricted these Indians to relatively small reservations in Minnesota, Wisconsin and Michigan, where they now live to the number of several thousands. They still receive small government annuities from early timberland sales.

[W. W. Warren, *History of the Ojibway Nation;* F. W. Hodge, ed., *Handbook of American Indians;* Frances Densmore, *Chippewa Customs.*]

WILLOUGHBY M. BABCOCK

Chisholm Trail, THE, was a cattle trail leading north from Texas, across Oklahoma to Abilene[qv], Kans. Much controversy has existed as to the origin of its name and even as to its exact location. It was apparently named for Jesse Chisholm, a mixed blood Cherokee, who followed a part of this route in freighting supplies and may have guided a detachment of soldiers over it soon after the close of the Civil War. The southern extension of the Chisholm Trail originated near San Antonio, Tex., though there is considerable doubt as to whether or not the Texas portion of it was ever known by that name. From here it ran north and a little east to the Red River which it crossed a few miles from the site of the present town of Ringgold, Tex. It continued north across Oklahoma, passing near the sites of the present towns of Waurika, Duncan, Marlow, Chickasha, El Reno and Enid to Caldwell, Kans. It therefore ran not far from the line of the 98th meridian. From Caldwell it ran north and a little east past the site of Wichita to Abilene, Kans. At the close of the Civil War the low price of cattle in Texas and the much higher prices in the North and East caused many Texas ranchmen to drive large herds north to market (*see* Cattle Drives). The establishment of a cattle depot and shipping point at Abilene, Kans., in 1867 brought many herds to that point to be shipped to market over the southern branch of the Union Pacific Railway[qv]. Many of these were driven over the Chisholm Trail which in a few years became the most popular route for driving cattle from Texas to the North.

The Chisholm Trail decreased in importance after 1871 when Abilene lost its pre-eminence as a shipping point for Texas cattle, due to the westward advance of settlement. Dodge City[qv] became the chief shipping point and another trail farther west, crossing the Red River near Doan's Store, Tex., became of paramount importance. The extension of the Atchison, Topeka and Santa Fé Railway[qv] to Caldwell, Kans., in 1880, however, again made the Chisholm Trail a most important route for driving Texas cattle to the North, and this position it retained until the building of additional trunk lines of railway south into Texas caused rail shipments to take the place of the former trail driving[qv] of Texas cattle north to market.

[Sam P. Ridings, *The Chisholm Trail;* Evan G. Barnard, *A Rider of the Cherokee Strip;* E. E. Dale, *The Range Cattle Industry.*]

EDWARD EVERETT DALE

Chisholm v. Georgia, 1793 (2 Dallas, 419). The heirs of Alexander Chisholm, citizens of South Carolina, sued the State of Georgia to enforce payment of claims against that state. Georgia refused to defend the suit and the Supreme Court, upholding the right of citizens of one state to sue another state, under Art. III, Sec. 2 of the Federal Constitution, ordered judgment by default against Georgia. No writ of execution was attempted because of threats by the lower house of the Georgia legislature. The Eleventh Amendment[qv] ended such actions. (*See also* States' Rights.)

[U. B. Phillips, *Georgia and State Rights;* Charles Warren, *The Supreme Court in United States History.*]

E. MERTON COULTER

Chiswell's Mines in the present Wythe County, Va., were known from the first discovery of that region, when the mines were operated by their owner, Col. John Chiswell. A fort built in 1758 was named Fort Chiswell and in 1772 it became the seat of the newly erected county of Fincastle[qv]. In 1776 the State of Virginia took over the mines. During the revolt in 1779 and 1780 of the loyalists in southwestern Virginia, a plot was formed to seize the mines, but it was thwarted by the patriots, who seized the plotters and confined them in the mines. From their treatment by Col. Lynch is derived the term "lynch law."[qv] The mines continued to produce throughout the Revolutionary War.

[Eckenrode, *Virginia in the Revolution.*]

LOUISE PHELPS KELLOGG

Chivington's Massacre. *See* Sand Creek Massacre or Battle, The.

Choctaw, THE, were one of the Five Civilized Tribes[qv] of the southern United States, formerly in southeastern Mississippi and southwestern Alabama. They were encountered in 1540 by DeSoto[qv]. After 1699, when Louisiana was founded, they became allied with the French although an English faction existed which brought on civil war between 1748 and 1750. After the French surrendered their territories in 1763 (*see* Paris, The Treaty of) Choctaws began to cross into Louisiana where a few of them still remain. Relations with the United States were uniformly friendly and, thanks to this fact and the personal eloquence of the great Choctaw chief Pushmataha, they refused in 1811 to join Tecumseh's[qv] coalition against the whites. In 1830, by the Treaty of Dancing Rabbit Creek[qv], they ceded their lands to the United States and accepted in exchange a large area in the southeastern part of the present Oklahoma to which the greater part of them migrated between 1831 and 1833 (*see* Indian Removals). Here they gradually evolved a government patterned somewhat after that of the United States which lasted until 1907 when their territory became an organic part of the new State of Oklahoma.

[Angie Debo, *The Rise and Fall of the Choctaw Republic.*]

J. R. SWANTON

Choctaw Land Frauds. After ceding their lands to the United States by the Treaty of Dancing Rabbit Creek[qv], Sept. 28, 1830, most of the Choctaws removed west of the Mississippi (*see* Indian Removals), those remaining behind being promised lands in Mississippi. Unscrupulous speculators acquired this Indian land script, on which they claimed title to $6,000,000 worth of government land. The fraud was exposed and the intended looting of the Federal treasury blocked. After dragging out from 1835 to 1846, the controversy was finally settled.

[Franklin L. Riley, Choctaw Land Claims, in *Publications of the Mississippi Historical Society*, VIII, 1904; J. F. H. Claiborne, *Mississippi, as a Province, Territory and State.*]

WALTER PRICHARD

Choctaw Trading House, Treaty of (Oct. 24, 1816), signed at St. Stephens[qv], Ala., provided for the purchase by the United States, for $10,000 in goods and a 20-year annuity of $6000, of the Choctaw[qv] lands, mostly in Alabama, east of the Tombigbee, south of the Tennessee and north of the line established by the Treaty of Mount Dexter (1805).

[American State Papers, *Indian Affairs*, Vol. II.]

MACK SWEARINGEN

Choctaw Trail designates any of several Indian paths through Choctaw country—central and southern Mississippi and western Alabama. Most important was a trail from the Natchez country (Mississippi River) to the Mobile area; another apparently ran roughly parallel but farther north. These met the Creek trails to Carolina called the "Great Trading Path."[qv] They were used by British traders and emigrants headed for Natchez[qv]. The French while occupying Mobile[qv] used a trail running northwestward. Another ran northeastward from the Natchez area to the Chickasaw country; this became part of the Natchez Trace[qv].

MACK SWEARINGEN

Cholera Epidemics. True cholera, whose endemic home is the delta of the Ganges, waited until the 19th century before crossing the Atlantic (1832). The devastation was terrible, the first assault of Asiatic cholera on Bellevue Hospital in New York being one of the main horrors of American medicine. It traveled along the waterways, for two years desolating a wide path from Canada to Yucatan. When cholera again came to this country (1848) it was quarantined at New York, but, escaping at New Orleans, invaded the Mississippi Valley, and was carried across the continent by the California gold-seekers (1849). For the third time, immigrant ships brought the epidemic to America, finding the door open in a less vigilant New York (1854). The fourth (1866) and fifth (1867) epidemics were less serious, and the sixth (1873), which again gained entrance through the portal of New Orleans, was the last.

[A Bibliography of Cholera, in John Shaw Billings' *The Cholera Epidemic in the United States.*]

VICTOR ROBINSON

Chouteau (P. Jr.) and Company was the successor to Pratte, Chouteau and Company. The latter was the Western Department of the American Fur Company[qv], which was sold out by John Jacob Astor to Bartholomew Berthold, Bernard Pratte, Pierre Chouteau, Jr., and Jean Pierre Cabanne in 1834. The company previously had been operated on a basis of an equal division of profits and losses with the parent company on returns from all posts on the Missouri River and its tributaries; those of the Mississippi below Prairie du Chien; posts in the Osage country in present Oklahoma; and in southwest Missouri. Some of the important forts controlled by this company were: Forts Pierre, Clark, Mackenzie, Union, Benton, Sarpy and John. Most of their business was on the Missouri River and its dependencies. The name of the company was changed in 1838 to Pierre Chouteau, Jr. and Company, with name Pierre being commonly abbreviated. The company carried on business until about 1866. P. Chouteau, Jr. and Company made a practice of distributing shares of the company among its most capable agents. (*See also* Fur Trade on the Upper Mississippi and Missouri Rivers.)

[Hiram Chittenden, *American Fur Trade of the Far West;* Chouteau mss. in Mo. Hist. Soc., St. Louis.]

STELLA M. DRUMM

Chouteau's Trading Posts. The Chouteau family had more extensive interests in the fur trade[qv] than the several posts established by them directly would indicate. Pierre Chouteau spent most of his time among the Indians. His brother Auguste attended to the purchasing of goods used by them in their trade and to the sale of the furs gathered therefrom. Trading largely among the Big and Little Osage[qv], the Chouteaus, in 1794, erected a post called Fort Carondelet, of considerable size and well fortified, in what is now Bates County, Mo. The Chouteau brothers were given, by the Spanish government, the exclusive right to trade with these Indians for a period of six years. At the expiration of this time Pierre Chouteau persuaded the Osage to move to the Arkansas River, where a fur-trading rendezvous was established, about 1802, at the junction of the Verdigris and Grand rivers in the present State of Oklahoma. In 1809, Pierre and his son, A. P. Chouteau, became stockholders in the St. Louis Missouri Fur Company[qv] and were restrained by agreement from trading on their private account. Auguste Chouteau continued to send out trappers on his individual account. By 1820 the elder Chouteaus had retired from active participation in the trade.

In 1822 Col. A. P. Chouteau occupied the trading post called "La Saline," where Salina, Okla., now stands. The following years he enlarged his operations and established a trading house just below the falls of the Verdigris. In 1836 he built a stockade fort, near the present town of Purcell, Okla., where extensive trade was carried on with the Comanche, Kiowa, Wichita[qqv] and allied tribes, until his death in 1838. These posts bore the name of Chouteau.

The only other trading post bearing the name was established by François G. Chouteau on an island three miles below the mouth of Kansas River. This was washed into the river in 1826 and another built about ten miles up the Kansas.

[Grant Foreman, *Pioneer Days in Early Southwest*, and *Advancing Frontier;* Hiram M. Chittenden, *American Fur Trade of the Far West.*]

STELLA M. DRUMM

Christian Commission, UNITED STATES, was formed in New York in 1861 to provide comforts and supplies to the armies and navies not furnished by the Federal Government. It received its support primarily from the churches. During the four years of the Civil War it collected more than $2,500,000 in cash, besides immense quantities of stores and clothing. (*See also* Sanitary Commission, United States.)

[Lemuial Moss, *Annals of the United States Christian Commission.*]

WILLIAM W. SWEET

Christian Endeavor, Young People's Society of, a Christian organization for young people of evangelical Protestant churches. The first society was founded Feb. 2, 1881, at the Williston Congregational Church, Portland, Maine, by Rev. Francis E. Clark. Its principles include open commitment to Christ, training in Christian service, loyalty to the Church and widespread Christian fellowship. It is interdenominational, international and interracial, and (1938) numbers 80,000 societies and 4,000,000 members, in more than 100 nations.

[Bert H. Davis, *Leadership through Christian Endeavor;* Amos R. Wells and Stanley B. Vandersall, *Christian Endeavor Essentials.*]

STANLEY B. VANDERSALL

Christian Science is the religion founded by Mary Baker Eddy (1821–1910) and represented by the Church of Christ, Scientist. The Christian Science denomination was founded by Mrs. Eddy at Boston in 1879, following her discovery of this religion and science in 1866 and her issuing of its textbook, *Science and Health with Key to the Scriptures,* in 1875. It consists of the Mother Church, the First Church of Christ, Scientist, in Boston, Mass., and branch churches or societies composed of local congregations.

Branch Churches of Christ, Scientist, and Christian Science Societies began to be organized in the 1880's. At the end of 1938 they numbered 2825, of which 2167 are in the United States. There are also sixty-five Christian Science organizations at universities or colleges.

Christian Science Sunday services consist mainly of a Lesson-Sermon, prepared readings from the Bible and the Christian Science textbook. Wednesday evening meetings include selected passages from the Bible and from the Christian Science textbook, and testimonies of healing from persons in the audience. Christian Science churches are also notable for the size of their Sunday schools.

The Christian Science buildings in Boston form an imposing group. They include the Original Church, erected in 1894, its large connected Extension, 1906, the Administration Building, 1908, and the monumental Publishing House, completed in 1933.

Mrs. Eddy's most important book, *Science and Health with Key to the Scriptures,* is published in English, French and German; also, in Braille. Some of her less important writings are published in ten languages; also, in Braille and Moon types. The Christian Science periodicals consist of the *Quarterly,* containing citations for Lesson-Sermons; the *Journal,* monthly in English, including directories of churches, reading rooms and practitioners; the *Sentinel,* weekly in English; the *Herald,* monthly or quarterly in different languages; and *The Christian Science Monitor,* an international daily newspaper issued in several editions.

[Lyman P. Powell, *Mary Baker Eddy, A Life Size Portrait;* E. Mary Ramsay, *Christian Science and Its Discoverer;* Sibyl Wilbur, *The Life of Mary Baker Eddy.*]

CLIFFORD P. SMITH

Christiana (Pa.) Fugitive Affair (1851). When an attempt was made to recover runaway slaves, a Maryland slave owner, Edward Gorsuch, was killed. Later, because he refused to assist in recovering the fugitives, Casper Hanway, a Quaker, was tried for treason, but acquitted.

[W. U. Hensel, *The Christiana Riot,* and *Treason Trials of 1851.*]

H. H. SHENK

Christina, Fort, was established by Peter Minuit and the Swedes who landed with him at "The Rocks" on March 29, 1638. It was the capital of New Sweden[qv] until 1643 and was made the seat of authority again in 1654. The following year it was surrendered to the Dutch (*see* New Netherland) who in turn surrendered it to the English in 1664. The town that grew around the fort was not only the first permanent white settlement in Delaware and the whole Delaware River valley, but was also the antecedent of the present city of Wilmington.

[Amandus Johnson, *The Swedish Settlements on the Delaware 1638-1664;* Anna T. Lincoln, *Three Centuries under Four Flags.*]

LEON DE VALINGER, JR.

Christmas, Puritan Attitude toward. The Puritans[qv] objected to the observance of Christmas on two counts: first on the ground of its pagan origin; second, they disliked even more the excesses which had grown up about its celebration. A law forbidding its observance was passed by the General Court of Massachusetts Bay (May 11, 1659) which stated that, "Whosoever shall be found observing any such days as Christmas or the like, either by forbearing labor, feasting, or any other way . . . shall pay for every such offense five shillings."

[W. W. Sweet, Christmas in American History, *The Chicago Theological Seminary Register,* January, 1934.]

WILLIAM W. SWEET

Christmas Seals. Adopting an idea applied in Denmark in 1904, Miss Emily P. Bissell, Delaware Red Cross secretary, sponsored a $3000 sale of stamplike seals at the 1907 Christmas season to support a cottage for indigent tuberculosis sufferers in Wilmington. The American Red Cross[qv] extended the sale nationally in 1908, and from 1920 it was an activity of the National Tuberculosis Association.

[Elizabeth Cole, *The Story of the Christmas Seal.*]

IRVING DILLIARD

Chrysler's Field (Canada), Battle of (Nov. 11, 1813). On Nov. 10, 1813, the American Army bent on capturing Montreal[qv] halted a mile east of Chrysler's farm on the north bank, overlooking the St. Lawrence River. Next morning Gen. James Wilkinson, commanding, delayed starting until sure that his front was clear. At about 11 A.M. the British gunboats began firing upon the American rear, 800 regulars, militia and Indians co-operating on land. Wilkinson directed Gen. John P. Boyd to drive the enemy back, employing about 2500 troops. They were poorly organized and ineptly led. Toward the end of the day, the Americans, after heavy casualties, retreated to their boats, leaving behind their dead and badly wounded. In proportion to their numbers the British had also suffered heavily, and made no efforts to pursue.

[James Ripley Jacobs, *Tarnished Warrior.*]

JAMES RIPLEY JACOBS

Church and State, Separation of. Nine of the thirteen American colonies had established churches. In Massachusetts, Connecticut and New Hampshire the Congregational Church[qv] was established by law; in Maryland, Virginia, North Carolina, South Carolina and Georgia, and in New York City and three neighboring counties, the Anglican Church[qv] was established.

With the formation of new state governments following the Declaration of Independence, separation of church and state came about more or less as a matter of course where establishment had been more a matter of theory than of fact. Such was the case in all the Anglican states except Virginia. Here the church had been strongly intrenched and a bitter struggle ensued. Baptists, Presbyterians, Methodists and Lutherans[qqv], assisted by such liberal statesmen as Jefferson and Madison, combined to fight establishment. Petitions flooded the Virginia Assembly from 1776 to 1779 and in the latter year a bill was passed cutting off state support. In this year also Jefferson's "Bill for establishing religious freedom" was introduced and after six years of bitter debate finally passed (Dec. 17, 1785).

In the New England states disestablishment was much longer delayed. The unpopularity of the Anglican Church, due to its large Tory[qv] membership, aided in its disestablishment. In New England, on the other hand, the Congregational Church was the church of the patriots.

The Revolution, nevertheless, brought with it a strong movement to separate church and state in New England, led by the Baptists. Though unsuccessful at the time, the agitation was continued, and with the growth of Methodism and Episcopalianism in New England after 1790, the nonconforming bodies united with a growing liberal element in Congregationalism to bring about separation. This was accomplished in 1818 in Connecticut, in 1819 in New Hampshire, but not until 1833 in Massachusetts.

[S. H. Cobb, *Rise of Religious Liberty in America;* J. C. Meyer, *Church and State in Massachusetts from 1740 to 1833;* W. T. Thom, *The Struggle for Religious Freedom in Virginia.*]

WILLIAM W. SWEET

Church Membership. Although the religious motive was strongly present in the establishment of a majority of the thirteen colonies, yet the economic motive was far more powerful in bringing individual colonists. This fact, together with the barriers placed in the way of the average person becoming a church member in a new country, meant that only a relatively small proportion of the colonial population was actually churched. At the close of the colonial period there were, according to careful investigation, 3105 congregations of all kinds in the English colonies. Of these 658 were Congregational, 543 Presbyterian, 498 Baptist, 480 Anglican, 298 Quaker, 251 Dutch and German Reformed, 151 Lutheran and 50 Catholic*qqv*. The German sectaries are not included, but their number was relatively small. New England was the best-churched section, though even here the proportion of church members to the total population was about one to eight. In the Middle colonies, where the German and Scotch-Irish*qqv* element was large and widely scattered and had come largely without ministers, the proportion was much smaller, probably not more than one to fifteen. In the Southern colonies the proportion was still less.

With the opening of the national period the churches which formerly had Old World connections achieved national organizations and began to think in terms of national need. This was particularly true of the Presbyterian, Methodist and Baptist bodies, and these were the groups most successful in following population westward, resulting in rapid growth. Thus the Methodists*qv* with but 15,000 members at the time of their organization into a separate church (1784) had grown to 740,459 by 1840. The Baptists numbered 740,026 in 1844. The Presbyterians at the time of their great division (1837) had more than 200,000. The Congregational and Episcopalian bodies, the two churches which had been established in nine of the colonies and for that reason had the largest colonial prestige, failed to develop any adequate method of following population westward and as a result lagged far behind. The great German and Irish immigration*qv* brought the Catholic membership to 600,000 by 1830; by 1860 it had increased to 4,500,000. The Protestant group to profit most from immigration was the Lutheran. In 1821 they numbered 41,201; by 1861 they had increased to 246,788, and by 1901 to 1,625,185, the latter figure showing the result of the large Scandinavian influx following the Civil War. In more recent years the Jews*qv* also have grown tremendously and now rank as one of the major religious bodies in America.

According to the last Federal religious census (1926) there were 44,382,189 adult church members in the United States in 213 denominations. The largest bodies are the Roman Catholics with 13,826,800 (18,605,003 including baptized children); Baptists 7,859,626; Methodists 7,237,449; members of Jewish congregations 2,930,332; Lutherans 2,826,658; Presbyterians 2,482,498; Protestant Episcopalians 1,366,262; Disciples of Christ 1,275,617; Congregationalists 859,911; Reformed (Dutch and German) 577,427; Latter Day Saints (Mormons) 474,973; Churches of Christ 433,714; United Brethren 358,824; Evangelical Synod (now united with the German Reformed) 314,518; Church of Christ Scientist 202,098. More recent statistics (estimates, 1933) place the total church membership in the United States at 60,812,874, a gain of 15.8% over a period of seven years.

[W. W. Sweet, *The Story of Religions in America;* C. Luther Fry, *The United States Looks at Its Churches; Census of Religious Bodies.*]

WILLIAM W. SWEET

Church Membership Suffrage was the means used by New England Puritans*qv* to control their theocracies against dissent. When the Puritans in the trading company of Massachusetts Bay*qv* retreated to America with their charter they established a theocracy*qv*, but without disturbing the outer shell of the trading company*qv* structure. They could maintain this theocracy successfully only so long as they could control the General Court of freemen*qv* or stockholders, which necessitated limiting freemanship to those who approved of the theocracy. This they could do by refusing to admit new freemen, but when pressure from dissatisfied non-freemen became too great, they decided to accept a limited number on condition of orthodox church membership. After the restoration the king demanded of

Massachusetts that the church membership qualification be removed, but although the colony made a gesture of complying, the requirement was not essentially altered. Through the influence of Massachusetts the colony of New Haven[qv] also adopted the principle of church membership suffrage. Among the other New England colonies it did not exist by specific regulation, although voters had to be in good standing in Connecticut and Plymouth[qqv]. By the fusion of Connecticut and New Haven in the charter of 1662 the narrow suffrage ended in the latter colony, as it did in Massachusetts when the charter was annulled in 1684.

[H. L. Osgood, *American Colonies in the Seventeenth Century*, I; I. M. Calder, *The New Haven Colony.*]

VIOLA F. BARNES

Church of England in the Colonies, The. The first successful English settlement in America was made by members of the established church at Jamestown in 1607. The church was provided for in the earliest plans for Virginia, and as soon as the colony was strong enough, it was legally established. All the other Southern colonies, except Maryland, were founded under the leadership of churchmen, and, in time, the Church of England was established in all of them, though this did not occur in North Carolina until 1765. Maryland was founded by a Roman Catholic proprietor, but the Protestant settlers there obtained control in the Revolution of 1689 and by 1702 had secured the establishment of the Church of England. In New York the church was established in the four leading counties, but not elsewhere. In the other Northern colonies it enjoyed no establishment and depended for support largely upon the English Society for the Propagation of the Gospel[qv] in Foreign Parts, founded in 1701.

During the 18th century the Church of England advanced in the colonies where it was not established and lost ground in those where it was—a phenomenon which corresponded with the general breakdown of colonial religious barriers that marked that century. The American Revolution deprived the church of its establishments in the South and of the aid of the S. P. G. in the North, exposed it to some popular opposition and confronted it with the problem of forming a national organization and obtaining a native episcopate.

[W. S. Perry, *History of the American Episcopal Church; Historical Collections Relating to the American Colonial Church;* W. W. Manross, *History of the American Episcopal Church.*]

W. W. MANROSS

Church of Jesus Christ of Latter Day Saints. *See* Mormons.

Church Trials. *See* Heresy Trials.

Church Union Movements. As early as 1648 the Cambridge Platform[qv] recognized the ideal unity of the church. Colonial governments attempted, in varying degrees, to enforce conformity to established churches or to penalize dissent. The establishment of legal equality for all sects by the Federal Constitution[qv] and the gradual disappearance of restrictive laws in the states put church union, like religion itself, on a purely voluntary basis.

The Plan of Union (1801) uniting the missionary work of Congregational and Presbyterian[qqv] churches was operative until 1837. Many interdenominational societies were formed for the promotion of missions, education, temperance and emancipation[qqv]. Co-operation for religious causes, often with the explicit approval of denominational authorities, produced the American Bible Society, Evangelical Alliance, Young Men's Christian Association, Young Women's Christian Association, Woman's Christian Temperance Union, International Sunday School Association, Young People's Society of Christian Endeavor and similar organizations of individuals[qqv]. Denominational boards formed co-operative councils in many fields. Certain denominations, especially the Episcopalians and Disciples of Christ[qqv], have constantly stressed union. Some of the divisions within the Lutheran, Presbyterian and Baptist[qqv] groups have been healed. Three Methodist[qv] bodies reunited in 1938. The Federal Council of Churches of Christ in America[qv] (1908) has been the most comprehensive agency of the American churches for united action.

[H. P. Douglass, *Church Unity Movements in the United States.*]

WINFRED ERNEST GARRISON

Churches, Attitude of, toward War. The colonial churches inevitably transplanted from Europe the current theories of war. Nonresistance and the incompatibility of war with Christianity were proclaimed by the Friends and some of the small German sects. The remainder accepted the Catholic and humanist view which discriminated between just and unjust war. The civil magistrate was primarily responsible for determining the justice of a war; the church attempted to soften its barbarities; the citizen did the fighting.

The Revolutionary cause was fervently championed by the Congregationalists and, to a lesser degree, by the Presbyterians, the Dutch and German Reformed clergy and the Roman Catholics. The Anglicans were torn by a clash of loyalties. The majority of the Friends and Mennonites, and some of the Methodists refused to support either side. The War of 1812 encountered the widespread opposition of the Congregationalists echoing the sentiment of New England. The Mexican War was sanctioned by the Methodists, Roman Catholics, and the Baptists and Presbyterians in the South. Clean-cut opposition came from the Friends, Congregationalists and the newly organized Unitarians. So zealously did the churches support both sides in the Civil War that most of them were disrupted (*see* Churches, Split of, by the Slavery Issue). Even the ranks of the nonresistant sects suffered some defections. The Spanish-American War was very popular. Almost the only attempts to stem the pro-war current in the churches were made by the Friends and the Unitarians. Preliminary surveys of the World War show that prominent clergy were overwhelmingly in favor of it. Of the mere handful of outspoken ministerial pacifists, over half came from the Unitarians, Congregationalists and Universalists. Since the World War, church opinion has swung far toward a pacifism[qv] at once idealistic and realistic.

[W. W. Sweet, *The Story of Religions in America;* W. W. Van Kirk, *Religion Renounces War.*]

CLAYTON S. ELLSWORTH

Churches, Established. *See* Church and State, Separation of.

Churches, Split of, by the Slavery Issue. At the opening of the Civil War three of the great American churches had already divided into Northern and Southern branches. A Presbyterian schism had occurred in 1837–38, dividing that body into Old School and New School, the New School being confined largely to the North. Though slavery had not been the principal issue, nevertheless it had played an important part in the division. In 1844–45 both Baptist and Methodist churches had divided squarely over the slavery issue and when the Civil War began each adhered to their own section in the struggle. Up to 1861 the Old School Presbyterians were still an intersectional church, and had excluded slavery as a subject for discussion in their General Assemblies. The New School had not done so, and as a result they were divided over slavery in 1857. The secession of the Southern states, however, brought division both to the Old School Presbyterians and to the Protestant Episcopalians, each forming independent denominations in the Confederate states. The slavery issue had been avoided by the Protestant Episcopalians in the General Conventions, and as a result there was an absence of bitterness on both sides. This fact made reunion relatively easy, following the end of hostilities.

The Roman Catholics experienced no divisions and very little controversy as a result of either slavery or the Civil War. This was due to the fact that the principal Catholic authority lay outside the nation and also to the fact that each Catholic diocese was largely independent. Other churches, like the Congregational, avoided splits because they were confined almost entirely to the North, while such bodies as the Quakers and some other small denominations had solved the slavery issue previous to the Civil War by excluding slave owners. The Disciples, though a religious body confined mostly to the border, experienced no real division, due to the looseness of their organization and the neutral position taken by their great leader, Alexander Campbell.

[Vander Velde, *The Presbyterian Churches and the Federal Union;* J. H. Norwood, *The Schism in the Methodist Episcopal Church, 1844.*]

WILLIAM W. SWEET

Churches and the World War. The beginning of the war found two Presbyterian elders with strong pacifist tendencies at the head of the American Government, Woodrow Wilson and William Jennings Bryan. Pacifist idealism also was strong among the American churches, their support of the war being secured by proclaiming that it was a "war to end war." With few exceptions church leaders supported every war policy of the Government. Each of the important churches formed wartime commissions, and a general War Time Commission was created by the Federal Council of Churches[qv], representing not less than thirty-five denominations. The Catholics also had a National War Council. Ministers from their pulpits urged enlistments; opened their churches for the work of war organizations; helped gather contributions for the numerous special war funds; preached propaganda sermons from outlines furnished by the Government; went to training camps and into the army and navy as chaplains and gave full support to the war work of the Y. M. C. A.[qv] and numerous other interchurch war agencies.

[Charles S. MacFarland, *The Churches of Christ in Time of War;* Gaius Glenn Atkins, *Religion in Our Times;* Ray H. Abrams, *Preachers Present Arms.*]

WILLIAM W. SWEET

Churubusco, Battle of (Mexican War, Aug. 20, 1847). Victorious at Contreras[qv], Scott the same day encountered Santa Anna's principal army at Churubusco, four miles below Mexico City. Mexican engineers had prepared scientifically constructed works of great strength covering the bridge over the Churubusco River and fortified a massive convent near by. These Scott assaulted simultaneously. The defenders resisted stubbornly, but after losing 6000 killed, wounded and prisoners, were routed and retreated to the capital. Scott reported 133 killed, 905 wounded and missing. Eighty American deserters, enlisted in a Mexican "Foreign Legion," were captured.

[Justin H. Smith, *The War with Mexico*, II.]

CHARLES WINSLOW ELLIOTT

Cíbola, a native name for the Zuñi[qv] country, first heard by Fray Marcos de Niza in 1539. His report (garbled and exaggerated in Mexico City) of "seven very great cities" in the North resulted in the Coronado expedition[qv]. As exploration advanced, the name Cíbola came to mean the entire Pueblo[qv] Indian country, and was extended to the Great Plains which, until late Spanish times, were called *los llanos de Cíbola.* As an administrative term, Cíbola was soon changed to New Mexico, but in one way the older name survived. The strange "cows" found on the plains were first called *vacas de Cíbola;* later this was shortened to *cíbolos* (buffalo).

[Bloom and Donnelly, *New Mexico History and Civics.*]

LANSING B. BLOOM

Cimarron, Proposed Territory of, known as the Public Land Strip, or No Man's Land, extended in longitude from 100° to 103°, in latitude from 36° 30′ to 37°.

Settled by squatters[qv] and cattlemen, the territory had no law, so to protect the squatter claims a movement was started to organize the country into Cimarron Territory. In March, 1887, territorial representatives drew up resolutions assuming authority for the territory. The proposal was referred to the Committee on Territories in Congress. There it remained. The area now constitutes the panhandle of Oklahoma.

[Rainey, *No Man's Land;* Thoburn, *History of Oklahoma.*]

ANNA LEWIS

Cincinnati was located opposite the mouth of the Licking River in the Symmes Purchase[qv] by three proprietors, Matthias Denman, Robert Patterson and John Filson. Israel Ludlow replaced Filson, who mysteriously disappeared in the fall of 1788. The first houses were built in the winter of 1788–89. The original name of Losantiville (*L* for Licking, *os* for mouth, *anti* for opposite, *ville* for city) was changed to Cincinnati (after the society of that name) by Gov. Arthur St. Clair, who made it the capital of the Northwest Territory[qv], 1790–1800. Fort Washington[qv] added to the importance of the little town, which had 2540 people by 1800. It was incorporated as a town in 1802 and as a city in 1819.

The early inhabitants were chiefly of New Jersey and Pennsylvania origin, but the population became more cosmopolitan as the city grew. By 1860 Cincinnati had 161,044 inhabitants, 45% of whom were foreign-born. The large German element, arriving in the decades 1830–60, played a particularly important part in the city's history.

The importance of Southern trade, and prejudice against the many illiterate free Negroes, made Cincinnati hostile to abolitionists[qv], a mob on one occasion destroying the press of Birney's *Philanthropist*[qv]. Know-Nothingism[qv], directed against the Germans and Irish, flared up in the 1850's, but soon subsided. In the Civil War Cincinnati, though losing its Southern trade, was loyal to the Union. In 1862, when threatened by Confederate advances, its citizens quickly organized to defend it, but the danger soon passed. Morgan's raid[qv] of 1863 went around the city.

Well located on the Ohio River to command Western and Southern markets, for many years Cincinnati rightly claimed the titles of "Queen City of the West" and "Porkopolis." In manufacturing it ranked third among American cities by 1860. But iron ore and coal were too remote, meat packing moved westward to the newer farming states, trunk-line railroads reduced the importance of the Ohio River and Cincinnati's leadership passed away.

[E. O. Randall and D. J. Ryan, *History of Ohio;* Charles T. Greve, *Centennial History of Cincinnati and Representative Citizens.*]

EUGENE H. ROSEBOOM

Cincinnati, Society of the. In June, 1783, shortly before the disbanding of the Continental Army[qv], an organization of its officers who had formed lasting friendships through service together was suggested by Gen. Henry Knox. At the headquarters of Baron von Steuben near Fishkill, N. Y., the organization was consummated, with Washington as the first president, and was named in honor of Cincinnatus, the Roman dictator, in allusion to the approaching return of the officers to civil pursuits. Its first object was to raise a fund for the widows and children of those slain in the Revolutionary War and it also hoped to promote a closer union among the states. Its membership consisted of the army officers and their eldest male descendants, or if direct descent failed, collateral descendants were eligible. It was divided into state societies, and there was a branch in France, which was destroyed by the Revolution in 1792. The Society aroused antagonism at first among ultra-republicans who believed that it was setting itself up as an aristocracy. Alexander Hamilton was the second president. Hamilton Fish (1808–93), son of Nicholas Fish, one of the founders, was president from 1854 until his death. Through failure of heirs, most of the state societies had disintegrated by 1900, but a revival of the general organization was effected in 1902.

[Francis Apthorp Foster, *Institution of the Society of the Cincinnati, Together with Resolutions, etc., of the General Society of the Cincinnati, 1783-1920.*]

ALVIN F. HARLOW

Cincinnati Riots (1884). The criminal courts had become corrupt in Cincinnati early in 1884, and when one Berners, a self-confessed and atrocious murderer, was convicted only of manslaughter, a mob attacked the jail on Friday evening, March 28, and burst open the main door with a huge timber; but Berners had been spirited out by a rear way. A company of militia hurried to the scene and drove off the rioters. On Saturday night mobs gathered again, broke into gun stores and armed themselves, attacked the jail and set fire to the courthouse, which was almost destroyed. Again troops drove the rioters away after a bloody battle. Sunday was disorderly, and that night mobs looted stores and shops. Troops with artillery were rushed from all parts of the state and threw up street barricades, where some hard fighting ensued. Not until the sixth day were the barricades removed and street-car service resumed. At least 45 persons had been killed and 138 injured.

[Lewis Alexander Leonard, *Greater Cincinnati and Its People.*]

ALVIN F. HARLOW

"Cipher Dispatches," THE, were code telegrams relative to the possible use of money to insure the votes of Florida and South Carolina for Tilden in the presidential campaign of 1876^{qv}. Their publication in 1878 helped to nullify the political effect of the reputedly questionable proceedings of the Republicans in winning the electoral votes of Louisiana, Florida and South Carolina.

[C. R. Williams, *Life of Rutherford B. Hayes.*]

ASA E. MARTIN

Circuit Courts. *See* Judiciary, The.

Circuit Riders (Ministerial). Circuit riding was devised by John Wesley for carrying on his religious movement in England. A circuit consisted of numerous preaching places scattered over a relatively large district served by one or more lay preachers. The original American circuit riders introduced Methodism into the colonies. Robert Strawbridge, who came to America about 1764, was the first in the long line. John Wesley sent eight official lay missionaries to America (1769–76), and several came on their own responsibility. By the end of the American Revolution there were about 100 circuit riders in the United States, none of whom was ordained. With the formation of the Methodist Episcopal Church[qv] (1784), Francis Asbury was chosen bishop, several of the circuit riders were ordained and the system was widely extended wherever settlements were springing up. It was found peculiarly adaptable to frontier conditions, since one man, equipped with horse and saddlebags, served a great many communities, a circuit often having as many as twenty-five or thirty preaching places. In this way the riders kept pace with the frontier, bringing the influence of religion to new and raw communities. The salary of the preachers was at first uniform, $64 a year, which by 1800 had become $100. Marriage was discouraged, for it usually caused withdrawal from the work. Peter Cartwright is the best known of the frontier preachers. His active career covered the first half of the 19th century, the scene of his labors being Kentucky, Tennessee, Ohio, Indiana and Illinois. The circuit system largely accounts for the even distribution of Methodism throughout the United States. Other religious bodies partially adopted it, particularly the Cumberland Presbyterians[qv].

[*Autobiography of Peter Cartwright the Backwoods Preacher*, edited by W. P. Strickland; W. W. Sweet, *The Rise of Methodism in the West.*]

WILLIAM W. SWEET

Circuits, Judicial, and Circuit Riding. When the Federal judicial system, under the Constitution, was established, the country was divided into three circuits (Eastern, Middle and Southern) to each of which two of the justices of the Supreme Court were assigned. They were required to hold the courts twice a year, sitting with district judges. During the first three years of its existence, the Supreme Court had practically no business to transact and the Chief Justice and his associates found employment in riding the circuits and trying cases at *nisi prius*. The roads and accommodations were bad and the duty proved to be onerous. The opening of the first courts in the spring of 1790 found, for example, Justice Iredell, of North Carolina, presiding in Boston. The justices complained, and President Washington wrote in August, 1791, that he hoped Congress would give "relief from these disagreeable tours" to hold twenty-seven courts from New Hampshire to Georgia. Some relief was granted in 1793 in a change by which only one justice was required to sit with a district judge; and thereafter the justices rode the circuits in turn, instead of being confined to fixed circuits. The development of the West added another and another circuit which meant yet more magnificent distances between court sites. The system was changed in 1869. Then circuit judges were appointed, most of whom traveled over several states. The bar, generally speaking, did not ride circuit with the Supreme Court justices or Federal circuit judges.

In the states, from the outset, circuit courts existed, and in the early days the judge, accompanied by many lawyers, rode large circuits. The system tended to develop lawyers of initiative, originality and resourcefulness. The "case lawyer" was a later product.

[Charles Warren, *The Supreme Court in United States History.*]

SAMUEL C. WILLIAMS

Circus, THE, is a development of the old Roman and mediæval types of amusement to fit American conditions. Before the Revolutionary War Jacob Bates displayed feats of horsemanship. During the 18th century circuses were more or less stationary, performing for some time in a semipermanent enclosure. Between horsemanship acts, clowns and jugglers performed and brilliant fireworks were shown. Rural conditions gave rise to the nomadic institution peculiar to America. So-called rolling shows made their appearance about 1800. By 1820 there were thirty or more of these primitive shows on the road. By 1828 Buckley and Weeks boasted 8 wagons, 35 horses and a canvas tent with a capacity of 800 people. The wagon show of the middle of the 19th century consisted of trapeze performances, horsemanship, clowns, tricks and animal acts. A trick mule, with a prize to any one who could ride him, climaxed the acting. Spaulding and Rogers operated the first rail circus in 1858.

Puritan feeling antagonistic to the circus led showmen to use Bible texts and terms. The lion cage was a den, and Solomon and the Queen of Sheba were impersonated. Cages were ornamented with Bible scenes. The menagerie accompaniment grew gradually in an attempt to get newer attractions as the result of competition. The two-ring circus came in 1869. Phineas T. Barnum and James A. Bailey during the last quarter of the century operated a three-ring circus called the "Greatest Show on Earth." In the 20th century a five-ring circus has developed.

About 1890 William F. Cody instituted the Wild West show rivaling the larger circus in interest and profit. Western cowboys performed, Indians danced and frontier scenes were re-enacted. With the advent of the aeroplane came the flying circus, consisting of a group of aeroplanes presenting a program of stunt flying.

[I. J. Greenwood, *The Circus.*]

EVERETT DICK

Cities, Colonial. Over 90% of the colonial people lived rural lives. The exploitation of rich natural resources called them to farms and plantations, to the forest and sea. The demands of commerce drew a few to urban centers. Five "cities," favorably located by geography, became the chief marts and ports of commerce, centers of culture and fashion, political and financial capitals. At the head of the list stood Boston[qv], for many years the largest town, rising from 7000 people in 1690 to 17,000 in 1740. After mid-century, Philadelphia[qv] forged far ahead with a count of about 40,000 in 1774, while Boston census at the same time was 20,000. Next to Philadelphia came New York City[qv] with 30,000 in 1774. In that year Newport, the chief port of commerce for the region of Rhode Island, numbered about 12,000. After 1750 rich planters from Carolina and wealthy merchants of Philadelphia summered at Newport[qv]. The only "city" in the South was Charleston[qv], a thriving port and town of a dominant political and social aristocracy. In Charleston, planters from the country had their town houses. Urban communities of less than 12,000 inhabitants included Salem, Providence and New Haven in New England and after mid-century Baltimore, Richmond, Wilmington (N. C.) and Savannah in the South.

[C. P. Nettels, *The Roots of American Civilization.*]

WINFRED T. ROOT

Cities, Growth of. In America during the colonial era there was relatively little urban growth. On the eve of the Revolutionary War there were only five communities with more than 8000 inhabitants and their combined strength was little more than 100,000 or only 3% of the total population. Nor was there much increase in the rapidity of city growth during the half century which followed the winning of independence. In 1820 there were only thirteen municipalities with over 8000 inhabitants, but a few of these were now attaining considerable size. New York, for example, had passed the 150,000 mark.

It was not until well into the twenties and thirties of the 19th century that the growth of American cities began to exceed that of the country as a whole. Immigrants began to flock in from Europe and many of them settled in the seaboard communities. The building of turnpikes and canals[qqv] stimulated internal trade. Forty-four cities were able to show more than 8000 population in 1840, and the largest ones were now becoming comparable with the great urban centers of Europe. Steamboat[qv] navigation on the Great Lakes and the larger navigable rivers gave added momentum to the development of the inland cities, and the railroads[qv], when they came, served to accelerate the pace.

The Civil War, while it lasted, placed a damper on city growth, but the setback was only for the moment. The march of agriculture, industry and trade across the face of the continent was resumed after the war, and city populations expanded in keeping with this progress. This growth kept up to the end of the century and beyond. In 1900 the percentage of the national population living in communities of over 8000 was 33%, in 1910 it was 38%, in 1920 it had risen to 44% and in 1930 it was slightly above 49%. The figures for 1940 will undoubtedly disclose that well over half the population of the United States has become urbanized.

The great urbanizing forces are still at work with undiminished vigor. The continued development of large-scale production, the greater facilities which the large city gives to industry in the way of a flexible labor supply, and the advantages derivable from a sizable labor market close at hand—these and the various social allurements of the city are still contributing to its growth. The increased productivity of agriculture is releasing men from the soil and it is to the cities that they go. This steadily strengthening urbanism is not an American phenomenon. It has its counterpart in nearly all other countries as well.

[J. G. Thompson, *Urbanization.*]

WILLIAM B. MUNRO

"Citizens' Alliances" were formed first in Kansas, and then in the neighboring states of Iowa and Nebraska, by townsmen who sympathized with the Farmers' Alliances[qv]. When the Supreme Council of the "Southern" Alliance met at Ocala, Fla., in December, 1890, it recognized the value of such support and assisted in the organization of these groups into the National Citizens' Alliance as a kind of auxiliary. Even more eager than the farmers for third-party action, members of the Citizens' Alliance were prominent in the several conventions that led to the formation of the People's party[qv], into which their order was speedily absorbed.

[H. R. Chamberlain, *The Farmers' Alliance.*]

JOHN D. HICKS

Citizens' Military Training Camps. Initiated in the summer of 1913 at Gettysburg, Pa., and Monterey, Calif., for 244 college undergraduates attending at their own expense, continued on the same basis in 1914 at Burlington, Vt., Asheville, N. C., Ludington, Mich., and Monterey for 667 students, the Citizens' Military Training Camp was widely publicized in 1915 when fostered at Plattsburg, N. Y., by Gen. Leonard Wood for business and professional men. It became part of the "preparedness" movement[qv]. In 1916 there were 12,200 enrolled at Plattsburg, Fort Oglethorpe, Fort Terry and Fort Wadsworth, and many who attended were the following winter commissioned in the embryo Officers' Reserve Corps[qv]. Re-established by the act of 1920 with transportation, rations and equipment furnished by the Government, these camps have enrolled more than 30,000 students annually, many of whom have earned commissions in the Officers' Reserve Corps.

[W. A. Ganoe, *History of the United States Army;* R. B. Perry, *The Plattsburg Movement.*]

ELBRIDGE COLBY

Citizenship may be defined as membership in a political community. During the colonial period, the American people were accustomed to calling themselves "subjects" of the English king, the term subject having a connotation appropriate to a monarchy. The English law, feudal in origin, made each person born within the colonies, save minor exceptions, a subject of the king. Through acts of Parliament and of the colonial assemblies, provisions were made whereby other persons, except certain classes disqualified on grounds of religious faith, could be naturalized as British subjects. With the signing of the Definitive Treaty of Peace of 1783[qv], and especially with the adoption of the Constitution[qv], the term "citizen" gained in favor as more descriptive of membership in a republican political community.

The Constitution recognizes a dual American citizenship, that of the United States and that of the state. It was not at first clear which carried the primary obligation. The earlier opinion, as expressed by Justice Story, was that "every citizen of a State is *ipso facto* a citizen of the United States." This view, that the state claim is antecedent, found acceptance in the Dred Scott Case[qv] of 1857. After the Civil War, however, the determination of the North to settle once and for all the status of the Negro led to the enactment of the Fourteenth Amendment[qv], which provided that "All persons born or naturalized in the United States, and subject to the jurisdiction thereof, are citizens of the United States and of the State wherein they reside." Thus, United States citizenship is now primary, that of the state derivative.

The Fourteenth Amendment embodies the English principle of *jus soli,* which fixes citizenship according to the place of birth. As interpreted by the American courts, not only are Negroes, born in this country, citizens of the United States, but so also are Orientals (U. S. v. Wong Kim Ark, 1898[qv]). The Indians, living in tribal relations, were not at first deemed to be "under the jurisdiction" of the United States in the sense of the Fourteenth Amendment (Elk v. Williams, 1884), but in 1924 Congress conferred citizenship upon all non-citizen Indians born within the territorial limits of the United States. The principle of *jus sanguinis,* which bases citizenship upon parentage, and which is widely accepted on the continent of Europe, has had some influence upon American policy. By Federal statutes, children born of American parents resident in foreign countries are presumed to be American citizens, though, by the act of 1907, such presumption will lapse unless on attaining the age of eighteen they record at an American consulate their intention to become residents of the United States and to retain their citizenship.

The Constitution, moreover, authorizes Congress to establish "an uniform rule of naturalization." Our Government has from the beginning been friendly to the idea of "acquired" citizenship. An early Federal pronouncement dignifies expatriation as "a natural and inherent right of all people." Hence, laws have been passed making provisions for naturalization[qv] of individuals, and special acts have conferred collective American citizenship (with certain exceptions) upon the inhabitants of Hawaii (1900), Puerto Rico (1917) and the Virgin Islands (1927)[qqv].

[F. A. Cleveland, *American Citizenship as Distinguished from Alien Status;* L. Gettys, *The Law of Citizenship in the United States;* Government Printing Office, *Naturalization, Citizenship, and Expatriation Laws;* C. H. Maxson, *Citizenship.*]

ROBERT PHILLIPS

Citrus Industry, The, including production, packing and marketing of oranges, grapefruit and lemons, got its start in China (*Citrus sinensis*). From 16th-century Spain came a bittersweet orange to Florida, where it spread as a wild fruit. The first orange trees in California grew at Mission San Gabriel (1804). In 1863 the Federal Government began a collection of citrus with the purchase of three varieties of oranges, a Maltese oval, a St. Michael and a Mandarin. The Bahia navel was imported in 1868, and the collection was augmented in 1871 by additional European specimens.

California now leads the industry, with its production of Valencia and navel oranges, lemons and grapefruit. The sweet, round orange is the most important citrus fruit in Florida; next in importance is the grapefruit; the tangerine and the Satsuma orange rank next; limes are grown in the extreme southern part of Florida. An extensive citrus culture, largely grapefruit, has developed since 1920 in Texas. Satsuma oranges are grown along the Gulf, in Alabama, Mississippi, Louisiana and Texas. There is also a growing citrus industry in Arizona.

By 1890 production of American citrus fruit had reached 4000 carloads. Since then the trend has been steadily upward. In 1936–37 the production of boxes of oranges by states was as follows: California, 29,827,000; Florida, 22,500,000; Texas, 2,000,000; Arizona, 220,000; other states, 391,000; a total of 54,938,000 boxes, an increase of 30,155,000 over the 1919–20 season. Grapefruit production by boxes was as follows in 1937–38: Florida, 14,600,000; Texas, 11,800,000; Arizona, 2,750,000; California, 1,728,000; a total for four states of 30,878,000 boxes, an increase of 24,585,000 over the 1919–20 season. Lemon production by California amounted to 7,597,000 boxes in 1936–37, an increase of 3,277,000 boxes over the 1921–22 season. During the 1930's the grapefruit canning industry has grown rapidly, the number of boxes used for canning in 1937–38 being, by states: Florida, 6,000,000; Texas, 5,200,000; Arizona, 625,000; California, 400,000; a total for four states of 12,225,000, an increase of 12,075,000 over the 1922–23 season.

Co-operative marketing prevails widely in California and Florida. The California Fruit Growers Exchange packs about 75% of the California crop. The general officials of the co-operatives look to the advertising and marketing; local packing houses pick the fruit, haul it to packing shed, wash, wax, sort, wrap and pack. Low-grade fruit is made into marmalade, jelly, peel, vinegar, citric acid, calcium citrate, oil of orange and lemon, etc.

Irrigation is practised to a limited extent in Florida and is necessary for moisture control in southern California. Groves in frosty sections have various types of heaters. Insect pests are checked by spray gun and fumigation tent, and are prevented from importation by inspection at state borders. Trees are fed with phosphates and nitrates. Owners of all but the largest tracts do much of the labor themselves; other laborers vary with the sections, being largely mestizos in California.

[R. G. Cleland and Osgood Hardy, *March of Industry; Bulletins* of the U. S. Dept. of Agriculture.]

ROBERT G. RAYMER

City Government. *See* Municipal Government.

City Manager Plan, THE, is a simplified form of municipal government which originated in Staunton, Va. (1908), but did not attract much attention until after its adoption in Dayton, Ohio, six years later. Then it spread rapidly, particularly in states which have the home-rule charter system (*see* Charters, City), until eventually it gained acceptance in several hundred cities, large and small. Its chief vogue, however, is in the smaller municipalities.

The essential features of the city manager plan are, first, a small council elected by the voters of the city on a nonpartisan ballot; and, second, the appointment by this council of a chief administrative officer known as the city manager who assumes full responsibility for the entire work of municipal administration. The manager is chosen for his administrative capacity; he holds office during the pleasure of the council, and is the most highly paid officer of the city government. In some cases a member of the council serves as titular mayor, but without any important administrative duties.

The city manager attends all meetings of the council, prepares the budget for the council's consideration and appoints all the administrative officials, with a few exceptions such as the city clerk and the members of the public library board. The city charter usually forbids all interference by members of the city council in the manager's routine work, but the council retains the power to enact the ordinances and to decide all questions of general policy. City managers may be chosen from outside the city and in many instances this policy has been pursued.

On the whole the city manager plan has operated successfully, but its success has been most uniform in the smaller municipalities. In the larger cities it has proved a more difficult problem to find competent managers and to keep the managerial office out of politics.

[T. H. Reed, *Municipal Government in the United States.*]

WILLIAM B. MUNRO

City Planning in the United States had its beginnings a long time ago. In 1692 William Penn devised a complete plan for his new city of Philadelphia, a plan which covered an area of about two square miles. A number of open spaces were reserved for public buildings and for parks while the rest of the tract was laid out with pencil and ruler in checkerboard fashion. Arterial highways and cross streets intersected one another at uniform intervals and at right angles.

More than a century later Maj. L'Enfant was brought over from Paris to plan the new national capital on the banks of the Potomac. This was a much larger enterprise with an area of about forty square miles. The French engineer varied the checkerboard plan by superimposing upon it a number of great diagonal avenues. Then came the upper portion of New York City, which was planned by a special commission in 1807. This commission merely cut up the area into 2000 city blocks, each exactly 200 feet wide, with serial numbers to designate all the newly planned avenues and streets. Other cities followed New York's unimaginative example until nearly all of them presented the same dull, drab symmetry.

About the beginning of the 20th century, however, city planning began to undergo a transformation both in scope and in technique. The public authorities commenced to realize that effective planning must take into account many things besides street layout: for example, the location of public buildings, transportation facilities, zoning, height of buildings and the facilitation of motor traffic. More weight must also be given to æsthetic considerations. Consequently in all the larger cities, and in most of the smaller ones, the local authorities were empowered to enact city planning ordinances and to establish planning boards with regulatory functions. The direction and nature of growth in virtually all American cities is now being guided by these boards. (*See also* Detroit, Woodward Plan of.)

[N. P. Lewis, *The Planning of the Modern City;* K. B. Lohman, *Principles of City Planning.*]

WILLIAM B. MUNRO

Civil Aeronautics Act (1938). The Civilian Aviation Act of 1926 established a Bureau of Commercial Aviation in the Department of Commerce, to map airways[qv], improve landing facilities and establish beacons and it also provided regulations for civilian flyers and for the operation of civilian air routes. The Post Office Department and the Interstate Commerce Commission[qqv] both exercised certain measures of control over air lines which carried mail, passengers and freight, as they did over railroads. The Lea-

McCarren Civil Aeronautics Act, which became law in June, 1938, created a Civil Aeronautics Authority of five members—to be appointed by the President—whose jurisdiction over aviation combines the authority formerly exercised by the Bureau of Commercial Aviation created in 1926, the Post Office and the Interstate Commerce Commission. A Safety Board of five members within the Authority's governance is also appointed by the President. The Authority regulates passenger, freight and mail rates and schedules, promulgates safety regulations, supervises the financial arrangements of air-line companies, passes upon all mergers and agreements between companies and may even designate and establish new airways. Existing air-mail[qv] contracts were terminated by the act, and the Post Office Department had the right to place mail upon any air line at rates approved by the Authority.

ALVIN F. HARLOW

Civil Liberties is a term generally used in the United States to indicate not only the idea of civil rights, privileges, prerogatives, franchises and freedom in general but also the concept of immunity or protection of individuals or groups from undue interference by the Government.

In England the idea of liberty was formulated particularly in the Magna Carta in 1215; in the Petition of Right in 1628; in the Habeas Corpus Act in 1679 and in the Bill of Rights signed in 1689. The concept was transferred to America by the Virginia charter of 1606 and by the charters of later colonies.

Subsequently, in the period from 1763 to 1775, when England undertook to increase its control over the American colonists, the latter objected strenuously. In the Declarations of Rights issued by the Stamp Act Congress in 1765 and the First Continental Congress in 1774, it was insisted that the colonists were entitled to all the rights and liberties of Englishmen[qqv]. In 1776 the Declaration of Independence[qv] held that "life, liberty, and the pursuit of happiness" were "inalienable rights" of men.

Meanwhile, the idea of civil liberties in America had been strengthened by legislative guarantees in at least eleven colonies. Six of the first state constitutions, drawn up during the Revolutionary War, contained elaborate bills of rights (*see* Bills of Rights, State). The national Constitution of 1787 included six guarantees of liberty but did not include a comprehensive bill of rights. As a result of popular demand, ten amendments, commonly called the Bill of Rights[qv], were added to the fundamental law in 1791.

The liberties guaranteed by the Bill of Rights and by the original Constitution include the prohibition of a state church; freedom of religion, speech and the press; the right of petition; liberty to assemble peaceably; the right to bear arms; protection against the quartering of troops; the right to a jury trial; immunity from unreasonable search and seizure, self-incrimination, double jeopardy, cruel and unusual punishments and excessive bail; the guarantee of just compensation for property taken by the Government by eminent domain; the guarantee that Congress will not deprive a person "of life, liberty, or property, without due process of law"; the privilege of the writ of habeas corpus; and the prohibitions of bills of attainder, ex post facto laws, grants of titles of nobility, religious tests for officeholders and convictions for treason except as defined in the Constitution.

The constitutional history of the United States abounds with illustrations of the different executive, legislative, judicial and popular interpretations of civil liberties at various times. Congress in 1798 and again in the World War period curbed freedom of speech and of the press by sedition laws. In the post-Civil War period the Ku Klux Klan Act[qv] sought to protect the civil liberties of Negroes. During the Civil War, President Lincoln suspended the writ of habeas corpus outside the war zone. The Civil Rights Cases and the Scottsboro Case[qqv] are examples of Supreme Court interpretations of the civil liberties of Negroes.

[T. M. Cooley, *Constitutional Limitations;* J. M. Mathews, *The American Constitutional System.*]

ERIK McKINLEY ERIKSSON

Civil Rights Act, The (April 9, 1866), was the first Federal statute to define citizenship and to safeguard civil rights within states. "All persons born in the United States and not subject to any foreign power, excluding Indians not taxed," were declared to be citizens of the United States. Such persons, "of every race and color," should have rights equal with white citizens for the security of person and property, in any state or territory. Jurisdiction over enforcement was given to Federal courts. The purpose of the act was to nullify the Black Codes[qv] of various Southern states. Since there was some doubt in Congress as to the constitutionality of the act, the Civil Rights section was later incorporated in the resolution framing the Fourteenth Amendment[qv]. After President Johnson vetoed the act (March 27, 1866) the opponents of the President won a two-thirds majority in Congress to override the veto, and thereafter Congress was in full command of Reconstruction[qv] legislation (*see* Civil Rights Cases; Force Acts).

[E. P. Oberholtzer, *A History of the United States since the Civil War*, Vol. I.]

C. MILDRED THOMPSON

Civil Rights Cases, 1883 (109 U. S. 3). Individuals are protected from violations of their civil rights on the part of the Federal authorities by the Bill of Rights[qv] in the Federal Constitution. They are protected from such violations on the part of state authorities by the Fourteenth Amendment[qv] and by the bills of rights in their respective state constitutions. The Civil Rights Cases clearly establish the fact that individuals have no constitutional protection—Federal or state—from violations of their civil rights on the part of other individuals. They may secure redress, but by court action, and under statutory rather than constitutional authorization. Furthermore, the statute must be a state, and may not be a Federal, one.

During the period of Reconstruction[qv], Congress adopted a series of acts known as the Force Acts[qv], of which the Civil Rights Act was one. For years Sen. Charles Sumner of Massachusetts had urged the adoption of such a measure; upon his death his erstwhile colleagues waived their doubts as to the measure's constitutionality, in their anxiety to pay tribute to a departed friend. This act (March 1, 1875), which was the last to be adopted in the group of Force Acts, sought to guarantee to all citizens of the United States full and equal enjoyment of the privileges of inns, theaters, restaurants, public conveyances, etc., and stipulated that such enjoyment should not be subject to any conditions applicable only to citizens of a particular race or color, or who had been in a previous condition of servitude. Suit was brought against certain proprietors—Stanley, Ryan, Nichols, Singleton and the Memphis and Charleston Railroad Company—for violation of the law.

The Court sustained the arguments of the defendants, who alleged that the act was unconstitutional. It was held that the denial of such privileges is not an indication of slavery or involuntary servitude; that the Fourteenth Amendment applies to states, not to individuals; that no law had been made by a state abridging rights or denying equal privileges to citizens of the United States, and that the acts complained of were committed by individuals, hence the cases did not come within the meaning of the Fourteenth Amendment. The decision, like that in the Slaughter House Cases[qv] ten years earlier, is one of permanent significance. If the Court had accepted the opposite view, the whole nature of the American constitutional system would have been changed in a manner and to an extent never contemplated by the Congress which proposed or by the states which ratified the War Amendments.

[Charles K. Burdick, *The Law of the American Constitution;* William A. Dunning, *Reconstruction, Political and Economic;* Andrew C. McLaughlin, *A Constitutional History of the United States;* J. G. Randall, *The Civil War and Reconstruction;* Charles Warren, *The Supreme Court in United States History;* W. W. Willoughby, *Constitutional Law of the United States.*]

W. BROOKE GRAVES

Civil Service, as distinct from military, naval and foreign service, is the term applied to those public employees who provide an administrative liaison between the state and the individual. All governmental units are thus operated by a civil service, with classified and unclassified divisions, expansion of which keeps pace with an increase in governmental functions. The classified service is characterized by appointment through competitive examination, salary standardization, permanent tenure, merit promotion and pension compensation; the unclassified service, on the other hand, is characterized by political appointment and rapid turnover in positions.

Corruption of civil service in the United States dates from 1789, but it was not until the Jacksonian era that political rotation of governmental posts became a widespread abuse which ultimately reached unprecedented proportions immediately after the Civil War. Then it was that reform organizations launched a campaign to make "civil service" synonymous with the "merit system"[qv]—a campaign which has been continued for more than fifty years. Civil service reform has been undertaken during four major periods in United States history—namely, the post-Civil War era, the post-Spanish-American War era, the post-World War era and the post-Depression era. Three major pressure groups[qv]—namely, the National Civil Service Reform League, the Civil Service Assembly of the United States and Canada, and the League of Women Voters[qv]—have concentrated their efforts on drafting better civil service laws, on improving relations between public employees and legislators, and latterly on improving relations between civil servants and citizens whom they serve.

Significant landmarks in Federal civil service reform have been the laws of 1853, 1855, 1871, 1883 and 1919. In 1853 and again in 1855 a simple system of "pass examinations" was inaugurated by Congress for Federal civil servants. In 1871 Congress gave the President power to determine a general system of personnel selection.

However, it was not until 1883, by the Pendleton Act[qv], which received the support of President Arthur, that a Civil Service Act of any moment was passed. This is still the basic statute. It has been supplemented by a major set of Civil Service Rules and Orders promulgated by President Theodore Roosevelt in 1903, which have been amended from time to time; and by the Classification Act of 1923. In 1919 war veterans were granted special preference. Congressional bills for complete reorganization of the existing civil service and for the extension of the merit system to first-, second- and third-class postmasters are pending as of 1938.

In 1883 New York adopted the first state Civil Service Act, the statute of which was later (1894) incorporated in the state constitution. Massachusetts followed in 1884; Wisconsin and Illinois in 1905 (the latter's statute amended in 1911); Colorado in 1907 (statute incorporated in the constitution, 1919); New Jersey in 1908; Ohio in 1912 (constitutional amendment; supplemented by a statute in 1913); California in 1913 (statute amended in 1929; incorporated in state constitution in 1934); Connecticut in 1913 (repealed in 1921; re-enacted in 1937); Kansas in 1915 (now defunct since 1920 for lack of funds); Maryland in 1920; Kentucky in 1936; Arkansas, Tennessee and Maine in 1937.

The same periods that have witnessed reform in Federal and state civil services have also seen similar reforms in municipalities. Approximately 450 cities (of the 960 having a population greater than 10,000) now use the merit principle for selection of personnel, though many of these confine merit appointments to police and fire services. Most cities operate their own statutes, but state commissions in Massachusetts and New Jersey directly control local civil services, while state commissions in New York and Ohio have partial local jurisdiction. About 40 of the 3056 counties have adopted the merit system to date (1939).

[Leonard D. White, *Trends in Public Administration.*]

FRANCES L. REINHOLD

Civil War, Economic Consequences of (North). Destructive as it was of material as well as of human values, the Civil War proved to be a great stimulus to the economic life of the North. Government contracts, paper-money inflation and a new protective tariff system[qqv] brought a rapid expansion of capital and a new prosperity to Northern industry, with large-scale industry increasingly common. Cotton manufacturing declined because of a shortage of raw material, but woolen manufacturing and the munitions and war supplies industries in general experienced sharp gains. The young petroleum[qv] industry was given an important place in the rapid growth of American capitalism. The telegraphs and railways[qqv] led the way to a new era of corporate consolidation. The later years of the war brought a new national banking system[qv] which promised a check upon the paper issues of the existing state banks. Out of these developments and, in addition, a frenzied stock-market speculation, came new fortunes that were often summed up as constituting a "shoddy" aristocracy.

To the common man this prosperity was not an unmixed boon. Agriculture experienced new gains with an expanded area and an increased use of farm machinery[qv]; this was often, however, at the price of overexpansion and debt. With wages lagging far behind a price rise that more than doubled the cost of living, labor found even less in which to rejoice; it therefore turned new energies toward organizing its forces in national craft unions. The burden of taxation was borne with little complaint. Excise taxes were levied upon as many articles as possible; tariff schedules reached in 1864 an average rate of 47%, partly offset by the internal revenue levies; income taxes came to be assessed upon all incomes in excess of $600 a year, with, however, less than a half-million persons affected. Thus was secured one fifth of the wartime needs of the Government. The rest was borrowed directly or indirectly; the war ended with a Federal debt of over $2,600,000,000. Yet the national wealth had been greatly increased and a new era of American capitalism was ahead.

[Fite, *Social and Industrial Conditions in the North during the Civil War.*]

ARTHUR C. COLE

Civil War, Economic Consequences of (South). The Civil War brought economic suffering, devastation and ruin to the South. As a result of the blockade[qv], the interruption of intercourse with the North and the strain of supporting the armed forces, the people were subjected to extreme privation. Large land areas were laid waste by military operations. Accumulated capital resources were dissipated. Railroads were either destroyed or allowed to deteriorate to the point of worthlessness. Live stock was reduced by almost two thirds. Slave property valued at about $2,000,000,000 was wiped out. Approximately one fourth of the productive white male population was killed or incapacitated. Land values were undermined; agricultural production was greatly retarded; trade was disrupted; banks and mercantile houses were forced into bankruptcy; the credit system was disorganized; and commercial ties with foreign nations were broken. (*See also* Reconstruction.)

The war also brought sweeping changes in the economy of the South. The destruction of slavery[qv] together with the devastation wrought by the conflict forced the plantation system to give way to a sharecropper, tenancy and small farm system. A central feature of this transition was the rise of the crop lien which tended to make necessary continued concentration on cotton cultivation. With the breakup of the plantations[qv] there occurred a great increase in the number and economic importance of the small towns and their inhabitants–merchants, bankers, lawyers and doctors.

The war also brought a diminution in the part the South has played in the determination of national economic policies. During the period since the war, tariff, monetary, railroad, banking and other such matters have generally been decided without any consideration for the wishes and needs of the South. The result has been what amounts to economic exploitation of the South by other sections of the nation.

[J. A. C. Chandler, ed., and others, *The South in the Building of the Nation*, especially Vols. V and VI; W. L. Fleming, *Documentary History of Reconstruction.*]

HAYWOOD J. PEARCE, JR.

Civil War, Financing Problems of the (Federal). When Salmon P. Chase reluctantly resigned from the Senate to become Secretary of the Treasury in March, 1861, the state of the Federal finances was not encouraging, especially in view of the impending war. During the preceding four years of the Buchanan administration the treasury had financed deficits annually through the flotation of government obligations, a factor which had shaken the confidence of investors in these securities. Chase, himself, at first, could only float additional loans to meet the essential expenditures of government.

Shortly, faced with the problem of financing the war, Secretary Chase decided on a tax program to cover the regular expenses of government, while the extraordinary expenses resulting from the war were to be financed by the sale of bonds and notes. During the fiscal year 1861, 64.3% of total net receipts came from taxes and only 35.7% from loans.

The situation changed radically in the next fiscal year. The customs law which had been enacted on Chase's recommendation did not yield sufficient revenue to cover even the ordinary expenses, and war expenditures, of course, increased rapidly. Moreover, the sale of government securities was not easy as it was usually required by law that such securities could not be put on the market below par, while the interest authorized was not sufficient to attract investors at par or above.

It was under these circumstances that Mr. Stevens and Mr. Spaulding of the House Ways and Means Committee were able to secure the passage of the first legal tender act[qv] (authorizing the issuance of $150,000,000 of greenbacks[qv]) on Feb. 25, 1862. Passage of this act was procured under the plea of dire necessity, although the opposition showed that by selling government obligations on the market for what they would bring the issuance of greenbacks could have been avoided.

In the fiscal year 1862 only 10.7% of total net receipts were obtained from taxes, whereas, of the remaining 89.3%, over one third came from non-interest-bearing obligations, mainly United States notes (greenbacks).

A second legal tender act was passed on July 11, 1862, and a third on March 3, 1863, each authorizing $150,000,000 of greenbacks. Further issues were avoided as a result of increased revenues from taxation with a concurrent and consequent improvement in the Government's credit. Thus, in the fiscal years 1863–66 the proportion of net receipts coming from taxes increased successively from 15.8% to 25.9% to 26.9% to 83% in the order given.

The reasons for the failure to tax more heavily in the earlier years of the war are easily explained. Secretary Chase was not experienced in finance and also contemplated a relatively short struggle. The Republican party[qv] was new and lacked solidarity. Internal taxes had not been levied for many years and the Republicans did not dare to risk the unpopularity that a heavy internal tax would probably have called forth. Accordingly, although heavier taxes early in the war would have been sounder financially, they were obviously not politically feasible until a later period.

[D. R. Dewey, *Financial History of the United States;* W. C. Mitchell, *A History of the Greenbacks.*]

FREDERICK A. BRADFORD

Civil War: General Orders No. 100 was a code comprising 157 articles "for the government of armies in the field" according to the "laws and usages of war." By order of Secretary Stanton, it was drawn up by Francis Lieber and a special board, and utilized by Union officers. The first code of its kind, it later formed the basis for German military field law during the Franco-

Prussian War and the conventions of the Hague Conferences[qv] of 1899 and 1907.

[Elihu Root, *Addresses on International Subjects.*]

FRANK FREIDEL

Civil War: Propaganda and Undercover Activities. The Abolition[qv] crusade and the proslavery reaction laid the psychological bases for the war. Upon the outbreak of the conflict, press and pulpit, North and South, further stirred the emotions of the people. In the South, propagandists devoted their efforts to asserting the right to secede and to proving that the aggressive North was invading Southern territory. In the North, the preservation of the Union, patriotism and the crusade against slavery were the major *motifs* in propaganda. On both sides, atrocity[qv] stories—largely concerned with the brutal treatment of the wounded, of military prisoners and of political dissenters—abounded. Southern efforts in propaganda lacked co-ordination, but in the North the radical Committee on the Conduct of the War[qv] gave official direction to the gathering and dissemination of atrocity stories which professed to reveal rebel depravity and to show the felonious and savage nature of the Southerners. The Sanitary Commission and the Union Leagues[qqv] were the chief unofficial agencies in this work. Both sides attempted to influence European opinion and Lincoln sent journalists and ecclesiastics to England and the Continent to create favorable sentiment.

Despite these efforts, many on both sides remained unconvinced. The Knights of the Golden Circle[qv] in the North were paralleled by numerous secret "peace societies" in the South. These organizations encouraged desertion; aided fugitive slaves, refugees and escaping prisoners; and occasionally attempted direct sabotage.

[W. B. Hesseltine, *Civil War Prisons;* G. Tatum, *Disloyalty in the Confederacy;* J. T. Adams, *America's Tragedy.*]

W. B. HESSELTINE

Civil War: Surrender of the Confederate Armies. The most important surrender after Appomattox[qv] was that of Joseph E. Johnston (C.) to William T. Sherman (U.) at the Bennett house near Durham Station, N. C., April 26, 1865. Parole was granted to 37,047 prisoners on the same terms Grant (U.) had given Lee (C.). Previously Sherman had joined Schofield (U.) at Goldsboro, N. C., on March 23, their combined force being about 80,000. Johnston, stationed before the town of Raleigh, had about 33,000 effective troops. On April 10, two days before the news of Appomattox arrived, Sherman advanced to Raleigh and Johnston retreated toward Greensboro, where he convinced President Jefferson Davis that further resistance, though possible, would merely entail prolonged suffering with ultimate subjection. The result was a conference between Sherman and Johnston on April 17–18, resulting in a memorandum to be submitted to Davis and the Governernment at Washington. The proposed surrender included President Lincoln's principles of reconstruction[qv] which, though far more reasonable than the ultimate congressional plan, were outside Sherman's authority to offer. The refusal of Secretary of War Stanton to accept these terms led Johnston, from motives of humanity, to agree to unconditional surrender. Not content with this outcome, Stanton published an embellished account of Sherman's action, made unjust accusations and created a national scandal.

The capitulation of the rest of the Confederate forces followed as a matter of course. On May 4 Richard Taylor (C.) surrendered to E. R. S. Canby (U.) at Citronelle, Ala., thus ending Confederate forces east of the Mississippi. Six days later Jefferson Davis was captured by James H. Wilson's (U.) cavalry near Irwinville, Ga., and was imprisoned at Fortress Monroe[qv]. The final act was the surrender of Kirby Smith (C.) and the trans-Mississippi troops to Canby at New Orleans on May 26. The total number surrendered and paroled from April 9 to May 26 was 174,223.

[J. F. Rhodes, *History of the United States.*]

FRED A. SHANNON

Civil War, The. The causes and preliminaries of the American Civil War (1861–65) are treated elsewhere in this work (*see* South, Civilization of the Old; Abolition Movement; Nashville Convention; Slavery; Missouri Compromise; Kansas–Nebraska Act; Republican Party; Campaign of 1860; Secession; Fort Sumter; The Confederate States of America). In understanding the background of the struggle it is essential to distinguish such broad factors as Southernism in terms of culture types, economic and political motives of the planter aristocracy, Southern defense reaction to Northern criticism, the whipping up of excitement by agitators on both sides, economic sectionalism (agrarian v. industrial tendencies), Northern thought-patterns as to democracy and slavery, Republican party strategy and the highly overemphasized issue of slavery in the territories. Sectional tension grew ominously in the 1850's and a major Southern crisis, accompanied by intense popular excitement, followed the election of Lincoln in November, 1860. By early February, 1861, the seven states of the Lower South had withdrawn from the Union and had begun the erection of the Southern Confederacy. After a period of inaction, the sending of an expedition by President Lincoln to relieve the Federal garrison at Fort Sumter in Charleston Harbor precipitated a Southern attack upon that fort, which was surrendered on April 13. This specifically was the opening of the war. Each side claimed that the other began it. Southerners argued that Lincoln's expedition was an invasion of a sovereign state; the Washington Government maintained that it meant no aggression in "holding" its own fort and that the "first shot" had been fired by the South.

Lincoln's inaugural address of March 4, 1861, had been conciliatory in tone; nevertheless his decision to retain Sumter, which necessitated sending food to the garrison, placed the opening "incident" in precisely that area where peace was most unstable and where emotion had been roused to greatest sensitivity. Fort Pickens[qv] in Florida, though similar in status to Sumter, presented no such menace of emotional outbreak. Lincoln's Sumter policy involved two main points: the sending of the provisioning expedition, and, after the fort had been fired upon, the call for 75,000 militia to be furnished by the states. This policy, while it produced a united North, served equally to unite the South; it was not until after Lincoln's call for militia that the four important states of the Upper South (Virginia, Arkansas, Tennessee and North Carolina) withdrew from the Union and joined the Confederacy. In this sense Lincoln's April policy, interpreted in the South as coercion, played into the hands of the secessionists while Buchanan's avoidance of an outbreak had supplied the setting for compromise efforts.

On the side of the Union there were twenty-three states with 22,000,000 people as against eleven states and 9,000,000 (including 3,500,000 slaves) within the Confederacy. In wealth and population as well as in industrial, commercial and financial strength the Union was definitely superior to the Confederacy. On the other hand the South had the advantage of bold leadership, gallant tradition, martial spirit, unopposed seizure of many Federal forts and arsenals, interior military lines and unusual ability among its generals. Its military problem was that of defense, which required far less men than offensive campaigns and widely extended hostile occupation. Between the two sections was a populous middle region (the Union slave states of Delaware, Maryland, Kentucky and Missouri; the area that became West Virginia; and the southern portions of Ohio, Indiana and Illinois) within which the choice of the people was for the Union while on the other hand there was cultural sympathy for the South and spirited opposition to the Lincoln administration (*see* Border States).

Legally the war began with Lincoln's proclamations: the proclamation of April 15, 1861, which summoned the militia to suppress "combinations" in the seven states of the Lower South, and the proclamations of April 19 and April 27, 1861, which launched a blockade[qv] of Southern ports. Internationally the Confederacy achieved recognition of belligerency, as in the British queen's proclamation of neutrality (May 13, 1861), but never achieved full standing in the sense of a recognition of independence by any foreign power. Nor did any foreign nation intervene in the struggle, though the British government seemed at times to be seriously contemplating it and the government of Napoleon III did offer mediation which was indignantly rejected by the United States (February–March, 1863).

Before Lincoln's first Congress met in July, 1861, the President had taken those measures which gave to Union war policy its controlling character. Besides proclaiming an insurrection, declaring a blockade and summoning the militia (definite war measures), he had suspended the habeas corpus[qv] privilege, expanded the regular army, directed emergency expenditures and in general had assumed executive functions beyond existing law. A tardy ratification of his acts was passed by Congress on Aug. 6, 1861 (U. S. *Statutes at Large,* XII, 326) and in 1863 these strongly contested executive measures were given sanction by the Supreme Court in a five-to-four decision sustained chiefly by Lincoln's own judicial appointees (*see* Prize Cases). In general, Lincoln's method of meeting the emergency and suppressing disloyal tendencies was not to proceed within the pattern of regular statutes, but to grasp arbitrary power by executive orders or proclamations, as in the Emancipation Proclamation[qv] (in which the President exercised a power which he insisted Congress did not have even in time of war), and his extensive program of arbitrary arrests[qv] wherein thousands of citizens were thrust into prison on suspicion of disloyal or dangerous activity. These arrests were quite irregular. Prisoners were given no trial (usually not even military trial); they were deprived of civil guarantees and were subjected to no regular accusations under the law. Such measures led to severe and widespread opposition to the Lincoln administration. In their denial of the habeas corpus privilege they were denounced as unconstitutional in a hearing before Chief Justice Taney (*ex parte* Merryman[qv], May, 1861), but in the Vallandigham case[qv] the Supreme Court, to which the Merryman case had not been brought, declined to interpose any obstacle to arbitrary arrest, thus in a negative way sustaining the President. (In 1866, however, the Court did overrule a wartime military commission in the Milligan case[qv].) Yet it cannot be said that Lincoln became in the 20th-century sense a "dictator." He allowed freedom of speech and of the press[qqv], contrary examples being exceptional, not typical. He tolerated widespread newspaper criticism of himself and of the Government, interposed no party uniformity, permitted free assembly, avoided partisan violence, recognized opponents in appointments and above all submitted himself, even during war, to the test of popular election. This testing resulted in marked Republican loss in the congressional election of 1862, while in 1864, though the situation looked very dark for the Republicans in August, the election in November brought in a considerable electoral majority.

In the military sense both sides were unprepared; had any conceivable policy of prewar preparedness been promoted (under the Southern secretaries of war of the 1850's) it could hardly have given the Union side that advantage which military writers often assume. The battle of Bull Run[qv] (July 21) was the only large-scale engagement in 1861. Though a Union defeat, it was, like most of the battles, an indecisive struggle. Except during the generalship of McClellan (U.), Meade (U.) and Grant (U.) the Southerners had the undoubted advantage of military leadership on the main eastern front; Lee's (C.) notable, though indecisive, victories of Second Bull Run, Fredericksburg and Chancellorsville[qqv] were won against Pope, Burnside and Hooker. At Antietam[qv], however, McClellan stopped Lee's Northern invasion of September, 1862, while the ambitious Confederate offensive of 1863 was checked at Gettysburg[qv]. In the West most of the operations were favorable to the Union side. This was especially true of the "river war" (resulting in the capture of Columbus, Forts Henry and Donelson, Nashville, Corinth and Memphis), the Federal half-victory of Shiloh; and more especially the important Union victories of 1863 at Vicksburg and in the Chattanooga area[qqv]. Later campaigns involved J. E. Johnston's (C.) unsuccessful operations against Sherman (U.) in upper Georgia, Sherman's capture of Atlanta and his famous raid through Georgia and the Carolinas, Sheridan's (U.) devastating operations in the Valley of Virginia, the Grant-Meade operations against Lee in Virginia (involving the costly battles of the Wilderness, Spotsylvania and Cold Harbor), the Hood-Thomas campaign in Tennessee and final operations in the Petersburg and Appomattox areas, which culminated in the fall of Richmond and the close of the war[qqv]. In the naval aspects Union superiority was impressively shown in the blockade of Southern ports which were eventually closed to the Confederacy's own warships, the capture and occupation of coastal positions, the co-operation of western flotillas with the armies, the seizure of New Orleans in April, 1862, the complete control of the Mississippi River after the fall of Vicksburg and Port Hudson in July, 1863, and the defeat and sinking of the Confederacy's proudest ship, the *Alabama*, by the *Kearsarge* (June 19, 1864)[qqv]. On the other hand Confederate cruisers and privateers did considerable damage to Union commerce (*see Alabama* Claims), the Union Navy failed in the operations against Richmond, and several ports (Wilmington, Charleston, Mobile) remained in Southern hands till late in the war. Galveston did not yield till after the war was over, June, 1865. Privateering was authorized by both sides but practised only by the Confederacy, and that chiefly in the first year of the war. The military decision in favor of the United States was registered in the surrender of Lee to Grant at Appomattox, April 9, 1865, and the surrender of J. E. Johnston to Sherman near Durham, N. C., on April 26. (For conditions within the Confederacy, *see* Confederate States of America.)

Methods of military recruiting and administration were amateurish, haphazard and inefficient. Conscription[qv] was used on both sides but by neither side with real effectiveness. Such factors as commutation money, bounties, bargaining in substitutes, draft riots[qqv], irregular popular recruiting, undue multiplication of military units, lack of a general staff and inadequate use of the very small regular army, marred the Union system of army administration. Somewhat similar difficulties existed also in the South. Guerrilla warfare[qv], though never a decisive factor nor a part of major strategy, was extensively practised. The administration of the War Department under Secretary Cameron (to January, 1862) was marred by fraud and corruption; under Secretary Stanton the system was improved, but profiteering and military blundering existed to a marked degree throughout the war. In addition, the Union cause was weakened by state control of national military processes, congressional interference (*see* Committee on the Conduct of the War), anti-McClellanism (involving the unwise abandonment of McClellan's peninsular campaign[qv] in the summer of 1862), confusion and circumlocution among divers army boards, councils and advisers, undue control of army matters by such men as Halleck and Stanton, extensive desertion[qv] and atrocious inadequacy in the care of hundreds of thousands of prisoners, the last-named abuse being chiefly due to utter breakdown in the exchange or cartel system. Negro troops[qv] were extensively used in the Union armies. The Confederate Government, late in the war, authorized their enrollment, but this was never put into practice.

What happened behind the lines would constitute a very elaborate story. Civilian relief was supplied by the United States Sanitary Commission[qv] (similar to the later Red Cross[qv]); war propaganda was spread by the Union League[qv] and the Loyal Publication Society; antiadministration effort was promoted by the Sons of Liberty and Knights of the Golden Circle[qqv]. Financial instability and monetary abnormality carried prices to fantastic heights in the South; in the North the disturbance was far less, but specie payments[qv] were suspended and treasury notes ("greenbacks"[qv]) depreciated to such an extent that the paper price of gold reached $2.84 in July, 1864. Taxation was heavy, yet a Federal debt of approximately three billions was accumulated. Federal bonds were marketed by the semiofficial efforts of Jay Cooke and Company[qv]. Currency and banking regulations were drastically modified by the establishment of the national banking system[qv]. Labor obtained from the war far less advantage than business entrepreneurs. Immigration[qv] was encouraged and the wartime increase of wages was not commensurate with the depreciation of the money system. Greed was widespread, stock speculation was rife, lobbying was rampant, contractors cheated the Government (*see* Civil War Contracts) and large numbers of men became unjustifiably rich. High wartime tariff[qv] laws gave ample protection[qv] to manufacturers. Various reforms and progressive schemes were delayed or wrecked by the war, but laws were passed for assigning free homesteads to settlers (*see* Homestead Movement, The), for encouraging Western railroad building (*see* Land Grants to Railways) and for Federal aid in the establishment of land-grant colleges[qv]. To a people once united but split asunder by the tragedy of war there came the inevitable horrors of war psychosis; this took manifold forms including un-Christian sputterings of hatred in the churches. One of the most savage of the wartime fanatics was "Parson" (W. G.) Brownlow of Tennessee. Yet Quakers[qv] and other honest religious objectors to war were given, by administrative procedure and later by law, the alternative of noncombatant service when drafted. Efforts of peace groups to end the war in 1864 received notable support from Horace Greeley (*see* Peace Movement in 1864), but, being associated with partisan politics, they met failure in every case; even the official efforts of high-placed statesmen met a like failure in the Hampton Roads Conference[qv] of February, 1865. War aims changed as the conflict progressed; the declaration of Congress on July 22, 1861, that the war was waged merely for the restoration of the Union was belied by the Radical Republicans[qv] who by 1864 had determined in the event of victory to treat the South as a subordinate section upon which drastic modifications would be imposed. One of the striking examples of wartime Radical policy was seen in the second confiscation act[qv] (July 17, 1862) which, against Lincoln's better judgment, decreed the forfeiture to the United States of the property of all adherents to the "rebellion." The relation of the war to the slavery question appeared in various emancipating measures passed by Congress, in Lincoln's Emancipation Proclamation as well as his abortive compensated emancipation scheme, in state measures of abolition, and finally in the antislavery amendment to the Constitution (*see* Thirteenth Amendment). (For international aspects of the struggle *see* *Trent* Affair; *Alabama* Claims; Civil War Diplomacy; Confederate States, Blockade of; Mexico, French in.) The distinction of Lincoln was discernible not in the enactment of laws through his advocacy, nor in the adoption of his ideals as a continuing postwar policy, nor even in the persuasion of his own party to follow his lead. Rather, the qualities which marked him as leader were personal tact (shown notably in a Cabinet crisis of December, 1862), fairness toward opponents, popular appeal, dignity and effectiveness in state papers, absence of vindictiveness and withal a personality which was remembered for its own uniqueness while it was almost canonized as a symbol of the Union cause. Military success, though long delayed, and the dramatic martyrdom of his assassination[qv] must also be reckoned as factors in the emancipator's fame. On the other side Southern memory of a cherished lost cause has been equally identified with the lofty perfection of Lee's personality.

To measure the war in terms of man power and casualties is a highly controversial task made doubly difficult by sectional pride, popular tradition, amateur history writing and inadequate statistics. Gen. Marcus J. Wright, a Confederate officer, after the war attached to the War Department, estimated Confederate man power at 600,000 to 700,000 men. Others, including T. L. Livermore and J. F. Rhodes, have put it much higher. Col. W. F. Fox, a careful military statistician, considered that the Union forces did not exceed 2,000,000 separate individuals. Comprehensive records are especially lacking on the Confederate side, while the better statistics on the Union side are in terms of enlistments and have been only conjecturally corrected to allow for numerous cases of reenlistment. Comparable units of military measurement have been hard to obtain in determining the totals involved in particular campaigns or battles, and inadequate attention has been given to the precise meaning of such terms as "effectives," men "present for duty," forces "actually engaged," etc. Grand totals include men in home guards, thousands who were missing and many other thousands who enlisted in the final weeks or were otherwise distant from fighting areas. On the Federal side in April, 1865, there were approximately a million men in the field, with two millions of the "national forces" not yet called out. The number of those subject to military call at the North was actually greater at the end of the war than at the beginning. Confederate dead have been estimated at 258,000, Union dead at 360,000. The stupendous economic and material loss has never been more than roughly estimated.

Aside from the obvious consequences of slaughter and destruction, the results of the war (or concomitants of the war and postwar period) involved suppression of the "heresy" of secession, legal fixation of an "indestructible" Union, national abolition of slavery, overthrow of the Southern planter class, rise of middle-class power in the South, decline of the merchant marine[qv], ascendancy of the Republican party, inauguration of a continuing high-tariff policy, far-reaching developments in terms of capitalistic growth associated with centralization[qv] of government functions and adoption of the Fourteenth Amendment[qv] (intended to consolidate party control by the protection of Negro civil rights but later applied as a shield to corporations). But with the mention of these factors the enumeration of long-time results is only begun. A full enumeration, impossible in these pages, would also include postwar intolerance, partisanship associated with the "bloody shirt" tradition, immense pension claims with their many abuses, a deplorable complex of "reconstruction" evils and excesses, carpetbag and scalawag corruption and, as the continuing result of all this, the "solid South."[qqv] Another way of viewing the whole subject is to consider what would have happened if no war had been fought, but such an inquiry is beyond historical testing. As of about 1900 it could be said that the wounds had been so far healed as to allow for a contented South within a reunited nation, but the antilynching filibuster of 1938 illustrated the persistence of sectionalism[qv] and the tendency of old intolerances to flare up more than seven decades after Appomattox.

[James Truslow Adams, *America's Tragedy;* Arthur C. Cole, *The Irrepressible Conflict, 1850-1865;* Edward Channing, *History of the United States,* VI; C. R. Fish, *The American Civil War;* D. S. Freeman, *R. E. Lee;* J. G. Randall, *Civil War and Reconstruction.*]

J. G. RANDALL

Civil War, The Navy in. On account of divided personnel, scattered forces and inadequate appropriations, the United States Navy was near to demoralization at the outbreak of the war. But the new Secretary, Gideon Welles, and the Assistant Secretary, Gustavus V. Fox, approached their task with intelligence and force.

The year 1861 was marked by a great disaster and two victories. The disaster, eight days after Fort Sumter was fired on, was the abandoning of the Norfolk Navy Yard[qqv]. The Federal Government not only lost eleven ships including the steam frigate *Merrimack,* but 3000 pieces of ordnance, 300 of them Dahlgren guns of the latest type. On the other hand, Admiral Stringham's squadron in August easily took the forts at the entrance to Hatteras Inlet, and DuPont's fleet in November captured two forts defending Port Royal, S. C.[qqv].

The year 1862 began with successful military and naval operations on the Tennessee and Cumberland rivers as Grant and Foote took Fort Henry and Fort Donelson[qqv], breaking the Confederate line of defense in the West, and saving Kentucky for the Union. On the Mississippi Foote's squadron co-operated with the army under Pope in taking Island No. 10[qv] and later advanced as far as Vicksburg. Farragut, at about the same time, coming from the Gulf with a strong seagoing fleet, succeeded in passing the strong forts of Jackson and St. Philip[qv] (April 24) and overpowering the Confederate Defense Squadron. New Orleans[qv] surrendered and the forts soon capitulated. This brilliant campaign prevented intervention on the part of France and possibly of England. On the Atlantic coast, the Confederate ironclad *Merrimack,* coming from Norfolk into Hampton Roads, destroyed the *Cumberland* and the *Congress* and threatened to break the Union blockade (March 8). But the *Monitor*[qv], arriving most opportunely, engaged the champion on the following morning and effectually checked her career.

In 1863, the Union ironclads increasing in numbers, naval attacks on Charleston[qv] became more determined. But even the *New Ironsides,* probably the strongest ship afloat, was unequal to the task. However, the blockade[qv] of South Carolina and other parts of the Southern coast was now highly effective. Of the first importance was the service rendered by Porter commanding the Mississippi Squadron[qv]. By his aid Grant, campaigning against Vicksburg, was able to cross the Mississippi and attack the city from the south and east. When he captured it (July 4) the Union controlled the entire Mississippi basin and split the Confederacy in two.

In 1864 the *Alabama*[qv] was sunk by the *Kearsarge* off Cherbourg, France (June 11). The *Alabama, Florida* and *Shenandoah*[qqv] were highly successful in their depredations on Northern commerce, and because all three had been built in British shipyards the United States claimed a heavy indemnity from England after the war (*see* Alabama Claims). On the 5th of August Farragut won his second decisive victory. With a fleet of wooden ships and ironclads he forced his way past Fort Morgan at the entrance to Mobile Bay[qv]. Later in the same morning he fought the Confederate ironclad *Tennessee* and compelled its surrender. Soon Mobile was barred from all approaches to the sea.

In 1865, on the 15th of January, the South's one remaining access to the sea was closed when the fleet commanded by Porter and the military forces by Terry took Fort Fisher[qv], the key to Wilmington, N. C. With the capture of Fort Fisher, a termination of the war favorable to the North was assured.

The service of the navy consisted in establishing an effective blockade; in carrying on joint operations with the army to capture strategic positions on the coast and to gain control of the Mississippi; and in pursuing and capturing the cruisers that preyed on Northern commerce. It was essential for the preservation of the Union.

[*Official Records of the Union and Confederate Navies.*]

CARROLL S. ALDEN

Civil War, Trade in Cotton during the. At the beginning of the Civil War the United States Government decided to permit a restricted trade in cotton in the districts held by the Union forces. This was done partly because of the foreign demand for cotton and partly to supply destitute Southerners with necessities. The trade was authorized by acts of Congress passed July 13, 1861, and July 2, 1864. In accordance with these laws, regulations were issued at various times, notably on Sept. 11, 1863, and on July 29, 1864, to control the trade. By them the commerce was restricted to treasury agents; private individuals and members of the military and naval forces were not allowed to participate in the traffic and there was to be no commercial intercourse with the Confederates. These rules covered the subject thoroughly, but owing to the profits involved they could not be enforced. Cotton at Boston was worth ten times as much as at the front and consequently Memphis and New Orleans, the principal trade centers, were infested with unscrupulous cotton buyers who proffered bribes for connivance in their illicit trade. Traders were thus allowed to purchase cotton from the Confederates in exchange for military supplies and to engage in private trade with them. Military expeditions, even, were sent out to get cotton for the traders: the Confederates would be warned of impending raids—in which they parted with cotton and in return received supplies that enabled them to maintain their forces.

The trade, legal and illegal, attained immense size. In the spring and summer of 1864 enough cotton went North to supply the factories, while each week $500,000 worth of goods was going South through Memphis. The results of the trade were harmful to the Union cause. According to Gen. Grant and other officers it prolonged the war at least a year.

[E. Channing, *History of the United States*, Vol. VI; J. F. Rhodes, *History of the United States from 1850 to 1877*, Vol. V; A. S. Roberts, Federal Government and Confederate Cotton, *American Historical Review*, Vol. XXXII, No. 2.]

A. SELLEW ROBERTS

Civil War and the Freedom of the Seas. During the American Civil War the United States "set on foot" a blockade[qv] of the Confederacy which was far from satisfying the most stringent requirements of international law set down in the Declaration of Paris[qv] (not ratified by the United States) and of previous diplomatic practice of the United States (*see* Foreign Policy). Further, the Supreme Court on appeal from prize courts developed the doctrine of continuous voyage[qv] one step beyond British practice during the Napoleonic Wars: it applied the doctrine to confiscate neutral property, contraband or no contraband, in transit between

Great Britain and British West Indian islands, when that property was ultimately destined, by a subsequent maritime leg of an essentially continuous voyage, to a blockaded Confederate port (*see Bermuda* Admiralty Case; *Springbok* Admiralty Case). When the property was ultimately destined by a subsequent terrestrial journey (via the neutral port of Matamoras, as in the case of the *Peterhoff*qv) continuously to the Confederacy, the Court did not construe the blockade to exist on land between the neutral country (Mexico) and the Confederacy, but it did confiscate the absolute contraband found on board.

Great Britain cheerfully acquiesced in the loose blockade and in the new interpretation of the doctrine of continuous voyage, which later gave her a valuable precedent with which to enforce, as against the United States, 1914–17, an imperfect blockade of Germany.

In the *Trent* caseqv the United States acknowledged the force, if not the justice, of a British protest, accompanied by an ultimatum, against forcibly taking rebellious American citizens off a British merchant ship on the high seas, an act analogous to British impressment of disobedient subjects (some of them naturalized American citizens) from American neutral vessels on the high seas during the Napoleonic Wars.

[James P. Baxter, 3rd, The British Government and Neutral Rights, 1861-1865, *American Historical Review*, XXXIV, 1928; Samuel Flagg Bemis, *A Diplomatic History of the United States;* F. L. Owsley, *King Cotton Diplomacy;* J. W. Pratt, British Blockade and American Precedent, *U. S. Naval Institute Proceedings*, XLVI, November, 1920.]

SAMUEL FLAGG BEMIS

Civil War Contracts. In the first year of the Civil War the Federal Government and a score of states were bidding against each other for war supplies, with disgraceful consequences. Too often the rule was to let the contract to the highest bidder, that is, to the one who would give the biggest cut to the officials and inspectors. Simon Cameron himself, as Secretary of War, apparently was not guiltless. It is a notorious fact that several of the great fortunes of the modern day had their origin in Civil War contracts. Colt's revolversqv, which sold at $14.50 on the market, brought $25 by army contracts, or $35 when bought by Frémont. Furthermore, goods of inferior quality often found readier sales than first-class products. Shoddy for clothing, sand for sugar, parched grain for coffee, brown paper for sole leather and worthless foreign guns for weapons were among the things foisted on the soldiers. After a year of this sort of orgy the War Department began serious efforts at reform, but the contract business remained slightly malodorous till the end of the war. The situation seems to have been not much better in the Confederacy. At any rate, there was much grumbling against contractors and blockade runnersqv.

[F. A. Shannon, *Organization and Administration of the Union Army.*]

FRED A. SHANNON

Civil War Diplomacy. The basic diplomatic policy of the United States during the Civil War was twofold: to prevent foreign intervention in behalf of the Southern Confederacy; and to gain the acquiescence of the great maritime powers, England and France, in the vast extension of maritime belligerent rights which was considered necessary in order to crush the South. The chief diplomatic figures in Northern diplomacy were Secretary of State William H. Seward, supported and advised by President Lincoln, Charles Francis Adams, minister to England, William Dayton, minister to France, John Bigelow, consul general in France and, after Dayton's death in 1864, minister in his stead, and Thomas Corwin, minister to the Juarez government of Mexico. The United States, of course, had its diplomatic representatives in all the other principal civilized nations. But since France and England were great maritime powers and none too friendly toward the United States at the time, they seemed to offer the only serious danger of foreign intervention, and at the same time they were the nations which had to be appeased because of aggression against their commerce in prosecution of the war against Confederate trade. So Federal diplomacy was largely concerned with these two nations as far as it related to the Civil War.

In the very beginning, Seward deliberately created the impression upon the British government that he was willing if not anxious for the United States to fight Great Britain should that country show undue sympathy for the Confederacy. The recognition of Confederate belligerencyqv before war had really begun—except the firing on Fort Sumterqv—gave Seward and Charles Francis Adams a tangible and even bitter grievance against both England and France. It resulted in Seward's issuing an ultimatum to England, threatening to break off diplomatic relations should England receive, even unofficially, the Confederate diplomatic agents. This grievance was constantly held up by Adams and Seward; and the launching of the Confederate cruisers (*see Alabama,* The; *Florida,* The; *Shenandoah,* The) and the building of the Confederate ramsqv in England—and France—gave other even stronger grounds upon which the American diplomats could complain. The sale of munitions and the colossal blockade-running[qv] business carried on with the Confederacy furnished further and constant complaints, particularly against England. French intervention in Mexico[qv] was an added score against France. The piling up of grievances by the United States against France and England, particularly the latter, cannot be overlooked as a powerful factor in making these two Western European powers extremely cautious with reference to even friendly intervention in the Civil War. It helped create the very definite belief that intervention meant a declaration of war by the United States. As for war, neither France nor England cared to pay such a price to see the United States permanently divided. These grievances of the United States were used to counteract the grievances of England and France in the blockade of their West Indian ports and the seizure of their merchant vessels, under the doctrine of "ultimate destination,"[qv] hundreds of miles from the Confederate coast when apparently destined to neutral ports. England, of course, was glad to see the re-establishing of the paper blockade[qv] and the doctrine of ultimate destination; but the methods employed in the seizure and search of scores of vessels, including the *Trent*[qv], created deep resentment in England, and Adams and Seward cleverly used the *Alabama* claims[qv] and other similar grievances as counterirritants.

The objective of Confederate diplomacy was to obtain foreign assistance in gaining independence. The Confederate government based its plans upon European dependence upon Southern cotton, at first; and finally upon the well-known desire of England to see a powerful commercial rival weakened, and of Napoleon III to see the champion of the Monroe Doctrine[qv] rendered impotent to frustrate his attempted annexation of Mexico. The Confederacy first sent William L. Yancey, Pierre A. Rost and A. Dudley Mann as joint commissioners to obtain European aid and recognition. Later Yancey resigned, the commission was dissolved, Mann was sent to Belgium as permanent commissioner and Rost to Spain. James M. Mason and John Slidell—taken prisoner by Wilkes and later released by the Federal Government on the demand of Great Britain—were sent to Great Britain and France respectively as Confederate diplomatic agents. The Confederacy sent John T. Pickett to the Juarez government in Mexico and Juan Quintero to the government of Santiago Vadaurri, governor-dictator of Nuevo Leon and virtual ruler of several of the neighboring border states of Mexico. The Confederate diplomats were ably supported by propagandist agents in both England and France. Edwin DeLeon and Henry Hotze were the chief propagandist agents. The Confederate diplomatic agents were informally received in May, 1861, in England; but after that Lord Russell refused even that much recognition under the pressure of Seward's ultimatum. However, the British government did continue to deal with the Confederate agents by means of correspondence. In Belgium, Spain, France, Mexico and even at the Vatican, Confederate diplomatic agents were received informally but freely. In fact, Slidell in France was on such good terms with Napoleon that the latter made a practice of intercepting messages to United States Minister Dayton for him.

The causes for the failure of the Confederacy to obtain foreign intervention were that the things to be gained by war on the part of England and France would not offset war losses. Europe had a surplus of cotton during the first year of the war; and after this surplus gave out, war profits, particularly in England, from cotton speculation, linen and woolen industries, munitions, blockade running and the destruction or transfer of the American merchant marine[qv] to British registry, dwarfed the losses among the cotton-mill operatives and removed the chief economic motives for intervention. It is also contended that the wheat famine in England made that country dependent upon the United States for its bread supply, and that this operated as an important factor in preserving the neutrality of the British.

[E. D. Adams, *Great Britain and the American Civil War;* E. M. Callahan, *Diplomatic History of the Southern Confederacy;* F. L. Owsley, *King Cotton Diplomacy.*]

FRANK L. OWSLEY

Civil War Munitions. The standard equipment of the Union Army was muzzle-loading Springfield or Enfield rifles and the type of cannon now so often found cluttering up courthouse lawns. Many early regiments, however, went to the front with nondescript arms of their own procuring. Other hundreds of thousands of rifles were furnished by contractors who took all the antiquated, castoff weapons which European governments could drag from the junk heaps of their armies. A large proportion of these, sold to the War Department at extravagant prices, had to be scrapped immediately. Others, which were issued to the soldiers, proved more dangerous to the man behind the breech than to the enemy before the muzzle. Before 1861 various American companies were making breech-loading repeating rifles which, by repeated testimony of experts, would fire fifteen times as rapidly as the best of muzzle-loaders, with equal accuracy and force, and with greater ease of manipulation. But the traditional backwardness of the War Department and its staff prevented the use of such improved weapons. All sorts of excuses, none of them valid, were conjured up against them. In the closing months of the war a new Chief of Ordnance, Alexander B. Dyer, equipped a few companies in the Southwest with repeating rifles, and with these weapons in their hands the men proved invincible. When the war was over the same arms were adopted for the regular army.

Throughout the war those persons responsible for its conduct preferred to set up huge armies with inferior guns to form a larger target for the enemy, rather than equip a smaller and more compact force with weapons of multiple effectiveness. Even Gatling guns^qv^, firing 250 shots a minute with frightful precision, were dismissed in cavalier fashion. A dozen of them were supplied to Gen. B. F. Butler, whose men proved their merits. But again, the weapon was not adopted for general use till after the war. Following a few initial blunders there was not much difficulty in procuring a plentiful supply of good muzzle-loading guns, or of powder and shot.

The munitions of the Confederacy were inferior to those of the North. Battlefield captures, raiding expeditions, imports from Europe and an increasing production from Southern munitions plants kept the troops armed. Largely cut off by the blockade^qv^ from European supplies, and with little industrial development, manufacturing plants had to be built and manned, and materials had to be obtained and prepared. While saltpeter and sulphur in the raw state were plentiful in the Confederacy, machinery and labor for conversion were generally lacking. Yet, in 1864, lead-smelting works, bronze foundries, a cannon foundry, rifle, carbine and pistol factories were operating (*see* Tredegar Iron Works). The big problem of supply was the lack of adequate transportation.

[F. A. Shannon, *Organization and Administration of the Union Army.*]

FRED A. SHANNON

Civil Works Administration, THE, was created by executive order in the winter of 1933–34 as a branch of the Federal Emergency Relief Administration^qv^, in order to launch an emergency program of public works projects, for the purpose of re-employing some 4,000,000 persons at regular wages until they could be absorbed by the Public Works Administration^qv^ or by private industry. This "civil works program" of local improvements required an abundance of labor and a minimum of materials, and included a wide variety of projects such as the maintenance and landscaping of roads and highways, repair of buildings and equipment of schools and universities, improvement of public parks and playgrounds, erosion control, pest control and the improvement of municipally owned water, gas and electric utilities. Public administrators, engineers and accountants handled the projects instead of private contractors, and the pay rolls were disbursed directly by the Federal Government. While critics occasionally questioned the social urgency of some of the projects, this experiment in public welfare temporarily boosted both the morale and the purchasing power of a large segment of population. About $900,000,000 was spent on this work, which was liquidated in the spring of 1934.

[F.E.R.A., *Monthly Reports*, December, 1933-July, 1934.]

MARTIN P. CLAUSSEN

Civilian Conservation Corps, UNITED STATES, is an organization created by acts of Congress March 31, 1933, and June 28, 1937, for the purpose of providing employment, particularly to young men, ages seventeen to twenty-three, who are unemployed and in need of employment, on projects which increase, preserve and restore the natural resources of the United States. The men enrolled in the Corps receive a basic cash allowance of $30 per month ($36 for assistant leaders and $45 for leaders), plus food, clothing, shelter, transportation, medical attention and education. They live in camps, each housing approximately 200 enrollees.

Approximately 200 major types of work are prosecuted on forest, park, agricultural and other types of lands. Indicative of the magnitude of the work is the fact that through March 31, 1939, approximately 8,500,000 man-days had been used in forest fire suppression and presuppression, more than 1,575,400,000 forest trees had been planted and 140,000 miles of roads and trails had been completed and maintained. Through March 31, 1939, approximately 2,180,000 men had served in the Civilian Conservation Corps (plus an additional 40,000 Indians and 20,000 territorials). Enrollment is for a period of six months, with a maximum service for young men of two years permissible.

[Annual Reports of the Civilian Conservation Corps.]

ROBERT FECHNER

Civilized Tribes, The Five. *See* Five Civilized Tribes.

Claiborne Settlement. Acting upon a trading license, William Claiborne established in 1631 a plantation upon Kent Island in the upper reaches of the Chesapeake Bay. The settlement was recognized as an outpost of Virginia and was represented in its General Assembly. This claim to prior occupation tended to invalidate Lord Baltimore's title according to the terms of the Maryland charter which passed the royal seal in 1632. In 1638 Gov. Calvert seized Kent Island, although during the civil war in England Claiborne temporarily regained control.

[M. P. Andrews, *Virginia, the Old Dominion;* J. H. Claiborne, *William Claiborne of Virginia.*]

MATTHEW PAGE ANDREWS

Claim Associations were frontier institutions designed to provide a quasi-legal land system in areas where no land law existed. Settlers who preceded the government surveyor into a new area and established their homes therein or who located on public land*qv* not yet offered at public auction sale made their improvements with no certainty of continued ownership. Before 1841 settlement in advance of survey and sale was contrary to law. Settlers had no protection against speculators buying their lands at the public auction; they had no protection against the "claim jumper"*qv* who sought to oust them and steal their improvements; nor had they means for registering, transferring or mortgaging their claims. Where squatters*qv* were fairly numerous it was natural that they should organize to protect their common interests. Claim associations or claim clubs appeared early in the 19th century and were found in practically every part of the public land area which received settlers before 1870. The squatters would come together, adopt a more or less stereotyped constitution or bylaws guaranteeing mutual protection to each claimant of 160 or 320 acres who met the simple requirements for improvements. Claim jumpers were dealt with in summary fashion by these associations. A "register" was selected who kept a record of all claims and their transfers, and a bidder was chosen to represent the group at the public auction sale.

The most important event in the life of the frontier was the government land auction and to it flocked the squatters, well armed and determined to defend their claims against any speculators who contemplated outbidding them. When the sale began, the bidder, flanked by the motley crowd of squatters, took a prominent position near the auctioneer, and as the squatters' sections were offered bid the government minimum price and no more. If higher bids were made, drastic action was at once taken, the offending speculator being treated as roughly as the claim jumper.

The claim associations' registry made it possible to buy and sell claims without the government patent and there frequently developed a large claim business, much of which was speculative. Early state and territorial law gave legal sanction to many of the practices of the associations, including the registering and transferring of claims. After the public auction and the establishment of state or territorial transfer laws the associations disappeared.

The Pre-emption Law of 1841*qv* legalized squatting upon surveyed lands and gave the settler the right of pre-empting his claim before the public sale, thereby protecting him against competitive bidding, but only if he could raise the funds to pay for the land. Claim associations were still necessary to give community sanction and force to the quasi land regulations in areas where no legal system existed. The heyday of the associations was in the 1840's and 1850's in Iowa, Kansas and Nebraska, where practically every township had its protective organization.

[B. H. Hibbard, *History of the Public Land Policies.*]

PAUL WALLACE GATES

Claim Jumper, THE, was one who drove a squatter*qv* from his claim or, in his absence, seized it. Next to the horse thief he was the most detested person on the frontier. The squatter's only recourse was to appeal to the local claim association*qv*, which undertook to rid the community of such undesirable characters.

[B. H. Hibbard, *History of the Public Land Policies.*]

PAUL WALLACE GATES

Claims, The Federal Court of, was created by Congress (1855) under its power to appropriate money to pay the debts of the United States. The court investigates contractual claims against the United States brought before the court by private parties, or referred to it by an executive department or by Congress. In some cases the decisions of the court are final, subject to appeal to the Supreme Court; in others, the court merely reports its findings to Congress or to the department concerned.

[F. W. Booth, The Court of Claims, *United States Daily*, Dec. 1, 3, 4, 5, 1928.]

P. ORMAN RAY

Clark, Fort (1813–19), was a frontier post erected, September, 1813, where Peoria, Ill., now stands. A wooden stockade mounting cannon, it was named in honor of George Rogers Clark. Although the force which built it withdrew before the end of 1813, it was garrisoned for at least considerable periods in 1814 and 1815. It was the scene of no serious conflicts, but it was an effective restraint upon hostile Indians during the War of 1812. Unoccupied, it was destroyed by Indians, partly in 1818, completely in 1819.

[E. E. East in *Peoria Journal-Transcript*, March 6, 1936, July 23, 1937.]

PAUL M. ANGLE

Clark, Fort (Mo.). *See* Osage, Fort.

Clark's Northwest Campaign (1778–79). During the early years of the Revolution the British exercised undisputed control over the country northwest of the Ohio River. Their most important center of influence was Detroit[qv], the headquarters of the posts and the key to the control of the fur trade and the Indian tribes. From Detroit emanated the influences which dominated the savages of the entire Northwest, and instigated the dispatching of uncounted war parties against the frontier settlements south of the Ohio. So terribly were the settlers of infant Kentucky harassed that they were considering abandoning the country altogether, when George Rogers Clark stepped forward as their leader and protector.

Clark perceived that Kentucky could best be defended by the conquest of Detroit, the center whence the raids were instigated. Too weak to make a frontal attack upon Detroit, or even upon Vincennes, he directed his first blow against the towns of the French in Illinois. Kaskaskia[qv] was occupied, July 4, 1778, and the remaining Illinois towns, and even Vincennes[qv], were easily persuaded to join the rebel standard. Upon learning of these developments, Lt. Gov. Hamilton of Detroit prepared to effect a counterstroke. Under great difficulties he marched upon Vincennes, which was retaken, Dec. 17; but instead of pushing on against Kaskaskia, Hamilton now dismissed his Indian allies and settled down for the winter.

The situation was thus placed in the balance and victory would favor the leader who struck first. Instantly perceiving this, Clark led his little army eastward across Illinois to tempt his fate at Vincennes. An untimely thaw flooded the prairies and drowned the river bottoms and the story of the difficulties encountered and vanquished surpasses many a flight of fiction. Even Clark himself said the recital of them would be too incredible for belief by any one not well acquainted with him.

A bullet through the breast of a British soldier apprised Hamilton of Clark's arrival. After an investment of thirty-six hours, Hamilton yielded his fort and garrison to the rebel leader, Feb. 24, 1779. Although Detroit, Clark's ultimate goal, was never attained, he retained his grip upon the southern end of the Northwest[qv] until the close of the war, and this possession proved an important factor in obtaining the Northwest for the United States in the Definitive Treaty of Peace of 1783.[qv]

[J. A. James, *Life of George Rogers Clark;* M. M. Quaife, *Capture of Old Vincennes.*]

M. M. QUAIFE

Class Struggle. The phrase "class struggle" refers to an alleged conflict between capitalist and wage-earning classes. The doctrine is identified with Karl Marx, founder of modern "scientific" socialism, who, with Friedrich Engels, first formally stated the concept in the *Communist Manifesto,* written in 1848 for the League of Communists. Marx contended that the determining factors of social evolution are economic, that the nature and functioning of social institutions—legal, political, religious, moral and literary—are in every epoch determined by the prevailing modes of production, exchange and distribution of wealth.

In this materialistically determined historical development, subsequent to the primitive community landownership, there has been a series of relentless class wars. Always the exploited, dispossessed class has rebelled against the possessing, exploiting class which is constantly fashioning new forms of production that are irreconcilable with existing forms. Thus feudalism was destroyed by the bourgeoisie and capitalism is expected to be overthrown by the revolutionary proletariat. The historical struggle is to culminate in a society freed from exploitation, oppression, class distinctions and class struggles.

The theory of the class struggle has been a dynamic influence in radical movements in every country. In the United States such organizations as the Socialist Labor party (1877), Social Democracy of America (1897), the Socialist party of America (1901), the Industrial Workers of the World (1905), the Communist party (1919), and the Communist Labor party[qqv] (1919) have been constructed around this theory. The national socialist movements of various countries have organized international workingmen's associations, including the First International (London, 1864); the Second International (Paris, 1889); and the Third International (Moscow, 1919).

[Karl Marx and Friedrich Engels, *Communist Manifesto;* H. W. Laidler, *The History of Socialist Thought.*]

GORDON S. WATKINS

Clayton Act of 1914, THE, was the result of a growing conviction that the Sherman Antitrust Law[qv] of 1890 did not reach some important evils of big business. The Sherman law was leveled mainly at the evils of monopoly and restraint of trade, and at the time it was passed the dominant method of combination was the business trust, where properties were transferred to trustees, a legal form different from the corporation[qqv]. In the years after the Sherman law, combinations began to organize as holding companies, interlocking directorates[qqv], under trade agreements of various kinds, and eventually as aggregations of nonrelated industries. A new situation had developed which the Clayton Act and the Federal Trade Commission Act[qv], passed the same year, were designed to cover. The Clayton law provided mainly prohibitions against practices which "substantially tended to lessen competition," or "substantially" tended to create monopoly, such as discrimination in prices among different producers, acquisition of stock by one company in another, the use of interlocking directorates where restraint was involved, and under certain conditions, a similar provision relative to banks. Another clause placed restrictions on the relation of common carriers to construction and supply companies. In some respects the rigors of the Sherman law were relaxed with respect to labor and agricultural organizations. In regard to labor, in some jurisdictions certain customary activities of unions were interpreted as restraints of trade. It was provided in the Clayton Act that nothing in the Federal antitrust statutes was to be construed to prohibit the existence of "labor, agricultural, or horticultural organizations, instituted for the purposes of mutual help . . . or to forbid or restrain individual members . . . from lawfully carrying out the legitimate objects thereof." Section 20 of the law prohibited the use of restraining orders or injunctions[qv] "unless necessary to prevent irreparable injury to property, or to a property right, of the party making the application, for which injury there is no adequate remedy at law."

[J. M. Clark, *Social Control of Business;* E. W. Crecraft, *Government and Business;* L. H. Haney, *Business Organization and Combination.*]

ISAAC LIPPINCOTT

Clayton-Bulwer Treaty, THE (1850), was a compromise arrangement resulting from the conflicting interests of Great Britain and the United States in Central America. In the late 1840's Great Britain, on the basis of claims dating from the 18th century, was occupying the Bay Islands, which belonged to Honduras, and also the eastern coast of Central America, as "protector" of the pseudo-kingdom of the Mosquito Indians (*see* Mosquito Question). After war broke out between the United States and Mexico the British government quickly saw that the assured American victory would stimulate American interest in a ship canal across the isthmus (*see* Squier Treaty). Therefore, on Jan. 1, 1848, British authorities, acting for the Mosquito king, seized the mouth of the San Juan River, the logical eastern terminus of any future canal in the region.

Strained relations at once developed between the two governments, though each assured the other that it had no selfish designs on the transit route. Negotiations in England having failed to end the dispute, Sir Henry Bulwer was sent to Washington, where, with Secretary of State John M. Clayton, he negotiated the treaty which bears their names. This provided that the two countries should jointly control and protect the canal which it was expected would soon be built somewhere on the isthmus. The introductory article, drafted by Clayton with the aim of ousting the British from Central America, pledged the two countries not to "occupy, or fortify, or colonize, or assume or exercise any dominion over Nicaragua, Costa Rica, the Mosquito Coast, or any part of Central America." The agreement was ratified July 4, 1850.

Almost immediately, however, the interpretation of the self-denying clause just mentioned became the subject of a bitter dispute between the two governments. The United States held that the pledge not to "occupy" required that Great Britain withdraw. The British replied that if the agreement had been intended to be retroactive this fact would have been definitely stated; and they failed to get out of the Bay Islands and the Mosquito territory. War again threatened, but Great Britain, valuing her cotton trade with the United States more than she did her claims in Central America, finally acquiesced in the American interpretation and withdrew in 1858–60.

The Clayton-Bulwer Treaty had become very unpopular in the United States, however, and when, after several decades, the canal was still unbuilt, popular demand grew for abrogation of the agreement, to make possible construction of an American-controlled canal. Finally, in 1902, the Hay-Pauncefote Treaty[qv] superseded the Clayton-Bulwer arrangement.

Critics have correctly charged that the latter, by taking Great Britain into American partnership in controlling the proposed canal, violated the spirit of the Monroe Doctrine[qv]. But it should be noted that the United States, by insisting upon a retroactive interpretation of the treaty, forced the British to give up long-existing territorial claims, which was a unique triumph for the Doctrine.

[M. W. Williams, *Anglo-American Isthmian Diplomacy, 1815-1915;* same, John Middleton Clayton, in *The American Secretaries of State and Their Diplomacy*, S. F. Bemis, ed., Vol. VI.]

MARY WILHELMINE WILLIAMS

Clayton Compromise, THE (1848), was the name given the plan drawn up by a bipartisan Senate committee headed by John M. Clayton for organizing Oregon and the Southwest. It excluded slavery from Oregon, prohibited the territorial legislatures of New Mexico and California from acting on slavery, and provided for appeal of all slavery cases from the territorial courts to the Supreme Court of the United States. It passed the Senate July 27, 1848, but was tabled in the House.

[G. P. Garrison, *Westward Extension, 1841-1850.*]

MARY WILHELMINE WILLIAMS

Clearing Houses. The first formal provision for a clearing-house association in the United States, that of New York City, was adopted on Sept. 13, 1853, by thirty-eight New York banks, and the first clearing of checks took place on Oct. 11. Clearing houses were subsequently established by the banks of Boston (1856), Philadelphia (1858), Chicago (1865) and St. Louis (1868). From the latter date on, growth in the number of clearing houses was rapid, with the result that associations of this character were soon to be found in all of the larger and a considerable number of smaller cities. At the time of reopening the banks, following the banking crisis of 1933[qv], there were more than 250 clearing-house cities in the United States.

Although the ostensible reason for the organization of clearing houses has been the clearing of checks, many of these associations have performed valuable collateral functions. Among the latter may be noted: (1) rendering assistance to weaker members in times of stress, (2) fixing uniform rates of interest and uniform collection charges, (3) examining members of the association and publishing statements of condition and volume of clearings, (4) gathering credit data for members and (5) issuing clearing-house loan certificates in times of strain.

A number of these functions were of more significance prior to the establishment of the Federal Reserve system[qv] than they have been since. In the fifty years prior to the World War, it is safe to say that the clearing-house associations of the United States were among the most efficient and valuable agencies connected with the conduct of American banking. Since 1914, various banking reforms have somewhat diminished the importance of their collateral functions. Nevertheless, clearing-house associations still continue to play an indispensable part in the operation of the American banking system.

[J. G. Cannon, *Clearing Houses;* W. E. Spahr, *The Clearing and Collection of Checks.*]

FREDERICK A. BRADFORD

Clearwater River, Battle on (July 11–13, 1877). During the Joseph campaign the hostile Nez Percé[qv] Indians under Joseph, White Bird and Toohulhulsote withdrew from Craig's Mountain and established camp on the Clearwater River, west of Kamiah, Idaho. Gen. O. O. Howard attacked with infantry, cavalry and artillery. The latter was ineffective. The battle was marked by charges and countercharges and established Joseph's position as head war chief. The Indian barricades were eventually carried and the Indians driven in retreat past Kamiah to the Lolo trail leading into Montana.

[H. H. Bancroft, *History of Washington, Idaho and Montana.*]

WILLIAM S. LEWIS

Clermont, THE (1807). *See* "Fulton's Folly."

Cleveland, Ohio. A trading post was located at the mouth of the Cuyahoga River as early as 1786; in the same year an Indian village named Pilgerruh was founded by three Moravian[qv] missionaries on a site ten or twelve miles upstream. In 1796 Moses Cleaveland, agent of the Connecticut Land Company[qv], which had acquired from Connecticut a large part of the Western Reserve[qv], laid out a town which was given his name. Granted a township government in 1800, made the seat of the new county of Cuyahoga in 1810, incorporated as a village in 1814, Cleveland in 1836 began its history as an incorporated city with a population of about 4000. Originally important commercially only as a post on the route from Pittsburgh to Detroit, with the opening of the Ohio Canal[qv]—to Akron in 1827 and to the Ohio River in 1832—it became an increasingly important outlet for products of the interior of the state, and for the Pennsylvania, West Virginia and Ohio coal that was soon brought in quantity to smelt the iron ore shipped from the Lake Superior mines. A railroad development, ambitiously planned in the 1830's but not realized until the 1850's, made additional contributions to the important iron industry of the Civil War period, since which time Cleveland has had the history of a rapidly expanding industrial city.

ARTHUR C. COLE

Cleveland Democrats, THE, were those Democrats who in Cleveland's second administration continued to support him after silverites, high-tariff men and other dissident elements had broken from his leadership. His insistence upon repeal of the Sherman Silver Purchase Act[qv] in 1893 and veto of the bill to coin the silver seigniorage on May 27, 1894, aroused an anger among the free-silver Democrats of the West and South which his successive bond issues to preserve the gold standard[qv] (1894–95) increased; his fight with a senatorial group over the Wilson Tariff Bill[qv], ending in an outspoken denunciation of their "perfidy," estranged protectionist Democrats; and he had the abiding ill will of Tammany[qv] members and David B. Hill's followers. In the Democratic National Convention of 1896 the Cleveland Democrats, led by William C. Whitney and William E. Russell, were decisively defeated (*see* Campaign of 1896); their refusal to accept the result brought about the formation of the National Democratic ("Gold Democratic"[qv]) party.

[Allan Nevins, *Grover Cleveland, A Study in Courage.*]

ALLAN NEVINS

Cliff Dwellers, THE, were a prehistoric race of Indians who built their dwellings under overhanging cliffs in rocky canyon walls. Most of the cliff dwellings are found within a hundred miles radius of the point where the boundaries of Colorado, Utah, New Mexico and Arizona meet. However, some have been reported as far north as Lodore Canyon, Colorado, and as far south as Sierra Madre, Mexico. The most important groups of these ruins are being preserved at Mesa Verde National Park. Other groups have been declared national monuments, e.g., Canyon de Chelly, Hovenweep, Montezuma Castle, Walnut Canyon and Navajo.

The cliff dwellers were an agricultural people raising corn, beans, melons and turkeys. Cisterns, ollas or water jars and irrigation systems give evidence of their struggle against an arid climate. The attacks of roving Indian enemies, disease, superstition and an increased aridity in the region caused the complete abandonment of these dwellings before the white man discovered America. Some of the present-day Pueblo Indians[qv] may be their descendants.

The cliff dwellings vary from single isolated rooms to large communal villages built solid to the roof of the cave. Several are three and four stories containing over 100 rooms. They are built of stone, much of it quarried and hewn with stone hammers, and adobe mortar and plaster. Many of the lower chambers are circular ceremonial rooms called kivas. Ceilings are timbered and these timbers enabled Dr. Douglass with his tree ring[qv] calendar definitely to date these ruins between 919 and 1273 A.D.

The dwellings are hundreds of feet above the floor of the canyon. Their inaccessibility made them safer from attack by enemies. Further protection was furnished by tall watchtowers built on the top of the mesas overlooking the canyons.

[F. H. Chapin, *The Land of the Cliff Dwellers;* National Park Service, *Mesa Verde National Park.*]

PERCY S. FRITZ

Climate. The influence of climate upon American history has been both economic and biological. Economic effects, such as variations in crops, are widely recognized as important historical factors. Biological effects, such as regional differences in human health and activity, have received little recognition. One of the obvious economic effects of climate has arisen through disasters, such as the floods[qv] of the Mississippi (1927) and Ohio (1936), the hurricanes[qv] that wrecked Galveston (1900) and Miami (1926) and the "Big Freeze" that put an end to orange growing in northern Florida (1894–95). Far more important, though less spectacular, is the way in which drought[qv] has repeatedly plunged thousands of families into poverty in the dry western plains, and has led to migration on a large scale. The great droughts of 1933–36 actually led California temporarily to flout the Constitution by excluding American citizens who came from the ruined "Dust Bowl"[qv] farther east. During the 19th century each major drought was followed by a major financial depression. Crop failures strained an imperfect financial structure to the breaking point. They have also been a powerful incentive to political agitation, as in the Populist Movement[qv] for free silver (1896). In fact, repeated droughts have tended to make the drier parts of the Great Plains[qv] a political hotbed, especially in North Dakota and Alberta, where unseasonable frosts combine with droughts to make the crops unreliable.

The effect of climate upon the health of man is even more important than its effect on the health of crops. Both effects depend upon the biological law that every living creature has an *optimum* climate, and cannot be at its best in any other. The best climate for human progress, however, depends upon the optimum not only for (1) health, but for (2) the suppression of dangerous parasitic organisms of all sorts, (3) the production of abundant crops with no danger of shortage, (4) the growth of plants supplying a wholesome diet for man and beast, as well as valuable raw materials and (5) freedom from disasters due to drought, flood, storm, etc. In the long run the first of these criteria, health, appears to be the most important. Where climate has the best direct effect upon health, however, it also ranks high in the other criteria. Putting all these conditions together we find the best American climates in three strips; namely, (1) the Atlantic coast from Maine to Maryland; (2) the southern Great Lakes region; (3) the Pacific coast from Puget Sound to southern California. The Pacific strip maintains its distinctive character for scarcely a hundred miles inland. The two eastern strips merge into a large peripheral area of good, but slightly less perfect climate. The strips and the peripheral area together extend from the Maritime Provinces, New England and New Jersey westward to the Mississippi and beyond. The best part of South America, in central Argentina, Uruguay and central Chile, is comparable to the edges of this peripheral area.

Historically, this distribution of climate has been of primary importance. It appears to be a main determinant of the general distribution of intensive agriculture, manufacturing, cities and the development of literature, education and science. Among the forty largest cities of America, eighteen (averaging 1,200,000 in population) lie directly in the narrow strips defined above, fourteen (700,000) in the eastern peripheral region and the corresponding part of South America, and only eight (700,000) in the remaining 95% of the two continents. Coal, waterways and land routes have influenced the situation of the cities, but climate is the main factor in their general location. The areas of favorable climate carry on practically all the more complex manufacturing industries. Only such relatively simple occupations as the making of cotton cloth and the preparation of raw materials for market, or such purely local industries as railroad yards, garages, printing establishments and bakeries are greatly developed outside the limits of the climates which closely approach the human optimum. For this reason the northeastern quarter of the United States, with an adjacent bit of Canada, forms a conspicuous historical unit which has often been politically at odds with other climatic areas, as in the case of its desire for a protective tariff[qv].

The northern parts of New England, New York, Michigan and Wisconsin, with adjacent parts of Canada, form another distinct climatic province. There the relatively conservative agricultural and commercial life is different from the hurry and bustle of the manufacturing zone. The fact that Maine and Vermont were the only Republican states in 1936 and that Quebec is the most conservative part of Canada illustrates the matter. Other factors of course play a large part in this, but the long, snowy and comparatively idle winters, the cool, short and very busy summers, the limited variety of crops and the difficulties imposed by cold weather upon machinery and transportation all combine to prevent such restless activity as is found in New York. Many people, to be sure, ascribe this difference to purely cultural causes. The geographer, however, finds that all over the world human society tends strongly to be organized in harmony with the physical environment. Cultural tendencies which are in harmony with the climate tend to persist, whereas tendencies which are at variance with the climate are sloughed off.

The Southern states illustrate this same point in a third climatic region. The development there of a small colonial aristocracy among a far larger number of poor white farmers was absolutely in harmony with the climate and with the plants which grow best in that climate. So, too, were the development of slavery[qv], the Civil War and the present contrast between North and South. Just as the long, cold winters act as a damper upon human activity in Quebec, so the long, hot summers act as a damper in the South. The heat does not make it impossible for white men to carry on manual labor in the South as many people suppose. The health of white men there, and in even warmer climates, is actually improved by working out of doors. Nevertheless, prolonged heat creates a strong disinclination to work. Therefore, the person who can refrain from work and enjoy the fruits of others' labor is envied. Hence the prevalent ideal has been to have some one else do the work, whereas in the most favored zone the social system is built around the physical fact that during most of the year the climate makes people feel like working.

Add now to this the influence of crops which thrive in the South but not in the North. In colonial days rice and especially tobacco, and in later times cotton[qqv], were crops of this kind that could be very profitably exported. They demand a far greater amount of monotonous labor in the hot sun than do corn, wheat and oats. Therefore, the urge to use indentured labor or slaves was far greater than in the North. At the same time, the warm climate made it possible to

Climate

keep such labor at work most of the year, and to support it at relatively small expense.

Thus in the South the biological effect of climate upon man and plants encouraged slavery and a social system which sharply distinguished between aristocratic slave-holding land owners and poor men with little land and no slaves. It would not be correct to say that the Civil War was caused by the climatic difference between North and South, but the conditions which caused the war could not have developed as they did if the climatic influences, both economic and biological, had been different. Although slavery is now gone, the disinclination to work engendered by prolonged heat still makes it more difficult in the South than in the North to become a skilled mechanic, or inventor, or to make progress in education, literature, science, industry and social organization. Thus, to the climatologist it appears inevitable that the historic development of the two sections will continue to be different.

West of these three eastern climatic regions lies the widely extended belt of grassy plains where deficiency of moisture prevents the growth of trees. There the extremes of heat and cold, moisture and drought are very great. Hence, not only are the crops unreliable, but the density of population is small and the market for manufactured goods is both small and unreliable. Moreover, the people often feel that they may move on at any time, and there is constant talk of political and economic change. These conditions create a social and economic atmosphere unfavorable to manufacturing. Thus, from far north in Canada to the borders of Mexico we have a long climatic province dependent mainly upon grain and cattle[qv]. Its problems are bound to be very different from those of either the East or the Far West.

Still farther westward the Rocky Mountain region is characterized not only by mining, but by dry climatic conditions which find expression in irrigation[qv] and in the raising of cattle or sheep. Hence, a very scanty population is either grouped in small and isolated units, or widely scattered on ranches. One historical effect of this has been to permit the Mormons[qv] to develop a unique social system almost unhampered by their neighbors. Another has been to separate the narrow strip of unusual climate along the Pacific coast from the rest of the country. Dryness has done more than mountains to preserve this separation. The rapid development of wealth, industry, science, education and new social movements on the Pacific coast could scarcely have followed its actual course without the help of the stimulating coastal climate and the isolation arising from the dryness of the Rocky Mountain area and the western plains.

North and south of the regions thus far described lie other huge climatic provinces. One of these, embracing most of Canada and Alaska, has had relatively little effect on history. Another, on the south, has been extremely important. When Columbus set sail from Spain the steady trade winds led him to hold a somewhat southerly course. For a hundred years thereafter most of the ships coming to America were similarly influenced by this climatic feature. Hence, Europe established contact with America in low latitudes, and in the part of the continent where the climate most favored the development of a relatively high primitive culture. On the plateaus of Mexico and Peru the dominant climatic elements are a warm, but not hot, summer with abundant rain, and a mild winter so dry that neither forests nor turfy grass will thrive. Hence the land is naturally free from forests without the help of the axe. Moreover, it is easy to cultivate. Not only are the grasses of a bunchy type which can easily be pulled up by hand, but summer floods from small mountain streams provide natural irrigation. In such a region agriculture is practicable even with no tools except a pointed stick and a clamshell or shoulder blade of a deer. More important still, this particular kind of climate was especially favorable to corn[qv], which is the outstanding native food plant of America. Then, too, the Mexican and Peruvian highlands, although depressingly monotonous, are so high and cool that they are fairly healthful and conducive to work. The enervating climate of the neighboring lowlands, either directly or through diet and disease, apparently had much to do with the decay of the Maya civilization after its brilliant intrusion from the highlands. In the highlands, the climate made it permanently possible for agriculture to become the foundation for a genuine civilization, with well established towns, regular trade routes, and many features of an advanced culture.

The presence of these relatively civilized people had an almost immeasurable effect on the early history of America. It determined the regions where the Spaniards could profitably search for gold and where they finally settled. It made it easy for them to master the Indians and make slaves of them. In climates where prolonged heat or monotony has an enervating effect people tend to alternate strongly between activity and careless indifference. In the best climates, on the contrary, people tend to be steadily active without great ups and downs. This is one of the most important climatic effects. Even in the highlands the tendency of the tropical Indians to relax after a brief effort assisted the Spaniards not only in conquering them, but in enslaving them. The enslavement resulted in extermination, or more often, in intermarriage. Thus there arose a new racial type, which has had a large share in determining the later history of Latin America.

One of the most interesting illustrations of the effect of climate upon history is found in the contrast between the relatively submissive Indians of tropical America and the warlike Indians farther north. The most virile of the latter may be represented by the Iroquois[qv] of New York who lived in the most stimulating climate of America. In harmony with this they were characterized by intense and constant activity, alertness and persistence. Such qualities, to be sure, depend on inheritance and training, but they are intensified by a climate where strong, but not undue contrasts of weather from day to day and season to season engender a state of nervous tension and at the same time promote physical health. In our own day, as we have seen, the climate from New England and New Jersey westward makes people always want to "do something," even if they have not fully thought out a plan. Indian wars and raids were an expression of a similar feeling, and in this respect were parallel to the feverish rush of modern New York and Chicago.

The quality thus expressed was an important element in delaying the settlement of the best part of North America and later in keeping the French out of what is now the United States. It also found expression in a surprisingly advanced form of political organization. It could not express itself in what is commonly called civilization because the climate which is best for human efficiency renders a fully sedentary, agricultural life impossible so long as iron tools are unknown. Without such tools extensive clearings cannot be made among the hardwood trees which are here dominant, and even a small field quickly becomes useless because choked with grass. Although the persistent energy of the Iroquois was thus denied expression along the lines of material culture, it was free politically. The Iroquois League with its representative form of organization was the highest expression of political capacity ever reached by the Indians. It enjoyed an extraordinary duration of two centuries (approximately 1570–1780). It is very doubtful whether it could have flourished so well in a less favorable climate, just as it is doubtful whether Harvard and Yale would hold their present prestige if they had always been located in an unstimulating climate.

This brings us to a final generalization as to the relation between climate and American history. Although many other factors introduce modifications, the degree of political stability varies as a rule in close harmony with the climate. The most stable portions of North America are the Northern states and southern Canada. The Southern states have staged one great uprising against the general government. Farther south we find Mexico repeatedly in the throes of revolution, and the governments of Central America, Colombia and Venezuela are still more unstable—not that revolutions necessarily occur in all tropical climates, but a tropical climate, even when fairly cool by reason of altitude, tends to break down people's self control, and make their activity spasmodic. When excited, they act too hastily, and then, becoming quickly exhausted, they submit to misgovernment without making persistent and effective efforts to correct it. Another historical effect of climate that must be noted is the remarkable contrast between the British who settled in southern New England from 1630 to 1643 and the larger number who settled at practically the same time in the West Indies. The first group, in a stimulating healthful climate, has progressed and increased. The other, in an unfavorable climate, has diminished not only in numbers, but in influence.

[Ellsworth Huntington, *Civilization and Climate; The Red Man's Continent*, in The Chronicles of America; and *World Power and Evolution;* Edward J. Payne, *History of the New World*, Vols. I and II; A. Grenfell Price, *White Settlers in the Tropics.*]

ELLSWORTH HUNTINGTON

Clinton and Montgomery, Forts, Capture of. *See* Highlands, The, 1777–81.

Clinton Riot, The, Sept. 4, 1875, was one of the worst disturbances during Reconstruction[qv] in Mississippi. Four whites and an undetermined number of Negroes were killed. It is important because President Grant refused to send the Army, thus allowing the whites to discard Radical Reconstruction.

[Charles Hillman Brough, The Clinton Riot, *Publications of the Mississippi Historical Society*, Vol. VI.]

MACK SWEARINGEN

Clipper Ships were long and narrow wooden sailing vessels, with lofty canvas. Their era lasted for a quarter of a century, from about 1843 to 1868, and gave to the world the greatest development of the sailing ship in speed and beauty. The word "clipper" has its origin, perhaps, in the verb "clip," meaning to run swiftly. The clipper ships were designed to do just that thing.

Tea from China quickly lost its flavor in the hold of a ship, and about 1843 the clippers began quicker delivery of that product. The discovery of gold in California[qv] induced many in the decade from 1849 to 1859 to take the voyage around Cape Horn[qv] in fast clipper ships. After carrying their cargoes of men and merchandise to California, the ships would either return to Atlantic ports for another such cargo, or would cross the Pacific to China in ballast, and load there with tea, silk and spices (*see* China Trade). The discovery of gold in Australia in 1851 also gave a great impetus to the building of clipper ships.

They were much more dependable than the old-type sailing vessel. In a heavy sea they strained less and were thus able to take better care of their cargoes; and they crossed belts of calm better than the low-rigged ships. The swift brigs and schooners built at Baltimore during the War of 1812 were known as Baltimore clippers[qv]; but the first real clipper was the *Ann McKim,* built there in 1832. Beginning about 1850 the California clippers increased rapidly in size, ranging from 1500 to 2000 tons register. Of this type the *Stag-Hound,* built in Boston in 1850, was the pioneer. Six of the clipper ships established speed records that have never been broken. Practically all of them were faster than the steamships of their day, and it was more than a quarter of a century before the steamship was able to break the record of the fastest clippers. Their great speed is attested by the fact that eighteen ships made passages from New York or Boston to San Francisco in less than 100 days. The four best passages were made by the *Flying Cloud*[qv], built in Boston in 1851, in 89, 89, 105 and 108 days, an average of 97¾ days. Then came the *Andrew Jackson,* built at Mystic, Conn., in 1855, in 89, 100, 102 and 103 days, an average of 98½ days. Those records were followed by the *Flying Fish,* built in Boston in 1851, in 92, 98, 105 and 106 days, an average of 100¼ days.

By 1855 the "extreme" clippers were succeeded by the "medium" clippers, vessels that did not carry so much canvas, but that could be handled by a smaller crew. Shortly after the close of the Civil War, American shipbuilding for oversea carrying trade declined. Although some clipper ships were built, the steamships[qv] gradually displaced them.

[A. H. Clark, *The Clipper Ship Era;* O. T. Howe and F. C. Matthews, *American Clipper Ships, 1835-1858;* Helen La Grange, *Clipper Ships of America and Great Britain, 1833-1869.*]

CHARLES GARRETT VANNEST

Clockmaking. Clocks were brought to America by the early settlers, and contemporary colonial artisans repaired them and probably made new ones. By the 18th century, at least, both household timepieces and belfry clocks were made to order. Fine examples of these are still cherished by collectors. Connecticut, whose population was outgrowing its agricultural resources before the Revolution, early developed several mechanical industries, including clockmaking. Its craftsmen received their skill from Holland, through New York, as well as from Great Britain. Finer timepieces had metal works, but wooden clocks were made in America soon after 1700. Being cheaper, they were in more demand and until the middle 1830's dominated the market. Itinerant vendors, like "Sam Slick,"[qv] peddled them, with tinware, through the country. Works were often sold separately from cases, and the more democratic shelf clocks supplanted the tall eight-day clocks of our grandfathers in the homes of the people. Even these, however, were long a luxury, the cheapest models costing fifteen dollars.

In the Connecticut Valley the use of interchangeable parts[qv] soon suggested itself to clockmakers, and early in the last century power machinery assembled in factories was used to shape wheels and other parts. Then quantity production began. The fact that Connecticut was already a brassworking center facilitated the transition to that metal. As a result American clocks, which could not be exported as long as they had wooden works affected by atmospheric changes, were soon sold throughout the world at prices incredibly low to foreigners. A long step toward this was the invention, about 1837, of one-day brass clocks, which could be manufactured for six dollars; in 1855 they were made to sell for seventy-five cents.

Notable pioneers who invented improvements which simplified and cheapened the American product were Ely Terry, who began making wooden clocks at Waterbury in 1793 and built up an extensive business at Thomaston, where the Seth Thomas clocks were subsequently manufactured; and Chauncey Jerome, once employed by Terry, who became the first large exporter and whose works developed into the New Haven Clock Company. Even earlier a family named Willard built up a business at Roxbury, Mass., which sold tall striking clocks and public timepieces in all parts of the country.

Steamboats and railroads made timepieces more necessary, foretelling the modern multiplication of time signaling and recording devices. It was not until the beginning of the present century, however, that electric clocks appeared prominently in manufacturing statistics.

Today about 10,000,000 clocks are made annually in the United States as compared with 10,000 in the first decade of the last century. More than 2,000,000 are electric clocks and nearly 7,000,000 alarm clocks. Connecticut still leads in this manufacture, followed by Illinois, Massachusetts and New York. Exports no longer play as important a part as formerly, though a half million or more alarm clocks are sold annually to foreigners.

[Chauncey Jerome, *History of American Clock Business;* Henry Terry, *American Clock Making;* William G. Lathrop, *The Brass Industry in the United States.*]

VICTOR S. CLARK

Closed Shop, THE. Demands that employers hire only union members arose at an early date. Such union rules appeared as early as 1799. Closed-shop demands in 1836 were attacked in the courts as conspiracies. Although in Commonwealth v. Hunt[qv] (1842), which legalized unions, the Massachusetts court upheld a closed-shop strike, even in 1939 a Federal court questioned the validity of such a strike. The National Labor Relations Act[qv] (1935) permits such agreements between employers and unions.

Campaigns for the closed shop were carried on by many unions after 1870. As union organization proceeded several types of arrangement relative to the employment of union men developed, among which were the open–union shop in which both union and nonunion men are employed, but the union is recognized and dealt with, as with the Congress of Industrial Organizations[qv] unions in the steel and automobile industries after 1937. The chief type of closed shop has been the closed shop with the open union. Here nonunion workers may be hired, but all subsequently must join the union. This policy, found among garment trades unions and the United Mine Workers[qv], characterizes unions in seasonal and competitive industries. The closed shop with the closed union, which permits the employer to hire only union men, has characterized the building and other trades in which skilled workers control and limit their supply.

Employers have usually resisted recognition of unions and the closed-shop demands. So-called open-shop drives, embarked upon by American employers, appeared about the beginning of the 20th century. After 1886 gains of many unions had forced employers to deal with labor organizations. About 1900 strong employer associations undertook an open-shop drive, or an antiunion campaign to restrain further union growth and throw off union control. Again, subsequent to the World War, during which organized labor made great headway, a nationwide campaign for the so-called American Plan, actually a drive for the open shop, began. This was prosecuted to the New Deal[qv] period.

[Commons and associates, *History of Labor in the United States;* C. R. Daugherty, *Labor Problems in American Industry;* L. Lorwin, *The American Federation of Labor.*]

HERBERT MAYNARD DIAMOND

Closure is a technical term in legislative procedure, applied to rules for the limitation of debate. The House of Representatives, because of its large membership, has found it necessary to curtail speeches by resorting to the five-minute rule with permission for a member to extend his remarks in the *Congressional Record*[qv], as a substitute for free debate. In 1917 the Senate adopted a mild closure rule which provided a one-hour limit for speeches when, upon petition signed by sixteen senators, the rule was invoked by a two-thirds vote. Since this rule did not prevent a filibuster near the end of the session nor "unrestrained garrulity" at other times, Vice-President Dawes in 1925 vigorously advocated reform; but nothing has yet (1939) been done to strengthen the 1917 rule. The only form of closure generally in use in state legislatures arises from motions for special orders, or for the previous question.

[Robert Luce, *Legislative Procedure;* W. F. Willoughby, *Principles of Legislative Organization and Administration.*]

W. BROOKE GRAVES

Coahuila and Texas, State of. On May 7, 1824, the Mexican Congress which established the federal system in Mexico united the former Spanish provinces of Coahuila and Texas, declaring that Texas might become a state when it acquired the necessary population and resources. The state was governed by a governor, a lieutenant governor, and a unicameral legislature of twelve members, in which Texas had first one member and ultimately three. The state constitution, effective in 1827, permitted a considerable degree of local political independence, but in state legislation and administration Texans were at a disadvantage. The union was ended by the Texas revolution[qv].

[G. P. Garrison, *Texas.*]

E. C. BARKER

Coal. *See* Anthracite; Bituminous.

Coal Mining and Organized Labor. One of the first coal miners' labor organizations in this highly seasonal industry, was a local unit formed in 1849. The American Miners' Association was formed in St. Louis in 1861, succeeded by the Miners' National Association founded at Youngstown, Ohio, in 1873, which was, in turn, succeeded by the National Federation of Miners in 1885. This latter organization, affiliated with the Knights of Labor[qv] in 1890, became one of the constituent elements of the United Mine Workers[qv].

The growth of the mine union movement was coincident with the growth of business and manufacturing. Labor was beginning to become articulate and to demand a larger share of the profits of industry. A strike in 1894 nearly destroyed the new miners' union, but one in 1897 in the bituminous coal[qv] field was successful and one in the anthracite[qv] field in 1902 gave the union bargaining power. By means of joint agreements with coal operators, wages, hours and working conditions were gradually improved and standardized. Union recognition and the check-off[qv] followed. Strikes, particularly in the bituminous field, were more frequent and increasingly bitter (*see* Colorado Coal Strikes; Herrin Massacre). As a result of concessions due to World War demands, the union had been able greatly to strengthen its bargaining power. The depression of 1920–21, with accompanying reduction in wages, produced a wave of strikes, particularly in West Virginia and in Indiana, Illinois, Kentucky and Kansas. In the prosperous years that followed, as wages were increased, hours shortened and working conditions improved, production costs increased. This was accompanied by an increase in captive (steel- and railroad-owned) mines, by consolidations with consequent elimination of small operators, and by increasing substitution of gas, oil and electricity for coal.

The World War had caused much more coal land to be opened for production than was needed to meet peace-time requirements. As in agriculture, the supply far exceeded the demand; there were too many mines and too many miners; increasing substitution of other fuels aggravated an already bad condition. Each time coal production costs increased, consumer substitution, likewise, increased. And so demand and supply fluctuated up and down with voluntary or forced adjustments, either by worker or operator or both. The New Deal[qv], in response particularly to the demands of the United Mine Workers, sought to stabilize and control the coal industry, first through the National Recovery Act and then by the Guffey Coal Acts[qqv], but this legislation neither increased the total volume of coal consumed nor the number of miners employed. Because of the conditions prevailing in the industry, which are so difficult to control or to anticipate, the miners have striven to secure an agreement guaranteeing an annual wage, but, as yet (1939), nothing in this direction has been agreed on.

[C. Evans, *History of the United Mine Workers.*]

THOMAS ROBSON HAY

Coast and Geodetic Survey, The United States (formerly designated as Survey of the Coast, and United States Coast Survey). When first proposed by President Jefferson and authorized by Congress on Feb. 10, 1807, the Survey of the Coast had as its mission the supplying to mariners of scientific data to aid navigation along the Atlantic coast. The Survey was placed under the Treasury Department, with Prof. Ferdinand Rudolph Hassler, an eminent Swiss scientist who had submitted the most acceptable plans, as its first superintendent.

Despite the clarity and simplicity of his plans, it was no easy matter for Hassler to execute them. His purchases of scientific instruments in England were delayed by the War of 1812. When finally he began his survey of primary base lines on Long Island and the New Jersey coasts in 1816, he was compelled by the amphibious nature of his task to employ army officers, naval officers and civilians as assistants. Personnel difficulties resulted in the temporary transfer of the Coast Survey from the Treasury to the Navy Department. In various years Congress failed to provide adequate funds. Delay in furnishing practical navigation charts led shipowners to precipitate congressional investigations.

From its initial handicaps, however, the Survey was freed in 1843 when Congress formally approved Hassler's scientific methods and adopted the "permanent plan of organization." Since 1843 the expansion of the United States across the continent and the accession of island dependencies have brought the total coast line under the Survey to approximately 100,000 miles. When land questions incident to the opening of the West imperatively demanded extensive inland surveys, Congress (June 20, 1878) enlarged the work of the Coast Survey to cover inland operations and the designation of the organization was changed to "Coast and Geodetic Survey." Since July 1, 1903, when the organization came under the Department of Commerce and Labor (now Department of Commerce), its duties have increased along with the growing interest of the Federal Government in problems of a social and economic nature. In 1925 it undertook seismological observations and investigations, to supply data on designing structures to reduce earthquake hazard; and under the air commerce act of 1926 it has issued aeronautical charts.

Thus today the activities of the Coast and Geodetic Survey are sixfold: (1) to survey and keep up to date charts of nearly 100,000 miles of coast line; (2) to determine geographical positions inland, connecting the coastal surveys and providing the framework for mapping and other engineering work; (3) to study tides and currents, furnishing datum planes to engineers and current tables to mariners; (4) to compile and furnish magnetic information essential to mariner, aviator, land surveyor, radio engineer; (5) to supply seismological data; and (6) to compile aeronautical charts for pilots of aircraft. The results of field investigations and surveys are analyzed in Washington and published as nautical and aeronautical charts, annual tables of predicted tides and currents, charts showing magnetic declination, annual lists of United States earthquakes, publications of geographical positions, "Coast Pilots," "Notices to Mariners" and manuals prescribing correct methods for its various classes of surveying. (*See also* Hydrographic Survey.)

[Florian Cajori, *The Chequered Career of Ferdinand Rudolph Hassler;* G. A. Webber, *The Coast and Geodetic Survey; The United States Coast and Geodetic Survey: Its Work, Methods and Organization,* Special Publication No. 23, Government Printing Office.]

RICHARD S. WEST, JR.

Coast Defense is a term applied to measures to defend coastal cities and important anchorages by guns, searchlights, submarine mines and obstacles to navigation against attack by aircraft and surface and submarine vessels. At the beginning of the Revolution, Boston was the only port in the revolting colonies provided with coast defenses. When the British evacuated it, March 17, 1776, they attempted to destroy the forts. The Americans recovered 250 cannon and rebuilt the defenses. Thanks to these defenses, Boston was the only important American port not taken or burnt during the remainder of the war. Fort Moultrie[qv], a new work at Charleston[qv], repulsed a British fleet, June 28, 1776. A system of coast defenses was begun in 1794. In the War of 1812 the successful defense of Fort McHenry[qv] at Baltimore, Sept. 14, 1814, furnished the theme of America's national anthem. On the following day, Fort Bowyer[qv] (now Fort Morgan) at the mouth of Mobile Bay defeated four British vessels and destroyed one of them.

New and more complete fortifications were begun in 1816–17. Most of the Southern forts were seized by the Confederates in 1861, and many of them became objectives of Federal military and naval expeditions. Admiral Farragut ran by Forts St. Philip and Jackson[qv] below New Orleans, April 24, 1862, and Forts Gaines[qv] and Morgan, Aug. 5, 1864; but the defenses of Charleston repulsed a Federal ironclad fleet, April 7, 1863. No American coast defense was attacked in the Mexican, Spanish-American, and World wars, and none in the Northern states in the Civil War. The present coast defense system was planned by the Endicott Board of 1885–86. It was revised by the Taft Board of 1905–6, and extended to naval bases, the Canal Zone, Hawaii and the Philippine Islands. A single unit is called a "harbor defense."

[Robert Arthur, *History of Fort Monroe.*]

S. C. VESTAL

Coast Guard, The. Its duties, which cover a wide range, include the enforcement of the navigation and other maritime laws of the United States, the rendering of assistance to vessels in distress, the saving of life and property, the destruction of derelicts, and the removal of obstructions and menaces to navigation. It also maintains the International Ice Patrol in the North Atlantic and the Bering Sea Patrol, and gives medical aid to deep-sea fishermen and the natives of Alaska.

Replacing two older organizations, the Revenue Cutter Service, and the Life Saving Service, the United States Coast Guard was established under a law approved by President Wilson on Jan. 28, 1915. On Aug. 4, 1790, Congress authorized a Revenue Cutter Service, to provide customs collectors with the aid of a sea-going military organization in discharging their duties. In 1871 Congress created the Life Saving Service. This was administered by the Revenue Cutter Service until 1878, when Congress established in the Treasury an independent bureau of the Life Saving Service. The United States Coast Guard, on its establishment in 1915, took over the duties of the two older services.

In peace time, it operates under the Treasury Department. In war time, it becomes part of the Navy, subject to the orders of the Secretary of the Navy. The Coast Guard has a present strength of about 10,000 and its floating equipment includes about 225 ships, ranging in size from large sea-going cutters to small harbor patrol craft.

[Darrel H. Smith and Fred Wilbur Powell, *The United States Coast Guard.*]

OLIVER MCKEE, JR.

Coasting Trade. From the beginning of British settlement in North America until after 1850, shipping along the coasts offered the principal means of transportation and communication between sections of the area. In the colonial period it served to distribute European imports as well as to exchange local products. With the growing diversity of sectional production, and the expansion of intersectional trade, coastwise shipping grew from 68,607 tons in 1789 to 516,979 tons in 1830 and 2,644,867 tons in 1860. Manufactured goods of the Northeast were exchanged for the cotton and tobacco of the South, while the surplus agricultural products of the Mississippi Valley came to the Atlantic coast by way of New Orleans. Following the completion of railroad trunk lines along the coast and across the Appalachians after 1850, passengers, merchandise and commodities of value went increasingly by rail, while such bulk cargoes as coal, lumber, ice, iron, steel and oil were shipped by sea. After 1865 the tonnage engaged in coastwise shipping continued to increase (4,286,516 tons in 1900, 10,049,000 tons in 1935), but not with the rapidity shown by rail and motor transportation. The years following 1870 witnessed bitter struggles between ship and railroad operators, characterized by rate wars, followed by agreements and growing control of coastwise trade by the railroads.

Coasting trade was reserved to British and colonial vessels by the Navigation Acts[qv] of 1651 and 1660; and with the formation of the Federal Union, the policy was continued, a prohibitive tax being placed on foreign built and owned ships in 1789, followed by their complete exclusion from coastwise competition under the Navigation Act of 1817[qv], which remains in force.

From 1800 until the Civil War, the schooner was the typical American coasting vessel, but after 1865 steamers and barges towed by steamers were used increasingly, until by 1920 the sailing vessel had largely disappeared.

[E. R. Johnson, T. W. Van Metre, G. G. Huebner, D. S. Hanchett, *History of Domestic and Foreign Commerce of the United States.*]

JOHN HASKELL KEMBLE

Coastwise Steamship Lines. American steamers made coastwise voyages as early as 1809, but the first regular lines were placed in operation in the sheltered waters of Long Island Sound and between Boston and the coast of Maine about 1825. Local services were established in the Gulf of Mexico by Charles Morgan in 1835, while the United States Mail Steamship Company opened a regular line from New York to Charleston, S. C., Havana, New Orleans and the Isthmus of Panama in 1848. In 1849 the Pacific Mail Steamship Company pioneered the route from Panama to San Francisco and Oregon. Prior to 1860 the railroads served chiefly as feeders for the steamship lines, but after the Civil War they offered serious competition. Although the coastwise lines remained active, they were forced to consolidate (Eastern Steamship Co., Atlantic, Gulf and West Indies Steamship Co.), and in some cases the railroads gained control of the steamships, as when the Southern Pacific Railroad acquired the Morgan line (1885). Increasing competition from railroads, motor busses and trucks, mounting operating costs and labor difficulties resulted in the withdrawal of a considerable part of the coastwise steamship service on the Atlantic and virtually all from the Pacific coast south of Alaska by 1937.

[Fred Erving Dayton, *Steamboat Days.*]

JOHN HASKELL KEMBLE

Cobb, Fort, was established by Maj. W. H. Emory, Oct. 1, 1859, on the Washita River, Indian territory. The Confederates occupied it for a time during the Civil War, but later abandoned it and the post fell into disrepair. Reoccupied by troops under Col. W. B. Hazen in November, 1868, to protect the nearby Indian agency (*see* Washita, Sheridan's Operations on), it was once more abandoned the following year in favor of Fort Sill[qv].

[W. S. Nye, *Carbine and Lance.*]

PAUL I. WELLMAN

Cochise Incident. *See* Apache Pass Expedition (Feb. 4–23, 1861).

Cod Fisheries, THE, of North America lie off the coasts of New England, Newfoundland and Labrador. The earliest explorers to the northeastern coast of North America noted the presence of the codfish. Cabot spoke of it, and in 1602 Gosnold gave Cape Cod its name because of the abundance of the fish in its waters. The earliest fishermen came from Spain and France, attracted by the lure of the bank fisheries off Newfoundland. In the 16th century Englishmen made frequent fishing voyages to the "banks."

Capt. John Smith's successful fishing venture in 1614 off the New England coast helped to establish the popularity of that region. Within a few years fishing colonies were established in Massachusetts (Cape Ann) and Maine (Monhegan Island and Pemaquid[qqv]). Massachusetts Bay[qv] early engaged in the codfishery. Within less than forty years after its settlement Boston was a busy trade center for fish.

England often exasperated the colonies by failing in treaties with France to accord a proper interest to the fisheries. In treaties from St. Germain (1632) to Ryswick[qqv] (1697), the French fisheries benefited. British colonists were particularly bitter in 1697 when Acadia was returned to France. The Treaty of Utrecht[qv] (1713) awarded Newfoundland and Nova Scotia (Acadia) to England, but France retained the island of Cape Breton and some fishing privileges.

The final defeat of France in the great colonial struggle with England, concluded by the Treaty of Paris[qv] (1763), left France only the fishing islands of St. Pierre and Miquelon and restricted fishing privileges. The New England cod fisheries expected to benefit by the triumph, but new discontent appeared when Parliament passed the Sugar Act[qv] of 1764. Its enforcement threatened to ruin the profitable trade with the French West Indies that was based on the exchange of the poorer grade of cod for sugar and molasses, which were manufactured into rum. Like the earlier Molasses Act of 1733[qv] this, too, was ineffective, largely because of smuggling[qv].

Codfishing suffered severely from the Revolutionary War, but expectations were held for its revival when the United States secured extensive fishing privileges from England in the Definitive Treaty of Peace[qv] (1783). This revival was delayed not only by the contraction of the market in Catholic Europe, but also by the immediate exclusion of Americans from trade with the British West Indies. Fishing bounties[qv] began to be paid in 1789, but did not become a real aid to the fisheries until considerably later.

The Peace of Ghent[qv] (1814) did not provide for the continuance of the fishing privileges which Americans had been enjoying in British colonial waters. The Convention of 1818[qv] attempted to settle the fisheries[qv] question, but it continued to be a sore spot in British-American relations until the award of the Hague Tribunal of Arbitration in 1910.

After the War of 1812 the cod and mackerel[qv] fisheries entered on a long period of expansion. The European market for salt codfish declined, but the domestic market more than offset this loss. The Erie Canal[qv] provided access to the Mississippi Valley, and introduction of the use of ice for preservation opened a wide domestic market for fresh fish (*see* Refrigeration). Tariffs from 1816 to 1846 on imported fish greatly helped New England fishermen to control the home market.

After the Civil War the cod lost the distinction of being the principal food fish of the American seas. From about 1885 the cod fisheries began not only to decline in relation to other American fisheries, but also in the amount of tonnage employed. Such cities as Boston and Gloucester in Massachusetts, and Portland in Maine, however, still serve as centers for an industry whose importance in American history is symbolized by Massachusetts' use of the "sacred codfish" as its emblem.

[Raymond McFarland, *A History of the New England Fisheries;* C. B. Judah, Jr., *The North American Fisheries and British Policy to 1713;* S. E. Morison, *Maritime History of Massachusetts, 1783-1860.*]

F. HARDEE ALLEN

Code Napoléon. One important reform resulting from the French Revolution was the unification and simplification of the French laws, prepared under Napoleon Bonaparte's direction and promulgated in 1804 as the "Code Civil," commonly called the "Code Napoléon." It served as the model for the "Digest of the Civil Laws" of Orleans Territory[qv], promulgated in 1808 and commonly called the "Old Louisiana Code," which, revised and amended in 1825 and 1870 as the "Civil Code of Louisiana," remains today the basic law of the State of Louisiana.

[Alcée Fortier, ed., *Louisiana;* Charles Gayarré, *History of Louisiana;* François Xavier Martin, *History of Louisiana;* Alcée Fortier, *History of Louisiana.*]

WALTER PRICHARD

Code Noir (Black Code) is the name commonly applied to the "Edict Concerning the Negro Slaves in Louisiana," issued by Louis XV in March, 1724, and promulgated in the colony by Gov. Bienville on Sept. 10, 1724. A large number of Negro slaves had been brought to the colony during the administrations of Antoine Crozat and John Law, and a definition of their legal status had become desirable. The "Code," consisting of fifty-four articles, fixes the legal status of Negro slaves and imposes certain specific obligations and prohibitions upon their masters. Regulations as to holidays, marriage, religious instruction, burial, clothing and subsistence, punishment and manumission of Negro slaves are prescribed in detail. The legal position and proper conduct of freed or free Negroes in the colony are defined. Article I of the "Code," rather curiously, decreed expulsion of Jews from the colony. Article III prohibited the exercise of any religious creed than the Roman Catholic and Article IV decreed confiscation for Negro slaves placed under the direction or supervision of any person not a Catholic. The essential provisions of the "Code" remained in force in Louisiana until 1803 and many of them were embodied in later American "Black Codes."[qv]

[C. Gayarré, *History of Louisiana;* A. Fortier, ed., *Louisiana.*]

WALTER PRICHARD

Code of the Laws of the United States, **The** (1934), is the official compilation, in a single volume of 3026 pages, of all acts of Congress in force on Jan. 3, 1935, arranged under fifty "Titles" or heads, such as aliens and citizenship, agriculture, banks and banking, commerce and trade, criminal code and procedure, internal revenue, public lands and railroads. It supplants not only the codification contained in the Revised Statutes of 1874 and 1878 but also the original Code of 1925 and seven volumes of "Supplements" published in 1926–34. The Code was prepared under the direction of the House of Representatives committee on the revision of the laws. No new law was enacted, and no old law repealed, by the Code; and its contents are declared to be "prima facie the law." The Code is usually cited as "U. S. C."

[Preface to *Code of the Laws of the United States,* 1925, 1934.]

P. ORMAN RAY

Codes of Fair Competition. This phrase technically, though not literally, describes the agreements negotiated under the authority of the National Industrial Recovery Act[qv] (N.R.A.) of June 16, 1933. Although not known as "codes," the rules of fair trade practice promulgated, after conferences with businessmen, by the Federal Trade Commission[qv] during the preceding decade were taken more seriously than previous codes of business ethics. But the sanctions supporting them were inadequate to assure their full effectiveness. On the other hand, violation of any provision of N.R.A. code was made a misdemeanor. This, and the penalty of being deprived of the blue-eagle[qv] symbol, encouraged general compliance. Although there were many qualifications in practice, the N.R.A. codes represented, in theory, agreements among members of particular branches of trade upon the rules or standards they would observe in the conduct of business, such agreements being subject to the approval of the President.

[L. S. Lyon and associates, *The National Recovery Administration;* J. M. Clark and others, The National Recovery Administration, Report of the Committee of Industrial Analysis, *House Doc. 158, 75 Cong., I Sess.,* Washington, 1937.]

MYRON W. WATKINS

Coeducation. During the colonial period girls were generally excluded from charity schools, free schools[qqv] and tax-supported town schools. However, there were certain communities which admitted them for instruction out of the regular school hours. Late in the colonial period and in the early national period they were generally admitted to the modified elementary schools, dame schools[qv] and tax-supported public free schools, as they had been earlier to many private charity schools. During the early national period many of the academies[qv] were coeducational in character because they were dependent upon tuition fees. When the academies were gradually replaced by public high schools[qv] girls were commonly admitted because high schools were tax-supported and equal educational privileges were taken for granted.

Coeducation in higher education first appeared in the Middle West, and before 1860 numerous colleges and state universities[qv] were open to women on terms of equality with men. It was firmly established by 1872, when the University of Michigan admitted women, and thereafter it became quite general. By this time the coeducational high school and the free-school system prevailed throughout the country.

[Thomas Woody, *A History of the Education of Women in the United States;* Paul Monroe, *The Founding of the American Public School System.*]

PAUL MONROE

Coercion Acts, **The**, also known as the Restraining Acts and, in part, as the Intolerable Acts[qv], were a series of four measures passed by the English Parliament in the spring and summer of 1774, partly in retaliation for such incidents as the *Gaspee* affair and the Boston Tea Party[qqv], but also partly as the enunciation of a more vigorous colonial policy. The Boston Port Act[qv], designed as a direct reply to the Tea Party, closed the harbor to all shipping until the town had indemnified the East India Company for the destruction of its tea and assured the king of its future loyalty, pending which Marblehead was made the port of entry. The Massachusetts Government Act[qv] deprived Massachusetts of its charter and the right to choose its own magistrates, reducing it to the status of a crown colony. An Act for the Impartial Administration of Justice[qv] provided that judges, soldiers and revenue officers indicted for murder in Massachusetts should be taken to England for trial, and lastly, the Quartering Act[qv] removed all obstacles to the billeting of troops in any town in Massachusetts.

[C. H. Van Tyne, *The Causes of the War of Independence;* G. E. Howard, *The Preliminaries of the Revolution.*]

FRANK J. KLINGBERG

Coetus-Conferentie **Controversy,** **The**, was a conflict in the 18th century between the progressive and the conservative parties in the Dutch Reformed churches, now the Reformed Church in America[qv]. The issue was American independence especially as related to the education and ordination of ministers and the power of discipline. Beginning in 1628 the churches had been under authority of the church in Holland, ministers generally being sent over by the classis (ecclesiastical jurisdiction) of Amsterdam. A century later positive movement for freedom began. An assembly known as a *coetus,* or informal classis, assuming some power, was formed in 1737. Its opponents gradually grouped themselves in a so-called *conferentie.* The controversy divided the ministers and the congregations. In 1771 a plan of union brought from Holland by the Rev. John H. Livingston reconciled the two parties and established virtually complete independence of the church in America.

[*Ecclesiastical Records of the State of New York.*]

W. H. S. DEMAREST

Cœur d'Alene Mission, THE, was a Roman Catholic Indian mission established, 1842, near the town of Cataldo, Idaho, by Father Nicholas Point and Brother Charles Huet, sent by Father Peter J. DeSmet. In 1877 the mission was removed to the vicinity of the town of Desmet, in the present Benewah County. The church gradually fell into decay, but was restored in 1929. The present church, a landmark, is Idaho's oldest structure reared by the hands of white men.

[Edward Cody, *History of the Cœur d'Alene Mission of the Sacred Heart;* Cornelius James Brosnan, *History of the State of Idaho.*]

CORNELIUS JAMES BROSNAN

Cœur d'Alene Riots, THE, in the lead and silver mines of northern Idaho, resulted from a strike of union miners in 1892. The mine owners protected nonunion labor with armed guards, and obtained injunctions against the unions. On July 11, 1892, armed union miners expelled nonunion men from the district, a mill was dynamited, and a pitched battle was fought. State and Federal troops took charge and martial law was proclaimed. In 1893 the local miners' unions were affiliated with the Western Federation of Miners[qv]. There were strikes in 1894 and 1899, when Federal troops suppressed violence. The Cœur d'Alene labor trouble gained national attention when Idaho's former governor, Frank Steunenberg, was killed, Dec. 30, 1905. The murderer, Harry Orchard, a former miner, claimed that the crime was instigated by officers of the Federation. He was chief witness for the state in the trial of "Big Bill" Haywood, secretary of the Federation, held in Boise in May, 1907. In 1908 Orchard was sentenced to be hanged, a punishment later commuted to life imprisonment. Haywood was acquitted, as was George A. Pettibone, the Federation's president, and the prosecution against Charles H. Moyer, member of the Federation's official board, was dropped.

[C. J. Brosnan, *History of the State of Idaho.*]

CORNELIUS JAMES BROSNAN

Coffee's Trading Posts were maintained by Holland Coffee and others under the name of Coffee, Calville and Company. In 1834 they located a post on the north bank of Red River, near the 99th meridian. Shortly thereafter they established another post on the same stream above the mouth of Walnut Bayou, in the present Love County, Oklahoma. As late as 1836 trading operations were carried on at both places, although the latter post was considered headquarters. During the late 1830's Coffee and his traders exercised a strong influence over the Indians and ransomed numbers of white captives brought from Texas.

[Grant Foreman, *Pioneer Days in the Early Southwest.*]

RUPERT N. RICHARDSON

Cohens v. Virginia, 1821 (6 Wheaton 264). The Supreme Court upheld its jurisdiction to review the judgment of a state court where, in a criminal case, it was alleged that the conviction violated some right under the Federal Constitution or laws (*see also* McCulloch v. Maryland; Osborn et al. v. U. S. Bank). This was one of Marshall's greatest opinions establishing national authority over the states.

[A. J. Beveridge, *The Life of John Marshall;* Charles Warren, *The Supreme Court in United States History.*]

CHARLES FAIRMAN

Coinage. The colonists never achieved a satisfactory coin currency. Spanish coins, the chief currency, were inadequate. In 1691 William Penn urged immigrants to bring one third of their property in coins. The scarcity was most acute in small change, the colonists being forced to "carrying Sugar and Tobacco upon their backs to barter for little Common Necessarys."

The efforts of the colonists to obtain coin from England and to find relief in such substitutes as wampum[qv] and beaver skins testify to the need, as well as their determined efforts to set up mints in the face of a shortsighted policy of suppression by the mother country. Virginia, Maryland and New York passed futile statutes for the establishment of mints. Only Massachusetts succeeded. In the latter part of the 17th century coins from her mint were widely popular. In an effort to keep them at home the colony gave them an excess legal value in British terms (*see* Pine Tree Shilling).

Release from English control in the Revolutionary period gave the colonies opportunity for state coinage. The Articles of Confederation[qv] actually sanctioned such coinage. From 1776 to 1789 state patents of coinage to private persons or direct minting by the states was widely prevalent. New Hampshire was attempting its own coinage in 1776. None of these projects got beyond coinage of a few copper pieces, although Massachusetts in 1786 provided for gold and silver as well as copper. One of the pieces from this mint was a "cent," 1/100 of the Spanish dollar[qv]. It was the first official coin on a decimal basis in history.

The national coinage system established in 1792 had unique features. It created *de novo* a coinage system for a nation, with new units, new principles of legal tender[qv] and a decimal system. The arts of coinage were unfamiliar, and the mint[qv], established in Philadelphia, made small progress. The costs of coinage were heavy. The ratio change in 1834 encouraged gold[qv] coinage, and a new mint, with horsepower, set up in 1836, initiated an era of coinage on a large scale. The subsidiary coinage laws[qv] of 1851 and 1853 and the new copper-nickel cent provision of 1857 called forth a tremendous volume of coinage.

For the first seventy years of the mint's existence counterfeiting[qv] was a national evil. Private coinage was not prohibited before the Civil War, and privately minted gold coins from Georgia, Colorado and California were widely used. The Civil War period was marked by the rivalry of copper, nickel and silver interests for preference in coinage materials, and the history of our coinage in the years after the war was marked by ugly political intrigue (*see* Silver Legislation).

The period since the Civil War has been marked by a continuous improvement in the efficiency of the mint, while the denominations, materials and physical qualities of the coins have been steadily improved, until the mint establishment has become one of the finest in the world, with the quality of its product unsurpassed.

[S. S. Crosby, *Early Coins of America;* D. K. Watson, *History of American Coinage;* Neil Carothers, *Fractional Money.*]

NEIL CAROTHERS

Coinage, Subsidiary. The establishment of subsidiary coinage in the United States has an importance far beyond its retail currency significance. At the time Alexander Hamilton devised the American coinage system, in 1792, the principles of subsidiary coinage were unknown. Since small silver coins were a necessity, silver had to be a standard. Since the world had been for 500 years slowly turning to gold as the major medium, gold had to be a standard. The double standard was Hamilton's only choice, although he himself and subsequent historians failed to realize it. This is the only explanation of a system which makes a five-cent "half-disme" a full legal tender piece with unlimited coinage.

The system was a failure. There could be no material coinage of gold at the fifteen-to-one ratio. The only source of silver bullion was from recoinage of the Mexican pieces in universal circulation, but they were so worn that recoinage meant a heavy loss. In 1834 a new ratio of sixteen to one was adopted, with a slight alteration in 1837. This ratio was designed to favor gold coinage. Its inevitable result would be a complete cessation of silver coinage. Certain temporary conditions actually encouraged small silver coinage for a time, but after 1840 the ratio gradually choked off silver coinage. When adverse conditions in Mexico reduced the flow of coins to this country, the rapidly expanding economic life of the United States faced a small-change famine. For ten years the country's retail currency was a dwindling mass of foreign coins worn beyond recognition.

In 1851 Congress created a three-cent piece of mixed silver and copper, to be made by the Treasury and sold to the public. England had stumbled accidentally and extra-legally into a single gold standard with subsidiary silver in 1816. Some understanding of its operation had reached America. This three-cent piece, devised for postage purposes, was a genuine subsidiary coin, although its creators only vaguely understood it.

By 1852 retail trade was paralyzed by the scarcity of small change. The business of hotels, ferries, railways and retail shops of all kinds was demoralized. The three-cent pieces poured into the gap. After two years of needless delay Congress passed in 1853 a subsidiary coinage law. It created five-cent, ten-cent, twenty-five-cent and fifty-cent silver coins, "debased" below their face values, to be made and sold for gold by the Treasury. It was the second subsidiary coinage system in history and the first system officially recognized as such.

A flood of the new coins poured into circulation, the mint running day and night. By 1857 the country had an abundant small change, after 250 years of scarcity. The British accounting and the Spanish currency disappeared.

[Neil Carothers, *Fractional Money.*]

NEIL CAROTHERS

Coinage Names. The nomenclature of colonial and United States coins^{qv} constitutes an interesting chapter in our history. The Spanish *reale,* the commonest coin of the colonies, one eighth of the Spanish dollar[qv], was equivalent to the six-penny "bit." In the 17th century it came to be known as the "bit." More than a century later the term was transferred to the new American coinage, and one quarter-dollar became "two bits." Historically "two bits" or "four bits" is the oldest monetary term in America. In Pennsylvania the *reale* was valued at 11 pence, the half-*reale* at 5½ and the two coins came to be known as a "levy" and a "fip." These terms were also transferred to the American coinage, and for many years a dime was a "levy," a half-dime a "fip." The smallest silver coin in the Louisiana territory was the *picaillon,* and our five-cent piece eventually became a "picayune." The word survives in our language.

A national coinage on a decimal basis resulted in an entirely new nomenclature. The term "dollar" was old when Shakespeare was making puns on it. The word came from Germany as "thaler," from the Joachimsthal silver mines. The English applied it to the Spanish *peso,* corrupting it to "dollar." But the terms "eagle," "disme," "cent" and "mille" were new. Historians have credited Gouverneur Morris with the invention of "cent" and possibly of "mille" and "disme," but the term "cent" was known earlier and he never used "mille" or "disme" in his writings on money. Only one other new term has appeared since 1792, the word "nickel" being used for years as the name of the "flying-eagle cent" and then being transferred to our five-cent piece.

[Neil Carothers, *Fractional Money.*]

NEIL CAROTHERS

Coins. In the 300 years of their history the American people have used as common currency an astonishing diversity of coins and paper money. During the entire colonial period there was a scarcity of coins, and the colonists used coins from any source. Small quantities of coins were brought by immigrants. The English brought shillings, sixpences, threepences, copper pence and halfpence. The Dutch brought *guilders* and *stivers,* the French *crowns, livres* and *picaillons,* the Swedes *dalers* and *skillings.* Pirates left in the ports coins from all the world, gold pieces from Spain, Portugal and Arabia, silver from Spain and Germany.

From the early 17th century the predominant coin was the Spanish dollar[qv] and its parts, the half, quarter, eighth and sixteenth. They poured into the country from 1650 until after 1850. For 200 years the commonest coin in America was the *reale,* the eighth of the Spanish dollar or "bit."[qv]

The scarcity of coins below the *reale* or sixpence was acute. There never was enough small change from 1607 to 1857. Massachusetts set up her own mint before 1700. Connecticut tried to coin her own copper pieces in 1738. In 1681 New Jersey legalized "Patrick's pence," copper pieces made by an Irish adventurer, and in 1722 England granted to William Wood the right to coin private copper pieces for the colonies. In the period of the Confederation a hodgepodge of private and state coins of copper were in circulation.

The currency confusion of the colonial period beggars description. Each colony legalized such coins as it chose and at such values in shillings and pence as it preferred. South Carolina in 1701 made legal tender thirteen varieties of coins. A traveler from Boston to Norfolk in 1750 might have had in his pouch paper notes, an English shilling and a sixpence or so, four or five Spanish *reales* and sixteenths, and a few copper Spanish *maravedis* and English halfpence. This assortment he had to revalue three times en route.

The establishment of a national coinage[qv] in 1792 added gold coins of $10, $5, and $2.50, a silver dollar, half-dollar, quarter-dollar, *disme* and half-*disme,* and two clumsy cent and half-cent pieces of pure copper. All the gold and silver pieces were unlimited legal tender. But Spanish coins remained the ordinary currency of everyday life.

After 1834 there was an abundant currency of gold[qv]. In 1849 a gold dollar was added, and this inconvenient piece enjoyed wide circulation. In 1851 a three-cent silver piece was added. In the three years of acute coin scarcity from 1851 to 1854 one-dollar gold coins, three-cent pieces and Spanish pieces worn beyond identification were the only small change (*see* Coinage, Subsidiary). The scarcity of small coins and the unpleasant physical qualities of Hamilton's pure copper pieces had created a universal prejudice against coins below sixpence.

All these adverse conditions were removed by two measures. An excellent subsidiary coinage of silver[qv] was created in 1853, with a half-dollar, quarter-dollar, dime and half-dime, and in 1857 the cent and half-cent of 1792 were replaced by a new one-cent piece of mixed nickel and copper, the "flying-eagle cent." With these measures the Spanish currency at last disappeared, and with it the two-centuries-old practice of keeping accounts in shillings and pence.

During the long Civil War period in which the people used fractional paper notes for small change the mint experimented with nickel, aluminum and bronze small coins (*see* Fractional Currency). The result was the creation of a five-cent nickel-copper coin, a three-cent nickel-copper coin, a two-cent bronze coin, and a one-cent bronze coin. The first and last of these are our present-day coins. These coins were the first to bear the inscription "In God We Trust."[qv] In the 1870's the people used as small change an assortment of three-, five-, ten-, fifteen- and twenty-five-cent notes; three-, five-, ten- and twenty-five-cent silver pieces; three- and five-cent nickel coins, and one- and two-cent bronze coins.

After 1875 coins gradually displaced the paper fractions. In that year Congress undertook to introduce a twenty-cent silver piece, a coin originally recommended by Jefferson in 1792. Also in this period the two-cent bronze coin, the three-cent nickel coin and the five-cent silver piece were abolished, while two unwise statutes forced into limited circulation an over-size silver "trade dollar"[qv] and the old and forgotten "standard" silver dollar[qv].

Since 1880 the common coin currency has been adequate and satisfactory. Various efforts to force the coinage of six-, three-, two-and-one-half and half-cent pieces have been unsuccessful.

[A. B. Hepburn, *History of the Currency;* C. J. Bullock, *Essays on Monetary History of the United States;* D. K. Watson, *History of American Coinage;* Neil Carothers, *Fractional Money.*]

NEIL CAROTHERS

Coin's Financial School was written by W. H. ("Coin") Harvey to convert to bimetallism[qv], at sixteen to one, people suffering from the hard times prevailing in 1894 (*see* Panic of 1893). It represented prominent bankers, editors and other gold monometallists as asking and taking instruction from "Coin, the smooth little financier." By graphic illustrations, homely allusions, glib arguments and the use of prominent names, the book obtained wide credence as a narrative of actual occurrences. Printed in cheap paper editions, it circulated very widely among farmers, debtors and other distressed classes, preparing many minds to receive Bryan's arguments.

[Allan Nevins, *Grover Cleveland, A Study in Courage.*]

JEANNETTE P. NICHOLS

Colbert's Gang was a band of whites, half-breeds and Chickasaw[qv] led by James Colbert. The band assisted the British in the defense of Mobile and Pensacola against the Spaniards in the Revolution; and later, by harrying the Spaniards from Chickasaw Bluffs, saved the east bank of the Mississippi for Great Britain and ultimately for the United States.

[D. C. Corbitt, James Colbert and the Spanish Claims to the East Bank of the Mississippi, *The Mississippi Valley Historical Review*, XXIV.]

R. S. COTTERILL

Cold Harbor (June 3, 1864). Following failures to smash and outflank Lee (C.) at Spotsylvania[qv], Grant (U.) on May 20 directed the Army of the Potomac[qv] southeast on a turning movement. Lee retired behind the North Anna[qv]. Grant recognized this position's strength and continued "side-slipping toward Richmond" by successive marches and deployments until the Confederates stood on a six-mile front without reserves, their right on the Chickahominy, their center at Cold Harbor. Estimating Confederate morale low and Lee's center weak, Grant ordered a direct drive, 60,000 men on 4000 yards frontage. The assault at 4:30 P.M., June 3, against well-entrenched lines cost 5600 casualties and failed completely. Grant dug in, held Lee in position until June 12, then resumed "side-slipping" and, crossing the James, threatened Richmond through Petersburg[qv].

[A. A. Humphreys, *The Virginia Campaigns of 1864 and 1865;* D. S. Freeman, *R. E. Lee.*]

ELBRIDGE COLBY

Cold Storage. *See* Refrigeration.

Collective Bargaining is the joint determination of the terms of employment by an organization of workers and an employer or association of employers through their duly authorized representatives. From joint conferences there issue trade agreements which cover such matters as wage rates, time and method of payment, physical conditions of work, the hiring and dismissal of employees and interpretation and enforcement. Under the common-law[qv] doctrine, inherited by the United States from England, combinations of workers to increase wages and reduce hours of labor were, until the middle of the 19th century, held to be illegal conspiracies against the public welfare. Attempts to make collective bargaining effective through the boycott and picketing have been greatly restricted under the Sherman Antitrust Act (1890) and the Clayton Antitrust Law (1914)[qqv].

From 1792 to 1850 collective bargaining was local in character because unions, such as the Typographical Society of New York (1794) and the Society of Journeymen Cordwainers of Philadelphia (1794), were local organizations. Subsequent to 1850, when the Typographical Union and other associations of skilled artisans organized into national unions, collective arrangements have generally been on a national basis. Collective bargaining is frequently industry-wide, covering most employers and workers in a given industry, as in coal mining in which joint negotiations are held between the United Mine Workers[qv] (1890), an industrial union, and the coal operators.

[J. R. Commons and J. B. Andrews, *Principles of Labor Legislation;* F. B. Sayre, *Cases on Labor Law.*]

GORDON S. WATKINS

Collector v. Day. Probate Judge Day of Barnstable County, Mass., having paid the Civil War income tax[qv] upon his salary under protest, brought suit to recover it and obtained judgment. The tax collector then sued out a writ of error. The United States Supreme Court in 1870 decided that it was not competent for Congress to levy a tax upon the salary of a judicial officer; the judgment obtained by Day was affirmed. (*See also* Taxation, Reciprocal Immunity from.)

[Lawrence B. Evans, *Cases on Constitutional Law.*]

ALVIN F. HARLOW

Colleges, Denominational, have been a distinctive feature in the development of higher education in the United States. Of the colonial colleges, all, with the possible exception of the College of Philadelphia, now the University of Pennsylvania[qv], were established by churches, primarily for the training of ministers. The period from the Revolution to the Civil War was by far the most fruitful in the founding of church colleges. During these years the churches dominated higher education in America, even the first state universities, with the exception of the University of Virginia[qv], being largely under the control of ministers. Between 1780 and 1829 forty permanent colleges were established, thirteen by Presbyterians, five by Congregationalists, six by Episcopalians, one by Catholics, three by Baptists[qqv], one by German Reformed and eleven by the states. In these early years Presbyterians and Congregationalists were the most influential in higher education, but beginning in 1830 the Baptists and Methodists entered upon an unprecedented era of college founding. By 1860 the Baptists had twenty-five colleges in nineteen states and the Methodists had established thirty-four permanent institutions.

Since the Civil War college founding by the churches has been much less rapid, but the movement has by no means disappeared. In more recent years the stronger denominational colleges have tended to become undenominational, though many still retain some relationship to the founding bodies.

[D. G. Tewksbury, *The Founding of American Colleges and Universities before the Civil War.*]

WILLIAM W. SWEET

Colleges and Universities, THE, of the United States, grew from about a dozen small colonial collegiate institutions, with only a few students, to several hundred colleges, with about 53,000 students, by 1860. Today approximately 1400 institutions of higher learning, with more than 2,000,000 students and almost numberless alumni, exist in this country.

There are three definite periods in the history of higher education in the United States: from the establishment of Harvard[qv] in 1636 to about 1860; from 1860 to the World War; and since the World War. The first of these periods was marked by the domination of the classics in a fixed collegiate curriculum. These subjects were standard in most of the American colleges for nearly two centuries; and their completion was required because of their alleged cultural values and the dignity which they were supposed to bestow upon college students. The second period may be said to have begun about 1869, when Charles W. Eliot became president of Harvard and introduced the elective system. During this period the classics began to yield to sciences and other subjects which were slowly given places in the curriculum. The third period roughly covers the past two decades, which have been marked by a tendency away from freedom of election to a measure of prescription.

The administration of higher education has, meantime, shown considerable change. Prior to 1860 most of the college presidents and trustees were clergymen or energetic members of denominational groups. It is significant that at least 40% of American college presidents prior to 1860 were born in New England, and that religion or denominationalism was one of the most potent influences in the movement to provide higher education.

Most of the early colleges were founded upon evangelical zeal and became agencies of denominational expansion. Also, it should be noted, the early colleges were frontier institutions, established to meet frontier needs. This purpose caused the American college to depart from its antecedents in Europe and to acquire features quite different from foreign institutions.

Higher educational institutions increased very rapidly down to 1860, legislatures granting charters to countless private ventures. But their mortality rate was very high due to financial difficulties, denominational competition, internal religious and political dissensions, unfavorable locations and natural disasters.

After the Civil War, when great fortunes were being amassed, business leaders were importuned for support and endowments, and gradually the change from ecclesiastical to lay control was made. This led to a change in collegiate curricula. The old classical tradition which had come down from the theologians and had so long prevailed began to give way and the religious purposes of higher education lost ground. This change was also hastened by the growth of the natural sciences as subjects of instruction, and the curriculum began to point towards business and the secular professions.

After the Revolution attempts were made to change some of the colonial colleges into state universities, but all such efforts failed. The most prominent instance was in 1816, in connection with Dartmouth College, which led to Daniel Webster's famous plea before the Supreme Court in 1819 (*see* Dartmouth College v. Woodward). The decision, which held that a charter is a contract which cannot be impaired by legislation, guaranteed the perpetuity of educational endowments. As a result, an energetic period of private and denominational higher educational effort followed. Another influence of the decision was to encourage the establishment of state universities[qv].

Interest in agricultural education began to grow before the middle of the 19th century. In the 1840's memorials were presented to Congress asking for the establishment of technical institutions for the training of students in agriculture, mechanics, architecture and road building. In 1862 Sen. Justin S. Morrill, of Vermont, was able to get through Congress a bill which appropriated public lands[qv] to the various states for the purpose of providing institutions that have come to be known as the land-grant colleges[qv]. The states and territories now receive Federal aid for the purpose of carrying on work in agriculture, mechanical arts, engineering and allied subjects (*see* Morrill Act).

Since about 1914 questions have been raised concerning the elective system, many of whose promises were found to be unfulfilled. There was a growing belief also that college students needed acquaintance with "a common intellectual world," and opportunities to develop more social intelligence. This tendency has taken the form of numerous experiments with required or elective orientation, general, overview or survey courses in the social and the natural sciences and, recently, even in the humanities. There has also been an increasing effort to guide students without hampering their initiative and to adjust the work of the college to their needs. This change has been due in part to the changed student personnel, to the necessity brought about by an increasingly complex world and to the recognition of individual differences. These modifications do not necessarily mean that the elective system has been abandoned, but rather that the principle of election has been adapted to changed conditions.

Higher education in the United States today includes institutions for men only, institutions for women only and coeducational institutions, professional and technical schools, teacher education institutions and junior colleges. The development of graduate work may be said to have begun with the opening of Johns Hopkins University in 1876. Graduate work is carried on in numerous colleges, but the Association of American Universities, largely an organization of graduate schools, now numbers only thirty-two institutions.

Enrollment in higher educational institutions has greatly increased since the World War. There are today approximately seven college students for every one in 1890, although the population of the United States has little more than doubled. In 1890 about half of the graduates of secondary schools went to college. With the number of high-school graduates so greatly increased in recent years, probably not more than one fifth of them now enter college.

[E. P. Cubberley, *Public Education in the United States;* Edgar W. Knight, *Education in the United States;* E. V. Wills, *The Growth of American Higher Education.*]

EDGAR W. KNIGHT

Collot's Journey (1796). Gen. Victor Collot came to Philadelphia after the British took possession of Guadeloupe, West Indies, where he had been governor. When litigation prevented his departure for France, he undertook a boat journey into the western country. He left McKeesport, Pa., June 6, 1796, visited the Ohio River settlements, made an excursion into the Illinois country[qv] and then turned back down the Mississippi to New Orleans[qv]. His journal illustrates the enlightened appreciation of the potentialities of the American West displayed by many of his countrymen of the period.

[Victor Collot, *Voyage dans l'Amerique Septentrionale.*]

EDGAR B. NIXON

Colombia, Canal Controversy with. The Hay-Herran Treaty[qv], signed between the United States and Colombia January, 1903, authorized the building of a canal across Panama under American auspices; but the Colombian Senate failed to ratify the agreement. The province of Panama, resentful over this failure, revolted in November, 1903, and, aided by the United States, established its independence (*see* Panama Revolution). The United States at once made a canal treaty with the infant republic (*see* Hay–Bunau-Varilla Treaty, The). Colombia, deeply hostile towards the United States for its part in the proceedings, repeatedly demanded amends. Finally, by an agreement made in 1921, the United States paid Colombia $25,000,000 for the loss of Panama.

[M. W. Williams, *The People and Politics of Latin America.*]

MARY WILHELMINE WILLIAMS

Colonial Agent, THE, was the representative sent to England by the colonies in America during the 17th and 18th centuries. Since the practice of maintaining an agent grew out of the exigencies of the times when communication was slow and uncertain, a representative formed an indispensable link between the mother country and her far-flung empire.

In the 17th century an agent went to England only on special missions. For instance, John Clarke was sent by Rhode Island to secure a charter for that community from the Restoration government. As soon as he had accomplished his arduous task, which took two years, he returned home. In the 18th century, however, when the business of colonial administration had greatly increased in volume and complexity, the agent, like the diplomat of today, remained at his post year after year. Benjamin Franklin was in England from 1757 to 1762 as agent of the Pennsylvania assembly.

The agent was not necessarily always a colonist; not infrequently an Englishman, especially interested in the American colonies, was appointed as, for example, the brilliant lawyer, Richard Jackson, who represented Connecticut during the Revolutionary period.

Though the agent was never an official member of the loose-jointed imperial machinery, yet his importance can hardly be overestimated. He served as a clearing house of information at a time when ignorance of colonial conditions was widespread; he attended hearings on various matters held by the Board of Trade and the Privy Council[qqv]; he prepared petitions embodying specific claims or requests; he worked on the perennial Indian problems; and he wrestled with boundary disputes which, because of prodigal land grants, caused endless difficulties.

It can be seen that many of these tasks were of a routine nature requiring only industry and an understanding of colonial aspirations. At times, however, emergencies arose which made unlimited demands on the resourcefulness and indeed the strength of the representative. After 1660 the home government tried repeatedly to revise or revoke altogether the colonial charters in the interest of more centralized government. As this would mean a serious curtailment of precious liberties, the agent was always instructed to fight such action as forcibly as possible. In 1730 a bill establishing a monopoly in West Indian rum, sugar and molasses was introduced into Parliament. This obviously favored the West Indian sugar planters at the expense of the New England merchants (*see* Trade, Triangular-Colonial). The struggle over this, the famous Molasses Act[qv], lasted three years and absorbed the New England agents and their West Indian rivals almost to the exclusion of everything else.

Nothing throws more light on the management of the British colonies in its early years than a study of the colonial agent. In and out of the offices of the Board of Trade he passed, conferring with an army of clerks, committee members and minor officials, attending hearings, talking with influential members of Parliament, chatting with friends and colleagues. Faithful, alert, friendly, an ambassador of frontier philosophy to the Old World, he did much to facilitate the administration of the first British empire.

[E. P. Tanner, Colonial Agencies in England, *Science Quarterly*, XVI, 1901; M. Appleton, Richard Partridge—Colonial Agent, *New England Quarterly*, V, No. 2, 1932.]

MARGUERITE APPLETON

Colonial Assemblies had their beginnings in the Virginia House of Burgesses called by Gov. Yeardley in 1619. The first Virginia assembly was an outcome of a new policy inaugurated after the Sandys-Southampton group gained control of the Virginia Company[qv]. It was unicameral[qv] in organization and was composed of the governor, his council and two burgesses elected for each of the towns, plantations and hundreds. Subsequently the units of representation were certain privileged towns or cities and the counties. Not until the latter part of the 17th century did the elected element separate from the parent assembly, resulting in a bicameral[qv] legislative body. From the beginning the Virginia assembly claimed and exercised the right to initiate legislation, and under Gov. Harvey vindicated the right to control taxation. After the withdrawal of

Colonial Assemblies

Gov. Berkeley from public life in 1652 the House of Burgesses exercised great authority scarcely checked by any outside interference except that embodied in the Navigation Act of 1651[qv], which placed certain limitations upon commercial intercourse. When Berkeley returned to power he failed to call elections, and retained the old assembly for many years prior to Bacon's Rebellion[qv] in 1676. Popular resentment of this means of attempting to control the legislative branch by the executive had the effect of restoring the representative character of the assembly.

Plymouth[qv] colony set up a popular assembly consisting of all qualified freemen[qv]. With the growth of out-settlements this evolved into a representative bicameral body. In Massachusetts Bay[qv] an effort was made by Gov. Winthrop and his supporters to concentrate legislative authority in the Court of Assistants[qv], with the Great and General Court limited to the activities of a court of election. This failed in face of the demand by deputies of the towns that the provisions of the royal charter should be fully observed. After experimenting with a primary assembly of all freemen of the company and with proxy voting, a representative bicameral system was evolved there as in Plymouth.

In Rhode Island[qv], after the federation of Providence, Portsmouth, Newport and Warwick, the towns were empowered to initiate legislation which was thereupon referred to the assembly; or, on the other hand, the assembly would refer measures to the towns for their approval or disapproval. The system was ineffective, and the charter of 1663 gave the assembly a dominating role in all matters of government.

Connecticut under its Fundamental Orders[qv] of 1639 had a General Court which was both a representative body and, upon sitting as a court of election, a primary assembly. The latter feature continued under the charter of 1662, although in the middle of the 18th century it disappeared in favor of local election of colonial officials. As in Rhode Island, the assembly was the real center of governmental authority and throughout the colonial period enjoyed great freedom from outside interference in the making of laws.

On coming into possession of his Maryland[qv] proprietary, Cecil Calvert, Lord Baltimore, called an assembly of freemen. However, he attempted to establish the principle that the proprietor alone might initiate legislation, and sent over drafts of a series of measures. The assembly rejected them, claiming sole powers of initiation, and passed a number of bills framed by its own members. Although these were rejected by Baltimore as in violation of his rights, he finally admitted the competence of the assembly to initiate laws, but insisted that all measures be submitted to him for acceptance or rejection.

During the 17th century law-making processes in Carolina[qv] were confused by the divergent aims of the eight proprietors and the settlers. The latter were determined to uphold the binding nature of the so-called Concessions and Agreement[qv] of 1665, which provided for a popularly elected assembly of freeholders. In opposition to this the proprietors attempted to enforce the feudal Fundamental Constitutions[qv] with its extraordinarily complicated law-making machinery, designed to guarantee proprietarial control of legislation.

Contemporaneously, New York under the Duke of York[qv] was ruled for many years without the aid of any popularly elected body, much to the dissatisfaction of the English-speaking population. However, with the retirement of Gov. Edmund Andros to England in 1680, the settlers refused to pay imposts, which made it necessary for the Duke either to send an army to subdue the people, or to grant an assembly. He chose the latter course in sending out Gov. Dongan; but the laws passed by the deputies were never ratified; and when James became king future assemblies were forbidden.

From the time of its founding Pennsylvania[qv] was provided with a popularly elected assembly. After the withdrawal of the charter of Massachusetts Bay in 1684, a process of consolidation took place in New England. With the establishment of the Dominion of New England[qv], the assemblies were suppressed and law-making powers were centered in the appointed Dominion council. New York, East New Jersey and West New Jersey[qqv], the two last with popularly elected assemblies, were also embodied in the Dominion before it collapsed in 1689.

During the 18th century the assemblies frequently came into collision with the governors (*see* Colonial Governors, The). In Massachusetts Bay such issues arose as those involving appropriations for a permanent establishment and for the building of forts and the control of the office of speaker of the house of representatives. In New York and in New Jersey, as the result of the maladministration of Cornbury, joint-governor of those provinces, the assemblies gained new powers over financial disbursements and administration generally. In Pennsylvania, with the beginning of the French and Indian War[qv] a controversy developed over the force of proprietorial instructions to the governor, as well as over the issue of paper money[qv], and the determination of the assembly, a unicameral body, to tax proprietorial lands. When Parliament threatened to compel all officeholders in Pennsylvania to take the required oaths rather than to affirm, in 1756 the Quaker majority in the assembly disappeared through resignations, with the result that for a short period harmony was restored between executive and legislature. Conflicts with the governors, as a rule, left the assemblies in a strongly entrenched position, in spite of the continued control of colonial legislation on the part of the Privy Council*qv*.

With the approach of the Revolution, breaches took place between the assemblies and their governors in all of the colonies except the two corporate colonies (Connecticut and Rhode Island), although the degree of friction varied from the violent manifestations in Massachusetts Bay to the not unsympathetic relations that subsisted between Gov. John Penn and the Pennsylvania assembly.

[H. L. Osgood, *The American Colonies in the Seventeenth Century*, and *The American Colonies in the Eighteenth Century.*]

LAWRENCE HENRY GIPSON

Colonial Charters. Royal charters represented the king's authorization of colonization under private enterprise and his definition of the relationship of the projected colony to the mother country. They were at the outset issued to two chief types of promoters, the trading company and the lords proprietors*qqv*, the former interested chiefly in trade, the latter in land as a source of profit. In the Restoration period, charters of incorporation which very closely resembled those previously given to trading companies were granted also to two already well-established squatter colonies, Rhode Island and Connecticut*qqv*.

Charters to trading companies vested powers of government in the company in England. That body could determine what officers, laws and ordinances were necessary for the colony, subject only to the condition that the laws must conform to those of England. In the proprietary charters*qv* the authority to govern was granted to the lord proprietor, who could determine the form of government, choose the officers and make the laws, subject to the advice and consent of the freemen*qv*. According to the corporation charters of Connecticut and Rhode Island, government was to be administered by governor, council and house of representatives; the latter chosen directly, the former indirectly by the people. In all types of charter the settlers who might go to the colonies were promised the rights and privileges of Englishmen*qv*, a phrase which, because of its vagueness, was to give considerable trouble later.

Toward the end of the 17th century the king began to find charters obstacles in the path of colonial control and tried to substitute the royal province*qv* for corporation and proprietary governments. In course of time he was almost completely successful, for by 1776 there remained only two proprietary provinces, Maryland and Pennsylvania*qqv*, and two corporation colonies, Connecticut and Rhode Island. Massachusetts*qv*, though operating under a charter, was governed in the 18th century as a royal province.

[H. L. Osgood, *American Colonies in the Seventeenth Century;* C. M. Andrews, *The Colonial Period in American History.*]

VIOLA F. BARNES

Colonial Commerce took various forms. There was the two-way commerce: that between a colony and the mother country, as was the case with respect to the tobacco trade; or that between two colonies or between a colony and a British or a foreign West India port, such as characterized the provision trade of Pennsylvania and the limited commercial relations of Connecticut. However, a triangular trade*qv* was a common, if not the most common, form that colonial commerce took. This might involve a colony, the African coasts and the West Indies, typified by Rhode Island's trade in rum, slaves and molasses; or involve a colony, a European country, such as Spain or Portugal, and Great Britain, as in the case of the trade of Massachusetts Bay in prime fish, in wines and British commodities; or a colony, Newfoundland and the West Indies, as was characterized by the trade of the same colony in merchandise, including rum, prize fish and molasses; or a Northern colony, a Southern colony and Great Britain, involving provisions, tobacco or rice from the Carolinas and British and European merchandise.

This commerce was carried on, as a rule, in American-built ships. When ships themselves were articles of commerce they were generally built in New England, loaded in a Southern port and then sent to their destination in England. The two greatest colonial commercial centers before the American Revolution were Boston and Philadelphia, each exercising a dominating influence over an extended region. However, New York controlled the business of that province and of western Connecticut and east New Jersey; Newport that of Rhode Island and of southern Massachusetts Bay; and Charleston that of South Carolina, Georgia and southern North Carolina. This commerce involved not only barter, specie transactions in Spanish or Portuguese coins and bills of exchange, but credit extensions on a great scale. For example, as the result of credit extensions to Virginia planters by British merchants before the outbreak of the Revolutionary War, the former were in many instances hopelessly involved in debt (*see* British Debts, The).

The commercial relations of the colonies with the outside world were subject to some restrictions from the beginning as the result of the comprehension of the plantations within the English realm, such, for example, as the prohibition of the export of English specie. However, the development of restrictions with particular reference to the colonies, outside of early restrictions by the crown on the sale of tobacco, is associated with the body of legislation known as the trade and navigation acts[qv], including the Woolen, the Molasses[qv], the Hat, the Iron[qv] and the Sugar Acts[qv]. Under these, certain colonial products, such as American woolens or beaver hats, could not enter into commerce; other products, placed on the enumerated list[qv], such as sugar, molasses, tobacco, dyewoods, indigo, cotton, rice, furs, ginger, copper, potash, hides, raw silk, ship-timber, naval stores and iron, could be carried directly only to the mother country or to another colony, with certain relaxations ultimately provided for the marketing in Europe of sugar and rice. Ships engaged in colonial commerce were confined, with certain exceptions in favor of prizes captured, to vessels of English, later British, or colonial construction and manned chiefly by those owing allegiance to the crown. All such vessels were required to have a British or colonial registry, to be commanded by British or colonial officers and to sail under British colors. Also it was incumbent upon colonial merchants who desired to import European commodities to do so through a British port, with the exception of a few specified articles such as salt for the New England and Newfoundland fisheries[qv], Madeira and Azores wines, and servants, provisions and horses from Ireland and Scotland.

[L. H. Gipson, *The British Empire before the American Revolution;* G. L. Beer, *Commercial Policy of England toward the American Colonies.*]

LAWRENCE HENRY GIPSON

Colonial Councils existed in all the colonies. In general they represented the same control as did the governor. In the royal provinces[qv] they were appointed directly by the crown, usually on recommendation of the Board of Trade[qv]. In the proprietary colonies[qv] they were appointed by the Proprietor, and in Massachusetts, Rhode Island and Connecticut the councils were elective. In the royal and proprietary provinces the members of the council served during good behavior. The governor could suspend members for cause, but they could be removed only by action of the crown or the proprietors.

Councils varied in size, although the standard practice tended to a uniform council of twelve in the royal provinces. Rhode Island had ten, Pennsylvania a council of eighteen and Massachusetts one of twenty-eight. Colonial councils acted as the upper house of the legislature and when so acting the governor was directed (1736) not to be present. The council together with the governor formed a supreme court of appeals in civil cases. Finally the council was an executive and administrative body for the governor, and many of his acts could be carried out only with the approval of the council. The duties of the council were specified in charters or in instructions to the royal governor, although custom gradually changed practices.

[Leonard Woods Labaree, *Royal Government in America.*]

O. M. DICKERSON

Colonial Currency. *See* Currency, Colonial.

Colonial Dames of America, The. Women are eligible for membership who are descended from some ancestor who came to reside in America prior to 1750, and who served his country in the founding of a town which has survived and developed, or who held an important position, or who contributed to the achievement of American independence. The society, organized in 1890, has as its objects the collection of relics and mementoes for preservation, the creation of interest in American history and the promotion of social fellowship.

FRANCES PARKINSON KEYES

Colonial Governors, The, were the chief civil officers in the American colonies before the Revolution. Some were appointed by the king as, for instance, the governor of the royal colony[qv] of Virginia; others were nominated by a proprietor (*see* Proprietary Provinces), such as William Penn, and were approved by the crown; and a few, those of the chartered colonies[qv], were elected by deputies of the freemen[qv] of the community.

Their duties were the usual ones of an administrative officer: defense, preservation of law and order, promotion of the general welfare. To these were added enforcement of the Navigation Acts[qv] and supervision of the collection of customs duties. And so necessary did those last-named functions seem to the home government, believing in the principles of mercantilism[qv], that even the governors of the chartered colonies were required to give oath and bond that they would execute the commercial laws.

The tasks of the executive of the chartered colonies were relatively simple. Chosen by his own people and linked by only nebulous bonds to the mother country, he suffered under no conflict of loyalties, and consideration of local interests easily took precedence over imperial policies.

The position of the governor of the royal or proprietary colonies, however, was always uncertain and often unpleasant. Saddled with definite instructions, he faced provincially minded and stubborn assemblies (*see* Colonial Assemblies). Therefore, he was forced to decide between either constant bickering and possible loss of salary—for the assembly controlled the purse strings—or jettisoning most of his instructions.

After the Restoration England attempted to reorganize her loose-jointed empire in order to establish uniform government in the colonies, but this was never accomplished. Consequently the colonial assemblies, overshadowing the governors, became the real executives and soon learned the art of self-government.

[G. L. Beer, *British Colonial Policy, 1754-1765;* O. M. Dickerson, *American Colonial Government.*]

MARGUERITE APPLETON

Colonial Governors – Instructions. Instructions were issued in the king's name by the Privy Council[qv] to every royal governor of a province. They elaborated and explained the general powers set forth in the governor's commission. They touched upon nearly every subject involved in colonial government—the council and assembly[qqv] and the governor's relations thereto, legislation, finance, justice, military and naval matters, as well as many other subjects such as religion and morals, Indian affairs, land distribution, alien groups and trade and commerce. Due to opposition on the part of the colonists or ignorance of colonial conditions on the part of the ministry, such instructions were often unenforced and unenforceable. But, as expressions of British authority, they definitely controlled the free development of colonial policies.

[L. W. Labaree, *Royal Instructions to British Colonial Governors, 1670-1776.*]

JULIAN P. BOYD

Colonial Judiciary, THE, was created in each colony by act of the assembly[qv] and followed the general pattern of English procedure. Each colony had a system of local courts to try petty offenses. There was a county court in most of the colonies to try major civil and criminal cases, which was presided over by one of the superior judges who travelled on circuit[qv]. There was a superior court made up of the superior court judges sitting *en banc* and presided over by a chief justice. Each colony had an attorney general.

In the royal provinces[qv] the chief justice and the judges of the superior court were at first appointed directly by the Crown. Every effort was made to secure competent men. In some cases well-trained lawyers were induced to emigrate to America to fill such vacancies, as was the case when William Atwood was appointed chief justice of New York (1701). Apparently, the first commissions were at the will of the crown, as were those of other important colonial officers. There were, however, no actual removals. The Act of Settlement had made English judges independent of the crown, with commissions during good behavior. Governors were authorized by instructions to fill vacancies when they occurred. Their instructions were not very clear on this point, except they were not to impose "any limitation of time" in any commissions they might issue. By the middle of the 18th century many judges had received commissions during good behavior. Gov. Clinton's appointment of William DeLancey as chief justice of New York attracted the attention of the Board of Trade[qv] to the obscurity of the instruction and in 1754, it instructed every governor that in future all judicial officers should be appointed "during pleasure only." In Pennsylvania the assembly enacted a law providing that judges could only be removed on address of the assembly (1759). This act was promptly disallowed in England (*see* Royal Disallowance).

The death of George II in 1760 terminated all judicial commissions, many of which had been granted by the governors during good behavior. The Board of Trade insisted that all renewals should be "at the pleasure of the Crown." This precipitated a controversy with the assemblies, which refused to pay judges unless their commissions read as formerly "during good behavior." Gov. Hardy of New Jersey had already renewed commissions under the former terms (1761). These commissions were held void by the Privy Council[qv] in England and funds were found to pay the judges so as to make them entirely independent of the local assemblies. This enforced solution of the question rankled with the Americans, as it deprived Englishmen in America of rights guaranteed to Englishmen in

England, and is one of the specific acts of tyranny charged against George III in the Declaration of Independence*qqv*.

[O. M. Dickerson, *American Colonial Government, 1696-1765*.]

O. M. DICKERSON

Colonial Newspaper, THE. The first newspaper in the American colonies, entitled *Publick Occurrences*qv, was published in Boston, Sept. 25, 1690, but, after a single issue, was suppressed by the authorities. The first regularly published newspaper was *The Boston News-Letter*qv, established in Boston, April 24, 1704. This was followed by other papers in Boston, then in Philadelphia, New York, Annapolis, Charleston, Newport and Williamsburg, all before 1750. By April, 1775, there were thirty-seven newspapers in eleven of the colonies on the Atlantic seaboard. The colonial newspaper was a small folio weekly, almost invariably of four pages, including foreign news on the first page, domestic news on the second, local news on the third and advertisements on the fourth. Political news and the proceedings of legislative bodies aroused a lively interest, and important documents and letters were often quoted at length, providing a means of disseminating information throughout the colonies, which more than any one cause welded the people together in their resistance to the mother country. Local news was negligible, and in fact the greatest amount of local information comes from the advertisements. Yet the history of no town could be written without access to its file of newspapers. Essays and poetry filled a considerable portion of the papers, especially the *Pennsylvania Gazette*qv, published by Benjamin Franklin in Philadelphia. Because of the scarcity of all but theological books, secular literature was almost unread in the colonies except through the newspapers. Outside of the Bible and the Almanac*qqv*, the newspaper was the only printed matter found in most colonial families.

[Isaiah Thomas, *History of Printing in America;* Check-list of files in *Proceedings* of American Antiquarian Society, 1913-27.]

C. S. BRIGHAM

Colonial Plans of Union (1643–1754). The separate founding of the colonies, coupled with difficulties of travel, prevented effective union until the Revolution. However, many proposals for union grew out of the common problems faced by the colonies. The most continuous problem was that of frontier defense against Indian attack. Rivalry with the Dutch and French aggravated this problem. Trade and boundary disputes emphasized the need of a common arbitrator. A common culture and allegiance suggested the reasonableness of unity. Moreover, the English home government, desiring to make the colonies an effective unit for imperial trade and defense, in some cases encouraged a union. The chief plans, which varied widely in origin and the number of colonies to be included, were: 1. The United Colonies of New England, 1643–1684qv. Massachusetts Bay, Plymouth, Connecticut and New Haven, united in a league largely for frontier defense. 2. Dominion of New England, 1688qv. The British crown made Sir Edmund Andros governor-general of all the New England colonies, New York, East and West Jersey. 3. Intercolonial Congress, 1689–91. New York, Massachusetts, Plymouth and Connecticut entered a temporary military league for frontier defense. 4. William Penn's "Briefe and Plaine Scheam" for Union, 1697. Penn's proposal for a loose confederation grew out of the conditions prevailing during King William's Warqv. 5. Union under the Earl of Bellomont, 1698–1701, who was commissioned governor of New York, Massachusetts and New Hampshire, and commander of the military forces of Connecticut, Rhode Island and the Jerseys. This step was taken by the crown because of colonial failure to co-operate in defense. 6. Hamilton's Plan, 1699, for frontier defense and production of naval supplies for the Royal Navy proposed by the deputy-governor of Pennsylvania. An intercolonial assembly was to levy a poll tax to finance the work which was to be done by British regulars. 7. A Virginian's Plan of Union, 1701, was an anonymous publication issued in London which advocated abolishing all the proprietary governments and uniting the colonies under an intercolonial congress and governor-general. 8. Robert Livingston's Plan, 1701. In a letter to the Lords of Tradeqv Livingston proposed that the colonies be grouped into three units, which would be co-ordinated by the Council of Trade for frontier defense. 9. Earl of Stair's Plan, 1721, submitted by the Earl of Stair to the Board of Tradeqv, was to include all the continental colonies and the British West Indies. There was to be a governor-in-chief appointed by the crown. An advisory council of two members from each colony was to assist this official. The governor and his council could levy assessments against the colonies for defense purposes. The scheme was to be established by action of Parliament. 10. The Lords of Trade Plan, 1721, was contained in a report given the king. It was essentially a brief outline of the Stair plan. 11. Daniel Coxe's Plan, 1722, appeared in a book of travel published in London.

It proposed a union of all the continental colonies under one governor, represented by a lieutenant in each colony. A great council composed of two delegates from each colony was to advise the governor and make the allotments of money and men needed for colonial defense. 12. The Kennedy-Franklin Plan, 1751, was published by Archibald Kennedy, receiver-general of New York, in a pamphlet dealing with Indian trade and frontier defense. These were to be directed by a superintendent to be assigned to the colonies by commissioners representing the colonial assemblies. Benjamin Franklin added some details which closely resembled his later Albany Plan. 13. The Albany Plan, 1754[qv]. This best known of all the colonial plans was largely the work of Franklin. It called for an intercolonial council with membership apportioned according to wealth and population. The president-general was to be appointed by the crown. Control of Indian affairs and frontier defense was to be under control of this royal officer and his council. The colonial legislatures rejected the plan and it was not pressed by the home government.

[Herbert L. Osgood, *The American Colonies in the Seventeenth Century* and *The American Colonies in the Eighteenth Century.*]

ROBERT MOULTON GATKE

Colonial Policy, The British, is technically that policy that was laid down or was evolved after the union of England and Scotland in 1707. This policy was based largely upon the earlier English policy, which envisaged the promotion of domestic industry, foreign trade, the fisheries and shipping, and the planting of crown lands in the New World with the establishment of colonial settlements, or the exploitation of the resources of America through such commercial companies as the Hudson's Bay Company[qv] and the South Sea Company. It also included the policy of encouraging the utilization of the vast labor resources of Africa in the establishment and maintenance of plantations for the production of so-called colonial staples (*see* Slavery).

The earliest manifestations of English colonial policy are embodied in the 16th-century patents to Gilbert and Raleigh[qv]; then in 1606 came those to the London and Plymouth companies[qqv] of Virginia in connection with which a settlement policy was laid down which, among other features, embodied the idea of direct crown control; but in 1609 this was modified in the charter of that year issued in favor of the Virginia Company substituting indirect for direct control and providing for a definite and extensive grant of land; this new policy also found expression in the creation of the Council for New England[qv] in 1620. Direct control, however, made its reappearance in 1624 when with the withdrawal of the political powers of the Virginia Company, Virginia took its place as the first of the so-called royal colonies under a system of government that permitted the survival of the colonial assembly[qv]. Nevertheless, this new policy was not to become basic until the beginning of the new century, for the year 1629 saw the appearance of the corporate colony of Massachusetts Bay[qv] with a charter that was sufficiently broad to permit the transfer of the government of the company to the New World, and 1632 that of the proprietaryship of Maryland with the granting to the Baltimore family of very wide powers. Thus three types of colonial government appeared as the result of the formulation of colonial policy—or perhaps one might suggest more accurately as the result of the failure of the Government to formulate a policy—royal, proprietary and charter[qqv].

Up to the Interregnum, colonial policy emanated from the crown and was directed by it. Then with the outbreak of the English Civil War the Long Parliament assumed control, acting mainly through a special commission or council provided for by the Ordinance of 1643, which gave to its president, the Earl of Warwick, the title of Governor-in-Chief and Lord High Admiral of all the English colonies in America (*see* Warwick Commission). Moreover, between the years 1645 and 1651 Parliament laid down various regulations which looked to a strict control of colonial commerce in favor of English shipping and manufactures. Nor did this parliamentary interference with the colonies cease with the Restoration, which not only gave validity to these restrictions but added to them in a series of measures beginning with the so-called First Navigation Act of 1660 and culminating in the very comprehensive Act of 1696 (*see* Navigation Acts). During the Commonwealth period Cromwell introduced a striking but temporary departure in colonial policy in 1654 with his ambitious plan known as the Western Design[qv] which had a twofold purpose: the acquisition of the Spanish empire in the New World and in this connection the removal of Northern English colonists to the warmer climes.

The growth in importance of the colonies led, moreover, to various experiments in their supervision such as the Laud Commission (*see* High Commission, Court of) appointed by Charles I, and the various councils of Charles II ending with the transference in 1675 of this function to the Lords of Trade[qv], a committee of the Privy Council[qv], which continued to function after a manner until in 1696 William III brought into existence the Lords Commissioners for Trade and Plantations, a body which survived until after the American Revolution and which in the main fully justified its existence.

Colonial policy in the 18th century was characterized not only by efforts to reduce the colonies to a uniform type—that of the royal colony—which met with considerable success, but also by increased restrictions upon colonial enterprise with such acts as the Woolen Act of 1699, the White Pine Acts, the Hat Act of 1731, the Sugar Acts[qv] of 1733 and 1764 and the Iron Act[qv] of 1750. With the middle of the 18th century an important modification of policy may be noted with the growing menace of French competition. Side by side with mercantilism[qv] (with the emphasis upon immediate economic gain), modern imperialism (with the emphasis upon power politics, territorial aggrandizement, centralization of authority and a unified Indian policy) made its appearance. With the collapse of French empire in North America (*see* Paris, The Treaty of) Parliament also turned its attention to securing a direct revenue from the colonies, passing for this purpose the Stamp Act of 1765 and the Townshend Acts of 1767[qqv]. Reliance upon these new policies helped to bring on a crisis in colonial affairs that led to the Revolution.

[*Cambridge History of the British Empire*, I; L. H. Gipson, *The British Empire before the American Revolution.*]

LAWRENCE HENRY GIPSON

Colonial Policy of United States. *See* Insular Possessions.

Colonial Settlements. Various little colonies were planted along the coastal ribbon of the Atlantic for different reasons. Government encouraged them to serve the economic needs of the nation, capitalists hoped for profit and people sought better opportunities. Tragedy stalked the efforts to colonize. Ships, abundant capital, many people were demanded to found a prosperous colony. The loss of life and money was tragic. Some ventures were stillborn, others were nursed through a puling infancy to maturity, a few grew lustily from birth.

Humphrey Gilbert landed with his company on Newfoundland's shores in 1584. A few months saw them sail away. Walter Raleigh[qv] in 1585 settled a few colonists on Roanoke Island (Carolina coast), but sustained effort failed to keep the venture alive. The time was not ripe and the cost was too heavy for private purses. The close of the war with Spain in 1604 freed England to turn to America. Joint-stock companies (*see* Trading Companies), combining capital and credit, entered into colonization. In 1607 the Plymouth Company[qv] tried a settlement on the Kennebec River (Maine), the London Company[qv] on the James River (Virginia). A rigorous winter and the death of the chief promoter sent the Kennebec settlers soon away (*see* Popham Colony, The). The Council for New England[qv] (1620) proved to be only a land company whose subgrants resulted in a few fishing, trading, lumbering camps on New England's shores. Against heavy odds the London Company persisted. During its existence about 5500 emigrants left England for Virginia[qv]; in 1625 a few over a thousand were living in the colony. The distress on a long voyage, disease, starvation and Indians in the colony took a deadly toll. Virginia lived to be the first permanent English colony, with a population of 5000 in 1634, rising to 50,000 in 1690.

England was not the only mother of colonies. In 1624 the Dutch West India Company sent over thirty families which founded New Amsterdam and Fort Orange (Albany)[qqv]. Forty years of effort showed a population of only about 8000. The Dutch were not a migrating people, and a grasping company attracted few settlers. In 1638 the New Sweden Company began Fort Christina on the Delaware with a few people, but New Sweden[qqv] never contained over a few hundred Swedes and Finns. Sweden's wars in Europe left her inadequate sources for colonial ventures. New Sweden ceased to be when captured by the Dutch in 1655.

The economic motive was not the only factor in colonial enterprise. Abundant land meant little without people. At first no urgent expulsive forces drove people away. Settlers were hard to secure until intolerable conditions sent them to the new land. This stream began in 1620 when the Pilgrims found their weary way to plant the colony of Plymouth[qv]. Villagers from northern England, denied freedom of worship, went to Holland for refuge, but finding Dutch life uncomfortable, they came to New England. The stream widened with the exodus of over 16,000 to New England during 1630–40 (*see* Great Migration, The). Various motives explain the migration, but primary was the purpose to establish in Massachusetts a city of God on Puritan lines (*see* Massachusetts Bay Company). Unable to reform the Anglican Church, visited with harsh royal authority, the Puritan leaders found the answer in Massachusetts. Villagers from Massachusetts Bay, in 1635, founded the colony of Connecticut[qv], where better land was available and a milder brand of Puritanism was practised. A small band of devoted Puritans began the colony of New Haven[qv] in 1638. In 1662 New Haven was merged with Connecticut and thirty years later the greater colony numbered about 18,000 people. Intolerable conditions in Massachusetts peopled Rhode Island[qv]. The Bay colony dealt severely with dissent. The radical views of Roger Williams drove him to find refuge in the settlement of Providence in 1636. The strange ideas of Mrs. Hutchinson and her followers brought exile, some settling at Portsmouth, others at Newport (*see* Antinomian Controversy, The). Rhode Island contained about 4000 souls by 1690. Massachusetts added Maine[qv] by purchase and secured Plymouth colony by merger and before 1700 the Bay province had over 50,000 people. New Hampshire[qv] was a slender little colony which harbored a few people under the proprietorship of Capt. John Mason. Maryland[qv] owed its genesis to Lord Baltimore, who under a royal charter in 1632 desired to find a refuge for Catholics and to build up a great landed estate. From small beginnings its population rose to 30,000 within sixty years.

After 1660 colonial expansion took on a renewed life. Again promoters sought profit and people better opportunities. The circle of English colonies was completed by the conquest of New Netherland[qv] in 1664, renamed New York[qv] and granted to the Duke of York. He subgranted New Jersey[qv] to Sir George Carteret and Lord John Berkeley. Carolina, granted to eight men by charter in 1663, divided into two colonies, North Carolina peopled from Virginia and South Carolina[qqv] settled by discontented planters from Barbados and persecuted Protestants from France and England. After thirty years of effort neither colony had over 3000 people. Quakerism, with its democratic and mystical principles, came into tragic collision with orthodoxy in both Old and New England. The Quakers[qv] found a welcome in Rhode Island and established their own colonies on the Delaware. In 1674 Berkeley sold West Jersey[qv], which finally came into the hands of the Quakers who settled along the Delaware at Burlington and other places. East Jersey[qv], purchased from the Carteret estate in 1680, soon fell under the control of a large board in which the Quakers were prominent. Before the century closed East Jersey counted less than 10,000, West Jersey about 4000. In 1681 William Penn received a charter for Pennsylvania[qv] where he tried a "Holy Experiment"[qv] in Quaker principles. The province became a haven of refuge for the persecuted, welcoming English, Welsh and Irish Quakers, and Germans. It grew lustily, having a population, inclusive of Delaware[qv], of over 12,000 within a decade. Delaware, granted to William Penn by the Duke of York, governed at first as part of Pennsylvania, in 1704 became a province with Penn as proprietor. Thus ends the founding of the original colonies except for Georgia[qv], which came into existence in 1732, in response to humanitarian motives. Georgia harbored debtors from English jails, and Lutheran exiles from Germany.

[C. M. Andrews, *Colonial Period of American History*, Vols. I-III.]

WINFRED T. ROOT

Colonial Ships, The, were very small. Sir Humphrey Gilbert's vessel, on which he lost his life, was one of ten tons. Newport's three ships, in which the first Virginians came to America, were of 100, 40 and 20 tons, respectively. The *Mayflower's*[qv] tonnage was 180, her keel length 64 feet, beam width 26 feet and depth from beam to keel 11 feet, while the full length was 90 feet. The *Dove,* and the *Ark*[qv], which carried Baltimore's company to Maryland, were of 50 and 400 tons, respectively.

On these vessels, passengers were weeks crossing the Atlantic. One ship made the journey in four weeks but the Pilgrims were ten weeks, the first Virginians and Calvert's party were four months and some Germans six months. Because of this delay, food and water were soon wretched. Biscuits and cereals were full of maggots and weevils. Water was covered with slime and became so nauseous that one had to hold his nose to drink it. Scurvy generally incapacitated one tenth of those on board. It was only when lemons and oranges were found to be specifics for scurvy that this condition was changed. Overcrowding, smallpox, seasickness, fevers, dysentery, cancer and mouth-rot added their quota to the misery and suffering of the transatlantic voyage.

Small vessels were soon being made in the colonies, often in the forests whence they were rolled on tree trunks to the water's edge. By 1676, 730 ships had been built in Massachusetts alone, and hundreds more in other New England colonies. It cost from six to ten pounds sterling for the voyage across the Atlantic and from forty to fifty dollars to go by ship from South Carolina to New York.

[James Lind, *Treatise on Scurvy;* C. B. Swaney, The Transatlantic Voyage in the Age of Sails, *Social Science*, Fall Number, 1937.]

CHARLES B. SWANEY

Colonial Society. The genius and temper of colonial society lay largely in the breed of the people who settled America. In the beginning New England and the South were settled by the English. A few Dutch and Walloons lived along the Hudson, a fewer Swedes*qv* along the Delaware. In general English institutions modified by American conditions formed the basis of the various colonial structures. England was not the only mother of colonies. The 18th century saw a great influx of foreigners. A population of about a quarter of a million in 1700 became over two million by 1775, of whom about a sixth were foreign born. In large numbers came the Scotsmen from Ulster in Ireland (*see* Scotch–Irish, The) and the Germans from the Rhine country. In smaller numbers came the Swiss, the French Huguenots*qv*, the Scotch Highlanders and a few Celtic Irish. The African reservoir was tapped to supply the colonies with servile labor, especially the South (*see* Slave Trade).

Nor was Europe a kindly mother. Intolerable conditions in Europe peopled the colonies. Not the privileged classes, but the poor, the distressed, the opponents of arbitrary authority migrated to the colonies. Devastating wars, bitter religious persecution, economic disabilities, the exactions of arbitrary princes, harsh legal codes were the forces of expulsion. America beckoned because it offered the opportunity for self-expression and human betterment. Abundant land provided room for all groups to fashion life in response to needs and desires and a broad and hostile ocean protected them from undue pressure from Europe.

English America became a laboratory of social experimentation. Religion played a large role in the unfolding of colonial society. In fact, colonization was a phase of the Protestant Reformation. The great secession from Rome broke Christianity into many factions. Unable to realize their religious principles at home, they took refuge in America. Their varying religious creeds were of an even greater variety than the racial stocks. England supplied the Puritans, Quakers, Baptists, Anglicans and others; Germany sent Lutherans, German Reformed and the Pietists (Mennonites, Dunkers, Moravians); Ulster the Scotch Presbyterians; France the Huguenots; Holland the Dutch Reformed*qqv*. Each group found room to give practical application to its peculiar beliefs. Massachusetts and Connecticut experimented in Puritan conceptions of life, Pennsylvania in Quaker principles, Georgia in humanitarian ideas, to mention only the major ventures. Ideals played a large part in the making of not one, but many societies.

In America there was at first no society prepared to receive the settlers, no institutions to lean upon. Here was plenty of land and raw nature. The colonists were forced to build social structures from the bottom. Nature knew no favorites and men were forced to be self-reliant and courageous. In time the frontier was overcome, a primitive society grew into an established order entrenched in institutions. In the 18th century there emerged in each colony a controlling aristocracy, in the North the rich merchants, in the South the wealthy planters. In Puritan New England they attended the Congregational Church, in the South the Anglican Church, both established by law. In Pennsylvania the Quakers dominated the colony. Each little colonial aristocracy was knit together by marriage ties. They enjoyed the wealth and leisure for refined living, for books and education. And they controlled politics.

America provided plenty of land, Europe plenty of people seeking refuge. With the growth of little aristocracies along the coast, there developed a democratic society composed of laborers, artisans, little shop-keepers in the port towns and villages, but more particularly of the farmers who pushed into the vacant lands of the interior. Beyond the coastal plain people lived under a maximum of labor and debt and a minimum of leisure. Here then were two societies in each colony, an aristocratic minority and a democratic majority, which touched each other at many points and the contacts produced friction. These conflicts were a major force in shaping society. The dissenting religious groups opposed the established churches in New England and the South and they resented Quaker domination in Pennsylvania. The Great Awakening*qv*, a burning religious revival which swept across the colonies in mid-century, split the Congregational and Presbyterian churches apart. These divisions were the evidence of conflicts between democratic and aristocratic tendencies.

Social cleavages showed themselves in various ways. The democracy of the interior protested against unfair representation in the controlling legislatures. They were angry because they received inadequate protection against the Indians. Frequent were the quarrels between the settlers and the absentee landlords and land speculators. Bitter were the contests between the creditor East and the democratic West over questions of currency and taxation. These antagonisms came to a dramatic conclusion in some colonies on the eve of the American Revolution. The Revolution itself not only emancipated America from Europe, but it also brought the democratic transformation of colonial society and politics.

[James Truslow Adams, *Provincial Society;* Curtis P. Nettels, *The Roots of American Civilization.*]

WINFRED T. ROOT

Colonial Wars. Although English, French and Spanish colonies in North America were repeatedly plunged into war by the outbreak of hostilities in Europe involving their parent states, the colonial wars, from the outset, were much more than mere New World phases of Old World conflicts. America's natural resources and the supposed advantages of owning American markets led Europeans to seek vast holdings here, and economic rivalries among the colonials themselves were intensified by racial and religious antagonisms. Louis XIV, concentrating on aggressions in Europe, gave little practical support to offensives in America; thus Frontenac, in King William's War[qv] (1689–97), resorted to the employment of Indian allies in ruthless border raids. Similar raids were utilized, chiefly by the French, in the subsequent conflicts: Queen Anne's War (1702–13), King George's War (1744–48) and the French and Indian War (1754–63)[qqv].

At the outset of hostilities, and in 1711, English colonials and English regulars tried, futilely, to capture Quebec[qv], the ultimate conquest of which by Wolfe, in 1759, is the best known of many dramatic episodes of these wars. English forces, chiefly colonial, captured Port Royal[qv] in 1690 and again in 1710, although not until the Treaty of Utrecht[qv] (1713) was Acadia[qv] confirmed to the English, becoming then their outpost, Nova Scotia. At Utrecht the French also yielded Newfoundland and their claims to the Hudson Bay territory. During "the long peace" following 1713 (actually marred by hostilities in America and the West Indies) France established Louisbourg[qv] on Cape Breton Island, a base of operations against English participation in North Atlantic fisheries and trade routes. The restoration of Louisbourg to France (1748) after its capture by New Englanders (1745) embittered many colonials, already indignant at England's tragic mismanagement of colonial volunteers in an expedition against Cartagena[qv] (1740). Other friction between England and her colonies was caused by the former's attempts to dominate military operations and the latter's failure to meet, fully or promptly, English requisitions for men, money and supplies, as well as by the colonies' persistence in trading with the enemy. Spain entered the conflict in the second war, exchanging blows with the English in Florida and South Carolina. When King George's War began Spain and England already were engaged in the War of Jenkin's Ear[qv]. Spain, a late entrant in the last colonial war, lost Florida to England. This conflict, the French and Indian War, was precipitated by English expansion westward and French advances into the Ohio Valley, the link between New France (Canada) and French Illinois and Louisiana[qqv]. Braddock's defeat[qv] (1755) near Fort Duquesne was followed by English disappointments and defeats at Crown Point, Niagara, Oswego, Ticonderoga[qqv] and elsewhere, until the turning of the tide in 1758, usually accredited to England's new war minister, William Pitt. By the Treaty of Paris[qv] (1763) France retained most of her West Indian Islands and some fishing bases off Canada; her other North American possessions east of the Mississippi, except the neighborhood of New Orleans, she ceded to England.

[G. M. Wrong, *The Conquest of New France;* W. Wood and R. H. Gabriel, *The Winning of Freedom;* S. M. Pargellis, ed., *Military Affairs in North America, 1748-1765;* S. M. Pargellis, *Lord Loudoun in North America;* F. Parkman, *A Half-Century of Conflict,* and *Montcalm and Wolfe;* T. C. Pease, *Anglo-French Boundary Disputes in the West, 1749-1763.*]

LOUISE B. DUNBAR

Colonies, Manufacturing in the. *See* Industries, Colonial.

Colonies, Vindication of the British, one of several tracts by James Otis, defending the colonies against British policy, appeared in 1765 when Otis engaged in a controversy with the Tory, Martin Howard. Specifically repudiating any thought of independence on the part of the colonists, Otis in this thirty-page tract insisted on their possession of the rights of Englishmen[qv], particularly that of self-taxation.

[C. F. Mullett, ed., *Some Political Writings of James Otis.*]

CHARLES F. MULLETT

Colorado was first visited by white men under the banner of Spain. Coronado[qv], seeking fabled wealth, penetrated the American Southwest. Returning, disillusioned, he probably touched the southeast corner of Colorado in 1541. New Mexico[qv], settled about 1600, then included the Colorado region. Spanish slave-catching and prospecting expeditions reached this country during the 17th century. In 1706 Ulibarri crossed the upper Arkansas, took formal possession for Spain and called the region Santo Domingo.

Frenchmen, from the Great Lakes region,

pushed toward the Rockies. The alarmed Spaniards countered. In 1719 and 1720 Valverde and Villasur[qv] led unsuccessful expeditions against the intruders. The Mallet[qv] brothers, in 1739, crossed Colorado territory and reached Santa Fé. With France eliminated in 1763 (*see* Paris, The Treaty of), Spain was again in undisputed possession of the Colorado region.

Through the Louisiana Purchase[qv], 1803, the eastern part of Colorado became American. Z. M. Pike[qv], first official explorer, led a small party up the Arkansas in 1806. Failing to climb the peak that bears his name, he turned south and built a log fort on the Conejos River. From here he was taken, as a prisoner, to Santa Fé[qv] and was finally released on the Louisiana border. His *Journal,* published in American, English, French, Dutch and German editions within four years, is an important historical sourcebook. The western boundary of the Louisiana Purchase was fixed in 1819 (*see* Adams-Onís Treaty). Through Colorado, it followed the Arkansas to its source and thence north to the 42nd parallel. S. H. Long, 1820, Frémont on his five expeditions, 1842–53, Gunnison, 1853, were official explorers who gave enlightening reports on the Colorado country[qqv].

Unofficial explorers, trappers and fur traders thoroughly examined the region from 1800 to 1840. These almost unknown Mountain Men[qv] are perhaps the most picturesque characters in Colorado history. They came in search of beaver skins and their annual summer rendezvous was at once a trade fair and a fiesta (*see* Trappers' Rendezvous). Pursuit of furs made them pathfinders. Depletion of beaver and invention of the silk hat ruined their trapping. They turned to buffalo robes. Barter with Indians created Bent's Fort[qv] and other trading posts in the region. This trade augmented the overland commerce to New Mexico that made the Santa Fé Trail[qv], which cut the southeast section of Colorado. The Mexican War brought Kearny's army over this trail and added the rest of Colorado Territory to the United States in 1848 (*see* Guadalupe Hidalgo, Treaty of).

Settlements in Colorado, established in the 1850's by New Mexicans, were typical Spanish towns, with dirt-roofed adobe houses[qv] enclosing a plaza. Irrigated agriculture and grazing were their economic bases. Need for Indian protection caused the establishment, in 1852, of Fort Massachusetts[qv], first United States military fort in Colorado.

Anglo-American settlement resulted from gold discoveries. News of finds at Cherry Creek, in 1858, caused the Pikes Peak Gold Rush[qv] of 1859. As a result of the reports, and of the panic of 1857[qv], some hundred thousand persons set out for the new Eldorado. Many turned back, disgusted at the meager prospects. Fortunately, real discoveries saved the movement from collapse. J. H. Gregory found lode gold near present Central City, May 6, 1859. Other discoveries followed. Mining camps and towns sprang up in the mountains, and outfitting towns at their eastern base. The influx of population brought need for government. Jefferson Territory[qv], locally organized in 1859, maintained some authority until replaced by Colorado Territory, created by Congress Feb. 28, 1861. Colorado troops sustained the Union in the Civil War, giving decisive aid in the battle of Glorieta[qv].

Refractory ores and Indian wars retarded growth in the 1860's. With the close of the Civil War, expulsion of the Plains Indians and the coming of the railroad, conditions improved. Founding of "colony" towns and opening of new mines increased population and helped bring statehood, Aug. 1, 1876. Development of the range cattle industry[qv], opening of the Ute reservation, and the discovery of great silver lodes at Leadville and Aspen furthered prosperity. Colorado's population of 39,864 in 1870 increased to 413,249 by 1890. Demonetization of silver and the Panic of 1893[qqv] brought distress. Abrupt reduction in silver output was offset by the rise of the great gold camp of Cripple Creek[qv]. Metal production reached its peak of $50,000,000 in 1900. Since then mining has rapidly declined. Farming became the leading industry. Canals and reservoirs increased irrigated acreage, with dry farming[qv] on the plains. Manufacturing and the tourist business added wealth.

[L. R. Hafen, *Colorado, the Story of a Western Commonwealth.*]

LEROY R. HAFEN

Colorado, Narrow-Gauge Railroads of. Beginning in the late 1860's Colorado became the center of the construction of narrow-gauge (three feet) railroads. In 1873 over half of the narrow-gauge mileage in this country was in Colorado. The Denver and Rio Grande[qv] was the pioneer, longest and best known narrow-gauge railway in the United States. Close study of the Festiniog Railway in Wales had convinced Gen. W. J. Palmer, first president of the Denver and Rio Grande, that a gauge of three feet was practicable in mountainous regions. Advantages cited for narrow-gauge construction were: lower costs of construction, operation and maintenance; greater curvature and higher gradients; larger pay loads in proportion to weight of rolling stock, and ability to penetrate areas closed to broad-gauge lines. Although many lines have been abandoned or broad gauged since the early 1890's, a considerable number are still in operation.

[J. H. Baker and L. R. Hafen, *History of Colorado.*]
GEORGE L. ANDERSON

Colorado Coal Strikes, THE, of 1903–4 and 1913–14, were produced by essentially the same causes: refusal of the operators to recognize the right of unionization and demands by the workers for higher pay and more healthful working conditions, as well as for the right to board, trade and seek medical attention wherever they pleased. The last demand grew out of the maintenance of "closed" camps and towns by the Colorado Fuel and Iron Company, the Gould-Rockefeller controlled operating companies, where none but company stores were permitted and into which only company-approved persons might enter.

The earlier strike, involving 10,000 workers, began on Nov. 9, 1903, following the refusal of the operators to confer with representatives of the United Mine Workers[qv]. Those in the northern field returned to work on Nov. 27, but the remainder continued on strike. After some loss of life and property the militia was sent to Trinidad and order was restored. In June, 1904, the troops were withdrawn, after which the strikers returned to work without having won any material advantages.

The strike of 1913–14 began on Sept. 23, 1913, following the refusal of the worker demands drawn up a week earlier. It involved a mixed reign of terror and civil war of several months' duration in the area between Walsenburg and Trinidad. The Ludlow massacre of April 20, 1914, in which many men, women and children were killed, was the most tragic event of the strike. Federal troops were sent into the area in May, 1914, order was gradually restored, strikers returned to work under more satisfactory working conditions, the state enacted legislation to prevent similar occurrences in the future and the Colorado Fuel and Iron Company adopted a more constructive labor policy.

[W. F. Stone, *History of Colorado.*]
GEORGE L. ANDERSON

Colorado River, Exploration of. In 1539 the Spaniard Ulloa reached the mouth of the Colorado, without knowing of the river's existence. Wrote he: ". . . we perceived the sea to run with so great a rage into the land that it was a thing to be marvelled at; and with the like fury it returned back again with the ebb . . . some great river might be the cause thereof." The actual discovery was made in August, 1540, by Alarcón, who, conquering the fierce tidal bore of the river's mouth, anchored and proceeded upstream in boats drawn by tow ropes. He reached a point near Lighthouse Rock, but did not make a junction with the overland expedition under Coronado[qv]. Two of Coronado's officers, Diaz and Cárdenas, reached the Colorado, and Cárdenas discovered the Grand Canyon[qv]. In the next two centuries exploration of the river was in the hands of the padres, who were more interested in souls than geography. Outstanding among the padres were the Franciscans, Garcés and Escalante, in the 1770's. It was Garcés who first made regular use of the name Colorado, doing so because, draining a red country, the stream was tinged with red during the spring melting of the snows.

In the early 19th century exploration was mostly by American trappers and fur traders. Gen. William Henry Ashley[qv], fur trader, descended the canyons of the Green River by "bullboat"[qv] in 1825 and supplied the first authentic information concerning the upper Colorado. At Ashley Falls he painted "Ashley, 1825" on a huge overhanging rock; the black lettering was still partly visible in 1911. In 1826 a British naval officer, Lt. R. W. H. Hardy, explored the lower Colorado and wrote the first dependable description of the country near the mouth. Most important of the trappers was James O. Pattie, whose narrative was vitiated and mutilated by the editor. Each pioneer contributed to the gradual accumulation of knowledge, in spite of the contradictions in their narratives.

With the establishment of a military post at the mouth of the Gila for the protection of California-bound gold seekers, the United States Government became interested in scientific exploration of the Colorado. The topographical engineers of the War Department sent several expeditions: Lt. G. H. Derby, 1850–51; Lt. J. C. Ives, 1857–58; Lt. G. M. Wheeler, 1871; and towering over all, the two expeditions of Maj. J. W. Powell, 1869 and 1871–72. Powell's work of blueprinting the stream has since been completed by the Geological Survey. A civilian, George A. Johnson, first ascended the river to the head of navigation, above the Black Canyon, in his steamer, the *General Jessup,* in 1858.

Most of the world's rivers are attractive routes for interior exploration and highways of settlement and commerce. Through most of its history the Colorado has been none of these things. It has been "a veritable dragon, loud in its dangerous lair . . . a formidable host of snarling waters." It has been anything but a friend and ally of man, and it is precisely this feature that has restrained man's interest and distributed exploration over three centuries. It is only in recent decades that man has utilized the waters of the Colorado for irrigation and other purposes.

[F. S. Dellenbaugh, *The Romance of the Colorado River;* L. R. Freeman, *The Colorado River.*]

FRANK EDWARD ROSS

Colorado River Aqueduct, THE, 242 miles long, estimated to cost $212,000,000, and scheduled for completion in 1939, was the first project initiated under the Hoover self-liquidating public works program. It will carry 1500 cubic feet of water per second for domestic use from the Colorado River to Los Angeles and other cities comprising the Metropolitan Water District. Boulder (Hoover) Dam[qv] power is used to lift the water about 1600 feet over the intervening mountains.

[Wilbur and Ely, *The Hoover Dam Contracts;* Reports of the Secretary of the Interior, 1930-32.]

NORTHCUTT ELY

Colorado River Projects. The Colorado River Compact, executed in 1922, under the chairmanship of Herbert Hoover, representing the United States, apportioned waters of the Colorado between the "Lower Basin" (Arizona, California and Nevada) and the "Upper Basin" (Colorado, Utah, New Mexico and Wyoming). It was the forty-seventh interstate compact[qv] authorized or ratified by Congress, and the first to apportion interstate waters.

Ratified by all parties except Arizona, it was approved by Congress as a six-state agreement in the Boulder Canyon Project Act (1928), which impressed the compact upon all projects built thereafter on the Colorado River system, and authorized construction of Boulder (Hoover) Dam[qv], the All American Canal[qv] and other Lower Basin projects. In 1930 Secretary of the Interior Ray Lyman Wilbur initiated a co-ordinated Lower Basin power and water program, which included an agreement settling water controversies in Arizona; contracts controlling use of Boulder (Hoover) Dam power in California and reserving waters for Arizona; power contracts for all Boulder (Hoover) Dam power, but reserving a "drawback privilege" on 36% of the energy for future use in Arizona and Nevada; and a repayment contract assuring construction of the All American Canal. Under that project, Boulder (Hoover) Dam has been constructed, and Parker Dam, the Colorado River Aqueduct[qv], Imperial Dam and the All American Canal are scheduled for completion before 1939. Other reclamation projects under construction (1939) are the Parker-Gila (Arizona), Bartlett Dam (Verde River, Arizona) and transmountain diversion (Colorado).

[Wilbur and Ely, *The Hoover Dam Contracts;* Reports of the Secretary of the Interior, 1930-32 inclusive.]

NORTHCUTT ELY

Colt Six Shooter, THE, the invention of Samuel Colt, was the first practical arm of its kind. With the rifle, it had its place in revolutionizing methods of warfare, and was an important link in the development of arms from the muzzle-loading musket to the magazine rifles and machine-guns of today.

Its manufacture began at Paterson, N. J., in 1836. Colt's patent, secured Feb. 25, 1836, covered the revolution and locking of the cylinder firmly in place, so that the chambers of the cylinder came in line with the barrel by simply pulling the hammer back to full cock. From the first, all the barrels were expertly rifled to give the greatest possible accuracy to the bullet. Although various models were produced at Paterson, the arms did not at first receive the endorsement of government officials, and the company failed in 1842.

A few Colt arms, used by army officers in the Seminole War and by Texas Rangers[qqv] during the border troubles, proved the worth of the "revolving pistol," and a supply was ordered by the Government in 1847. As Colt had no factory at that time, the first 2000 or 3000 were made for him at the plant of Eli Whitney in New Haven, Conn. These were heavy revolvers of .44 caliber and soon became the standard of the United States Army and the Texas Rangers. Colt resumed the manufacture of revolvers at Hartford, Conn., in 1848. From 1856 to 1865 there were 554,283 of the powder and ball revolvers manufactured at the Hartford factory. Large quantities of these arms were used during the Civil War by both Union and Confederate troops. All Colt revolvers, up to the early 1870's, were made to shoot loose powder and lead bullets, the powder being ignited by a percussion cap. From that period, envelope cartridges, enclosing powder and bullet, were used until the advent of metallic ammunition.

Colt six shooters played a prominent part in the development of the West. When first used in Indian fighting the six shooter was a surprise weapon, as the savages did not look for more than one shot and when opposed by a single-shot arm it was their custom to draw fire and then rush the settler while he was reloading.

The six shooter won its popularity in the West because it was easily carried, accurate and of high capacity. Sheriffs, cowboys[qv] and plainsmen quickly became expert marksmen. It was an ideal weapon for mounted rangers and cattlemen, and was used for hunting as well as for defense. The extinction of the buffalo[qv] can be laid, in part, to the efficiency of the six shooter in the hands of hunting horsemen.

SAMUEL M. STONE

Columbia, Burning of. Sherman's army reached Columbia, S. C., Feb. 17, 1865, on its famous march through the Carolinas[qv]. The fact that Columbia was the capital city of the state which was held peculiarly responsible for the war, and the desire of the Union soldiers for vengeance, probably account for the burning of the city, which occurred that night. Sherman's assertion that the fire spread from bales of cotton ignited by evacuating Confederates under Gen. Wade Hampton is not acceptable, for the cotton appears to have been drenched by fire engines long before the fires of the night of Feb. 17 gained headway. The house fires, reported to have been started by Union soldiers, originated on the windward side of the long-extinguished cotton in the middle of a very wide street and swept over that street and eastward across the city. It is probable that only by confining his men to camp could Gen. Sherman have prevented the conflagration. He later asserted that he would not have done that to save the city. In his memoirs Sherman wrote: "Having utterly ruined Columbia, the right wing began its march northward."

[D. D. Wallace, *History of South Carolina*, III.]

D. D. WALLACE

Columbia College, established by royal charter on Oct. 31, 1754, as the College of the Province of New-York, was known from the beginning as King's College. The first president, Rev. Samuel Johnson, D.D., began instruction with a class of eight students in the schoolhouse in the rear of Trinity Church. In 1760 the college moved into a new building on what is now Park Place, New York City. Rev. Myles Cooper of Oxford, who succeeded Johnson as president in 1763, developed the college and conformed it as much as possible to English patterns, adding a medical school in 1767. Upon the occupation of New York by the American army at the outbreak of the Revolution, the building was taken over for use as a military hospital, all teaching ceased, and the students were dispersed. The corporation maintained its existence, however, and was rechartered, in 1784, as Columbia College under the Regents of the University of the State of New York. This form of government proving unsatisfactory, in 1787 an act was passed confirming the royal charter of 1754, and vesting the property and franchises of King's College in the trustees of Columbia College in the city of New York, under which charter it has continued to operate. The medical faculty was revived in 1785, but discontinued in 1813, its work being carried on by the College of Physicians and Surgeons, which was again incorporated in the college in 1860. During the first half of the 19th century the enrollment remained at about 100 annually, with a small faculty and a traditional curriculum. The administration of Charles King (1849–64) saw the establishment of the Law School (1858), the Medical School (1860), the School of Mines (1864), the enlargement of the faculty and curriculum and the awakening of the university idea. During King's administration the college was moved (1857) from its original site to Madison Avenue and 49th Street. Under Pres. Frederick A. P. Barnard (1864–89), Columbia achieved university status, which was confirmed by the revised corporation statutes of 1891; the first graduate school, that of Political Science, was established in 1880; women were permitted to study for Columbia degrees (1883) and the library began to grow in size and usefulness. Under Seth Low, president from 1889 to 1901, Columbia was moved (1897) to its present site on Morningside Heights, and the graduate faculties of Philosophy (1890) and Pure Science (1892) established. Columbia University now (1939) includes, in addition to the schools above mentioned, Barnard College (1889), Teachers College (1898); Schools of Architecture (1881), Pharmacy (1904), Journalism (1912), Business (1916), Dental and Oral Surgery (1916) and Library Service (1926); Bard College (1928) and the New York Post-Graduate Medical School (1931). Barnard College, Teachers College, College of Pharmacy and Bard College are financially independent but affiliated corporations.

[*A History of Columbia University.*]

MILTON HALSEY THOMAS

Columbia Fur Company, THE, founded about 1822 and operating in the countries of the Sioux and Omaha, had, by 1827, gained a place of such strength as to become a serious competitor of the western branch of John Jacob Astor's American Fur Company[qv]. Accordingly, negotiations were completed, during the summer of that year, which made the smaller company a part of the Astor firm. The former Columbia Fur Company thereafter transacted business under the name of the "Upper Missouri Outfit" and confined its operations to the territory above the mouth of the Big Sioux.

[H. M. Chittenden, *The American Fur Trade.*]

CARL P. RUSSELL

Columbia River, Exploration and Settlement. The estuary of the Columbia was first seen, described and mapped in 1775 by Capt. Bruno Hezeta, who named it Bahia de la Asumpcion, though Spanish maps showed it as Ensenada de Hezeta. In 1792 Capt. Robert Gray of Boston sailed ten miles up the river proper and six miles up Gray's Bay, naming it Columbia's River after his ship. The same year W. R. Broughton of Vancouver's[qv] party surveyed and charted to Cottonwood Point, 119 statute miles from the ocean.

In 1800 Lagasse and LeBlanc reached the upper river from the Rocky Mountains. Lewis and Clark[qv], in 1805, explored from the mouth of the Yakima to Cottonwood Point, 214 miles. In 1807 David Thompson explored for 111 miles, from the mouth of Blaeberry Creek to the Columbia River's source in Columbia Lake; and in 1811 Finan McDonald navigated from Kettle Falls to Death Rapids, 255 miles. In the same year Thompson navigated the entire river.

Prior to the great wagon train of 1843, settlements had been started along the river in over forty localities. The posts of the fur traders included those of the North West Company, the Astorian posts[qqv] and those of independent traders. Among the earliest were Fort Clatsop (1805) and Chouteau's post (1807). Other settlements were Fort Colville (1825); Willamette Valley, an agricultural settlement (1829); Bonneville's cantonment (1832); Whitman Mission (1836); and Cœur d'Alene (1842)[qqv]. After 1843 the wagon train rapidly opened the country, and subsequently the steamboat, railroads and highways have transformed the wilderness into a prosperous and populous region.

[H. H. Bancroft, *History of the North West Coast,* and *History of Oregon.*]

J. NEILSON BARRY

Comanche, The, were a tribe, or a group of tribes more or less closely related, belonging to the Shoshonean stock. There were once twelve divisions of the Comanches, the most important being the Yamparika, Kotsoteka, Nokini, Kwahadi and Penateka.

The Comanches appeared in New Mexico early in the 18th century. Soon they drove the Apaches[qv] out of the South Plains country. By the middle of the century they were causing the Spaniards at San Antonio considerable annoyance, and thereafter, for a century and a quarter they harried the frontier settlements of Texas. By 1840, when they had reached the limit of their southward migration, the Comanche country was the South Plains from the Arkansas River to the San Saba River in Texas. At peace with the Comanches lived the Kiowas[qv] in the northern part, and the Wichitas and other Caddoan peoples in the southeastern part, of the vast domain the Comanches claimed. War parties of Comanches frequently raided settlements as far north as the Platte River and as far south as Durango. They were not a numerous people; 20,000 souls, in 1800, and 10,000, in 1850, represent liberal estimates.

A reservation for Comanches, maintained in Texas from 1855 to 1859, did not lessen their marauding operations (*see* Washita, Sheridan's Operations on). A larger reservation assigned to them in southwestern Oklahoma, in 1867 (*see* Medicine Lodge, Treaty of), was not occupied by the more warlike divisions until they were driven in by troops eight years later (*see* Red River Indian War).

Superb horsemen, nomadic and warlike, the Comanches constituted the greatest human factor in retarding the settlement of the South Plains.

[Rupert N. Richardson, *The Comanche Barrier to South Plains Settlement.*]

RUPERT N. RICHARDSON

Combine, The, is a farm machine that makes harvesting and threshing a single process. It was developed by 1828, but not perfected until the 1870's. Between 1870 and 1873 the United States Patent Office recorded the invention of six harvester-threshers; and by 1880 the combine was commercially established.

Until 1920 this machine was used primarily on the west coast, because fair weather and dry grain were considered essential to its operation. High grain prices and the popularity of labor-saving devices after the World War brought the combine to the states of the Middle West where large-scale farming was being practised. About this same time a desire for efficiency in the harvesting of soybeans brought the harvester-thresher into extensive use.

Early in the 1930's a small or baby combine was perfected. Weighing about two tons, selling for less than $500, and covering twenty acres per day, these machines have brought increased efficiency to small farms. Great numbers of farmers are now able to own and operate combines with a resulting saving of labor. Consequently the substitution of machine-power for man-power has reduced labor requirements and increased the effectiveness of each laboring unit.

[W. M. Hurst and W. R. Humphries, Harvesting with Combines, United States Department of Agriculture *Farmers Bulletin*, 1761.]

BENJAMIN F. SHAMBAUGH

Comic Strips and Funny Papers were a natural extension of the robust humor of the 1870's and 1880's, abetted by an expanding newspaperdom, bent on circulation and experimenting with color printing. James Swinnerton drew comic bear pictures for the San Francisco *Examiner* in 1892, and the New York *Daily News* printed an isolated comic strip as early as 1884, but the forerunner of the colored "funny paper" was R. F. Outcault's "Origin of a New Species," which appeared, Sunday, Nov. 18, 1894, in the New York *World*. In 1896 Hearst lured Outcault, who meanwhile devised the "Yellow Kid," highly popular bad-boy character, to the New York *Journal*. The ensuing battle, with both newspapers printing Sunday "Yellow Kid" pages, and attendant sensationalism, provoked the term, "yellow journalism."^qv^

Early comic characters, such as Happy Hooligan, Buster Brown, Foxy Grandpa, Little Jimmy, Hans and Fritz and Nemo, if not elevating, were relatively harmless; yet critics soon denounced the funny paper's influence, and in 1907 the International Kindergarten Union asked parents to bar it from their homes. Power over circulation, however, was manifest when strips set styles, and on the fortieth anniversary of Outcault's first page, the New York *Times* alone among important newspapers still resisted them. Brisbane rated comic strips second to news in the elements of "a successful newspaper," surveys showed a majority of readers had favorites, while the dispute of two Washington newspapers over rights to Andy Gump was carried to the United States Supreme Court.

Syndicates grew around leading strips and bought them away from one another as a fortune-making business developed from Mutt and Jeff, Jiggs, Toonerville Folks and others. As many as 2500 newspapers used some 250 strips and single panels from 75 agencies. At its peak, Hearst's *Comic Weekly: Puck*, distributed by 17 newspapers with a circulation reaching 5,500,000, alone ran 50 comics in its 32 pages. One syndicate claimed a circulation of more than 50,000,000. Comic section advertising skyrocketed from a $360,000 business in 1931 to more than $16,500,000 in 1937, cost per page reaching $17,000.

Meantime the strips generally changed from comics to serial picture stories, presenting everything from domestic affairs and Negro life to high adventure and crime. Many found them more degrading than ever, but syndicates employed linguists to prepare the strips for increasing demand over the world; when Orphan Annie's dog was lost, Henry Ford telegraphed her creator to do all he could to find it. If juvenile delinquency could be traced to some, Briggs' "Days of Real Sport" was a genuine contribution to humor. Perspective reveals the comics as a machine age's folk tales with Popeye supplanting Paul Bunyan and the popular characters literally being handed down from one drawing board to another.

[A. M. Lee, *The Daily Newspaper in America;* W. G. Bleyer, *Main Currents in the History of American Journalism;* Frank Weitenkampf, *Bookman*, July, 1925; *News Week*, Dec. 1, 1934; Rube Goldberg, *Saturday Evening Post*, Dec. 15, 1928; D. F. McCord, *American Mercury*, July, 1935; J. K. Ryan, *Forum*, May, 1936; B. Price, *World's Work*, August, 1931; *Fortune*, April, 1937; S. M. Smith, *Pictorial Review*, January, 1935; R. L. Neuberger, *New Republic*, July 11, 1934; *Literary Digest*, Dec. 12, 1936, also April 7, 1934; L. Thompson, *Saturday Review of Literature*, Nov. 13, 1937; *Editor & Publisher*, July 21, 1934; William Murrell, *A History of American Graphic Humor*, 1865-1938.]

IRVING DILLIARD

Commander in Chief. The Constitution makes the President the commander in chief of the Army and Navy of the United States, and of the state militia when called into the service of the United States. The powers that the President may actually exercise in this capacity are not, however, explicitly defined, and the Supreme Court has held, in Ex parte Milligan^qv^, that their extent must be determined "by their nature and by the principles of our institutions." This means, in general, that although Congress may decide the general military policy and must provide for the armed forces, the President has almost complete control of such forces as are provided, and may exercise this control in such a way as to formulate important domestic and foreign policies. President Polk thus used his power as commander in chief virtually to force a war with Mexico, President Cleveland to break a railway strike in Chicago (*see* Pullman Strike of 1894), President Coolidge to supervise elections in Nicaragua, and there are numerous other instances that demonstrate how broad this power has become in practice and to what extent its exercise depends upon the President's own interpretation of his responsibility under the Constitution.

[Clarence A. Berdahl, *War Powers of the Executive in the United States;* The Powers of the President as Commander in Chief, *Foreign Policy Association Information Service*, Vol. IV, no. 10, July 10, 1928; C. C. Tansill, War Powers of the President of the United States with Special Reference to the Beginning of Hostilities, *Political Science Quarterly*, Vol. XLV, pp. 1-55, March, 1930.]

CLARENCE A. BERDAHL

Commander in Chief of the British Forces in North America was a position of highest importance in the last half of the 18th century, held by Horatio Sharpe (1754), Braddock (1755), Shirley (1755–56), Loudoun (1756–57), Abercromby (1758), Amherst (1758–63) and Gage (1763–75); and, with more limited control, Howe (1775–78), Clinton (1778–82), Carleton (1783 f.), etc. Responsible to the crown and appointed by the crown, these commanders were supervised directly by the ministry. Supreme in American military supervision and significant in financial expenditures, the duties of the position involved an astonishing scope of responsibility and power, touching many aspects of American life.

[Stanley Pargellis, *Lord Loudoun in America;* Clarence Carter, ed., *The Correspondence of General Thomas Gage.*]

ALFRED P. JAMES

Commerce. *See* Trade, Domestic; Trade, Foreign.

Commerce, Court of. This court, created by act of Congress, June 18, 1910, was intended to provide a specialized tribunal for a constantly growing and increasingly complex volume of litigation, and to expedite the course of justice. It consisted of five judges appointed by the President for five-year terms, on the expiration of which, new members were to be assigned by the Chief Justice of the United States from among the circuit judges. In broad terms, its jurisdiction covered all civil suits arising under the Interstate Commerce Act, the Elkins Act, the orders of the Interstate Commerce Commission[qqv], etc. Its early decisions created a popular impression that the court was unduly solicitous for railroad interests and inclined to hamper effective regulation by the Interstate Commerce Commission. A strong congressional minority had opposed its creation in 1910 and there was a growing demand two years later for its abolition. When one of its members, Judge Robert W. Archbald, was impeached, convicted of corruption and removed from the bench Jan. 13, 1913, the demand became so imperative that Congress dissolved the court, Oct. 22, 1913.

[I. L. Sharfmann, *The Interstate Commerce Commission.*]

W. A. ROBINSON

Commerce, Department of, was created, by an act of Congress, Feb. 14, 1903, "to foster, promote, and develop the foreign and domestic commerce, the mining, manufacturing, shipping, and fishery industries, the labor interests, and the transportation facilities of the United States." This law was modified by an act of March 4, 1913, establishing the Department of Labor[qv]. The Department of Commerce in the narrower sense came into being at the latter date. But many of the functions of the department are as old as the Federal Government and many of its agencies, under various names, were organized early in our history.

After the formation of the Department of Labor in 1913, the Department of Commerce retained the Bureaus of the Census[qv], Corporations, Fisheries, Foreign and Domestic Commerce, Lighthouses, Navigation, and Standards[qv], and the United States Coast and Geodetic Survey[qv] and Steamboat Inspection Service. Lighthouse service[qv] and aids to navigation were authorized by law as early as 1789. The first census was taken in 1790. Coast and geodetic surveys, vital to shipping and defense, were authorized in 1807. The statistical work of the Bureau of Foreign and Domestic Commerce has been traced to an office established in the Treasury Department[qv] in 1820. The beginnings of the varied research and experimental work of the Bureau of Standards were authorized as early as 1830. A Commissioner of Fish and Fisheries was appointed in 1871. The Bureau of Navigation was established in 1884.

Under Mr. Hoover, as Secretary of Commerce and later as President, the department acquired jurisdiction over the Patent Office and the Bureau of Mines (1925), greatly expanded the work of many of its agencies (notably the Bureau of Standards and the Bureau of Foreign and Domestic Commerce) and added new services such as the Aeronautics Division (later the Bureau of Air Commerce), the Radio Division and the Federal Employment Stabilization Board.

Many services falling under the broad statutory definition of the department's functions remained in other departments or under independent agencies such as the Interstate Commerce Commission[qv]. On the other hand, some of the agencies under the jurisdiction of the Department of Commerce, such as the Bureau of the Census, performed general functions equally relevant to the work of other departments. During the presidency of Franklin D. Roosevelt, the historic problems of differentiation and co-ordination were accentuated by the increasingly varied and vital responsibilities of Government. Changes affecting the Department of Commerce included the transfer, in 1938, of the work of the Bureau of Air Commerce to the newly organized Civil Aeronautics Authority.

[U. S. Department of Commerce and Labor, *Organization and Law of the Department of Commerce and Labor*, Washington, 1904; U. S. Department of Commerce, *The Department of Commerce: Condensed History, Duties, . . .*, Washington, 1913.]

WITT BOWDEN

Commerce Clause, THE JUDICIAL HISTORY OF THE, properly begins with the famous case of Gibbons v. Ogden[qv] (1824) in which Chief Justice Marshall defined commerce as intercourse. On the basis of this definition, the Supreme Court has held that Congress' power to regulate commerce among the states is the power to govern commercial intercourse among them. This power of Congress Marshall considered to be plenary and unaffected by the states and their powers.

When Roger B. Taney became Chief Justice, the Court assumed a view more congenial to states' rights[qv], and the rule was laid down that there is a field of jurisdiction which is exclusively reserved to the states (*see* License Cases, 1847). However, the supremacy of Federal power was asserted again four years later when the Court maintained that where the subject matter is local in character the states may act, but only until Congress chooses to legislate. Whatever subjects of commerce are in their nature national, or admit only of uniform regulation, must be left to the exclusive control of Congress (Cooley v. Bd. of Wardens[qv], 1852).

Until the Civil War most interstate commerce was by water, and few questions of jurisdiction arose between the Federal and state governments. But the construction of railroads[qv] throughout the United States created new problems. Illinois undertook to regulate that part of an interstate journey which was entirely within the state. This exercise of state power the Supreme Court held unconstitutional (Wabash St. L. and P. Ry. Co. v. Illinois[qv], 1886). In order that the railroads might not be wholly unregulated, Congress in 1887 established the Interstate Commerce Commission[qv].

The growth of the regulatory power of Congress in the field of commerce after 1887 was rapid. The Sherman Antitrust Act[qv] in 1890 extended the power of Congress to prohibit combinations in restraint of trade[qv] among the states. This act was early given a judicial interpretation which greatly restricted its scope (U. S. v. E. C. Knight Co.[qv], 1895), but in subsequent decisions came to represent an important exercise of the Federal regulatory power. The act was applied to combinations of labor as well as capital (Loewe v. Lawlor[qv], 1908), a step which aroused the opposition of the trade unions[qv] and led in 1914 to the passage of the Clayton Act[qv]. At the same time Congress established the Federal Trade Commission[qv].

The field of transportation was gradually confided by Congress to the supervision of the Interstate Commerce Commission. Beginning with the Elkins Act[qv] in 1903, a series of measures strengthened the powers of the commission and enabled it to assume jurisdiction of steamship and railroad companies, express and sleeping-car companies, motor bus and motor truck concerns, power transmission lines, telephone and telegraph lines and oil pipe line companies when engaged in interstate commerce. The Supreme Court in the late 1890's ruled that the commission could forbid discriminatory and unreasonable rates but did not admit the right to impose any definite rate or schedules on a railroad. The rule was laid down that a common carrier was entitled to a fair return upon the value of the property dedicated to the public use (Smyth v. Ames[qv], 1898). When Congress in 1906 authorized the commission to fix rates for the future (*see* Hepburn Act), the courts had to determine a basis upon which the value of the property of a common carrier was to be ascertained. In other words, the judges were obliged to delve into the realm of economic theory to discover a rate basis[qv] which could be applied.

Meanwhile, conflicts arose between the commerce power and the reserved powers[qv] of the states. Within the legitimate exercise of the police power[qv], the states might forbid the running of freight trains on Sunday, prohibit the importation within their borders of diseased cattle, and enact many other laws designed to promote the health, safety, and moral welfare of citizens. But in 1918 a majority of the justices of the Supreme Court refused their assent to an act of Congress prohibiting the transportation in interstate commerce of goods the product of child labor[qv]. The field of production was therefore to be considered as falling within the reserved powers of the states (Hammer v. Dagenhart[qv]). However, the Supreme Court had already admitted a large sphere of police power to Congress. The Mann White Slave Act[qv] and the act forbidding the distribution of lottery tickets through interstate commerce were police regulations.

The Transportation Act of 1920[qv] assumed the judicial rulings already laid down in behalf of the power of Congress. Among these was the rule that "wherever the interstate and intrastate transactions of the carriers are so related that the government of the one involves the control of the other," Congress is entitled to regulate both classes of transactions (Shreveport Case[qv], 1914). The extension of Federal power to the regulation of the business of the commission men and of the livestock dealers in the great stockyards of the country was upheld by the Supreme Court (Stafford v. Wallace[qv], 1922). In this case the Court held that stockyards are not a place of rest or final destination but a throat through which the current of commerce flows. While the Supreme Court clung to its decision in the child-labor case, it upheld an act of Congress forbidding the transportation in interstate commerce of goods made by convict labor[qv] into any state where the goods are to be sold or used in violation of its laws. This decision assumed that where state policy condemned a practice the power of Congress might be put forth to prevent interstate commerce from frustrating the policy (Kentucky Whip and Collar Co., v. Illinois Central R. R. Co., 1937).

While the Supreme Court was permitting these extensions of Federal power, it was confronted with a case involving the validity of the National Industrial Recovery Act[qv], in which Congress sought to delegate to the President control over the entire field of production where it affected interstate commerce. The N.I.R.A. was overturned not only as an unconstitutional delegation of power to the President but also as an invasion of the reserved powers of the states (Schechter Poultry Corp. v. U. S.[qv], 1935). Two years later the Court receded markedly from the position it had taken not only in the latter portion of this decision but also from its position in the child-labor case. In upholding the validity of the National Labor Relations Act[qv], a majority of the justices agreed that manufacturing, although carried out wholly within a state, may affect interstate commerce in such a way that it comes within the scope of Federal power (N.L.R.B. v. Jones and Laughlin Steel Corp.[qv], 1937).

The judicial interpretation of the commerce clause has taken many bypaths since the decision of John Marshall more than a century ago. Most of these have been pointed out by states' rights, and it is only as the philosophy of particularism has succumbed to the nationalizing tendencies of the last two generations that the Supreme Court has been able to return to the fundamental principles of the decision in Gibbons v. Ogden.

[E. S. Corwin, *The Constitution and What It Means Today*, 6th ed.]

WILLIAM S. CARPENTER

Commerce Commission. *See* Interstate Commerce Commission, The.

Commercial Cable Company, THE, founded in 1883 by John W. Mackay and James Gordon Bennett, was the principal competitor of the Western Union[qv] in the field of communications. In 1884 it laid two transatlantic cables to compete with those leased by the latter from the American Telegraph & Cable Co., and its land lines were operated in conjunction with the Postal Telegraph[qv], most of whose stock it controlled.

[I. M. Tarbell, *The Nationalizing of Business.*]

WHEELER PRESTON

Commercial Committee (Revolutionary), THE, was one of the principal standing committees of the Continental Congress[qv]. Originating as the "Secret Committee," appointed (Sept. 19, 1775) to make purchase of powder, its functions were little by little enlarged until it became the chief agency of Congress in the extensive business of exchanging American products for arms and ammunition abroad, having its own agents both in America and in Europe. It was reconstituted July 5, 1777, with the name Committee of Commerce (although oftener called the Commercial Committee), and again Dec. 14, 1778. During its career the committee was more than once under the fire of severe criticism. Its chief figure was Robert Morris, who, as Superintendent of Finance (1781), took over most of its functions. (*See also* Revolutionary Committees.)

[Jennings B. Sanders, *Evolution of Executive Departments of the Continental Congress, 1774-1789.*]

EDMUND C. BURNETT

Commission Government is a system of municipal government in which all executive and legislative powers are concentrated in the hands of a small elective board, usually of five members. The plan, in its present form, was originated by Galveston, Tex., during an emergency caused by the tidal flood which partially destroyed that city in 1900 (*see* Galveston Storm, The). It was not intended to be a permanent scheme of city government, but having proved successful it was retained after the emergency had passed. Attracting attention in other parts of the country, the commission plan spread northward and in due course was adopted by several hundred cities, most of them small communities. During more recent years, however, it has lost ground. Many cities have abandoned the commission plan in favor of city manager government[qv] or have restored the older mayor-and-council type of government.

The essence of the plan is its simplicity. The voters elect a commission, usually of five members, on a nonpartisan ballot. One of the commissioners serves as chairman and may bear the title of mayor but he has no independent executive powers. All questions of general policy are decided by the commissioners as a group. They enact the ordinances, determine the tax rate, vote the appropriations, and so on. But each individual commissioner takes immediate charge of an administrative department and for this purpose all the administrative work of the city is consolidated into five departments.

The commission plan has demonstrated the value of simplification in city government; on the other hand it has disclosed some organic defects. Chief among these is the absence of unified executive authority. It provides a five-headed mayoralty which often becomes divided within itself. So far as large cities are concerned, moreover, a legislative body of only five members is not deemed to be adequately representative.

[W. B. Munro, *The Government of American Cities.*]

WILLIAM B. MUNRO

Commission Merchants and Factors. The factor or commission merchant was one of the significant figures in the early commercial life of the country. Legally "a factor is an agent employed to purchase or sell goods on commission in his own name, or in the name of his principal," and is distinguished from a broker in that he "is entrusted with the possession, management, control and disposal of the goods to be bought or sold."

The factorage system was introduced into the colonies soon after the dissolution of the Virginia Company[qv] (1624); developed through the colonial and early national periods; and probably was of most importance from 1815 to 1860. During these years the great staple crops of cotton, tobacco, sugar and rice[qqv] were produced in the South for distant markets in the Northeast and Europe, from whence were received manufactured goods and supplies. Commission merchants, either possessed of large capital or able to procure it from the banks, advanced money during the period of production to planters and manufacturers, in return for which the products of farm and factory were consigned to them for sale. The planter and manufacturer were thus freed from the expense and trouble of selling and could devote their time, capital and energy to the production of goods.

The chief disadvantages of the system were: 1, that the merchant might be more interested in a quick rather than a profitable sale; and 2, that frequently the proceeds of the sales did not equal the sum advanced by the merchant, leaving the planter or manufacturer in debt. Southern planters had the added grievance that since most goods were imported by Northern merchants and a substantial portion of the produce handled by the same agents, the profits of their trade were going to a rival section. Consequently there were numerous attempts by Southerners to build up direct trade connections between Europe and the Southern ports, and from 1850 to 1860 an attempt by Southern planters to deal directly with the European manufacturer without any intermediary at all, thus eliminating the Southern and European as well as the Northern merchant. All of these attempts failed, and it was only the development of the commodity exchanges, the tremendous increase of industrial capital and the improved methods of transportation and communication, that ended the dominant position of the commission merchant in American economy.

[L. C. Gray, *History of Agriculture in the Southern United States to 1860;* N. S. Buck, *The Development of the Organization of Anglo-American Trade.*]

T. P. GOVAN

Committee for Industrial Organization. *See* Congress of Industrial Organizations.

Committee Form of Government during the American Revolution. *See* Revolutionary Committees.

Committee of the States, THE. The Articles of Confederation[qv] empowered Congress to appoint a committee consisting of one delegate from each state, "to be denominated 'A Committee of the States,'" to sit in the recess of Congress and to exercise such powers as Congress, "by the consent of nine states, shall from time to time think expedient to vest them with"; with the one proviso, that the committee should not be authorized to do any act requiring the voice of nine states.

Once only, in June, 1784, was the Committee of the States called into existence. Early in August certain members, who had opposed the appointment of the committee, withdrew, leaving the committee without a quorum (nine), and the committee was not thereafter able to reassemble.

[Edmund C. Burnett, The Committee of the States, in American Historical Association, *Annual Report*, 1913, Vol. I.]

EDMUND C. BURNETT

Committee of the Whole, THE, consists of all the members of a legislative chamber, but organized as a committee and thus enabled to operate under less rigid procedures than if sitting formally as a house. A smaller number is required for a quorum, there is more freedom of debate, there is usually no roll call or other record vote, and in other ways it is easier to do business in Committee of the Whole. Although now discontinued by the United States Senate and by several state legislatures, it is regularly used by the national House of Representatives.

[D. S. Alexander, *History and Procedure of the House of Representatives;* W. F. Willoughby, *Principles of Legislative Organization and Administration.*]

CLARENCE A. BERDAHL

Committee of Thirteen, THE (1850), was a select committee of the Senate agreed to on April 18 upon motion of Sen. Henry S. Foote of Mississippi, to which were to be sent the compromise resolutions of Senators Henry Clay of Kentucky and John Bell of Tennessee. The original provision that the committee should mature a scheme of compromise for the adjustment of all the pending issues of slavery was dropped out as unnecessary. Chosen by ballot on April 19, the committee, with Clay as chairman, included six Democrats and seven Whigs; three of the former and four of the latter were from the slave states. On May 8 the committee reported, offering two bills: an omnibus bill*qv* providing for the admission of California and for the territorial organization, without the Wilmot Proviso*qv*, of Utah and New Mexico, together with a settlement of the disputed Texas boundary, and a bill to terminate the slave trade*qv* in the District of Columbia. A lengthy amendment to the fugitive slave law*qv* was also submitted. (*See also* Compromise of 1850.)

[J. B. McMaster, *History of the People of the United States*, VII.]

ARTHUR C. COLE

Committee of Thirteen, THE, of the United States Senate was constituted Dec. 18, 1860, under resolution of Sen. Powell of Kentucky, to consider the compromise proposals of Sen. Crittenden*qv*. It included leaders of different groups —Seward and Wade, Republicans; Davis and Toombs, Secessionists; Crittenden, Powell and Hunter, for the Border States*qv*. The Committee rejected by a vote of 7 to 6 the test compromise proposal concerning slavery in the territories, and made no recommendation to the Senate. (*See also* Committee of Thirty-three.)

[James Ford Rhodes, *History of the United States, 1850-1877*, Vol. III.]

C. MILDRED THOMPSON

Committee of Thirty-three, THE, of the United States House of Representatives, was constituted Dec. 6, 1860, one member from each state, on motion of Mr. Boteler of Virginia. This committee to consider Crittenden's compromise*qv* measures operated at the same time as the Senate Committee of Thirteen*qv*, but independently of it. No decision was reached, and no report made.

[James Ford Rhodes, *History of the United States, 1850-1877*, Vol. III.]

C. MILDRED THOMPSON

Committee on Public Information, THE, was set up by executive order of President Wilson, April 14, 1917. Formally it was the Secretaries of State, War and Navy with Mr. George Creel as civilian chairman. Actually it was the latter and a far-flung organization abroad and at home presenting the war issues by pamphlets, films, cables, posters, speakers (Four-Minute Men*qv*). Its function was informational, not censorship. The first year's budget was supplied by the President ($1,600,000); the second year by an appropriation of $1,250,000.

[G. Creel, *How We Advertised America;* G. S. Ford, *On and Off the Campus.*]

GUY STANTON FORD

Committee on the Conduct of the War, THE, was a joint committee of Congress to inquire into the management of the Civil War. It was organized on Dec. 20, 1861, and continued until ninety days after the close of the Thirty-eighth Congress, i.e., June, 1865. Sen. Wade of Ohio was chairman. The other members were: for the Senate, Chandler (Michigan) and Andrew Johnson (Tennessee); for the House, Gooch (Massachusetts), Covode (Pennsylvania), Julian (Indiana) and Odell (New York). Most of the members belonged to the radical wing of the Republican party*qv*, and grew more out of sympathy with the Lincoln administration as the war progressed. In 1864 the functions of the committee were extended to include investigation into contracts and expenditures, as well as military affairs. The eight published volumes of the committee, including reports, testimony and papers, deal chiefly with military campaigns and the competency of commanding officers. Of the generals who commanded the Army of the Potomac[qv] all except Grant were investigated by this committee.

[W. W. Pierson, Jr., The Committee on the Conduct of the Civil War, in *American Historical Review*, XXIII.]

C. MILDRED THOMPSON

Committees of Correspondence, organized as part of the transitional Revolutionary machinery to facilitate the spread of propaganda and coordinate the patriot party, were of three general types. Samuel Adams was the promoter of the first local committees on Nov. 2, 1772, and within three months Gov. Hutchinson reported that there were more than eighty such committees in Massachusetts. On March 12, 1773, Virginia organized the second type, the colony committees which were in reality standing committees of the legislature. The third type and the most important was the county committee which was chosen by the local units and acted as the agent of the central colonial committees. The importance of these committees as channels for the creation and direction of public opinion during the preliminaries of the Revolution can hardly be overemphasized. They exercised at times judicial, legislative and executive functions and, containing the germ of government, gave rise to the later committee system.

[E. D. Collins, Committees of Correspondence in the American Revolution, *Annual Report*, American Historical Association, 1901, Vol. I; H. M. Flick, The Rise of the Revolutionary Committee System, *History of the State of New York*, Vol. III.]

A. C. FLICK

Committees of Safety carried on and extended the work of the Revolutionary Committees of Correspondence[qv], and with the breakdown of constitutional modes of government, anarchy might have prevailed had not these extralegal committees developed to guide and stabilize the Revolutionary movement. The Second Continental Congress[qv] on July 18, 1775, recommended the establishment of such committees in the various colonies to carry on the all-important functions of government. Many of these committees had been active since 1774 and with the sanction of Congress they rapidly developed into a unified system which supplied the armies with men and equipment, apprehended Tories[qv] and carried on other exacting and unceasing duties of government. With the adoption of state constitutions[qv] the committees were largely replaced by constitutional agencies, New Hampshire and Connecticut alone continuing their committees throughout the war. So useful, however, had the committees proved themselves to be that many of them continued unofficially throughout the greater part of the war.

[Agnes Hunt, *The Provincial Committees of Safety of the American Revolution.*]

A. C. FLICK

Commodities as Money were found in use chiefly in the colonial period where there was a scarcity of coin or other suitable currency. By 1700 the use of commodity currencies was giving way to coin payments in the towns and cities, although remaining common for some years in the rural districts.

Commodities which were used as money consisted of wool, cattle and corn in New England, tobacco in Maryland and Virginia, lumber and tobacco in New York, beaver skins in Pennsylvania, New York and New England, and rice, pitch and corn in the Carolinas. In several cases colonial legislatures declared certain commodities legal tender[qv] in the payment of debts. Trade with the Indians led to the use of wampum[qv]—under a variety of local names—as currency in practically all of the colonies.

[N. Carothers, *Fractional Money;* J. L. Laughlin, *The Principles of Money.*]

FREDERICK A. BRADFORD

Commodities Exchange Act, The (1936), was passed by Congress to prevent and remove obstructions and burdens upon interstate commerce resulting from market manipulation and excessive speculation upon exchanges dealing in agricultural commodities. (*See also* Securities and Exchange Commission.)

[Public-No.675—74th Congress; *United States News*, July 20, 1936, p. 14, Oct. 5, 1936, p. 3.]

P. ORMAN RAY

Commodity Exchanges. The enormous expansion of markets after 1850 required the formation of organizations which could handle exchanges of commodities on a large scale. The buyers and sellers of commodities in every city and market of large commercial importance formed these boards of trade or chambers of commerce[qv] as they are sometimes called. The Chicago Board of Trade was organized in 1848. The New York Produce Exchange was formed in 1850. The Merchants Exchange of St. Louis had the characteristics of a modern exchange about 1854. The New York Cotton Exchange was organized in 1870 and the New York Coffee Exchange in 1882.

[American Produce Exchange Markets, *The Annals of the American Academy of Political and Social Science*, Vol. XXXVIII, No. 2.]

FRED M. JONES

Commodity Prices. As revealed by indices of wholesale prices, commodities in the United

States have experienced three major price swings during which they reached their highest levels in 1814–15, 1864–65 and 1919–20. In these periods they were about 65% (1814) to 150% (1864 and 1920) above the levels prevailing a few years prior to the peaks.

The rapid upward movement of prices must be largely attributed to currency disturbances. The expansion and depreciation of state bank issues following the expiration of the charter of the First United States Bank (1811), the issuance of Treasury notes to aid in financing the War of 1812, and the suspension of specie payments[qqv] in 1814 combined to cause the first peak. The depreciation of the greenbacks[qv] issued in financing the Civil War accounts for the height of the peak in the 1860's and the credit expansion which accompanied the World War largely explains the high point in 1919–20.

Decades of irregularly declining prices followed each period of inflation. Not until 1848 was the turning point from such a decline reached after the early 19th-century inflation. Following the high prices of the 1860's the decline continued until about 1896, when a gradual increase began, became greatly accelerated in 1915, and finally culminated in the peak prices of 1919–20. The turning point in the decline of prices following the World War is not yet (1939) clearly established.

Over shorter periods of time, commodity prices have for the most part followed the so-called cycle of general business activity, constituting symptomatic indicators of the speculative excesses which characterize periods of prosperity. There are, however, important exceptions to this rule. In the decade of the 1920's commodity prices did not share in the upward movement which typified security prices.

As the prices of commodities have fluctuated between higher and lower levels inequalities in price movements have appeared. Prices of agriculture products have been notably sensitive, exhibiting a more rapid and violent movement than the general average of commodity prices or than the prices of industrial products. The unequal pressure or benefit of price movements upon debtors and creditors, agriculture and industry has occasioned much political activity as evidenced by the organized opposition to the First and Second United States Banks, the post Civil War free-silver controversy, which came to focus with the organization of the People's party in 1892, and the reaction to the post World War deflation, which culminated in the devaluation of the dollar (1934) and large-scale silver purchases under the Silver Purchase Act of 1934[qqv].

[Warren, Pearson and Stoker, *Wholesale Prices for 213 Years*, Cornell University Agricultural Experiment Station.]

WILLIAM A. NEISWANGER, JR.

Commodore. A naval title applied to captains commanding, or having commanded, squadrons. They were authorized to fly a broad pennant distinctive of that rank, although until 1862 the rank itself did not legally exist in the United States Navy. The rank is next above captain and corresponded to that of a brigadier general of the army. With minor exceptions the rank was abolished in 1899.

DUDLEY W. KNOX

Common Lands in early New England towns were either lands held in common by the proprietors in which the individual owners had fractional rights and carried on farming in accordance with open field practices, or, more generally, undivided and unallotted land on the outskirts of the New England settlements, used for pasturage and woodland. In the latter part of the 17th century newcomers insisted on sharing these undivided lands with the proprietors, but the rights of the "noncommoners," as the newcomers were called, were seldom recognized. Statutes in the 18th century and court decisions upheld the town proprietors.

[A. Maclear, *Early New England Town;* R. H. Akagi, *Town Proprietors of the New England Colonies.*]

RICHARD B. MORRIS

Common Law, originally custom and usage, became the law "common" to all the people of England by judicial enforcement. Thus it originated in England, but has come to consist in great part in the principles which have been declared and developed in the decisions of the courts when adjudicating upon the private law in countries of Anglo-Saxon origins. It is usually not incorporated in the constitution or written statutes of a country but is the term generally used to describe that system of fundamental law which is in force among English-speaking peoples as contrasted with Roman Law and derivative systems based on an enacted code. The early settlers of the United States claimed, and were in fact supposed, to have brought with them to America their inherent common-law rights of person and property. It is the English common law which thus is recognized throughout the United States as the common law of the country and is the fundamental basis of our institutions of government.

The common law is enforced primarily by the governments of each of the states and territories. It has been influenced to some extent by the Code Napoleon^{qv} in its development in the State of Louisiana due to the original French settlement there. It is, of course, subject to repeal or amendment by statute, but primarily the common law has been developed and extended by the state and Federal courts, past and present.

In those states where the common law has been codified, these codes consist in large part of a restatement of common-law doctrines and their later development up to the time of codification. In addition, the common-law rights of the individual, as generally accepted, have been stated to a greater or lesser extent at various times in American history. Among these statements is that in the Declaration of Independence[qv] which says that all men "are endowed by their Creator with certain unalienable rights, that among these are life, liberty, and the pursuit of happiness." Also the Bill of Rights[qv] or the first ten Amendments to the United States Constitution and the bills of rights in the various state constitutions[qv] are in whole or in large part made up of statements of common-law rights and of methods of protecting these rights which are inborn, inherent and inalienable, and not granted by any government, according to Anglo-Saxon and American theory. Thus, the American governments, national and state, are merely the added protection to the common-law rights which the citizens already possess.

[T. E. Holland, *Jurisprudence;* W. W. Willoughby and L. Rogers, *An Introduction to the Problem of Government;* R. Pound, *Spirit of the Common Law.*]

WILLIAM STARR MYERS

Common Sense, a tract by Thomas Paine, was published in Philadelphia, January, 1776. In contrast to writers who denounced British tyranny but insisted on colonial loyalty, Paine described reconciliation as only "an agreeable dream." He maintained that, being of age, the colonies were qualified for independence and that their future interest demanded it. While many men had similar beliefs, none had so graphically stated the case. With its circulation of 120,000 in the first three months, the tract greatly fertilized the independence spirit which flowered so brilliantly in July, 1776.

[M. D. Conway, ed., *The Writings of Thomas Paine.*]

CHARLES F. MULLETT

Commonwealth v. Hunt. This case, decided by the Supreme Court of Massachusetts in 1842, held the Boston Journeymen Bootmakers Society, defendant, to be a lawful organization. Previously, associations of workers had been judged unlawful conspiracies (*see* Philadelphia Cordwainers' Case). The doctrine of conspiracy rests upon the assumption that an act which is innocent and legal when performed by an individual becomes dangerous and illegal when performed by a group. The historical significance of the case lies in the fact that it marks the legal recognition of labor unions as lawful institutions, provided the methods of attaining their ends are "honorable and peaceful."

[Francis B. Sayre, *Cases in Labor Law.*]

GORDON S. WATKINS

Communications, International. Save for some cross-border roads and trails, the United States, prior to 1850, depended on waterways for communication with other countries (*see* Waterways, Inland; Shipping, Ocean). Even today, though much trade and travel with Canada and Mexico are via rail and highway, the steamship is still our chief international carrier, despite promising developments in aircraft.

Our first international rail connection (1851) linked Montreal and Boston via Rouse's Point, N. Y.; in 1853 the Montreal–Portland route was completed; and by 1879 the Grand Trunk controlled tracks to Chicago via Toronto. By 1910 the Canadian Pacific, Canadian Northern (now Canadian National), Northern Pacific and Great Northern had border crossings between the "Soo" and Vancouver, and rails crossed into Mexico at three places. Motor bus routes, largely postwar, in 1935 entered Canada at thirteen points. In 1919 commercial air flights began across Puget Sound, and the Navy's flying boat NC–4[qv] made the first Atlantic crossing, followed in the same year by the British dirigible R–34. In 1928 the *Graf Zeppelin* made the first *commercial* flight of lighter-than-air craft to the United States. Meanwhile the Kelly Act (1925) had provided for air-mail contracts (subsidies), and by 1926 services had been started; by 1930 they had been extended to Canada and most of Latin America. In 1937 transpacific air service was inaugurated (*see* China Clipper, The), and in 1939 transatlantic air service began. On the Canadian and Latin-American routes 154,091 passengers were carried, 1936–37.

For international transmission of news and messages, the United States depended on private and public postal services which, with the development of packet lines after 1800, were fairly regular. By 1850 New York–Halifax telegraph[qv] service was opened, and was extended via cable[qv] to Europe temporarily in 1858 and permanently in 1866. There are now (1939) twenty-one cables across the Atlantic alone. Telephone[qv] service began with Canada before 1900. Speech was transmitted experimentally by radio telephone to Paris in 1915; in 1921 telephone cable was laid to Cuba and in 1927 telephone service was opened with London and Mexico. By 1938, 93% of the world's telephones were interconnected. Supplementing telephone, telegraph and cable communication is international short-wave radio for transmission of messages and broadcasting of radio programs; and since 1929 American long-wave programs have been sent by private wire to Montreal and Toronto for rebroadcast.

FRANK A. SOUTHARD, JR.

Communism is a social system in which wealth and the agencies for producing, distributing and exchanging wealth are owned in common. Movements seeking communal ownership have included the numerous utopian schemes beginning with Plato's *Republic* and reappearing periodically to the middle of the 19th century (*see* Communities), and the modern socialistic schools which had their inception with the publication of the *Communist Manifesto* by Karl Marx and Friedrich Engels in 1848 (*see* Class Struggle). At the present time the term communism generally indicates the Marxian revolutionary movement that seeks the overthrow of capitalism. This phase of communism stems from the Bolshevik Revolution in Russia in 1917.

Contemporary communism in the United States derives its inspiration and ideology from Marxism, which believes in the class struggle, the economic interpretation of history, the inevitable realization of communism, the disappearance of the state and world revolution. The communist movement was formally organized in 1919, when the Communist party of America and the Communist Labor party were formed from certain dissident left-wing elements of the Socialist party[qv] of America. Driven under ground for a time, the movement reappeared in 1921 as the Workers (Communist) party, which assumed political leadership of revolutionary forces. In industry the Trade Union Unity League, affiliated with the Red (Moscow) International of Labor Unions, was organized. Likewise, the Young Communist League was formed.

The movement has been hopelessly divided from the beginning. The Communist party and the Communist Labor party could not agree on unity. In 1928 the Communist League of America, consisting of Trotsky sympathizers opposed to Stalin, was created; and in 1929 there was organized the Communist party of the United States of America, comprising those who believed the methods urged by Moscow were unsuited to American conditions. Recently all communist groups have sought to capture the American labor movement by boring from within or forming centers of influence in the American Federation of Labor and the Congress of Industrial Organization[qqv]. The communist movement has never gained significant numerical strength in this country, due partly to a lack of unity but primarily to the fact that its ideology finds little fertile soil here.

[Max Eastman, *Marx, Lenin and the Science of Revolution;* Karl Kautsky, *The Ecomonic Doctrines of Karl Marx;* H. J. Laski, *Communism.*]

GORDON S. WATKINS

Communities. Among the earliest settlements that were deliberate communistic experiments were the shortlived community founded by Plockhoy, a Dutch Mennonite, on Delaware Bay in 1662; the Labadist[qv] Community of Protestant Mystics, founded in northern Maryland in 1680; the Mennonite Community at Germantown, Pa., founded in 1683; and the community of "The Women in the Wilderness" in Pennsylvania, in 1694. After the disappearance of the latter, Conrad Beissel, who had expected to join it, adopted the Dunker[qv] religion and founded, in 1732, the Ephrata Community[qv].

The first of the Shaker Communities[qv], which now (1939) number twenty-seven and are scattered over seven states, was the Jerusalem Community, founded in 1786 by Jemima Wilkinson at Gates County, N. Y. The main branch of Shakers were followers of Ann Lee; their first permanent community was established in 1787 at Mt. Lebanon, N. Y. Other important Shaker societies are at Watervliet, N. Y., Union Village, Ohio, and East Canterbury, N. Y.

Two communities, the Harmony Community and the Zoar Community[qqv], were founded by groups of Separatists from Württemberg, Germany, led by George Rapp and Joseph Blaumiler, respectively. The Harmony Society was originally, in 1805, in Butler County, Pa.; in 1814 the Harmonists removed to Indiana; and in 1825 they located at Economy, Pa. Zoar was founded in Ohio in 1817 and maintained its community organization until 1898.

Other religious communities were those of Perfectionists, led by Noyes at Oneida, N. Y., Brooklyn, N. Y., and Wallingford, Conn.; the Hopedale Community, Massachusetts (1842–57); the Amana Community in New York, and later in Iowa (1842–); the Bishop Hill Colony in Illinois (1848–62)[qqv]; the Mormon Community at Orderville, Utah (1874–84), and the communities of the Huterian Brethren.

The nonreligious communities in America

have been experiments in some economic or social philosophy. An example of the former was Robert Owen's unsuccessful communistic experiment at New Harmony,[qv] Ind., which he purchased from the Rappists in 1825.

In 1841 a group of Boston intellectuals established a literary community known as West Rexburg Community. In 1842, when the entire community was converted to Fourierism[qv], they transformed their society into a Fourierist "phalanx," which was called the Brook Farm Association[qv]. Other Fourierist communities were the Wisconsin Phalanx (1844–50) and the North American Phalanx, New Jersey (1843–56).

Other settlements founded on social or economic communism were at Teutonia, Pa. (1843), Icania, Iowa (1848–98), Equity, Ohio (1830–32), Eutopia, Ohio (1847–51), Modern Times, Long Island, N. Y. (1851–60), Steelton, N. J. (1915–), the Ruskin Commonwealth, Tennessee, and later Georgia (1894–1901), New Llano, Calif., and later Louisiana (1914–), and Fairhope, Ala.

[Wm. Alfred Hinds, *American Communities.*]

H. H. SHENK

Community Chests, a system for raising and apportioning funds for social welfare through a single annual campaign, started in Ohio in 1913. The system has spread widely, 419 cities conducting such campaigns in 1937. Of these, 317 raised $63,927,265.

[Elwood Street, *Social Work Administration;* Association of Community Chests and Councils, New York, *Community Chest Campaigns.*]

FRED A. EMERY

Commutation Bill, The (1783). Delegates from nine states in the Continental Congress[qv] concurred, March 22, 1783, in a resolution commuting the half-pay promised officers of the army on disbandment into a lump sum equal to five years' full pay, to be discharged by certificates bearing 6% interest. New Hampshire and New Jersey voted negatively. (*See also* Newburgh Addresses.)

[George Bancroft, *History of the United States;* Richard Hildreth, *History of the United States.*]

CHARLES WINSLOW ELLIOTT

Compact Theory, The, involves the idea that the basis of government is in the agreement of the people. Its appearance in America coincides with the first settlements and it is implicit in the Mayflower Compact[qv]. Church covenants and trading company charters[qqv] gave support to the compact philosophy. Thomas Hooker in his *Survey of the Summe of Church Discipline* (1648) declared that the foundation of authority in both church and state is in the consent of the people. The idea of compact is therefore equally valid as the basis of ecclesiastical and civil government. But the 17th century theologians found no means of interpreting the compact, except by divine revelation. It was left for John Locke[qv] to find in natural law a means of interpretation. Following Pufendorf, the guide of Locke, an Ipswich clergyman named John Wise in 1717 developed the compact theory in the light of the newer currents of thought. It was not long before the New England clergy were appealing to natural law and the social compact to dismiss absolutism on both sides of the Atlantic. Their homilies undoubtedly paved the way for the adoption of the compact idea in the revolutionary philosophy. Jefferson as he compiled the Declaration of Independence[qv] could with truth declare that the ideas it contained were hackneyed. The theory as it existed in 1776 in America was distinctly more individualistic than the English prototype. Locke envisaged the reversion of power upon the dissolution of the compact to the whole community but many Americans were not satisfied unless the individual, from whom the rights were originally granted, regained possession upon the exercise of the right of revolution.

[W. S. Carpenter, *The Development of American Political Thought.*]

WILLIAM S. CARPENTER

Compagnie de L'Occident (Western Company), also known as the "Mississippi Company" or "Mississippi Bubble,"[qv] was organized by John Law in 1717 for exploiting the resources of Louisiana. The scope of its activities was expanded, and in 1719 it became the Compagnie des Indes (Company of the Indies), which retained control of Louisiana until 1731.

[A. Fortier, *Louisiana,* Cyclopedic, II.]

WALTER PRICHARD

Companionate Marriage. M. M. Knight first used the term "companionate" in 1924, to mean a marriage entered for the sake of companionship rather than children. Judge Benjamin Lindsey then (1927) proposed legal recognition of "companionate marriage" by permitting divorce by mutual consent to childless couples, while retaining the usual divorce procedures for others. No American state has yet carried out this proposal. Strictly used, the term implies no change in the marriage laws, nor any license to cohabitation without marriage.

[B. B. Lindsey and W. Evans, *The Companionate Marriage.*]

JOSEPH K. FOLSOM

Company of One Hundred Associates, The (less frequently called the Company of New France), was a privileged commercial company established by Richelieu in 1627 for the colonization of New France or Canada. Its charter required the company to send colonists to Canada for the next fifteen years; to provide for them for three years; and thereafter to furnish them enough cleared land for their support. In return the company was given political power over the colony, seigneurial control of the land and monopoly of trade excepting the whale and cod fisheries. Since the company was more interested in trade than in colonization the colony failed to prosper and the charter was revoked in 1663.

[H. P. Biggar, *The Early Trading Companies of New France.*]

SISTER MARY BORGIAS PALM, S.N.D.

Compromise Movement of 1860, The, was an attempt, following the election of Lincoln (*see* Campaign of 1860), to check the movement towards secession[qv] and to avert war, by meeting the grievances of the South in regard to slavery. It emanated from the Border States[qv] and took form first in the Crittenden Resolutions[qv] for amendment to the United States Constitution. When Congress rejected the Crittenden Compromise[qv] the movement continued in the Border Slave State Convention[qv] of February, 1861. No agreement was reached upon the chief demand of the South, the recognition of property rights in slavery in the territories.

[James Ford Rhodes, *History of the United States, 1850-1877.*]

C. MILDRED THOMPSON

Compromise of 1850, The, a designation commonly given to five statutes enacted in September, 1850, following a bitter controversy between the representatives of the North and of the South. The controversy reached a fever heat during the weeks following the assembling of Congress in December, 1849, while the election of a speaker under the customary majority rule was prevented by the unwillingness of the Free Soil[qv] members, who held the balance of power, to be drawn into an arrangement with either of the two major parties. In the course of the prolonged balloting criminations and recriminations passed between the hotheaded spokesmen of the two sections. Pointing to indications that the principle of the Wilmot Proviso[qv] might be enacted into law and receive the signature of President Taylor, Southerners insisted as a matter of right upon the recognition of the Calhoun[qv] doctrine that under the Constitution all the territories should be deemed open to slavery. There was talk of secession[qv] unless this principle was recognized in fact or as a basis for some adjustment. Plans were under way for the discussion of a satisfactory Southern program at a Southern convention called to meet at Nashville[qv] in June.

In the face of increasing sectional strife Henry Clay returned to the United States Senate and on Jan. 29, 1850, suggested a series of resolutions intended to provide the basis for the prompt adjustment of the main questions at issue between the two sections. His resolutions were shortly referred to a select committee of thirteen[qv] of which he was made chairman. Its report (May 8), which covered the ground of Clay's resolutions, recommended an "omnibus bill" providing for the admission of California under its free state constitution, for territorial governments for Utah and New Mexico[qqv], silent on slavery, and for the settlement of the boundary dispute between Texas and the United States (*see* Texas Cession of 1850). It also recommended a bill for the abolition of the slave trade in the District of Columbia and an amendment to the fugitive slave law[qqv].

The hope of compromise was tied up with the fate of the omnibus bill. Clay rallied to his support the outstanding Union men, including Daniel Webster, Lewis Cass, Henry S. Foote and Stephen A. Douglas; the latter became the active force in the promotion of the necessary legislation. President Taylor wanted the admission of California but no action on New Mexico and Utah until they should be ready to become states; he was, therefore, a formidable obstacle to the plans of the compromisers until his death on July 9. Even the active support of his successor, however, did not offset the fact that the idea of compromise "united the opponents instead of securing the friends" of each proposition.

Compromise as such had clearly failed; the ground which it had contemplated was covered in five statutes each formerly included as sections of the proposed omnibus bill. The act establishing a territorial government for Utah (Sept. 9) contained the important "popular sovereignty"[qv] clause providing that any state or states formed out of this territory should be admitted with or without slavery as their constitutions should prescribe. An identical clause was appended to the New Mexico territorial act (Sept. 9), which also resolved the conflict between Texas and the Federal Government over the Santa Fé region by a cession, with compensation to Texas, to the newly created territory. On the same date the act admitting California under its constitution prohibiting slavery in the new state was approved. The Fugitive Slave Act of Sept. 18, 1850[qv], which amended the original statute of Feb. 12, 1793, provided for the appointment of special commissioners to supplement the regular courts empowered after a summary hearing to issue a certificate of arrest of a fugitive "from labor," which authorized the claimant to seize and return the fugitive (with a fee of $10 when the certificate was issued and of only $5 when denied); in no trial or hearing was the testimony of the alleged fugitive to be admitted as evidence nor was a fugitive claiming to be a freeman to have the right of trial by jury; Federal marshals and deputy marshals were to execute the warrants under a heavy fine for refusing and were made liable for the full value of fugitives who escaped their custody; these officials were empowered to call to their aid when necessary any bystanders or *posse comitatus;* finally, any person wilfully hindering the arrest of a fugitive or aiding in his rescue or escape was subject to heavy fine and imprisonment, as well as to heavy civil damages.

These statutes were shortly presented to the country as a series of compromise measures. They did not, however, magically calm the sectional storm. In the North there was widespread denunciation of the "iniquitous" features of the Fugitive Slave Act and deliberate declaration that its enforcement would never be tolerated. At the same time the conservative forces organized a series of Union meetings and pleaded the obligations of the North to pacify the South. In the latter section the other four enactments precipitated the most serious disunion crisis that the country had ever faced. In the states of Georgia, Mississippi and South Carolina the "Southern Rights," or secession, forces were checkmated only by the most strenuous efforts of the Union or Constitutional Union elements. Both sides foreswore old party labels and fought under their new banners to win control over the official state conventions that were ordered. The Southern Rights forces lost in the first test fight in Georgia (*see* Georgia Platform) and had to carry this moral handicap in the remaining contests. It was not until 1852 that the country at large made clear its acquiescence in what at length became known by the oversimple label, "The Compromise of 1850."

[J. B. McMaster, *History of the People of the United States*, Vol. VIII; J. F. Rhodes, *History of the United States since the Compromise of 1850*, Vol. I.]

ARTHUR C. COLE

Compromise Tariff of 1833, THE, ended the dangerous national crisis produced by South Carolina's nullification[qv] of the high tariff acts of 1828 and 1832 (*see* Calhoun's *Exposition*). Sponsored by Henry Clay, this measure provided for systematic reduction of duties until July 1, 1842, when a uniform rate of 20% would be established. Patriotism, Northern fears of drastic tariff reductions, and states' rights[qv] perturbations in regard to the Force Bill[qv] helped to ensure the passage of the Compromise. The bill mollified South Carolina and started a lower tariff trend that was not definitely reversed until after the outbreak of the Civil War.

[C. G. Bowers, *The Party Battles of the Jackson Period;* G. G. Van Deusen, *The Life of Henry Clay.*]

GLYNDON G. VAN DEUSEN

Compromises of the Federal Constitution, THE. To a great extent the whole work of the Convention of 1787[qv] was a compromise among the views, more or less local or sectional, of the populations of the thirteen different states which recently had been colonies of Great Britain. In fact, at the close of the Revolution the National Government consisted of little more than a league of thirteen independent and autonomous nations. It was the question of strengthening this league or creating an entirely new national government that caused most of the debate in the convention.

On May 29, 1787, Edmund Randolph of Virginia submitted the so-called Virginia Plan which aimed to create an entirely new national government that should operate upon the citizens as individuals and, in large part, disregard the autonomy of the separate states. This alarmed the states' rights people and on June 15 William Paterson of New Jersey laid before the convention the so-called New Jersey Plan. This provided for a revision of the Articles of Confederation[qv] and an increase in the powers of the National Government of that day. But that Government was to operate upon the states as such, and not upon individual citizens. Of course, both sides of the question were immediately involved in the determination of the form of the national legislative body and the representation therein. At the suggestion of delegates from Connecticut the compromise was agreed upon that the national legislative body, or Congress[qv], should consist of two Houses, in one of which (the Senate) the states should have equal representation and in the other (the House of Representatives) the representation should be based upon population.

This at once brought up the question of the representation of the slave population of the states. The Northern states claimed that the

Negroes were property, hence should not be counted among the inhabitants for the purposes of apportionment. The Southern states claimed that they were individuals, hence should be included. These arguments on both sides, which were inconsistent with the usual convictions of the respective sections, were compromised by the provision that representatives should be apportioned among the states "according to their respective numbers" which shall be determined by adding to the whole numbers of free persons "including those bound to service for a term of years and excluding Indians not taxed, three-fifths of all other persons" (Constitution, Art. I, Sec. 2, Par. 3).

The third of these most important compromises was concerned with the slave trade[qv]. It was desired by the Northern states that this trade be prohibited, but that Congress be empowered to pass navigation acts and otherwise regulate commerce. South Carolina and Georgia wished a continuation of the slave trade but feared the national control of navigation acts and commerce. This in turn was compromised by granting to Congress the power to pass navigation acts and otherwise regulate commerce, but that it should be prohibited from taxing exports. On the other hand, the Northern states consented to a continuance of the slave trade for twenty years, or until 1808. As a further concession it was recommended that until that year a tariff of ten dollars a head be levied upon all Negroes imported, while a clause was added to insure the recovery of fugitive slaves[qv]. This compromise secured absolute free trade between the states with the entire control of commerce in the hands of the Federal Government. The price to be paid was a postponement for twenty years of the abolition of the foreign slave trade.

[John Fiske, *Critical Period of American History;* Max Farrand, *The Records of the Federal Constitution of 1787.*]

WILLIAM STARR MYERS

Comptroller General of the United States, THE, is head of the general accounting office created by the Budget and Accounting Act of 1921[qv]. He is appointed by the President and Senate for a fifteen-year term, and is removable only by Congress. His office is charged with performance of the auditing functions previously performed by sundry other officials, with the task of devising and installing an up-to-date system of accounting for all government offices, and with the duty of reviewing all financial transactions of administrative officers and agencies, which he must disallow if found not to be in accord with law.

[W. F. Willoughby, *The Legal Status and Functions of the General Accounting Office.*]

P. ORMAN RAY

Comptroller of the Currency. This office was created by the act of Feb. 25, 1863, providing for the organization of national banks[qv] and was retained in the revised law of June 3, 1864. The law provided that the Comptroller of the Currency be appointed by the President, upon recommendation of the Secretary of the Treasury, for a term of five years. His duties were to take charge of plates and dies used in printing national bank notes, to examine national banks, and to make an annual report to Congress. From Aug. 10, 1914, to Feb. 1, 1936, the Comptroller also served as an ex-officio member of the Federal Reserve Board, and he acts as a director in the Federal Deposit Insurance Corporation[qqv].

[F. A. Bradford, *Money and Banking.*]

FREDERICK A. BRADFORD

Comstock Lode, THE, Virginia City, Nev., from its discovery in 1859 to its decline in 1879, held the spotlight of the world. During this period more than $500,000,000 in silver and gold were taken from these mines.

To mine this ore great hoisting machines, giant pumps, heavy stamps, drills, cables and hundreds of other things were manufactured. To drain hot water from underground reservoirs, Adolph Sutro[qv] completed a five-mile tunnel from the floor of the Carson River to the Comstock mines in 1878. To extract the silver from the rock, the old Mexican patio method was first used; later, the amalgamating process was employed for the reduction of the ore.

Water, for the 40,000 inhabitants of Virginia City and vicinity, was brought from Marlette, an artificial lake, thirty miles away in the Sierra Nevada Mountains, through pipes, tunnels, flumes and a large inverted siphon. The pipe and siphon were made, piece by piece, in San Francisco, to fit around mountains, to cross Washoe Valley and to extend up the Virginia Mountains.

The discovery of the Big Bonanza[qv] in the California Consolidated Mine, 1873, made multimillionaires of John W. Mackay, James G. Fair, James C. Flood, William S. O'Brien, William Sharon and William C. Ralston.

San Francisco was the residuary legatee of the Comstock wealth. With this money palatial homes were built; banks, the San Francisco Stock Exchange, and dozens of other businesses were established.

[Eliot Lord, *Comstock Mining and Miners.*]

EFFIE MONA MACK

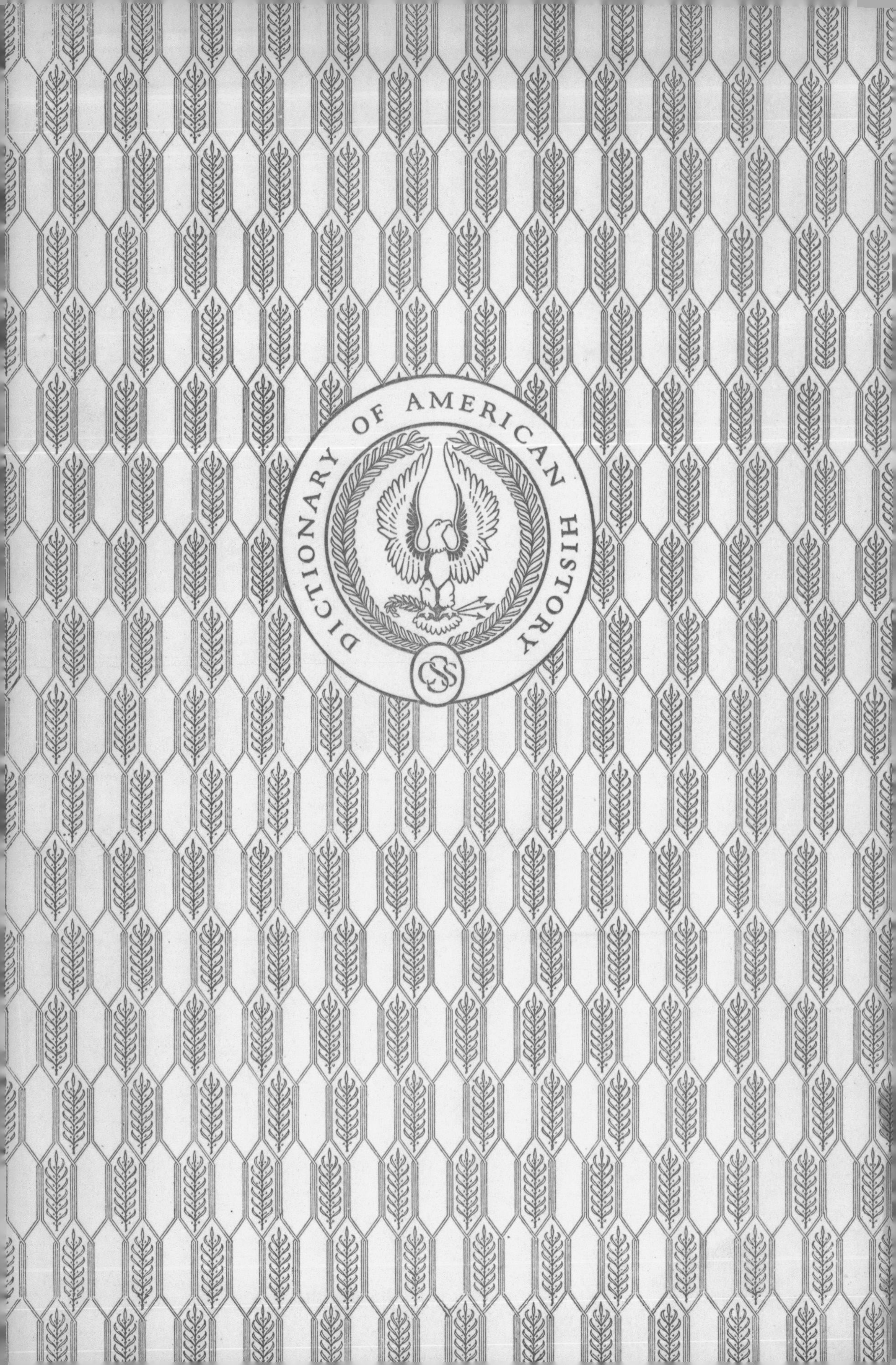
DICTIONARY OF AMERICAN HISTORY
CSS